1,000,000 Books

are available to read at

Forgotten Books

---◆---

www.ForgottenBooks.com

---◆---

Read online
Download PDF
Purchase in print

ISBN 978-1-5280-4228-4
PIBN 10917386

This book is a reproduction of an important historical work. Forgotten Books uses state-of-the-art technology to digitally reconstruct the work, preserving the original format whilst repairing imperfections present in the aged copy. In rare cases, an imperfection in the original, such as a blemish or missing page, may be replicated in our edition. We do, however, repair the vast majority of imperfections successfully; any imperfections that remain are intentionally left to preserve the state of such historical works.

1 MONTH OF
FREE
READING

at
www.ForgottenBooks.com

By purchasing this book you are eligible for one month membership to ForgottenBooks.com, giving you unlimited access to our entire collection of over 1,000,000 titles via our web site and mobile apps.

To claim your free month visit:
www.forgottenbooks.com/free917386

English
Français
Deutsche
Italiano
Español
Português

www.forgottenbooks.com

Mythology Photography **Fiction**
Fishing Christianity **Art** Cooking
Essays Buddhism Freemasonry
Medicine **Biology** Music **Ancient**
Egypt Evolution Carpentry Physics
Dance Geology **Mathematics** Fitness
Shakespeare **Folklore** Yoga Marketing
Confidence Immortality Biographies
Poetry **Psychology** Witchcraft
Electronics Chemistry History **Law**
Accounting **Philosophy** Anthropology
Alchemy Drama Quantum Mechanics
Atheism Sexual Health **Ancient History**
Entrepreneurship Languages Sport
Paleontology Needlework Islam
Metaphysics Investment Archaeology
Parenting Statistics Criminology
Motivational

JOURNAL

OF THE

ROYAL

STATISTICAL SOCIETY.

(Founded 1834.)

INCORPORATED BY ROYAL CHARTER 1887,

VOL. LV.—YEAR 1892.

LONDON:

EDWARD STANFORD, 26 AND 27, COCKSPUR STRF
CHARING CROSS, S.W.

1892.   /., LONDON.

NOTICE.

———

CONTENTS.

Vol. LV.—Year 1892.

March, 1892.

June, 1892.

MISCELLANEA :—

JOURNAL

OF THE

ROYAL

STATISTICAL SOCIETY.

𝔉ounded 1834.

𝔍ncorporated by 𝔕oyal 𝔔harter 1887.

VOL. LV.—PART I.

MARCH, 1892.

LONDON:

EDWARD STANFORD, 26 AND 27, COCKSPUR STREET,
CHARING CROSS, S.W.

1892.

ROYAL STATISTICAL SOCIETY,

No. 9, Adelphi Terrace, Strand, W.C., London.

NOTICES TO FELLOWS.

March, 1892.

The Council desire to call the attention of the Fellows to the fact that notwithstanding the change in the name of the Society by the addition of the word "Royal," they are still, in using letters after their names, signifying the membership of the Society, only entitled under Rule 6, to use the letters F.S.S.

Annual Subscriptions are due in advance, on the 1st of January in each year. A Form for authorising a Banker or Agent to pay the Subscription Annually will be forwarded by the Assistant Secretary, on application. When convenient, this mode of payment is recommended. Drafts should be made payable to the order of "The Royal Statistical Society," and crossed "*Drummond and Co.*"

To be included in the Ballot at any particular Ordinary Meeting, the Nomination Papers of Candidates for Fellowship, must be lodged at the Office of the Society, at least six days before the date of such Meeting.

Fellows who may desire to receive Special and Separate Notices of each Paper to be read before the Society at the Ordinary Meetings, should indicate their wishes to the Assistant Secretary.

The Ordinary Meetings of the Society are now held, by permission of the Lords of the Committee of Council on Education, in **The Lecture Theatre of the Museum of Practical Geology, 28, Jermyn Street, S.W.**

Fellows are entitled to a copy of the Catalogue of the Library and the Index to the Catalogue. They may be had on personal application at the office, or will be forwarded upon the payment of carriage (1s. per parcel post). Fellows residing abroad or in the colonies are requested to send the necessary amount to cover postage, according to postal circumstances. (Weight, 3 lb. 14 oz. and 2 lb. 10 oz. respectively.)

The Library and the Reading Room are open daily for the use of Fellows from 10 A.M. to 5 P.M., excepting on Saturdays, when they are closed at 2 P.M.

Fellows borrowing books from the Library are requested to be good enough to return them with as little delay as possible, but without fail at the expiration of a month, and without waiting for them to be recalled.

Fellows changing their Addresses are requested to notify the same to the Assistant Secretary, so that delay or error in forwarding communications, or the *Journal,* may be avoided.

By Order of the Executive Committee

ROYAL STATISTICAL SOCIETY·

AN OUTLINE OF ITS OBJECTS.

THE *Royal Statistical Society* was founded, in pursuance of a recommendation of the British Association for the Advancement of Science, on the 15th of March, 1834; its objects being, the careful collection, arrangement, discussion and publication, of facts bearing on and illustrating the complex relations of modern society in its social, economical, and political aspects,—especially facts which can be stated numerically and arranged in tables;—and also, to form a Statistical Library as rapidly as its funds would permit.

The Society from its inception has steadily progressed. It now possesses a valuable Library of more than 27,000 vols. and a Reading Room; Ordinary Meetings are held monthly from November to June, which are well attended, and cultivate among its Fellows an active spirit of investigation; the Papers read before the Society are, with an abstract of the discussions thereon, published in its *Journal*, which now consists of fifty-four annual volumes, and forms of itself a valuable library of reference.

The Society has originated and statistically conducted many special inquiries on subjects of economic or social interest, of which the results have been published in the *Journal*, or issued separately.

To enable the Society to extend its sphere of useful activity, and accomplish in a yet greater degree the various ends indicated, an increase in its numbers and revenue is desirable. With the desired increase in the number of Fellows, the Society will be enabled to publish standard works on Economic Science and Statistics, especially such as are out of print or scarce, and also greatly extend its collection of Foreign works. Such a well-arranged Library for reference, as would result, does not at present exist in England, and is obviously a great *desideratum*.

The Society is cosmopolitan, and consists of Fellows and Honorary Fellows, forming together a body, at the present time, of nearly *one thousand one hundred* Members.

The Annual Subscription to the Society is *Two Guineas*, and at present there is no entrance fee. Fellows may, on joining the Society, or afterwards, compound for all future Annual Subscriptions by a payment of *Twenty Guineas*.

The Fellows of the Society receive gratuitously a copy of each part of the *Journal* as published quarterly, and have the privilege of purchasing back numbers at a reduced rate. The Library (reference and circulating), and the Reading Room, are open daily for the convenience of Members.

Nomination Forms and any further information will be furnished, on application to the *Assistant Secretary*, 9, *Adelphi Terrace, Strand, W.C., London.*

CALENDAR FOR THE SESSION 1891-92.

1891	MON.	TUES.	WED.	THURS.	FRI.	SATUR.	SUN.	1892	MON.	TUES.	WED.	THURS.	FRI.	SATUR.	SUN.
NOV.	...	...	...	...	...	...	1	MAY	...	...	...	...	...	...	1
	2	3	4	5	6	7	8		2	3	4	5	6	7	8
	9	10	11	12	13	14	15		9	10	11	12	13	14	15
	16	**17**	18	19	20	21	22		16	**17**	18	19	20	21	22
	23	24	25	26	27	28	29		23	24	25	26	27	28	29
	30								30	31					
DEC.	...	1	2	3	4	5	6	JUNE	...	...	1	2	3	4	5
	7	8	9	10	11	12	13		6	7	8	9	10	11	12
	14	**15**	16	17	18	19	20		13	14	15	16	17	18	19
	21	22	23	24	25	26	27		20	**21**	22	23	24	25	26
	28	29	30	31					27	28	29	30			
1892 JAN.	...	...	...	...	1	2	3	JULY	...	...	...	...	1	2	3
	4	5	6	7	8	9	10		4	5	6	7	8	9	10
	11	12	13	14	15	16	17		11	12	13	14	15	16	17
	18	**19**	20	21	22	23	24		18	19	20	21	22	23	24
	25	26	27	28	29	30	31		25	26	27	28	29	30	31
FEB.	1	2	3	4	5	6	7	AUG.	1	2	3	4	5	6	7
	8	9	10	11	12	13	14		8	9	10	11	12	13	14
	15	**16**	17	18	19	20	21		15	16	17	18	19	20	21
	22	23	24	25	26	27	28		22	23	24	25	26	27	28
	29								29	30	31				
MAR.	...	1	2	3	4	5	6	SEP.	...	...	...	1	2	3	4
	7	8	9	10	11	12	13		5	6	7	8	9	10	11
	14	**15**	16	17	18	19	20		12	13	14	15	16	17	18
	21	22	23	24	25	26	27		19	20	21	22	23	24	25
	28	29	30	31					26	27	28	29	30		
APR.	...	...	...	...	1	2	3	OCT.	...	...	...	...	...	1	2
	4	5	6	7	8	9	10		3	4	5	6	7	8	9
	11	12	13	14	15	16	17		10	11	12	13	14	15	16
	18	19	20	21	22	23	24		17	18	19	20	21	22	23
	25	**26**	27	28	29	30			24	25	26	27	28	29	30
									31						

The dates of the Ordinary Meetings of the Society, at which Papers are read and discussed, are marked in the Calendar above by **Black Figures**.

The Chair will be taken at 7.45 p.m., precisely.

These Meetings are now held, by permission of the Committee of Council on Education, in **The Lecture Theatre of the Museum of Practical Geology, 28, Jermyn Street, S.W.**

THE ANNUAL GENERAL MEETING

WILL BE HELD ON THE 28TH JUNE, 1892, AT 5 P.M., AT 9, ADELPHI TERRACE.

ROYAL STATISTICAL SOCIETY.

Programme of the Session 1891-92.

THE

MONTHLY MEETINGS

ARE HELD ON THE

THIRD TUESDAY IN THE MONTHS OF NOVEMBER—JUNE,

(EXCEPT APRIL,)

In the LECTURE THEATRE of the MUSEUM OF PRACTICAL GEOLOGY,

28, JERMYN STREET, S.W., at 7.45 p.m.

Tuesday,	Nov.	17.	Tuesday, March 15.	
„	Dec.	15.	„ April	26.
„	Jan.	19.	„ May	17.
„	Feb.	16.	„ June	21.

The following Papers have been read (March, 1892):—

The President's Opening Address. By F. J. MOUAT., M.D., LL.D. (Delivered 17th November.)

"Enumeration and Classification of Paupers, and State Pensions for the Aged." By CHARLES BOOTH. (Read 15th December.)

"The Recent Agricultural Depression, as exhibited in the · Rental of an Oxford College and the Financial Position of a leading London Hospital." By L. L. PRICE, M.A., and J. C. STEELE, M.D. (Read 16th February.)

"Tonnage Statistics of the Decade 1880-90." By JOHN GLOVER. (Read 15th March.)

The following Papers have been offered; and from these and from others that may yet be offered, a selection will be made by the Council:—

"The Imperial Census of India of 1891, Administrative and Statistical." By J. A. BAINES, Census Commissioner for India.

"Income Tax and Population." By F. B. GARNETT, C.B.

"The Extension of Women's Employment in Textile Manufactures." By W. A. S. HEWINS, B.A.

"Comparative Efficiency and Earnings of Workmen in different Countries." By J. S. JEANS.

"The United States Census of 1890." By GEORGE B. LONGSTAFF, M.A., M.D.

"An Inquiry into the Statistics of the Consumption of Milk and Milk Products in the United Kingdom." By R. HENRY REW.

Papers have also been promised by M. TROÏNITSKY, of St. Petersburg, and Dr. GUILLAUME, of Berne, Honorary Fellows. That of Dr. Guillaume is entitled "Le nouveau bulletin d'information des décès en Suisse."

5

STANFORD'S LIBRARY MAPS.

REVISED AND CHEAPER ISSUE.

The Publisher begs to announce the issue of **New and Revised** Editions of these fine Maps, which have hitherto held the first place as Maps for the Libraries of Gentlemen, Public Offices and Libraries, or for Commercial purposes.

The Maps have undergone a thorough revision to bring them up to date, and the cost of production having been considerably reduced by the use of new machinery, it has been decided to make a substantial reduction in the prices at which they have hitherto been sold to the Public, in the hope of extending their circulation and usefulness.

The Maps of which New Editions are now ready are :—

EUROPE. Scale, 50 miles to 1 inch. Size, 65 by 58 inches.

ASIA. Scale, 110 miles to 1 inch. Size, 65 by 58 inches.

AFRICA. Scale, 94 miles to 1 inch. Size, 58 by 65 inches.

NORTH AMERICA. Scale, 83 miles to 1 inch. Size, 58 by 65 inches.

SOUTH AMERICA. Scale, 83 miles to 1 inch. Size, 58 by 65 inches.

AUSTRALASIA. Scale, 64 miles to 1 inch. Size, 65 by 58 inches.

The Prices of each of these Maps will in future be as follows :—

Four Sheets, Coloured, 35s.
Mounted on Rollers and Varnished, 45s.
Mounted to fold in Morocco Case, 60s.
Mounted on Spring Rollers, £5.

The other Maps in Stanford's Library Series are :—

THE WORLD ON MERCATOR'S PROJECTION.
ENGLAND.   **CANADA.**
SCOTLAND.   **UNITED STATES.**
IRELAND.   **AUSTRALASIA.**
LONDON.   **AUSTRALIA.**

For particulars of Price, Size, &c., see STANFORD'S CATALOGUE OF MAPS, ATLASES, &c., *sent post free for 3d.*

EDWARD STANFORD, 26 & 27, COCKSPUR STREET, LONDON, S.W.

ROYAL STATISTICAL SOCIETY.

Binding of the Journal.

Arrangements have been made with the Printers to bind the annual volumes of the *Journal* in cloth (in the style of the Catalogue and Index to the Library), at a cost of One Shilling per volume, conditionally on six to twelve volumes being sent at a time. Fellows wishing to have their *Journals* thus bound, should therefore send them (carriage prepaid) to the *Offices of the Society*, 9, Adelphi Terrace, Strand, W.C. (*not* to the Printers). To avoid delay, Fellows are requested to send their *Journals* to the offices *as soon as possible*, as they will only be forwarded to the Binders when there are six copies ready to be bound.

These terms apply to the binding of the present and of preceding volumes.

Fellows who wish to avoid the trouble of sending their *Journals* to London, can have the cases sent down to them at the same price (exclusive of carriage). The weight of one single cover is about 5 ounces.

Fellows who desire it, can have the several parts of the *Journal* retained and forwarded annually, bound in a single volume, at their expense. Or, by special instruction from any Fellow, the December part only may be retained and bound up with the other parts when received from the Fellow.

7

ROYAL STATISTICAL SOCIETY.

LIST OF THE SOCIETY'S PUBLICATIONS.

Note.—Sets—or Copies of any number—of the *Journal*, or of the other Publications of the Society (if not out of print), can be obtained of the publisher, E. Stanford 26, and 27, Cockspur Street, Charing Cross, London, S.W., or through any bookseller.

	Price.
Journal (published quarterly)— Vols. 1—54. 8vo. 1838-91	5s. each part*
General Analytical Index to Vols. 1—50 of the Journal (1838-87). In 4 parts. 8vo.— (i) For the First Fifteen Volumes (1838-52) (ii) For the Ten Volumes (1853-62) .... (iii) For the Ten Volumes (1863-72) .... (iv) For the Fifteen Volumes (1837-87) ...	3s. 6d. each part
First Report of a Committee on Beneficent Institutions. I. The Medical Charities of the Metropolis. 68 pp. 8vo. 1857	2s. 6d.
Statistics of the Farm School System of the Continent (reprinted from the *Journal*, with a Preface and Notes). 63 pp. 8vo. 1878 ...	1s.
Catalogue of the Library (New)— iv + 573 pp. Cloth, super royal 8vo. 1884	10s.
Index to the Catalogue of 1884— i+372 pp. Cloth, super royal 8vo. 1886	10s.
Jubilee Volume— xv + 372 pp. Cloth, 8vo. 1885	10s. 6d.
List of Fellows, Rules and Bye-Laws, Regulations of the Library, and Outline of the Objects of the Society, &c. Corrected annually to 31st December. 8vo.	Issued gratuitously

Price of back Numbers of the Journal, &c., to Fellows only.

Fellows only, can obtain sets—or single copies of any number—of the *Journal*, or copies of the other Publications, at the Society's Rooms, 9, Adelphi Terrace, Strand, W.C.

By different resolutions of the Council, the prices charged to Members are as follows:—(a.) back numbers of the *Journal* of the Society, three-fifths of the publishing price; (b.) each part of the General Index to the *Journal*, 2s. 6d.; (c.) the Jubilee Volume, 5s.

NOTE.—One or two numbers of the *Journal* are now out of print.

* Before 1870 the price varied.

8

ROYAL STATISTICAL SOCIETY.

Founded 15th March, 1834, Incorporated 31st January, 1887.

LIST OF THE FORMER

Patron and Presidents

OF THE SOCIETY.

Patron.

	Period.
HIS ROYAL HIGHNESS THE PRINCE CONSORT, K.G.	1840–61

Presidents.

The Most Noble the Marquis of Lansdowne, F.R.S.	1834–36
Sir Charles Lemon, Bart., M.P., LL.D., F.R.S.	1836–38
The Right Hon. the Earl Fitzwilliam, F.R.S.	1838–40
The Right Hon. the Viscount Sandon, M.P.	1840–42
(afterwards Earl of Harrowby.)	
The Most Noble the Marquis of Lansdowne, K.G., F.R.S.	1842–43
The Right Hon. the Viscount Ashley, M.P.	1843–45
(afterwards Earl of Shaftesbury.)	
The Right Hon the Lord Monteagle..................	1845–47
The Right Hon. the Earl Fitzwilliam, F.R.S.	1847–49
The Right Hon. the Earl of Harrowby...............	1849–51
The Right Hon. the Lord Overstone	1851–53
The Right Hon. the Earl Fitzwilliam, K.G., F.R.S.	1853–55
The Right Hon. the Earl of Harrowby, K.G., D.C.L.	1855–57
The Right Hon. the Lord Stanley, M.P.	1857–59
(now Earl of Derby.)	
The Right Hon. the Lord John Russell, M.P., F.R.S.	1859–61
(afterwards Earl Russell.)	
The Right Hon. Sir J. S. Pakington, Bart., M.P., G.C.B...	1861–63
(afterwards Lord Hampton.)	
Colonel W. H. Sykes, M.P., D.C.L....................	1863–65
The Right Hon. the Lord Houghton, D.C.L., F.R.S.	1865–67
The Right Hon. W. E. Gladstone, M.P., D.C.L.	1867–69
W. Newmarch, Esq., F.R.S., Corr. Mem. Inst. of France..	1869–71
William Farr, M.D., C.B., D.C.L., F.R.S.	1871–73
William A. Guy, M.B., F.R.S......................	1873–75
James Heywood, M.A., F.R.S., F.G.S.	1875–77
The Right Hon. George Shaw Lefevre, M.P.	1877–79
Thomas Brassey, M.P.............................	1879–80
(now the Right Hon. Lord Brassey.)	
The Right Hon. Sir James Caird, K.C.B., F.R.S.........	1880–82
Robert Giffen, C.B., LL.D.	1882–84
Sir Rawson W. Rawson, K.C.M.G., C.B.	1884–86
The Right Hon. George J. Goschen, M.P., F.R.S.	1886–88
T. Graham Balfour, M.D., F.R.S.	1888–90

9

NOTICE.

THE Council of the Royal Statistical Society wish it to be understood, that, while they consider it their duty to adopt every means within their power to test the facts inserted in this *Journal*, they do not hold themselves responsible for their accuracy, which must rest upon the authority of the several Contributors.

Vol. LV.]   [Part I.

JOURNAL

OF THE ROYAL STATISTICAL SOCIETY,

MARCH, 1892.

Death of Sir James Caird, P.C., K.C.B., F.R.S., LL.D.,
Past President of the Society.

In opening the proceedings at the ordinary meeting on the 16th February, the President said:—

I regret that it is my painful duty to make known to you the death of one of our most distinguished members, the late Sir James Caird, another victim of the mysterious pestilence which has removed so many of our leading men. He joined the Society some thirty-five years since, occupied the chair from 1880-82, and furnished some valuable communications to our transactions on the important branch of economics of which he was probably the greatest exponent of our time, and to which his life was devoted. He possessed in an exceptional degree the merit of being a worker as well as a thinker, hence his views commanded very general assent, and were of more than ephemeral interest in their application.

This is not the proper occasion to enlarge upon his merits as a statist, which will be duly dealt with in our transactions hereafter.

The RECENT DEPRESSION *in* AGRICULTURE *as shown in the* ACCOUNTS
of an OXFORD COLLEGE, 1876-90.

By L. L. PRICE, ESQ., M.A.

[Read before the Royal Statistical Society, 16th February, 1892.
The President, Dr. F. J. MOUAT, F.R.C.S., LL.D., in the Chair.]

CONTENTS:

LIST OF TABLES.

CONTENTS—*Contd.*

I.—*Introductory Remarks.*

FOR some time the agricultural industry of this country has been
depressed; and, as year by year has gone by, the prospect, instead
of becoming brighter, has only seemed to grow more and more
gloomy. But during the last year or two a feeling of reviving
confidence has begun, gradually and intermittently, to spread
among the agricultural classes, and the opinion is now widely
entertained that the depression has finally reached, if it has not
already passed, its lowest point. The present time, therefore,
would seem to be opportune for endeavouring to trace the course
of the depression, to gauge its intensity, and to investigate its
results; and such an endeavour will be made in the following
paper. The work has already been executed on a large scale by
competent authorities, and it is by comparison only a modest
enterprise which is here essayed. It is to exhibit the course and
to measure the effects of the depression, as illustrated by the
accounts of an Oxford college.

There are, however, some grounds for believing that even this
limited endeavour, however imperfectly it may be fulfilled, may
not prove entirely useless. In some respects, at any rate, what
has occurred within these comparatively narrow limits may be
regarded as typical of the incidents of a larger area. The estates

of a college are often dispersed in various parts of the country, as they are generally the gifts of many benefactors at different times; and, although this is perhaps to a less degree the case with the college with which this paper is concerned, and its chief estates are, with one important exception, situated at no great distance from Oxford itself, it is nevertheless an owner of property in eleven [1] counties. A college, therefore, can hardly have been fortunate enough to escape by the lucky accident of the peculiar situation of its property the effects of agricultural depression; and yet it may well have suffered more seriously in some districts and some classes of its property than in others, and its estates may be regarded as tolerably representative of the general results of the changing conditions of agriculture in the country as a whole. The particular college with which we are now to deal may be considered as typical on another ground also; for, in respect of the revenue derived from its corporate property, and of the acreage of its estates, it may be said to occupy a position intermediate between the richest and the poorest colleges in the University of Oxford.

Perhaps, however, the chief reason for hoping that the information contained in this paper may not be destitute of value is that the accounts on which it is based have been, with minor exceptions, kept according to an uniform system, and the estates to which they relate have undergone few changes during the period which it is proposed to bring under review. The accounts of the Oxford colleges have, like those of the colleges at Cambridge, been published year by year for some little time, and they contain important and interesting material for the statistical student. But they necessarily relate to totals rather than to the items of which those totals are composed, and there is reason for believing that the different colleges follow different methods of classification and arrangement in arriving at the totals presented under the various headings of the published accounts. Although, therefore, the comparison between the accounts of the same college in different years may be made with some confidence, the comparison of the accounts of one college with those of another, and the addition of the totals of the various items, as they appear under the same head in the accounts of different colleges, so as to form a grand total, may be vitiated by a difference in the methods of arriving at those totals which have been adopted by different colleges. Examples might be furnished in illustration, but I will now content myself with entering a caution against any indiscriminate use of the ~es given in these published accounts. The accounts, on the hand, of a single college, which will be taken as the basis of

IX. ne of these counties it is only an owner of tithe, and in another it minal rent from the small piece of land in its possession.

the present paper, are free from such a defect. They have been kept in accordance with an uniform system, and they relate to estates which, with few exceptions, have remained unaltered during the period under review. They afford the means of discovering the way in which the totals given in the published accounts are made up; and, while they furnish information which has not hitherto been generally published, it may, I hope, without any breach of confidence, be submitted to the Royal Statistical Society in the particular shape in which it will be presented in this paper.

II.—*The Period of Time selected for Investigation.*

The period of time, which it will be convenient to bring under review, will embrace the fifteen years extending from 1876 to 1890. This period will, I think, adequately comprise the duration of the agricultural depression. It will include the effects, at any rate, of its commencement, and it may fairly be hoped that its termination will not be found to have been excluded. The well-known agricultural writer, Mr. W. E. Bear, writing in 1888 on "The British "Farmer and his Competitors," stated that the country had then "been suffering from agricultural depression in its acute stage for "fully nine years." "For some time before 1879," he added, "there were complaints of the unremunerativeness of farming; "but in that year veritable disaster was experienced, and although "the failure of crops has never been quite as complete since, lean "harvests have been more common than fat ones, and prices have "been generally falling." The statistics employed by him in the course of his little book commenced in many cases with the year 1877; and, by selecting 1876 as our *terminus à quo*, we may reasonably be confident, in the case of the estates with which we are dealing, that we have gone back sufficiently far to discover the state of affairs prior to the changes caused by the depression. If anything, until 1878 the rental of the college had tended slightly in an upward direction as compared with 1874, which may perhaps be regarded as the true beginning of the series of bad seasons and of losses in farming, and the arrears had decreased in amount; and, by commencing with the year 1876, we avoid the disturbing effects of some changes in the acreage and the conditions of tenure of some of the land which we shall have to consider.

For similar reasons the year 1890 may be taken as the *terminus ad quem*. It is the last year for which the college accounts are as yet completed; and it is generally agreed in agricultural circles that farmers were then beginning to entertain, and not without reason, more decidedly cheerful views of their future prospects. The "Statist" newspaper, indeed, as far back as 1887, in its review of the year 1886, noticed a "recovery" in the price of wheat, and remarked that this recovery showed that "at last, "after many years of depression, the usual circumstances which "bring about improvement in such cases are beginning to be "present." But the review of the following year was unfavourable in tone. The average price of wheat had fallen to nearly 28s. a quarter, and a lower quotation than any recorded in the present century before this year had been reached; and the agricultural industry was, the newspaper stated, "still in a very "deplorable state." By 1889, however, signs of improvement were more decidedly manifest, and the improvement has since continued. The "Economist," reviewing the trading and commercial history of 1889, declared that there was sufficient evidence to "indicate that our farmers, as a whole, fared better in 1889 "than they had done for many years before." And of 1890 the same newspaper remarked that "one satisfactory feature of the "year's business" was that "our farmers fared better than they "had done for many years." "It is significant," it added, "of "an improved state of things that the demand for farms was "better last year than it had been for a long time before." The accounts, which we are about to examine, tend to confirm this encouraging view, and show that it is not too sanguine a supposition to believe that the agricultural industry of the country has certainly reached, if it has not passed, the lowest point of depression; that landlords and farmers have adjusted themselves to the altered conditions; and that, if a decided recovery from the fall of prices is an unreasonable expectation, a further fall is now, at any rate, improbable. Let us then proceed to consider the course of the depression as shown in the accounts between 1876 and 1890 of the college of which I have had the honour for the last few years to be treasurer. And first the situation, extent, and character of tenure of the various estates should be briefly indicated.

III.—*Description of the College Estates.*

The total acreage of the landed estates belonging to Oriel College, Oxford, on 1st January, 1872, was thus stated in the report of the Universities Commission (1874):—

	A.	R.	P.
A. Corporate property :—			
(1.) Lands let on beneficial lease .... =	943	3	14
(2.) „ at rack rent .... =	5,049	3	38[2]
(3.) Copyholds for lives .... =	34	—	2
B. Trust property :—			
Lands let at rack rent .... =	157	3	18
Total acreage .... =	6,185	2	32

---

[2] By an error of arithmetic reckoned by the Commissioners as 5,050a. 2r. 33p.

This return was defective in consequence of some clerical errors and some omissions, and the quantities differed in the case of several of the separate estates from those which were subsequently ascertained by more accurate surveys.   The return, as amended in 1881 by the insertion of the omissions and the substitution of the corrected quantities, showed the acreage of the estates at the time of the Commission to be as follows :—

		A.	R.	P.
A. (1.) Lands let on beneficial lease	=	956	1	13
(2.) „ at rack rent	=	5,142	3	25
(8.) Copyholds for lives	=	34	3	10
B. Lands let at rack rent	=	158	1	8
Total acreage	=	6,292	1	16

In 1874 the college sold part of one of its estates, and in the early months of 1876 it disposed entirely of another, while it added in the former year to a third by the purchase of some 100 acres. At the beginning, therefore, of the period under review in this paper the total acreage would stand nearly as follows :—

		A.	R.	P.	*	A.	R.	P.
Acreage in 1872	=	6,292	1	16		220	1	28
Deduct sold* since 1872	=	324	–	3		103	2	15
		5,968	1	13		324	–	3
Add bought since 1872	=	99	3	28				
Total acreage in 1876	=	6,068	1	1				

Between 1876 and 1890 some further changes occurred.   The college sold portions of two estates, and it added by purchase to three.   It also acquired for its full corporate use an additional small estate; and, if these changes alone are taken into account, the total acreage in 1890 would stand as under :—

A.	R.	P.			A.	R.	P.		A.	R.	P.
A 13	3	39	Acreage in 1876-77	=	6,068	1	1	B	48	1	24
5	3	36	Deduct sold (A) since 1876-77	=	20	2	3		11	–	22
–	1	28							–	1	32
–	–	20			6,047	2	38		4	2	14
20	2	3	Add bought (B) since 1876-77	=	64	2	12		64	2	12
			Total acreage in 1890	=	6,112	1	10				

But in the interval between 1876 and 1890 additional exactitude in the measurement of the quantities contained in the various estates was secured, in a large degree in consequence of the publication of the sheets of the Ordnance Survey, and the total acreage of the college estates in 1890 seems to be really 6,142 a. 1 r. 5 p. This total is shown in the following table (Table I), where the distribution of the acreage among the various estates is exhibited, together with the counties in which they are respectively situated, their corrected acreage in 1872 (at the time of the Universities Commission), their acreage in 1876-77, in 1881 (a date when many of the fresh surveys of the estates made about this time had been completed), and lastly in 1890. The table is followed by another (Table II) showing the rental of the college lands for successive years, according to estates, from 1876-77 to 1890. The different estates are in each case indicated by numbers :—

TABLE I.

Num-ber.	County.	Corrected Acreage, 1872.			Acreage, 1876-77.			Acreage, 1881.			Acreage, 1890.			Remarks
		A.	R.	P.	A.	R.	P.	A.	R.	P.	A.	R.	P.	
A 1	Yorkshire...	14	3	33	14	3	33	14	3	33	14	3	33	
2	Oxon	13	3	25	13	3	25	13	3	25	15	1	35*	
3	„	181	2	25	181	2	25	181	2	25	188	3	32*	
4	Lincolnshire	9	–	5	9	–	5	9	–	5	8	2	37*	
5	Oxon	1,555	3	4	1,335	1	16	1,335	1	16	1,346	1	9*	220a. 1r. 28p. sold in 187
6	„	—			—			—			4	2	14	Came into hand in 1883
6 A	„	103	2	15	—			—			—			Sold in 1876
7	Berks	2,630	2	24	2,630	2	24	2,630	2	24	2,641	3	10	11a. 22p. bought in 1887
8	Northants...	—			—			—			—			Quantity not known, but s
9	Wilts	1	2	–	1	2	–	1	2	–	1	2	–	Garden let to rector
10	Bucks	24	2	8	24	2	8	24	2	8	24	2	8	Woodland
11	Oxon	702	–	32	802	–	20	850	2	4	867	1	32*	99a. 3r. 28p. bought in 1 / 48a. 1r. 24p. „
12	„	181	2	5	181	2	5	181	2	5	180	2	33*	
13	„	118	1	13	118	1	13	118	1	13	119	1	25*	
14	Somerset	589	–	1	589	–	1	575	–	2	568	2	17*	13a. 3r. 39p. sold in 1878
15	„	7	1	18	7	1	18	1	1	22	–	3	14	5a. 3r. 36p. „ '78 / 1r. 28p. „ '84 / 20p. „ '87
	Total	6,184	–	8	5,909	3	33	5,938	1	22	5,983	3	19	
B 16	Kent...........	158	1	8	158	1	8	158	1	8	158	1	26	Trust property
	Total	6,292	1	16	6,068	1	1	6,096	2	30	6,142	1	5	

TABLE II.

	1876-77. Year to Lady Day.			1877-78.			1878-79.			1879-80.			1880-81.			1881. Second Half Year.			1882. Year to Michaelmas.		
	£	s.	d.	£	s.	d.	£	s.	d.	£	s.	d.	£	s.	d.	£	s.	d.	£	s.	d.
1	50	–	–ᵇ	50	–	–ᵇ	50	–	–ᵇ	50	–	–ᵇ	50	–	–ᵇ				50	–	–
2	40	1	–	60	1	–	60	1	–	60	1	–	40	1	–	30	–	6	60	1	–
3	220	–	–	220	–	–	223	15	–	213	15	–	200	–	–	100	–	–	200	–	–
4ᵈ																					
5	1,772	19	8	1,768	16	8	1,770	15	2	1,620	15	2	1,604	15	2	783	–	2	1,501	15	2
6ᵉ																					
7▲	3,160	1	6	3,161	–	–	3,159	7	–	2,755	18	–	2,553	15	–	1,102	10	–	2,347	13	–
7▣	407	7	6	421	15	5	398	19	5	408	1	11	397	8	11	199	3	3	384	17	5
7c	750	–	–	750	–	–	750	–	–	675	–	–	600	–	–	300	–	–	500	–	–
8	2	13	6	2	13	6	2	13	6	2	13	6	2	13	6	2	13	6	2	13	6
9ʳ	12	–	–	12	–	–	12	–	–	12	–	–	12	–	–				12	–	–
10ʰ	8	2	10	2	–	–	2	10	–	2	10	–	2	10	–				2	10	–
11	1,639	2	10	1,773	8	10	1,775	8	4	1,651	11	4	1,617	10	10	787	2	10	1,556	1	10
12	303	8	–	303	8	–	303	8	–	303	8	–	303	8	–	151	14	–	303	8	–
13ⁱ	270	–	–	270	–	–	270	–	–	270	–	–	270	–	–	135	–	–	270	–	–
14	1,590	13	6	1,554	16	–	1,591	1	–	1,562	11	–	1,540	13	6	749	6	9	1,513	18	6
15	102	15	3	116	7	3	93	2	4	93	2	4	94	2	4	45	18	6	95	2	4
Total	10,279	5	6	10,466	6	8	10,462	15	9	9,681	7	3	9,307	18	3	4,386	9	6	8,800	–	9
16	193	–	–	193	–	–	193	–	–	193	–	–	179	–	–	82	10	–	165	–	–
Total	10,472	5	6	10,659	6	8	10,655	15	9	9,874	7	3	9,486	18	3	4,468	19	6	8,965	–	9

	1883.			1884.			1885.			1886.			1887.			1888.			1889.			1890.		
	£	s.	d.	£	s.	d.	£	s.	d.	£	s.	d.	£	s.	d.	£	s.	d.	£	s.	d.	£	s.	d.
1	100	–	–ᶜ	50	–	–	50	–	–	42	9	–ᵇ	63	–	–	62	–	–	62	–	–	62	–	–
2	60	1	–	60	1	–	60	1	–	60	1	–	60	1	–	60	1	–	60	1	–	60	1	–
3	200	–	–	200	–	–	200	–	–	192	10	–	180	–	–	180	–	–	180	–	–	180	–	–
4ᵈ																								
5	1,515	12	8	1,425	12	8	1,293	2	8	1,295	12	8	1,232	19	8	1,115	19	8	1,083	19	8	1,033	19	8
6ᵉ	13	–	–	13	–	–	13	–	–	13	–	–	13	–	–	13	–	–	13	–	–	13	–	–
7▲	2,346	7	6	2,307	7	6	2,207	3	–	2,115	9	–	1,889	3	4	1,885	14	–	1,821	19	4	1,830	9	4
7▣	383	5	5	366	9	5	355	8	5	353	14	11	353	16	5	355	8	5	351	8	5	350	12	5
7c	500	–	–	500	–	–	510	–	–	{ 510	–	–ᶠ	510	–	–	510	–	–	510	–	–	510	–	–
										41	12	0ᶠ	25	9	8	24	13	5	24	13	5	24	13	5
8	2	13	6	2	13	6	2	13	6	2	13	6	2	13	6	2	13	6	2	13	6	2	13	6
9ʳ	12	–	–	12	–	–	12	–	–	12	–	–	12	–	–	12	–	–	12	–	–	12	–	–
10ʰ	2	10	–	2	10	–	2	10	–	2	10	–	2	10	–	2	10	–	2	10	–	2	10	–
11	1,554	2	10	1,521	8	10	1,479	8	10	1,456	8	10	1,424	13	10	1,299	19	1	1,261	11	10	1,251	1	10
12	303	8	–	303	8	–	245	–	–	245	–	–	245	–	–	245	–	–	245	–	–	245	–	–
13ⁱ	270	–	–	270	–	–	270	–	–	270	–	–ᵈ	270	–	–	175	10	–	175	10	–	175	10	–
14	1,490	13	6	1,534	14	2	1,618	3	6	1,770	15	6	1,646	8	–	1,647	18	–	1,647	18	–	1,648	18	–
15	97	6	8	142	15	4	125	13	4	94	10	3	118	–	7	93	19	2	92	13	8	97	3	–
Total	8,851	1	1	8,712	–	5	8,444	4	3	8,478	7	5	8,047	16	–	7,686	6	3	7,536	17	10	7,499	12	2
16	165	–	–	165	–	–	165	–	–	160	–	–	160	–	–	145	–	–	130	–	–	130	–	–
Total	9,016	1	1	8,877	–	5	8,609	4	3	8,638	7	5	8,207	16	–	7,831	6	3	7,666	17	10	7,629	12	2

ᵃ In 1886 the year of account was changed from Michaelmas to Midsummer.
ᵇ Year reckoned to Michaelmas.   ᶜ Two years' rent.
ᵈ Let with tithe for 1s. a year to vicar.   ᵉ Let to the provost at a quit rent of 6l. until 1883.
ᶠ Additional land purchased.   ᵍ Year to Lady Day.
ʰ Right of shooting let for this rent, which runs to Lady Day.   ⁱ Let on lease until 1888.

IV.—*General Result of the Depression.*

The first of these tables shows, as will be seen, an increase in the acreage of the college estates from 6,068 a. 1 r. 1 p. in 1876-77 to 6,142 a. 1 r. 5 p. in 1890, while the second table exhibits a diminution in rental from 10,472l. 5s. 6d. to 7,629l. 12s. 2d. during the same period. The broad result, therefore, of the agricultural depression has been a fall of 27 per cent. in the rental, with an increase in the acreage. But the full effects of the depression can only be accurately gauged by a more detailed examination of the separate estates; and, before this detailed examination is made, it will be instructive to compare the division of the acreage according to the nature of the tenure at the two periods :—

TABLE III.

	1876-77.			1890.		
	A.	R.	P.	A.	R.	P.
Lands let at rack rent	5,402	–	32	5,500	–	26
„ on beneficial lease....................	506	–	29	418	1	7
„ in augmentation of benefices	46	3	12	31	–	30
Copyholds	15	5	38	14	2	28
Woodland	57	–	1	104	1	6
Cottages and allotments	89	2	9	73	2	28
Total acreage .... =	6,068	1	1	6,142	1	5

The same classification is applied to the different estates in the following tables :—

TABLE IV.—1876-77.

Number.	Lands Let at Rack Rent.			Lands Let on Beneficial Leases.			Let to Augment Benefices.			Copyholds.			Woodlands.			Cottages and Allotments			Total.		
	A.	R.	P.	A.	R.	P.	A.	R.	P.	A.	R.	P.	A.	R.	P.	A.	R.	P.	A.	R.	P.
1	—			—			14	3	33	—			—			—			14	3	33
2	13.3		25	—			—			—			—			—			13	3	25
3	181	2	25	—			—			—			—			—			181	2	25
4	—			—			9	–	5	—			—			—			9	–	5
5	1,29	1	8	—			—			15	–	18	20	2	39	1	–	36	1,335	1	16
7	2,18	2	1	387	2	37	—			—			33	1	22	26	–	4	2,630	2	24
9	8	2	–	—			—			—			—			—			1	2	–
10	—			24	2	8	—			—			—			—			24	2	8
11	789	3	8	—			—			–	2	17	· —			11	2	35	802	–	20
12	181	2	5	—			—			—			—			—			181	2	5
13	118	1	13	—			—			—			—			—			118	1	13
14	469	1	23	93	3	24	22	3	14	—			2	3	–	–	–	20	589	–	1
15	5	3	36	—			—			–	3	8	—			–	2	14	7	1	18
Total...	5,243	3	24	506	–	29	46	3	12	16	1	38	56	3	21	89	2	29	5,909	3	33
16	158	1	8	—			—			—			—			—			158	1	8
Total...	5,402	–	32	506	–	29	46	3	12	16	1	38	56	3	21	89	2	29	6,068	1	1

TABLE V.—1890.

Number.	Lands Let at Rack Rent.	Lands Let on Beneficial Leases.	Let to Augment Benefices.	Copyholds.	Woodlands.	Cottages and Allotments.	Total.
	A. R. P.	A. R. P.	A. R. P.	A. R. P.	A. R. P.	A. R. P.	A. R. P.
1	14 3 33	—	—	—	—	—	14 3 33
2	15 1 35	—	—	—	—	—	15 1 35
3	188 3 32	—	—	—	—	—	188 3 32
4	—	—	8 2 37	—	—	—	8 2 37
5	1,302 1 39	—	—	18 3 11	25 - 14	4 3.25	1,346 1 9
6	4 2 14	—	—	—	—	—	4 2 14
7	2,184 2 15	387 2 37	—	— *	33 2 12	35 3 26	2,641 3 10
9	1 2 -	—	—	—	—	—	1 2 -
10	—	—	—	—	24 2 8	—	24 2 8
11	834 2 12	—	—	- 2 17	—	32 1 8	867 1 32
12	180 2 33	—	—	—	—	—	180 2 33
13	119 1 25	—	—	—	—	—	119 1 25
14	494 2 2	30 2 10	22 1 33	—	21 - 12	—	568 2 17
15	—	—	—	- 1 -	—	- 2 14	- 3 14
Total..	5,341 3 -	418 1 7	31 - 30	14 2 28	104 1 6	73 2 28	5,983 3 19
16	158 1 26	—	—	—	—	—	158 1 26
Total..	5,500 - 26	418 1 7	31 - 30	14 2 28	104 1 6	73 2 28	6,142 1 5

* Quantity not known, but probably very small.

From these tables it is evident that the amount of land let at rack rent has increased, and that let under beneficial leases and in augmentation of benefices has diminished; and such a change would, in the natural sequence of events, have been followed by an increase in the rental; for the annual reserved rent, as it is called, under the system of beneficial leases represents a lower sum than the rack rent, and a fine is paid on the renewal of the lease expressly as a premium for the enjoyment of the tenure at a rental which is comparatively low, and land let with the avowed intention of augmenting the value of a living is not likely to be let at a rack rent. Both these points are, in fact, illustrated by Table II. The estate numbered 1 in that table forms the rectorial glebe of the parish in which it is situated. It consists of some cottages and some farm buildings, and until 1886 was let by the college as rectors to the vicar of the parish at a rental of 50l. per annum. On his decease, and the presentation of a new vicar, the college took this glebe into its own hands, and the present rental is 62l. The estate, again, numbered 14 is situated near Bath, and consists partly of one large farm, partly of two small farms and a number of market gardens and cottages, and partly of residential houses. The rental of the estate increased by more than 100l. between 1876 and 1890, although the acreage diminished by a sale in 1878; but the explanation is though extent to be found in the fact that some of the property, which was formerly let under beneficial lease, is now let at rack rent.

V.—*The Beneficial Leasehold System.*

In this connection a curious example of the manner in which a prophecy may seem to be proved false by the subsequent course of events, but may have been in reality justified, may be discovered by referring to the anticipations formed at the time of the Universities Commission of 1872. A return of the property of the college was made on 1st January, 1872, and the annual income accruing from the college estates was thus stated :—

		£	s.	d.
A. Corporate property—				
From lands let on beneficial leases	=	1,164	10	6
„ at rack rent	=	8,255	14	9
From copyholds for lives...........................	=	5	15	—
		9,426	—	3
B. Trust property—				
From lands let at rack rent	=	178	8	—
Total...............................	=	9,604	8	3

This total did not include a sum of 50*l.* derived from the property numbered 1 in the tables previously given, or a sum of 12*l.* arising from the property numbered 9; and the addition of these two sums would increase the total to 9,666*l.* 8*s.* 3*d.* It was stated also in the return that deductions had been made for " fixed " charges paid by the college," though not for " repairs, insurance, " collection, or income tax." An estimate was then attempted of the " prospective increase of income," and such an increase was considered to be probable in the case of the estates let on beneficial leases, and, to a small extent, also with regard to the copyholds for lives. " Assuming," the return stated, " that none of the beneficial " leases are renewed, the estimated increase of income derivable " from the falling in of these leases, and the increase of the reserved " rents will be :—

		£	s.	d.
On or before the 31st December, 1875, about.......................		35	12	—
During the five years ending 31st December, 1880, about....		474	15	—
„	'85, „	306	15	—
	'90, „	—	—	—
„	'95, „	694	—	—

" These several sums are cumulative."[3]

---

[3] The return also stated that the 5,019 acres of corporate property, which were ⁞ rack rent, were let at an average rent of 1*l.* 12*s.* 10*d.* an acre. The fixed ᶠor which deduction was made, included land tax, tithe, and quit rents.

The Commissioners themselves in their report described the
character of the tenure under beneficial leases in the following
terms : " Its distinctive feature," they stated, " is this, that only a
" small part, in most cases only a nominal part, of the annual value
" of the property leased is represented in the form of yearly rent, the
" remainder being paid for by the lessee in the way of fine, forfeit,
" or premium, and that at fixed periods *in anticipation* of the term
" in respect of which this peculiar payment is made.   As the
" colleges," they proceeded, were " restrained " by statute or Act of
Parliament from granting leases for more than a limited period,
it was the practice to extend the term to its full duration at
periodical intervals in consideration of a fine.   This system the
Commissioners described as " evidently detrimental to the pecu-
" niary interest of the colleges," and declared that its result was that
the "yearly income of the college" was "uncertain and pre-
" carious ; and that at all times a large part of the fee-simple
" value of the estate under beneficial lease " was " the property of
" the lessee and must virtually be bought back before the college "
could " enjoy the full annual value."   At the time when they
reported, the " quantity of land let on beneficial leases " was
" large;" but " much progress," they stated, had " been made
" during recent years towards a better method of leasing, either
" by increasing the yearly reserved rent, or by running out the
" leases, and letting the property at rack rent."   As the result of
that process they estimated that the prospective increase in the
income of the university and colleges of Oxford (exclusive of one
college for which the necessary materials for calculation were not
furnished) would be :—

		£	s.	d.
For the five years ending 1875	....	11,088	13	5
„	'80	....	21,921	2	3
	'85	....	39,868	7	2
„	'90	....	25,963	2	1

But the fulfilment of this larger prophecy may perhaps be inferred from the manner in which the anticipations made with
reference to a single college have since been realised.   By 1890,
according to the calculations given above, the income derived from
the landed estates of this college should, on the assumption that
the beneficial leases were not renewed, have increased by 817*l.* 2*s.*,
and by 1895 by 1,511*l.* 2*s.*; and in the year in which the calculation was made (1872) the net annual rack rent value of the
lands let on beneficial leases was estimated at about 2,513*l.*, as compared with an actual revenue of 1,164*l.* 10*s.* 6*d.*, or a difference of
1,348*l.* odd.   Since 1872 the acreage of the lands let on beneficial
leases has diminished from 956a. 1r. 13p. to 418a. 1r. 7p., although

in the case of one estate (numbered 7ʙ in Table II) the lease is
still renewed, and, in the case of other holdings comprised in the
estate numbered 14, some of the leases were renewed in 1878, and
are now running out. But the fall in the rental of the lands let
on rack rent occasioned by the agricultural depression has been so
great as to neutralise the effects of the termination of the beneficial
leases; and the rental of the college, which was estimated at
9,604*l*. 8*s*. 3*d*. (or, more accurately, 9,666*l*. 8*s*. 3*d*.) in 1872, after
rising to 10,472*l*. 5*s*. 6*d*. in 1876-77, in spite of a decrease of
acreage, fell to 7,629*l*. 12*s*. 2*d*. in 1890, or 2,000*l*. below the figures
of 1872, and nearly 3,000*l*. below those of 1876-77, while the
acreage exhibited a small increase as compared with that of
1876-77, and no large decrease as compared with that of 1872.
The rental derived from lands let on beneficial leases in 1890 may
be eliminated in the following manner :—

	£	s.	d.
No. 7ʙ............................. =	350	12	5
Pt. of No. 14 .... =	112	17	–
Total .... =	463	9	5

And the income derived from copyholds existing in the same year
would be—

	£	s.	d.
Pt. of No. 5 .... =	1	18	8
„ 7 .... =	–	5	–
„ 11 .... =	–	10	10
Total .... =	2	14	6

These two sums amount to 466*l*. 3*s*. 11*d*., leaving a sum of
7,163*l*. 8*s*. 3*d*. for lands let at rack rent (including cottages and
allotments), as against 8,255*l*. 14*s*. 9*d*., or, more accurately,
8,317*l*. 14*s*. 9*d*. in 1872.

VI.—*Detailed History of some Individual Holdings.*

This change in the character of the tenure of some of the
college property must be taken into account before the full
measure of the agricultural depression can be determined; and
perhaps that measure is more evidently shown by an investigation
of the circumstances of the separate estates. That numbered 1 in
the tables has been already described. No. 2 is a small farm in
the neighbourhood of Oxford, the rent of which has remained unaltered since Lady Day, 1852, with the exception that the college
has recently so far modified the conditions of tenure as to undertake to pay half, instead of, as formerly, the whole, of the rates.
No. 4 consists of the rectorial glebe of a parish in Lincolnshire,

which is let to the vicar at a nominal rent of a shilling a year. No. 6 is a field near Oxford, let to the tenant of No. 2. It was formerly let to the Provost of the college at a quit rent, and he sub-let it at a rent of 17*l.* until Michaelmas, 1882, when it passed into the hands of the college. No. 8 is a small parcel of land let to the vicar of a college living in Northamptonshire, and No. 9 is another piece let to the rector of another living, situated in Wilt-shire. Under No. 10 the sum paid for the right of shooting in a wood is given, and No. 15 consists of a few cottages near Bath. Nos. 5, 7, 11, and 14 are the four estates of considerable size which are in the possession of the college, and to these special attention must be given. But Nos. 3, 12, 13, and 16 are, like Nos. 5, 7, and 11, purely agricultural estates, and therefore serve also to illustrate the nature and effects of the depression. Nos. 3, 12, and 13 are situated at no great distance from Oxford itself, and No. 16 is a property in Kent, the revenues of which belong entirely to a trust administered by the college.

The land comprised in No. 3 was described by the college agent in a report made in 1861 as "varying a good deal" in "quality." "A great portion of the arable," he stated, consists of a "heavy loam," and is "wet" and "rather expensive of culti-"vation, but productive of pretty good crops;" and part of it is "lighter and more friable, and is useful corn and stock land." The grass portion of the farm is "naturally of good quality" in part, but "is liable to floods." Especially was this the case with some sixteen acres, which the agent described as "very rough "pasturage," and not of much "value." The present acreage of the holding amounts to 188a. 3r. 32p., as compared with 181a. 2r. 25p. in 1876; but this difference is chiefly due to the more exact measurements of the Ordnance Survey, although a small purchase of a cottage and land, amounting to 1r. 32p., was made in the intervening period. At the time of the survey the arable portion of the farm amounted to 109 acres, and the pasture to 78 acres. The rent was 220*l.* in 1876-77, and in 1890 it had fallen to 180*l.* In 1874 it had been 190*l.*, and had been raised to 220*l.* in order to afford interest at 4 per cent. on an outlay of 750*l.* in improvements. The present tenant came into possession just before the disastrous year of 1879, and on his entrance the rent was raised from 220*l.* to 227*l.* 10*s.*; but the higher rent was only paid for two half-years, and in January, 1880, it was agreed to make an abatement of 27*l.* 10*s.* from the rent for three years from Michaelmas, 1879. In this, as in many other cases, a temporary abatement passed into a permanent reduction, and, in spite of the purchase of the cottage which was mentioned above as an addition to the farm in 1886, the rent was again reduced to 180*l.* There is a heavy tithe on the land commuted at 62*l.* 17*s.* 3*d.*, and this has been hitherto paid by the tenant.

The estate numbered 12 on the tables is, like the one last mentioned, in part only the possession of the college, and in part its revenues belong to a trust which the college administers. It also consists of land which is partly liable to floods at times. Its acreage has remained unaltered since 1876-77, and the apparent difference in quantity is entirely due to the greater accuracy of the Ordnance Survey. The arable and the pasture are almost exactly equal, the former being 87 and the latter 88 acres. The college agent described the farm in 1886 as a "very useful and desirable "holding, with a comfortable house and homestead," and land of "useful quality." Before the agricultural depression it was let at a rent of 303*l.* 8*s.*, the acreage being 180a. 2r. 33p., and the tenant paying the tithe, which was commuted at 27*l.* 7*s.* Owing to the desirable character of the farm, no reduction was made in the rent until 1884, when it was lowered to 245*l.*, the tenant still continuing to pay the tithe. He, like the tenant in the previous case, commenced his tenancy immediately prior to 1879, and by Lady Day, 1881, his arrears amounted to 75*l.* 17*s.* These arrears continued without increase or diminution until 1884, when a remission was made by which they were extinguished, and the rent was lowered. But by 1886 arrears again made their appearance in the rent account, amounting to 50*l.* at the end of that year, and the college then undertook to pay the tithe. The arrears, however, continued to increase until, by the end of 1888, they amounted to half a year's rent, but for the following two years they have remained stationary.

The third of the four individual holdings, which we are now considering, consists of 119a. 1r. 25p., of which 95 acres are arable and 20 acres pasture, but some 10 acres of the farm are absorbed in wood and waste. In 1858 the land was described as "principally "a light sandy loam, and not generally productive of heavy crops; "but its nearness to Oxford," the report of the college agent went on to state, "renders it a desirable occupation and consequently "valuable." The gross annual value was estimated at that time at 210*l.*, but since then the college has effected considerable improvements at the homestead, and has built a new house. The farm was let on a lease for twelve years from Michaelmas, 1876, at a rent of 270*l.*, and, together with another farm which is still held on a lease near Bath, it formed an exception to the practice, nearly universal in the case of the college farms, of yearly tenancies. But the lease, though nominally in existence for twelve years, became practically inoperative before its termination, and the pressure of adverse times was too powerful to be resisted by any legal covenant. The present rent is nearly 100*l.* below that which was fixed in 1876, and land let at 2*l.* 6*s.* an acre fifteen years ago is now let at less than 1*l.* 10*s.*, being a reduction of some 35 per cent. But the reduction has in reality been effected by more gradual stages. Before 1879 had passed an abatement of 27*l.*, or 10 per cent., had been made. In 1880-81 arrears of 57*l.* 16*s.* 7*d.* had arisen, and, in spite of a remission of 27*l.* again in 1881, and yet again in 1882, had only diminished to 50*l.* at the end of the latter year. In 1883 25*l.* were remitted, and the arrears decreased to that extent. In 1884 50*l.* were remitted and the arrears extinguished. In 1885 an abatement of 60*l.* was made; in 1886 and 1887, of 70*l.*; and in 1888, six months before the expiration of the lease, the rent was reduced to 175*l.* 10*s.*

The estate numbered 16 is situated in Kent. At the beginning of the period under review it yielded a rent of 193*l.*, and the tenant paid the tithe; at the end it yielded a rent of 130*l.*, and the college paid the tithe, and scot, amounting to 37*l.* 12*s.* at the commuted figures. The reduction in this case on a farm of smaller acreage than the last has been more than 100*l.*, or some 44 per cent. The farm is situated between five or six miles from an important market town and railway junction, and there is another station nearer to it. But it lies at some distance from the high road, and is approached by a private roadway, which requires for its maintenance considerable outlay from year to year. The soil was described in 1881 by the college surveyor as being throughout " a very strong heavy loamy clay on a pure clay subsoil," and the arable portion, amounting to some 26 acres, was stated to be " very expensive to cultivate, and very uncertain of crops in " wet seasons," but " capable of producing large crops of corn in dry " and favourable years." Some dozen acres were cultivated to hops.

VII.—*Account of Four Large Estates.*

The detailed history of these four detached holdings, which, like most of the college farms, are of a mixed character of cultivation, including arable and pasture, will furnish a representative type of what has occurred elsewhere; and we may now proceed to a more brief and general notice of the circumstances of the four principal estates belonging to the college, and numbered 5, 7, 11, and 14 on the tables. Of these the first three are purely agricultural, and the last, as was stated before, consists partly of farms, partly of market gardens and cottages, and partly of residential houses. It will, however, in this last case, be possible to trace the changes in the rental of the only farm of any size; and in that of the first two estates the acreage has remained unaltered, with a very small exception, for which allowance can easily be made, and even the different holdings have in the latter of these two instances

continued practically unchanged. In the case of No. 11 the estate
has been increased by a purchase in the period between 1876 and
1890, and the holdings have altered. In succeeding tables the
acreage of each holding, and the rent at the beginning and end of
the period under review will be given, and the different holdings
will be distinguished by letters :—

TABLE VI.— (*No.* 5.)

Holding.	Rent, 1876-77.	Rent, 1890.	Acreage, 1876-77.	Acreage, 1890.
	£ *s.*	£	A. R. P.	A. R. P.
A ....{	12 –	} 380	{ 218 1 35	} 631 3 7
B	220 –			
	415 –		408 – 29	
C	617 10	300	403 1 36	452 – 28
D	200 –	90	112 1 6	66 1 36
E	162 –	132	101 3 19	106 – 26
F	69 –	50	45 – 10	43 2 39
Total	1,695 10	952	1,289 1 15	1,300 1 18

The difference in the total acreage of this estate is very small,
and is due to more accurate surveys, and to the fact that some
small copyholds have come into hand; but, in spite of this small
increase, the rental has fallen 743*l.* 10*s.*, and, in the case of the
first two holdings, the college now pays the tithe, commuted at
168*l.* 8*s.* 5*d.*, which was borne by the tenants at the commencement
of the period under review. If this circumstance be taken into
consideration, together with the fact of a remission for two or
three years past of 12*l.* from the rent of the holding lettered E,
the total fall in the rental of this estate will amount to some
50 per cent. The estate is situated in Oxfordshire, and some of
the land is stony and cold.

The next estate, which is the largest possession of the college,
is situated in the valley of the upper Thames, in Berkshire. It
consists of three portions, distinguished in the tables at 7A, 7B, 7C.
7B is let on a beneficial lease, and may be separately considered;
7C has been slightly increased by a purchase, which may be omitted
in order to facilitate comparison; and, in the case of 7A, a small
addition has recently been made to the rent of one of the holdings,
in consideration of the erection of two new cottages, and this
addition may also be left out of account. A belt of heavy clay
extends across the lower portion of 7A, and the college has drained a
part of this land during the depression, and has engaged in large
expenditure on various improvements throughout the estate. The
holdings, although all the tenants with one exception have changed,
have remained practically unaltered, and the comparison between

the rent at the beginning and end of the period can therefore be made with ease.   The college has paid the tithe throughout :—

TABLE VII.—(*No. 7.*)

Estates.	Holdings.	Rent, 1876-77.	Rent, 1890.	Acreage, 1876-77.	Acreage, 1890.
		£ *s.*	£	A. R. P.	A. R. P.
7A	A	649 10	{ 136 165 85	} 422 2 14	{ 213 3 39 152 3 37 57 2 11
	B	619 –	250	377 3 29	386 2 8
	C	628 –	·350	356 1 34	379 1 37
	D	562 –	300	288 – 7	284 1 12
	E	444 –	300	239 1 8	235 3 17
	F	70 –	40	25 1 30	27 3 37
	G	18 –	12	9 – –	9 3 4
		2,990 10	1,638	1,718 3 2	1,748 2 2
7C	H	750 –	510	429 3 21	433 1 23
		3,740 10	2,148	2,148 2 23	2,181 3 25

The fall in rental here for the farms let at rack rent has amounted to 1,592*l.* 10*s.* on a rental of 3,740*l.* 10*s.*, or upwards of 43 per cent.

VIII.—*A Corn Rent.*

The estate numbered 7B, which forms part of the property, but was reserved for separate consideration, is let on a system once very common in the case of college property, but now rapidly becoming extinct.   The holding is a beneficial leasehold, and the reserved rent consists partly of a fixed money payment, and partly of certain quantities of wheat and malt.   The bursars of the various colleges in Oxford meet twice a year, in April and October, at a "Corn Rent dinner," when the "Clerks of the Market" communicate to them the "best" price at which a transaction in wheat, barley, and malt has been effected in the Oxford market on a previous market day.   Adam Smith, in a notable passage,[4] comparing the respective qualifications of money and other commodities as measures of value, remarks that "when a landed " estate " " is sold with a reservation of a perpetual rent, if it is " intended that the rent should always be of the same value, it is " of importance to the family in whose favour it is reserved that " it should not consist in a particular sum of money."   "The rents," he proceeds to state, "which have been reserved in corn have " preserved their value much better than those which have been

[4] " Wealth of Nations," Book I, chap. v.

c 2

" reserved in money, even where the denomination of the coin has
" not been altered. By the 18th of Elizabeth it was enacted,
" that a third of the rent of all college leases should be reserved
" in corn, to be paid either in kind or according to the current
" prices at the nearest public market. The money arising from
" this corn rent, though originally but a third of the whole, is in
" the present times, according to Dr. Blackstone, commonly near
" double of what arises from the other two sources." So wrote
Adam Smith in 1776, and the practice described in his pages still
prevails; and in the case of the particular holding we are now
considering, which consists of a mansion, pleasure grounds, and
farm, with an acreage of 387a. 2r. 37p., part of the rent is thus
determined. A fine is paid on the renewal of the lease, amounting
in 1872 to 735*l.*, in 1879 to 700*l.*, and in 1886 to 600*l.* The
reserved rent consists of a fixed money payment, and "2,048
" gallons of good sweet and well winnowed wheat, and 2,000
" gallons of good sweet and well aired barley malt," "or in lieu of
" the said corn, the just price thereof after the rate or price of the
" best wheat and malt that is or shall be sold in the market of
" Oxford the next market day before the same rent shall become
" due and payable without fraud or deceit." This reserved rent
has remained unaltered since 1876, and the figures in Table II
show that the changes in prices have brought about a fall from
407*l.* 7*s.* 5*d.* in 1876-77, and 421*l.* 15*s.* 5*d.* in 1877-78, to 350*l.* 12*s.* 5*d.*
in 1890, or a decrease of 14 per cent. compared with the rental of
1876-77, or 17 per cent. as compared with that of 1877-78. As
part of the reserved rent consists of a fixed sum of money, this
should be deducted from the total rent in order to ascertain the
true percentage of the fall due to the changes in the corn rent
alone. The figures would then stand for 1876-77 at 182*l.* 19*s.*,
and for 1877-78 at 197*l.* 7*s.*, and for 1890 at 126*l.* 4*s.*, and the fall
would be 30 per cent. on the corn rent of 1876-77, or 36 per cent.
on that of 1877-78. The fall in the average tithe rent charge
during the same period has been from 110*l.* 14*s.* 11*d.* in 1876,
109*l.* 16*s.* 11¼*d.* in 1877, and 112*l.* 7*s.* 5¼*d.* in 1878, to 78*l.* 1*s.* 3½*d.* in
1890, or a fall of 32*l.* 13*s.* 7½*d.* as compared with 1876, 31*l.* 15*s.* 8*d.*
as compared with 1877, and 34*l.* 6*s.* 1¾*d.* as compared with 1878.
The fall in the corn rent, therefore, has been greater; and the
best prices on special days recorded in the Oxford market do not
of course correspond with the average prices ascertained for the
purposes of the Tithe Commutation Acts. But the comparison of
the two sets of prices is given in the following table, together with
the highest price of wheat officially recorded for the year (ending
at Michaelmas), and the average price of wheat for successive
years, as stated in the published returns :—

TABLE VIII.—O = *October*; A = *April*.

Year.	Price of Wheat per Bushel.								Price of Barley.			
	Oxford.		Tithe.		Highest.		Average.		Oxford.		Tithe.	
	s.	*d.*	*s.*	*d.*	*s.*	*d.*	*s.*	*d.*	*s.*	*d.*	*s.*	*d.*
1876 O	6	8¼	5	9¼	6	1¼	5	8½	5	–½	4	4¾
'77 A	7	3	7	1¼	8	7	6	11½	5	7½	4	11½
O	8	6							6	1½		
'78 A	7	8½	5	9½	6	11¾	6	2	5	6	5	–¼
O	6	10½							6	5		
'79 A	5	9	5	5¾	6	2¼	5	2¾	4	6	4	3
O	7	–¾							6	6¾		
'80 A	6	6	5	6½	6	3½	5	8¼	5	–	4	1½
O	6	4½							5	3		
'81 A	6	6	5	8	6	10¾	5	7	4	–¾	3	11¾
O	6	9							4	3		
'82 A	6	10½	5	7½	6	4¾	5	9½	3	6	3	10¾
O	5	6							5	3		
'83 A	6	–	5	2¼	5	5¾	5	2½	4	3	3	11¾
O	6	1½							5	4½		
'84 A	5	–	4	5½	5	2¼	4	8¾	4	3¾	3	10
O	4	6							5	4½		
'85 A	4	7½	4	1¼	4	9	4	1½	4	3	3	9
O	4	1½							5	–		
'86 A	4	3	3	10½	4	1¾	3	10¼	3	9	3	3¾
O	3	9							4	6		
'87 A	4	6	4	–¾	4	6½	4	1¼	3	3	3	2
O	4	–							4	3		
'88 A	4	3	3	11¾	4	9	3	11¼	4	3	3	5¾
O	4	6							4	1½		
'89 A	4	–	3	8½	4	–¼	3	9	3	9	3	2¾
O	4	1½							4	4½		
'90 A	4	–	4	–¼	—		—		4	4½	3	5¾
O	4	–							3	9½		

This table shows that in only five cases has the price of wheat, for the purposes of the corn rent, fallen below the tithe average, and in one case the price of barley has so fallen.. In nearly every instance, as might be expected, the corn rent price has exceeded the average for tithe, and sometimes the excess has been large. In ten cases it has even exceeded the highest recorded price of wheat for the year ending at Michaelmas, although, on the other hand, in seventeen it has fallen below this. In four cases it has fallen below the average price of wheat for the year, and in one instance it has exactly coincided with it.

IX.—*Four Large Estates—Continued.*

And now, returning from this digression, we may tabulate the results of the depression as they have affected the third of the large estates of the college (that numbered 11):—

TABLE IX.—(*No.* 11.)

Holding.	Rent, 1876-77.	Rent, 1890.	Acreage, 1876-77.	Acreage, 1890.
	£ *s.*	£ *s.*	A. R. P.	A. R. P.
A	61 –	—	32 3 1	—
B	525 13	370 –	287 – 28	306 2 12
C	215 –	216 15	119 1 21	145 – 26
D	226 –	140 –	121 3 19	124 – 28
E	198 –	150 –	99 2 3	114 – 37
F	130 –	127 –	58 – 15	83 3 14
G	100 –	80 –	49 2 30	50 3 19
	1,455 13	1,083 15	768 1 37	824 3 16

In this estate, which is situated not far from Banbury, in
Oxfordshire, some changes have taken place besides mere redistri-
bution of the acreage between the different farms. 48 a. 1 r. 24 p.
were added by purchase in 1877, and the rent of the holding
lettered C was increased by 120l. 14 a. 3 r. 36 p., formerly part of
another small holding not included in this table, were added to E
in 1882, and the rent raised in consideration to the amount of 30l.
8 a. 1 r. 16 p. were taken from F in 1886 and added to the ground
let by the college in allotments, and the rent was in consequence
reduced by 13l. In addition to these changes, account must be
taken of the facts that the tenant of B was paying 10l. interest on
arrears at the beginning of the period, and that the tenant of D
has received an abatement of 20l. from his rent for the last three
or four years, and that it is now permanently reduced to 120l. In
order, therefore, to measure the real extent of the depression, the
rental of 1876-77 should be increased by 120l. for the purchase in
1877, and 10l. for the interest on arrears, making thus a new total
of 1,585l. 13s. The rent of E, to which 30l. was added in 1882,
has fallen from 203l. at that date to 150l. in 1890, being a fall of
25 per cent.; and a proportionate deduction should be made from
the 30l., leaving 22l. 10s. to be subtracted from the rental of 1890
in order to eliminate the effects of the change in acreage. The
rent of F has remained unaltered since the decrease of acreage in
1886, and therefore the full sum of 13l. may be added on this
account to the rental of 1890, while 20l. should be deducted from
it on account of the remission made to D. Adding 13l. and sub-
tracting 42l. 10s., the rental of 1890 will appear as 1,054l. 5s., as
compared with 1,585l. 13s. in 1876-77, representing a fall of
531l. 8s., or about 33⅓ per cent.

Lastly, if we take the chief farm, which is in fact the only one
of considerable size, on the estate numbered 14, we find that in
1876-77 the rent was 555l. for 321 a. 20 p. In 1878 22 a. 1 r. 18 p.
were added to the holding, and 4 a. 2 r. 25 p. were taken away,

leaving a total addition of 17a. 2r. 33p; and the total rent was put at 570*l.* The farm was then held on a lease for twelve years, commencing with 1874. It is situated on one of the hilly slopes near Bath, and it was not spared by the disastrous year of 1879. In the year 1879-80 37*l.* were remitted from the rent; in 1881 it was reduced to 500*l.* for a period of three years, and the reduction was continued until the expiration of the lease in 1886, when 21a. 12p. were taken out of the holding. This deduction left a total acreage of some 4 acres less than the farm had contained in 1877-78, and a new lease was concluded for another period of twelve years, at a rent of 380*l.*, being some 175*l.* less than the rent of 1877-78, and representing a reduction of some 32 per cent., or, on a rough calculation for the decrease of acreage, 30 per cent.

X.—*Summary of the Results of the Depression.*

We may now bring together into one table the results, which we have been separately examining, with reference to the rack rent farming tenancies among the college property. This table will show the rent (omitting shillings and pence) at the beginning and the end of the period under review, the percentage of reduction, and the rent per acre:—

TABLE X.

Number.	Rental.		Per-centage of Reduction.	Rent per Acre.			Remarks.
	1876-77.	1890.		1876-77.	1890.		
	£	£		£ s.	£ s.	d.	
3	220	180	17	1 4	- 19	-	Tenant has paid tithe
5	1,880	940	50	1 9	- 14	6	College paid tithe in 1890, but not in 1876-77
7 A C	} 3,740	2,148	42	1 15	1 -	-	College has paid tithe
11	1,585	1,054	33½	1 18	1 6	6	No tithe
12	332	245	25	1 17	1 7	-	College paid tithe in 1890, but not in 1876-77
13	270	175	35	2 6	1 10	-	No tithe
14	555	380	31	1 15	1 4	-	Tenant has paid tithe
16	233	130	44	1 9	- 16	6	College paid tithe in 1890, but not in 1876-77
Total ..	8,815	5,252	40	1 14	1 -	-	

In this table it will be noticed that in two cases the tenant still paid the tithe in 1890, and that in three the college in 1890 discharged this payment, which was borne by the tenant at the beginning of the period. Allowance has been made for the changes caused in the latter class of cases by increasing the rent paid at the beginning of the period by the tithe at the time, calculated according to the official average. But, in order to obtain really similar conditions for all the estates comprised in the table, and to ascertain the true average rent per acre for all the rack rent farms of any size amongst the college property, the tithe calculated according to the average should be added to the rental at both periods in those cases where the tenant bore this charge in 1876-77, and continued to bear it in 1890. The result of this would be to make the fall from 40 to 41 per cent., and the rent per acre a little over 1*l.* in 1890, as compared with 1*l.* 15*s.* in 1876-77. As we have noticed in detail in particular instances, allowance has been made in the table for any changes in the acreage of the different estates, and therefore it is with some confidence that the assertion may be hazarded of a fall in rent of 40 to 41 per cent.

XI.—*Arrears and Abatements.*

But this fall of 40 to 41 per cent. does not represent the full consequences of the depression; for abatements have been made in successive years to meet contingencies which, it was hoped, would prove to be of a temporary nature, and the arrears of rent outstanding at the close of each financial year have undergone considerable fluctuations. In Table XI these arrears will be shown, together with the increase or decrease in their amount at the close of one year compared with that at the close of another; and this will be followed by another table, giving the rental, the abatements, the increase or decrease of arrears, and the resulting receipts from the landed estates of the college year by year. In order to arrive at the figures more easily, the estate numbered 16, the revenues of which do not form part of the corporate revenue of the college, but belong entirely to a trust, has been omitted.

TABLE XI.

	1875-76.	1876-77.	1877-78.	1878-79.	1879-80.	1880-81.
	£ s. d.	£ s. d.	£ s. d.	£ s. d.	£ s. d.	£ s. d.
Arrears at close of year	531 7 –	551 9 1	258 12 2	1,437 3 4	3,004 1 11	2,535 1
Increase (+) or decrease (–)	....	+ 20 2 1	– 292 16 11	+ 1,178 11 2	+ 1,566 18 7	– 469 –

	1881. Second Half.	1882.	1883.	1884.	1885.
	£ s. d.	£ s. d.	£ s. d.	£ s. d.	£ s. d.
Arrears at close of year	3,342 9 1	3,286 8 –	2,532 18 5	2,091 18 6	2,244 9 5
Increase (+) or decrease (–)	+ 807 7 10	– 56 1 1	– 753 9 7	– 440 19 11	+ 152 10 11

	1886.	1887.	1888.	1889.	1890.
	£ s. d.	£ s. d.	£ s. d.	£ s. d.	£ s. d.
Arrears at close of year	3,267 11 –	3,078 12 5	1,375 2 4	1,056 1 8	940 16 2
Increase (+) or decrease (–)	+ 1,023 1 7	– 188 18 7	– 1,703 10 1	– 319 – 8	– 115 5 6

TABLE XII.

	1876-77.			1877-78.			1878-79.			1879-80.			1880-81.		
	£	s.	d.	£	s.	d.	£	s.	d.	£	s.	d.	£	s.	d.
Rental	10,279	5	6	10,466	6	8	10,462	15	9	9,681	7	3	9,307	18	3
Abatements	36	5	–	20	10	–	255	11	–	905	8	6	322	3	–
	10,243	–	6	10,445	16	8	10,207	4	9	8,775	18	9	8,985	15	3
Arrears .... add + deduct — }	– 20	9	1	+ 292	16	11	–1,178	11	2	– 1,566	18	7	+ 469	–	8
	10,222	11	5	10,738	13	7	9,028	13	7	7,209	–	2	9,454	15	11

	1881. Second Half.			1882.			1883.			1884.			1885.		
	£	s.	d.	£	s.	d.	£	s.	d.	£	s.	d.	£	s.	d.
Rental	4,386	9	6	8,800	–	9	8,851	1	1	8,712	–	5	8,444	4	3
Abatements	86	10	–	47	15	–	673	16	–	277	4	11	470	4	1
	4,299	19	6	8,752	5	9	8,177	5	1	8,434	15	6	7,974	–	2
Arrears .... add + deduct — }	–807	7	10	+ 56	1	1	+753	9	7	+440	19	11	–152	10	11
	3,492	11	8	8,808	6	10	8,930	14	8	8,875	15	5	7,821	9	3

	1886.			1887.			1888.			1889.			1890.		
	£	s.	d.	£	s.	d.	£	s.	d.	£	s.	d.	£	s.	d.
Rental	8,478	7	5	8,047	16	–	7,686	6	3	7,536	17	10	7,499	12	2
Abatements	327	5	3	1,548	18	10	411	4	–	108	8	4	44	11	11
	8,151	2	2	6,498	17	2	7,275	2	3	7,428	9	6	7,455	–	3
Arrears .... add + deduct — }	–1,023	1	7	+ 188	18	7	+ 1,703	10	1	+319	–	8	+115	5	6
	7,128	–	7	6,687	15	9	8,978	12	4	7,747	10	2	7,570	5	9

XII.—*The Year* 1879.

The fact, which is brought into greater prominence perhaps than any other in these tables, is the disastrous character of the year 1879. In 1879-80 the rental, which had amounted to 10,466*l.* 6*s.* 8*d.* in 1877-78, and 10,462*l.* 15*s.* 9*d.* in 1878-79, fell to 9,681*l.* 7*s.* 3*d.* This represented a fall of nearly 800*l.*, or some 8 per cent., in a single year, and since that time, with the exception of trifling increases in two years, of which a ready explanation can be found in special circumstances—in the case of the first, partly in the accident of a change in reckoning the year of account of one

estate, and partly in the addition of a new property—in the case of
the second, in the latter cause entirely—the diminution in rental,
though steady and unintermittent, has been, by comparison with
1879-80, gradual and moderate. In that year of 1879 also the
abatements, which in 1877-78 had reached the modest figure of
20*l.* 10*s.*, and had increased in 1878-79 to 255*l.* 11*s.*, rose to
905*l.* 8*s.* 6*d.*—a sum which has only been once approached, and
then it was exceeded, in the subsequent period. On that occasion,
in 1887, the large deduction for abatements was due to the final
settlement of the affairs of an outgoing tenant, whose serious
difficulties had really begun in 1879. In fact an examination of
the rent accounts of many, if not most, of the individual tenants
would yield similar results; and the arrears outstanding at the
close of the year 1879-80, which had diminished to the amount
of 292*l.* 16*s.* 11*d.* in 1877-78, and increased to the extent of
1,178*l.* 11*s.* 2*d.* in 1878-79 (the beginning of the bad year), were
swollen to the extent of 1,566*l.* 18*s.* 7*d.*, and amounted in all to
3,004*l.* 1*s.* 11*d.*, or upwards of a third of the rental. Since then
they have, with the exception of additions in three years, which
are small by comparison with that of 1879-80, tended downwards,
until at the end of 1890 they amounted to 940*l.* 16*s.* 2*d.*, as compared with 531*l.* 7*s.* at the beginning of the period under review,
and 258*l.* 12*s.* 2*d.* in 1877-78. The arrears at the close of 1877-78,
when they had reached the lowest point before 1879, represented a
fortieth of the rental, and in 1890, when they reached the lowest
point after 1879, a little more than an eighth, but in 1879-80 itself
they amounted to almost a third. The total result of the year
1879-80 was to produce receipts from the landed estates of the
college, after deducting abatements, and taking account of the
change in the arrears, which amounted to 7,209*l.* 2*d.*, as compared
with 9,028*l.* 13*s.* 7*d.* in the previous year, and 10,738*l.* 13*s.* 7*d.*
in 1877-78. This represented a fall of 1,800*l.* on the receipts of
1878-79, and 3,500*l.* on those of 1877-78; in other words, of 20 per
cent. on the receipts of the former, and of 34 per cent. on those of
the latter year. In the following year, that of 1880-81, the receipts
increased to 9,454*l.* 15*s.* 11*d.*, a higher figure even than that of
1878-79, although the rental had diminished in comparison with
both 1878-79 and 1879-80; and this increase was due to diminished
arrears and lessened abatements. With oscillations from year to
year, sometimes upwards and sometimes downwards, as compared
with the preceding year, the receipts have fallen, until in 1890
they reached the sum of 7,570*l.* 5*s.* 9*d.*: but even this sum, though
a fall of some 25 per cent. on the receipts of 1876-77, exceeded the
receipts of 1879-80 by some 300*l.* to 400*l.* The calamitous consequences of 1879 could scarcely be more strikingly demonstrated,

and it was evidently no exaggeration to say that in English agriculture " in that year veritable disaster was experienced."

The abatements and arrears exhibited in the foregoing tables are, with scarcely any exception, connected with the agricultural tenancies comprised in the landed estates of the college, and in the following table the abatements will be shown as they relate to those particular estates. This table will be followed by another, in which the arrears outstanding in respect of the several estates at the close of the year will be given, and in two further tables the same process will be applied to the individual holdings of the largest agricultural estate in the possession of the college (that numbered 7 in the previous tables.)

TABLE XIII.

	1876-77.	1877-78.	1878-79.	1879-80.	1880-81.	Second Half of 1881.	1882.	1883.
	£ s.	£ s.	£ s.	£ s. d.	£ s. d.	£ s.	£ s.	£ s. d.
3	—	—	—	—	—	—	—	—
5	—	15 -	60 -	91 4 -	142 2 -	54 10	6 18	75 - -
7	2 -	—	194 2	544 3 -	129 10 -	—	—	496 14 6
11	—	—	—	166 10 -	14 - -	—	9 -	43 - -
12	—	—	—	—	15 8 6	—	—	—
13	—	—	—	27 - -	—	27 -	27 -	25 - -
14	—	—	—	57 - -	—	—	—	—
Total	2 -	15 -	254 2	885 17 -	300 15 6	81·10	42 18	639 14 6
Abatements in Table XII	36 5	20 10	255 11	905 8 6	322 3 -	86 10	47 15	673 16 -

	1884.	1885.	1886.	1887.	1888.	1889.	1890.
	£ s. d.	£ s. d.	£ s. d.	£ s. d.	£ s. d.	£ s. d.	£ s. d.
3	—	—	—	—	—	—	—
5	54 10 -	82 6 9	61 10 -	379 15 -	52 15 -	12 - -	18 8 -
7	41 16 5	104 6 - {	*44 10 3 / 62 10 -	*623 _9 5	} 309 18 4	—	—
11	53 - -	223 11 4	88 - -	418 - -	20 - -	72 12 -	20 - -
12	77 18 6	—	—	—	—	—	—
13	50 - -	60 - -	70 - -	70 - -	—	—	—
14	—	—	—	—	—	—	—
Total	277 4 11	470 4 1	326 10 3	1,491 4 5	382 13 4	84 12 -	38 8 -
Abatements in Table XII	277 4 11	470 4 1	327 5 3	1,548 18 10	411 4 -	108 8 4	44 11 11

* Settlement with outgoing tenant.

TABLE XIV.

	1875-76.	1876-77.	1877-78.	1878-79.	1879-80.	1880-81.
	£ s. d.	£ s. d.	£ s. d.	£ s. d.	£ s. d.	£ s. d.
3	—	—	—	—	—	—
5	—	—	—	531 11 10	794 1 10	369 12 6
7	100 - -	250 - -	100 - -	629 8 -	1,699 12 7	1,465 7 1
11	196 3 6	146 3 6	146 3 6	276 3 6	497 11 6	558 19 1
12	149 3 6	147 18 3	—	—	—	75 17 -
13	—	—	—	—	—	57 16 7
14	—	—	—	—	—	—
Total	445 7 -	544 1 9	246 3 6	1,437 3 4	2,991 5 11	2,527 12 3
Arrears in Table XI	531 7 -	551 9 1	258 12 2	1,437 3 4	3,004 1 11	2,535 1 3

	Second Half of 1881.	1882.	1883.	1884.	1885.
	£ s. d.	£ s. d.	£ s. d.	£ s. d.	£ s. d.
3	—	—	—	—	—
5	446 5 -	665 17 9	575 - -	437 10 -	336 5 -
7	1,780 10 8	1,658 5 9	895 11 -	850 - -	1,142 10 -
11	892 12 7	798 3 9	860 9 11	772 10 11	650 19 9
12	75 17 -	75 17 -	75 17 -	—	—
13	61 8 10	50 - -	25 - -	—	—
14	—	—	—	—	—
Total	3,256 14 1	3,248 4 3	2,431 17 11	2,060 - 11	2,129 14 9
Arrears in Table XI	3,342 9 1	3,286 8 -	2,532 18 5	2,091 18 6	2,244 9 5

	1886.	1887.	1888.	1889.	1890.
	£ s. d.	£ s. d.	£ s. d.	£ s. d.	£ s. d.
3	—	—	—	—	—
5	408 15 -	358 8 9	271 8 -	6 8 -	19 - -
7	1,900 18 -	1,859 18 4	150 - -	240 - -	—
11	871 4 4	692 18 4	801 8 7	674 19 4	784 10 5
12	50 - -	92 10 -	122 10 -	122 10 -	122 10 -
13	—	43 18 1	—	—	—
14	—	—	—	—	—
Total	3,230 17 4	3,047 13 6	1,345 6 7	1,043 17 4	926 - 5
Arrears in Table XI	3,267 11 -	3,078 12 5	1,375 2 4	1,056 1 8	940 16 2

TABLE XV.

	1876-77.	1877-78.	1878-79.	1879-80.	1880-81.	Second Half of 1881.	1882.
	£	£ s. d.	£ s.	£ s.	£ s.	£ s. d.	£ s. d.
A	—	—	65 -	158 15	—	—	—
B	—	—	51 12	145 8	—	—	—
C	—	—	—	44 -	—	—	—
D	—	—	56 -	50 -	75 -	—	—
E	2	—	21 10	100 -	21 10	—	—
F	—	—	—	7 -	15 -	—	—
G	—	—	—	1 10	3 -	—	—
H	—	—	—	37 10	15 -	—	—
Total	2	—	194 2	544 3	129 10	—	—

	1883.	1884.	1885.	1886.	1887.	1888.	1889.	1890.
	£ s. d.	£ s. d.	£ s.	£ s. d.	£ s. d.	£ s. d.	£ s. d.	£ s. d.
A	270 - -	—	83 16	—	—	259 18 4	—	—
B	—	—	—	—	623 9 5	—	—	—
C	—	41 16 5	—	44 10 3	—	50 - -	—	—
D	225 - -	—	17 10	17 10 -	—	—	—	—
E	1 14 6	—	—	45 - -	—	—	—	—
F	—	—	—	—	—	—	—	—
G	—	—	3 -	—	—	—	—	—
H	—	—	—	—	—	—	—	—
Total	496 14 6	41 16 5	104 6	107 - 3	623 9 5	309 18 4	—	—

TABLE XVI.

	1875-76.	1876-77.	1877-78.	1878-79.	1879-80.	1880-81.	Second Half of 1881.	1882.
	£	£	£	£ s.	£ s. d.	£ s. d.	£ s. d.	£ s. d.
A	—	—	—	—	270 - -	270 - -	270 - -	270 - -
	—	150	100	407 18	772 15 6	750 - -	730 - -	885 4 7
	—	—	—	—	56 17 1	27 17 1	63 - 8	85 11 2
	100	—	—	—	300 - -	417 10 -	417 10 -	417 10 -
	—	100	—	221 10	—	—	—	—
	—	—	—	—	—	—	—	—
	—	—	—	—	—	—	—	—
	—	—	—	—	300 - -	—	300 - -	—
Total	100	250	100	629 8	1,699 12 7	1,465 7 1	1,780 10 8	1,658 5 9

	1883.	1884.	1885.	1886.	1887.	1888.	1889.	1890.
	£ s.	£	£ s.	£ s. d.	£ s. d.	£	£	£ s. d.
A	—	—	—	189 1 8	559 18 4	—	—	—
	750 -	850	950 -	1,350 - -	950 - -	—	—	—
	145 11	—	—	200 - -	150 - -	—	—	—
	—	—	192 10	161 16 4	200 - -	150	240	—
	—	—	—	—	—	—	—	—
	—	—	—	—	—	—	—	—
	—	—	—	—	—	—	—	—
	—	—	—	—	—	—	—	—
Total	895 11	850	1,142 10	1,900 18 -	1,859 18 4	150	240	—

These tables show that the loss sustained by the college through abatements and arrears was, with small exceptions, connected with its agricultural tenancies, and they illustrate once more the effects of the year 1879. At the beginning of the period covered by the tables the arrears, amounting to 445*l.* 7*s.* (as compared with a total sum for arrears of 531*l.* 7*s.*, of which 79*l.* concerned an estate afterwards sold) had arisen in connection with three holdings only; and at the end of the period the arrears, which then amounted to 926*l.* 5*d.*, concerned four holdings. In two cases these farms were identical with those of which the rent was in arrear at the beginning of the period, and, of the total sum of 926*l.* 5*d.*, 784*l.* 10*s.* 5*d.* had arisen in connection with one estate, and, of the two farms on that estate responsible for this amount, the arrears amounted to 458*l.* 4*s.* 4*d.* in the case of one. But in 1879-80 the figure for arrears in Table XIV is 2,991*l.* 5*s.* 11*d.*, out of a total sum of 3,004*l.* 1*s.* 11*d.*; and to this sum the three chief agricultural estates contributed their respective shares. To the sum of 2,527*l.* 12*s.* 3*d.* in the following year five out of the seven estates contributed. Table XIII, in which the abatements made in successive years are shown, furnishes similar evidence. In 1876-77 these amounted to 2*l.*, and concerned only one farm; in 1890 they amounted to 38*l.* 8*s.*, and were granted to three tenants on two estates, and in two cases similar sums had been given for two or three years previously, while in one of these two cases the abatement has since been exchanged for a permanent reduction. But in 1879-80 the abatements amounted to 885*l.* 17*s.*, and were given to the tenants on five of the seven estates.

Perhaps, however, the nature and effects of the year 1879 can be seen more clearly in the figures of Tables XV and XVI. In 1876-77 the abatements amounted to the small sum of 2*l.*, in 1877-78 they disappeared altogether, and in 1889 and 1890 they again amounted to *nil.* But in 1879-80 they were granted to the tenants of all the farms on the estate, and they represented a sum of 544*l.* 3*s.* on a rental of 3,261*l.*, or some 16 or 17 per cent. This sum was only exceeded in 1887, when the settlement of the affairs of an out-going tenant, whose difficulties, as we previously stated, commenced in 1879, was concluded. In 1883 the sum was approached, and in this case an attempt was made to meet the difficulties of other tenants who had also suffered in 1879. The arrears, again, which had been 100*l.* at the close of 1875-76, and also at the close of 1877-78, amounted to 1,699*l.* 12*s.* 7*d.* at the close of 1879-80. Five out of the eight farms were concerned in these arrears; and, of the three remaining, one was a very small holding, and another was small by comparison. In 1875-76, on the other hand, only one farmer was in arrears, and in 1888 and

1889 the same was the case, while by 1890 the arrears had entirely
disappeared.   In 1886 they amounted to 1,900*l.* 18*s.*, and in 1887
to 1,859*l.* 18*s.* 4*d.*; but these figures were immediately prior to
the settlement of the affairs of two of the tenants mentioned
before in connection with the abatements.   For the year 1886 one
was responsible for the sum of 1,350*l.*, and the other for 189*l.* 1*s.* 8*d.*;
in 1887 the arrears of the latter amounted to 559*l.* 18*s.* 4*d.*, and of
the former to 950*l.*   In 1879-80 the arrears of the one, which had
amounted to 100*l.* in 1877-78, and to 407*l.* 13*s.* in 1878-79, increased
to 772*l.* 15*s.* 6*d.*, and the arrears of the other amounted to 270*l.* as
compared with *nil* before.   In the second half of the year 1881 the
arrears of 1879-80 were again exceeded; but this seems to have
been partly due to the change which was then made in reckoning
the year of account.   The arrears of 1879-80 were coincident with
a total rental of 3,261*l.*, and they therefore amounted to 50 per
cent. of the rental; in 1886, when the difficulties originating in the
former year were approaching a settlement, arrears of 1,900*l.* 18*s.*
coincided with a rental of 2,447*l.*, and amounted to more than
77 per cent. of the rental; in 1887, when the final adjustment of
these difficulties may be considered to have been reached, the arrears
amounted to 1,859*l.* 18*s.* 4*d.* with a rental of 2,222*l.*, or some 84 per
cent.   In fact, if we take into consideration the allowance of
623*l.* 9*s.* 5*d.* made in 1887, we have the extraordinary result that
the rental fell short of the total arrears and abatements by
261*l.* 7*s.* 9*d.*   But these arrears were, as we have seen, largely due
to the years 1879-80, and the true loss falling on any one year can
only be reached by a comparison with the figures of preceding
years.   Applying, then, to Tables XV and XVI the same process
as that employed for all the landed estates of the college, we have
the following table :—

TABLE XVII.

	1876–77.	1877–78.	1878–79.	1879–80.	1880–81.
	£ *s.*	£ *s.*	£ *s.*	£ *s. d.*	£ *s. d.*
Rental	3740 10	3,739 10	3,784 6	3,261 – –	2,977 – –
Abatements	2 –	—	194 2	544 3 –	129 10 –
Arrears	3,738 10 −150 –	3,739 10 +150 –	3,540 4 −529 8	2,716 17 – −1070 4 7	2,847 10 – +284 5 6
	3,588 10	3,889 10	3,010 16	1,646 12 5	3,081 15 6

TABLE XVII—*Contd.*

	Second Half of 1881.	1882.	1883.	1884.	1885.
	£ s. d.	£ s. d.	£ s. d.	£ s. d.	£ s.
Rental	1,384 – –	2,668 – –	2,668 – –	2,628 – –	2,538 –
Abatements	—	—	496 14 6	41 16 5	104 6
	1,384 – –	2,668 – –	2,171 5 6	2,586 3 7	2,433 14
Arrears	–315 3 7	+122 4 11	+762 14 9	+45 11 –	–292 10
	1,068 16 5	2,790 4 11	2,934 – 3	2,631 14 7	2,141 4

	1886.	1887.	1888.	1889.	1890.
	£ s. d.	£ s. d.	£ s. d.	£	£
Rental	2,447 – –	2,222 – –	2,136 – –	2,148	2,148
Abatements	107 – 3	623 9 5	309 18 4	—	—
	2,339 19 9	1,598 10 7	1,826 1 8	2,148	2,148
Arrears	–758 8 –	+40 19 8	+1,709 18 4	–90	+240
	1,581 11 9	1,639 10 3	3,536 – –	2,058	2,388

From this table it will be seen that the receipts in 1879-80 were only 1,646*l.* 12*s.* 5*d.*, as compared with 3,010*l.* 16*s.* in the previous year, and 3,889*l.* 10*s.* in the year before that. This represented a fall of nearly 46 per cent. in a single year, and in the succeeding year, despite of diminished rental, there was a recovery of over 99 per cent., owing to the decrease in abatements and arrears. Only twice since 1879-80 have the receipts fallen to so low a figure—in 1886 and 1887, when, as we before stated, the difficulties arising in the case of two tenants reached their final adjustment. In 1890 the receipts, though more than 1,200*l.* below those of 1876-77, and 1,500*l.* below those of 1877-78, exceeded those of 1879-80 by the extent of 743*l.*, with a rental amounting to 2,148*l.* as compared with 3,261*l.* 17*s.*, in 1879-80. In 1876-77 the deductions to be made for abatements and arrears were only 152*l.* on a rental of 3,740*l.* 10*s.*; in 1890 there was an addition of 240*l.* to be made; but in 1879-80 the deductions amounted to some 50 per cent. On one farm (that lettered A) the arrears amounted to as much as half the rent, in spite of an abatement of more than a fourth of the rent, and the receipts, without deduction for rates or repairs, were only 111*l.* 5*s.*, or about 20 per cent. of the rent. The cash received was in fact only 100*l.* On B the rent was 525*l.*, the arrears increased during the year to the extent of 364*l.* 17*s.* 6*d.*, and an abatement was made of 145*l.* 8*s.*, making a total deduction of 510*l.* 5*s.* 6*d.*, and leaving a balance of 14*l.* 14*s.* 6*d.*, while the property tax and the bills for repairs executed by the tenant amounted to just that sum. Here no cash at all was received during the financial year. In the case of a third farm 100*l.* represented the cash receipt on a rental of 450*l.* Again, then, it seems that it was in no sense an exaggeration for Mr. Bear to declare that in 1879 "veritable disaster" was experienced in English agriculture. Nor, it must be remembered, can the true net receipts of an estate be determined without taking into account the outlay on rates and taxes, on repairs and maintenance, on insurance and management, and on donations and subscriptions, such as are expected from a landlord, for educational and other objects. It will be interesting to endeavour to ascertain these expenses, as far as may prove to be possible, for the year 1879-80, on the largest agricultural estate in the possession of the college. Detailed particulars of the rental, the abatements, and the arrears, of the rack-rented farming tenancies on this estate have been furnished in previous tables.

XIII.—*The Expenses of an Estate.*

The total rental for the whole estate, including cottages and allotments, amounted in 1879-80 to 3,907*l.* (omitting shillings and pence). The total abatements amounted to 544*l.*, leaving a balance of 3,363*l.* From this a sum of 1,074*l.* required to be deducted on account of the increase in the arrears during the year; and in this way an apparent net receipt of 2,289*l.* is reached. The rates, taxes, and tithe for the estate amounted to 473*l.*, of which 7*l.* were paid in drainage rates, 66*l.* in property tax, and the remainder (400*l.*) in tithe. The repairs of an ordinary character involved an expenditure of 124*l.*, and those of a less ordinary nature an outlay of 233*l.*, making a total sum of 357*l.*

Thus an eighth of the gross receipts was absorbed in the payment of taxes and tithe, and an eleventh in the execution of repairs. The expenses of insurance of the farm buildings amounted to some 25*l.*, and the cost of the management of the property, so far as it was possible to assign that cost specifically to any one estate, to some 58*l.*, while 32*l.* were devoted to subscriptions and donations of a customary character. The total expenditure under these various items amounted to 945*l.*, and this, deducted from 2,289*l.*, left a net receipt of 1,344*l.*, out of a gross rental of 3,907*l.*, or about a third. As much as two-thirds, therefore, of the rental of this estate were intercepted on its way from the tenant to the landlord, and in this deduction no account is taken of the share of the general expenses of managing the college property with which this one estate should be credited, if it were possible to do so. Nor again has account been taken of expenditure of a capital nature on permanent improvements, which was undertaken in

previous years by means of borrowed money.   It is difficult to
determine the amount of interest, and of repayment of principal,
which should be charged to each separate estate under this head.
But it would seem to be well within the margin to reckon upon at
least 900*l.*, and the deduction of this further sum would leave the
net receipt at some 450*l.*, were it not that in that year of 1879-80,
in addition to a receipt of 10*l.* for stone and gravel of an ordinary
character, a fine of 700*l.* was paid on the renewal of the lease of
the beneficial leasehold mentioned in an earlier part of this paper.
Reckoning this payment as a receipt of the year, although it is
strictly of the nature of a capital receipt, and the year ought
perhaps to be credited with no more than a seventh part, and
including, on the other hand, amongst the expenses the charge for
the debt, the net receipt would still be some 1,150*l.* on a rental of
4,617*l.*, or less than a fourth.   I have taken out the figures for the
other years of the period in a similar way; but they are not, I
think, of sufficient instructiveness to be given in a table.   I will
therefore content myself with a comparison of the three years
1877-78, 1879-80, and 1889.   The first of these years is the second,
and the other the last but one of those comprised in the period
under review; and I have selected these years because they seem
to be of a more ordinary and representative character than either
the first or the last.

TABLE XVIII.

	1877-78.	1879-80.	1889.	
	£	£	£	
Rental	4,401	3,907	2,776	
Miscellaneous receipts	22	10	4	From sale of stone.
	4,423	3,917	2,780	
Abatements	4	544	....	
	4,419	3,373	2,780	
Arrears	+ 157	− 1,074	− 89	
	4,576	2,299	2,691	
Rates, &c.	1,169	945	969	
	3,407	1,354	1,722	
Charge for debt	900	900	700	
	2,507	454*	1,022	* 700*l.* to be added for fine.
Rates, taxes, and tithe	472	473	372	
Repairs : ordinary	210	124	235	
„ extraordinary	402	233	222	
Insurance	22	15	29	
Agency, law, &c.	41	58	84*	* 23*l.* = special expenses connected with loan.
Donations, &c.	22	32	27	
	1,169	945	969	

TABLE XIX.

	1876-77.			1877-78.			1878-79.			1879-80.			1880-81.		
Repairs.	£	*s.*	*d.*	£	*s.*	*d.*	£	*s.*	*d.*	£	*s.*	*d.*	£	*s.*	*d.*
Ordinary	670	12	1	617	10	8	484	14	8	555	2	–	658	6	10
Extraordinary	1,372	17	6	597	8	4	624	12	9	738	6	9	608	8	8
Total	2,043	9	7	1,214	19	–	1,109	7	5	1,293	8	9	1,261	15	1

	1881. Second half.			1882.			1883.			1884.			1885.		
Repairs.	£	*s.*	*d.*	£	*s.*	*d.*	£	*s.*	*d.*	£	*s.*	*d.*	£	*s.*	*d.*
Ordinary	228	3	8	725	3	8	678	10	5	758	3	10	688	11	4
Extraordinary	146	10	–	808	–	1	490	8	9	695	17	6	774	8	6
Total	374	13	8	1,533	3	9	1,168	19	2	1,454	1	4	1,462	19	10

	1886.			1887.			1888.			1889.			1890.		
Repairs.	£	*s.*	*d.*	£	*s.*	*d.*	£	*s.*	*d.*	£	*s.*	*d.*	£	*s.*	*d.*
Ordinary	623	7	11	733	17	11	782	11	9	628	14	9	501	12	8
Extraordinary	852	3	–	931	18	5	453	1	5	473	1	7	312	–	7
Total	1,475	10	11	1,665	16	4	1,235	13	2	1,101	16	4	813	12	10

Table XVIII shows that, while rates, taxes, and tithe have diminished with the decrease of rental, the outlay upon repairs has not; and in fact it is the case that on the college estates generally the depression has brought with it no relief, but rather additional pressure, on the score of repairs. As the beneficial lease-hold system came to an end, considerable expenditure was necessitated in order to bring the farms into order, and to maintain and improve the buildings. Before this task had been accomplished the depression came; and partly for this reason, and partly in consequence of changes in the system of cultivation, and amongst other things the conversion of arable into pasture, the years of depression have been years of varying but considerable outlay. Table XIX will show the expenditure on repairs executed out of revenue during the period under review.

In addition to this, the college has expended, or contracted loans with a view to expending, borrowed money to the amount of 7,250*l.* on the erection and improvement of cottages and farm buildings, and on the execution of draining and fencing operations, during the period under review in this paper. It has also paid interest, and repaid principal, on debt previously incurred for these objects, and has reduced the capital outstanding of the loans for improvements by one-half, from 22,000*l.* odd to some 11,000*l.*

XIV.—*Concluding Remarks.*

In conclusion, two points of interest may be briefly noticed. During the period under review several acres of arable have been laid down to permanent pasture, and the most serious fall in rental has taken place on the estate which contained the largest proportion of arable land. On this estate, numbered 5 in Table X, the reduction in rent has been some 50 per cent., and the proportion of the land in arable was to the whole acreage of the estate as 10 to 13. But on the other hand the proportion of arable on the estate numbered 7, which is the largest piece of property belonging to the college, was less than a half (and this has since been reduced to about a third by the conversion of arable to pasture), and yet the fall in rental has been 42 per cent., or more than that on the third of the three great estates of the college, where, with a fall of only 33⅓ per cent, the quantity of arable was more than three-fourths of the total acreage. On the first estate the rent is about 14*s.* 6*d.* an acre, and the college now pays the tithe; on the second the average rent is 1*l.*, and the college continues its former practice of paying the tithe; on the third there is no tithe at all, and the rent is about 1*l.* 6*s.* 6*d.* an acre. No doubt these facts, coupled with the conversion of several acres of arable into permanent pasture, show that the fall in the price of corn has been a potent factor in the depression; but they also show that other circumstances may affect the result.

The other fact, which it may perhaps be of some interest to record, is that, of the tenants of the college included in Table X, eight were tenants in 1876-77, and twelve have become tenants since that year. Of these, however, four belong to the same family as the former tenants, on whose deaths they succeeded to the occupancy of the farms. The college has been fortunate enough to have had no farm thrown upon its hands during the whole continuance of the depression.

The Agricultural Depression *and its* Effects *on a* Leading London Hospital. *By* J. C. Steele, M.D.

[Read before the Royal Statistical Society, 16th February, 1892.
The President, Dr. F. J. Mouat, M.D., F.R.C.S., in the Chair.]

The diminished value of arable land consequent on the agricultural depression which has existed with unremitting severity in most parts of the country for the past twelve or fourteen years, has probably been felt less by hospitals for the sick than by any other class of public institutions. This is accounted for by the facts that the vast majority of hospitals are indebted for their existence and maintenance to voluntary contributions, and that they have rarely had opportunities of investing surplus capital in land, while until very recently[1] the disabling clauses of the Statute of Mortmain precluded them from receiving bequests of landed property. In the case of endowed charities of long standing, where a portion, and in some instances nearly the whole of the revenue is derived from arable property, the consequences have been more or less disastrous to the wellbeing of the institutions, and have induced the executive in many instances to adopt measures of a compensatory character to which they had hitherto been strangers. The chief of these expedients is of course an appeal to public generosity, the mainspring of all philanthropic endeavours, and when these wants are sufficiently made known and understood, it has rarely happened that such appeals for help in time of trouble have not been met with an adequate response from an approving public.

The institution to which I intend to refer as having suffered materially from the continual agricultural depression is Guy's Hospital, founded in 1724 at the sole costs of the testator, whose property consisting almost entirely of personalty, realized in the year 1732 a sum amounting to 220,000*l.*[2] The proceeds on the completion of the hospital were invested from time to time under the Act of Incorporation in the purchase of real estate in the counties of Essex, Hereford, and Lincoln, and it appears to have been the aim of successive trustees less to extend the area of the property, than to complete the several estates and render them more valuable and convenient for occupation by purchases, sales, and exchanges. The bequest of William Hunt, of Petersham, in 1829, amounting to 193,000*l.*, enabled the trustees still further to improve the property, by an expenditure of upwards of 13,000*l.*, while 24,000*l.* was spent in the purchase

[1] The Mortmain and Charitable Uses Act, 1891.
[2] " Report of the Commissioners for Inquiring into Charities," 1837.

of freehold and leasehold property in the neighbourhood of the hospital. The remainder of the money was retained to comply with the requirements of Mr. Hunt's will, which necessitated the building of an additional hospital, and the maintenance of 100 beds in addition to the 400 provided for by the will of the founder. The gross income from the landed property in the year 1835, as stated by the Commission of Inquiry, amounted to 22,434*l.*, which when apportioned to the separate counties allowed the following subdivision of rental :—

	£
Estates in Essex	7,788
„ Herefordshire	7,367
„ Lincolnshire	7,279

To this must be added income from property in Southwark, comprising both leasehold and freehold, which then amounted to 2,298*l.*, and dividends from consols amounting to 4,945*l.*, making a gross income of 29,677*l.*, exclusive, of course, of the necessary outgoings. In a table in the Appendix, taken from the Commissioners' report, we can form an adequate idea of the income and outgoings on the several estates at this time. This table is taken on an average of six years, ending Lady Day, 1836, and shows the annual revenue of the hospital from all sources to have amounted to 30,491*l.*, while the total outgoings on the estates, and some fixed payments in perpetuity in accordance with the testamentary requirements of the founder, made up a sum of 9,708*l.*, leaving a clear annual balance available for hospital purposes close upon 21,000*l.* The average number of patients annually under treatment at this period did not exceed 3,120, and considering that the Hunt bequest necessitated the governing body to find accommodation for 500 persons, under pain of the legacy being transferred to St. Thomas's Hospital, the mean residence of the patients must have far exceeded the average limits of the present time.

Twenty-five years after the period referred to by the Inquiry Commission, a report by the Treasurer of the hospital at that time, makes the gross rental of the country and town estates in 1856 to amount to 32,187*l.* 16*s.* 7*d.*, and the extent of the land under cultivation to 23,704 acres, allocated in the following manner :—

	Acres.	Rental.			Increase per Cent.
		£	*s.*	*d.*	
Herefordshire	10,465	9,173	14	6	24
Lincolnshire	5,173	10,770	17	7	48
Essex	8,066	9,820	19	6	26
Southwark	—	2,422	5	-	—

By a gradual and steady increase in the land value, as well as

by a judicious extension by purchase and rebuilding of the Southwark property, the income on the several estates amounted in 1872
(as appears from the published statement of the Treasurer), to
46,870*l.*, while the area of land under cultivation also underwent
considerable alteration.   The accompanying figures best explain
these alterations in the three counties and in Southwark:—

	Acres.	Rental.			Increase per Cent.
		£	*s.*	*d.*	
Hereford	9,490	12,152	17	—	32
Lincoln	6,391	14,870	6	6	38
Essex	8,785	12,109	10	1	23
Southwark	—	7,737	19	8	—

The higher rental from the Lincolnshire property, when compared with the others as regards acreage, is accounted for by its
containing within its enclosure a township or hamlet consisting of
a couple of hundred houses and cottages, two-thirds of which
belong to the estate.   Up to this period there could be little
difference of opinion as to the wisdom displayed in the original
investments, which after a period of a century and a half may
be computed to have realized nine times their original value.

We now come to consider the gradual and steady depreciation
of the value of the land, and its effect on the hospital finances.
This can be best estimated from a perusal of the large table in the
Appendix, which gives a summary of income and expenditure on
the country estates for a period of seventeen years ending Lady
Day, 1891, together with an abstract of the number of in-patients
under treatment each year, and the mean residence of each in days.
As it is mainly with the land question we are dealing, I will limit
myself to a contrast between the first three and the last three years
of the series respectively as it affects income derived from
country property only, the difference between the gross and net
rental representing the outgoings before the money became available for hospital purposes.   The calculations are made on an
average of years, the first statement representing the mean rental
of the years 1875-76-77 :—

	Gross Rental.	Net Rental.	Increase per Cent.
	£	£	
Hereford	13,227	8,863	9
Lincoln	15,472	12,797	4
Essex	12,517	9,390	3

Throughout the period in question, and coincident with the
diminution of available income, there is a notable increase of

liabilities and outgoings, due sometimes to accidental and unforeseen causes, but mainly to outlay on property which must.be maintained notwithstanding its unremunerative character.   Much of this consists of outmarsh reclaimed from the sea on the coasts of Lincolnshire and Essex, as well as of river banks, formerly scoured by the tides, all of which periodically require reparative attention.

In contrast with the foregoing table, the following figures, representing an average of the income from land for the past three years, 1889-90-91 show the extent of the depreciation at the present time :—

	Gross Rental.	Net Rental.
	£	£
Hereford	11,051	6,405
Lincoln	10,875	7,528
Essex	6,247	3,856

	Loss on Gross Rental.		Loss on Net Rental.
Hereford	16 pr. ct.	Hereford	28 pr. ct.
Lincoln	29 ,,	Lincoln	41 ,,
Essex	50 ,,	Essex	59 ,,

It is generally conceded that the decline in land value has been greater in wheat growing counties like Lincoln and Essex than in those further west such as Hereford, which depends more on its pasturage and the growth of other cereals.   The land in Essex has been peculiarly unfortunate, as sixty years since it returned a larger revenue than either of the two other estates, while the rental from Lincolnshire would have shown a corresponding depreciation had it not been for the residential property on the estate.   The depreciation first made itself felt in the year 1881, and since then the rental has been steadily declining.   In the same year the governing body was reluctantly compelled to curtail the accommodation for patients, and to take exceptional measures with the view of increasing the sources of income.   The most prominent of these was, by borrowing money and by private subscription, and a few years afterwards by calling public attention to the pressing needs of the establishment, and the necessity for its maintenance as a great curative institution for the poor of South London.   After a time the appeal was generously responded to, the result enabling the executive to maintain not less than 500 beds in constant occupation, and to carry out some important sanitary and structural alterations absolutely necessary in a building erected long before any other having a like object now in use in the metropolis.   A column in the first table on p. 48 in the Appendix gives a numerical summary of the patients treated in the hospital from 1875 to 1891 inclusive. from which it may be seen that notwithstanding the curtailment of the accommodation, which in 1882 reduced the number of in-patients to 4,923, the annual returns go on increasing, and during the past two years actually outstrip the numbers under treatment in the earlier years, which may be considered the golden age of the hospital. This fact requires explanation, and it is given in an adjoining column of the table, which represents the mean stay of the patients in hospital for each year consecutively. Judging from the practice of the general hospitals which notify these matters, the residence of the patients appears to range between 25 and 30 days, the mean stay over all being about 30 days. In former times, and in fact up to the year when a marked reduction in the amount of accommodation took place, the patients' mean residence at Guy's was considerably greater than in that of any general hospital in London which published observations, being seldom less than 40 days. Since 1881, when the limit of accommodation was reduced, and the mean stay of the patients was estimated at 39·5 days, there is noticed a steady diminution in the length of residence throughout the remaining years of the series. During the past year the stay has been reduced to 27·5 days, and in the year prior to that to 27·3 days. This means a rapid admission and discharge, and benefit to a greater number; whether the benefit is of an equally permanent character to that derived from a longer residence may be matter of opinion.

The problem how to make good deficiency of income occasioned by agricultural depression in the case of a large hospital hitherto supported by its own endowment, is not difficult to solve. If it is to continue to pursue the same beneficent objects, it must be indebted to voluntary help, and not to local government agencies. It is quite possible that a charitable institution, like any other, in the face of a diminishing income, may reduce its power of doing good to a level with its resources, but this Procrustean notion in the case of a time honoured medical charity is hardly likely to find favour either with the public or with those to whom its management is entrusted. Individual enterprise and philanthropic co-operation have been the keystone of success of all our medical charities, causing them to be the boast of our own, and the admiration of foreign countries, and it would be a manifest misfortune if in the future, circumstances should occur to render them even partially dependent on State help. It says much for the hopeful confidence which the managers of the various medical charities in London possess in their institutions, that they should go on increasing the work, notwithstanding (according to a competent authority)[3] there is an annual deficit in their conjoint incomes of not less than 30,000l. annually. There is one feature of

[3] *The Hospital,* 19th December, 1891.

hospital expenditure which is liable to be overlooked when appeals are diffusely advertised for their maintenance. This refers to the increased cost at which hospitals are conducted in comparison with what was the case twenty or thirty years ago. The tables submitted exemplify this, and the figures are borne out by the records of other hospitals, where the cost of administration and maintenance may be shown to have risen from 20 to 50 per cent. during the period. The increase in cost can be readily accounted for by the privileges which the sick now enjoy, in comparison with their predecessors of a previous generation, with respect to food, medical efficiency, nursing, and other hygienic requirements thought necessary for their comfort and rapid recovery. As no exception has been taken to the additional outlay by the friends and contributors to hospitals, it may be assumed that the changes have met with general approval. On the other hand, if the medical charities of the country are to continue their dependence and maintenance on voluntary assistance alone, it is only reasonable to expect that they should be free from those restrictions to their utility which, however necessary they may be with respect to commercial industries, are totally out of place when applied to charities. In a paper published in the transactions of this Society⁴ for the past year, I referred to the recent imposition of local rates upon hospitals as a burden from which they had been exempted by the practice of little short of three centuries, but in consequence of what is usually considered to have been a judicial blunder on the part of the Court of Appeal, they are now held to be liable. It is hardly conceivable that in a country where the spirit of legislation has ever been on the alert to remove every impediment that might interfere with the benevolent instincts of the people, a decision on a matter totally irrespective of charitable institutions should become to be recognised as a principle of common law. The hospitals in this country have a special history, inasmuch as they are all the offspring of voluntary effort to relieve the commonwealth of a huge responsibility in attending to the medical requirements of the sick poor, without seeking compensation in any way from the public exchequer. In Scotland and in Ireland the hospitals are freed from these restrictions, and in the colonies, and in fact in most civilized countries, they are not only free from taxation, but are largely subsidised by the municipal or imperial authorities in accordance with their respective needs. The subject is one loudly demanding consideration by the legislature, and it is earnestly to be hoped that Parliament, which has never failed to deal justly as well as mercifully with the charities, will pronounce judgment on this question by passing a declaratory Act by which their ancient privileges would be restored to them.

⁴ June, 1891.

The following Statement shows the Income of the Hospital, the Outgoings of the Estates, and Annual Payments, taken on an Average of Six Years ending Lady Day, 1836.

INCOME.

	£	s.	d.
Rent, fee farm rent, and annuity of 125l. from the Stationers' Company	24,302	4	2
Casual profits	1,428	2	—
Dividends	4,577	10	—
Received from parish patients	183	4	10
	30,491	**1**	**—**

OUTGOINGS ON ESTATES.

		£	s.	d.	£	s.	d.
Quit rents, annuities, and fines					665	13	8
Rates and taxes					521	1	—
Land tax					1,210	—	4¾
Building and repairs					3,365	1	4
Sea and river banks					373	14	2¼
Fencing and planting					473	12	10
Abatements to tenants					979	15	1¼
Receiver's expenses					1,083	4	5¾
Total outgoings on the estates					8,672	2	11¾
Payments to Christ's Hospital, Tamworth Almshouses, &c., by founder's will		530	5	8			
Payments to Hunt's annuitants		264	9	9			
Interest on money borrowed		241	14	11			
					1,036	10	4
Balance available for hospital purposes					9,708	13	3¾
					20,782	7	8¼
					30,491	**1**	**—**

Income and Outgoings of the Estates and Annual Payments for the Year ending Lady Day, 1879.

INCOME.

	£	s.	d.
Rent, fee farm rent, and annuity of 125l. from the Stationers' Company	47,667	4	6
Casual profits	2433	4	4
Dividends	123	2	8
Legacies	295	12	5
Parish patients	143	6	6
	50,662	10	5

OUTGOINGS ON ESTATES AND ANNUAL PAYMENTS.

	£	s.	d.	£	s.	d.
Quit rents, annuities and fines				677	15	3
Rates and taxes				354	5	9
Land tax				896	2	10
Building and repairs				4,345	11	9
Sea and river banks				271	2	6
Fencing and planting				441	17	3
Abatements to tenants				55	6	9
Receiver's expenses				1,780	10	2
Stipends, donations to schools, &c.				452	3	8
				9,274	15	11
Payments to Christ's Hospital, Tamworth Almshouses, &c.	525	-	-			
Interest on money borrowed	18	14	8	543	14	8
				9,818	10	7
Available for hospital purposes				40,843	19	10
				50,662	10	5

Income and Outgoings on the Estates for 1891 (Year ending Lady Day).

INCOME.	£	s.	d.
Rent, fee farm rents, and Stationers' Company	34,309	16	10
Casual profits	1,178	15	10
Dividends	68	14	6
Parish patients	175	7	—
Out-patients	730	16	4
Paying patients	2,941	9	7
Lady pupils' fees (for board and lodging)	1,031	14	—
Hospital Sunday Fund	246	2	6
„ Saturday Fund	588	5	—
Interest on Special Appeal Fund	2,170	5	9
	43,441	7	4

OUTGOINGS ON ESTATES AND ANNUAL PAYMENTS.	£	s.	d.		£	s.	d.
Quit rents, &c.	1,714	11	1				
Rates and taxes	432	2	8				
Land tax	842	17	9				
Building and repairs	4,288	1	8				
Sea and river banks	300	4	6				
Fencing and planting	226	16	3				
Abatements to tenants	1,695	12	8				
Receiver's expenses, &c.	1,289	5	3				
Stipends and donations to schools, &c.	215	19	5				
Total outgoings on estates					11,005	11	3
Payments to Christ's Hospital, Tamworth Almshouses, &c.	525	—	—				
Interest on money borrowed	796	5	—				
					1,321	5	—
Total of outgoings and payments					12,326	16	3
Available for hospital purposes					31,114	11	1
					43,441	7	4

* These sources of income, amounting to 7,708*l.* 13*s.* 2*d.*, were not available in 1879.

Abstract of the Account of Income and Expenditure of Guy's Hospital as made up for the Year ending 25th March, 1879.

	£	s.	d.
Rents for the year ended Michaelmas			
Rent, free farm-christmas, 1878 (after deducting allowances to tenants and others, works executed, and other expenses)	40,948	15	7
Legacies	295	12	5
Parish patients	143	6	6
	41,387	14	6
Balance, being deficiency for the year	354	17	2
	41,742	11	8

Cr.	£	s.	d.			
By Drugs, surgical instruments, &c.	5,735	10	11			
" Bread	929	3	9			
" Meat	3,453	15	2			
" Butter, &c.	573	9	1			
" Diet, including milk, tea, sugar, poultry, &c.	3,021	19	—			
" Malt liquor	644	—	1			
" Board of medical residents	671	12	11			
" Fuel	1,216	14	8			
" Gas, &c.	1,010	17	5			
" Bed furnishings, &c.	1,584	15	11			
" Repairs	4,653	1	—			
				£	s.	d.
" Hospital site—rent				445	5	—
rates and taxes				1,300	13	3
	1,835	18	3			
" Occasional dinners—audit	71	3	10			
" Museum and school buildings	525	3	8			
" Salaries of officers	6,087	1	7			
" Pensions and allowances	843	6	2			
" Servants' wages—male servants and nurses	5,928	7	9			
" Petty expenses	45	6	10			
" Soap and water	82	3	1			
" Stationery	197	5	4			
" Laundry	453	15	11			
" Wines and spirits	567	16	3			
				£	s.	d.
" Annuities payable under Founder's will				525	—	—
" Interest on money borrowed				18	14	8
" New buildings				1,052	—	—
	1,595	14	8			
" Burials	14	8	7			
	41,742	11	8			

Abstract of the Account of Income and Expenditure of ——'s Hospital as made up for the Year ended 31st March, 1891.

Dr.

	£	s.	d.
To Rents of estates for the year ended Michaelmas and Christmas, 1890 (after deducting allowances to tenants and others, works executed, and other expenses, &c.)	24,551	15	11
" Lady pupils' fees	1,031	14	–
" Parish and pauper patients	175	7	–
" Paying in-patients	2,941	9	7
" out-patients	730	16	4
" Hospital Saturday Fund	588	5	2
" Sunday	246	2	6
" Dividend and interest on investments of "Special Appeal" fund	2,170	5	9
	32,435	16	1
" Balance, being deficiency for the year	6,783	13	8

	£	s.	d.
Amount transferred from "Special Appeal" fund during the year	7,803	18	2
Less deficiency as above	6,783	13	8
Balance of income and expenditure account, as per accounting statement	1,020	4	6

Cr.

	£	s.	d.	£	s.	d.
By Drugs, surgical instruments and appliances				5,120	1	7
" Bread				483	–	6
" Meat				2,157	19	1
" Butter, &c.				540	–	4
" Diet, miscellaneous, inclusive of milk, tea, sugar, poultry, fish, and vegetables				3,255	18	7
" Malt liquor				57	2	5
" Board of medical residents				650	–	11
" Fuel				1,208	5	3
" Gas, &c.				730	3	11
" Bed furnishings, &c.				1,347	8	4
" Repairs				3,251	5	6
" Hospital site—rent	443	5	–			
" " rates and taxes	1,575	1	7	2,020	6	7
" Legal expenses				311	–	10
" Museum and school buildings				415	15	11
" Salaries—Medical	1,470	–	–			
" " Pharmaceutical	576	8	4			
" " Other departments	2,285	10	1			
" Board and salaries and washing for matron and sisters, and board for lady pupils				4,331	13	5
" Pensions and allowances				1,779	–	3
" Servants' wages—Male servants				735	15	10
" Board and wages, and washing for nurses, probationers, and all female servants				5,229	15	6
" Petty expenses				45	17	1
" Soap and water				254	8	3
" Stationery				319	2	7
" Laundry				912	3	6
" Uniforms				302	10	6
" Wines and spirits						

GUY'S HOSPITAL. *Statement of Income and Expenditure,* 1875 to 1891.

[For the compilation of this and the accompanying tables, I am indebted to Mr. Henry Williams, Clerk and Accountant to the Hospital.]

Year.	Country Estates.		Town Property.		Un-assured Sources of Income, &c.	Net Income available for Hospital Expenditure.	Special Expenditure.	Hospital Expenses.	Total Disbursements.	In-patients under Treatment each Year.	Days in Residence.
	Gross.	Net.	Gross.	Net.							
	£	£	£	£	£	£	£	£	£		
1875	41,840	30,919	7,549	6,533	794	38,246	525	36,650	37,175	5,776	39·8
'76	41,679	31,179	7,977	7,188	3,013	41,370	537	36,704	37,241	5,854	38·6
'77	41,993	31,396	8,313	7,567	726	39,689	528	40,652	41,180	5,722	37·3
'78	40,367	30,486	7,888	7,186	683	38,355	580	46,332	46,912	5,544	39·5
'79	42,005*	33,421	7,844	7,177	784	41,382	543	41,198	41,741	5,718	37·9
'80	41,379	33,809	8,109	7,657	499	41,965	554	39,767	40,321	5,727	39·2
'81	40,842†	25,983	8,071	7,512	462	33,957	791	35,107	35,898	5,189	39·3
'82	39,399	24,439	8,111	7,340	2,095	33,874	972	33,972	34,944	4,923	36·7
'83	37,885	26,281	7,924	7,150	468	33,899	902	35,498	36,400	5,150	34·4
'84	35,186‡	18,646	7,993	7,277	6,103	32,026	1,120	35,300	36,420	5,121	33·1
'85	33,592	20,612	7,806	7,193	9,535	37,340	1,275	33,542	34,817	4,956	34·4
'86	31,938	20,736	7,622	7,050	6,250	34,036	1,504	32,569	34,103	4,963	33·1
'87	29,631	19,504	7,560	6,852	5,047	31,403	1,815	31,521	33,336	5,204	31·4
'88	31,210	19,905	7,639	6,865	5,853	32,623	1,521	33,541	35,062	5,453	30·2
'89	28,797	18,652	7,728	7,154	6,945	32,751	1,385	36,469	38,654	5,828	28·4
'90	28,191	17,495	7,634	7,016	7,483	31,984	1,353	37,332	38,685	6,189	27·3
'91	27,550	17,222	7,678	7,035	8,173	32,430	1,321	37,898	39,219	6,131	27·5

* Large sale of timber this year. † Heavy "sluice" expenses on Lincolnshire estate.
‡ This and two following years serious collapse of sea-wall in Lincolnshire.

Average Income for Three Years ending Lady Day, 1878.

	Gross.	Net.
	£	£
Herefordshire..............	13,227	8,863
Lincolnshire	15,472	12,797
Essex	12,517	9,390
	41,216	31,050

The same Property, Three Years ending Lady Day, 1891.

	Gross.	Net.
	£	£
Herefordshire	11,051	6,405
Lincolnshire	10,875	7,528
Essex	6,247	3,856
	28,173	17,789

	Loss on Gross Rental.	Loss on Net Rental.
	Per cent.	Per cent.
Herefordshire	29	28
Lincolnshire	33	41
Essex	50	59

DISCUSSION *on* MR. PRICE'S *and* DR. STEELE'S PAPERS.

MR. F. B. GARNETT said he was sure that the Society was greatly
indebted to the authors of the two papers for the light which they
had afforded on the subject of agricultural depression in particular
cases. He had himself had some familiarity with the subject, and
took a great interest in it. It occurred to him that it might be
useful to endeavour to compare the results which had been shown
with regard to the properties of Oriel College, Oxford, and Guy's
Hospital respectively with the recorded valuations of lands
generally for the same period. The returns of the Local Government Board, which only gave the total gross and rateable value of
all properties, were unfortunately of no assistance, but the Inland
Revenue Returns afforded information of the value of "lands"
separately from other properties assessed for the income tax. The
observation of Mr. Price, that the year 1879 was the most disastrous
in regard to the depreciation in value of landed property, might
seem at first sight to be irreconcilable with the statement in the
last (thirty-fourth) report of the Commissioners of Inland Revenue,
to the effect that "the gross assessments on annual value of land
(in the United Kingdom) assessed under Schedule A were at their
highest in 1879," when they amounted to 69,548,796*l.* This
statement required to be qualified by reference to the statement in
the Commissioners' twenty-fourth report, by which it was shown
that while there was a nominal increase in the value of "land," as
shown by the assessment for 1879-80, a considerable decline is
really apparent, inasmuch as actual repayments of duty in respect
of admitted claims arising out of depreciation of landed property
or agricultural distress and discharges from assessment, as un-
collectable for the same causes, were made to such an extent as
represented an assessment of 996,240*l.*, which. after abating the
increase recorded by the first assessments, shows a net decline
on the value of lands in 1879-80, as compared with 1878-79, of
842,000*l.* The Commission also noticed in their twenty-fourth
report that there was a great falling off in the improvement of the
value of land shown by the assessment of 1879-80, as compared
with the improvement on the previous year of new valuation, viz.,
1876-77. As a matter of fact, early in 1879 it had become apparent
that landed property was very much depreciated, and he himself,
in August in that year, had, as secretary to the Board of Inland
Revenue, issued general instructions as to the extent to which
effect might be given in the new assessment for 1879 to reductions
of rent. This was followed by the issue, under authority from the
Treasury, of special regulations under which allowances were to be
made on account of the then present agricultural depression. He
thought it might be useful as an appendix to the two papers, if a
table were given containing the figures extracted from the published reports relating to the assessments from 1876-77 to 1889-90,
showing the actual assessed value of lands in the United Kingdom

for each year, with the increase or decrease over the preceding year, and of the estimated capital value of repayments or abatements so far as given in the reports. It would be seen that the assessed value of lands had fallen from 69,548,796*l.* in 1879-80, to 58,153.900*l.* in 1889-90, being a diminution in the assessment of 11,394,896*l.* Dr. Steele had approached his subject from the different point of view that, in all charitable institutions, when income was diminishing, the first impulse was to look for ways and means to supplement the deficiency. He concurred with Dr. Steele in regretting that alterations had been made in the manner of dealing with some charitable institutions in regard to the exemptions heretofore allowed them.

Annual Value of "Lands" Assessed for Income Tax from 1876-77 *to* 1889-90, *with the Increase or Decrease each Year for the United Kingdom.*

Year.	Annual Value Assessed.	Increase or Decrease of Annual Value as Compared with Pre- ceding Year.	Decrease of Assessment below 1879-80.	Estimated Annual Value Represented by Repay- ments and Abatements.	Estimated net Annual Value after Reductions.	Estimated net Decrease below Assessed Value in 1879-80.
1876–77	69,438,632	+ 2,420,000	....	....	....	....
'77–78	69,324,989	− 113,643	....	....	....	....
'78–79	69,265,311	− 59,678	....	....	....	....
'79–80	69,548,796	+ 283,485	....	996,240	68,552,556	....
'80–81	69,291,973	− 256,823	256,823	1,035,040	68,256,933	1,291,863
'81–82	68,811,032	− 480,941	737,764	1,243,104	67,567,928	1,980,868
'82–83	65,957,322	− 2,853,710	3,591,474	not stated	....	....
'83–84	65,442,227	− 515,095	4,106,569	,,	....	about 5,265,000
'84–85	65,039,166	− 403,061	4,509,630	,,	....	
'85–86	63,268,679	− 1,770,487	6,280,117	732,000	62,536,679	7,012,117
'86–87	62,483,149	− 835,530	7,115,647	690,000	61,743,149	7,805,647
'87–88	61,253,522	− 1,179,627	8,295,274	1,150,000	60,103,522	9,445,274
'88–89	58,755,134	− 2,498,388	10,793,662	604,800	58,150,334	11,398,462
'89 90	58,153,900	− 601,234	11,394,896	544,000	57,609,900	11,938,896

Mr. CLARE SEWELL READ said he thought the last speaker might be answered by saying that he did not think Mr. Price had said the year 1879 was the one in which there was the greatest reduction of the income of his college, or in the rental of land. But a farmer would feel his losses, not in 1879, but in the following year, 1880, then he would ask his landlord for a reduction, which he might not obtain for another two or three years. This seemed to be the effect on the hospital figures. On that point he might remark that some landlords did not meet their tenants soon enough. He remembered, in 1879, incurring a good deal of censure from some landlords in Norfolk by telling them to be sure and give to their old tenants that reduction which they would have to give to new ones: the result being that where the reduction was made many a tenant was saved. He hoped he might say, without offence, that he thought neither a college nor a hospital were the best landlords, for the simple reason that they could not possibly be residential.   As a tenant farmer, and also a landowner himself, he was convinced that a good resident proprietor was a considerable benefit to a neighbourhood.   He thought the papers pointed to a very melancholy effect on the small owners of land; they had heard the depreciation which had taken place in the income from unencumbered estates, such as the estates belonging to these institutions generally were; but what must be the effect on private properties which were in any way encumbered?   The result in his own county of Norfolk and the adjoining counties was that at least half the gentlemen who were resident on their estates twenty-five years ago had ceased to be so.   The hall and sporting were generally let to Londoners, and in many cases the owner lived in one of the small farm-houses on the estate, or was educating his children as cheaply as he could on the continent.   There was a great cry now about stopping the migration of agricultural labourers into the towns; but they could obtain a living there, while the owner and the farmer, as a rule, could not.   He believed that the small landowners who had encumbered estates were in even a worse plight than the farmers.   He was sorry to find that the College at Oxford, previously to the last Act, made the tenant pay the tithe: this was a direct contradiction of the express purpose of the Act of 1836.   He found his own position as a tenant farmer better than that as a landowner: he had had reductions made in his rent without asking, but he dare not ask the mortgagee to reduce the interest.   As a yeoman, he contended that all the ills of the landlord and of the tenant were concentrated on him in that capacity, and he therefore had the greatest possible doubt as to the financial success which would attend the Government scheme of creating small holdings.

Mr. W. E. BEAR thought the great merit of the two papers just read consisted in their being a record of actual facts and not of estimates.   Very often they got estimates, and by able men, of the reduction of rent in certain districts, but these were not based entirely upon the writers' own experiences, as were the statements of Mr. Price and Dr. Steele.   With respect to the apparent discrepancy between the returns, the highest assessments being for 1879, the year when depression reached the climax in the arable districts, he did not quite see why this should be regarded as a discrepancy, as it was quite possible for a sudden change to take place.   He thought no one who knew anything about agriculture would say 1879 was the height of prosperity, either for landlords or tenants.   Farmers had felt the depression creeping on, but it was not generally acknowledged until the year 1879 brought out facts that no one could dispute.   Before 1879 there were very few reductions in rent.   There were some temporary remissions in 1878, and even in 1879, but very few permanent reductions.   At that time he protested strongly against temporary remissions, because they gave farmers no real hope; they were a kind of charitable relief.   The permanent reductions had to be made, but they were unfortunately made to new men, instead of to the old tenants.

Mr. A. E. BATEMAN said that Table VIII was one which concerned work which for many years he had had to do with at the Board of Trade, before the recent transfer of the corn returns to Major Craigie's able hands at the Board of Agriculture. Mr. Price had said the Oxford corn rents were above the tithe average, and it was certainly worth notice that the College made a very good bargain when they were authorised to base a part of their rents upon the *best* price of a bushel of wheat and malt. In every market there was a great difference in the wheat brought in, and a still greater difference in barley. There was malting barley and grinding barley, and there had been many complaints made to the Board of Trade that the tithe averages excluded a great deal of tail corn that did not come to market, and were unduly raised by parcels of corn which were sold several times over. In the case of Oxford, tail corn certainly did not come into the calculation, and he was surprised to find the Oxford corn rents, based on the highest prices of the day, did not work out even more beyond the average than they did. During the years covered by Mr. Price's paper, the Oxford prices of the best bushel were 8 per cent. above the average, while barley was 20 per cent. above, and to that extent the Oxford colleges had been very well off. The only other point which he would mention was in Dr. Steele's paper, with regard to his complaint of the high local rates being paid by hospitals. About thirty years ago the legislature passed an Act entitling every society which did not teach or amuse, to have the houses it occupied exempt from local rates, and under that the Royal Statistical Society was almost entirely exempt. He hoped the hospitals would be able to get that Act extended to them.

Mr. J. R. BRECKON said that Dr. Steele alluded to the period when the hospital's income was curtailed by the decrease in the revenue from land, and a special endeavour was made to obtain voluntary contributions. In the town where he lived, Sunderland, the population was largely made up of the working classes, and such workpeople contributed more than half the ordinary receipts of the infirmary. This was a source of income that was constantly increasing, and it appeared to him a proper subject for considera-tion whether the principle that had been so effectually carried out at Sunderland could not be more generally applied throughout the country. He thought it desirable that the working people should take an interest in the hospital management, and, as was the case at Sunderland, have their representatives on the committee. The other point to which he wished to allude was the sum paid for malt liquor in 1879 and 1891, namely, 644*l*. in the first year, against 57*l*. in the latter, while the sum spent on wines and spirits fell from 567*l*. to 326*l*. Whether this suggested that any special exertions had been applied to bring about that reduction, he did not know, but nevertheless he thought it was a most gratifying fact.

Mr. S. B. L. DRUCE said that he would re-echo what Mr. Bear had said as to the value of the two papers, because they gave actual facts. Having been on the Duke of Richmond's Commission, he was aware how difficult it was to get at facts relating to actual farms and estates: they could only be got at voluntarily. He agreed with what Mr Price and Dr. Steele had brought out from the accounts of Oriel College and Guy's Hospital, that the year 1879 was a year of veritable disaster, the *black year* of English farmers. As Mr. Read pointed out, the actual effect of the year could not be ascertained until after its termination; this was clearly seen by the accounts of Guy's Hospital, where the results of 1879 were not fully felt till 1881. Another point clearly brought out by both papers was that arable land had suffered a great deal more than pasture land. He had himself reported, in 1882, that of all the fifteen counties over which his inquiries extended—the Eastern and Eastern Midlands—Essex had fared the worst, and Dr. Steele's paper confirmed this. That paper also showed that Lincolnshire had suffered very severely, and in his list that county stood third in order of depression, the second being Huntingdon, which was not here dealt with. One fact that struck him in the tables referring to the Oriel College estates was, that there had been a large increase in the amount of land set apart by the college for cottages and allotments during this period under discussion: it had nearly doubled in fourteen years. He was not one of those who held that there were but very few allotments in this country previously to the passing of the Allotment Act in 1887; he and Major Craigie had, on the contrary, found that a large number existed in 1875 and 1876, but he was bound to say the number had very considerably increased since the passing of the Act. This was a specific piece of evidence which showed that the labourers had not felt the depression so much as the farmers and landlords, and in this connection he would cite the following remarkable figures, which a large farmer in Berkshire gave from his own books, at the Farmers' Club a few days ago. The gentleman in question all through farmed the *same* land, and the same quantity, viz., 1,400 acres:—

	1871.	1891.
	£	£
Rent	2,800	1,712
Labour	2,990	2,884

Before sitting down, he would like to congratulate Oriel College on not having had any farm thrown on its hands during the depression, and on this, which (he hoped Mr. Read would not take exception) showed that the college could not be altogether a bad landlord, namely, that of the twenty present tenants of the college, eight were actually the same as at the beginning of the depression, and four more were members of families other members of which were then tenants of the college.

Mr. D. F. BASDEN said he would like to refer to the causes of the depression. It commenced about the beginning of the period covered by the paper (1876) or shortly before. Farmers had been depending, and depend still, on their crops and stock for making their profit. Prior to the period under review the price of corn had been high, which enabled the farmer to make a profit and employ more capital.   He was able also to employ more artificial manure and more labour, so that the land improved in quality, and larger crops were raised.   The depression arose from three causes : (1.) Unfavourable seasons occurring simultaneously with importation of foreign corn, the latter bringing prices gradually down from 60*s.* to 30*s.* a quarter; (2.) The increased importation of foreign cattle, which made markets unreliable; (3.) The losses of the farmer reduced his working capital, and the quality of the land suffered proportionately, as he could no longer keep the same quantity of stock on the land, nor purchase expensive artificial dressings for the soil, while just before this time Mr. Joseph Arch went through the country and agitated amongst the agricultural labourers for an increase of wages and no piece-work.   In consequence, farmers had to employ less men for the same pay, and the land was therefore less cared for.   These three things coming together were, he believed, very largely the cause of the depreciation in agriculture.

Sir RAWSON RAWSON said that the papers read this evening ought to bring a crumb of comfort to Irish landlords, who, like himself, had been obliged, either voluntarily or by law, to make such large reductions in the rentals of their tenants, since they learnt that their English comrades had suffered equally.   He himself had a farm in one of the eastern counties of Ireland, and he had thought himself very badly off in having to reduce the rent under voluntary agreements by 44 per cent.   Yet Oriel College and Guy's Hospital had been obliged to reduce some of their leases by 50 and 56 per cent.

Mr. L. L. PRICE, in reply, said he might perhaps be allowed to read some portions of a letter received from the college agent, Mr. Robert Castle, who possessed a very extensive experience of the management of the estates of the Oxford Colleges and other owners.   Mr. Castle wrote, that from his "experience of the results of the agricultural depression in the case of other colleges and private estates, he thought that Oriel College might be taken as a fair average typical one."   He added, "I am sorry I shall not be able to be present at the meeting, for I think it due to your college to point out the ready way it has recognised facts, however unpleasant, the good feeling and relations it has maintained all through with its tenants, and with the labourers on its estates, and the public spirit and sense of duty with which it has all through these trials persevered in carrying out permanent improvements on the estates, both to land and buildings, so that the estates are without doubt in a better and more satisfactory state at the present time, both as to farm houses and buildings, labourers' cottages and general cultivation, than they had ever been, and much, I think, above the average in each respect; and this, I think, should be borne in mind when the large expenditure which has been made is taken into consideration."   He (Mr. Price) would like to say that though a college might not be the best landlord, it was also probably not the worst; he was aware, as Mr. Read had remarked, that it could not be resident.   It could not therefore see or execute immediately minor repairs which, if carried out at the time, would benefit the estate; but on the other hand, it compared generally with great landlords who did not derive the whole of their income from their landed estates; and, therefore, when it became a question of carrying out certain repairs or of making certain remissions, the case did not come home in the same way as it might in the case of a small landlord. He agreed fully with what Mr. Bear had said about temporary remissions, and he believed that Oriel College had tried to make permanent reductions as early as possible. The chief increase in the allotments since the Act had taken place on one estate, the others had existed for some years previously before the Act was passed. With regard to the non-payment of tithe, the effect of the Tithe Act was to produce a change in only two of the college estates. It was true that, at the beginning of the period under review, the college did not pay the tithe, but in that it only followed a practice which was very general. Before the Act had been passed, it had altered the practice in every case except those two estates.

Dr. STEELE said he quite agreed with Mr. Price that they had turned the corner with regard to agricultural distress. At all events they heard from their land agents that the farmers were paying their rents more regularly than before. Unlike Oriel College, Guy's Hospital had had four or five farms thrown on their hands: four of these the governors, through their agent, had cultivated, and to good profit. He thought the question relative to the best manner of investing money bequeathed to hospitals or educational establishments would form a good subject for analysis and discussion in the Society. He was glad to hear a favourable expression of opinion with regard to the rating of hospitals. They had suffered much from this cause since 1866, up to which time, from the reign of Elizabeth, they had been exempt, but now the charities paid between them 30,000*l*. and 40,000*l*. a year in rates in London alone. The annual deficit of hospitals ranged from 20,000*l*. to 50,000*l*.; he had put it down in the paper at 30,000*l*., and this was about the sum they jointly paid on account of rates. Mr. Breckon had remarked on the great reduction in the expenditure on alcohol, this was shown in the tables of every hospital in London. Milk had, in fact, taken the place of alcohol, and the quantity of milk consumed amounted now to a pint a day, and sometimes a quart a day for each patient. He had taken a great interest in the question of inducing the working classes to support hospitals. They had till now been very badly supported by working people, possibly because they did not get an adequate *quid pro quo* in the shape of letters of recommendation, and also from not being allowed to put their members on the board of management. He thought if this last were done they would probably take more interest in the success of the institutions, as in Glasgow, with which he was best acquainted, workmen contributed 14,000*l*. annually to medical charities, while in London the street and shop collections only realised 18,000*l*. He would much like to see an improvement in that respect.

DISCUSSION *on* MR. BOOTH'S PAPER: ENUMERATION *and* CLASSIFICA-
TION *of* PAUPERS *and* STATE PENSIONS *for the* AGED. (*Printed
in the Journal for December*, 1891, vol. liv, part iv).

MR. W. VALLANCE said 'he rose with considerable diffidence and
embarrassment to address the meeting, not having had the opportunity of considering the paper in detail and analysing its figures.
With reference to the statement[1] that medical relief only is
counted as pauperising the sick person and the head of the
family, whilst the addition of relief in food is held to pauperise
the whole family, he might observe that the rule of classification
was that in medical relief the sick person only is counted, whilst
in other relief the head of the family is enumerated, with the
addition of the wife, child, or children on whose account the
relief is given. There was no doubt that the present statistical
records of pauperism were more or less incomplete, but so grave
had been the defects discovered in the earlier system, although
apparently more complete, that the Poor Law Board fell back upon
a single day's enumeration twice yearly for their figures. He
greatly feared that the forms for monthly and half-yearly returns
suggested on pp. 627 and 628 would be found unworkable. At the
same time it might be possible, in each year, to so arrange a
"statistical register" as to afford in parallel columns the requisite
classification and analysis which would admit of yearly totals being
reached, and which would obviate the possibility of duplication.
Upon the subject of old age pensions he would prefer not to offer
a remark at the present stage. The proposal involved principles
so entirely at variance with those hitherto generally accepted, that
it demanded a graver consideration than he had been able yet to
give it. It was a reversal of the principle that whilst in a free
country a man was free to trade with his labour, he should be held
to be responsible for his present and future maintenance ; so also,
that if a man contracted marriage, he did so, or was supposed to
do so, with the knowledge that the responsibilities he thereby freely
accepted he would be held liable to discharge. He confessed to
being afraid of the general result of a system which would lead
men to look forward to a public provision in the future, and not to
feel restraint imposed upon them in earlier life. He had himself
been bold enough to prepare a scheme—not of old age pension—
but of aid and encouragement to the voluntary exercise of thrift,
and which, in brief, was a scheme for the supplementation of a
certain limited form of voluntary savings out of earnings by corresponding subscriptions by employers : the advantages which he
claimed for this being, among others, that it would afford to an
insurer an encouragement to thrift by the doubling of his own
deposits, that it imposed the burden of supplementation upon those
who receive the benefit of the insurer's labour, that it secured to

[1] *Journal of the Royal Statistical Society*, vol. liv, p. 625 (December, 1891).

an insurer's family a provision in the event of his death before 65, that it measured the provision exactly to the measure of thrift, and that it provided, if old age arrived, for an ultimate pension. He would not say more than that on the general scheme of pensions, he felt he was on very thin ice, and would rather sit down and listen to others more able than himself to discourse upon it.

Mr. C. S. LOCH said he had had the advantage of seeing the paper before the meeting, and as he took a view opposed to that of Mr. Booth, he would at once refer to the early part of the paper. The paper consisted of two parts, of which the first three sections were one and the last another. Under those circumstances he proposed to run through various points in it. He knew that to deal with this question at all thoroughly under present conditions was extremely difficult. It seemed to him that they were in some danger of treating the question of statistics in a rather partial and unscientific manner. The use of statistics was to throw into concrete and clearly defined quantities what were generally treated as generalisations, and he thought that in the latter part of his paper Mr. Booth had rather drifted into a statement of more or less sentimental statistics. Directly they left the purely statistical statement they had to deal with a great many causes, and the application of their principles required essentially one characteristic—that those who were turning their attention to causes should be so versed in the actual administration as to know what the limits should be of any proposals that were made. They would also learn, so to speak, the intensity of the causes. In both these points he thought there was fear of failure. Next, he felt that there was a certain arbitrariness in the management of the figures. What was wanted in this matter of pauperism was a chart or table showing the movement in or out. Drink had been regarded as the principal cause, but he did not think they could so isolate it; and when they got to working through the various pp. 607—9, they found the total was very much larger when they added drink as a secondary cause. He did not think they could dissever the one from the other; life was too much mixed. He confessed that he did not quite follow Mr. Booth in his method of dealing with the Stepney figures. He had to do with a union where the outdoor relief was very largely reduced, and he found himself in this dilemma—that the number of applications in the course of the year was out of all proportion to the number of applications in the day. The consequence was he had to come to some sort of blend between the old and the new. That seemed to be a very difficult system to follow. It would have been easy to have said "Here are two systems: one creates paupers, and the other does not;" but Mr. Booth had taken the wine of five vintages and mixed it with that of 1889, and said, "Here is my average table." But he (Mr. Loch) did not think it was an average. It would have been much better to have waited and taken other unions, and then draw the deductions. With regard to the suggested tables on pp. 627 and 628, he was in the presence of Mr. Vallance desirous to say very little; but he had himself tried to compile something like a speci-

men paper, and after considering the form suggested by Mr. Booth,
he could not help thinking that the divisions of in-door and out-
door would have to be largely modified. There was one point on
p. 625 which he thought was worth attending to. Mr. Booth said:
" Combining the two we get 134 per cent.; or, in other words, we
find we have to multiply by 2·34 in place of 3·5 as assumed by
Mr. Dudley Baxter." He had looked up the present pauperism
figures, and he found that if they took those figures and applied
the system to them they got not 2·34, but 2 as the multiplier.
That made a great difference in the figures. Very much more
explanation was necessary with regard to the table on p. 631 if they
were to make any real use of the figures. Mr. Booth had made a
subtraction sum. He had put together all the paupers of the
country and set against it the old age pauperism. In the pauperism
of the country there were first of all the children, the insane, &c.,
but in the old age pauperism there were no children or insane;
the consequence was the two things did not correspond. They
ought to have the list of paupers for every five years, and then
they would see clearly what the pauperism was as against increasing
age. If the pauperism was at the same level, they would get the
corresponding sets of figures, but with results quite different from
those that Mr. Booth brought out. Next, Mr. Booth had not laid
any stress whatever upon the causes of pauperism, and that was a
crucial blot in his argument. No reference really had been made
to out-door relief of any serious character. If they were setting
aside absolutely this out-door relief question the less said about it
the better. A large proportion of this out-door relief should not
be brought into the account at all. Turning to the question of
pensions, if Mr. Booth had put his suggestions before the Poor
Law Commissioners when pauperism was so large his proposal
might have been adopted. The number of paupers for whom there
should be legislation could be largely reduced. As a matter of
fact, every year there had been a steady reduction of old age
pauperism. The whole system proposed was an elaborate super-
imposition of a new poor law, which would leave the old poor
relief going on as at present up to 60 or 65 years of age, and after
that there would be the pensions, but there was no promise in the
paper of an introduction of better administration of the poor law.
It was all very well to say credit was due to Mr. Bland Garland
and others, but those people knew that this sort of thing did not
help good administration. To him it was a serious matter that
these things should go forward upon figures which he did not
think from a statistical point of view could back the proposal.

The Right Hon. LEONARD COURTNEY, M.P., said he felt very
much like the late Lord Beaconsfield; he was on the side of the
angels, and he recognised there was a certain sphere he was unwilling to tread. Still he would, in the very fewest possible
minutes make but two or three observations that did occur to him.
Now Mr. Loch had said that this proposal was one to get rid
of the trouble of a very small proportion of persons who are
supported by the State over 65, and for the sake of that small

minority they were going to tend to pauperise the very large majority. The fact which struck him most forcibly in hearing this paper was the extreme proportion of those over 65 who were already pauperised. Thirty-eight per cent., according to one calculation—say, two persons out of every five—were receiving some kind of aid from the State; and although this figure is said to be excessive, and might possibly be reduced, Mr. Booth's own figures only reduce it to something like 35 per cent., and this is the very oppressive statistical fact in the paper. Nobody can be content with this vision of that immense proportion of elderly people receiving aid from the rates. It is true that a very considerable proportion of those ranked as paupers are only paupers by way of receiving medical relief or some casual assistance which does not affect their daily life. He would have liked a statistical statement of that number, so that they might get at the true proportion of the pauperised mass. But even with the greatest reduction, they would find left a very considerable number to make them anxious as to the present and the future. He did not understand why Mr. Bland Garland and Mr. Jones should be looked upon as persons whom it was impossible to imitate, and he strongly deprecated the suggestion that some kinds of virtue were too great, and that therefore they must take to regularising vice. It is impossible that all persons can in this or that fashion conform to the highest life. Not only are the poor always with us, but we must make up our minds to have them always with us; not only are they improvident, but they must be always improvident. Therefore let us take them as they are. He protested against all these arguments, and deprecated the reference to the two above-mentioned gentlemen as persons whose influence might not extend and whose example might not be copied beyond the sphere of Bradfield and Whitechapel. One of the most pathetic suggestions in the paper was with reference to the fate of women who are so dependent on men. They receive enough to go on with from day to day, and their future is left entirely uncared for; and this does not apply only to the poorest class. Though it might look incurably absurd, the true cure for that bad side of our social relations lies in women's suffrage. He did not suggest that giving woman a vote would make her self-supporting, but he put it forward as suggesting this, that one great thing we have to get hold of if we want to recast the organisation of our life is to consider that woman is to be a more self-subsisting animal, a person whose future should be dependent somewhat on herself, and not to be regarded as someone to be taken in hand by a male. Once get every father, husband, brother to look upon a woman as a person whose future ought to be capable of self-support, not as one falling helpless if left alone, and a very considerable reform of the problem of pauperism will be effected. He thought the last part of Mr. Booth's paper the most disputable. It requires not so much a knowledge of statistics as of human nature to weigh it. The dread of want is a tremendous element in human action. It has been said that all action depends on two things—love of pleasure or dread of want; but here the dread of want has to be

contrasted with the love of present pleasure, and we find too
often it is ineffectual to sustain thrift. The point suggested in
Mr. Booth's paper is that if you get rid by a State provision of the
necessity of having regard to the dread of want, you will perhaps
develop a greater anxiety for future pleasure. You are going to
say with respect to everybody, "You need not look upon the future
as involving sheer want; we will take all care away from you by
providing that from 65 you shall have a State provision, and we
hope this will encourage you to save." Those who do not save
now are to be impelled by this to save something. He did not
meet with human beings so constituted himself, and did not believe
he would be so constituted if put to the test. He felt there was a
great margin of people now hovering about those who do descend
upon public relief who have made some sort of a provision by
joining clubs, by saving, or even by the education in well-being of
their children, having always before them that as a cardinal duty
and an object of exertion. Is there not some risk of bringing
below the present margin of self-support those who are now above
it? and by giving them the comfortable feeling that they will
never be in want of bread, will not the motive to exertion be
diminished? Some years ago there was a witness before the
committee on Canon Blackley's scheme, whose evidence he
(Mr. Courtney) had read with considerable interest. A cabman,
born in a workhouse, lived a tolerably jolly life till he became old
and got nothing. He was asked how it was he had not looked
forward to the future, and he answered in almost poetic language
something in this fashion: "Can a butterfly even think there is
going to be a winter?" Will the motive to thrift be diminished
if an adequate claim to stave off the terror of want be provided as
a right for every citizen? He could not see his way to any other
conclusion, and in testing the question asked himself, What is the
kind of society you would create? Is it a better one to struggle
after to inspire each person with a sense that on him or her lies
the responsibility of the future and the necessity of making provision for it? or would it be improved by taking away this horror
of the fag-end of life, which is extremely powerful now among
many, and might with adequate teaching and example leaven the
mass?

Professor MARSHALL said that in talking to German friends,
if he wanted to prove that England could show as good studies of
contemporary social history as Germany could, his first example
was always taken, not from the work of leisured professional
economists, but from that of one of the busiest of business men,
Mr. Charles Booth. Germany had derived great benefit from the
practice of its Government of constantly inviting suggestions
from experts; and as the English Government did not do this so
frequently, it might be well that bodies of experts, and in particular
this great Society, should be forward in volunteering suggestions,
especially such as had a basis of experience behind them, their
practicability and utility having been already proved by volunteer
experiment. The paper just read offered an excellent opportunity

for doing this; and he ventured to hope that the Council would see
their way to urging the Local Government Board to act, at all
events in a tentative and experimental way, on some of Mr. Booth's
suggestions. He would now pass to a defect in poor law statistics,
for which the Government could not be held responsible. It arose
from the fact that people put down their ages as they wished them
to be thought to be, not as they actually were. When a man was
trying to earn an honest and independent living, he tried to conceal
his grey hairs, because they diminished his market value. But
when he was inclined to rely on public or private charity, he
generally represented himself as older than he was. It was probable
that a very great number of those who were entered in poor law
returns as over 65, were really under 60. If this were so,
Mr. Booth's calculations would need three corrections: Firstly,
the real evil was not quite as great as even he represented.
Secondly, when rigid proofs of age were required, the expense of
his scheme would be diminished. But thirdly, the number of
those who are past work and need a pension as much as those who
are really over 65, but who would be excluded from the benefits of
Mr. Booth's scheme, would be much larger than he takes it to be.
Possibly next to the general relation in which this pension scheme
stands to the existing poor law, he would observe that the general
teaching of history was that when any great social reform was
first introduced, the first essential was perfect simplicity; and in
order to get simplicity, a broad clear unambiguous line had to be
drawn, even though it did not closely correspond to the actual
conditions of life. This had been the case with poor law reform.
The evils with which the 1834 Act had to contend were so great,
and the men and the machinery by which it had to be carried out
were so inadequate for their task, that it was then necessary, and
because necessary therefore right, to draw broad clear lines round
those who were to receive public relief. These broad lines
assumed that public charity disgraces, but private charity does
not disgrace a man, and that public charity ought to be given
only to the destitute and only in proportion to destitution, without any reference to character or previous thrift. Both of these
assumptions were probably necessary to enable the 1834 Act to
render the splendid services to the country which it did render;
and he had no feeling but gratitude to the framers of the Act.
The time had however now come for inquiring whether these
two assumptions were true. He himself did not believe that
they were. People who took his view were often charged with
favouring lax administration. But that was not the case. As
between lax and rigid administration of the poor law, he was
on the side of rigid. But he thought the question for the future
was between discriminating and indiscriminating poor relief; and
he was on the side of discrimination. If the present poor
law was to be retained with all its faults, except that it was
to be polished by the addition of a pension scheme, he thought
Mr. Booth's plan was the best that had been suggested, for it was
the simplest and would work with less friction than others. In
common with others it would promote thrift by making it more

possible to save enough to escape the need of appealing for charity,
it would not interfere with the main work of benefit societies, and
it would strengthen the best trade unions which made liberal
benefit grants. For many of these unions were finding that as the
average age of their members increased, the number of the
superannuation benefit became almost intolerable, and public
pensions would leave more of their provident funds for other
purposes. But on the other hand Mr. Booth's scheme brought
out more clearly than any other the inconsistency of the present
relations between public and private charity. If Mr. Booth's plan
were adopted, there would be two public insurance schemes
working side by side. The income of both would be derived from
taxes, including rates. Everybody would contribute to both, but
the rich much more largely than the poor in either case. But on
the one hand, even if a man had lived a dissolute life he might yet
after 65 draw out of the new public insurance fund many times as
much as he had paid in without incurring any kind of stigma;
and on the other hand, a man who had lived as a good citizen and
done all he could when in work to provide for time of need, but
had yet been unable to maintain himself completely till the age of
65, could not get back a single penny of what he had himself paid
into the old insurance fund, without being stigmatized as a pauper
for the rest of his days; and to crown the absurdity, if he received
the money from a semi-public charity organisation society, to the
funds of which he had never contributed, he would then escape
the taint of pauperism. Such broad lines of division might have
been necessary in the past, but they were untrue lines; and we
were rich enough and had leisure enough to spend the money and
the time required for drawing divisions more in accordance with
reason and the actual facts of the case. He quite agreed with Mr.
Courtney that self respect and independence of character were of
far more real value to the English working classes than all the
money they had received in poor relief. But he held that the
present poor law, by putting on the same footing those who had
and those who had not tried to provide against a day of need,
tended to diminish those virtues; or at least not to promote them
as much as might be done by a poor law that was more reasonable, more discriminating, more generous, but not laxer than the
present one. He thought there should be no hesitation in taxing
all classes for any public purpose that could not be attained by
any other end. But since every tax cost more to the people than
it brought to the State, a man was injured by paying in taxes
a sum of money the net proceeds of which were to be returned to
himself. And he thought that was a weak point in Mr. Booth's
scheme, which involved the levying of very heavy taxes out of
which money would be paid back to all, whether they were in want
or not; and he would prefer that the new public pension scheme and
the old poor law should be assimilated and combined. Assuming
there to be no unnecessary waste, the rich might be fairly called
on to contribute freely to the expense of such an increased staff
as will be required to carry out an extended poor law in a more
discriminating way, and with some reference to the antecedents

and especially to the past thrift of those who applied for it. He did not think that the burden of providing for the deserving poor should fall entirely on charity organisation. societies. Other rich people besides the subscribers to these societies should be made to pay their share. We all owed the greatest gratitude to the officers of those societies for their splendid work; but they had undertaken more than they could manage, because they did much that ought to be paid for by taxes and rates which fell upon the whole of the wealthier classes, both those who were and those who were not selfish. No doubt this was partly unavoidable with the existing poor law; but the charity organisation societies seemed to him to make a mistake in trying to narrow rather than extend the help which the deserving poor got from the poor law. There was an immense field that properly belonged to private agencies: it needed more than all the money and more than all the energies which unselfish people were willing and able to supply : and much of that was left undone because besides their proper work private agencies were doing what should be done at the expense of all alike. The question whether a person in need came in contact with a charity organisation society and got help from it or applied to the poor law officer, and was called a pauper, was often decided by mere accident.

On the motion of Mr. Bourne the discussion was adjourned to the following Tuesday.

The discussion was resumed on 22nd December, but before it was opened, Mr. Booth said he wished to correct two errors in his paper which had been pointed out by Mr. Vallance. On p. 625 it was stated, "The doctor's visit and his medicine are not counted as pauperising more than the sick persons and the responsible party (father or husband); but if any form of food be added, though it be intended strictly for the invalid, the addition is held to pauperise the whole family." It should be that it only pauperises the responsible party and the sick person, unless the sick person be the responsible party, in which case it pauperised the whole family. Then with regard to the age of 60 (p. 630), Mr. Vallance had pointed out that that was not the legal age, but it rested with the guardians by usage. Perhaps some guardians present would tell the meeting whether there was any probability of old paupers overstating their age, as Professor Marshall thought this might involve a very great error.

Mr. STEPHEN BOURNE said he owed an apology to the meeting for not proposing to treat the subject from a statistical point of view. He regretted that he had not had time to look into the figures, but he did not for one moment presume to think that Mr. Booth's figures were open to very minute criticism in order to ascertain how far they represented the actual state of things. It seemed to him the *crux* of the whole question was the proposition embodied in the concluding pages of the paper, one which was novel in the form it assumed, but not at all novel in the thing it proposed to attain. He held a very decided notion as to that and kindred schemes

which had been proposed. They must, however, all be indebted to
Mr. Booth for his valuable facts, for they were not previously prepared to believe that there was such a large amount of pauperism
among the old people of the country. It was a lamentable thing
to think that the wage-earners and food providers, and to a very
large extent the wealth earners of the country, should in their old
age require either Government assistance or the aid of charity.
His feeling was that Mr. Booth's scheme was not workable. The
very large amount of money it would require would about treble
the income tax that was at present paid, and he was rather inclined
to think that this amount was not over estimated—probably the
reverse. Whatever scheme was proposed to carry out the object,
the bulk of the expense would not fall upon those who would avail
themselves of its provisions. He certainly thought all who attained
the age might themselves apply it to charity, for there were very
few, even in the most exalted classes of society, who had not some
relatives who would be glad to receive it. That was one point of
weakness which characterised Canon Blackley's original scheme.
Unfortunately it seemed to be sometimes considered that the merit
consisted in the bestowal of charity, rather than in caring to know
where it went. He believed that the large amount of money that
would have to be collected would be the first impediment, even
supposing the country agreed to raise so much by taxes. Speaking
as an old Government official formerly engaged in collecting the
revenue, he did not think that the Customs duties fell in fair proportion on the larger portion of the community. For instance, he
himself paid an insignificant amount on tobacco and alcohol, and
if the people could only see the temperance reform spreading
throughout the land, they would find the amount of Excise
tumbling down. Mr. Booth did not place the evil so high as many
others did, but certainly it was the source of some portion of the
poverty that existed among the aged poor. How was the scheme
to be worked? There would be a great difficulty in fixing the
true age of the recipient. The difficulty in proving the age of a
very large portion of the population was very lamentable, and
there would be a constant incentive to make out the age greater
than it really was. If the scheme were carried out, they would find
that there would be a general rush to assume a greater age than
the true one, and the enormous expense and difficulty of investigating all those cases would, to his mind, surpass the difficulty of
ascertaining whether the proposed recipients were worthy of consideration in the disposal of the present out-door relief. Then
again it would operate to a certain extent as an impediment to
emigration. Those who went to the colonies would feel that
there was a great loss to them of the provision secured at home.
As an old servant of the State he knew that the fact of having a
pension secured kept him in the service long after he would
otherwise have left it, and a large portion of the population would
reject the offers made to them to leave the old country and settle
in new places. There was a great amount of sentiment in this
matter, but he did not think it would be worth while for the sake
of that sentiment to adopt so large and expensive a scheme as that

proposed, involving so much labour and pains. If a man had laboured for the benefit of the country, spending his time, thought and energy in promoting the interests of the country, there ought not to be any feeling of disgrace or discredit about accepting a recompense in old age. They were running into a very great error in decrying judicious out-door relief and praising up in-door relief. The latter broke up family ties and cost the country a great deal more than was necessary, whereas out-door relief did something to assist other existing provisions. He therefore felt that the cost of guarding against fraud would far surpass that which was required to discriminate those who deserved help under the present system by means of out-door relief. No doubt a large portion of those who sought relief were undeserving members of society, but that relief itself was a matter of positive duty. However much a man might have contributed to his present misery, they could not leave him to starve. He ventured to think that Mr. Booth's scheme would not meet with acceptance from the large mass of economists and philanthropists.

. Rev. Canon BLACKLEY said he felt at the previous meeting that he should be quite content to make no further use of the invitation kindly given to him by the Society than to sit still and congratulate himself on the remarkable advance of public opinion since he first started on this proposal fourteen years ago. But there were some points in the paper that he thought it was only reasonable he should touch upon. Mr. Booth referred to certain suggestions made by Mr. Chamberlain and a Parliamentary committee, but he thought that anything they had put forward could hardly yet be called a proposal, for our statesmen and parliamentary men were quite wise enough not to commit themselves for the present to any particular scheme whatever. It was quite enough for them to press, as they are doing, upon public attention the enormous importance of this matter. He did not think that within any short time they would have any definite distinct proposal put before the public. He understood that Mr. Booth simply put forward the proposal he had explained as something in other people's minds. He therefore did not take it as adopted by Mr. Booth as his final view. His own (Canon Blackley's) first proposal was that every person of every class should be compelled to lay by a certain minimum provision in very early days. He had a Parliamentary committee to examine the question about the years 1885, 1886, and 1887, and that committee received very strong objections from the friendly societies against the sick pay part of his proposal. That part only of the proposal could interfere with the great friendly societies, and it was only the great friendly societies that ever ventured to enter the field against him, because the bad societies simply made a stalking horse of the great ones, their own unsoundness depriving them of any *locus standi*. The friendly societies made very violent objection to any interference with their sick pay. Their average sick pay was 12*s.*, and his proposal was only for a minimum of 8*s.*, but practically they did not provide for pensions at all, and therefore his proposal as to pensions could never be proved to interfere with friendly society action. But even if his pension proposal did affect (as it would not) the good of some particular society, the good of the whole nation should be considered first. The Parliamentary committee refused to entertain the idea of compulsory sick pay, and the National Provident League joined him in thinking it was a very advisable thing to bow his head to the storm; but then he thought they might reasonably go to the leaders of the friendly societies and say, "we give up the sick pay altogether, and as our pension proposals do not interfere with pensions you do not give, we ask you to join us in getting for our old people in their old days something that will keep them." He met with no response. He asked their assistance, but he never had an answer. While the subject was in debate he came upon another question which had not occurred to him at first. Mr. Bourne had stated that he was obliged to Mr. Booth for putting before them the great extent of old age pauperism. That was not very complimentary to him (Canon Blackley), who had published the fact years previously; for, curious to say, Mr. Booth put it at the very figure as his own —42·7 per cent. It was also a remarkable thing that that evidence was put before the Parliamentary committee seven years ago, and he took great pains to get the committee to give a recommendation to the Government that the inquiry he had made on a limited scale should be made on a general one, so that the country might know exactly what the measure of its old age pauperism was. Now there could be no question about the result, because it had been arrived at by two independent persons, with two independent methods. The providing of pensions for the aged was infinitely more important than providing sick pay. Mr. Booth put aside the German system with these remarks, "There are, I think, fatal objections in the complicated nature of these schemes and in the practical impossibility of exercising any compulsion of this character on our people." Now the pension system was not complicated, and further it was assumed in the paper that there was a practical impossibility of exercising any compulsion to make people provide for themselves, while it proposed as not impracticable to exercise an enormous new compulsion of the thrifty to provide gratuitous universal pensions for the wasteful. He thought that the completion of a scheme of that sort in Germany, once established was sure, and now unalterable, and there was no practical impossibility in the way of carrying out anything of the sort. Mr. Chamberlain's idea was that a compulsory scheme was not for the present to be thought of and therefore he put forward a voluntary one, and asked for State aid. He (Canon Blackley) never asked for State aid, but he said it was not unreasonable, because it took away the argument of our working people being unable to provide for old age. No reasonable man, knowing what our working people could earn in youth, would call it generally impossible for some provision to be made. The third scheme was that of old people having a pension conditional only upon the fact that they reached a certain age. That would certainly do away with in-door pauperism in some cases, but to his mind the pauperism would remain all the same. He could not agree with a scheme by which people who might be very unworthy should be given in early life an absolute claim to an old age pension to which they had paid nothing whatever. That scheme would give double out-door relief to everyone who now desired out-door relief and 5s. a week to everyone who did not want it at all. He contended that that was pauperisation, and would make paupers of people who got for nothing what they had not contributed to. For the present he thought they should be content to go step by step. If they established State aid, the nation would gradually learn in its wisdom to press upon public attention the importance of saying that if the State offered security and cheapness to everyone who did something for himself, then the wasteful and unwilling should be made to give their contribution, but if they began by establishing a pension for everyone that was old, they were making the prevention of pauperism for ever impossible, because in giving it to the old of the present day, they would give the younger a legal right which could never be taken away from them, and in a vast number of cases it would discourage and prevent the people from making any provision for themselves. Now he would show how he thought something might be done. There should be no pro-posal to give everyone at 65 years of age 5s. a week, but if the proposal was to make every young person give something towards his own pension, then those now too old to insure might be pensioned off, and would die out. That would do something to prevent the pauperisation of the masses, and to help the present old folk out of their misery. Therefore he said that to confer a universal gratuitous pension claim would make it impossible after-wards to introduce any measure of satisfactory thrift, whereas if they directed attention first to giving a good voluntary scheme and then later on a compulsory one, then they could deal with all the old and pauperised, and the taxpayers who would other-wise be called upon to pay that enormous charge, would be delivered from a monstrous and continual injustice, and the people who received that unjust levy would be saved from eternal degradation.

Mr. T. FATKIN said that if he thought 40 per cent. of the rising generation of working men would be paupers at 70 years of age, he would conclude that the improvident in early and middle life had a better chance of long life than thrifty working men. But the habits of working men now are different to what they were twenty-five years ago. Of the 14,000,000 males now living in England and Wales, 4,700,000 are (according to Dr. Ogle) under 20 years of age, 8,200,000 between 20 and 65, 460,000 between 65 and 70, and 660,000 over 70 years of age. If 40 per cent. of these latter, *i.e.*, 264,000, are now unprovided for, what are the prospects of the 8,200,000 now between 20 and 65? In Mr. Fatkin's opinion they have four times more money saved than the same number of working men who were living at those ages twenty years ago. The population had increased during those twenty years, but that does not affect the question. The

great increase in business in friendly societies since 1875 is the
result of wise legislation in that year. He thought that, as
regards building societies, more money belonging to the working
classes had been financed by these societies during the past
twenty-five years than has been financed either by Government
or trustees' savings banks. He granted that much money had
been lost, and will still be lost unless Parliament enacts further
statutory safeguards. Mr. Ludlow says that the Building Societies
Act of 1874 is too weak, and that "the opposition of one society
of exceptional magnitude has, it is understood, been the great
obstacle" to more stringent measures. He (Mr. Fatkin) would
venture to say that that society was not in Yorkshire. Twenty
years ago the Commissioners of Friendly Societies estimated the
capital of investing members at 15,000,000*l.*; the aggregate subscribed capital of 124 of the largest societies in England was
then 8,000,000*l.* Now the amount of funds in building societies is
put down as 51,000,000*l.*, but the amount is nearer 100,000,000*l.*,
and he had no hesitation in asserting that three-fourths of this
belongs to the working classes. As an illustration of the difference
between the registrar's returns and his own estimates, he would
take the figures for the society he represented, and for the accuracy
of which he could vouch. Twenty years ago investing members had
invested with the Leeds Permanent Building Society 350,000*l.*;
now they had 1,600,000*l.* Many working men invest their savings
weekly in building societies until they amount to such a sum as
enables them, with the society's assistance, to purchase one or
more houses. For instance, the borrowing members owe his
society 1,600,000*l.* upon mortgage of property for which they
have given 3,000,000*l.* Consequently the borrowing members
have 1,400,000*l.* of their own capital in the property, which sum
had been previously invested in the society, and therefore the
members have a capital of at least 3,000,000*l.*, whereas the
registrar returns this at 1,600,000*l.* Moreover, 75 per cent. of
this belongs to the working classes. The same proportionate
increase has been going on in connection with savings banks,
co-operative and friendly societies, &c. The savings of the working classes between the ages of 20 and 65 are worth not less than
200,000,000*l.* If these statements cannot be proved to be wrong,
he would like to ask the meeting whether it is not more necessary
in the interests of the working classes to direct the attention of
the legislature as to how this amount is being financed, rather
than how the working classes shall be taxed to support the
improvident in the future. He objected as much as anyone to
too much maternal government interference, but as manager of a
society in which nearly 15,000 working men are putting all their
savings, he had the authority of his board to say that they court
and desire any inquiry into their accounts by any persons
appointed by Government. He had not such a high opinion of
the manner in which the Government transacts its own financial
business, as to lead him to think it impossible for his private
undertaking to finance the savings of the working classes as well
as, and more economically than the Government; but the latter

is the proper tribunal to put statutory obligations on all societies as to how their business should be conducted.

Mr. J. H. ALLEN (Guardian of St. Pancras) said he had been a guardian for some years, and Chairman of the Out-relief Committee, so it was supposed that he ought to know something of the subject in hand. He was not going to criticise Mr. Booth's figures, but there were one or two points that he would like to call attention to before proceeding to the question of old age pauperism. On p. 612 Mr. Booth said : " So that the total number of persons living on 31st December who had obtained relief during the twelve months was 8,706, or 3,649 more than were counted on 1st January, being an addition of 70 per cent. on all classes of in-door paupers together." That was the most startling news he had ever heard for St. Pancras, and he thought it was rather mis. leading. As a matter of fact he might say that the number of in-door poor had varied very slightly during the last few years. For the week ending 5th December, 1891, the in-door poor numbered 5,085; in 1890 the number was 5,054. The out-door poor for the week ending 5th December, 1891, was 1,510, and for 1890, 1,550, so that the in-door poor had increased by 31, and the out-door poor had decreased by 40. Moreover it must always be borne in mind that of late years a considerable number of persons had taken advantage of the poor law infirmaries, and they now sent a large number of persons to training homes, convalescent homes, seaside homes, which was not even dreamt of being done some years ago. With regard to the out-door relief question, he wished to add a few figures. In the year 1871, when trade was going up by leaps and bounds, and the population was very much less than it was now, the amount of out-door relief was 32,000*l.* a year. In 1891, when trade certainly was not going up by leaps and bounds, and the population was larger, the amount of out-door relief was 6,500*l.* per annum. He ventured to say that not a single poor person had been injured by that; on the contrary, they were physically, morally, and socially infinitely better than they were before. Somers Town was a perfect paradise now to what it was then. He quoted these facts to show that though 25,000*l.* a year had been withdrawn from the labouring population, yet it was admitted on all hands that the parish was in a better condition than it was formerly. Now with regard to old age pensions, he took it that everyone, high or low, would like to have a pension guaranteed by the State for old age, and if he were one of the labouring population he should certainly go for Mr. Booth's scheme tooth and nail; but he did not think the scheme had been properly put before the public, who would have to pay directly about 17,000,000*l.* He would like first of all to know what was being done at the present time by the working classes in the way of saving for themselves. He would also like to know the amount of money invested at the present time by the working classes in post office banks, savings banks, building societies, and co-operative societies, and also what the trades unionists and friendly societies thought of the scheme. He remembered being at a meeting at Toynbee Hall some years ago, when the members of those societies said they were perfectly able to manage those things themselves, and would not have any interference from the State. He would also like to quote from a speech of Mr. B—— at one of the railway societies' meetings a short time ago. He said: "I understand that in the savings banks, especially of these railway companies, there are no fewer than 20,000 depositors, and that the amount of money deposited by them is over 1,500,000*l*." For all that the meeting knew, that movement was going on. It therefore seemed to him that they ought to pause very seriously before they attempted to put a stopper on such a splendid movement. It was perfectly well admitted' that a man who had by his own frugality and forethought, put by for his old age, was an infinitely better citizen and left a far better influence behind him than one who had allowed himself to depend entirely on the State or the parish for his old age. He imagined that what Mr. Booth wanted to know was whether the guardians agreed with his scheme or not. He, for one, did not agree with the scheme at all, and he would state the reason why. He considered that a wise and judicial administration of the poor law, leaving the working classes at perfect liberty to work out their own independence, was an infinitely better system than all the State aid in the world. He also considered that Mr. Booth's scheme was nothing more than a huge out-door relief system, and a large out-door relief was condemned by the report of the commissioners for 1834 in one of the most far-seeing reports ever issued. Still he did not like to pooh pooh a scheme simply because he did not agree with it himself. There could be no doubt that the scheme had come before the public, and they had got to face it. It might be that some such scheme as Mr. Booth's would be forced upon them by a majority of well meaning persons whether they liked it or not; therefore it seemed to him that those who were in the minority, if they could not squash it altogether, should try and make it as little objectionable as possible. Of the two schemes at the end of the paper he should prefer the first, always supposing that that hateful clause No. 5 was cut out of it altogether. To quote the words of the board of guardians of St. George's-in-the-East, it would be pauperisation indeed; it would discourage at once friendly societies and charity societies, and it would cut at the root of parental and filial affection. A great deal more might be said about the enormous improvements that had been made in the administration of late years: about why it was that although 2,000,000*l*. had been spent annually on the poor law and 4,000,000*l*. on charity, yet the results were so small; but he would conclude by thanking Mr. Booth for his paper.

Dr. W. OGLE said that Mr. Booth aimed at two objects, the substitution of maintenance by pension for maintenance in a poor house, and the removal from the receipt of such pension of the stigma of pauperism. For himself he could not see that any stigma whatsoever was attached to poverty, or to its necessary consequence, maintenance at the expense of others. Probably there

were cases—though Mr. Booth had shown that the proportion of
these was not so large as supposed—in which poverty was the
result of vice or idleness; but there were also cases in which
wealth was the result of methods of money making that would not
bear investigation by a strict moralist; and, if they were to generalise for all poverty from its exceptional cases, they must do the
same for wealth; with the result that poverty and wealth alike
would have to be regarded as disgraceful. Moreover if any stigma
did really attach to pauperism, he failed to see how that stigma
would be erased by Mr. Booth's plan of universal pensions. The
supposed disgrace of maintenance from the rates consisted in the
receipt of public money which the recipient had not previously
contributed himself; and this definition would apply just as fully
to the receipt of an old age pension by a labourer, as to his receipt
of out-door or in-door relief under the present system. He had
heard it said that the labourer or artisan would have contributed
indirectly if not directly to the fund from which his pension would
be paid, and that by virtue of such contribution all stigma would
be removed from its receipt. But the same was true, or at any
rate was equally true, of the fund from which in-door or out-door
relief is given under the poor law system; and if the mere fact
of indirect contribution, however inadequate, removed all disgrace
in the one case, it must be equally efficacious in the other; and yet
we were told that the receipt of a pension would be honourable,
while the receipt of poor law relief was a disgrace! In all cases
where the contributions made, directly or indirectly, by any
individual to the fund from which the proposed pensions were
to be provided were inadequate to supply one such pension,
the recipient—disguise the fact under what name you please—
would still remain a pauper to the extent of the excess of his
pension above his contributions; and that fact would not be
affected in the slightest degree by the further fact that other men,
who had contributed adequately, or more than adequately, to the
fund were having their contributions, or part of their contributions
returned to them. Take an example. Let A and B be two men
of the same age; and let the additional taxes paid by A, in order
to carry out this scheme, be such that when he reaches 65 their
sum would be equivalent to a pension of 25*l.* a year for the rest of
his life; while B contributes such amounts as would just give him
at that age an annual 1*l.* When they both reach 65, A is to
receive 13*l.* a year out of the 25*l.* which he has supplied; B is also
to receive 13*l.*, 1*l.* contributed by himself, the other 12*l.* by A. To
the extent of those 12*l.* B—call him what you please—is in reality
a pauper; and the fact that A has 13*l.* of his own money returned
to him makes no difference whatsoever. Or take another illustration. Supposing he (Dr. Ogle) met a man in great want, and
regardless of the advice of charity experts, offered him half-a-
crown. An eleemosynary taint might be said to attach to the
receipt of that half-a-crown; but would that taint be in the least
degree washed away, if, when he gave the man his half-a-crown, he
also give himself another by transferring a coin from his right
hand pocket to his left? He could understand and sympathise

with the feeling that might prompt the man at once to decline
his proffered alms; but he was utterly unable to understand,
and indeed he would feel nothing but contempt for the man who
having that feeling could nevertheless accept the money, if the
nature of the transaction were but disguised by such a transparent
covering as he had supposed. But it might be said if by this little
artifice you prevented the poor man's self esteem from being
wounded, why not adopt it? First and mainly because he objected
most strongly to all shams and all cunning devices to hide the
true nature of things and make black appear white; and secondly,
and in a minor degree, because the proposed device in this case
would be most costly; because—to go back to his illustration—
the half-a-crown in the process of transference from one of his
pockets to another would be converted into a florin. For it was
not to be supposed that this scheme of universal pensions could be
carried out without enormous cost of management. When account
was taken of the necessity of strictly investigating the ages of
claimants, of preventing personation, of insuring the conveyance
of the weekly dole to the right recipients, a large proportion of
whom would be decrepit and bedridden, and so unable to apply in
person for their money; and when it was further borne in mind
that it is held to be essential, in order to remove all appearance of
pauperism, that all this intricate detail of business shall be carried
out without the assistance of that local machinery by which the
poor law is now administered; when all this was taken into consideration, it would be seen that the expense of management
would be a very serious item in the total expenditure. Yet in
Mr. Booth's estimate not one penny was allowed for this. He
simply took the number of persons now living of 65 years of age
or over and multiplied it by 13, and so got his 17 millions as the
total annual cost; whereas when he considered on the other side of
the account what might be saved from the poor law expenditure, he
took as his basis the whole 8½ millions spent, of which no less than
3 millions are really spent on management and incidental expenses,
1¼ millions upon lunatics, and only 4¼ millions upon actual poor
relief. Nor should it be forgotten that these 17 millions at most
only represented the actual amount of the proposed pensions at the
present time; and that as the population grew so also would the
number of pensions, and consequently the number of millions to be
annually expended; and, further, that even as regards the present
cost there was much doubt whether the 17 millions would cover the
pensions of all the claimants. For, if there were one fact more
clearly taught than another to those who had much to do with
censuses, it was that a very large proportion of persons do not know
their precise age, and that even those who do are ready to misstate
it for the most trivial reasons; so that we might feel certain that
when once it is realised that the age of 65 gives right to a pension,
the number of persons of that age would make a sudden leap upwards; and, as one much interested in the recent census, he could
but express his satisfaction that the returns were collected before
this paper was read.

Mr. W. M. ACWORTH said it had been his misfortune as a layman and not a statistician to have to study the statistics of the poor law, and he thought that anyone who had done so would be grateful to Mr. Booth for pointing out the unsatisfactory way in which the Local Government Board figures were drawn up. For all practical purposes a lunatic was surely an in-door pauper. But he more frequently appeared as an out-door paupei, because, though in a public institution supported out of the rates, he was not in an establishment under the control of the guardians. But a person in a private certified home, supported by charitable contributions, was classed under the provisions of a special Act of Parliament as an in-door pauper. Surely it was desirable that the Local Government Board should be asked to draw up a more logical classification. The real organic distinction was between a person who lived in his own home and had his wages or his savings or his cadgings supplemented by the poor law, and one who was maintained entirely by the poor law. Practically the discussion had been on the question of pensions. Mr. Booth had put forward two main reasons for accepting his pension scheme. One was that the scheme might practically be considered as final; the other was that when 40 per cent. of the population over 65 were paupers, it was time to do something. Was the scheme final? Had people over 65 who were unable to maintain themselves a greater claim in the eyes of public opinion to be maintained without the stigma of pauperism, than the people who were unable to maintain themselves owing to sickness? If they depauperised people over 65 by giving them a pension, would they not be called upon to depauperise all people in the poor law infirmaries in London, in which there were at the present time twice as many patients as in the voluntary hospitals? They too, might, it seemed to him, claim to be depauperised. 17 millions was a large sum, but it might be worth while giving even 17 millions if it was a final scheme. But it might be said that very few working men lived to 65, and was there not a possibility that the working men's representatives in Parliament would move down the age five years, or say that the price of bread had gone up, and that the amount ought to be 7s. a week? Then as to the next point, they were told they must spend the 17 millions because 40 per cent. of the population over 65 were practically paupers. He did not much believe in that 40 per cent. The basis of the generalisation was so very small that everybody must feel a certain amount of suspicion in accepting it. He had in his hand a pamphlet issued by Mr. Loch. It mentioned four country unions in which the total number of paupers over 60 were 472, 254, 61 and 73. The population of the first three unions was practically the same, and the population of the last was about half as much again. So that in two country unions such as Bradfield and Linton, alike in general circumstances, in the one case with a population of 18,000 they had 73 paupers over 60, and in the other with a population of 12,000 they had 472 paupers over 60. Now could anybody generalise from figures made up in that fashion? The percentage of pauperism to the total population over 60 was in Linton 33 per cent., in Midhurst 18 per cent., in Brixworth 5 per cent., and in Bradfield 4 per cent. If it was possible to arrive at a state of things in which only 4 per cent. of the population over 60 required relief, evidently there was no need to apply heroic remedies. Surely no one would propose to embark on an expenditure of 17 millions to deal with 4 per cent. of the population. St. George's-in-the-East was probably the poorest union in England. The Strand was not amongst the poorest. Twenty years ago the percentage of pauperism in St. George's-in-the-East was 41 per cent., now it was 19 per cent. In the Strand twenty years ago it was 26 per cent., now it was 40 per cent. Surely the moral of that was that the number of paupers—in other words the number of people—to whom it is supposed to be necessary to give pensions, was absolutely a matter of poor law administration. Until they knew what the poor law administration was, and what it was going to be, it was impossible to generalise from a percentage arrived at from the figures for England at large as to what was the actual amount of preventible pauperism, and what was the most appropriate mode of preventing it.

Mr. F. HENDRIKS said that he wished to avail himself of the ten minutes allotted to speakers on this occasion, to offer a few observations upon the financial and economical results which would flow from the adoption of Mr. Booth's recommendation of universal pensions for the aged over 65. In the first place, he could not see that his figures were justified statistically. So far from 17,000,000l. a-year being the initial charge, it would be at least 26,000,000l. Mr. Booth had taken the population aged 65 of England alone, and had omitted that of Scotland and Ireland. But England's male population was only about 74 per cent. of the total male population of the United Kingdom. Then again the figures required correction to bring them up to present date, seeing that the population of England had increased something like 14 per cent. in the last decennial period of census enumeration. He was convinced that if it were statistically examined, it would be found that the net sum to be paid to male pensioners alone, aged 65, of course free of income tax, would be 26,000,000l. How was that to be provided for? It must either be by an increased income tax or by an augmentation of the poor law taxation of lands and houses, unless the whole fiscal system of the country were altered. Now the income tax at the present time, at 6d. in the £, produced only 12,800,000l. per annum, consequently the rate of taxation to meet pensions of 26,000,000l. at the outset, would have to be about 1s. in the £ beyond the present rate, or 1s. 6d. instead of 6d. What economical results could be expected from that? It would exceed the charge of the national debt, and consequently the rate of interest at which the Government could borrow in future would be very materially altered, and the effects on the economical condition of the country would be disastrous. He held that the scheme was perfectly impossible. In the three years coincident with the Crimean war, the income tax never averaged more than 1s. 3d. in the £, but that was only a temporary tax, and yet it was felt to be a grevious burden on the country at the time, although it soon after fell as low as 4*d*. in the £. Yet, according to the pension proposal, there was to be a permanent tax of 1*s*. 6*d*. in the £ to begin with, and he held that that was a *reductio ad absurdum*. He did not believe either in the rhyme or reason of State pensions: he thought they would be destructive to the three virtues that distinguished England—thrift, self-help, and charity. Those three virtues would receive so grievous a blow that he did not think they would ever recover. He must protest against the observation made by Mr. Booth about the present poor law. Of course they were not there to quarrel about a mere phrase, but when a phrase was taken in conjunction with the context it became important. He referred to the description Mr. Booth applied to the present poor law as a "socialistic law." He denied *in toto* that it ever was so. It was framed in a spirit of pure benevolence; it was passed to substitute something for the charity which had previously been dispensed by the Church and the monasteries on the aged and worn out poor. It was as impossible then as it is now to find the effectual means for this out of private charity. When they were left to voluntary charity, it might be got in retail, but it never was got in wholesale. It was with the founders of the poor law in Queen Elizabeth's time a statesmanlike object to prevent the uncertain effect of private and merely voluntary charity, and to substitute for that not a socialistic law, but a poor law by which the really deserving poor would be relieved by national and compulsory charity. The latter term might sound paradoxical, but it could be defended. He would illustrate it by the case of the famine relief some years ago in Ireland. They all paid for that as a compulsory charity, and through taxation it was made proportionate to the various means of the contributors. The English poor law never was in its inception a socialistic law, and it was not so at the present time.

Mr. EDWIN R. SPEIRS wished to say a few words with regard to the proposition made by Mr. Booth. He thought that the scheme placed before them now was the very best one before the country at the present time. Why he considered it so was because he believed it would be a great mistake to have a compulsory system of assurance when there was every indication that the working classes were doing that kind of thing for themselves. In the second place he thought that Mr. Booth had taken the first step towards separating the thrifty and the thoughtful people from the improvident and lazy. The great mistake that had been made in the poor law was that the unfortunate poor had to mix with those who were indolent and those who had been leading bad lives. The nation should separate the paupers, and place those who were unfortunate in houses apart from the others. We would then have a separation of the good from the bad, and consequently our support and sympathy would go into the proper quarter. He also thought it would be an injustice to the vast majority of the community to introduce a compulsory system of assurance, because in a great many cases it would be unfair for people to be taxed for that purpose. The mortality, for instance, of the Cornwall miners showed that very few of them reached the age of 60. The mortality among earthenware manufacturers, glass blowers, paper stainers, etc., was also so great that very few would reach the age of 65 to receive the benefits of the pension scheme. It would therefore be a great injustice to tax these people for something that they would not live long enough to enjoy. They had been asked if Mr. Booth's scheme was a final one. He thought it would be ridiculous to imagine that it was so. If Mr. Gladstone or Lord Salisbury came to the meeting and took his oath to any scheme to fit in with the present condition of affairs, and said it would be final, he (Mr. Speirs) for one would get up and say he did not believe it. They must go on improving their scheme as the world improved. There cannot be finality in such measures.

Mr. JOHN LLOYD (Hon. Secretary of the National Provincial League) said that at a meeting of the Brixton Liberal Association at which he gave a short address the other evening, a motion was put from the chair to the effect that it was desirable that the State should *assist in providing* pensions for the aged, but the meeting instead unanimously passed the resolution that the State *should provide* pensions. His own view was that the State ought to provide one moiety and the people themselves the other. It seemed to him that while he and those who shared his views were trying to put a stepping stone in the stream of pauperism, in order in some way to bridge it over, Mr. Booth tried to take a leap right across; and in trying to do too much, there was considerable risk of failure and of falling in the middle. The league suggested that the State should act as a trustee for the working classes; that the State should husband and take care of some of the money of the people which they had paid during their long lives in taxes, and return it to them in old age. There would be no pauperism in that. The country would not allow the present state of things to continue, this large army of aged paupers to exist amongst us. A change must come, and they were all called upon to try to devise the best scheme they could. Although different friendly societies and other associations had done an immense deal of good for the working classes, little had been done for aged persons, and scarcely anything for women. In 1820-30 he found, on looking through old country papers, that there were a large number of women's friendly societies in existence, but they had now entirely disappeared, and nothing seemed to have taken their place. He hoped that though they might not be able to make the costly bridge which Mr. Booth proposed, they would certainly have a stepping stone placed half way across the great river of pauperism, and that without further loss of time.

Mr. M. N. ADLER said that many friendly societies issued tables for pensions payable at a certain age, but very few members availed themselves of them. There were 6 million members of well regulated friendly societies granting sick pay and death pay, and 6 million members of industrial societies, but he doubted

whether there were 6,000 members of these societies who had provided for old age pensions. Of the Foresters it was stated that
not three out of half a million had voluntarily provided for a
pension. That being the case, he thought that all those arguments
founded upon working men being willing whilst still young to
make provision for old age which not half of them would attain
fell to the ground. They were not prepared to lock up their
savings in this way, and preferred to provide for more urgent
claims.

Mr. BOOTH, in reply, said that in attempting to go over the
whole subject he would try not to omit any points that had been
raised against him. If he did omit any he might perhaps make
it up by mentioning some which had been raised elsewhere. He
would divide the subject into two, treating the first three parts of
his paper as one thing, and the last part as another thing. With
regard to parts one to three, he would like first to reply to
Mr. Allen, who objected to his statement on p. 612, that the number
of persons who had obtained relief during the twelve months was
8,706, or 3,649 more than were counted on 1st January, being an
addition of 70 per cent. on all classes of in-door paupers together.
It did not mean that there had been that increase in the pauperism,
but merely that in attempting to state the annual volume of
pauperism in St. Pancras they had to add 70 per cent. That was
considerably less than at Stepney, but at the same time it had no
particular bearing on the administration of one place or the other.
The statement commonly made was that they ought to multiply
by 3½, whereas at St. Pancras it proved that they only had an
increase of three-quarters; therefore it was a favourable rather
than an unfavourable return. Mr. Loch complained that instead of
dealing with Stepney twice over, contrasting or combining Stepney
now with what it was many years ago, he ought to have worked
from several unions. It had been found very difficult to obtain an
equally complete account even of St. Pancras. He would however
readily admit that what he had done was very incomplete. He
felt that it would be perfectly impossible to arrive at a really
satisfactory statement by private inquiry, and that nothing but
a Government inquiry could do it. By the great kindness of
Mr. Elliott of the Local Government Board he obtained some
sort of comparison between different unions, and it was very
evident that the variation was so great that even if they took
twenty unions and worked them out they could not be perfectly
satisfied that the result would represent the whole country.
He did not think the figures given were at all satisfactory; they
were a perfect quagmire through which he had waded to the
best of his ability. He did not think the conclusion he had
arrived at was very much out, and it was similar to that which
Canon Blackley arrived at from an area also comparatively small.
He thought that Canon Blackley would take the same view as he
himself did, that a private individual could not do what was
needed. He had received an interesting letter from Mr. Aveling,
the clerk to the Paddington guardians, in which he said that in

Paddington they had adopted a system of case papers, and each case was numbered consecutively. The pauper carried his paper through the different institutions to which he might be transferred, and upon readmission he took up the same number again. That was an instance of how easily the thing might be carried out if the Government added a little pressure to the good will of the local bodies. The system of case papers there mentioned was certainly a very good one. As to part iv, Mr. Courtney hinted in a very gentle way that fools stepped in where angels feared to tread, and claimed himself to be on the side of the angels, but later on Mr. Courtney spoke of that wisdom which to the Greek was foolishness, and that showed that there were two possible ways of looking at a thing. Mr. Loch spoke of part iv as "sentimental statistics." Those statistics were by no means as hard and clear and firm as they should be, he wished he could have made them clearer and firmer. When he finished the first three parts he had doubted whether he ought to go any further, but he came to the conclusion that it was desirable the thing should be thrashed out. There seemed to him there was enough material for a very good discussion, and he thought that position had been proved. He did not at all object to being attacked. There were those who minimised the evil, represented at that meeting chiefly by Mr. Acworth. There seemed however no doubt that the numbers of old paupers were very great, counting as paupers everybody who received relief however small. He was inclined to think that if they knew the whole truth, it would be found that a very large number of those who received relief, received very little, but still they were in receipt of public relief. He did not doubt that good administration had a good effect, but in the first place all it did was to cause other forms of help to take the place of help from the rates. At Stepney they had practically given up out-door relief, but there were a great number who were so poor that when they were dead the parish had to bury them. Was it not possible that there might be a certain drift in town towards certain parishes? He believed it was so in districts where there was a great deal of endowment, and he felt sure that there would be a tendency to drift away from a well administered *régime* to another parish. Therefore they could not be certain that the evil was not so much cured as altered in its distribution. It had been suggested to him that Mr. Burt's return was taken on 1st August, and that there was no time in the year when the unions were so empty as at the beginning of August. That perhaps might be set against the possibilities of exaggeration with regard to age. Perhaps Mr. Allen would tell them whether the ages given in Mr. Burt's return could be relied upon.

Mr. ALLEN said he could not give an answer off-hand.

Mr. BOOTH said that Dr. Ogle spoke about the stigma of pauperism, and said that wealth might be disgraceful as well as poverty, but people without means who had to go before the guardians were in an entirely different position from those who

had pensions, however those pensions were obtained. Mr. Courtney
said that no one could be trusted to save if the fear of want was
not present. He thought that was a most astounding statement.
People saved in order to get capital for business and for their
children, and after that they saved for their own comfort. He
wished to lay stress upon the underlying character of the proposal
advocated, and in that way he found little difficulty in agreeing
with much that his opponents had said.

A vote of thanks to Mr. Booth terminated the proceedings.

MISCELLANEA.

CONTENTS:

I.—*The Russian Famine.* By E. LEVASSEUR. (Translated from the *Journal de la Société de Statistique de Paris*, January, 1891.)

IN making this communication to the Society I am relying on the publications of the Central Statistical Commission of Russia, of which our colleague of the International Statistical Institute, M. Troinitsky, is the director. The most recent publication, which I received yesterday, bears the title, *General Results of the Russian Harvest of* 1891. It contains not only the results of this harvest, but a comparison with those of the three preceding years, according to governments and districts, and shows the production of cereals, potatoes, hay and straw in 1891.

As everyone knows, Russia occupies the whole of the eastern half of Europe; for its surface, as to which all writers are not in strict agreement, is, according to my estimate (based on the returns of General Strelbitsky), 5,477,000 square kilometres,[1] and that of Europe is 10 million square kilometres. But the sixty governments (of which ten make up the old kingdom of Poland) considered in the official returns, deal only with an area of 5,016,000 square kilometres, Finland and the European portion of the Caucasian provinces being excluded.

Comparing the general results of the year 1891 with those of the quinquennial period 1883-87,[2] we have the following table:—

[1] This is Levasseur's estimate of the area of that part of Russia which is comprised within the geographical boundaries of Europe; an area which does not correspond with that of political *European Russia.*

[2] These results are published in *La Récolte moyenne dans la Russie d'Europe,* 1883-87; published by the Central Statistical Commission, but they deal only with the fifty governments of Russia proper: in the table the ten Polish provinces have been added.

	Mean 1883-87. Millions of		1891, Millions of		Difference. ——— Millions of Bushels.	Ratio of the Harvest of 1891 to the Mean of 1883-87.
	Tchetverts.	Bushels.	Tchetverts.	Bushels.		
Cereals.						
Winter wheat....	12·6	72·7	12·0	69·2	− 3·5	95
Summer „	29·5	170·2	18·5	106·7	− 63·5	62
Rye	118·5	683·7	90·7	523·3	−160·4	76
Barley	26·2	151·2	25·4	146·6	− 4·6	96
Spelt	1·3	7·5	1·0	6·3	− 1·2	85
Buckwheat	10·5	60·6	7·5	43·3	− 17·3	71
Millet	8·6	49·6	6·2	35·8	− 13·8	72
Peas	2·4	13·9	2·7	15·6	+ 1·7	112
Maize	3·9	22·5	4·9	28·3	+ 5·8	125
Total	213·5	1,231·9	169·0	975·1	−256·8	79
Oats....................	93·3	538·3	77·5	447·2	− 91·1	83
Grand total....	306·8	1,770·2	246·5	1422·3	−347·9	80
Potatoes	83·0	478·9	69·1	398·7	− 80·2	83

Compared with the average for 1883-87, the deficit of cereals (including peas) which serve for the use of man is therefore, according to this table, 257 million bushels, or 21 per cent. If we include oats, which are used as food in Russia both for men and animals, the deficit is 348 million bushels,[3] *i.e.,* 20 per cent.[4] Comparing it, as the Russian Central Statistical Commission has done with the last three harvests, 1888-90, the deficit for the cereals (including peas) is about 21 per cent.; as compared with the first of these years, which is the best that up to the present has been recorded in Russia, it is 30 per cent.

[3] Compared with 1888 there is a deficit of 30·2 per cent.
   „   '89   „   10·4   „
   „   '90   „   21·2   „

[4] The Central Statistical Commission has calculated the mean weight of cereals of all kinds per head of inhabitants in the country districts (*i.e.,* without taking into account the population of the towns), with the following result:—

              In 1889................. 723 lbs. of cereals per head.
                „   '90................. 855   „
                „   '91................. 622   „

In Russia, wheat and maize having much less importance than rye and oats, we can estimate the mean weight of cereals at 48 lbs. per bushel, and the production per head is—
        In 1889, 15·1 bushels; 1890, 17·9 bushels; 1891, 12·4 bushels.

In France the production of all kinds of cereals is about 260 million hectolitres (see *La France et ses Colonies,* by E. Levasseur, vol. ii, p. 43), or 715¼ million bushels, which gives about 18·7 bushels per head, if we calculate on a population of 38¼ millions (*i.e.,* the total population, towns included). It must be noticed, in comparing these figures with those of Russia, that the proportion for France would be much greater if we calculated only on the rural population. To convert these bushels into pounds, we should here take 52 as the factor instead of 48, because the principal crop in France is wheat, which is heavier than rye; we thus have 1,014 lbs. per head. Land is more highly cultivated in France than in Russia, and consequently the average production is greater.

It may be asked how far these figures are reliable. I answer, to the same extent as the returns of most other European States. They are collected on the spot by local administrators, and worked up by competent authorities. Like harvest returns generally, they are the outcome, not of enumerations, but of estimates; they are consequently only approximate. People can of course refuse to believe in them from a pre-conceived scepticism; but then we must give up speaking of good or bad harvests in any country, and refrain from passing any opinion on agricultural wealth, for opinions of this nature can in every country be founded with precision only on statistical data. We can check these figures and criticise them, but only by comparing them with other figures, furnished also by statistics on harvests of a similar nature, obtained during several years from the same localities, and by bringing to bear upon the official returns information obtained through private sources or by means of the press. This is what has been done, and I believe, on the whole, that the comparative measure here given of the harvest of 1891 is sufficiently well grounded to enable us to calculate fairly the consequences. Whether the deficit be 300 or 350 million bushels, it is in either case enormous.

The causes of this failure are well known. The winter had been very hard, the late spring frosts were severe, and the cold, penetrating the ground unprotected by snow, killed the seeds; when the summer did come, the drought lasted long, and was aggravated by a persistent east wind.

The whole of Russia has not suffered to the same extent. Thus in the extreme south the harvest appears to have been good in the Caucasian provinces: but these do not form part of European Russia, and their crops are not included in the foregoing table. The grand duchy of Finland is also excluded. In short, the area of the sixty governments (including the Asiatic portions of Perm and Ufa, since their harvests are included in the total) on which the statistics bear is 5,016,030 square kilometres, and the population about 92 million souls in the middle of 1891.

This huge area covers many regions differing essentially in climate and soil. In Poland the harvest was up to the average, slightly inferior to that of 1890, but superior to that of 1889, and in this quarter there will be no scarcity.

Production per Head.*

Governments.	1890.	1891.	Governments.	1890.	1891.
	lbs.	lbs.		lbs.	lbs.
Kalisz	745	694	Radom	777	617
Kielce	780	684	Siedlce	891	761
Lomjo	622	460	Suwalki	753	736
Lublin	950	751	Warsaw	689	651
Piotrkov	505	361			
Plock	934	941	Poland	747	657

* In this and the two following tables, the net weight of cereals and peas per head of *rural* population only is given, the quantity set apart for seed having been deducted.

Almost all the governments situated immediately to the east of Poland—those of Little Russia, the Baltic provinces, and those which extend to St. Petersburg and Moscow—have on the whole a crop superior to that of 1890; those in the centre of Greater Russia—Yaroslav, Moscow, Smolensk, Kaluga—have suffered from the calamity, but its severity only begins to be appreciable in the two latter, to the south of Moscow.

Production per Head.

	1890.	1891.
	lbs.	lbs.
Kaluga	566	457
Moscow	429	367
Smolensk	817	702
Yaroslav	790	736

But it is in the south-eastern governments, in the basin of the Don and of the lower and middle Volga, that the disaster is most severe. If we draw a line on the map from Odessa to Moscow, and from Moscow to Vyatka, we see that all the districts bounded on the one hand by this line and on the other by the Ural mountains and river, the Caspian Sea, the Ponto-Caspian depression, and the Black Sea, have suffered most cruelly. With the exception of Ufa and Ekaterinoslav (which have a better harvest), the crops are everywhere inferior to those of 1890; there is a deficit of nearly 70 per cent. in the government of Tamboff, and it is still greater in Orenburg, where the total production however is less. In Voronej it reaches such proportions that we should hesitate to accept the figures were they not contained in an official publication The harvest here was 13·7 million tchetverts in 1888, 6·6 million in 1889, and 14·9 million in 1890. Last year it was only 2·8, so that the rural population, instead of gathering in 1,505 lbs. per head as in 1890, had only 66 lbs. in 1891. This government exported; now it must import, if it can.

Production per Head.

	1890.	1891.	Percentage.
	lbs	lbs.	lbs.
Kazan	529	139	26
Kursk	1,144	549	48
Orel	1,130	649	57
Orenburg	534	80	15
Penza	664	404	61
Ryazan	900	345	38
Samara	675	222	33
Saratoff	981	429	44
Simbirsk	773	303	41
Tamboff	1,327	420	31
Tula.................	1,211	680	56
Voronej	1,505	66	4
Vyatka	705	451	64
	—	—	39

[To these thirteen governments might have been added those of Kaluga, Nijni-Novgorod to the north, and Astrakhan to the south. This has not been done, because the deficit is there less than in those we have tabulated.]

These thirteen governments which have suffered the most severely form a compact area, which, from one end to the other— from Kursk on the south-west to Vyatka on the north-east—has a length of more than 1,400 kilometres, whose area, 1,031,000 square kilometres, is almost double that of France, and whose population, according to the official estimate for 1886, is 27,647,000.

Area and Population of the Thirteen Governments which have suffered most.
(Official Estimate of 1886.)

[000's omitted.]

	Square Kilometres.	Population.		Square Kilometres.	Population.
Kazan	63·7	2,162,	Simbirsk	49·5	1,606,
Kursk	46·4	2,355,	Tamboff	66·6	2,759,
Orel	46·7	1,050,	Tula	30·9	1,464,
Orenburg	191·2	1,317,	Voronej	65·9	2,664,
Penza	38·8	1,550,	Vyatka	153·6	2,937,
Ryazan	42·1	1,867,			
Samara	151·0	2,570,			
Saratoff	84·5	2,346,	Total	1030·9	27,647,

This vast region has the uniform aspect of a plain, low towards the east on the left bank of the Volga and higher on the right bank, in Greater Russia, which is a plateau of about 250 metres (825 feet) in height, slightly undulating, and even forming a shallow basin through which the Don and its principal tributaries meander. It is bounded on the east by a chain of picturesque hills of from 300 to 350 metres (1,000 to 1,150 feet), at the base of which flows the Volga. The mean temperature of this plain varies from + 8° (centigrade) in the south to + 2° in the north, which is about the same temperature as that of Sweden. The winters are as severe as those of Finland, from − 8° to − 14° (centigrade) in January, but by way of compensation the summers are as warm as the centre and south of France, + 19° to +24°. There is little rain, the mean annual fall being 40 to 50 centimetres (16 to 20 inches); the number of rainy days at Kazan is only 90. June is the wettest month. This region is by nature sparsely wooded towards the centre, besides which the peasants have themselves cut down the trees, either for firewood or in order to utilise the land for cultivation. Government has endeavoured to put a stop to this deforestation, but the law enacted seems inadequately enforced, and it is only in the steppes of the south that its efforts to plant have met with any measure of success. The absence of large trees is one cause of the dryness, for it leaves this flat country without the slightest protection against the burning south winds and the east winds—glacial in winter, and always dry. This is why this portion of Russia has suffered more than the other parts from the spring frosts, the dryness of the east winds, and the absence of summer rains.

The harvest of 1890 had given in these provinces 657 million bushels; in 1891 it only yielded 359 millions, a deficit of 298 millions, or 45 per cent. Of the total deficit of 348 million bushels for the whole of Russia, these thirteen governments account for 298, or 85 per cent.

Total Quantity of Cereals in 1890 and 1891.

	1890. Millions of		1891. Millions of	
	Tchetverts.	Bushels.	Tchetverts.	Bushels.
Kazan	6·0	35	3·2	18
Kursk	11·0	63	6·5	38
Orel	9 3	54	6·1	35
Orenburg	4·5	26	2·8	16
Penza	4·5	26	3·6	21
Ryazan	7·2	42	3·9	23
Samara	7·9	46	4·0	23
Saratoff	8·4	48	4·8	28
Simbirsk	5·4	31	3·3	19
Tamboff	14·3	83	6·4	37
Tula	7·9	46	5·3	31
Voronej	14·9	86	2·8	16
Vyatka	12·4	72	9·4	54
Total	113·6	657	62·1	359

It should be noted that this district includes the greater part of the "black land," the region most fertile in cereals, and for that very reason the population is denser there than elsewhere (27 per square kilometre; the mean density of European Russia is 16).

A deficit of 20 per cent., *i.e.*, one-fifth of the produce of a country, is in all cases sufficiently alarming. When this fifth represents 348 million bushels, the evil is considerably aggravated because it is the more difficult to remedy. It would require 6,000 ships of a tonnage of 2,000 tons to bring the quantity required to Russia.

If this deficit had occurred in some country where the average wealth per head was large, such a country could, up to a certain point, buy with its savings a sufficient quantity of food to stave off famine. Thus in 1879-80 France was able to buy in two years the equivalent of 86 million hectolitres of grain and flour, and found more than 1,500 million francs to pay for them. This is not the case with Russia, where, apart from a certain number of proprietors who enjoy a large income, and the inhabitants of the great industrial centres, the mass of the peasants live on the annual produce of the soil, without laying by. Many of them are even debtors to the treasury, since they do not pay their taxes regularly, and are besides burthened with public debts.

Independently of the sum necessary to acquire 348 million bushels, which represent probably not less than 60,000,000*l.*, and of the number of ships required to carry the grain to Russian ports, we must take into account the internal means of transport by which it would be carried to the empty markets.

Now, in spite of the development of Russian railways during the last thirty years, there are still very many gaps, as there are only now (1890) 17,591 miles of railway over an area of a little more than half Europe (exclusive of Finland and Caucasia).[5]

In reality, to preserve the people from famine, Russia will not require to import anything like 350 million bushels.

It may be said that the Russians divide their grain harvest into four principal parts: the first for their own nourishment, the second for that of their animals, the third for the manufacture of alcohol, and the fourth for exportation.

Since 1879 Russia has exported on an average 300 million roubles' worth of cereals and flour,[6] which is more than one-fifth of the value of the whole crop,[7] but rather less than the fifth of the quantity gathered in, since it is especially the dearest cereal, wheat, which is exported.[8] On the 28th July the export of rye was prohibited, but the delay granted enabled foreigners to lay in a portion of their stock. Since the 3rd November all exportation of cereals has been forbidden.

In 1889·90 the receipts from the tax on drinks, which is principally derived from the distilleries, counted for more than 270 million roubles in the budget. M. Broch estimated in 1880-81 that the consumption of alcohol in Russia was 3,600,000 hectolitres (80 million gallons), and Mulhall in his new dictionary puts it down at 4 million hectolitres (91 million gallons). In calculating the return at 25 per cent. for rye and maize, and supposing that these two cereals form one half of the raw material, there would be about 8 million hectolitres (22 million bushels) of grain employed in this manufacture. The high price of grain will hamper the distilleries, and, besides, the government can exercise a powerful influence. Thus there is on this side also an economy possible; but the treasury would suffer in consequence; the return from one of the principal sources of its revenue would be seriously diminished.

Cattle consume the greater part of the oats, and also a portion of the inferior grains. They are also fed on straw and hay; but

---

[5] The total length of European railways was about 83,000 miles in 1890. Great Britain has 100 kilometres of railway for every 1,000 square kilometers, France 64, and Russia 5 only. It must also be noted that in Russia the railways are very unequally distributed, and that the region affected by the famine is more opened up than the northern portion of the empire.

[6] 427 million roubles in 1888, 375 in 1889, 308 in 1890.

[7] The evaluation of the harvests of the years 1884-89 has varied between 1,714 and 1,343 million paper roubles.

[8] In 1889, when the total harvest was 1,589 million bushels, Russia exported 300 million bushels, of which 104 millions were wheat, 67 oats, 52 rye, 45 barley, &c. According to official statistics, Russia appears to have exported on the average, from 1883 to 1889, 49·8 per cent. (*i.e.*, one-half) of the wheat crop, 66 per cent. of the maize, 37 per cent. of the barley, 19 per cent. of the oats, and 9 per cent. only of the rye, although the latter is the principal crop: this is because the population lives chiefly on this latter cereal.

straw is as scarce as grain, and the drought has burnt up the meadows and much diminished the hay harvest. From want of food to give them, many of the peasants will sell their animals or eat them to sustain themselves—a second possible economy, but one to be regretted. The value of the animals will decline, as generally happens in such cases; horses and oxen are already offered at very low prices in certain districts. When the famine is over many years will be required to repair the losses which it will have caused to the live stock of Russia.

Will the reduction under these three heads be sufficient to make the food stock supply the wants of the inhabitants? The Russians live principally on rye; nine-tenths of the net crop (*i.e.*, after having subtracted the quantity necessary for seed for next year's harvest) are generally required for home consumption. But it is precisely the rye crop which is most deficient; 523 million bushels have been harvested instead of 684 millions; 161 millions are wanting. If we estimate the average consumption per head at 2·5 hectolitres (6·9 bushels), 640 million bushels would be required to feed 92 million people (a number which I consider probable as being now the population of these sixty governments), and the deficit is still 117 million bushels. But the whole population does not live on rye, since other grain is consumed. This explains how the Minister of Finance, calculating on other data and by a different method, estimates the deficit at 85,500,000 pouds only (about 60 million bushels), and concludes that on the whole Russia has produced enough for her wants. The deficiency of rye is, apparently, therefore from 60 to 120 millions, say 85 million bushels, which must be replaced by some other food. How much can importation supply before the next harvest? What other food can be procured to replace the bread? How will places at a distance from railways be supplied? What influence will the scarcity have on prices? These are questions into which we will not enter at present. We will conclude by saying that privations must engender disease and increase the death-rate. It is unfortunately certain that in such conditions there will be fewer marriages, fewer births, and, above all, more deaths in 1892 than there were in 1890. It is with a feeling of profound sadness and compassion that we think of the sufferings which these millions of human beings will endure through climatic conditions which it was out of their power to avert. But since the evil is inevitable, it is better to meet it fairly than to turn aside, and try to measure its extent in order to seek the better afterwards the remedies which may mitigate the pernicious results; this is a task that devolves upon statisticians.

The Russian government understands the situation; it has already taken measures in consequence, and it watches with care. Private charity is doing its part, and is on the increase. I do not intend here to detail what the one and the other have done up till now to help so many unfortunates to tide over a year of dearth, and it is not for us to counsel them as to what is still to be done; before the Statistical Society we confine ourselves to exposing the true state of affairs.   R. H. H.

II.—*Religious Census of India*, 1891.

	Total.	Males.	Females.
Total : India	288,159,672	—	—
A. *Provinces—*			
Censused...........................	221,094,277	112,500,870	108,593,407
Registered	261,910	Sex not	recorded.
Total	221,356,187	—	—
B. *States—*			
Censused...........................	· 66,112,769	34,216,083	31,896,686
Registered	690,716	Sex not	recorded.
Total	66,803,485	—	—

	Total.	Provinces.	States.
Religions—			
Hindu	207,654,437	155,031,299	52,623,138
Musulman	57,365,214	49,594,442	7,770,772
Christian............................	2,284,191	1,491,489	792,702
Jain	1,416,109	494,483	921,626
Sikh...................................	1,907 836	1,407,971	499,865
Buddhist	7,131,057	7,095,094	35,963
Parsi	89,887	76,935	12,952
Jew	17,180	14,655	2,525
Aniaristic (Forest Tribes)	9,302,083	5,867,355	3,434,728
Minor religions*	289	267	22
Unreturned	38,763	20,287	18,476
Total	287,207,046	221,094,277	66,112,769

* Minor includes unclassible entries, as Theist, Deist, Atheist, Agnostic, indifferent, of no religion, &c., &c.

J. A. BAINES.

III.—*Commercial History and Review of* 1891.

THE following is taken from the supplement to the *Economist* of 20th February, 1891, in continuation of similar extracts for previous years :—

" Perhaps the most noteworthy feature of our trade in 1891 is the vitality it has displayed under exceptionally adverse circumstances. Not only here, but almost universally, the year was one of financial prostration, the result of previous excesses. All lending nations have had heavy losses to bear, and been forced to economise ; while those countries that had been living upon borrowed money, finding they could get no further credit, have been compelled to do without many things they had previously been able to obtain only too easily. With the financial incidents of the year we shall deal more fully later on. Here it is sufficient to note how their tendency has been at all points to restrict business, which has had further to contend against the depressing influence of bad harvests, of currency complications, and of hostile tariff legislation. There would certainly have been no cause for surprise if, under such conditions, we had failed quite to maintain the volume of our trade. But, as a matter of fact, there was no shrinkage. As to our foreign trade, the record is as follows:—

Imports.

	1891.	1890.	Increase or Decrease.	
	£	£	£	Per ct.
Half year ending 30th June	212,292,000	206,927,000	+ 5,365,000	+2·5
31st December	223,399,000	218,959,000	+ 9,440,000	+4·4
Year	435,691,000	420,886,000	+14,805,000	+3·5

Exports of British and Irish Produce.

	1891.	1890.	Increase or Decrease.	
	£	£	£	Per ct.
Half year ending 30th June	124,066,000	127,556,000	− 3,490,000	−2·7
„ 31st December	123,206,000	135,974,000	−12,768,000	−9·4
Year	247,272,000	263,530,000	−16,258,000	−6·2
Total imports and exports	682,963,000	684,416,000	− 1,453,000	−0·2

Here an increase in the value of our imports as compared with 1890 is more than offset by a falling off in that of our exports, and the total of imports and exports combined shows a fractional decline. When, however, the returns are more closely analysed, it is found that while the increase in the value of the imports is mainly due to the larger quantities we received, the falling off in the exports is to some extent attributable not to diminished shipments, but to the lower prices at which these are entered. The details of this analysis will be found in another column (see Appendix I), and from it we derive the following statement, which shows how the volume of our foreign trade last year compares with 1890 and previous years:—

Volume of Our Foreign Trade. Increase or Decrease per Cent. as compared with previous Years.

	Imports Retained for Home Consumption.	Exports of Home Produce.	Imports and Exports.
	Per cent.	Per cent.	Per cent.
1891....................	Increase 4·34	Decrease 5·30	Increase 0·25
'90....................	Decrease 0·31	„ 0·51	Decrease 0·39
'89....................	Increase 11·25	Increase 3·71	Increase 8·08
'88....................	„ 3·42	„ 4·64	„ 3·94
'87....................	„ 5·07	„ 4·80	„ 4·93
'86....................	Decrease 0·37	„ 5·33	„ 1·94
'85....................	Increase 3·28	Decrease 3·84	Decrease 0·26

It is worth noting that the increase in the quantity of foreign commodities we imported for home consumption in 1891 was mainly in the raw material for our textile manufactures, and that it was not for us therefore as with some other European nations, who, owing to the failure of their own harvests, were compelled to import very large additional quantities of food products which happily they were able to obtain with comparative ease owing to the extraordinarily abundant harvest in the United States and Canada. And as regards the exports, it must be remembered that trade with the east was hampered by exchange difficulties consequent upon the frequent and rapid fluctuations in the price of silver, and that we had poured such large quantities of our goods into the United States during the latter part of 1890 in order to avoid the higher duties of the McKinley tariff that some temporary curtailment of our shipments thither was inevitable. The actual falling off was from 32,077,000*l.* in 1890 to 27,544,000*l.* in 1891, and if we add to that a decrease of about 5¼ millions in our exports to the southern and central American States, who, being unable to borrow, could not buy from us, the great bulk of the decrease is accounted for. Thus, on the whole, our foreign trade in 1891 was wonderfully well maintained, while there can be no doubt that our home trade assumed larger dimensions. Of that perhaps the best evidence is afforded by the traffic returns of our railway companies. Taking the fifteen chief English lines whose accounts are summarised in Appendix II, the comparison with 1890 is as follows :—

	Passengers and Parcels.		Merchandise.		Minerals.	
	1891.	1890.	1891.	1890.	1891.	1890.
	£	£	£	£	£	£
First six months	12,380,600	12,276,000	9,263,100	8,998,600	6,876,800	6,540,300
Second „	15,322,300	14,870,900	9,711,100	9,597,400	7,053,000	7,015,900
Total for year	27,702,900	27,146,900	18,974,200	18,596,000	13,928,800	13,556,200
Increase or decrease first six months....	+104,600 = 0·9 per cnt.		+264,500 = 2·9 per cnt.		+335,500 = 5·1 per cnt.	
Increase or decrease second six months	+451,400 = 3·0 „		+113,700 = 1·2 „		+37,100 = 0·5 „	
Total increase or decrease for year	+556,000 = 2·0 per cnt.		+378,200 = 2·0 per cnt.		+372,600 = 2·8 per cnt.	

The growth in merchandise and mineral traffic here shown is proportionately smaller than the average of immediately preceding years, as will be seen from the following :—

Increase in Railway Receipts.

	Merchandise.	Minerals.	Merchandise and Minerals Combined.
	Per cnt.	Per cnt.	Per cnt.
1891	2·0	2·8	2·3
'90	2·8	4·1	3·3
'89	7·0	6·1	6·6
'88	4·1	2·8	3·5
'87	1·6	8·6	2·5

Still, although the rate of progress slackened in 1891, there was an expansion, which, taken in conjunction with the stationariness of our foreign trade, makes it evident that the volume of our home trade must have undergone a further enlargement. In some branches of industry, such for instance as the textile trades, and some departments of our metal trades, that growth in the home consumption can be clearly traced, and although in others, such as the pig iron and coal trades, there was curtailment instead of expansion, yet the volume of business as a whole undoubtedly increased.

" There is, however, one feature of the statistics, both of our home and our foreign trade, which is calculated to cause some anxiety. They show that we lost ground during the latter half of the year. Thus the decline in the value of our exports, which was no more than 2·7 per cent. in the first half of the year, increased to 9·4 per cent. in the latter half; and in the railway traffic receipts, while the first half of the year yielded an increase of 2·9 per cent. in merchandise and 5·1 per cent. in minerals, in the second half the increases were only 1·2 per cent. and 0·5 per cent. respectively. That is a backsliding which is somewhat ominous, and clouds the prospect for the current year.

" When we pass from a consideration of the amount of business done to that of the profit earned upon it, there is every reason to believe that in this respect 1891 compares unfavourably with its predecessor. It is notorious, of course, that in all branches of finance business this was the case. And although there are no means of measuring exactly the profits of general trade, all evidence points to the conclusion that they were sensibly curtailed. For one thing 1891 was a year of slowly declining prices. Here is how our 'index number,' which registers the combined movements of a number of chief commodities, compares with previous years :—

'Index Number,' representing the Combined Prices of Twenty-two Leading Commodities.

1st January, 1892	2133
„ July, '91	2199
„ January, '91	2224
„ July, '90	2259
„ January, '90	2236
„ July, '89	2161
„ January, '89	218
„ July, '88	2 1
„ January, '88	30
„ „ '87	059
„ „ '86	023
„ „ '85	098

From this it will observed that the general level of prices was fully 4 per cent. lower at the end of 1891 than it was at the beginning. There was, it is true, a distinct rise in the prices of nearly all food products; the price of Scotch pig iron was forced up by the manipulation of a London syndicate; and owing to the deficiency of the Indian crop, a very sharp rise took place in jute. These advances, however, which were in no way beneficial to manufacturers or traders, only emphasise the decline which is recorded in nearly all other leading commodities. There was certainly, as we have previously said, a reduction in the prices of imported raw material, and here it may be well to show what was the overhead movement in the prices of our imports and exports for the year. The method of arriving at this is set forth in Appendix II, and the results brought out are:—

Prices of Imports and Exports. Average Rise or Fall as compared with previous Years.

	Imports Retained for Home Consumption.	Exports of Home Produce.	Imports and Exports.
	Per cnt.	Per cnt.	Per cnt.
1891	+ 0·50	− 0·93	− 0·08
'90	− 1·38	+ 6·41	+ 1·78
'89	+ 1·14	+ 2·32	+ 1·61
'88	+ 2·89	+ 0·90	+ 2·04
'87	− 1·72	− 0·52	− 1·22
'86	− 5·67	− 5·35	− 5·53

The contrast here shown between 1890 and 1891 is very marked. In 1890 the prices of our imports declined, while those of our exports advanced, whereas in 1891 we paid overhead higher prices for our imports, and got lower prices for our exports. But while that was the broad result, it is necessary to note that the greater cost of our imports last year was wholly due to the higher prices of foodstuffs. For our imports of articles of food of all kinds we had to pay no less than 9,534,000*l.* more than they would have cost us had we been able to obtain them at the same prices as in 1890. On the other hand the raw material for our textile manufactures cost us 4,757,000*l.* less than it would have done if the prices of 1890 had been maintained, the gain being mainly in cotton and wool. In the same way we gained fully 1,000,000*l.* from the lower cost of imported metals, and in nearly all other branches of imports there was a similar saving. But while in the end cheap material must benefit manufacturers, the time of falling prices is always a trying one for them. The stocks of material they must hold are constantly depreciating and dragging down the prices of the finished products, so that when they come to put their goods on the market they have to sell at rates regulated not by the prices for raw material they actually paid, but by the lower prices current at the time of sale. How adversely the cotton trade was affected in this way is shown by the fact that the net profits of the Oldham spinning companies amounted last year to only 10,763*l.*

as compared with 376,041*l.* in 1890 and 220,587*l.* in 1889. And although other branches of our textile industries did not fare anything like so badly, they nearly all felt a somewhat similar pinch. In its effect upon profits, moreover, the influence of the fall in prices was accentuated by the difficulty of making compensating reductions in the working expenses. The cost of labour, indeed, tended rather to increase than diminish, and although the necessity of reducing wages is now being felt, employers are slow to provoke the contests with the workmen, to which attempts to enforce reductions must inevitably give rise.

"From what has already been said, it may be gathered that to our working population the past year was one of moderate prosperity. It cannot be said that their condition continued to improve as it had done in 1889 and 1890. These were years in which, while wages rose rapidly, the cost of living was somewhat reduced. In 1891, however, there was, with comparatively few exceptions, an advance in the prices of provisions; and although during the early part of the year some further additions were made to wages, the increase was relatively small and partial, and was not in all cases maintained till the close. During the latter part of the year also there was not such full employment for labour as there had been. The trade societies who report monthly to the Labour Correspondent to the Board of Trade upon the condition of the industries with which they are connected, have made returns which show that at the end of last year 4·37 per cent. of their members were out of work, as compared with 3·05 per cent. at the end of 1890, and 1·7 per cent. at the close of 1889. On the other hand, however, we find that the amount of pauperism continued to decrease, the figures for the past ten years being :—

England and Wales.

End of December.	Total Number of Paupers.	Number in every 1,000 Inhabitants.	End of December.	Total Number of Paupers.	Number in every 1,000 Inhabitants.
1891	675,175	23·2	1886	751,884	27·3
'90	695,821	24·2	'85	743,478	27·3
'89	713,247	25·1	'84	723,671	26·9
'88	738,388	26·2	'83	714,704	26·8
'87	758,146	27·2	'82	740,907	28·1

Some portion of the falling off in the number of paupers which has been shown during recent years may be due to more stringent administration, for under the new system of local government finance there is a pecuniary inducement to guardians to apply the workhouse test more rigidly. The past year, however, can hardly have been affected in this way more than its immediate predecessors, and the smaller proportion of pauperism it shows may therefore be taken to indicate that the working population maintained a fair degree of prosperity, although in this connection it should be observed that the reduction in the pauper roll last year was greater in the agricultural than in the manufacturing districts.

As another indication of the condition of the mass of the people we have the statistics of the consumption of dutiable articles, the record for the past three years being :—

Quantities Retained for Home Consumption.

		1891.	1890.	1889.
Tea	lbs.	202,456,800	194,008,500	185,621,800
Coffee	cwts.	261,100	256,200	259,309
Tobacco	lbs.	61,094,800	59,342,500	57,026,400
Wines	galls.	14,855,800	15,018,800	14,158,900
Spirits, home	proof galls.	30,744,200	29,410,400	27,183,400
„ foreign	galls.	8,385,500	8,961,300	8,599,600
Beer.......................	barrels	31,667,300	31,236,800	29,823,800

Consumption, it will be seen, did not increase so rapidly in 1891 as it did in 1890, and it must be borne in mind that the impetus given to the consumption of luxuries such as spirituous liquors and tobacco during a period of high wages continues to operate for some time after there has been a change for the worse in the industrial position. Still, although the statistics would not warrant the conclusion that the condition of the working classes was as progressively good in 1891 as in 1890, they may fairly be taken to indicate that there was no material change for the worse. And very similar is the teaching of the returns of the savings banks, which are as follow :—

	January.				
	1892.	1891.	1890.	1889.	1888.
	£	£	£	£	£
Amount at credit of trustee savings banks	42,672,538	43,336,098	44,861,448	45,959,856	47,156,131
Amount at credit of Post Office savings banks....	71,660,245	67,760,621	63,020,925	58,614,600	53,904,127
Total	114,332,783	111,096,719	107,882,873	104,574,456	101,060,258
Increase over previous year	8,236,064	3,214,346	3,307,917	3,514,198	3,524,721

"Of what is still the most important branch of our industry—agriculture—the record of the past year is a favourable one. According to the official statistics the yield of the wheat crop was $2\frac{1}{2}$ bushels over the ordinary average, and that of barley just a shade over the average, while oats are only a quarter of a bushel under the average. And for all their cereal produce farmers obtained higher prices than they had done for a number of years. The failure of several of the European harvests, and especially that of Russia, which spread famine through the land and led to the prohibition of wheat exports, caused a great rise in prices, and although the whole of the advance was not maintained, still on the average it was very considerable, and represented a very

substantial monetary gain to producers.   Whether the farmers did
as well with their cattle and sheep may be doubted.   Cattle did,
indeed, as a rule, fetch higher prices, but, under the competition of
imported foreign mutton, all but the very best qualities of sheep
sustained a sharp drop.   On the whole, however, the agricultural
industry probably fared better in 1891 than it had done for many
years previously, and the present outlook for it is decidedly
encouraging.   The movements in the prices of cereals are shown
in the following tables :—

*Gazette Average Price of Wheat (per Imperial Quarter) in United Kingdom
immediately after Harvest, 1885-91, and Total Average Gazette Price
of Calendar Years.*

Periods.	1891.	1890.	1889.	1888.	1887.	1886.	1885.
	s. d.	s. d.	s. d.	s. d.	s. d.	s. d	s. d.
After harvest........................	40 11	35 9	31 2	36 4	29 11	33 1	32 4
Calendar year average	37 –	31 11	29 9	31 10	32 6	31 –	32 10

Comparative Gazette Prices of Grain.

Week.	Wheat.			Barley.			Oats.		
	1891.	1890.	1889.	1891.	1890.	1889.	1891.	1890.	1889.
	s. d.	s. d.	s. d.	s. d.	s. d.	s. d.	s. d.	s. d.	s. d.
Aug. 1............	38 6	35 –	30 8	25 7	23 4	19 11	21 9	20 4	20 6
8............	38 9	36 3	30 11	26 6	24 5	19 10	21 5	20 5	19 5
15............	39 4	35 6	30 9	26 4	25 4	19 5	21 2	20 3	19 5
22	39 8	36 5	30 5	24 4	26 2	19 6	21 4	20 1	18 11
29............	40 3	35 9	31 2	26 3	31 3	24 6	21 3	19 2	19 6
Sept. 5............	40 11	34 6	31 –	27 7	30 11	29 9	21 9	19 1	19 2
12............	41 5	33 7	30 2	29 3	30 3	32 5	21 8	18 8	17 2
19............	41 2	32 1	29 5	28 11	29 11	28 11	21 1	17 9	17 2
26............	36 5	31 6	29 1	28 1	29 9	29 –	19 1	17 8	16 11
Oct. 3............	34 5	31 2	29 3	28 –	29 5	29 4	18 10	17 5	16 8
10............	34 4	30 11	29 4	28 10	29 3	29 8	18 5	17 5	16 8
17............	34 10	30 10	29 10	28 11	29 7	30 4	18 7	17 3	16 4
24	34 9	31 –	30 4	29 6	29 10	30 11	18 10	17 3	16 11
31............	35 2	31 6	30 3	29 11	29 7	31 3	18 8	17 3	16 8
Nov. 7........ ...	35 11	32 1	30 8	30 7	29 5	31 –	19 5	17 3	17 1
14............	36 7	32 8	30 2	30 11	29 3	30 4	20 6	17 6	17 –
21............	37 2	32 9	30 –	30 11	28 11	29 11	21 4	17 8	17 4
28............	38 9	32 7	30 1	31 3	29 –	29 9	22 4	17 8	17 6
Dec. 5............	39 1	32 3	30 2	30 11	28 9	30 2	23 4	17 10	17 7
12............	38 11	32 2	30 2	30 9	28 5	29 10	22 2	17 10	17 11
19............	37 10	32 4	30 1	30 1	28 8	30 4	21 7	17 6	18 2
26............	36 10	32 3	29 10	29 6	28 5	30 6	21 4	17 11	18 2

" Passing reference has been made to the effect of the McKinley
Act upon our trade with the United States.   Of that ill-advised
piece of legislation we have now, in all probability, experienced
the worst effects.   The immense stocks of goods accumulated
prior to the passing of the Act should by this time be pretty well

worked off, and the purchases which were suspended until they were cleared off are now being renewed. But the effects of the new fiscal legislation by continental States has yet to be felt. From the customs arrangements entered into between Germany, Austria-Hungary, Belgium, and Italy, with the partial participation of Switzerland, we are more likely to gain than to lose. These new arrangements, which include a reduction of certain duties and improved transit regulations, are, it is hardly necessary to say, conceived primarily in the interests of the contracting States; but as we can claim the most-favoured-nation treatment from all of those powers, we shall possibly reap some advantage from them. It is different with the legislation of France. That is of the most ultra-protectionist character; and while it is certain to prove more injurious to France herself than to any other nation, it cannot fail to restrict trade. We may, indeed, secure a footing, at the expense of France, in other countries, such, for instance. as Spain, which will now impose upon French products higher duties than upon ours. But Spain also is proposing materially to increase her customs duties, and Portugal has already done so. These tariff alterations, and the conflicts to which they are certain to give rise, must inevitably unsettle trade; and although we may here and there gain advantages at the expense of those who are waging an industrial war against one another, the general disorganisation of commerce is a thing to be deplored. There are already, however, indications that the protectionists have carried their policy to such extremes that a reaction may be expected. A few weeks' experience of the operation of the French tariff is causing a revolt on the part of consumers, and in the discussion upon the subject which took place in the Chamber the other day, M. Léon Say ventured to predict that if only time were given for the new tariffs to produce all their bad effects it would become impossible to maintain them. He may probably be too sanguine, but just as there has been a revulsion against a high tariff policy in Germany and Austria-Hungary, so there may be on the part of France, which has apparently been carried further in that direction than her people, now that they are experiencing its results, are inclined to go.

"Of the trade prospects of the current year it is unfortunately not possible to speak very hopefully. There are some encouraging features, such, for instance, as the cheapness of the raw material for our manufactures. Prices of commodities, moreover, are now so low that there is less margin for a further fall. On the other hand, however, this very cheapness is forcing producers to reduce working expenses, and it is not unlikely, therefore, that labour disputes will be even more numerous this year than they were in 1890 and 1891, although that is saying a great deal. Further, some of our foreign customers are not unlikely to be even less able to buy from us than they were in 1891, for whereas we began that year under engagements to supply some of them with more money, these engagements have been fulfilled, and now our purse is closed against them, with no prospect of being opened again for sometime to come. This applies mainly to South American States, but elsewhere financial difficulties threaten to lessen the demand for our products. Our Australian colonies, for instance, have been buying largely from us with the money we have been constantly lending them. Now, however, from circumstances partly of their own creating, and partly extraneous to them, they find that they cannot raise money with anything like the same freedom as formerly, and are being driven to live more upon their own resources. The ultimate result of that cannot fail to be beneficial. It will cause them to be more self-dependent, and to endeavour to make fuller use of their productive powers. We look to it to lead to an increase of exports from these colonies hither, but also, and that is the main point for our manufacturers, to a reduction of their imports, which are mainly from this country. Our trade with them, in short, will now be rather a natural trade than one artificially fostered by lavish lending on the one side and borrowing on the other. It will be a healthier trade for that reason, but for a time, so far as exports hence are concerned, a more restricted trade. Looking nearer at hand, we see Spain, Portugal, Italy, and Greece, all struggling with serious financial embarrassments, and Russia reduced to extremities by the failure of her crops and the famine expenditure that it has entailed. And the violent fluctuations in silver which had so disturbing an effect upon our trade with India and the East last year have, unfortunately, still to be reckoned with. These are not conditions under which we can look for an expansive foreign trade, and we are warned by the statistics of railway traffic, to which we have already referred, that latterly our home trade has been showing less elasticity. That continues to be the teaching of the traffic returns for the current year, and it is supported by the reports made by trade societies to the Board of Trade. Whereas in January, 1891, out of twenty-two societies reporting, seven characterised their trade as 'very good,' seven as 'good,' seven as 'moderate,' and only one as 'bad.' this month out of nineteen societies reporting eighteen speak of trade as 'moderate,' and only one as 'good.' The industries which these societies represent are, of course, affected by the condition of our foreign as well as our home trade, and we must not assume that the change in the latter is as great as the change in the character of the reports. Still, they must be taken as indicating a kind of languor in the home markets, and when we add that sooner or later this year we shall be plunged into the turmoil of a general election, which always leads to a temporary restriction of business, we have probably said enough to explain why we think the present trade outlook is not over bright.

"To the financial prostration which has characterised 1891 we have already alluded. During the year some progress has undoubtedly been made in the work of liquidation bequeathed to it by its predecessor. Over-commitments have been reduced, losses written off, and a good deal of rottenness removed. Very much, however, still remains to be done. It cannot, for instance, be said that we have approached any nearer to a settlement of Argentine affairs. The Rothschild committee's moratorium scheme has proved a failure, and nothing has yet been devised to take its place. And while no progress has been made in this direction new troubles have come upon us. Our investments in Brazil have become impaired by a series of revolutions which have shown how very little political stability that country possesses. Uruguay has defaulted, and although, by methods which cannot be characterised as either honest or straightforward, the bondholders have been coerced into concurrence in a scheme of reconstruction, it remains to be seen whether the republic will be less unfaithful in regard to her new engagements than she has been with the old. Portugal also has been driven to compound with her creditors, and Spain and Greece are at their wits' end to find the means to continue the payment of the interest upon their debts. Our Australian colonies too, although no sane person would dream of classifying them with such bankrupt or semi-bankrupt States, have betrayed a financial weakness which has seriously affected their credit; and the failures of a number of Australian so-called banks and building and land companies have involved British investors in heavy losses. At home too we have had a series of discreditable disclosures in regard to bankrupt joint-stock companies—such, for instance, as the Hansard Union—while confidence in the misnamed 'trust' companies has been well nigh destroyed by the revelations made as to the losses sustained through reckless and incompetent management. The more modern of these companies have indeed been at the root of many of the evils from which we are now suffering. They have constituted themselves the channel through which the money of investors has been squandered in South America and elsewhere in a way which would have been impossible without their intervention. People have believed in a 'trust' company, and surrendered their money to it, who would never have entertained for a moment the idea of themselves taking up such rubbish as the securities in which the 'trust' actually did place their funds. To earn promoters' profits they have been active in foisting upon the public shares in industrial and other enterprises of a shady character. In order that their founders might realise usurious profits they have chosen to run excessive risks, and, lest the true nature of their operations should become known, they have refused to give their shareholders any information with regard to their investments. Some light has been thrown upon their transactions by the explanations which the directors of several of them have been compelled to make in order to account for the heavy losses incurred, and a good deal more insight into their affairs will doubtless yet be afforded in the same way. Here, however, it is enough to note how largely instrumental they have been in fostering the excesses of previous years, and how much they are to blame for the evils to which these have given rise. For the time being the public have lost all confidence; they are either avoiding the stock markets altogether, or investing only in gilt or semi-gilt-edged securities. This caution may have been carried too far, as reactions usually are, but it cannot be said to be unjustified, and it is likely to continue throughout the current year at all events.

It is hardly necessary to say that in such circumstances our ne v
capital commitments last year were on a relatively small scale.
The amount of the new capital applications was 104,595,000*l.*,
which compares with the total in preceding years thus :—

	1891.	1890.	1889.	1888.
	£	£	£	£
1st quarter	30,549,000	30,243,000	54,846,000	34,691,000
2nd ,,	24,808,000	59,510,000	49,866,000	74,957,000
3rd ,,	16,936,000	39,103,000	34,526,000	22 951,000
4th ,,	32,302,000	13,709,000	48,198,000	27,570,000
	104,595,000	142,565,000	189,436,000	160,149,000

"And classifying the issues of 1891 we have the following statement :—

	£
Home and colonial Government and corporation issues	23,000,000
Foreign government and corporation issues	22,000,000
Railways (home and foreign)	16,000,000
Trusts and financial companies	9,000,000
Breweries	3,250,000
Mines	3,250,000
Banks	3,000,000
Miscellaneous	25,000,000
	104,500,000

"Included in the 22,000,000*l.* of foreign loans floated in 1891 is
the Russian loan of 19,775,000*l.*, of which pract'cally none was
taken up here, and of the 25,000,000*l.* included under the head
'miscellaneous,' part consisted of rearrangements of the capital of
private firms in which the outside public participated, if at all,
to only a small extent, while of the remainder a large portion was
not subscribed. The actual new capital commitments were therefore, as we have said, comparatively small, and the actual money
calls as will be seen from the following table, amounted to only a
little more than a half of the total for the previous year.

	Capital Created and Issued.			Actual Money Calls.		
	In England.	England and Elsewhere.	Total.	In England.	England and Elsewhere.	Total.
	£	£	£	£	£	£
In 1891...	80,239,270	24,355,640	104,594,910	66,809,596	9,234,200	76,043,796
,, '90....	125,898,000	16,667,000	142,565,000	120,717,000	20,290,000	141,007,000
,, '89 ..	178,980,000	28,107,000	207,087,000	152,012,000	15,791,000	167,804,000
,, '88....	140,758,000	19,497,000	160,255,000	125,864,000	11,388,000	137,252,000
,, '87...	96,770,000	14,439,000	111,209,000	84,161,000	9,507,000	93,668,000
,, '86....	93,946,000	7,927,000	101,873,000	70,342,000	17,134,000	87,476,000
,, '85...	55,558,000	22,414,000	77,972,000	62,824,000	15,051,000	77,875,000
,, '84...	91,520,000	17,511,000	109,031,000	74,255,000	16,348,000	90,603,000
,, '83....	69,650,000	11,500,000	81,150,000	63,600,000	13,300,000	76,900,000
,, '82....	95,300,000	50,250,000	145,550,000	62,150,000	32,500,000	94,650,000

" Currency questions were well to the fore last year. Towards the end of February Mr. Goschen, in a speech at Leeds, called attention to the insufficiency of the cash reserves held by our banks, and intimated that he had a scheme of currency reform which he intended to proceed with as soon as possible. His exposition of the dangers arising from the smallness of the cash basis upon which our huge fabric of banking credit has been reared deeply impressed the public mind, and in deference to the feeling aroused the joint-stock banks took measures to strengthen their position, and agreed to the publication of monthly or quarterly accounts, so that people might see how they habitually stood. The result of that publicity has been very beneficial, and has led the joint-stock banks as a whole to increase considerably their balance at the Bank of England. What has been done in this direction may be gathered from the following statement :—

	End of December, 1891.			End of December, 1890.		
	Liabilities to Public.	Cash in Hand and at Bank.	Proportion of Cash to Liabilities	Liabilities to Public.	Cash in Hand and at Bank.	Proportion of Cash to Liabilities.
	£	£	Per cnt.	£	£	Per cnt.
London and Western ...	27,125,600	4,407,700	16·3	26,958,600	3,984,200	14·8
Union	15,728,300	2,532,200	16·1	16,809,700	2,814,400	16·8
London Joint Stock	12,824,800	1,310,100	10·2	14,165,100	1,165,700	8·1
City	8,979,300	1,040,600	11·6	9,677,300	783,300	8·1
London and S. Western	5,393,100	882,200	16·3	4,897,600	721,800	14·8
„ County	37,492,000	4,862,800	12·9	39,296,100	4,981,700	12·7
Imperial	4,214,100	392,500	9·3	4,251,000	421,600	9·9
Alliance........................	5,243,100	659,100	12·6	5,403,300	594,300	10·9
Consolidated..................	3,659,400	509,800	13·9	3,799,800	621,300	16·3
	120,659,700	16,597,000	13·7	125,258,500	16,088,300	12·9

" In all probability, too, had Mr. Goschen, while public opinion was warm on the subject, proceeded with his promised measure of reform, he might have effected some further improvements. Mainly, however, through Parliamentary exigencies this was not done, and nothing more was heard of his scheme until December, when at a meeting convened by the London Chamber of Commerce he outlined a plan for displacing the gold in circulation by an issue by the Bank of England of 1*l*. notes, the emissions between 38,000,000*l.*, which is the present amount of issue, and 50,000,000*l.* to be made one-fifth against securities, and four-fifths against gold, while for all notes in excess of 50,000,000*l.* gold was to be held. He proposed also that as a substitute for the extra-legal method of meeting crises by a suspension of the Bank Act, the bank should be empowered, as soon as its stock of gold should reach 30,000,000*l.*, to increase its fiduciary issue in time of extreme pressure, on condition that it charged a high rate for its advances, and paid over to the State all save a small portion of the profits earned upon the excess issues. The chief defect of this scheme is, that although it might largely increase the stock of gold in the issue department, it would not add a single penny to the reserve in the banking department, which is the main object to be aimed at. It is hardly necessary, however, to criticise the scheme, since, owing to the antagonism of bankers and the obstructive attitude of the Gladstonian party, there is no probability of its passing through Parliament. The only legislation that there is any chance of carrying through is a tentative measure, merely authorising the bank to issue 1*l.* notes on the same conditions as it now issues notes of a larger denomination, and to confer upon it power to increase its fiduciary issues in the manner proposed by Mr. Goschen, but without any restriction as to the amount of gold it must hold before it can begin to exercise that power. That would leave many currency questions unsettled, and would also leave undetermined the question as to how the banks are to be induced or compelled to keep adequate cash reserves. It would, however, pave the way for future reforms, and would impart to our monetary system an amount of elasticity in which it is now very greatly lacking.

" The course of the money market in 1891 was a more than usually chequered one. At the beginning of January the bank rate stood at 5 per cent., but owing to the weakness following upon the strain of the Baring crisis the market was easy, and within a month the bank rate was reduced first to 4 per cent., then to 3½ per cent., and ultimately to 3 per cent., at which it stood till almost the middle of April. Throughout nearly the whole of this period, however, gold had been flowing out of the bank, and in order to check the drain, the rate was raised to 3½ per cent. This not proving sufficiently effective, and there being the prospect of further large withdrawals, another advance to 4 per cent. was made on 6th May, followed a week later by a movement to 5 per cent. This raised the value of money here so decidedly above its level on the continent and in the United States that gold poured in upon us, and that all the more quickly, because the bank had simultaneously advanced its buying price for the metal. The open market, therefore, rapidly gave way, and after fruitlessly attempting to stem this movement, the bank towards the end of June lowered its rate to 4 per cent., then a fortnight later to 3 per cent., and finally, after another interval of two weeks, to 2½ per cent. No sooner, however, had this point been reached than gold began again to flow away in considerable quantities, the absorption being mainly by Germany and Holland. Towards the end of September this had gone so far that the bank had to raise its rate to 3 per cent. Early in November a further advance to 4 per cent. took place, but in the second week in December this step was partially retraced, and the rate lowered to 3½ per cent., at which it remained till the close of the year. Throughout the whole year the determining factors in fixing the bank rate were the international movements of bullion, of which the most conspicuous were the large influx from the United States during the earlier months, and the subsequent steady demand on continental account, partly in connection with the accumulation of gold by the Austro-Hungarian Government, preparatory to a resumption of specie payments. The home demand for money was uniformly quiet, and gave rise to no pre-occupations. But a struggle for gold continued from January to December, the bank being compelled every now and again to make a strong effort to attract supplies, but finding it impossible to retain them, because no sooner did it build up its reserves than the market rates fell away, and a fresh efflux began. The inability of the bank to control the market has thus been made more marked than ever, and has been the cause of more frequent changes in the bank rate than in any previous year since 1875. The following is our usual ten years' record of rates :—

	1891.	1890.	1889.	1888.	1887.	1886.	1885.	1884.	1883.	1882.
Change bank rate	12 p.ct.	11 p. ct.	8 p. ct.	9 p. ct.	7 p. ct.	7 p. ct.	7 p. ct.	7 p. ct.	6 p. ct.	6 p. ct.
Highest "	5	6	6	5	5	5	5	5	5	6
Lowest "	2½	3	2½	2	2	2	2	2	3	3
Average "	3/5/11	4/10/4	3/14/10	3/6/3	3/6/-	3/-/4	2/16/9	2/19/2	3/11/6	4/2/8
Average market rate best three months' bills	2/10/-	3/13/11	2/15/6	2/7/-	2/7/3	2/1/-	2/-/9	2/8/1	3/-/8	3/7/3
Market below bank	15/11	16/5	19/4	19/3	18/9	19/4	16/-	11/1	10/10	15/5

European Rates of Discount per Cent. per Annum, 1891.

Cities.	Beginning of Months of 1891.												
	Jan.	Feb.	Mar.	April.	May.	June.	July.	Aug.	Sept.	Oct.	Nov.	Dec.	Avge.
London.													
Bank rate	5	3	3	3	3½	5	2½	2½	2½	3	4	4	3·26
Open market	3¾	1⅝	3	2¼	3¾	3¾	1⅝	1⅛	2¼	3	3½	2⅞	2·50
Paris.													
Bank rate	3	3	3	3	3	3	3	3	3	3	3	3	3·00
Open market	3	2⅛	2¾	2⅞	2⅞	2⅛	2½	2⅛	2¼	2¾	2¾	2½	2·58
Vienna.													
Bank rate	5½	4½	4	4	4	4	4	4	5	5	5	5	4·50
Open market	5½	4⅛	3⅝	3⅝	3	3⅞	3½	3⅝	4½	5	5	4⅞	4·15
Berlin.													
Bank rate	5½	4	3	3	3	4	4	4	4	4	4	4	3·87
Open market	4¾	2¾	2⅝	2⅝	2⅝	2⅝	3¼	3	2⅞	3⅝	2⅞	2⅝	3·00
Frankfort.													
Bank rate	5½	4	3	3	3	4	4	4	4	4	4	4	3·87
Open market	4⅝	2¾	2⅞	2⅝	2¾	2¾	3⅝	3⅝	3	3⅜	3¼	2⅞	3·18
Amsterdam.													
Bank rate	4½	3½	3	3	3	3	3	3	3	3	3	3	3·17
Open market	4½	2⅞	2⅝	2¾	3	2⅛	2⅝	2¾	2¾	3	2¾	2⅝	2·91
Brussels.													
Bank rate	3	3	3	3	3	3	3	3	3	3	3	3	3·00
Open market	2⅞	2⅛	2⅝	2⅝	2⅝	2⅜	2⅛	2⅝	2⅝	2¾	2¾	2¼	2·66
Hamburg.													
Bank rate	5½	4	3	3	3	4	4	4	4	4	4	4	3·87
Open market	4¾	2⅝	2¾	2⅛	2⅝	2½	3⅛	3¼	2⅞	3⅜	3⅛	2⅝	3·01
St. Petersburg													
Bank rate	5½	5½	5½	5½	5½	5½	5½	5½	5½	5½	5½	5½	5·50
Open market	4¼	4¼	4	4	3¾	4	3¾	3¾	4	5	5¼	6½	4·21

" Upon the movements in the silver market during the year Messrs. Pixley and Abell report as follows :—' The price of silver was very steady at the commencement of the year at about 48*d.*, and continued so until the end of the month, when advices from New York seemed to point to the improbability of further legislation.   Continued American sales then ensued, causing decline. Indian and continental inquiries sufficed to absorb supplies, but the quotation slowly fell back to 43⅜*d.*   By June nearly all Indian inquiry has ceased, but important special orders for the continent coming on a somewhat scantily supplied market quite prevented any fall, and by July dealings had taken place at over 46*d.*   From this point, until practically the end of the year, there was steady decline.   Both Spain and Japan were important buyers, but usually at declining rates.   The large amounts sent to India early in the year had caused over supply, and it was not until November that bazaar requirements saw a resumption of shipments, but these lasted a rather short time as regards Bombay, and Calcutta' then became the chief importer.   At the end of last year stocks of silver in New York were very large, and during the past twelve months most of the visible supply has been absorbed.   This being the case, and seeing that the United States treasury have been steady purchasers of 4,500,000 ozs. per month for more than a year, it seems curious that silver, in so good a position statistically, should not be higher, and we believe we are right in attributing the flattening influence to the greatly increased amount of silver lead arriving here from Australia and elsewhere.   The same reason will account for the remarkable excess of silver exports over imports during 1891, no notice having been taken of the silver arriving in this way.'   With reference to our imports of silver-bearing ores here referred to, the *Economist* has published the following statement for the four years ending 1890 :—

Imports of Silver Ore or Ore of which the greater part in Value is Silver.

	From Foreign Countries.	From British Possessions.	Total.
	£	£	£
1890...............	1,291,000	1,346,000	2,637,000
'89...............	1,061,000	1,168,000	2,229,000
'88...............	809,000	687,000	1,496,000
'87...............	750,000	628,000	1,378,000
	3,911,000	3,829,000	7,740,000

" For 1891 the value of silver imported in this form was probably between 2¼ and 3 millions.   It is very doubtful, however, whether these imports have really had the flattening influence upon the market which Messrs Pixley and Abell attribute to them. The main factor in forcing down the price of the metal has, in our opinion, been the unwise attempt of the United States to create an artificial market for it, by compelling the Treasury to purchase 4,500,000 ounces a month.   It is quite evident that this policy is leading to serious financial difficulties.   The Treasury cannot go on indefinitely inflating the currency with millions of notes issued against its purchases of silver without driving gold out of the country. Gold is the only portion of the currency which has a value abroad equal to its value at home, and it is the portion, therefore, that will inevitably be displaced if the Treasury continues pouring out new masses of paper money. But if gold is driven out, the Treasury will be unable to maintain the parity between gold and silver, and the whole mass of the silver currency will become debased. Seeing that it is to this that things are tending, and believing that sooner or later the Treasury will be compelled to suspend its purchase of silver, all holders of the metal have been anxious to get rid of their stocks, and it is to this pressure to sell upon a sensitive and demoralised market that the heavy fall in the price of the metal during the past year is mainly due. How prices fluctuated during the year will be seen from the subjoined table :—

Monthly Fluctuations in Price of Bar Silver.

	1891.		1890.		1889.		1888.		1887.	
	d.	*d.*	*d.*	*d.*	*d.*	*d.*	*d.*	*d.*	*d.*	*d.*
January	$48\frac{3}{4}$	$46\frac{7}{8}$	$44\frac{7}{8}$	$44\frac{1}{8}$	$42\frac{11}{16}$	$42\frac{3}{8}$	$44\frac{9}{16}$	$44\frac{1}{4}$	$47\frac{1}{8}$	$46\frac{1}{4}$
February........	$46\frac{3}{4}$	$44\frac{1}{8}$	$44\frac{5}{8}$	$43\frac{11}{16}$	$42\frac{3}{4}$	$42\frac{1}{2}$	$44\frac{3}{16}$	$43\frac{13}{16}$	47	$46\frac{5}{16}$
March	$45\frac{5}{16}$	$44\frac{3}{8}$	$44\frac{3}{8}$	$43\frac{3}{4}$	$42\frac{5}{8}$	$42\frac{1}{4}$	$43\frac{3}{4}$	43	$46\frac{7}{16}$	$44\frac{5}{16}$
April	45	$43\frac{7}{8}$	48	$43\frac{7}{8}$	$42\frac{5}{16}$	$42\frac{1}{16}$	$42\frac{7}{8}$	$42\frac{1}{2}$	$44\frac{9}{16}$	$43\frac{1}{4}$
May	$45\frac{1}{8}$	$44\frac{1}{4}$	$47\frac{1}{8}$	46	$42\frac{1}{4}$	$41\frac{13}{16}$	$42\frac{5}{8}$	$41\frac{5}{8}$	$43\frac{1}{4}$	$43\frac{7}{16}$
June	46	$44\frac{1}{4}$	49	$46\frac{1}{4}$	$42\frac{3}{16}$	42	$42\frac{1}{2}$	42	$44\frac{1}{4}$	$43\frac{11}{16}$
July...............	$46\frac{3}{8}$	$45\frac{5}{8}$	$50\frac{7}{8}$	$47\frac{9}{16}$	$42\frac{5}{16}$	42	$42\frac{5}{16}$	42	$44\frac{7}{16}$	$43\frac{7}{8}$
August	$46\frac{1}{8}$	$45\frac{1}{16}$	$54\frac{1}{8}$	$50\frac{3}{4}$	$42\frac{9}{16}$	$42\frac{1}{4}$	$42\frac{1}{8}$	$41\frac{15}{16}$	$45\frac{1}{4}$	$44\frac{1}{4}$
September	$45\frac{5}{16}$	$44\frac{3}{4}$	$54\frac{5}{8}$	50	$42\frac{11}{16}$	$42\frac{3}{8}$	$44\frac{3}{16}$	$42\frac{1}{16}$	45	$44\frac{7}{16}$
October	45	$44\frac{1}{16}$	$51\frac{1}{2}$	$48\frac{1}{8}$	$43\frac{1}{2}$	$42\frac{5}{8}$	$42\frac{3}{8}$	$42\frac{7}{8}$	$44\frac{3}{4}$	$43\frac{13}{16}$
November	$44\frac{1}{16}$	$43\frac{1}{2}$	$48\frac{3}{4}$	45	$44\frac{3}{8}$	$43\frac{1}{8}$	$43\frac{1}{8}$	$42\frac{7}{8}$	$43\frac{15}{16}$	$43\frac{5}{8}$
December	$44\frac{1}{4}$	$43\frac{1}{2}$	$49\frac{1}{2}$	$47\frac{1}{4}$	$44\frac{3}{8}$	$43\frac{3}{4}$	$42\frac{7}{8}$	$42\frac{5}{16}$	$45\frac{1}{8}$	$43\frac{13}{16}$
Yearly avge.	$45\frac{1}{16}$		$47\frac{11}{16}$		$42\frac{11}{16}$		$42\frac{7}{8}$		$44\frac{5}{8}$	
Highest price	$48\frac{3}{4}$		$54\frac{5}{8}$		$44\frac{3}{8}$		$44\frac{9}{16}$		$47\frac{1}{8}$	
Lowest ,,	$43\frac{1}{2}$		$43\frac{11}{16}$		$41\frac{13}{16}$		$41\frac{5}{8}$		$43\frac{1}{4}$	

"As the crisis of 1890 was of a financial rather than of a commercial character, its effect was naturally felt during the past year far more in the financial than in the commercial world. The stock exchange felt it keenly. Overshadowing all the influences which arose during the year to affect business, either favourably or adversely, was the fact that the market had been prostrated in the autumn of 1890 by a blow which had shaken public confidence, and left a large weight of securities ready to be unloaded upon the market whenever anything like an opportunity for liquidation should present itself. The mere knowledge that such was the position was calculated to prevent the restoration of confidence and to postpone the opportunity of realisation without very severe loss. At all events, recovery from such events as the collapse of Argentine credit and of the Barings at least takes time, and the year 1891 did not suffice to bring it about. The depressing influence was practically never once shaken off. Greatly restricted business, as is evidenced by the fact that the bank clearings on stock exchange pay days barely reached three-quarters of the amount they attained in 1890, was the feature of the year, and except in the American railroad department, quotations at the end of the year were very considerably lower than at the beginning, especially in the South American and Portuguese stocks. The very highest class of securities, British funds, did not suffer greatly, for the reason that the circumstances of the year were such, as may easily be imagined, as to guide capital into only the safest of investments, at the expense of the more speculative securities. But we have not to look very far down the list before discovering the effect of the year's caution, for in colonial loans there is a general decline, brought about principally by the refusal of investors to take up the new issues offered by the principal Australian colonies, who one after another received rebuffs by the failure of their loans, which rendered the year one of the most unfavourable in the annals of colonial finance. In the English railway department practically the only exceptions to the general decline which took place was in the case of the Metropolitan underground lines, and in the Midland, these railways having done comparatively well during the year. The other lines, generally speaking, although maintaining their traffic receipts, were unable to contend as successfully against increased expenses, arising principally from augmented wages bills. The Scotch lines, on the whole, found more favour in the eyes of the stock exchange in 1891 than they did in the previous year, an important factor in bringing about the change being the cessation of parliamentary warfare, and the arrangement of the terms of a very comprehensive working agreement. But the weakest spot in the stock exchange business of the year was undoubtedly to be found in the foreign department. Many of the European government securities receded markedly. Portuguese led the way, and the country is now taking steps to formulate some arrangement with her creditors. Italy, towards the close of the year, made a promise of drastic retrenchment, but not before it had become absolutely necessary; whilst Greece and Spain both lapsed into serious financial difficulties, and Russia, after launching a huge loan in Paris, had to ignominiously recall part of it to relieve the financiers there of a burden much too heavy for them to bear. But the course of European financial affairs, dark as the picture was, compared favourably with those of South America. The position in Argentina, in spite of all efforts to bring about an improvement, has become during the year not better, but worse, and the fall in the securities which took place in the latter part of 1890, after the revolution and the Baring collapse, was eclipsed by the still heavier decline which continued throughout the whole of 1891. Uruguayan securities naturally fell, in face of the unreasonable agreement which was rushed through for the reduction of the interest on the debt. Chili was engaged in civil war during the greater part of the year, and the vagaries of the Brazilian government brought about the deposition of the president after an uprising which at one time threatened to have serious results.

Fortunately, the investments of the northern half of the American continent, in which our stock exchange is principally interested, were not subjected to such disastrous influences as those of the southern. American, and with them Canadian, rails all rose considerably during the year, the main reason being the bountiful wheat crop, which contrasted strangely with the poor results of the European harvest. Amongst miscellaneous stock exchange securities, however, we find depression. Bank shares gave way, for the year was unfavourable for banking business in many respects; breweries were adversely affected by the famous Sharp *v.* Wakefield decision, and the financing trust companies' stocks declined very heavily, owing to the admittedly serious depreciation in the securities they hold. In the mining market prices gave way through sheer dulness, in spite of great improvement shown month by month in the gross output of gold in the Randt district, and in spite of another attempt to manipulate the copper market, which caused a temporary advance not only in the price of the shares, but in the price of the metal also. Thus, in almost all directions depression characterised the business of the Stock Exchange in 1891."

APPENDIX I.

Our Foreign Trade of 1891 compared with that of 1890.

In the two following tables we have valued the imports of 1891 at the average prices of 1890, and compared the total thus obtained with the aggregate values given in the Board of Trade returns for 1890 and 1891 respectively. A comparison of the computed total for 1891 with the actual total for 1890 shows whether the quantities of our various imports and exports have increased or diminished; and similarly, a comparison of the computed with the actual totals for 1891 shows how much we have lost or gained by the fall in prices. Framed in this way the tables are:—

1. *Imports.*

	1891.		1890.
	Value in Trade and Navigation Returns.	Value Calculated at Prices of 1890.	Values in Trade and Navigation Returns.
	£	£	£
Living animals	9,246,000	9,094,000	11,216,000
Articles of food and drink	175,515,000	166,516,000	162,639,000
Tobacco	3,415,000	3,219,000	3,543,000
Metals..	23,080,000	24,071,000	23,711,000
Chemicals, dye stuffs, and tanning } substances	7,314,000	7,175,000	8,190,000
Oils	7,340,000	7,696,000	6,992,000
Raw materials for textile manu- } factures	89,215,000	93,973,000	85,239,000
Raw materials for sundry industries } and manufactures	40,035,000	41,738,000	41,666,000
Manufactured articles	65,082,000	67,002,000	63,218,000
Miscellaneous ,, ...	14,936,000	14,180,000	14,008,000
Parcel post.....................................	561,000	560,000	503,000
Total imports...........................	435,691,000	435,224,000	420,885,000
Deduct re-exports	61,797,000	63,210,000	64,349,000
Net imports	373,894,000	372,014,000	356,536,000

2. *Exports of British Produce.*

	1891.		1890.
	Value in Trade and Navigation Returns.	Value Calculated at Prices of 1890.	Values in Trade and Navigation Returns.
	£	£	£
Living animals	672,000	767,000	871,000
Articles of food and drink	10,687,000	10,384,000	11,235,000
Raw materials	21,342,000	22,110,000	21,538,000
Yarn of all kinds	17,988,000	18,893,000	19,345,000
Textile fabrics of all kinds	88,030,000	87,212,000	98,113,000
Metals and machinery	55,050,000	56,305,000	61,665,000
Apparel and articles of personal use..	11,331,000	11,379,000	11,285,000
Chemicals and chemical and medi- } cinal preparations	8,882,000	8,229,000	8,948,000
All other articles	32,194,000	33,183,000	34,541,000
Parcel post.....................................	1,095,000	1,100,000	1,000,000
	247,272,000	249,562,000	263,542,000

From Table 1 it will be seen that the value of our net imports in 1890 was 356,536,000*l.*, while our imports in 1891, if valued at the same prices as were paid in 1890, would have cost us 372,014,000*l.* It is evident therefore that the quantity of goods imported by us last year was considerably greater than in 1890, the increase being 15,478,000*l.*, or about 4·3 per cent. Our exports, however, declined. If we had sold the goods shipped by us last year at the same prices as in 1890, they would have realised 249,562,000*l.*, and comparing this with the 263,542,000*l.* which represents the value of our exports in 1890, there is a decrease of 13,980,000*l.*, or about 5·3 per cent., which is the measure of the falling off in the volume of last year's export trade. Combining imports and exports, we find an increase in the volume of our foreign trade last year (exclusive of re-exports) which works out at about 0·2 per cent., the figures being :—

	£
Value of net imports and exports in 1891, calculated at the prices of 1890	621,576,000
Actual value of net imports and exports in 1890	620,078,000
Increase	1,498,000
	= 0·2 per cent.

Next, as to values. Our net imports in 1891 cost us 373,894,000*l.*, whereas, if we had paid for them the same prices as in 1890, they would have cost us 372,014,000*l.* It is obvious therefore that the prices of 1891 were higher on the average than those of 1890 by just about 0·5 per cent., and that owing to this fact we had to pay 1,880,000*l.* more for our imports than would have sufficed to buy the same quantity of products in 1890. At the same time, our exports brought lower prices. Had we got the same prices for our goods as in 1890, the values of last year's exports would have amounted to 249,562,000*l.* Their actual value, however, was only 247,271,000*l.*, the average fall in the price of our exports being thus about 0·9 per cent. There was thus a double loss on the year's trading in consequence of the movements in prices—a loss of 1,880,000*l.* on our imports, because we bought them dearer than in 1890, and a loss of 2,291,000*l.* on our exports, because we were not able to get for them such good prices as in 1890.

APPENDIX II.

Railway Traffic Receipts in 1891 *and* 1890.

Subjoined is an analysis of the traffic receipts of fifteen of the principal English railways during the past two years :—

First Half-Year.

[00's omitted.]

	Passe1 Parcels, &c		Merchandise.				Live Stock.	
	1891.		1891.	1890.	1891.	1890.	1891.	1890.
	£	£	£	£	£	£	£	£
and N. Western	2,130,2	2,135,4	2,014,8	1,950,6	1,240,7	1,189,7	89,9	96,0
estern	1,835,7	1,814,9	1,176,0	1,116,0	1,080,8	1,027,0	67,9	67,4
	1,231,9	1,198,0	1,603,2	1,551,4	1,402,3	1,248,8	43,9	40,2
tern	948,6	937,2	1,088,0	1,093,9	1,246,4	1,282,9	53,0	50,9
re & Yorkshire.	827,4	814,9	826,8	807,1	430,0	418,2	19,3	19,3
orthern	728,9	717,1	655 0	629,7	398,2	360,1	25.9	25,0
astern	922,7	903,6	562,8	544,6	249,3	244,6	45,8	49,2
and S. Western.	1,019,9	1,021,4	349,4	341,2	141,1	121,0	16,8	16,2
tern	680 0	704,3	172,8	164,7	84,0	79,0	5 7	5,9
and Brighton	802,6	803,8	169,4	168,8	113,0	106,1	6,4	6,6
ster and Sheffield	253,0	243,1	389,3	382,9	279,5	269,2	9,0	8,8
Chatham, and }	426,1	427,9	77,1	74,8	60,5	53,3	2,3	2,8
taffordshire........	105,2	101,8	111,8	107,7	116,5	110,2	1,9	1,9
litan	312,8	298,6	10,2	9,9	10,2	8,9	3	2
ndon	155,6	154,0	56,5	55,3	23,3	21,3	8	1,0
	12,380,6	12,276,0	9,263,1	8,998,6	6,875,8	6,540,3		391,4
or decrease } 90 }								

Second Half-Year.

[00's omitted.]

and N. Western	2,633,4	2,576,5	2,058,4	2,049,2	1,265,4	1,243,4	134,7	132,5
estern	2,298,4	2,224,2	1,197,5	1,189,2	1,079,0	1,087,4	81,3	79,2
	1,502,4	1,442,8	1,719,2	1,657,3	1,475,7	1,420,3	61,2	54,4
astern	1,221,7	1,213,1	1,124,5	1,134,9	1,248,2	1,325,4	56,5	55,9
ire & Yorkshire.	957,0	926,4	834,3	832,2	444,7	430,4	21,5	21,0
orthern	896,9	863,5	693,1	691,2	406,1	401,2	21,1	24,0
rn	1,232,7	1,183,9	591,4	589,4	269,5	265,9	35,7	35,1
ld S. Western.	1,243,9	1,193,6	378,5	366,2	143,2	141,3	22,5	22,2
tern	848,3	841,8	207,4	196,0	87,1	84,1	9,1	8,3
and Brighton....	1,024,2	997,5	196,5	186,2	120,2	118,7	7,3	7,1
ster and Sheffield	311,6	295,0	435,5	429,0	302,6	296,0	8,1	8,0
Chatham, and }	552,3	535,7	92,6	87,9	61,1	59,8	3,7	4,6
taffordshire........	121,5	115,5	113,1	111,9	115,9	110,4	2,1	2,0
litan	315,4	303,3	10,5	10,5	10,7	10,7	2	
don	161,6	158,1	58,6	56,3	23,6	22,9	1,3	
	15,322,3	14,870,9	9,711,1	9,597,4	7,053,0	7,015,9	466	
or decrease } 90 }	+ 451,4		+ 113,7		+ 37,1			

at
idle
uary,
, against

IV.—*Prices of Commodities in* 1891. *By* A. SAUERBECK, ESQ.

THE following table shows the course of prices of forty-five commodities during the last fourteen years as compared with the standard period of eleven years 1867-77, which in the aggregate is equivalent to the average of the twenty-five years 1853-77 (see the Society's *Journal*, 1886, pp. 592 and 648):—

Summary of Index Numbers, 1867-77 = 100.

	Vegetable Food (Corn, &c.).	Animal Food (Meat, &c.).	Sugar, Coffee, and Tea.	Total Food.	Minerals.	Textiles.	Sundry Materials.	Total Materials.	Grand Total.	Silver.*	English Wheat Harvest.†	Average Price of Consols.‡	Average Bank of England Rate.‡
1878	95	101	90	96	74	78	88	81	**87**	86·4	108	95 3/16	3 3/4
'79	87	94	87	90	73	74	85	78	**83**	84·2	64	97 1/2	2 3/8
'80	89	101	88	94	79	81	89	84	**88**	85·9	93	98 3/8	2 1/2
'81	84	101	84	91	77	77	86	80	**85**	85·0	97	100	3 1/2
'82	84	104	76	89	79	73	85	80	**84**	84·9	100	100 1/2	4 1/8
'83	82	103	77	89	76	70	84	77	**82**	83·1	93	101 3/16	3 7/10
'84	71	97	63	79	68	68	81	73	**76**	83·3	107	101	3
'85	68	88	63	74	66	65	76	70	**72**	79·9	111	99 1/4	3
'86	65	87	60	72	67	63	69	67	**69**	74·6	96	100 3/4	3
'87	64	79	67	70	69	65	67	67	**68**	73·3	114	101 3/4	3 3/10
'88	67	82	65	72	78	64	67	69	**70**	70·4	100	101	3 3/10
'89	65	86	75	75	75	70	68	70	**72**	70·2	107	98	3 6/10
'90	65	82	70	73	80	66	69	71	**72**	78·4	110	96 1/2	4 5/10
'91	75	81	71	77	76	59	69	68	**72**	74·1	111	95 3/4	3 3/10
Average 1882-91	71	89	69	77	73	66	74	71	**74**	77·2	105	99 1/2	3 5/10
'78-87	79	95	76	84	73	71	81	76	**79**	82·1	98	99 1/2	3 3/10

* Silver 60·84 per oz. = 100. † Harvest 28 bushels per acre = 100.
‡ Consols and bank rate actual figures, not index numbers; consols 2¾ per cent. from 1889.

The index number for all commodities was 72, or the same as in the two preceding years, though a very close calculation would have made the last two years somewhat lower than 1889, viz., 1891 = 71·6, 1890 = 71·7, 1889 = 72·3. That the difference was not greater in view of the general state of affairs is due to the higher prices of corn, and the still high level of coffee and coals. Vegetable food (corn, &c.) was ten points or 15 per cent. higher, while animal food and sugar, coffee and tea, did not in the aggregate show much change. The rise of four points for all food, however, was neutralised by a fall of three points for materials. Among these there was a decline in the case of minerals, which would have been larger had not Scotch pig iron—one of the standard sorts—been artificially upheld by speculators,[1] and the

[1] Comparison of Scotch pig iron with competing sorts and steel rails:—

pri	1889.	1890.	1891.	
	s. d.	*s. d.*	*s. d.*	
pig iron	47 9	49 7	47 2	5 per cent. lower than 1890
orough No. 3	43 –	47 7	40 –	15 "
....	55 –	58 5	49 9	
rails	5*l.*	[illegible]	[illegible]	19 "

greatest fall took place for textiles, viz., about 10 per cent., from 66 to 59, which is the lowest annual figure on record. Sundry materials were on the average unchanged, and call for no comment.

The monthly fluctuations of the average index numbers of all the forty-five descriptions of commodities were thus (1867-77 = 100):—

December, 1889	73·7	September, 1890	72·2	June,	1891....	71·8
January, 1890....	73·2	October,	72·9	July,	„	71·6
February, „	72·7	November, „	71.2	August,	„	71·9
March, „	71·5	December, „	71.1	September, „		71·7
April, „	71·2	January, 1891....	71·1	October,	„	70·7
May, „	70.8	February, „	71·5	November, „		71·4
June, „	70·5	March, „	71·7	December, „		71·4
July, „	71·2	April, „	72·4	January, 1892....		70
August, „	72·8	May, „	72·8	February, „		70

After the fall in 1890 the course of prices during 1891 would according to these figures appear uneventful, but as in the case of the annual average prices, we have to distinguish between corn on the one side and minerals and textiles on the other. The separate index numbers are given in the following (1867-77 = 100):—

	1889.	1890.			1891.			1892.
	December.	March.	June.	December.	March.	June.	December.	February.
Corn, &c.	65	62	68	68	73	77	77	71
Minerals	88	80	79	78	77	77	74	71
Textiles	71	67	65	62	60	58	58	58
All other articles	73	74	72	73	73	73	73	73

The figures show a decline for corn in the early part of 1890, an improvement later on, and a rapid rise in 1891 owing to the failure of the Russian and French crops, and the unsatisfactory harvest in several other European countries. On the other hand minerals and textiles fell on the average uninterruptedly during the last two years, and stand now 19 per cent. lower than in December, 1889. Among minerals, coals remained high, and they have only lately given way, but iron, copper, and lead fell heavily. The decline for textiles extended principally to cotton, wool, silk, and hemp; and the three first are now very near the lowest level ever known.[9] Flax maintained its price, but jute after a heavy drop in 1890 experienced a violent rise during the last six months in consequence of a very short crop. Other articles—twenty-two out of forty-five descriptions—remained in the aggregate unchanged.

Silver, with the exception of a short-lived rally in the middle of the year, followed a downward course, and touched in February,

* Cotton middling American went down to 3$\frac{11}{16}$d. in February, 1892, against 3$\frac{1}{8}$d. in 1848; from 1849 to 1890 it had never been under 4$\frac{3}{8}$d. per lb.

1892, the unprecedentedly low price of 41⅜d. oz., against 41⅝d. the lowest quotation in 1888. The principal causes are probably to be sought in the large production, in the sale of accumulated stocks, and in the incapability of the East to take large quantities except at low prices.

The movements of prices reflect to some extent the unsatisfactory state of trade in most countries, and particularly of the three great industries, iron, cotton, and wool. The course of production of these articles may be gathered from the following figures :—

	Iron.		Cotton.		Wool.	
	Production of United Kingdom, United States, and Germany only.	Average Price of Scotch Pig.	Total Supply in Europe and North America per Season.	Average Price of Middling American.	Supply of Colonial and River Plate only per Season.	Average Price of Port Philip Average Fleece.
	Tons.	*s.* and *d.*	Bales.	*d.* per lb.	Bales.	*d.* per lb.
1879	10,964,000	47	6,537,000	$6\frac{7}{16}$	1,285,000	$18\frac{3}{4}$
'80	14,313,000	54·6	7,685,000	$6\frac{4}{5}$	1,377,000	$21\frac{1}{4}$
'81	15,202,000	49·1	8,454,000	$6\frac{7}{16}$	1,443,000	$19\frac{1}{2}$
'82	16,591,000	49·4	8,043,000	$6\frac{1}{8}$	1,534,000	$19\frac{1}{4}$
'83	16,594,000	46·9	9,409,000	$5\frac{3}{4}$	1,603,000	19
'84	15,511,000	42·1	8,267,000	6	1,668,000	$18\frac{1}{4}$
'85	15,146,000	41·10	7,594,000	$5\frac{1}{4}$	1,684,000	$16\frac{1}{4}$
'86	16,221,000	39·11	8,549,000	$5\frac{1}{4}$	1,814,000	$15\frac{1}{2}$
'87	18,001,000	42·3	9,079,000	$5\frac{1}{4}$	1,786,000	$15\frac{3}{4}$
'88	18,826,000	39·11	9,134,000	$5\frac{9}{16}$	1,978,000	$15\frac{3}{4}$
'89	20,451,000	47·9	9,314,000	$5\frac{11}{16}$	2,116,000	$17\frac{1}{4}$
'90	21,765,000	49·7	9,969,000	6	2,016,000	16
'91	20,032,000*	47·2	10,869,000	$4\frac{11}{16}$	2,385,000	$14\frac{3}{4}$
'92, Feb.	—	40·3	—	$3\frac{11}{16}$	—	$12\frac{1}{2}$

* United Kingdom, 1891, estimated at 7,300,000; United States, 8,280,000; and Germany, 4,452,000 tons.

The output of iron, it will be seen, had to be reduced by about 8 per cent. last year after a rapid development, but the stocks in this country at least are now very moderate. The European and North American supply of cotton reached an enormous figure, to which has still to be added the consumption of India, last year 1,179,000 bales, against 597,000 in 1885, and 267,000 bales in 1879. This year's production will probably not be much smaller, while in the case of wool, after a considerable increase, a fresh addition is anticipated. The large quantities of cotton and wool had to be forced into consumption at a time of general stagnation and lack of enterprise at constantly falling prices, inflicting large losses on producers, dealers, and manufacturers. Notwithstanding this, excessive stocks of cotton were left on hand. And as these ind tries were and are still affected by large supplies and a fall, so th ute industry is now handicapped by a short supply and a rise of e raw article, the equivalent of which cannot be realised for the nufactured goods. Some other industries did not fare much better, but there are also exceptions, and the shipbuilding trade and some branches of engineering in this country were reported to have been fairly prosperous. Freights have however fallen considerably, and this may affect shipbuilding.

The European export trade generally suffered from the effects of the new American tariff, from the shrinkage of the South American trade, and the decline of the Eastern exchanges.

There has been a great combination of adverse influences: the natural reaction from a period of trade development (1888-89), of over production and over speculation in some branches, the protracted financial crisis taking ever greater dimensions and causing enormous losses, the McKinley Bill, the fall of silver, the famine in Russia, bad harvests in several other countries, and the dearness of bread. The only redeeming feature was, thanks to the higher prices, the comparatively better position of the agricultural population in those countries that had fair or good harvests, particularly in the United States, and of the labouring classes where wages had not fallen. But the depression and the shortening of time in many manufacturing districts has now thrown many people out of employment, and the tendency of wages is downwards.

The following figures give in each case the average index number of ten years (see the Society's *Journal*, 1888, pp. 155 and 156, and the dotted line in the diagram of the *Journal*, 1886):—

1838–47	93	1875–84	87	1879–88	78
'48–57	89	'76–85	85	'80–89	76
'58–67	99	'77–86	82	'81–90	75
'68–77	100	'78–87	79	'82–91	74

These show the gradual change of prices in average periods. The number of 72 in 1891 was 28 per cent. below the standard period of 1867-77, 9 per cent. below the period 1878-87, but only 3 per cent. below the average of the last ten years.

The arithmetical mean of the forty-five index numbers, which for the last two years was 72, has, as in former years, again been subjected to two tests:—

Firstly, by using the same index numbers of the separate articles, but calculating each article according to its importance in the United Kingdom, when the mean for 1891 is 71·9 against 72·1 in 1890.

Secondly, by calculating the quantities in the United Kingdom at their actual values (the production on the basis of my price tables, the imports at Board of Trade values, and consequently a considerable portion according to a different set of prices) and at the nominal values on the basis of the average prices from 1867-77. In this case the mean is 74·5 against 74·2 in 1890.

The result of the second calculation differs somewhat from that obtained by ordinary index numbers, and this is due to the high export price of coals, which article forms a large item in the trade of the country, if the commodities are taken according to quantity, and to the fact that in a falling market the declarations of the value of imports are naturally higher than the actual prices obtained.

The following table gives the figures which have served for the second test (see also the Society's *Journal*, 1886, pp. 613—19) :—

Movements of Forty-five Commodities in the United Kingdom (Production and Imports).

	Estimated Actual Value in each Period.	Nominal Values at Average Prices of 1867-77, showing Increase in Quantities.	Movement of Quantities, 1848-50 = 100.	Movement of Quantities from Period to Period.	Ratio of Prices according to this Table, 1867-77 = 100.
	Mln. £'s and dec.	Mln. £'s and dec.			
Avge. 1848-50	219·8	294·8	100	—	74·6
„ '59-61	350·1	382·7	130	30% over 1849	91·5
„ '69-71	456·6	484·6	164	27% „ '60	94·2
„ '74-76	537·8	538·4	183	—	99·9
„ '79-81	489·7	578·5	196	19% over 1870	84·6
'84-86	445·7	610·1	207	—	73·0
1887..............	423·1	627·7	213	—	67·4
'88..............	443·2	640·8	217	—	69·2
'89..............	492·3	680·7	231 ⎫		72·3
'90..............	499·4	673	228 ⎬ 18% over 1880		74·2
'91*	517·1	694	235 ⎭		74·5

* 1891 subject to correction after publication of the complete agricultural and mineral produce returns.

The nominal values at the uniform prices of 1867-77 show the exact movement of quantities in the aggregate. The quantities during the last three years were on the average 18 per cent. larger than in 1880, and 131 per cent. larger than in 1849.

*Average Prices of Commodities.**

No. of Article	0	1	2	3	4	5	6	7	8	1—8	9
		Wheat.		Flour.	Barley.	Oats.	Maize.	Potatoes.*	Rice.		Beef.
Year.	Silver.†	English Gazette.	American.	Town Made White.	English Gazette.	English Gazette.	American Mixed.	Good English.	Rangoon Cargoes to Arrive.	Vegetable Food. Total.	Prime.
	d. per oz.	s. and d. per qr.	s. and d. per qr.	s per sack (280 lbs.).	s. and d. per qr.	s. and d. per qr.	s. per qr.	s. per ton	s. and d. per cwt.		d. per 8 lbs.
1877	54 7/8	56·9	55	45	39·8	25·11	27 1/2	130	10	—	61
1878	52 9/16	46·5	48	38	40·2	24·4	25	155	10	—	61
'79	51 1/4	43·10	48	36	34	21·9	23 3/4	180	9·7	—	55
'80	52 1/4	44·4	51	39	33·1	23·1	25 3/4	130	9·1	—	58
'81	51 11/16	45·4	52	40	31·11	21·9	27 3/4	85	8·4	—	56
'82	51 5/8	45·1	48·6	40	31·2	21·10	31	95	7·5	—	60
1883	50 9/16	41·7	45	36	31·10	21·5	27 3/4	105	8·1	—	61
'84	50 11/16	35·8	36·6	31	30·8	20·8	25 1/4	75	7·8	—	58
'85	48 5/8	32·10	35	29	30·1	20·7	23	75	7	—	52
'86	45 3/8	31	35	28	26·7	19	21	80	6·7	—	49
'87	44 5/8	32·6	34	28	25·4	16·3	21 1/2	85	6·10	—	43
1888	42 7/8	31·10	37	30	27·10	16·9	23 1/2	80	7·1	—	48
'89	42 11/16	29·9	35	29	25·10	17·9	20	80	7·3	—	47
'90	47 11/16	31·11	35·6	29	28·8	18·7	20	70	7·3	—	47
'91	45 1/16	37	40	33	28·2	20	28	92	7·11	—	47
Average 1882-91	47	35	38	31 1/2	28 1/2	19	24	84	7 1/2	—	51
'78-87	50	40	43 1/2	34 1/2	31 1/2	21	25	102	8	—	55 1/2
'67-77	58 1/4	54 1/2	56	46	39	26	32 1/2	117	10	—	59
Index Numbers (or Percentages) of Prices, the Average of 1867-77 being 100.											
1877	90·2	104	98	98	102	100	84	111	100	797	104
1878	86·4	85	86	83	103	94	77	132	100	760	104
'79	84·2	80	86	78	87	84	73	111	96	695	93
'80	85·9	81	91	85	85	89	79	111	91	712	98
'81	85	83	93	87	82	84	85	73	83	670	95
'82	84·9	83	87	87	80	84	95	81	74	671	102
1883	83·1	76	80	78	82	82	85	90	81	654	104
'84	83·3	65	65	65	79	78	78	64	77	571	98
'85	79·9	60	62	63	77	79	71	64	70	546	88
'86	74·6	57	62	61	68	73	65	69	66	521	83
'87	73·3	60	61	61	65	63	65	73	68	516	73
1888	70·4	58	66	65	71	64	72	69	71	536	81
'89	70·2	55	63	63	66	69	61	69	72	518	80
'90	78·4	59	63	63	73	72	61	60	72	523	80
'91	74·1	68	71	72	72	77	86	79	79	604	80

* The annual prices are the averages of twelve monthly or fifty-two weekly quotatio potatoes of eight monthly quotations, January to April and September to December.

† Index numbers of silver as compared with 60·84*d.* per ounce being the parity between gol and silver at 1 : 15½ ; not included in the general average.

Average Prices of Commodities—Contd.

10	11	12	13	14	15	9—15	16A	16B	17	18A*	18B*
Beef.	Mutton.		Pork.	Bacon.	Butter.		Sugar.			Coffee.	
Mid-dling.	Prime.	Mid-dling.	Large and Small, Average.	Water-ford.	Fries-land, Fine to Finest.	Animal Food. Total.	British West Indian Refining.	Beet, German, 88 p. c., f.o.b.	Java, Floating Cargoes.	Ceylon Planta-tion, Low Mid-dling.	Rio, Good Channel.
d. per 8 lbs.	*d.* per 8 lbs.	*d.* per 8 lbs.	*d.* per 8 lbs.	*s.* per cwt.	*s.* per cwt.		*s.* per cwt.	*s.* per cwt.	*s.* per cwt.	*s.* per cwt.	*s.* per cwt.
49	69	54	51	75	127	—	24½	25½	30	102	77
49	68	55	50	74	122	—	20	21½	25	101	62
45	64	52	48	72	107	—	19	21¼	24	90	58
49	66	54	55	76	125	—	20½	21½	25½	87	61
48	69	57	54	76	123	—	21¼	22	26½	80	49
51	72	60	51	74	125	—	20	21½	25½	65	39
51	78	61	49	72	123	—	19	20¼	24½	76	43
49	64	53	48	70	120	—	13¼	13¼	17½	62	47
44	56	47	45	68	111	—	13½	14¼	17½	60	39
40	62	50	45	67	100	—	11¾	11¾	14¼	68	46
36	52	42	43	61	103	—	11¾	12½	14½	90	78
39	58	47	40	61	100	—	13	12¾	16	80	64
39	63	50	43	66	102	—	16	16½	19	95	76
38	59	45	42	62	100	—	13	12½	15¼	101	83
40	58	42	39	63	106	—	13½	13½	15½	101	76
42½	61	49½	44½	66½	109	—	14½	15	18	80	59
46	64½	53	49	71	116	—	17	18	21½	78	52
50	63	55	52	74	125	—	23	24	28½	87	64

Index Numbers (or Percentages) of Prices, the Average of 1867-77 being 100.

10	11	12	13	14	15	9—15	16A–16B		17	18A*	18B*
98	109	98	98	101	102	710	106		105	117	120
98	108	100	96	100	98	704	88		88	116	97
90	102	95	92	97	86	655	86		84	103	91
98	105	98	106	103	100	708	89		89	100	95
96	109	104	104	103	98	709	92		93	92	77
102	114	109	98	100	100	725	87		89	75	61
102	116	111	94	97	98	722	84		86	87	67
98	102	96	92	95	96	677	56		62	91	74
88	89	85	87	92	89	618	59		62	69	61
80	98	91	87	91	80	610	50		50	78	72
72	83	76	83	82	82	551	52		51	104	122
78	92	85	77	82	80	575	57		56	92	100
78	100	91	83	89	82	603	69		67	109	119
76	94	82	81	84	80	577	54		54	116	130
80	84	76	75	85	85	565	57		54	116	119

Average Prices of Commodities—Contd.

19A*	19B*	19	16—19	1—19	20	21	22	—	23
Tea.			Sugar, Coffee, and Tea.		Iron.		Copper.		Tin.
Congou, Common.	Average Import Price.	Mean of 19A and 19B.	Total.	Food. Total.	Scotch Pig.	Bars, Common.	Chili Bars.	English Tough Cake.	Straits.
d. per lb.	*d.* and dec. per lb.				*s.* and *d.* per ton	£ per ton	£ per ton	£ per ton	£ per ton
7¾	15·98	—	—	—	54·4	6¾	68	75	68
7¾	15·29	—	—	—	48·5	5⅝	62	67	61
9	14·68	—	—	—	47	5¾	58	64	73
8¾	13·47	—	—	—	54·6	6¾	63	68	88
6⅛	12·82	—	—	—	49·1	5¾	62	67	93
5	12·58	—	—	—	49·4	6¼	66	71	102
5¾	12·46	—	—	—	46·9	5¾	63	67	93
6¼	11·78	—	—	—	42·1	5⅛	54	59	81
6⅛	12·06	—	—	—	41·10	4⅞	43	47	87
6⅓	11·77	—	—	—	39·11	4⅜	40	44	98
5	10·58	—	—	—	42·3	4⅜	44	47	112
4	10·99	—	—	—	39·11	4⅞	81	78	117
4¼	10·79	—	—	—	47·9	6¼	51	54	93
4⅛	10·65	—	—	—	49·7	6⅜	54	59	94
5⅛	10·76	—	—	—	47·2	5⅝	51	55	91
5¾	11⅓	—	—	—	44½	5⅓	55	58	97
6¾	12¾	—	—	—	46	5⅓	55	60	89
11¼	17¼	—	—	—	69	8¼	75	81	105

Index Numbers (or Percentages) of Prices, the Average of 1867-77 being 100.

118	* 69	* 93	81	410	1,917	79	82	91	—	65
106	69	89	79	361	1,825	70	68	83	—	58
97	80	85	82	349	1,699	69	70	77	—	69
97	78	78	78	353	1,773	79	82	84	—	84
84	58	75	66	335	1,714	71	70	83	—	89
68	45	73	59	303	1,699	71	76	88	—	97
77	49	72	60	307	1,683	69	70	84	—	89
73	56	68	62	253	1,501	61	62	72	—	77
65	58	70	64	250	1.414	60	59	57	—	83
75	58	69	64	239	1,370	58	56	53	—	93
113	44	62	53	269	1,336	61	56	59	—	107
96	36	64	50	259	1,370	58	59	108	—	111
114	38	63	50	300	1,421	69	76	68	—	89
123	40	62	51	281	1,382	72	77	72	—	90
118	49	62	56	285	1,454	68	68	68	—	87

Average Prices of Commodities- Contd.

No. of Article	24	25	26	20—26	27	28	29A	29B	30A	30B	31
	Lead.	Coals.			Cotton.		Flax.		Hemp.		Jute.
Year.	English Pig.	Wallsend Hetton in London.	Average Export Price.	Minerals. Total.	Middling Uplands.	Fair Dhollerah.	St. Petersburg 12 Head Best.	Russian, Average Import.	Manilla Fair Roping.	St. Petersburg Clean.	Good Medium.
	£ per ton	s. per ton	s. and dec. per ton		d. per lb.	d. per lb.	£ per ton	£ per ton	£ per ton	£ per ton	£ per ton
1877........	20⅓	20	10·17	—	6 5/16	5 3/16	45	43	28	35	17½
1878........	16⅝	18	9·46	—	6⅛	4 15/16	39½	40	25	29	17
'79........	15⅛	18	8·77	—	6 5/16	5	34	35	27	25	16½
'80........	16⅓	15½	8·95	—	6 15/16	5¼	35	40	30	23	18¾
'81........	15⅛	17	8·97	—	6 7/16	4⅜	32½	33	43	24	18½
'82........	14⅓	17	9·14	—	6⅝	4 5/16	29½	30½	46	24	15
1883........	12⅞	18	9·35	—	5¾	3⅞	30	30½	46	26	14¼
'84........	11¼	16½	9·29	—	6	3 15/16	29½	30¾	38	29	13½
'85........	11⅝	16½	8·95	—	5⅝	4¼	34	35	35	29	12
'86........	13¼	16	8·45	—	5⅛	3 9/16	35	35	29	29	11½
'87........	12⅞	16	8·32	—	5⅜	3 9/16	32	31½	34	29	12¼
1888........	13⅞	16½	8·41	—	5 9/16	3⅞	29	28	·37	26	13¼
'89........	13	17½	10·21	—	5 15/16	4⅛	28	28	50	26	15
'90........	13¼	19	12·62	—	6	3 15/16	27	26	39	26	13¼
'91........	12⅓	19	12·16	—	4 11/16	3¼	28	26	32	24	13
Average 1882-91	13	17¼	9¾	—	5¾	3⅞	30	30	38½	27	13¼
'78-87	14	16¾	9	—	6	4¼	33	34	35½	26½	15
'67-77	20⅓	22	12½	—	9	6¾	46	47½	43	35	19

Index Numbers (or Percentages) of Prices, the Average of 1867-77 being 100.

Year.	24	25	26	20—26	27	28	29A, 29B	30A, 30B	31
1877........	100	91	81	589	70	77	94	81	92
1878........	81	82	76	518	66	73	84	69	90
'79........	74	82	70	511	70	74	73	67	87
'80........	80	70	72	551	77	78	79	68	99
'81........	74	77	72	536	71	65	70	86	98
'82........	71	77	73	553	74	64	64	90	79
1883........	63	82	75	532	64	58	65	92	75
'84........	55	75	74	476	67	59	64	86	71
'85........	57	75	72	463	62	63	73	82	63
'86........	65	73	68	466	57	53	75	74	61
'87........	63	73	67	486	62	53	68	81	64
1888........	68	75	67	546	62	58	61	81	70
'89........	63	80	82	527	66	61	60	97	79
'90........	65	86	101	563	67	58	56	82	70
'91........	61	86	97	535	52	48	57	72	68

Average Prices of Commodities—Contd.

32B	33	34	27—34	35A	35B	38
Wool.		Silk.				Oil.
Merino, Adelaide, Average Grease.	English, Lincoln Half Hogs.	Tsatlee.	Textiles Total.		River Plate Salted.	Palm.
d. per lb.	*d.* per lb.	*s.* per lb.		*d.* per lb.	*d.* per lb.	£ per ton
9⅛	16¼	20	—		7¾	40
9⅛	15	16½	—		6¾	38
8⅛	12⅛	16	—		6¾	34
10⅝	15⅛	15	—		7⅛	32
9¼	12⅜	15¾	—		7	32
9	11¼	15¾	—		7	35
8⅛	10	15⅞	—		7	41
8⅛	10	14½	—		7	36
6¾	9⅞	12¾	—		6⅛	30
6⅝	10	13¾	—		5¾	24
7	10⅝	14⅛	—		6¼	22
7	10⅞	13	—		4⅞	22
8¼	11	13½	—		5	25
7½	11	14	—		5⅛	27
6⅞	9¾	13	—		5⅛	26
7½	10¼	14	—	7½	6	29
8⅝	11¾	15	—	8⅛	6¾	32½
9⅞	19¾	23	—	9	7	39

Index Numbers (or Percentages) of Prices, the Average of 1867-77 being 100.

94	82	87	677	101	100	94	103
93	76	72	623	94	92	84	97
88	63	69	591	92	91	82	87
103	77	65	646	105	97	86	82
92	63	68	613	100	95	89	82
92	57	68	588	100	94	107	90
89	51	68	562	100	94	103	105
85	51	63	546	100	94	94	92
73	50	55	521	95	94	76	77
70	51	60	501	85	94	63	61
72	54	63	517	86	94	61	56
72	53	57	514	73	87	71	56
82	56	59	560	70	84	72	64
76	56	61	526	70	81	71	69
70	49	57	473	66	81	75	67

Average Prices of Commodities—Contd.

No. of Article }	89	40ᴀ		1—45
		Oil.		
Year.	Olive.	Linseed.		Grand Total.
	£ per tun	£ per ton		
1877........	49	28		
1878........	49	26		
'79........	46	27		
'80........	41	27		
'81........	38	26		
'82........	37	23		
1883........	36	20		
'84........	40	20		
'85........	39	22		
'86........	38	20¼		
'87........	34	20¼		
1888........	36	18¼		
'89........	35	20		
'90........	41	23		
'91........	43	21		
Average 1882–91	38	21		
'78–87	40	23		
'67–77	50	20		

Year										Grand Total
1877........	98	92	96 *	78	100	75	100	1,037	2,303	4,220
1878........	98	85	73	76	107	76	87	969	2,110	3,935
'79........	92	89	59	74	107	86	75	934	2,036	3,735
'80........	82	90	60	80	111	100	89	982	2,179	3,952
'81........	76	85	58	71	104	93	89	942	2,091	3,605
'82........	74	75	48	69	95	90	91	933	2,074	3,773
1883........	72	68	52	72	80	86	88	920	2,014	3,697
'84........	80	69	52	71	68	83	82	885	1,907	3,408
'85........	78	73	55	60	75	72	81	836	1,820	3,234
'86........	76	69	47	53	71	69	76	764	1,731	3,101
'87........	68	65	45	54	68	66	70	735	1,738	3,074
1888........	72	63	52	52	71	66	74	737	1,797	3,167
'89........	70	69	46	55	68	62	84	744	1,831	3,252
'90........	82	73	45	66	61	59	79	756	1,845	3,227
'91........	86	70	45	70	63	66	73	762	1,770	3,224

* Petroleum as compared with the average from 1873-77 only.

V.—*Agricultural Returns of* 1891.

[THE following is summarised from the Report of the Director
of the Statistical Department on the Returns now published for
the year 1891 of the Board of Agriculture.]

The total area of arable land in the United Kingdom has again
diminished during the year 1891, and this time by 318,520 acres,
while the permanent pasture has increased by 452,238 acres, so
that the whole area under cultivation has increased by 133,718 acres.
The increase in permanent pasture is, however, in part due to an
amended classification, certain areas now being for the first time
considered as pasture which were formerly included in the category
of mountain and heath land. Of the arable land, the only two
divisions to show any increase are the areas devoted to hops and
to small fruit, the hops now covering 1,590 acres more than in
1890, and the small fruit 13,405 acres, a very considerable increase.
The corn crops have diminished by 130,740 acres. As regards
live stock, cattle and sheep show a large increase during the year,
while, owing to a decrease of nearly 13 per cent. in Ireland, the
number of pigs is smaller than in 1890.

*Acreage under the different Crops, and Live Stock in the United Kingdom
in 1891 and 1890.*

Acreage.	1891.	1890.	1891 compared with 1890.	
			Increase.	Decrease.
	Acres.	Acres.	Acres.	Acres.
Total cultivated area	48,179,473	48,045,755	133,718	—
Total of permanent pasture	27,567,663	27,115,425	452,238	—
„ arable land	20,611,810	20,930,330	—	318,520
Corn crops	9,443,509	9,574,249	—	130,740
Green „	4,510,653	4,534,145	—	23,492
Clover, &c., under rotation	6,013,685	6,097,210	—	83,525
Flax	76,477	99,326	—	22,849
Hops	56,145	54,555	1,590	—
Small fruit	60,138	46,733	13,405	—
Bare fallow	451,203	524,112	—	72,909
Live Stock.	Number.	Number.	Number.	Number.
Horses	2,026,170	1,964,911	61,259	—
Cattle	11,343,686	10,789,858	553,828	—
Sheep	33,533,988	31,667,195	1,866,793	—
Pigs	4,272,764	4,362,040	—	89,276

One of the most marked features of the agricultural depression
has been the gradual decrease in the acreage of the arable land and
the contemporaneous but larger increase in the pasture. About
one half of this latter increase is land which twenty years ago was
under the plough. Twenty years ago the arable land in Great
Britain was to the pasture as 3 : 2; now the acreage of each is

almost exactly the same. The following table shows the acreage of the arable area of Great Britain at intervals of ten years, with the acreage of the permanent pasture, and the total accounted for annually as cultivated land.

Acreage of the Principal Crops in Great Britain at Ten-Year Periods.

[000's omitted.]

Year.	Corn Crops.	Green Crops.	Clover, Grasses under Rotation.	Other Crops.	Bare Fallow.	Total Arable Land.	Permanent Pasture.	Grand Total.
	Acres.	Acres.	Acres.	Acres.	Acres.	Acres.	Acres	Acres.
1871....	9,675,	3,738,	4,370,	77,	543,	18,403,	12,435,	30,839,
'81....	8,848,	3,511,	4,342,	71,	796,	17,568,	14,643,	32,212,
'91....	7,925,	3,298,	4,717,	116,*	429,	16,485,	16,434,	32,919,

* Including 59,000 acres of small fruit not previously distinguished.

The percentage of the arable land of Great Britain under each crop at the same intervals is given as under:—

Number of Acres per 1,000 of Arable Land under each kind of Crop.

Distribution of Surface.	1871.	1881.	1891.
	Acres.	Acres.	Acres.
TOTAL of arable land	1,000	1,000	1,000
TOTAL corn crops	526	504	481
„ all other crops	474	496	.519
Wheat..	194	160	140
Barley...	130	139	128
Oats..	148	165	176
Rye	4	2	3
Beans	29	25	22
Peas..	21	13	12
Potatoes	34	33	32
Turnips and swedes	118	116	116
Mangold..	19	20	22
Cabbage, kohl-rabi, and rape	10	8	10
Vetches or tares...............	17	14	14
Fallow or minor crops	39	58	39
Clover and rotation grasses	237	247	286

The area devoted to wheat in Great Britain was in 1891 less by 79,000 acres than in 1890, this deficiency representing nearly three-fourths of the total reduction (108,000 acres) of the corn crop area. The greater part of this decrease has taken place in the *grazing* counties; it amounts to 14 per cent. in Scotland, 10 per cent. in Wales, and 9½ per cent. in the south-western counties, while in the rest of England the decrease is only 2 per cent. Cambridge is the only county which can show any considerable increase in the wheat area, viz., 1,721 acres. In Scotland the diminished area has been almost entirely replaced by barley. The area under oats shows a diminution of 21,000 acres in Scotland, 7,000 acres in Wales, but an increase of 25,000 acres in England. Potatoes also cover a greater area in England, as do hops. In Ireland the area of every kind of corn crop has decreased, except beans, the greatest deficiency being in the acreage of wheat, which is less in 1891 than in 1890 by nearly 12,000 acres, or 12½ per cent. The acreage of potatoes has also decreased by 27,500 acres, but the acreage of turnips and swedes has slightly increased.

A new feature of the returns for Great Britain for 1891 is an investigation into the area devoted to woods and plantations. Returns were given in 1872, 1881, and 1888, but as these were all more or less defective, they cannot therefore be properly compared with those of the present year. There is an apparent advance (the area of woodland surface in 1872 was given as 2,187,000 acres, in 1881 2,458,000, in 1888 2,561,000, and now in 1891 as 2,695,000 acres). But that most of this is due to better registration, is apparent from the fact, that although the increase since 1881 is 237,000 acres, yet the area of the plantations—this term being used to denote woods planted during the last ten years, *i.e.*, since 1881—is only 103,000 acres, while trees have been felled from considerable areas during the interval. The area of woods and plantations in England is now returned at 1,518,321 acres, in Wales at 174,967 acres, in Scotland 905,759 acres, and in Ireland 311,351 acres.

It is noteworthy, moreover, that two-fifths of the surface of 103,000 acres planted in the last ten years are returned from Scotland alone, while practically half of the 41,000 acres of new plantations in that country occurs in the counties of Aberdeen, Inverness, and Ross and Cromarty. In England the counties where most planting would seem of late to have been done are Devon and Hants in the south, and Yorkshire, Northumberland, and Cumberland in the north.

The county of Hants now stands in the returns as possessing the largest area of woodland in England, or 122,574 acres, Sussex with 122,073 comes second, while it may be worth noting that the four counties of Hants, Sussex, Surrey, and Kent, forming the south-eastern corner of England, possess between them nearly a fourth of the English woods and plantations, showing over 11 per cent. of the surface thus occupied, in contrast with 4 per cent. as the mean for the rest of the country.

In Scotland, Inverness accounts for 169,000 acres of woodland. This area is far the largest in Great Britain. It is considerably in excess of the surface returned as under all forms of crops or grass in that county, and nearly equal to a fifth part of the whole Scottish woodlands.

If the Irish record of woods and plantations annually shown in the returns for that country, and now amounting to 311,351 acres, be added to the aggregate now obtained for Great Britain, and to the figures obtained from the Isle of Man and Channel Islands, the woodland area of the United Kingdom may be taken as 3,007,569 acres.

The following table shows the advance in live stock in Great Britain during the last twenty years :—

Live Stock in Great Britain.

[000's omitted.]

	Horses.	Cattle.	Sheep.	Pigs.
1871	1,254,	5,338,	27,120,	2,500,
'81	1,425,	5,912,	24,581,	2,048,
'91	1,488,	6,853,	28,733,	2,889,

Turning now to the imports of agricultural produce, the most remarkable feature in the returns is that the value of the animals and animal products in 1890 for the first time exceeds the value of the cereals. The most important increase is in the importation of fresh mutton, which in 1870 and 1880 was absolutely *nil*, whereas in 1890 it had reached the total of 1,656,000 cwt. Imports of fresh beef have increased in almost as large proportions—from 12,000 cwt. in 1870 to 1,855,040 cwt. in 1890. These large increases in dead meat have been accompanied by a decrease in the imports of live sheep, and more especially pigs, though more cattle have arrived in this country. While only 4,000 pigs were brought into the United Kingdom from abroad, 603,000 passed from Ireland into Great Britain in the year 1890.

Imports of Grain and Animal Products (United Kingdom).

[000's omitted.]

	Quantities.			Values.		
	1870.	1880.	1890.	1870.	1880.	1890.
				£	£	£
Wheat.................. cwt.	30,901,	55,262,	60,474,			
Flour .... ,,	4,804,	10,558,	15,773,			
Maize .... ,,	16,757,	37,225,	43,438,	34,170,	62,857,	53,485,
All other corn, meal, and flour ,,	21,640,	31,128,	35,935,			
Butter and margarine .... cwt.	1,159,	2,326,	3,108,			
Cheese.................. ,,	1,041,	1,776,	2,144,	11,170,	19,468,	22,086,
Eggs .... No.	430,842,	747,409,	1,234,950,			
Cattle .... ,,	202,	390,	643,			
Sheep .... ,,	670,	941,	358,	4,655,	10,239,	11,216,
Pigs...................... ,,	96,	51,	4,			
Beef (fresh) .... cwt.	12,	727,	1,855,			
Mutton .... ,,	—	—	1,656,	3,367,	16,430,	20,225,
Bacon, hams, pork ,,	824,	5,744,	5,300,			
Other dead meat.. ,,	321,	1,095,	1,114,			
Total value, all animal products	—	—	—	19,192,	46,137,	53,527,

In spite of the rainy summer, the crops in Great Britain were in bulk above the average in 1891; although, owing to the smaller area, the harvest yielded a quantity somewhat less than in 1890, there was nevertheless a larger yield per acre of wheat. Barley and oats yielded rather less than in 1890. It is generally reported that all the corn crops were in 1891 light and inferior in quality and condition; also that an unusually large proportion of grain was shed in the fields.

Summary of Agricultural Produce Statistics (Wheat, Barley, and Oats) in England, Wales, Scotland, and Great Britain, for 1891.

WHEAT.

	Estimated Total Produce.		Acreage.		Estimated Average Yield per Acre.	
	1891.	1890.	1891.	1890.	1891.	1890.
	Bshls.	Bshls.	Acres.	Acres.	Bshls.	Bshls.
England	68,694.456	69,442,417	2,192,398	2,255,694	31·33	30·79
Wales	1,461,740	1,712,541	61,590	68,669	23·73	24·94
Scotland	1,971,067	2,199,526	53,294	61,973	36·98	35·49
Great Britain	72,127,263	73,354,484	2,307,277	2,386,336	31·26	30·74

BARLEY.

England	60,900,824	62,250,366	1,772,432	1,775,606	34·36	35·06
Wales	3,438,620	3,621,793	117,101	119,780	29·36	30·24
Scotland	7,789,651	8,061,642	223,265	215,792	34·89	37·36
Great Britain	72,129,095	73,933,801	2,112,798	2,111,178	34·14	35·02

OATS.

England	69,786,175	72,104,034	1,672,835	1,648,153	41·72	43·75
Wales	7,698,529	8,116,344	234,055	241,199	32·89	33·65
Scotland	34,901,557	39,967,668	992,239	1,013,646	35·17	39·43
Great Britain	112,386,261	120,188,046	2,899,129	2,902,998	38·77	41·40

The Irish returns of cereals are estimated in cwt., and the production of the three principal cereals is given as follows in the Report of the Registrar-General for Ireland:—

	Area.		Produce.		Yield per Acre.	
	1891.	1890.	1891.	1890.	1891.	1890.
	Acres.	Acres.	cwts.	cwts.	cwts.	cwts.
Wheat	80,870	92,341	1,401,127	1,413,964	17·3	15·3
Oats	1,215,896	1,221,013	18,833,576	17,796,312	15·5	14·6
Barley	177,066	182,058	3,310,459	3,057,257	18·6	16·8

Potatoes, in spite of a diminished area (753,000 acres in 1891, against 781,000 in 1890), produced last year in Ireland 3,036,586 tons (4 tons per acre), against 1,810,429 in 1890. The remarkable feature of the potato crop is the proportion of *champions* grown in the country. It was first introduced in quantity into Ireland after the failure of the potato crop of 1879, and it now takes up 79·7 per cent. of the acreage under that tuber.

Sufficient foreign statistics of the harvest of 1891 are not yet available for comparison with the English, but it may be useful to summarise the average produce per acre of the principal corn producing countries of the world in the following table. For Russia, unfortunately, no statistics as to the area under the different crops are available of a later date than 1883-87. The acreage does not however vary greatly from year to year, and if we assume that the area under cultivation has remained the same during 1888, 1889, and 1890, as during 1883-87, it appears that the annual yield of *wheat* in Russia was in 1888, 9·92; in 1889, 5·99; and in 1890, 7·14 English bushels per acre. For *barley* the figures for the same years were respectively 12·29, 9·00, and 12·70; for *oats*, 15·11, 13·59, and 15·02; and for *rye*, the staple grain of the country, 10·60, 8·27, and 10·10 bushels per acre.

Estimated Average Yield per Acre of Wheat, Barley, and Oats in certain Countries, in English Imperial Bushels per Acre.

	Wheat.			Barley.			Oats.		
	1888.	1889.	1890.	1888.	1889.	1890.	1888.	1889.	1890.
United Kingdom[a]...	27·97	29·89	30·66	33·03[b]	32·37[b]	35·23[b]	37·95	39·75	41·54
Australasia[c]	10·51[d]	10·98	9·28	19·47[d]	22·19	18·63	24·44[d]	28·72	25·62
Austria	17·16	13·76	—	19·89	15·78	—	22·03	16·91	—
Hungary	19·24	12·61	19·50	18·04	13·45	20·61	21·22	16·82	21·05
Canada[f]	—	14·05	17·71	—	25·58	23·03	—	31·63	29·41
Denmark	30·60	—	—	30·77	—	—	30·84	—	—
France	15·75[c]	17·13[c]	—	19·68	20·15	—	25·33	25·16	—
Germany	19·47	18·03	21·48	23·41	20·53	24·49	27·75	24·71	28·80
Holland.....	31·73[c]	—	—	45·60[c]	—	—	41·21[c]	—	—
India	9·17	9·23	9·67	—	—	—	—	—	—
Sweden	—	22·54	—	—	25·80	—	—	23·71	—
United States	10·80	12·47	10·73	20·67	—	—	25·20	26·53	19·21

[a] Exclusive of the Channel Islands and the Isle of Man.   [b] Including bere.

[c] In most of the Australasian colonies the returns are for the twelve months ending in March of the years subsequent to those stated.

[d] Exclusive of South Australia.   [e] Including spelt.

[f] Provinces of Ontario and Manitoba only.   [g] In 1887.

R. H. H.

VI.—*Strikes and Lock-outs in* 1890.

[THE following is condensed from the report of Mr. J. Burnett, Labour Correspondent to the Board of Trade].

The years 1889 and 1890 have undoubtedly been the two best for trade for several years past, as is admitted even by many trade union secretaries. In 1837 a revival of trade began, which continued till the middle of 1890, after which period the demand for labour began to fall away again. All the more important branches of trade shared in the general prosperity. Several trade unions have furnished returns showing the percentage of men affiliated to them who were unemployed during each month, and the following interesting table, deduced from these returns, brings out clearly the general prosperity in the two years mentioned:—

Monthly Percentage of Unemployed Members of certain Trade Societies.

Month.	1887.	1888.	1889.	1890.	1891.
January	9·9	6·8	3·3	1·75	3·05
February	10·3	7·8	3·1	1·44	3·37
March	8·5	7·0	2·8	1·40	2·60
April	7·7	5·7	2·2	1·70	2·85
May	6·8	5·2	2·0	1·96	2·69
June	8·5	4·8	2·0	1·96	2·98
July	8·0	4·6	1·8	1·88	2·86
August	8·5	3·9	1·7	2·28	3·28
September	8·3	4·8	2·5	2·28	4·23
October	7·5	4·4	2·1	2·60	4·48
November	8·6	4·4	1·8	2·60	—
December	8·5	3·1	1·5	2·40	—

The work-people participated to a very great extent in this prosperity, as the results of their demands secured them a considerable increase of wages together with a decrease in the number of hours of labour per week.

The most important strike of the year in point of numbers occurred in March, when 107,484 miners of the Yorkshire, Lancashire, and Midland coal districts struck for an advance of wages of 10 per cent. This lasted only seven days, and ended in favour of the workmen. It may be noticed that in this month, when the proportion of unemployed labourers reached its lowest point, there were three other strikes in which more than 5,000 employés participated. The railway servants' strike in Scotland was by no means the largest from the point of view of the number of men employed, but its effects being felt immediately, and at the busiest time of the year, it attracted more attention than several others. The two following tables give the particulars of the strikes involving over 5,000 work people in 1890 and 1889:—

1890.

Industry.	Date.	Locality.	Number of Men Affected.	Object.	Result.
Dock labourers	27 Feb.—31 March	Liverpool and Birkenhead	20,000	For advance in wages and employment of union men only	Unsuccessful
Brick barge men	1 March.—28 April	Thames and Medway	8,811	For return to previous prices	Partly successful
Coal mining	15—24 March	York, Lancs, and Midlands	107,484	For advance in wages	Successful
Engineers	17—26 March	Newcastle and district	20,000	For reduction in hours	„
Boot and shoe trade	31 March—5 May	London	10,000	For provision of proper workshops	„
„	12 June—14 July	Norwich	7,000	Disagreement as to items of a new price list	„
Steel manufacture	28 July—17 Aug.	Glasgow and district	7,000	Against reduction of wages	Unsuccessful
Woollen manufacture	16 Dec.—29 April, 1891	Manningham, Bradford	5,000	„	„
Railway servants	21 Dec.—31 Jan., 1891	North British, Caledonian, Glasgow and S.W.	5,728	For advance in wages and reduction in hours	„

1889.

Industry.	Date.	Locality.	Number of Men Affected.	Object.	Result.
Seamen and firemen	Jan.—Feb.	Various ports	49,000	For increase in wages	Partly successful
„	3 June—July	„	49,000	For advance in wages	„
Nail makers and anchor smiths	8—15 July	East Worcestershire	15,000	„	Successful
Dock labourers	13 Aug.—14 Sept.	London, E.	12,000	For increase of pay and alteration of conditions	„
Lightermen and barge men	22 Aug.—14 Sept.	Thames	12,000	For advance in wages and sympathy with dockers	„
Timber carriers, &c.	28 Nov.—4 Dec.	Bristol	5,000	For advance in wages and objection to unloading of foreign vessels by their own crews	Partly successful
Bedstead makers	2 Dec.—12 Dec.	Birmingham and district	5,100	For advance in wages	Successful
Firewood cutters	30 Dec.—2 Jan., 1890	London	5,000	„ prices	„

The trades in which the greatest number of strikes occurred were the following :—

	1890.	1889.		1890.	1889.
Cotton manufacture	135	137	Carpenters and joiners....	20	14
Dock, &c., labourers	102	86	Seamen and firemen........	17	43
Coal mining	86	111	Printing trade	9	25
Shipbuilding..................	64	107	Provision ,, ...	4	35
Woollen manufacture....	44	26	Bedstead making	3	35
Boot and shoe makers....	42	24	Coal transport	—	27
Engineering	30	77	Miscellaneous	399	361
Stone masons	25	5			
Tailors	25	7			
Worsted and stuff manufacture............	23	25		1,028	1,145

The numbers for the two years cannot, however, be compared with each other, owing to the different arrangement adopted for recording the strikes. In 1889 it was found difficult to distinguish between the number of separate and distinct strikes and the number of establishments affected; whereas in 1890 a strike, whether general or local, is made the unit. For example, the strike of seamen and firemen at the beginning of 1889 affected 17 ports, and counts in the total for 17 strikes; while the coal miners' strike in 1890 only counts as one, although the number of localities affected was 50. A more accurate comparison may be made by saying that in 1889 3,164 distinct establishments were affected, and in 1890 4,382, supposing, where no information is given, that only one establishment is concerned.

The distribution of strikes, according to the county in which they took place, is as follows :—

	1890.	1889.		1890.	1889.
London............................	91	143	South Wales..................	79	49
Yorkshire........................	195	145	North ,, ...	9	4
Lancashire	187	164	Total Wales	88	53
Stafford..........................	32	31			
Durham	23	48	Lanark	45	57
Warwick	22	51	Forfar	28	34
Monmouth	20	2	Renfrew............................	13	41
Gloucester and Somerset	14	120	Remainder*	70	114
Remainder*	132	119	Total Scotland	156	246
Total England	716	813	Total Ireland............	68	33

* Including the strikes which affected more than one county.

One of the most noteworthy features in the returns is the number of unsuccessful strikes during 1890 as compared with 1889, the percentage of unsuccessful strikes having advanced from 18·1 to 31·3 per cent. The coal miners' strike in 1890 adds over 100,000 to the number of successful workpeople, and thus raises their average abnormally.

	Number of Strikes.				Number of Persons Affected (so far as ascertained).			
	1890.		1889.		1890.		1889.	
	Number.	Per Cent.	Number.	Per Cent.	Number.	Per Cent.	Number.	Per Cent.
Total strikes	1,028	100·0	1,145	100·0	392,981	100·0	322,000	100·0
Successful	384	37·4	476	41·6	213,867	54·4	93,524	29·0
Partly successful...	230	22·4	368	32·1	66,029	16·8	177,476	55·1
Unsuccessful	322	31·3	207	18·1	101,902	25·9	40,472	12·6
Result not known	92	8·9	94	8·2	11,183	2·9	10,528	3·3

The object of most of the strikes was an advance in wages, this reason by itself causing 436 out of the whole 1,028 strikes, or more than 42 per cent. The causes of the strikes, with their results, may be classified thus :—

	Total.	Suc-cessful.	Partly Suc-cessful.	Unsuc-cessful.	Result not known.
Wages—					
For advance	436	182	119	92	43
„ and reduction in hours	28	11	6	6	—
„ and combined with unionism	8	—	5	2	1
„ and other concessions	42	15	17	9	1
Against reduction	83	34	14	30	5
For introduction and adherence to scales of prices and wages settle-ments..................	42	23	4	10	5
Hours—					
For reduction	23	10	6	5	2
Working arrangements—					
Against alteration in working arrange-ments, rules, holidays, meal times, &c....................	53	15	10	24	4
For alteration and improvement in	101	37	22	34	8
Against introduction or for abolition of fines, deductions, &c....................	10	5	4	1	—
Unionism—					
Objection to working with or employ-ment of non-unionists.....................	59	14	3	34	8
Defence of unionist colleagues, rules, customs, &c.........................	30	13	1	15	1
Against introduction or for limitation of apprentice, boy, and female labour	11	3	—	7	1
Disputes with fellow work people as to demarcation line of work	17	6	6	5	—
Disputes with fellow work people, &c., as to prices, wages, &c.	8	—	1	7	—
Defence of or objection to fellow work people (apart from unionism)	35	9	1	23	2
Defence of or objection to officials	13	2	4	5	2
Sympathy with other disputes or strikes	19	4	1	12	2
Cause not known......................	10	1	1	1	7
	1,028	384	230	322	92

The average duration per head of all strikes was 19·88 days.

The methods by which the strikes were settled is interesting, and a comparison brings out the fact that over 50 per cent. were settled by conciliation or arbitration :—

Total number of strikes	1,028
. Settled by conciliation..	527
„ „ (by mediation)	15
„ arbitration	33
„ . submission of work people	173
„ hands being replaced..............................	89
„ conciliation and submission	28
„ and hands replaced	11
„ submission (by mediation)	2
„ and hands replaced	47
, „ disappearance or withdrawal of cause of } dispute without mutual arrangement .... }	11
No details obtained as to settlement.................................	92

It is difficult to estimate the loss of money incurred, owing to the absence of information concerning some of the establishments affected. In 373 strikes, affecting 1,785 establishments, the weekly loss of wages by work people is put down at 261,296*l.*, while 193 strikes laid idle 680 establishments, having a fixed capital of 32,113,263*l.* The outlay of the employers of 853 establishments (affected by 181 strikes) in payment of fixed charges, such as rates, rent, salaries, &c., and in cost of stopping and re-opening the works, was 151,343*l.* As regards the work people, the estimated loss of wages during strike was 578,895*l.*; the total weekly gains in wages to those affected were 17,974*l.*, and the losses 1,068*l.* Employers' associations spent 41,780*l.* in fighting thirteen strikes, whereas trade unions spent 88,809*l.* in support of strikes.

So far as ascertained the lock-outs numbered only twelve. In seven of these the employers were successful, and in another they were partially successful. In ten of these cases (the only ones for which particulars are given) the total number of men locked out amounted to 264 only.

The information as to foreign strikes is obtained from the public press and from occasional publications of the Foreign Office. With the exception of the United States, however, the returns are so meagre, only the more important finding their way into the newspapers, that it is useless giving them here. The United States returns are collected by *Bradstreets*, and are fairly reliable, so that the following comparison is useful :—

Strikes in Great Britain and the United States, 1890.

	Great Britain.	United States.		Great Britain.	United States.
Bakers	7	9	Pottery trades	9	3
Building and kindred trades	113	260	Printing „	9	24
			Shipbuilding	64	6
Cabinet and furniture making	18	18	Textile	241	56
			Transport—		
Cigar and tobacco trades	—	78	Land	33	87
Clothing trades	78	93	Seafaring and water-side labour	113	16
Glass „	2	14	Miscellaneous	92	76
Leather „	11	16			
Metal „	137	91			
Mining and quarrying	101	80		1,028	927

R. H. H.

VII.—*Pauperism in* 1890-91.

[The following is taken from the Twentieth Annual Report of the Local Government Board.]

Pauperism, during the year ended Lady Day, 1891, has again decreased in England and Wales, and this in spite of the exceptionally severe weather during the winter. The total number of persons relieved on the 1st January, 1891, was 780,457, against 793,246 in January, 1890, and in July, 1890 and 1889, the numbers were respectively 739,003 and 757,189, these numbers being, as is always the case, less than the numbers for January. The decrease has however by no means been continuous (though, as will be seen in the second table, the ratio per 1,000 to the estimated population has with few exceptions declined steadily): the minimum number relieved on the 1st July was 701,375 in 1876, and on the 1st January 732,532 in 1877. After this period the number has oscillated considerably, and the decline has been continuous since 1888. The two following tables show the pauperism on the 1st January and 1st July in England and Wales, at intervals of five years, and the ratio per 1,000 of estimated population. In the second table the "mean number" of paupers is the arithmetical mean of the numbers relieved on the 1st July and 1st January of the particular year (ending Lady Day) to which the numbers refer.

Pauperism from 1860 to 1891.

Year.	Number Relieved on 1st January.				Number Relieved on 1st July.			
	In-door.	Out-door.	Deduct.*	Total.	In-door.	Out-door.	Deduct.*	Total.
1860	117,309	728,085	519	841,875	102,223	710,290	674	811,839
'65	140,174	835,490	892	974,772	121,700	770,046	455	891,291
'70	169,471	915,727	377	1,084,821	144,594	843,663	385	987,872
'75	155,655	662,557	390	817,822	134,238	612,268	441	746,065
'80	194,651	649,387	184	843,854	172,458	600,249	174	772,533
'85	194,732	594,289	119	788,902	172,739	575,846	175	748,410
'89	204,903	612,432	145	817,190	175,361	581,973	145	757,189
'90	200,482	592,983	219	793,246	173,458	565,732	187	739,003
'91	198,218	582,413	174	780,457				

* This number represents those who received both in-door and out-door relief on the days mentioned, and who are therefore counted in the in-door and out door totals; also those non-settled paupers whose relief had been transferred to the accounts of the unions to which it was chargeable.

Mean Number of Paupers of all Classes.

Year ending Lady Day.	In-door.		Out-door.		Total.	
	Number.	Ratio per 1,000 of Estimated Population.	Number.	Ratio per 1,000 of Estimated Population.	Number.	Ratio per 1,000 of Estimated Population.
1850....	123,004	7·0	885,696	50·4	1,008,700	57·4
'55....	121,400	6·5	776,286	41·7	897,686	48·2
'60....	113,507	5·8	731,126	37·1	844,633	42·9
'65....	131,312	6·3	820,586	39·3	951,899	45·6
'70....	156,800	7·1	876,000	39·4	1,032,800	46·5
'75....	146,800	6·2	654,114	27·6	800,914	33·8
'80....	180,817	7·1	627,213	24·7	808,030	31·8
'85....	183,820	6·8	585,118	21·6	768,988	28·3
'89....	192,105	6·7	603,512	21·1	795,617	27·8
'90....	187,921	6·5	587,296	20·2	775,217	26·7
'91....	185,838	6·3	573,892	19·5	759,730	25·8

As regards the distribution of pauperism in England and Wales, it was greatest in the south-western division, amounting there (on the 1st January, 1891) to 40·8 per 1,000 of the estimated population; it was least in the north-western, only 17·8 per 1,000. The individual counties, however, in which it was greater, were Norfolk and Dorset (45·8 and 44·8 per 1,000 respectively); in Lancaster and York (West Riding) it was 17·3 and 18·0 per 1,000. With one exception (London) the number of out-door paupers in every county was much greater than the number of in-door. As regards the first, Dorset and Norfolk again come out with the largest ratio (39·2 and 38·3), and Lancaster (11·4 per 1,000) is again the lowest, while in London it is only 11·6. The ratio of in-door paupers is far greater in London than any other county, viz., 13·9; the next two in order being Berks and Kent, with 8·8 per 1,000 each, Cornwall and Nottingham having only 4·0 per 1,000.[10] The conditions are very much the same on the 1st July, except that the ratio is generally from 0·5 to 1 per 1,000 lower than in January. In July, however, London's ratio of out-door paupers is less than that of Lancaster, being little over 10 per 1,000.

[10] These are *union* counties.

The following table is interesting, as showing the fluctuations in the number of persons in receipt of poor relief according to the season.

Number of Paupers (exclusive of Lunatics and Vagrants) in receipt of Relief in England and Wales on the Last Day of each Week in 1890.

| Month. | Week. | Number of Paupers. | | Total. | Increase. | Decrease. |
		In-door.	Out-door.			
January	1st	193,202	522,385	715,587	2,340	—
„	2nd	194,035	527,716	721,751	6,164	—
„	3rd	194,492	531,229	725,721	3,970	—
„	4th	195,258	533,792	729,050	3,329	—
„	5th	194,924	535,417	730,341	1,291	—
February	1st	194,516	536,211	730,727	386	—
„	2nd	194,231	537,108	731,339	612	—
„	3rd	193,495	537,795	731,290	—	49
„	4th	193,013	538,276	731,289	—	1
March	1st	192,397	539,390	731,787	498	—
„	2nd	189,300	536,554	725,854	—	5,933
„	3rd	186,967	534,049	721,016	—	4,838
„	4th	184,277	526,577	710,854	—	10,162
April	1st	180,270	514,893	695,073	—	15,781
„	2nd	179,702	511,923	691,625	—	3,448
„	3rd	179,018	511,965	690,983	—	642
„	4th	178,141	511,272	689,413	—	1,570
„	5th	175,434	509,653	685,087	—	4,326
May	1st	173,993	597,649	681,642	—	3,445
„	2nd	172,636	506,060	678,696	—	2,946
„	3rd	169,509	504,200	673,709	—	4,987
„	4th	168,757	501,992	670,749	—	2,960
June	1st	168,691	501,522	670,213	—	536
„	2nd	167,435	501,509	668,944	—	1,269
„	3rd	166,205	500,383	666,588	—	2,356
„	4th	165,131	499,010	664,141	—	2,447
July	1st	164,705	495,866	660,571	—	3,570
„	2nd	164,599	495,584	660,183	—	388
„	3rd	164,788	494,561	659,349	—	834
„	4th	164,595	493,765	658,360	—	989
„	5th	164,078	493,362	657,440	—	920
August	1st	164,403	492,529	656,932	—	508
„	2nd	164,895	492,754	657,649	717	—
„	3rd	165,176	493,248	658,424	775	—
„	4th	164,952	492,525	657,477	—	947
September	1st	164,884	492,264	657,148	—	329
„	2nd	165,205	491,393	656,598	—	550
„	3rd	166,138	491,331	657,469	871	—
„	4th	167,765	491,211	658,976	1,507	—
October	1st	168,919	487,203	656,122	—	2,854
„	2nd	170,574	483,483	654,057	—	2,065
„	3rd	172,414	485,133	657,547	3,490	—
„	4th	173,947	485,380	659,327	1,780	—
„	5th	175,528	487,484	663,002	3,675	—
November	1st	176,991	487,975	664,966	1,964	—
„	2nd	178,396	490,010	668,406	3,440	—
„	3rd	179,701	491,273	670,974	2,568	—
„	4th	182,380	493,619	675,999	5,025	—
December	1st	183,909	495,961	679,870	3,871	—
„	2nd	185,877	499,066	684,943	5,073	—
„	3rd	188,162	503,668	691,830	6,887	—
„	4th	188,361	507,460	695,821	3,991	—

The total number of those over 60 years of age who were in receipt of relief was 286,867, classified as follows:—

Ages.	In-door.	Out-door.	Total.
60—65	13,372	27,808	41,180
65—70	15,807	46,433	62,240
70—75	16,809	60,899	77,708
75—80	12,384	48,495	60,879
80 and upwards	9,752	35,108	44,860
	68,124	218,743	286,867

There were 76,228 pauper lunatics chargeable to the poor rate on the 1st January, 1891, of whom 51,795 were in county or borough asylums, 1,630 in registered hospitals and licensed houses, 16,990 in workhouses or asylums of the Metropolitan Asylums Board, and 5,813 residing with relatives, &c. The number has increased steadily every year from 30,130 in 1859. Besides these there were 1,556 lunatics chargeable to county and borough rates.

Considering now the expenditure on the poor, the following table shows that the rate per head of population, and the rate in the £ on rateable value, of the expenditure on poor relief, have decreased during the last ten years:—

Year ending Lady Day.	Estimated Population.*	Expenditure on Relief of the Poor.	Rate per Head on Population.	Rate in Pound on Rateable Value.
		£	*s.* *d.*	*s.* *d.*
1881	25,714,288	8,102,136	6 3½	1 2·3
'82	26,061,736	8,232,472	6 3¾	1 2·1
'83	26,413,861	8,353,292	6 4	1 2·2
'84	26,770,744	8,402,553	6 3¼	1 2·1
'85	27,132,449	8,491,600	6 3	1 2·0
'86	27,499,041	8,296,230	6 −½	1 1·5
'87	27,870,586	8,176,768	5 10½	1 1·2
'88	28,247,151	8,440,821	5 11¾	1 1·6
'89	28,628,804	8,366,477	5 10¼	1 1·4
'90	29,015,613	8,434,345	5 9¾	1 1·5

* This estimate is based on the censuses of 1871 and 1881, not 1891; and as the population is in reality considerably lower than it was expected, the rate per head in the later years given here is somewhat below the reality. The population in the middle of 1890, based on the census of 1881, and the preliminary return for 1891 was estimated at 28,762,287, and the rate per head of population was therefore 5*s.* 10¾*d.*

London spends far more on its paupers than any other union county, the total amount being 877,404*l.*, this being more than double the amount (382,580*l.*) spent by Lancaster. Rutland spends only 4,913*l.* The rate per head is 10*s.* 9*d.* in London, 7*s.* 6¾*d.* in Hertford, 7*s.* 5½*d.* in Hereford, 3*s.* 10*d.* in Lancaster, 3*s.* 9¼*d.* in Cumberland, 3*s.* 6¼*d.* in York (West Riding), and 3*s.* 5*d.* in Durham.

The cost per head on the mean number of paupers of *all classes* was, in London (year ended Lady Day, 1890) 21*l.* 16*s.* 1*d.*: double the amount for England and Wales generally (10*l.* 17*s.* 7¼*d.*);

the cost per head on the mean number of *out-door* paupers was, in London, 4*l.* 17*s.* 1*d.*; in England and Wales, 4*l.* 11*s.* 7¾*d.*

The returns from the fever hospitals under the management of the Metropolitan Asylums Board during the year were as follows:—

	Cases.	Deaths.
Scarlet fever	6,530	510
Diphtheria	1,073	316
Enteric fever	588	93
Typhus	24	5
Small pox	26	3

During 1890 forty committees were formed, with the authorization of the Local Government Board, for the purpose of finding and superintending homes for orphan or deserted children in different parts of the country. On the 1st January, 1891, 1,495 children were boarded out under the provisions of the "Boarding-out Order, 1889," and 3,145 children under the "Boarding of Children in Unions Order."

Boards of guardians sent 375 orphan or deserted children to Canada, at a cost to the poor rates of 4,190*l.* 16*s.*, and 72 other persons were also assisted to emigrate to Canada, Australia, India, or New Zealand, at a charge to the poor rates of 271*l.* 10*s.*

Poor Rate Receipts and Expenditure, 1889-90. *England and Wales.*

Receipts (other than from Loans).

	£
From poor rates	15,820,594
„ county and borough councils	1,030,489
Payments under Section 121 of the Local Government Act, 1888, and Treasury subventions	444,754
All other receipts (less receipts from other local authorities)	493,373
	17,789,210

Expenditure (not Defrayed out of Loans.)

RELIEF OF THE POOR—

	£
Maintenance	1,899,648
Out relief	2,453,860
Lunatics in asylums or licensed houses	1,221,719

Workhouse or other loans repaid and interest thereon—

	£
Principal repaid	328,434
Interest	276,893

	£
	605,327
Salaries, remunerations, rations, and superannuations	1,394,687
Miscellaneous	859,104
	8,434,345
PAYMENTS for or towards the county, borough, or police rate	6,238,420
OTHER PURPOSES UNCONNECTED with relief to the poor	3,062,949
	17,735,714
MEDICAL RELIEF	326,657

The poor rate expenditure in the metropolis for the year ended 31st December, 1890, was as follows :—

PAUPERS—	£	£
Maintenance of in-door paupers	272,218	
„ pauper children	163,996	
„ insane poor	199,771	
School fees for out-door pauper children	1,834	
Vagrants : expenses under Houseless Poor Acts	16,263	
		654,082
MEDICAL RELIEF—		
Medicine and medical and surgical appliances		19,180
PAID OFFICERS—	£	
Salaries	243,262	
Rations	72,577	
Compensation for loss of office	2,359	
		318,198
TOTAL for purposes immediately connected with the relief of the poor		991,460
REGISTRATION fees		10,692
VACCINATION fees and expenses		12,713
MAINTENANCE of small-pox and fever patients		11,296
AMBULANCE expenses		12,194
TOTAL		1,038,355

R. H. H.

VIII.—*Fires in London and the Metropolitan Fire Brigade in the Year* 1891.

THE following particulars are taken from the Report of the Chief Officer, Mr. J. Sexton Simonds, to the Fire Brigade Committee of the London County Council, in continuation of similar notices for previous years :—

" The number of calls for fires, or supposed fires, received during the year has been 4,164. Of these 1,029 were false alarms, 243 proved to be only chimney alarms, and 2,892 were calls for fires, of which 193 resulted in serious damage, and 2,699 in slight damage.

" These figures only refer to regular calls for fires, or supposed fires, involving the turning out of firemen, fire engines, fire escapes, horses, coachmen, and pilots; they do not include trifling damages by fires which were not sufficiently important to require the attendance of firemen; neither do they include the ordinary calls for chimneys on fire, which are separately accounted for further on.

" The fires of 1891, compared with those of 1890, show an increase of 337; or compared with the average of the past ten years, an increase of 691.

" The following table gives the result both in actual numbers and percentages :—

Year.	Number of Fires.			Percentages.		
	Serious.	Slight.	Total.	Serious.	Slight.	Total.
1866........	326	1,012	1,338	25	75	100
'67........	245	1,152	1,397	18	82	100
'68........	235	1,433	1,668	14	86	100
'69........	199	1,373	1,572	13	87	100
'70........	276	1,670	1,946	14	86	100
'71........	207	1,685	1,842	11	89	100
'72........	120	1,374	1,494	8	92	100
'73........	166	1,382	1,548	11	89	100
'74........	154	1,419	1,573	10	90	100
'75........	163	1,366	1,529	11	89	100
'76........	166	1,466	1,632	11	89	100
'77........	159	1,374	1,533	10	90	100
'78........	170	1,489	1,659	10	90	100
'79........	159	1,559	1,718	9	91	100
'80........	162	1,709	1,871	9	91	100
'81........	167	1,824	1,991	8	92	100
'82........	164	1,762	1,926	9	91	100
'83........	184	1,960	2,144	9	91	100
'84........	194	2,095	2,289	9	91	100
'85........	160	2,110	2,270	7	93	100
'86........	151	1,998	2,149	7	93	100
'87........	175	2,188	2,363	7	93	100
'88........	121	1,867	1,988	6	94	100
'89........	153	2,185	2,338	7	93	100
'90........	153	2,402	2,555	6	94	100
'91........	193	2,699	2,892	7	93	100

Average for Ten Years.

1881-90	162	2,039	2,201	7·5	92·5	100
'91........	193	2,699	2,892	6·7	93·3	100

"The number of fires in the metropolis in which life has been seriously endangered during the year 1891 has been 192; and the number of these in which life has been lost has been 47.

"The number of persons whose lives have been seriously endangered by fire is 268; of these 207 were saved, and 61 lost their lives. Of the 61 lost, 31 were taken out alive, but died afterwards in hospitals or elsewhere, and 30 were suffocated or burned to death.

     *   *   *   *   *

"The number of calls for chimney fires has been 1,651. Of these 518 proved to be false alarms, and 1,133 were for chimneys on fire. In these cases there was no attendance of engines, but only of firemen with hand-pumps.

"The number of journeys made by the fire engines and hose vans of the brigade has been 32,795, and the total distance run has been 65,800 miles. These figures do not include hose carts and escapes, which are run by hand.

"The quantity of water used for extinguishing fires in the

metropolis during the year has been nearly 19 million gallons, or about 84,000 tons. Of this quantity, about one-third of the whole was taken from the river, canals, and docks, and the remainder from the street pipes.

" During the year there have been 5 cases of short supply of water, 8 of late attendance of turncocks, and 3 of no attendance, making altogether 16 cases in which the water arrangements were unsatisfactory.

" As long as the supply of water is intermittent in some parts of the metropolis, difficulties must occasionally arise, but each year the area under constant service is increasing, and the cases in which the water arrangements are unsatisfactory show a proportionate decrease.

" The services rendered by the metropolitan police and the city police have, as usual, been invaluable. The assistance of the salvage corps has also on all occasions been most heartily accorded.

" The strength of the brigade is as follows :—

55	land fire engine stations.	13	hose and coal vans.
4	floating or river „	6	waggons for street duties.
51	hose cart stations.	8	street stations.
179	fire escape „	132	watch boxes.
9	steam fire engines on barges.	706	firemen, including chief officer, superintendents, and all ranks.[11]
47	land steam fire engines.		
78	six-inch manual fire engines.	25	men under instruction.
17	under six-inch manual fire engines.	17	pilots.
35½	miles of hose.	73	coachmen.
105	hose carts and reels.	133	horses.
8	steam tugs.	73	telephones between fire stations.
13	barges.	55	alarm circuits round fire stations, with 502 call points.
12	skiffs.		
215	fire escapes.	21	telephones to police stations.
9	long fire ladders.	8	telegraphs } to public and other
9	ladder vans.	55	telephones } buildings.
2	„ trucks.	14	bell-ringing fire alarms to public and other buildings.
1	trolly for ladders.		
2	trollies for engines.		

" The number of firemen employed on the several watches kept up throughout the metropolis is at present 125 by day and 325 by night, making a total of 450 in every twenty-four hours; the average number of men available for general work at fires by night is 320.

" The number of accidents to members of the brigade recorded during 1891 is as usual heavy; but this is invariably the case when the work is well done.

" There have been during the year 395 cases of ordinary illness, and 109 injuries, making a total of 504 cases, of which many were serious, and 6 resulted in death.

*   *   *   *   *

" The total number of calls during the year, including those for actual fires, supposed fires, chimney fires, and supposed chimney

---

[11] The post of second officer is at present vacant.

fires, has been 6,815, or nearly 19 a day, all of which have been attended by firemen with suitable appliances.

" Of the 1,029 false alarms received during the year, 450 have been malicious calls sent through the fire alarm call posts. These malicious alarms constitute a serious public danger, as they cause engines and escapes to be away from their stations at times when they may be required for actual fires. Unfortunately the persons who give the false alarms are very seldom detected in the act, there having been only 15 arrested during last year.

" The total number of attendances with engines at fires, or supposed fires, has been 9,945.

" In addition to attending fires, the brigade has kept 164,250 watches of twelve hours each, has made 35,922 hydrant inspections and 84,662 fire plug tablet inspections, has maintained all the machinery and appliances of the establishment in working order, written many thousand reports and letters, and carried on a variety of other work.

*　　*　　*　　*　　*

、 " The number of men who have been taken on and trained during the year is 102."

*　　*　　*　　*　　*

The following particulars (*a*, *b*, *c*) are obtained from the tables appended to the report, viz. :—

(*a*) The fires classified according to occupations, arranged in the order of frequency of occurrence ; to which are added, for the purpose of comparison, the corresponding figures for the three previous years :—

Number.	Occupations.	Number of Fires.			
		1891.	1890.	1889.	1888.
1	Private houses	718	632	580	494
2	Lodgings	451	428	361	277
3	Victuallers	82	57	70	68
4	Unoccupied	49	35	22	25
5	Boot and shoe makers	47	38	42	38
6	Greengrocers and fruiterers	45	27	18	36
7	Grocers	44	46	45	34
8	Tailors, clothiers, and outfitters	43	80	31	36
9	Oil and colourmen	36	43	44	45
10	Printers	36	27	20	19
11	Offices	35	21	14	27
12	Engineers and machinists	34	24	19	10
13	Bakers	34	35	80	31
14	Builders	34	26	85	20
15	Under repair and building	33	87	35	24
16	Confectioners and pastrycooks	32	82	21	25
17	Cabinet makers	32	21	23	20
18	Chandlers	31	15	17	18
19	Farming stock	31	15	10	18
20	Drapers	30	39	21	80
21	Tobacconists	29	25	25	22

Number.	Occupations.	Number of Fires.			
		1891.	1890.	1889.	1888.
22	Coffee houses	28	26	35	29
23	Stables	26	33	37	13
24	Warehouses	26	12	19	9
25	Booksellers, binders, and stationers	24	16	13	11
26	Furniture makers and dealers	21	18	18	14
27	Corn dealers	19	12	17	13
28	Dairymen	19	13	12	8
29	Laundries	19	16	15	11
30	Public buildings	18	10	13	7
31	Refreshment rooms	18	16	20	19
32	Carpenters and workers in wood	17	7	18	8
33	Chemists	16	15	16	7
34	Railways	16	17	8	6
35	Butchers	15	14	16	14
36	Milliners and dressmakers	15	18	14	11
37	Cheesemongers	14	15	6	4
38	Hotels (including club houses)	13	26	17	27
39	Wardrobe dealers	13	8	6	9
40	Lamp and oil merchants	12	1	1	2
41	Mantle makers	12	10	5	6
42	Brewers	11	4	4	1
43	China and glass dealers	11	7	12	9
44	Hatters	11	9	11	7
45	Looking glass and picture frame makers	11	7	5	5
46	Schools	11	11	6	5
47	Surgeons	11	7	3	5
48	Carriers	10	6	2	4
49	Fishmongers	10	13	15	8
50	Fried fish shops	10	11	16	11
51	Hairdressers	10	9	14	12
52	Ironmongers	10	4	12	9
53	Provision merchants	10	5	7	2
54	Timber ,,	10	4	5	5
55	Wheelwrights	10	4	6	7
	Remainder, varying from 9 to 1	2,413 479	—	—	—
		2,892	2,555	2,338	1,988

(*b*) The fires classified under the causes to which they have been assigned, and arranged in the order of frequency of occurrence :—

Causes.	Number of Fires.
1. Unknown	886
2. Lamps (not gas) and lights (thrown down)	585
3. Gas (in various ways)	264
4. Defective (or improperly set) flues, hearths, stoves, &c.	204
5. Sparks from fires, &c.	195
6. Candles	150
7. Hot ashes	104
8. Children playing with fire, matches, &c.	101
9. Overheating of flues, ovens, furnaces, boilers, &c.	79
10. Airing linen and drying stoves	77
11. Boiling over, or upsetting of fat, pitch, &c.	61

12. Foul flues, &c. 38
13. Gas stoves, portable, overheating of, goods falling on........................ 23
14. Smoking tobacco 18
15. Vapour of spirits in contact with flame 18
16. Lucifer matches.. 17
17. Lime slaking by rain and otherwise 15
18. Fireworks 10
19. Fumigating 7
20. Doubtful... 6
21. Fire, clothes coming in contact with 6
22. Spontaneous ignition.. 5
    Miscellaneous, varying from 3 to 1.................................... 23

            Total 2,892

(c) The following table, giving the totals of the fires for each day of the week for the last ten years, shows on the average that the largest number of fires occurs on Saturday and the smallest number on Monday. The annual average number of fires for the last ten years is 2,291:—

Years.	Sunday.	Monday.	Tuesday.	Wednesday.	Thursday.	Friday.	Saturday.	Total.
1882....	285	246	296	267	281	274	277	1,926
'83....	297	334	309	318	269	295	322	2,144
'84....	296	330	304	335	338	340	346	2,289
'85....	331	319	321	338	326	300	335	2,270
'86....	294	293	294	317	306	304	341	2,149
'87....	327	297	352	336	357	292	402	2,363
'88....	288	273	267	295	299	272	294	1,988
'89....	318	281	363	305	384	337	350	2,338
'90....	334	362	382	385	347	338	407	2,555
'91....	413	397	445	367	396	446	428	2,892
Total...	3,183	3,132	3,333	3,263	3,303	3,198	3,502	22,914

IX.—*Fires in Paris.*

As a comparison of the work of the fire brigades in the two largest cities of Europe cannot but prove interesting, we take the following from the *Journal de la Société de Statistique de Paris* for *February*, 1892, whose information is based on the returns of the officers of the Paris Fire Brigade. The details of London fires in 1890 will be found in the *Journal of the Royal Statistical Society* for *March*, 1891—the French returns being a year behind our own —but wherever possible the figures for London are given below for the sake of comparison.

The number of fires in Paris during 1890 was 1,052, plus 1,504 chimney fires and 219 false alarms. Of the 1,052 fires no less than 821 were extinguished without the aid of the engines (762 by

means of pails of water, and 59 by sand and wet rags); 134 were
put out with the help of one engine, and 97 by more than one.
These last were the more serious fires. In London in that year
there were 2,555 fires (of which 153 were serious), 1,087 chimney
fires, and 991 false alarms. In the cases of chimney fires there
were no engines used, only hand pumps.

Number of Fires in each Month, Paris and London, 1890.

	Paris.					London.		
	Fires.	Chimney Fires.	Total Fires.	False Alarms.	Total Calls.	Fires.	False Alarms.	Total Calls.*
January	111	209	320	23	343	201	83	284
February	93	307	400	14	414	217	87	304
March	77	214	291	27	318	182	63	245
April	77	165	242	29	271	207	68	275
May	69	35	104	18	122	233	85	318
June	42	33	75	8	83	182	81	263
July	82	22	104	20	124	159	81	240
August	71	23	94	15	109	162	87	249
September........	77	28	105	18	123	233	82	315
October..........	99	77	176	25	201	232	102	334
November........	99	108	207	15	222	237	89	326
December	155	283	438	7	445	310	83	393
Total	1,052	1,504	2,556	219	2,775	2,555	991	3,546

* Excluding chimney fires.

This table thus brings out that in 1890 there were 1,503 more
fires in London than in Paris, though in the latter city there
were fewer chimney fires—1,087 against 1,594: Captain Shaw's
report, however, does not give the number of chimney fires in each
month. Both cities agree in having a maximum in December, but
the effect of the different seasons is much more pronounced in
Paris. This is mostly due to the chimney fires, which reach 283
in December and only 22 in July. It would be interesting to
know whether the chimney fires in London show the same fluctuations. In London the minimum occurs in July; Paris, in that
month, instead of a minimum which the other figures would lead
one to expect, shows a secondary maximum, possibly due to the
illuminations and fireworks of the 14th.

The losses caused by fire are estimated at 9,226,327 frs.
(369,050*l.*). 792 fires caused a loss of less than 1,000 frs. each,
the total damages being 124,127 frs.; whereas, in the remaining
260 cases, the damage was over 1,000 frs., and the total loss
9,102,200 frs. From 1875 to 1884 the average amount of damage
from each fire was 8,910 frs., now (1885-90) it is only 6,111 frs.
[According to the above figures, however, it was in 1890 8,770 frs.]

These evaluations are only approximate, as the damages are
generally mentioned at the time to the firemen by the owner, who
sometimes has a tendency to exaggerate his losses. The owners
have declared that in 1,035 cases the premises were insured, and

the contents in 831 ; that there was no insurance on the premises in 12 cases, nor on the contents in 216 places. In the remaining cases the firemen could obtain no information.

One feature of the Parisian returns is the classification of the fires according to the floor of the building in which they originate :—

In the cellar	135	On the 5th floor	59
On the ground floor	299	„ 6th „	49
„ 1st „	203	„ 7th „	4
„ 2nd „	116		
„ 3rd „	115		1,052
„ 4th „	72		

The causes of fire are given as follows :—

Faulty construction	170	Handling dangerous sub-stances	62
Lighting	270		
Heating	118	Malice	3
Matches	52	Unknown	294
Imprudence of smokers, drunkards, &c.	25		
Exercise of occupations	58		1,052

After the alarm had been given the time which elapsed before the attack on the fire began was—

5 minutes in 921 cases		30 minutes in 1 case
10 „ 94 „		35 „ 1 „
15 „ 23 „		40 „ 1 „
20 „ 6 „		45 „ 1 „
25 „ 3 „		1 hour 15 „ 1 „

The time elapsed between attacking the fire and its complete extinction was as follows :—

5 minutes in 675 cases		1 hour – minutes in 25 cases
10 „ 70 „		1 „ 15 „ 12 „
15 „ 62 „		1 „ 30 „ 6 „
20 „ 44 „		1 „ 45 „ 3 „
25 „ 45 „		2 „ – „ 6 „
30 „ 36 „		2 „ 15 „ 3 „
35 „ 19 „		2 „ 30 „ 4 „
40 „ 10 „		2 „ 45 „ 1 „
45 „ 18 „		3 „ – „ 1 „
50 „ 9 „		3 „ 30 „ 1 „
55 „ 1 „		4 „ 30 „ 1 „

The firemen, in 14 cases of fires, giving way of houses, immersions in the Seine or in wells, have brought out 34 people; 8 of these were dead before the men arrived, while 26 were saved by their intervention. The London fire brigade in the same year saved 151 lives; 31 were taken out alive, but died from the results of the fire, and 30 were suffocated or burnt to death.

The whole organisation of the service is one of the attributes of the Minister of War, but the direct administration is in the hands of the Prefect of Police. It consists of two battalions of six companies, lodged in twelve barracks, each of which contains 3 officers and about 140 men. They are commanded by a colonel, who has under him 51 officers and 1,693 men. The barracks are connected by means of the telegraph with the head quarters. The telegraphic system belonging to the service has a total length of wire of 409,566 metres (254 miles), and 203 call apparatus; it is exclusively managed by the men. A number of public alarms, now in process of installation, will render the calls still more speedy. The system at the present moment serves 112 public alarms by means of 95,033 metres of wire, besides 182 private alarms with 171,984 metres of wire.

Comparative Summary of the Fires, Improvement of the Service and Expenses.

Date.	Number of Men.*	Area.	Population.	Number of Inhabitants to One Fireman.	Budget.	Fires.
		Acres.			£	
1841....	808	8,495	935,261	1,145	29,349	203
'57....	889	8,495	1,278,705	1,438	33,876	298
'60....	1,238	19,271	1,537,486	1,241	41,700	445
'67....	1,498	19,271	1,848,075	1,233	59,105	690
'79....	1,690	19,271	2,126,230	1,258	72,926	878
'90....	1,693	19,271	2,379,582	1,405	106,994	1,052

* Excluding officers.

R. H. H.

X.—*Railway Returns*, 1890.

A COMPARISON of the Returns for 1890 and 1889 shows that the traffic (both passenger and goods) on all the principal railways has increased in the United Kingdom, but that the expenses connected with the working of the railways have increased in a greater proportion, so much so that the net receipts are in some cases lower than in 1890, while the proportion per cent. of expenditure to receipts has increased in the whole kingdom by about 2 per cent. Scotland is the greatest sufferer in this respect—in one company, the Caledonian, this proportion has risen from 47 to 52 per cent. Only one railway does not show this increase, and that is the Metropolitan, in which the proportion is lower than in any other of the seventeen principal railways given below, viz., 43 per cent. The only other railway whose expenditure is less than 50 per cent. of its gross receipts is the London, Brighton, and South Coast. Full details for 1891 are not yet published, but on the large railways the expenditure last year again increased more than the receipts. The accounts of the Scotch railways are almost all made up to 31st January, hence the full effect of the strike on the three principal Scotch railways in December, 1890, and the following January, appears in the accounts for 1890.

The expenses show an increase under all heads; the only remarkable features being the compensation for personal injuries and the legal and parliamentary expenses. Under the first of these heads Scotland paid more than double the amount she paid in 1890, while England and Wales paid 25 per cent. less. For the second item Scotland paid 77,186*l.* in 1890, against 40,977*l.* in 1889, and Ireland 25,966*l.*, against 8,775*l.* in 1889.

The increased expenditure has of course affected the dividends, which have been as follows during the last three years on the principal railways:—

Rates of Dividend per Cent. per Annum.

	1889.		1890.		1891.	
	First Half.	Second Half.	First Half.	Second Half.	First Half.	Second Half.
Great Eastern	1½	4	2	4	1½	3½
„ Northern	3½	6¼	3½	6	3¼	5½
„ Western	5½	8	5¼	7¾	5	7½
Lancashire and Yorkshire	4¼	4¾	4	4½	3½	4¼
London and North Western	6¾	8	6¾	7¾	6¼	7¾
„ and South „	4½	7½	4¾	7¼	4¼	7¾
„ Brighton, and South Coast	4¼	10	4¼	9¾	3¼	9¾
„ Chatham, and Dover	3¼	4½	4½	4½	3½	4½
Manchester, Sheffield, and Lincolnshire	1¼	5½	–¾	4¾	–¼	4
Metropolitan	3	2¾	3	3	3¼	–
Midland	5¼	6¾	5½	7	5¾	7
North Eastern	6¼	8¼	6¾	7¾	6	7
South „	3	6¾	3¼	6¼	2¼	6
Caledonian	5	5¼	5	3¾	4	–
Glasgow and South Western	4	4	4	3½	3¾	–
North British	1¾	3½	1¾	1½	1	–
Great Southern and Western of Ireland	5	5	4½	5	5	–

The following table shows the receipts and expenditure of the principal railways in the United Kingdom in 1890 and 1889; the figures are extracted from the Railway Returns presented to Parliament for those two years. [Similar information for 1891 will be found on p. 109]:—

Receipts and Expenditure of the Principal Railways in the United Kingdom, 1890 and 1889.

| | Miles Open | Gross Receipts [000's omitted.] | | | | | | Working Expenses [000's omitted.] | | Net Receipts [000's omitted.] | | Proportion per Cent. of Expenditure to Receipts. | |
| | | Passengers | | Goods | | Total. | | | | | | | |
		1890.	1889.	1890.	1889.	1890.	1889.	1890.	1889.	1890.	1889.	1890.	1889.
		£	£	£	£	£	£	£	£	£	£		
Great Eastern	1,099	2,102,	1,976,	1,742,	1,693,	4,199,	4,001,	2,310,	2,137,	1,889,	1,865,	55	53
" Northern	824	1,655,	1,582,	2,337,	2,301,	4,060,	3,944,	2,326,	2,213,	1,734,	1,731,	57	56
" Western	2,481	4,006,	3,802,	4,536,	4,473,	8,760,	8,470,	4,521,	4,193,	4,239,	4,276,	52	50
Lancashire and Yorkshire	522	1,731,	1,642,	2,518,	2,481,	4,368,	4,221,	2,450,	2,286,	1,918,	1,935,	56	54
London and North Western	1,877	4,718,	4,508,	6,667,	6,512,	11,591,	11,218,	6,229,	5,817,	5,362,	5,401,	54	52
" and South	835	2,216,	2,114,	1,010,	986,	3,249,	3,311,	1,899,	1,791,	1,530,	1,520,	55	54
" Brighton, and South } Coast	435	1,801,	1,728,	608,	589,	2,572,	2,499,	1,261,	1,185,	1,311,	1,314,	49	47
" Chatham, and Dover	184	964,	945,	283,	279,	1,430,	1,419,	763,	730,	667,	689,	53	51
Manchester, Sheffield, and } Lincolnshire	322	556,	516,	1,428,	1,413,	2,257,	2,193,	1,174,	1,093,	1,082,	1,100,	52	50
Metropolitan	38	626,	615,	41,	37,	706,	693,	302,	300,	404,	397,	43	43
Midland	1,382	2,654,	2,519,	5,989,	5,666,	8,727,	8,270,	4,711,	4,338,	4,015,	3,931,	54	52
North Eastern	1,612	2,157,	1,985,	4,946,	4,679,	7,290,	6,842,	4,053,	2,643,	3,273,	3,219,	56	53
" South	393	1,553,	1,515,	509,	505,	2,304,	2,261,	1,169,	1,112,	1,135,	1,149,	51	49
Caledonian	875	1,227,	1,150,	1,911,	1,894,	3,292,	3,201,	1,706,	1,520,	1,586,	1,681,	52	52
Glasgow and South Western	347	507,	493,	655,	663,	1,201,	1,187,	655,	617,	546,	569,	55	52
North British	1,086	1,229,	1,115,	1,855,	1,953,	3,129,	3,024,	1,608,	1,437,	1,521,	1,586,	51	47
Great Southern and Western } of Ireland	543	405,	398,	388,	380,	796,	782,	439,	407,	357,	375,	55	52

The following summary tables, giving the whole capital, traffic, working expenditure, net receipts, and rolling stock of all the railways in England and Wales, Scotland, and Ireland, are taken from the Railway Returns for 1890:—

CAPITAL.

[000's omitted.]

	England and Wales.	Scotland.	Ireland.	Total United Kingdom.
	£	£	£	£
Authorised capital................................	833,049,	129,398,	42,083,	1 004,529,
By shares and stocks....................	606,912,	101,514,	30,066,	738,492,
„ loans and debenture stock	226,137,	27,884,	12,017,	266,037,
Paid up stock and share capital	542,289, 28,360,	95,744, 20,106,	26,927,	664,959, 48,466,
Ordinary.....................................	271,268, 8,197,	44,623, 12,833,	16,179,	332,070, 21,079,
Guaranteed...............................	82,469, 6,080,	13,626, 2,722,	2,702,	98,797, 8,801,
Preferential	188,552, 14,084,	37,495, 4,502,	8 045,	234,092, 18,585,
Capital raised by loans and debenture stock	197,745, 8,508,	24,396, 50,	10,372,	232,513, 8,558,
Loans	7,007,	1,211,	1,122,	9,340,
Debenture stock............................	190,738, 8,508,	23,185, 50,	9,250,	223,173, 8,558,
Total capital paid up and raised by loans and debenture stock	740,034, 36,868,	120,140, 20,156,	37,299,	897,472, 57,024,
Subscriptions to other companies	28,842,	2,012,	302,	31,156,

Note.—The figures in *italics* show the amounts (included in the roman figures) by which the capital of the railways has been nominally increased.

TRAFFIC.

		England and Wales.	Scotland.	Ireland.	Total United Kingdom.
Length of line open on 31st December, 1890	miles	14,119	3,162	2,792	20,073
Double or more	,,	9,094	1,292	603	10,989
Single	,,	5,025	1,870	2,189	9,084
Passengers conveyed (exclusive of season and periodical tickets)	No.	[000's omitted.]			
		721,115,	75,216,	21,413,	817,744,
1st class	,,	24,535,	4,308,	1,345,	30,187,
2nd ,, ...	,,	57,664,	862,	4,334,	62,860,
3rd ,, ...	,,	638,916,	70,046,	15,735,	724,697,
Holders of season or periodical tickets	,,	1,164,	68,	26,	1,259,
Goods traffic—					
Minerals	tons	184,818	29,801	1,147	215,765
General merchandise...........	,,	74,319	9,872	3,150	87,342
Distance travelled by trains	miles	262,542*	37,342†	13,581‡	313,465§
Passenger trains.................	,,	139,736	18,479	8,452	166,667
Goods and mineral trains	,,	122,327	17,026	4,272	143,626

* Including 479,000 miles run by mixed trains.   ‡ Including 856,000 miles run by mixed trains
†   ,,   1,838,000   ,,   §   ,,   3,172,000   ,,

[000's omitted.]

	England and Wales.	Scotland.	Ireland.	Total United Kingdom.
	£	£	£	£
Receipts (gross) from passenger traffic	29,208,	3,469,	1,651,	34,328,
Passengers	25,128,	2,834,	1,837,	29,299,
1st class	2,637,	386,	171,	3,194,
2nd ,, ...	2,278,	47,	320,	2,646,
3rd ,, ...	18,164,	2,190,	789,	21,143,
Season or periodical tickets	2,049,	210,	57,	2,316,
Excess luggage, parcels, carriages, horses, dogs, &c.	3,507,	443,	167,	4,117,
Mails	573,	193,	147,	912,
Receipts (gross) from goods traffic	35,976,	4,819,	1,425,	42,220,
Merchandise	19,782,	2,496,	1,023,	23,30
Live stock	898,	216,	263,	1.
Minerals	15,296,	2,107,	140,	1.
Miscellaneous, rents, tolls, navigation, steamboats, &c.	3,089,	262,	49,	
Total receipts from all sources of traffic	68,273,	8,550,	3,125.	

WORKING EXPENDITURE AND NET RECEIPTS.

[000's omitted]

	England and Wales.	Scotland.	Ireland.	Total United Kingdom.
	£	£	£	£
Maintenance of way, works, &c.	5,900,	729,	408,	7,037,
Locomotive power (including stationary engines)	10,205,	1,175,	467,	11,846,
Repairs and renewals of carriages and waggons	3,310,	460,	140,	3,909,
Traffic expenses (coaching and merchandise)...........................	11,272,	1,318,	452,	13,042,
General charges...................................	1,523,	181,	93,	1,796,
Rates and taxes	1,957,	215,	79,	2,251,
Government duty	304,	25,	—	329,
Compensation for personal injuries, &c.	119,	40,	66,	226,
Compensation for damage and loss of goods	193,	21,	6,	220,
Legal and parliamentary expenses	238,	77,	26,	341,
Steamboat, canal, and harbour expenses	1,558,	63,	13,	1,634,
Miscellaneous, not included in the above	361,	156,	15,	532,
Total working expenditure........	36 965,*	4,460,	1.764.	43,189.*
Total receipts as given above	68.273,	8,550,	3,125,	79,949,
Net receipts	21,308,	4.090,	1,362,	36,760,
Proportion per cent. of expenditure to receipts	54,	52,	56,	54,

* Exclusive of 53,185*l*. received by the North London Company for working other lines.

ROLLING STOCK *on* 31*st December*, 1890.

	England and Wales	Scotland.	Ireland.	Total United Kingdom.
	No.	No.	No	No.
Locomotives	13 731	1,814	692	16,237
Carriages, waggons, trucks, &c.	458,165	115,737	17,557	591,459
Carriages used for conveyance of passengers only	31,374	4,136	1,558	37,068
Other vehicles attached to passenger trains	11,337	1,561	915	13,813
Waggons of all kinds used for the conveyance of merchandise, live stock, and minerals	402,942	108,810	14,663	526,415
Other carriages or waggons on the railways, not included in the above	12,512	1,230	421	14,163

R. H. H.

XI.—*English Literature in* 1891.

THE following particulars are taken from the *Publishers'*
Circular of the 2nd January, 1892, in continuation of a series of
similar extracts for previous years :—

" From the table we present, as is usual at the end of the year,
it appears that the total sum of publications and new editions of
the past year is very slightly less than the sum of the figures for
1890. A comparison of the various departments shows that in
divinity and sacred literature the production has been about 10 per
cent. less than in the previous year. In classical and school books
also the figures are a little less for 1891 than for 1890 ; while
in works for young people 1891 shows a decrease as compared
with its predecessor. This may be partly accounted for by the
fact that it is often very difficult to settle wheth r a work of
imagination is a ' juvenile book ' or intended for grown up people.
The total that is found under the head of novels and new editions
of novels—1,216, or about four a day for every working day—is
so extraordinary, that a few might well be spared to rank among
volumes for younger readers. In law books we note a considerable increase of number. In political and social science, on the
other hand, books are fewer, and in the fine arts and illustrated
volumes fewer still. Books of travel are in greater number for
1891 than they were for 1890; as also works on biography. The
past year has been one of great activity in publishing monographs
on distinguished persons. In poetry we observe a slight increase.
Year-books and volumes of magazines remain about the same as
last year, while in medicine and surgery there do not seem to have
been so many books published. Essay literature and ' miscellaneous ' works (such as cannot easily be placed in any category),
taking the two classes together, present results almost identical
with those of last year.

" The sum of new books proper, in all departments, for 1891,
is just fifteen over that of the preceding year.

Analytical Table of Books Published in 1891.

	Jan.	Feb.	Mar.	April.		Nov.	Dec.	Total of Books on each Subject for the Year.
eology, sermons, iblical }	* 40	39	39	44		57	43	520
	† 11	12	10	13		15	9	107
								627
ucational, classi-l, and philogical }	* 45	67	68	39		54	43	587
	† 9	6	7	12		16	7	107
								694
nile works and les }	* 16	9	7	8		62	23	348
	† 1	2	1	1		22	3	99
								447
vels, tales, and ther fiction }	* 62	77	61	52		111	79	896
	† 13	25	21	14		23	24	320
								1,216
w, jurisprudence, }	* 3	2	11	8		4	7	61
	† —	7	7	2		6	6	48
								109
itical and social economy, trade nd commerce }	* 5	4	11	7		18	9	105
	† 1	3	6	—		2	2	31
								136
, science, and lustrated works }	* 5	6	5	1		13	9	85
	† 4	1	1	—		5	2	31
								116
ages, travels, id geographical search }	* 13	10	9	16		23	36	203
	† 2	1	5	4		11	3	68
								271
tory, biography, c. }	* 20	24	23	30		44	42	328
	† 3	6	10	10		12	9	85
								413
try and the rama }	* 8	5	13	9		14	13	146
	† 8	3	5	1		5	8	55
								201
r - books and erials in volumes }	* 56	28	16	15		41	42	310
	† —	—	—	1		1	—	6
								316
icine, surgery, c. }	* 7	16	4	17		8	16	120
	† 1	5	—	3		4	4	55
								175
es-lettres, essays, onographs, &c. }	* 11	11	13	11		20	13	131
	† 9	7	18	7		10	5	123
								254
cellaneous, including pamphlets, sermons }	* 33	47	36	53		60	62	589
	† 3	3	11	19		18	10	142
								731
	389	426	413	397		674	529	
								5,706

* New books.

" The analytical table is divided into fourteen classes; also new books and new editions.

Divisions.	1890.		1891.	
	New Books.	New Editions.	New Books.	New Editions.
Theology, sermons, biblical, &c................	555	153	520	107
Educational, classical, and philological....	615	88	587	107
Juvenile works and tales.....................	443	95	348	99
Novels, tales, and other fiction	881	323	896	320
Law, jurisprudence, &c.	40	39	61	48
Political and social economy, trade and } commerce .... }	87	22	105	31
Arts, sciences, and illustrated works.......	54	19	85	31
Voyages, travels, geographical research ..	188	69	203	68
History, biography, &c.	294	97	328	85
Poetry and the drama...........................	114	74	146	55
Year-books and serials in volumes	318	1	810	6
Medicine, surgery, &c.	143	50	120	55
Belles-lettres, essays, monographs, &c. ...	171	191	131	123
Miscellaneous, including pamphlets, } not sermons .... }	511	100	589	142
	4,414	1,321	4,429	1,277
	5,735		5,706	

Newspaper Statistics.—The following is taken from the *Newspaper Press Directory* for 1892:—

'· There are now published in the United Kingdom 2,255 newspapers, distributed as follows :—

England—
London 461
Provinces 1,302
——— 1,763
Wales... 95
Scotland....................................... 206
Ireland 167
Isles 24

Of these there are—

138 daily papers published in England.
6 　　　　　,,　　　　Wales.
20 　　　　　　　　　Scotland.
19 　　　　　　　　　Ireland.
2 　　　　　　　　　British Isles.

On reference to the first edition of this useful directory for the year 1846, we find the following interesting facts—viz., that in that year there were published in the United Kingdom 551 journals; of these 14 were issued daily—viz., 12 in England and 2 in Ireland; but in 1892 there are now established and circulated

2,255 papers, of which no less than 185 are issued daily, showing that the press of the country has more than quadrupled during the last forty-six years. The increase in daily papers has been still more remarkable ; the daily issues standing 185 against 14 in 1846. The magazines now in course of publication, including the quarterly reviews, number 1,901, of which more than 473 are of a decidedly religious character, representing the Church of England, Wesleyans, Methodists, Baptists, Independents, Roman Catholics, and other Christian communities."

XII.—*Notes on Economical and Statistical Works.*

The Industrial and Commercial Supremacy of England. By the late James E. Thorold Rogers. London: T. Fisher Unwin, 1892.

This volume has a melancholy interest; for its publication, we are told in the preface, is the fulfilment of an intention which had been formed in the lifetime of the author, and was so far frustrated by his death that the lectures, of which this work is composed, were still in their original shape and had not been corrected for commission to print. It was the practice of his father, Mr. Arthur Rogers writes, to repeat a course of lectures before they were published, and in this instance the repetition had been prevented by death. The lectures are, accordingly, printed substantially as they were delivered in the University of Oxford, although some allusions of a local or personal nature have been omitted. The order of delivery has been followed throughout; but the editor observes that there is no " special connection " between some of the lectures. They seem, he states, to have " aimed rather at expounding the methods " employed by his father in his historical studies than at " announcing new facts or enunciating new theories." They contain "almost all the hitherto unpublished comments on the economic history of England delivered in public " by the Professor. They go some way towards completing the work of a laborious life; for we believe that material for the final accomplishment of the monumental task undertaken in Professor Rogers' *History of Prices* has been happily left behind, and his other writings—his *Six Centuries of Work and Wages,* his *First Nine Years of the Bank of England,* and his *Economic Interpretation of History*—form, together with the volume now before us, a more popular statement of the chief results of the elaborate researches set forth in detail in the larger work. Taken together, these additions to our economic literature constitute a whole of which any single writer might well be proud. They represent an immense mass of most painstaking inquiries undertaken in a department of research which was comparatively unknown or neglected before Professor Rogers commenced his studies. In no limited or superficial sense he may be regarded as the pioneer of such historical investigations in England; and it would be difficult to measure the extent of the influence which, directly or indirectly, he has exercised on the general course of economic thought.

In the volume before us we have the opinions and comments of a bold and original mind on many topics of importance, accompanied in every instance by an application of the historical records of the past to the illumination of the present. The characteristic qualities of the Professor are manifest in every lecture; and readers, who may be inclined to resent what may be regarded as his defects, will remember that they are the defects of his virtues, which it would need much to outweigh. Width of erudition may atone for frequent discursiveness, and the positive and sweeping character of some of his utterances may be attributed to the influence of a strong personality, which could certainly not be reproached with any unwillingness to seek for, or examine, evidence. Landlords, for example, are condemned in no measured terms for raising rents before the Franco-German war, and their subsequent losses are freely ascribed to their previous imprudence; but the works of improvement carried out, and the development of agricultural science and practice fostered, by some members of their class are frankly acknowledged, and Professor Rogers is far from regarding with favour the proposals of Mr. Henry George for confiscating rent.

The discursiveness of many of the lectures, and the vast quantity and varied character of the material which they contain, render it a task of extreme difficulty to furnish a summary or analysis of the volume before us. It comprises two courses of lectures: the first consisting of eight, and the second of twelve lectures. The first may perhaps be distinguished from the second as dealing more largely with the past than the present; but, where the author traces the history of the past, he generally mingles with it his comments on the present; and, where he is concerned mainly with the present, he views it in the light of the knowledge he has gained of the past. The question of bimetallism, for instance, is tested partly by reference to the currency agitations of 1825; and the advantages of trades unions are shown by tracing the joint-stock principle in labour to its early origin. However, in the first course of lectures the author appears to be dealing more closely with the various ways in which the industrial and commercial supremacy of England has been slowly built up—and to this part the title on the cover, which differs from that on the title page, would more fittingly apply. In the second course he discusses various topics of present interest. In the opening lecture of the first course he traces the development of industrial skill in England; and here, as in a later lecture on immigration, he shows how largely it was due to the influence of foreign settlers. In the second lecture he deals with the conditions of economic progress; and in the third with "the progress of English population and the causes thereof." In this lecture he reviews the evidence which had led him to hold that the population of England and Wales was "almost stationary" during the fourteenth, fifteenth, and sixteenth centuries, and "amounted to between two and a quarter and two and a half millions." The evidence is derived from four sources :—(1) The average product of agriculture; (2) a return in 1377 of the number of persons liable to a poll tax then imposed; (3) an actual census of some hundreds in Kent taken in the reign of Henry VIII ; (4) the houses contained in various surveys made of a college estate towards the end of the sixteenth century. At the end of the seventeenth century population had more than doubled, and this process was repeated in the eighteenth, although Malthus was, Professor Rogers holds, influenced by special and passing circumstances of his times. In the next lecture he traces the development of credit agencies ; and here, as in his account of the early years of the Bank of England, he draws some instructive inferences from the fluctuations in the prices of stocks. In the following lecture the development of transit is considered ; in the sixth the history is traced of chartered trading companies, such as the East India Company, the Bank of England, and the South Sea Company ; and in two concluding lectures the "joint stock principle" in capital and labour is examined. The arguments for and against limited liability are forcibly stated in the former, and the history, action, and aims of trades unions are set forth in the latter.

In the second course of lectures contained in the volume Professor Rogers deals first with some points of economic theory, which he criticises throughout in a trenchant manner. The economic doctrine of waste, and the economic theory of rent, are subjected to a severe scrutiny, which may, however, be said to be more unfavourable to the latter than to the former. The ambiguity of the term "unproductive labour" is shown, and the history of its successive use by the Physiocrats, by Adam Smith, and by Mill, is traced. The Ricardian theory of rent is pronounced erroneous because it misplaces the emphasis on prices instead of on profits. In this lecture Mr. Rogers gives some striking figures of the comparative rise in the rents of pasture, arable, and building sites. Contrasted with the fourteenth century, the rent of arable land has increased eighty-eight times as compared with a rise in pasture of nine times, and the rise in urban rent has of course been far greater. The two following lectures deal with the same subject of land, the first treating of contracts for the use of land, and the second of the comparative advantages of large and small holdings. Professor Rogers doubts the wisdom of the policy of consolidating farms. He then proceeds to discuss movements of labour under two heads of emigration and immigration, and in the following lecture the topic of bimetallism is handled under the title—movements of currency. In the eighth lecture he returns to the subject of land under the title of peasant agriculture and manufactures, and gives an historical account of the different forms of tenure. In the following two lectures the relations of home trade to domestic and international competition are considered, and in the last two lectures of the course a sketch is furnished of the economic legislation passed during the century, from 1815 to 1841, and thence forward to 1885.

Methods of Industrial Remuneration.   By David F. Schloss.
London : Williams and Norgate, 1892.

In this book Mr. Schloss has performed a work which will be
of very great service to economic students.   In his own words he
has "attempted to present a faithful delineation of the wage-system
in all its forms, and of the several modifications introduced with a
view to the improvement of that system."   We venture to think
that he has been singularly successful in this attempt, and that
no such careful and minute analysis of the varieties of industrial
remuneration has ever been presented to the public before.   From
a failure to discriminate clearly between these different methods of
payment, and to attend to small distinctions, however unimportant
they may at first sight seem, a considerable amount of confusion
has infected the reasonings of many writers, and led them to form
untenable judgments on insecure evidence.   This has perhaps
been especially the case with regard to profit sharing and co-operative production, and, accordingly, Mr. Schloss's critical examination
of the promise and performance of these projected reforms on the
established wages system is not the least valuable part of his
book.   He devotes to it about half of the volume.   He supplies
some cogent reasons, which deserve the most careful examination,
to show why the adoption of profit-sharing has found so little
favour with employers and employed, and has been emphatically
condemned by perhaps the shrewdest body of working men in the
country—the members of the co-operative societies.   They have,
as he aptly points out, engaged in the work of production as well
as of distribution with no little success, and the difficulty in the
former case of superseding the employer, on which great stress has
been laid by eminent economists, has, he thinks, perhaps been
exaggerated.   The failure of co-operative production—in the
common, though limited, sense of the term—has been rather due
to a faulty system of industrial remuneration, and this faulty
system is the very basis of that system of profit-sharing which
economists, who have disapproved of co-operative production
have commended as exhibiting the merits without the failings of the
larger scheme.   Mr. Schloss shows by a statistical examination of
the actual instances of profit-sharing how small and, in many
cases, how illusory is the share of profits obtained by the workmen
who, according to the theory of the matter, have themselves, by
dint of the stimulus to increased exertion or avoidance of waste,
produced the increase of profit in which they only partially share.
He argues that by some modification of the established wages
system, without any sharing in profits as such, the same desirable
result of an increase of output might be secured, and the workmen
might obtain a larger proportion of the increase, without any of
the fettering conditions, which often make the receipt of their
share in the profits earned in the past conditional on their remaining in the service of the same business firm for the future.   A
bonus or premium may be given, he points out, for qualitative
as well as for quantitative excellence of work, in the shape of what
he calls progressive wages, paid either to individuals or collectively
to a body of workmen.   In the first part of his book Mr. Schloss

considers this method of progressive wages together with other varieties of the wages system. He distinguishes them as time-wages, piece-wages, task-wages, collective time, piece, task and progressive-wages, contract-work, and co-operative-work. He shows by instructive examples how often an element of piece-wages may enter into time-wages, and how often the reverse may be the case. He examines with scrupulous fairness the objections entertained to piece-wages by large classes of workmen ; and he discusses with minute and discriminating care the various questions connected with sub-contracts and the so-called "sweating system." Throughout the book he gives illustrations of each method of remuneration from facts of his own observation and inquiry, and to this feature much of its value is due.

Di Alcuni Indici Misuratori del Movimento Economico in Italia. By L. Bodio. Roma: 1891.

The economic condition of Italy forms one of the most interesting subjects of study at the present time. The emigration of Italians to the Argentine Republic and to other American States, the immigration of Italians into France, where they are apparently viewed with somewhat the same feelings as those entertained towards the immigrant Jews in London, the early beginnings of factory organisation in Italy itself, which presents the same features of very long hours and unhealthy conditions as those which marked the period before factory legislation in England, the distress inflicted on the agricultural classes by Indian competition since the opening of the Suez Canal, the tariff contests with France, the financial difficulties of the government, and the poverty of large sections of the population, are some of the points which attract attention, and on most, if not all, Dr. Bodio throws considerable light, though it be the "dry light" of the dispassionate observer and collector of facts, in the instructive volume before us. For the ability of Italian economists and statisticians is as great and as widely known and recognised as the distress of the country is notorious. Dr. Bodio is the head of the statistical department of the State; and in this volume he has collected from official and other sources some statistical data, which have been revised and amplified in a second edition, of the economic condition of Italy. The work is divided into five sections. In the first the author deals with the number of the population, their hygienic and sanitary condition, the existing provision for education, whether primary, or secondary and technical, or higher, the character and resources of the various eleemosynary institutions, the position of the mutual aid and co-operative societies, and, lastly, the extent of crime. The second section is entitled *Statistica Economica;* and the agricultural and industrial statistics, the trade with the West, the mercantile marine, the roads and railways, the postal and telegraphic service, and the credit system, receive attention. In the third part the financial situation of Italy, both of the central and the provincial and communal governments, is presented. In the following part the military and naval forces are reviewed ; in the fifth the growth in private

wealth during recent years is traced; and the sixth and concluding part con'ains general tables setting forth the data which have
been separately examined in the preceding sections.

In an introduction Dr. Bodio states that he commences his
statistics, which, he says, may be summarily described as *L' Italia
in cifre*, with the year 1862. The population of Italy in 1890
numbered 31,233,220 persons, as compared with 28,459,628 in 1881,
and an estimated population (including Venice) of 25 millions in
1861. Emigration, which is chiefly directed towards America,
has grown from 19,756 emigrants in 1876, to 195,993 in 1888, and
has then declined to 104,733 in 1890. According, however, to
figures collected from the other European States, Italy only stands
for 6·98 per 1,000 inhabitants in 1888, the year of the largest
volume of emigration, as compared with 8·99 for Scotland, 15·14
for Ireland, 9·59 for Sweden, and 10·84 for Norway. The hygienic
condition of the people has undoubtedly improved, and the rate of
mortality has fallen from 30·06 per 1,000 (without distinction of
sex or age) in 1862-66, to 26·39 in 1890. There has been a decline
in infant mortality, and in the number of deaths from certain
prevalent diseases, such as malarial fever, though Italy scarcely
compares favourably in the matter of health with other European
countries. As regards educational progress, the number of pupils
at the elementary schools has grown from 1,008,674 in 1861-62 to
2,307,982 in 1887-8. The increase has been greatest in the towns;
and the number of pupils per 100 inhabitants was still in 1887-88
only 7·51 for Italy as compared with 14·49 for France, 10·09 for
Belgium (in the public schools alone), 14·28 for Holland, 16·06 for
Switzerland, 12·51 for Austria, 17·83 for Prussia, and 16·39 for
England and Wales (in the public schools alone). The number of
students at the universities has increased from 10,381 in 1866-67 to
16,578 in 1888-89. The amount of crime against persons tends to
diminish, while that of offences against property tends rather to
increase. But Italy occupies an unenviable position compared
with other European countries in the statistics of homicides, the
figures of persons charged and condemned being in 1888 8·42 per
100,000 inhabitants, as against 1·46 in France, 0·80 in Germany,
6·57 in Spain, 2·16 in Austria, 0·38 in England, 0·52 in Scotland,
and 0·86 in Ireland.

Passing to what he distinguishes as *Statistica Economica*,
Dr. Bodio examines first the agricultural and then the industrial
statistics of his country. The production of wheat, of rice, and
of the vine, has on the whole increased during the period brought
under review, while that of barley and oats has apparently
diminished. The number of horses and mules, asses and cattle,
seems to have increased, and that of sheep, goats, and pigs to have
decreased. Industrial statistics, are, it appears, somewhat difficult
to ascertain with sufficient detail and exactitude, but Dr. Bodio
supplies such as are available. In the matter of railways the
length in kilometres has grown from about 2,189 in 1861 to 13,277
in 1871; the number of post offices has doubled in the period
from 1862 to 1890, and the number of letters sent by post has
increased from 72 millions in 1863 to 128 millions in 1889-90.

But the maximum in this last respect was apparently reached in 1887-88, and since that date there has, it seems, been some decline. The different institutions of credit are next examined, and special attention is naturally given to the operations of the Bank of Naples and the Bank of Sicily. The co-operative credit societies and the popular banks, which are one feature of Italian society, also receive attention, and they have grown in numbers from 64 in 1871, to 692 in 1888, many having been established in 1886. They appear to transact no inconsiderable business.

In his third section Dr. Bodio passes to the examination of the national and local finances. In 1881 there was a surplus of some considerable amount, but by 1885-86 it had been exchanged for a deficit, and every subsequent year has presented the same ominous feature of finance, while, in 1888-89 the deficit amounted to as much as 234 million liras. In 1889-90 it has decreased to 74 millions. The revenue has, Dr. Bodio shows, grown from 480 millions in 1862 to 1,562 millions, and the expenditure from 926 to 1,637 millions. The subject considered in the next section, the war establishment, has been largely responsible for this increased expenditure. The army has been augmented from 476.045 men in 1865 to 2,848.308 in 1891, the obligation to serve having been introduced in 1875, when the forces amounted to 893,580; and the military expenditure absorbed in 1891 281 million liras. The Italian navy is, of course, one of the most important and efficient in Europe. In the fifth section of his book, Dr. Bodio presents some data on the growth of private wealth; and on the difficulty of ascertaining, arranging, and interpreting these. he lays just stress. He refers to the similar calculations of Dr. Giffen in England, and Dr. Soetbeer in Prussia. but his observations scarcely admit of an analysis which will do them adequate justice, and we must refer the readers of the *Journal* to Dr. Bodio's volume.

Les Habitations Ouvrières en Belgique. Par le B⁰ⁿ· Hippolyte de Royer de Dour. Bruxelles: Société Belge de Librairie, 1890.

This work was successful in obtaining a prize offered for the best Belgian treatise on the means of improving the condition— moral, intellectual, and physical—of the working classes and the poor; and among the adjudicators of the prize was the late eminent economist M. Emile de Laveleye. The scope of the work has been somewhat enlarged in the course of its execution, and, commencing with the idea of merely grouping together the information which he had collected on the character and origin of the actual efforts which had been made in Belgium to improve the dwellings of the working classes, the author has embraced in his consideration the part played in the matter by public authorities and by sanitary reformers, the resources offered by legislation, the conclusions formulated by congresses and inquiries, the different means of facilitating the ownership of property by workmen, the suitable modes of lodging, the results achieved by associations of workmen, by societies, and by charitable organisations, and the particular solution of the various questions raised which he himself favours.

These points are discussed in the first part of the volume, and in the second he examines the recent legislation passed on the subject, by which *comités de patronage* were established, whose express function it was to concern themselves with this particular question. In the first chapter of the first part the general aspects of the matter are reviewed, and the importance of his dwelling as a factor in the workman's life is duly emphasised. The notice attracted by the question in other countries is shown, and the writer then passes to the consideration of his own country. The action of the public authorities, the various investigations which have been instituted, and congresses which have been held, the efforts of different associations and the course of legislation, are carefully studied. In the third chapter the moral aspects of the question, and the relative advantages and drawbacks of blocks of dwellings and separate tenements, receive attention ; and in the fourth the importance of diffusing the ownership of property is emphasised, the part played by education in inducing this result is shown, and the various organisations which promote the possession of property by the working classes are pointed out. The fifth chapter is devoted to statistics giving the results of actual efforts which have been made by working men's or co-operative societies, by the enterprise of employers, by societies expressly formed for providing sanitary and inexpensive dwellings, by individual initiative, and by public authority. The whole volume is a storehouse of information assiduously collected, and carefully arranged, on a subject of great importance, and is plentifully illustrated with drawings showing the detailed construction of different types of dwellings.

Statistik der deutschen Arbeiter-Kolonien für 1887-89. Von Dr. G. Berthold. Berlin : M. Priber, 1891.

In this pamphlet Dr. Berthold continues his investigations into the condition and results of the workmen's colonies in Germany. In two previous pamphlets he had dealt with the years 1885-86 and 1886-87, and in the present work he embraces the two years 1887-89. Such a careful statement of actual facts, illustrated as it is by several statistical tables, is an opportune contribution to the discussion started in this country by General Booth's well-known scheme; for the "farm-colony" in the proposal of the leader of the Salvation Army finds its parallel in these German workmen's colonies, as the town-shelter does in the relief stations and shelters established in the German cities through the efforts of Pastor von Bodelschwing and others. At the shelters there are labour-bureaux ; but, if the applicant cannot procure work through their means, he may proceed to a colony, where he will find work of the nature of agricultural labour, carpentry, and the like. Dr. Berthold in an introduction shows that these colonies now number twenty-four in all, and that in twenty of them, for which he supplies full particulars, accommodation is provided for 2,395 persons, and that up to March, 1889, since the opening of the first colony at Wilhelmsdorf in 1882, 31,145 persons had been received and 29,457 discharged. He gives also the figures for the three years 1888, 1889, and 1890 of those admitted and those refused admission month by month, from which it seems that the admissions increase towards winter, and diminish towards summer. He then proceeds to furnish some detailed information about each of the twenty colonies; and, after some general comments, the pamphlet concludes with a series of statistical tables, dealing first with each particular colony, and then collectively with the full number of twenty in some cases and with sixteen in others. These tables show, among other facts, the average duration of stay in the colony, the number of persons who return when once discharged, and the reasons for discharge; and in an appendix a detailed description is given of the individual colonists in three of the colonies. Besides this information some data are furnished in an earlier part of the pamphlet of the expenditure and the revenue of the colonies, many of which have been, largely or in part, supported by grants from the local authorities. A fair proportion of those who leave seem to obtain employment, amounting to 27 per cent. in 1885-86, 24 in 1886-87, and 20 in 1887-89. But a considerable number, representing 54 per cent. in 1885-86, 57 in 1886-87, and 60 in 1887-89, appear to depart at their own wish, while a small number are sent away for misconduct or drunkenness, or the like. Whether the colonies have or have not diminished the number of vagrants is doubtful, as the number of re-admissions is large, and the increase in the winter months of the admissions is significant. But on all these points Dr. Berthold furnishes such information as is available, and in many particulars it is remarkably full and detailed.

Jahrbücher für Nationalökonomie und Statistik. Jena: Gustav Fischer.

Heft 1, Band III, contains an interesting statistical article by *Dr. Paasche*, entitled Die Entwickelung der britischen Landwirtschaft unter dem Druck ausländischer Konkurrenz; Die Bedeutung der Gilden für die Entstehung der deutschen Stadtverfassung, by G. von Below; Die zweite Lesung des Entwurfes eines Bürgerlichen Gesetzbuches für das Deutsche Reich (continued), by Assessor Greif; Die Revision des Deutschen Patentgesetzes, by C. Gareis; Die Verwaltung der Stadt Berlin in den Jahren 1882-88, by E. Loening.

Heft 2, Band III, contains: Landgemeinden und Gutsbezirke in den östlichen Provinzen Preussens, by E. Loening; Die Silberfrage in den Vereinigten Staaten Nordamerikas, by S. M. Lindsay; Novelle zum preussischen Armengesetz, by E. Loening; Die Urteile der deutschen Handelskammern über die Novelle zur Gewerbeordnung nach den Jahresberichten für 1890, by R. Van der Borght; Die Zunahme der Bevölkerung in den hauptsächlichsten Kulturstaaten während der letzten Dezennien (from official sources); Die Brotpreise in Berlin im Jahre 1891, by E. Hirschberg.

XIII.—PERIODICAL RETURNS.

REGISTRATION OF THE UNITED KINGDOM.

No. I.—ENGLAND AND WALES.

MARRIAGES—To 30TH SEPTEMBER, 1891.

BIRTHS AND DEATHS—To 31ST DECEMBER, 1891.

A.—*Serial Table of* MARRIAGES, BIRTHS, *and* DEATHS, *returned in the Years* 1891-85, *and in the* QUARTERS *of those Years.*

Calendar YEARS, 1891-85:—*Numbers.*

Years	'91.	'90.	'89.	'88.	'87.	'86.	'85.
Marriages No.	—	223,028	213,865	203,821	200,518	196,071	197,745
Births......... ,,	913,836	869,937	885,944	879,868	886,331	903,760	894,270
Deaths .... ,,	587,666	562,248	518,353	510,971	530,758	537,276	522,750

QUARTERS *of each Calendar Year,* 1891-85.

(I.) MARRIAGES:—*Numbers.*

Qrs. ended last day of	'91.	'90.	'89.	'88.	'87.	'86.	'85.
March........ No.	49,057	40,905	41,006	40,276	38,836	39,202	39,111
June .... ,,	52,543	59,180	55,741	51,684	52,637	50,325	52,054
September ,,	58,553	57,143	53,820	51,603	49,746	48,565	49,476
December ,,	—	65,800	63,298	60,258	59,299	57,979	57,104

(II.) BIRTHS:—*Numbers.*

Qrs. ended last day of	'91.	'90.	'89.	'88.	'87.	'86.	'85.
March........ No.	229,953	225,640	220,296	223,766	219,162	230,330	231,955
June .... ,,	238,825	220,060	227,641	224,112	226,338	231,087	222,142
September ,,	224,089	220,769	220,341	214,651	222,835	224,332	218,558
December ,,	220,969	203,468	217,666	217,339	217,996	218,011	221,615

(III.) DEATHS:—*Numbers.*

Qrs. ended last day of	'91.	'90.	'89.	'88.	'87.	'86.	'85.
March........ No.	158,099	165,318	139,344	149,976	143,123	156,653	147,721
June .... ,,	171,555	128,625	124,434	124,918	128,488	125,359	132,340
September ,,	116,469	122,515	122,362	107,881	125,232	125,366	114,308
December ,,	141,543	145,790	132,213	128,196	133,915	129,898	128,381

M 2

Annual Rates of MARRIAGES, BIRTHS, *and* DEATHS, *per* 1,000 PERSONS LIVING *in the Years* 1891-85, *and in the* QUARTERS *of those Years.*

Calendar YEARS, 1891-85 :—*General Ratios.*

YEARS	'91.	Mean '81-90.	'90.	'89.	'88.	'87.	'86.	'85.
Estmtd. Popln. of England in *thousands* in middle of each Year....	29,081,	—	28,762,	28,447,	28,135,	27,827,	27,522,	27,220,
Persons Married	—	14·9	15·5	15·0	14·4	14·4	14·2	14·5
Births	31·4	32·5	30·2	31·1	31·2	31·9	32·8	32·9
Deaths...............	20·2	19·1	19·5	18·2	18·1	19·1	19·5	19·2

QUARTERS *of each Calendar Year,* 1891-85.

(I.) PERSONS MARRIED :—*Ratio per* 1,000.

Qrs. ended last day of	'91.	Mean '81-90	'90.	'89.	'88.	'87.	'86.	'85.
March	13·7	11·9	11·5	11·7	11·5	11·3	11·6	11·7
June...................	14·5	15·4	16·5	15·7	14·7	15·2	14·7	15·2
September	16·0	14·9	15·8	15·0	14·6	14·2	14·0	14·4
December	—	17·6	18·2	17·7	17·0	16·9	16·7	16·6

(II.) BIRTHS :—*Ratio per* 1,000.

Qrs. ended last day of	'91.	Mean '81-90.	'90.	'89.	88.	'87.	'86.	'85.
March	32·1	33·4	31·8	31·4	31·9	31·9	33·9	34·6
June...	32·9	33·2	30·7	32·1	31·9	32·6	33·7	32·7
September	30·6	31·9	30·5	30·7	30·3	31·8	32·3	31·9
December	30·2	31·5	28·1	30·4	30·6	31·1	31·4	32·3

(III.) DEATHS :—*Ratio per* 1,000.

Qrs. ended last day of	'91.	Mean '81-90.	'90.	'89.	'88.	'87.	'86.	'85.
March	22·0	21·6	23·3	19·9	21·4	20·9	23·1	22·0
June...................	23·7	18·7	17·9	17·5	17·8	18·5	18·3	19·5
September	15·9	17·3	16·9	17·1	15·2	17·9	18·1	16·7
December	19·3	19·1	20·1	18·4	18·1	19·1	18·7	18·7

B.—*Comparative Table of* Consols, Provisions, Coal *and* Pauperism *in each* Quarter *of* 1889-90-91.

Quarters ending	Average Prices of: 2¾*l.* per Cent. Consols (for Money) per 100*l.* Stock.	Discount charged by the Bank of England.	Wheat per Quarter in England and Wales.	Meat per Pound at the Metropolitan Meat Market (by the Carcase), with the *Mean* Prices. Beef.	Mutton.	Coal (Seaborne) in the London Market per Ton.	Pauperism. Quarterly Average of the Number of Paupers Relieved on the *Last Day* of each Week. In-door.	Out-door.
1889	£ *s.* *d.*	£	*s.* *d.*	*d.* *d.* *d.*	*d.* *d.* *d.*	*s.* *d.*		
Mar. 31	98 10 –	3·41	29 11	3¼—6⅛ 4¾	3½—7⅞ 5¾	16 4	197,363	558,527
June 30	98 11 6	2·59	29 3	3⅛—7¼ 5⅜	4⅞—8⅞ 6⅞	14 6	178,019	529,366
Sept. 30	97 19 2	3·20	30 –	3⅛—7¾ 5⅝	5⅜—9⅜ 7⅜	15 9	170,072	512,156
Dec. 31	97 2 2	5·02	29 11	3⅛—7⅛ 5⅛	6⅛—9⅞ 8	19 5	184,399	512,707
1890								
Mar. 31	97 4 9	5·34	29 10	3⅛—7⅛ 5⅛	6⅞—10⅜ 8⅝	19 4	192,316	533,577
June 30	97 15 9	3·19	32 8	3⅛—7⅛ 5⅜	6⅜—9¼ 7⅞	17 9	172,686	506,303
Sept. 30	96 – –	4·30	34 4	3½—7⅜ 5½	6⅞—9⅛ 8	18 8	165,091	493,107
Dec. 31	94 19 4	5·29	31 10	3½—7⅛ 5⅛	7—9⅛ 8⅛	19 3	178,858	492,131
1891								
Mar. 31	96 16 6	3·35	32 11	3⅞—7¼ 5⅝	6⅛—8⅞ 7¾	19 5	186,337	514,189
June 30	95 10 5	3·80	39 6	4¼—7½ 5⅞	5⅜—8⅜ 7	18 2	172,510	490,721
Sept. 30	95 10 11	2·54	38 11	4¼—7¾ 6	5¼—8⅞ 7⅛	18 8	164,799	474,575
Dec. 31	95 0 8	3·57	36 8	4⅜—7½ 6	5¼—8⅞ 7⅛	18 1	179,495	474,350

C.—*Special Average Death-Rate Table:*—Annual Rate *of* Mortality *per* 1,000 *in* Town *and* Country Districts *of* England *in each Quarter of the Years* 1889-91.

	Area in Statute Acres.	Population Estimated in the middle of 1891.	Quarters ending	Annual Rate of Mortality per 1,000 in each Quarter of the Years: 1891.	Mean '81-90.	1890.	1889.
T Districts. All tri th as tion Sub-Dis- -fourths of ion of which, ted in 1891, ithin the boun- Urban Sanitary existing in 1886	3,678,263	18,602,555	March ..	22·8	22·4	24·4	20·6
			June	24·7	19·3	18·7	18·3
			Sept.	16·8	18·8	18·5	18·5
			Dec.	20·3	20·5	22·0	19·7 9,099
			Year	21·1	20·3 ,02	,596 6,710	16,050 7,745
			Year	18·5	,3,092	21,793	25,144
Co y Districts. All th tra E n aining Regis- b-Districts of and Wales— g within the ition of Town	33,561,088	10,478,492	March ..	20·7	23,600	13,343	14,979
			June	21·	10,297	8,358	11,052
			Sept.	14			
			Dec.	1 21	11,284	7,675	10,672

D.—*Special Town Table:*—POPULATION ; BIRTH-RATE *and* DEATH-RATE *in each Quarter of* 1891, *in* TWENTY-EIGHT *Large Towns.*

Cities and Boroughs.	Estimated Population in the Middle of the Year 1891.	Annual Rate to 1,000 Living during the Thirteen Weeks ending							
		4th April. (1st Quarter.)		4th July. (2nd Quarter.)		3rd October. (3rd Quarter.)		2nd January. (4th Quarter.)	
		Births.	Deaths.	Births.	Deaths.	Births.	Deaths.	Births.	Deaths.
Twenty-eight towns	9,405,108	32·0	23·0	33·3	26·2	31·5	18·1	31·5	21·2
London*	4,221,452	31·9	22·6	31·8	23·8	30·6	17·4	30·9	20·5
Brighton	115,606	26·3	19·6	27·0	18·2	25·6	14·2	24·1	19·2
Portsmouth	160,128	35·1	24·2	30·9	23·2	28·9	14·3	28·9	16·4
Norwich	101,316	35·1	22·3	32·3	20·1	31·0	15·1	30·8	20·9
Plymouth	84,464	32·3	25·0	29·8	21·8	30·4	19·9	28·4	24·6
Bristol	222,049	29·9	24·3	31·2	20·4	29·1	14·2	29·6	23·3
Wolverhampton	82,799	34·8	21·0	35·7	27·1	32·1	20·2	33·4	28·2
Birmingham	429,906	32·8	22·4	35·5	28·0	33·0	16·8	32·5	19·5
Leicester	142,581	30·4	21·0	35·9	27·3	33·3	19·2	31·8	16·4
Nottingham	212,662	26·7	18·1	31·5	25·0	28·4	15·4	28·1	17·7
Derby	94,496	28·7	16·2	34·0	24·7	29·3	14·9	27·8	18·8
Birkenhead	99,597	30·3	23·3	32·5	22·0	32·9	17·1	33·6	19·2
Liverpool	517,116	29·9	22·9	34·9	31·8	34·2	22·4	33·4	26·2
Bolton	115,253	34·2	23·2	35·7	25·1	31·8	18·5	34·1	20·6
Manchester	506,469	34·5	28·4	35·4	33·7	33·7	19·9	32·7	24·2
Salford	198,717	29·7	24·2	38·2	31·1	34·7	20·3	35·1	22·1
Oldham	132,010	27·3	24·9	34·8	33·3	29·2	19·2	29·1	21·6
Blackburn	120,496	32·4	28·6	36·0	32·0	34·1	20·1	31·7	21·3
Preston	107,864	37·7	30·8	38·1	29·1	35·0	26·7	33·9	23·2
Huddersfield	95,656	23·2	26·6	25·8	30·6	24·1	17·3	22·9	16·1
Halifax	83,109	28·5	29·7	27·5	30·8	24·5	14·5	25·3	16·9
Bradford	216,938	25·9	19·5	31·1	30·7	28·0	16·7	26·5	19·2
Leeds	369,099	34·1	24·2	36·1	28·3	32·9	18·6	33·0	20·4
Sheffield	325,304	35·3	22·2	38·3	34·0	34·8	18·7	36·7	19·8
Hull	200,934	32·6	19·2	35·2	26·6	34·2	18·0	33·4	18·3
Sunderland	131,302	39·2	22·6	38·9	23·3	35·4	24·1	35·2	28·9
Newcastle	187,502	41·7	26·1	37·3	23·1	35·2	20·3	33·9	28·8
Cardiff	130,283	39·8	24·7	36·6	22·8	34·8	16·6	37·3	26·0
Edinburgh	261,970	27·1	21·8	30·3	21·6	26·3	16·1	27·5	25·5
	567,143	38·8	31·2	38·0	25·8	33·3	19·1	32·4	27·0
Qrs. ended *last day of*	347,312	29·5	30·1	30·3	23·4	27·9	21·6	24·6	29·8
March									
June									
September									
December									

* ...³ of this table, London includes the Strand Union workhouse at
25 ...Union workhouse at Mitcham, and the metropolitan hospitals
15·... ...le Registration London.

March .... ³
June 25
September .... 15·...
December .... 19·3

E.—*Divisional Table:*—MARRIAGES *in the Year ending* 30*th September; and* BIRTHS *and* DEATHS *in the Year ending* 31*st December,* 1891, *as Registered Quarterly.*

1	2	3	4	5	6	7
			MARRIAGES in Quarters ending			
DIVISIONS. (England and Wales.)	AREA in Statute Acres.	Enumerated POPULATION, 1891 (Unrevised).	31st December, 1890.	31st March. 1891.	30th June, 1891.	30th September, 1891.
		No.	No.	No.	No.	No.
ENGLD. & WALES....*Totals*	37,239,351	29,001,018	65,790	49,057	52,543	58,553
I. London	74,692	4,211,056	10,254	8,022	8,195	10,570
II. South-Eastern	3,991,604	2,867,476	5,763	3,911	4,598	5,046
III. South Midland	3,238,579	1,863,666	3,724	2,281	2,575	3,174
IV. Eastern	3,136,622	1,575,260	3,584	2,034	2,243	2,498
V. South-Western	4,997,695	1,908,934	3,840	2,961	3,313	3,233
VI. West Midland	3,964,632	3,244,634	7,879	5,501	5,846	6,408
VII. North Midland........	3,535,223	1,806,089	4,003	2,915	3,506	3,385
VIII. North-Western........	1,951,126	4,665,916	10,150	8,798	9,040	10,520
IX. Yorkshire	3,726,829	3,218,747	7,680	5,762	5,830	6,752
X. Northern	3,528,621	1,863,120	4,175	3,610	3,834	3,564
XI. Monmthsh. & Wales	5,093,728	1,776,120	4,738	3,262	3,563	3,403

8	9	10	11	12	13	14	15	16
	BIRTHS in each Quarter of 1891 ending				DEATHS in each Quarter of 1891 ending			
DIVISIONS. (England and Wales.)	31st March.	30th June.	30th September.	31st December.	31st March.	30th June.	30th September.	31st December.
	No.	No.	No.	No.	No.	No.	No.	No.
ENGLD. & WALES....*Totals*	229,953	238,825	224,089	220,969	158,099	171,555	116,469	141,543
I. London	35,727	33,498	32,222	32,556	24,833	24,605	18,069	21,252
II. South-Eastern	20,003	20,063	19,428	18,946	13,901	12,830	9,333	11,620
III. South Midland........	13,756	14,654	13,367	13,222	9,080	8,872	6,190	7,423
IV. Eastern	12,245	12,922	11,936	11,974	7,923	7,679	5,612	6,507
V. South-Western	13,435	13,935	13,180	12,747	10,658	8,953	6,790	9,099
VI. West Midland	26,428	27,599	25,528	25,412	17,480	18,881	12,596	16,050
VII. North Midland........	14,220	15,090	13,940	13,843	8,829	11,462	6,710	7,745
VIII. North-Western........	38,175	40,451	37,942	37,888	28,381	33,092	21,793	25,144
IX. Yorkshire	24,784	27,229	25,151	24,780	17,420	23,600	13,343	14,979
X. Northern	16,489	17,665	16,741	15,878	9,673	10,297	8,358	11,052
XI. Monmthsh. & Wales	14,691	15,719	14,654	14,223	9,921	11,294	7,675	10,672

F.—*General Meteorological Table,*

[Abstracted from the particulars supplied to the

1891. Months.	Temperature of									Water of the Thames	Elastic Force of Vapour.		Weight of Vapour in a Cubic Foot of Air.	
	Air.			Evaporation.		Dew Point.		Air—Daily Range.						
	Mean.	Diff. from Average of 120 Years.	Diff. from Average of 50 Years.	Mean.	Diff. from Average of 50 Years.	Mean.	Diff. from Average of 50 Years.	Mean.	Diff. from Average of 50 Years.		Mean.	Diff. from Average of 50 Years.	Mean.	Diff. from Average of 50 Years.
	°	°	°	°	°	°	°	°	°		In.	In.	Grs.	Gr.
Jan......	34·1	−2·6	−4·3	32·7	−4·3	30·6	−4·3	9·6	+0·1	...	·171	−·030	2·1	−0·3
Feb.......	38·5	−0·3	−0·9	37·3	−0·3	35·2	0·0	14·5	+3·5	...	·205	−·002	2·3	−0·1
Mar. ...	40·3	−0·8	−1·2	37·3	−1·8	33·6	−2·2	13·4	−1·3	...	·193	−·030	2·2	−0·3
Means...	37·6	−1·2	−2·1	35·8	−2·1	33·1	−2·2	12·5	+0·8	...	·190	−·017	2·2	−0·2
April ...	44·2	−1·9	−2·7	39·2	−4·5	36·9	−3·4	17·4	−0·9	...	·219	−·032	2·5	−0·4
May......	50·3	−2·2	−2·3	47·0	−1·9	43·5	−1·5	19·7	−0·7	...	·283	−·016	3·2	−0·2
June ...	60·4	+2·1	+1·5	50·1	+1·5	52·4	+1·7	20·9	−0·1	...	·394	+·023	4·4	+0·2
Means...	51·6	−0·7	−1·2	45·4	−1·6	44·3	−1·1	19·3	−0·6	...	·299	−·008	3·4	−0·1
July......	60·3	−1·4	−1·8	56·3	−1·3	53·2	−0·9	20·1	−0·9	...	·406	−·011	4·5	−0·2
Aug. ...	58·6	−2·3	−2·8	55·8	−1·5	53·3	−0·7	17·8	−2·1	...	·407	−·010	4·5	−0·2
Sept. ...	59·1	+2·6	+2·1	55·8	+1·9	52·8	+1·7	19·6	+1·4	...	·400	+·021	4·5	+0·2
Means...	59·3	−0·4	−0·8	56·0	−0·3	53·1	0·0	19·2	−0·5	...	·404	·000	4·5	−0·1
Oct.......	50·9	+1·4	+1·2	48·6	+0·8	46·2	+0·5	14·8	+0·2	...	·313	+·006	3·5	−0·3
Nov. ...	43·1	+0·7	−0·4	41·8	+0·3	39·9	+0·4	10·5	−0·9	...	·246	·000	2·8	0·0
Dec. ...	41·1	+2·1	+1·5	39·3	+1·1	37·1	+0·8	11·1	+1·8	...	·221	+·005	2·6	0·0
Means...	45·0	+1·4	+0·8	43·2	+0·7	41·1	+0·6	12·1	+0·4	...	·260	+·004	3·0	−0·1

Note.—In reading this table it will be borne in mind that the sign (−) minus signifies

About London the mean daily temperature of the air was generally below its average of sixty years from 1st October to the 10th of November, being particularly so on the 30th and 31st of October, when it was as much as 7°·5 and 9°·6 respectively below its average, the mean daily deficiency for these forty-one days being 0°·6; from 11th to 20th November it was above, particularly so on the 19th, when it was as much as 11°·2 above, the mean daily excess being 3°·5; from 21st to 30th November it was below, the mean daily deficiency being 4°·1; from 1st to 16th December it was generally above, being particularly so on the 4th, 5th, and 10th, when it was as much as 10°·8, 10°, and 8°·4 respectively above; the mean daily excess for the sixteen days ending 16th December being 4°·1; from 17th to 25th December it was below, being particularly so from the 19th to the 25th, when it was as much as 12°·6, 13°, 13°·6, 16°·2, 13°·9, 14°·1, and 11°·1 respectively below its average; the mean daily deficiency for the nine *for the Year ended 31st December, 1891.*

Registrar-General by JAMES GLAISHER, Esq., F.R.S., &c.]

Degree of Humidity.		Reading of Barometer.		Weight of a Cubic Foot of Air.		Rain.		Daily Horizontal Movement of the Air.	Reading of Thermometer on Grass.					1890. Months.
									Number of Nights it was			Low-est Read-ing at Night.	High-est Read-ing at Night.	
Mean.	Diff. from Aver-age of 50 Years.	Mean.	Diff. from Aver-age of 50 Years.	Mean	Diff. from Aver-age of 50 Years.	Amnt.	Diff. from Aver-age of 76 Years.		At or below 30°.	Be-tween 30° and 40°.	Above 40°.			
		In.	In.	Grs.	Grs.	In.	In.	Miles.				°	°	
87	0	29·961	+·200	562	+8	1·56	−0·31	302	21	9	1	12·0	44·1	January
88	+3	30·282	+·483	563	+10	0·05	−1·51	158	17	11	0	25·3	39·1	Feb.
77	−4	29·642	−·107	549	−1	2·14	+0·60	381	10	20	1	20·6	41·0	March
84	0	29·962	+·192	558	+6	Sum 3·75	Sum −1·22	Mean 280	Sum 48	Sum 40	Sum 2	Lowest 12·0	Highst 44·1	Means
76	−4	29·793	+·052	548	+5	0·72	−1·02	263	10	19	1	25·9	43·5	April
78	−1	29·607	−·178	537	−3	2·69	+0·62	246	1	16	14	28·0	46·4	May
75	0	29·841	+·030	530	−2	0·96	−1·03	244	0	4	26	37·4	57·0	June
76	−2	29·747	−·032	538	0	Sum 4·37	Sum −1·43	Mean 251	Sum 11	Sum 39	Sum 41	Lowest 25·9	Highst 57·0	Means
78	+2	29·759	−·034	529	+1	3·39	+0·84	254	0	5	26	37·0	54·5	July
83	+7	29·646	−·137	529	0	3·72	+1·36	293	0	2	29	36·4	54·0	August
80	−1	29·834	+·028	532	−1	0·82	−1·55	255	0	3	27	38·5	57·0	Sept.
80	+3	29·746	−·048	530	0	Sum 7·93	Sum +0·63	Mean 267	Sum 0	Sum 10	Sum 83	Lowest 36·4	Highst 57·0	Means
84	−5	29·608	−·106	537	−3	4·32	+1·58	310	3	18	10	20·2	50·0	October
88	−3	29·670	−·071	546	−2	2·01	−0·34	230	13	13	4	24·0	41·5	Nov.
86	−3	29·804	+·011	551	−2	2·67	+0·71	374	13	15	3	15·4	43·2	Dec.
86	−4	29·694	−·056	545	−2	Sum 9·00	Sum +1·95	Mean 305	Sum 29	Sum 46	Sum 17	Lowest 15·4	Highst 50·0	Means

days ending 25th December being 11°·8; and from 26th to 31st December it was above, being as much as 9°·1, 10°·7, and 12°·5 respectively above its average on the 29th, 30th, and 31st, the mean daily excess for the six days being 6°·4.

The mean temperature of the air for December was 41°·1, being 2°·1 and 1°·5 above the average of one hundred and fifty and fifty years respectively; it was 11°·3, 3°·5, and 0°·3 higher than in 1890, 1889, and 1888 respectively.

The mean high day temperature of the air for December was 46°·5, being 2°·2 above the average of fifty years; it was 13°·2, 4°·8, and 0°·9 higher than in 1890, 1889, and 1888 respectively.

The mean low night temperature of the air for December was 35°·4, being 0°·6 above the average of fifty years; it was 10°·2 and 2°·9 higher than in 1890 and 1889 respectively, and 0°·2 lower than in 1888.

No. II.—SCOTLAND.

BIRTHS, DEATHS, AND MARRIAGES, IN THE YEAR
ENDED 31ST DECEMBER, 1891.

I.—*Serial Table:—Number of* BIRTHS, DEATHS, *and* MARRIAGES *in Scotland, and their Proportion to the Population estimated to the Middle of each Year, during each Quarter of the Years* 1891-87 *inclusive.*

	1891.		1890.		1889.		1888.		1887.	
	Number.	Per Cent.	Number.	Per Cent.	Number.	Per Cent.	Number.	Per Cent.	Number.	Per Cent.
1st Quarter—										
Births	31,563	3·17	30,124	2·96	29,830	2·97	30,481	3·04	30,589	3·11
Deaths........	22,471	2·26	23,316	2·29	19,609	1·95	20,824	2·08	20,036	2·04
Marriages ..	6,952	0·70	6,687	0·66	6,318	0·63	5,942	0·59	6,249	0·63
Mean Temperature }	38°·2		40°·1		38°·6		36°·5		38°·6	
2nd Quarter—										
Births	33,395	3·31	31,789	3·09	32,294	3·18	32,088	3·20	32,698	3·29
Deaths........	20,804	2·07	19,607	1·91	18,213	1·79	18,048	1·80	18,685	1·88
Marriages ..	7,206	0·72	7,079	0·69	6,546	0·64	6,318	0·63	6,083	0·61
Mean Temperature }	47°·9		49°·5		51°·0		47°·5		49°·6	
3rd Quarter—										
Births	30,738	3·02	30,300	2·92	30,277	2·95	30,037	2·96	30,602	3·04
Deaths........	16,809	1·65	16,668	1·60	16,787	1·63	14,919	1·47	16,885	1·68
Marriages ..	6,560	0·64	6,480	0·62	6,257	0·61	5,892	0·58	5,643	0·56
Mean Temperature }	55°·7		55°·4		54°·6		53°·3		55°·7	
4th Quarter—										
Births	30,269	2·97	29,317	2·82	30,369	2·96	30,627	3·02	30,486	3·03
Deaths........	23,464	2·30	19,387	1·87	18,594	1·81	17,371	1·71	18,894	1·88
Marriages ..	7,231	0·71	7,195	0·69	7,197	0·70	7,129	0·70	6,876	0·68
Mean Temperature }	41°·9		41°·5		42°·6		43°·4		39°·9	
Year—										
Population .	4,033,180		4,110,547		4,077,070		4,034,156		3,991,499	
Births	125,965	3·12	121,530	2·95	122,770	3·01	123,225	3·05	124,375	3·12
Deaths........	83,548	2·07	78,978	1·92	73,203	1·80	71,161	1·76	74,500	1·87
Marriages ..	27,949	0·69	27,441	0·67	26,318	0·65	25,281	0·63	24,851	0·62

*ecial Average Table:—Number of Births, Deaths, and Marriages in Scotland and
'he Town and Country Districts for each Quarter of the Year ending 31st
mber, 1891, and their Proportion to the Population; also the Number of
'timate Births, and their Proportion to the Total Births.*

ths.	Illegitimate Births.						Marriages.		
Ratio. One in every	Number	Per Cent	Ratio. One in every		Per Cent.	Ratio. One in every	Number.	Per Cent.	Ratio. One in every
33	2,416	7·7	13·0		2·19	46		0·68	148
31	984	7·5	13·4	9,888	2·41	41	3,213	0·78	128
29	239	6·0	16·7	2,678	2·28	44	898	0·76	131
32	488	7·1	14·0	4,542	2·09	48	1,446	0·67	150
36	685	9·9	10·1	4,747	1·90	53	1,210	0·48	206
46	25	3·6	27·8	616	1·94	52	185	0·58	172
‥AND 30	2,475	7·4	13·5		2·07	48		0·72	140
ipal towns 28	973	6·9	14·4	9,399	2·36	42	3,470	0·87	115
' „ 28	236	5·6	17·9	2,565	2·19	46	888	0·76	132
' „ _ 29	536	7·5	13·3	4,097	1·95	51	1,298	0·62	162
35	687	9·4	10·6	4,202	1·67	60	1,476	0·59	170
47	43	6·4	15·7	541	1·72	58	74	0·24	424
AND 33	2,302	7·5	13·3		1·65	61		0·64	155
pal towns 32	890	7·0	14·2	7,215	1·79	56	3,413	0·85	118
„ 30	239	6·1	16·4	2,062	1·74	57	843	0·71	141
„ 33	486	7·5	13·3	3,477	1·64	61	1,230	0·58	172
and rural 37	646	9·3	10·7	3,499	1·38	78	1,018	0·40	250
⁓ „ 42	41	5·4	18·4	556	1·75	57	56	0·18	566
rter— AND 34	2,344	7·7	12·9		2·30	48		0·71	141
pal towns 32	914	7·3	13·7	10,102	2·51	40	3,273	0·81	123
„ 32	246	6·6	15·2	2,911	2·46	41	843	0·71	141
„ 33	439	6·8	14·6	5,008	2·36	42	1,433	0·68	148
and rural 37	707	10·3	9·7	4,920	1·94	52	1,553	0·61	164
ır „ 44	38	5·2	19·1	523	1·65	61	129	0·41	246

	Scotland.	Principal Towns.	Large Towns.	Small Towns.	Mainland Rural.	Insular Rural.
as of 1891 (un- l figures)	4,033,103	1,589,874	468,533	840,288	1,008,464	125,944
d to the middle '1	4,040,839	1,594,847	470,125	841,529	1,008,504	125,834

III.—*Bastardy Table:*—*Proportion of* ILLEGITIMATE *in every Hundred* BIRTHS *in the Divisions and Counties of* SCOTLAND, *during each quarter of the Year ending 31st December,* 1891; *with the Corresponding Figures for* 1890 *added for Comparison.*

Divisions and Counties.	Per Cent. for the Quarters ending 1891.				Per Cent. for the Quarters ending 1890.			
	31st March.	30th June.	30th Sept.	31st Dec.	31st March.	30th June.	30th Sept.	31st Dec.
SCOTLAND	7·7	7·4	7·5	7·7	8·2	7·2	7·5	7·3
Divisions—								
Northern	6·7	7·9	6·3	7·7	8·8	7·5	7·4	6·4
North-Western	4·8	5·9	5·6	6·5	6·1	6·3	5·7	5·0
North-Eastern	14·3	13·2	12·8	13·5	14·5	11·9	12·5	13·3
East Midland	8·1	8·2	8·0	7·7	8·4	8·2	7·3	7·7
West Midland	6·1	5·8	6·5	6·3	6·2	5·6	5·7	5·5
South-Western	6·2	5·8	6·1	6·1	6·4	5·8	6·2	5·9
South-Eastern	7·4	7·4	6·9	7·8	7·9	6·8	7·5	7·3
Southern	11·2	11·6	12·8	13·2	16·0	11·3	13·2	12·3
Counties—								
Shetland	2·5	5·6	6·6	4·6	2·3	2·2	2·2	3·6
Orkney	6·6	7·9	6·6	6·4	1·6	7·2	4·8	5·3
Caithness	10·7	9·9	7·3	12·1	17·0	10·9	13·1	8·9
Sutherland	3·2	6·7	4·1	5·2	7·8	6·5	4·3	7·6
Ross and Cromarty	3·3	4·6	4·4	5·0	4·9	4·2	4·8	2·7
Inverness	6·3	7·2	6·9	8·2	7·3	8·3	6·6	7·3
Nairn	13·7	11·1	15·2	8·9	18·2	7·8	8·0	6·6
Elgin	14·1	13·5	14·0	14·1	15·2	9·0	12·5	14·4
Banff	15·2	16·0	13·3	12·9	15·2	15·6	14·8	14·1
Aberdeen	14·5	12·4	13·0	13·3	14·1	11·8	12·1	13·0
Kincardine	12·6	14·9	8·0	15·3	15·1	9·9	12·4	14·3
Forfar	10·1	9·4	8·7	8·4	10·7	10·0	7·8	9·8
Perth	6·8	9·1	8·7	8·4	9·5	9·0	8·7	7·9
Fife	6·2	6·3	6·3	6·1	5·4	5·1	6·1	5·2
Kinross	9·4	6·5	11·3	4·7	2·3	7·8	12·9	6·2
Clackmannan	4·8	5·9	8·1	5·4	3·8	8·6	4·7	4·0
Stirling	5·7	5·8	6·1	6·2	6·9	5·9	6·2	6·2
Dumbarton	5·9	4·2	6·4	5·6	5·4	4·1	4·4	4·2
Argyll	6·9	8·5	7·8	7·4	7·0	7·5	6·3	5·9
Bute	9·8	8·3	5·4	7·1	3·0	6·6	8·4	6·9
Renfrew	4·0	5·0	4·4	4·7	5·4	4·2	5·4	5·3
Ayr	6·8	6·4	7·6	7·1	7·2	6·5	7·2	6·5
Lanark	6·5	5·9	6·1	6·2	6·4	6·0	6·1	5·8
Linlithgow	5·2	10·1	5·5	4·6	6·6	6·3	7·7	7·2
Edinburgh	7·6	6·9	6·9	7·9	7·8	6·7	7·8	7·3
Haddington	6·3	8·7	6·8	6·3	9·2	8·4	5·6	5·8
Berwick	11·2	9·9	9·7	13·3	10·1	8·6	8·9	9·0
Peebles	8·7	4·5	11·5	13·4	7·9	2·5	2·9	7·8
Selkirk	8·9	4·9	4·7	8·9	8·9	6·1	5·6	6·4
Roxburgh	8·0	7·8	9·6	10·0	14·4	7·4	9·8	9·8
Dumfries	11·7	12·2	12·1	11·6	18·4	11·0	12·4	12·6
Kirkcudbright	13·9	11·8	13·4	14·3	14·8	10·4	15·3	11·0
Wigtown	11·8	15·1	18·0	19·1	14·3	14·7	17·0	17·1

IV.—*Divisional Table:*—MARRIAGES, BIRTHS, *and* DEATHS *Registered in the Year ended 31st December,* 1891.

(Compiled from the Registrar-General's Quarterly Returns.)

1	2	3	4	5	6
DIVISIONS. (Scotland)	AREA in Statute Acres.	POPULATION, 1891. (*Persons.*)	Marriages.	Births.	Deaths.
		No.	No.	No.	No.
SCOTLAND .... *Totals*	19,639,377	4,033,103	27,949	125,965	83,548
I. Northern	2,261,622	118,250	502	2,748	2,021
II. North-Western........	4,739,876	163,757	758	8,973	2,941
III. North-Eastern	2,429,594	433,551	2,746	13,058	7,327
IV. East Midland	2,790,492	628,964	4,160	18,099	12,583
V. West Midland	2,693,176	314,862	1,862	9,405	6,431
VI. South-Western........	1,462,397	1,560,931	12,300	55,153	35,775
VII. South-Eastern	1,192,524	609,487	4,500	18,149	12,432
VIII. Southern	2,069,696	203,301	1,121	5,385	4,038

No. III.—GREAT BRITAIN AND IRELAND.

SUMMARY *of* MARRIAGES, *in the Year ended 30th September,* 1891; *and of* BIRTHS *and* DEATHS, *in the Year ended 31st December,* 1891.

(Compiled from the Quarterly Returns of the respective Registrars-General.)

COUNTRIES.	[000's omitted.]		Marriages.	Per 1,000 of Population.	Births.	Per 1,000 of Population.	Deaths.	Per 1,000 of Population.
	Area in Statute Acres.	Population, 1891. (*Persons.*)						
	No.	No.	No.	Ratio.	No.	Ratio.	No.	Ratio.
England and Wales .... }	37,239,	29,001,	225,953	7·8	913,836	31·5	587,666	20·3
Scotland	19,639,	4,033,	27,913	6·9	125,965	31·2	83,548	20·7
Ireland	20,323,	4,706,	21,375	4·5	107,883	22·9	86,053	18·3
GREAT BRITAIN AND IRELAND }	77,201,	37,740,	275,241	7·3	1,147,684	30·4	757,267	20·1

Note.—The numbers against Ireland represent the marriages, births, and deaths that the local registrars have *succeeded* in recording; but how far the registration approximates to absolute completeness, does not at present appear to be known. It will be seen that the Irish ratios of marriages, births, and deaths are much under those of England and Scotland.—ED. S. J.

Trade of United Kingdom, 1891-90-89.—*Distribution of Exports* from United King according to their Declared Real Value; and the Declared Real Value (Ex-duty Imports at Port of Entry, and therefore including Freight and Importer's Profit.*

Merchandise (*excluding Gold and Silver*) Imported from, and Exported to, the following Foreign Countries, &c.	1891.		1890.		
	Imports from	Exports to	Imports from	Exports to	Imports from
	£	£	£	£	£
I.—FOREIGN COUNTRIES.					
Northern Europe; viz., Russia, Sweden, Norway, Denmark & Iceland, & Heligoland	43,829,	12,920,	43,427,	13,260,	47,720,
Central Europe; viz., Germany, Holland, and Belgium	71,615,	35,653,	69,368,	37,094,	71,365,
Western Europe; viz., France, Portugal (with Azores, Madeira, &c.), and Spain (with Gibraltar and Canaries)	58,732,	24,760,	60,660,	25,169,	60,688,
Southern Europe; viz., Italy, Austrian empire, Greece, Roumania, Bulgaria, & Malta	12,345,	11,357,	11,497,	12,577,	10,964,
Levant; viz., Turkey, Asiatic and European (including Cyprus), and Egypt	16,084,	10,336,	13,197,	10,157,	13,745,
Northern Africa; viz., Tripoli, Tunis, Algeria and Morocco	1,762,	1,161,	2,090,	1,149,	2,003,
Western Africa	600,	1,025,	1,101,	1,610,	1,027,
Eastern Africa; with African Ports on Red Sea, Aden, Arabia, Persia, Bourbon, and Kooria Mooria Islands	714,	1,521,	941,	1,283,	780,
Indian Seas, Siam, Sumatra, Java, Philippines; other Islands	4,638,	3,464,	3,308,	2,792,	5,038,
South Sea Islands	59,	176,	51,	200,	59,
China and Japan, including **Hong Kong**	6,996,	11,873,	7,118,	13,231,	8,317,
United States of America	104,510,	27,545,	97,357,	32,077,	95,340,
Mexico and Central America	1,899,	2,841,	1,884,	2,901,	1,661,
Foreign West Indies, Hayti, &c.	249,	2,323,	320,	3,059,	248,
South America (Northern), New Granada, Venezuela, and Ecuador	735,	2,360,	687,	2,264,	603,
„ **(Pacific)**, Peru, Bolivia, Chili, and Patagonia	4,679,	3,039,	4,524,	4,246,	4,546,
„ **(Atlantic)** Brazil, Uruguay, and Argentine Republic	8,096,	13,694,	8,821,	17,909,	7,521,
Whale Fisheries; Grnlnd., Davis' Straits, Southn. Whale Fishery, Falkland Islands, and French Possessions in North America	150,	85,	112,	80,	108,
Total—Foreign Countries	337,692,	166,083,	326,463,	181,008,	331,733,
II.—BRITISH POSSESSIONS.					
British India, Ceylon, and Singapore	41,782,	34,674,	41,377,	37,450,	44,336,
Austral. Cols.—N. So.W., Victoria & Queensld.	18,535,	18,466,	17,182,	16,556,	16,106,
„ „ So. Aus., W. Aus., Tasm., N. Zealand, & Fiji Islands	12,727,	7,031,	12,174,	6,438,	10,714,
British North America	12,607,	7,245,	12,444,	7,228,	12,184,
„ W. Indies with Btsh. Guiana & Honduras	2,762,	3,109,	2,989,	3,834,	3,657,
Cape and Natal	6,187,	7,954,	6,096,	9,110,	6,118,
Brt. W. Co. of Af., Ascension and St. Helena	1,778,	1,693,	1,076,	871,	915,
Mauritius	268,	258,	265,	320,	422,
Channel Islands	1,202,	759,	959,	727,	938,
Total—British Possessions	97,848,	81,189,	94,562,	82,534,	95,390,
General Total £	435,540,	247,272,	421,025,	263,542,	

Trade of United Kingdom, for the Years 1890-86.—*Declared Value of the Total Exports of Foreign and Colonial Produce and Manufactures to each Foreign Country and British Possession.*

Merchandise Exported to the following Foreign Countries, &c.	[000's omitted.]				
	1890.	1889.	1888.	1887.	1886.
I.—FOREIGN COUNTRIES.	£	£	£	£	£
Northern Europe; viz., Russia, Sweden, Norway, Denmark, & Iceland, & Heligoland	5,507,	5,660,	4,849,	4,507,	3,592,
Central Europe; viz., Germany, Holland and Belgium	23,504,	25,735,	24,177,	24,640,	22,566,
Western Europe; viz., France, Portugal (with Azores, Madeira, &c.), and Spain (with Gibraltar and Canaries)	9,459,	8,879,	10,508,	8,034,	7,914,
Southern Europe; viz., Italy, Austrian Empire, Greece, Ionian Islands, and Malta	1,356,	1,478,	1,461,	1,341,	1,560,
Levant; viz., Turkey, Roumania, Syria and Palestine, and Egypt	727,	705,	619,	706,	868,
Northern Africa; viz., Tripoli, Tunis, Algeria, and Morocco	128,	151,	124,	118,	119,
Western Africa	180,	149,	168,	145,	166,
Eastern Africa; with African Ports on Red Sea, Aden, Arabia, Persia, Bourbon, and Kooria Mooria Islands	—	—	—	—	—
Indian Seas, Siam, Sumatra, Java, Philippines; other Islands	54,	88,	72,	48,	62,
South Sea Islands	—	—	—	—	—
China, including **Hong Kong** and Japan ...	473,	524,	463,	869,	566,
United States of America	14,272,	13,585,	12,314,	10,692,	10,783,
Mexico and Central America	157,	157,	163,	123,	126,
Foreign West Indies and Hayti	1,055,	963,	881,	741,	886,
South America (Northern), New Granada, Venezuela and Ecuador	92,	99,	78,	81,	69,
„ **(Pacific),** Peru, Bolivia, Chili, and Patagonia	347,	412,	378,	283,	253,
„ **(Atlantic),** Brazil, Uruguay, and Argentine Confed.	491,	795,	561,	458,	489,
Other countries (unenumerated)	184,	145,	132,	120,	121,
Total—Foreign Countries	57,986,	59,525,	56,948,	52,906,	50,140,
II.—BRITISH POSSESSIONS.					
British India, Ceylon, and Singapore	1,774,	1,540,	1,485,	1,653,	1,371,
Austral. Cols.—New South Wales and Victoria, So. Aus., W. Aus., Tasm., and N. Zealand	2,464,	2,742,	3,186,	2,526,	2,622,
British North America	1,047,	1,286,	1,135,	1,112,	1,152,
„ W.Indies with Btsh.Guiana & Honduras	420,	388,	380,	329,	278,
Cape and Natal	675,	802,	495,	461,	323,
Brt. W. Co. of Af., Ascension and St. Helena...	89,	79,	75,	66,	71,
Mauritius	26,	29,	34,	29,	31,
Channel Islands	193,	209,	230,	223,	210,
Other possessions	48,	57,	75,	44,	36,
Total—British Possessions	6,736,	7,132,	7,095,	6,443,	6,094,
General Total ....£	64,722,	66,657,	64,043,	59,349,	56,234,

IMPORTS.—(United Kingdom.)—**For the Years 1891-90-89-88-87.**—*Declared Real Value (Ex-duty), at Port of Entry (and therefore including Freight and Importer's Profit), of Articles of Foreign and Colonial Merchandise Imported into the United Kingdom.*

[000's omitted.]

Foreign Articles Imported.	1891.	1890.	1889.	1888.	1887.
	£	£	£	£	£
Raw Matls.—*Textile*,&c. Cotton, Raw ...	46,081,	42,757,	45,269,	39,401,	39,897,
Wool	29,727,	28,586,	30,301,	27,652,	25,983,
Silk*	14,148,	14,032,	15,387,	13,793,.	13,302,
Flax	2,775,	2,856,	3,066,	2,992,	2,708,
Hemp and Jute	7,341,	7,868,	8,694,	6,710,	5,847,
Indigo	1,043,	1,521,	1,783,	1,704,	1,673,
	101,115,	97,620,	104,500,	92,252,	89,410,
„ „ *Various*. Hides	2,437,	2,514,	3,074,	3,002,	3,132,
Oils	2,639,	2,468,	2,618,	2,197,	2,326,
Metals	23,030,	23,711,	22,085,	23,243,	16,618,
Tallow	1,772,	1,729,	1,645,	1,433,	1,074,
Timber................	14,929,	17,127,	19,826,	14,645,	11,989,
	44,807,	47,549,	49,248,	44,520,	35,139,
„ „ *Agrcltl*. Guano	138,	167,.	191,	202,	186,
Seeds	7,554,	6,872,	7,947,	7,579,	6,992,
	7,692,	7,039,	8,138,	7,781,	7,178,
Tropical,&c.,Produce. Tea	10,775,	9,998,	10,023,	10,216,	9,859,
Coffee and Chic...	3,508,	4,058,	4,411,	3,659,	4,334,
Sugar & Molasses	20,031,	18,261,	22,653,	18,260,	16,515,
Tobacco	3,416,	3,543,	3,974,	2,821,	3,400,
Rice	2,793,	2,549,	2,689,	2,314.	1,878,
Fruits	6,960,	6,723,	6,215,	6,146.	5,771,
Wines	5,995,	5,891,	5,909,	5,386,	5,468,
Spirits	2,343,	2,128,	1,859,	1,759,	2,012,
	55,821,	53,151,	57,733,	50,561,	49,246,
Food .... Grain and Meal.	61,571,	53,045,	50,808,	50,675,	47,819,
Provisions	52,508,	51,198,	47,454,	41,775,	40,526,
	114,079,	104,243,	98,262,	92,450,	88,345,
Remainder of Enumerated Articles	66,857,	66,517,	65,103,	58,939,	52,630,
Total Enumerated Imports	390,371,	376,119,	382,984,	346,503,	321,948,
Add for Unenumerated Imports (say)	45,320,	44,767,	44,227,	40,079,	39,987,
Total Imports	435,691,	420,886,	427,211,	386,582,	361,935,

     * "Silk," inclusive of manufactured silk, " not made up."

EXPORTS.—(United Kingdom.)—**For the Years 1891-90-89-88-87.**—*Declared Real Value, at Port of Shipment, of Articles of* BRITISH *and* IRISH *Produce and Manufactures Exported from the United Kingdom.*

[000's omitted.]

BRITISH PRODUCE, &c., EXPORTED.	1891.	1890.	1889.	1888.	1887.
	£	£	£	£	£
MANFRS.—*Textile.* Cotton Manufactures..	60,250,	62,079,	58.826,	60,325,	59,577,
„ Yarn	11,190,	12,352,	11,711,	11,656,	11,379,
Woollen Manufactures	18,452,	20,422,	21,840,	19,991,	20,585,
„ Yarn	3,910,	4,089,	4,342,	4,052,	3,970,
Silk Manufactures	1,745,	2,230,	2,507,	2,666,	2,326,
„ Yarn	515,	478,	509,	388,	439,
Linen Manufactures	5,031,	5,716,	5,777,	5,553,	5,455,
„ Yarn	898,	866,	839,	887,	939,
	101,991,	108,232,	105,851,	105,518,	104,670.
„ *Sewed.* Apparel	5,150,	5,036,	4,977,	4,659,	3,941,
Haberdy. and Mllnry.	1,999,	2,113,	2,251,	2,322,	2,349,
	7,149,	7,149,	7,228,	6,981,	6,290,
METALS, &c. Hardware	2,525,	2,765,	2,988,	3,167,	2,920,
Machinery	15,820,	16,413,	15,255,	12,933,	11,146,
Iron	26,875,	31,582,	29,153,	26,373,	25,000,
Copper and Brass	4,368,	5,058,	3,787,	3,391,	3,005,
Lead and Tin	1,175,	1,315,	1,282,	1,430,	1,147,
Coals and Culm	18,895,	19,020,	14,794,	11,341,	10,176,
	69,658,	76,153,	67,259,	58,635,	53,394,
Ceramic Manafcts. Earthenware and Glass	2,970,	3,113,	3.240,	3,104,	2,911,
Indigenous Mnfrs. Beer and Ale	1,704,	1,877,	1,858,	1,706,	1,678,
and Products. Butter	124,	138,	144,	146,	156,
Cheese	47,	48,	49,	51,	57,
Candles	315,	262,	231,	199,	181,
Salt	595,	653,	539,	487,	525,
Spirits	1,271,	1,250,	1,176,	1,187,	1,018,
	4,056,	4,228,	3,997,	3,726,	3,615,
Various Manufcts. Books, Printed	1,389,	1,325,	1,295,	1,245,	1,175,
Furniture	593,	647,	—	—	—
Leather Manufactures	4,229,	4,279,	2,787,	2,683,	2,460,
Soap	577,	535,	503,	482,	451,
Plate and Watches	391,	404,	438,	392,	329,
Stationery	916,	968,	965,	909,	831,
	8,095,	8,158,	5,988,	5,711,	5,255,
Remainder of Enumerated Articles	37,332,	42,354,	37,230,	33,847,	30,886,
Unenumerated Articles	16,021,	14,156,	17,299,	16,212,	14,377,
TOTAL EXPORTS	247,272,	263,543,	248,092,	233,734,	221,198,

Note.—This and the three preceding tables are condensed from the December numbers of the Accounts relating to Trade and Navigation of the United Kingdom.

PPING.—(United Kingdom.)—*Account of Tonnage of Vessels Entered and leared with Cargoes, from and to Various Countries, during the* Years *ended ecember,* 1891-90-89.

Countries from whence Entered and to which Cleared.	Total British and Foreign.					
	1891.		1890.		1889.	
	Entered.	Cleared.	Entered.	Cleared.	Entered.	Cleared.
	Tons.	Tons.	Tons.	Tons.	Tons.	Tons.
OREIGN COUNTRIES.						
ia { Northern ports	1,478,096	1,143,145	1,508,054	1,153,659	1,787,349	1,243,619
{ Southern „	797,101	251,574	889,262	211,719	930,603	204,132
en	1,556,485	1,270,064	1,542,865	1,246,573	1,592,338	1,200,601
ay	1,171,293	899,575	1,159,981	803,112	1,152,634	742,419
lark................................	376,442	1,086,421	365,928	1,018,471	348,498	1,064,859
any	1,974,764	3,782,367	1,944,907	3,485,666	1,982,872	3,512,456
and	1,790,742	1,902,070	1,836,907	1,803,281	1,872,415	1,827,850
ium	1,454,371	1,474,902	1,495,715	1,461,290	1,369,572	1,197,079
ce................................	2,191,863	4,028,542	2,126,373	3,961,517	2,122,184	3,533,130
n	2,232,083	1,421,538	2,891,455	1,392,799	2,626,536	1,270,798
ugal ....:	133,225	446,683	153,176	457,498	152,486	458,336
....	237,467	2,232,207	261,726	2,417,396	273,479	2,317,742
rian territories	47,975	97,991	46,136	72,344	66,112	79,941
ce................................	108,735	155,947	110,933	153,911	91,318	140,884
nania	374,408	175,677	376,096	122,386	268,544	86,904
ey	283,610	341,617	278,161	406,047	298,528	446,463
t	447,304	976,001	350,387	915,743	300,719	912,627
ed States of America ...	5,255,570	3,618,191	5,544,836	3,349,880	5,212,581	3,228,754
ico, Foreign West } dies, and Central } nerica ....}	73,880	392,094	91,152	441,494	83,165	406,560
il	130,554	893,276	174,606	764,909	196,502	765,749
....	19,448	43,296	46,806	56,015	41,679	44,998
....	267,462	369,133	184,009	403,088	205,353	287,716
a	152,623	90,663	127,956	84,322	140,525	57,627
r countries	1,111,401	1,485,255	1,255,822	1,984,192	1,074,077	2,367,328
tal, Foreign Countries	23,666,987	28,578,229	24,713,249	28,169,312	24,190,069	27,398,572
RITISH POSSESSIONS.						
h American Colonies	1,320,818	816,683	1,444,170	814,903	1,446,770	812,212
Indies, including } ylon, Singapore, and } auritius ....}	1,519,890	1,879,419	1,297,783	1,894,557	1,458,661	1,830,438
ralia and New Zealand	747,069	1,054,173	716,714	973,701	597,612	954,087
t Indies	97,341	269,790	112,839	283,518	140,420	279,053
nel Islands....................	321,223	50,235	354,151	276,095	334,880	240,709
r possessions	427,456	1,364,911	341,194	1,444,997	349,408	1,533,810
tal, British Possessions	4,433,797	5,635,211	4,266,851	5,687,771	4,327,751	5,650,309
L FOREIGN COUNTRIES BRITISH POSSESSIONS.						
lve Months { 1891	28,100,784	34,213,440	—	—	—	—
ended { '90.......	—	—	28,980,100	33,857,083	—	—
ecember, { '89........	—	—	—	—	28,517,820	33,048,881

GOLD AND SILVER BULLION AND SPECIE. —(United Kingdom.)
—*Declared Real Value of*, IMPORTED AND EXPORTED *for the Years* 1891-90-89.

[000's omitted.]

Countries.	1891.		1890.		1889.	
	Gold.	Silver.	Gold.	Silver.	Gold.	Silver.
Imported from—	£	£	£	£	£	£
Australia	4,280,	144,	2,097,	197,	4,169,	28,
S. America, Brazil, Mexico, W. Indies }	4,535,	2,171,	4,412,	2,527,	2,801,	2,146,
United States	7,675,	3,984,	2,594,	4,058,	2,569,	3,976,
	16,490,	6,299,	9,103,	6,782,	9,539,	6,150,
France	1,637,	1,527,	4,848,	2,022,	1,673,	2,281,
Germany, Holland, Belg., and Sweden }	920,	1,253,	3,979,	1,122,	2,895,	388,
Portugal, Spain, and Gibraltar }	6,454,	66,	1,875,	134,	64,	164,
Malta and Egypt	41,	28,	515,	187,	676,	150,
China, with Hong Kong and Japan }	1,141,	3,	582,	56,	658,	—
West Coast of Africa	178,	35,	151,	29,	170,	27,
All other Countries	3,364,	105,	2,515,	54,	2,011,	25,
Totals Imported	30,275,	9,316,	23,568,	10,386,	17,686,	9,185,
Exported to—						
France	5,539,	761,	813,	458,	1,692,	126,
Germany, Holland, Belg. & Sweden }	7,841,	405,	1,881,	154,	998,	47,
Portugal, Spain, and Gibraltar }	1,095,	4,036,	4,189,	660,	2,394,	51,
	14,475,	5,202,	6,883,	1,272,	5,079,	224,
B. India, China, Hong Kong and Japan }	1,500,	7,082,	2,802,	8,456,	1,669,	9,621,
United States	3,163,	9,	1,012,	629,	10,	31,
South Africa	—	11,	750,	61,	2,891,	242,
S. America, Brazil, Mexico, W. Indies }	2,658,	80,	1,855,	151,	4,097,	322,
All other Countries	2,432,	731,	1,005,	321,	1,209,	226,
Totals Exported	24,228,	13,115,	14,307,	10,890,	14,455,	10,666,
Excess of imports	6,047,	—	9,261,	—	3,231,	—
„ exports	—	3,799,	—	504,	—	1,481,

BRITISH CORN.—*Gazette Average Prices* (ENGLAND AND WALES), *Weekly for 1891.*

Weeks ended on Saturday.	Wheat.		Barley.		Oats.		Weeks ended on Saturday.	Wheat.		Barley.		Oats.	
1891.	s.	d.	s.	d.	s.	d.	**1891.**	s.	d.	s.	d.	s.	d.
Jan. 3	32	7	28	5	17	9	July 4	38	9	26	9	21	1
„ 10	32	8	28	5	17	6	„ 11	38	7	26	2	20	11
„ 17	32	9	28	6	17	9	„ 18	38	3	26	1	21	6
„ 24	32	11	28	6	18	–	„ 25	38	6	25	7	21	9
„ 31	32	8	28	10	18	–							
							Aug. 1	38	9	26	6	21	5
Feb. 7	32	5	28	5	18	–	„ 8	39	4	26	4	21	2
„ 14	32	3	28	–	18	–	„ 15	39	8	24	4	21	4
„ 21	32	3	27	9	18	–	„ 22	40	3	26	8	21	3
„ 28	32	4	27	5	18	2	„ 29	40	11	27	7	21	9
March 7	32	7	27	7	18	5	Sept. 5	41	8	29	3	21	8
„ 14	33	2	27	9	18	6	„ 12	41	2	28	11	21	1
„ 21	34	5	27	5	18	6	„ 19	36	5	28	1	19	1
„ 28	35	3	27	11	18	6	„ 26	34	5	28	–	18	10
April 4	36	5	27	10	18	11	Oct. 3	34	4	28	10	18	5
„ 11	37	9	27	4	19	3	„ 10	34	10	28	11	18	7
„ 18	39	–	27	9	19	6	„ 17	34	9	29	6	18	10
„ 25	40	1	27	11	20	3	„ 24	35	2	29	11	18	8
							„ 31	35	11	30	7	19	5
May 2	41	1	28	1	20	7							
„ 9	41	4	28	9	21	1	Nov. 7	36	7	30	11	20	6
„ 16	39	11	27	11	20	9	„ 14	37	2	30	11	21	4
„ 23	39	6	27	1	20	11	„ 21	38	9	31	3	22	4
„ 30	40	1	26	9	21	1	„ 28	39	1	30	11	22	4
June 6	40	5	28	3	21	1	Dec. 5	38	11	30	9	22	2
„ 13	40	2	27	2	21	3	„ 12	37	10	30	1	21	7
„ 20	39	6	26	6	21	2	„ 19	36	10	29	6	21	4
„ 27	39	–	28	3	21	–	„ 26	36	6	29	4	20	9

BRITISH CORN.—*Gazette Average Prices* (ENGLAND AND WALES), *Summary of, for 1891, with those for 1890, added for Comparison.*

Average for	Per Imperial Quarter, 1891.						Per Imperial Quarter, 1890.					
	Wheat.		Barley.		Oats.		Wheat.		Barley.		Oats.	
	s.	d.	s.	d.	s.	d.	s.	d.	s.	d.	s.	d.
January	32	8	28	6	17	9	30	1	31	6	18	4
February	32	3	27	10	18	—	29	9	31	8	18	6
March	33	10	27	8	18	5	29	9	30	6	18	6
First quarter	32	11	28	—	18	1	29	10	31	3	18	5
April	38	3	27	8	19	5	29	10	29	8	18	4
May	40	4	27	8	21	10	32	2	28	1	19	4
June	39	9	27	6	21	1	32	8	25	4	19	9
Second quarter	39	5	27	7	20	9	31	9	27	8	19	2
July	38	6	26	1	21	3	33	8	24	1	19	7
August	39	9	26	2	21	4	36	1	26	1	20	—
September	38	5	28	6	20	2	32	11	30	2	18	3
Third quarter	38	11	26	11	20	11	34	3	26	9	19	3
October	35	—	29	6	18	9	30	11	29	6	17	4
November	37	10	31	—	21	7	32	3	29	2	17	5
December	37	6	29	11	21	5	32	3	28	6	17	9
Fourth quarter	36	9	30	2	20	7	31	10	29	1	17	6
THE YEAR	37	—	28	2	20	1	31	11	28	8	18	7

REVENUE OF THE UNITED KINGDOM.

Net Produce in QUARTERS *and* YEARS *ended 31st* DEC., 1891-90-89-88.

[000's omitted.]

QUARTERS, ended 31st Dec.	1891.	1890.	1891.		Corresponding Quarters.	
			Less.	More.	1889.	1888.
	£	£	£	£	£	£
Customs	5,497,*	5,422,	—	75,	5,879,	5,516,
Excise	7,342,*	7,120,	—	222,	7,015,	7,870,
Stamps	3,200,*	3,360,	160,	—	3,480,	2,960,
Taxes	25,	30,	5,	—	40,	35,
Post Office	2,560,	2,490,	—	70,	2,390,	2,360,
Telegraph Service	645,	615,	—	30,	590,	515,
	19,269,	19,037,	165,	397,	19,394,	19,256,
Property Tax	1,110,	1,180,	70,	—	1,110,	1,010,
	20,379,	20,217,	235,	397,	20,504,	20,266,
Crown Lands	160,	160,	—	—	160,	160,
Interest on Advances	111,	211,	100,	—	113,	114,
Miscellaneous............	914,	656,	—	258,	801,	727,
Totals	21,564,	21,244,	335,	655,	21,578,	21,267,
			NET INCR. £390,			

YEARS, ended 31st Dec.	1891.	1890.	1891.		Corresponding Years.	
			Less.	More.	1889.	1888.
	£	£	£	£	£	£
Customs	19,587,*	19,816,	229,	—	20,423,	19,927,
Excise	24,710,*	25,335,	625,	—	24,625,	25,660,
Stamps	12,885,*	13,580,	695,	—	12,770,	13,130,
Taxes	2,420,	2,975,	555,	—	2,975,	2,945,
Post Office	10,030,	9,670,	—	360,	9,460,	8,890,
Telegraph Service	2,450,	2,425,	—	25,	2,255,	2,040,
	72,082,	73,801,	2,104,	385,	72,508,	72,592,
Property Tax	13,325,	12,870,	—	455,	12,480,	13,695,
	85,407,	86,671,	2,104,	840,	84,988,	86,287,
Crown Lands	430,	430,	—	—	430,	420,
Interest on Advances	222,	348,	126,	—	286,	334,
Miscellaneous............	2,893,	3,079,	186,	—	3,259,	3,132,
Totals	88,952,	90,528,	2,416,	840,	88,963,	90,173,
			NET DECR. £1,576,			

* Exclusive of transfers to local taxation account.

LONDON CLEARING; CIRCULATION, PRIVATE AND PROVINCIAL.

The London Clearing, and the Average Amount of Promissory Notes in Circula ENGLAND *and* WALES *on Saturday in each Week during the Year* 1891; SCOTLAND *and* IRELAND, *at the Dates, as under.*

[0,000's omitted.]

	ENGLAND AND WALES.				SCOTLAND.					
DATES. Saturday.	London: Cleared in each Week on the preceding Wednesday.	Private Banks. (Fixed Issues, 2,73).	Joint Stock Banks. (Fixed Issues, 2,02).	TOTAL. (Fixed Issues, 4,75).	Average for Four Weeks ending	£5 and upwards.	Under £5.	TOTAL. (Fixed Issues, 2,68).	£5 and upwards	Under £5.
1891.	£	£	£	£	1891.	£	£	£	£	£
Jan. 3......	125,62	1,07	1,25	2,32	Jan. 3...	1,88	4,56	6,44	3,96	3,14
„ 10......	151,74	1,09	1,27	2,36						
„ 17......	163,68	1,06	1,26	2,32						
„ 24......	141,69	1,04	1,23	2,27						
„ 31... ..	144	1,03	1,22	2,25	„ 31...	1,77	4,21	5,98	3,82	3,00
Feb. 7......	142,16	1,02	1,23	2,25						
„ 14......	124,86	1,00	1,23	2,23						
„ 21......	173,99	1,00	1,23	2,22						
„ 28......	124,37	1,00	1,21	2,21	Feb. 28...	1,74	4,19	5,93	3,77	2,89
Mar. 7......	168,23	1,01	1,23	2,24						
„ 14......	118,77	1,01	1,23	2,24						
„ 21......	153,36	1,01	1,23	2,24						
„ 28......	146,00	1,03	1,27	2,30	Mar. 28...	1,70	4,19	5,89	3,77	2,80
April 4......	100,65	1,07	1,31	2,38						
„ 11......	134,12	1,08	1,31	2,39						
„ 18......	156,18	1,07	1,29	2,36						
„ 25......	126,28	1,06	1,28	2,34	April 25...	1,74	4,33	6,07	3,81	2,82
May 2......	153,17	1,06	1,30	2,36						
„ 9......	137,77	1,06	1,32	2,38						
„ 16......	146,56	1,06	1,33	2,39						
„ 23......	117,74	1,04	1,30	2,34	May 23...	2,11	4,70	6,81	3,83	2,78
„ 30......	106,22	1,02	1,27	2,29						
June 6......	145,14	1,02	1,26	2,28						
„ 13......	110,88	1,00	1,23	2,23						
„ 20......	139,00	99	1,21	2,20	June 20...	2,11	4,68	6,79	3,54	2,62
„ 27......	108,40	99	1,21	2,20						
July 4......	158,45	1,01	1,23	2,24						
„ 11......	134,33	1,02	1,23	2,25						
„ 18......	135,37	98	1,21	2,19	July 18...	1,89	4,60	6,49	3,43	2,58
„ 25......	113,89	97	1,19	2,16						
Aug. 1......	103,66	96	1,19	2,15						
„ 8......	124,49	97	1,19	2,16						
„ 15......	107,44	95	1,17	2,12	Aug. 15...	1,85	4,47	6,32	3,43	2,61
„ 22......	135,87	94	1,15	2,09						
„ 29......	101,64	93	1,15	2,08						
Sept. 5......	131,20	93	1,15	2,08						
„ 12......	98,47	92	1,14	2,06	Sept. 12...	1,87	4,50	6,37	3,35	2,61
„ 19......	128,88	92	1,14	2,06						
„ 26......	109,03	94	1,16	2,10						
Oct. 3......	138,61	1,00	1,22	2,22						
„ 10......	132,93	1,04	1,25	2,29	Oct. 10...	1,85	4,58	6,43	3,57	2,80
„ 17......	104,62	1,04	1,27	2,31						
„ 24......	135,52	1,03	1,26	2,29						
„ 31......	109,52	1,03	1,26	2,29						
Nov. 7......	153,21	1,04	1,27	2,31	Nov. 7...	1,94	4,72	6,66	4,02	3,06
„ 14......	109,80	1,02	1,27	2,29						
„ 21......	142,95	1,03	1,28	2,31						
„ 28......	115,21	1,03	1,28	2,31						
Dec. 5......	149,58	1,02	1,23	2,25	Dec. 5...	2,25	4,95	7,20	3,89	3,06
„ 12......	113,68	99	1,22	2,21						
„ 19......	142,55	99	1,22	2,21						
„ 26......	120,18	98	1,22	2,20						

BANK OF ENGLAND.

Pursuant to the Act 7th and 8th Victoria, cap. 32 (1844)

[0,000's omitted.]

Liabilities. Notes Issued.	DATES. (Wednesdays.)	Government Debt.	Notes in Hands of Public. (Col. 1 minus col. 16.)	Minimum Rates of Discount at Bank of England.
£ Mlns.	1891.	£ Mlns.	£ Mlns.	Per cnt. (End of 1889) 5
39,80	Jan. 7	11,02	25,06	7 Jan. 4
40,68	,, 14	11,02	24,67	
40,47	,, 21	11,02	24,22	21 ,, ... 3¼
40,79	,, 28	11,02	24,00	28 ,, ... 3
40,81	Feb. 4	11,02	24,33	
39,15	,, 11		24,06	
38,38	,, 18		23,86	
38,73	,, 25		23,62	
38,56	Mar. 4		24,22	
38,68	,, 11		23,95	
38,77	,, 18		23,81	
38,58	,, 25		24,70	
37,84	April 1		24,87	
37,41	,, 8		25,00	
36,74	,, 15		24,76	15 April...... 3¼
37,23	,, 22		24,55	
36,66	,, 29		24,86	
36,17	May 6		25,03	6 May 4
36,39	,, 13		24,95	13 ,, ... 5
37,27	,, 20		24,58	
39,57	,, 27		24,64	
41,60	June 3		25,02	3 June...... 4
42,40	,, 10		24,80	
43,17	,, 17		24,85	17 ,, ... 3
43,52	,, 24		25,46	
43 74	July 1		26,46	1 July 2½
42,85	,, 8		26,52	
41,87	,, 15		26,46	
43,42	,, 22		26,19	
42,71	,, 29		26,27	
42,66	Aug. 5		26,82	
42,61	,, 12		26,45	
42,43	,, 19		26,21	
42,03	,, 26		25,89	
41,84	Sept. 2		26,07	
42,00	,, 9		25,73	
41,70	,, 16		25,48	
41,17	,, 23		25,29	23 Sept. ... 3
40,59	,, 30		26,23	
39,25	Oct. 7		26,19	
38,64	,, 14		25,87	
38,18	,, 21		25,85	
37,65	,, 28		25,43	28 Oct. 4
37,26	Nov. 4		25,72	
38,24	,, 11		25,42	
38,30	,, 18		25,16	
38,87	,, 25		25,00	
38,98	Dec. 2		25,39	
39,29	,, 9		25,16	9 Dec. 3¼
39,96	,, 16		25,16	
38,87	,, 23		25,63	
38,10	,, 30		25,65	

—WEEKLY RETURN.

for Wednesday in each Week, during the Year 1891.

[0,000's omitted.]

Liabilities					DATES.	Securities	
Capital and Rest		Deposits.		Seven Day and other Bills.	(Wednesdys.)		
Capital.	Rest.	Public.	Private.			Government.	Other.
£ Mlns.	£ Mlns.	£ Mlns.	£ Mlns.	£ Mlns.	1891.	£ Mlns.	£ Mlns.
14,55	3,46	5,03	33,72	,16	Jan. 7	11,24	30,15
14,55	3,47	3,75	33,95	,19	„ 14	9 58	29,53
14,55	3,50	5,96	32,69	,21	„ 21	9,45	30,40
14,55	3,51	7,65	30,77	,21	„ 28	9,45	29,64
14,55	3,54	8,22	29 59	,23	Feb. 4	9,45	29,26
14,55	3,54	9,59	29,20	,23	„ 11	11,45	29,60
14,55	3,57	11,59	28,16	,22	„ 18	12,44	30,03
14,55	3,52	13,03	28,47	,21	„ 25	12,44	31,19
14,55	3,78	12,25	29,81	,21	Mar. 4	11,84	33,39
14,55	3,68	11,78	29,09	,21	„ 11	11,84	32,33
14,55	3,92	12,93	29,06	,23	„ 18	11 84	33,24
14,55	3,93	13,73	29,06	,19	„ 25	11,84	35,19
14,55	3,91	12,67	28,59	,17	April 1	11,84	34,72
14,55	3,11	8,15	30,44	,18	„ 8	11,84	31,72
14,55	3,14	7,71	29 86	,22	„ 15	11,84	30,64
14,55	3,15	8,38	28,84	,19	„ 22	11,84	30,07
14,55	3,14	8,02	28,88	,21	„ 29	11,84	30,54
14,55	3,15	8,08	28,33	,25	May 6	11,84	30,26
14,55	3,18	6,25	30,18	,20	„ 13	9,94	31,97
14,55	3,20	7,15	31,28	,17	„ 20	9,94	32,57
14,55	3,21	6,40	32,98	,19	„ 27	9,94	31,32
14,55	3,17	6,28	33,34	,20	June 3	9,94	29,94
14,55	3,19	6,90	33,62	,20	„ 10	9 94	29,76
14,55	3,20	7,07	34,93	,19	„ 17	9,94	30,56
14,55	3,20	7,03	34,75	,19	„ 24	9,94	30,59
14,55	3,23	6,87	35,17	,18	July 1	9,94	31,81
14,55	3,41	4,20	37,80	,22	„ 8	12,42	30,77
14,55	3,42	3,50	37,15	,22	„ 15	12,42	30,46
14,55	3,44	4,12	36,79	,18	„ 22	12,12	29,69
14,55	3,45	4,36	35,54	,18	„ 29	11,84	28,82
14,55	3,50	3,32	34,98	,19	Aug. 5	11,84	28,39
14,55	3,52	3,82	34,66	,20	„ 12	11,84	28,30
14,55	3,54	4,20	33,25	,19	„ 19	10,32	28,39
14,55	3,55	4,84	32,86	,18	„ 26	10,31	28,06
14,55	3,77	4,32	32,40	,20	Sept. 2	10,16	28,36
14,55	3,78	5,29	31,67	,24	„ 9	10,16	28,09
14,55	3,78	4,62	31,86	,19	„ 16	10,16	27,56
14,55	3,80	5,19	31,11	,23	„ 23	10,16	27,96
14,55	3,79	5,44	31,60	,18	„ 30	10,16	30,09
14,55	3,09	4,81	31,22	,27	Oct. 7	12,66	27,36
14,55	3,12	3,62	32,31	,22	„ 14	12,66	27,40
14,55	3,13	5,52	29,97	,18	„ 21	12,36	27,60
14,55	3,13	4,49	29,70	,19	„ 28	12,26	26,56
14,55	3,13	4,33	29,78	,19	Nov. 4	12,26	27,12
14,55	3,14	4,36	29,66	,18	„ 11	11,86	26,06
14,55	3,15	4,90	27,72	,17	„ 18	10,15	25,97
14,55	3,15	4,91	28,58	,17	„ 25	9,45	26,66
14,55	3,11	5,22	30,28	,20	Dec. 2	10,16	28,40
14,55	3,13	5,39	29,67	,17	„ 9	10,16	27,58
14,55	3,14	5,48	30,05	,17	„ 16	10,16	27,53
14,55	3,14	5,71	29,08	,20	„ 23	10,16	28,51
14,55	3,17	5,40	30,65	,17	„ 30	10,16	30,68

FOREIGN EXCHANGES.—*Quotations as under*, LONDON *on Paris, Hamburg, and Calcutta;—and New York, Calcutta, and Hong Kong, on* LONDON, *for* **1891.**

1	2	3	4		5	6	7		8		9
			Calcutta.						Price per Ounce.		
DATES. (Thursdays)	London on Paris. 3 m. d.	London on Hamburg 3 m. d.	London on Calcutta.		Indian Council Bills. Minimum Price per Rupee.	New York on London. 60 d. s.	Hong Kong on London. 4 m. d.		Gold Bars (Fine).		Standard Silver in Bars.
1891.			*s.*	*d.*	*d.*	Per cnt.	*s.*	*d.*	*s.*	*d.*	*d.*
Jan. 15	25·41½	20·55	1	6⅛	18 7/16	4·84½	3	5¾	77	9½	48¾
„ 29	25·36¼	20·50	1	6 3/16	18¼	4·85	3	5⅝	77	10½	47¾
Feb. 12	25·37½	20·52	1	5⅜	17⅞	4·86	3	3⅛	77	10½	46½
„ 26	25·42½	20·53	1	5	17 1/16	4·85	3	2⅞	77	10	44¼
Mar. 12	25·45	20·55	1	5	17 7/32	4·85¼	3	3	77	10	45 1/16
„ 26	25·41¼	20·53	1	5	17 1/16	4·86	3	2¼	77	9½	44¾
Apl. 9	25·40	20·58	1	5⅛	17⅛	4·86	3	2⅜	77	9½	44¾
„ 23	25·46¼	20·56	1	4 15/16	16¾	4·85	3	2	77	9	44½
May 7	25·47½	20·68	1	5 1/32	16 15/16	4·84¾	3	2½	77	9	44½
„ 21	25·60	20·69	1	4 11/16	16¾	4·83½	3	2⅛	77	9	44 9/16
June 4	25·50	20·65	1	4⅞	16 15/16	4·84¾	3	2¼	77	9½	44 5/16
„ 18	25·46¼	20·60	1	4¾	16⅞	4·85½	3	2½	77	9½	44 9/16
July 2	25·45	20·56	1	5 3/16	17⅜	4·85½	3	2¾	77	9	45¾
„ 16	25·40	20·54	1	5⅜	17 9/16	4·84½	3	3⅜	77	9½	46
Aug. 6	25·45	20·53	1	5 3/16	17 13/32	4·83¾	3	3	77	10½	45½
„ 20	25·45	20·53	1	5 3/16	17 9/32	4·83¾	3	2¾	77	11	45 5/16
Sept. 3	25·46¼	20·52	1	5⅛	17 7/32	4·81¾	3	2¾	77	11	45 1/16
„ 17	25·50	20·54	1	5⅛	17 3/32	4·81¼	3	2⅜	77	10½	44⅞
Oct. 8	25·50	20·55	1	4 13/16	16 29/32	4·79¾	3	2	77	11½	44 13/16
„ 22	25·47½	20·54	1	4 13/16	16 15/16	4·80¾	3	2	77	11	44½
Nov. 5	25·41¼	20·55	1	4¾	16¾	4·80¾	3	1⅝	77	10¼	43⅞
„ 19	25·38¾	20·55	1	4⅝	16 23/32	4·81	3	1 9/16	77	10¾	43 3/16
Dec. 10	25·37½	20·51	1	4 9/16	16⅝	4·81¾	3	1½	77	10¾	43⅝
„ 24	25·38¾	20·51	1	4⅝	16⅝	4·81¾	3	1⅜	77	11	43¾

XIV.—*Additions to the Library.*

*Additions to the Library during the Quarter ended 15th March, 1892,
arranged alphabetically under the following heads:—*(a) *Foreign
Countries;* (b) *India and Colonial Possessions;* (c) *United Kingdom
and its Divisions;* (d) *Authors, &c.;* (e) *Societies, &c.* (*British*);
(f) *Periodicals, &c.* (*British*).

Donations.	By whom Presented.
(a) Foreign Countries.	
Argentine Republic—	
Comercio exterior. Datos trimestrales del, Año 1891. No. 71	The National Department of Statistics
Higiene. Anales del Departamento Nacional de Higiene, Año I. Oct.—Dec., 1891	The Department
Buenos Ayres. Boletin mensual de Estadistica Municipal. Oct., Nov., 1891	The Municipal Statistical Bureau
Instituto Geografico Argentino. Boletin del, Tomo xii, Cuadernos 1—10, 4 parts, 8vo., 1891-92....	The Institute
Austria and Hungary—	
Eisenbahn-Statistik. Hauptergebnisse der österreich-ischen, im Jahre 1890. 8vo......	The Statistical Department, Ministry of Commerce.
Post- und Telegraphenwesens. Statistik des österreichischen, im Jahre 1890. Mit einer statistischen Uebersicht über die Post und den Telegraphen in Europa. 8vo.	The Statistical Department, Ministry of Commerce.
Sanitätswesens, Statistik des, für 1888......	The Central Statistical Commission
Sparcassen, Statistik der, für 1889. 4to.	The Central Statistical Commission
Statistische Monatschrift. Oct., 1891, Jan., 1892......	The Central Statistical Commission
Waaren-Ausfuhr aus dem allgemeinen österreichisch-ungarischen Zollgebiete im Jahre 1890. 4to.	The Central Statistical Commission
Statistische Uebersichten betreffend den Auswärtigen Handel des Zollgebiets. Oct.—Dec., 1891	The Statistical Department, Ministry of Commerce
Zollgebiete. Werthe für die Mengeneinheiten der im Jahre 1890, im österreichisch-ungarischen, ein- und ausgeführten Waaren. 8vo.	The Statistical Department, Ministry of Commerce
Hungary—	
Magyarorszag Aruforgalma Ausztrival es mas Orszagokkal. (Monthly Trade Returns.) July,1891	The Royal Hungarian Statistical Bureau
Statistisches Jahrbuch für Ungarn, 1888, Heft 2. Sanitätswesen. 1889, Heft 5, Handelsverkehr. 1890, Heft 3, Landwirthschaft	The Royal Hungarian Statistical Bureau
Ungarns Waarenverkehr mit Oesterreich und anderen Ländern für das Halbjahr vom Monate Jänner bis Ende Juni, 1891 ; xi Jahrgang	The Royal Hungarian Statistical Bureau
Prague. Bulletin hebdomadaire de la Ville de Prague et des Communes-faubourgs. (Current numbers)....	The Statistical Bureau
Belgium—	
Annales des Travaux Publics de Belgique. Tome xlix, cahier 2 (contains "Statistique des mines, minières, carrières, &c., pour 1890"). Diagram, 8vo. 1891....	The Administration of Mines
Mouvement, Commercial avec les Pays Etrangers. Dec.—Feb., 1891-92	The Bureau of General Statistics
Brussels. Bulletin hebdomadaire de Statistique Démographique et Médicale. (Current numbers)....	Dr. E. Janssens
Hasselt. Exposé de la situation administrative de la Ville. Exercice 1890-91. 8vo.	The Burgomaster

Donations—Contd.

Donations.	By whom Presented.
(a) Foreign Countries—*Contd.*	
China. Customs Gazette, No. 91. July—Sept., 1891. 4to.	Sir Robert Hart, G.C.M.G.
Denmark—	
Importation et Exportation, production d'eau-de-vie et de sucre de betteraves en 1890. 4to.	The Royal Danish Statistical Bureau
Nationalökonomisk Tidskrift, 1892. Hefte 1, 2.............	The Danish Political Economy Society
Egypt—	
Chemins de Fer, Télégraphes et Port d'Alexandrie. Rapports du Conseil d'Administration sur les Exercices 1879, 1880, 1883-90. 10 vols.. sm. 4to.....	W. F. Halton, Esq.
Daira Sanieh. Rapports par le Conseil de Direction de la, sur la situation des années 1885, 1889, et 1890. 3 vols., 4to.	R. Hamilton Lang, Esq., C.M.G.
Dette Publique. Comptes Rendus des Travaux de la Commission de la, pendant 1889 et 1890. 2 vols., 8vo.	Alonzo Money, Esq., C.B.
Domaines de l'Etat. Rapports présentés par les Commissaires des Domaines, à l'appui des Comptes définitifs des recettes et des dépenses des Exercices 1883, 1887, 1888, et 1889 et des comptes provisoires des Exercices 1884, 1888, 1889, et 1890. 4 vols., 4to.	M. Ed. Bouteron
Enseignement Public. Exposé des Réformes effectuées pendant 1885 ou en cours d'éxecution dans l'. 8vo.	
Enseignement Public en Egypte. 4ᵉ et 5ᵉ Rapports, années 1888 et 1889. 2 vols., 8vo.	Yacoub Artin Pacha
Public Works Ministry. Irrigation. Reports of the Administration of the Department of, for 1889 and 1890. 2 vols., diagrams, 8vo.	Colonel Scott Moncrieff
Sanitaires et d'Hygiène Publique. Administration des Services, Bureau de Statistique. Rapport annuel, 1889. Diagrams, 4to.	Dr. Engel
Services Sanitaires, &c. Bulletin hebdomadaire. (Current numbers)..	The Department
Suez. Compagnie Universelle du Canal Maritime de, Rapport et situation financière, Exercice 1890. 4to.	The Company
France—	
Agriculture. Bulletin du Ministère de l'. 10ᵉ année, Nos. 7 et 8. 11ᵉ année, No. 1. 8vo. 1891-92....	The Ministry of Agriculture
Annuaire Statistique de la France. VIIᵉ année, 1884. 8vo.	M. Vannacque
Bulletin Consulaire Français, Aug., 1890—Oct., 1891. 15 parts, 8vo.	The Editor, British Trade Journal
Commerce de la France. Documents Statistiques sur le, Aug.—Nov., 1888-90. 4 parts, 8vo.	
Commerce de la France avec ses Colonies et les Puissances Etrangères. Tableaux généraux pour les années 1881, 1884, 1885, 1886, 1888, 1889, et 1890. 7 vols., la. 4to.............	The Director-General of Customs
Finances, Ministère des, Bulletin de Statistique et de Législation comparée. Dec., 1891, Jan., 1892. Table des matières, 1887-91	The Ministry of Finance

Donations—Contd.

Donations.	By whom Presented.
(a) Foreign Countries—*Contd.*	
France—*Contd.*	
Justice Criminelle et Justice Civile et Commerciale. Comptes généraux de l'Administration de la, pendant 1886. 2 vols., 4to	M. Yvernès
Travaux Publics. Ministère des—	
Album de Statistique Graphique de 1890-91. Diagram-maps, 4to.	
Bulletin de Statistique et Législation comparée. Oct., Nov., 1891	The Ministry of Public Works
Industrie Minérale et Appareils à vapeur en France et en Algérie. Statistique pour 1890, avec un Appendice concernant la Statistique minérale internationale. Diagram-map, 4to.	
L'Economiste Français. (Current weekly numbers)	The Editor
Le Monde Economique. (Current weekly numbers)	,,
Polybiblion. Revue Bibliographique Universelle—	
Partie Littéraire. Dec.—Feb., 1891-92	
Partie Technique. Dec.—Feb., 1891-92	
Le Rentier. Journal Financier Politique. (Current numbers)	,,
Journal des Economistes—	
Jan., 1892. Le marché financier de 1891 : *A. Raffalovich.* Les marines marchandes et la Protection : *D. Bellet*	
Feb. La Participation aux Bénéfices: *M. Block.* Mouvement Agricole : *G. Fouquet*	,,
Revue d'Economie Politique—	
Dec., 1891. Organisation de la grande Industrie en Autriche : *E. Schwiedland.* Montesquieu économiste : *J. Oczapowski*	
Jan., 1892. Les nouvelles compagnies de colonisation privilégiées : *P. Cauwès.* Origines de l'Economie Politique : *A. de Miaskowski.* Législation sur les Fabriques en Angleterre : *Miss V. Jeans.* La politique sociale de la Belgique : *C. Favre.* Emile de Laveleye : *E. Mahaim*	The Publishers
Ecole Libre des Sciences Politiques, Annales. Jan., 1892. Les Finances de la guerre de 1796 à 1815 : *S. de la Rupelle.* La France économique vers le milieu du XVIIe Siècle : *H. Pigeonneau*	The Institution
Société de Statistique de Paris, Journal—	
Dec., 1891. Division de la propriété en France, avant et après 1789 : *M. Gimel.* Les brevets d'invention : *T. Loua*	
Jan., 1892. La Disette en Russie : *E. Levasseur.* Nos Etudiants : *T. Loua.* Les Statistiques Judiciaires : *A. de Malarce*	The Society
Feb. Le denombrement de 1891 : *V. Turquan.* Recrutement de l'armée française en 1890 : *T. Loua.* Les Incendies à Paris en 1890 : *V. Miquel*	
Germany—	
Deutsches Handels-Archiv. Sept., 1890—Nov., 1891. 16 parts, 4to.	The Editor, British Trade Journal

Donations—Contd.

Donations.	By whom Presented.
(a) Foreign Countries—*Contd.*	
Germany—*Contd.*	
Monatshefte zur Statistik des Deutschen Reichs. Nov., Dec., 1891	
Seeschifffahrt. Statistik der, für 1890. Zweite Abtheilung. 4to.	The Imperial Statistical Bureau
Verkehr auf den deutschen Wasserstrassen im Jahre 1890. 4to.	
Waarenverkehr des deutschen Zollgebiets mit dem Auslande im Jahre 1890. Theil 2. 4to.	
Prussia. Preussische Statistik—	
114. Die Sterblichkeit nach Todesursachen und Altersklassen der Gestorbenen, sowie die Selbstmorde und die tödtlichen Verunglückungen in 1889. Fol.	The Royal Prussian Statistical Bureau
115. Die Ergebnisse der Ermittelung des Ernteertrages für 1890. Maps, fol.	
Berlin—	
Bevölkerungs-und Wohnungs-Aufnahme vom 1 Dec., 1885, in der Stadt Berlin. Heft 2. 4to.....	
Volkszählung vom 1 Dec., 1890. Einstweilige Ergebnisse der, in der Stadt Berlin. Diagram, map, 8vo.	The Statistical Bureau of Berlin
Geburts- und Sterblichkeits-Verhaeltnisse der Stadt Berlin. Jahr 1891. Sheet	
Eheschliessungen, Geburten, Sterbefälle und Witterung. (Current weekly numbers)	
FRANKFORT. Jahresbericht über die Verwaltung des Medicinalwesens, die Kranken-Anstalten und die œffentlichen Gesundheitsverhaeltnisse der Stadt. Jahrgang 1890. 8vo.	The Statistical Bureau of Frankfort
Archiv für Soziale Gesetzgebung und Statistik. Band iv, Heft 4, 1891. Studien zur Fortbildung des Arbeitsverhältnisses : *H. Herkner.* Die Thätigkeit der preussischen Ortspolizeibehörden als Organe der Gewerbeaufsicht : *K. Frankenstein.* Die Gesetzgebung zu Gunsten der Bergarbeiter in Deutschland und Oesterreich : *L. Verkauf.*...............	The Editor
Jahrbücher für Nationalökonomie und Statistik ... Dritte Folge. Band iii, Heft 1. 8vo. Jena, 1892. (Selection from Contents.) Die Entwickelung der britischen Landwirthschaft unter dem Druck ausländischer Konkurrenz : *Dr. Paasche.* Die Bedeutung der Gilden für die Entstehung der deutschen Stadtverfassung : *G. von Below*......................	Gustav Fischer, the Publisher
Greece. Population. Recensement général à la date 15—16 Avril, 1889. 2ᵉ partie. Tableaux. 18 + 167 pp. 4to. Athènes, 1890	The Statistical Bureau
Italy—	
Annali di Agricoltura, 1891—	
187. Concorso a premi per la preparazione de vini da pasto. Plates......................	The Director-General of Agriculture
188. Atti della Commissione consultiva per la Pesca, Sessione 1891	

Donations.	By whom Presented.
(a) Foreign Countries—*Contd.*	
Italy—*Contd.*	
Annali di Agricoltura, 1891—*Contd.*	
189. Atti della Commissione consultiva per la Fillossera. Map	The Director-General of Agriculture
Annali di Statistica. Statistica Industriale. Fasc. 35. Provincia di Napoli. Map	
Bollettino di Legislazione e Statistica Doganale. Nov.—Dec., 1891	
Bollettino del Ministero degli Affari Esteri. Nov., 1891	
Bollettino mensile delle situazioni dei Conti degli Istituti d' Emissione. Oct.—Dec., 1891	The Director-General, Statistical Department of the State
Bollettino di Notizie sul Credito e la Previdenza. Oct., Nov., 1891	
Bollettino settimanale dei Prezzi di alcuni dei principali Prodotti Agraria e del Pane. (Current weekly numbers)	
Bollettino Sanitario, Direzione della Sanita Pubblica. Oct., Nov., 1891	
Sanita. La ricerca del Gittajone... Plate, la. 8vo. 1892	
Statistica del commercio speciale di Importazione e di Esportazione. Nov., 1891	
L'Economista. (Current weekly numbers.) 1892	The Editor
Giornale degli Economisti—	
Jan. 1892. Di un errore del Cournot nel trattare l' economia politica colle matematica: *V. Pareto.* La specie e le razze	
Feb. Prime linee di una teoria generale dell' assicurazione: *F. Sartori.* La nuova tariffa doganale italiana: *A. de Marco.* Il totalizzatore applicato agli indici del movimento economico: *E. Benini*	"
Mexico—	
Hacienda y Credito Publico. Memoria de, corre-spondiente al año economico de 1888-89. La. 8vo.	The Editor, British Trade Journal
Noticias de la amonedacion practicada en las Casas de Moneda de la Republica en Julio, Agosto, Septiembre, y en el primer trimestre del año fiscal 1891-92. Sheets. 1891	The Statistical Bureau
Netherlands—	
Statistiek der geboorten, en der sterfte naar den leeftijd en de oorzaken van den dood in Nederland over July—Sept., 1891. Sheets	The Netherlands Legation
Statistiek van den in-, uit-, en doorroer over het Jaar 1888, 1889, and 1890. 6 vols., fol.	Dr. Verkerk Pistorius
Bijdragen van het Statistisch Instituut. No. 3. 1891. Zevende Jaargang. (Selection from Contents.) Arbeidersbudgets (met Beilage en 80 Staten)	The Institute
Paraguay. Revue du Paraguay. Sept.—Nov., 1891	The Statistical Bureau
Roumania. Population. Mouvement de la, de Roumanie pendant 1889. 4to.	The Ministry of Agriculture, &c.

Donations—Contd.

Donations.	By whom Presented.
(a) Foreign Countries—*Contd.*	
Russia—	
Agricultural Year-Book 'for 1891. Part 2. (In Russian.) Diagram-maps, 8vo. '	The Department of Agriculture
Agriculture. Résultats généraux de la récolte en Russie, 1891. Diagram-maps, sm. 4to.	The Central Statistical Committee
Aperçu du Commerce Extérieur de la Russie par les Frontières d'Europe et d'Asie en 1890. (In Russian.) Fol.	
Commerce Extérieur de la Russie par la frontière d'Europe et la côte caucasienne de la Mer Noire. Sept.—Nov., 1891	The Statistical Bureau, Customs Department
Commerce Extérieur de la Russie. Tableaux comparatifs, année 1890. (In Russian.) Fol...............	
Diagram-map showing the condition of Winter Crops, Nov., 1891. Sheet	
Diagram-maps showing prices of Rye and Oats in European Russia on 1st Nov., 1st Dec., 1891, and 1st Jan., 1892. Sheets	The Department of Assessed Taxes
Finance. Règlement définitif du Budget de l'Empire pour l'Exercice 1890. Rapport présenté au Conseil de l'Empire par le Contrôleur de l'Empire. 8vo.	The Controller
Journal of the Ministry of Finance. (In Russian.) (Current numbers.) 1891	The Ministry of Finance
Prostitution, La, d'après l'enquête du 1ᵉʳ (13) Août, 1889. 8vo. 1891	The Central Statistical Committee
Finland—	
Industri-Statistik, år 1889. Senare delen. Fabriker och Handtverkerier...............	
Jernvägs-Statistik . . . för år 1890. (Railways.) Map and diagram. 8vo.	
Lots-och Fyrinrättningen . . . för år 1889. (Shipwrecks.) 8vo. 1891	Sir R. W. Rawson, K.C.M.G., C.B.
Postsparbanken . . . för 1890. (Post Office Savings Banks.) 8vo.	
Société de Géographie de Finlande. Fennia. 4. Bulletin de la. Maps and plates. 8vo. 1891	The Society
Spain—	
Comercio de Cabotaje. Estadística General del, entre los Puertos de la Península ó Islas Baleares en 1890. Fol.	The Director-General of Indirect Taxation
Comercio Exterior. Resumenes Mensuales de la Estadística del, Nov.—Dec., 1891............... ...	
Comercio Exterior. Resumenes Mensuales de la Estadística del, Nos. 10—24, Sept., 1890—Nov., 1891. 15 parts. 8vo.	The Editor, British Trade Journal
Sociedad Geográfica de Madrid. Boletin. Oct.—Dec., 1891	The Society
Sweden—	
Bidrag till Sveriges Officiela Statistik—	
G. Fångvården, 1890. (Prisons, &c.)...............	The Central Statistical Bureau, Stockholm
L. Statens Jernvägstrafik, 1890. (Railways.)	
M. Postverket, 1890. (Postal.) ·	

Donations—Contd.

Donations.	By whom Presented.
(a) Foreign Countries—*Contd.*	
Sweden—*Contd.*	
Bidrag till Sveriges Officiela Statistik—Contd.	
N. Jordbruk och Boskapsskötsel, 1891. (Agriculture)	
P. Undervisningsväsendet, 1887-88. (Education)	The Central Statistical Bureau, Stockholm
Q. Statens Domäner, 1890. (Forests, &c.)	
S. Allmänna Arbeten, 1890. (Public Works)	
Switzerland—	
Bulletin hebdomadaire des mariages, naissances et des décès dans les Villes de la Suisse. (Current numbers.) 8vo.	The Federal Statistical Bureau
Population. Mouvement de la, en Suisse pendant 1890. 4to. Berne, 1891	
Aargau—	
Aargauische Statistische Mittheilungen für 1891. 1. Die aarg. Kreditinstitute im Rechnungsjahre 1889-90. 2. Landwirthschafts-Statistik pro 1890. Fol.	
Bodenwerth, Bodenvertheilung, Bodenverschuldung, und Bodenbesteuerung im Aargau. Eine steuerstatistische Studie. 8vo.	The Statistical Bureau
Die Verwaltung und Buchführung bei kleineren Sparkassen. 8vo.	
Schweizerischen Handels- und Industrie - Verein. Bericht über Handel und Industrie der Schweiz im Jahre 1890. 4to.	The Association
United States—	
Agriculture. Report (No. 91) on the Crops of 1891, and on Freight Rates of Transportation Companies. Diagrams. 8vo.	J. R. Dodge, Esq.
Army. Report of the Surgeon-General of the, for the fiscal year 1890-91. 8vo......	The Surgeon-General
Census [1890] Bulletins. Nos. 127. Population of Colorado. 133. Population of Louisiana. 134. Population of California. 136. Population of Tennessee. 137. Population of North Dakota. 138. Population of Alabama. 139. Population of Kentucky. 140. Schools for the Deaf in United States. 142. Transportation by Water on the Pacific Coast. 143. Agriculture. Hops. 144. Population of Florida. 145. Population of Illinois. 148. Population of Texas. 149. Railway Statistics. 151. Railway Statistics. 154. Paupers in Almshouses in 1890, classified by age and sex. 152. Statistics of Churches. 153. Irrigation in Montana. 155. Railway Statistics. 156. Iron and Steel Industries of New England States. 157. Irrigation in Idaho	The Superintendent of Census
Extra Census [1890] Bulletins. 12. Statistics of Farms, &c. Illinois. 13. Agriculture. Tobacco. Maps. 15. Statistics of Farms, Homes and Mortgages. Tennessee. 16. The same for Alabama, Illinois, Iowa, and Kansas	

Donations—Contd.

Donations.	By whom Presented.
(a) Foreign Countries—*Contd.*	
United States—*Contd.*	
Commerce. Annual Report in regard to Imported Merchandise entered for consumption in the United States, with Rates of Duty and Amounts of Duty collected during 1890-91. 8vo.	The Bureau of Statistics, Treasury Department
Comptroller of the Currency, Annual Report of the, for 1890-91. 2 vols. 8vo.	The Comptroller of the Currency
Education. Report of the Commissioner of, for 1888-89. 2 vols. Diagrams. 8vo.	
Education Bureau. Circulars of Information, 1891. Nos. 1. Higher Education in Indiana. 8. Sanitary Conditions for Schoolhouses. 7. Promotions and Examinations in Graded Schools. 8 parts. Plates.	The Bureau of Education
Education Bureau. Special Report on Public Libraries. Part 2. Rules for a Dictionary Catalogue. Third edition. 1891. 8vo.	
Finances. Annual Report of the Secretary of the Treasury on the state of the, for 1891. 8vo.............	The Secretary of the Treasury
Foreign Commerce. Annual Report on, for the year 1890-91. 8vo..............	The Bureau of Statistics, Treasury Department
Imports and Exports. Summary Statement of, Oct.—Dec., 1891.............	
Mint. Annual Report of the Director of the, for the year ended 30th June, 1891. 8vo.	The Director of the Mint
Observations made during 1886 at the United States Observatory. Plates. 4to. 1891	The Superintendent
CONNECTICUT. State Board of Health. Monthly Bulletin, Nov.—Jan., 1891-92	The State Board of Health
MASSACHUSETTS. Births, Marriages, and Deaths. Forty-ninth Report on the Registry and Return of, for 1890, with Returns of Divorces in 1890	The Secretary of the Commonwealth
MINNESOTA. Statistics of Minnesota for 1877, being the Ninth Annual Report of the Commissioner of Statistics. 8vo.	Horace G. Wadlin, Esq., Boston
MISSOURI. First and Fifth Annual Reports of the Bureau of Labour Statistics for 1879 and 1883. 2 vols., 8vo.	
New York State—	
Chamber of Commerce. 123rd Annual Banquet of the, Nov. 17th, 1891. Speeches made on the occasion. 8vo.	H. W. Cannon, Esq.
Another copy	G. R. Gibson, Esq.
Labor. Eighth Annual Report of the Bureau of Statistics of, for 1890. Parts 1 and 2. 8vo.........	The Commissioner
Library Bulletin. Legislation No. 2. Comparative Summary and Index of State Legislation in 1891. [With Appendix showing the Receipts and Expenditure of the different States of the Union in 1890.] 8vo.	The State Library
OHIO. Fourth Annual Report of the Bureau of Labor Statistics for 1880. 8vo, ...	H. G. Wadlin, Esq.
Banker's Magazine. Dec.—Feb., 1891-92	The Editor
Bradstreet's Journal (Current weekly numbers)	,,
Californian Illustrated Magazine. Vol. i. No. 3. Feb., 1892. La. 8vo.........	The Publisher

Donations.	By whom Presented.
(a) Foreign Countries—*Contd.*	
United States—*Contd.*	
Commercial and Financial Chronicle. (Current weekly numbers)	The Editor
The Forum, Dec., 1891. The Jewish Persecution, its Financial and International Aspects : *A. Leroy-Beaulieu.* Plan for a Permanent Bank System : *H. White.* Bank-Note Circulation, Mr. Harter's Plan : *H. W. Cannon.*	H. W. Cannon, Esq.
Investor's Supplement to Commercial and Financial Chronicle, Jan., 1892	The Editor
Political Science Quarterly. Vol. vi, No. 4. Dec., 1891. The Single Tax : *C. B. Spahr.* Sociology as a University Study : *F. H. Giddings.* The Social Contract Theory : *D. G. Ritchie*	The Publishers
Quarterly Journal of Economics. Vol. vi, No. 2. Jan., 1892. Capital and Interest : *S. M. Macvane.* Evolution of Wage Statistics : *C. D. Wright.* The Prussian Income Tax : *J. A. Hill*	,,
American Academy of Political and Social Science. Annals. Vol. ii, No. 4, Jan., 1892. The Demand for Public Regulation of Industries : *W. D. Dabney.* Study of Municipal Government : *F. P. Pritchard.* Instruction in French Universities : *L. S. Rowe*	The Academy
American Economic Association Publications. Vol. vi, Nos. 4 and 5. Municipal Ownership of Gas in the United States : *E. W. Bemis.* No. 6. State Railroad Commissions and how they may be made effective : *F. C. Clark.* Map, 8vo. 1891	The Association
American Geographical Society. Bulletin. Vol. xxiii, No. 4, part 1, Dec., 1891. Plate, 8vo..........	The Society
American Statistical Association Publications. Vol. ii, No. 15, Sept., 1891. The Eleventh Census : *Hon. R. P. Porter.* Criminal Statistics : *R. P. Falkner*	The Association
Bradstreet Company, 1891. A Record—not a Prospectus [giving Failures in North America in 1890 and 1891]. 16 pp., 12mo.........................	The Company
Columbia College. Studies in History, Economics, and Public Law. Vol. i, No. 3. History of Municipal Ownership of Land on Manhattan Island to ... 1844 : by *G. A. Black.* Plans, 8vo. 1891....	Columbia College
Franklin Institute. Journal. Dec.—Feb., 1891-92	The Institute
Uruguay. Anuario Estadistico de la Republica Oriental del Uruguay. Año 1890. Plates and diagrams, la. 8vo.	The Statistical Bureau
International. Bulletin International des Douanes. Nos. 15—22. 8vo. Brussels, 1891-92	The Board of Trade
(b) India and Colonial Possessions.	
India, British—	
The Tribes and Castes of Bengal. By *H. H. Risley.* Anthropometric data. 2 vols., 8vo. Calcutta, 1891	The Record Department, India Office

Donations—Contd.

Donations.	By whom Presented.
(b) India and Colonial Possessions—*Contd.*	
India, British—*Contd.*	
Trade by Land with Foreign Countries. Monthly Accounts. 1891-92; Nos. 5—7 .... Trade and Navigation. Monthly Accounts. 1891-92. Nos. 7—9	The Department of Finance and Commerce, Calcutta
Indian Engineering. (An illustrated weekly journal.) (Current numbers.) 1891-92	P. Doyle, Esq., C.E., the Editor
Canada, Dominion of—	
Agriculture and Colonization. Report of Select Standing Committee on. 8vo., 1891	J. G. Bourinot, Esq., C.M.G.
Banks acting under Charter, Monthly Statements for Nov.—Dec., 1891..................	N. S. Garland, Esq.
Life Insurance Companies. Preliminary Abstract of the business of Canadian, for 1891. 8vo.	
Public Accounts for the year 1890-91	
Sessional Papers. Session 1891, vols.—	
iv. Report on Inland Revenues for 1889-90. Inspection of Weights, Measures, and Gas. Adulteration of Food. Report of the Minister of Agriculture for 1890	
v. Report on Canadian Archives, 1891. Reports on Western Hemisphere Trade, and on Experimental Farms for 1890	
vi. Annual Report of Dairy Commissioners for 1890. Reports of High Commissioner and Agents for 1890. Mortuary Statistics of Principal Cities for 1890. Criminal Statistics for 1889-90. Report on Jamaica Exhibition, 1891	
vii. Report of the Department of Marine for 1889-90. Report on Steamboat Inspection for 1890. Export Cattle Trade. Deck Loads of Timber and Deal..................	
viii. Reports of the Department of Fisheries for 1890, and of Inspectors for 1890. Plates and maps	J. G. Bourinot, Esq. C.M.G.
x. Report of Minister of Public Works for 1889-90. Maps........................	
xi. Report of Minister of Railways and Canals for 1889-90. Canal Statistics for 1890. Railway Statistics for 1890	
xii. Report of Superintendent of Insurance for 1890. Business of Canadian Life Insurance Companies for 1890. Report on Penitentiaries for 1889-90........................	
xiii. Reports of Department of Militia and Defence, of Secretary of State, of Civil Service Examiners, of Department of Printing and Stationery, and of Librarians of Parliament for 1890-91. Civil Service List, 1890	
xiv. Report of Postmaster-General for 1889-90. Report of Department of Interior for 1890. Report of Geological Survey Department for 1890...........	
xv. Reports on Indian Affairs, and North-West Mounted Police for 1890	

Donations—Contd.

Donations.	By whom Presented.
(b) India and Colonial Possessions—*Contd.* **Canada, Dominion of—***Contd.* xvi. Superannuations. Canadian Pacific Railway. Elections, &c. .... xvii. Trade between United States and Canada. Spanish American Treaty. Exports of Potatoes. Fisheries, &c. Iron Trade, &c. Map, 8vo.	J. G. Bourinot, Esq., C.M.G.
MANITOBA. Report on Crops and Live Stock, No. 31....	The Agricultural Department
Insurance and Finance Chronicle. (Current numbers)....	The Editor
Cape of Good Hope— Argus Annual and South African Directory, 1892. 25th year of publication	The Colonial Secretary, Cape Town
Census, 1891. [Final] Return of Population, showing for each Census District the number of Persons, Male and Female, classed according to the six main races. Sheet	The Director of Census
Grenada. Census of 1891. Report and Abstract of the, with graphic tables and notes thereon. Fol.........	C. H. Johnson, Esq., the Compiler
Natal— Customs. Annual Report of the Collector of, for 1890-91. Fol................ .... Customs Guide. No. 1. October, 1891. 8vo............ Shipping and Trade Returns for the last six months of 1891. Fol................	R. I. Finnemore, Esq.
New South Wales— Agriculture. Rust in Wheat, Report of the Conference on. Plan, fol. 1891	The Director of Agriculture
Statistical Register for 1890 and previous years. 8vo....	T. A. Coghlan, Esq.
New Zealand. Mining Industry. Reports on the. Plates, fol. 1891	The Minister of Mines
Queensland— Census of 1891. Preliminary Statement of. Map, fol................ Supplement to the Government Gazette (containing Vital Statistics). (Current numbers) .... Vital Statistics, 1890. Thirty-first Annual Report by the Registrar-General. Fol.	The Registrar-General
South Australia— Census of 1891. Part 1. Summary Tables. Fol. .... Statistical Register for 1890. Part 3, Production; 7, Religious, Educational, and Charitable Institutions. 2 parts, fol.	L. H. Sholl, Esq., Superintendent of Census
Public Library, Museum, and Art Gallery. Reports of the Board of Governors and of the standing Committees for 1890-91. Plates, fol.	Robert Kay, Esq.
Straits Settlements. The Perak Government Gazette. (Current numbers.) 1891-92	The Government Secretary

Donations—Contd.

Donations.	By whom Presented.

(b) **India and Colonial Possessions—***Contd.*
Victoria—
Census of 1891. Birthplaces of the People. Religions of the People. 2 parts, fol. ....   H. H. Hayter, Esq., C.M.G.
Friendly Societies, Thirteenth Annual Report on, for 1890. Fol. ....

Public Library, Museums, and National Gallery of Victoria. Report of Trustees for 1890. La. 8vo.....   The Librarian
Public Library, Museums, &c. Rules and Regulations. 8vo. 1891. ....

Statistical Register of the Colony for 1890. Part 7, Law, Crime, &c. ....   H. H. Hayter, Esq., C.M.G.
Victorian Year-Book for 1890-91, in 2 vols. Vol. i, 8vo. ....

Royal Society of Victoria—
Proceedings. Vol. iii, new series, plates, 8vo., 1891 (contain " Anthropology in Australia :" *A. W. Howitt.* The New Britain Currency or Shell   The Society
Money: *R. H. Rickard*) ....
Transactions. Vol. ii, part 1, 1890, and vol. iii, part 1, 1891. 2 vols., plates, 4to. ....

Australia. The Year-Book of Australia for 1886 and   E. Granville, Esq., 1890. 2 vols, 8vo., maps, &c. 1886-90 ....   J.P., the Editor

---

(c) **United Kingdom and its several Divisions.**
United Kingdom—
A Collection of Parliamentary Papers on Education, Crime, Trade, Railways, the Colonies, &c., for the   A. L. Roberts, Esq.
Sessions 1890-91. 8vo. and fol. ....

Board of Trade Journal. Dec.—Jan., 1891-92 ....
Labour Statistics. Statistical Tables and Report on Trades Unions. Fourth Report, years 1889 and 1890. [C-6475.] 1891 ....
Strikes and Lock-Outs of 1890. Report on the, by the Labour Correspondent to the Board of Trade.   The Board of Trade
[C-6476.] 1891.............. ....
Statistical Abstract for the several Colonial and other Possessions in each year from 1876-90. 8vo. [C-6456.] 1891 ....
Trade and Navigation. (Current Monthly Returns)....

Great Britain. Agricultural Returns of Great Britain, with Abstract Returns for the United Kingdom,   Major P. G. Craigie
British Possessions and Foreign Countries, 1891. [C-6524.] 1891 ....

England—
Births and Deaths in London, and in twenty-seven other Great Towns. (Current Weekly Returns) ....
Quarterly Return of Marriages to Sept., Births and   The Registrar-Gene-
Deaths to Dec., 1891. No. 172 ....   ral of England
Births, Deaths, and Marriages in England (1890). 53rd Annual Report of the Registrar-General of. [C-6478.] 8vo. ....

Donations.	By whom Presented.
(c) United Kingdom and its Divisions—*Contd.*	
England—*Contd.*	
British Museum, Catalogue of Printed Books. 6 parts, fol. 1891	The Trustees of the Museum
LONDON COUNTY COUNCIL. Fires in London. Report of the Chief Officer of the Fire Brigade on, during 1891. 8vo.	J. Sexton Simonds, Esq., Chief Officer
Ireland—	
Births and Deaths in Dublin, and in fifteen of the principal Urban Sanitary Districts. (Current Weekly Returns)	The Registrar-General of Ireland
Quarterly Return of Marriages to June, Births and Deaths to Sept., 1891. No. 111	
Marriages, Births, and Deaths. 27th detailed Annual Report of the Registrar-General on, during 1890. [C–6520.] 1891	
Education. Appendix to the 57th Report of the Commissioners of National Education for 1890. 8vo. [C–6411–I.] 1891	W. R. J. Molloy, Esq.
Scotland—	
Births, Deaths, and Marriages in the eight principal Towns. (Current weekly and monthly returns)	The Registrar-General of Scotland
Births, Deaths, and Marriages, Quarterly Return of, registered in the quarter ending 31st Dec., 1891	
Births, Deaths, and Marriages. Thirty-fifth detailed Annual Report of the Registrar-General of. [Abstracts of 1889.] [C–6452.] 8vo. 1891	
GLASGOW. Census, 1891. Old Glasgow and its Statistical Divisions, as at 5th April, 1891. Greater Glasgow as constituted by the City of Glasgow Act, 1891. Map, 8vo.	Dr. J. B. Russell
(d) Authors, &c.	
ARTIN (YACOUB PACHA). L'Instruction Publique en Egypte. viii + 214 pp., 8vo. Paris, 1889	The Author
BERTHOLD (DR. G.). Statistik der deutschen Arbeiter-Kolonien für 1887-89. Mit Rückblicken auf die Entwicklung und Bedeutung derselben seit 1882. 150 pp., 8vo. Berlin, 1891	,,
BODIO (L.). Di alcuni indici misuratori del movimento economico in Italia. (2ª edizione riveduta ed ampliata). 150 pp. 4to. Roma. 1891	,,
BOSCO (AUGUSTO). La Delinquenza in Italia. 19 pp. 8vo. Firenze, 1891	..
DALLA VOLTA (RICARDO). La riduzione delle ore di lavoro e i suoi effetti economici. v + 134 pp., 12mo. Firenze, 1891	,,
FINDLAY (GEORGE). The Working and Management of an English Railway. Fourth edition, revised and enlarged. 8 + 354 pp., plates, 8vo. 1891	,,
FYFE (PETER). The Progress of Death in Scotland and her Counties since 1855. A comparison. 14 pp. Diagrams, 8vo. Glasgow, 1892 (2 copies)	,,

Donations—Contd.

Donations.	By whom Presented.
(d) **Authors, &c.**—*Contd.*	
GRIMSHAW (THOMAS W.) Irish Progress during the past ten years, 1881-90. 33 pp., 8vo. Dublin, 1891	The Author
HAGGARD (F. T.). A plea for Agriculture and the Agricultural Classes of the United Kingdom. 16 pp., 8vo. Tunbridge Wells, 1891	,,
HARDY (RALPH PRICE). Old Age Pensions. Old Age Pensioning, with reference to certain proposed schemes, and to the existing Poor Law provision. 16 pp., 8vo. 1891	,,
JONES (H. R. BENCE). Annual Supplements to Willich's Tithe Commutation Tables for 1891 and 1892. 2 parts, 8vo. 1891-92	,,
JORDAN (WILLIAM LEIGHTON). The Standard of Value. Sixth edition. 167 pp., 8vo. 1889	
KARDORFF - WABNITZ (WILH. VON). Die deutsche Landwirthschaft und ihre Zukunft. 22 pp., 8vo. Berlin, 1891	,,
Loch (C. S.)—	
Old Age Pensions and Pauperism. An inquiry as to the bearing of the Statistics of Pauperism quoted by the Rt. Hon. J. Chamberlain, M.P., and others, in support of a scheme for national pensions. 59 pp., 8vo. 1892	,,
Charity Organisation. iv + 106 pp., 8vo. 1892	
MARTIN (JOHN BIDDULPH) "The Grasshopper" in Lombard Street. xx + 328 pp. Plates and portraits. La. 8vo. 1892	,,
Mathieson (F. C., and Sons)—	
The Statutory Trust Investment Guide. 216 pp., 8vo. 1891	Messrs. Mathieson and Sons
Mathieson's Highest and Lowest Prices. 1892 issue. 43 pp., 8vo. 1892	
MILLIET (E. W.). Summarischer Bericht über die Sparkassenfrage. 18 pp., 4to. [Berne.] 1891	The Author
RAFFALOVICH (ARTHUR). Le Marché Financier en 1891, précédé d'une étude sur les rapports de l'Etat et de la Bourse. xii + 202 pp., 8vo. Paris, 1892	,,
RAWSON (SIR RAWSON W.). Our Commercial Barometer for 1890-91. 2 parts, 8vo. 1891-92	,,
RENTOUL (ROBERT REID). The Reform of our Voluntary Medical Charities : some serious considerations for the Philanthropic. xii + 139 pp., 8vo. 1891. Another copy presented by the author.	Messrs. Baillière, Tindall, and Cox
SCHLOSS (DAVID F.). Methods of Industrial Remuneration. xx + 287 pp. 8vo. 1892	The Author
Statesman's Year Book, statistical and historical annual of the States of the World for 1892. Edited by J. Scott Keltie. 29th annual publication. xxxii + 1152 pp., maps, 8vo. 1892	The Editor
VENN (JOHN). The Logic of Chance, an Essay on the foundations and province of the theory of probability, with especial reference to its logical bearings and its application to moral and social science and to statistics. Third edition. xxix + 508 pp. 8vo. 1888	The Author

Donations—Contd.

Donations.	By whom Presented.
(d) Authors, &c.—*Contd.*	
WAGNER (DR. H.). Extract from "Die Bevölkerung der Erde," relating to the Area and Population of China, Corea, Japan, and Asiatic Turkey. Map., 8vo. Gotha, 1891	The Author
(e) Societies, &c. (British).*	
Anthropological Institute of Great Britain and Ireland. Journal. Vol. xx, Nos. 1 and 2, vol. xxi, Nos. 1 and 3. Plates. 8vo. 1890-92	The Institute
British Economic Association. The Economic Journal. Vol. i, No. 4. Dec., 1891. (Contents.) Introductory Lecture on Political Economy : *F. Y. Edgeworth.* The Alleged Differences in the Wages of Men and Women : *S. Webb.* The Coal Question : *F. Brown.* The New Theory of Interest: *W. Smart.* Evolution of the Socialist Programme in Germany : *G. Adler.* Labour Troubles in New Zealand : *W. T. Charlewood.* Attempt to Estimate the Circulation of the Rupee : *F. C. Harrison.*..............................	The Association
Economic Review, The. Vol. ii, No. 1. Jan., 1892. (Contents.) Poor Relief in Italy : *F. S. Nitti.* Plea for Pure Theory : *Rev. W. Cunningham.* Women ·Compositors : *S. Webb* and *A. Linnett.* A Social Policy for Churchmen : *Rev. T. C. Fry.* Mazzini's Political Philosophy : *Rev. A. Chandler.* Malthusian Anti-Socialist Argument : *E. Cannan.* Use and Abuse of Endowed Charities : *Rev. L. R. Phelps.*..................	Messrs. Percival & Co., the Publishers
Cobden Club— Wages and Hours of Labour, by Sir Lyon Playfair. 12mo. 1891 .... Leaflet No. 94. Fiscal Federation Protection System. 1891	The Club
East India Association. Journal. Vol. xxiv, No. 1. 1892	The Association
Friendly Society of Ironfounders. 82nd Annual Report for 1891, also current Monthly Reports	Sir R. W. Rawson
Glasgow Philosophical Society. Proceedings. Vol. xxii. 1890-91. Plates. 8vo. 1891. (Selection from Contents.) Relations of Thomas Carlyle to Political Economy : *J. Bonar.* Inquiry into the Nature of Heredity : *W. Wallace.*.......	The Society
Howard Association. Report, October, 1891, and Leaflets relating to Prisons, Prisoners, &c. 8vo.	The Association
Hull Incorporated Chamber of Commerce and Shipping. Annual Report of the Council, 1890-91. 8vo.	C. M. Kennedy, Esq.
Institute of Bankers. Journal. Dec.—Feb., 1891-92........	The Institution
Institution of Mechanical Engineers. Proceedings. Nos. 4 and 5. Plates. 8vo. 1891............................	··
London Chamber of Commerce— Journal. Dec.—Jan., 1891-92 .... Year-Book of Commerce for 1890-91 and 1892. Edited by Kenric B. Murray. 2 vols. 8vo. 1890-91	Kenric Murray,·Esq., the Editor

* Foreign and Colonial Societies will be found under the various Countries or Possessions to which they belong.

Donations—Contd.

Donations.	By whom Presented.
(e) Societies, &c. (British)—*Contd.*	
London Conciliation Board. First Annual Report for 1891. 8vo.	The Secretary of the Board
London Hospital. General Statement of the Number of Patients under Treatment in the Hospital during 1891. Sheet	W. J. Nixon, Esq.
Manchester Unity. The Oddfellows' Magazine for Feb., 1892. Portrait. 8vo.	The Secretary
Royal Agricultural Society. Journal. Third series. Vol. ii, part 4, No. 8. 8vo. 1891	The Society
Royal Geographical Society. Proceedings. Jan.—Mar., 1892	,,
Royal Irish Academy. Transactions. Vol. xxix, part 17. 4to. 1891	The Academy
Royal United Service Institution. Journal. Dec.—Feb., 1891-92	The Institution
Royal Society. Proceedings. Vol. l, Nos. 303, 304. 1892	The Society
Society of Arts. Journal. (Current numbers.) 1892	,,
Surveyors' Institution. Transactions. Vol. xxiv. Part 4. 1892	The Institution

(f) Periodicals, &c. (British).*		
Accountant, The	Current numbers	The Editor
Athenæum, The	,,	,,
Bankers' Magazine, The	,,	,,
British Trade Journal, The	,,	,,
Building Societies and Land Companies' Gazette, The	,,	,,
Commercial World, The	,,	,,
Darkest Russia: A Journal of Persecution	,,	,,
Economist, The	,,	,,
Fireman, The	,,	,,
Insurance and Banking Review, The	,,	,,
,, Post, The	,,	,,
,, Record, The	,,	,,
Investors' Monthly Manual, The	,,	,,
Iron and Coal Trades' Review, The	,,	,,
Machinery Market, The	,,	,,
Nature	,,	,,
Policy-Holder, The	,,	,,
Review, The	,,	,,
Sanitary Record, The	,,	,,
Shipping World, The	,,	,,
Statist, The	,,	,,
Surveyor, The	,,	,,

* Foreign and Colonial Periodicals will be found under the various Countries or Colonies in which they are issued.

Purchases.

Authors, &c.—

Bastable (C. F.). The Commerce of Nations. viii + 216 pp. 8vo. 1892

Del Mar (Alexander). History of Money in Ancient Countries from the Earliest Times to the Present. xxxiv + 358 pp. 8vo. 1885.

Fyfe (H. H.). Annals of our Time. Parts 1, 2 of vol. iii. 8vo., 1892.

Mulhall (M. G.). Dictionary of Statistics. viii + 632 pp. Plates, la. 8vo. 1892.

Rogers (James E. Thorold). The Industrial and Commercial History of England (Lectures delivered to the University of Oxford). Edited by his son, Arthur G. L. Rogers. xi + 473 pp. 8vo. 1892.

Salmon (James). Ten Years' Growth of the City of London [1881-91]. Report, Local Government and Taxation Committee of the Corporation, with the Results of the Day-Census, 1891. 139 pp. Map and plates, 8vo. 1891.

Simmonds (P. L.). A Handbook of British Commerce; being a descriptive and statistical account of the various articles forming the Import and Export Trade of the United Kingdom. viii + 204 pp., 8vo. 1892.

White (Arnold). The Destitute Alien in Great Britain; a series of papers dealing with the subject of Foreign Pauper Immigration. Arranged and edited by. 191 pp., 8vo. 1892.

Wilkinson (J. Frome). Pensions and Pauperism, with Notes by T. E. Young. 127 pp., 8vo. 1892.

Nouveau Dictionnaire d'Économie Politique. Livr. 16, 1892.

Palmer's Index to the Times. Quarter ending 31st Dec., 1891.

Vierteljahrschrift für Volkswirtschaft, Politik, und Kulturgeschichte. 29er Jahrgang. Band i, 1 hälfte. (Contents.) Studie über das sogenannte Staatsabstractum: *J. v. Held.* Der russische Wechselkurs im letzten Jahrzehnt: *N. S.* Das Abzahlungs-Geschäft und die neuesten Vorschläge zu seiner Regelung: *W. Hausmann.* 8vo. Berlin, 1892.

Periodicals, &c.—

Almanach de Gotha, 1892.

Annuaire de l'Economie Politique et de la Statistique, 1891.

Banking Almanac, 1892.

British Almanac and Companion, 1892.

County Council Companion, 1892.

Directory of Directors, 1892.

Financial Reform Almanac, 1892.

Ham's Inland Revenue Year-Book, 1892.

Howe's Directory of Charities, 1892.

India Office List, 1892.

Kelly's Handbook, 1892.

Metropolitan Year-Book, 1892.

Stock Exchange Year-Book, 1892.

Vacher's Parliamentary Companion (Current monthly numbers).

Parliamentary Papers—

Agricultural Statistics of Ireland for 1890.

British Army. General Annual Return for 1890.

Belgian Councils of "Prud'hommes." Report on, 1891.

Building Societies. Annual Return for 1890.

Civil Service Commission, 35th Report, for 1890.

Colonial Tariffs, List of, 1891.

Corn Sales, Report of Select Committee on, 1891.

Purchases—Contd.

Parliamentary Papers—*Contd.*

Friendly Societies. Report of the Chief Registrar for 1890.

Gas Companies' (Metropolis) Accounts for 1890.

India. Financial Statement for 1891-92.

Italy, Report on Private Wealth in, 1891.

Local Taxation Returns for 1889-90.

Members of Parliament, Lists, &c., of, from 1705 to 1885.

Metropolitan Hospitals, Second Report of Royal Commission on, 1891.

Metropolitan Water Companies, Accounts for 1890.

Mining Royalties, 2nd and 3rd Reports of the Royal Commission on, 1891.

Prisons in Scotland, Report on, for 1891.

Provision for Old Age in Foreign Countries, Report on, 1891.

Railway Accidents during 1890.

Railway Servants' Hours of Labour, 1891.

Relief of the Poor in Scotland in 1890-91.

Salmon and Freshwater Fisheries. Return for 1890.

Shipping Casualties in 1889-90.

Strikes and Lock-outs, Report on, 1891.

Switzerland, Report on Insurance against Sickness in, 1891.

Town Holdings, Report of the Select Committee on, 1891.

Trade Statistics for 1854-90.

Wages, Report on the Relation of, to Cost of Production, 1891.

Weights and Measures, Report on Inspection of, 1891.

Vol. LV.]

[Part II.

JOURNAL

OF THE ROYAL STATISTICAL SOCIETY,

JUNE, 1892.

TONNAGE STATISTICS *of the* DECADE 1880-90.

By JOHN GLOVER, ESQ.

[Read before the Royal Statistical Society, 15th March, 1892.
The President, DR. F. J. MOUAT, LL.D., in the Chair.]

CONTENTS:

General Observations.

THE Society's *Journals* for March, 1863, June, 1872, and March, 1882, contain papers which I had the honour to read, relating to the progress of shipping during three previous decades. The paper I am about to read relates to the last decade, and so will complete in the Society's *Journal* a record for forty years. My first paper recorded that the total entries and clearances at ports in the United Kingdom were in 1850 under 40 million tons; and the tables submitted to-night show, that in 1890 the same entries and clearances had quadrupled, having grown to more than 164 millions of tons. The increase during the last decade with which I dealt, viz., that of 1870-80, was from 73 million tons to 133 million tons, an increase of 60 million tons; or, to put it otherwise, an increase which exceeded the whole entries and clearances of 1860—they were under 59 million tons. After a development so vast between 1870 and 1880, it would not have been an unreasonable conjecture, that some pause might have been expected during 1880-90. But in spite of many circumstances which might have slackened the growth of our maritime trade, the enormous figures for 1880, viz., 133 million tons, grew to over 164 million tons in 1890.

In the preparation of the tables I am about to submit, I have adhered as closely as possible to the construction of my previous tables, so that the comparisons, for what they are worth, are made with the same things. If I remember rightly, some reflections were made in the discussion on my last paper on the method of comparing at intervals so long as that of a decade. Since then, I have seen a good deal of "grouping" of the maritime statistics into three years and other periods, but the results did not satisfy me that any such arbitrary grouping enabled the figures to convey the instruction they contained. It is no unusual thing in the experience of the Fellows of this Society to see figures made to support theories which they do not teach; also to see them used on opposite sides of a great controversy. Comparisons of fixed dates at long intervals, without any arbitrary selection, appear to me to form a better basis for conclusions. I therefore adhere to the comparison of decades, and of beginnings and ends of decades; except in those cases in which, for the decade under immediate treatment, I give the facts for the whole of the ten years, leaving each year to tell its own tale.

As to the general character of the decade, I may say it was remarkable in many respects. Like its predecessor, it was free from any maritime war; our flag was never belligerent. The Egyptian operations were carried through with very slight disturbance to the freight markets, and made demands too limited to show what transport resources our steamer fleet places at the disposal of the government. The price of coal was 50 per cent. higher in 1890 than in 1880. But the average price for the decade was less than during either of the two decades preceding. It was not to be expected that the shipping industry would escape the labour troubles which afflicted nearly all other trades, especially towards the end of the period. They led to the formation of what is known as the Federation of Shipping of the United Kingdom, by the help of which (for the present at all events) the ship owners have preserved for themselves and their captains and officers, that control over the navigation of their vessels which is essential to the safety of life and property on the high seas. It was by no means a peaceful decade so far as regards political agitations. There was indeed much political agitation; and much public interest was excited by the statements and counter statements made on shipping affairs. There was much inquiry— a Select Committee in 1880, a Royal Commission on Tonnage in 1831, a Royal Commission on Loss of Life at Sea in 1884, and the

Load Line Committee; a Select Committee on Life Saving Appliances in 1887, a Committee on Pilotage in 1888, and a Departmental Committee on the Life Saving Appliances Act in 1889, and another Departmental Committee in 1890 on the subject of Bulkheads. No less than 34 Bills were introduced to Parliament, but of these only 15 became Acts, the most important of which were the Carriage of Grain Act, 1880, the Payment of Wages Act, 1880, and the Load Line Act, 1890.

Tested either by value or by the estimated weight carried, the imports and exports of the decade show a large increase. The value for 1890 was 749 millions, compared with 697 millions in 1880, 547 millions in 1870, and 375 millions in 1860; so that between the latter date and 1890 the value doubled. An indication of this growth is given by the figures for a few of the more bulky articles enumerated in—

TABLE I.—*Showing the Quantities of certain Articles Exported and Imported in* 1860, 1870, 1880, *and* 1890.

[000's omitted.]

	1860.	1870.	1880.	1890.
Exports—				
Coal........................ tons	7,821,	11,702,	18,729,	28,738,
Iron and steel........ ,,	1,442,	2,825,	3,792,	4,001,
Salt .... ,,	696,	764,	1,061,	726,
Imports—				
Corn .... cwts.	52,000,	74,103,	134,172,	155,620,
Rice......................... ,,	1,535,	4,077,	7,889,	5,957,
Wool .... lbs.	148,000,	263,250,	463,508,	633,028,
Wood .... loads	2,727,	4,460,	6,430,	7,212,
Sugar .... cwts.	8,817,	15,304,	20,654,	26,994,
Pyrites .... tons	93,	411,	658,	656,
Guano..................... ,,	141,	280,	80,	27,
Petroleum .... galls.	—	6,859,	38,793,	105,080,
Oil seed cake .... tons	—	158,	241,	282,

The increase of 10 million tons in the coal export, compared with that of 1880, explains how our increased fleet finds outward cargoes. Cheap coal forms the base of our position as maritime carriers; but I mark it as a distinctly disadvantageous fact, that whereas the average price in Cardiff was 9s. 6d. per ton in 1880, it had been forced up to 14s. 3d. in 1890. The excess of only 200,000 tons in the iron export of 1880, compares badly with the increases of the previous decades, and is no doubt explained by the hostile tariffs of other States, for it was very cheap here for most of the period under review. The decrease in the export of salt, from 1,051,240 tons in 1880, to 726,021 tons, is very regrettable. During the previous decade the export had grown from 764,707 tons to 1,051,240 tons, equal to 37·5 per cent. The loss in 1890 compared with 1880 is over 30 per cent., bringing the export to less in 1890 than it was in 1870. This loss of more than 300,000 tons of export cargo is very disadvantageous to our shipping; and it is rather difficult to see how it can be good for the Salt Union to have sent so much custom to other sources of supply, through the high price they fixed.

In the import figures in Table I the only important decrease is in the article of rice. We imported nearly 100,000 tons less in 1890 than in 1880. It is said, and I fear these figures prove the allegation, that the continental ports are beating us in the rice trade. London has especially suffered loss on this article. It can be discharged, stored, cleaned, and handled so much cheaper in the Dutch and German ports than in London, that many cargoes which used to come here now go to the continent, and the London workers, and dock companies, and traders generally lose the benefit of handling them. The ship owners are not so much concerned in this item of decrease, because they carry the cargoes to the continental ports instead of to our own ports, and are there subjected to much lower charges than they would incur in either London or Liverpool.

So far as concerns tonnage questions, the other items of import in Table I are satisfactory. Wool shows a large increase from 463 to 633 million lbs. Wood—another article occupying much tonnage space in relation to value—increased from 6,430,021 loads to 7,212,850 loads. Sugar advanced during the decade from 20,654,988 cwts. to 26,994,733 cwts.; though I must qualify this fact with the observation that the increasing proportion of beet sugar in our consumption yields little employment to our shipping, as beet comes from the near countries, France, Holland, Belgium, and consequently occupies our vessels less than voyages with cane sugar from the East and West Indies formerly did. The enormous growth in the item of petroleum, from 39 to 105 million gallons, will also be noted. The most important item in the import table, both in itself and as affecting tonnage questions, is that of grain. It will be observed that the figure for 1890 is double that of 1870. In the latter year our import was 3,705,175 tons; in 1880 it was 6,708,626 tons; in 1890 it was 7,781,048 tons. I should perhaps not err, if I were to say that the obtaining of this vast extent of human food from other countries is the miracle of modern commerce.   Had any of our early Fellows ever hinted that a time would come in which there would arise the development of wants so vast; or that the English people would create wealth adequate to pay for such supplies; or that they would have under their own flag the ships necessary for its maritime transport—the one statement would have seemed only more incredibly absurd than the other. I never heard or read of any other group of human beings who either wanted so much, or who could have paid for it; and, certainly, no other State ever had the means for its maritime transport.

I add here, as a factor vitally affecting freight and tonnage questions, that great fluctuations occur in the sources from which these grain supplies come; for while the voyage from the Atlantic and Russian ports may occupy only three weeks, that from Australia may exceed three months, and from the Pacific ports more than four months. It is obvious how fluctuations in the sources of such supplies explain some of the more serious disturbances to which the freight markets are subject. I have therefore made an effort to show them for the decade in Table II for the article of wheat only:—

TABLE II.—*Showing the Total Quantities of Wheat and Wheat Meal and Flour Imported into the United Kingdom during each Year of the last Decade, where it came from, and the Percentage Variation in the Supply from each source in each Year, and in the Ten Years.*

	United States of America (Atlantic Ports) and Canada.	Per-centage of Total for the Year.	United States of America (Pacific Ports) and Chili.	Per-centage of Total for the Year.	Russia.	Per-centage of Total for the Year.	British India.	Per-centage of Total for the Year.	Germany.	Per-centage of Total for the Year.	Australasia.	Per-centage of Total for the Year.	Austrian Territories.	Per-centage of Total for the Year.	Argentine Federation.	Per-centage of Total for the Year.	Other Countries.	Per-centage of Total for the Year.	Total.
	Tons.		Tons.		Tons.		Tons.		Tons.		Tons.		Tons.		Tons.		Tons.		Tons.
1881	1,731,701	50·56	871,688	19·61	204,465	5·97	366,896	10·72	187,467	4·01	168,968	4·74	55,391	1·61	1	—	95,384	2·78	3,435,961
'82	1,485,506	38·59	900,361	23·30	488,963	12·49	423,158	10·95	243,391	6·55	148,902	3·83	79,149	2·05	1	—	94,382	2·44	3,864,903
'83	1,314,280	32·66	786,388	19·53	671,402	16·69	563,449	13·98	239,963	5·96	138,442	3·44	88,323	2·20	6,964	0·16	216,939	5·39	4,058,894
'84	1,263,739	40·47	561,946	17·99	274,841	8·81	399,047	12·79	141,835	4·55	265,686	8·51	78,188	2·50	10,539	0·34	125,904	4·04	3,190,068
'85	1,118,178	28·92	864,471	22·36	603,063	15·60	608,713	15·75	169,770	4·39	270,536	6·99	95,287	2·47	16,761	0·43	119,815	3·09	3,866,681
'86	1,372,018	44·15	710,553	22·87	186,636	6·06	551,569	17·74	106,739	3·43	40,569	1·27	70,738	2·28	13,836	0·45	54,418	1·75	3,107,176
'87	1,958,665	53·05	566,674	18·07	278,287	7·54	425,494	11·53	107,030	2·89	67,708	1·83	69,530	1·88	50,921	1·38	67,930	1·84	3,692,239
'88	979,311	26·42	548,858	14·81	1,080,066	29·13	409,434	11·05	218,699	5·90	118,336	3·19	103,657	2·79	88,011	2·38	160,506	4·33	3,706,879
'89	806,568	22·02	692,006	18·90	1,077,886	29·40	460,867	12·58	184,690	5·04	71,466	1·95	115,103	3·14	1,926	0·05	252,958	6·92	3,664,570
'90	960,890	25·20	608,147	15·95	979,263	25·69	455,580	11·95	99,784	2·62	149,442	4·18	69,408	1·82	141,900	3·72	337,959	8·87	3,819,373
Total	12,987,706	—	7,010,387	—	5,888,849	—	4,663,906	—	1,699,368	—	1,442,653	—	894,778	—	330,143	—	1,526,355	—	36,983,443
Percentage of total for the ten years ...	35·80		19·32		16·09		12·85		4·57		3·98		2·27		0·91		4·21		100

In this table it is noticeable that the supplies from the Atlantic ports are nearly double those from any other quarter, and that, if we include the Pacific supplies, more than 55 per cent. of our total imports during the decade came from the West. Russia follows at a long distance with 16 per cent. of the total, and India with less than 13 per cent. But the variations from the same source in different years is still more remarkable. From the Atlantic sources we received as much as 53 per cent. of our whole import in 1887, but the next year it fell to 26 per cent.—one half, and in 1889 to˙22 per cent.

The proportion of the Pacific supply was highest in 1882—23 per cent., and was under 16 per cent. in 1890. The variation is large, but less than that of the Atlantic.

The Indian supply was the steadiest of the decade—the nearest to its average; but it was under 11 per cent. in 1881, and in 1886 nearly 18 per cent.

The total tonnage result of all the goods imported and exported has been computed by my friend Mr. John Williamson of Liverpool, and communicated by him to the Chamber of Shipping of the United Kingdom. His estimate for 1880 was that it amounted to 53 million tons, and for 1890 76,544,237 tons; in other words, the work to be done, the goods to be carried in and out in the service of the United Kingdom, grew from 53 million tons in 1880, to 76½ million tons in 1890—an increase of 44 per cent. This represents what I call the demand for carrying capacity. The growth is enormous! The tables immediately following show the effect of this demand on the shipping returns.

Table III.—*Showing the Total Entries and Clearances at Ports in the United Kingdom for the Years* 1850, 1860, 1870, 1880, *and* 1890.

[000's omitted.]

Year.	Tons.	Increase.	Increase per Cent.
1850	39,634,	—	—
'60	58,707,	19,072,	48˙12
'70	73,198,	14,491,	24˙68
'80	133,250,	60,052,	82˙04
'90	164,340,	31,089,	23˙33

In reading my last paper, I was obliged to say that owing to some uncertainty regarding the entries and clearances coastwise, it was possible that there might be some mistake regarding the increase of 60 million tons between 1870 and 1880. It will be observed, however, that on that increase the year 1890 shows a further increase of 31 million tons. Table IV, which I am about to read, shows, with the same qualification, that half of this 31 millions is increased coasting trade; from which it would appear that coasting traffic by sea is holding its own, despite the competition of railways at so many points.

TABLE IV.—*Showing the Total Tonnage Entered and Cleared Coastwise.*

[000's omitted.]

Year.	Tons.	Increase.	Increase per Cent.
1850....................	25,129,	—	—
'60....................	34,017,	8,888,	35·37
'70....................	36,558,	2,540,	7·47
'80....................	74,514,	37,956,	106·55
'90....................	90,056,	15,542,	20·86

The figures regarding our foreign trade are shown in the following tables:—

TABLE V.—*Showing the Total Tonnage Entered and Cleared at Ports in the United Kingdom, in the Foreign Trade only, in* 1850, 1860, 1870, 1880, *and* 1890.

[000's omitted.]

Year.	Tons.	Increase.	Increase per Cent.
1850....................	14,505,	—	—
'60....................	24,689,	10,184,	70·21
'70....................	36,640,	11,950,	48·40
'80....................	58,736,	22,095,	60·30
'90....................	74,283,	15,547,	26·47

TABLE VI.—*Showing the Tonnage Entered and Cleared in the Foreign Trade, with Cargoes only, in the same Years.*

[000's omitted].

Year.	Tons.	Increase.	Increase per Cent.
1850....................	12,020,	—	—
'60....................	20,837,	8,817,	73·35
'70....................	31,624,	10,786,	51·76
'80....................	49,678,	18,054,	57·08
'90....................	62,836,	13,157,	26·48

Though the percentage of increase for 1890 is considerably less in the Tables V and VI, it is satisfactory to observe that the actual increase in the foreign trade is 15½ million tons in 1890 compared with 1880; or if the vessels in ballast be excluded, it is over 13 million tons. The foreign trade however is partly done by foreign vessels; and in the next tables we ascertain how much of the work was done by English, and how much by foreign ships.

TABLE VII.—*Showing the Amount of British Tonnage Entered and Cleared with Cargoes only, and in Ballast, from and to Foreign Countries and British Possessions.*

[000's omitted.]

Year.	With Cargoes only.			With Cargoes and in Ballast.		
	Tons.	Increase.	Increase per Cent.	Tons.	Increase.	Increase per Cent.
1850	8,039,	—	—	9,442,	—	—
'60	12,119,	4,080,	50·75	13,914,	4,472,	47·36
'70	22,243,	10,123,	83·52	25,072,	11,157,	80·18
'80	35,885,	13,642,	61·37	41,348,	16,276,	64·91
'90	46,406,	10,520,	29·32	53,973,	12,624,	30·53

TABLE VIII.—*Showing the Amount of Foreign Tonnage Entered and Cleared, with Cargoes and in Ballast, at Ports of the United Kingdom.*

[000's omitted.]

Year.	With Cargoes only.			With Cargoes and Ballast.			Proportion of Total Foreign Entries and Clearances to	
	Tons.	Increase.	Increase per Cent.	Tons.	Increase.	Increase per Cent.	Total Entries and Clearances.	British Entries and Clearances.
1850....	3,981,	—	—	5,062,	—	—	34·89	53·61
'60....	8,718,	4,737,	118·00	10,774,	5,711,	112·00	43·63	79·58
'70....	9,381,	663,	7·00	11,568,	793,	7·00	31·57	46·13
'80....	13,793,	4,412,	47·00	17,387,	5,819,	53·00	29·61	42·05
'90....	16,429,	2,636,	19·12	20,310,	2,923,	16·81	27·34	37·63

The facts disclosed regarding the tonnage in our foreign trade are satisfactory, though the increase is less than in the previous decade. The entries and clearances with cargo grew from nearly 50 million tons in 1880 to nearly 63 million in 1890; and of the increased 13 millions, 10½ million tons appear to be British, and a little more than 2½ million tons appear to be foreign. The growth of 13 million tons in our foreign transactions, following on a decade in which the growth was 18 million tons, is only less remarkable than the fact that our own flag was able to respond to such demands to the extent of 24 million tons increase in the twenty years, and explains the further fact that, notwithstanding foreign tonnage in our trade increased 7 million tons in the same period (though little more than 2½ millions in the last decade), the proportion of foreign to British has declined. The decline has been continuous since 1860, when it was 79·58; in 1870, 46·13; in 1880, 42·05; and in 1890, 37·63.

The relative position of the various foreign flags in our trade has undergone some important changes since 1880.   This appears in—

TABLE IX.—*Showing the Tonnage of Sailing and Steam Vessels with Cargoes only, and their Nationalities, Entered and Cleared at Ports in the United Kingdom, in the Years* 1850, 1860, 1870, 1880, *and* 1890.

Nationality.	1850.	1860.	1870.	1880.	1890.
British	8,039,308	12,119,454	22,243,039	35,885,868	46,406,250
Norwegian	331,664	948,212	1,975,575	2,914,407	3,792,739
German......................	—	1,797,747	1,433,595	2,576,819	3,354,754
Dutch	240,444	445,556	436,214	1,049,377	1,768,904
Danish	285,263	618,681	623,798	1,158,572	1,485,616
Swedish......................	125,649	366,700	591,985	1,310,707	1,448,559
French	369,624	616,410	785,658	1,133,630	1,271,181
Spanish	46,328	128,181	293,800	584,721	1,154,290
Belgian	71,775	112,537	305,384	461,078	696,121
Russian......................	163,254	242,673	538,443	470,336	456,621
Italian	—	275,688	811,903	884,206	364,321
American	1,215,225	2,734,381	1,134,215	882,277	272,735
Austrian	—	316,511	356,701	260,923	100,914
Other countries	1,132,140	115,187	94,370	106,029	263,070
Total foreign	3,981,366	8,718,464	9,381,641	13,793,082	16,429,825
Total British and foreign	12,020,674	20,837,918	31,624,680	49,678,950	62,836,075
Proportion of foreign	33·2	41·9	29·7	27·8	26·15
Proportion of British	66·8	58·1	70·3	72·2	78·85
	100·0	100·0	100·0	100·0	100·00

It will be observed that I have not placed the flags in alphabetical order, but in the order of highest tonnage.   Norway has kept its place, for the last three decades, at the head of all the foreign flags in the trade of the United Kingdom.   Germany is second, as in the decade 1870-80.   Sweden was third in 1880, but has declined to the fifth place, and Holland becomes third.   Denmark was fourth in 1880, and keeps its place.   The French flag was fifth in 1880.   Great expectations were begotten by the system of bounties adopted by France in 1881, to which I refer later; but the increase of the French flag in our trade being only 137,551 tons in 1890 compared with 1880, she fell to the sixth place among the foreign flags in 1890.   The observable decreases in the decade are the Austrian; the Italian, from 884,206 tons in 1880, to only 364,321 tons in 1890; and, greatest of all, the American, from 882,277 tons in 1880, to 272,735 tons in 1890.   This is the most remarkable fact in this table.   In 1860 the American flag occupied the first place in the foreign tonnage of the kingdom, in 1890 it had fallen to the eleventh. In 1860 its figure of 2,734,381 tons, compared with only 12,119,454 tons of our own; and the next foreign flag was nearly a million tons behind it. In 1890 its figure dropped to 272,735 tons, while our 12 millions had become 46 million tons.

The changes in Table IX are further explained by:—

TABLE X.—*Showing the Tonnage of Steam Vessels only, with Cargoes only, Entered and Cleared at Ports in the United Kingdom, with their different Nationalities, in* 1860, 1870, 1880, *and* 1890.

Nationality.	1860.	1870.	1880.	1890.
British	3,976,852	11,825,002	27,052,131	42,127,266
German	344,959	399,673	1,149,645	2,523,635
Dutch	122,838	161,062	875,774	1,645,283
Spanish	87,088	180,119	518,726	1,114,086
Danish	29,652	92,561	536,417	1,029,044
French	42,699	206,602	552,758	984,550
Norwegian	18,115	27,952	138,276	917,105
Swedish	16,165	62,556	593,175	826,692
Belgian	58,849	288,095	457,338	692,994
Russian	20,717	98,561	46,697	145,218
American	8,809	4,852	139,070	108,558
Italian	432	3,765	7,796	67,319
Austrian	300	6,704	None	36,833
Other countries	27,541	19,138	53,253	237,177
Total foreign	728,164	1,551,640	5,071,925	10,328,494
Total British and foreign	4,705,016	13,376,642	32,124,056	52,455,760
Proportion of foreign	15·5	11·6	15·9	19·69
„ British	84·5	88·4	84·1	80·31
	100·0	100·0	100·0	100·00

In my last paper I directed attention to the increase in foreign steamer entries and clearances, from 1½ million tons to 5 million tons; but in the last decade the increase is larger still, viz., from 5 million tons to more than 10 million tons. It is due to ourselves, however, at once to add that the bulk of this tonnage is built in this country, and a considerable, though unknown, portion of it is owned by British subjects. The limited liability Act is further facilitating this process, by enabling ships entirely owned by foreigners to be registered as British by the simple formality of vesting the property in a registered limited liability company, all the shareholders in which can be foreigners. So that we have really devised means whereby foreigners can have our flag if they like. So long as no questions of belligerency arise, I am not prepared to say that any very serious objections can be taken to this. But the circumstances are conceivable in which ships owned by foreigners, but carrying the English flag, might involve us in serious complications.

TABLE XI.—*Showing the Total Tonnage of Steam Vessels Entered and Cleared in the United Kingdom in the Years* 1840, 1850, 1860, 1870, 1880, *and* 1890.

Year.	Total Tons of Steam Vessels.	Of which British.	Percentage of British.	Increase per Cent. of British Steam.
1840	791,555	663,048	83	—
'50	2,209,847	1,802,955	81	171
'60	4,967,473	4,186,620	84	132
'70	15,072,331	13,341,058	88	228
'80	37,213,942	30,976,037	83	132
'90	61,685,009	49,023,775	79	58

The facts disclosed in this table down to 1880 were emphasised in my last paper as furnishing a story of maritime progress which, so far as I knew, had no parallel. An increase from under $2\frac{1}{4}$ millions to $61\frac{1}{2}$ in forty years is astonishing, but its progressive steps are more so. $2\frac{1}{4}$ millions in 1850 became nearly 5 million tons in 1860. By 1870 the 5 millions had reached 15, a growth of 10 million tons in that decade; and by 1880 the 15 millions had become 37 million tons, an increase of 22 millions, at which point some slackening in the pace might have been naturally looked for; but instead we find a still larger growth, viz., 24 million tons between 1880 and 1890 increasing 37 millions to over $61\frac{1}{2}$ million tons. Not less remarkable is the fact that throughout this vast increase the British proportion did not vary 5 per cent. When the steam entries were under one million—83 per cent. of them was done by our flag, grown to $61\frac{1}{2}$ million tons—$79\frac{1}{2}$ per cent. is done by our flag still.

I have so far spoken of the tonnage of goods carried, and the tonnage of entries and clearances. I now proceed to give some particulars of the fleet by which this work is done.

TABLE XII.—*Showing the Number and Tonnage of Vessels belonging to the United Kingdom.*

Year.	Number.	Net Tonnage.	Rate of Increase.
1850..................	25,984	3,564,833	—
'60..................	27,663	4,658,687	30·7
'70..................	26,367	5,690,789	22·1
'80..................	25,185	6,574,513	15·5
'90..................	21,233	7,945,071	20·8

The reduction in the number of vessels under our flag, to which

I directed attention in my last paper, has made further considerable progress. This is shown by a decline of nearly 4,000 vessels
in the number of our fleet between 1880 and 1890. The smaller
number, however, consisted of ships so much larger, that the
tonnage had grown from 6½ to nearly 8 million tons. As a mere
increase in tonnage this would not account for the increase of
work done; but the explanation appears when we inquire further,
what proportion of the fleet consisted of steamers, and what of
sailing vessels? This is shown in Table XIII.

TABLE XIII.—*Showing the Number of Sailing and Steam Vessels Registered
as belonging to the United Kingdom, with their Average Size, in* 1850,
1860, 1870, 1880, *and* 1890.

Year.	Sailing Vessels.				Steamers.			
	Number of Vessels.	Tonnage.	Increase or Decrease.	Average Size.	Number of Steamers.	Tonnage.	Increase per Cent.	Average Size.
			Per cnt.					
1850....	24,797	3,896,359	—	130	1,187	168,474	—	140
'60....	25,663	4,204,360	23·7	164	2,000	454,327	170	227
'70....	23,189	4,577,855	8·8	198	3,178	1,112,934	145	350
			Decrease.					
'80....	19,938	3,851,045	15·8	198	5,247	2,723,468	144	518
'90....	13,852	2,907,405	24·5	210	7,381	5,037,666	85	682

From Table XIII it appears that while we have about 4,000
vessels fewer under our flag than in 1880, the decline in the number
of sailing ships since that date exceeds 6,000; and that the loss in
number is only reduced to 4,000 by the fact that more than 2,000
steamers were added during the decade. The sailing tonnage
decreased nearly a million tons; but against this loss we have to
set off an increase in steamer tonnage of 2,314,198 tons; or in
other words we parted with 24½ per cent. of our sailing tonnage,
and added nearly 85 per cent. to our steamer tonnage. The
additions to our sailing fleet in recent years have been either very
small craft for coasting purposes, or very large iron and steel
vessels chiefly for the Pacific grain trade, the failure to make the
Panama Canal having led to the opinion that the Pacific trade is
secured against steamer competition for many years. It is observable however that the number of sailing ships under our flag is
little more than half the number we had in 1860, and that the
decline has been rapidly accelerating every decade since. I may
add here that the growth of the Norwegian flag in our trade is to
a considerable extent the result of our having sold so many of our
sailing vessels. They have been the chief buyers. Agitations made
their employment by English owners impracticable; but large
numbers of these ships are constantly trading to our ports under
the Norwegian flag. The steamer increase is very remarkable.

It was by far the largest increase compared with any previous decade; that of 1880 showing 1,610,534 tons over 1870; that of 1890 showing 2,314,198 tons over 1880. In my last paper I gave some reasons for the opinion that the ordinary computation of steamer tonnage as equal to three times the amount of sailing tonnage was an under estimate of the fact. I am still of that opinion. But using this measure, it follows that the mere increase in steamer tonnage during the last decade is equal to 7 million tons of sailing tonnage, while the amount of sailing tonnage under our flag now is less than 3 million tons. It also follows, that whereas our effective carrying power in 1870 (reckoning 1 steam as equal to 3 sailing tons) was 8 millions, and in 1880 12 millions, this had grown in 1890 to 18 million tons—an increase of 50 per cent. in the decade. This explains how the work of 164 million tons of entries and clearances in 1890, compared with 133 million tons in 1880, was done with a smaller number of vessels under the flag than we had since 1840. The voyages indicated by the entries and clearances at ports in the United Kingdom, however, do not show the whole work done by our flag. It performs a large amount of cross or intermediate service between foreign countries, which makes no mark whatever on our navigation returns. Some idea of this may be gathered by observing the degree in which other States are obliged to employ foreign tonnage, and the proportion which our flag bears therein. This appears in—

TABLE XIV.—*Showing the Proportion of the Entries and Clearances in the Foreign Trade of the Countries named under the National Flag, the British Flag, and other Foreign Flags.*

Date of Return.	Country.	Entries and Clearances under			Total Foreign.	Total Foreign in my last Paper.
		National Flag.	British Flag.	Other Foreign Flags.		
		Per cnt.	Per cnt.	Per cnt.	Per cnt.	Per cnt.
1889....	Russia	7.3	55.1	37.6	92.7	86.5
'90....	United States	22.1	52.8	25.1	77.9	78.7
'89....	Italy.................	24.8	48.4	26.8	75.2	61.0
'89....	Holland	30.5	52.0	17.5	69.5	69.3
'89....	Sweden	33.7	22.1	44.2	66.3	64.6
'89....	France	36.1	40.6	23.3	63.9	72.0
'89....	Germany	42.4	36.6	21.0	57.6	62.4
'89....	Norway	63.1	16.3	20.6	36.9	30.0

From Table XIV it would appear that more of the trade of the following States is being done by foreign tonnage now than ten years ago, viz.: Russia, Italy, Sweden, and Norway; also that only France and Germany are carrying a larger proportion of their own trade than appeared at my last investigation, and that the United States and Holland stand about where they were in this matter. It will be noted that of the entries and clearances in

Russia, the United States, and Holland, more than half are made by our flag; while the entries and clearances under the British flag are 48·4 per cent. in Italy, 40·6 in France, and 36·6 in Germany, from which it is safe to remark that more of the work of Russia, France, Italy, Holland, and the United States is done by our flag than by the flags of those States.

It will also be observed that English tonnage is double that of any other foreign flag in the United States, and nearly so in Italy. It is treble that of any other flag in Holland. In Russia the British proportion is 55·1, other foreign flags 37·6. In France 40·6 British, other foreign flags 23·3. In Germany, British 36·6, other foreign flags 21 per cent. In Sweden and Norway other foreign flags exceed our percentage. The proportion of foreign tonnage in the trade of Russia, which was 86·5 in 1879, had become 92·7 in 1889; that of the United States varied only from 78·7 to 77·9. France, with the help of bounties on its shipping, and differential duties on direct imports and exports, succeeded in decreasing the proportion of foreign tonnage in its trade from 72 to 63·9 per cent. In the case of Italy, however, and in spite of much friendly help from the government to its flag, the proportion of foreign tonnage grew from 61·0 to 75·2 per cent.

For the better appreciation of these comparisons with other flags, I show in—

TABLE XV.—*The Tonnage of the Merchant Vessels of the Countries named.*

Country.	1880.*			1890.†		
	Tonnage Registered as Seagoing.	Of which Steamer.	Percentage of Steamer.	Tonnage Registered as Seagoing.	Of which Steamer.	Percentage of Steamer.
United Kingdom	6,519,772	2,720,551	41·7	7,945,071	5,037,666	63·4
Greater Britain...	1,927,399	228,531	11·8	1,743,017	376,040	21·6
Total British Empire .... }	8,447,171	2,949,282	34·9	9,688,088	5,413,706	55·9
Norway	1,526,689	51,674	3·4	1,611,398	168,081	10·4
United States	1,352,810	156,323	11·6	946,695	197,680	20·9
Germany	1,171,286	196,343	16·7	1,320,721	617,911	46·8
Italy	1,005,972	72,666	7·2	824,474	182,249	22·1
France	932,853	255,959	27·4	932,735	492,684	52·8
Sweden	530,803	83,659	15·7	504,679	134,970	26·7
Holland	339,155	58,597	17·3	247,058	109,954	44·5
Denmark	251,958	48,799	19·3	289,217	103,824	35·9
Belgium	71,191	59,536	83·6	70,221	65,951	93·9
	7,182,717	983,556	13·7	6,747,199	2,073,254	30·7

* The years of the foreign States are—Norway 1878, United States 1880, Germany, Italy, France, Sweden, Holland, Denmark, and Belgium 1879.

† The years of the foreign States are—United States 1890, all the others 1889.

From Table XV it appears that there was an actual decrease of foreign tonnage during the decade under the flags mentioned, viz., from 7,182,717 to 6,747,199 tons. But the foreign steam tonnage had more than doubled, rising from 983,556 to 2,073,254 tons. Computing this on the usual rule of 3 to 1 for steamers, the result is an effective carrying power in 1890 of nearly 11 million tons against 9 millions in 1880. The total growth of effective carrying power under the flag of the British Empire, computing in the same way, was from 14¼ millions in 1880 to 20½ million tons in 1890 : in other words an increase of 50 per cent. in the decade.

It is observable also that while the total tonnage of all these enumerated States is under 7 million tons, that of the British Empire exceeds 9½ million tons; and that while all the steamer tonnage of these States is a little over 2 million tons, that of the United Kingdom alone exceeds 5 millions, and that of the Empire approximates to 5¼ millions.

The United States appear to have diminished both in sail and steam tonnage. France, Italy, Holland, and Denmark doubled their steamer tonnage, and Germany and Norway trebled their steamer tonnage.

Other States have been doing a great deal, but our addition of steamer tonnage since 1880 exceeds the total of steamer tonnage existing under all these other flags in 1890, as shown by the remarkable figure of 2,073,254 tons for all foreign, and 5,413,706 tons for the British Empire alone.

The enormous amount of work done by our flag for our own and other States, as shown in the foregoing tables, is the efficient source of that invisible export which helps so largely to make up for the excess value of imports over exports, about which we have heard so often in this Society.

It is coming to be understood how a quarter of a million men on board vessels at sea, carrying goods to markets where they sell for so much more than the cost at the place of shipment as covers the freight charges and profit, are producing the equivalent of an export value for the flag by which the goods are carried, just as much as if the same number of men were employed in cotton mills ashore instead of on board ships afloat; and that the result is as real an addition to the value of our export trade, as if the labour were spent in cotton manufactories instead of in carrying machines. I recently referred again to the remarkable paper read to the Society in 1882 by Mr. Giffen, in which he made an estimate of what this invisible export was equal to. Computing the 1890 tonnage figures on Mr. Giffen's data, I find it equal to 90 millions sterling, which may help to the appreciation of the important

place our carrying business occupies in relation to the disparity
in value between exports and imports.

Those who have done me the honour to follow me so far
through the proofs of growing tonnage wants, both in our own and
other countries, and of the degree in which our flag is supplying
these wants, will be ready to ask, what is being done to sustain
this remarkable position ?   This question I am able to answer by
information regarding new ships, for which I am indebted to the
officials of Lloyd's Registry of British and Foreign Shipping, whose
assistance and courtesy I gratefully acknowledge.   From a statement which I have, but the details of which I hardly thought it
necessary to print in full, it would appear that the production of
new vessels for 1890 exceeded that of any previous year.
Excluding vessels under 100 tons, it appears by " Lloyd's Register
" Book " that the new vessels produced in 1890 were :—

	Tons.
In the United Kingdom	1,197,235
„ the United States	140,878
„ Germany	102,465
„ British colonies	44,540
„ France	34,562
„ Norway	27,153
„ Holland and Belgium	26,133
„ Sweden	12,692
Total tons	1,585,658

our proportion being equal to 75 per cent. of the whole—more
satisfactory probably from the national point of view than from
that of the shipowners.

During the decade steel has almost supplanted the use of iron
in shipbuilding.   This is shown clearly in Table XVI :—

TABLE XVI.—*Showing the Number and Gross Tonnage of New Vessels built in the United Kingdom classed by "Lloyd's Register" during each of the Years 1881-90.*

Years.	Steel.				Iron.				Wood.				Total.				Grand Total.	
	Steam.		Sailing.		Steam.		Sailing.		Steam.		Sailing.		Steam.		Sailing.			
	No.	Tons.	No.	Tons.	No.	Tons.	No.	Tons.	No.	Tons.	No.	Tons.	No.	Tons.	No.	Tons.	No.	Tons.
1881....	19	38,792	8	3,167	391	612,040	50	73,686	6	885	84	8,911	416	651,717	187	85,764	553	737,481
'82....	50	105,441	8	12,477	432	714,489	67	107,745	11	945	65	5,250	493	820,875	140	125,472	633	946,347
'83....	87	146,136	15	15,703	545	782,807	66	113,298	5	484	67	5,276	637	929,427	148	134,277	785	1,063,704
'84....	73	112,288	18	12,376	276	484,109	92	137,341	14	1,074	85	7,465	463	597,471	190	157,182	653	754,653
'85....	85	124,337	26	31,884	131	134,375	117	160,296	14	762	90	8,349	230	257,474	233	200,529	463	458,003
'86....	105	155,366	20	28,984	104	79,715	55	102,259	17	1,045	71	6,030	226	236,126	146	137,273	372	373,399
'87....	192	359,705	13	18,008	59	41,908	28	48,500	6	563	49	4,209	257	393,176	90	70,717	347	463,893
'88....	320	611,574	30	53,883	60	36,995	14	22,792	10	1,944	30	2,643	390	660,513	74	79,318	464	739,831
'89....	438	877,530	52	99,072	81	45,805	10	19,669	5	322	27	2,508	519	923,657	89	121,249	608	1,044,906
'90....	469	921,491	56	107,578	91	39,226	4	5,294	3	784	16	1,479	563	961,501	76	114,351	639	1,075,852

It will be observed that in 1881 only 19 steel steamers were built, and 391 of iron; but in 1890 the number of steamers built of steel had increased to 469, and the number built of iron had fallen to 91. So in 1881 only 3 sailing vessels were built of steel, and 50 of iron; but in 1890 56 steel sailing ships were built, and only 4 iron. The production of wooden vessels is now limited to very small craft, and has ceased to be of any importance; but steel appears to have displaced iron, even with more rapidity than that with which iron displaced wood.

All the new tonnage, however, is not additional carrying power, much of it being required to replace the vessels which, from various causes, such as wrecks, sales to foreigners, &c., disappear from our registry every year. The extent of this disappearance is much greater than could be imagined, and I therefore give the figures for each year of the last decade in—

TABLE XVII.—*Showing the Tonnage Removed from the Registers of the United Kingdom in each Year from* 1881 *to* 1890.

Year.	Sail.		Steam.		Total Removed from Registers.	
	Vessels.	Tons.	Vessels.	Tons.	Vessels.	Tons.
1881	1,022	281,897	260	158,358	1,282	440,255
'82	919	258,695	296	188,443	1,215	447,138
'83	917	274,579	286	189,620	1,203	464,199
'84	826	225,397	265	157,193	1,091	382,590
'85	1,501	229,498	348	170,712	1,849	400,210
'86	1,236	210,781	314	178,308	1,550	389,089
'87	1,012	240,505	348	169,757	1,360	410,262
'88	787	240,922	321	178,426	1,108	419,348
'89	708	205,384	324	188,388	1,032	393,772
'90	765	223,349	338	212,785	1,103	436,134
Total	9,693	2,391,007	3,100	1,791,990	12,793	4,182,997
Average	969	239,100	310	179,199	1,279	418,299

From the above it would seem that nearly 1,000 sailing ships, and 300 steamers, have been removed from the registers during each year of the decade. In the year 1885, when agitation was high, it will be seen that no less than 1,849 removals from the registers took place. I commend this fact to the consideration of all whom it concerns. The average removals during the decade are no less than 1,279 per annum, and the average tonnage removed exceeds 400,000. These annual removals from our flag would furnish a respectably sized fleet for some of the smaller States.

Table XVIII.—*Showing the Number of Total Wrecks during the Years stated, which occurred to British and Foreign Vessels on or near to the Coasts of the United Kingdom; and the Number of Total Losses arising from Collision included therein.*

	1881.	1882.	1883.	1884.	1885.	1886.	1887.	1888.	1889.	1890.
Wrecks involving total loss..	705	606	551	473	371	380	421	401	367	353
Total losses from collisions included in the above figures..	69	80	56	66	80	70	83	82	72	72

That the number of wrecks in 1890 should be only half those of 1881, must be considered highly satisfactory; also the steady tendency throughout the decade for it to become less. It is regrettable, however, that the total losses from collision show no corresponding decline; on the contrary, we find 353 wrecks in 1890, yielding more total losses from collision than the 705 wrecks of 1881.

This is perhaps the class of sea casualty which more than any other is dependent on human agency. The Board of Trade publishes elaborate rules to prevent collisions at sea, and all the officers in charge of ships hold Board of Trade certificates of their competency to navigate—yet these collisions happen! It is disappointing to see this cause of disaster still operating so heavily, and it forces the question: Why does not the general reduction in loss from other causes show here also? What is the explanation? Is it the rules that are in fault, or the certificated officers? Or are we to conclude that, while traffic at sea is getting safer so far as all other causes of disaster are concerned, this frequency of collisions is to be regarded as inevitable, and that no reduction may be looked for? I am most reluctant to accept any such conclusion. It is also clearly not the opinion of the courts, for in most of the law suits, in which sea collisions end, the judicial authorities find one side or the other to blame, and order payment. But as the sole object of the rules is to prevent collisions, it seems clear that the rules fail to attain their object, and the continuance of collisions to such an extent suggests doubt as to whether our policy in this matter is not based on unsound principles. I have long entertained grave doubts about it; but if the rules had prevented collisions I would have concealed my doubts. At present the chief results are litigation and penalties; the collisions themselves go on. The money penalties do not fall on those whose errors cause the collisions, and whose greater care might so often

avoid them.   Besides, these penalties are so uncertain in their
operation, and sometimes so heavy, that the innocent persons who
have eventually to pay, are forced to provide against the possibility
by insurance, by which the operation of the penalties, as such, is
of course defeated.   One of our law courts is kept pretty constantly occupied with collision suits, to the great advantage of the
legal profession.   That again, however, does not stop the collisions,
but only adds to their ultimate cost, and to the loss of the public
in the final result.   It was indeed one of the acute legal discoveries
of the decade, that "collision" was not "a peril of the sea,"
because it was the result of the action of human discretion and
will.   I confess, however, that it is the only peril of the sea which
I fear when I am at sea.   This is neither the place nor the time
to further pursue this subject; but I direct attention to this
matter as standing in regrettable contrast with the improvements
so marked in our maritime affairs generally; and as one which
must be most unsatisfactory to the department responsible for the
rules which have not prevented collisions at sea.

The number of men employed in our maritime trade appears in—

TABLE XIX.—*Showing the Number of Men Employed in Sailing and Steam
Vessels belonging to the United Kingdom, and distinguishing British
from Foreign Seamen.*

Year.	Men in		Total.	Of which British.	Foreign.
	Sailing Vessels.	Steamers.			
1850	142,730	8,700	151,430	—	—
'60	145,487	26,105	171,592	157,312	14,280
'70	147,207	48,755	195,962	177,951	18,011
'80	108,668	84,304	192,972	169,692	23,280
'90	84,008	129,366	213,374	186,147	27,227

It is not surprising to find so large a decrease in the men
afloat in sailing vessels.   Their greatly reduced number made that
result inevitable.   The increase of 45,000 men afloat in steamers
since 1880 was also to be expected, from the large increase in the
steamer fleet.   The total increase is not so large as it appears, as
I understand the figure for 1890 includes masters, which the
earlier returns did not.   The proportion of foreigners is remarkably large, though not much in excess of that in 1880.   'It is
singular, however, that there should be work for 27,227 able-
bodied men, which our teeming population should not supply.   It
is a curious commentary on the "out-of-work" theories on which
so much philanthropic effort is based.   The above figures do not
include Lascars and Asiatics, who are largely employed in the
Indian trade.   Adding these, the total men employed under our

flag in 1890 was 236,108, of course excluding those in the Royal Navy. It would appear from these figures that, if we make a reasonable deduction for the fact that the captains are included in the 1890 return, there can be very few more British sailors employed in 1890 than there were in 1880, when our fleet was so much smaller. The increased size of vessels, and much labour-saving machinery on board, has no doubt further economised human labour; but our larger operations required more men, and they seem to have been found among the foreigners, Lascars and Asiatics. This must be admitted to be a regrettable fact. I am afraid its causes must be looked for in the agitations concerning maritime affairs of the last two decades. Statements of the most incorrect and misleading character, directly contradicted by the official returns, have been often made, and were repeated quite recently. These no doubt affect the opinion of the seafaring classes, and dispose many who might become sailors to seek employment on shore, and so make the necessity for manning our ships with 50,000 foreigners and Asiatics. These are to be had in any numbers, and are more sober, more amenable to discipline than many of the "union" men, whose *morale* has been sapped by desertion having been made easy, and by being perpetually instructed to believe that their employers, being capitalists, are their natural enemies. How otherwise can we explain that with far safer and more commodious ships, with much better food, with higher wages, the English sailor should make it necessary for English shipowners to employ 50,000 foreigners and Asiatics to get our work done? That is a problem which I venture earnestly to commend to all who really have the interests of our sailors at heart. It is regrettable enough to have our food grown to the extent it is grown by foreign labour: I cannot admit that there is any necessity whatever for such an amount of foreign labour to be employed in carrying it.

I directed attention in my last paper to the steady decrease in the number of apprentices' indentures enrolled. In 1880 the number was 3,501. In 1890 it had fallen to 2,167. This is only further confirmation of what I have said about seamen. There is no class of labour in this country, and, so far as I know, in any other country, so protected by government regulations and interference. The shipowners cannot engage or pay off a seaman except at a government office, or in the presence of a Government official sent on board the ship, on payment of an additional fee. The engagement and the account on discharge must all be made on government forms provided for the purpose; the limit of time within which wages must be paid in the presence of the official is exactly defined; so that, so far as nursing and coddling go, the seaman ought to be the best conditioned labourer in the country. Yet, despite all this, for twenty years past agitations have been rife; and during a time when our ships have improved so much as to out-distance all competitors in the maritime trade of the world, the number of apprentices has decreased, and the number of foreigners in this carefully protected labour has nearly doubled.   These facts should, I think, raise doubt as to whether, on this matter, our action—however well intended—is really based on sound principles; whether it would not be better for the government to interfere less · between employer and employed in this, as in other trades.   In any case, I mark it as a very unsatisfactory element in our maritime position, whatever be its causes, that, despite the admitted difficulties of finding employment for our people on shore, our work at sea should be done to such an increasing extent by foreigners.

The subject of the loss of life at sea was exhaustively treated in an able paper read before this Society by my friend Mr. Thomas Scrutton in December, 1885.   I therefore do not propose to say much on it.   By using great totals, and by skilful grouping, the statistics on the subject had been misused—unintentionally I am sure.   Periods of known bad weather had been ignored.   The dissection of the totals, however, corrected much of the misapprehension, and forced some forgotten considerations into the controversy which practically settled it.   First, that the loss of life at any period must be taken in relation to the number of lives at risk at that period; to the known weather facts; and to the magnitude of the maritime work being done.   Secondly, that it would always remain possible to say truly that there was preventible loss of life at sea.   There is much preventible loss of life on land also.   So long as it suits us to occupy a quarter of a million of imperfect men afloat, they are certain to commit faults, errors, and crimes even, which will make it possible to say quite truthfully that preventible loss of life at sea continues.

I mentioned in my last paper that the Registrar-General, whose figures of mortality in relation to strength I then quoted, expressed the opinion that they aggravated the mortality of seamen afloat. It was found on subsequent investigation that some of the deaths were recorded twice, and that many deaths on board colonial and fishing vessels had been included, the crews of which vessels were not included in the strength on which the rate of loss was computed.   There was much doubt also as to what constituted the strength of the mercantile marine.   The figures used have only been estimates, not ascertained facts; indeed, the latter seem to be hardly ascertainable.   The Registrar-General, no doubt for some good reason, has discontinued the record from which I last quoted, so that I am unable to give a continuation of the figures for the last decade on his authority. I may add, however, that in a return of the loss of life at sea, dated 17th March, 1891, in continuation of Parliamentary Paper No. 3875, the corrected figures of the total deaths from drowning in 1881 are given. The loss of life for that year had been stated as 3,475, the corrected figures are 3,084. This would seem to show that the surmise of the Registrar-General touching the exaggeration of the deaths was justified.

The official statement on the subject of loss of life at sea is published in the abstracts relating to shipping casualties by the Board of Trade for the year 1889-90, dated July, 1891, No. C-6468. Summarising these, Mr. Swanston, the secretary to the Marine Department, says: "The loss of life by wreck and casualty in " vessels belonging to the United Kingdom was 1,297 in 1889-90, " or 709 less than in 1888-89, 246 less than in 1887-88, 628 less " than in 1886-87, and 735 less than the average for the ten " years preceding 1886-87."

But it appears that even here, as elsewhere, we must beware of totals. This loss of life must itself be dissected to get at any reliable opinion on the matters which legislation in the United Kingdom can directly affect. For Mr. Swanston himself adds in the report from which I am quoting, that "the number of lives lost " in 1888-89 was swelled by the large number of Indian passengers " (703) lost in the ss. *Vaitarna*, of Glasgow, 64 tons, which was " missing on a coasting voyage in India." And, as affecting the life loss in vessels belonging to British possessions abroad he also adds: "The lives lost in 1887-88 were swelled by 495 Chinese " passengers lost in the *Wah Yeung*, of Hong Kong, and 131 " passengers lost in a ferry boat on the river Hooghly, and in " 1886-87 were swelled by 735 Indian passengers lost in the " missing steamer *Sir John Lawrence.*" The disturbing character of these Chinese and Indian passenger figures will be obvious to all statisticians, and fully justifies the qualifications made by Mr. Swanston respecting them.

At the same time, I do not think Mr. Swanston's statement adequately represents the improvement that has taken place. I have therefore prepared a table which shows the total tonnage of British vessels entered and cleared at ports in the United Kingdom only from 1881-90, the lives of seamen lost during the same period, and the proportion of life lost per 100,000 tons to the total tonnage entered and cleared. This at all events is based on facts, not on estimates, and I give the comparative ratios, which speak for themselves.

TABLE XX.—*Showing from 1881 to 1890 the separate Tonnage of British Sailing and Steam Vessels Entered and Cleared at Ports in the United Kingdom, the Lives Lost, and the Proportion per 100,000 Tons between the Lives Lost and the Work done.*

Year.	Sailing Vessels.			Steam Vessels.		
	Total Tonnage of British Vessels Entered and Cleared at Ports in United Kingdom.	Lives Lost.	Proportion of Lives Lost to Total Tonnage Entered and Cleared.	Total Tonnage of British Vessels Entered and Cleared at Ports in United Kingdom.	Lives Lost.	Proportion of Lives Lost to Total Tonnage Entered and Cleared.
			Per 100,000 tons			Per 100,000 tons
1881...	32,486,115	1,854	4·17	82,448,250	468	0·57
'82....	31,165,021	1,508	4·84	87,541,294	916	1·05
'83....	30,033,734	1,146	3·81	94,921,999	779	0·82
'84....	27,916,938	1,200	4·30	96,646,187	492	0·51
'85....	27,912,934	540	1·93	98,844,770	718	0·73
'86....	26,582,738	734	2·76	99,108,556	155	0·16
'87....	26,722,539	773	2·89	103,857,831	646	0·62
'88....	26,138,700	687	2·63	112,061,218	581	0·52
'89....	25,361,467	557	2·20	114,747,913	418	0·36
'90....	23,338,193	480	2·06	118,511,100	482	0·41

N.B.—The tables of lives lost are made up annually to 30th June. The tables of tonnage entered and cleared are made up annually to 31st December.

The figures under "Lives Lost" are the total number of crew lost at sea by wreck and casualty in vessels of all kinds belonging to the United Kingdom, excluding fishing vessels.

As regards sailing vessels first. It will be noted that the tonnage was nearly 32½ millions in 1881, and under 23½ millions in 1890; the lives lost in the first year were 1,354, and in the latter only 480; the ratio being 4·17 per 100,000 tons in 1881, and only 2·06 in 1890. So that a decreased trade by sailing vessels ended in, not merely a decreased loss, but in a reduction in the ratio of loss from 4·17 to 2·06, or 50·6 per cent.; a large reduction both in actual number and in ratio. As regards steamers, it will be also noted that the tonnage in 1881 was nearly 82½ millions, and in 1890 118½ millions; the lives lost in the first year were 468, and in the last 482; the ratio being 0·57 in 1881 and 0·41 in 1890. The increase in the traffic was equal to 43·6 per cent.; the decrease of life lost was equal to 28 per cent.

The reported deaths among masters and seamen from all causes in 1889 were 13·1 per 1,000 of the strength, comparing with 19 per 1,000 in 1879, and the average annual rate of 23·2 per 1,000 during the twenty-eight years preceding.

I think it will be admitted that these statements regarding diminishing life loss at sea are most satisfactory. The superior safety of steam vessels is most apparent. The greater control over their movements possessed by steamers, is a constant factor working for safety. The tendency is growing for even the largest steamers to rely almost entirely on their engines, and very little

on sails. It is very remarkable to hear, as we now frequently
hear, of engines running for thousands of miles without being
stopped for any purpose whatever.

It is just to add that the decreasing loss of life in sailing
vessels is most important. The character of our sailing fleet is
improving. The small old wooden vessels are disappearing from
the register, as I have shown, at the rate of about 1,000 a year;
and the new sailing tonnage consists for the greater part of steel
and iron ships of large tonnage, and most superior type.

The question of bounties offered by certain foreign States
excited much interest in the early years of the decade, particularly
those sanctioned by the French Act of the 29th January, 1881.
The French tonnage figures, to which I have already referred,
hardly seem to justify either the hopes excited by this Act in
France or the fears that it produced here. A report made by
Lord Lytton to the Marquis of Salisbury gives the following
figures as the total bounty paid, both for the construction and
running of vessels in the year named :—

		Frs.	
1881	......	1,931,793	
'82	......	10,999,201	
'83	......	11,625,588	
'84	......	13,074,299	
'85	......	8,696,431	
'86	......	10,583,965	
'87	......	11,000,000	
'88	......	9,000,000	Estimates.
'89	......	9,000,000	

The French estimates do not distinguish the annual sums set
apart as bounties for construction from those earned in navigation.
In asking for the last two figures in the above list, the Minister
attributed the smallness of the amount to the notable falling off in
the building of ships at French yards. The bounty on the
construction of ships was enacted without any limit of time;
that for running was established for ten years, and expired in
January, 1891; it has been temporarily renewed, and is expected
to be renewed again for a long period.

TABLE XXI.—*Showing the Number and Net Tonnage of Vessels that
passed through the Suez Canal in* 1870, 1880, *and* 1890.

Year.	Number of Vessels.	Net Tonnage.	Transit Receipts.	Mean Net Tonnage per Vessel.	Proportion of British Vessels to Total Tonnage.
			frs.		
1870	486	436,609	5,159,327	898	—
1880	2,026	3,057,421	39,840,487	1,509	79·97
1890	3,389	6,890,094	66,984,000	2,033	77·37

It will be observed that during the last decade the tonnage considerably more than doubled, and that the proportion of British tonnage, notwithstanding the great increase shown, is only slightly less than in 1880. The next State to our own in proportion of canal traffic in 1890 was Germany, with 7·12 per cent., about one-tenth of the English; France follows with 5·31 per cent.; Holland with 3·61 per cent. France had the second place, but in the last three years, despite the bounties, her proportion of the traffic has decreased, and she now occupies the third place.

It is satisfactory to be able to add, that the controversy between the English shipowners and the canal company, and the subsequent agreement to which it led in 1883, after the rejection by Parliament of the provisional arrangement made by Mr. Childers, have resulted in the removal of the unpleasantness and friction which then existed in canal affairs, and in the establishment of a state of things by which both the company and the shipowners have benefited. It is only just to the company to say that the traffic has been much better managed. The organisation of night transit by the extensive use of the electric light, by providing the channel with lighted buoys and beacons, in connection with other improvements, has reduced the time of transit from about forty-eight hours in 1883, to twenty-two hours in 1890. These improvements, and the extra staff involved, were effected at considerable cost to the company. The reductions in the transit dues provided for in the agreement were all duly made, and from 1885 the pilotage charge was abolished. This item had brought the company a revenue close upon 100,000*l*. in 1883. Large sums of money have been expended in deepening and widening the canal. The company has gained by this wise and far seeing policy, adopted with some reluctance in 1883. The revenue in 1890 was larger than in any previous year, and in 1891 showed a still further increase, having risen to 85 millions of francs.

In my last paper I alluded to the changes likely to result if the Panama canal were completed, of which, at that time, there appeared some prospect. Its failure has been one main cause of the recent construction of so many large steel sailing ships, based on the expectation that the northern Pacific grain trades are nearly safe against serious steamer competition for the remainder of this century at least. After the heavy losses sustained in the attempt to pierce the Isthmus by M. de Lesseps, it seems doubtful that the European public will at any early date risk more capital in the effort. Indeed one has only to think of the losses which have been, and are still being suffered in canal and dock enterprises nearer home, to be satisfied that the Pacific traffic must go for a long time *viâ* Cape Horn, unless the United States Government should

decide to provide funds for one of the schemes for getting through
the Isthmus.

The last fact relating to the decade which I propose to name is
the Load Line Act of 1890. The subject had been under occasional consideration by Lloyd's Registry since 1870.   In 1873,
Mr. Martell, the chief surveyor to the Registry, prepared and submitted to the Royal Commission on Unseaworthy Ships, then
sitting, a series of freeboard tables. These were based upon the
principle of every vessel having a certain proportion of spare buoy-
ancy according to its structure.   In 1875 and 1880 further steps
were taken; and in the latter year especially, after extensive
information had been accumulated of the load lines in actual use,
the Committee of Lloyd's Registry instructed their chief surveyor
to frame tables suitable for the various types of vessel. These tables,
however, after much criticism, underwent further amendment in
1882 and 1883, and in 1885 were referred to a departmental committee of experts, by which they were finally adopted, and are now
known as the Load Line Committee's Tables. With modifications,
they were substantially the tables prepared by Lloyd's Registry;
and as issued by the Load Line Committee, were accepted by the
Board of Trade in August, 1885, and by the Committee of Lloyd's
Registry in September, 1885. The use of these tables, however,
was in a restricted sense voluntary, until the Load Line Act was
passed in June, 1890, and became compulsory in December of that
year.   Previous to the passing of the Act, about 2,200 vessels had
been voluntarily submitted by the owners to Lloyd's Registry to
be marked in accordance with the tables. This extent of voluntary
approval cleared the way for the Act, and enabled its provisions to
be brought into operation with less friction than might have been
expected.   Freeboards have been already assigned to about 6,500
British vessels by "Lloyd's Register." I understand that the Board
of Trade has assigned about 2,200 freeboards, and other authorised
bodies about 800; leaving to be dealt with somewhere about 1,000
vessels, many of which are permanently engaged abroad, and some
of which are gradually coming in from long voyages. This accounts
approximately for the vessels liable under the Act; all the smaller
craft—ships under 80 tons register employed solely in the coasting
trade, fishing vessels and pleasure yachts—being exempted.

I record the settlement of the load line during the decade,
and the facts relating to the preparation, modification, adoption,
and legislation of these tables, as proof of the extreme care with
which this State interference with the liberty of shipowners has
been very gradually established; of the loyalty with which it has
been accepted by the shipowners themselves, many of whom had
urged its adoption; and, lastly, of the skill and wisdom of the

officials and experts concerned, especially of Mr. Martell, the author of the first series of tables already named. It is needless to add that the tables are neither final nor perfect; so that if the future should bring some new types of vessel to which they are inapplicable, such structures would be considered and dealt with on their merits.

In concluding my papers on this subject in 1872 and in 1882, I referred to the natural growth of this great shipping industry as the conclusive reason for the State letting it severely alone. In the decade 1870-80, under the influence of a well meant philanthropy, considerable interference was sanctioned. Fortunately, at an early period of the last decade, an influential voice from within the Board of Trade itself proclaimed that this legislation was a delusion, and that its chief permanent result had been an army of surveyors, costing the country about 1,000*l.* per week. So it happened that during the last decade, in spite of much proposed interference, very little was enacted. I mention the fact as creditable both to the present and to the last Government. The department concerned knows, and the public—certainly the wiser part of the public—is beginning to see that in the use of our great mineral resources for maritime business the largest possible liberty to the shipowner is our soundest policy. The facts I have submitted to-night show what enormous progress has been made without the restrictions which some people thought indispensable. I have only on this point therefore to reiterate the opinion expressed in 1872 and 1882, to the effect that as our State does not give, and is not asked to give, either bounties or favours, or privileges, of any kind to its flag, it should not hamper it with restrictions in its unrestricted competition with other flags. Indeed, what I have named as to the failure of the Board of Trade regulations to prevent collisions at sea, and as to the increasing numbers of foreigners in our service, rather suggests the necessity for inquiry, with a view to less artificial arrangements, on both of these most important subjects.

It would seem unnecessary to emphasise the financial and political importance of this trade to the country. The capital invested, the employment given both on shore and afloat, and the value annually produced are so many considerations which explain the envy of other States, though they are only beginning to be very gradually appreciated in our own. But by far the most important aspect from which this tonnage question can be regarded is its intimate connection with our supplies of food. This I may indeed emphasise; the facts are so difficult to grasp, so little known, that so long as the ordinary Englishman finds bread and meat on his table, he is contented to know that the one comes from the butcher and the other from the baker, and makes as little further inquiry as an ancient Hebrew would have made as to the supplies of manna in the wilderness. But the degree of our dependence on food brought over sea is constantly increasing. It is not merely that our population is larger than it was fifty years ago, but that the larger population—in spite of all allegations to the contrary now and then made—is so much better off, has so much more to spend, eats so much more, and drinks more, besides wearing more and better clothes and living in better houses. The limited area of these islands cannot supply half the present inhabitants at their present rate of consumption. Two-thirds of our daily bread is dependent on sea carriage, but it is carried in our ships so easily and cheaply that the consumers generally are quite unconscious of the fact. In 1890, the imported value of five articles—corn (of all kinds), meat, butter, cheese, and eggs, was equal to 2 millions sterling per week. To put other nations under tribute for the supply of our wants to this vast extent, and to be able to pay for the supplies, I have already called the miracle of modern commerce. The increased work required of our flag is largely consequent on these demands for foreign food. It is noteworthy also that some of our nearest European neighbours are following our example in this matter. Their heavy duties on the import of foreign corn have not been able to keep it out, though they have kept the prices to consumers in France and Germany at an elevation above the English prices measured exactly by their import duties. Fortunately our teeming population has suffered no such disadvantage. Our free trade policy has thus benefited mankind everywhere, by stimulating the production and cheapening the cost of human subsistence, while the reduction in the cost of sea carriage has made supplies from the most distant sources so freely available, as practically to place the surplus food of the world at the disposal of the European populations. Sir Robert Peel had an idea that the freight from America would be too dear to enable American grown wheat to compete seriously with English. In a famous cabinet memorandum which he presented to his colleagues before the repeal of the corn laws, he assured them that no quantity of wheat could probably be delivered from the United States at a less cost than 45*s*. per quarter. Against this prediction I only mention the fact that in one year during the last decade, viz., in 1887, with the average price of wheat at 32*s*. 6*d*., we carried from the United States to the United Kingdom 8 million quarters. To such a degree has the steamer, the railway, and the telegraph changed the conditions of this question, and falsified the prediction on which Sir Robert Peel obtained the assent of his Cabinet to his great measure.

It is not the province of statisticians to prophesy, and this would be the last place to venture. But it is strictly within the province of the statistician to mark the growth of facts, and it can hardly be denied that the change from being a self supporting nation, as we were fifty years ago, to being absolutely dependent on foreign growers and open sea communications for two-thirds of our daily bread, forces into our policy a new factor of the first magnitude. It is not the balance of power in Europe which concerns us now, but how we can feed our people. Other nations are in quite different circumstances. Their interests and policy are not necessarily ours. In addressing the German Parliament in December last (the "Times," 11th December), General von Caprivi made the following significant observations, in defending the continuance of the German corn duties:—

" The corn laws were necessary for the protection of German " agriculture, although it is certain that they have not had the " effect expected from them. It is nevertheless certain that their " existence prevents an agricultural crisis, of which it would be " impossible to overrate the evil consequences. *A parallel with* " *English conditions is not possible.* . . . . . The chief reason, " however, for the necessity for the maintenance of agriculture is " exclusively a question of State. I am convinced that such a " cultivation of grain is indispensable to us as will, in case of need, " suffice to feed even our increasing population in time of war, and " that the State which cannot exist from its own agricultural pro- " duce, is on the downward path."

Fortunately the English and German conditions are not parallel, otherwise we should not only be on the downward path, but already near to the bottom, and of this there are no signs. On the other hand, we must not ignore the fact—a fact that has never hitherto existed in the history of our race—viz., that 38 millions of human beings living in a group of islands, depend on sea communications for two-thirds of their daily bread! Is it too much to expect that these islanders, and their parliament, and their statesmen, and even their philanthropists, should appreciate the fleet by which they are fed, in a degree second only to that other fleet by which their shores and empire are defended ? Is it too much to say that these are the considerations by which English policy—fiscal and foreign alike—ought to be mainly governed ?

DISCUSSION *on* MR. GLOVER'S PAPER.

SIR RAWSON W. RAWSON said all Fellows must be grateful to Mr. Glover for this valuable collection of facts, and hoped that younger Fellows than himself would hear him finish his fifty years' report of the tonnage of the kingdom. He differed a little from Mr. Glover as to the view he took of the value of a single year for comparison, for he was rather disposed to group a few years together for comparative purposes. In this instance it so happened that 1880 was a year in which our trade—both import and export—sprang up "in a leap and a bound" from the preceding three years' depression. Consequently Mr. Glover, in wishing to show the great advance during the last decade, had done himself an injustice. The tonnage imports in 1880 were 14 per cent. above those of the preceding year, and their values 13 per cent. higher; whilst the tonnage exports were 12 per cent., and their values 15 per cent. higher. Those who followed the course of events knew what an immense difference that made in the trade of the year. There were different ways of showing a contrast between one period and another. To compare 1880 with 1890 told little, because 1879 and 1881 might be quite different from 1880; and, in fact, this was the case, for after 1880 there came a reaction and a falling off in everything. There were three different methods of comparison, and he thought the soundest was to take all the years of the decade together and average them: thus the whole trade of one decade was compared with that of another. The end of a decade—say the last three years, might also be taken; but a single year should never be taken, since you could never depend on it as affording ground for fair comparison. Another method was to take the year itself, the year preceding, and the year following. Which of these methods should be used depended very much on the object in view. Mr. Glover showed that between 1870 and 1880 there was an increase of 57 per cent. in the tonnage entered and cleared with cargoes in the foreign trade, and an increase of 26 per cent. between 1880 and 1890, showing that in the last decade the increase was only one-half what it was in the preceding one. But if you took the ten years together, and compared the decade ending 1870 with that ending 1880, the advance was 60 per cent., and the decade between 1880 and 1890 it was 46½ per cent. There were many remarkable changes in the figures of 1880 in Table I, which prevented any fair comparison with the decade of which 1880 was made the representative. With reference to Mr. Glover's remarks on the salt trade, he had inquired into the price of that article as affecting the export trade. In 1870 it was 10s.; in 1880, 11s. 6d.; and in 1890, 18s.; and, consequently, the export of this article from England had been knocked on the head. A strong proof in support of his objection to a single year was afforded by Mr. Glover's statement, that wool showed a large increase, from 463 to 633 million pounds; in the year before 1890 it was 701 millions: and in 1891 it was 715 millions. What then was the value of a comparison between these single years?

Colonel HILL said he could not attempt to criticise the mode in which the statistics had been presented, but could endorse every word of eulogium on a paper so valuable, not only to the Society, but to the important branch of British commerce with which it dealt, viz., shipowning. The first thing that struck him was the wonderful expansiveness of British trade. It was only by a continuance of such expansion that shipowners could now hope for any profitable return on their investments. He thought the mere fact of the enormous increase in the number of vessels rendered it almost impossible that any regulations could altogether prevent collisions at sea. He had taken a great interest in the question of the supply of seamen. There could be no doubt the nurseries from which seamen had been supplied were one by one falling away. The sailing vessel was being supplanted by the steamer. He saw from the returns at Lloyds that in the fishery trade, whence large numbers of the very best sailors used to be drawn, steam was asserting its supremacy, and destroying even that source of supply. If shipowners and the Admiralty were to combine they would be able to train up a much larger number of sailors, who might be usefully employed in taking the places of the foreigners now found on our ships in such alarming numbers. It might not now be deemed proper to insist upon shipowners taking boys to sea in their steamers, but, personally, he would have no objection to see an enactment made to that effect. No doubt a good deal had been done by those who were supposed to have the sailors' welfare at heart, of a nature to deter men from going to sea. Only a few days ago he had seen an article in an Irish paper which, speaking of the remarks he (Colonel Hill) had made at the Associated Chambers of Commerce, hoped they would not be made an excuse for making further inroads on the " pittance of the sailor." He maintained that sailors were better looked after than any other class : they had better wages, better food, and their comfort was studied in every possible way. As to legislation, they all agreed that the less they had the better it would be for shipping; and there could be no stronger reason adduced for the avoidance of restrictive legislation, than the facts Mr. Glover had brought forward as to the enormous increase and proud position of the British carrying trade and its magnificent fleet.

Mr. CLARKE HALL said he should be very glad if shipowners could find it profitable to take apprentices ; but he was afraid that it was not a profitable investment, and therefore they could hardly be expected to take them for the good of the public.

Sir EDWARD HARLAND regretted that he had not had the advantage of hearing the earlier part of the paper. It appeared to him that the fact of the number of collisions being almost stationary, while losses from other causes decreased, admitted of a ready, though not a satisfactory explanation. The cause was the much larger class of vessels now trading, and the speed at which they went. Nowadays ships carried on in all weathers, whereas formerly they were content to lay to during a gale or fog; but a steamer could not afford to do this. He hoped that many of the melancholy calamities from such collisions might be materially lessened if the recommendations of the Bulkhead Committee, called together last year by the Board of Trade for the consideration of the safety of ships, could be followed, if to a limited extent only, by shipowners. He was sure that they had yet to learn the simple and inexpensive mode pointed out in that report, and he believed that quietly, but if not, then by means of legislation, some of the recommendations would be adopted. He referred to a more accurate and scientific method of subdividing ships built of iron or steel, so that, in case of a collision, the uninjured parts should be amply sufficient to keep the vessel afloat. Being a shipowner as well as a ship builder, he regretted that owners fifty years ago got the law repealed requiring ships to carry a certain number of apprentices. He could understand shipowners of that time objecting to what was rather a severe impost, but, as a result, the supply of seamen had become so injuriously affected that he doubted whether anything short of compulsion, *i.e.*, legislation, would secure anything like an adequate supply of seamen again; though of course it would be preferable that shipowners should see this for themselves, especially sailing shipowners, as it was generally considered that the men learnt the duties of their calling better in a sailing ship. He himself thought a great deal of valuable work could be learnt in steamers, and he would much prefer a man who had served his apprenticeship on a steamer, to a loafer off the quays, or some foreigner probably not half as well taught. Therefore he would not hesitate to ship boys on his steamers, feeling that he was thereby producing a nursery for the more modern requirements. With regard to shipping generally, he regarded this enormous increase in our tonnage as a direct result of our coal-fields. These were the source of the wealth of the country, and made it possible to live in the very artificial condition of having two-thirds of our food brought from the Antipodes. As soon as the coal supply decreased, so that we could no longer afford to waste it in gigantic furnaces manufacturing for everybody all over the world, then England would retire again into a very third-rate position among nations. He thought something should be done to prevent the waste of coal or its exportation to foreign countries; for he looked upon the possession of it as the key to the whole of our marvellous position.

Mr. J. S. JEANS said he had intended to call attention to the last point raised by Sir E. Harland, as he could fully appreciate the great importance of coal to our maritime industry. He would like to have seen Mr. Glover refer also to the causes of the enormous development of our shipping trade. Among such causes the question of coal was *facile princeps*. Mr. Glover had mentioned that the total export tonnage carried by our ships was something

like 75 million tons yearly, and he might have added that of this
quantity some 30 million tons, or not quite half, were coal, which
guaranteed a large amount of double freight.   But the development of our shipping industry was also dependent on other
elements on which he would have liked to hear Sir E. Harland or
Mr. Glover touch.   One was our peculiarly advantageous position
with respect to the manufacture of cheap iron and steel.   There
could be no doubt that next to coal this was the basis of the whole
matter; and he thought that the shipping development of the last
decade owed more to the substitution of steel for iron than to any
other cause—excepting, indeed, the expansion of the coal exports.
The necessities of our food supply had compelled shippers to look
for cheap transportation, and had developed the inventive talents
of the country in the form of triple and quadruple expansion
engines.   Had it not been for our industrial necessities he doubted
whether that development would have taken place.   With respect
to the decline in the shipping and shipbuilding of the United
States, while he was in Philadelphia, about eighteen months ago,
he had learned from one or two of the leading shipbuilders on the
Delaware that the reason of that decline was largely the substitution of iron and steel for wood.   So long as timber was the
material used for building ships, the United States could fairly
well compete with us, but when it came to be a question of iron
and steel, into the production of which labour entered to so large
an extent, they ceased to be in the running.   They still, however,
produced a very large tonnage annually of wooden ships that were
used for their lake and river trade.   He had also ascertained of
late that considerable attention was being given on Lake Superior
to the production of iron and steel vessels of the type known as
whale backs, which were intended to be sent right down from
Duluth, through Lake Superior, the Sault St. Marie Canal, and the
Lower Lakes to Europe.   In one case at least they had sent a
large cargo of grain to Liverpool by such means.   There were
shipbuilders in the United States who looked to this as the system
of the future for the export of grain supplies, and it was possible
we might witness an important development in that direction
before long.

Mr. STEPHEN BOURNE said that on the last occasion when
Mr. Glover read a paper it fell to his lot to open a discussion,
and to start the point with regard to the selection of a single year
at the end of a decade rather than the average of two or three,
which was the system he advocated.   On that occasion Mr. Glover
was rather fortunate in the particular years for comparison, but on
the present occasion it turned rather to his disadvantage.   The
increase in tonnage in 1880 was a quarter of the increase during
the whole decade of which 1880 was the last year, consequently
had Mr. Glover taken 1871 and 1881 instead of 1870 and 1880, the
figures would have shown a much smaller increase for the first
decade, and a larger increase on the one just ended.   Still as he
had always taken each tenth year as it had come, it was perhaps
best to continue the same system, only it should be borne in mind

that the results were not to be too strongly dwelt on. The advantage of a little friendly criticism on the last occasion was manifested in this, as Mr. Glover had now embodied several tables giving each year separately. Mr. Glover had shown that the British tonnage entered and cleared with cargoes was 46,406,000 tons in 1890; had he taken 1891 this would have been only 45,534,000. This was a point to which attention might be drawn, that the preponderance of British tonnage was not being kept up as it would appear from Table VII, for in 1891 we had 870,000 tons less British shipping in our entries and clearances, while there were 350,000 tons more foreign. Attention had been called to the enormous increase in petroleum; but here again the statement given did not represent the full increase, for in 1891 50 per cent. more petroleum was imported than in the year preceding. He could not quite agree with Mr. Glover in thinking it was a matter of danger for us to be dependent on foreign countries for our food supply. He thought it was the greatest security for the maintenance of peace that countries should be mutually dependent on each other, and the greatest possible means of promoting civilisation throughout the world. It was the great magnitude of our business that would tend to preserve the peace of this country, because there was no possibility of the whole world being in arms against us at the same time, and the numerous sources from which we derived our supplies would prevent any one country from doing us serious injury. He cordially joined in thanking Mr. Glover for a most interesting and valuable paper, one that was certainly amongst the best of the session.

Mr. A. E. BATEMAN wished to make a remark on two passages in the paper. Mr. Glover had said that "the increasing proportion of beet sugar in our consumption yields little employment to our shipping, as it comes from the near countries, and consequently occupies our vessels less than voyages with cane sugar from the East and West Indies formerly did;" and again, "I add here, as a factor greatly affecting freight and tonnage questions, that great fluctuations occur in the sources from which these grain supplies come, for while the voyage from the Atlantic and Russian ports may occupy only three weeks, that from Australia may exceed three months, and from the Pacific ports more than four months." Seventy years ago people were content to record the number of ships entering and clearing at a port or in a country. For many years the tonnage had been recorded, but we had not yet began to record how far the tonnage travelled. At the last meeting of the International Statistical Congress, M. Kiaer, the talented head of the Norwegian Statistical Department, tried to institute the registration of the ton-mile, *i.e.*, the number of tons per 1,000 miles travelled. It made a great difference in freight earnings whether a vessel of 1,000 tons came from Havre or from Australia. Though any such system of recording distance would give a great deal of trouble, he felt bound to mention what was desired by the Institute of International Statistics, namely, the record of the "carrying energy" of shipping as shown by the tonnage carried by distance.

Mr. G. G. CHISHOLM said he would refer to what Mr. Glover called the "miracle of modern commerce." He had said the dependence of this country on food brought from abroad was constantly increasing, but he (Mr. Chisholm) did not think that the statistics quite bore out the statement down to the latest period. He had grouped the imports of wheat and flour in five-year periods since 1831, and he found that in every period there had been an increase over the previous one until the period 1881-85 inclusive. In that period the total amount of wheat and flour imported amounted on the average to 76,780,000 cwts. annually (taking 80 cwts. of flour as equivalent to 100 of wheat). In 1886-90, however, the average was 75,930,000 cwts., or rather less, and that indicated that there had in the last quinquenniad been no tendency to increase the amount of imports. There were various grounds for believing that the agricultural depression had come to an end, which implied that if the imports of wheat and flour did increase in future, it would not be to so alarming an extent as hitherto. It was quite true that the experience of the present year seemed to belie that anticipation; but 1891 had been an exceptional year. The harvest of the United States had furnished a much greater yield per acre than any of the preceding eleven years, namely 15·3 Winchester bushels, against the previous maximum (1882) of 13·6, and against the average of 12·06 for the twelve years 1880-91; and this coincided with a great expansion in the last year in the wheat area of the United States. This area fluctuated during the period in question for the most part between 36,000,000 and 38,000,000 acres; it was 36,000,000 in 1890 and 39,900,000 in 1890-91. One other point he would mention. Mr. Glover and Sir Rawson Rawson had alluded to salt and the apparent effect of the Salt Union in enhancing prices, and thus reducing trade. Salt was one of those articles which might be described as ballast cargoes, which shippers were willing to send out at a moderate rate in order to get the ships to a destination where they would get a homeward cargo. The chief market for salt was India. Now it appeared that the import of salt from the United Kingdom into India had declined from 6,218,000 cwts. in 1886-87 to 3,617,000 cwts. in 1889-90. From Germany in the same years the import into India rose from 460,000 to 1,816,000 cwts., and the whole effect did not appear to end there. The value of the exports from India to Germany rose from about 310,000*l.* in 1885-86 to 1,913,000*l.* in 1889-90 (gold values at the average rate of exchange of the rupee for each year), an increase of more than sixfold in four years. It was quite possible that the increased export of salt from Germany to India, enabling ships to go out there with a ballast cargo, fostered the homeward trade from India to Germany; so that the action of the Salt Union in forcing up prices had a doubly bad effect on our trade.

Mr. G. J. SWANSTON said that Mr. Glover had alluded to the interference of the authorities in connection with shipping matters. It seemed to him that the period of great improvement to which

the tables bore testimony, was really the period of such interference as had occurred. The Mercantile Marine Act was passed
in 1850, and the Merchant Shipping Act in 1854: these were the
Acts which would probably be regarded as commencing the interference with the mercantile marine; the figures put before them
that evening showed, however, that the immense development in
our mercantile marine might be dated from the year 1850, and
had continued down to the present time. With regard to the rule
of the road at sea, the only part taken by the Board of Trade in
the matter—he spoke subject to correction—was to formulate the
views of a considerable number of people who had studied the
subject. These rules were not made by the Board of Trade, but
the Board had taken an active part in putting the regulations into
shape and securing their universal adoption. With regard to the
employment of foreigners, that was a matter altogether beyond the
Board of Trade, and he was not aware that the legislature had
since the passing of the Merchant Shipping Act, 1854, interfered
with the proportion of foreign seamen carried.

Mr. GLOVER, in reply, thanked the Fellows for their patient
attention to the wonderful story he had placed before them, and
those who had taken part in the debate for their too friendly
appreciation of his work. As Sir Rawson Rawson had pointed
out, a comparison of separate years instead of decades might have
still further emphasised the progress made during the last decade,
but he had preferred to adhere to the plan of his previous papers,
in spite of the fact that the year 1880, with which 1890 is compared, was one of quite exceptional development. The observations
of Sir Rawson Rawson however had this important advantage, viz.,
they showed that the marvellous story Mr. Glover had related was
not exaggerated, but might have been made stronger still by
another treatment of the figures. He felt much obliged to Sir
Rawson Rawson for pointing this out. Mr. Glover agreed with
Sir Edward Harland as to the causes of many of the collisions,
but could not accept his view that we may expect them to be
materially lessened by the adoption to some limited extent of the
recommendations of the Bulkhead Committee. Such adoption
might have a tranquillising effect on the nerves of the passengers
on board large swift mail steamers. No doubt some kinds of ships
could be made nearly unsinkable, and that consistently with their
special uses. That ships generally could be made so consistently
with their uses as ordinary goods carriers Mr. Glover did not
believe. He would regret therefore if serious inquiry regarding
the whole subject of collisions should be deferred on any expectations that changes in the bulkhead arrangements would have much
effect. In reducing the number they could have no effect whatever.
The causes of so many collisions being well known, as Sir Edward
Harland had pointed out, their treatment requires re-consideration
in Mr. Glover's opinion for this, if for no other reason, that the
present treatment does not prevent collisions. It is satisfactory
only to the lawyers, who are kept supplied with costly suits and
wealthy litigants, for the most part underwriters. Mr. Jeans

would find the causes of growth in English shipping business,
and the relation thereof to our mineral resources, fully treated in
Mr. Glover's previous papers. He had thought it desirable to
make the relation of shipping to "our food supplies" the main
point of the present paper. Perhaps Mr. Jeans would allow him
to point out that the 75,000,000 tons of goods estimated to have
been carried by our flag in 1890 does not represent export tonnage
only as stated by Mr. Jeans, but export and import together. This
fact only confirms Mr. Jeans's conclusion that our minerals are the
basis of the whole matter. It is to be added however that this
75,000,000 tons represents the work done for our own kingdom
only, and recorded in our own returns of entries and clearances;
it does not include any portion of the immense work done by our
flag for other States, some idea of which is given in Table XIV.
Mr. Glover thanked Mr. Bourne for his remarks. Where it
seemed necessary to prevent any important error he had given the
figures for each year, while continuing the comparison of decades.
He observed that Mr. Bourne did not seem to see any danger in
the degree of our dependence on foreign countries for food, and
thought the fact was a great security for the maintenance of
peace, and the greatest possible means of promoting civilisation
throughout the world. This seemed to Mr. Glover too optimist a
view concerning so serious a matter as two-thirds of the "daily
bread" of 38,000,000 of human beings living on islands, and
absolutely dependent on sea communications. Whether this be
so or not, however, Mr. Glover thought it important that these
islanders should know the facts, and take care that they get due
consideration from their politicians and statesmen. Mr. Bateman
directed attention to an important defect in our present returns,
and to the suggestion of M. Kiaer as to some effort being made to
secure the registration of the ton-mile. It is quite certain that the
present returns do not represent the "carrying energy" under our
flag. Mr. Glover did not think there would be any serious difficulty
in making vessels give a return of the miles they had travelled and
the tons of merchandise they had carried since their last clearance
outwards from an English port. Mr. Bateman's suggestion was
well deserving of consideration. Mr. Swanston seemed to think
Mr. Glover unduly apprehensive about Government interference
in shipping affairs. Mr. Glover however was of opinion that the
controversies of the last two decades clearly showed the tendency
to interfere, and regulate, and direct and inspect everything,
instead of leaving those responsible to act on their responsibility
to the common law. The controversies had prevented many
foolish proposals from becoming law, and illustrated the absolute
need of the legislature refusing all interference with trade until
the need be demonstrated by special inquiry and the most carefully
verified facts.

An INQUIRY *into the* STATISTICS *of the* PRODUCTION *and* CONSUMPTION
of MILK *and* MILK PRODUCTS *in* GREAT BRITAIN.

By R. HENRY REW, ESQ.

[Read before the Royal Statistical Society, 26th April, 1892.
The President, Dr. F. J. Mouat, LL.D., in the Chair.]

FROM a social point of view as affecting an important part of the
national food supply, not less than from an agricultural point of
view, it will be admitted that it is desirable to ascertain what are
the production and consumption of milk and milk products in this
country. Both agriculturally and socially the milk supply has of
late years acquired increased importance. The deposition of
wheat growing from the place of honour as the chief object of
British husbandry, and the increase (by about 4 million acres in
the past twenty years) of permanent pasture, have elevated dairy
farming to a degree which seems the greater by reason of the
depression into which corn growing has seemed to sink. On the
other hand it may also be said that the tendency of the present
generation in the direction of temperance has aided not only—
as may be assumed—to increase the consumption of milk as a
beverage, but also to direct attention to its supply as a matter of
vital concern to the health and well-being of the community
at large.

It were greatly to be desired that the inquiry which is undertaken in this paper should result in an answer demonstrating
accurately the quantity of milk, butter, and cheese respectively
produced and consumed at the present time in this country. It
would be highly satisfactory if we could, for what would be
practically the first time, reduce the attainable figures to reasonable
statistical certainty. Possibly it may be expected that this paper
will conclude with some such result, but it will be best at once to
disappoint such an expectation. This paper will have to end,
as it begins, with a note of interrogation; it is an "inquiry"
throughout.

But if the results are not conclusive, and if at the end we have
still to admit that the data are insufficient to permit of dogmatising
either as to consumption or production, the hope may yet be
permitted that some little light will be found to have been shed
upon the details of a difficult subject, which has hitherto perhaps

not received the attention which it might fairly claim from statisticians.

The subject of milk production will be admitted by all who have examined it to be one of extreme complexity. Perhaps in no other branch of food production is the difficulty of arriving at precise facts so great. In the case of meat there is no doubt considerable trouble, yet even there the range of error is, comparatively speaking, limited. In the case of corn and other crops the data for ascertaining the yield are tangible, and although necessarily any general conclusions can only be arrived at by estimates, yet every practical man who undertakes to make an estimate for a given area, has at least some opportunities of forming an accurate opinion. He has at any rate the facts before him. But in the case of milk it is different. Unfortunately it is still true that in many instances the farmer himself hardly knows —except approximately—what the annual production of his herd is. The habit of keeping "milk records" has much increased of late years, but it is still by no means general. And if it be difficult to ascertain from an individual farmer what his own production is, how much more difficult is it for him to estimate the production of his neighbours? He cannot, as in the case of a field of wheat, look over the hedge and judge for himself. I cannot but feel therefore that there is much force in what one of my correspondents wrote, viz., "You ought to obtain a return from every farmer," and if the practicability of that remark were only equal to its truth, it would be conclusive.

I cannot do better on this point than quote the opinion of Sir John Lawes. He writes:—

" The subject is full of complication, and even to ascertain " what is the average yield of a dairy of cows is most difficult. " You may obtain no doubt how much milk a man sells or produces, " but one man brings up calves, another (and this is much more " important) purchases cows just after or just before calving; " some bring in their heifers, which always yield less milk, some " only use cows. I have no doubt that you will obtain some " useful information."

As Sir John Lawes points out, one of the initial difficulties which beset the inquirer is the wide range of the unit of production. There are tolerably well known limits within which the quantity of wheat per acre, or the percentage of carcase per bullock, must fall, but the idiosyncrasies of a cow in its possible yield are almost incalculable. The effective production of milk by a single cow ranges from *nil* (in the case of a cow which only rears her calf), to 1,000 or 1,200 gallons, or even more in exceptional instances.

The problem to be attacked consists of two parts—(*a*) production, (*b*) consumption—which obviously overlap each other.

(*a*) Given an ascertained number of cows in Great Britain at a certain date yielding or capable of yielding milk, what is the total quantity of milk which they will produce in the year, and, further, what proportions of such total quantity are made into butter and cheese respectively?

(*b*) What is the average annual consumption per head of population of (i) milk, (ii) butter, (iii) cheese in Great Britain; and how much of each is home produce, the quantities imported, and the population being known?

For the sake of definiteness, I have thought it better to endeavour to arrive in the first place at a result for a particular year—taking 1890. The total number of "cows and heifers in "milk or in calf" as returned on 4th June, 1890, was for the United Kingdom as follows :—

		Per Cent. United Kingdom.
England	1,832,950	46·4
Wales	282,159	7·1
Scotland	422,881	10·7
Great Britain	2,537,990	
Ireland	1,400,426	35·4
Isle of Man and Channel Islands	17,804	0·4
United Kingdom	3,956,220	100·0

The attempt to fix the average yield of each of these cows obviously involved, in the first place, an appeal to practical men. A large number of circulars were accordingly sent out to farmers in all parts of the country, and a considerable proportion of them were duly filled up and returned. Many of my correspondents have taken much trouble in giving information, and to all of them I beg to tender my sincere thanks. The circular was divided into two parts, one for estimates and the other for "records." In the first part I asked, *inter alia*, for an estimate of the gross average yield of milk per cow per annum in the district, and a further estimate of the amount (to be deducted therefrom) used for rearing calves. In the other part of the circular I asked for similar information respecting the particular herd of the person addressed. There were various other details asked for which need not at the present moment be referred to. The replies which were received vividly displayed the variety of conditions and circumstances which have to be taken into account. First of all there is the calf, who is the innocent cause of untold complications. Milk is now so essentially an article of human food that we have almost lost sight of the original claim of the calf. As a matter of fact, however, there are still an appreciable number of what we may call old-fashioned cows, who do no more than rear their calves. Thus one of my Herefordshire correspondents replied to the inquiry as to how much milk per cow is used in his district for rearing calves, "all, as a rule;" and this answer I believe fairly applies to the greater part of that county. Again, a Lincolnshire correspondent wrote : " In Lincolnshire a large number of calves are bought from " dairy counties and reared for beef. A cow rears on an average " two or three calves per annum." On the other hand, the practice which possibly most widely prevails and yearly increases, is for the cow practically not to rear a calf at all, the whole of her milk, with only an infinitesimal deduction, going to market. The common, and, I believe, increasing, use of prepared foods and skim milk for calves has probably tended materially to augment what may be termed the effective production of milk in dairy districts.

The yield of milk from individual cows varies enormously. A table is given in the Appendix (No. I) showing for all the animals in one herd, the number of days in milk and the quantity (in lbs.) of milk yielded after each calf. This is kindly furnished by Mr. I. N. Edwards, of St. Albans, who has for many years kept accurate records of his herd of shorthorns. It will be seen that the length of time during which a cow continuously gave milk ranged from 112 to 471 days, and the quantity of milk given by one cow during one lacteal period from 1,458 lbs. to 11,162 lbs.[1] The age of the animal affects the yield. Mr. J. F. Hall, of Sharcombe, Wells, writes that he found from records in his Jersey herd that the average yield of 38 heifers, with their first and second calves (under four years old), for 42 weeks—which was the average period of lactation—was 503 gallons, while with 13 older animals the average yield for 41 weeks—the average period of lactation in their case—was 584 gallons. Mr. George Gibbons, of Tunley, Bath, states that two-year-old heifers would give only two-thirds of the average for older cows.

The earlier writers on agriculture who referred to the production of milk appear to have drawn general conclusions from insufficient premisses. In George Culley's well-known "Observa-"tions on Live-Stock" (fourth edition, 1807) it is stated, in reference to the shorthorn cow of that day, that "there are

---

[1] For readiness of reckoning it may be assumed that 10 lbs. = 1 imperial gallon. The precise equivalent as commonly calculated is 10 lbs. 4·2 ozs. = 1 gallon.

" instances of cows giving 36 quarts[2] of milk per day, and of
" 48 firkins of butter being made from a dairy of twelve cows; but
" the more general quantity is 3 firkins per cow in a season and
" 24 quarts of milk per day." These estimates are, however,
probably rather loose. The yield of 24 "quarts" (4⅘ imperial
gallons) per day must have referred to a comparatively short
period after calving.

Coming to a later period, the following appears in
Mr. J. F. W. Johnston's " Lectures on Agricultural Chemistry
" and Geology " (second edition, 1847) :—

" Good ordinary cows in this country yield, on an average,
" from 8 to 12 quarts a day. The county surveys state the
" average daily produce of dairy cows to be in—

	Quarts.		Quarts.
Devonshire	12	Lancashire	8 to 9
Cheshire	8	Ayrshire	8

" But the best Ayrshire kyloes will yield an average of 12½ quarts
" daily during ten months of the year (Ayton).

	Quarts.
The yearly produce of the best Ayrshire kyloes is stated by Mr. Ayton, at	4,000
Of average Ayrshire stock, at	2,400
Good shorthorns, grazed in summer, and fed on hay and turnips in winter, yield (Dickson)	4,000
Mixed breeds in Lancashire (Dickson)	3,500
Large dairy of mixed long and shorthorns at Workington Hall, taking an average of four years (Mr. Curwen)	3,700

" Cross breeds in many localities are found more productive in
" milk than pure stock of any of the native races of cattle."

These figures are of some interest, but they scarcely afford
sufficient data for making a statistical comparison.

So far as I am aware the first serious attempt to arrive at an
estimate of milk production and consumption was that made by
Mr. John Chalmers Morton in a paper read before the Society of
Arts on 13th December, 1865. Unfortunately the scope of that
paper was restricted to London, and so far therefore as the milk
production of the country generally is concerned it affords little
help.

I copy, however, at the end of this paper (Appendix II), for
the sake of its intrinsic interest, a table which was given by
Mr. Morton, showing the number of cows kept, their daily rations
of food, and their estimated daily production of milk for fourteen
dairies, of which twelve were described as "strictly town dairies."

[2] No doubt the "quart" here referred to is the old "wine quart," five of which
went to an imperial gallon. This is certainly the case in the quantities given by
Mr. Johnston.

Beyond noting that the average production "per stall"[3] per diem, so far as estimates are given (*i.e.*, in eleven instances), was about 11 quarts, it is not necessary to refer to it here.

Ten years later Mr. Morton, in an article in the "Journal of the "Royal Agricultural Society" for 1875 (vol. xi, 2nd series), reckoned the average annual quantity of milk drawn from each cow in England at 420 gallons. He stated that this was "most likely "more than is yielded annually by the average cow beyond the "requirements of its calf," and added that, "considering the "comparatively low production of Hereford, Devonshire, and "Sussex, and some other counties, the quantity of milk to be "dealt with in English dairies upon the whole is probably not "more than 650 millions of gallons annually," which would be about 400 gallons per cow. Referring however to the cheese-making counties of Cheshire, Stafford, Warwick, Derby, Gloucester, Somerset, and Wilts, he assumed that the average there would be 480 gallons per cow. Three years later (1878), in the journal of the same Society (vol. xiv, 2nd series), Mr. Morton made an estimate of the milk production of Great Britain. He calculated that the whole number of "cows and heifers in milk or in calf," enumerated in the agricultural returns, would yield "rather more "than 440 gallons apiece within twelve months." From this however he deducted one-sixth as taken by the calf, so that the effective production of milk per cow would be reduced on this estimate—for Great Britain—to say 370 gallons. Again, in 1885, Mr. Morton made another estimate in his handbook on "The "Dairy of the Farm." In this case he estimated the gross production of milk of each of the cows and heifers enumerated in the returns for the United Kingdom at only about 320 gallons apiece, deducting from this one-twelfth for calves, thus making a net estimate of 294 gallons.

In 1879 Professor J. P. Sheldon, in his work on dairy farming, estimated the gross production of milk per cow for the United Kingdom at 440 gallons, deducting one-eighth for rearing and fattening calves, or say 385 gallons net effective production. In a more recent work ("The Farm and the Dairy," 1889), Professor Sheldon remarks that he is disposed to raise his estimate by 20 gallons, "because a good deal of attention has been paid in "the interval"—*i.e.*, from 1879 to 1889—"to the improvement of "the milking properties of cows," thus bringing his net estimate to 403 gallons.

---

[3] The expression "per stall" is used by Mr. Morton, because in these cases as soon as a cow fell off in her yield she was replaced by another, so that the "stall" always contained a cow in full milk. The length of time during which an individual cow occupied the "stall" varied from six to twelve months.

In 1888 the late Mr. James Howard published an estimate of the annual value of the farm produce of the United Kingdom based on the official figures for the three years 1885-87. He put the total production of milk at 550 million gallons, that of cheese at 2,710,000 cwt., and that of butter at 1,918,660 cwt., but without giving any details of the calculation. If we work out these figures (allowing 303 million gallons as made into cheese and 564 million gallons as made into butter), we find that they represent approximately an effective annual production of milk per cow for the United Kingdom of about 360 gallons.

Mr. R. E. Turnbull, of Brampton, Cumberland, made in 1890 some elaborate calculations of the production and consumption of milk and milk products for the United Kingdom. Taking the number of cows and heifers in milk as 2,875,000, he estimates the average annual yield of milk per head at 40 cwt. (say 448 gallons, or about 390 gallons, after allowing for the calves), making a gross yield of 115 million cwt. (say 1,287 million gallons). This he divides as follows:—For household use, 37,805,000 cwt.; butter, 40 million cwt.; cheese, 22 million cwt.; calves, 15,195,000 cwt.

It will be convenient to recapitulate these various estimates in tabular form.

Estimates of Average Production of Milk per Cow in the United Kingdom, made by different Authorities.

Authority.	Date.	Gross Yield.	Deduct for Calves.	Net Yield.
		Galls.		Galls.
Morton	1885	320	$\frac{1}{13}$	294
Sheldon {	'79	440	$\frac{1}{8}$	385
	'89	460	$\frac{1}{8}$	403
Howard	'88	—	—	360
Turnbull	'90	448	$\frac{1}{8}$	393
Mean	—	—	—	367

It would be difficult to show more concisely than appears in the above brief table the uncertainty which prevails on this subject. When it is remembered that an estimate of the total quantity of milk produced in these islands would differ by about 400 million gallons according as the highest or the lowest of these standards was adopted, it will be admitted that it is desirable that some attempt should be made to reconcile these varying authorities. It will probably be a matter of some surprise to find the high authority of the late Mr. Morton attached to an estimate (that of 1885) which is so much lower than is usually associated with his name. This, as above mentioned, appears in a little book on "The Dairy of the Farm," and the following is the passage

(p. 13) containing the estimate. After mentioning that the number of cows and heifers in milk or in calf in the United Kingdom was 3,724,528 in 1884, he goes on :—

" With all deductions for those breeds which do little more
" than rear their calf, and for those breeds where the whole milk
" is devoted to the raising of stock and the fatting of veal, and
" considering, on the one hand, the small yield of some breeds, and
" on the other the large quantity produced by cows now fed
" especially for the yield of milk, we may assume that the
" 3,724,528 cows yield nearly 1,200 million gallons annually."

Before going further we may usefully glance at a few data referring to foreign countries.

In a volume lately published by the French Ministry of Agriculture ("Statistique Agricole de la France," 1882), it is stated that :—

" According to the census of 1882, the 5,019,670 cows in France
" furnished 1,500,531,230 gallons of milk, valued at 56,280,000*l.*,
" the mean annual produce of a milch cow (large, medium, and
" small race) thus being 330 gallons."

The mean annual produce of a milch cow ranges, it appears from this publication, in different departments, from 144 to 704 gallons.

In Switzerland the annual production of milk is stated by Professor Anderegg of Berne[4] at about 319,482,000 gallons, which is thus utilised :—

		Gallons.	Per Cent.
Consumed in a raw state		77,000,000	24
Manufactured—			
Condensed milk	33,000,000		
Butter and cheese	154,482,000		
		187,482,000	58
For feeding stock (swine, calves)		55,000,000	18
		319,482,000	100

Taking the number of cows at 552,447, the annual production per head would be 578 gallons.

In a Foreign Office Report (No. 101, of 1888) some interesting particulars are given of twenty-three co-operative dairy farms in Denmark in 1886, including elaborate tables showing the details of feeding and of production, with the cost of each. From this it appears that the average annual yield of milk per cow for the whole number (1,200) supplying these dairies was 283 gallons.

In a report for the year 1888 of the State of New York Dairy

---

[4] In an article quoted in the "Milch Zeitung" of 11th April, 1890.

Commissioner (quoted in Foreign Office Report, C–5895—46) statistics are given in reference to 1,061 cheese factories and creameries, whereat the milk of 10,934 cows was dealt with, and it appears that the average amount of milk yield per cow " during " the season " was about 320 gallons.

In the annual report of the United States Secretary of Agriculture for 1889, it is observed that the Dairy Commissioner of Iowa is reported as having stated that the average cow in that State gives 3,000 lbs. (300 gallons) of milk annually.

It is needful to bear in mind that returns from factories are of uncertain statistical value, inasmuch as it is impossible to tell if the whole—and, if not, what proportion—of the yield of each cow is sent to the factory.

Before proceeding to a consideration of the present probable average yield in this country, it may be of interest to refer for a moment to one or two maxima. Instances of an individual yield per cow of 1,000 gallons and upwards are by no means uncommon. The highest record in this country which I have observed is given in Professor Long's•" Dairy Annual," and is that of a shorthorn cow owned by Mr. H. L. Cripps, which gave 1,650 gallons between 20th May, 1888, and 7th April, 1889. This, however, has been quite eclipsed by an American record reported in the Chicago "Breeder's Gazette" of 18th February, 1891. A Holstein-Frisian cow named Paulina Paul finished a " butter test " on 7th February, having, it is stated, during the previous twelve months, yielded 1,153 lbs. 15¾ oz. of butter from 18,669 lbs. 9 oz. (say, 1,860 gallons) of milk.

These exceptional cases, however, are of little value, except as curiosities. It is of more interest to refer to a few instances of what may be taken as fairly typical records of dairy herds in this country extending over several years. These are given in a table (Appendix III). These records are, of course, in the nature of maximā, as they refer to herds specially kept for milk, while the mere fact of records being carefully kept is an indication that the management is above the average. For what it is worth, however, it may be mentioned that the average annual yield per cow, several different breeds being represented, is 666 gallons.

Turning now to the figures which I have collected bearing on the main question under consideration, the following table gives a summary of those which have reached me, so far as they are capable of being presented in statistical form :—

Summary of Returns received from Farmers in Great Britain, giving Estimates of Average Milk Yield per Cow in the Districts specified.

	County or District.	Prevailing Breed.	Gross Annual Yield per Cow.	Used for Calves.	Net Yield.
			Galls.	Galls.	Galls.
1	Beds	Shorthorns*	625	208	417
2	,, ...	,,	525	—	—
3	,, ...	,,	456	57	399
4	Berks	,,	810	160	650
5	Bucks	,,	600	56	544
6	,, ...	,,	600	56	544
7	,, ...	,,	525	25	500
8	Cheshire	,,	500	50	450
9	,, ...	,,	500	12	488
10	,, ...	,,	600	30	570
11	,, ...	,,	450	20	430
12	Cumberland	,,	660	110	550
13	,, ...	,,	500	80	420
14	,, ...	,,	550	80	470
15	Derbyshire	,,	600	30	570
16	Stafford	,,	450	25	425
17	Dorset	Devons and Shorthorns........	600	84	516
18	Essex	Shorthorns	675	None	675
19	Gloucester	,,	450	20	430
20	,, ...	,,	500	14	486
21	,, ...	,,	560	40	520
22	Hants	,,	500	25	475
23	,, ...	,,	650	150	500
24	,, ...	,,	600	60	540
25	Hereford	Herefords	90	60	30
26	,, ...	,,	400	133	267
27	Herts	Shorthorns	500	250	250
28	Hunts	,,	625	208	417
29	Kent	,,	720	200	520
30	Leicester	,,	600	20	580
31	Lincoln	,,	575	300	275
32	,, ...	,,	500	200	300
33	Monmouth	,,	500	20	480
34	Norfolk	Polled	300	10	290
35	Northampton	Shorthorns	500	400	100
36	,, ...	,,	400	46	354
37	Northumberland	,,	700	10	690
38	Notts	,,	450	40	410
39	Salop	,,	440	21	419
40	,, ...	,,	600	50	550
41	,, ...	,,	400	200	200
42	Somerset	,,	450	12	438
43	,, ...	,,	475	35	440
44	Stafford	,,	450	10	440
45	,, ...	,,	548	45	503
46	Sussex	,, and Channel Islands	500	40	460

* The " breed " mentioned in each case does not imply that the cattle are all pedigree stock, but that they have generally the character of the breed, usually with some admixture of blood. In many cases, for instance, the term " Grade " Shorthorns " is used, and in others where it is not used it is evidently intended to be understood.

Summary of Returns received from Farmers in Great Britain—Contd.

County.	Prevailing Breed.	Gross Annual Yield per Cow.	Used for Calves.	Net Yield.
		Galls.	Galls.	Galls.
47 Warwick	Shorthorns	530	30	500
48 ,,	,,	750	83	667
49 ,,	,,	900	100	800
50 Isle of Wight	,,	400	None	400
51 Wilts	,,	500	25	475
52 Yorkshire	,,	912	182	730
53 ,,	,,	700	15	685
54 ,,	,,	600	80	520
WALES.				
55 Montgomery	Herefords	300	10	290
56 ,,	Crosses, Welch, &c.	400	200	200
57 ,,	Herefords	300	75	225
SCOTLAND.				
58 Aberdeen {	Cross	600	300	300
	Shorthorns	750	80	670
59 ,,	Crosses	600	300	300
60 ,,	,,	500	330	170
61 Arran	Ayrshire	180	90	90
62 S. Ayrshire	,,	550	110	440
63 W. ,,	,,	550	45	505
64 Berwick	,, and Crosses	375	175	200
65 Clackmannan	Shorthorns	400	133	267
66 E. Forfar	Cross	550	412	138
67 Kirkcudbright	Ayrshire	400	40	360
68 Lanark	,,	600	10	590
69 Selkirk	Cross	800	20	780
70 Wigton	Ayrshire	500	25	475
71 ,,	,,	480	15	465
72 Coupar Angus	Crosses	300	250	50
73 Sanquhar	Ayrshire	380	20	360
74 S.W. Scotland	,,	600	30	570
Mean for Great Britain	—	528·75	93·07	435·07

The returns here summarised represent some forty-five districts, and I may say confidently that all of those farmers whose estimates are here given are well competent to judge of the ordinary production in their respective districts. The returns represent a wide diversity of farm practice. In a few cases the quantity estimated to be used for calf rearing has had to be approximately calculated from explanations. It will be borne in mind that the "net yield" represents the actual quantity available as "commercial milk." The mean net yield of milk per cow works out for Great Britain from these estimates at 435·07 gallons, or considerably more than any of the estimates yet accepted. There is no doubt good ground for believing that the production of milk per cow has appreciably increased of late years, in consequence of improved methods of feeding and greater attention to the details of dairy farming. I do not propose, however, as will be explained subsequently, to adopt this without modification as a standard for the whole country, but, so far as it goes, the result squares with probabilities.

The following table gives returns of actual yields from fifty owners of herds of dairy cattle in various districts. The "number "of cows" in the third column is the number of "cows and heifers "in milk or in calf" on 4th June, 1890, and consequently so returned for the purpose of the agricultural returns:—

Table showing the Number of Cows and Heifers in Milk and in Calf on 4th June, 1890, and the Year's Milk Yield in certain Individual Herds.

	County or District.	Breed.	Number of Cows.	Year's Milk Yield (after deducting Calves).	Average Yield per Cow.
				Galls.	Galls.
1	Beds	Shorthorns	40	13,200	330
2	,, ...	,, ...	27	15,000	555
3	Berks.....................	Jerseys and shorthorns........	14	7,000	500
4	Bucks	Shorthorns	30	9,654	322
5	,, ...	,, ...	175	73,669	421
6	,, ...	Ayrshire	51	8,000	156
7	,, ...	Jerseys	11	4,503	409
8	Gloucester ....{	Shorthorns and Channel Islands.................	} 56	29,379	524
9	,, ...	Shorthorns	50	21,190	424
10	Hants ....{	Channel Islands and cross-breds	} 20	11,100	555
11	,, ...	Jerseys and shorthorns........	28	7,300	260
12	Hereford	,, ...	16	3,000	187
13	,, ...	Guernseys	8	1,900	237
14	Herts.....................	Shorthorns	22	8,740	397
15	Leicester	,, ...	30	12,965	432
16	Lincoln	,, ...	30	21,000	700
17	,, ...	,, ...	60	27,000	450
18	Norfolk.................	Red polls	22	10,266	467
19	Northampton	Shorthorns	24	10,950	456
20	,,	,, ...	56	18,582	332
21	Northumberland	,, and cross-breds	46	30,000	652
22	Notts.....................	,, ...	30	12,227	408
23	Salop.....................	,, ...	78	37,740	484
24	,, ...	,, ...	60	35,400	590
25	Stafford.....................	,, ...	58	28,465	491
26	,, ...	,, ...	21	10,400	495
27	Surrey	Ayrshire	80	40,000	500
28	Sussex	Jerseys and shorthorns........	89	38,000	427
29	,,	,, ...	27	7,840	290
30	Warwick	Shorthorns	25	16,500	660
31	Isle of Wight	Guernseys	30	16,250	542
32	Wilts.....................	Jerseys	8	3,873	484
33	,,	Shorthorns	24	13,000	542
34	Yorks.....................	,, ...	18	8,568	476
35	,, ...	,, and Guernseys...	56	41,000	732

Table showing the Number of Cows and Heifers in Milk—Contd.

County or District.	Breed.	Number of Cows.	Year's Milk Yield (after deducting Calves).	Average.
WALES.			Galls.	Galls.
36 Montgomery.... {	Shorthorns, Ayrshire, West Highland, Herefords, and crosses .... }	62	12,000	193
SCOTLAND.				
37 Aberdeen	Polled Angus	25	3,600	144]
38 ,, ...{	Shorthorns, crosses, and polled .... }	18	6,000	333
39 Ayrshire	Ayrshire	70	30,800	440
40 ,, ...	,, ...	70	27,250	389
41 East Forfar	Crosses	5	675	135
42 Kirkcudbright	Galloways	35	3,000	86
43 Lanark	Ayrshire	40	22,183	555
44 Selkirk	,, and cross..............	57	39,900	700
45 Wigton	,, ...	110	47,610	433
46 ,, ...	,, ...	100	52,828	528
47 Sanquhar	,, ...	40	21,830	546
48 Stirling................	,, ...	20	8,547	427
49 Glasgow	,, ...	97	63,535	655
50 Midlothian	Cross shorthorns	32	44,408	1,388
Totals	—	2,201	1,037,827	471

The mean available yield of milk per cow on these records is 471 gallons, and it will be seen that here again the figures have a wide range. Generally speaking, however, it may be assumed that such records are only available in the case of herds kept especially for milk production, and consequently we should expect to find the yield somewhat high. On the other hand, however, there is no doubt that the average yield in each case is pulled down to a certain extent by the fact that many of the cows or heifers enumerated may have contributed very little to the year's supply.

As regards Scotland, reference may be made to an article by Mr. John Speir in the "Transactions of the Highland and Agri-"cultural Society" for 1886, which contains much interesting information on dairy practice across the border. He confines his observations almost entirely to the "ten dairying counties," and, as regards these, the following estimate of the number of cows in each county which may be appropriated to each branch of dairy production is worth quoting:—

Estimate of the Number of Cows in each of the Ten "Dairying Counties" of Scotland, apportioned to the Various Branches of Dairy Production.

County.	Milk.	Butter.	Cheese.	Rearing.	Family Use.	Total.
Argyll	3,106	3,000	10,000	6,000	1,000	23,106
Ayr	5,700	6,500	33,926	—	—	46,126
Bute	1,343	2,000	—	—	—	3,343
Dumbarton	5,000	2,491	—	—	—	7,491
Dumfries	2,000	200	2,727	10,000	3,750	18,677
Lanark	13,000	12,200	12,015	—	—	37,215
Kirkcudbright	750	200	5,030	7,000	1,509	14,489
Renfrew	8,700	5,400	2,031	—	—	16,131
Stirling	2,250	4,000	1,706	3,000	—	10,956
Wigtown	1,500	1,500	18,090	—	—	21,090
Outside	14,000	13,376	—	—	—	27,376
	57,349*	50,867	85,525*	26,000	6,259	226,000

* These totals are incorrectly given in the original table.

These figures refer to 1885, and they account, as will be seen, for 226,000 out of the total of 419,210 appearing in the agricultural returns for that year as the number of cows and heifers in milk or in calf in the whole of Scotland.

As regards the yield per cow, Mr. Speir writes:—

"Ayrshires, which are the class of cows in universal use in the "dairying districts of the west, usually give about 600 gallons of "milk without any forcing . . . With judicious management and "liberal fare, from 620 to 650 gallons per annum has been yielded "by good average stocks. Many farmers say they have more. "I have before me at the present time the quantities sold from "three dairies in the immediate neighbourhood of Glasgow, where "the apparent yield is an annual production of from 680 to 730 "gallons. Under these circumstances I am led to believe the "amounts were calculated from the average number kept. In "some cases at least these cows were seldom bulled, and of course "milked more than the regular time. Over and above this, as one "cow got fat or went dry, another new calved one was put in her "place, so that such figures do not give a just idea of the average "production of an Ayrshire herd. A production of 620 gallons at "8½d. will, at present values, equal, with one calf, about 22l. 10s., "and it may be considered as pretty near the average production "of fairly good stocks without going to extremes one way or the "other."

It will be observed that these figures refer only to dairy herds, that is, according to Mr. Speir's estimate, to only some 54 per cent. of the cows included in the agricultural returns.

I cannot say very much about Ireland, and for the few data which I have obtained I am indebted mainly to Professor Carroll of Glasnevin, Dr. Moorhead of Errigle, Colonel des Barres of

Tallow, and one or two other gentlemen who have also kindly afforded information which however is not in a form which can be usefully tabulated, even if it were adequate.

It is notorious that much has been done of late years in Ireland, by the instrumentality of the Government dairy schools, and by the establishment of creameries and milk factories, to stimulate milk production as an industry. I have from two districts estimates of 560 and 450 gallons respectively as the average yield per cow. No doubt the fact that a very large quantity of Irish milk is used for rearing calves would go to pull down the average for the country. But, on the whole, in the absence of fuller information, I must assume that the results, from the point of view of milk production, in the calf rearing districts are counterbalanced by those obtained in the butter making and milk selling districts. I have not therefore taken Ireland as being to any appreciable extent a disturbing element in the calculation, but have followed the example of former estimators, and adopted one standard of yield for the whole of the United Kingdom.

Coming now to a consideration of the standard to be adopted, I would first of all recall the fact that we have eliminated the calf. Former estimates have, as a rule, taken the gross yield and then deducted a certain proportion for the calf. No doubt it comes to the same thing in the end, but it may tend to clearness to endeavour to bear in mind that milk taken by the calf cannot be considered as coming into a calculation of milk production at all. To reckon calves as "consumers" seems to me rather confusing. Now, according to the table of estimated yields, the average would work out at 435 gallons per cow. I am disposed to think that this errs on the side of excess. It contains several instances of low net yields where the calf swallows a goodly share of the milk; as, for instance, in Lincoln, 40 and 52 per cent. respectively; in Shropshire, 50 per cent.; and in Northampton, 80 per cent. But, for the simple and natural reason that it is easier to obtain returns about milk from those who are chiefly engaged in its production, I do not think the returns from the non-dairying districts bear a sufficiently large proportion to the total. On the whole, therefore, I believe, after a careful consideration of such facts as I have been able to obtain from all sources, that if we deduct 10 per cent. from the figure given by the table the result will very fairly approximate to the truth. This gives us, therefore, roundly, 400 gallons as the standard net average available yield of milk per cow for the United Kingdom.

Referring for a moment to former estimates, I find that the mean of the latest calculations of the four authorities quoted above would be, for the United Kingdom, 367 gallons. I believe, however, that the progress made of late years in dairying matters,

and the greater attention given to the breeding and feeding of
cattle for milk production, would account for some increase, and I
am glad to find myself in almost exact agreement with Professor
Sheldon's estimate of 1889.

The total number of cows or heifers .in milk or in calf in the
United Kingdom in 1890 was 3,938,416, but I do not think it can
be assumed that all of these are effective producers of milk either
for calf rearing or consumption. There is on any given date a
certain proportion of the cows in every herd dry, either for calving
or fattening. The former are, as a matter of course, included in
the returns, and it is possible that many of the latter, though
they ought strictly speaking to be excluded, are reckoned among
the cows and heifers returned. As regards the proportion of cows
in a herd actually in milk at a given date, I gather from statements made by a few of my correspondents that it might be
reckoned at something like 80 per cent. It seems to me that it
would be misleading to take the whole number of cows and heifers
in the agricultural returns into the calculation without allowing
for a proportion which are always non-productive. I therefore
venture to deduct under this head 10 per cent. from the number
of cows and heifers as returned.

The figures therefore stand thus :—

Number of cows and heifers "in milk and in calf," 4th June, 1890	3,938,416
Deduct 10 per cent. as non-productive	393,841
	3,544,575
Total production (in imperial gallons) of milk in the year 1890, at an estimated average net yield of 400 gallons per cow	1,417,830,000

Before leaving for awhile this branch of the subject, it may be
interesting to show the number of cows in the country in each of
the past twenty-six years, together with the population and the
proportion of cows to population. It will be seen that relatively
the production of milk has decreased, unless the falling off in
the ratio of cows to population has been counterbalanced by an
increased individual yield per cow. Comparing quinquennial
periods, there were in Great Britain in 1866-70 82·1 cows per
1,000 of population, and in 1886-90 there were only 77·9. The
absolute number of cows had increased, but not sufficiently to keep
pace with the growth of population. The latest return (for 1891),
however, is more encouraging, showing as it does the largest
number of cows on record. In Ireland, of course, the circumstances differ essentially. There the period 1886-90 showed a
higher proportion (290·8) of cows to population than any of the
four preceding quinquennial periods, but this was due, not to an
increase in the number of cattle, but to the decrease of population.

Year	GREAT BRITAIN [000's omitted]				IRELAND [000's omitted]				UNITED KINGDOM, exclusive of Channel Islands and Isle of Man. [000's omitted]			
	Number of Cows in Milk or in Calf.	Population Estimated to the Middle of each Year.	Number of Cows per 1,000 of Population.	Quinquennial Averages.	Number of Cows in Milk or in Calf.	Population Estimated to the Middle of each Year.	Number of Cows per 1,000 of Population.	Quinquennial Averages.	Number of Cows in Milk or in Calf.	Population Estimated to the Middle of each Year.	Number of Cows per 1,000 of Population.	Quinquennial Averages.
1866	1,884,	24,557,	76·7		1,483,	5,520,	268·7		3,367,	30,077,	111·9	
'67	2,038,	24,853,	82·0		1,521,	5,482,	277·5		3,559,	30,335,	117·3	
'68	2,144,	25,156,	85·2	82·1	1,476,	5,461,	270·3	275·1	3,620,	30,617,	118·2	116·7
'69	2,135,	25,470,	83·0		1,506,	5,444,	276·6		3,641,	30,914,	117·8	
'70	2,162,	25,793,	83·8		1,529,	5,419,	282·5		3,691,	31,206,	118·3	
'71	2,091,	26,127,	80·0		1,545,	5,387,	286·8		3,636,	31,514,	115·4	
'72	2,155,	26,467,	81·8		1,552,	5,369,	289·0		3,717,	31,836,	116·8	
'73	2,238,	26,787,	83·5	82·2	1,528,	5,337,	286·3	288·1	3,766,	32,124,	117·2	116·1
'74	2,274,	27,203,	84·0		1,491,	5,299,	288·9		3,765,	32,502,	115·8	
'75	2,253,	27,560,	81·7		1,530,	5,279,	289·8		3,783,	32,839,	115·2	
'76	2,226,	27,922,	79·7		1,533,	5,278,	290·5		3,759,	33,200,	113·2	
'77	2,207,	28,290,	78·0		1,532,	5,286,	288·1		3,739,	33,576,	111·1	
'78	2,208,	28,662,	77·0	77·7	1,484,	5,282,	281·0	281·3	3,692,	33,944,	108·8	109·3
'79	2,255,	29,037,	77·7		1,465,	5,266,	278·1		3,721,	34,308,	108·5	
'80	2,242,	29,420,	76·2		1,398,	5,203,	268·7		3,640,	34,623,	105·1	
'81	2,270,	29,789,	76·2		1,392,	5,146,	268·6		3,662,	34,935,	104·9	
'82	2,267,	30,106,	75·3		1,399,	5,101,	274·3		3,666,	35,207,	104·1	
'83	2,306,	30,427,	75·8	77·3	1,402,	5,019,	279·3	276·5	3,708,	35,446,	104·6	105·6
'84	2,391,	30,752,	77·8		1,356,	4,966,	273·0		3,747,	35,718,	104·9	
'85	2,530,	31,079,	81·4		1,417,	4,928,	287·5		3,947,	36,007,	109·6	
'86	2,538,	31,411,	80·8		1,419,	4,893,	290·0		3,957,	36,304,	109·0	
'87	2,536,	31,746,	79·9		1,394,	4,841,	287·9		3,930,	36,587,	107·4	
'88	2,450,	32,084,	76·4	77·9	1,385,	4,781,	289·7	290·8	3,835,	36,865,	104·5	105·6
'89	2,434,	32,426,	75·1		1,364,	4,794,	288·1		3,798,	37,160,	102·2	
'90	2,538,	32,772,	77·4		1,400,	4,692,	298·4		3,938,	37,464,	105·1	
'91	2,657,	33,122,	80·2	—	1,442,	4,681,	308·1	—	4,099,	37,803,	108·4	—

In this connection it is interesting to note that the proportion of cows and heifers in milk or in calf to the total number of cattle in the United Kingdom has shown on the whole a tendency to decrease during the past twenty years. In England, Wales, and Scotland respectively the absolute number of animals engaged in milk production was larger in 1891 than in any year on record, but relatively to the total herds less than it was at the commencement of the period. In Ireland milch cattle were not only absolutely less, but relatively they showed a greater decline than in any other division of the United Kingdom. This is shown in the following table :—

Table showing the proportion of Cows and Heifers in Milk or in Calf to the Total Number of Cattle in each of the Years 1866-91.

[000's omitted.]

Year.	England.		Wales.		Scotland.		Ireland.	
	Cows.	Per Cent. of Cattle.	Cows.	Per Cent. of Cattle.	Cows.	Per Cent. of Cattle.	Cows.	Per Cent. of Cattle.
1866	1,291,	39·0	223,	41·2	370,	39·5	1,488,	39·6
'67	1,411,	40·7	245,	44·9	382,	39·0	1,520,	41·1
'68	1,505,	39·8	255,	43·0	384,	36·5	1,463,	40·4
'69	1,499,	40·4	256,	43·5	380,	37·3	1,504,	40·3
1870	1,529,	40·7	256,	42·3	376,	36·1	1,529,	40·2
'71	1,461,	39·8	251,	42·0	380,	35·5	1,546,	38·9
'72	1,523,	39·0	251,	41·6	392,	34·9	1,550,	38·2
'73	1,581,	37·9	260,	40·4	397,	34·6	1,528,	36·8
'74	1,614,	37·5	264,	39·7	396,	34·3	1,491,	36·1
'75	1,595,	37·8	261,	40·0	397,	34·8	1,530,	37·2
'76	1,574,	38·6	259,	40·7	393,	34·7	1,533,	37·2
'77	1,558,	39·1	254,	41·2	395,	35·8	1,521,	38·1
'78	1,568,	38·9	253,	41·6	388,	35·4	1,484,	37·2
'79	1,605,	38·9	262,	40·7	389,	35·9	1,465,	36·0
1880	1,593,	38·3	261,	39·8	387,	35·2	1,397,	35·6
'81	1,621,	38·9	260,	39·7	389,	35·5	1,391,	35·2
'82	1,618,	39·6	260,	40·3	390,	36·1	1,399,	35·1
'83	1,651,	39·2	260,	39·9	395,	36·1	1,402,	34·2
'84	1,715,	38·5	267,	39·2	409,	36·8	1,356,	32·9
'85	1,831,	38·9	280,	39·5	419,	35·6	1,417,	33·5
'86	1,837,	38·5	283,	39·3	417,	36·0	1,419,	33·9
'87	1,842,	39·8	283,	40·6	412,	36·8	1,392,	33·5
'88	1,765,	40·5	275,	41·3	410,	36·9	1,385,	33·8
'89	1,752,	40·2	272,	40·8	409,	35·6	1,364,	33·3
1890	1,833,	39·7	282,	40·0	423,	35·7	1,400,	33·0
'91	1,917,	39·4	295,	38·9	445,	36·4	1,442,	32·4

form

Taking the present total milk production then as 1,43·5 if the gallons, we have next to endeavour to estimate how over these is used for making cheese or butter. And here it will be difficult to get very far without taking into consideration the question of consumption.

First of all as regards the quantity of milk sold as such. It is a matter of common observation that the quantity of milk produced in the country and sold in the towns has during the past thirty years increased. Every traveller by rail has noted the outward and visible signs of the expansion of this trade in the battalions of cans—technically known as " churns "—which daily come and go along all the country lines of railway. Milk now comes to London, for instance, every day from about a dozen different counties, much of it travelling from 100 to 150 miles.

Not quite the whole of this railway trade in milk represents increased consumption—although the greater part of it may probably be so reckoned. It sprang up in the first instance out of the disappearance of large numbers of the old town cowsheds. At the time of the reading of Mr. Morton's paper (above referred to) before the Society of Arts—*i.e.*, twenty-five years ago—the number of cows kept in London was estimated to have decreased within a short time from 24,000 to 10,000. They are now estimated at 8,500. No doubt the increase of population in other large towns has had a corresponding effect. Happily just at the time when it became on many grounds necessary to draw the town supplies of milk from long distances, the invention of refrigerators rendered possible its conveyance by rail without deterioration.

By the courtesy of the general managers of seven of the nine great lines of railway having termini in London, I am able to give the quantity of milk brought by rail to the metropolis over their systems during the year 1890. In two instances in which the figures have not been supplied I have made an estimate based on calculations made by Mr. G. Barham, who has an intimate acquaintance with the London milk trade.

In order to show the growth of the trade, I have given the figures for the year 1864 as obtained by Mr. Morton in 1865. I have also given for the sake of comparison in three instances the figures referring to 1887 obtained by Mr. George Gibbons, and given by him in a paper read before the Economic Section of the British Association in 1888.

Table showing the Quantity of Milk brought into London by different Lines of Railway in the Years mentioned.

Railway.	1864.	1887.	1890.
	Imperial galls.	Imperial galls.	Imperial galls.
Great Northern	209,896	—	4,370,624
Midland	—	6,436,920	7,000,000
Great Eastern	1,020,492	—	4,547,036*
Great Western	500,000†	8,500,000	9,778,815
South Eastern	186,092	—	1,268,800
London, Chatham, and Dover	—	—	23,108
London and South Western	400,000	5,640,193	5,743,436
London and North Western	85,616	—	7,000,000‡
London, Brighton, and South Coast..	54,004	—	700,000‡
Total	—	—	40,431,819

* To Liverpool Street and stations within 12 miles of London.

† 1865 ; given in Mr. Gibbons's paper read before the Economic Section of the British Association in 1888.

‡ Estimated ; no information supplied by companies.

It would be interesting if it were possible to give figures for the whole of the rail-borne milk as nearly complete as those of the milk conveyed to London. I ventured to solicit returns of the total quantity of milk carried by the railway companies mentioned above, but I am bound to admit that the request was one which necessarily involved so much labour that I was scarcely justified in making it. I am therefore the more sensible of the kindness of the general managers of the Great Western, the Midland, and the Great Eastern Railways in taking considerable trouble to send me the full returns for their systems. These figures are as follows :—

Table showing the Quantity of Milk conveyed over the Railways named during the Year 1890.

Railway.	Mileage (1889).	Quantity Carried.
		Imperial galls.
Great Western	2,477	12,985,748
Midland	1,375	11,080,000
Great Eastern	1,100	4,713,111
Total	4,952	28,778,859

The total length of the railways of England and Wales in 1889 was 14,034 miles, so that these three lines between them represent more than one-third of the railway system of the country. It would be misleading to attempt with only these data to form an estimate of the total quantity of rail-borne milk, but if the same quantity per mile were carried over all lines as over these three, the gross quantity would be some 85 million gallons per annum, or about 233,000 gallons per day.

To return to the question of London milk supply, we have seen that the railways bring in about 40 million gallons per annum (nearly 110,000 gallons per day). But there is still a considerable quantity of milk produced in the metropolitan area. The deputy clerk of the London County Council (Mr. Alfred Spencer) has kindly furnished me with the following figures:—

Number of licensed cowshed premises in the county of London	620
Number of separate cowsheds upon such premises	850
Estimated average accommodation in each cowshed....	15 cows.
„ actually kept in each cowshed	10 „
„ daily yield of milk per cow—	
In summer....................................	10 quarts.
„ winter	8 „
Estimated average *daily* supply of milk from cows kept in London	20,000 imperial gallons.

In 1886 Mr. Spencer and Dr. Winter Blyth prepared a paper on the preservation of the purity of milk, which was read before the Society of Medical Officers of Health. It contained the following passages:—

" In 1884 one of us . . . obtained from the railway depôts, from " farms and from other sources the necessary statistics, with the " following results:—

" (a) *By rail.*—The average quantity brought up by rail to all " the railway stations in London which receive milk, was found to " be, on a day in the summer of 1884, 88,603 imperial gallons, and " on a day in the winter, 78,956 imperial gallons.

" (b) *By road.*—The deliveries to London by road that could " be ascertained, was a daily average quantity of 958 gallons in " summer and 818 gallons in winter.

" (c) *From London cowhouses.*—The supply of milk from the cows " kept in London was found to be about 26,250 imperial gallons on " a day in summer, and 21,000 gallons on a day in winter.

" Taking in each case the mean of the summer and winter " supply, and to this quantity adding 1,708 gallons from miscel- " laneous sources, the total daily supply of milk to the metropolis " was found to be as follows:—

	Gallons per Day.	Per Cent.
By rail	83,779	76·2
„ road	888	0·8
London cowsheds	23,625	21·5
Miscellaneous....................	1,708	1·5
Total	110,000	100·0

"The total population of the metropolis was estimated by the
"Registrar-General to be, in the middle of 1884, 4,019,361; hence
"the average daily consumption of 110,000 gallons of milk dis-
"tributed among that number of people, gives a quantity per head
"of about 4 ozs. (⅕ pint)."

As regards the rail-borne milk, the figures which I have given
above enable us to bring the supply from that source down to
date. The supply from road and miscellaneous sources we may
take to be the same now as in 1884, but the supply from the
London cowsheds has, in Mr. Spencer's opinion, decreased to
20,000 gallons per day. Thus corrected, the present annual milk
supply of London would be as follows:—

	Gallons per Day.	Gallons per Annum.	Per Cent.
By rail	110,712	40,431,000	83·1
From cowsheds	20,000	7,300,000	15·0
By road and miscellaneous	2,527	923,000	1·9
Total	133,239	48,654,000	100·0

Taking the present population (1891) of London as 4,211,056,
this gives an annual consumption per head of only 11·55 gallons
(0·25 pint per day). We cannot accept this as typical of the
country at large. Mr. Spencer observes that the consumption per
head in London is "undoubtedly lower" than in the provinces,
and he mentions the very much larger quantity of condensed milk
which is used, especially in the poorer neighbourhoods.

There are one or two factors which would affect this calculation, but of which it is not possible to estimate the precise value.
Perhaps the most considerable is the use of condensed milk, which,
of course ought to be added to the supply. It is impossible
to obtain any reliable data by which the quantity of condensed
milk manufactured and used in this country can be estimated.
The quantity imported was in the year 1890 407,426 cwts.,
which would represent perhaps about 13 million gallons of milk.[5]
The amount annually produced in this country may, at a very
rough estimate, be reckoned at about 200,000 cwts., representing,
say, 6 million gallons of milk. The exportation of condensed milk
was in 1890 162,037 cwts., of which 61,491 cwts. represented home
produce and 100,546 cwts. foreign and colonial produce. Possibly
therefore the consumption of milk—as condensed milk—in this
country, amounts to nearly 19 million gallons per annum, of which
perhaps London takes—at a rough estimate—about one-third.

[5] The ratio of condensed milk to whole milk, is based on a calculation which
has been kindly supplied by Mr. F. J. Lloyd, F.C.S.

Then again there has of late years grown up a considerable trade in skim or "separated" milk. It is impossible to take this into consideration, and throughout this paper I have dealt strictly with whole milk. But there is no doubt that the problem has been complicated by the fact that a proportion of the milk produced now-a-days is "contrived a double debt to pay," viz., on the one hand to the butter consumer, and on the other hand to the milk consumer. This separated milk is said to be a good and economical food, and we must therefore hope for its further utilisation (so long as it is sold openly, and not used to dilute whole milk), notwithstanding that from a statistical point of view its extended sale adds a fresh terror to the construction of any estimates of milk consumption.

As regards the consumption of milk in the country generally, I think no one has gone into the subject with so much care as Mr. Morton, and he placed it at one-fifth of a pint per head per diem as lately as 1875, founding his estimate on a careful collection of data made ten years previously. In 1885, however, he increased his estimate to one-fourth of a pint, remarking ("The Dairy of "the Farm," p. 14) that the consumption of milk "has very "greatly increased of late years."

I have been able to obtain some figures showing the average daily delivery of milk per family by retailers in a few fairly typical localities. From these I have calculated the consumption per head on the basis of five persons per family.

Statistics of Milk Consumption, taken from the Books of Milk Retailers in Various Districts.

Description of District.	Approximate Number of Families served.	Average Consumption per Day per Family.	Average Consumption per Head.	
			Per Day.	Per Annum.
		Pints.	Pints.	Galls.
1 West end of London	4,000	3·750	0·750	34·218
2 North of London	2,000	3·250	0·650	29·656
3 Manchester	—	2·666	0·533	24·318
4 „ (middle class district)	146	1·500	0·300	13·687
5 „ (working „)	200	1·000	0·200	9·125
6 Small country town	90	1·624	0·325	14·828
7 Putney and Wandsworth	700	2·286	0·457	20·838
8 Small town (health resort)	500	3·000	0·600	27·375
9 East end of London (1 gallon of milk divided into 37 portions)	—	0·432	0·086	3·923

It is obviously impossible to give the true mean of these figures, but if we take each of the nine cases as typical, and give each an equal value, we get an average daily consumption per family of 2·17 pints, and per head of 0·43 pint, and an average annual consumption per head of 19·75 gallons.

With reference to No. 9 (the east end of London) it is necessary to explain that the figures are based on the fact that a gallon of milk is divided on an average into thirty-seven portions, each portion being, I believe, fetched by the consumer. I have assumed that each family consumes one of these portions every morning and evening. It will be seen that even on this assumption the consumption per head is infinitesimal, and it reveals incidentally a significant fact in connection with the dietary of the poor. I may perhaps add that the gentleman who was good enough to procure me that particular return is one of the highest authorities on the London milk trade.

I am disposed to think that this table represents what may be considered a trustworthy and valuable class of evidence, though I am afraid it is not sufficient to stand by itself as giving a standard for the country generally. I have obtained another set of figures which may throw a little further light on the subject. These are returns from eighteen public institutions in or near London—none of them being hospitals or places where there is a medical dietary—showing the average daily consumption of milk, cheese, and butter per head. To these I have added figures taken from the books of a large west end boarding house. I am much indebted to those who have the control of these various establishments for the courtesy and readiness with which my inquiries have been replied to.

Average Daily Consumption per Head of Milk, Cheese, and Butter at certain Public Institutions, &c.

Description of Inmates.	Number of Inmates.	Milk per Head.	Cheese per Head.	Butter per Head.
		Pints	oz.	oz.
1 { Children	195	} —	0·13	0·15
Adults	10			
2 { Children	165	} 0·57	—	—
Adults	10			
3 Children	500	0·80	—	—
4 Boys, 8 to 14 years	280	—	0·29	0·14
5 { Children	505	} 0·40	0·23*	0·31
Adults	45			
6 Boys	50	0·23	0·82	0·82
7 { Children, average age 12 years	180	1·25	1·00	1·00†
,, ,, 7 ,,	140	1·00	Nil	1·00†
Adults ,, 27 ,,	39	0·75	1·14	1·14
8 Boys, 14 to 18 years	220	0·39	—	0·71
9 ,,	254	0·37	0·16	0·79
10 { Children	220	} 1·00	—	0·71
Adults	25			
11 { Children (infants)	566	0·88	—	1·00
Adults	70	0·69	0·57	1·14
12 Girls	—	1·00	—	—
13 { Children (deaf and dumb)	282	0·75	—	—
Adults	48	1·00	1·14	1·71
14 { Females, 11 to 76 years (deaf and dumb)	47	0·33	—	1·00
15 Aged men, 67 to 90 years	95	0·29	0·57	1·14‡
16 Girls	—	0·85	—	1·14
17 Children, average age 12 years	230	0·50	—	1·00
18 { Children	2,163	} 0·36	—	—
Adults	186			
19 Adults §	20	0·51	0·40	1·28
MEAN { per day	—	0·66	0·54	0·90
		Galls.	lbs.	lbs.
per annum	—	30·11	12·32	20·53

* Cheese not given daily.   † Butter four days per week.
‡ Margarine.   § London west end boarding house.

The figures are no doubt exceptional, and it would not be at all safe to take them as a basis for a general calculation. So far as milk is concerned it is obvious that the consumption would be high in well managed institutions whose inmates are mainly children. We can but wish that all children had as much milk as those in most of these institutions, but it would be absurd to assume that it is so.

From a large number of dietaries collected all over the country by Dr. Edward Smith five and twenty years ago, and published in a report to the Poor Law Board in 1867, it appeared that the average quantity of milk consumed weekly by labourers' families ranged from 178 ozs. in North Wales, and 120 ozs. in West-moreland, to three-quarters of an ounce in Gloucestershire, but the mean of forty counties was about 0·3 pint per day per head, or about 13·7 gallons per annum. This too it must be remembered applied to rural districts where milk is (and at that time was perhaps even more generally than now) given in part payment of, or supplementary to, wages.

Turning now, before we go further, to milk products, it is to be observed that a very large proportion of the demand for cheese and butter is supplied from abroad. The net imports (*i.e.*, after deducting exports) per head of population for the year 1890 were: butter and margarine, 8 lbs. 8 ozs.; cheese, 6 lbs. 1 oz. A table is given in the Appendix (IV) showing the constant increase in the consumption per head of population of foreign dairy produce in this country. This must indicate one of two things—either that the home production of butter and cheese is diminishing, or that the demand per head has increased, and the increase has been entirely met from abroad.

There is some ground for the belief that both cheese and butter-making are decreasing in this country. One of my correspondents who has wide knowledge and long experience of the whole subject —Mr. T. Carrington Smith, of Staffordshire—writes:—

"During the last few years the sale of whole milk for con-
" sumption in London and other large towns has increased rapidly.
" Year by year the manufacture of cheese is decreasing, while the
" production of butter is also less, though in a considerable degree
" its manufacture for the time being is increased or decreased
" in accordance with the demand and prices current in the local
" markets."

There are very few data from which to estimate the present pro-duction of cheese and butter in the United Kingdom. Mr. Morton arrived at an estimate by assuming that the whole of the milk produced in the counties of Chester, Stafford, Warwick, Derby, Gloucester, Somerset, and Wilts, was used for cheese making. Other estimators have, presumably, followed a similar course, though this method—rough and ready as it is—does not touch the most difficult part of the problem—that of butter.

I made an attempt to obtain from my correspondents some estimates and figures which might have formed the basis of a cal-culation, but though many of them have been good enough to give interesting information, I find that it is impossible to arrive at any result which would be at all useful.

The late Sir James Caird, in 1878 ("R.A.S.E. Journal,"vol. xiv), reckoned the total home production of cheese and butter at 3 mil-lion cwts. (150,000 tons).

In Mr. Mulhall's recently published "Dictionary of Statistics," the annual production of cheese in the United Kingdom is stated to be 40,000 tons, or one-third of the consumption. In another place in the same work the annual production of butter and cheese in the United Kingdom is stated to be 110,000 tons, and the annual total consumption of both these articles, 328,000 tons, or 19 lbs. per head of population. The authority for these calculations is not mentioned.

In a paper read by Professor Carroll, of the Glasnevin School, at the Dairy Conference in Dublin in 1887, the annual production of butter in the United Kingdom was put at 90,000 tons, and the consumption at 205,000 tons, or 13 lbs. per head.

Professor Sheldon (in "The Farm and the Dairy," 1889) puts the annual make of cheese at 100,000 tons, and that of butter at 90,000 tons.

Mr. W. E. Bear, in "The British Farmer and his Competitors," basing his calculations on Professor Sheldon's estimate, arrives at the following result for the years 1876 and 1886 respectively:—

	Estimated Home Produce.		Net Imports.	
	Total.	Per Inhabitant.	Total.	Per Inhabitant.
Butter, &c.—	cwts.	lbs.	cwts.	lbs.
1876	1,785,700	6·05	1,636,379	5·52
'86	1,918,660	5·85	2,848,850	7·16
Cheese—				
1876	2,520,000	8·53	1,486,266	5·01
'86	2,710,000	8·27	1,728,253	5·14

The only chance of getting any approximation to the truth, it seems to me, is to look at the subject from the point of view of consumption. What is the probable consumption of cheese and butter?

The following is a calculation, published November, 1891, by Professor Long :—

	Per Head.	Value.	
	lbs.	s.	d.
Consumption of imported butter	9·4	7	4
„ home made butter	5·6	5	6
	15·0	12	10
„ imported cheese	5·7	2	4½
„ home made cheese	7·9	3	7½
	13·6	6	0

Mr. Morton (in 1885) estimated the daily consumption of home produce per head at ½ oz. of cheese and ¼ oz. of butter. This would represent an annual consumption per head of 2 lbs. 13⅝ oz. of cheese, and 5 lbs. 11¼ oz. of butter, exclusive of imports. Mr. John Algérnon Clarke, quoted by Professor Sheldon, put the total annual consumption per head at 15 lbs. of cheese, and 14 lbs. of butter.

The late Mr. H. J. Little, writing on the condition of the agricultural labourers in 1878, reckoned the consumption of butter per labourer's family at ½ lb. per week. Butter was then reckoned at 1s. 6d. per lb. and it was supplemented by 1 lb. of lard at 10½d. per lb. Now that butter is so much lower in price, probably the same family would take 1 lb. per week, or say rather more than 10 lb. per head per annum. In the same article the weekly consumption of butter by an unmarried farm labourer was estimated at ½ lb. per week, or 26 lbs. per annum.

The figures which were given above of the consumption at various institutions gave the mean per head as 12 lbs. of cheese and 20 lbs. of butter.

Taking all the facts into consideration, I venture to put the probable total consumption per head of butter and cheese in the United Kingdom at the present time as follows:—

Butter—15 lbs. per annum or 0·66 oz. per day.
Cheese—12   ,,   0·53   ,,

It will be remembered that this includes a foreign supply of 8·8 lbs. of butter and 6·1 lbs of cheese per head per annum.

As regards the consumption per head of milk, three calculations from very different data have been given in this paper. We must dismiss altogether the average (30·25 gallons) given in the table referring to public institutions. It is, as I have already remarked, and as might be expected, altogether exceptional as regards milk. There remain the two quantities given by the figures referring to the London milk supply (11·55 gallons), and by those obtained from milk sellers in various localities (19·75 gallons). It will be observed that the calculation referring to London milk is perhaps the closest and most reliable which I have been able to give, resting as it does almost entirely on ascertained figures. Unfortunately, for reasons previously given, we cannot rely on it as typical of the country at large. Nor, in the face of the London figures, should we be justified in adopting universally the figure given by the milk sellers' returns. Taking everything into consideration, I venture to suggest that an average of 15 gallons per head cannot be very far wrong as the annual milk consumption of the people of the United Kingdom. This amounts to a daily consumption of one-third (0·33) of a pint per day per head, as compared with Mr. Morton's latest estimate (1885) of one-fourth of a pint per head.

Taking therefore the annual production (on the basis of 1890) as previously stated, at 1,417 million gallons, we may reckon it to be consumed as follows :—Milk, 570 million gallons ; butter, 617 million gallons (representing 105,000 tons of butter); cheese 224 million gallons (representing 100,000 tons of cheese); miscellaneous (condensed milk &c.), 6 million gallons.

The total consumption per head of dairy produce, with the amount of milk represented thereby, is shown in the following statement :—

	Consumption per Head.			Total Quantity of Milk represented (in thousands of gallons—000's omitted).		
	Home Produce.	Foreign Produce (*Net* Imports).	Total.	Home Produce.	Foreign Produce.*	Total.
	Galls.	Galls.	Galls.	Galls.	Galls.	Galls.
Milk	15	—	15	570,000,	—	570,000,
	lbs.	lbs.	lbs.			
Butter	6·2	8·8	15	617,000,	884,000,	1,501,000,
Cheese	5·9	6·1	12	224,000,	232,000,	456,000,
Miscellaneous, condensed milk, &c... }	—	—	—	6,000,	13,000,	19,000,
	—	—	—	1,417,000,	1,129,000,	2,546,000,

* The quantity of milk represented by the cheese and butter imported is based on the same ratio as that of the home produce.

In calculating the ratio of milk to cheese and butter respectively, I have assumed throughout this paper that 1 lb. of cheese represents one gallon, and 1 lb. of butter represents 21 pints. I have collected a number of records from various sources—English and foreign—(with which it is not necessary to encumber this paper) which go to justify in their average results the adoption of this standard.

In conclusion, while admitting that the results arrived at are only tentative, I hope that they may serve in some measure to throw some light on a difficult subject. In the attempt which I have made to bring these figures before the Society, I have received help, as I have previously acknowledged, from many quarters. But to no one am I so deeply indebted as to Major Craigie, who from the first inception of this paper to its final completion, has afforded me invaluable assistance and advice, and indeed but for whose encouragement I should have been disposed to shrink from the task.

I may add one word more, which by a natural association of ideas may appropriately follow a reference to the Director of the Statistical Department of the Board of Agriculture. It is this: Is it too much to hope that ere long we may look for some better official help in solving a problem which is of the deepest interest, not only to statisticians but to agriculturists and to social economists? The Board of Agriculture has already given ample proof of its energy, and the demands upon its activity have not been light since its establishment. Yet I venture to hope that it may ere long, whether in connection with the Agricultural Returns or by a special inquiry, be able to give us, for the first time complete and reliable information as to the production of milk and milk products in this country.

APPENDIX.

TABLE I.—*Copy of Milk Register* (1890) *of St. Albans Dairy Herd of Pure Bred the Quantity of Milk (in lbs.)*

[In the case of purchased animals the record can be only given for the time during extends over the

Name of Cow.	First Calf.		Second Calf.		Third Calf.		Fourth Calf.	
	Days in Milk.	Pounds of Milk Yielded.	Days in Milk.	Pounds of Milk Yielded.	Days in Milk.	Pounds of Milk Yielded.	Days in Milk.	Pounds of Milk Yielded.
Home bred.								
ueen of Fame 3rd	266	4,723	236	5,002	389	7,190	275	6,570
ady Whiteflank 2nd	197	2,467	176	1,935	235	5,082	268	5,596
ocalist 6th	280	3,614	351	3,890	300	4,513	265	3,853
aphne 6th..............	279	4,081	330	5,812	246	4,574	334	9,273
lexandria 8th	263	4,041	251	4,102	248	4,465	272	4,853
lvira 8th	386	5,414	319	4,221	270	3,771	316	4,512
weetheart 46th........	327	3,937	271	4,688	244	4,333	219	4,053
mily Foggathorpe	363	5,349	308	5,973	269	4,473	251	5,784
ocalist 5th	310	4,210	367	5,434	167	5,197	379	5,944
uby 11th	366	4,566	263	5,020	270	4,593	—	—
ay Duchess 20th....	248	3,795	249	3,848	253	4,120	—	—
estris 123rd	432	4,854	320	5,795	—	—	—	—
,, 124th	326	4,123	284	5,358	—	—	—	—
livette	400	4,129	214	3,705	—	—	—	—
rinket........................	277	3,360	—	—	—	—	—	—
Purchased.								
ay Duchess 18th....	—	—	252	6,180	330	5,264	280	6,140
estris 68th	—	—	—	—	229	5,371	332	6,157
,, 82nd	—	—	—	—	308	5,998	281	5,997
lvira 7th	—	—	—	—	—	—	196	4,297
aphne	—	—	—	—	—	—	280	5,578
atchless 5th...........	—	—	—	—	—	—	280	7,753
ountess of Wragby	—	—	—	—	—	—	—	—
atchless 16th	—	—	—	—	—	—	—	—
ay Duchess 17th....	—	—	—	—	—	—	—	—
ady Whiteflank	—	—	—	—	—	—	—	—
ater Nymph	—	—	—	—	—	—	—	—
ame	—	—	—	—	—	—	—	—
livia	—	—	—	—	—	—	—	—
estris 37th	—	—	—	—	—	—	—	—
harm	—	—	—	—	—	—	—	—
Average	308	4,177	279	4,731	275	4,921	282	5,757

APPENDIX.

Shorthorns, showing for all the Cows in the Dairy the Number of Days in Milk and Yielded after each Calf.

which they have been in the herd, while in the case of those bred at home it whole life.]

	Pounds of Milk Yielded.	Sixth Calf.			Days in Milk.	Pounds of Milk Yielded.
		Days in Milk.	Pounds of Milk Yielded.			
	7,002	266	7,237		—	·
	2,573	—	—		—	·
	3,090	—	—		—	·
	—	—	—		—	·
	—	—	—		—	·
	—	—	—		—	·
	—	—	—		—	·
	—	—	—		—	·
	—	—	—		—	·
	—	·	—		—	·
	—	—	—		—	·
	—	—	—		—	·
	—	—	—		—	·
	5,872	314	7,815		—	·
	5,734	469	11,162		—	·
	8,481	372	10,010		—	·
	6,680	112	2,215		—	·
	3,618	140	1,458		—	—
	7,995	280	7,588		—	—
	6,349	238	5,878		411	7,909
	3,051	258	5,591		—	—
224	4,047	220	5,357		—	—
423	10,825	—	—		—	—
	—	251	6,037		322	7,580
	—	341	9,170		—	—
	—	254	4,371		—	—
	—	—	—		196	4,144
	—	—	—		186	2,746
	5,410	270				

II.—*Table giving the Daily Rations of a Cow, and in some cases the Actual but generally the Estimated Daily Return of Milk in Fourteen instances, examined by Mr. J. C. Morton in 1865, Twelve of which were strictly Town Dairies.*

[Extracted from No. 682, vol. xiv, of the "Journal of the Society of Arts," 15th December, 1865.]

Number.	Cows Milked.	Cows Bought per Annum.	Loss on Sales per Stall.	Daily Winter Rations of a Cow.					Daily Produce of Milk per Stall.
				Grains.	Hay.	Distillery Wash.	Roots.	Meal or Cake.	
	No.	No.	£	Bshl.	lbs.	Galls.	lbs.	lbs.	Qts.
1	108	160	7	1½	15	—	30	3 (F)	9½
2	80	150	2	1½	—	—	—	4	12
3	40	40	—	1	14	—	40	2 (F)	10
4	68	76	—	1	—	—	42	—	9½
5	10	—	—	1½	12	—	60	2 (F)	—
6	100	150	—	¾	9	—	56	3	—
7	20	—	—	1	6	—	56	3	—
8	—	—	—	1	14	—	28	Pint condiment	12
9	50	100	—	1	12	—	28	Peck bran	12
10	—	—	—	1½	9	—	28	Pint meal	9½
11	—	—	—	1½	15	—	30	—	12
12	50	75	—	1	14	—	25	5	10
13	—	—	—	1½	7	—	60	4	9
14	—	—	—	1½	11	6	42	3	10

Note.—The summer ration is grass, as much as they will eat, grains, and a little meal.

(F) This indicates that in these cases the meal or cake was given only to fattening cows; in others it was given continually.

Records of the Average Yield of Milk per Annum in a Number of Dairy Herds for different Years.

	County.	Breed.	Years.	Number of Cows in Milk.	Average Yield.
					Galls.
f Westminster	Cheshire	Shorthorn	1886	{ —	621
				{ —	635
....	„	„	'87	{ —	677
				{ —	574
....	„	„	'88	{ —	758
				{ —	611
....	„	„	'89	{ —	609
				{ —	580
„	„	„	'90	{ 42	714
				{ 41	609
ey Mason	Norfolk	Red Polls	'86–87	23	491
„	„	„	'87–88	26	415
„	„	„	'89–90	20	420
garton of Tatton	Cheshire	Dutch....................	1887	5	715
„	„	„	'88	5	974
„	„	„	'89	6	781
„	„	„	'90	6	736
„	„	Dairy shorthorns	'89	9	704
„	„	„	'90	14	634
„	„	Kerries	'90	6	355
Paget	Notts	Dairy shorthorns ...	'88	13	636
....	„	„ ...	'89	14	688
....	„	„	'90	11	765
hall........................	Northumberland	Dairy shorthorns and cross-bred .... }	'84	{ —	814 cows
				{ —	686 heifers
....	„	„	'85	{ —	772 cows
				{ —	732 heifers
....	„	„	'86	—	863 cows
....	„	„	'87	{ —	930 cows
				{ —	800 heifers
....	„	„ ...	'88	{ —	906 cows
				{ —	741 heifers
. Paget, Bt. M.P.	Somerset	Shorthorns	'86	—	605
„	„	„	'87	—	532
„	„	„	'88	45	578
rhead .... {	Errigle, county Cavan, Ireland .... {	Cross - bred and shorthorn, and old Irish cow, and a few Ayrshires and Kerries .... }	'87	24	482
„	„	„	'88	26	543
„	„	„	'89	22	600
„	„	„	'90	28	616*
Dairy School {	County Cork, Ireland	Shorthorn and Ayrshire crosses .... }	४	४ 30	691
„	„	„	७०	28	717

IV.—*Quantity per Head of the Population of the Imports of Butter (including Margarine) and Cheese into the UNITED KINGDOM in the Years specified.*

Year.	Butter and Margarine.	Cheese.	Year.	Butter and Margarine.	Cheese.
	lbs.	lbs.		lbs.	lbs.
1867	4·2	3·3	1879	6·7	5·8
'68	4·0	3·2	'80	9·5	5·7
'69	4·6	3·5	'81	6·6	5·9
'70	4·2	3·7	'82	6·9	5·4
'71	4·7	4·3	'83	7·3	5·7
'72	4·0	3·7	'84	7·7	6·0
'73	4·5	4·7	'85	7·4	5·7
'74	5·6	5·1	'86	7·4	5·3
'75	5·0	5·6	'87	8·4	5·5
'76	5·6	5·2	'88	8·4	5·7
'77	5·5	5·5	'89	9·4	5·7
'78	5·9	6·5	'90	9·1	6·3

V.—*Quantities of BUTTER and CHEESE Imported into the United Kingdom in each of the Years specified, with the Quantity of Milk represented in each case, estimated on the Basis of One Pound of Cheese to One Gallon of Milk, and One Pound of Butter to Twenty-one Pints of Milk.*

Year.	Imports of Butter (including Margarine).	Quantity of Milk Represented.	Imports of Cheese.	Quantity of Milk Represented.
	cwts.	Galls.	cwts.	Galls.
1866	1,165,081	343,783,814	872,342	97,702,304
'67	1,142,262	335,825,028	905,476	101,413,312
'68	1,097,539	322,676,466	873,377	97,818,224
'69	1,259,089	370,172,166	979,189	109,669,168
1870	1,159,210	340,807,740	1,041,281	116,623,472
'71	1,334,783	392,426,202	1,216,400	136,236,800
'72	1,138,081	334,595,814	1,057,883	118,482,896
'73	1,279,566	376,192,404	1,356,728	151,953,536
'74	1,619,808	477,798,522	1,485,265	166,349,680
'75	1,467,870	431,553,780	1,627,748	182,307,776
'76	1,659,492	487,890,648	1,531,204	171,494,848
'77	1,637,403	481,396,482	1,653,920	185,239,040
'78	1,796,517	528,175,998	1,968,859	220,512,208
'79	2,045,399	601,347,306	1,789,721	200,448,752
1880	2,326,305	683,933,670	1,775,997	198,911,664
'81	2,047,341	602,180,745	1,840,090	206,090,080
'82	2,169,717	637,896,798	1,694,623	189,797,776
'83	2,334,473	686,385,062	1,799,704	201,566,848
'84	2,475,436	727,778,184	1,927,139	215,839,568
'85	2,401,373	706,003,662	1,833,832	205,389,184
'86	2,431,540	714,872,760	1,734,890	194,307,680
'87	2,789,274	820,046,556	1,836,789	205,720,368
'88	2,811,176	826,485,744	1,917,616	214,772,992
'89	3,169,532	931,842,408	1,907,999	213,695,888
1890	3,107,713	913,667,622	2,144,074	240,136,288
'91	3,371,037	991,048,878	2,041,317	228,627,504

Discussion *on* Mr. Rew's Paper.

Mr. George Barham said the paper was bristling with facts, and so full of tables and information that he had been unable to grasp the subject sufficiently during the short time it was being read, and regretted that he had had no opportunity of reading the paper before coming into the room, but he thought they would all agree that they were much indebted to Mr. Rew for the large amount of work and patience he had displayed in collecting so much information. It wound up with what he thought a useful suggestion, namely, that the Board of Agriculture might materially assist dairy farmers, who, he believed, had suffered as much as others during the recent depression. As a dairy farmer himself, he could bear testimony to the great value of the Board of Agriculture, and he thought the time was now ripe for it to ask for returns on the subject. Mr. Rew had said that 10½ quarts of milk would make 1 lb. of butter; this was exceedingly good management even with a Laval cream separator, and he thought that on an average the quantity of milk required was nearer 15 quarts. Mr. Rew had also said that the length of time during which a cow continuously gave milk varied from 112 to 174 days. This period was sometimes considerably exceeded; in fact he had known instances of a cow remaining in milk for three years continuously, and giving a fairly large quantity during the whole time. In other countries it was known that where cows had been spayed they had maintained their milk supply for a very long period. The figures quoted from Mr. Culley bore out the impression that English shorthorn cows formerly gave much more milk than at present. There were instances of cows giving 36 quarts a day, but he doubted whether such a result could be obtained at present. Mr. Culley had also mentioned a dairy of 12 cows which yielded 48 firkins of butter, though he presumed this would refer to the best dairy cows. He believed that forty years ago, at Rhodes's dairy at Islington, for example, cows were sent away for slaughter when they yielded less than 10 quarts daily. Holstein cows yielded more milk than shorthorns, and some gentlemen would remember that a cow gained the prize at Amsterdam with 36 quarts in a day. It was very difficult to obtain any reliable information as to the consumption of milk per head of the population; and although he had long been connected with the production and sale of milk, he had scarcely any idea of what the average consumption was. In hospitals and infirmaries it was consumed largely, as also in rich people's houses. In poor people's houses, on the contrary, the milk supply was always the first to be curtailed when economy became necessary. Prisoners formerly had cocoa with milk every morning, but at present, since the prisoners had been taken over by the central authority, only a few pints were consumed among hundreds of prisoners. There was evidently room for a large increase in this branch of farming, and efforts should be made to encourage it, not only in the interests of young children in large towns, but also in the interest of the dairy farmer.

Mr. S. B. L. DRUCE said it was a matter of great congratulation to people in London, that they were now able to get their milk direct from the country at a moderate cost. Ten years ago he had found that milk was being sent to London by the Midland Railway from the other side of Derby, at the rate of 1*d.* a gallon, and, as Mr. Rew had pointed out, the quantity sent by rail had considerably increased since that time. In many parts of the country, too, facilities were given to dairy farmers to send their milk to other large towns, as, for instance, some farmers in Derbyshire towns sent their milk as far as Newcastle. He had long thought that the trade in separated milk ought, in the interests of the poor of this metropolis, to be encouraged. At first, like many other persons, he was himself rather tempted to disparage separated milk; but he could not agree with those who maintained that all the goodness was gone out of it. He could not of course say that separated milk would do all the good that whole milk did; but he thought it would be a great advantage if, especially in the summer months, poor children and women in our crowded towns could obtain such a wholesome drink as separated milk at a cheap rate; it would at all events be better than gin. One of the first persons to introduce the sale of separated milk as such into London was, he believed, Lord Vernon. In establishing his depôts in several poor localities, this nobleman had conferred a great benefit on the poor of London, and he could not help throwing out the suggestion to Mr. Barham, who had also done something in the same direction, but for the middle class, that he might develop this branch of the milk trade. He thought the public in London were greatly indebted to the large dairy companies, to whom it was mainly owing that the milk as now sold in London was so pure and wholesome. He had been much struck with the statement in the paper, that although the number of cows had increased of late years, yet they had not increased sufficiently to keep pace with the population; so that the number of cows per 1,000 of the population was less during the period 1886 to 1890 than it had been during 1866 to 1870. That dairy farming had, at all events during the earlier period of the depression, suffered less than any other branch of farming (a fact admitted by farmers at large), was borne out by the paragraph in the paper in which it was stated that the number of animals engaged in milk production was larger in 1891 than in any year on record. Relatively, however, to the total herds the number was less than twenty years ago, and this, he thought, showed that there was still a wide field for the further development of dairy farming in this country, and he could only hope that this valuable paper might lead to some steps being taken in that direction.

Mr. H. M. PAUL said his remarks would have reference to the importation of butter and cheese. It had been shown conclusively by Mr. Rew that the amount imported was about equal to the amount made in the United Kingdom, and that there had been an increase in these importations. . During the five years 1861-65 the quantity of butter and margarine imported, according to the official figures, was 3·9 lbs. per head of population, while in 1886-90 it was 8·5 lbs. In this connection the question arose : what was being done at home? Was the manufacture of butter and cheese at home really being stimulated to the greatest extent? It was noteworthy that whereas up till 1886 butter and margarine were combined in the official returns, they were given separately after that date. Similarly the importation of cheese had increased, for whereas during the five years 1861-65 these were 2·9 lbs. per head, in 1886-90 they had reached 5·7 lbs. per head. To those who desired to see the development of Greater Britain it was a subject of consolation that the imports from our colonies should increase. So far those from the Australasian colonies had been small. In 1891 there were received thence about 43,000 cwts. of butter, and 29,000 cwts. of cheese; but it was believed that with the greater development of the factory system these imports would be materially increased. It should also be borne in mind that the supplies from the colonies reached this country just when the quantity received from other countries, and the home production, during our winter months, were curtailed. The quality of Australasian cheese and butter was good, and while the price obtained for the former was equal to that for the best Canadian, 126s. per cwt. had been paid for the butter in the wholesale market during the past winter.

Mr. E. G. EASTON had hoped, when he first saw that the Society was to consider the subject, that the economical side would not be overlooked. It was a matter which had two sides, and Mr. Rew had marvellously kept the economical side out of the paper. He had hoped that the consideration of the health and well-being of the community would be discussed. The matter might be summed up briefly by taking the number of cows in milk to produce a given quantity each; but in considering the quantity consumed by each individual, the question arose as to what *was* milk. A certain quantity of butter was given, but farmers sometimes made the butter, and then sent the milk to London: it was therefore possible that the statistics of those particular districts might answer a double purpose. With regard to separated milk, no trade had made such gigantic strides during the last three or four years, since the introduction of separators. He would suggest for Mr. Rew's consideration that there were many tons of milk which had answered the butter factor, and then been sent up to London and elsewhere, and answered other purposes as well. It had been said that separated milk was a wholesome drink; anyone would admit that, but it was in fact the wealthier classes who would drink it, and not the mass of the poor, who would always want the best article. Another important factor, to which he

feared Mr. Rew had scarcely done justice, was condensed milk.
The importation of this article grew alarmingly, but he was glad to
think that of late years Ireland was beginning to turn her attention to this trade, and would doubtless in a few years take away
a great deal of the continental trade in this article. He had no
idea Mr. Spencer had fixed the average production of milk per
cow at so low an average; his own experience was that it was a
good deal higher, in fact that the average in most cowsheds was
10 quarts a day. He had hoped the Society would bear in mind
the economical side of the question, as there were 8,000 establishments for the sale of milk in London, half of which in the course
of a generation would be prohibited from dealing in it on sanitary
and other grounds.

Mr. H. FABER said that he would make a remark on the
particular side of the question in which he was interested,
namely, the importation of butter to this country. He understood Mr. Barham's view to be that the consumption of milk per
head in this country was so small, that there was a likelihood of a
great development of that consumption, and therefore of the milk
trade in this country. But with the increase in the population,
and the increase in the consumption of milk, it must be admitted
that it was quite impossible that the cows of this country should at
any time be able to supply the people with all the milk, butter,
and cheese which they required. England was essentially an
industrial country; a very large proportion of the population was
employed in consuming food, and not producing it, therefore
if its industry were kept up at the present high rate, it would be·
impossible to produce the food necessary, particularly in the case
of dairy products. Nearly half the butter imported into this
country came from Denmark. This importation had greatly
increased of late, but had now probably reached its maximum. In
the last six or seven years the export of butter from Denmark had
quadrupled, and this was due to the action of the co-operative
dairies to which the whole milk was sent from the small farmers,
the separated milk being returned, so that whereas previously
whole milk was consumed as an article of diet, separated milk had
now taken its place, enabling the people to export the butter. He
quite agreed with the gentleman who advocated the use of
separated milk: it was certainly the most economical way of using
it, and considering that out of the total solids, or nourishing
constituents of milk, which were about 12 per cent., roughly
speaking, only 3½ per cent. were taken for the butter, and nearly
9 per cent. left, it was obvious that the nourishing qualities of
separated milk were not much below those of whole milk.

Sir RAWSON W. RAWSON said he thought this paper likely to
be of great advantage to statisticians for the information it contained; to the agricultural population for the suggestions it embodied, and to the Board of Agriculture for the recommendations
offered as to further information which it would be desirable to
collect. He did not know whether he understood Mr. Barham to

say that the average produce of the cow at the present time was
less than formerly.

Mr. BARHAM replied that he believed that the produce of a cow
now was less than it was forty years ago, but more than it was
fifteen years ago.

Sir RAWSON RAWSON could not understand why with the care
devoted to the improvement of the breeds, and with the increased
means of supplying food at all seasons, there should be no
increased production. If it were true, the cause should be ascertained why, instead of advancing as we were in almost every other
kindred matter, we should be retrogressing in this. Since he had
returned to England, he had been glad to observe a great increase
in the consumption of milk by classes which formerly consumed
spirits and beer. The Aerated Bread Company's shops spread
over the metropolis were the greatest blessing to this town. He
rejoiced at the increase in the imports of butter and cheese, if it
arose from the diminution of the production of those articles here
in consequence of the increased consumption of milk. Cheese and
butter could be brought across the seas : milk could not, and he
hoped therefore that the farmer would find it pay him best to send
his milk to the towns and centres of consumption, instead of
making it into butter and cheese.

Mr. C. W. GRAY, M.P., said that the answer to the question
asked by the last speaker—how it was that the supply of milk
products had fallen off—depended simply on whether a profit could
be made out of the industry or not. For some reason or other there
was not much money to be made out of milk production at present in
England. He thought that the British farmer, as a rule, understood his business quite as well as any on the globe. Many people
attributed the ills which had befallen the farmer during the last
twenty years to the farmer himself. Formerly he was held up as
an example to all the world, but now it had become the fashion to
run him down. A little while ago, he was told that to make milk
production pay, he ought to keep a great number of cows; now it
appeared that this was all wrong, and that to do well they ought
to keep two cows only. It was extremely difficult for the British
farmer to compete successfully with the foreigners who sent their
milk products to this country. He would like to see some
thoroughly practical man go over to these competing countries,
Denmark especially, and see how it was that they were able to
flood the English market with this produce at less cost than
our own farmers.

Mr. T. J. PITTAR pointed out that while ten years ago our
supplies of butter and cheese from foreign countries represented
16,000,000 sterling, in 1891 it had risen to nearly 20,000,000*l*., an
increase of nearly 24 per cent. Considering the countries whence
this supply was obtained, it appeared that from Denmark the
value of the quantity sent over had increased in that time by about

190 per cent., whereas from France, which formerly contributed a
much greater proportion of our supply than Denmark, the increase
was only about 24 per cent.   In the same time the population had
only increased by 8·6 per cent.   It appeared therefore that the
British manufacturers were allowing themselves to be cut out by
the foreigners.   This confirmed what other speakers had mentioned, that abroad, as in Denmark, the dairy farmers had
managed to make milk and milk products exceedingly profitable.
Condensed milk last year was imported to the value of 900,000*l.*,
representing 440,000 cwts., an increase of something like 10 per
cent. on the imports of the previous year; this also pointed to
the increase of the foreign supply of these products as against
the decaying supply of this country, because the increase in
the population in a single year is something less than 1 per cent.

Major P. G. CRAIGIE said that they were all extremely indebted
to one of the younger Fellows of the Society—Mr. Rew—who
had brought forward such an interesting collection of facts, of
which so much might afterwards be made.   It was very desirable
to stimulate the interest of younger members to make original
inquiries, such as had been perseveringly made by Mr. Rew, into
some of the dark questions of statistics.   The consumption and
production of milk was a question on which, in view of the great
diversity of estimates, he had himself always been afraid to venture
on any very definite statement.   A paper like the present was
therefore welcome to all who studied our food supply.   It had been
said that evening that the Board of Agriculture ought to obtain
and furnish precise statistical details on this subject; but he
thought he could best answer the suggestion that much was to
be immediately expected in this direction, by quoting Mr. Rew's
own paper, where it was made very evident that the majority
perhaps of farmers themselves did not know accurately the
quantity of milk their herds produced per annum.   A cow was
not continually productive throughout the year, and it would
be, he feared, impossible to ask in the annual returns every owner
of cattle to state how much milk every individual cow produced in
the year.   With the present machinery such minute inquiries
could not be undertaken.   He was therefore particularly anxious
to see voluntary investigators breaking ground in a new direction,
where voluntary effort would be, as matters stood, more effective
than official returns.   He would like to call Mr. Rew's attention to
the returns for the year 1866.   In any reference to statistics of
the number of animals in this country, it must be remembered that
1866 was the first and really the experimental year of our now
annual agricultural returns.   Naturally the figures collected were
less complete than the later *data*, and in the table used to-night it
would be noticed they differed from almost all the succeeding
years.   He thought it well therefore to omit 1866 in any serial
statement based on the agricultural returns, and begin with 1867
only.   With reference to the imports of dairy produce, he had in
his hand a very remarkable diagram, prepared by a German
writer, and published in the *Milch Zeitung* for the benefit of

continental producers, showing the enormous imports of this country, both of butter and cheese. This diagram was meant to suggest, and did suggest, to continental producers that England was *the* market for the dairy produce of the world. He hoped that further research and inquiry, such as had been suggested that evening, would bring out why and under what conditions various foreign countries were able, with profit to themselves, to export so much to this country.

Mr. A. E. BATEMAN said he could quite confirm what Major Craigie had said as to the statistics of 1866. In that year the Board of Trade began collecting the statistics of live stock and acreage, in consequence of the cattle plague, and there were difficulties in collecting the returns in the first year, which made the figures for 1866 less reliable than those of subsequent years. Table V in the Appendix gave the importations of butter, including margarine. About one-third of this importation was margarine, which in America was called "bull butter." A second column in the table gave the quantity of milk supposed to be equivalent to these imports of butter and margarine, but the latter being "bull butter" did not represent milk at all; it represented suet or internal fat of animals. The above-mentioned table therefore required an explanatory note. The Mige-Mouries process of making margarine, which was the one first adopted, was based on the discovery that an ill-fed cow who had formerly been well fed, would go on giving milk for some time by using up the internal fat which she had accumulated in her happier days. Hence the notion of purifying this fat and using it for butter without it ever having been milk. A certain quantity of margarine was no doubt made in this country both from imported and pure home grown suet and oleo, besides the 60,000 tons of margarine annually imported from abroad. The margarine question had always been a great difficulty in butter-producing countries. Denmark, having an important butter trade, had been very firm in repressing margarine, but complaints were now made with regard to the butter from France and other countries having margarine in it. A small percentage of margarine mixed with butter was very difficult to test.

Mr. J. H. SHERWIN said he would like to ask Mr. Rew whether he was quite sure that all the gallons mentioned in the returns he had obtained were imperial gallons, and not barn gallons, the latter having twice the capacity of the former. Mr. Rew had stated that $10\frac{1}{2}$ quarts of milk would make 1 lb. of butter. He thought that the reason why the production of butter had fallen off in this country was because the farmer found it did not pay. A barn gallon of milk sold in a large market, as Birmingham, fetched 1s. 5d. in summer, and 1s. 9d. in winter, whereas the $10\frac{1}{2}$ quarts made into 1 lb. of butter fetched 1s. 4d. It was therefore more profitable to sell the raw material. He would further suggest that it was very doubtful whether one-third of a pint was the average consumption per head of population. He had found out that the

consumption per head in his own family, without any stint whatever, was two-thirds of a pint per day, and he thought it hardly
possible that for the whole of the population it could be one-third
of a pint.

Mr. R. H. REW, in reply, regretted that the results he had been
able to bring forward were not more conclusive, but he should be
satisfied if what he had done might at some future time prove of
assistance to anyone who took up the subject. With regard to
what Mr. Gray had said, he had not attempted to advise farmers,
and he did not think that farmers generally wanted much advice.
As to the alleged decrease in the production of a cow as compared
with former years, the figures quoted from Mr. George Culley
referred to 1807. He was not quite sure whether Mr. Culley
referred to a particular district, but he rather thought not. As
Mr. Druce pointed out, the number of cows per 1,000 of the
population had incontestably decreased, and this showed that,
assuming the production of a cow to be the same, the milk production had decreased. But his figures tended to show that the
production from the cow had increased.   His figures were the
highest yet accepted, viz., a standard of 400 gallons per cow, after
deducting the requirements of the calf. Another point referred
to by Mr. Barham was the quantity of milk required to make 1 lb.
of butter. He thought there was good ground for taking up the
position he (Mr. Rew) had. Only a few days ago he read an
article by Mr. T. F. Hall, who stated that from Jersey cows 8
quarts was a fair average to take. The Jersey cow was now a
considerable factor in milk production, and if the above were true
of Jerseys generally, it would pull down the average. He thought
it impossible that any of his correspondents had made the mistake
of confusing barn gallons with imperial gallons; he could only
say that he had taken the greatest precaution to ask for imperial
gallons only. As regards the agricultural returns for the year
1866, they were no doubt admittedly unreliable, and it would be
better, perhaps, to ignore them. He had reckoned margarine as
equivalent to butter in the table of imports, partly because it was
impossible — except for two or three recent years — to separate
them, but chiefly because every pound of margarine presumably
displaced a pound of butter, and therefore represented in competition and in consumption practically the same thing for statistical purposes.

The ENUMERATION of PAUPERS—a CORRECTION.

By CHARLES BOOTH, ESQ.

THE following extracts from "Pauperism and the Endowment of "Old Age," the volume just issued by Mr. Charles Booth, refer to errors which occurred in the figures given in the Paper on the subject published in the December number of the *Journal*:—[1]

From Part I, chapter vi.

"The figures, if they were in themselves correct, would show "that the paupers counted for six months were, thirty-five years "ago, rather less than two-and-a-half times the number on one "day. It is probable that this was then an exaggeration, and "would be still more so now.

"This probability is borne out by the evidence of a parlia- "mentary return, made in 1881 at the instance of Mr. J. R. Hollond, "then member for Brighton, which seems to have been entirely "overlooked and forgotten by those who have been content to "quote and requote the figures used by Mr. Dudley Baxter. This "return, which is signed by Mr. Purdy, as statistical secretary to "the Local Government Board, gives the 'number of persons "'relieved as paupers (exclusive of vagrants) during the half- "'year ended with Lady-day, 1881, in each union county of "'England,' and may be compared with the return of the number "in receipt of relief on the 1st January in that year. The com- "parison shows a total of 1,291,424 for the six months, against "803,303 on the single day, or an addition to the number on one "day of 61 per cent.

"The following table shows how the 61 per cent. is distributed "between in-door and out-door relief (stating the lunatics separately "as in a different category, and assuming that 6 per cent.[2] is for "them a sufficient percentage of addition):—

	Counted 1st January.	Counted for Six Months.	Percentage Addition.
Lunatics	62,954	66,731	6 p. ct.
In-door poor	172,722	299,788	74 ,, } 65½ p. ct.
Out-door ,, ...	567,450	924,905	63 ,,
Total............	803,126	1,291,424	61 p. ct.

Vol. liv, p. 621. 1891.[1]
The actual percentage of increase at Stepney.

" The difference between the 61 per cent. addition, according
" to Mr. Hollond's return of 1881, and the 134 per cent. according
" to Mr. Dudley Baxter's version of Mr. Purdy's figures in 1857,
" may be accounted for in three ways—

" (1.) Error in the earlier count.
" (2.) Difference in the time of year chosen for the 'one
" ' day' return.
" (3.) Changes in the character of pauperism since 1857.

" (1.) As to possible error in the earlier count, St. Pancras
" furnishes some evidence. Both at Stepney and at St. Pancras
" the officials have continued making up the half-year's figures in
" the old way, and by the kindness of the guardians I have had
" access to the books in which the returns are preserved. A
" comparison of the figures in Mr. Hollond's return with the
" figures in these books shows, at Stepney, an exact agreement,
" but at St. Pancras, while the books show 24,048, the return gives
" 20,618 as the true number. At St. Pancras, I understand, no
" attempt was usually made to strike off duplicate entries due to
" the passing of paupers from institution to institution, if indeed
" re-entries in the same institution were allowed for, and thus
" the current figures involved an error which had probably been
" characteristic of many of the returns on which Mr. Purdy must
" have based his figures in 1857, but on which it seems he did not
" entirely rely. At Stepney the workhouse system is more simple,
" and exceptional care has been taken to avoid any duplication,
" and thus the return made for Mr. Hollond contains exactly the
" same figures as appear in their own books, and may be accepted
" as correct.

" (2.) The effect of a different time of year is very evident.
" The number in receipt of relief on the 1st of January is at
" its largest, and consequently the addition to be made for
" others relieved in the twelve months will be at its smallest.
" Mr. Hollond's figures are compared with the 1st January.
" Mr. Dudley Baxter's are compared with those on the 1st of
" July. The difference between the numbers in January and in
" July is about 10 per cent. Allowing for this difference, if we
" take for Mr. Hollond's return the 1st July as the starting point,
" in place of 61 per cent. we get 79 per cent.

" (3.) There have been many changes since 1857. Out-door
" relief has been less loosely given; the proportion of the old has
" undoubtedly increased, and an altered policy with regard to
" children and the sick may have assisted in making the character
" of pauperism generally more stable.

" The difference is nevertheless so great between 61 per cent.
" (or 79 per cent.) and 134 per cent., and the question so important,
" that I am glad to know that a return to cover the twelve months
" ending Lady-day, 1892, has been moved for, and will be made
" by the Local Government Board. Meanwhile Mr. Hollond's
" return represents the latest and best official evidence on the
" subject.

" But both these percentages refer to a six months' count, and
" give no positive information as to the numbers for a whole year.
" We have to add something, but it is difficult to say how much;
" and just as a good deal depends upon what day is chosen in
" arriving at the percentage of increase for six months, so the
" addition to be made for the second half-year will depend much
" on which six months have been counted first.

" At Stepney, starting with those in receipt of relief at the
" end of April, and working backwards, we find that we have to
" add on the whole 130 per cent. to reach the six months' total for
" the winter half-year ending on Lady-day, and to the six months'
" total we have to add 29 per cent. to give the year's total. At
" Ipswich, comparing those relieved on 1st January with the whole
" number relieved (also during the winter half-year), the addition
" is found to be 92 per cent., and to the six months' total 40 per
" cent. must be added to give that for twelve months.[3]

" The number of paupers for six months and twelve months
" compared is as follows :—

	Counted on One Day.	Counted for the Winter Six Months.	Counted for Twelve Months.
Stepney Ipswich	1,087 (1st May) 895 (1st Jan.)	2,530 or 130 % additional 1,723 „ 92 „	3,259 or 200 % additional 2,406 „ 169 „
		Average, 112 per cent.	Average, 185 per cent.

" If we may venture to apply a similar rate of progress to
" Mr. Hollond's six months' figures, we should have—number of
" paupers for all England :—

Counted on One Day.	Counted for Six Months.	Counted for Twelve Months.
740,172* (1st January)	1,224,693* or 65½ % addl.	1,581,303 or 110 % addl.

* Lunatics deducted.

[3] Lunatics are excluded from these figures, but no deduction has been made for deaths.

" I am able to compare this estimate with actual returns from
" Paddington and Ashby, as well as Stepney and Ipswich, but in
" this comparison I have deducted the deaths that have occurred
" amongst those relieved, for it is evident that those who die
" during the year should not be included in an estimate of existing
" pauperism. I assume that the dead as well as the living are
" included in Mr. Hollond's return, and, guided by the facts at the
" unions I have examined, I adjust the figures by assuming a
" death-rate of 6 per cent. The table is arranged to show in-door
" and out-door poor separately :—

*A Year's Pauperism, excluding Lunatics and Vagrants, and deducting those who Died
during the Year.*

Parish.	Year.	In-door.			Out-door and Medical.			Total.		
		Number on One Day.	Number for Twelve Months.	Per Cent. of Increase.	Number on One Day.	Number for Twelve Months.	Per Cent. of Increase.	Number on One Day.	Number for Twelve Months.	Per Cent. of Increase.
Stepney	1889	925	1,905	106	162	1,142	637	1,087	3,047	182
Paddington {	'90 and '91 (mean)	} 1,083	2,478	129	510	1,888	270	1,593	4,866	180
Ashby-de-la-Zouch }	1889	122	224	84	565	916	62	687	1,140	67
Ipswich	'91	290	568	96	605	1,737	187	895	2,305	158
		2,420	5,175	114	1,842	5,683	209	4,262	10,858	155
All England (estimated) }	1881	172,722	370,039	114	567,450	1,118,891	97	740,172	1,488,930	101

" This table shows in a very remarkable manner the more constant
" character of country as compared with city pauperism, especially
" as regards out-door relief; and, taking this into account, there
" is nothing improbable in the estimated figures here given for
" all England, which point to a probable addition of more than
" 100 per cent. on the in-door, and rather less than 100 per cent.
" on the out-door, or on the average of about 100 per cent. all
" round.

" On the information which I had before me when I wrote the
" paper on this subject for the Royal Statistical Society last
" December, before seeing Mr. Hollond's 1881 return, I assumed
" that for in-door pauperism an addition of 85 per cent., including
" lunatics, or 106 per cent. excluding them, might fairly be made,
" but that for out-door pauperism double this rate would not be
" too much. This last assumption, though true of the unions I

" had examined, and perhaps true of city pauperism generally,
" is plainly not true of country pauperism, and consequently the
" hypothetical figures I put forward at that time involved a con-
" siderable error.   It now seems that, if we take the whole country,
" the percentage to be added to obtain the annual figures for out-
" door pauperism is actually less than that needed for in-door
" pauperism, and an analysis of Mr. Hollond's return shows con-
" clusively that it is in the country districts, where out-relief is
" most freely given, that it is also most stable in character.   In
" towns, and especially where out-relief is checked, there is usually
" a great development of medical or other forms of temporary
" assistance given to those in trouble; and as the people relieved
" in this way vary from month to month, the total numbers on the
" books are much swollen in the course of a year.

    " The revised estimate which I now put forward of 100 per
" cent. to be added on the whole, in-door and out—and probably
" rather more than this rate in-door and rather less than this rate
" out-door—differs very widely from the 3 or 3½ times laid down
" by Mr. Mulhall and Mr. Baxter.   It does not pretend to exact-
" ness, and should be used with some reserve pending the com-
" pletion of the present official inquiry."

From Part II, chapter ii.

    " We have seen that for pauperism of all ages, excluding
" lunatics, it is probably necessary to double the number relieved
" on one day to arrive at the total number relieved in a year.   But
" as people grow older they become more settled in their habits,
" and a larger and larger proportion of those who occasionally
" accept relief either enter the house to stay there or receive
" out-relief in a permanent form.   The deduction for the deaths
" occurring amongst those relieved during the year also chiefly
" affects the old.   The result is that instead of doubling the
" number on one day, we do not need to add more than from
" 30 to 50 per cent.   This rate is considerably less than I esti-
" mated when addressing the Royal Statistical Society in Decem-
" ber last.   The estimate made at that time was admittedly
" supposititious; that now put forward is based on actual count
" in five unions, and though still open to question, as the basis
" is not broad enough for safety, is certainly nearer the truth
" The following table gives the percentages for the five unions in
" which an actual enumeration has been made :—

Percentages to be added to the Number of Paupers, as Counted on One Day, to arrive at the Total Numbers for a Whole Year (Lunatics excluded and Deaths deducted).

Union.	In-door.		Out-door (Ordinary).		Medical.		Combined.	
	All Ages.	Over 65.	All Ages.	Over 65.	All Ages.	Over 65.	All Ages.	Over 65.
	Per cnt.	Per cnt.	Per cnt.	Per cnt.	Per cnt.	Per cnt.	Per cnt.	Per cnt.
Stepney	106*	37	32	Nil	657	861	182	69
Paddington..............	129	23	65	11	1,091	508	180	32
Ipswich	96	82	93	23	1,256	1,860	158	53
Bradfield.............. {	No return	} 45 {	No return	} 27 {	No return	No return	No return	} 38
Barton-upon-Irwell	„	23	„	Nil	„	300	„	12†

* Division of Stepney :—Under 16, 42 per cent.; 16 to 60, 308 per cent.; 60 to 65, 60 per cent.; 65 and upwards, 37 per cent. = 106 per cent.

† There was a heavy mortality amongst the old at Barton. If deaths are not deducted, the percentage for in-door becomes 53 per cent., and for out-door 14 per cent., or in all combined 31 per cent.

" Guided by the actual percentages at the different ages shown " by count at Stepney, we may perhaps assume that the total " addition of 100 per cent. would be allotted as under to the " different ages :—

Under 16 .... 40 per cent.	⎫	
16 to 60 { In-door, 286 per cent. / Out-door, 310 „ } 305 „	⎬ 100 per cent.	
60 to 65 .... 60 „		
Over 65 .... 40 „	⎭	

" Applying these percentages to the figures of pauperism on " one day, we are able to construct the following table. As these " figures do not pretend to accuracy, I treat in-door and out-door " alike, and do not attempt to distinguish between the sexes. It " is, however, probable that the out-door figures are rather over- " stated, and we know that of those relieved outside the work- " house a very large proportion are women.

A Year's Pauperism, 1890-91 (*excluding Lunatics and Vagrants*).

	In-door.				
	Under 16.	16—60.	60—65.	Over 65.	Total.
Number of paupers on 1st July, 1890*	47,069	35,670	13,372	54,752	150,863
Estimated additions for twelve months	40 % 18,827	286 % 102,112	60 % 8,023	40 % 21,901	100 % 150,863
Total	65,896	137,782	21,395	76,653	301,726

	Out-door.				
	Under 16.	16—60.	60—65.	Over 65.	Total.
Number of paupers on 1st July, 1890*	178,258	110,688	27,808	190,935	507,689
Estimated additions for twelve months	40 % 71,303	310 % 343,326	60 % 16,686	40 % 76,374	100 % 507,689
Total	249,561	454,015	44,494	267,309	1,015,378

* Divided by ages according to Mr. Burt's return of 1st August, 1890.

In-door and Out-door (combined).

	Under 16.	16—60.	60—65.	Over 65.	Total.
Number of paupers on 1st July, 1890	225,327	146,358	41,180	245,687	658,552
Estimated additions for twelve months	40 % 90,130	305 % 445,438	60 % 24,709	40 % 98,275	100 % 658,552
Total	315,457	591,796	65,889	343,962	1,317,104

" If, pending better information, this table may be taken to
" represent the facts or a reasonable approximation to them, we
" can go a step further, and show what proportion of our popula-
" tion at each age are to be accounted paupers.

	Population.	Paupers.*	Ratio to Population.
			Per cnt.
Under 16	11,144,021	315,457	2·8
16—60	15,722,273	591,796	3·8
60—65	812,028	65,889	8·1
Over 65	1,322,696	343,962	25·9
Total	29,001,018	1,317,104	4·5

* Pauper lunatics excluded.

" When the results of the promised inquiry are published by
" the Local Government Board we shall know what degree of error
" is shown by the figures given above. It may meanwhile be
" accepted as probable that the ratio of paupers to population, if
" on the average it is 4½ per cent., will be for those from 16 to 60
" (the naturally self-supporting years of life) less than 4 per cent.,
" but that for those between 60 and 65 the rate will rise to about
" 8 per cent., while for those over 65 it is probably more than
" 25 per cent."

MISCELLANEA.

CONTENTS:

I.—*The Medals of the Royal Statistical Society.*

THE medals of the Society are two in number, the Guy Medal and the Howard Medal.

THE GUY MEDAL.

This medal was established in 1891, and is intended to encourage original research in statistics, under conditions contained in the rules appended to this notice. It may be of gold, silver, or bronze; is open to statists of all countries, is not confined to any particular year, and the award is determined by the Council in the manner indicated in the rules.

The medal for 1892 has been awarded by the Council to Mr. Charles Booth, for his investigations into the life and labour of the poor in London, as contained in his papers read before the Society, and their expansion in the separate works subsequently published by him on the subject.

THE HOWARD MEDAL.

The Howard Medal was founded in 1873, the centenary of the appointment of John Howard as High Sheriff of the county of Bedford, and is intended to reward the most meritorious essay on some selected subject of social statistics, under conditions contained in the regulations also appended to this notice.

The matters to be investigated were originally confined to those illustrated in the life and work of Howard, but as this was found to narrow and restrict the field of inquiry injuriously, it was determined to extend the subjects to all branches of sanitary and scientific research tending to the safety of life and promotion of health generally.

The subject selected for the session 1892-93 is "Perils and Protection of Infant Life, with statistical illustrations where practicable." As this question will doubtless be investigated in the labour inquiry now in progress, the present is deemed to be a fitting time to collect and digest as much information as may be procurable on the bearing of occupations and surroundings on life and health, particularly at the earliest period of life, when the mortality in certain classes is known to be abnormally great, but of which the exact causes are imperfectly known at present.

Further particulars or explanations regarding both medals can be obtained from the Assistant Secretary at the offices of the Society.

FREDERIC J. MOUAT, *President.*

JOHN B. MARTIN,
A. E. BATEMAN, } *Honorary Secretaries.*
P. G. CRAIGIE,

Rules for the Award of "The Guy Medal."

1. The Guy Medal of the Royal Statistical Society, founded in honour of the distinguished statistician whose name it bears, is intended to encourage the cultivation of statistics in their strictly scientific aspects, as well as to promote the application of numbers to the solution of the important problems in all the relations of life in which the numerical method can be employed, with a view as far as possible to determine the laws which regulate them.

2. The medal may be of gold, silver, or bronze; the first to be granted for work of a high character founded upon original research; the two latter for work founded on existing data. In any case the results to be first given to the world through this Society.

3. There shall be no obligation to award either a gold, silver, or bronze medal annually; but each year at the ordinary monthly meeting of the Council in April, the members shall be invited to submit the names of any authors of papers read before the Society or of work done in its interest, during the current or immediately preceding session, whom they may consider entitled to a medal of either class; that any such proposals, with the grounds on which they are made, shall be circulated to each member of Council at least a week before the Council meeting in May, when all proposals shall be considered and decided by resolution of a majority of at least two-thirds of the members then present, or the final consideration and determination may be adjourned, if necessary, until the Council meeting in June.

4. A medal may be awarded to others than Fellows of the Society.

5. The Council shall also have power at any time to grant a medal to anyone deemed worthy of such distinction by reason of special and extraordinary services to statistical science, although not strictly falling within the foregoing regulations, provided that the proposal for such an award shall in the first instance be favourably considered by the Executive Committee, and recommended by them to the Council; that notice of the proposal be placed upon the agenda for the Council meeting, and that the award shall be made by the vote of a majority of not less than two-thirds of the members present.

Rules for the Award of " The Howard Medal."

1. That a medal, to be called "The Howard Medal," shall be presented in the name of the President, Council, and Fellows of the Royal Statistical Society, to the author of the best essay on some subject in "social statistics," selected by the Council.

2. That the medal be a bronze medal, contained in a case, having on one side a portrait of John Howard, on the other a wheatsheaf, with suitable inscription.

3. That the subject of the essay shall be selected by the Council at their ordinary meeting in May, and at the anniversary meeting of the Society the title of the said essay shall be formally announced.

4. That the essays be sent to the Council of the Royal Statistical Society, 9, Adelphi Terrace, Strand, W.C., London, on or before 30th June of the year following the announcement of the subject of the essay. Each essay to bear a motto, and to be accompanied by a sealed letter, marked with the like motto, and containing the name and address of the author; such letter not to be opened, except in the case of the successful essay.

5. That no essay exceed in length 150 pages of the *Journal of the Royal Statistical Society*.

6. That the Council shall, if they see fit, cause the successful essay, or an abridgment thereof, to be read at a meeting of the Royal Statistical Society, and shall have the right of publishing the essay in their *Journal* one month before its appearance in any separate independent form; this right of publication to continue till three months after the award of the prize.

7. That the Executive Committee for the time being, or any special committee the Council may appoint in June of the year of competition, shall examine the essays, and report their decision to the Council at their meeting next preceding the ordinary meeting held in November of each year.

8. That the President shall place the medal in the hands of the successful candidate, at the conclusion of his annual address, at the ordinary meeting in November, when he shall also re-announce the subject of the prize essay for the following year.

9. Competition for this medal shall not be limited to the Fellows of the Royal Statistical Society, but shall be open to any competitor, providing the essay be written in the English language.

10. That the Council shall not award the prize except to the author of an essay, in their opinion, of a sufficient standard of merit; and that no essay shall be deemed to be of sufficient merit that does not set forth the facts with which it deals—in part, at least, in the language of figures and tables, and that distinct references be made to such authorities as may be quoted or referred to.

II.—*M. Charles Keleti.*

WE regret to record the loss of one of the most distinguished of our Honorary Fellows: M. Charles Keleti, whose death took place on the 30th May. M. Keleti has been the Chief of the Royal Hungarian Statistical Bureau since 1867, in which year it was created as a section of the Ministry of Agriculture and Commerce; but since then it has been developed and is now a separate department. It was at the International Statistical Congress of Buda-Pesth in 1876, that the Fellows of this Society had the best opportunity of appreciating him and the work he had done; and none of those who were present on that occasion will forget the welcome extended to them by the Hungarians as a nation, and by M. Keleti and his department. M. Keleti has always taken a prominent part in all questions of international statistics, and attended several of the congresses which took place before 1876, and after this last congress in his own city, he was President of the "Commission permanente de Statistique," now superseded by the International Statistical Institute. He was elected an Honorary Fellow of the Royal Statistical Society in 1874, and has throughout evinced his sympathy with us, by invariably sending to our library the numerous and valuable reports of his Bureau, prepared under his direction, besides his own publications, and by taking part in our jubilee celebration in 1885.

III.—*Area and Population.* By EMILE LEVASSEUR.

PART I.—*The States of Europe.*

THE most important work, and that which deservedly enjoys the greatest authority, on the area and population of the States of Europe and of the other parts of the world, is *Die Bevölkerung der Erde*, which is published as a supplement to the *Mittheilungen von Dr. Petermann*, and of which the first edition was published in 1872, and the eighth in August, 1891. Besides this special investigation, there are also the *Almanach de Gotha*, which, like the *Mittheilungen*, is published by the Geographical Institute of Justus Perthes, and the *Statesman's Year-Book*, both annual publications, which are too well known by statisticians, and too much appreciated by the public, to require any commendation. They give the area and the population under the articles devoted to each country. The *Geographisch-Statistische Tabellen*, which were first issued by Otto Hübner, and which have been continued by Dr. Juraschek, give also each year the superficies and the population of the different States; the same information is also given in M. Maurice Block's *Annuaire de l'Economie Politique et de la Statistique*. In 1886 and 1887 I published in the *Bulletin* of the *International Statistical Institute* an article on the area and population of the countries of the world, of which the figures relating to the States of Europe were contributed by the Directors of the Statistical Bureaux of these States. A short summary will also be found in the *Annuaire du Bureau des Longitudes*, and a fuller one in my *Précis de la Géographie de l'Europe*. The figures given for the same year in these different publications are not always in strict agreement. These differences do not however necessarily indicate an error. There is doubtless but one true figure for the area and the population of a country on any particular day, but when this is not known exactly two approximations may be given, which may be equally probable though not identical.

The following table which I have prepared from the third volume of *La Population Française*, is therefore not a criticism on the figures furnished by these other publications, but a further contribution to our knowledge of the subject. The public generally imagine area and population to be two numerical notions which it is easy for governments to determine with perfect precision, and that one has but to take the figures with absolute confidence from the official returns. Writers themselves, in this matter, mostly do the same, and the figures contained in their works generally agree solely because one has copied from the other. The following tables, and the notes which accompany them, call attention to a few differences,—slight, it is true—but they will emphasise the fact that the figures for the area and population, although among the most complete that are furnished by statistical science, should, like all other knowledge, be only accepted with caution.

I will preface the table in question with the following general remarks on area and population :—

1. In several countries the official figure of the area of a country is taken from the ordnance survey; but this survey does not include in all cases (especially in France) the whole of the territory and inland waters, and, on the coast, small bays, harbours, and estuaries of rivers; geographers themselves are not unanimous as to what waters should be included in the area of a country. In other States the official or semi-official area has been measured on topographical maps drawn on a large scale; but the result may vary according to the scale of the map and the skill of the surveyor. Several States again have contented themselves with adopting the measurements taken by individuals, especially those of General Strelbitsky and of the Geographical Institute of Gotha. Also the best works on the subject sometimes give from one year to another different valuations for the same country. To take but one example, and that from one of the States of Europe where this kind of study is much practised, and from a book which is an authority on the subject, the area of the German empire as given in the different series of *Die Bevölkerung, &c.*, is as follows: In 1872, 540,302 sq. kiloms.; in 1874, 540,612; in 1876, 540,631; in 1878, 539,829; in 1880, 540,477; in 1882, 540,518; in 1891, 540,419. General Strelbitsky gave it as 540,800 sq. kiloms. The differences are inconsiderable; they are greater for France,[1] for Italy, England, &c.[2]

2. The population of a country is found by means of censuses, and in the intervening periods by calculating the excess of births

---

[1] See *La France et ses Colonies.* By E. Levasseur, vol. i, p. 2.

[2] See also *Statistique de la superficie et de la population des Contrées de la Terre*, p. 9, showing differences amounting to several millions of sq. kiloms. for the Argentine Republic.

over deaths; very few countries possess the means of taking account of emigration and immigration. The results of the censuses are not of irreproachable exactitude; nevertheless they are, with few exceptions, preferable to all other estimates, and they are generally adopted by statisticians and geographers. But European States do not all take a census of their population regularly; Turkey has never taken any at all: several take them only at intervals of ten years. All these are so many causes of error or of divergence in an estimate of the total population of Europe. A satisfactory result cannot be obtained by adding together the results of the different censuses, because of the diversity of the times at which they have been taken. To be able, therefore, to add the populations together, I have brought them, by means of calculation, and with the aid of the rate of actual increase, up to what would be the probable figure at the end of the year 1890.

3. I have now to state the reason for the order which I have adopted in grouping the States. All such groupings are necessarily somewhat arbitrary, and the author is always subject to criticism. That which I have made use of for more than twenty years in my *Précis de Géographie,* and which I have retained here, is, despite its imperfections which I admit, simple, and in my opinion agrees more with the geographical situation than those groupings which are found in other works. To give but one example from a very important work, I prefer it to the method adopted in *Die Bevölkerung, &c.,* which places Belgium in central Europe, Sweden in the north-western group, and France in the south-western group.

TABLE 1.

States and Colonies.	Area (in Thousands of sq. kiloms.).	Population. (Millions of Inhabitants at the end of 1890.)	Density. (Number of Inhabitants per sq. kilom.)
Western Europe.			
United Kingdom of Great Britain and Ireland, with the Channel Islands ([1])	314·6	37·9	120
Holland ([2])	33·0	4·6	139
Belgium ([3])	29·6	6·1	206
Grand Duchy of Luxemburg	2·6	0·2	76
France ([4])	536·5	38·3	72
Monaco	0·02	0·01	—
Western Europe	916·3	87·1	95
Central Europe.			
German Empire ([5])	540·6	49·4	91
(Prussia)	(348·3)	(29·9)	—
Switzerland ([6])	41·3	2·9	70
Liechtenstein	0·16	0·009	60
Austria-Hungary (exclusive of Bosnia and Herzegovina) ([7])	625·5	41·3	66
Central Europe	1,207·6	93·6	77

TABLE 1—*Contd.*

States and Colonies.	Area (in Thousands of sq. kiloms.).	Population. (Millions of Inhabitants at the end of 1890.)	Density. (Number of Inhabitants per sq. kilom.)
Southern Europe.			
Andorra	0·4	0·006	13
Portugal ([8])	89·3	4·5	50
Spain ([9])	497·1	17·2	34
Gibraltar (to England)	0·005	0·02	40
Italy ([10])	286·6	30·2	105
Saint Marino	0·06	—	—
Malta (to England)	0·3	0·2	—
Greece ([11])	65·1	2·2	33
Turkey ([12])	168·5	5·2 ?	31
Bosnia, Herzegovina, and Novi-Bazar (administered by Austria)	58·4	1·5	25
Bulgaria (*with* Eastern Roumelia) ([13])	96·6	3·1	33
Servia ([14])	48·1	2·1	43
Montenegro	9·1	0·2	22
Roumania ([15])	131·0	5·4	41
Southern Europe	1,450·6	71·8	50
Eastern Europe.			
Russian Empire ([16])	5,477·0	98·0	18
Northern Europe.			
Sweden ([17])	442·8	4·8	11
Norway ([18])	325·3	2·0	6
Denmark ([19])	144·4	2·3	16
Spitsbergen and other arctic islands (Jan Mayen, Bear Islands, &c.)	70·5	0·0	—
Northern Europe	983·0	9·1	9
Total for EUROPE	10,034·4	359·6	35·8

Explanatory Notes.

(1). UNITED KINGDOM.—This area includes inland waters; it is that which the compilers of *Die Bevölkerung, &c.*, have adopted from the English census, and it is almost identical with that of General Strelbitsky (314,200). The figure 312,931 was supplied to me by Dr. Ogle, Superintendent of Statistics in the General Register Office; it is that given in the Ordnance Survey, and has been used by me in the *Stat. de Superficie, &c., de la Terre.* The population as calculated by the Registrar-General was about 38,600,000: the number given, 37,900,000, is the provisional result of the census of 1891. Thus the calculated population was in excess of the actual population by more than 500,000.

(2). HOLLAND.—The area of Holland, according to the measurements of the new survey (1889), is 32,538·3 sq. kiloms., and with the rivers and lakes (461·6 sq. kiloms.) 32,999·9 sq. kiloms.

According to the census of 31st December, 1889, there were
4,511,415 inhabitants.

(3). BELGIUM.—The Belgian survey gives an area of 29,457
sq. kiloms.; but the rivers, which are not included therein, have a
superficies of about 192 sq. kiloms. The last census (5,520,009
inhabitants) dates from 1880; 6,100,000 is the estimated population
for 1890.

(4). FRANCE.—The area of France, as given in the *Annuaire
du Bureau des Longitudes*, is 528,400 sq. kiloms.; but this area,
calculated from the survey, does not comprise certain waste lands,
and is less than the area (533,000 sq. kiloms.) measured by General
Strelbitsky, on a map drawn to the scale 1 : 320,000; and than that
(536,500 sq. kiloms.) measured by the Geographical Department of
the Army on a map drawn to a scale of 1 : 80,000. The figures
calculated by the Geographical Department of the Army are
provisional. [For the different estimates of the area of France, see
La France et ses Colonies, vol. i, p. 2.] The census of 1891 gives a
population (resident) of 38,343,150 inhabitants.

(5). GERMAN EMPIRE.—*Die Bevölkerung, &c.*, gives (on p. 1)
540,419 sq. kiloms. as the area, exclusive of the inland bays and
the German portion of the Lake of Constance. I prefer the
official figures, 540,597 (without Heligoland), as given in the
Stat. Jahrbuch des Deutschen Reichs (1891). The census of the
1st December, 1890, gives a population of 49,424,135 inhabitants.

(6). SWITZERLAND.—The official figure of the area is 41,347 sq.
kiloms., which includes the Swiss portions of the lakes of Geneva
and of Constance. The *Annuaire Stat. de la Suisse* (1891) gives
it as 41,390. The census of the 18th December, 1888, gave a
population of 2,933,334 inhabitants.

(7). AUSTRIA AND HUNGARY.—The area, according to the official
survey, was of Austria, 300,024 sq. kiloms.; of the countries
under the crown of Saint Stephen, 325,338 sq. kiloms.; total,
625,362 sq. kiloms. A planimetrical measurement made upon a
map drawn to the scale, 1 : 75,000, by Mr. Penck, gave the figure
625,557. The provisional results of the census of the 31st December,
1890, gave 23,835,261 inhabitants for Austria, and 17,449,705 for
Hungary; total, 41,284,966. With Bosnia, Herzegovina, and the
annexed portion of the sandjak of Novi-Bazar (58,460 sq. kiloms.,
and 1,489.091 inhabitants), the total area of the Austro-Hungarian
monarchy is 683,978 sq. kiloms., and its population 42,774,057 souls.

(8). PORTUGAL.—In the *Bulletin de l'Inst. Internat. de Stat.*
(1886-87), I set down the area of Portugal (excluding Madeira
and the Azores) at 88,869 sq. kiloms., according. to Councillor
Madeira Pinto. General Strelbitsky puts it at 89,100. A new
official survey, inserted in the *Annuario Estadistico* of Portugal
(1884), gives the area as 89,372 sq. kiloms. The estimated population in 1881 was 4,306,554 inhabitants in Europe; I estimated
the population in 1890 at 4,500,000.

(9). SPAIN.—497,244 sq. kiloms. is the official measurement
calculated by the Geographical and Statistical Institute, which
is about 3,000 sq. kiloms. less than that calculated by General
Strelbitsky. The census of 1887 gave the population of Spain as

17,257,432 inhabitants (including the Balearic Islands, but excluding the Canary Islands).

. (10). ITALY.—The Italian Military Geographical Institute has calculated that the area of Italy is 286,588 sq. kiloms., which number replaces the old official estimate of 296,323 sq. kiloms. General Strelbitsky found it to be 288,540 sq. kiloms. According to the General Statistical Bureau of the kingdom of Italy, the population, calculated on the births, deaths, and emigration returns, was 30,158.000 inhabitants at the end of the year 1890.

(11). GREECE.—The area of Greece, according to official documents, was, first 63,581 sq. kiloms. then 65,662 sq. kiloms. I take it as 65.119 (64,689 if we exclude the small islands near the coast, which form part of the nomarchies of the mainland), according to General Strelbitsky's measurements. The provisional results of the census of 1889 give the population as 2,217,000 inhabitants.

(12). TURKEY.—Neither the area nor the population of Turkey are exactly known. I have taken for the former 168,533 sq. kiloms., as reckoned by the Geographical Institute of Gotha (*Die Bevölkerung, &c.*), less than that which I gave (174,139) in the *Stat. de Superficie, &c., de la Terre.* In that work I estimated the population at 4,137,000 inhabitants. M. Cuinet (*La Turquie d'Asie*) estimated it at 4,798,685. *Die Bevölkerung, &c.*, gives it as 5,600,000. I consider this last estimate rather too high, and have therefore put the population as 5,200,000.

(13). BULGARIA.—I had given the area of Bulgaria and Eastern Roumelia as 99,872 sq. kiloms., but have now taken the new planimetrical measurement of M. Trognitz (*Die Bevölkerung, &c.*), which is 96,660 sq. kiloms. The census of the 1st January, 1888, gave the population as 3,154,375 inhabitants.

(14). SERVIA.—For this country I have also taken the new planimetrical calculation of Trognitz, 48,100 sq. kiloms. The provisional results of the census of the 31st December, 1890, gave the population as 2,157,477 inhabitants.

(15). ROUMANIA.—The figure 5,400,000 is an hypothetical estimate given for want of more precise information. It appears however that from an estimate made in Roumania, the population in 1888 (excluding the Dobruja) would probably be 5,331,000 inhabitants.

(16). RUSSIA.—In the *Stat. de Superficie, &c., de la Terre* I set down the area of the Russian empire in Europe as 5,477,089 sq. kiloms. *Die Bevölkerung, &c.*, gives it as 5,337,784 sq. kiloms. in its general table, p. xii, but this does not include Nova Zembla (the area of which is 91,070 sq. kiloms., according to my *Superficie, &c.*, and 91,814 according to *Die Bevölkerung, &c.*), and it takes for i south-eastern European limit the Ponto-Caspian depressi General Strelbitsky, who, like myself, takes for the Europ limits the crests of the Ural mountains, the Ural river, and the crests of the Caucasus, gives in the new edition (1889) of his work 5,515,057 sq. kiloms., including the sea of Azof, the area of which is 37,605 sq. kiloms.; excluding this sea, we have 5,477,452 sq. kiloms., the figure I have here adopted. In 1885 the population

x 2

of this country was estimated at 92,947,000 inhabitants. I have estimated it for 1890 at 98,000,000.

(17). SWEDEN.—The official area of Sweden is 442,818 sq. kiloms. According to General Strelbitsky it is 450,574 sq. kiloms. According to the population registers, the number of inhabitants of Sweden on the 31st December, 1889, was 4,477,400.

(18). NORWAY.—The old official area was 318,195 sq. kiloms. General Strelbitsky found it to be 325,422. A new official survey gives 325,285 sq. kiloms.; this is the figure which I have adopted. The official estimate of the population in December, 1888, was 1,990,000 inhabitants.

(19). DENMARK.—I had calculated the area of Denmark (including the Faroë Islands and Iceland) at 142,464 sq. kiloms. *Die Bevölkerung, &c.*, estimates it at 144,397 sq. kiloms.; and this is the figure I have here adopted. The provisional results of the census of 1890 give the population of Denmark as 2,172,205, and that of Iceland and the Faroë Islands at about 82,200; total 2,254,405.

PART II.—*The Five Divisions of the World.*

Authors differ more with regard to the area and population of Africa, Asia, Oceania, and America than they do with regard to these particulars for Europe. It is natural that it should be so, since the inhabitants of Europe are in general more advanced, and have been longer civilised than those of the other parts of the world. If the total area of Europe, of which nearly the entire territory belongs to civilised States, having mostly surveys and topographical maps, is open to question, that of the other parts of the world must of necessity be of far greater uncertainty. This area, for the majority of countries, is only obtained by means of calculations made by geographers upon maps which are relatively upon a small scale. The same remark applies to population, because the number of States out of Europe which take regular censuses is small, besides which, several of these censuses are deserving of but limited confidence. As more than half the population of the globe is only ascertained by means of the vague estimates of geographers or of travellers, the figure of the population of the earth can be but an approximate quantity. I have considered the area and population of the five divisions of the world in the *Stat. de Superficie, &c., de la Terre (Bull. de l'Inst. Internat. de Stat.,* 1886-87), and a summarised table was published in the *Ann. Bur. des Longitudes,* and detailed tables were given in my *Précis de Géographie, &c.* Since the last edition of this *Précis, Die Bevöl-kerung, &c.*, by Wagner and Supan, has appeared. In the following table I give (i) the figures which I have myself adopted (these will be found in the *Ann. Bur. des Longitudes* for 1892, and in the appendix to the third volume of *La Population Française*); (ii) the figures given in the three publications which are the greatest authorities on this subject, viz., *Die Bevölkerung, &c.*, 1891; *The Statesman's Year-Book,* 1891; and *Geographisch-Stat. Tabellen,* 1891-92. Explanatory notes follow the table:—

TABLE 2.

Countries	I. According to La Population Française (vol. iii, Appendix) and Ann. du Bur. des Longitudes for 1892.		II. According to Die Bevölkerung der Erde, viii, 1891.		III. According to the Statesman's Year-Book, 1891 (after E. G. Ravenstein).			IV. According to Otto Hubner's Geograph. Stat. Tabellen aller Länder der Erde, 1891-92.	
	Area (in Millions of sq. kiloms.).	Population (in Millions).	Area (in Millions of sq. kiloms.).	Population (in Millions).	Area (In Thousands of Square Miles).	Area (In Millions of sq. kiloms.).	Population (in Millions).	Area (in Millions of sq. kiloms.).	Population (in Millions).
Europe	10·0	360	9·7	357·4	3,555	9·2	360·2	9·7	358·2
Africa	30·5	158	29·2	164·0	11,514	29·8	127·0	29·8	206·1
Asia	42·2	824	44·2	825·9	14,710	38·1	850·0	44·6	860·3
Oceania	11·1	8·8	7·7 (Australia, Continental, and Tasmania)	8·2	3,288	8·5 (Australasia)	4·7	8·9 (Australia and Oceania)	5·3
America { North	23·7 } 42·4	88 }	38·3	121·7	6,446 }	16·7	89·3	38·8 }	124·5
America { South	18·7	34 }			6,837	17·7	36·4		
Oceanic Islands	—	—	1·9	7·42	—	—	—	—	—
Polar Regions	—	—	4·5	0·08	4,889	12·7	0·3	4·5	0·08
	136·2	1,497	135·5	1,479·7	51,239	132·7	1,467·9	135·8	1,554·5

Explanatory Notes on the Table.

EUROPE.—I. Europe, as it appears in Table 1, has for its limits : to the east, the Kara river, the principal crest of the Ural mountains, the Ural river, and the Caspian Sea as far as the peninsula of Apcheron; to the south-east, the crest of the Caucasus. It comprises, in the Ægean Sea, Lemnos and the islands to the north; to the south of the Ægean Sea, Crete. It includes, on the north, Iceland, and the polar islands situated between the extreme meridians of Europe—Nova Zembla, Spitzbergen, Jan Mayen, &c. It does *not* include Franz-Joseph Land, of which the area is entirely unknown. The area of this part of the world thus bounded is, according to my calculation, 10,034,285 sq. kiloms.

In 1886 the population of Europe was estimated by me at 347,060,000. The figure of 360.000,000, which represents this population in 1890, has been obtained either directly from the censuses of the years 1890 and 1891, or indirectly by calculating the population of the countries of which the censuses were too old (see p. 300). The European population is known from the censuses and from the annual movement of population of most of the States. Turkey, however, furnishes no such information, and a few States, like Roumania and Portugal, furnish it only at long intervals.

II. Wagner and Supan, in the last edition of *Die Bevölkerung, &c.*, attribute to Europe an area of 9,729,861 sq. kiloms. In adding to this figure Iceland and the polar regions, which they place in another group, we have a total of 10,046,000 sq. kiloms. In a special table (p. 52) they give as the superficies of Europe, including Iceland, Nova Zembla, and the Sea of Marmora, 10,010,566 sq. kiloms. General Strelbitsky, in the new edition of his work on the area of Europe, gives 10,010,922. Between my estimate, that of General Strelbitsky, and that of Wagner and Supan, there is but a slight difference (22,000 sq. kiloms. at most).

The number of the population which is given by Wagner and Supan (357,400,000) is formed almost of the same elements as the number 360,000,000; the difference is caused principally by Russia—the European population of which I have put at 98,000,000, whereas Wagner and Supan have given but 96,000,000 —and Turkey.

III. The figures given by Mr. J. Scott Keltie at the beginning of the *Statesman's Year-Book* are borrowed from a work by Mr. E. G. Ravenstein, and are not followed by any explanatory notes. The volume gives the population as 380,200,000, but this is an error, and the figure should be 360,200,000 (as corrected by Mr. Ravenstein).

IV. The greater part of the returns relating to area and to population that are given in the *Geogr. Stat. Tabellen*, now edited by M. Juraschek, are the same as those given in the *Alm. de Gotha*, and are therefore almost identical to those contained in *Die Bevölkerung, &c.*

AFRICA.—I. Africa includes Madeira, the Azores, and the islands situated to the south of the Cape of Good Hope. The area which I have assigned to Africa (30,500,000 sq. kiloms.) is almost the mean of the three numbers which I gave in the *Stat. de Superficie de la Terre:* 31,431,089—which is the total of the separate estimates given for each country by the best authorities on the subject (and which I have given in the table on p. 321 of the first volume of *La Population Française)*—30,121,000, and 29,914,000. These two last numbers are the result, the first, of a planimetrical measurement made upon a map drawn to the scale of 1 : 10,000,000, and the second of a calculation of the spherical trapeziums or portions of trapeziums comprised between two meridians and two parallels on this same map. This number, 30,495,600, is also given in the Appendix to the last edition of my *Précis de Géographie, &c.*

The total number of the inhabitants of Africa is unknown, the figures given by statisticians are purely hypothetical, and this must be clearly understood at the outset. Still, to obtain an estimate of the total population of the earth, we must make this hypothesis, by adding to populations that are known or partially known, the most probable figures for the vast territories of which the population is not known. I had supposed, with other writers, that Africa had a population of about 200,000,000 inhabitants (197,000,000 is given in the *Stat. de Superficie de la Terre,* 1886), but a more critical examination of the economic conditions under which the populations of the interior live, has led me to believe that this figure is too high. Travellers—hitherto only in small numbers—who have visited these parts are generally inclined to over-rate the density of the population, because they almost always, either by land or water, follow the trading routes, where the population is generally denser than elsewhere. For these reasons, therefore, I have thought it desirable to reduce the probable population of Africa to 153,000,000. The details as to the area or population of the different States or regions of this part of the world, as also for Asia, Oceania, and America, will be found in the Appendix to the last edition (1891) of my *Précis de Géographie, &c.*

II. Wagner and Supan have given the superficies of Africa, calculated upon an English map drawn to the scale of 1 : 5,977,382, and including the islands off the coast of the Gulf of Guinea, as 29,207,100 sq. kiloms.; but the other islands, notably Madagascar (592,000 sq. kiloms.), are not comprised in this total.

The number, 164,000,000, of inhabitants which they give does not therefore correspond to the population of all the territory which I have designated as Africa.

III. This population is that which Mr. Ravenstein calculated in the *Proceedings* of the Royal Geographical Society (January, 1891), by reducing to 3·6 inhabitants per sq. kilom., the mean density of equatorial and southern Africa.

IV. Juraschek, who includes Madagascar and the neighbouring islands in Africa, gives its area as 29,825,848 sq. kiloms., and the population as 206,112,000 inhabitants.

Asia.—I. I had estimated the area of Asia, excluding the East India Islands, at 42,000,000 sq. kiloms. (*Stat. de Superficie de la Terre*), then at 41,345,000 sq. kiloms. (*Précis de Géographie, &c.*). A careful study of *Die Bevölkerung, &c.,* has, however, led me to take the number 42,186,000.

The figure of the population of Asia depends to a great extent upon the number of inhabitants attributed to China; this latter number at the best is but a very uncertain estimate. I had given 789,000,000 as the population of this continent (*Stat. de Superficie de la Terre*, and *Précis de Géographie, &c.*, p. 309), but I then had for India only the returns of the census of 1881, which gave the population as 257,500,000; I remarked, however (p. 158 of the *Précis*), that the probable population of these possessions in 1885 would be about 280,000,000. From the provisional results of the census of 1891 it appears to be 294,000,000; consequently the present total population of Asia should be not 789,000,000 (as I had calculated), but 824,000,000.

II. Wagner and Supan, profiting by the works of General Strelbitsky and of M. Trognitz, give the area of Asia as 44,142,658 sq. kiloms. But the Sunda Islands and the Philippine Islands, the area of which is 1,994,000 sq. kiloms., are included therein, and in my opinion they should not be considered as forming part of Asia. Besides, for the polar regions (the archipelago of New Siberia, Wrangel Island, &c.) I have added 38,000 sq. kiloms. The area is thus brought up to 42,186,000 sq. kiloms.

I have adopted this number, which is the result of measurements more exact than were those formerly made by myself. Siberia and Russian Turkestan have, according to this new measurement, 16,830,663 sq. kiloms., instead of 16,231,000 (see *Précis, &c.*, p. 309); the English possessions about 4,070,000 sq. kiloms., instead of 3,765,000, &c.

The population of Asia is, according to Wagner and Supan, 825,954,000, but in taking from this the population of the islands which I have considered as forming part of Oceania, it is reduced to 786,000,000. Wagner and Supan estimate the population of the Chinese empire at 361,000,000; I have taken it as 400,000,000 (the *Alm. de Gotha* for 1891 gives it as 402,000,000, and the *Statesman's Year-Book* as 404,000,000). They estimate the population of Turkey in Asia at 15,500,000; I have taken the figure calculated by M. Cuinet in *Turquie d'Asie*, which is 21,500,000. Again, they consider the population of Kafiristan, &c., to be 4,000,000; I take it to be only 500,000. They give the population of independent Arabia at 2,500,000; I give it as 3,500,000. The French possessions they estimate at about 19,000,000, while I consider their population to be 14,500,000. They give, according to the provisional results of the census of 1891, the total population of all the English possessions in Asia as 294,500,000; I had given, in accordance with the returns of 1885, 257,500,000, for which figure, in my new calculation, I have substituted that of 294,000,000. They estimate the population of Siam at 9,000,000, adding that estimates vary from 5,500,000 to 12,000,000; my own is 5,800,000. The other differences are of less importance.

III. Ravenstein (*Proceedings* of the Royal Geographical Society, January, 1891) merely gives, without details, the total area and population. According to an amended estimate which he has made, he considers that the population should be 850,000,000 instead of 830,000,000; this figure appears to me too high.

OCEANIA.—I. Under the name of Oceania I have included all the islands in the Pacific ocean and in the seas forming part of it, and situated between the continent of Asia (which includes the Japanese islands) and the American continent (including the islands along the coast). I have divided it into three parts—the Malay archipelago, extending from the Straits of Malacca to New Guinea (exclusively); Australasia, which name, borrowed from English nomenclature, is more correct since the development of European colonisation, than the old one of Melanesia; and Polynesia, which includes the groups of islands formerly known as Micronesia, and the greater part of Old Polynesia. In Australasia is included Australia, the smallest of the continents in my opinion, the largest of the islands according to others.

I think it desirable to explain to the reader my reasons for thus defining Oceania, since other geographers take a different view. The division of the earth into five parts is a simple plan; it corresponds to the division of the sea into five oceans. It is handy for geographers and for teaching, and should therefore be retained. It is to avoid complicating these divisions that I have considered the polar regions of the north as forming part of the three continents which are nearest to them. It is also for the sake of clearness and for an analogous reason that I have defined Oceania as above. All divisions of this kind are somewhat arbitrary, because Nature in this case, as in many others, has not everywhere created limits which are beyond discussion. It is certainly not necessary to consider the Hawaiian Islands and Australia as being in the same part of the world; it is however permissible to unite in one group all the islands which are scattered over the great ocean. It should also be remarked that if we take the Malay archipelago away from Oceania, as do generally the German geographers, the insular world contained in the great ocean is cut in two, and the least populated of the five parts of the world is diminished in order to increase the number of inhabitants of the most densely populated continent; a division of the earth having but 4,000,000 of inhabitants would be out of all proportion to the others. Physically speaking, if the fauna of the western Malay islands resembles that of Asia, the fauna of the eastern islands is similar to that of New Guinea. As regards ethnography, the number of Malays in Indo-China is too small for it to be necessary to consider the peninsula and the islands as forming part of the same division of the world. From the political point of view, the islands do not belong to the same powers which own Indo-China. The name "Indies" which the Dutch possessions bear, is applied to the West Indies as well as to this archipelago; it is therefore not a sufficient reason for its geographical annexation to Asia. It is to be remarked besides that Wagner and Supan do not use the word Oceania, although custom has adopted it, and that they divide the continents and islands of the earth into seven divisions.

II. Wagner and Supan include only in this group the Australian continent and Tasmania.

III. The *Statesman's Year-Book*, under the name of Australasia, appears to include the two regions which I have described as Australasia and Polynesia.

IV. Juraschek, under the names of Australia and Oceania, includes Oceania without the Malay archipelago.

AMERICA.—I. According to my definition, North America includes, besides the continent to the north, the polar archipelago and Greenland, and to the south the West Indies as far as and including Trinidad, which is situated off the coast of South America. I had estimated its area in 1886 as 23,400,000 sq. kiloms.; a new calculation which I made in 1891 gave it as 23,700,000.

For the population of the British possessions in North America, I had given in my *Précis,* 4,323,000, figures based upon different censuses taken from 1881 to 1886. The English *Statistical Abstract* estimated the population in 1889 as 5,273,000, but the census of 1891 gives a figure slightly below this estimate, and I have had but to add 77,000 to the number 4,323,000 which I had previously given. The total population of North America is thus brought up to 88,000,000 inhabitants.

As regards South America, the areas by means of which I have obtained the total of 18,752,000 sq. kiloms. differ but slightly from those which I had calculated in 1886, the total of which was 18,300,000 sq. kiloms.; they are taken principally from the official documents of the States situated in this part of the world.

II. Wagner and Supan give the area of North America as 19,810,200 sq. kiloms., but they do not include the American polar archipelago, Greenland, Central America, nor the West Indies. They give the area of South America as 17,732,130 sq. kiloms., based upon planimetrical measurements made by the Geographical Institute of Gotha, and they claim thereby to have been able to rectify the official returns; but they have not included the Falkland Islands and South Georgia.

The population which they give for America, namely, 79,600,000 for North America, 3,200,000 for Central America, 5,500,000 for the West Indies, and 33,330,000 for South America, do not differ materially from my figures.

III. The area given for North America by Mr. Ravenstein does not include the polar archipelago nor Greenland, but even taking into account this difference of classification, his estimate appears to me insufficient. The population of the two divisions on the contrary (89,300,000 and 36,400,000) seems in my opinion slightly too high.

IV. The area given by Juraschek is exactly that of *Die Bevöl-kerung, &c.;* the population differs but slightly.

ISLANDS IN THE OCEAN.—Under this title Wagner and Supan group archipelagos and islands which I have distributed among the five parts of the world:—(i.) a large portion of the islands of Oceania, New Guinea, and the adjacent islands, Melanesia, New Zealand, Micronesia, Hawaiian Islands, Polynesia; (ii.) the islands in the Indian Ocean, Madagascar, Réunion, Mauritius and adjacent islands, Kerguelen Islands, &c.; (iii.) the islands in the Atlantic, Azores, Madeira, Canaries, Cape de Verd Islands, &c.

POLAR REGIONS.—Under this title Wagner and Supan, Raven-stein and Juraschek include Greenland and the other polar regions of the north. They do not count the lands of the southern polar regions (except that Wagner and Supan class South Georgia with the islands of the Atlantic), their area not being known.

IV.—*Emigration and Immigration in 1891.*

THE emigration and immigration returns for 1891 are especially important. Until 1890 a return of the foreigners arriving on our shores was obtained from the *Alien Lists* only for the ports of London and Hull, but in the middle of that year, the Act (which dates from the time of William IV) was enforced in all ports. Dr. Giffen's present return to the Board of Trade consequently includes for the first time the numbers, according to these lists, of the aliens who disembarked in Great Britain during the whole of the preceding year. It is divided into two parts, the first dealing with the emigration between the United Kingdom on the one hand, and countries out of Europe, and not bordering on the Mediterranean, on the other; the second dealing with the passenger movement between this country and the continent, and the extent of alien immigration into the United Kingdom. In considering this latter question however, it must be borne in mind that the larger portion of the alien immigrants are simply *en route* to America.

I.

The trans-oceanic movement from and to the United Kingdom may be summarised in the following table :—

TABLE I.

	1891.	1890.	1889.
Total emigrants, including foreigners	334,543	315,980	342,641
„ immigrants „	151,369	155,910	147,398
Excess of emigrants	183,174	160,070	195,243
British and Irish emigrants................	218,507	218,116	253,795
„ immigrants ...,........	103,037	109,470	103,070
Excess of British and Irish emigrants	115,470	108,646	150,725

Thus the emigration from our shores was last year greater than in 1890, but less than in 1889 ; but the same table shows that the increase was almost entirely due to the emigration of foreigners, the number of British and Irish remaining practically stationary.

Besides this, the increase is entirely owing to *emigrants*, in the narrower sense of the word, for the number of cabin passengers, who may be taken to consist of tourists and business men, slightly declined; the whole increase being among the steerage passengers. Owing to a decreased British and Irish immigration, the excess of emigrants of these nationalities has increased.

" Table II brings into notice certain well marked characteristics peculiar to the several elements of the British and Irish emigration. Thus English emigration is more widely diffused than Scotch or Irish; 63 per cent. thereof was directed, it is true, to the United States in 1891, yet still it contributed largely to the total native emigration to British North America, Australia, the Cape, and other places. Of Scotch emigration in 1891, over 69 per cent. was to the United States, and of Irish emigration no less than 91·5 per cent.; and these are about the proportions maintained for some years. It may further be observed that while among English and Scotch adult emigrants, married persons are half as numerous as the single; among Irish adults only one person in ten is married. Consequently we have, as has frequently been observed, a very small proportion of children among Irish emigrants, viz., 9 per cent. only, or little more than half the proportion obtaining usually among English and Scotch emigrants."[3]

TABLE II.—*Numbers, Nationalities, and Destinations of Passengers leaving the United Kingdom for Places out of Europe in 1891, in Vessels under the Passengers' Acts; including also Passengers for Places out of Europe in Vessels not under the Acts, as far as recorded.*

Nationality.	To United States.	To British North America.	To Austral- asia.	To Cape of Good Hope and Natal.	To all other Places.	Total.
English	87,581	17,881	14,549	8,545	9,325	137,881
Scotch............................	15,376	2,370	2,459	448	1,537	22,190
Irish	53,438	1,327	2,539	97	1,035	58,436
Total British and Irish	156,395	21,578	19,547	9,090	11,897	218,507
Foreigners	95,621	12,174	410	1,596	2,474	112,275
Not distinguished	—	—	—	—	3,761	3,761
Grand total	252,016	33,752	19,957	10,686	18,132	334,543

Besides these, 3,133 emigrants left for the United States and other trans-oceanic countries *viâ* continental ports (Amsterdam, Antwerp, Rotterdam, and Havre). The number in 1890 was 3,102.

[3] This paragraph and the other portions in inverted commas are taken *verbatim* from the " Report to the Board of Trade on Emigration and Immigration from and into the United Kingdom in 1891."

TABLE III.—*General Statement of Emigration and Immigration between the United Kingdom and Places out of Europe and not bordering on the Mediterranean Sea, from* 1871 *to* 1891.

	Emigration.		Immigration.		Excess of Emigrants over Immigrants.	
	Total.	British and Irish only.	Total.	British and Irish only.	Total.	British and Irish only.
1871	252,435	192,751	53,827	—	198,608	—
'72	295,213	210,494	70,181	—	225,032	—
'73 ...	310,612	228,345	86,416	—	224,196	—
'74 ...	241,014	197,272	118,129	—	122,885	—
'75	173,809	140,675	94,228	—	79,581	—
'76	138,222	109,469	93,557	71,404	44,665	38,065
'77	119,971	95,195	81,848	63,890	38,123	31,305
'78	147,663	112,902	77,951	54,944	69,712	57,958
'79	217,163	164,274	53,973	37,936	163,190	126,338
1880	332,294	227,542	68,316	47,007	263,978	180,535
'81	392,514	243,002	77,105	52,707	315,409	190,295
'82	413,288	279,366	82,804	54,711	330,484	224,655
'83	397,157	320,118	100,503	73,804	296,654	246,314
'84	303,901	242,179	123,466	91,356	180,435	150,823
'85	264,385	207,644	113,549	85,468	150,836	122,176
'86	330,801	232,900	108,879	80,018	221,922	152,882
'87	396,494	281,487	119,013	85,475	277,481	196,012
'88	398,494	279,928	128,879	94,133	269,615	185,795
'89	342,641	253,795	147,398	103,070	195,243	150,725
1890	315,980	218,116	155,910	109,470	160,070	108,646
'91	334,543	218,507	151,369	103,037	183,174	115,470

" Some remarks may now be made on the oscillations observable in the trans-oceanic passenger movement, to which attention has been drawn in previous reports. First, then, reviewing the total outward current of emigration during the last twenty years, we find that in 1872 this was nearing a maximum point, which was reached in 1873, with a total numbering 310,000, that thence there was a continuous descent to a minimum of 120,000 in 1877, and that this was again followed by an upward movement to a still higher maximum (413,000) in 1882, the completion of the downward and upward movement taking ten years; then from 1882 there is again a downward movement, but this is sooner arrested, viz., at a minimum of 264,000 in 1885, after which the upward movement re-commences till a further maximum (398,000) is reached in 1888, the whole movement upwards and downwards having been of shorter range than the previous one, and completed in six years. As to the last three years, 1889, and again 1890 showed diminishing numbers (the total being however as high as 316,000 even in the latter year), while the larger figures of 1891 seem to mark a renewed upward tendency. A similar examination of the total British and Irish emigration only shows closely corresponding oscillations.

"In regard to *immigration*, a similar upward and downward movement has hitherto been observed; the maxima and minima being reached two or three years later than those of *emigration*; thus there was a swing from a high to a low point, and back to a high point in the period 1874-84, followed by a downward movement till 1886, since which year there has been a gradual increase in numbers; but while the increase in the outward current came to an end in 1887-88, both total immigration and that of British and Irish only continually increased throughout the years 1887-90, and did not begin to decrease till 1891.

"The figures representing the excess of total and of native emigration over immigration will be found to follow the same cycles as those of gross emigration, and need not be examined in detail. The last maximum point was reached in 1887, and in the years 1888, 1889, and 1890 the numbers showed continuous diminution, followed in 1891 by a decided recovery in total emigration, and a slight recovery in British and Irish emigration only.

"Upon the whole then, it would seem that 1890 marked the lowest point of a short cyclical movement from a maximum of emigration reached in 1887-88, and that an upward movement commenced in 1891. Whether and how far this is the beginning of a new movement upwards, which will continue in the present and next succeeding years, or whether it is only a slight increase during a period of comparative stationariness in both inward and outward currents, remains to be seen.

"It is of course not claimed that exact regularity in the recurrence of these cyclical movements can be predicted, but the close connection between fluctuations in the current of emigration, and the periodic waves of general trade prosperity and depression is so well marked (as has frequently been pointed out in these reports), that, whether there is a true law of periodicity or not, the oscillations should at least be carefully observed.

"In connection with this point it will be of interest to compare with the figures for the United Kingdom the latest available statistics of trans-oceanic emigration from certain other European countries, as shown in the following table (compiled from Norwegian, Swedish, and German official returns), which, in some of its bearings will serve as a link between the two parts of this report. The emigration from Spain and Italy, though considerable, is not included, as being chiefly directed to the States of South America, with which we are less concerned.

Years	Number of Trans-Oceanic Emigrants.				
	From Norwegian Ports.	From Swedish Ports.*	German Emigrants from all Ports.	Non-German Emigrants from German Ports.	British and Irish Emigrants from the United Kingdom.
1882	32,891	—	203,585	62,524	279,366
'83	24,447	25,678	173,616	57,363	320,118
'84	16,185	17,664	149,065	68,986	242,179
'85	15,227	18,222	110,119	66,247	207,644
'86	17,324	27,913	83,225	99,827	232,900
'87	25,722	46,252	104,787	92,989	281,487
'88	26,160	45,561	103,951	106,886	279,928
'89	15,556	28,529	96,070	106,808	253,795
'90	13,368	—	97,103	168,471	218,116
'91	—	—	115,392	196,080	218,507

* To the United States only.

"The Scandinavian emigration is seen to follow very closely the course of the British and Irish emigration, but this cannot be said either of the German emigration (which shows an almost continuous decrease till 1889, followed by a slight increase in 1890, and a considerable increase in 1891) or of the non-German emigration from German ports (which shows an almost continuous increase, though the addition of these two sets of figures for each year would give totals varying in some accordance with the British and Irish statistics).

"The non-German emigration from German ports (Hamburg, Bremen, and Stettin) is chiefly made up of Austrians, Hungarians, and Russians. The Austrians and Hungarians numbered both in 1890 and in 1891 over 55,000, almost all for the United States; the Russians about 86,000 in 1890, and 110,000 in 1891, of whom 64 per cent. in 1890, and 86 per cent. in 1891, were stated to be bound for the United States, and the remainder chiefly for Brazil.

"Some statistics may also be given, from official returns for the United States, of European *immigration* into that country, which accounts for the great bulk of the emigration from northern Europe. It should be explained that the word immigrants is used in these returns to denote only those alien arrivals who are believed by the American authorities to have the intention of permanently settling in the United States.

Number of European Emigrants into the United States.

Years ended 30th June.	Number.	Years ended 30th June.	Number.
1882	646,764	1887	481,453
'83	521,154	'88	536,524
'84	452,206	'89	432,819
'85	351,488	'90	443,225
'86	328,535	'91	543,985

" These figures show an oscillatory movement in close agreement with that observed in regard to emigration from the United Kingdom in the same years. They too also point to a continued increase in general emigration from the north of Europe during the year now current, an inference strengthened by the United States' (preliminary) return of the total number of immigrants of all nationalities that arrived at the chief ports in that country during the calendar year 1891, which is given as 590,666, the corresponding figures for 1890 having been 491,026."

II.

The information as to the movement of passengers between the United Kingdom and continental ports is obtained from various sources; first, from the information furnished by the different shipping companies, the Belgian State Mail Packets, and the railway companies; secondly, from the lists furnished under the Alien Acts (these now include lists at all the principal and many of the minor ports of the United Kingdom; lists are also obtained from all continental ports, including those on the Mediterranean and Black Sea); thirdly, from the reports of the British consuls abroad; fourthly, from the Jewish Boards of Guardians here, and similar bodies in other countries; and fifthly, from the police authorities in different parts of the kingdom.

1. The number of passengers from continental ports to the United Kingdom was in 1891 504,445; the number from the United Kingdom to continental ports was 418,003, leaving a balance inwards of 86,442. Assuming that this excess consists of foreigners only, we have still to deduct from this number the excess of emigrant foreigners over immigrants who leave the United Kingdom for trans-oceanic ports. The foreign emigration (Table II) amounts to 112,275 persons, and the immigration to 47,197, showing an excess of emigrants of 65,078, so that the excess of arrivals of foreigners into the United Kingdom from all places is 21,364.

" This is a maximum figure as to the immigration of foreigners into the United Kingdom in 1891. In the records dealt with, the whole passenger movement is accounted for, and on the assumption that there is no emigration of British and Irish persons *viâ* the continent, the result must be correct within very narrow limits. The only doubt that could arise would be from any incompleteness in the data, and on this head, on account of the interest taken in the subject, it may be useful to state that (1) as regards the movement between the United Kingdom and places out of Europe, the data are the passenger lists obtained in the course of administering the Passenger Acts, and which are controlled for administrative purposes by officers of the Board of Trade and the Customs, and (2) as regards the movement between the United Kingdom and continental ports, the data are returns voluntarily supplied to the Board of Trade by the shipping companies carrying on the traffic; as to which also, though the returns are not compulsory, no doubt can really exist, all the

companies concerned having made returns, with the exception
of three or four unimportant foreign companies only. A remark
on this last point in last year's report appears to have been mis-
understood, as throwing doubt on the practical completeness and
trustworthiness of the returns, but there should be no doubt on
this point. The exceptions are quite unimportant, and as far as
the balance shown is concerned there need be no hesitation in
using the account as approximately correct enough for all practical
purposes."

In 1890 the number of passengers arriving was 450,000, and
the number departing 393,000, leaving a balance inwards of
58,000; deducting the excess of trans-oceanic foreign emigrants,
the net balance inwards was about 8,000; there is thus an increase
of some 13,000 according to this source of information.

2. The total number included in the alien lists for 1891 is
136,772, which includes all those who arrive from the continent
for permanent settlement. Of these 136,772 alien immigrants, no
fewer than 98,705 had through tickets to America, leaving a
balance of 38,067 only. [As a matter of fact some 112,000 left
the United Kingdom; it is therefore evident that about 13,000
who arrived without through tickets, also proceeded to non-
European places.] Again, there are to be deducted 9,757 (principally Norwegians, Swedes, and Danes) who arrive here to enter
as crews of ships leaving the United Kingdom. The nationalities
of the remainder, 28,270, are as follows :—

Russians and Poles	12,607
Norwegians, Swedes, and Danes	4,647
Germans	5,817
Dutch	911
French	1,453
Italians	734
Other nationalities	2,101
	28,270

Of the 12,607 Russians and Poles, it is known that 2,000 were
sent out of the country by the Jewish Board of Guardians alone,
and allowing for others who went away independently, we cannot
arrive at a total of more than 10,000 Russians and Poles who
remain. Considering the ports of London and Hull, there has
been an increase during the year 1891 of arrivals over the number
in 1890. For other ports, the last six months only of 1890 can be
considered, as it was only in the middle of that year that complete
returns from all ports were obtained for the first time.

The following table shows the number of aliens who arrived in
London, Hull, and other ports during each month of the years
1890 and 1891 :—

TABLE IV.

Month.	London.		Hull.				Other Ports.			
			Aliens *en route* to America or other Places.*		Aliens not stated to be *en route* to America or other Places.		Aliens *en route* to America or other Places.†		Aliens not stated to be *en route* to America or other Places.	
	1890.	1891.	1890.	1891.	1890.	1891.	1890.‡	1891.	1890.‡	1891.
January	622	627	618	747	11	94	—	1,339	—	839
February	802	802	1,385	2,019	51	240	—	1,626	—	1,144
March	819	959	5,874	7,820	7	175	—	3,279	—	1,708
April	783	997	5,273	9,390	42	115	—	3,525	—	1,356
May	1,453	1,174	7,592	8,158	165	133	1,152	2,706	3,505	1,271
June	1,691	1,998	6,057	8,797	174	289	1,760	3,901	2,656	1,890
July	1,742	2,618	3,561	5,133	263	268	1,819	3,883	1,756	2,084
August	1,669	2,352	3,861	6,322	300	330	2,166	3,509	1,419	2,047
September	1,480	2,375	5,373	6,136	197	262	2,017	4,444	1,248	1,585
October	1,110	1,208	3,378	3,991	182	349	1,733	2,112	1,172	1,546
November	1,257	1,303	2,840	3,383	140	208	2,047	2,980	1,100	1,347
December	834	1,063	1,215	1,027	152	212	1,245	2,462	1,083	1,115
Total	14,262	17,476§	47,027	62,923	1,684	2,675	—	35,766	—	17,932

* In 1890 the whole of the aliens given under this head were *en route* to America; in 1891 17 were *en route* to other places.

† In 1890 the whole of the aliens given under this head were *en route* to America; in 1891 99 were *en route* to other places.

‡ In the earlier months of 1890 alien lists were obtained from London and Hull only.

§ This figure includes 16 aliens arrived at London *en route* to America and other places. The number is so small that it is considered inexpedient to make a separate column. Practically the immigrants from Europe into London are without through tickets.

Comparison of totals with those of previous years :—

Comparison of Totals with those of Previous Years.

	1891.	1890.	1889.	1888.
Arrivals in London (destination not stated)	17,460	14,262	9,846	10,887
Arrivals in Hull—				
(a.) *En route* to America and other places	62,923	47,027	41,595	62,901
(b.) Destination not stated	2,675	1,684	364	215

The number arriving at the different ports, and not stated to be *en route* to America, in 1891, has been as follows (excluding seamen) :—

Port.	Adults	Children	Total.
London	12,992	2,299	15,291
Grimsby	1,847	375	2,222
Hull	1,484	148	1,632
Hartlepool, West	629	125	754
Tyne ports	2,474	274	2,748
Leith and Grangemouth	1,273	100	1,373
Other ports	4,076	174	4,250
Total	24,775	3,495	28,270

Of this total, no less than 15,926 came from Hamburg, and of these again 12,034 were Russians and Poles, leaving consequently only 573 Russians and Poles who came from other European ports.

"3. The information next referred to is that derived from Her Majesty's consuls at European ports. Careful watch has been kept throughout the year by consular officers at those ports, especially at Hamburg, Riga, Memel, and Libau, on movements of population likely to result in increased alien immigration into the United Kingdom, and reports on the subject have been furnished from time to time. These reports leave no doubt that throughout the year there flowed westwards through Germany a large stream of emigrants from Russia (mainly Jews), who were making their way to sea ports, especially Hamburg, the majority in the hope of proceeding to America. Many were possessed of very small or no means, and these were often helped forward from place to place by local Jewish relief committees. A large proportion of the emigrants were said to be women (with their children) on the way to join their husbands, who had gone on in advance to make a home elsewhere."

It appears from information furnished by the British consuls abroad, that the great majority of the emigrants from Russia through Germany, had no intention of going to the United Kingdom: still, the consuls were instructed to issue warnings to such emigrants that there was no likelihood of their obtaining a living over here. These Russian Jews were (in June, 1891) arriving in Berlin at the rate of 700 a day, and as far as possible were being dealt with by the Jewish relief committee.

"The consul at Riga and the consul-general at Hamburg furnish fuller details, and it will be of interest to record here some extracts from their reports; as to Riga itself the numbers are not large. Mr. Consul Wagstaff writes, under date 8th January, 1892: 'Regularly throughout the summer a few Hebrew families left this port by the weekly steamer for Lübeck, in all about 300 persons, and some 15 others for Stettin. On arrival at these ports they were cared for by the Jewish relief committees, and helped forward on their journey, their ultimate destination being unknown, but from what I was able to learn, only a small proportion were bound to the United Kingdom.' In regard to Libau, the consul forwards a dispatch from Mr. Vice-Consul Hill, who says: 'Since my last report on this subject, there has undoubtedly been a very large emigration of families of the Hebrew persuasion from this place, possibly to the extent of several hundred families; but as these, for the greater part, have left this place—travelling overland from here to Memel, or else by ship from here to Polangen, and thence to Memel—it is absolutely beyond my power to determine the exact number. Under my immediate cognisance, as emigrants from Libau to the United Kingdom, I have had no application either for information or particulars. Warnings as to the bad state of trade, the existence of strikes in the United Kingdom, &c., were given in the newspapers at my request at the commencement of the summer of 1891. At the present time, however, one does not hear anything as to the further expulsion of the Jewish population of this port, so that for the time being it appears that there is rather less excitement on the subject.'

"Mr. Consul-General Dundas's report from Hamburg, dated 30th January, 1892, after referring to the natural diminution in the volume of emigration during the winter months, contains the following general remarks in reference to the class of alien emigrants proceeding to the United Kingdom: 'Of those who have left this city for ports in the United Kingdom it is very difficult to assert positively that any are destitute, or what proportion can be so classed, as it is not possible to ascertain their actual circumstances, and the only means of forming any opinion is by their general appearance, and by the fact of whether they had assisted passages or not. But it may safely be said that the class leaving for the United Kingdom and not proceeding further are pretty much the same as formerly, a considerable proportion being, if not destitute, at least little better; and those whose final destination is beyond, are of a better class and in better circumstances.' Mr. Dundas adds: 'The total number of emigrants who sailed out of this port for trans-Atlantic countries from the 1st January to the 31st December, 1891, amounted to 144,332 souls. Of these, 94,394 were conveyed direct, and 49,938 departed by indirect routes. Of this latter number there are no means of verifying the proportion which passed through the United Kingdom, but it may reasonably be assumed that the bulk, or nearly so, of the indirect emigrant traffic did pass that way. Neither do the returns here record the number of emigrants who leave this port for the United Kingdom with the intention of there seeking employment, these being regarded. not as emigrants, but as passengers only.'

"4. The principal agency from which information has been obtained is the London Jewish Board of Guardians. Its annual reports show the extent of the work done in London both through the agency of this body itself and also by means of a joint committee originally established in connection with the Mansion House Fund of 1882, but now known as the Russo-Jewish and Jewish Board of Guardians Joint Committee. From these reports, as well as from returns specially supplied to the Board of Trade, tables covering a series of years have been compiled. It appears from these tables that there was undoubtedly some increase of destitution in London which the charitable agencies had to deal with, and that this increase was largely due to the increased arrival of destitute immigrants. The number of applications for relief to the Jewish Board of Guardians alone was 4,722 in 1891, as compared with 3,569 in 1890; the number of cases relieved 4,474, as compared with 3,351; and the number of new cases only 2,092, as compared with 1,319. The number of applications for relief to the joint committee was 618 in 1891, as compared with 391 in 1890, and the number of new cases only 366, as compared with 205 in 1890. In the case of both bodies there is accordingly a very considerable increase. The numbers emigrated were:—By the Jewish Board of Guardians 1,043 cases, comprising 1,591 individuals, as compared with 621 cases and 1,004 individuals in 1890; and by the joint committee 210 cases, comprising 521 individuals, as compared with 161 cases and 415 individuals in 1890. A large number of the persons thus dealt with were sent back to the continent, and the remainder were emigrated, principally to America."

5. Reports have also been collected from the Commissioner of Police of the Metropolis, and from the chief constables in the principal towns. In London a larger number was reported to have arrived than during the previous year, but statistics are wanting. For Manchester no figures can be given. In Liverpool there are from 1,000 to 1,200 alien Jews, of whom some 140 are *destitute;* at Leeds the probable estimated Jewish population of the borough is 11,000 (there are about 800 destitute *aliens*), and there was here an increase of rather under 500 during the year; at Birmingham there were in 1891, 345 Russians and Poles (a slight decrease since 1886). In many of the towns the indigent Jews are entirely relieved by the Jewish boards of guardians.

Upon the whole, therefore, the Russian-Polish immigration into the United Kingdom for settlement has been but very little over 10,000 in 1891. At the same time the increase has been very considerable since 1890, during which year the immigration had only been some 5,000 to 6,000.

V.—*Sea Fisheries of the United Kingdom.*

A FEW years ago the systematic collection of fishery statistics was commenced in England and Wales by the Board of Trade, the first return being made in the spring of 1885, and Scotland followed the example very shortly afterwards. The statistics for 1891 thus give the information for six complete years, so far as concerns England, Wales, and Scotland, and for four years for Ireland. The returns are made for most districts by the coastguard officers, but at the large ports it is necessary to employ special officers. The statistics apply solely to fish first landed on our coasts, and therefore exclude all that has been imported from foreign countries, and also all that has previously been landed elsewhere in the United Kingdom; it must be noted also that the values given are landing values only, nothing being added for the expenses of transit, curing, &c.

Considering the whole period of which we now have some definite knowledge, it may be stated broadly that the value of the fish annually landed in England and Wales has considerably increased, while the quantity has somewhat diminished. In Scotland the quantity has increased, though irregularly, during the period, the value rising steadily since 1887; while in Ireland the amount shows considerable fluctuations, the maximum being in 1889, since which year the quantity has diminished. The variations in value of the fish landed in Ireland do not correspond to the fluctuations in quantity, as will be seen from Table I; but this is accounted for in the three countries by the steady rise in value during the whole period.

TABLE I.—*Statement showing the Quantity and Value of Fish (excluding Shell Fish), and the Total Value of Fish (including Shell Fish) returned as Landed on the Coasts of the United Kingdom, distinguishing England and Wales, Scotland, and Ireland, during each of the undermentioned Years, so far as the particulars can be given.*

Years.	England and Wales.	Scotland.	Ireland.	Total United Kingdom.
	Quantity (excluding Shell Fish).			–
	cwts.	cwts.	cwts.	cwts.
1886	6,412,433	4,718,145	} No returns	—
'87	6,029,481	5,043,529		—
'88	6,348,072	4,756,936	402,245	11,507,253
'89	6,464,564	5,416,012	801,654	12,682,230
'90	6,100,630	5,362,115	798,631	12,261,376
'91	5,966,076	5,283,764	611,078	11,860,918
	Value (excluding Shell Fish).			
	£	£	£	£
1886	3,688,079	1,403,391	} No returns	—
'87	3,778,958	1,330,394		—
'88	3,948,013	1,339,577	183,528	5,471,118
'89	3,862,389	1,430,631	317,931	5,610,951
'90	4,368,552	1,559,612	362,804	6,290,968
'91	4,491,018	1,753,987	295,643	6,540,648
	Total Value (including Shell Fish).			
	£	£	£	£
1886	3,957,075	1,476,259	} No returns	—
'87	4,103,459	1,396,963		—
'88	4,212,957	1,411,306	191,186	5,815,449
'89	4,168,930	1,493,578	334,044	5,996,552
'90	4,742,612	1,627,461	373,849	6,743,922
'91	4,870,572	1,829,786	308,627	7,008,985

TABLE II.—*Quantity of Fish first Landed in the United Kingdom in 1891.*

	England and Wales.			Total.	Scotland.	Ireland.	Total United Kingdom.
	East Coast.	South Coast.	West Coast.				
	cwt.	cwt.	cwt.	cwt.	cwt.	cwt.	cwt.
Soles	61,287	10,808	10,593	82,688	17,739*	3,814	104,241
Turbot	47,594	5,892	3,889	56,875	5,024	1,242	63,141
Prime fish not separately distinguished	43,728	10,627	970	55,325	229	—	55,554
Total prime fish ..	152,609	26,827	15,452	194,888	22,992	5,056	222,936
Cod	307,631	8,663	44,217	360,511	501,392	44,072	905,975
Haddock............	1,727,969	179	12,400	1,740,548	725,792	20,899	2,487,239
Hake	16,432	31,041	92,472	139,945	—†	38,447	—†
Halibut	81,231	—	7	81,238	19,152	—†	—†
Herrings.............	979,816	87,687	139,004	1,206,457	3,421,818	101,774	4,730,049
Ling	76,353	4,497	12,701	93,551	176,345	15,909	285,805
Mackerel	16,278	124,112	228,097	368,487	1,743	299,934	670,164
Pilchards	—	96,321	2,594	98,915	—†	—†	—†
Plaice	647,915	44,378	19,029	711,322	78,982‡	—†	—†
Sprats	104,316	11,283	103	115,702	3,615	5,799	125,116
Whiting	—†	—	—†	—†	71,138	14,878	—†
All other, except shell fish	560,096	160,767	133,649	854,512	260,795	64,310	2,433,634
Total	4,670,646	595,705	699,725	5,966,076	5,283,764	611,078	11,860,918
	No.	No.	No.	No.	No.	No.	No.
Crabs	3,745,240	632,431	233,899	4,611,570	2,805,250	275,896	7,692,716
Lobsters..................	93,065	530,937	106,296	730,298	667,244	211,668	1,619,210
Oysters	33,688,000	4,331,000	6,066,000	44,085,000	353,200	901,680	45,339,880
	cwt.	cwt.	cwt.	cwt.	cwt.	cwt.	cwt.
Other shell fish	399,134	45,790	88,568	533,492	309,405	11,378	854,275

TABLE III.—*Value of Fish first Landed in the United Kingdom in 1891.*

	England and Wales.			Total.	Scotland.	Ireland.	Total United Kingdom.
	East Coast.	South Coast.	West Coast.				
	£	£	£	£	£	£	£
Soles	386,718	73,910	56,518	517,146	30,214*	15,560	562,920
Turbot	175,179	20,022	13,805	209,006	17,211	3,973	230,190
Prime fish not separately distinguished	98,064	45,094	2,261	145,419	1,248	—	146,667
Total prime fish	659,961	139,026	72,584	871,571	48,673	19,533	939,777
Cod	209,971	6,244	32,090	248,305	188,010	19,244	455,559
Haddock..............	876,400	107	7,628	884,135	375,538	13,081	1,272,754
Hake	10,651	18,815	53,388	82,854	—†	15,386	—†
Halibut	176,697	—	22	176,719	17,154	—†	—†
Herrings..............	424,338	28,359	50,784	503,481	918,872	39,336	1,461,679
Ling	51,482	3,247	9,303	64,032	56,024	6,023	126,079
Mackerel	14,931	124,442	222,311	361,684	1,459	144,041	507,184
Pilchards	—	24,815	646	25,461	—†	—†	—†
Plaice	611,129	40,577	18,610	670,316	67,180‡	—†	—†
Sprats	9,208	3,582	44	12,834	308	502	13,644
Whiting	—†	—†	—†	—†	29,509	6,951	—†
All other, except shell fish	400,871	99,802	88,953	589,626	51,260	31,556	1,763,972
Total	3,445,639	489,016	556,363	4,491,018	1,753,987	295,643	6,540,648
Crabs	28,367	21,152	2,792	52,311	15,384	2,759	70,454
Lobsters	4,105	24,953	5,386	34,444	31,366	7,123	72,933
Oysters	119,555	9,157	13,329	142,041	1,568	1,251	144,860
Other shell fish	106,181	13,976	30,601	150,758	27,481	1,846	180,085
Total shell fish	258,208	69,238	52,108	379,554	75,799	12,984	468,337
Total value of fish landed	3,703,847	558,254	608,471	4,870,572	1,829,786	308,627	7,008,985

* Lemon soles.   † Included in "all other"   ‡ Includes flounders and brill.

Tables II and III give the quantity and values of the principal
kinds of fish landed in England and Wales, Scotland, and Ireland
during the past year. It will be noticed that in England and
Wales there is not a single one of the more important fish which
does not occur in great majority on one or other of the three coasts.
Soles, turbot, cod, haddock, halibut, herrings, ling, plaice, sprats,
crabs, and oysters come from the east coast, while the quantity of
these fish furnished by the other coasts is very small and in many
cases insignificant. Pilchards and lobsters come from the south
coast, while on the west hake and mackerel predominate. Haddock
forms a larger proportion of the weight than any other fish landed
in England, but for the United Kingdom the weight of herrings
is nearly double that of haddock, this being due to the enormous
take of the former in Scotland, whence nearly 3,500,000 cwts. of
herrings are procured, forming 65 per cent. of the fish landed north
of the Tweed. As regards value, the take of both herrings and
haddock in the United Kingdom is worth more than 1,000,000*l.*
annually, while soles, mackerel, and cod are each valued at half a
million sterling. The total value is just over 7,000,000*l.* There
has been for every sort a slight rise of price in 1891; in some
cases this rise has been very great, especially for halibut (1*l.* 10*s.*
to 2*l.* 3*s.* 6*d.* per cwt.), mackerel (from 13*s.* 9*d.* per cwt. in 1889
to 15*s.* 5*d.* in 1890, and 19*s.* 7½*d.* last year), and, above all, herrings
(4*s.* 10½*d.* per cwt. in 1889 to 7*s.* 2*d.* in 1890, and 8*s.* 4½*d.* in
1891).

As regards the ports or districts, by far the largest quantity
(over 60,000 tons, valued at more than 1,000,000*l.*) was landed at
Grimsby, London coming next, although before 1889 it occupied
the first position. The amount landed in the metropolis has, however, fallen off considerably since 1887, in which year the value
was almost 1,100,000*l.*, while last year it was 600,000*l.* The most
important districts, and the quantity landed in these districts in
1891, are given in Table IV. The fishing industry at Neyland is
quite a new one; it is said that the fish have changed their ground
within the last few years. No returns were made here in 1886;
the value in 1887 was 7,562*l.*, and in 1890 it had risen to
305,402*l.*

TABLE IV.—*Quantity and Value of Fish Landed at the principal Ports or Districts in England and Wales in 1891.*

Port or District.	Quantity, *excluding* Shell Fish.	Value, *including* Shell Fish.	Port or District.	Quantity, *excluding* Shell Fish.	Value, *including* Shell Fish.
	Tons.	£		Tons.	£
Berwick	2,542	47,172	Folkestone	1,331	24,154
North Shields..	11,447	149,321	Hastings	1,742	23,320
Scarborough....	6,749	86,617	Brixham	3,073	57,854
Hull	29,557	429,743	Plymouth........	8,968	147,366
Grimsby	62,942	1,188,763	Penzance	4,158	77,692
Boston	6,250	63,527	St. Ives	5,696	43,450
Yarmouth	23,828	306,625	Neyland	13,254	265,178
Lowestoft	28,639	483,736	Milford	6,929	110,761
London	46,242	602,206	Hoylake	464	18,337
Whitstable*	37	87,452	Liverpool	1,593	30,144
Ramsgate	1,639	66,402	Fleetwood........	2,198	39,020

* The fish landed at Whitstable is almost exclusively shell fish.

The monthly take depends of course upon what fish are in season, the variations occurring principally with mackerel, herrings, and pilchards. The most important months in 1891 were April and November, whereas formerly May and October furnished the greatest quantity. It is a curious fact, however, that on the west coast the take of oysters in the close season (May to August) enormously exceeds the take in the remaining months of the year, and to such an extent that, though the west coast yields on the whole but a small proportion of the oysters first landed on our coasts, yet the quantity landed in England and Wales during the summer months is above the quantity taken up in the spring. The figures are as follows:—

TABLE V.—*Quantity and Value of the Oysters first Landed on each of the Coasts of England and Wales during each Month of the Year 1891.*

1891.	East Coast.		South Coast.		West Coast.		England and Wales.	
	Number.	Value.	Number.	Value.	Number.	Value.	Number.	Value.
	1,000's	£	1,000's	£	1,000's	£	1,000's	£
January........	3,455	13,140	436	946	74	217	3,965	14,303
February	2,489	9,499	366	826	64	177	2,919	10,502
March	1,989	8,876	264	633	45	122	2,298	9,631
April	1,578	6,189	972	1,562	64	178	2,614	7,929
May	1,859	4,953	366	771	700	1,480	2,925	7,204
June	1,295	3,323	243	527	1,640	3,490	3,178	7,340
July	1,233	3,248	126	302	1,671	3,566	3,030	7,116
August	2,591	7,358	229	535	1,288	2,751	4,108	10,644
September....	4,284	17,708	294	677	345	859	4,923	19,244
October........	5,856	20,734	502	1,060	68	178	6,426	21,972
November....	3,599	11,716	318	828	66	186	3,983	12,730
December	3,460	12,811	215	490	41	125	3,716	13,426
Total	33,688	119,555	4,331	9,157	6,066	13,329	44,085	142,041

The imports in 1891 were 2,363,711 cwts., valued at 2,839,253*l.* (an increase of 67,737 cwts., and 27,798*l.* over 1890); the exports of British and Irish produce were valued at 1,709,829*l.* last year, against 1,795,267*l.* in the year before. In the exports were included 951,153 barrels of herrings (the greater part going to Germany), while in 1890 there were 1,150,175 barrels.

Comparing the English fisheries with the foreign, it appears (so far as a comparison can be made) that a greater value of fish is landed on our shores than on those of other countries which give annual returns. Though the years of the returns differ, yet the values are all very much the same as they were in the previous year, consequently the relative importance remains much the same. The value of the fisheries in France (1889) was 3,853,000*l.*; Norway (1890), 1,234,000*l.*; Canadian Dominion (1890), 3,691,000*l.*; whereas in the United Kingdom (1891) the value (including Scotch and Irish salmon) was 7,570,000*l.*

VI.—*The United States Census of* 1890.

IN no country is such an elaborate census taken as in the United States of America, and it may perhaps be said also that in no country is it of more importance that so many subjects should be dealt with, as owing to the absence of registration generally, this decennial enumeration forms the only means of ascertaining the condition of the people. On the last occasion the work was even larger than usual, as in 1880 the tenth decennial census was taken, and that year consequently marked an epoch in the history of the country. But owing to the quantity of new investigations undertaken in 1890—under the superintendence of the Hon. R. P. Porter—the volume of facts embodied in the reports will more than equal that of 1880, and there will be no less than twenty-five volumes of 1,000 pages each when the work is completed. Mr. Porter last autumn gave an address on the eleventh census before the American Statistical Association; and it is from this that the following remarks on some of the new features are taken.

In the first place, the work has been enormously simplified by the use of the electrical tabulating machine invented by Hollerith. A new form of population schedule was distributed among the people, a family schedule being used as far as possible, and several questions were added which had not hitherto been asked, *e.g.*, concerning the children, aliens, &c. There were consequently about 20 millions of these schedules. When these had all been collected, the information contained in each was transferred to cards, divided into a certain number of compartments by means of holes punched in the centre of the compartments. These cards are then placed on a horizontal board pierced with as many holes as there are compartments on the card, and so situated that each hole is under the centre of a compartment. Under each of these holes is a tube partly filled with mercury which communicates, by means of wires from the bottom of the tubes, with the index of a

counter.   Above the card is a second horizontal movable board, on
the lower side of which are springs terminated by blunt needles,
these being arranged so as to dip into the tubes.   When the upper
board is lowered, these needles dip into the mercury through all
the holes punched in the card, and an electric current is thus set
up which moves the index of the counter; where no hole in the
card has been punched opposite a tube, the spring above the needle
becomes compressed so that the latter does not pierce the card,
and nothing is registered.   By this method, the number of tables
that can be produced with a given amount of labour is very largely
increased.   At each handling, some seventy different combinations
of facts as regards general population can be produced, and four
or five handlings practically exhaust the information on the
schedules.   General Walker in 1880 was unable to tabulate
conjugal condition; this is one example of what will be done by
the help of the machine.   One of the most striking features is
the speed attained.   The cards were all punched in six months; a
clerk can pass 10,000 cards through a machine in one day, and in
October last, 100 clerks with 100 machines were tabulating
1 million cards daily.   The saving in time and labour is obvious.

Dr. Billings, in charge of the vital statistics, and Mr. F.
H. Wines, who is preparing the statistics of pauperism and crime,
are also using the machine for their tables.

Mr. Porter has made a calculation as to the percentage of
errors introduced into the results by the use of the electrical
machine, and finds their number to be far less than with the
old method.   Some 200,000 cards chosen at random after being
punched were compared with the original schedules, and from this
examination, Mr. Porter concludes that one hole in about 1,500 is
incorrectly punched.   Three-fourths of these are due to the hole
having accidentally not been punched at all, and the machine
invariably rejects such cards.   If however the holes are punched
inconsistently, *e.g.*, a child under 10 years old may be set down as
a carpenter, this appears on the resultant slip, and can easily be
corrected.   The remaining errors are therefore trifling in number,
and are "consistent," as for instance a man's age may be set down
as 29 instead of 25.   These last are really the only errors which
cannot be detected.

Owing to the absence of any federal registration of births
and deaths in the United States, there are practically no vital
statistics for the country generally.   Some few individual States
and localities have laws in force making such registration obligatory; and their importance is beginning to be recognised by
others.   An endeavour has been made by the census enumerators
to collect statistics of mortality, and though every effort may be
made to supply deficiencies, the result can scarcely be accepted
with absolute confidence in the absence of full records.   Still
useful results will doubtless be brought out, especially for those
States which have for any length of time registered the births,
marriages, and deaths.   The most important new features in this
branch may be summarised as follows :—

(1.) "A special study of the birth and death-rates, and of the principal causes of death in twenty-four of our largest cities, to show where the highest and lowest death-rates prevail, and what the relations of these are to topography, drainage, character of inhabitants, overcrowding, poverty, and other environments.

(2.) "A special study of the influence of race upon fecundity and mortality, including studies of the birth and death-rates of mulattoes as distinguished from negroes on the one hand, and whites on the other, and of the principal European races which have contributed to the population of this country.

(3.) "A special study of the relations of occupation to death-rates, and to particular causes of death, as shown by a detailed study of figures derived from the records of our largest manufacturing cities for a period of five years, in addition to the data of the whole country for the census year which were obtained by the enumerators.

"The records obtained from States and cities maintaining a compulsory system of registration of deaths are much larger than those obtained in previous censuses, and cover an aggregate population of over 17,000,000. The death records of this population for the census year in the State of New Jersey, in New York city, Brooklyn, Richmond county, Winchester county, King's county, and part of Queen's county (New York), and in Boston, Philadelphia, Baltimore, and the district of Columbia, and for a somewhat lesser period of time in Chicago, St. Louis, and Cincinnati, have been tabulated. The total number of deaths thus recorded, the records of which are especially accurate and complete, is 740,884. These records in connection with those for the census year furnish a continuous record of deaths for these localities for a period of six years, which will afford more reliable information than anything which has heretofore been published with regard to the vital statistics of this country."

The last sentence is sufficient to show the backward condition of vital statistics in the States.

A report is also published on the social statistics of cities, dealing with the following points for each city of more than 10,000 inhabitants : altitude, cemeteries, drainage, fire, government, licences, parks, police, public buildings, streets, street lighting, and waterworks.

A complete census of the different churches in the United States has for the first time been obtained. The information required has in almost every instance been procured by means of circulars addressed to the clerks or secretaries of the various denominational associations. These returns embrace full statistics of every sect existing in the States, down to Confucianists, Salvationists and the Theosophical Society.

With regard to the wealth, debt, and taxation, the division of the census over which Mr. Porter presided under General Walker in 1880, the work has been carried out on much the same lines, but the details are much fuller.

Perhaps the most important of all the new features of this census, apart from the use of the electrical tabulating machine, is the endeavour to collect statistics of the number and amount of mortgages in the union. It is, to begin with, an inquiry which would naturally arouse much hostility from people who, in a free country, object to the State's prying into their affairs, and the census commissioners must have entered on this task with a great deal of trepidation. It was recognised that it was impossible to put questions in the schedules asking owners for particulars as to the extent to which their property was mortgaged, &c. Such a course would have immediately aroused hostility, and might even have endangered the accuracy of the other returns. As it was, the inquiry was simply reduced to the question whether an occupier owned or rented his farm or home, and in the former case whether or not it was free from debt. A special staff of some 2,500 agents was employed to make an abstract of every mortgage placed on record during the last ten years in the United States. The cost of this inquiry will amount to not less than $2\frac{1}{2}$ million dollars.

"The two important features[4] brought out in this inquiry are the amount of mortgages placed on record each year for ten years, and the amount of the existing debt. It would of course be absurd to accept the amount of the uncancelled mortgages as the amount of debt in force. Such an exhibit would manifestly be a gross exaggeration unworthy of confidence. The extent of this defect in the records has been ascertained by the census office in 102 counties, representing all parts of the country, and in 61 of these counties that have been tabulated the face of the uncancelled records exaggerates on the average the true amount of the debt by 71 per cent. It was therefore decided to make a transcript of the record in every case for ten years, and ascertain therefrom the average life of a mortgage.

"Preliminary experiments by special agents of the census office pointed to the use of the average life of mortgages, with an allowance for partial payments as promising results much nearer the truth, near enough, at any rate, to be fairly conclusive as to the amount of existing indebtedness. This plan is approximately correct, and under perfectly uniform conditions would produce accurate results. An objection that can be raised against it is that mortgages are not uniform in amount and number recorded each year. These variations, however, when large amounts of debt are considered, are not as great as may be supposed, and under careful observation and corrective treatment, lose much of their influence for error. If the average life of all mortgages under such circumstances is four years, and the total amount of the mortgages recorded within the last four years is taken as equivalent to the amount of indebtedness existing at the present time, it is evident that many paid mortgages created within the four years are included within the amount, and that many unpaid mortgages created more than four years ago are not included. In such cases it is true, if the average life of mortgages is correctly represented, that the mortgages of the life period of four years now paid are exactly equal to the mortgages made previously to the life period

- [4] *The Eleventh Census.* An Address delivered before the *American Statistical Association* by the Hon. R. P. Porter.

and now unpaid, so that the total recorded debt of the life period stands for the amount of debt in force.

" Our agents were therefore instructed to transcribe for every real estate mortgage acknowledged and received within the ten years ended 31st December, 1889 (except mortgages made by public and quasi public corporations), the following facts: The State and county in which the mortgaged real estate is situated; the year in which the acknowledgment was made; corporations, both as mortgagors and mortgagees, classified as savings banks (including loan and trust companies, but not including savings banks), building and loan associations, insurance companies, mortgage corporations, and all others; the original amount of the debt; the actual rate of interest, or, if not ascertainable from records, the customary rate at the time; the number of incumbered acres and city or village lots; and also for the cancelled mortgages of 1880-83, the full dates of acknowledgment and cancellation. For the purpose of checking this inquiry, special investigations were conducted in 102 counties, well distributed throughout the United States, and representing every phase of American life and industry. In these counties the same facts were taken from the records as in other counties, and also for all uncancelled mortgages as far back in time as any appreciable number of them were found in force, the names and addresses of the parties. Schedules were sent these persons, and in each one of these counties an exact statement of existing debt has been compiled. The enormous cost would preclude this method for the whole country, but work in what is termed "inquiry" counties has been of great service in correcting the work elsewhere. The "inquiry" counties also reveal the purposes for which the debt was incurred. By far the largest proportion of real estate mortgaged debt has been incurred to secure the purchase of lands, and cost of improvements stands second in importance. The security of purchase money is generally 50 to 75 per cent. of the real estate mortgage debt of the people of a county, and improvements generally represent from 10 to 20 per cent. of the debt.

" The following table summarises the results of this inquiry as far as possible to date :—

	Alabama.	Iowa.	Kansas.	Tennessee.	Illinois.
Number of mortgages recorded during 1880-89	93,828	520,448	654,243	93,282	612,249
Amount of mortgages recorded during 1880-89	$91,099,623	$439,936,354	$498,658,903	$100,212,257	$870,699,940
Number of mortgages in force. January 1, 1890	35,331	252,539	298,880	39,470	297,247
Amount of mortgages in force, January 1, 1890	$39,027,983	$199,774,171	$248,146,826	$40,421,396	$384,299,180
Number of acres encumbered, January 1, 1890	6,008,636	16,312,176	26,590,795	3,035,816	10,751,244
Number of lots encumbered, January 1, 1890	14,213	163,712	265,462	32,957	287,878
Number of acres encumbered, during 1880-89	16,175,153	33,864,721	58,510,089	7,269,279	21,578,919

	Alabama.	Iowa.	Kansas.	Tennessee.	Illinois.
Number of lots encumbered, during 1880-89	34,649	303,556	544,934	65,566	602,152
Percentages of debt recorded, 1880-89 ; in force, January 1, 1890	42·84	45·41	48·76	40·34	44·14
Percentage of assessed acres encumbered, January 1, 1890..............	21·67	46·96	61·59	11·72	81·04
Equated life of mortgage (in years)	2·73	4·92	3·38	2·81	4·02
Range of interest rates (per cent.)	1—40	1—20	1—60	1—12	1—18
Amount *per capita* of mortgages in force January 1, 1890	$26	$104	$170	$23	$100

" So much for the inquiry relating to recorded real estate indebtedness. The result of the direct inquiry as to the debt on farms and homes is not yet complete. The average farm and home debt, shown by tabulation of partial returns from counties distributed throughout the union, is $1,288 for farms and $924 for homes. If these averages hold good for the United States there is an existing debt in force of $2,500,000,000 on the farms and homes of the United States occupied by owners and incumbered. Only some rough results of this inquiry are now known. It is probable that the number of families occupying and owning mortgaged farms and homes does not exceed 2,250,000, leaving perhaps 10,250,000 families that hire their farms and homes, or occupy and own them free of incumbrance. The total number of families occupying farms is supposed to be about 4,750,000, so that about 7,750,000 families occupy homes."

With regard to agriculture, several new industries are now made the subject of an inquiry, such as horticulture, viticulture, irrigation, the production of sugar, and the peculiar conditions of farm occupancy in the Southern States. Manufactures have received special attention, and an endeavour has been made to ascertain the true proportion of labour and wages employed in actual production : a classified wage-table is also added. The superintendent has been enabled by law to withdraw the manufacturing schedules from the enumerators, and charge the collection of the data upon experts. Special censuses have consequently been made of the following industries amongst many others :— Chemical industry, clay and pottery, coke and glass, distilled spirits used in the arts, manufactures, and medicine, electrical apparatus and appliances, gas, lumber mills, printing, publishing, salt, shipbuilding, slaughtering and meat packing, &c. Mines and mining are also exhaustively treated, and statistics of the production of every mineral in the States are recorded. Fifteen bulletins will be published on the fisheries, special attention being paid to the carp, to which six of the fifteen bulletins are devoted. Railroad statistics are being prepared, both for the ten years ended 1889 and for the single year ended June, 1890. Another inquiry made for the first time by the eleventh census, is that of transportation by water. "Everything was sought for that would enable the census office to furnish a complete presentation of all that was worth knowing concerning the industry of transportation by water as conducted by American craft," and "the statistics cover every class of floating construction, from the push boat on the Little Kanawha to an Atlantic liner, and from a barge on the Dismal Swamp canal to a steamer trading with the Orient." Special census bulletins are also being issued concerning Alaska and the Indians; in the case of many of these, special enumerators were employed to collect the information (which includes a statement of their condition as well as their numbers) for individual tribes, as for instance the Cherokees, the Pueblos, &c.

Mr. Porter concludes his address by expressing a strong hope that the Government will establish a permanent census bureau, and it would certainly be an advantage in a country where the taking of the census is a work of such an enormous labour; it would probably take over also most of the work done here in the Registrar-General's office. The Senate seems to have considered the idea favourably up to the present, and Mr. Porter says: "In accordance with a resolution of the Senate, I am preparing a report and Bill for a permanent census bureau, which if enacted will remedy much of the decennial census trouble, and put a great public work on a business basis. Such a bureau would not only be an immense saving to the Government, especially since the introduction of mechanical tabulation, but it would keep active and competent minds continually working out improvements in census methods; it would keep a nucleus of trained census clerks and capable mathematicians; it would admit of certain branches of work being done annually at a cost of a few million circulars and a small amount expended for tabulation; it would give sufficient time to perfect the work of enumeration, and it would give general satisfaction to all who are earnestly in search of correct statistics of our nation's population and wealth."

The following is the very comprehensive list of the subjects treated in this census :—

I. *Population.* —Characteristics, conditions, distribution, and parentage; occupations.

II. *Vital and Social Statistics.*—Mortality and vital statistics; social statistics; statistics of special classes; pauperism and crime.

III. *Education and Church Statistics.*—Education and illiteracy; religious bodies in the United States.

IV. *Valuation, Taxation, Public Expenditures, and Indebtedness.*— Valuation and taxation; receipts and expenditures; indebtedness.

V. *Farms, Homes, and Mortgages.*— Recorded indebtedness; ownership of farms and homes and indebtedness thereon.

VI. *Agriculture.* — Irrigation; tobacco; farms, cereals, grass lands, and forage crops; the fibers, forestry, and sugar; live stock on farms and dairy products; wool and miscellaneous; horticulture, including truck farming, floriculture, seed farming, nurseries, and tropic and semi-tropic fruits; viticulture; live stock on ranges; live stock not on farms.

VII. *Manufactures.*—General statistics of manufactures; statistics of specified industries; manufactures in cities; lumber and saw mills, timber products; slaughtering and meat packing; chemical manufactures and salt; clay and pottery products; coke and glass; cotton manufactures; dyeing and finishing of textiles; electrical industries; manufactured gas; iron and steel; printing, publishing, and periodical press; wool manufactures, including woollen goods, worsteds, felt goods, carpets other than rag, wool, hats, hosiery, and knit goods; shipbuilding; silk and silk goods; agricultural implements; paper mills; boots and shoes; leather, tanned and curried; brick yards; flour and grist mills; cheese, butter, and condensed milk factories; carriages and wagons; leather, patent and enamelled.

VIII. *Mines and Mining.*—Mineral industries in the United States; iron ore; gold and silver; copper, lead, and zinc; quicksilver; manganese; petroleum and natural gas; aluminium; coal; stone; precious stones; mica; mineral waters; minor materials.

IX. *Fish and Fisheries.*—Statistics of fisheries by geographical divisions; statistics of fisheries by name; scientific and popular names of fishes, with their geographical distribution; illustrations of the principal food fishes of the United States; condensed description of fish by species; statistical summary for each species for the United States; directory of principal firms and corporations engaged in the fishing industry of the United States.

X. *Transportation.*—Railroads; statistics for the year ended 30th June, 1890; statistics for ten years ended in 1889; lake, ocean, and river transportation; canals; transportation on the Pacific coast; express business; street railways.

XI. *Insurance.*—Fire, ocean marine, inland navigation and transportation, and tornado insurance business; life insurance, showing the business of level premium, assessment, and co-operative companies; miscellaneous insurance, including the business of accident, burglary, and theft guarantee, hail, live stock, plate glass, and real estate title guarantee, steam boiler, surety, and wind storm insurance companies; fraternal and other beneficiary associations.

XII. *Indians.*—Report and statistics of the condition of Indians living within the jurisdiction of the United States, 1890, taxed and untaxed.

XIII. *Alaska.*—Population and resources of Alaska.

XIV. *Veterans of the Civil War* —(Seven volumes, of 1000 pages each; publication not yet authorised.)

XV. *Statistical Atlas.*—(Publication not yet authorised.)

VII.—*Reform of the Currency in Austria-Hungary.*[*]

For thirty years (1848 to 1878), with only one break (of half a year, November, 1858, to April, 1859), the paper money of Austria-

* See the following Government papers, Vienna, Court Press, 1892:—

1. Denkschrift über den Gang der Währungsfrage seit dem Jahre 1867. (18 pp.)

Hungary was inconvertible, and (whether State notes or bank notes) was during that time more or less depreciated in comparison with the silver standard. In the autumn of 1878 the depreciation of notes and the agio on silver ceased.[6] The silver gulden no longer fetched more than the paper. Paper and coin together were evidently not more than enough for the wants of the people, for, if the heavy fall in the gold value of silver since 1870 explains the rise of paper to par, something more is needed to explain the rise of the silver gulden above its mint price,—a singular phenomenon which was seen in 1879, and has continued since.

A few figures from the "Statistical Tables in illustration of the question of the Standard," will help to show what happened.

The total circulation of State notes[7] and bank notes amounted at the end of the year—

1870 .... To 649,006,679 millions of gulden,[8] of which 54 per cent. were State notes.

'78 .... To 652,801,389, of which 55 per cent. were State notes.

'79 .... „ 629,789,926, „ 49 „

'91 .... „ 834,066,311, „ 45 „

(Tables, p. 160.)

In the same years the two mints coined as follows :—

1870.	Gold	3,940,719.	Silver	5,453,554
'78.	„	5,391,306.	„	28,829,476
'79.	„	5,189,596.	„	66,682,821
'91.	„	5,986,641.	„	6,298,337

(Tables, pp. 84 and 85.)

In the beginning of 1879 the importation of silver for coining, which was then "free,"[9] reached such a point, that in March of that year the Government suspended free coinage; and the suspension still continues.

It is calculated (see Minutes of Commission, 1892, p. 51, 2, Bunzl) that there are in existence in the empire 210 millions of silver gulden, of which 30 are in circulation, the rest in the coffers of the banks.

According to another estimate (Minutes of Commission, p. 84, 1,

2. Denkschrift über das Papiergeldwesen der Oesterreichisch-ungarischen Monarchie. (51 pp.)

3. Statistische Tabellen zur Währungs-Frage der Oest.-ungar. Monarchie. (446 pp.)

4. Stenographische Protokolle über die vom 8 bis 17 März, 1892 abgehaltenen Sitzungen der nach Wien einberufenen Währungs-Enquête-Commission. (298 pp.)

5. Gesetzentwürfe betreffend die Regelung der Valuta und die Convertirung einiger Kategorien der Staats-schuld, 16 pp. *Motive*, 54 pp.

[6] See *Motive* (in Supplement of the Bills), p. 9.

[7] The State notes represent a State debt, and usually bear interest; the Bank notes are the ordinary notes of the Austrian-Hungarian Bank, which the bank has for some time been perfectly able to cash if the State had allowed it.

[8] The silver gulden at the ratio 15½ to 1 = 1s. 11½d.; with silver at 3s. 6d. an ounce it is = 1s. 4¼d.

[9] *I.e.*, "claimable as a right," to be done on private account on payment of the mint charge.

Jeitteles) the amounts in 1891 were 250 silver gulden and 85 gold, the proportion being then (as in most years) about 25 per cent. of gold to 75 of silver.

Instead of simply authorising cash payments and resuming free coinage, the Imperial Government has taken advantage of the situation to propose a reform of the currency by the adoption of a gold standard. It summoned a commission of inquiry in March of this year, and laid before it the following questions:—

1. What standard should be taken as the basis for a reform of the currency?

2. If the gold standard is adopted, should there be allowed also a subordinate circulation of silver, and to what extent?

3. Should there be allowed a circulation of Treasury bonds, payable in current money, not of forced currency, and bearing no interest; and under what conditions?

4. What principles should be taken as guides for the calculation of the gold equivalent of the present gulden?

5. What unit of coinage should be chosen?

The commission consisted of thirty-six members, including bank directors, merchants, railway directors, lawyers, heads of chambers of commerce and agriculture, editors, and professors, from all parts of the empire. There are such familiar names as Hertzka, Juraschek, Lieben, Mataja, Karl Menger. In addition, there were present as official assessors, finance minister Steinbach (who was chairman of the meetings) and his colleagues Böhm-Bawerk, Winterstein, Kapf, Mensi, and Gruber. Each member of the commission was called on to deliver his opinion in a set speech on each of the points submitted; and there followed in many cases a cross-examination of the speaker by such of the hearers as differed from him or found difficulty in gathering his meaning. The drift of the coming Bills seems to have been generally anticipated. On the first question there was practically no difference of opinion: though Austria had hitherto possessed a single silver standard (alone among European nations), and though it was a country of comparatively poor people, many of whom had never seen a gold coin, the commissioners one after the other declared for a single gold standard. Bimetallism found few to praise it, and fewer to urge its adoption,[10] though at the congress at Paris in 1878, and the monetary conference at Paris, 1881, the Austrian representative had declared for bimetallism. On other points there was less harmony. It was much debated, for example, whether, for the determination of the gold equivalent of the gulden (Qu. 4), there should be taken the quotation ruling at the time of the passing of the law, or the same with allowance for any unusual disturbance, or an average over some considerable period before. There were divergent opinions about the unit of the coinage, many speakers upholding the time-honoured gulden,[11] some contending that a

---

[10] But see *Protokolle*, pp. 175—90 (Professor Milewski, of Krakau) and pp. 191—97 (Professor Pilat, of Lemberg). The former displayed, like many others of the Commissioners, a wide knowledge of English authorities.

[11] *Protokolle*, p. 217, i (Professor Menger), p. 45 (Professor Braf, of Prague).

smaller unit would tend towards cheapness and even to thrift.[12] The professors and the practical men did not avoid an occasional passage at arms.[13] But the Bills, as laid before the two Parliaments, are very closely in keeping with the views prevailing at the commission, and the Government cannot be accused of failing to give every due consideration to the opinions of experts before putting their hand to legislation. They have consulted foreign as well as home financiers. They have contrived to keep the details of their plans secret till the moment was ripe. They have (it is understood) made no little provision already of the necessary gold.

Towards the end of May in this year their plans were at last laid before the two Parliaments in the shape of six Bills. The first of these Bills proposes the establishment of a gold standard, the unit of account to be a crown, divided into 100 heller. The actual gold coins are to be 20-crown pieces and 10-crown pieces of the fineness of 900 parts gold to 100 copper. Out of a kilogramme of gold of the prescribed fineness shall be coined 147·6 20-crown pieces and 295·2 10-crown pieces. The 20-crown piece would then have the full weight of 6·775067 grammes and the fine weight of 6·09756; of the 10-crown piece in proportion. The crown of account would be, roughly speaking, equal to 10*d.* of English money and 1 fr. 5 c. of French. It would be only about half the value of the present gulden.

After prescribing the design, size, and assay, the Bill lays down that the remedy shall be the difference between full weight and 6·749 grammes in the case of the 20-crown and 3·37 in case of the 10-crown pieces. But gold coins made light by the ordinary wear and tear of circulation shall be received by the State offices at full nominal value for withdrawal. The mint may coin gold for private account at a charge not exceeding 3 per cent. for the 20 and 5 per cent. for the 10-crown pieces, and this "free coinage" is deemed essential on principle to the adoption of a standard as such.[14] Besides these two gold pieces, the Austrian ducat (= 9*s.* 5*d.*) will still be coined for commerce, but not the 8 and the 4 gulden pieces (introduced in 1870).

The silver gulden, ¼ gulden, and 2 gulden pieces shall remain for the present in circulation at the following rating: 2 gulden = 4 crowns, 1 gulden = 2 crowns, ¼ gulden = 50 heller. There shall be issued also[15] new silver pieces of 1 crown and ½ crown, nickel pieces of 20 heller and 10 heller, and bronze of 2 heller and 1 heller. The coinage of silver, nickel, or bronze is not to be conducted on private account. The silver coins are to be in fineness 835 parts silver to 165 copper. The silver, nickel, and bronze coins are to be received at all public offices at their nominal value, the silver without limit, the others to the amount of 10 crowns. Between members of the public, silver is not to be legal tender

---

[12] *Protokolle*, p. 54 (Dr. Bunzl, of Vienna), p. 59 (Herr Dub, of Rothschild's), p. 72 (Dr. Zgorski, of the Galicia Land Bank).

[13] See the discussion after Professor Menger's speech, *Protokolle*, pp. 217—23.

[14] *Motive*, p. 17.

[15] As token money.

beyond 50 crowns, nickel beyond 10 crowns, bronze beyond 1 crown. Worn silver, nickel, and bronze coins are to be withdrawn for re-coinage at the expense of the State.

The fractional currency at present in circulation will be called in at the discretion of the administration, which will fix a date beyond which these pieces will no longer be exchanged for new currency. At present they are to be so rated:—

20 kreutzer piece	= 40 heller	4 kreutzer piece	= 8 heller
10 "	= 20 "	1 "	= 2 "
5 "	= 10 "	$\frac{1}{10}$ "	= 1 "

Levantine (or Maria Theresa) dollars of 1780 will continue to be coined on private account for foreign commerce. The coining of them costs about $\frac{1}{2}$ per cent.; and, as the mint charge is $1\frac{1}{2}$,[16] this is a very profitable business for the mint.

The paper money is to be accepted as at present, till its corresponding coins have been called in; and the paper gulden is to rank (see above) as = 2 crowns. The time for the obligatory and universal adoption of the new currency will be determined by later legislation. Till then it shall be at the option of everyone to pay in the new currency or the old at the above rating of the two.

The above Bill shall become law with the passing of the second : viz., the Bill for a treaty between the Austrian and Hungarian ministries in regard to the currency standard of the country. The said second Bill repeats the terms of the first Bill in regard to the gold standard and the gold coins to be issued in accordance therewith. It leaves the amount of the coinage to the discretion of the several mints. Practically it is a re-statement of the first Bill with a few special clauses demanded by the different special circumstances of the two countries concerned. The redemption of State notes to the amount of 312 millions of gulden is to be effected by a joint arrangement of the two States, in accordance with which 70 per cent. of the cost shall be borne by the Austrian and 30 by the Hungarian Government. The treaty is to determine at the end of 1910, and if a year before this term it is denounced by either party, the currency made and put into circulation under the treaty is to remain valid for two years at the least. If there is no such denunciation the treaty is to remain in force for another ten years. The treaty Act is to take effect, like the other laws, from the date of passing.

The third Bill is very brief, and relates to the arrangements to be observed in fulfilling of such existing pecuniary obligations between individuals and obligations to the customs departments as were to be fulfilled in Austrian or Hungarian gold currency. They may be fulfilled either with the old or the new pieces at the rate of 42 of the old gold gulden to 100 crowns of the new, " in order that the intrinsic value of the sums to be paid may not be altered." (Article II.)

---

[16] *Motive*, p. 29. *Cf. Tabellen*, p. 24 (Handelsmünzen) and p. 88. The average for twenty-four years of the value in gulden is over 2 millions a year, at the old rate of 2 gulden to the piece. It reached 10 millions in 1876.

The fourth proposes an addition to Article 87 of the statutes of the Austrian-Hungarian Bank to the following effect: "The bank is under obligation to pay bank notes at any and every time at its chief offices in Vienna and Buda-Pesth for legal gold coins at the nominal value and for bar gold, according to the legal mint rate of the crown standard. The bank is entitled at the same time to get the bars tested and assayed by its own experts at cost of the person offering them, as well as to deduct the coinage dues fixed and notified by the Governments."

The fifth Bill gives powers to the Austrian Minister of Finance to take up a loan bearing 4 per cent. interest in gold, to procure gold for the new coins, on account of the State. The amount to be so procured is to be equal to 183,456,000 Austrian gold guldens; it is to be melted down and re-coined as soon as received, and then kept in the State treasury or in the coffers of the national (Austrian-Hungarian) bank. The control of this treasure is to be in the hands of the Debt Commissioners of the Imperial Parliament, who are to make an annual report on the subject.

The sixth Bill relates to the conversion of the 5 per cent. untaxed State Debt warrants (payable in notes), the 5 per cent. debentures of the Vorarlberg State Railway (payable in silver), and the 4¾ per cent. of the Crown Prince Rudolf Railway (payable in silver). These are to be converted into a uniform untaxed debt paying 4 per cent. in gold.

Appended to the Bills is a Statement of Reasons (*Motive*) given clearly and briefly. After referring to the work of the Commission, this document calls attention to the opportunity now given for the funding of the floating debt, and the warrants of short-dated mortgages on public revenues (*Partial-hypothekar-anweisungen*[17]), and for the conversion of the funded debt.

The need of the reformed currency, and the probable benefits of it to home and foreign trade, are described, with due mention of the special difficulty of carrying out such reforms in an empire like Austria-Hungary. The chief currency hitherto has been State paper (representing an unfunded debt) and bank notes, with a forced circulation not really demanded by the bank itself, both of them a result of political exigencies now no longer existing. The fate of silver since 1879 is recalled to memory in order to establish the conclusion that a return to cash payments must not be a return to payments in silver. To be in a line with other nations, Austria must have the same basis for her currency as the others; and this is not silver but gold. To introduce the double standard would involve her in the difficulties of determining the ratio of the value of gold and silver. But silver will remain as token money, and even for the present there will be no violent dethronement of it as legal tender. The name of the new coins is defended on the ground that as new it must have a distinctive character; and yet the name must have a familiar sound in all the parts of the polyglot empire. The "Krone" has long been a

---

[17] Especially *Salinenscheine*. *Cf.* Tables, pp. 442—44; *Denkschrift über das Papiergeldwesen*, p. 32.

popular name for the half gulden. There was a gold "Krone" in use thirty years ago, though not coined in any considerable quantity since 1859 (see Tables, p. 86).

The two serious difficulties anticipated by the Commission in their discussions were, how to get rid of the old silver, and how to procure the new gold. Both seem fairly met by the Bills before the Parliament, and, if these become law, and if peace continues, the effect may be to give to Austria-Hungary a currency as sound as any in Europe. Even if peace should not last, the empire will find it easier to encounter her enemies with a good currency than with a bad. If peace were broken when the operation was only in its first stages, no doubt the Government might be strongly tempted to use the mint treasure as a war treasure; but they have already (June, 1892) given a pledge to the Reichsrath to use it for none but its declared purpose; and in all probability events will allow them to carry out their great measure in its integrity.

VIII.—*Notes on Economical and Statistical Works.*

Pauperism and the Endowment of Old Age. By Charles Booth. London: Macmillan and Co., 1892.

It is now many years since Mr. Booth has been engaged in his endeavours to throw light upon the social condition of the inhabitants of London, and more especially of the East End. After a long period of patient labour, spent in extracting the materials from the records of the poor law officials in Stepney and St. Pancras and various country unions, he has been enabled to lay before us an estimate of the amount of pauperism in England, and to formulate a scheme of universal pensions, not in the vague fashion in which it is constantly spoken of, but basing his arguments on the facts and figures which he has collected. These estimates and proposals are contained in the volume before us, together with numerous illustrations of the poverty and crime existing in the metropolis. The book is divided into two parts: "Pauperism, a picture" (as he well describes it), and the "Endowment of Old Age, an argument." The greater part is an enlargement of the paper read before this Society last December, and it is therefore unnecessary to refer in detail to the portions dealing with Stepney and St. Pancras. Several pages are devoted to some selected "stories of Stepney pauperism," which present a vivid picture of the distress and vice existing in this part of London, and exhibit to a striking extent the influence of "association." The author also considers the means at present adopted, apart from parish relief, for assisting the poor by charity, and in this connection it is impossible to overrate the work done by the Charity Organisation Society. By way of comparison with these London unions, we have a chapter on pauperism at Ashby-de-la-Zouch. The chief difference consists in the number of out-door paupers as compared with in-door, the percentage of the whole population being 1·54 and 0·31 respectively at Ashby on the 1st of January, 1891, while the percentages at Stepney on the same date were

0·24 and 1·52. It must however be remembered that in the latter union out relief has been almost abolished.

Since Mr. Booth read his paper in December last, he has been able to take into account the results arrived at in Mr. Hollond's Parliamentary Return (1881), and partly in consequence of this he has been led to modify somewhat his estimate of the percentage to be added to the pauperism of a single day in order to arrive at the total for the whole year. A discussion of this, as well as of the amount of *old age* pauperism, appears on another page,[18] and it is sufficient to note here that the percentage of persons over 65 relieved has been reduced from nearly 40 to 30 per cent. of the whole population above that age. The author gives two examples of "good administration of the present poor law," namely, the unions of Bradfield and Brixworth, in which out relief has been as far as possible denied, with the happiest results both to paupers and ratepayers. In fact in the latter portion of the book, when he comes to consider the amount to be saved from the rates by the adoption of a State pension, he is evidently influenced by the results achieved in these two unions.

The chapter that will perhaps be most eagerly read is that on the "endowment of old age," although without the preceding portions of the book this portion could scarcely have been written, and although these earlier portions have cost far more labour, and are really the more valuable, inasmuch as they lay before us real facts and not proposals only. In considering the best method of supporting the aged poor, Mr. Booth deals first with the suggestions of Canon Blackley, Mr. Chamberlain, Mr. Fatkin, and Mr. Vallance; and after pointing out the objections to these, comes to his own scheme of providing universal pensions as being the only one by which none are *forced* to set apart a portion of their earnings, and by which the taint of pauperism is abolished. He next considers the various objections that have been brought against this plan, and after meeting them, gives an outline of the method he would suggest for the payment of the pensions. In the first place, the age of any person claiming the pension is to be established by the registrar of the district in which he resides. To this effect the claimant must produce evidence by means of witnesses from the places where he has lived during the last ten years; thus, as "identification for sixty-five years is impracticable," Mr. Booth would "treat all evidence as to age as a matter of hearsay only, and suggest no attempt at proof." This somewhat loose identification seems to afford ample opportunity for anyone to overstate his age. To pay the registrar (or registrars if he has resided in more than one district during the last ten years) "the amount of the fees (which need not exceed 10s. to 20s. in all) could be deducted from the first payments of pension at the rate of 2s. 6d. a week till paid." This to a pauper with only 5s. a week seems a very serious deduction which does not appear altogether necessary.

Appendices include (*a*) statistical tables of Stepney pauperism; (*b*) a summary of Stepney stories, showing the cause of each

[18] p. 287, &c.

person's dependence on the parish, arranged under the author's system of denoting the cause by an initial letter, with a summary of the work done by the Charity Organisation Society at Stepney; (c) forms suggested for periodic returns; and (d) particulars of the proposals for providing pensions, as formulated by the National Providence League and the Poor Law Reform Association. A new feature is the publication of the book simultaneously in two forms, one at 5s. and a people's edition at 6d. This attempt to make the poorer people acquainted at the earliest possible moment with their actual condition and the projects for their relief, deserves to meet with all success.

Elements of Economics of Industry.   By Alfred Marshall. London: Macmillan and Co., 1892.

Thirteen years ago Professor Marshall published, together with his wife, a manual, which bore the title of the *Economics of Industry*. That volume contained in brief the theory which has since been developed at length in the first volume of the recently issued *Principles of Economics*, but it also contained some account of industrial movements, such as trades unions, co-operation, and conciliation, to which there is no counterpart in the larger work. The present volume consists in the main of an abridgment of the *Principles*, and it follows the arrangement of this book rather than that of the old *Economics of Industry*, which it now supersedes. But it so far resembles the older book that a chapter of great importance is appended on trades unions. In that chapter the author preserves a just balance between the views of the advocates and the opponents of these institutions; and he is especially happy in pointing out the ulterior effects of certain lines of action which might be, and indeed often are, overlooked by employers or workmen concerning themselves with the immediate issues of the moment, but are disclosed by economic analysis. The other part of the volume can be best described in Professor Marshall's own language. He says that it is an "attempt to adapt" the first volume of the *Principles* "to the needs of junior students." "The necessary abridgment," he adds, "has been effected not so much by systematic compression, as by the omission of many discussions on points of minor importance, and of some difficult theoretical investigations. For it seemed that the difficulty of an argument would be increased rather than diminished by curtailing it and leaving out some of its steps. The argumentative parts of the *Principles* are therefore as a rule either reproduced in full or omitted altogether; reference in the latter case being made in footnotes to the corresponding places in the larger treatise. Notes and discussions of a literary character have generally been omitted." The old *Economics of Industry* has long occupied a very high place, and the new is likely to take, if it be possible, a higher. But a regret may perhaps be expressed that, like the *Principles* and the old *Economics of Industry*, it is as yet only a first volume of an unfinished work; and therefore the student, whether junior or advanced, has to look forward to the future for the treatment of some of the topics usually handled in an economic treatise.

An Introduction to the Theory of Value. By William Smart.
London: Macmillan and Co., 1891.

In this little book Mr. Smart has given a clear and concise
account of the theory of value expounded by the chief representatives of the school of writers commonly known as the Austrian
School. The theory, he states, is "that enunciated by Menger
and Jevons, and worked out by Wieser and Böhm-Bawerk." It
regards utility as the all important element in determining value,
and lays stress on the final or marginal utility. To the element
of cost of production emphasised by the older English economists
it will only allow a subordinate place, and it maintains that the
true process is from product to cost rather than from cost to
product. That is to say, these Austrian writers, who have lately
attracted a considerable amount of attention both in this and
other countries, hold that the value of commodities, &c., is determined from the side of demand rather than that of supply. Unlike
Jevons they make but a sparing use of mathematics proper, though
they affect arithmetical illustrations; but they push the main
ideas to be found in his book further and develop them more
systematically. In this outline of their theory there are examples
of the greater fulness and more thorough method which they have
brought to the exposition of the idea of marginal utility. A
distinction is established between "subjective" and "objective
value," which they regard as independent, though closely connected, conceptions. The useful is treated as a larger class
including the smaller class of the valuable; as value "must
emerge at some particular limiting point of utility." This leads
directly to the conception of marginal utility, and Mr. Smart shows
how the conception may be applied to the difficult and complicated
cases of goods which may be put to different uses, and of what he
calls "complementary goods," which are several in number, but
contribute to one satisfaction, and are, in short, a group of goods.
It may perhaps be questioned whether the Austrian economists
have solved the problem of value—and this Mr. Smart allows—
whether they have fully appreciated the work of writers like
Ricardo and Mill, and whether they have not exaggerated one
very important side to the undue neglect of the other; but there
can be no doubt of the ability with which they have put forward
their views, of the immense importance of the discussion, which
touches the very centre of economics, and of the lucidity which
characterises Mr. Smart's summary of their theory. In a brief
compass he has given an adequate account of opinions which it is
not easy to state at once clearly and shortly; and, in doing so, he
has rendered no small service to English economic students, who
are enabled to read in their own language the chief results of the
inquiries of a distinguished body of foreign economists.

The Commerce of Nations. By C. F. Bastable. London:
Methuen and Co., 1892.

This book forms one of a series entitled "Social Questions of
To-day." There are indeed few questions which are now more
eagerly discussed than that of Free Trade and Protection, to which

a large portion of the book is devoted, and there is perhaps none on which erroneous opinion is so easy and so prevalent. Professor Bastable has already shown his capacity to deal with this vexed question from a scientific standpoint in his *Theory of International Trade*, which was noticed in this *Journal* some few years since; and in the present volume he has effected a happy combination of theory and facts. We have rarely, if ever, seen the various arguments in favour of protection more fully or fairly stated, or more completely refuted. Professor Bastable begins by sketching the outline of the theory of international trade. He then proceeds to pass in review the mercantile system, and to trace the transition from this to modern protection. The English customs system, and the system, so opposed, of the United States are next examined, and their history is given in its main stages. In the following chapters the reform of continental tariffs in a free trade direction from 1815 to 1865 and the subsequent reaction to protectionism from 1865 to 1890 are investigated, and the similar action in the matter of customs duties of our own colonies is also explained. The author then proceeds to scrutinise the claims and pretensions of protection, the arguments of an economic, or social, or political character advanced in its behalf, the other expedients besides import duties, such as bounties, which it sometimes adopts, the serious drawbacks and complexities and evils which are incidental to its practical operation, and the degree to which proposals for reciprocity, or retaliation, or commercial federation, which have attained no little popularity, are tainted by its characteristic fallacies, and involve similarly mischievous consequences. In short Professor Bastable has in this little volume executed with admirable skill and thoroughness a task of urgent social importance.

Threadneedle Street: a reply to " Lombard Street." By Arthur Stanley Cobb. London: Effingham Wilson and Co., 1891.

This book is a contribution to the discussion on the question of our cash reserves, to which the Baring crisis and the proposals put forward by the Chancellor of the Exchequer have recently attracted fresh attention. The purport of the book is to urge that the duty of maintaining a sufficient reserve rests with the great London banks rather than, as popular opinion inclines to believe, with the Bank of England; and, as that opinion is largely due to the influence of the late Mr. Bagehot, who called his book *Lombard Street*, Mr. Stanley Cobb styles his attempt to show on the contrary that it has not been proved "that it is the duty of the Old Lady of Threadneedle Street to save Lombard Street bankers the trouble and expense of keeping cash reserves," *Threadneedle Street*. He maintains that Peel's Act, by separating the Issue from the Banking Department, placed the banking department on the same footing as respects the duty of keeping a sufficient reserve to meet its liabilities as any other bank, and that it only has towards the public the responsibility—no more and no less—of a large and influential banking institution. The bank is not, so far as the Banking Department is concerned, a public institution, but is carried on for the benefit of its proprietors. It does not retain any privilege of "exclusive" banking. It keeps the Government balances for which, like any ordinary bank, it is responsible; and its management of the debt does not create any obligation on the part of the Government to preserve its other functions and character. The suspension, however, of Peel's Act in times of pressure encourages bankers to rely upon the reserve of bullion in the Issue Department, and to avoid the expense of keeping sufficient reserves of their own. This was not intended by the authors of the Act, and is a violation of the contract for securing the convertibility of the bank note. The reason of the pressure on the Banking Department at the Bank of England which occurs in these times of panic, is not, Mr. Cobb holds, the existence of one as opposed to many reserves, so much as the disposition on the part of other banks at such a time to hoard their resources and to decline to grant the accommodation previously given, because they fear that their reserves will not be sufficient to enable them to meet the extra demands that may be made upon them. But of the insufficiency of these reserves taken together there can be little doubt; and Mr. Cobb adds to the urgency of the case established by Mr. Goschen's figures. He shows that the so-called cash reserves, which appear in bank accounts, can only be made available, like money at call, by inconveniencing, and perhaps embarrassing, some one else—in this case some other bank. The proportion of cash reserves to deposits he puts at 2·2 per cent. in 1890, as compared with 3·9 per cent. ten years before—a diminution of over 43 per cent. He next proceeds to examine the remedies suggested by Mr. Goschen, and he singles out as of practical importance the publication of accounts and the issue of 1*l*. notes. The first he thinks useless, unless the character of the deposits—whether held at call or at short notice—is known; and that even then public opinion would probably not be very operative in producing an increase of the central reserve, as so much might filter through on its way. The publication of fuller accounts of the deposits at the Bank of England, and especially of the bankers' balances, he regards as very useful as a barometer to assist the effective regulation of the rate of discount. The issue of 1*l*. notes and the formation by this means of a second reserve he considers wrong, because it would throw all the responsibility on the discretion of one bank, without the wholesome influence at present exercised in restraining rash over-lending by the uncertainty of the time when Peel's Act will be suspended. And so he would prefer what he calls the "setting aside by the banks of a *minimum* proportion of cash reserve to liabilities towards an insurance fund against the evils of excessive competition." A percentage of 2½ per cent. would give a reserve of this nature of 16,250,000*l*., which might be kept in the custody of the Bank of England wholly apart from its ordinary business, and advances be made from it at a rate not less than 10 per cent. on "approved securities." Mr. Cobb ends his book by pointing out the urgency of the question, and arguing that the failure of one of the large joint stock London banks would throw the Baring crisis into the shade by the magnitude of the interests affected and the width of the suffering caused.

Illegitimacy and the Influence of Seasons upon Conduct. By Albert Leffingwell. London: Swau, Sonnenschein, and Co., 1892.

The present volume, so the author states in his preface, "contains the first treatise in the English language upon the subject of illegitimacy," although on the continent "this phase of social phenomena has attracted considerable attention." The treatise is founded upon, and illustrated by, statistical tables drawn from official sources. It discloses a remarkable uniformity in the presence of this feature of society in special districts from year to year and even from decade to decade. "Of each 1,000 births in Scotland, there are almost twice as many illegitimate as in England and Wales, and more than three times as many as in Ireland." Different sections of the three countries exhibit similar variations; and in English counties, for example, where an abnormally high rate prevailed as far back as 1842, it has, broadly speaking, prevailed ever since; and in counties, where the average was then less than for all England, it is less to-day. Dr. Leffingwell shows that the causes which might be supposed to produce a relative excess of illegitimacy, such as poverty, ignorance, and the contamination of great cities, do not appear in this position in the statistical tables, and he himself is inclined to lay greater stress on religion, legislation, and legal impediments to marriage, and heredity or the influence of race and ancestry. He then gives some evidence of the age and class of the women who contract relations likely to produce illegitimate births, and of the extent to which these births are concealed. He concludes by observing that the rate has been slowly declining for many years both in the United Kingdom, and abroad in the greater part of Europe. In another essay, which is included in the same volume, he points out with the aid of statistics how certain classes of crime and certain kinds of conduct seem to affect certain seasons of the year more than other periods. Towards midsummer suicides, crimes against person, murder and homicidal assaults, crimes against chastity, attacks of insanity, and births, especially of an illegitimate character, apparently tend to increase.

Conférences sur la Statistique et la Géographie Économique faites en 1889-90 à la réunion des officiers sous les auspices de M. le Ministre de la Guerre et de la Société de Statistique de Paris. Paris: V. Rozier, 1891.

The French Minister of War, desirous to spread a knowledge of industrial and commercial statistics in the army, instituted negotiations, which resulted in a number of meetings in Paris on the Saturdays between the 23rd November, 1889, and the 22nd February, 1890, under the joint auspices of the Government and the Statistical Society of Paris; and the report of the proceedings at these meetings is contained in the volume now before us. The meetings were fourteen in number, and were divided into two series, of which the first was devoted to the treatment of general questions, such as the object and history of statistics, the methods of statistical investigation, and the organisation of statistical bureaux in France and other countries. The second series, numbering eleven meetings, discussed subjects falling under the head of economic statistics and geography; and among the subjects handled were wine, the production and sale of cereals, salt and sugar, the production and sale of meat throughout the world, cattle and stock in France, the agricultural districts of France, the foreign commerce of France, her textile industries, her woods and forests, her coal, iron, and steel. Officers of the Army of high position and distinguished statisticians attended the meetings; and papers of value were contributed to the proceedings.

The important general questions discussed at the first three meetings were intrusted to the competent hands of MM. Levasseur, Cheysson, and Bertillon. M. Levasseur commenced with the topic of the object and history of statistics. He stated that statistics was at once an instrument and a record of knowledge, and he devoted his considerations to the latter aspect of the study. The social sciences were, he said, sciences of observation rather than reasoning; and, owing to the diversity and changeability of the phenomena with which they had to deal, they required a great number of observations in order to disentangle a law from the facts. Accordingly certain methods were needed, and these statistics supplied. Among the hundred or more definitions of the study, he contented himself with the one which described it as the numerical study of social facts. These facts might be grouped in three classes—administrative facts, such as taxes, the recruiting of the army, the statistics of which might attain a high degree of certainty; facts which, without belonging to the first class, were registered by the State, and included the movement of the population and foreign trade, and depended on the degree of exactitude which characterised the registration; and, thirdly and lastly, facts which required some special action to ascertain them, and were neither *administratif* nor registered regularly by the administration, such as mineral and metallurgic statistics. After pointing out the dangers to be specially avoided in collecting and interpreting statistics, M. Levasseur proceeded to trace its history from the remote beginnings in the past, and, with greater detail, from Achenwall in Germany and Petty in England, the one, the father of descriptive statistics, and the other, the employer of "political arithmetic." He concluded by extracting from his well known work on the French population a classification of statistical material. At the second meeting M. Cheysson handled the subject of the methods of statistics. He first considered the collection of facts, whether by monographs, or inquiries. He then passed on to the question of the arrangement and interpretation of the facts which had been collected, of which he distinguished two main varieties—the numerical and the graphic, with its diagrams and cartograms, differently shaded or coloured, and its lines of varying length, and curves. M. Bertillon at the third meeting gave an account of the arrangements and work of the different statistical departments established in France and other countries, especially when regarded from the standpoint of the military importance and value of the information which they collected, or might collect.

To the second series of discussions contributions were made by MM. de Foville, Levasseur, de Zolla, Pigeonneau, Melard, and Keller. M. de Foville treated of the statistics of wine. France, Spain, and Italy, he showed, produced each about a quarter of the total wine supply of the world, and were followed in order by Austria-Hungary, Portugal, Germany, Turkey, Greece, the region of the Danube, and Switzerland. Accordingly he devoted his attention to the three countries first enumerated, and especially to France. He showed how disastrous had been the effect of the phylloxera in the last decennial period of 1878-89; and that its ravages had reached their worst in the districts which were still most productive. There were six chief centres of production in France—the valley of the Marne, of the Seine, of the Loire, of the Charente, of the Gironde, and of the Aude and Hérault. He did not despair of the future in spite of the phylloxera; for, though a panacea for this pest remained to be discovered, there were measures by which the plant might be protected when threatened, be aided in its resistance when attacked, and have its place supplied by hardier varieties when destroyed. The other topics discussed at the remaining meetings afforded equally instructive material, which appears to have been collected with no less care and interpreted with no less practised skill and discretion. The whole was designed to form the basis of examination for the officials of the French army; but the limits of space will not allow more than a summary to be furnished here. The production of cereals was treated by M. Levasseur under the headings of the documentary sources of information, the amount of production in France as shown by maps and other diagrams, the trade in wheat, and the changes in its prices at different epochs in France, and the production of cereals in other countries, and in conclusion some reflections were offered on the tariff policy pursued with reference to the cereals. M. de Foville examined into the production and use of salt and sugar, and M. Zolla into that of meat. The agricultural districts of France were described by M. Pigeonneau, and the same professor investigated the foreign trade of France, and its textile industries. The volume concludes with an account of the French woods and forests by M. Melard, and of coal and iron in France by M. Keller.

Jahrbücher für Nationalökonomie und Statistik. Jena: Gustav Fischer.

Heft 3, Band iii contains the following:—Wert, Kosten, und Grenznutzen, by E. Böhm-Bawerk; a review of Herman Paasche's work *Zuckerindustrie und Zuckerhandel der Welt*, by C. Hager; Die Verleihung der Korporationsrechte nach der zweiten Lesung des Bürgerlichen Gesetzbuches, by J. Conrad; Gesetz vom 7 Juli, 1891, betr. die Beförderung der Errichtung von Rentengütern; Gesetz vom 11 Juli, 1891, betr. die Königlichen Gewerbegerichte in der Rheinprovinz; Statistik der Krankenversicherung der Arbeiter im Deutschen Reiche für 1889, by A. Wirminghaus; Der englische Aussenhandel seit 1880, by M. Diezmann; Zur Arbeiterwohnungsfrage, by Flesch; Die Schwankungen des Diskonts und des Silber-

preises im Jahre 1891 und der Vorjahre; Preisaufgaben der Rube-
now-Stiftung.

Heft 4, Band iii:—Agrarstatistische Untersuchungen, by J.
Conrad; Die Valutaregulierung in Oesterreich-Ungarn, by Carl
Menger; Zur neuesten Litteratur über die Verstaatlichung des
Grund und Rodens, by Karl Diehl; Litteratur zur Währungsfrage,
by Robert Zuckerhandl; Die zweite Lesung des Entwurfes eines
Bürgerlichen Gesetzbuches für das Deutsche Reich (Fortsetzung),
bv Assessor Greiff; Das Grossherzoglich Hessische Gesetz über
die Brandversicherungs-Anstalt für Gebäude vom 28 Sept., 1890,
by Zeller; Das preussische Wildschadengesetz vom 11 Juli, 1891,
by Wilhelm von Brünneck; Budget Frankreichs im Jahre 1891, by
Max von Heckel; Das Niveau der Warenpreise in den Jahren
1886-90; Die Statistik des Tabulargrundbesitzes in Galizien, by
W. Steslowicz.

Heft 5, Band iii:—Die Valutaregulierung in Oesterreich-Ungarn
(Fortsetzung), by Carl Menger; Stadtrecht und Marktrecht, by
W. Varges; a review of L. Goldschmidt's *Handbuch des Handels-
rechtes*, 3 Aufl. I. 1, by Richard Ehrenberg; Studien zur preus-
sischen Einkommensteuer. Untersuchungen über das geltende
Recht und seine Fortbildung, by J. Jastrow; Die zweite Lesung des
Entwurfes eines Bürgerlichen Gesetzbuches für das Deutsche
Reich, by Assessor Greiff (continued); Der Gesetzenwurf betr.
die Feststellung der Kronen-Währung in Oesterreich-Ungarn, by
Carl Menger; Die Entwickelung des Reichsversicherungsamtes,
by Ludwig Fuld; Stenographische Protokolle über die vom 8 bis
17 März abgehaltenen Sitzungen der nach Wien einberufenen
Währungs-Enquete-Kommission, by Robert Zuckerhandl.

IX.—*Additions to the Library.*

*Additions to the Library during the Quarter ended 16th June, 1892,
arranged alphabetically under the following heads:—*(a) *Foreign
Countries;* (b) *India and Colonial Possessions;* (c) *United Kingdom
and its Divisions;* (d) *Authors, &c.;* (e) *Societies, &c. (British);*
(f) *Periodicals, &c. (British).*

Donations.	By whom Presented.
(a) Foreign Countries.	
Argentine Republic—	
Comercio exterior. Datos trimestrales del, año 1891. Nos. 72 and 73. 8vo.	The General Statistical Bureau
Higiene Publica. Anales de, Vol. i, No. 1. 8vo. 1892....	Dr. E. R. Coni
Buenos Ayres—	
Anuario Estadistico de la Ciudad de Buenos Aires. Año I. 1891. 8vo.	The Municipal Statistical Bureau
Boletin mensual de Estadistica Municipal. Dec., 1891; Jan.—Mar., 1892	
Recensement de la ville de, [1887]. Analyse du Tome ii. 8vo.	Sir Rawson W. Rawson, K.C.M.G., C.B.

Donations.	By whom Presented.
(a) Foreign Countries—*Contd.*	
Argentine Republic—*Contd.*	
Sociedad médica argentina. Revista de la, Publicacion bimestral. Vol. i, No. 2. Marzo, 1892. Plate, 8vo.	The Society
Austria and Hungary—	
Consulats-Behörden. Jahresberichte der k. und k. österr.-ungar. 11 parts, 8vo. 1891	The Statistical Department, Ministry of Commerce
Handel des Zollgebiets. Statistische Uebersichten betreffend den auswärtigen, im Jahre 1891 und Jan.—April, 1892. 8vo.	
Handels. Bericht über die Erhebung der Handelswerthe und Haupt-ergebnisse des auswärtigen, im Jahre 1890 in vergleichung mit den Vorjahren. Fol.	
Statistische Monatschrift—	
Jan. Die überseeische österreichische Auswanderung in 1889 und 1890.....................	
Feb. Der internationale Austausch der durch die Volkszählung gewonnenen Individualdaten über die Staatsfremden. Die Sterblichkeit in den grösseren Städten Oesterreichs, 1891	The Central Statistical Commission
Mar. Arbeitsstatistik. Oesterreich-Ungarns Aussenhandel, 1891. Statistik des Binnenverkehres	
Staatshaushalt in den Jahren 1887 und 1888. Der Oesterreichische. Fol.	
Strafrechtspflege. Die Ergebnisse der, im Jahre 1888.	
Unterrichts-Anstalten, Statistik für 1889-90. Fol.	
Waaren-Einfuhr in das allgemeine Oesterr.-Ungar. Zollgebiet im Jahre 1890. Fol.	
Denkschrift über den gang der Währungsfrage seit dem Jahre 1867. Fol. 1892	
Denkschrift über das Papiergeldwesen der österreichisch-ungarischen Monarchie. Fol. 1892	
Statistische Tabellen zür Währungs-Frage der Oesterreichisch-ungarischen Monarchie. Diagrams, fol. 1892	Dr. Ignaz Gruber, Vienna
Währungs - Enquête - Commission. Stenographische Protokolle über die vom 8 bis 17 März 1892 abgehaltenen Sitzungen der nach Wien einberufenen. La. 8vo. 1892	
Oesterreichisches Statistisches Taschenbuch, bearbeitet nach amtlichen Quellen. 8vo. 1890.....................	J. S. Keltie, Esq.
HUNGARY. Magyarorszag Aruforgalma Ausztriaval es mas Orszagokkal. (Monthly Trade Returns.) (Current numbers)	The Royal Hungarian Statistical Bureau
BUKOWINA. Mittheilungen des Statistischen Landesamtes des Herzogthums. Heft 1. 8vo. 1892........	The Statistical Bureau
VIENNA. Die Polizeiverwaltung Wiens im Jahre 1885. 8vo.	Sir R. W. Rawson
BRÜNN. Summarischer Bericht der Handels- und Gewerbekammer in Brünn ... wahrend 1891. 8vo.	
PRAGUE. Bulletin hebdomadaire de la Ville de Prague et des Communes-faubourgs. (Current numbers)....	The Statistics Bureau
Belgium—	
Armée Belge. Statistique médicale pour l'année 1890. La. 8vo.	The Belgian Government

Donations—Contd.

Donations.	By whom Presented.
(a) Foreign Countries—*Contd.*	
Belgium—*Contd.*	
Instruction Publique. Statistique générale de l', en Belgique [pendant 1876-85]. 2° Partie. Diagrams, maps, 4to.	Sir R. W. Rawson
Mouvement Commercial avec les Pays étrangers. Mar.—May, 1892	The Bureau of General Statistics
Travaux Publics. Annales des, Tome xlix. Cahier 3. 8vo. 1892. (Contains "Legislation du Travail des femmes, des adolescents et des enfants dans les établissements industriels")	The Administration of Mines
BRUSSELS. Bulletin hebdomadaire de statistique Démographique et Médicale. (Current numbers)....	Dr. E. Janssens
Chili. Sinopsis Estadistica y Geografica de Chili en 1889 y 1890. 2 vols., 8vo.	C. T. Maude, Esq., H.M. Chargé d' Affaires
China—	
Customs Gazette, No. 92. Oct.—Dec., 1891. 4to.....	
Lighthouses, Light-Vessels, &c. List of, for 1892. Maps	Sir Robert Hart, G.C.M.G.
Trade, Returns of, and Trade Reports for 1891. 4to.	
Denmark—	
Agriculture, Superficie, emploi de la terre et sémences le 16 Juillet, 1888. 4to.	The Royal Statistical Bureau
Justice civile, 1886-90. 4to.	
Danmark i 1890. Supplementbind til Danmarks Statistik. Hefte 1—5. 8vo. 1890	Sir R. W. Rawson
Nationalökonomisk Tidskrift, 1892. Hefte 3	The Danish Political Economy Society
Egypt—	
Commerce Extérieur de l'Egypte pendant 1891	
Douanes Egyptiennes. Rapport du Directeur-Général sur l'Exercice de 1891.	A. Caillard, Esq.
Finances. Budgets provisoires du Gouvernement Egyptien pour les Exercices 1888 et 1892. 2 vols.	
Finances. Compte général du Gouvernement Egyptien pour l'exercice 1891. 4to.	A. Boinet Bey
Finances. Comptes généraux de l'administration des Finances rendus pour les Exercices 1883, 1885, 1889, et 1890. 4 vols. fol.	
Postes Egyptiennes. Administration des, Rapport sur l'Exercice 1891. 8vo.	The Director-General of the Post Office
Services Sanitaires, &c. Bulletin hebdomadaire. (Current numbers)	The Department
Shipping. Returns showing arrivals and clearances of commercial vessels at port of Alexandria in 1880-91. Sheets	Rear-Admiral R. M. Blomfield
Bo~avaux des, pendant 1891. 4to. bunaux Indigènes. Rapport statistique sur les	
Rect~ture. Bulletin du Ministère de l'. Nos. 2 To~ 892. 8vo.	The Ministry of Agriculture

Donations.	By whom Presented.
(a) Foreign Countries—*Contd.*	
France—*Contd.*	
Albums de Statistique graphique de 1886, 1887, 1888, et 1889. 4to.	Sir R. W. Rawson
Atlas de Statistique Financière, 1889. La. 4to.	J. S. Keltie, Esq.
Coloniales, statistiques, pour 1888	
Finances, Ministère des, Bulletin de Statistique et de Législation comparée. Feb.—April, 1892	The Ministry of Finance
Navigation Intérieure. Recensement de la Batellerie. Année 1891. 4to.	The Ministry of Public Works
Revue générale d'Administration, Mars, 1892 (containing " Denombrement de Population en 1891 ")	M. V. Turquan
Travaux Publics. Ministère des, Bulletin de Statistique et Législation comparée. Dec., 1891, Jan., 1892	The Ministry of Public Works
L'Economiste Français. (Current weekly numbers)	The Editor
Le Monde Economique. (Current weekly numbers)	"
Polybiblion. Revue Bibliographique Universelle—	
Partie Littéraire. Mar.—May, 1892	
Partie Technique. Mar.—May, 1892	
Le Rentier. Journal Financier Politique. (Current numbers)	..
Revue Géographique Internationale. Feb. et Mar., 1892	
Journal des Economistes—	
Mar. La pacification des rapports du capital et du Travail : *G. de Molinari.* L'Incidence des Droits Protecteurs : *P. des Essars.* Les Houillères du Nord et du Pas-de-Calais : *G. François*	
April. Concurrence entre les compagnies d'assurances sur la vie americaine et les compagnies françaises: *E. Rochetin.* L'Impôt sur les transactions de Bourse en Autriche : *A. Raffalovich.* Le Monde de la Finance au 17ᵉ Siècle : *C. Jannet.*	"
May. Mouvement agricole: *G. Fouquet.* Crédit agricole et populaire : *E. Cohen.* Tarifs par zones des Chemins de Fer de l'Etat en Hongrie : *D. Korda.* Mines de Soufre de la Sicile : *J. W. M.*	
Revue d'Economie Politique—	
Feb. Traités de Commerce entre l'Allemagne, l'Autriche-Hongrie et l'Italie : *D. A. Peez.* La Monnaie mesure de valeur : *C. Menger.* Origine et abolition des droits sur les céréales en Angleterre : *L. Brentano*	
Mar. Enseignement de l'Economie Politique dans les Universités des Pays de langue allemande : *H. Saint Marc.* Projets de loi français et italien concernant l'arbitrage et les Conseils de Prud' hommes : *V. Mataja.* Mendicité et assistance par le Travail en Allemagne : *E. Fuster.* La vie des ouvriers de fabriques dans le grand Duché de Bade : *H. Herkner*	The Publishers
April. Essai historique sur la legislation industrielle de la France : *M. Sauzet.* L'Enquête de la Commission du Travail en Angleterre : *J. Rae*	

2 A

Donations—Contd.

Donations.	By whom Presented.
(a) Foreign Countries—*Contd.*	
France—*Contd.*	
Ecole Libre des Sciences Politiques, Annales. VIIᵉ année. No. 2. April, 1892. Les finances russes, le passé, le présent, l'avenir: *R. G. Levy*	The Institution
Société de Géographie, Comptes rendus des Séances. No. 6. 8vo. Paris, 1892 (contains remarks of the Donor on Population of England)	M. E. Levasseur
Société de Statistique de Paris, Journal—	
Mar. La machine électrique à recensement: *E. Cheysson.* Le recensement de 1891: *E. Levasseur.* La population de la Grande Bretagne: *D. Bellet.* La Russie economique: *A. Raffalovich*	
April. Avenir de la richesse agricole en France: *A. Coste.* Commerce de France: *T. Loua.* La Bière: *J. P. Roux*	The Society
May. Les lois d'assurance ouvrière, les accidents du Travail: *Dr. Vacher.* Les encaisses des banques d'emission depuis 1881: *P. des Essars*	
Conférences sur la Statistique et la Géographie Economique faites en 1889-90. 8vo. 1891	M. E. Levasseur
Germany—	
Bevölkerung. Stand und Bewegung der. des Deutschen Reichs und fremder Staaten in 1841-86. Diagrams and maps, 4to. 1892	
Handel, Monatliche Nachweise über den Auswärtigen, des deutschen Zollgebiets. Jan.-April, 1892. 8vo.	
Vierteljahrshefte zur Statistik des Deutschen Reichs—	
Heft 1. Die Bevölkerung des Deutschen Reichs nach der Volkszählung vom 1 Dec., 1890. Eheschliessungen, Geburten und Sterbefälle in 1890. Steinkohlen-Bergbau in 1881-90. Seeschiffahrt in 1890. Auswanderung in 1891. Krankenversicherung der Arbeiter in 1890	The Imperial Statistical Bureau
Heft 2. Gemeinden und Wohnplätze von mindestens 2,000 Einwohnern nach der Volkszählung 1 Dec., 1890. Häuser und Haushaltungen, 1 Dec., 1890. Produktion der Bergwerke, Salinen und Hütten, 1891. Erzeugung von Roheisen während 1872-91. Einfuhr, Ausfuhr, und Durchfuhr, 1891	
PRUSSIA. Geburten, Eheschliessungen und Sterbefälle im Preussischen Staate während 1890. 4to.	The Royal Prussian Statistical Bureau
Berlin—	
Eheschliessungen, Geburten, Sterbefälle und Witterung. (Current weekly numbers) Tabellen über die Bewegung der Bevölkerung der Stadt Berlin im Jahre 1890. La. 4to.	The Statistical Bureau of Berlin
DRESDEN. Mittheilungen des Statistischen Amtes der Stadt Dresden. I Jahrgang. Nos. 1—4. 1891. Fol.	The Statistical Bureau of Dresden
FRANKFORT. Handelskammer zu Frankfurt am Main. Jahres-Bericht für 1891. 8vo.	The Chamber of Commerce
GDEBURG. Magdeburgische Statistik. Hefte 2—4, Bewegung der Bevölkerung im Jahre 1886-88. Heft The Wohnungs- und Haushaltungsverhaeltnisse volkerung. 4 parts, diagrams, &c. 8vo.	Sir R. W. Rawson

Donations—Contd.

Donations.	By whom Presented.

(a) Foreign Countries—*Contd.*

Germany—*Contd.*

Allgemeines Statistisches Archiv. 2er Jahrgang, 1891-92. I Halbband. (Selections from contents.) Statistik und Selbstverwaltung: *Dr. E. Mischler.* Die Jahresschwankungen in der Häufigkeit verschiedener Bevölkerungs- und moralstatistischer Erscheinungen: *Dr. K. Becker.* Die Statistik der Zwangsversteigerungen landwirthschaftlicher Anwesen: *Dr. A. Cohen.* Ueber Sammlung und Verwertung des durch die Arbeiterversicherung gebotenen sozialstatistischen Materials: *Dr. G. v. Mayr.* Russlands Bedeutung für den Weltgetreidemarkt: *Dr. O. Mertens.* 8vo. Tübingen, 1892 .... — Dr. G. von. Mayr

Archiv für soziale Gesetzgebung und Statistik. Band 5, Heft 1. 1892. (Contents.) Der wirtschaftliche Fortschritt, die Voraussetzung der sozialen Reform: *G. S. Gaevernitz.* Die staatlich unterstütze auswanderung im Grossherzogthum Baden: *E. von Philippovich.* Die Lohn-und Arbeitsverhältnisse der Münchener Kellnerinnen: *A. Cohen.* — The Publisher

Jahrbücher für Nationalökonomie und Statistik. Hefte 2—5, 1892. 8vo ....

Greece—

Population. Mouvement de la, pendant 1889 et 1890. 4to. ATHENS. Bulletin de mortalité pour la ville d'Athènes, Jan.—Feb., 1892 .... — The Statistical Bureau

Guatemala—

Exposicion universal de Paris, 1889. Informe por el comisionado especial del gobierno. La. 8vo. .... Exposicion universal de Paris, 1889. Recompensas obtenidas por la República. 8vo. .... Memoria de la Secretaria de Fomento á la Asamblea nacional legislativa en sus sesiones ordinarias de 1892. La. 8vo. .... — „

Italy—

Agricoltura. Notizie e studi sulla, Produzione e commercio del Vino in Italia e all' Estero. 1892 .... Annali di Statistica. Statistica Industriale della Provincie di Siena, Bergamo, e Grosseto. 3 parts, maps. 8vo. 1892 .... Bollettino del Ministero degli Affari Esteri. (Current numbers) .... Bollettino mensile delle situazioni dei Conti degli Istituti d' Emisione. (Current numbers) .... Bollettino di Notizie sul Credito e la Previdenza. (Current numbers) .... Bollettino settimanale dei Prezzi di alcuni dei principali Prodotti Agraria e del Pane. (Current weekly numbers) .... Bollettino Sanitario, Direzione della Sanita Pubblica. (Current numbers) .... Statistica del commercio speciale di Importazione e di Esportazione. Jan.—April, 1892 .... — The Director-General, Statistical Department of the State

Donations—Contd.

Donations.	By whom Presented.

(a) Foreign Countries—*Contd.*

Italy—*Contd.*

Cause di Morte. Statistica delle, in tutti i comuni del Regno, confronti con alcuni Stati esteri. .Anni 1889-90. La. 8vo. ....

Elettorale, Statistica, 1889-90

Igiene e la Sanità pubblica nel Regno. Circa i fatti principali riguardanti, nell' ultimo trimestre 1891 e gennaio 1892. La. 8vo. .... — *The Director-General, Statistical Department of the State*

Istruzione elementare. Statistica dell', per l'anno scolastico 1888-89. La. 8vo. ....

Istruzione elementare. Condizioni della, in Italia e del suo progresso dal 1861 in poi. Diagrams and maps. 8vo. 1890 .... — *Sir R. W. Rawson*

Popolazione. Movimento dello Stato civile. Anno xxix, 1890. 8vo............ —

Società cooperative di Credito e Banche popolari, le Società ordinarie di Credito, le Società ed Istituti di Credito agrario e gli Istituti di Credito fondiario nell' anno 1889. 8vo. .... — *The Director-General, Statistical Department of the State*

L'Economista. (Current numbers) .... *The Editor*

Giornale degli Economisti—

March. La teoria dei prezzi dei Signori Auspitz e Lieben e le osservazioni del Prof. Walras: *V. Pareto.* Il problema della popolazione, critica dei sistemi: *F. Virgilii.* La "clearing house" postale: *G. B. Salvioni*..

April. Cenni sul concetto di massimi edonistici individuali e collettivi: *A. Bertolini e M. Pantaleoni.* Il Bilancio dello stato: *E. Pisani*........................

May. Considerazioni sui principii fondamentali dell' economia politica pura: *V. Pareto.* L'Economia politica negli Stati Uniti nell' America settentrionale: *L. Cossa.* Il riordinamento della circolazione fiduciaria: *A. de Marco* ....

Giornale delle Camere di Commercio e degli Istituti di Credito. Anno III. Jan.—May, 1892. 8vo. ....

Padova. L' anno accademico 1890-91 nella università di Padova. Relazione dal Rettore Prof. C. F. Ferraris. 8vo. 1891 .... — *The Author*

Japan. Tokyo-Fu. Weekly Reports of Deaths in. (Current numbers) .... — *The Prefect of Tokyo-Fu*

Mexico—

Amonedaciones e introducciones de metales preciosos á las Casas de Moneda. Año fiscal de 1890-91. Fol. Exportaciones en el año fiscal de 1890 a 1891. Fol..... — *The Statistical Bureau*

Netherlands—

Bevolking. Statistiek van den Loop der, van Nederland over 1890. 8vo........................ . ... — *The Netherlands Legation*

Caisse d'Epargne Postale des Pays-Bas. Extrait du rapport sur le service de la, en 1890. 4to...................... — *The Director of Savings Banks*

Statistiek der geboorten, en der sterfte naar den leeftijd en de oorzaken van den dood in Nederland over Oct.—Dec., 1891: Sheets............... — *The Netherlands Legation*

Donations.	By whom Presented.
(a) **Foreign Countries**—*Contd.* **Paraguay.** Revue du Paraguay. (Current numbers)	The Statistical Bureau
Roumania. Judieiara, Statistica, din Romania pe anul 1886. 4to. 1891	The Director of Statistics
Russia— Agriculture. Importation, Exportation, Prix et Consommation des Céréales et données sur la récolte et la vente à l'étranger. (In Russian.) Diagram-maps, 8vo. 1889	Sir R. W. Rawson
Diagram-maps shewing prices of Rye and Oats in Russia in Europe on 1st Jan., 1st Feb., 1st March, and 1st April, 1892. Sheets	The Department of Assessed Taxes
Finland— Befolknings-Statistik, 31st Dec., 1880. (Census.) Part 1. 4to......... Befolknings-Statistik, 1880-88. (Movement of Population.) 8 vols. 4to. and la. 8vo. .... Blinde, Döfstumme och Sinnessjuke. Statistik öfver, 1883. (Lunacy, &c.) La. 8vo. .... Elementarläroverkens i Finland. Underdånig Berättelse öfver, Tillstånd ogh Verksamhet, 1884-90. (Elementary Education.) 2 parts......... Elementarläroverkens i Finland. Statistisk Öfversigt af, Tillstånd och verksamhet, 1884-85—1888-89. (Education.) 5 parts. La. 8vo. .... Fångvården, 1884-89. (Prisons.) 6 vols. La. 8vo. Folkundervisningen i Finland, Statistik öfver, utgifven af Öfverstyrelsen för Skolväsendet. 1884-85—1889-90. 6 parts. La. 8vo. .... Förmögenhets-Förhållanden, 1881. (Revenues) .... Handel och Sjöfart, 1881-88. (Trade and Shipping.) 4 vols. La. 8vo. .... Industri-Statistik, 1884-89. (Industries.) 10 vols. Jernvägs-Statistik, 1884-89. (Railways.) 6 vols. Jernvägsstyrelsens. Bihang till, i Finland Berättelse för 1889. Map. La. 8vo. .... Kronoskogarne, 1885, 1888. 2 vols. 8vo. .... Landmäteriet, 1885-89. 5 parts. La. 8vo. .... Lots-och Fyrinrättningen, 1885-88. 4 vols. La. 8vo. Medicinalverket, 1884-89. (Public Health.) 6 vols. Ofversigt af Finlands Ekonomiska Tillstånd, 1881-85. (Economic condition.) La. 8vo. .... Post-Statistik, 1885-89. (Postal.) 5 vols. La. 8vo. Postsparbanken, 1887-89. (Post Office Savings Banks.) 3 parts. 8vo. .... Sparbanks-Statistik, 1883-85. (Savings Banks.) 8vo. Statistisk Årsbok för Finland, 1887-90. (Statistical Year-Book.) 3 vols. 8vo. .... Väg-och Vattenbyggnaderna, 1885-88. 4 parts....... *Livonia*— Agrarverhältnisse. Materialien zur Kenntniss der livländischen, mit besonderer Berücksichtigung der Knechts- und Tagelöhner- Bevölkerung. La. 8vo. 1885	Sir R. W. Rawson

Donations—Contd.

Donations.	By whom Presented.

(a) Foreign Countries—*Contd.*

Russia—*Contd.*

Livonia—Contd.

Bauer-Verhältnisse. Materialien zur Kenntniss der livländischen. La. 8vo. 1883 ....

Landvolksschulwesens in Livland. Materialien zur Kenntniss des evangelish-lutherischen. 1884 ....

REVAL. Ergebnisse der Revaler Handelsstatistik aus den Jahren 1885-89. 8vo................................

Riga—

Geburten, Sterbefälle und Ehen der Stadt Riga. Material zur Statistik der, in 1881-85. 4to. ....

Handelsstatistik. Ergebnisse der Rigaer, aus den Jahren 1881-85. Diagrams. La. 4to. ....

Handels - Beiträge zur Statistik des Rigaschen, Jahrgang 1886, 1887, 1888, und 1890 (abth. 1). 4 vols. La. 4to. ....

Infectionskrankheiten in Riga. Statistik der, für die Jahre 1883-87. Plan. 4to. ....

Schulstatistischen Enquête in Riga. Resultate der am 17 Feb., 1883, ausgeführten. La. 8vo.............

Statistisches Jahrbuch der Stadt Riga. I. . 8vo. ....

} Sir R. W. Rawson

Servia. Recensement de la Population, 31 Dec., 1890. Résultats préliminaires, et 1ᵉʳᵉ Partie, Fasc. 1, 2; 2ᵉ Partie, Fasc. 1. 8vo. and 4to. 1891-92 ....

} The Statistical Bureau

Spain—

Censo de la Poblacion de España, 1877. Resultados generales del. La. 8vo. ....

} J. S. Keltie, Esq.

Censo de la Poblacion de España en 31 Dec., 1887. Tomo I. La. fol. ....

} Geographical and Statistical Institute

Comercio Exterior. Resumenes mensuales de la Estadistica del. Nos. 24—28, 1892......................

} The Director-General of Indirect Taxation

Sociedad Geográfica de Madrid. Boletin. Jan.—April, 1892 The Society

Sweden and Norway—

Bidrag till Sveriges Officiela Statistik—

B. Rättsväsendet, 1890. (Judicial Statistics, Civil)

C. Bergshandteringen, 1890. (Minerals, &c.) ....

D. Fabriker och Manufakturer, 1890. (Industries)

E. Inrikes Sjöfart och Handel, 1890. (Inland Shipping and Trade)................................

F. Utrikes Handel och Sjöfart, 1890. (Foreign Trade and Shipping)............................

} The Central Statistical Bureau

K. Helso- och Sjukvärden, 1890. (Lunacy) ....

L. Statens Jernvägstrafik, 1890. (Railways) ....

N. Jordbruk och Boskapsskötsel, 1890. (Agriculture)

P. Undervisningsväsendet, 1885, 1888-89. (Education) ....

Statistisk Tidskrift. Nos. 2, 3, 1891; No. 1, 1892.

} The Central Statistical Bureau, Stockholm

NORWAY—

Annuaire Statistique de la Norvège. 11ᵉ année, 1891. 8vo. ....

Meddelelser fra det Statistiske Centralbureau. 9ᵉ Bind, 1891. (Journal of the Bureau.) 8vo.....

} The Central Statistical Bureau, Christiania

Donations.	By whom Presented.
(a) Foreign Countries—*Contd.*	
Sweden and Norway—*Contd.*	
NORWAY—*Contd.*	
Norges Officielle Statistik—	
142. Fiskerier, 1890. (Sea Fisheries)...................	
143. Sundhedstilstanden, &c., 1889. (Health)	The Central Statisti-
144. Fattigstatistik, 1889. (Poor Relief.)	cal Bureau, Christ-
145. Sindssygeasylernes, &c., 1890. (Lunacy)	iania
146. Kommunale Finantser, 1888. (Finance)	
CHRISTIANIA. Statistiske Meddelelser angaaende Christiania By. 5ᵗᵉ aargang. 1891	The Municipal Sta- tistical Bureau
Switzerland—	
Bulletin hebdomadaire et Bulletin mensuel des mariages, naissances et des décès dans les Villes de la Suisse. (Current numbers.) 8vo.	
Emigration de la Suisse pour les pays d'outre-mer en 1891. 4to.	The Federal Statisti- cal Bureau
Journal de Statistique Suisse, 1891, No. 4; 1892, No. 1. 4to.	
United States—	
Agriculture. Monthly Reports on Crops, &c. (Current numbers)	J. R. Dodge, Esq.
Bureau of American Republics. Bulletin No. 31. Costa Rica. Map and plates, 8vo. 1892	The Bureau
Census Bulletins. Nos. 158. Manufactures, District of Columbia. 159. Churches. 160. Railway Statistics. 162. Finances of Maine. 163. Irrigation in Nevada. 164. Railway Statistics. 165. Population of places having one thousand inhabitants or more in 1890. 166. Mineral Products of the United States, 1880-89. 167. Fisheries of the Pacific States. 168. Production of cast-iron pipe foundries. 169. Manufactures: The Wool Industry. 170. Manufactures, City of St. Louis. 171, 172. Railway Statistics. 175. Population by color, sex, and general nativity, 1890. 176. Summary of national, state and local indebtedness. 178. Agriculture: Irrigation in Oregon. 179. Transportation by water in the United States. 183. Population by color, sex, and general nativity, 1890	R. P. Porter, Esq., Superintendent of Census
Extra Census Bulletins. 17. Insurance Business of the United States. 18. Farms, Homes, and Mortgages. Ownership and Debt in Kansas and Ohio. 20. Farms and Mortgages in Nebraska	
Finances. Annual Report of the Secretary of the Treasury on the state of the, for 1891. 8vo.............	The Secretary of the Treasury
Foreign Commerce and Navigation, Immigration and Tonnage. Annual Report on, for the year ending 30th June, 1891. 8vo.	
Imports, Exports, Immigration, and Navigation. Quarterly Report for the Quarter ending 30th Sept., 1891. (No. 1, 1891-92.) 8vo......................	The Bureau of Sta- tistics, Treasury Department
Imports and Exports. Summary Statement of, Jan. —April, 1892	
Statistical Abstract of the United States for 1891	

Donations—Contd.

Donations.	By whom Presented.
(a) **Foreign Countries**—*Contd.*	
United States—*Contd.*	
Marine Hospital Service. Annual Report of the Supervising Surgeon-General for the year 1890-91.	The Surgeon-General
Observations made during 1887 at the U. S. Naval Observatory. Diagrams, 4to. 1892	The Observatory
Railways. First and Second Annual Reports on Statistics of, in the United States to the Interstate Commerce Commission for the years (ending 30th June) 1888-89. Also advance copy of the Third Report for 1890. 3 vols., maps. 8vo..........................	Sir R. W. Rawson
CONNECTICUT. State Board of Health. Monthly Bulletin, Feb.—April, 1892	The Board of Health
ILLINOIS. Statistics of Coal in Illinois, 1891, with reports of State Inspectors of Mines. Map, 8vo.....	John S. Lord, Esq.
New York State—	
Tribute of the Chamber of Commerce to the memory of John Jay Knox, 3rd March, 1892. Portrait.	G. R. Gibson, Esq.
Museum. Annual Report of the Regents for 1890. Plates, 8vo.	New York State Library
Museum Bulletin. Vol. i, No. 1. March, 1892	
PENNSYLVANIA. University Publications. Vol. iii, No. 2. The Theory of Dynamic Economics. By S. N. Patten. 8vo. 1892	Prof. S. N. Patten
Smithsonian Institution—	
Annual Report of the Board of Regents for the year ending 30th June, 1890, with Report of the National Museum. 2 vols. Plates, 8vo.	The Institution
Bibliography of the Algonquian Languages. Plates, 8vo. 1891	
Catalogue of Prehistoric Works east of the Rocky Mountains. Plates, 8vo. 1891	The Bureau of Ethnology of the Institution
Omaha and Ponka Letters. 8vo. 1891....................	
Contributions to North American Ethnology. Vol. vi. The Cegiha Language. 4to. 1890.....	
Banker's Magazine. (Current numbers)	The Editor
Bradstreet's Journal. (Current weekly numbers)	,,
Commercial and Financial Chronicle. (Current weekly numbers)	..
Investor's Supplement to Commercial and Financial Chronicle, Mar. and May, 1892...................................	
Political Science Quarterly. Vol. vii, No. 1, March, 1892. (Selection from Contents.) The Finances of the Confederacy: *J. C. Schwab.* Irish Land Legislation, I: *W. A. Dunning.* Boehm-Bawerk on Capital: *H. White*	,,
Quarterly Journal of Economics. Vol. vi, No. 3. April, 1892. (Contents.) University Settlements: *E. Cummings.* The fundamental error of "Kapital und Kapitalzins:" *F. B. Hawley.* The Bank of Venice: *C. F. Dunbar*	The Publisher
Yale Review, The, a Quarterly Journal of History and Political Science. Vol. i, No. 1, May, 1892. (Selection from Contents.) German Tariff Policy, Past and Present: *H. Villard* and *H. F. Farnam.* Legal Theories of Price Regulation: *A. T. Hadley.* Labor Troubles between 1834 and 1887: *E Woollen.* 8vo.	,,

Donations.	By whom Presented.
(a) Foreign Countries—*Contd.*	
United States—*Contd.*	
American Academy of Political Science, Annals—	
Mar. Theory of Value: *F. von Wieser.* Basis of Interest: *D. M. Lowrey* .... May. The Australian System of Voting in Massachusetts: *R. H. Dana.* Indian Education: *F. W. Blackmar*	The Academy
American Economic Association Publications. Vol. vi, Nos. 1 and 2. Report of Proceedings at their Annual Meeting, 1890. Vol. vii, No. 1. The Silver situation in the United States: *F. W. Taussig*............	The Association
American Geographical Society. Bulletin. Vol. xxiii, No. 4, part 2, 1891; vol. xxiv, No. 1, March, 1892. Plates	The Society
American Philosophical Society, Proceedings. Vol. xxix, Nos. 136 and 137. 8vo. 1891.........	..
American Statistical Association, Publications—	
Dec., 1891. Census Enumeration in Prussia: *C. C. Plehn.* Plea for the Average: *G. K. Holmes* .... Mar., 1892. Statistics of Crime in Massachusetts: *F. G. Pettigrove.* Development of Statistics of Religion: *E. F. de Flaix.* Net Profits of Manufacturing Industries in Massachusetts: *F. B. Hawley.* Classification of Trade Statistics: *F. C. Hicks.* Proposed Statistical Legislation: *R. P. Falkner*	The Association
Columbia College. Studies in History, Economics, &c. Vol. i, No. 4. Financial History of Massachusetts: *C. H. J. Douglas.* 8vo. 1892	The College
Franklin Institute. Journal. (Current numbers)	The Institute
CHICAGO. Royal Commission for the Chicago Exhibition, 1893. Handbook of Regulations, and General Information. 1st edition, April, 1892. 12mo.	Sir Henry Wood, M.A.
International—	
Bulletin International des Douanes. (Current numbers.) 8vo. Brussels, 1891-92	The Board of Trade
Congrès Monétaire International, tenu à Paris, les 11—14 Septembre, 1889. Compte-rendu "in extenso" et Documents. 8vo. 1890.........................	Sir R. W. Rawson
(b) India and Colonial Possessions.	
India, British—	
Moral and Material Progress and Condition of India. Statement of, during 1890-91. (220.) 1892...........	The India Office
Trade by Land with Foreign Countries. Monthly Accounts. 1891-92; Nos. 8 and 9 .... Trade and Navigation. Monthly Accounts. 1891-92. Nos. 10 and 11.........................	The Department of Finance and Commerce, Calcutta
Trade of British India with British Possessions and Foreign Countries. Statement for 1886-87 to 1890-91. [C—6646.] 1892.........................	The India Office

Donations—Contd.

Donations.	By whom Presented.
(b) **India and Colonial Possessions—***Contd.*	
India, British—*Contd.*	
Reports on Somali Land and the Harrar Province, by Major F. M. Hunter and Lieutenant J. D. Fullerton. Maps and plans. 8vo. Simla, 1885	Sir R. W. Rawson
Bengal—	
Report on the Administration of Bengal, 1890-91. General Report on Public Instruction for 1890-91. Maps. Fol..	His Ex. The Lieutenant-Governor of Bengal
Indian Engineering. (Current numbers)	The Editor
Canada, Dominion of—	
Census of 1891. Bulletins. Nos. 1, 2, Population of Province of Ontario. 3. Population of Eastern Maritime Provinces. 4. Population of Province of Quebec. 5. Population of Manitoba, N.W. Territories, and British Columbia. 6. Dwelling Places of the People. 7. Live Stock in N.W. Territories. 8. Manufactures. 9. Religions. 8vo.	George Johnson, Esq.
Banks acting under Charter, Monthly Statements of, Jan.—Mar., 1892....................	N. S. Garland, Esq.
Agriculture. Report of Minister of, for 1891	
Archives. Report on Canadian, 1891. Map	
Auditor-General. Report of, for 1890-91	
Civil Service List of Canada, 1891	
Civil Service. Report of Royal Commission on, 1892	
Debates of House of Commons. Session 1891. 3 vols.	
Dividends unpaid up to end of 1891	
Estimates for the year ending 30th June, 1893............	
Geological Survey Department. Report for 1891........	
High Commissioner for Canada. Report for 1891	
Inland Revenues. Report on, for the years 1890-91....	
Insurance Companies. Reports for 1891	J. G. Bourinot, Esq., C.M.G.
Journal of the Senate. Vol. xxv. Session 1891	
Journals of House of Commons. Session 1891............	
Marine. Report of Department of, for 1890-91	
Militia and Defence. Department of, Report for 1891	
Mortuary Statistics of Cities and Towns for 1891	
Penitentiaries. Report on, in Canada, for 1890-91	
Public Works. Report of Minister of, for 1890-91	
Postmaster-General. Report of, for 1890-91	
Railways and Canals. Report on, for the year 1890-91	
Shareholders in Chartered Banks on 31st Dec., 1891.	
Secretary of State. Report of, for 1891	
Trade and Navigation. Tables of, for the year 1890-91.	
MANITOBA. Report on Crops and Live Stock, No. 32.	The Agricultural Department
Insurance and Finance Chronicle. (Current Numbers)....	The Editor
Toronto University. Studies in Political Science. First Series, No. 3. Conditions of Female Labour in Ontario: *J. T. Scott.* 8vo. 1891	Prof. W. J. Ashley
Cape of Good Hope—	
Acts of Parliament of the Colony. Session 1891. Fol.	The Colonial Secretary

Donations—Contd.

Donations.	By whom Presented.
(b) India and Colonial Possessions—*Contd.* **Cape of Good Hope—*Contd.*** Census of 1891. Returns of Agricultural Machinery, Implements, and of Agricultural Produce, &c. Sheets .... Civil Service List and Calendar for 1892. 8vo. .... Votes and Proceedings of Parliament, Session 1891, with Appendices I (in three volumes), and II. Fol. and 8vo.	The Colonial Secretary
Mauritius. Civil List for 1892. Sm. 4to. 1892	,,
Newfoundland. French Treaty Rights in Newfoundland. The case for the Colony stated by the People's Delegates. Map, 8vo. 1890	Sir R. W. Rawson
New South Wales— Agricultural Gazette. Parts 1 and 2, 1892 .... Agriculture. Report of the Conference of Fruit Growers, with Appendices. 8vo. 1891......................	The Director of Agriculture
Census and Industrial Returns Act of 1891. Information respecting. Fol...... Census of 1891. Tables A. Population of each Division of the Colony. B. Ages of the People. C. Increase of Population in each Division of Colony since 1881. Sheets .... Statistical Register for 1891 and previous years. Part 1, Shipping. Part 2, Commerce. Part 3, Financial and Monetary........................	T. A. Coghlan, Esq., Government Statistician
Statistical Register for 1890 and previous years. 8vo.	The Agent-General for N. S. Wales
New Zealand— Report on the Statistics of New Zealand, 1890, with map and appendices. 8vo. .... Statistics of the Colony for 1890, with Abstracts from the Agricultural Statistics of 1891. Fol................	The Registrar-General
WELLINGTON Harbour Board. Annual Reports, &c., for 1891. Fol.	The Secretary to the Board
Queensland. Supplement to the Government Gazette (containing Vital Statistics). (Current numbers)	The Registrar-General
Saint Lucia. Census Report of the Island of Saint Lucia, 1891. Fol.	The Colonial Secretary
South Australia. Statistical Register, 1890. Fol.	The Government Statist
Straits Settlements. The Perak Government Gazette. (Current numbers.)	The Government Secretary
Tasmania— Census of 1891. Part 1. Population, Dwellings, Land. Part 2. Ages of the People. Fol...................... Statistics of the Colony for 1890. Fol. .... Tasmanian Official Record, 1892. Third year of issue. Maps and diagrams. 8vo........................	R. M. Johnston, Esq., Government Statistician

Donations—Contd.

Donations.	By whom Presented.
(b) India and Colonial Possessions—*Contd.* **Victoria—** Australasian Statistics for 1890. Fol............................... Census for 1891. Ages of the People, Parliamentary Representation, Education of the People, Conjugal Condition of the People, Inhabitants and Homes. Sheets, &c., fol.	H. H. Hayter, Esq., C.M.G., Government Statist
The Bankers' Magazine and Journal of the Bankers' Institute of Australasia. Vol. v. Nos. 8 and 9. 1892. Plates, 8vo.	The Editor
Royal Society of Victoria. Transactions. Vol. ii, part 2. 4to., plates. 1891	The Society
(c) United Kingdom and its several Divisions. **United Kingdom—** Board of Trade Journal. (Current numbers)	The Board of Trade
Emigrants' Information Office. Handbooks, 1888 ... Maps, 8vo.	Sir R. W. Rawson
Mineral Statistics of the United Kingdom for 1891. [C-6657.] Maps, fol.	The Home Office
Mint. Twenty-Second Annual Report of the Deputy Master of the Mint, 1891. [C-6674.] 8vo.............	The Deputy Master of the Mint
Navigation and Shipping. Annual Statement for 1891. [C-6663.] 1892............................. Trade and Navigation. (Current Monthly Returns)	The Board of Trade
Great Britain. Agricultural Produce Statistics of Great Britain for 1891. Map, 8vo. [C-6617]	The Board of Agriculture.
England— Births, Deaths, and Causes of Death. Annual Summary of, in London and other Great Towns, 1891.... Births and Deaths in London, and in twenty-seven other Great Towns. (Current weekly returns) .... Quarterly Return of Marriages to Dec., 1891, Births and Deaths to Mar., 1892. No. 173	The Registrar General of England
British Museum, Catalogue of Printed Books. 8 parts, fol. 1892	The Trustees of the Museum
Medical Officer. Supplement to Twentieth Annual Report of Local Government Board, containing Report for 1890 of the. Plates, 8vo. [C-6461]	The Medical Officer
Mersey. Report on the present state of the navigation of the river, 1891. Map, 8vo.	Admiral Sir G. H. Richards, K.C.B.
BIRMINGHAM. Report on Health of, for 1891, and on ... Adulteration of articles of food and drink. Plan and diagram, 8vo.	The Medical Officer of Health
LIVERPOOL. Free Public Library, Museum, and Walker Art Gallery. Thirty-ninth Report of the Committee for 1891. 8vo...........................	The Librarian
Ireland— Births and Deaths in Dublin, and in fifteen of the principal Urban Sanitary Districts. (Current weekly returns)	The Registrar-General of Ireland

Donations.	By whom Presented.
(c) United Kingdom and its Divisions—*Contd.* **Ireland—*Contd.*** Quarterly Return of Marriages to Sept., Births and Deaths to Dec., 1891. No. 112	The Registrar-General of Ireland
DUBLIN. Metropolitan Police. Statistical Tables for 1891. Fol.	The Commissioner of Police
Scotland— Births, Deaths, and Marriages in the eight principal Towns. (Current weekly and monthly returns) .... Births, Deaths, and Marriages, Quarterly Return of, registered in the quarter ending 31st Mar., 1892 .... Births, Deaths, and Marriages. Supplement to monthly and quarterly returns of, in 1891; also Vaccination Returns relative to children born in 1890	The Registrar-General of Scotland
EDINBURGH. Accounts published in 1891. Fol.........	The City Chamberlain

(d) Authors, &c.

BADEN-POWELL (B. H.). The Land-Systems of British India, being a manual of the Land-Tenures and of the Systems of Land-Revenue Administration prevalent in the several provinces. 3 vols. 8vo. Maps. Oxford, 1892	The Clarendon Press
BARKER's Trade and Finance Annual, 1886-87. 2nd edition. Maps. 8vo. [1886].....................	Sir R. W. Rawson
BEGG (ALEXANDER). The great Canadian North-West ; its past history, present condition, and glorious prospects. 135 pp., 8vo. Montreal, 1881	
BENEDETTI (I. DE). Brevi Cenni intorno alla Legislazione per la protezione della proprieta industriale nei principali paesi del mondo. Norme e consigli agl' inventori e industriali italiani. 86 pp., 8vo. Roma, 1886	
BESOBRASOF (W.). Études sur l'Economie Nationale de la Russie. 3 vols. Plates, 8vo. St. Pétersbourg, 1883-86	
BOOTH (CHARLES). Pauperism ; a picture, and the endowment of old age, an argument. viii + 355 pp., 8vo. 1892	The Author
CARLYLE (J. E.). African Colonies and Colonization, with notices of recent annexations. 82 pp., maps, 8vo. Glasgow, 1885	Sir R. W. Rawson
CERNUSCHI (HENRI). Seven Pamphlets on Bimetallism. 8vo. 1878-87	The Author
CHADWICK (EDWIN). Evils of Disunity in Central and Local Administration, especially with relation to the metropolis, and also on the new centralisation for the people . . . 125 pp., 8vo. 1885	Sir R. W. Rawson
COGHLAN (T. A.). The Wealth of Australasia. 17 pp., 8vo. Sydney, 1891	The Author
COHN (GUSTAV). Die Arbeitszeit der englischen Eisenbahnbediensteten auf Grund der amtlichen Materialien erörtert. 31 pp., 8vo. Berlin, 1892	„

Donations—Contd.

Donations.	By whom Presented.
(d) **Authors, &c.**—*Contd.*	
COLLET (Miss CLARA E.). Prospects of Marriage for Women. 16 pp., 8vo. 1892	W. Whitaker, Esq.
COOPER (JOSEPH). Graduated Tables to Ordinary and Industrial Life Assurance. 4 parts. Farnworth, 1892	The Author
Dictionary of Political Economy. Edited by R. H. Inglis Palgrave. Part 2. Beeke-Chamberlayne. 8vo. 1892	The Editor
DRU (LEON) et (E.) LEVASSEUR. La Récolte de 1891 en Russie et l'Exposition française à Moscou. 56 pp., map, 8vo. Paris, 1892	M. E. Levasseur
FENTON (JAMES J.). An Australian Federal Debt. In slip. Melbourne, 1892	The Author
FOLGER (HERBERT). The Growth of Tariff Associations. 36 pp., diagrams, 8vo. 1892	"
GABELLI (ARISTIDE). Roma e i Romani. Terza edizione. 83 pp., 8vo. Roma, 1883	Sir R. W. Rawson
GIBSON (GEORGE). Wall Street. The utilities and ethics of speculation. The Stock Exchange as an economic factor. International finance. 39 pp., 8vo. 1891	The Author
GREY (Earl), K.G., &c. The Commercial Policy of the British Colonies and the McKinley Tariff. 79 pp., 8vo. 1892	Messrs. Macmillan & Co.
HAGUE (GEORGE). On the moral and metaphysical element in Statistics. 10 pp., 4to. [Ottawa.] 1891	The Author
HAZELL (WALTER) and HODGKIN (H.). The Australasian Colonies : Emigration and Colonisation. Report of Inquiries made by, during a visit to Australia, Tasmania, and New Zealand, Dec., 1886—April, 1887. 89 pp., 8vo. 1887	Sir R. W. Rawson
HOWELL (E. J.). Mexico : its progress and commercial possibilities. x + 203 pp. Map. 8vo. 1892	The Author
ISSAIEU (A. A.). Mauvaise récolte et famine en Russie. (In Russian.) 45 pp., 8vo. St. Petersburg, 1892.	"
JOHNSTON (R. M.). The Attack on the Credit of Australasia. 17 pp., 8vo. 1892	W. Whitaker, Esq.
JURASCHEK (DR. FRANZ VON.). Übersichten der Weltwirtschaft. Lieferung 5, 6. 12mo. Berlin, 1892	The Author
KRAL (DR. FRANZ). Geldwert und Preisbewegung im Deutschen Reiche, 1871-84, mit einer Einleitung über die Methode der statistischen Erhebung von Geldmenge und Geldbedarf. viii + 111 pp., 8vo. Jena, 1887	Sir R. W. Rawson
Levasseur (E.)— La Population Francaise. Tome iii (Livre 4, Lois de la Population et l'équilibre des nations). 569 pp., diagrams, la. 8vo. Paris, 1892. Superficie et Population: les Etats d'Europe. Division de la Terre en cinq parties du monde. 16 pp., 4to. Paris, 1892	The Author
LOUA (TOUSSAINT). La France Sociale et economique d'après les documents officials les plus récents. 119 pp., la. 8vo. Paris, 1888	Sir R. W. Rawson
McCLINTOCK (EMORY). On the effects of selection, an actuarial essay. 87 pp., 8vo. New York, 1892	The Institute of Actuaries
MARSHALL (ALFRED). Elements of Economics of Industry, being the first volume of Elements of Economics. xiv + 416 pp., 8vo. 1892	Messrs. Macmillan

Donations.	By whom Presented.
(d) Authors, &c.—*Contd.*	
MATHERS (EDWARD P.). The Gold Fields revisited, being further glimpses of the Gold Fields of South Africa. viii + xxvi + 352 pp. Maps. 8vo. Durban, 1887	
MAYR (G.) e (G. B.). SALVIONI. La Statistica e la Vita Sociale. Seconda Edizione. lxxxi + 589 pp. Maps and diagrams. 8vo. Torino, 1886	Sir R. W. Rawson
MAZZOLA (UGO). L'Assicurazione degli operai nella Scienza e nella Legislazione Germanica. viii + 432 pp. 8vo. Roma, 1886	
MENZIES (WILLIAM J.). America as a field for investment. 24 pp. Map. 8vo. Edinburgh, 1892	Messrs. Blackwood & Sons
MORSELLI (ENRICO). Critica e Riforma del Metodo in Antropologia fondate sulle leggi statistiche e biologiche dei valori seriali e sull' esperimento. 178 pp., la. 8vo. Roma, 1880	Sir R. W. Rawson
MOXON (THOMAS B.). Memorandum upon the Bimetallic Proposals submitted to the Manchester Chamber of Commerce. 27 pp., 8vo. Manchester, 1892	The Author
NIEROP (A. H. VAN) and (E.) BAAK. De Nederlandsche Naamlooze Vennootschappen. Jaargang 1891. Tiende Jaargang. lix + 422 pp., 8vo. Zwolle. [1892]............	The Authors
Ourém (Baron d')— Notice sur les Institutions de Prévoyance au Brésil. vi + 174 pp. 8vo. Pau, 1883 .... Etude sur la représentation proportionelle au Brésil. 84 pp. 8vo. Paris, 1887 .... Brésil. Notice générale sur les Sessions Parlementaires de 1888 et 1889. 2 parts. 8vo. Paris, 1890-91	J. S. Keltie, Esq.
PANTALEONI (MAFFEO). Teoria della Pressione tributaria e metodi per misurarla. Parte Prima, Teoria della Pressione Tributaria. 78 pp. 8vo. Roma, 1887	
PISANI (EMANUELE). La Statmografia (nuovo metodo di scritture per bilancio). Applicazione alle aziende pubbliche. 6 + xxiv + 93 pp. 8vo. Siracusa, 1886....	Sir R. W. Rawson
RASERI (E.). Materiali per l'Etnologia Italiana ... 206 pp. La. 8vo. Diagrams. Roma, 1879	
RAU (S.). L'Etat militaire des principales puissances étrangères au printemps de 1883. 3e edit. 527 pp. 8vo. Paris, 1883..	J. S. Keltie, Esq.
RECLUS (ELISÉE). Nouvelle Géographie universelle. La Terre et les hommes. Vol. xvi. Les Etats-Unis. Maps and plates. La. 8vo. Paris, 1892	The President, Dr. F. J. Mouat
STOLZE (F.) und (F. C.) ANDREAS. Die Handelsverhältnisse Persiens, mit besonderer Berücksichtigung der deutschen Interessen. 86 pp. Map, 4to. Gotha, 1885	J. S. Keltie, Esq.
STUART (C. A. VERRIJN). Een belangrijk feit op het gebied der Nederlandsche bevolkingsstatistiek. 32 pp., diagrams. 8vo. [Amsterdam.] 1892	The Author
SUFFLING (ERNEST R.). The Land of the Broads. Illustrations and map. 8vo. Stratford [1892]	Wm. Burt, Esq.
SUPAN (ALEXN.). Die Verschiebung der Bevölkerung in den industriellen Grossstaaten Westeuropas im letzten Jahrzehnt (1881-91). 8 pp. Maps. 4to. 1892........	The Author

Donations—Contd.

Donations.	By whom Presented.

(d) Authors, &c.—*Contd.*

SUTCLIFFE (JOHN). The Financial Crises of 1866 and 1890. 24 pp. 8vo. Manchester, 1892 .... } The Author

TOMMASI-CRUDELI (CORRADO). Il Clima di Roma. Conferenze fatte nella Primavera del 1885 ... Plates and maps. ix + 158 pp. 8vo. Roma, 1886 .... } Sir R. W. Rawson

VIRGILII (FILIPPO). Economia Politica. 17 pp. 4to. Milano, 1892 .... } The Author

(e) Societies, &c. (British).[*]

British Association. Report of the Sixty-first meeting of the Association held at Cardiff in August, 1891. Plates, 8vo. 1892 .... } The Association

British Economic Association. The Economic Journal. Vol. ii, No. 5. March, 1892. (Contents.) Relativity of Economic Doctrine: *Rev. W. Cunningham.* Notes on a recent Economic Treatise : *L. L. Price.* Geometrical methods of treating exchange-value, monopoly and rent: *H. Cunynghame.* Origin of the law of diminishing returns, 1813-15 : *E. Cannan.* Trusts in the United States: *J. Jenks.* Origin of the eight hours system at the Antipodes: *H. H. Champion.* Influence of opinion on Markets : *A. Ellis* .... } ,,

Economic Review. Vol. ii, No. 2. April, 1892. (Selection from Contents.) Pensions for the Aged: *Rev. W. M. Ede.* Economical administration of Law: *S. L. Holland.* Some results of the great Dock Strike : *Rev. J. G. Adderley.* Dialogue on Co-operation: *J. M. Ludlow.* 8vo. 1892· } The Publisher

Central Association for dealing with Distress caused by Mining Accidents. Report upon the re-insurance of the Fatal Accident Risks of Miners' Permanent Funds. By F. G. P. Neison and J. H. Schooling. 45 pp., 8vo. 1891 .... } F. G. P. Neison, Esq.

East India Association. Journal. Vol. xxiv, Nos. 2 and 3. 1892 .... } The Association

Friendly Society of Ironfounders. (Current Monthly Reports) .... } Sir R. W. Rawson

Great Eastern Railway. Official Guide to the. Maps and illustrations, 8vo. 1892..................... } W. Birt, Esq.

Institute of Actuaries. Journal. Jan. and April, 1892. 8vo. .... } The Institute

Institute of Bankers. Journal. March—June, 1892 .... The Institution

Institute of Brewing. Transactions. Vol. v, No. 4. March, 1892. Sixth Session, 1891-92. 8vo. .... } The Institute

Institute of Chartered Accountants in England and Wales. Charter of Incorporation, Bye-Laws, and List of Members. 12mo. 1892 .... } ,,

Institution of Civil Engineers. Minutes of Proceedings. Vol. cvii. (Contains "Sale of Water by Meter in Berlin: *W. Gill.*) Plates, 8vo. 1892 .... } The Institution

Institution of Mechanical Engineers. Proceedings. Feb., 1892. Plates, 8vo. .... } ,,

[*] Foreign and Colonial Societies will be found under the various Countries or Possessions to which they belong.

Donations—Contd.

Donations.	By whom Presented.
(e) Societies, &c. (British)—*Contd.*	
London Chamber of Commerce. Journal. April—May, 1892	The Chamber of Commerce
Manchester Literary and Philosophical Society. Memoirs and Proceedings. Fourth series. Vol. 5, No. 1. 1891-92. Plates, 8vo.	The Society
Peabody Donation Fund. 27th Annual Report of the Trustees for 1891. 4to.	J. Crouch, Esq.
Royal Agricultural Society. Journal. Third Series. Vol. iii, Part 1. Portrait, 8vo. 1892	The Society
Royal Asiatic Society. Journal. Jan. and April, 1892. Plates, 8vo.	„
Royal College of Physicians. List of the Fellows, Members, Extra-Licentiates, &c. 8vo. 1892	The College
Royal Geographical Society. Proceedings. April—June, 1892	The Society
Royal Institution of Great Britain. Proceedings. Vol. xiii, part 2, No. 85. Plates, 8vo. 1892. Also List of Members, 1891	The Institution
Royal Medical and Chirurgical Society. Medico-Chirurgical Transactions. Vol. lxxiv. Plates, 8vo. 1891	The Society
Royal National Life-Boat Institution. Annual Report, &c. 1892. 8vo.	The Institution
Royal United Service Institution. Journal. Mar.—May, 1892	„
Royal Society. Proceedings. Vol. 1, Nos. 305 and 306. 1892	The Society
Society of Arts. Journal. (Current numbers.) 1892	„
Surveyor's Institution. Transactions. Vol. xxiv. Parts 5—12. 1892	The Institution
Travelling Tax Abolition Committee. The Gazette of the. Vol. ii, Nos. 14—30. 2 parts, 8vo. 1884-92	The Committee
(f) Periodicals, &c. (British).[*]	
Accountant, The .... Current numbers	The Editor
Athenæum, The .... „	„
Bankers' Magazine, The......................... „	„
British Trade Journal, The .... „	„
Building Societies and Land Companies' Gazette, The .... „	„
Commercial World, The......................... „	„
Darkest Russia : A Journal of Persecution .... „	„
Economist, The .... „	„
Fireman, The .... „	„
Insurance and Banking Review, The .... „	„
„ Gazette .... „	„
„ Post, The .... „	„
„ Record, The .... „	„
Investors' Monthly Manual, The .... „	„
Iron and Coal Trades' Review, The .... „	„
Machinery Market, The......................... „	„

[*] Foreign and Colonial Periodicals will be found under the various Countries or Colonies in which they are issued.

Donations.		By whom Presented.
(f) Periodicals, &c. (British)—*Contd.*		
Nature .... Current numbers		The Editor
Policy-Holder, The	,,	,,
Review, The	,,	,,
Sanitary Record, The	,,	,,
Shipping World, The	,,	,,
Statist, The	,,	,,

Purchases.

Authors, &c.—

Cobb (Arthur S.). Banks' Cash Reserves. Threadneedle Street : a reply to "Lombard Street" (by the late Mr. Walter Bagehot). x + 179 pp., 8vo. 1891.

Leffingwell (Albert, M.D.). Illegitimacy and the influence of Seasons upon Conduct. Two studies in Demography. viii + 160 pp., map and diagrams, 8vo. 1892.

Noback (Friedrich). Münz-, Maass- und Gewichtsbuch. Das Geld-, Maass- und Gewichtswesen, die Wechsel- und Geldkurse, das Wechselrecht und die Usanzen. Zweite Auflage ... xii + 1234 pp., 8vo. Leipzig, 1879.

Smart (William). An Introduction to the Theory of Value on the lines of Menger, Wieser, and Böhm-Bawerk. viii + 88 pp., 8vo. 1891.

Soetbeer (Adolf)—
Litteraturnachweis über Geld und Münzwesen insbesondere über den Wahrungsstreit, 1871-91. iv + 322 pp., 8vo. Berlin, 1892.
Edelmetall-Produktion und Werthverhältniss zwischen Gold und Silber seit der Entdeckung Amerika's bis zur Gegenwart. Diagrams, 141 pp., 4to. Gotha, 1879.

Spender (J. A.). The State and Pensions in Old Age, with an introduction by A. H. D. Acland, M.P. xxvi + 165 pp., 8vo. 1892.

England. Royal Gardens, Kew. Bulletin of miscellaneous information. Jan.—April, 1892, with two Appendices. 8vo.

Germany. Vierteljahrschrift für Volkswirtschaft, Politik und Kulturgeschichte. Band i, Heft 2. Die Durchschnittsprofitrate auf Grundlage des Marx'schen Wertgesetzes : *J. Lehr.* Handwerk und Arbeit in geschichtlicher Betrachtung : *C. Meyer.* Die Volkswirtschaft seit Adam Smith : *F. C. Philippson.* Band ii, Hälfte 1. Zur Reform des preussischen Herrenhauses : *G. Siegel.*

Russia. St. Petersburger Kalender für 1892. 164 Jahrgang. 414 pp., map, 8vo. St. Petersburg, 1892.

Parliamentary Papers—

Corn Prices. (84.) 1892.
Deer Forests, Scotland. (452.) 1891.
Friendly Societies. Reports on, 1891.
Hours of Adult Labour in Colonies. (115.) 1892.
Labour. Reports on, in different countries. 1892.
Local Taxation Returns (England) for 1890-91.
Metropolitan Hospitals. Analysis of Evidence before Select Committee on, 1891.
Mines. Summaries of Reports on, for 1891.
Redemption of Tithe Rent Charge. Reports on. [6606.] 1892.
Tramways. Return relating to, 1891.

Vol. LV.]   [Part III.

JOURNAL

OF THE ROYAL STATISTICAL SOCIETY,

SEPTEMBER, 1892.

REPORT *of the* COUNCIL *for the* FINANCIAL YEAR *ended 31st December,*
1891, *and for the* SESSIONAL YEAR *ending 28th June,* 1892,
presented at the FIFTY-EIGHTH ANNUAL GENERAL MEETING *of
the* ROYAL STATISTICAL SOCIETY, *held at the Society's Rooms,*
9, *Adelphi Terrace, Strand, London, on the 28th of June,* 1892.

THE Council have the honour to submit their Fifty-eighth
Annual Report.

The roll of Fellows on the 31st December last as compared
with the average of the previous ten years was as follows—

Particulars.	1891.	Average for the previous Ten Years.
Number of Fellows on 31st December	1,019	939
Life Members included in the above	172	154
Number lost by death, withdrawal, or default	80	58
New Fellows elected	36	84

Since the 1st January last, 16 new Fellows were elected, and
the number at present on the list is 1,001.

Deaths during the past Year, June, 1891—*June,* 1892.

	Date of Election.
Aldam, William, J.P., D.L.........................	1841
Baker, George	1884
d Bourne, William, A.I.A.	1886
Bramwell, The Right Hon. Lord, F.R.S.	1886
c d p (4) Caird, The Rt. Hon. Sir James, K.C.B., F.R.S.	1857
c Campbell, Sir George, K.C.S.I., M.P., D.C.L.	1874

c Indicates those who had served on the Council.
d Indicates those who had been Donors to the Library.
p Indicates those who had contributed Papers, with the number.

Deaths during the past Year—Contd.

		Date of Election.
	Carpenter, Frederick	1886
	Cleveland, His Grace the Duke of, K.G.	1850
	Crompton-Roberts, C. H.	1880
	Goddard, Frederick R.	1877
d	Johnson, Edmund	1871
d	Knox, Hon. John Jay	1890
	Manwaring, George	1890
	Morton, James	1873
	Runtz, John	1879
	Smith, John Fisher	1879
c	Smith, The Right Hon. W. H., M.P.	1867
d	Solomon, Hon. Michael, C.M.G.	1884
	Webster, James Hume	1873
	Wells, W. Lewis	1873

c Indicates those who had served on the Council.
d Indicates those who had been Donors to the Library.

Of the above, the greatest loss to the Society was that of the Right Hon. Sir James Caird, one of its former Presidents, and a Trustee. His contributions[1] to our Transactions were devoted to the land question and to agriculture in their political, economical, and social relations, and are valuable land marks in the history of a subject of paramount importance to all civilised countries, and to our own in particular. It was in the collection and digest of information in this branch of economics that he exhibited the highest characteristics of a statistician—scrupulous accuracy, painstaking industry, and the strictest impartiality—which established for him a great reputation, and acquired for him an authority which he retained to the end of his life.

Since the writing of the above, intelligence has been received of the death of one of our honorary members, M. Keleti, of Buda Pesth, chief of the Royal Hungarian Statistical Bureau. He took an active part in the late International Statistical Congress, and presided over that held in the capital of Hungary in 1876, as well as over the last meeting of the Permanent Commission which was held in Paris in 1878. His work will be noticed at greater length hereafter.

The financial condition of the Society continues to be satisfactory, as exhibited in the accompanying table, in which the particulars are contained for the twenty-five years 1867-91 :—

[1] Two inaugural addresses, chiefly devoted to the land question, and two papers in agricultural statistics, dealing with that subject in a masterly manner.

Year.	Annual Subscriptions. £	Composi-tions. £	Journal Sales. £	Journal. £	Library. £	Year.
1867....	603	21	105	365	34	1867
'68....	622	21	109	293	17	'68
'69....	617	42	103	279	7	'69
1870....	670	21	112	314	15	1870
'71....	657	63	115	317	15	'71
'72....	739	189	141	318	6	'72
'73....	832	189	167	384	17	'73
'74....	918	252	140	461	40	'74
'75....	928	105	133	449	18	'75
'76....	1,054	168	159	524	75	'76
'77....	1,117	252	151	474	49	'77
'78....	1,197	294	169	580	32	'78
'79....	1,300	126	176	671	34	'79
1880....	1,317	273	202	573	80	1880
'81....	1,305	84	145	609	37	'81
'82....	1,291	189	227	553	60	'82
'83....	1,361	126	150	585	49	'83
'84....	1,447	294	207	645	38	'84
'85....	1,462	63	188	625	27	'85
'86....	1,583	231	180	735	32	'86
'87....	1,621	126	188	609	87	'87
'88....	1,686	334	171	711	59	'88
'89....	1,678	126	229	623	146	'89
1890....	1,764	84	155	567	68	1890
'91....	1,707	42	146	582	172	'91

a Includes purchase of Government stock.   b Includes sale of 1,000l. stock.   c Includes expense of moving to new premises.

d Includes Dr. Guy's legacy of 250l.   e Includes cost of Jubilee Volume.

f Includes cost of Catalogue and Index, and of Charter.   g Includes cost of part iv of Index to Journal.

h Includes Mrs. Lovegrove's legacy of 100l.   i Includes outlay for Guy Medal and for binding the "Times."

The losses by death and withdrawal during the past year, amounting to 80, were unusually heavy, and were not recouped by the number of new members joining. This has, however, in no way crippled the means of usefulness of the Society, as all sums necessary to maintain the institution in a state of efficiency, and to meet such extraordinary expenses as have arisen, particularly during the past year, have been found, and devoted to those purposes. For example, the drainage of the building was in an unsatisfactory and insanitary state, which had to be rectified chiefly at the expense of the Society, from the conditions of the lease, which has still a short time to run. A portion of the cost was borne by the landlord.

The cost of placing the Library in a satisfactory state was also abnormally heavy, as mentioned in the report of the last year. The termination of the tenure of our chief tenants has deprived us of a small source of income, which it is not intended to replace, as the accommodation thus released is needed for our own wants.

A brief estimate of receipts and expenditure for the current year is submitted for the first time, to indicate the resources available for the continuance of our work, due provision being made for all such outlay as is likely, in ordinary circumstances, to arise. It includes the increase of salaries, the cost of editing the Journal, the outlay for medals, the payment for works not completed at the end of the past year, with a fair margin for contingencies.

Estimate of Receipts and Payments in 1892.

Receipts.	£	Payments.	£
		Ordinary Expenditure—	
		Rent (less Sublet)	250
Dividends	78	Rates and Taxes	45
		Fire, Lights, and Water........	55
		Furniture and Repairs	15
		Salaries, &c.	533
Subscriptions	1,625	Journal	570
		Ordinary Meeting Expenses...	32
		Advertising	60
Compositions	42	Postage	85
		Stationery and Printing	75
		Library	100
Journal Sales	160	Medals	25
		Incidental Expenses..............	70
			1,915
Advertisements in Journal	20	Extraordinary Expenditure—	
		Drainage Repairs	111
Total	1,925	Completion of Binding "Times" .... }	35
Balance from 1891	412		
			2,061
			276
	2,337		2,337

The Society re-assembled in November, and the papers read and the members elected at each of the monthly meetings have been as follows :—

SESSION 1891-92.

First Ordinary Meeting, Tuesday, 17*th November,* 1891.

The President, DR. FREDERIC J. MOUAT, F.R.C.S., LL.D., in the Chair.

The following were elected Fellows :—

Joseph Cooper.	Rev. William Douglas Morrison.
William Denne.	Fredk. William Forbes Ross, M.B., C.M.
James Lawrence.	Pandit Har Bilas Sarda, B.A., M.R.A.S.
Robert George Maxwell.	David F. Schloss.

The President delivered an Inaugural Address.

A cordial vote of thanks to the President for his Address was moved by Sir Rawson W. Rawson, seconded by Mr. F. Hendriks, supported by Mr. F. F. Guy, and carried unanimously.

Second Ordinary Meeting, Tuesday, 15*th December,* 1891.

The President in the Chair.

The following were elected Fellows :—

Oscar Berry.	Arthur Wellesley Harris, M.R.C.S., L.S.A., D.P.H.
Daniel Biddle, M.R.C.S., L.S.A., &c.	John Oates, F.S.A.A.
Harold A. Stuart.	

Mr. Charles Booth read a Paper on "Enumeration and Classi-"fication of Paupers, and State Pensions for the Aged."

In the discussion which followed, the undermentioned took part: —Mr. W. Vallance, Mr. C. S. Loch, The Right Hon. Leonard Courtney, M.P., and Professor Alfred Marshall. As the discussion was not completed, on the motion of Mr. Stephen Bourne, seconded by Sir Rawson W. Rawson, it was adjourned to the following Tuesday.

Adjourned Meeting, Tuesday, 22*nd December,* 1891.

The President in the Chair.

The Discussion on Mr. Booth's Paper was resumed by Mr. Stephen Bourne, and continued by Canon Blackley, Mr. T.

Fatkin, Mr. J. H. Allen, Dr. W. Ogle, Mr. W. M. Acworth, Mr. F. Hendriks, Mr. E. R. Speirs, Mr. John Lloyd, Mr. M. N. Adler, and Mr. Charles Booth in reply.

On account of the lamented death of His Royal Highness the Duke of Clarence and Avondale, the Third Ordinary Meeting, fixed for the 19th January, 1892, was postponed, and a letter of condolence was addressed to H.R.H. the Prince of Wales, the Honorary President of the Society, which was graciously acknowledged.

Fourth Ordinary Meeting, Tuesday, 16th *February,* 1892.

The President in the Chair.

The following were elected Fellows:—

George Washington Bacon, F.R.G.S.	Hubert Richardson.
William Henry Hey.	Francis Hansard Rivington.
Charles Henry Johnson, B.A.	Charles Samuel.

Mr. L. L. Price read a Paper on "The Recent Depression in "Agriculture as Shown in the Accounts of an Oxford College, "1876-90."

Dr. J. C. Steele read a Paper on ".The Agricultural Depression, "and its Effects upon a Leading London Hospital."

In the discussion which followed, the undermentioned took part:—Mr. F. B. Garnett, Mr. Clare S. Read, Mr. W. E. Bear, Mr. A. E. Bateman, Mr. J. R. Breckon, Dr. W. Cunningham, Mr. S. B. L. Druce, Mr. D. Basden, and Sir Rawson W. Rawson.

Fifth Ordinary Meeting, Tuesday, 15th *March,* 1892.

The President in the Chair.

The following were elected Fellows:—

Frederick William Bell.	William Lawson Dash, J.P.
Arthur Trobridge.	

Mr. John Glover read a Paper on "Tonnage Statistics of the "Decade 1880-90."

In the discussion which followed, the undermentioned took part:—Sir Rawson W. Rawson, Colonel Hill, M.P., Mr. J. Clark

Hall, Sir Edward Harland, M.P., Mr. J. S. Jeans, Mr. Stephen Bourne, Mr. A. E. Bateman, Mr. G. G. Chisholm, and Mr. G. J. Swanston, C.B.

Sixth Ordinary Meeting, Tuesday, 27th April, 1892.

The President in the Chair.

The undermentioned were elected Fellows:—

Robert A. Hadfield.	James Carlisle McCleery.
Stanley Anderton Latham.	Westley Richards, J.P.

Charles Marshall Wates.

Mr. R. Henry Rew read a paper on "An Inquiry into the "Statistics of the Production and Consumption of Milk and Milk "Products in Great Britain."

In the discussion which followed, the undermentioned took part:—Mr. George Barham, Mr. S. B. L. Druce, Mr. H. Moncrieff Paul, Mr. E. G. Easton, Mr. H. Faber, Sir Rawson W. Rawson, Mr. C. W. Gray, M.P., Mr. T. J. Pittar, Major P. G. Craigie, Mr. A. E. Bateman, and Mr. J. H. Sherwin.

Seventh Ordinary Meeting, Tuesday, 17th May, 1892.

The President in the Chair.

The undermentioned were elected Fellows:—

Harald Faber.	Hans George Leslie Shand.

Mr. J. S. Jeans read a paper on "The Recent Movement of "Labour in Different Countries in Reference to Wages, Hours of "Work, and Efficiency."

In the discussion that followed, the undermentioned took part: Sir Charles Dilke, Mr. John Burnett, Mr. G. Howell, Mr. W. H. Hey, Mr. D. F. Schloss, Sir R. W. Rawson, Mr. F. J. Vincent, Mr. E. Trow, and Dr. F. J. Mouat.

The occurrences of the past year which are deemed deserving of permanent record, are noted in the brief narrative which follows, and are intended to show the present state and future prospects of the Society.

The arrangements regarding the purchase of books for the library, the placing of the valuable file of the "Times" in a thoroughly satisfactory condition for study and reference, and the improvement of the accommodation available for investigations in statistical and collateral subjects, briefly referred to in the report of the Session of 1890-91, have all been carried into effect; and it is hoped will be largely utilised both by the Fellows of the Society, and by such members of the legislature and other properly accredited persons as are interested in such matters. Every aid to facilitate such researches will be, and is indeed already, afforded by the present competent permanent staff of the Society, who are frequently referred to, and whose thorough practical knowledge of the unrivalled resources of our library will, it is hoped and believed, bring additional members to our ranks, when its intrinsic value is fully realised.

The rearrangement of the permanent salaried staff has fully answered the expected increase in the efficiency of the work assigned to it, and all the changes mentioned above have been accomplished within the limits of the current income of the Society. Thus, while that income has been somewhat diminished by a decrease in the number of Fellows, and the expenditure was augmented by the permanent improvements above referred to, a small reduction of expenditure has been secured by some of the literary work formerly paid for, having been performed by the paid executive as a portion of their current duties. It has been deemed inexpedient to increase the unexpended balance at the end of the session by unimportant economies, so long as any of the purposes for which the Society exists are unfulfilled, and the means of utilising its resources are not curtailed in a manner that can be of no permanent use.

The question of the increase of subscriptions by additions to the ranks of the Society has not been lost sight of, and among other measures intended to attain that end has been the institution of the Guy medal referred to in last year's report. This medal has been executed by Mr. Harry Bates, A.R.A., and is a work of art of considerable merit, for which the thanks of the Council were communicated to the artist. The statutes appended to this report show the nature and purposes of the award, with the rules regulating it, and the Council have much satisfaction in announcing the first fruit of a measure which it is believed will be of great advantage hereafter, to the Society and to statistical science. The Guy gold medal has been awarded to Mr. Charles Booth, for his eminently valuable, original, and prolonged researches upon one of the most difficult problems of social science —the labour and life of the poor of this vast metropolis, and the best means of raising their condition, without the violation of the economic laws underlying all forms of charity and beneficence in their influence on the well-being, conduct, and character of the poor.

The competition for the Howard medal, which has been in abeyance for the last few years, has been revived, and the subject selected for the next essay is upon a question which has attracted much attention for some years past, and is well deserving of careful study, that of infant life and its perils and protection. Infant life is believed to be exposed to many avoidable risks which may be mitigated or removed by a knowledge of the causes upon which they depend, regarding which much more accurate information is required than is now possessed. The rules for the competition are also contained in the Appendix to this report. The basis of the subjects considered suitable for examination from a statistical standpoint has been considerably extended, and is no longer restricted to such topics as are immediately connected with the life and labours of John Howard.

Not the least noteworthy of the incidents of the past year has been the resignation of the office of Editor of the *Journal* of the Society by Dr. Robert Giffen, after performing gratuitously, with signal advantage to statistical science and to the Society, the responsible and difficult duties of that office. Dr. Giffen has occupied the post for sixteen years, and it is the opinion of the Council that very much of the high position occupied by the Society in public estimation at home and abroad is due to the ability, eminence as a statistician, and literary excellence of the work of the late Editor.

To the vacant office, on the recommendation of Dr. Giffen, who has had experience of his work generally and of his special capacity for the work of Sub-Editor, the Council have appointed Mr. Reginald Hooker, who has been since March, 1891, the Assistant Secretary of the Society. The salary formerly attached to the post has been renewed in Mr. Hooker's case, and a small consultative committee has been appointed to aid him with advice when he may need it, without fettering his action or diminishing his personal responsibility and authority.

" As the report of the Demographic Section of the recent congress held in London has not yet been published, it cannot be reviewed by the Society.

The Society was well represented at the meetings of the International Statistical Institute held in Vienna in September last.

The cordial thanks of the Council have been tendered, on behalf of the Society, to the Auditors for their honorary services in auditing the Treasurer's accounts for the past year.

Permission to hold the Ordinary Meetings of the Society in the Theatre of the Museum of Practical Geology, in Jermyn Street, has been continued through the courtesy of the Education Department, and the Council have again conveyed to the Lords of the Committee of Council on Education their thanks for the accommodation thus afforded.

The Council, in conclusion, venture to hope that their action in all the matters above noted will meet with the approval of the Fellows and show that no effort has been spared to maintain the reputation and continue the usefulness of the Society. Whilst the diminution in the number of new members is a matter of regret as diminishing its resources, much of it is due to the fluctuations naturally incident to an old institution, and some has probably been caused by the establishment of other associations performing part of the same work, a contingency to which all branches of modern science are liable, as the boundaries of knowledge extend, and as each department needs subdivision for more effective treatment. Another probable rival is the multiplication of scientific journals appearing at short periods, and at small cost, which doubtless tempt workers in every department of research to publish the results of their labours as quickly as possible, to prevent their being anticipated by others in the rapid movements of research in our times. The more rapid the advance, and the more complex the problems pressing for solution, the more need of the application of the numerical method to harmonise the results, and to eliminate the errors to which all scientific inquiries are liable; hence there is no ground for apprehension as to the future of statistics, or of the institutions devoted to their pursuit.

The following list of Fellows proposed as President, Council, and Officers of the Society for the Session 1892-93 is submitted for the consideration of the meeting :—

COUNCIL AND OFFICERS FOR 1892-93.

PRESIDENT.

CHARLES BOOTH.

COUNCIL.

Arthur H. Bailey, F.I.A.	John Scott Keltie, F.R.G.S.
Alfred Edmund Bateman, C.M.G.	Charles Malcolm Kennedy, C.B.
Henry R. Beeton.	Robert Lawson, LL.D.
Stephen Bourne.	*C. S. Loch, B.A.
*J. Oldfield Chadwick, F.R.G.S.	John Biddulph Martin, M.A.
Hyde Clarke.	Richard Biddulph Martin, M.A.
Major Patrick George Craigie.	Francis G. P. Neison, F.I.A.
Rev. Wm. Cunningham, M.A., D.D.	William Ogle, M.A., M.D., F.R.C.P.
Prof. F. Y. Edgeworth, M.A., D.C.L.	R. H. Inglis Palgrave, F.R.S.
Thomas Henry Elliott.	*Sir Wm. C. Plowden, K.C.S.I., M.P.
*The Rt. Hon. Visct. Grimston, M.P.	Sir Francis Sharp Powell, Bart., M.P.
*Rowland Hamilton.	*Richard Price-Williams, M.Inst.C.E.
Frederick Hendriks, F.I.A.	*L. L. Price, M.A.
Noel A. Humphreys.	John Rae.
Frederick Halsey Janson, F.L.S.	Ernest G. Ravenstein, F.R.G.S.

Those marked * are new Members of Council.

TREASURER.

Richard Biddulph Martin, M.A.

HONORARY SECRETARIES.

John Biddulph Martin, M.A. | Alfred Edmund Bateman, C.M.G.
Major Patrick George Craigie.

FOREIGN HONORARY SECRETARY.

John Biddulph Martin, M.A.

The abstract of receipts and payments, and the balance sheet of assets and liabilities on 31st December, 1891, are subjoined, together with the report of the Auditors on the accounts for the year 1891 :—

(I.)—ABSTRACT *of* RECEIPTS *and* PAYMENTS *for the* YEAR *ending* 31st DECEMBER, 1891.

RECEIPTS.		£	s.	d.	PAYMENTS.			£	s.	d.
Balance in Bank, 31st December, 1889 ... } £256 17 6					Rent £316 17 6					
					Less sublet ...... 123 15 –					
								193	2	6
Balance of Petty Cash .		30	17	8	Rates and Taxes			57	19	8
„ Postage Account }	4 13 5				Fire, Lights, and Water			53	6	4
					Repairs, Furniture, &c...............			67	18	8
		292	8	2	Salaries, Wages, and Pension ...			477	5	11
Dividends on 2,900*l.* Consols Stock		77	15	4	Journal, Printing...... £522 19 6					
					„ Annual Index 5 5 –					
Subscriptions received:—					„ Shorthand Reporters } 18 18 –					
58 Arrears .... £121 16 –					„ Literary Services } 35 2 –					
740 for the year 1891 .... } 1,554 – –								582	4	6
15 in Advance ...... 31 10 –					Ordinary Meeting Expenses			30	15	10
—		1,707	6	–	Advertising			58	6	11
813					Postage and delivery of Journals..			85	4	6
					Stationery and Sundry Printing...			64	5	6¼
					Library.....................................			171	15	6
					Incidental Expenses			49	8	2¼
								1,891	14	1
2 Compositions............................		42	–	–	Mr. H. Bates, A.R.A., for the Guy Medal ....}			65	–	–
Journal Sales		145	10	10				1,956	14	1
Advertisements in Journal		8	13	6	Balance per Bank Book ....} £371 17 6					
		2,268	13	10	Balance of Petty Cash 35 – 8					
Mrs. Lovegrove's Legacy		100	–	–	„ Postage ... 5 1 7					
								411	19	9
Total		£2,568	13	10	Total £2,368 13 10					

(Signed)   " A. H. BAILEY,

" J. O. CHADWICK, F.C.A., } *Auditors.*"

" *25th February,* 1892.   " SAM. DYER NIX, F.C.A., }

(II.)—BALANCE SHEET *of* ASSETS *and* LIABILITIES, *on* 31*st* DECEMBER, 1891.

LIABILITIES.	£ s. d.	£ s. d.
Harrison and Sons—		
For Journal	159 9 6	
„ Printing and Stationery	26 12 3	
Street Bros., for Advertisements	6 8 6	
Taxes to April, 1892 ...	38 19 3	
Miscellaneous	40 9 4	
		266 13 10
15 Annual Subscriptions received in advance		31 10 -
		298 3 10
Balance in favour of the Society* ..		6,702 13 4
		£7,000 17 2

ASSETS.	£ s.
Cash Balances	411 19
2,900*l.* New 2¾ per cent. Consols costing	2,760 14
Property: (Estimated Value of)—	
Books in Library......... £1,500	
Journals in Stock 1,500	
Pictures, Furniture, and Fixtures......... 500	
	3,500 -
Lease of Premises (cost) 500	
Less amount written off for time expired (seven years) 280	
	220 -
Arrears of Subscriptions recoverable (say)	88 4
Sundry Debtors.....................	19 19

(Signed)   " A. H. BAILEY,

" J. O. CHADWICK, F.C.A., ⎱ *Auditors.*"

" 25*th February*, 1892.   " SAM. DYER NIX, F.C.A., ⎰

(III.)—BUILDING FUND (ESTABLISHED 10*th July*, 1873), BALANCE SHEET, *on* 31*st* DECEMBER, 1891.

LIABILITIES.	£ s. d.
Amount of Fund Invested from last Account	284 5 6
Dividends received during 1891......	7 12 8
	£241 18 2

ASSETS.	£
Invested as per last Account in Metropolitan Consolidated 3½ per Cent. Stock, in the name of the Treasurer, Richard B. Martin, Esq.—	

	Stock.	Cost.
	£228 10 9	284 5
Balance since invested		7 12

(Signed)   " A. H. BAILEY,

" J. O. CHADWICK, F.C.A., ⎱ *Auditors.*'

" 25*th February*, 1892.   " SAM. DYER NIX, F.C.A., ⎰

"Report of the Auditors for 1891.

"*The Auditors appointed to examine the Treasurer's Accounts of the Society for the Year* 1891,

"Report:—

"*That they have compared the Entries in the Books with the several Vouchers for the same, from the 1st January to the 31st December,* 1891, *and find them correct, showing the Receipts (including a Balance of* 292*l.* 8*s.* 2*d., from* 1890) *to have been* 2,368*l.* 13*s.* 10*d., and the Payments* 1,956*l.* 14*s.* 1*d., leaving a Balance in favour of the Society of* 411*l.* 19*s.* 9*d. at the 31st December,* 1891.

"*They have also had laid before them an Estimate of the Assets and Liabilities of the Society at the same date, the former amounting to* 7,000*l.* 17*s.* 2*d., and the latter to* 298*l.* 3*s.* 10*d., leaving a Balance in favour of the Society of* 6,702*l.* 13*s.* 4*d., exclusive of the present value of the absolute Reversionary Interest bequeathed to the Society by the late Dr. Guy.*

"*The amount standing to the credit of the Building Fund at the end of the year* 1891, *was* 241*l.* 18*s.* 2*d., of which* 234*l.* 5*s.* 6*d. was invested in* 223*l.* 10*s.* 9*d. Metropolitan Three and a Half per Cent. Stock, in the name of the Treasurer, R. B. Martin, Esq., thus leaving a balance of* 7*l.* 12*s.* 8*d. since invested.*

"*They have verified the Investments of the Society's General Funds and Building Fund, and also the Banker's Balance, all which were found correct.*

"*They further find that at the end of the year* 1890 *the number of Fellows on the list was* 1,063, *which number was diminished in the course of the year to the extent of* 80, *by Deaths, Resignations, and Defaulters, and that* 36 *new Fellows were elected, leaving on the list on the 31st December,* 1891, *one thousand and nineteen* (1,019) *Fellows of the Society.*

(Signed) "A. H. Bailey,
"J. O. Chadwick, F.C.A., } *Auditors.*"
"Sam. Dyer Nix, F.C.A.,

"*25th February,* 1892.

APPENDIX.

Rules for the Award of "The Guy Medal."

1. The Guy Medal of the Royal Statistical Society, founded in honour of the distinguished statistician whose name it bears, is intended to encourage the cultivation of statistics in their strictly scientific aspects, as well as to promote the application of numbers to the solution of the important problems in all the relations of life in which the numerical method can be employed, with a view as far as possible to determine the laws which regulate them.

2. The medal may be of gold, silver, or bronze; the first to be granted for work of a high character founded upon original research; the two latter for work founded on existing data. In any case the results to be first given to the world through this Society.

3. There shall be no obligation to award either a gold, silver, or bronze medal annually; but each year at the ordinary monthly meeting of the Council in April, the members shall be invited to submit the names of any authors of papers read before the Society or of work done in its interest, during the current or immediately preceding session, whom they may consider entitled to a medal of either class; that any such proposals, with the grounds on which they are made, shall be circulated to each member of Council at least a week before the Council meeting in May, when all proposals shall be considered and decided by resolution of a majority of at least two-thirds of the members then present, or the final consideration and determination may be adjourned, if necessary, until the Council meeting in June.

4. A medal may be awarded to others than Fellows of the Society.

5. The Council shall also have power at any time to grant a medal to anyone deemed worthy of such distinction by reason of special and extraordinary services to statistical science, although not strictly falling within the foregoing regulations, provided that the proposal for such an award shall in the first instance be favourably considered by the Executive Committee, and recommended by them to the Council; that notice of the proposal be placed upon the agenda for the Council meeting, and that the award shall be made by the vote of a majority of not less than two-thirds of the members present.

Rules for the Award of "The Howard Medal."

1. That a medal, to be called "The Howard Medal," shall be presented in the name of the President, Council, and Fellows of

the Royal Statistical Society, to the author of the best essay on some subject in "social statistics," selected by the Council.

2. That the medal be a bronze medal, contained in a case, having on one side a portrait of John Howard, on the other a wheatsheaf, with suitable inscription.

3. That the subject of the essay shall be selected by the Council at their ordinary meeting in May, and at the anniversary meeting of the Society the title of the said essay shall be formally announced.

4. That the essays be sent to the Council of the Royal Statistical Society, 9, Adelphi Terrace, Strand, W.C., London, on or before 30th June of the year following the announcement of the subject of the essay. Each essay to bear a motto, and to be accompanied by a sealed letter, marked with the like motto, and containing the name and address of the author; such letter not to be opened, except in the case of the successful essay.

5. That no essay exceed in length 150 pages of the *Journal of the Royal Statistical Society.*

6. That the Council shall, if they see fit, cause the successful essay, or an abridgment thereof, to be read at a meeting of the Royal Statistical Society, and shall have the right of publishing the essay in their *Journal* one month before its appearance in any separate independent form; this right of publication to continue till three months after the award of the prize.

7. That the Executive Committee for the time being, or any special committee the Council may appoint, in June of the year of competition, shall examine the essays, and report their decision to the Council at their meeting next preceding the ordinary meeting held in November of each year.

8. That the President shall place the medal in the hands of the successful candidate, at the conclusion of his annual address, at the ordinary meeting in November, when he shall also re-announce the subject of the prize essay for the following year.

9. Competition for this medal shall not be limited to the Fellows of the Royal Statistical Society, but shall be open to any competitor, providing the essay be written in the English language.

10. That the Council shall not award the prize except to the author of an essay, in their opinion, of a sufficient standard of merit; and that no essay shall be deemed to be of sufficient merit that does not set forth the facts with which it deals—in part, at least, in the language of figures and tables, and that distinct references be made to such authorities as may be quoted or referred to.

PROCEEDINGS *of the* FIFTY-EIGHTH ANNUAL GENERAL MEETING.

The PRESIDENT, DR. F. J. MOUAT, LL.D., *in the Chair.*

MR. JOHN B. MARTIN (Hon. Secretary) read the circular convening the meeting.

The minutes of the last ordinary meeting were read and confirmed.

The Report of the Council was taken as read.

The PRESIDENT said he might mention, as it was not contained in the report, that the meeting in June was not held because Mr. Baines, although he had arrived in England, had not obtained all the information necessary for the paper, and could only have given it in an imperfect form. It was therefore thought better to postpone it. The competition for the Howard medal, which had been in abeyance for the last few years, had been revived, and the subject for the next essay was the State of Infant Life and its Perils and Protection. Infant life was believed to be exposed to many avoidable risks, which might be mitigated or removed by a knowledge of the causes on which they depended, with regard to which much more accurate information was required than was at present obtainable. The rules had been slightly altered, and they were therefore reprinted with the regulations for the Guy medal in the Appendix to the report in order that they might receive the formal sanction of the meeting. Not the least noteworthy incident of the past year was the resignation of the office of editor of the *Journal* by Dr. Robert Giffen, after holding it for eighteen years with a degree of efficiency which had been of great advantage to the Society, and of considerable benefit in extending a knowledge of the work of the Society amongst other nations. The Council had recorded their opinion of the very high position which the Society had obtained in public estimation owing to the great ability and eminence as a statistician and the literary excellence of the work of the editor. The vacant office had been filled by the appointment of the Assistant Secretary, Mr. Hooker, who had shown his capacity for the work by the manner in which he had performed the duties of sub-editor during the last year. He did not know that it was necessary to make any further remarks in continuation or addition to those contained in the report. It covered the whole ground, and showed where the weak points were. As they were losing some of their members, there might be some defect in the mode of election which probably might be discovered and remedied by his successor and those who would act with him during the ensuing year, but he did not consider the Society was at all in an unsatisfactory state, because a considerable number of those who had retired were gentlemen who had taken no active part in the proceedings, or exhibited any interest in the work of the Society. He concluded by moving that the Report of the Council, the

Abstract of Receipts and Payments, the Balance Sheet of Assets and Liabilities, and the Report of the Auditors for 1891 be adopted, entered on the minutes, and printed in the Journal.

Mr. F. HENDRIKS seconded the motion. He considered the report most satisfactory, and was sure that it would be so considered by the Fellows at large. Very much was due to the pilot who had steered their vessel during the past year.

Mr. ELLIOTT said before the resolution was put he should like to call attention to two points which he thought might be usefully borne in mind in the coming year, especially by the younger members. The first point noticed in the report was that the number of new members joining during the year was the smallest number added to the Society's roll for the last twenty-two years. That was a distinctly unsatisfactory feature. They could not help members leaving, but they might do something to induce new members to join. In the second place he noticed that the receipts from the sale of the Journal were lower than they had been for the last eleven years, which was again a distinctly unsatisfactory feature. It could not arise from the fact of the Journal being less worth reading than it was eleven years ago, for it was larger and contained as much and more good matter than it did then. It might possibly be due to some fault on the part of the Society in bringing the Journal under the notice of the book-buying public, and they might not perhaps be quite keeping up with the times in that respect. He felt conscious that he was as responsible as anybody else for these defects, but thought it might be useful to call attention to the matter.

The resolution was then put and carried unanimously.

The PRESIDENT said the next formal business was to approve the appointment by the Council of its Trustees. The death of Sir James Caird rendered it necessary to appoint a third, and the appointment by the Council required the sanction of the general meeting. He would therefore move "that this meeting approves of the proposed appointment by the Council of James Heywood, Esq., the Right Hon. Sir John Lubbock, Bart., and John Biddulph Martin, Esq., to be Trustees of the real and personal property of the Society, with the exception of the leasehold house in which its business is carried on, which is to be conveyed to the Society."

Mr. HYDE CLARKE said he thought it was desirable not to forget that they were now an incorporated Society, and that it was very questionable whether it was necessary to have trustees at all, or whether it would not be better to place the funds in the name of the Society.

The PRESIDENT said he scarcely thought that could be done now, because the same subject could not be discussed again in the same session in which it had once been determined and decided by the Council. This question therefore must be deferred, or it might be brought forward again next year. He would therefore put the resolution, when, if it were carried, the matter would be handed over to the new Council for them to take steps to carry it into legal effect.

The resolution was then put and carried unanimously.

The PRESIDENT said he was happy to inform the meeting that the proposed list of Council and Officers for the ensuing session was unanimously adopted. He begged to propose that the thanks of the meeting be given to the Scrutineers.

Carried unanimously.

The PRESIDENT then formally announced the subject of the essay for the Howard Medal for 1893, viz., "Perils and Protection of Infant Life, with statistical illustrations where practicable."

Mr. R. HAMILTON then proposed "that a cordial vote of thanks be awarded to the President, Council, and Officers for their services during the past session." He felt that not only would a long speech on such a matter be rather tiresome, but it would be like gilding refined gold to attempt to add anything with regard to the conspicuous merits of the President and officers during the past year.

Mr. J. OLDFIELD CHADWICK had much pleasure in seconding the resolution, and would not add anything to it. The record of their meetings was quite sufficient speech to all the Fellows of the Society.

The resolution was put and carried unanimously.

The PRESIDENT said so far as he was personally concerned he returned his most sincere thanks for the honour. They had passed through an exceptional year in many respects, having undergone a considerable change in the manner of procedure, &c. With regard to the suggestions of Mr. Elliott, no doubt some means should be adopted which he hoped would be more successful than they had been in the past for attracting new members and getting a sufficient supply of papers and matters for discussion. This had been a chronic complaint for many years which now seemed to have culminated, and it would be very necessary to take some steps in the matter. The income and expenditure were now very nearly equal, and therefore if any unexpected emergency arose there would scarcely be funds enough to carry on with, whereas if they could secure a permanent roll of 1,000 members, it would enable the Society to undertake all the work it contemplated, unless any very unforeseen contingency arose. He was quite sure the other officers and Council were equally grateful to the Fellows for their appreciation of what they had been able to do during the past year. He was quite certain that in the gentleman now elected to the office he had had the honour to hold, they had chosen one far more capable than he could pretend to be of conducting the proceedings with a success which he hoped would mark his reign.

State Experiments *in* New Zealand.

By Sir Robert Stout, K.C.M.G.

The Colony of New Zealand has made several experiments in the art of government that may be of interest to older countries. The word " socialism " has been used in connection with them, but this term has so many varied and even opposite meanings that it were unwise to characterise such experiments by any special term. Indeed Professor Adams of the Cornell University has declared that it is an intellectual blunder to say that all extensions of the functions of government are in the direction of socialism. M. Leroy-Beaulieu on the contrary asserts that the term socialism is properly applied to an extension of the State functions. Whatever term may however be applied to the State experiments I am about to mention, the result cannot fail to be interesting. In these days when social questions have become so absorbing, the different roads that seem to have been travelled—and that are still journeyed over—in the democracies of the United States of America and in the southern colonies of Britain are worthy of note. For in the Australasian colonies many things are undertaken by the government which in the United States are left to private enterprise, and indeed one of the most noticeable features in the governments of these colonies is the extent to which they undertake or interfere with business ventures. And, judging by the utterances of many leading Americans on the subject, one is apt to conclude that the results of such non-interference have been far from satisfactory, for we hear a great deal about "millionnaires," "mono-"polies," and "trusts" and even of corruption and "rings." both in State legislatures and in municipal corporations, all of which may be said to be unknown amongst us. We have however, in our heavy public debts, burdens to carry, from which many of the States of the Union are free; and the communities of these colonies may have perhaps less elasticity and resource than their American *confrères*. To enable us to determine which is the best course for the democracy to pursue, many things would require to be taken into consideration. But it is not my purpose, in this paper, to attempt this, nor even to defend the system we have adopted in New Zealand. My design is the more modest one of stating the facts and indicating some of the more immediate and direct consequences, premising that the ultimate and indirect results cannot perhaps yet be seen nor estimated. I have mentioned results, but, after all, results very rarely come up to the expectations of those who are responsible for them. In democracies as in other States these are often disappointing. If, for example, one were to write down the hopes of those who struggled for reform in the early years of this century, and to picture the future that the chartists dreamed of, and then to write down the results of the extension of the franchise, of free government, of the abolition of privileges, would it not be seen that the millennium of the reformers is still in the far distance? Free government has been attained, but it has not brought in its train the benefits that were expected. Human nature is not easily changed; and the passing of statutes has not always led to social advancement. This consideration may deaden the enthusiasm of the impatient radical by showing that reforms can only come slowly, and that their consequences may not appear for years after they have been achieved, but still who would now say that the English Reform Bills were wrongly conceived or improperly enacted? In the colonies we are pioneers, but as the great American poet has said—

"We take up the task eternal and the burden and the lesson."

The State in New Zealand has undertaken the following functions:—

(1.) Free primary education, with assistance to secondary and higher education in the form of land grants, &c., &c.
(2.) A telephone system.
(3.) Telegraphs in addition to the usual postal arrangements.
(4.) Railways.
(5.) Water races for irrigation and for mining.
(6.) Life insurance and annuities.
(7.) Trusteeship and administration of property.
(8.) Guaranteeing of titles to land.
(9.) Labour bureaux.
(10.) Co-operative contracting.
(11.) Advisory functions to farmers, &c., &c.

The State does much more in New Zealand than all these things. There are the usual administrative functions performed by the New Zealand government which other governments perform, such as defence, police, lighthouses, harbours, beacons, justice, &c., &c. I have preferred to point out some things that are usually not performed by a general municipal government. There has been, it will be seen, a considerable extension of State functions, and this extension of functions has not been confined to what may be termed the general government of the colony. It extends also to municipalities. In most towns that have been incorporated, the municipality owns both the gas and the water-works.   The tramways pay a rental to the local authority, but there is reserved the option of purchase. There are some privately owned gasworks it is true, but the tendency is for the municipality to become its own supplier of gas, water, libraries, bath houses, &c., &c.; in fact of all things that may be necessary for the health and recreation of the citizens.

1. *Education.*

All primary schools are free, and in them a sound English and commercial education can be obtained.   Education is secular and compulsory, and the cost to the State for the year ending 31st March, 1892, was for public schools 340,463*l*. 16*s*. 11*d*., for native schools 14,215*l*. 10*s*. 7*d*., industrial schools 9,856*l*. 18*s*. 8*d*., deaf mutes 3,149*l*. 19*s*. 8*d*., and the cost of general administration was 2,040*l*. 1*s*. 2*d*. The number of pupils of all ages on the school rolls was at the end of 1891, 119,523.

The administration is under a Minister of Education, who has to guide him and advise him an inspector-general and a secretary. The minister's function however is more advisory or directory than administrative, for practically the administration is left to boards and committees, and it may be useful to point out how these committees and boards are elected.   Beginning with com-mittees : The householders and parents of children attending the school elect yearly a school committee of 5, 7, or 9 members according to the numbers of children in a district.   A meeting is held, and the election takes place at the meeting.   The school districts are small; very rarely is there more than one school in a district.   These school committees have the general supervision of educational matters, subject always to the board.   There are thirteen boards.   These consist of 9 members, who hold office for three years; 3 members retire each year, and they are elected by the school committees in each educational district, so that their election is not direct by citizens, but mediate through school committees.   They have the power after consulting the committees of appointing and dismissing teachers.   The inspectors are appointed by them, buildings are erected and looked after by them, and they perform the main administrative work of the educational districts, subject always to the advice of the com-mittees.   The committees look after the more petty and local wants of the schools.   The system has worked fairly well, and the standards required of the pupils are equivalent to the standards in the education code of England.   There are practically seven standards, and a boy or girl who has passed these is well equipped for the business of life.   The highest standard is an education a little above the highest English elementary standard. Steps are being taken to introduce technical education. This already exists in some schools in the shape of woodwork, agriculture, chemistry, science, &c., &c. The State also maintains industrial schools. These are for neglected children or children whose parents have fallen from the paths of rectitude; or children who have committed some offence. There are at present four industrial schools, but the boarding out system is adopted, with the result that not many children are kept in these schools compared with the number on the rolls. As soon as possible children are boarded out to families, and after being trained, are sent to work either to assist farmers or to a trade, &c., &c. There is also a deaf and dumb school, conducted on the articulation and lip reading system, and aid has been given towards the erection of an institute for the blind. The deaf mute school has been exceedingly successful. It may be necessary to add that New Zealand has ample secondary schools in every educational district. The total number of secondary schools is twenty-two. Most of these are under the inspection of the State, having their governing boards partially appointed by the government or by education boards. Three or four of them are under the management of ecclesiastical bodies. The secondary schools look really to the matriculation and scholarship examinations of the University as the test of their work. The subjects required and marks given for these are as follows :—

For the Matriculation Examination :—

(1.) English.—Grammar and composition, with *précis* writing.

(2.) Arithmetic.—Fundamental rules, vulgar and decimal fractions, proportion, and square root.

(3.) Algebra.—To simple equations, inclusive, with easy problems.

(4.) Euclid.—Books I and II.

(5.) Latin.—Translation at sight of easy passages from Latin into English, translation of easy passages from English into Latin, and questions on grammar.

(6.) Greek.—As in Latin.

(7.) French.—As in Latin.

(8.) German.—As in Latin.

(9.) History.—History of England, from the accession of William III to the accession of Victoria.

(10.) Geography.—Political and physical.

(11.) Elementary Mechanics.—The elements of statics, dynamics, and hydrostatics.

(12.) Elementary Physics.—Heat, sound, light, and electricity.

(13.) Elementary Chemistry.—The non-metallic elements and the atomic theory.

(14.) Elementary Biology.—(The papers will contain questions on both zoology and botany, but candidates will not be required to answer questions in more than one of these subjects.)

Zoology.—Elements of animal physiology.

Botany.—Elements of the morphology and physiology of flowering plants, including the main characteristics of the chief native and introduced natural orders.

A candidate must pass in at least seven subjects, except those who take Latin or Greek, who shall be required to pass in six subjects only. Every candidate shall be required to pass in English, arithmetic, and at least one of the following languages—Latin, Greek, French, German.

The subjects for Junior Scholarships are :—

        (1.) Latin.
        (2.) Greek.
        (3.) English.
        (4.) French.
        (5.) German.
        (6.) Mathematics.
        (7.) History and geography.
        (8.) Natural and physical science.

The requirements for the Scholarship Examination are, in addition to the matriculation, the following :—

(1.) Latin.—Translation at sight from and into Latin, and questions on history and antiquity.

(2.) Greek.—As in Latin.

(3.) English.—Paraphrase, mensuration, and explanation of passages selected from the works of any of the standard English writers; general questions on etymology, grammar, and the uses of words; also a short essay on some easily understood subject.

(4.) French.—Translation at sight from and into French of a more difficult kind than the exercises set in the matriculation paper.

(5.) German.—The same as French.

(6.) Mathematics—

(a.) Arithmetic (the whole subject), and algebra to quadratic equations inclusive; also ratio, proportion, variation, the progressions, permutations, and combinations.

(b.) Euclid, Books I, II, III, IV, and VI, and plane trigonometry, to solution of triangles inclusive, with easy transformations and examples.

(7.) History and Geography.—A paper on outlines of the history of England from the accession of Elizabeth, with especial reference to the colonies, and on geography, political and physical.

(8.) Natural and Physical Science.—Any of the following :—

(a.) Chemistry.—The chief physical and chemical characters of the following elements, and of their more important compounds: oxygen, hydrogen, carbon, nitrogen, chlorine, bromine, iodine, fluorine, sulphur, phosphorus, silicon, sodium, potassium, calcium, magnesium, zinc, aluminium, iron, manganese, chromium, lead, silver, copper, mercury, tin, gold, platinum; the laws of chemical combination; equivalents; the atomic theory; atomic value (valency); the general nature of acids, bases, salts; the elements of qualitative analysis.

(b.) Magnetism and Electricity.—Properties of magnets; magnetic field; magnetic induction; magnetic laws and units; elementary facts of terrestrial magnetism; electrical attraction and repulsion; conduction and insulation; electrostatic induction; distribution of electricity on conductors; simple electrostatic laws; electrostatic units; friction machines; condensers; common forms of voltaic batteries; heating, chemical, and magnetic effects of electric currents; electromagnetic units; galvanometers; Ohm's law and its simple applications; measurement of resistance and of electromotive force.

(c.) Sound and Light.—Production and propagation of sound; intensity; pitch; quality; velocity of sound in uniform media; reflection of sound; vibration of strings, and of the air in pipes; resonance; beats; the diatonic scale; production and propagation of light; photometry; velocity of light and modes of determining it; reflection and refraction; formation of images by plane and spherical mirrors and by simple lenses; the prismatic spectrum; optical instruments and vision.

(*d.*) Heat.—Expansion of solids, liquids, and gases; thermometry; liquefaction and solidification; vaporisation and condensation; properties of vapours; hygrometry; latent heat; specific heat; calorimetry; conduction; convection; the mechanical equivalent of heat.

(*e.*) Elementary Mechanics of Solids and Fluids.—Composition and resolution of statical forces; mechanical powers, ratio of the power to the weight in each; centre of gravity; laws of motion; laws of motion of falling bodies; hydrostatics.

(*f.*) Botany—(1.) The morphology, histology, physiology, and life history of saccharomyces, bacteria, protococcus, closterium, spirogyra, penicillium, mucor, saprolegnia, peziza, agaricus, a fucoid, nitella (or chara), marchantia, a moss, a fern, pinus, and the bean plant. (2.) The general morphology and classification of angiospermous flowering plants, with especial reference to the following natural orders : orchideæ, liliaceæ, gramineæ, polygonaceæ, scrophularaceæ, boragineæ, ericaceæ (including epacrideæ), compositæ, rubiaceæ, umbelliferæ, onagraceæ, rosaceæ, leguminosæ, malvaceæ, caryophyllaceæ, cruciferæ, and ranunculaceæ; the modification of roots, stems, leaves, &c., to different purposes; parasitism; fertilisation of flowers, and modes of dispersion of seeds.

The university, which is an examining institution, has affiliated to it three teaching colleges : the Auckland university college, the Canterbury college, and the Otago university. The New Zealand university provides for the granting of degrees and of scholarships. The examiners are mainly appointed in England. It receives an annual grant of 3,000*l.*, besides having some small landed endowments. The colleges mentioned have also obtained substantial government aid, and the Auckland university college receives annually 4,000*l.* as a money grant. It will be seen therefore that so far as education is concerned the State has made provision for the education of its youth from the infant school to the university.

2. *Telephones; and* 3. *Telegraphs.*

There are 2,592 telephones in New Zealand. This is a larger number than there are for example in the more thickly populated colony. of Victoria; and the telephone system is being yearly extended. We can use telephones now in many parts for 50 miles. The charge per telephone is 5*l.* a year. It may not be necessary to mention the postal department, but in 1891 the average number of letters per head was 37·70. The postage is 2*d.*, except in towns, where it is 1*d.* There were also book packets delivered and posted, 7,170,761 ; newspapers delivered and posted, 18,501,911. The parcel post is in operation. During the past year the parcels posted were 162,282. The letters posted amounted to 23,867,402, and delivered, 23,745,462 ; total letters, 47,612,864. Money orders paid 160,279, of the value of 582,661*l.* 16*s.* 7*d.*, and issued 195,239, of the value of 651,989*l.* 19*s.* 6*d.* The postal notes sold were 214,334 of the value of 78,808*l.* 10*s.*, and paid 212,645, of the value of 76,865*l.* 1*s.* 6*d.* There are 1,240 post and telegraph offices, 65 telephone exchanges, and 2,603 miles of telephone wires, and 13,235 miles of telegraph wire.   No private telephones are allowed in the colony; all must be under State control and State supervision, nor are private telegraph wires permitted; all belong to the State.   In connection with the postal department there is a post office savings bank.   This was only begun in 1867, and it has mounted up so that there was to credit on 31st December, 1891, 2,695,447*l.* 11*s.* 6*d.*   The average amount of deposit was per head 4*l.* 5*s.* 7*d.*   The number of accounts was 104,467, and the interest credited for the year was 104,098*l.* 17*s.*   The revenue of the postal and telegraph department up to 31st December, 1891, was 320,058*l.* 1*s.* 3*d.*, and the expenditure 268,343*l.* 1*s.* 1*d.*   There are three cables connecting the north and south island.   The cable connecting Australia with New Zealand belongs to the Eastern Telegraph Extension Company, but it is proposed to connect Australia with a New Zealand owned cable.   If the Canadian people were to lay a transpacific cable, I believe New Zealand might be induced to grant a small subsidy to it.

4. Railways.

The railways were begun by the colony as a whole in 1870. Prior to that date, but under the federal form of government which New Zealand possessed, called the provincial system, there had been provincial railways.   Railways had been begun in Canterbury, in Southland, in Otago, and in Auckland.   In 1870 there was a general public works scheme started for the whole colony, and there are now 1,869 miles of railway open for traffic.   The total cost has been 14,656,691*l.*, and the revenue earned last year was 1,115,431*l.* 10*s.* 10*d.*, the expenditure 706,517*l.* 6*s.* 2*d.*; leaving 2*l.* 15*s.* 9*d.* per cent. on the cost.   It may be useful to note two things that have happened in New Zealand.   The demand for railways became so great that the general government could not meet all the demands, especially for what may be termed side lines. An Act was passed in 1877 giving power to a district to allow a company to construct such lines, and giving the company rating power to enable it to pay for the cost of construction.   District railways as they were called were constructed under this provision, but the general government had in the end to purchase these lines. It had given a guarantee of 2 per cent. on the cost of construction, and it was found very difficult to work these district railways with the main lines.   There was a continual conflict of authority, and an unsatisfactory mode of arrangement in dealing with rates. Then another system of railway construction was started in 1880 on what was called the land grant system.   The government gave to private companies certain blocks of land proportioned to the cost of the line. It was arrived at in this way : They were to get one-third of the cost in a land grant, provided the expenditure did not exceed a certain amount per mile. Under this system the Wellington and Manawatu line of 84 miles, and the Kaihu line of 16½ miles were constructed. The latter has fallen into the hands of the government, and the former is still managed by a company. There is also a line on this system called the Midland railway (late East and West Coast Middle Island railway). The fact is this system was introduced because the government were afraid to become liable for the loans that were required to construct these lines. It was discovered that by the means of land grants the borrowing of money by the colony would not be necessary, whilst the colony would be benefited by having these lines constructed. It seems to me however doubtful if this system has been any gain to the colony. The Wellington and Manawatu line for example was not constructed through difficult country, but a great part of it is through rich lands, and the large endowment in the shape of land grants given to the company would have gone a considerable way towards its construction. It is also a connecting line between the seat of government and the West Coast and Napier lines, and the policy of leaving it to a private company to form such a connecting line between two government railway systems can hardly be approved. To show the goods and passengers carried, the following statistics may be of interest. The traffic for the past thirteen years has been as follows :—

Year.	Miles.	Revenue.	Expenditure.	Tonnage.	Parcels, &c.	Cattle, Sheep, &c.	Passengers.	Season Tickets.
		£	£		No.	No.	No.	No.
1879–80	1,172	762,573	580,010	1,108,108	180,331	285,209	2,967,090	5,077
'80–81	1,277	836,454	521,957	1,377,783	286,865	390,704	2,849,561	6,499
'81–82	1,319	892,026	523,099	1,437,714	316,611	343,751	2,911,477	7,207
'82–83	1,358	953,347	592,821	1,564,793	341,186	477,075	3,283,378	8,621
'83–84	1,396	961,304	655,990	1,700,040	359,896	686,287	3,272,644	9,036
'84–85	1,477	1,045,712	690,026	1,749,856	347,425	729,528	3,232,886	8,999
'85–86	1,613	1,047,419	690,340	1,823,767	349,428	858,662	3,362,266	10,717
'86–87	1,727	998,768	699,072	1,747,754	372,397	942,017	3,426,403	11,821
'87–88	1,758	994,843	687,328	1,735,762	399,109	940,209	3,451,850	11,518
'88–89	1,777	997,615	647,045	1,920,431	399,056	919,392	3,132,803	11,817
'89–90	1,809	1,095,570	682,787	2,073,955	405,838	1,068,575	3,376,459	12,311
'90–91	1,842	1,121,701	700,703	2,086,011	413,074	1,348,364	3,433,629	13,881
'91–92	1,869	1,115,432	706,517	2,066,791	430,216	1,153,501	3,555,764	16,341

There are about 4,600 *employés* in the government service connected with the railways. There have been very few accidents on the lines. No severe accidents have happened ; the most serious was caused by the wind blowing a train over an embankment on the Rimutaka incline. There have been no collisions, and for the past year not a single passenger has been killed.

5. *Water Races.*

The government has spent a large sum of money on water races. These have been expended mainly with the object of bringing water to gold fields, for the purpose of sluicing or of other modes of gold working, and for the carrying away of *débris* from mines. The total amount spent for water races has been 350,439*l*. 6*s*., and the total profit during the thirteen years since they have been constructed has been from sales of water and gold duty 65,967*l*. 17*s*. 3*d*. This has been done by the general government. Water races have been constructed by local bodies—county councils—for New Zealand has a complete system of local government, that is, it has municipalities for towns and counties for large districts, and road boards for smaller parts of counties. Some counties, however, have no road boards, the whole of the local affairs being managed by the county council. There are in Canterbury alone at least 3,500 miles of water races. They are used for irrigating the land and watering stock, and they have been eminently successful. They are open races, the water being taken

TABLE I.

Name of Office.	Number of Years of Business in the Colony.	Accounts Closed.	Assurances and Endowments.		Annuities.	
			Number.	Amount.	Number.	Amount per Annum.
				£		£ *s.* *d.*
The Australian Mutual Provident Society	29	31 Dec., 1890	1,832	493,867	4	169 16 –
The Colonial Mutual Life Assurance Society (Limited)	7	,,	533	180,932	1	36 4 6
The Equitable Insurance Association of New Zealand....	6	,,	—	—	—	—
The Equitable Life Assurance Society of the United States	6	,,	141	32,749	—	—
The Mutual Assurance Society of Victoria (Limited)	7	,,	126	26,970	—	—
The Mutual Life Association of Australasia	14	,,	753	185,475	—	—
The National Mutual Life Association of Australasia (Limited)	11	30 Sept., 1890	563	143,199	—	—
The New York Life Insurance Company	4	31 Dec., 1890	65	25,116	—	—
The Life Insurance Department of the New Zealand Government	21	,,	2,744	684,242	17	890 6 3
Totals	—	—	6,757	1,772,550	22	1,096 6 9

from the rivers fed from the snows of the Southern Alps. As the Canterbury plain has a considerable fall, about twenty feet per mile, there has been no trouble in carrying the water in the races. There have been some races constructed in Otago, but it is in Canterbury that irrigation has been mainly developed.   Its peculiar climatic conditions require such aid to agriculture, being bounded on the west by the Alps, the vapour-carrying westerly winds do not bring moisture across these ranges. The rainfall of Canterbury is more limited than that of almost any other district in New Zealand. Assistance has also been given by the government to mining in various ways. This has generally been done by constructing roads by bonuses, and grants in aid of prospecting.

6. *Life Insurance and Annuities.*

The government life insurance department was started in the year 1870. It has therefore had an existence of about twenty-one years. At the end of 1891 its total accumulated funds were 1,872,797*l*. The number of policies in existence was 29,226. The rate of premiums is less than the ordinary private life offices. It

TABLE I.

uring the Year, including Policies he Colony.		Policies discontinued during the Year, including Policies transferred from the Colonies.		Number of existing Policies at end of Year.	Gross Amount Insured by Policies at end of Year.
Premiums.					
Single.	Annual.	Number.	Amount.		
£ *s. d.*	£ *s. d.*		£ *s. d.*		£ *s. d.*
1,636 19 6	15,658 10 8	1,170	333,855 — —	15,704	4,941,826 — —
312 13 4	4,943 8 11	550	173,150 — —	2,785	933,255 11 11
—	—	34	19,873 18 2	65	14,476 1 10
—	951 17 11	158	59,050 — —	915	465,653 — —
—	878 12 3	185	37,561 13 2	935	239,024 17 11
70 11 —	6,035 6 2	495	132,682 19 —	2,962	768,137 16 2
177 7 6	4,182 18 6	297	81,920 — —	2,330	590,656 — —
—	1,190 11 10	43	19,000 — —	207	85,591 — —
8,464 12 5	20,489 1 1	1,877	466,341 — —	28,102	7,544,030 — —
10,662 3 9	54,330 7 4	4,809	1,323,434 10 4	54,025	15,582,650 7 10

has an absolute government guarantee, and the result has been that through its operation life insurance has become much extended in New Zealand. It is very difficult to get accurate details of the amount insured per head in the various countries. The average amount of life insurance per head of the population of New

TABLE II.—*Statement of*
Policies Issued and Discontinued

Year 1891.	ASSURANCES.									
	Whole Life and Term Assurances.					Endowment Assurances.				
	Num-ber.	Sum Assured.	Rever-sionary Bonus.	Annual Premium.		Num-ber.	Sum Assured.	Rever-sionary Bonus.	Annual Premium.	
				Ordinary.	Extra.				Ordinary.	Extra.
		£	£	£ s. d.	£ s. d		£	£	£ s. d.	£ s. d.
:ies in force 31st Decem-r, 1890	17,172	5,171,537	195,783	133,862 16 3	1,092 4 6	10,292	2,345,831	67,979	84,844 18 5	898 14 9
as allotted as 31st Decem-r, 1890	—	—	282,678	—	—	—	—	113,761	—	—
business, 1891	1,588	444,607	—	10,764 15 -	273 18 2	1,288	249,109	—	9,122 19 10	144 16 3
Total :ies discon-iued during 91	18,760	5,616,144	478,461	144,627 11 3	4,365 2 8	11,580	2,594,941	181,740	93,967 18 3	1,043 11 -
	1,114	323,026	37,871	8,717 16 4	311 11 11	603	134,941	14,261	5,217 15 3	61 - 7
l policies in rce at 31st :cember, 1891	17,646	5,293,118	440,590	135,909 14 11	4,053 10 9	10,977	2,459,999	167,479	88,750 3 -	982 10 5

Particulars of Policies Discontinued

	Num.	Sum	Rever.	Ordinary.	Extra.	Num.	Sum	Rever.	Ordinary.	Extra.
:ath	177	62,484	7,224	1,842 8 2	89 8 10	56	13,070	1,279	590 18 4	6 12 4
aturity	—	—	—	—	—	49	13,573	2,375	793 6 10	5 7 8
urrender	165	48,209	2,919	1,268 9 7	58 7 8	108	23,134	1,458	810 13 3	3 - 8
„ of bonus	—	—	16,876	—	—	—	—	5,273	—	—
apse	771	212,133	10,852	5,014 11 -	141 2 3	390	85,164	3,876	3,000 16 6	39 15 5
xpiry of policy	1	200	—	3 - 8	—	—	—	—	—	—
„ pre-mium	—	—	—	554 10 7	10 8 4	—	—	—	—	—
ellaneous	—	—	—	34 16 4	12 4 10	—	—	—	92 2 4	6 4 6
Total	1,114	323,026	37,871	8,717 16 4	311 11 11	603	134,941	14,261	5,217 15 3	61 - 7

Progress of Business of the Government Insurance

med	31,049	9,455,801	612,605	250,569 4 9	9,729 4 3	20,065	4,704,718	227,749	170,420 13 11	2,352 15 11
id	13,403	4,162,683	172,015	114,659 9 10	5,675 13 6	9,088	2,244,719	60,270	81,670 10 11	1,370 5 6
in force	17,646	5,293,118	440,590	135,909 14 11	4,053 10 9	10,977	2,459,999	167,479	88,750 3 -	982 10 5

NOTE.—The ordinary premium is the premium at the true age; the

Zealand is, however, 25*l.*, that is at the end of 1891. This is compared with Australia's 22*l.*, Canada's 10*l.*, United States' 1c and the United Kingdom's about 12*l.* I do not know if my figur of comparison are absolutely correct : they are the best that cou be obtained here. They have been furnished to me by the ve

Business at end of Year 1891.

during the Year 1891.

Simple Endowments, Investments, &c.			Annuities.							
Number.	Sum Assured.	Annual Premium.	Number.	Annual Premium.	Annuity.	Number.	Sum Assured	Reversionary Bonus.	Ordinary.	Extr
	£	£ s. d.		£ s. d.	£ s. d.		£	£	£ s. d.	£ s.
536	26,662	1,139 1 6	102	10 16 –	5,668 14 4	28,102	7,544,030	263,762	219,857 12 2	4,990 19
—	—	—	—	—	—	—	—	396,439	—	—
35	6,185	260 14 11	23	—	1,040 17 8	2,934	699,901	—	20,148 9 9	417 14
571	32,847	1,399 16 5	125	10 16 –	6,709 12 –	31,036	8,243,931	660,201	240,006 1 11	5,408
89	3,230	151 3 11	4	—	362 11 4	1,810	461,197	52,132	14,086 15 6	372
	29,617	1,248 12 6	121	10 16 –	6,347 – 8	29,226	7,782,734	608,069	225,919 6 5	

—	—	—	4	—	362 11 4	237	75,554	8,503	2,363 6 6	96 1
22	583	33 11 –		—	—	71	14,156	2,375	826 17 10	5 7
62	2,302	105 – 7	—	—	—	335	73,645	4,377	2,184 2 5	61 8
—	—	—	—	—	—	—	—	22,149	—	—
5	345	12 12 4	—	—	—	1,166	297,642	14,728	8,027 18 10	180 17
—	—	—	—	—	—	1	200	—	3 – 8	—
—	—	—	—	—	—	—	—	—	554 10 7	10 8
—	—	—	—	—	—	—	—	—	126 18 8	18 9
89	3,230	151 3 11	4	—	362 11 4	1,810	461,197	52,132	14,086 15 6	

Department since date of Establishment to 31st Decem

Extra premiums	5,036 1 2	
Reduction of premium by bonus, &c.	230 19 6	
	231,186 7 1	

extra, the additional premium imposed for any reason whatsoever.

able actuary of the government insurance department. He has compared the returns of the Board of Trade in England from the English offices, the English preliminary census, and various books. The average number of policies per 1,000 of the population is here 87, in Australia 70, in Canada 29, in the United Kingdom 26, in the United States 18. The average amount insured per policy is as follows :—

New Zealand	288
Australia	317
Canada	344
United Kingdom	480
United States	565

This will show that life insurance is very widely diffused in New Zealand, and that a lower stratum is tapped. The department has been well and faithfully administered, but no doubt what has made it so successful is that there has been an absolute government guarantee. The rates, are as I have said, somewhat

TABLE III.—LIFE ASSURANCE. REVENUE OF NEW ZEALAND BUSINESS.—*Showing th their New Zealand Business, and of the Life Insuranc*

Name of Office.	Date when Financial Year ended.	Premiums (New).	Premiums (Renewals).	Consideration for Annuities.
		£ s. d.	£ s. d.	£ s. d.
The Australian Mutual Provident Society	31 Dec., 1890	14,438 19 1	136,644 1 2	1,636 19 6
The Colonial Mutual Life Assurance Society (Limited)	,,	4,058 7 7	19,080 8 5	300 — —
The Equitable Insurance Association of New Zealand	,,	—	442 6 5	—
The Equitable Life Assurance Society of the United States	,,	902 15 —	17,332 16 4	—
The Mutual Assurance Society of Victoria (Limited)	,,	594 16 10	7,508 19 1	—
The Mutual Life Association of Australasia	,,	5,047 7 10	19,824 8 1	—
The National Mutual Life Association of Australasia (Limited)	30 Sept., 1890	3,736 6 6	15,132 2 8	—
The New York Life Insurance Company	31 Dec., 1890	887 6 5	2,292 12 6	—:
The Life Insurance Department of the New Zealand Government	,,	21,325 3 8	195,213 9 1	7,071 3 11
Totals	—	50,991 2 11	413,471 3 9	9,008 3 5

* Including 612l. 17s. 11d., excess of expenditure.

lower than those of other offices. Generally speaking they are a fraction lower than the lowest of the other offices, but what might naturally be expected to follow has happened ; the division of profits has not been so great as in some of the Australian offices that have higher rates. However, during the five years ending December, 1890, the surplus, after valuation by the London actuaries, Messrs. Bailey, Hardy, and King, was found to be 239,475*l.* There are at least eight other offices competing for business in New Zealand. The one with the largest number of policies is the Australian Mutual Provident. It is the oldest office in New Zealand, having been in operation for forty-one years in Australia, and here thirty years. The total number of policies in the colony was, in the year 1890, 54,025; the total amount insured being 15,582,650*l.* 7*s.* 10*d.* I have to give (in Table I) the results for 1890, as those for 1891 will not be ascertained for a month or two yet.

Keeping however to the government business, it may be noted that the total revenue now is 330,895*l.* The total business can be gathered from Table II.

In conducting its business the government acts like an ordinary

Revenue of the various Life Assurance Companies operating in the Colony in regard to Department of the Government, for the Year 1890.

Interest.			Other Receipts.			Total Revenue.			Remissions for Investment, and Transfers from Head Office and Branches.			Funds at beginning of Year.			Total Revenue Account.		
£	s.	d.	£	s.	d.	£	s.	d.	£	s.	d.	£	s.	d.	£	s.	d.
79,865	12	7	25	11	4	282,611	3	8	56,273	18	7	1,259,201	19	2	1,548,087	1	5
1,736	16	1	—			25,175	12	1	—			67,844	8	10	93,020	—	11
—			—			. 412	6	5	—			—			1,055	4	4*
2,525	2	3	9	15	—	20,770	8	7	—			46,612	15	6	67,383	4	1
1,539	14	1	4	4	—	9,647	14	–	—			5,892	—	3	15,539	14	3
3,469	18	2	1	10	6	28,343	4	7	—			62,304	14	1	90,647	18	8
6,436	2	11	33	8	7	25,338	—	8	454	4	10	102,428	18	8	128,221	4	2
50	—	–	1	6	7	3,231	5	6	—			nil			3,402	18	–†
89,795	18	2	19	15	5	313,425	10	3	—			1,582,447	17	11	1,895,873	8	2
185,419	4	3	95	11	5	658,985	5	9	56,728	3	5	3,126,732	14	5	3,843,230	14	—

† Including 171*l.* 12*s.* 6*d.*, excess of expenditure.

life insurance company. It sends out lecturers and agents and enters into active competition for obtaining "lives." In the larger towns there are branch offices; but in the smaller towns the post offices act as agents. It will be seen from Table III that the government department has not crushed out the private companies.

I have given in the first table the number of years that the various offices have done business in this colony. The government intend to develop the life insurance department to enable pension schemes to be carried out by an annuity system. This will apply first to government officers, but no doubt will soon be extended to others in the community. The funds obtained by the government through the insurance department are invested in government bonds and also lent out on mortgage to individuals. Two conditions are invariably insisted upon in mortgages, that no loan shall exceed half the value of the property, nor shall one loan be of a larger amount than 5,000*l.*, and then on freehold only. Looking at life insurance as a mode of thrift and investment, it will be seen that during the past twenty-one years much has been done in New Zealand in this direction. Friendly societies have, however, not been injured. Their total number is 357, and their total assets 451,573*l.*, the membership being 26,379. They include the usual friendly societies in England: Manchester Unity, Oddfellows, Foresters, Rechabites, American Order of Oddfellows,

ABLE IV.—*Showing the Business of the Post Office Savings Banks in New Zealand Year by*

Totals for Colony in	Number of Post Office Savings Banks Open at the close of the Year.	Number of Deposits Received during the Year.	Total Amount of Deposits Received during the Year.	Average Amount of each Deposit Received during the Year.	Number of Withdrawals during the Year.	Total Amount of Withdrawals during the Year.	Average Amount of each Withdrawal during the Year.	Excess of Deposits over Withdrawals during the Year.
			£ s. d.	£ s. d.		£ s. d	£ s. d.	£ s. d.
1891	311	176,971	1,842,987 15 2	10 8 3	111,603	1,693,515 9 3	15 3 3	149,472 5 11
'90	296	162,938	1,658,543 3 5	10 3 6	106,868	1,500,437 9 5	14 - 9	158,105 14 -
'89	294	153,920	1,515,281 11 3	9 16 10	99,185	1,457,081 5 -	14 13 9	58,200 6 3
'88	290	145,355	1,544,747 7 11	10 12 6	96,204	1,387,471 1 10	14 8 5	157,276 6 1
'87	283	136,197	1,312,151 1 5	9 12 8	89,962	1,182,409 7 6	13 2 10	129,741 13 11
'86	271	137,989	1,248,305 6 11	9 - 11	89,182	1,336,287 6 4	14 19 8	
'85	256	131,373	1,341,001 3 2	10 4 1	84,832	1,264,305 8 3	14 18 -	76,695 14 11
'84	213	129,279	1,227,909 11 4	9 9 11	80,800	1,195,931 - 11	14 16 -	31,978 10 5
'83	222	127,600	1,178,474 4 1	9 4 8	78,405	1,205,719 18 3	16 10 6	
'82	207	129,952	1,325,852 2 11	10 4 -	69,308	1,142,599 - 1	16 9 8	183,253 2 10
'81	190	125,855	1,189,012 2 7	9 8 11	60,137	902,195 1 8	15 - 1	286,817 - 11
'80	178	81,660	864,441 18 10	10 11 9	57,446	780,504 13 4	13 11 8	83,937 5 6
'79	165	71,865	812,399 11 11	11 6 1	54,698	876,180 19 3	16 - 4	
'78	147	69,908	762,084 12 -	10 18 -	42,746	742,053 14 3	17 7 2	20,030 17 9
'77	138	60,953	681,294 13 2	11 3 6	39,363	667,023 7 5	16 18 10	14,271 5 9
'76	124	57,295	664,134 12 6	11 11 9	39,486	696,261 7 4	17 12 8	
'75	119	56,129	657,653 4 -	11 14 4	36,977	729,759 17 9	19 14 8	
'74	103	62,627	699,249 14 3	13 5 8	29,778	620,155 8 0	20 16 5	79,094 5 6
'73	97	39,223	580,542 5 5	14 16 2	21,268	425,908 3 5	20 - 5	154,634 2 -
'72	92	31,681	430,877 - -	13 12 -	17,254	313,176 7 11	18 3 -	117,700 12 1
'71	81	24,642	312,338 18 4	12 13 6	14,773	261,347 16 3	17 13 9	50,991 2 1
'70	70	20,489	264,328 5 7	12 18 -	11,934	209,509 13 2	17 11 1	54,818 12 5
'69	59	17,133	240,898 5 9	14 1 2	9,292	180,518 4 1	19 8 7	60,380 1 8
'68	55	13,014	194,535 11 6	14 18 11	6,365	107,094 17 3	16 16 6	87,440 14 3
from 1st Feb., to 31st Dec., 1867	46	6,977	96,372 7 10	13 16 3	1,919	26,415 18 9	13 15 3	69,956 9 1

and one or two smaller societies.   It may be said that the government insurance may weaken other modes of saving.   It has not, as I have said, injured friendly societies, and Table IV will show that savings banks deposits have increased.   I give only those in post office savings banks.   There are other savings banks which also show a good business.

It cannot be expected that the result of this extension of government insurance can be seen at present.   It is only as years roll on when the competition for work and food becomes more intense, that the value of these wise provisions will be appreciated. Having such a department as the government insurance, it will facilitate experiments in old age pension schemes.   A scheme for that has been elaborated, and no doubt before anything is done in England some attempt will be made to solve the difficult problem of making some provision for labourers in their old age.

7. *Trusteeship.   Administration of Property.*

I now come to government trusteeship—the administration of property, &c.   This was a new department created in 1871. Before this date there had been provision for administering intestate estates where there were either no relatives in the colony

ear, from the Date they were Established, in February, 1867, *to the 31st December,* 1891.

Excess of Withdrawals over Deposits during the Year.	Cost of Management during the Year.	Average Cost of each Transaction, Deposit, or Withdrawal.	Interest for the Year.	Number of Accounts Opened during the Year.	Number of Accounts Closed during the Year.	Number of Accounts remaining Open at close of the Year.	Total Amount standing to the Credit of all Open Accounts, inclusive of Interest to the close of the Year.	Average Amount standing to the Credit of each Open Account at close of the Year.
£ s. d.	£	s. d.	£ s. d.				£ s d.	£ s. d.
—	5,000	- 4·16	104,098 17 -	25,131	17,873	104,467	2,605,447 11 6	25 16 -
—	5,000	- 4·45	92,819 - 6	23,719	17,256	97,208	2,441,876 8 7	25 2 4
—	4,000	- 3·79	84,809 17 1	21,778	15,521	90,745	2,191,451 14 1	24 2 11
—	4,000	- 3·97	78,080 6 -	21,307	16,543	84,488	2,048,441 10 9	24 4 10
—	4,000	- 4·24	67,363 15 3	20,368	15,515	79,724	1,813,084 18 8	22 14 10
87,881 19 5	4,000	- 4·23	65,925 9 6	21,671	16,757	74,871	1,615,979 9 6	21 11 8
—	4,000	- 4·44	62,228 3 11	20,661	16,421	69,957	1,638,035 19 5	23 8 4
—	4,000	- 4·57	57,381 13 7	20,228	16,447	65,717	1,499,112 - 7	22 16 3
117,245 14 2	4,000	- 4·66	56,046 17 3	20,386	15,967	61,936	1,409,751 16 7	22 15 2
—	4,000	- 4·82	54,909 18 11	21,014	14,505	57,517	1,470,950 13 6	25 11 5
—	3,500	- 4·52	42,204 19 -	25,059	12,718	51,008	1,232,787 16 9	24 3 4
—	3,500	- 6·04	32,822 12 4	16,137	12,217	38,667	903,765 16 10	23 7 6
63,781 7 4	3,000	- 5·69	31,715 18 2	15,401	12,786	34,747	787,005 19 -	22 12 11
—	2,500 .	- 5·33	31,664 12 9	13,005	9,634	32,132	819,071 8 2	25 9 9
—	2,500	- 5·98	29,193 14 6	11,235	8,591	28,761	767,375 17 8	26 13 7
32,146 14 10	2,500	- 6·20	28,762 4 7	11,255	9,472	26,117	728,910 17 5	27 14 4
72,106 13 9	2,500	- 6·44	28,565 3 5	11,273	8,681	24,334	727,295 7 8	29 17 9
—	2,250	- 6·55	26,935 6 8	10,346	5,736	21,742	770,886 18 -	35 9 -
—	1,800	- 7·14	20,106 16 10	7,382	3,816	17,132	664,807 5 10	33 16 1
—	1,556	- 7·63	14,711 - 5	6,205	3,188	13,566	490,066 7 -	36 2 5
—	1,351	- 8·23	11,291 10 10	4,615	2,383	10,549	357,654 14 6	33 18 1
—	1,264	- 9·36	9,243 3 11	4,304	2,277	8,317	295,372 1 7	35 10 3
—	1,186	- 10·77	7,412 8 -	3,839	1,801	6,290	231,311 5 3	36 15 5
—	789	- 9·77	4,880 7 3	3,282	1,186	4,252	163,518 15 7	38 9 1
—	892	1 10·18	1,241 5 -	2,520	364	2,156	71,197 14 1	33 - 5

TABLE V.— *Return showing the Number and Value of Estates remaining in the Public Trust Offices at the close of the Years* 1889, 1890, *and* 1891.

Class.	Number of Estates on			Value of Estates on				Number on 31st March, 1892.	Value on 31st March, 1892.
	31st December, 1889.	31st December, 1890.	31st December, 1891.	31st December, 1889.	31st December, 1890.	31st December, 1891.			
				£ s.	£ s.	£			£
Intestacies No. 1	788	752	794	42,958 10 ⎫ 32,396 — ⎭	75,305 —	83,381	974	87,480
„ 2								
Real estates	106	109	114	22,363 10	23,496 10	24,190	114	24,439
Lunatic estates	213	137	181	34,548 10	32,918 10	34,913	214	34,581
Wills and trusts No. 1	126	138	168	235,090 10	251,624 —	256,800	172	266,700
„ 2	138	150	175	131,963 —	166,423 10	158,360	178	161,000
Native reserves	93	99	100	339,041 —	340,869 —	344,692	100	347,492
W.C. settlement reserves	293	293	293	349,213 —	349,462 —	350,289	293	351,987
Miscellaneous	1,176	813	1,091	207,839 10	215,011 10	183,402	1,140	187,484
	2,939	2,491	2,916	1,393,413 10	1,455,110 —	1,436,027	3,185	1,461,163

or relatives who could not or who did not choose to undertake the administration of the estate. In the year mentioned, however, there was started a public trust office, and its transactions have grown very large. For example, on 31st March, 1890, there were being administered 2,491 estates, of the value of 1,393,413*l.* This included wills 288, native reserves 392, intestacies 752, real estates 109, lunatic estates 137, and the office is gradually growing. At the end of 1891, 2,916 estates, of the value of 1,436,027*l.*, were in process of administration, and on the 31st March, 1892, the number of estates had mounted up to 3,185, of a value of 1,461,163*l.* Table V will show the growth of business for the three past years.

A new departure has been made during the past year in reference to administration.

A law has been passed that if there is no provision specially declaring how investments are to be made, then the moneys from various estates may be invested together in the various securities named, viz. :—

(1.) Government securities of the United Kingdom or of any colony or dependency thereof.
(2.) Debentures issued as mortgages executed by any local body in the colony secured upon rates, or upon real estate, up to one half the value.
(3.) Mortgages of real estate up to one half the value.
(4.) Fixed deposits in any bank if same has been created or established by any Act of the Colonial Parliament or by Royal Charter, or in the post office or other savings bank established in New Zealand under any Colonial Act.

In the case of any such investments the department guarantees the money invested, but the interest is not to exceed to the beneficiaries 5 per cent. on amounts not exceeding 3,000*l.*, or 4 per cent. up to 20,000*l.* To secure the department against loss, a ½ per cent. may be made payable to a guarantee fund.

It will be seen that in small estates beneficiaries will obtain 5 per cent., and in large estates 4 per cent., if no special investment has been provided for in the will or trust settlement.

The public trust office also pays its accounts in cash and not in cheques on the bank of New Zealand, which is the New Zealand banker. This is practically making it a bank on a small scale, and the business is yearly developing. With this recent alteration in the law as to the State guaranteeing a certain rate of interest, I believe that the business of the office

will very largely increase.   The following table will show the
cash transactions of the office :—

PUBLIC TRUST OFFICE.   *Statement of Cash Received and Paid from
30th June, 1873, to 31st December, 1891.*

Year.		Receipts.			Payments.		
		£	s.	d.	£	s.	d.
30th June, 1874	Cash	42,094	7	8	37,042	5	6
„ '75	„	54,003	16	4	49,866	17	6
„ '76	„	66,467	15	8	61,234	3	6
„ '77	„	63,579	15	2	58,074	11	1
„ '78	„	118,625	12	10	106,338	2	4
„ '79	„	69,976	17	11	73,992	5	1
„ '80	„	41,813	12	3	41,218	13	11
„ '81	„	68,262	9	2	73,002	19	3
„ '82	„	71,319	19	4	65,076	7	1
31st Dec., '82	„	45,018	10	6	46,379	3	9
„ '83	„	90,119	13	1	97,024	12	3
„ '84	„	116,136	15	9	102,288	14	2
„ '85	„	196,094	9	8	196,401	12	5
„ '86	„	125,984	5	3	134,646	9	9
„ '87	„	109,030	13	11	107,698	9	9
„ '88	„	146,715	15	10	140,777	1	3
„ '89	„	183,336	12	11	196,626	3	10
„ '90	„	143,386	10	8	129,385	11	4
„ '91	„	171,190	10	8	168,235	15	1
		1,923,158	4	7	1,885,309	18	10

The total number of estates has been 25,042.   There is a
growing feeling in favour of utilising the trust office, because
of its absolute security.

The person who has a small sum to leave for the benefit of
his widow or children, if he leaves it in the trust office, will
know that though the interest may not be large, yet that the
beneficiaries will receive it regularly, and that the capital will
be safe.   It has been held that the public trustee has the same
liabilities as other trustees.   He may be guilty of either breaches
of trust or neglect, and for these he may be sued by those injured
and the office must indemnify them.   The administration has been
a gain to the State, as there has been reaped a profit of 18,000l.
up to the end of 31st December, 1891, which has been passed to
the ordinary revenue of the colony, and after paying all expenses,
losses, &c., there is a further sum of 30,000l. to credit, including
dividends and balances unclaimed, after allowing for re-funds.
There are in New Zealand two private companies doing the same
kind of work—managing properties, obtaining probate of wills, &c.
They have not long been in existence, and their transactions as yet,
so far as trusteeships are concerned, have not been very extensive.

8. *Guaranteeing Titles.*

What is known as the Torrens system of land transfer has been adopted in New Zealand. This system is well known in Australia, and all that need be said about it is that the State on certain conditions guarantees titles to land. A guarantee fund has been accumulated, and so far hardly any claims have been made on it; it now amounts to about 80,000*l*. This may be attributed to two things, (1) the care of the examiners of titles, and (2) that New Zealand was not old when the system was brought into operation. All new lands sold by the government come under the Land Transfer Act. Year by year the land which was under the old system of registration—which was a complete system of registration, only without the government guarantee—is gradually being brought under the land transfer system.

9. *Agricultural Department.*

The government performs the function of an advisory board to farmers and others. Under this head it has special officers who give instruction and aid to farmers in reference to dairy produce, and fruit and forest culture. It sends its dairy inspectors around to instruct people how to carry on cheese and butter factories. The inspectors also give lectures to farmers as to the mode of preparing milk and cream for butter and cheese making, lectures are also delivered on fruit culture and on tree planting. There are stock inspectors, rabbit inspectors, and veterinary inspectors. These stock inspectors see that flocks are kept free from disease. At present there is, happily, no disease in cattle, sheep, or horses. The inspectors also see that the rabbits are kept down, being either poisoned or trapped, and the extent of this pest may be measured by the fact that the export of skins for the past year was 14,302,233, weighing 2,025,978 lbs., of the value of 126,251*l*. The veterinary officer also advises farmers as to the nature of and remedies for disease, and how to treat stock, and in this way the agricultural department assists in developing the production of the colony.

10. *Labour Bureaux.*

There have been established throughout the colony what are termed labour bureaux. They are in the principal towns, and are under the charge of government officers, assisted by the police department, whose duty it is to receive applications for work, and to endeavour to obtain employment for those requiring it. They communicate with farmers, pastoralists and others, and the local officer arranges to forward those out of employment to where work is to be had. If any are without means, they are provided with free passes on the railway, and otherwise assisted until they obtain work. The government has always some work going on, and the unemployed may be sent on to the public works. It has been in operation since June, 1891, and for the twelve months it has found employment for 2,974 people—2,000 going to private persons and 974 to government works. Its cost has been trifling, only 339*l.* for salaries, and 1,700*l.* for railway fares and travelling expenses. It is proposed to start one or two State farms, so that if required work may be found for the casually unemployed. This labour bureau also works in with factory inspection, for the Factories' Act is very stringent in its provisions, especially as to ventilation, proper convenience for the meals of the workpeople, and strict surveillance as to hours. The main provisions are as follows :—

Extracts from " Factories Act, 1891."

All factories must be registered; a factory being defined as follows :—

"'Factory or work-room' means any office, building, or place in which three or more persons are engaged, directly or indirectly, in working for hire or reward in any handicraft, or in preparing or manufacturing articles for trade or sale, and any office, building, or place in which steam or other mechanical power is used for the purpose of manufacture;

" But where the operations of any manufacturer are carried on, for safety or convenience, in several adjacent buildings grouped together in one enclosure, these shall be classed and included as one factory for the purposes of registration and the computation of registration fees."

Inspectors are appointed, who have the following powers :—

"(1.) To enter, inspect, and examine at all reasonable hours, by day and night, a factory or work room, and every part thereof, when he has reasonable cause to believe that any person is employed therein, and to enter by day any place which he has reasonable cause to believe to be a factory or work room;

"(2.) To take with him in either case a constable into a factory or work room in the execution of his duty;

"(3.) To require the production of the certificate of registration held by the occupier of any factory or work room, or any other book, notice, record, list, or document which such occupier is by this Act required to keep, and to inspect, examine, and copy the same, or any notice or other document required to be kept or exhibited therein;

"(4.) To make such examination and inquiry as may be necessary to ascertain whether the enactments relating to public health and of this Act are complied with so far as respects the factory or work room and the persons employed therein;

"(5.) To examine, either alone or in the presence of any other person, as he thinks fit, with respect to matters under this Act, every person whom he finds in a factory or work room, or whom he has reasonable cause to believe to be or to have been within the preceding two months employed in a factory or work room, and to require such person to be so examined, and to sign a declaration of the truth of the matters respecting which he is so examined."

In every factory there must be kept—

"(a.) A record of the names of all persons employed in such factory or work room, together with the ages of all persons who are under 20 years of age; and

"(b.) A record of the particular kind of work of each and every person employed in such factory or work room;

"And such record shall be produced for inspection by the inspector when demanded."

There are strict sanitary provisions :—

"Every factory or work room shall be kept in a cleanly state, and free from effluvia arising from any drain, privy, or other nuisance. Where members of both sexes are working in the same factory or work room, there shall be a separate water closet or privy for each sex.

"A factory or work room shall not be so overcrowded while work is carried on therein as to be injurious to the health of the persons employed therein, and shall be ventilated in such a manner as to render harmless, as far as is practicable, all the gases, vapours, dust, or other impurities generated in the course of the manufacturing process or handicraft carried on therein that may be injurious to health. The owner or occupier of every factory or work room shall provide a supply of fresh drinking water.

"A factory or work room in which, in the opinion of the inspector, there is a contravention of this section, and which opinion is signified in writing under the hand of the inspector, shall be deemed not to be kept in conformity with this Act.

"The inspector may from time to time determine, as to each factory or work room, what space of cubic and superficial feet shall be reserved, appropriated, and maintained for the use of each person working therein, according to the nature of the work, but so that such space shall not be less than or in excess of that prescribed from time to time by regulations; and shall, by notice in writing to the occupier, require such space to be reserved and appropriated accordingly within a time to be fixed by such inspector; and shall in like manner require that every such space is properly lighted and ventilated, and maintained and kept free from any materials or goods or tools other than those in use or required by the person for whom such space is so reserved and appropriated.

"No person under 18 years of age, and no woman shall, except on half-holidays, be employed continuously in any factory or work room for more than 4¼ hours without an interval of at least half an hour for a meal.

"No females or persons under 16 years of age employed in a factory or work room shall be permitted to take his or her meals in any room therein in which any manufacturing process or handicraft is then being carried on, or in which persons employed in such factory or work room are then engaged in their employment, unless such factory or work room is of open construction, and is certified to by the inspector as being properly exempted from this provision.

"Subject to the last preceding section the occupier of every factory or work room in which more than six females are employed shall provide a fit and proper room in or near to such factory or work room, in which such females or persons employed therein may take their meals without the provisions of this Act being contravened; but in cases where, from the small number of persons employed, the size of the factory or work room, or the nature of the employment, the inspector thinks that any room or place of shelter which is sufficiently secure from the weather and from public view will suffice as a place in which meals may be taken, he may, by writing under his hand, sanction the use of such room or place of shelter as a place in which meals may be taken.

"If an occupier fails or neglects to provide such room or place of shelter he shall be deemed to act in contravention of this Act.

"The Governor in Council may from time to time declare any manufacturing process, handicraft, or employment to be noxious for the purposes of this Act, and, where any manufacturing process, handicraft, or employment has been declared by the Governor in Council to be noxious for the purposes of this Act, no person employed in the factory or work room in which any such manufacturing process, handicraft, or employment is carried on shall be permitted to take his or her meals in any room therein in which such manufacturing process, handicraft, or employment is then being carried on, or in which persons employed in such factory or work room are or have been in the course of the day engaged in their employment.

"If in a factory or workshop where grinding, glazing, or polishing on a wheel, or any process is carried on by which dust is generated, and by the workers inhaled to an injurious extent, and it appears to an inspector that such inhalation could be to a great extent prevented by the use of a fan or other mechanical means, the inspector may direct a fan or other mechanical means of a construction proper for preventing such inhalation to be provided within a reasonable time; and if the same is not provided, maintained, and used the factory or workshop shall be deemed not to be kept in conformity with this Act.

"A woman, or person under 18 years of age, shall not be employed in any part of a factory or work room in which wet spinning is carried on unless sufficient means be employed and continued for protecting the workers from being wetted, and (where hot water is used) for preventing the escape of steam into the room occupied by the workers.

"A factory or work room in which there is a contravention of the provisions of this section shall be deemed not to be kept in conformity with this Act."

There are various other provisions as to bakehouses, &c.

Perhaps the most important parts of the Act are as to the age of *employées.* They are—

"A woman, or person under 18 years of age, who works in a factory or work room, whether for wages or not, either in a manufacturing process or handicraft, or in cleaning any part of a factory or work room used for any manufacturing purposes or handicraft, or in cleaning or oiling any part of the machinery, or in any other kind of work whatsoever incidental to or connected with any manufacturing process or handicraft, or connected with the article made or otherwise the subject of any manufacturing process or handicraft, shall, save as is otherwise provided by this Act, be deemed to be employed within the meaning of this Act.

"For the purposes of this Act an apprentice shall be deemed to work for hire.

"No person shall to the extent mentioned in the second schedule to this Act be employed in the factories or work rooms or parts thereof mentioned in that schedule.

"Notice of the prohibition in this section shall be affixed in all factories or work rooms to which it applies.

"No person shall employ in any factory or work room any boy under the age of 16 years for more than 48 hours in any one week. No person shall employ in a woollen mill any female for more than 48 hours in any week, nor between the hours of 6 o'clock in the afternoon and 7 o'clock in the morning. No person shall employ in any other factory or work room any female between the hours of 6 o'clock in the afternoon and 8 o'clock in the morning, or for more than 8 hours in any one day.

"No child shall be employed in any factory or work room.

"A person under the age of 16 years shall not be employed in a factory or work room unless the occupier of the factory or work room has obtained a certificate in the prescribed form of the fitness of such person for employment in that factory or work room.

"A certificate of fitness for employment for the purposes of this Act may be granted by the inspector for the district, and shall be to the effect that he is satisfied, by the production of a certificate of birth or other sufficient evidence, that the person named in the certificate of fitness is of the age therein specified and fit for the employment.

"All factories or work rooms in the same line of trade and in the district of the same inspector, or any of them, may be named in the certificate of fitness for employment if the certifying inspector is of opinion he can truly give the certificate for employment therein.

"The certificate of birth which may be produced to such inspector shall either be a certified copy of the entry in a register of births kept in pursuance of 'The Registration of Births and Deaths Act, 1875,' of the birth of the person, and such certificate of birth shall be given by the registrar without fee, or a statutory declaration made by some competent person as to the age of the person for whom it is desired to obtain a certificate of fitness for employment.

"No girl under 15 years of age shall work as type setter in any printing office : Provided that nothing in this clause contained shall apply to the case of any girl at the time of the passing of this Act engaged in type setting in any printing office.

"In the case of a woman, or any person under 18 years of age, any forfeiture on the ground of absence or leaving work shall not be deducted from or set against a claim for wages, or other sum due for work done before such absence or leaving work, except to the amount of the special damage (if any) which the occupier of the factory or work room may have sustained by reason of such absence or leaving work."

Every woman, and every person under 18 years of age, must have, as to holidays—

"(1.) Christmas Day, New Year's Day, Good Friday, Easter Monday, and Her Majesty's birthday ; and

"(2.) Every Saturday afternoon from 1 of the clock in the afternoon: Provided that in any city, borough, or town district where it may be found inconvenient that work should cease on Saturdays as before mentioned, the council or town board may, by special order, from time to time appoint any other working day in the week on which women and persons under the age of 18 years shall have a holiday from 1 of the clock in the afternoon; or such special order may provide and appoint separate working-days in the week on which different classes or sets of workers, being women and such persons as aforesaid, shall have a holiday from 1 of the clock in the afternoon; and upon any such special order becoming operative, this Act shall operate in respect of all persons affected by such special order as if the day or separate day named therein had been mentioned in this Act in place of the word 'Saturday.'

"(3.) Nothing in this Act shall be deemed to prevent the employment of females or persons under the age of 18 years in printing offices on Saturdays or any other half holiday up to the hour of half-past four in the afternoon, nor the substitution of two other days for Easter Monday and Her Majesty's birthday in the case of female type setters.

"Wages shall be paid by the occupier to every woman and person as aforesaid employed in a factory or work room in respect of every such holiday, and at the same rate as paid on ordinary working-days."

The factories or work rooms in which the employment of persons is restricted are :—

"SECOND SCHEDULE (before referred to).

"*Factories or Work Rooms in which the Employment of Persons is restricted.*

"(1.) In a part of a factory or work room in which there is carried on—
(a.) The process of silvering of mirrors by the mercurial process, or
(b.) The process of making white lead,
a person under 18 years of age shall not be employed.

"(2) In the part of a factory in which the process of melting or annealing glass is carried on, a male person under 14 years of age, and a female person under 18 years of age, shall not be employed.

" (3.) In a factory or work room in which there is carried on—

(a.) The making or finishing of bricks or tiles not being ornamental tiles, or

(b.) The making or finishing of salt,

a girl under 16 years of age shall not be employed.

" (4.) In a part of a factory or work room in which there is carried on—

(a.) Any dry grinding in the metal trade,

(b) The dipping of lucifer matches,

a person under 16 years of age shall not be employed.

" (5.) In any grinding in the metal trades other than dry grinding, or in friction cutting, a child shall not be employed."

The definition of a child is—

" ' Child' means a boy under the age of 13 years and a girl under the age of 14."

In some places the bureau and the factory inspector work together. Following up the system of labour supervision, a scheme of co-operative contracting has been devised—of course this is only in operation in government works. It may be explained in this way : Suppose there are some men out of employment, and the government has for example a piece of railway construction to perform—say earthwork—the government sets out a piece of work for a gang of men. It may be many chains in length and it may include rock cutting. The government provides free of cost all requisites such as tents and tools, except shovels, spades and axes. The cost of repairing plant and tools is borne by the men, explosives are provided by the government, but the cost is deducted from the amount payable to the men. The main conditions may thus be summarised : Suppose there is a gang of ten men, they elect one of their number to act as head man of their party ; he receives all money due for the work done, signs receipts for it, and is responsible for the proper carrying out of the work. If he is found to neglect his duty or is otherwise unsuitable, the officer in charge may appoint another head man out of the party. If any of the party are absent from work they have a sum deducted from the money coming to them (they are paid by the piece) equivalent to the time absent according to the average rate made per day since last payment. The officer in charge has power to discharge from the work any men who neglect their duty or otherwise misconduct themselves, but the party cannot discharge any of their number without the consent of the officer in charge, nor can the party select their own ten men ; they must take the ten men as they come. The officer in charge is an arbitrator or referee in case of any dispute in the gang. If any one is prevented attending work through illness, his place is left open until the subsequent progress payment, that is for the month, and if he cannot come himself he may send a substitute, assuming his illness still continues. If anyone leaves work except through illness, he has no claim after the day he stops work, nor can he be received back again into the same gang without the consent of all concerned. The men are paid by the piece, but all are paid an equal amount whether all can do the same work or not. The system has worked exceedingly well. All the profits that used to go to the contractor now go to the men, because the government pay the same price as they would have to pay contractors. The result has been that the men have been able to earn on an average from one to two shillings per day more than they would have been paid by a contractor. In fact the contractor's profit has gone into the pockets of the men, and with no injury to the government, for the work has not cost the government one penny more than it would have under the ordinary contracting system.

Many other experiments have been made in New Zealand, but I have selected the foregoing to illustrate how government functions have been extended. To carry them out no taxation on the people has been necessary. The government security, no doubt, has been the main thing that has made them a success. It is not fitting to dwell on other things that New Zealand has accomplished. I may only say that year by year our exports are increasing, and we have shown that we can carry on our government without further aid from the London money lender. No doubt we are heavily indebted. Our net public debt amounts to 37,677,619*l.* Part of this immense sum was spent on war, part on railways, part on immigration, and part on the purchase of the land from the Maories—for the colony has recognised the title of the aborigines—but as against the great debt we have large landed estates, railways, water races, roads, lighthouses, and all the many requisites modern civilization demands. So far, our State has been free from corruption of any kind, and the spending of such large sums has, no doubt, developed our resources to a large extent. Without railways we could not have exported such quantities of wheat and other products. Our exports last year amounted to the large sum of 9,566,397*l.*, a not inconsiderable amount for a population of 650,000 men, women, and children. Our internal trade has largely developed. Our total products amount to at least 24,000,000*l.* I do not intend, however, to speak of New Zealand's general progress. Our record is not a bad one considering we have only just celebrated our jubilee. No doubt our climate counts for much. We have not the severe winters of England, far less the months of snow and frost experienced in Canada and the Northern United States, nor do we experience their summer heat, and we have neither the droughts of Australia nor its floods. It is fairly I think open to question if private enterprise, unaided by the State, could have accomplished in fifty years what has been done through State action, and if our taxation must necessarily be large to pay our interest, yet our resources are equally extensive. There is no tendency to create millionnaires such as are common in America, but I do not know if this will be a loss to our people, I rather think it will be a gain. There are other experiments we are bent on making, as, for example, to solve the difficult problem of equality of sacrifice in taxation, and to limit the area of holdings of land ; but these hardly bear on the questions I have been discussing. I have mentioned what we have done, and I have also stated that the indirect results cannot yet be estimated. So far we seem an enterprising and a thriving people. Competition in business is as active as in America. We are law abiding, and there is certainly growing up amongst us a reverence for the government and obedience to law that do not exist in many democracies. The growth of the State conscience is no doubt always slow, but it has begun to develop here, and the fact that the State is doing so much for the people may tend to make this growth more vigorous and stable.

The ADDRESS *of the* PRESIDENT *of the* ECONOMIC SCIENCE *and*
STATISTICS SECTION *of the* BRITISH ASSOCIATION, *held at* EDIN-
BURGH, 1892.

By the HON. SIR CHARLES W. FREMANTLE, K.C.B.

I SUPPOSE that few Presidents of any Section of this Association begin
the preparation of their addresses without taking at least a mental
retrospect of the work of their predecessors. I have turned with
great interest to the address delivered by the late Lord Neaves,
who occupied this chair in 1871, when the Association last met in
Edinburgh. Lord Neaves rightly held that the subject of statistics
is ancillary to the main subject of the Section, Economic Science,
and his immediate predecessor, the lamented Professor Stanley
Jevons, pointed out at Liverpool in 1870 that even "the name
" 'statistics' in its true meaning denotes all knowledge relating to
" the condition of the State or people." I propose to devote the
main portion of my Address to a subject to which I have devoted
much attention, and which is intimately connected with the
welfare of an important section of our people, and I shall hope to
point out the means which may be taken to promote their welfare
without leading them, as Lord Neaves expressed it in his concluding words, "to dispense with ordinary and necessary prudence."
It is impossible to exaggerate the change which has taken place
since the date of Lord Neaves' address in the ideas of the public
as to its responsibilities in regard to what is called charity. While
it recognises that much which was then held to be "charity" is
nothing more than justice to the poorer classes, its sense of the
dangers of pauperisation has been greatly intensified, and it justly
regards many of the charitable methods which would then have
been unhesitatingly advocated as not conducive to their best
interests. I venture to claim a considerable part of the change
which has taken place as due to the efforts of the Charity Organisation Society, which had then been recently founded, and of which
I have the honour this year to be chairman. I claim that the
Society has made men everywhere think, and think seriously, of
the duty incumbent upon them not only of giving, but of giving
with care and discrimination, and that it has enlisted in the
service of their poorer brethren an army which, besides being
always ready to be prudently generous, is in a thousand cases
willing to ensure, by personal effort, that charitable help shall be

wisely and kindly dispensed. Such personal effort realises what was well described centuries ago in the Talmud as "the doing of " kindness," and is developing "a system founded not on rights " but on sympathy, dealing not in doles but in deeds of friendship " and of fellowship, and demanding a giving of oneself rather " than of one's stores." It has naturally followed that collateral subjects, such as the promotion of thrift and the better regulation of benevolent and benefit societies, have during the last twenty years received a greatly increased amount of enlightened attention.

Before proceeding however to the main subject of my Address, let me briefly refer to two questions more directly connected with the special work to which the greater part of my official life has been devoted.

The first of these is the restoration of the gold coinage, a question which has for many years past exercised the minds of successive Chancellors of the Exchequer and has been a stumbling block to bankers and the commercial world. It had long been felt that the machinery provided by the law, as laid down in the old proclamations and embodied in the Coinage Act of 1870, was of necessity powerless to maintain the gold currency in an efficient condition. The law provided that "where any gold coin of the " realm is below the current weight ... every person shall, by " himself or others, cut, break, or deface any such coin tendered to " him in payment, and the person tendering the same shall bear the " loss;" but as there was no penalty for the disregard of this obligation, it became practically inoperative. Gold coins, however much below the least current weight, passed freely from hand to hand, and bankers received them from their customers and paid them away again. Only the Bank of England and a few other public departments obeyed the law, with the result that the principal sufferers were the banking establishments, who in the course of business pay large amounts of gold coin into the Bank of England, and were obliged to submit to the loss on all coins found to be light. The banks, in self-defence, naturally paid in as many full-weight coins as possible, and put the light again into circulation. Not more than 1,500,000*l*. of light coin, therefore, was annually withdrawn, and it was calculated that, at last, of the sovereigns in circulation as many as 46 per cent., and of the half sovereigns no fewer than 70 per cent., were below the least current weight. A Bill was brought in in 1884 for the withdrawal of light coins by the State and for the substitution for the half sovereign of a ten-shilling piece of the intrinsic value of 9*s*., so that a fund might be provided to cover the expense of the operation and of the future maintenance of the currency in a proper condition; but this Bill was not proceeded with. Of the subsequent Bills introduced none became law, until in 1889 an Act was passed withdrawing light gold coins of former reigns, and these coins were finally called in under a proclamation issued in November, 1890. The entire operation was effected at a cost of about 50,000*l.* It is curious to note that this is the first instance in which gold coin has been decried in this country, for the guinea and half guinea had never been declared uncurrent, and doctors and others might have contended that their fees were still represented by coins which were legal tender. The Act of 1889, with the subsequent proclamation, having served its purpose by clearing the circulation of all the older gold coinages, there only remained coins of the present reign to deal with. The Coinage Act of 1891 provides for the withdrawal of light gold coin by the State at its full nominal value, and will apply equally to coins which will hereafter become light as to those which have already fallen below the legal weight. No one can now or in the future suffer for tendering a light sovereign or half sovereign more than for making a payment with a worn half crown or shilling, and any Victorian gold coin tendered at the Bank of England, provided that it has not been defaced and that its weight has not been fraudulently reduced, is received and exchanged. For the present, coins must be sent in in parcels of 100*l.* It is unnecessary to dwell upon the advantage which these arrangements have conferred, and will confer, upon the public. In 1842-45, when the previous withdrawal of light gold took place, the coin was only paid for by weight at the Mint price of 3*l.* 17*s.* 10½*d.* per ounce, and many were the misunderstandings and bitter complaints to which the conditions of withdrawal gave rise. No inconvenience or alarm, on the other hand, is likely to attend the measures necessary under the Act of last year, which make it possible to effect the gradual withdrawal of the light coin without friction. To 1st July last the amounts withdrawn were: sovereigns 5,150,000*l.*, and half sovereigns, 3,850,000*l.* It had been estimated that the average deficiency of weight in each sovereign would be 2·57*d.*, and in each half sovereign 2·65*d.*, and the actual deficiency found has been 2·65*d.* in the case of sovereigns and 2·93*d.* in the case of half sovereigns. After the first withdrawals have been effected it is probable that the deficiency will become less, as a certain amount of much worn coin had no doubt been accumulated in banks in anticipation of the passing of the Act. As far as the work has as yet proceeded, however, the cost of withdrawing 1,000,000*l.* in sovereigns has been found to be 11,056*l.*, and of withdrawing 1,000,000*l.* in half sovereigns 24,418*l.* A sum of 400,000*l.* was set aside by the Act for the expenses of the withdrawal, which will be sufficient at this rate to meet the loss on 26,593,000*l.* Elaborate investigations were conducted by the late Professor Jevons in 1868, by Messrs. Inglis Palgrave and J. B. Martin in 1882, and by the Mint in 1888, with a view of ascertaining the total amount of light gold in circulation in the United Kingdom. Time does not admit of my analysing the results here, and indeed, so far as actual facts are concerned, the problem can never be solved, as a large number of coins become light each year, and the restoration of the currency, therefore, can never be complete. I might perhaps mention, as an interesting fact, that the Mint examination just referred to showed the gold coins circulating in Scotland to be less worn than those in circulation in England and Wales, owing no doubt to the general use in the north of 1*l.* notes.

The other question connected with the currency to which I wish to refer, is one which since the last meeting of the Association has been much discussed, and which, though it has not as yet been the subject of legislation, is of primary importance.

In December last, the Chancellor of the Exchequer, in an address at the London Chamber of Commerce, described the changes which he thought it would be desirable to make in the currency system of this country for the purpose of increasing the central store of gold. The Baring crisis and difficulties which accompanied it, and in particular the necessity for obtaining 3,000,000*l.* in gold from the Bank of France at very short notice, had drawn the attention of the business community to the fact that the existing metallic reserve was very small in relation to the enormous structure of credit founded upon it, and that it might be found to be wholly insufficient. Mr. Goschen's proposal was to allow the bank to issue 1*l.* notes, requiring four-fifths of any additional amount of issue so created to be covered by gold, while only the remaining fifth would be allowed to be issued against securities. The effect of this scheme, if 1*l.* notes proved popular, would have been to increase the total amount of the central store of gold, and also to increase the proportion borne by the gold in the issue department of the Bank of England to the note issue covered by it. At the same time the profits upon the fiduciary portion of the additional issue would have sufficed to defray the cost of that issue without additional charge to the public. The Chancellor of the Exchequer considered that if a substantial increase were by these means secured in the gold in the issue department, it would be safe to allow the bank, in times of crisis, an elastic power of issuing further notes against securities, upon conditions stringent enough to secure this privilege from abuse. This elastic power of increased note issue was intended to take the place of the illegal suspensions of the Bank Act which had on several occasions been found necessary in the past.

This scheme was the subject of much discussion both in the press and in banking and business communities. There appeared to be a general consensus of opinion that an increase in the central store of gold was very desirable, but there was difference of opinion as to the manner in which that increase might best be brought about. Objection was also felt by many bankers, and by a large part of the general public in the south of England, to the issue of 1*l.* notes.

The conditions of the concluding session of the late Parliament were not favourable for dealing with a large scheme of currency reform, and as it was evident that the scheme proposed would not receive such unanimous support as would make it possible to pass it without very full discussion and consideration, the Chancellor of the Exchequer did not bring his proposals before the House of Commons in the shape of a Bill.

I make no apology for devoting a large part of this Address to the subject of old-age pensions, although I am inclined to condole with my hearers and myself on the necessity of discussing a question which has now been for many months before the public, and which may by this time be considered to have been worn somewhat threadbare. But the question is surely a great and important one, on the wise solution of which the welfare of a not inconsiderable part of our population may materially depend, and one, therefore, which should certainly find a place in the discussions of this section of the British Association.

All honour, let me say in the first place, to Canon Blackley, the pioneer of the movement so closely identified with his name and labours! Canon Blackley was, and is, in the opinion of many thoughtful people, only in advance of his age, and deserving of the credit of seeing that without compulsion no system of national insurance worthy of the name can be carried into effect. His scheme, with others subsequently proposed, was considered by a committee of the House of Commons originally appointed in 1885, and reappointed in the Parliaments of 1885 and 1886, "to inquire " into the best system of national provident insurance against " pauperism." The report of the committee, issued in August, 1887, stated that their inquiry had "practically narrowed itself " into an examination of one particular scheme," namely, Canon Blackley's, "which had manifestly impressed itself, whether " favourably or unfavourably, upon the minds of witnesses, to the " exclusion of all other proposals." It might "be briefly described," they reported, as a scheme "for the compulsory insurance of all " persons, of both sexes and of every class, by the prepayment " between the ages of 18 and 21 years of the sum of 10*l.* or

" thereabouts into a national friendly or provident society,
" thereby securing to the wage-earning classes 8s. per week sick pay
" and 4s. per week superannuation pay after the age of 70 years."
In pronouncing their opinion on the scheme, the Committee first
called attention to the evidence they had received from working
men and large employers of labour in favour of enforced contributions to a national insurance fund, the latter class of witnesses
describing the benefits which had resulted from the establishment
of such funds among persons in their own employment.   They
then proceeded to record the objections to the scheme laid before
them from the administrative and actuarial points of view, to the
difficulty of enforcing the payments to the fund, to the exclusion
of all but wage earners from benefit, to the discontent which would
be felt by the upper and middle classes at being called upon to
contribute, and, finally, to the proposal for compulsion, which they
considered "open to very strong objections."   It is clear, I think,
that we are not prepared, at any rate at present, for the adoption
of so sweeping a measure.

Canon Blackley has, indeed, since expressed his willingness to
admit the idea of State aid towards pensions in accordance with
the proposals of the National Provident League, with which he is
connected; but he appears disposed to admit this and other
deviations from his original plan only as stepping stones towards a
general system of compulsory contributions.

I next turn to Mr. Chamberlain's scheme.   **Mr. Chamberlain**
and the voluntary committee of members of the House of
Commons with whom he is associated propose to establish a State
pension fund, to which Parliament should be asked to make an
annual grant, to be supplemented by contributions from local
rates.   The scheme is applicable to both men and women, and
contains provisions for the payment of certain sums into the Post
Office Savings Bank before the age of 25, and certain further
sums during each of the succeeding forty years, which would
entitle men to pensions of 13l., and women to pensions of 7l. 16s.
per annum at 65.   There are other provisions for the cases of
widows of persons dying before 65, and for other contingencies.
There can be no doubt that this is a serious and businesslike
attempt to grapple with the problem before us, but it seems open
to the objection that it only touches the fringe of the question.
By it only the willing fish would be swept into the net, while
the too numerous small fry, anxious to elude the cast of the
fisherman, whose especial object it nevertheless is to secure them,
are allowed to swim away at their ease in the sea of thriftlessness
and prospective pauperism.   No one who knows the mental
attitude and habits of thought prevalent among a large proportion

of the working classes, can have failed to note the force of the resistance which they are too often inclined to oppose to any attempt, however gentle, to bring them into the disagreeable position of making definite arrangements even for the immediate future, and of practising anything like systematic self denial. The inveterate dislike to looking forward, the hopefulness that in some cases seems actually to grow as misfortunes thicken, the daily evidence that "muddling on" often does not in fact lead to any decisive or irretrievable catastrophe—all these contribute to encourage a "happy-go-lucky" existence, and to fortify the belief that without any special effort life may not improbably be lived without great distress, and in due time brought to a fairly satisfactory end. With these fatalistic views and ideas, can we wonder that there is so little thought of the morrow? It is to be feared that such a scheme as Mr. Chamberlain's, notwithstanding the manifest advantages which it offers, would not be widely adopted except by the comparatively small number of prudent people who are already prepared to make the effort necessary to secure a provision for their old age.

Many other schemes of more or less importance and interest have been put forward. Some are ingenious; some appear to contemplate the problem from one point of view only; others are, I had almost said, fantastic. An able and useful work by Mr. J. A. Spender, published in February last, and entitled "The "State and Pensions in Old Age," with a preface by Mr. Arthur Acland, M.P., discusses the merits of the more important proposals which had then been made, and contains much valuable information.

Among the contributions to the literature of the subject should be mentioned a pamphlet by the Rev. T. W. Fowle, rector of Islip, with the title "The Poor Law, the Friendly Societies, and Old "Age Destitution—a proposed Solution." Mr. Fowle advocates the gradual extinction of out-door relief within a period not exceeding twenty-five years, and the allocation to the friendly societies of the sum thus saved, which he reckons, including cost of management, at 3,000,000*l.* per annum, on condition that they should in return guarantee a sufficient maintenance to all their members permanently disabled by sickness or old age. He further proposes that, in consideration of this subsidy, the societies should be required to be, or to become, efficient, and to subject their tables, investments, and rules to the sanction of a Government authority. I do not think the societies would consent to this arrangement. It would doubtless have the eventual effect of putting them all on a solvent basis, except those whose financial position is clearly hopeless, and whose extinction might be contemplated, as Mr. Fowle contends, with equanimity. But such an interference with the affairs of the societies generally would be resented, and their opposition to it, and to any general scheme of pensions which would affect their position and objects, could hardly be considered unnatural or altogether selfish, composed as they are in the main of the flower of the working classes, keenly alive to the advantages of their independence, and to the evils which any infringement of it might entail.

A striking instance of the feeling in this matter is afforded by the speech of the Grand Master of the Manchester Unity of Oddfellows at the annual congress of delegates held at Derby in June last. Speaking of old age pensions, Mr. Bytheway said: " For the State to assume that a man in these days was not in a " position to earn for himself sufficient to put by to keep himself " in old age without assistance from the State, would have a most " demoralising effect, and would be impolitic on national grounds, " and calculated to destroy that independence of character that " had done so much in the past history of our country to raise " and elevate the people, and encourage thrift upon the only true " basis—industry, self help, and self denial, and therefore to create " a strong self reliance in its train of good results. If the lazy or " drunken were to fare alike with the temperate and industrious, " this would not encourage thrift; and by giving pensions all " round it would certainly not be an encouragement to the better " members of society, but would act in a contrary direction. The " suggestion that the medium for granting State pensions should " be through the agency of friendly societies perhaps more imme-" diately concerned them. As they had built up for themselves a " position, and accumulated large funds by the exercise of liberty " in managing their own affairs, he would not advise running the " risk of losing this liberty and selling their own birthright for " a mess of pottage, and having the right of self management " curtailed by any intermeddling on the part of the State, which " would be sure to follow if State aid were accepted by them in " their aggregate capacity as Oddfellows. Any friendly society " accepting such aid would, no doubt, very soon be subject to State " control; in fact, having expended public money, Government " would only be doing its duty by claiming complete supervision of " the affairs of any society so aided. Whatever form the national " pension scheme took, it meant an enormous burden being cast " upon the country, and the rate and tax payers would have to " supply the means to a very great extent. The lowest estimate " would mean many millions per annum. In fact the members of " the Manchester Unity would be in the position of not only " providing for themselves but contributing to a greater number

" in the aggregate who, through laziness, dissipation, and want of
" thought to provide for a rainy day, neglected all the opportunities
" afforded by such societies as theirs, or by any other means, to
" make any provision at all for the future. This struck at the
" very root and foundation of friendly societies, and would even-
" tually endanger, if not destroy, all such institutions, as it would
" be unjust that the careful and watchful should pay for the reck-
" less and vicious, and even be punished by having to provide for
" their maintenance. . . . He himself thought that any scheme
" should be self supporting, and that the public funds should not
" be drawn upon to provide pensions. The country had been
" made what it was by individual character, and friendly societies
" had done very much to form that character among the hard
" working population, and might now be regarded as bulwarks of
" strength to it."

At another point in the working man's social scale, we find
the following resolution passed by the executive of the London
Dockers' Union in March last. While its political economy is
perhaps not so good as that of the Oddfellows, and its language is
stronger, it breathes the same spirit of dislike of interference with
the management of a pension fund: "That this executive com-
" mittee of the Dockers' Union hereby declares its opinion that
" any section of pension fund not being directly controllable by
" payees should not be countenanced in any way. We are of
" opinion also that it is an insidious attempt to perpetrate an
" unjust taxation upon wages. Also a means of retaining a large
" portion of the workers' earnings for employers' own benefit;
" while the possible good of such a system is so remote, the
" longevity of the toilers so low an average, and industrial
" mortality so high through insufficient wage and unhealthy
" environment, that we consider it opposed to economic fairness
" and a curtailment of remuneration, relieving capital and property
" of burdens at the expense of the already overtaxed and under-
" paid workmen."

Nor is the dislike to interference confined to schemes of State
aid, for we read that in February last a well known manufacturing
firm in Lancashire offered to subscribe 1,000*l.* a year towards a
sick and pension fund for their workpeople, and that the proposal
was rejected by a majority of more than two to one, on the ground,
no doubt, that it would be prejudicial to the perfect freedom of
the latter.

Among the other schemes, Mr. Vallance, the clerk of the
Whitechapel Board of Guardians, the value of whose contributions towards the science of poor law administration and cognate
subjects has been so widely acknowledged, suggests that wage

earners should be encouraged to put by small weekly sums, to be met by similar sums contributed, under legal enactment, by their employers, with a view to the formation of a bonus at death, if happening before 65, or of pension after that age. The well known objection to all such schemes is that an employer might be tempted in some shape practically to deduct from wages the amount which he would be called upon to contribute.

The proposal of Mr. T. Fatkin, secretary and manager of the Leeds Permanent Benefit Building Society, points to the investment of savings, under the management of municipal bodies, in local securities yielding a higher rate of interest than that given by the Government, the compound interest on which at 3 or $3\frac{1}{4}$ per cent. would give greater benefit to the investor. This scheme, again, is one of which it is obvious that advantage would only be taken by persons firmly resolved to make some provision for the future.

I need not specially refer to other schemes which have been recommended, with the exception of that of Mr. Charles Booth, whose views on any subject connected with the welfare of the poor must always command the highest respect. Mr. Booth has made a proposal which from its comprehensive boldness has astonished many of his admirers, and which, coming from any other quarter, would, I venture to say, have been generally characterised, if not as Utopian, at least as affording to our social and political intelligences, in their present imperfect state of development, no food for serious discussion. It is nothing less, as is well known, than a scheme for universal pensions, or general endowment of old age. With his usual straightforwardness Mr. Booth at the outset informs his readers[1] that as there are at present 733,000 women and 590,000 men, or about 1,323,000 persons in all, above 65 years of age in England and Wales, a universal pension list for those parts of the United Kingdom alone would amount, at 13*l.* each, to 17,000,000*l.* per annum. This sum is reduced by an anticipated contribution of 4,000,000*l.* from the local authorities in consideration of the reduction which would be effected in the rates, and the total amount to be provided by imperial taxation for carrying the scheme into effect throughout the United Kingdom is estimated at 16,000,000*l.* per annum. Mr. Booth anticipates that such a sum could be raised without difficulty by direct and indirect taxation, which latter might include increased duties on sugar and drink, "provided there be any desire that the thing should be done." I should fear that the means proposed would be quite sufficient to counteract any such desire, and Mr. Booth is unquestionably right

[1] "Pauperism—a Picture; and Endowment of Old Age—an Argument." London: Macmillan and Co., 1892, p. 64.

in adding that "if the project does not so far commend itself to "the community as to make the necessary sacrifice welcome, no "sensible statesman could be expected to take it up."

But even if there should be any such widely expressed desire, let us see whether the scheme should commend itself in any degree to our matured ideas of self government or to our long experience of the working of the poor law and charitable and other agencies. It is proposed that every man and woman in the United Kingdom should, after 65, receive a pension—duke and dock labourer, countess and costermonger. Every person, whatever his or her position or antecedents, whether good or bad, rich or poor, thrifty or reckless, is to be treated in precisely the same way. No man, however wealthy or neglectful of his plainest duties to society, however drunken or improvident, as soon as he has reached the magic age, is to be debarred from the right to receive his pension. Is there any merit, I would ask, in living to 65? and cannot a man or woman who has attained that age be almost as great a discredit to society as at any preceding time of life? Surely the mere fact of attaining a certain age should not obliterate the equally certain fact, it may be, that a man's whole career has been a negation of his duty as a citizen and even as a decent human being. Nor can I pass over as futile some of the many objections to the scheme which Mr. Booth mentions, and with which he deals. Among these are that the hard working and thrifty would pay for the idle and worthless, and that it is unjust as well as impolitic that the undeserving and those who have done nothing to help themselves should benefit equally with the thrifty and deserving. Mr. Booth contends (I quote his own words) that as "according to "the present law every drunken, immoral, lazy, ill tempered old "man or woman now existing has a right to demand the shelter of "the workhouse," there can therefore be no harm in according to such people a weekly allowance of 5s., which is in effect less than they would cost in the workhouse. I think the difference between the two cases is obvious. The financial results of each arrangement to the payer of rates and taxes may be nearly identical, but surely we ought to look further than this and see to it that the deserving citizen is not confronted with the spectacle of his undeserving brother living upon an allowance which he has done nothing to earn, in as perfect freedom as himself, and with every advantage, so far as the law goes, which he himself enjoys. I do not think this would be a very edifying state of things, nor one likely to promote thrift. To this second point Mr. Booth only answers that "it is even more subtly dangerous to inquire into a "man's character than into his means, if the benefit to be received "is to be kept free from all taint of pauperism." I confess that it disturbs me little, as I conceive it would disturb our disreputable friend still less, to add the taint of pauperism to the many worse taints with which he has . been polluted, and to which he has become indifferent, during a long and ill spent life. If he could look forward to his pension, as Mr. Booth proposes, would he feel a glow of moral superiority and of conscious pride in his manhood ? Hardly. His motto would only vary the epicurean "let us eat "and drink, for to-morrow we die," to "let us eat and drink, for "to-morrow" (that is, when we complete our 65th year) "we "shall get pensions of 5s. a week." But in regard to his prospective pensioners generally, however deserving, Mr. Booth admits "that a provision for old age, obtained compulsorily under the "law, and paid out of taxation, would carry with it none of the "moral benefit which would attend the winning of a pension by "direct personal sacrifice . . . nor would it directly minister "to independence of character," though he contends, in a somewhat too sanguine spirit, as it appears to me, "that no one would "make less voluntary effort to save because of it, and that many "would increase their exertions in this direction." I should have thought that, on the contrary, looking to the widespread inclination to prefer provision against sickness to insurance for old age, which is a well known feature in the habits of the working classes, and to which the arrangements of the friendly societies bear such striking witness, the mere fact of having a pension of 5s. a week to fall back upon would be sufficient to deter most of them from making further provision for the declining years which they may never live to see. Granted, however, that the advantages of a universal pension scheme from taxation were fully shown, there still remain several points touched upon by Mr. Booth which should make the cautious mind pause before consenting to its adoption. For instance, Mr. Booth says: "It is not to be forgotten "or disguised that year by year the sum needed" (for pensions) "must steadily increase, faster very likely than the rate of increase "of the whole population. . . . Happily, wealth is increasing "faster than population." When it is considered that the initial cost is estimated at 16,000,000l. per annum, this is a very disquieting suggestion, and quite sufficient in itself to make the boldest hesitate before plunging into such a sea of uncertainty. Then the administrative details of carrying the scheme into effect would necessarily be somewhat complex; and Mr. Booth shows that when the official army of registrars and superintendent registrars has been set in motion, the arrangements for fixing the age of the applicant made, and the precautions against fraudulent claims in two places taken, a great deal of difficult and harassing work will have been done. He contends, indeed, that the system is simple as compared with any scheme of national insurance, but he says enough to show that, as might be expected, a very considerable amount of trouble both to officials and claimants will be inevitable. And, finally, he makes no provision for the expenses of the scheme, which, he thinks, need not exceed from 10s. to 20s. in each case, suggesting that this amount "could be deducted " from the first payments of pension at the rate of 2s. 6d. a week " till paid." It is to be feared that, looking to the necessity which there certainly would be, especially in towns, of keeping a constant watch over each case to prevent fraud, such as the drawing of a pension after the decease of the pensioner, the services of registrars would be in pretty continuous demand, and those services would have to be paid for.

But it may be said that national pension schemes have been set on foot in other countries, and that there is no reason why we should be behindhand in the good work. It is true that in Germany three insurance laws have been passed, and according to Mr. Wilhelm Bode—whose article in the "National Review" of March last should be read by all interested in the question—the latest, that for old age and sickness, is by far the most unpopular. It is generally called the "Klebegesetz," or "sticking law," from the immense number of stamps which it is necessary to use in carrying its provisions into effect, and its administration appears to have been found intolerable. A report on the working of the law during the first year (1891) made by Herr von Bötticher in the German Reichstag in February last, shows that there were 173,668 claims for old age pensions under this law during the year, of which 132,917 were allowed, the average amount of pension being 125 marks, or 6l. a year. It is to be observed that these persons obtained pensions without having contributed anything to the insurance fund. Mr. Bode states that Herr von Bötticher congratulated himself that a larger number of persons called upon to insure had not absconded, and that the discontent caused by it was not greater, adding that no wish was felt in the country for a continuation of social reform laws. This latest social law certainly does not appear to have been attended with encouraging results. Already a popular movement for its repeal has made some way in Bavaria, but there is, of course, but little prospect of getting rid of it at present. Meanwhile the self-help societies have either ceased to exist or have been greatly crippled, and Mr. Bode can only hope that they will one by one come back, and that the energy of German manhood, sapped by the compulsory system, will return, and the dishonesty which it fostered die out. His article concludes with an earnest appeal to England not to encumber herself "with any big scheme of any impatient State socialist,"

but to remain, " what she has been so long, the chosen land of the
" free—of the men who help themselves." I think such an appeal
should touch us nearly.

In June, 1891, a Bill was presented to the French Chamber of
Deputies by M. Constans, then Minister of the Interior, and
M. Rouvier, Minister of Finance, for the creation of a " Caisse
" Nationale des Retraites Ouvrières," or pension fund for the
benefit of workmen and others employed in trade, farm labourers,
and domestic servants of both sexes, whose income does not exceed
3,000 frs. (120*l.*) per annum. All persons in this position will be
considered to be willing to take advantage of the benefits of the
fund, unless they make a declaration of unwillingness before the
mayor of their place of residence. It is proposed that the fund
should be formed by equal contributions from the depositor and his
employer, which are either to be paid into the newly established
" Caisse," or into duly authorised provident societies already
existing, and by an addition to be made by the State equal to
two-thirds of those contributions. The latter are to consist of
not less that 5 c. nor more than 10 c. per working day contributed
both by the workman and his employer; and, taking the average
number of actual working days in the year at 280, so as to allow
for holidays, slackness of work, and sickness, it is calculated that,
after thirty years of continuous saving, 5 c. per day put by from
each source, and invested at 4 per cent., should amount to a
pension of 180 frs., and 10 c. per day to a pension of 360 frs. per
annum. These amounts not being considered sufficiently high to
tempt the class whom it is desired to benefit, it is proposed, as
mentioned above, that the State should materially add to them.
The term of years over which the contributions are to spread is
limited to thirty, as, owing to compulsory army service, it is
considered that contributors will hardly have settled down to
steady work before the age of 25, and that but few persons would
be willing to continue the necessary payments beyond the age of
55 or 56. On arriving at the time for pension, the contributor
must be able to prove that his income is not more than 600 frs. per
annum. The Bill also contains provisions for life insurance, the
State contributing towards the payment of the annual premiums;
for the payment of their pensions to contributors who have become
permanently incapacitated through sickness; and for the relief of
those who may be obliged on account of accident to interrupt their
payments into the fund. Several other Bills have been brought
forward by independent deputies with analogous objects, into the
details of which time will not permit me to enter. It is interesting, however, to note that some of the methods proposed for
raising the funds necessary to enable the State to grant pensions

are hardly such as would commend themselves to our ideas ; as, for instance, the proposal in a Bill presented by several deputies that all collateral successions to property should be suppressed, and that a sliding scale of succession duty should be fixed, rising from 1 per cent. on sums below 10,000 frs. to no less than 75 per cent. on sums above 1,000,000 frs. Hardly less interesting is the suggestion of another enthusiastic legislator that, at the central office of the pensions department, to be placed in the Louvre, there should be a museum in which a "golden book" should be kept for inscribing the names of donors of not less than 100 frs. to the pension fund, while the generosity of donors of 10,000 frs. should be recorded on a marble tablet, and that of princely sub-scribers of not less than 100,000 frs. by a bust.

In Italy the question of establishing a national pension fund has also been widely discussed, and in past years several schemes have been proposed to the legislature. A Bill is now before the Chamber providing for the establishment of a central governing body, whose duty it would be to administer funds partly subscribed by authorised savings banks or other self-help societies and by individuals, and partly by the State from various specified sources. Every Italian, man or woman, certified to belong to the working classes, may subscribe to the fund, but not more than 500 lire, or 20*l.* per annum, and every person who has subscribed for not less than twenty years is to be entitled at 60 to a pension, the amount of which is to be determined by the amount of contributions made to the funds with the addition of compound interest. No pension may exceed 20*l.* per annum. Provision is also made, in the case of the subscriber's death, for the payment to his representatives of all contributions and interest. It is evident that this scheme does not go very far in the direction of establishing a general old age pension fund.

In April, 1891, the Danish Legislature passed a law, giving every Danish subject, man and woman, the right to a pension at 60 years of age. Exception is made of persons who have been convicted of crime, who have fraudulently made over their property to relations or others, who have brought themselves to distress by extravagance or evil living, who have during the preceding ten years received relief from the poor law (assistance publique), or who have been convicted of mendicity. Applications for pensions are to be addressed to the parish (commune), who will make all inquiries, and fix the amount of the relief to be granted, which may be in money or in kind. The relief may be withdrawn if the pensioner should become ineligible through misconduct or spend his pension improperly, and, if he marries, his pension is *ipso facto* withdrawn, and he becomes chargeable to the poor law.

It will be seen therefore that there is in Denmark no sentimental objection to an inquiry into an applicant's moral character and pecuniary position such as Mr. Booth so strongly deprecates, and that the so-called pensions are but an extension of the system of what we should call out-door relief. The pension is to be derived from the parish, subject to certain conditions as to the applicant's place of birth, or, if the place of birth cannot be determined, from the poor law, and the State contributes half the expenses of the parishes in distributing the relief, provided that those expenses do not exceed 1,000,000 crowns (55,000*l.*) in each of the years 1891-95, and 2,000,000 crowns (110,000*l.*) in subsequent years. No appeal lies against the decision of the communal authorities.

It is evident that, as only one of the three schemes last mentioned is in operation, they cannot as yet be fully judged, but I venture to question whether there is anything which we could think of following here. In this country there is, no doubt, a holy horror of the workhouse, but there is also a perhaps unreasonable prejudice in favour of "going as you please," and a scarcely less pronounced aversion, upon the whole reasonable and certainly characteristic to being what the French would call "administered." I can hardly imagine my countrymen, of any class or disposition, subjecting themselves to a regular system of Government interference in affairs of which the management, or mis-management for the matter of that, they have always considered to be a Briton's birthright. Let us ask ourselves, after looking at the question in all its bearings, whether we must not give up the idea of anything like compulsion in matters of thrift, if indeed we must not also give up the idea, when it came to the point, of anything in the nature of Government help and intervention.

But is there, then, no way in which help can be rendered to our deserving poor? Must the present state of things go on, and the public conscience continue to be shocked at the sight of thousands of old people lapsing hopelessly into pauperism? Let us examine the present state of things, and look a little into its causes. How is old age pauperism brought about? There is doubtless a not inconsiderable part of our population which might make at least some provision for old age, but which prefers the careless living from hand to mouth, and considers subscription to a burial club the only claim which the future has upon it. As I have already said, even where there is some thought of the morrow, inveterate habit leads many bread winners to think more of the immediate than of the comparatively distant future, and to provide rather against the risk of accident or illness by joining a sick club than against the remote prospect of destitution when the day of work is over. When all this is conceded there must remain, no doubt, many cases of unforeseen and undeserved misfortune, in which old age overtakes the toiler without his having had a chance of making provision for it—cases where wages have hardly ever been such as to allow of saving, where families have been large and sickly, where the struggling widow, work and pinch how she might, has had difficulty in keeping the wolf from the door. These are the hardships with which we must all sympathise—these are the sorrows we should all wish to relieve. Putting unavoidable misfortune aside, however, for the moment, let us consider whether our present system is such as to offer the maximum amount of encouragement to self help and self reliance, and the minimum amount of encouragement to an easy going frame of mind which looks forward .to pauperism with equanimity. What are the prospects, generally speaking, of the average worker who has made no provision for his old age? He sees the system of out-door relief in full operation; he knows that unless and until he becomes utterly helpless and friendless, a dole will be made to him which will keep him from starvation, and he learns to look forward to that dole without repugnance and without dismay. The circumstances under which it is allotted to him make but little change in his family arrangements. His able bodied children, if he has any, are seldom called upon by the guardians to make any great sacrifice for him, and he sinks down into a more or less contented, but complete and hopeless, pauperism. I say that a community which tolerates and maintains such a system incurs a grave responsibility, and, so long as it makes no effort to improve it, has no right to wax impatient at the crying evil of old age pauperism. And if a change in the system is possible, surely we ought to consider whether it cannot and ought not to be made before we seek by heroic measures to set aside arrangements susceptible of gradual improvement, and substitute for them a state of things which would perpetuate many of the worst evils of dependence. If we had reason to believe that the poor law could only be administered in the manner indicated above, we should perhaps be justified in at once looking outside it for means to improve the condition of our aged poor. But the very reverse is the case. We have abundant evidence that by firm and patient administration, the condition of whole districts in regard to pauperism may be radically changed, to the great benefit, material and moral, of the poorer inhabitants. During the last twenty years experiments in this direction have been made both in urban and rural districts, not conceived in the spirit of empiricism or caprice, but undertaken as the result of ripe experience and with a single eye to the real interests of the poor, which have been attended with complete success. The tendency of the reforms effected has been, as is well known, towards a great reduction, and in some cases the total abolition, of out-door relief. In the winter of 1869-70 the guardians of Whitechapel, one of the poorest districts in London, had forced upon them the necessity of reviewing their position. Up to that time, in the words of Mr. Vallance, the clerk to the guardians :—

"The system may be said to have been that of meeting apparent "existing circumstances of need by small doles of out-door relief, "the in-door establishments .... being reserved for the destitute "poor who voluntarily sought refuge in them. Able bodied men "who applied for relief on account of want of employment were "set to work under the Out-door Relief Regulation Order, and in "return for such work, were afforded out-door relief in money and "kind. Under this system, the administration was periodically "subjected to great pressure; so much so that the aid of the "police had not infrequently to be invoked to restrain disorder "and afford necessary protection to officers and property. Police "protection was even at times required for the guardians during "their administration of relief."

In such circumstances, it is not to be wondered at that the guardians should have earnestly endeavoured to reform " a system "which was felt to be fostering pauperism and encouraging idle- "ness, improvidence, and imposture, while the 'relief' in no true "sense helped the poor." They gradually restricted out-door relief in "out-of-work" cases, and subsequently in other cases also. Sick persons, widows, and the aged and infirm were only relieved out of the workhouse on conditions strictly applicable to their individual cases. The latter class were not so relieved unless it was proved that they had been thrifty and had no children or other relations legally or morally liable to support them and able to do so, and even they ceased to be a charge on the rates after the establishment of the Tower Hamlets Pension Fund, which was formed for the express purpose of saving the really deserving poor from the poor law. The result has been that out-door relief has gradually ceased to exist in Whitechapel, and that no cases, other than those of sudden or urgent necessity relieved by the relieving officer in kind, have been added to the out-door relief lists for more than twenty years. Notwithstanding this, the number of in-door paupers has not increased. Inquiry was made into every case in which out-door relief was withdrawn during the two years ended Lady Day, 1875, from able bodied widows and deserted women, the most helpless of all classes, with the result that out of 167 cases, comprising 600 individuals, 77 were found to be doing as well as, or better than when in receipt of out-door relief without further assistance, 52 were obtaining an independent living after having received assistance from charitable agencies or other sources, 10 had been admitted to the workhouse, 18 had apparently left the district, 2 had died, and 8 only, owing to vicious habits or the refusal of the assistance offered, were believed to be not doing well. It will thus be seen that of the 167 cases, no less than 129 had been taken from the ranks of pauperism, with the best results to themselves, to say nothing of the rate-payers, and with moral results to the community at large which cannot be described in detail here, but which must be obvious. Mr. Loch, the secretary of the Charity Organisation Society, in his work " Old Age Pensions and Pauperism,"[2] has given details showing what the results have been of a similar poor law policy in two other poor Metropolitan unions—Stepney and St. George's-in-the-East—the latter, taken as a whole, being the poorest of all. the unions in London, and comparing them with the unions of the Strand and Bethnal Green. He has also shown the results of careful administration in unions the very opposite to the London districts above mentioned, namely the rural unions of Brixworth in Northamptonshire, and Bradfield in Berkshire, as compared to the two similar unions of Linton in Cambridgeshire, and Midhurst in Sussex. The facts brought out by these two sets of comparisons are striking and conclusive. In unions in which there has been a careful administration of the poor law for a period, more or less, of twenty years, it has been proved that the proportion of paupers over 60 to population can be reduced in the country to about 4 per cent., and in London, judging by its poorest union, by more than half the present number. Can it be doubted that in these cases the bugbear of old age pauperism has already been faced and in a great measure dispelled, and is there any reason, beyond the force of habit and a *vis inertia* which surely might be grappled with, why both town and country guardians should not follow the example set them by the pioneers of this movement, and by a common effort subdue the common enemy? Let us not, with the experience we have to guide us, be led astray in this matter, though some of our philanthropists and political economists seem inclined to countenance a large increase of public expenditure in connection with the relief of the poor. Among the many nostrums for the cure of the disease under which the State is supposed to labour, is a proposal by Mr. Bartley, M.P., embodied in the " Old Age Provident Pension Bill," which he brought in during the last session of Parliament. Mr. Bartley proposes that every

---

[2] " Old-Age Pensions and Pauperism." An Inquiry as to the Bearing of the Statistics of Pauperism quoted by the Right Hon. J. Chamberlain, M.P., and others in support of a scheme for National Pensions. London: Swan, Sonnen-schein and Co., 1892.

person (man or woman) of 65, who is not a criminal or drunkard, and who is unable to earn the wages of his calling, shall be entitled to a pension of 7s. per week from the local authority, which is to be the county council, provided that he has never received poor law relief. If he has purchased an annuity from the post office or some friendly society, or paid a lump sum for the purchase of a deferred annuity from the post office, or is prepared to pay a lump sum of not less than 10l. to the local authority, or has partially provided for himself in other ways, to the satisfaction of the local authority, he is to be entitled to a pension of 3s. 6d. per week, with the addition of an extra amount according to the payments which he has made. And further, there are to be pensions, if the local authority should see fit, of 3s. 6d. per week even for the persons declared ineligible, provided that they can show unavoidable illness or misfortune. The necessary funds are to be raised by a special rate to be called the " pension " rate." I need not do more than call attention to these provisions to show how disastrous such a law would be. The burden which would be imposed on the county councils of deciding upon the merits or demerits of each case ; the wide discretion allowed in the award of pensions, even to the criminal and drunkard, if only what can be construed into "unavoidable misfortune." can be proved; and the danger that absolutely different constructions of the law would prevail in different localities—all combine to make it next to impossible but that its operations should be fatal to the exercise of thrift, and should bring back in redoubled force many of the evils of extensive out-door relief, with greatly increased burdens on the ratepayer. Among the political economists I regret to say that an eminent professor, and what is more (I speak with bated breath), a former president of this Section, has thrown his great weight into the scale of wide, if not lavish, distribution of out-door relief. I am not quite sure that I understand Professor Marshall's position, but he propounds in the " Economic Journal " sixteen questions which he thinks should be considered before any large scheme is undertaken for the relief of the aged, and which seem incidentally to show his antagonism ot most of what I had thought to be the generally accepted maxims of poor-relief.

But let it not be supposed that advocates of a firm and careful administration of the poor law consider it the only thing required to prevent or deal with all cases of old age pauperism. In the best regulated unions, especially in towns, there will always be cases—too many, alas !—of highly deserving old people who are unable to maintain themselves, and of whom no just person could bear to think as condemned to out-door relief, and still less to incarceration in a workhouse. These are precisely the cases which

. are best brought out where out-door relief has either been entirely abolished or is quite the exception. For these—and experience in well managed unions has shown how comparatively few they are—there surely remains the exercise of a well ordained charity which will step in and prevent a consummation so much to be deprecated. Children and other relations, who under a loose system of poor-relief are too apt to consider that in one shape or other their parents and aged kinsfolk may naturally be left to the tender mercies of the poor law, are brought together and induced to contribute to their support, and pension societies, such as the Tower Hamlets Pension Committee, the local pension committees of the Charity Organisation Society, and the like, are willing and anxious to come to the rescue. Nor is this organised assistance to those whom the late Duke of Albany called " the aristocracy of the " poor," of use to the recipients only. In hundreds of cases which have come under my own knowledge in east London, for instance, it has been the means of inspiring in men and women a holy zeal for charity which, without any hateful feeling of patronage on the one side, or of cringing dependence on the other, gives a scope, such as none other can supply, for a true friendship between rich and poor, and blesses both the giver and the receiver. I have endeavoured to show, in these few and necessarily brief remarks about one of the great social questions which occupy men's minds to-day, that for the promotion of the best interests of our aged poor, there may be a "more excellent way" than a vast organisation of State aided pensions. May we work out this and other similar problems, as Englishmen do, calmly, wisely, and to good effect!

But turning to our immediate duty as members of this Section, let us endeavour to ascertain what we can do to inculcate and foster sound views on these and similar subjects. In the proceedings of this British Association for the Advancement of Science we may see how intimately the work of Section F is related to that of the sections in which the physical and mechanical sciences are studied. The extraordinary advances which have of late years been made in the application of science to industry have materially added to the wealth of the working classes, and that wealth is more easily earned than in the past. But their knowledge of the great economic laws upon which true progress must depend has not kept pace with their increased resources; nor can this be the case until they are able to grasp the principles of our subject. It may fairly be urged that the advance in physical science is drawing its relations to economic science closer day by day. May we not be about to witness some of the

enormous developments caused by the substitution of machinery
for hand labour which we have for some time past been led to
expect?   The rapid exhaustion of coal fields, to which Sir Robert
Ball has recently again called attention, is leading to the utilisation
of power from other sources, a question with which the President
of Section G will doubtless deal.

We are told that the falls of Niagara develop a force of $4\frac{1}{2}$ million horse power, or the equivalent of all the steam power used in
the world, and that steps have been taken for the immediate utilisation from this source of 100,000 horse power, or the equivalent
of one forty-fifth part of the steam power of the globe.   Advances
such as these in the utilisation and transmission of energy must,
by extending the means of production, profoundly affect the wage
earning capacity of the workman, and consequently the general
relations between employers and employed; and it is the privilege
of members of this Section to prepare their countrymen for the
altered condition under which they may be called upon to live and
work.   They must never be weary in setting before all sections of
the community the necessity of being ready to face such momentous
changes as those which I have indicated, and, if I may be permitted
to borrow an illustration from electrical science, I would say that
their duty is analogous to that of the " transformers," of which so
much has lately been heard.   They deal less with energy itself
than with its control, but their function is so to change forces of
unwonted "potential," that those forces may cease to be dangerous
and disruptive, and may be made to weld the various efforts of
humanity into coherence and strength.

An Inquiry *into the* Trustworthiness *of the* Old Bills *of*
Mortality.

By Dr. William Ogle, M.D., F.R.C.P.

The London Bills of Mortality are usually said, on the authority
of Captain Graunt, to have begun in 1592-93; but Maitland,
writing in the middle of the last century, puts back their commencement to the year 1562. "In that year," he writes, "a
" grievous pestilence raged in this city; therefore in order to know
" the increase and decrease of the same, 'twas judged necessary to
" take an account of the number of burials, which being the first of
" the kind that was ever taken in *London*, it commenced on the first
" of *January, Anno* 1562,[1] and ended the last of *December*, 1563;
" whereby it appears that the number total buried within the City
" and Suburbs in that year, amounted to 23,630, whereof of the
" Plague 20,136."[2] This same bill had also been given by Stowe,[3]
who was living in the year to which it relates, and whose account
contains the further information that the area covered by the bill
consisted of 108 parishes " in the citie and liberties thereof," and
of eleven other parishes " adjoining to the same citie."

As this bill for 1563 is for the exact year of 365 days, it is
plain that it cannot have been obtained by summation of successive weekly bills. Nevertheless, it appears from passages in
Stowe's "Memoranda," published by the Camden Society,[4] that
weekly returns were prepared at that time, for Stowe gives the
number of deaths from the plague for each week from 3rd July,
1563, to 26th July, 1566. It is curious, however, that in one of
this long series of weekly returns the period covered is not an
exact week of seven days, but only a period of six days, namely
from[5] 18th July to 23rd July inclusive; and it therefore appears
not impossible that such variations may have been made in the
length of periods covered by the weekly returns as would allow

---

[1] *I.e.*, 1563 as we should date it; the year at that time ending in March.
[2] Maitland's "History of London" (1756), p. 736.
[3] Stowe's "Ann." (edit. 1631), p. 657. Stowe gives the total as 23,660 or
30 more than Maitland.
[4] Camden Society, 1880, "Gairdner," pp. 128 and 144.
[5] The omission of one day from this bill had the effect of making the last
weekly return in the year end on 31st December; but there must have been previous alterations in the weekly returns if they commenced on 1st January; for the
days from 1st January to 17th July inclusive are not divisible by seven.

a general bill to be constructed from them for the exact year from 1st January to 31st December.

Maitland says that he had seen this general bill for 1563 in the library of Sir Hans Sloane; and as that library passed into the possession of the British Museum, I hoped to have found it in that wilderness of books. In this, however, I was disappointed; but in the course of my search I lighted by accident[e] on a bill of still greater age. This bill, which is for a week "syns the "xvi[th] day of November unto the xxiii day of the same month," is unfortunately without the date of the year; but is catalogued doubtfully as being about 1512. Why this precise year was selected I have been unable to discover, but I am assured by experts in such matters that the handwriting is indisputably of the earlier part of the sixteenth century. The precise date, however, is not a matter of much importance. It is sufficient for the present to have shown that the bills of mortality in London go back much farther than has been usually supposed, and were not unknown even in the earlier part of the sixteenth century.[7]

By whom those earlier returns were compiled can only be surmised; but in all probability they were drawn up by the same agency as the later bills, namely, the Company of Parish Clerks, who had been incorporated by Henry III as the Brotherhood of St. Nicolas, and who, so far as can be seen, would have been the only body in possession of the necessary information as to burials.

As the main object of the bills was to give information concerning the plague, their publication discontinued with its cessation, to be renewed however when fresh outbreaks occurred; and thus up to the year 1603 the bills only appeared intermittirgly. But in that year the publication became permanent, and has continued without break to the present day. Although however the publication of the bills was thus intermittent, it does not appear to be equally certain that the materials were not collected continuously by the parish clerks; for that this company collected in after years much information concerning the mortality which they did not include in their published returns is certain, and, moreover, a very large proportion of the weekly returns given by Stowe

---

[e] Egerton MSS. 2603, f. 4. See Appendix A.

[7] Since the above was written, a learned work ("History of Epidemics," Cambridge, 1891) has been published by Dr. Creighton, in which are given many new and interesting particulars as to the bills of mortality of the sixteenth century. The Egerton bill, on which Dr. Creighton had also lighted, is attributed by him with much probability to 1532, in which year an Order of Council was issued calling on the mayor to furnish a bill of the deaths from plague. The bill which Dr. Brewer ascribed to the year 1528, is shown conclusively by Dr. Creighton to belong to 1585. Dr. Creighton also gives particulars of a long series of weekly bills from 1578 to 1583, discovered by him among the papers of Lord Burghley at Hatfield.

covers a period, viz., from 23rd June, 1564, to 26th July, 1566, when the great outbreak of plague of 1563 had come to an end, and during the whole of which scarcely a death from that disease occurred in London.

It appears probable, therefore, that the parish clerks made continuous returns to their company of the burials in their respective parishes, but that it was only in times of pestilence that they were called on by the Government to make those returns public; and that the figures given by Stowe for the period when plague was absent were obtained by him not from any public returns, but direct from the company's register or books.

The earlier bills existed only in manuscript; it was not until 1625 that they were issued in print; the Company of Parish Clerks having in that year "obtained a decree, or act, under the " seal of the High Commission Court or Star Chamber, for the " keeping of a printing press in their hall in order to the printing " of the weekly and general bills within the City of London and " liberties thereof; for which purpose a printer is assigned by the " Archbishop of Canterbury. And on the 18th of July that year, " a printing press was accordingly set up, and an order then made " that from thenceforth the weekly reports of the burials, within " the circuits aforesaid, should be printed, with the number of " burials against every parish, which till that time had not been " done." [3]

Although only the City and its liberties are mentioned in the foregoing order, as a matter of fact the area comprised in the bills was by no means thus limited. Even in 1603, when the bills first became continuous, in addition to the parishes of the City and its liberties, certain out parishes in Middlesex and Surrey were included, and further parishes were added to the list in 1604, 1606, 1626, and 1636. The only addition made in the next century was of St. Mary-le-Strand, with the Duchy of Lancaster, which was taken in in 1726. No addition whatsoever was made in the nineteenth century up to 1849, in which year the old bills of the parish clerks came to an end, having been practically superseded since 1840 by the new bills published under the authority of the Registrar-General, and covering a very much wider area. The details of the successive additions to the bills, old and new, are given in an Appendix (B) to this paper. It is important to notice the existence of such changes, because otherwise the error may be made—and indeed has often been made—of supposing that the total deaths in the successive returns are throughout deaths in one and the same area.

* "A Collection of the Yearly Bills of Mortality from 1657 to 1758 inclusive" (1759), p. 9.

Besides these changes in the area covered by the bills, there were also notable changes from time to time in the particulars given.

The weekly bills when they first became continuous gave the number of burials only in the aggregate for the whole area, and not separately for each parish; males and females were not distinguished; the causes of death, excepting the plague, were not stated, nor were the deaths classified by ages.

These deficiencies were gradually remedied; parishes being distinguished in 1625,[9] sexes and causes in 1629, and ages, in the general if not in the weekly bill, in 1728. The number of christenings (Appendix C) appears to have been given from the commencement, at any rate in the Annual Bill. Although these several particulars only made their appearance in the bills at the dates just given, they seem to have been collected by the parish clerks from the beginning, but not published; for Graunt,[10] writing in the latter half of the seventeenth century, notes that "although the "general yearly bills have been set out in the several varieties "afore mentioned, yet the original entries in the hall-books were "as exact in the very first year, as to all particulars, as now, and "the specifying of casualties and diseases was probably more."

The mode in which the bills were composed is thus described by the same writer : "When any one dies, then, either by tolling "or ringing of a bell, or by bespeaking of a grave by the sexton, "the same is known to the searchers, corresponding with the said "*Sexton*. The *Searchers* hereupon (who are ancient matrons, "sworn to their office) repair to the place where the dead Corps "lies, and by view of the same, and by other enquiries, they "examine by what *Disease* or *Casualty* the Corps died. Here-"upon they make their report to the *Parish Clerk*, and he, every "*Tuesday* night, carries in an Accompt of all the *Burials* and "*Christnings* happening that week, to the *Clerk* of the *Hall*. "On Wednesday the general Accompt is made up and printed, and "on *Thursday* published and dispersed to the several families who "will pay four shillings *per Annum* for them."

This account of the manner in which the data for the weekly bill were obtained is perhaps not quite so clear as might be wished. The natural interpretation of it, however, would be that the searchers ascertained, so far as they could, the causes of death, and reported the results of their inquiries to the parish clerk, who

---

[9] It is, however, to be noted that, as the information was obtained from each parish separately, there were always the means of giving the deaths by parishes ; and that as a matter of fact they were so given in the earliest weekly bill now extant, namely, the bill in the Egerton manuscripts at the British Museum.

[10] Graunt's "Observations," &c., 5th edit. (1676), p. 17.

obtained either from the sexton or from the parish register the number of burials, and combining the two, made his return to the clerk of the Hall. But, if this were so, it would seem hardly possible, excepting in rare cases of very gross carelessness, that the number of burials in the week in a given parish should have been wrongly returned, and especially impossible that more burials should be returned as having happened in the week than was actually the case. Yet a comparison of the annual bills with the parish registers of burials shows that such must have been a frequent occurrence. For, as I shall have occasion presently to point out in more detail, the number of burials as given in the register is frequently in excess of the number given in the annual bill, and still more frequently falls short of it; I think it therefore very probable, as the only explanation I can see of these discrepancies, that very often the searcher must have been trusted to return not only the causes of death, but also the number of burials; and that such return sometimes included deaths of persons who were afterwards not buried in the parish graveyard, and more frequently omitted deaths of persons who were so buried, but concerning which the searcher received no information.

Be this however as it may, the untrustworthiness of the bills was soon recognised. Graunt, writing in 1665, estimates [11] that in the years of plague—the very disease for information concerning which the bills had been instituted—the deaths caused by it were understated by 25 per cent. And that the returns generally, so far as they depended upon the reports of the searchers, must have been excessively untrustworthy, may be inferred with much certainty from a chance passage in which he speaks of these old women as performing their office "after the "mist of a cup of ale," and as ready to conceal anything which the friends of a deceased person might wish to hide if they received "the bribe of a two-groat fee instead of one," which appears to have been their proper fee at that period. [12]

Attacks of this kind made it necessary for Mr. Bell, who was then the clerk to the Parish Clerks' Company, to say what he could in defence of the bills; and consequently in the preface to "The General or Whole Year's Bill," for the year 1665, he thus expresses himself: " Searchers are generally ancient women, "and I think are therefore most fit for their office. But sure I am "they are chosen by some of the eminentest men of the Parish to "which they stand related; and if any of their Choosers should "speak against their abilities they would much disparage their "own judgements. And after such choice they are examined

---

[11] Graunt, *op. cit.*, p. 49.   [12] *Op. cit.*, p. 34.

' touching their sufficiency, and sworn to that office by the *Dean of*
" *Arches*, or some Justice of the Peace, as the cause shall require. As
" for the Clerks' returns I dare affirm that they were never more
" punctual in the discharge of their duties than at this day." And
he goes on to say that they like the Searchers are sworn, " and I
" presume there cannot be a stricter obligation than an oath to
" bind any person." As this was all that Mr. Bell could find to
say in answer to the serious charges against the accuracy of the
bills, we may conclude with much certainty that those charges were
substantially true, and that the bills in the middle of the seventeenth
century were grievously deficient. Nor do they appear to have
improved in later times. Thus in " A Collection of the Yearly
" Bills of Mortality from 1657 to 1758 inclusive," published in 1759,
the anonymous editor, who was clearly a man of ability and of
painstaking accuracy, thus expresses himself : " There is another
" material defect which affects both baptisms and burials . . . This
" arises from the neglect of parish clerks and their deputies in not
" making exact returns to the common-hall. From some large
" parishes no account is sent for weeks together, and the account
" for several is sometimes inserted in one weekly bill. If this was
" done without any omissions the account would come right at the
" end of the year; but omissions in many, there is good reason to
" believe, are never supplied or corrected. This is often to be
" ascribed to negligence, but it is sometimes owing to disputes
" between the clerk in orders and the officiating clerk, that the
" bills of births and burials are neither so regularly kept nor so
" accurately returned as they ought to be. What allowance is to
" be made for these omissions can be hardly settled; but it is
" judged that they are not inconsiderable." [13]

Similarly, Maitland, writing in 1756, says that " The Bill of
" Mortality of the City of London is certainly one of the most
" defective of its kind," and even so late as 1835, when the old
bills were just coming to their end, we find the writer of the
article " Bills of Mortality," in the " Penny Cyclopædia," re-
iterating the old complaint of the evil habits of the searchers.
" On the death," says the writer, " of an individual within the
" prescribed limits, intimation is sent to the searchers, to whom
" the undertaker or some relative of the deceased furnishes the
" name and age of the deceased and the malady of which he died.
" No part of this information is properly authenticated, and it
" may be true or false. The appointment of searcher is generally

[13] *Op. cit.*, p. 6. The writer is believed to have been Dr. Birch, as much of
the preface exists in manuscript in the papers of that gentleman now in the
British Museum. (The copy in the Museum was given by Dr. William Heberden,
who received it from the editor.)

" made by the churchwardens, and usually falls upon old women,
" and sometimes on those who are notorious for their habits of
" drinking. The fee which these official characters demand is
" one shilling, but in some cases two public authorities of this
" description proceed to the inspection, when the family of the
" defunct is defrauded out of an additional shilling. They not
" unfrequently require more than the ordinary fee, and owing
" to the circumstances under which they pay their visit, their
" demands are generally complied with. In some cases they even
" proceed so far as to claim as a perquisite the articles of dress in
" which the deceased died. Such are the means at present
" employed in collecting medical and political statistics in the
" metropolis of England."

Whether these and the earlier charges against the searchers
were true we have now no means of ascertaining, but this we may
most confidently assert, that, quite independently of any intentional
dishonesty on the part of these " ancient women," statements of
causes of death collected by them in the way described, and without further verification, are of very little, if of any, real value.
In the case only of very obvious diseases, of diseases that are
attended by external symptoms easily recognised and not easily
confounded with the symptoms of other ailments, can much
reliance be placed on such haphazard diagnosis as ocular inspection of the body by an unskilled searcher, even if sworn to the
office by the Dean of Arches? The charges, however, made
against the parish clerks, that they were careless and inaccurate
in making their returns to the Clerk of the Company, admit of
examination; for many of the parish registers are in existence,
and some of these have been published, and we can compare the
number of burials in such parishes as given in the bills with the
number as entered in the register. The result of a considerable
number of such comparisons which I have made, has been to show
that the two rarely tally. Out of one hundred and twenty comparisons made by me between the annual return in the bills and
the entries in a parish register, there were only twenty occasions,
that is once in six times, in which bill and register gave the same
number.

In all the remaining hundred instances there was a discrepancy,
and sometimes a very large one. The balance was sometimes on
one side, sometimes on the other; that is to say the number of
deaths given in the bill sometimes exceeded, sometimes fell short
of, the number of entries in the register; and, as these errors
occurring indifferently in contrary directions tended of course to
correct each other, the total amount of error was but slight when
a sufficiently long series of years was taken into account.

For instance, the bills for the ten years 1657-66 show for the five parishes of St. Peter's Cornhill, St. Michael's Cornhill, St. Dionis Backchurch, St. Thomas the Apostle, and St. Mary Aldermary, an aggregate of 1,879 burials, while the registers only show an aggregate of 1,843.

Burials from 22nd December, 1656, to 18th December, 1666.

Parish.	Bills.	Register.
St. Peter's, Cornhill	410	418
St. Michael's, Cornhill	362	332
St. Thomas the Apostle	408	402
St. Dionis, Backchurch........................	357	352
St. Mary, Aldermary	347	339
	1,879	1,843

The years indicated in the above table take in the great plague year, 1665, and it is to be noted that, notwithstanding the alarm and general confusion caused by that visitation, the figures for that year tally in the two records in a more than average degree. There were in that year 586 burials in these parishes according to the bills, and 580 according to the parish registers.

Then came the great fire, destroying many of the parishes. But for two of the above mentioned parishes I have continued the comparison to the end of the century, with the following result:—

Burials from 21st December, 1669, to 17th December, 1700.

Parish.	Bills.	Register.
St. Peter's, Cornhill	1,020	1,062
St. Dionis, Backchurch........	934	961
	1,954	2,023

In this period the balance is on the side of the registers, the deficiency in the bills being nearly $3\frac{1}{4}$ per cent.; but if the figures be added to those of the earlier period in the same century, the total of the bills comes to 3,833, while the total by the register is 3,866, the deficiency in the bills being therefore on the whole account less than 1 per cent.

A similar result is obtained by a comparison of bills and registers in the next century, as the following table shows, in which the bills for the ten years 1744-53 show in six parishes an aggregate of 1,092 burials, while the registers show 1,097, or almost the same number, the deficiency in the bills being again less than 1 per cent.

Burials from 13*th December,* 1743, *to* 11*th December,* 1753.

Parish.	Bills.	Register.
St. Peter's, Cornhill	168	158
St. Michael's, Cornhill	161	172
St. Thomas Apostle	99	114
St. Dionis, Backchurch..............	268	310
St. Mary, Aldermary............................	194	164
St. John Baptist, Wallbrook	202	179
Total	1,092	1,097

On the whole, then, judging from these samples, we are justified in assuming that the bills in the seventeenth and eighteenth centuries, though they give figures for single years and for individual parishes that rarely tally exactly with those derived from the registers, nevertheless, when taken in the aggregate and for a sufficient series of years, are fairly accurate transcripts of the parish registers.

But when we pass on to the nineteenth century the state of things appears to have got worse. I have not, it is true, made any direct comparisons between the bills and the parish registers in this century, but an examination of the bills themselves renders it practically certain that the returns had become very untrustworthy. Again and again there occur years in which some or other parish makes no return at all. Thus Bridewell Precinct made no return from 1806 to 1814; the Savoy, none in 1814, nor from 1816 to 1819; St. John, Wapping, made no return in 1815; St. Ann's, Soho, in 1821 and 1823; St. Leonard's, Shoreditch, in 1826; and St. George's, Hanover Square, altogether ceased to make a return from 1824 onwards. Moreover, the returns themselves, when made, fluctuate from year to year in so extraordinary a manner that it is impossible, without very strong evidence to the contrary, to admit their approximate accuracy. For instance, the burials in St. Leonard's, Shoreditch, after averaging about 900 a year pretty regularly, drop suddenly in 1822 to 372, rising in the next three years to 1,046, 1,058, 1,666, respectively; then in 1826 not being given at all, and then again suddenly rising to 2,195 in 1827.

St. Mary, Whitechapel, returns 429 burials in 1820, then 1,004 in 1821, and then drops again in 1822 to 586. Similarly inexplicable fluctuations occur in the returns from other parishes, such as St. George's-in-the-East, St. George's Hanover Square, and St. John's Clerkenwell. Of course, in times of great pestilences, such as occurred in the sixteenth and seventeenth centuries, enormous differences might reasonably be expected to occur, and, as a matter of fact, did occur, in the number of burials in consecutive years; but there have been no pestilences such as these in the nineteenth century, and the fluctuations in the bills are vastly too great and too irregular to be accounted for by variations in any of the diseases with which we are familiar. The conclusion, therefore, seems forced upon us that the old bills of mortality had become in the nineteenth century much less accurate than they had been in earlier times, and that any estimates of mortality based upon these will almost certainly, owing to the frequent neglect of parishes to make any return at all, be very far short of the reality. A single example will show this : St. George's, Hanover Square, as above stated, made no return from 1824 onwards; but the burials in this one parish had averaged 857 annually in the preceding nine years, so that the neglect of this one parish caused a deficiency of 857 burials in the year, or a not inconsiderable proportion of the whole number given for London in the bills.

Thus much then as to the degree in which the figures in the old bills of mortality may be supposed to tally with the number of burials as given in the parish registers. The question, however, necessary though it was to inquire into it, really becomes almost unimportant when the very much more serious defects in the bills arising from other causes are taken into consideration.

These defects, stated shortly, are as follows : the figures given in the bills are for burials, not for deaths; they are for burials only of members of the Established Church, excluding therefore all Roman Catholics and all the various kinds of non-conformists ; lastly they do not include all the burials even of members of the Established Church, but only of such of these as were buried in the parish churches and cemeteries;[14] "by which means," as Maitland observes, many burial grounds belonging to the Church of England, such as St. Paul's Cathedral, Westminster Abbey, " the Temple Church, St. Peter's ad Vincula, the Rolls and " Lincoln's Inn Chapels, the Charter House and divers others " belonging to hospitals " are excluded from the reckoning.

What proportion of burials of the Church of England population took place in these private burial grounds I have no means of estimating. Probably it was no very serious proportion of the whole; still the number was not inconsiderable, for I find that there were buried 1,112 persons at Chelsea Hospital[15] in the twenty years from 1781 to the end of the century; at St. Peter's ad Vincula there were 14 burials in each of the years 1729 and

[14] " History of London," ii, 740.
[15] Burial register of Chelsea Hospital, in General Register Office, No. 38.

1730,[16] while in Westminster Abbey,[17] the only other one of these burial places concerning which I have been able to find information, there were buried 400 persons in the last twenty years of the seventeenth century (1681-1700), and 210 in the last twenty years of the eighteenth century (1781-1800).

Of much more serious import is the fact that a large number of persons who died within the limits of the bills of mortality were carried away to be buried in the country. In some of the parish registers the names of these persons and the place to which they · were carried to be buried have been entered by the clerk or church-warden, and it is surprising to see, considering the difficulties of transport in those days, what a large number of corpses were carried to considerable distances, both from and to London, for burial.

This fact, and also the further important fact that the number carried out far exceeded the number carried in, was noted by Maitland, who states, "I have for divers years observed that " the number of persons carried from London to be inhumed in " other parts of the country, is greater than that of those brought " from all other places in the kingdom[18] to be buried in this city " and suburbs." And the careful compiler of the collection of· bills of mortality published in 1759 is more explicit in his statement, and has taken pains to form an estimate of the amount of deficiency in the bills thus brought about.[19] " Another defect in the " bills," he says, " not so generally attended to, is that the number " of persons carried into the country to be buried is not brought " into account in them. Many are frequently removed from one " parish to be buried in another that are both within the bills, " which makes no difference upon the whole. But great numbers " are carried from parishes in town to be buried in the country. " This number has probably increased, as the fashion of having " country houses has more prevailed. A few indeed who die else- " where are brought to be buried in parishes within the bills; but " the number of these is very disproportionate to those who are " carried out. A distinct account of this matter ought to be kept " in the several parishes, but seldom is kept with any exactness.

"In one of the largest and most populous parishes in West- " minster, in which as careful a register is made as in any, the " account is found to stand thus:—

[16] See bills of mortality for these years. St. Peter's ad Vincula was put into the bill in 1729; "But a contest arising between the inhabitants of the Tower· " Liberty without and within the Tower, whether the church of St. Peter's ad " Vincula was parochial or not, the question was tryed in the Court of King's " Bench at Westminster in 1730, when it was determined in the negative, which " occasioned this church to be left out of the bills of mortality soon after." MS. 4213, 1. British Museum.

[17] Register of Westminster Abbey.

[18] *Op. cit.,* ii, p. 742.

[19] *Op. cit.,* p. 5.

"Buried here each year, at an average, for the last ten years 1,074

"Carried out to be buried every year, on an average 261

"Brought in every year, at an average . ... `124`

    "Of these, at least one-sixth are children of the⎱

      "parish out at nurse in the neighbourhood,⎱   104

      "and to be considered as persons living and ⎰ 20⎰

      "dying in the parish ....⎰

"Difference between those carried out and brought in................ 157

                                            1,074

"Total of persons dying in the parish each year 1,231

"This may be of some use in forming a judgment of the rest;
"and yet this is far from being perfect. Those who are brought
"in to be buried are carefully registered, those who are carried
"out are not so. Such are entered by themselves in the burial
"account as come to the knowledge of those whose business it is
"to attend to these matters; but of these many are heard of but
"by accident, and some not at all.

"Supposing the number of persons carried away and not
"brought to account to be one-sixth (which I think comes as near
"the truth as any supposition we can make), this will make the
"whole number of deaths to be one-fifth more than are registered
"in the bills.

"If the state of deaths which are not registered in the bills be
"the same or nearly the same in this parish as in others, the
"defect in this article may with some degree of probability be
"supplied." And then he goes on to deal with other defects with
which at present we are not concerned.

It appears, therefore, according to this estimate, which was
clearly made with much care, and against the reception of which
I can see no reason, that, simply owing to this one cause of
omission, we must add 20 per cent. each year to the total number
of deaths given in the bills.

Nor is this all; for there still remains another cause of defect
which, so far as I can judge, was of about the same magnitude.
The bills were intended only to "comprehend persons belonging to
"the Church of England, and buried according to its service," and
though "some few among the poorer sort, both of papists and
"dissenters, who live at a distance from their respective burial
"grounds, and cannot bear the expence of being carried thither,
"are buried according to the rites of the Church of England,
"and by that means have a place in the weekly bills,"[20] such was
only an exceptional occurrence, and the great mass of Roman
Catholics and of the non-conformists were buried in their own
cemeteries, and were altogether unrecognised in the bills.

[20] *Op. cit.*, pp. 4 and 5.

What proportion of the population belonged to the Roman
Catholic and the non-conforming communities it is not easy to
estimate. Indeed, we may feel pretty certain that the proportion
varied very greatly from time to time. For instance, in the latter
half of the seventeenth century the authorities appear to agree in
saying that the number of dissenters declined very greatly; and
many of the non-conformist ministers, especially of the Presbyterians, joined the Church of England, and often, as Tillotson,
Butler, Secker, rose to great eminence in it. Bishop Burnet,
speaking in the House of Lords, said that at a moderate computation the non-conformists had declined one-fourth, if not one-
third. This, however, does not help us much, as we do not know
what was the proportion before this falling off of a fourth or
a third.[21] It is, however, said that "a computation was made by
the direction of Compton, Bishop of London, soon after the
revolution, of the number of dissenters, taking in papists and all
others, and that made them to be as one to ten.[22] If the decline
of one-fourth or one-third of which Bishop Burnet spoke, was from
this proportion, the non-conformists at the end of the seventeenth
century must have been no more than one in fifteen.

As to the proportion in the next, that is, the eighteenth
century, the information is still very uncertain. Thus Maitland,
writing in 1756, says that some persons estimated that one half
was the proportion, but this he thinks is a great mistake, and he
himself holds that not more than 1 in 7½ was either a Catholic
or a Dissenter;[23] and by an examination of the burial registers in
many of the non-conformists' cemeteries, he considers that in 1729
the number of persons buried either in these cemeteries, or in
private burial grounds belonging to the Church of England was
3,038.[24] As, however, the burials as given in the bill for that
year were 29,722, the omission of 3,038 would only amount
in round numbers to 1 in 11. The estimate made by the
editor of the collection of bills, written after Maitland, and
with full knowledge and quotation of his calculation, puts the
proportion at 1 in 6, and this estimate I am disposed to accept
as the more probable, partly because I am impressed by the
great carefulness with which this writer deals with his figures,
and partly because such limited means of inquiry as I have been
able to apply tally more nearly with this estimate than with that
of Maitland. Thus I chanced to find that in the London parishes
of St. Mary Aldermary, and St. Thomas the Apostle, the church-
warden or some other official had taken the trouble to enter in

[21] *Cf.* Abbey and Overton, "English Church in Eighteenth Century," i, 480.
[22] "Burnet's History of His Own Time," v, 187, *note* (Oxford edit., 1823).
[23] "History of London," p. 746.   [24] *Op. cit.*, p. 742.

their parish registers, under the date Lady Day, 1733, a list of the houses in their respective parishes, with the names of the occupiers, the number of their families, and whether they were church people or non-conformists; and in the register of St. Mary Aldermary, a similar list is given eighteen months later. So far as can be ascertained from these lists, the catholics and dissenters formed about 28 per cent. of the total population, or more than 1 in 4. Of course it is possible that these two small parishes may have been exceptional, and not truly representative of the bulk. I have no reason, however, to suppose this to have been the case (see Appendix D). I have also tried to estimate the proportion by an examination of those burial registers of non-conformist communities in London that are in the custody of the Registrar-general. Unfortunately, however, this collection does not include all the non-conformist registers, nor are there any of the Roman Catholics. All therefore that I have been able to ascertain with certainty is that the number of burials in those non-parochial cemeteries was very large; I counted up in those registers to which I had access 2,067 burials in 1780, and 2,329 in 1790. If to these be added the burials in those non-conformist registers which are not now forthcoming, and those of Roman Catholics, and we remember that the total number of burials in 1790 given in the bills for that year was only 18,038, it will be seen that the estimate of 1 in 6 is by no means improbable. It merely supposes that in addition to the 2,329 counted by me, there were 1,279 others of which I was unable to obtain evidence.

If, then, we accept this estimate of the proportion of the population of London who in the eighteenth century were outside the Church of England, we shall have to correct the total of burials given in the bills of mortality in that period, which, as we have seen, have already had to be raised by 20 per cent. for the burials of those who were carried out to be buried in the country, by a further 20 per cent.; and the double correction will now amount to no less than 44 per cent.

Even if it be thought that the estimate of the non-conformist population in the eighteenth century has been set too high, and we take the lowest estimate on record, namely, that of Maitland, who gives 1 in 7½ as his calculation, we shall still have to apply a correction of close upon 39 per cent. in order to convert the number of burials as given in the bills into the number of deaths of all persons independently of religious persuasion.

It matters very little which of these two estimates we adopt; either of them shows sufficiently that a very inadequate idea of the mortality of London in the eighteenth century is furnished by the number of burials as given in the bills.

In the nineteenth century the deficiencies in the bills were probably even greater than they had been in the eighteenth; for while the previous causes of defect remained equally in operation, there was added to them an increasing negligence on the part of the parish clerks in making their returns. In the three years that preceded the publication of the new bills by the Registrar-general, namely, in 1837-38-39, the number of parishes that were defaulters varied from thirteen to fifteen; and the consequence of this increasing negligence, was that the total burials declined gradually, and almost uninterruptedly, in spite of the increase of the population as shown in the census returns, from over 28,000 in 1832 to less than 15,000, or scarcely more than half the previous total, in 1840, and in 1846 actually fell to less than 12,000.

We have fortunately the means of estimating with very closely approximate accuracy the extent to which the burials, as given in bills for 1839 and 1841 fell short of the actual number of deaths. For in these years the old bills and the annual reports of the Registrar-general overlap, and the mode in which the annual reports for those two years were drawn up, enables us to extract from them, with sufficiently approximative accuracy, the deaths registered within the area of the old bills. The bills gave 16,685 burials in 1839, and 14,599 in 1841. The deaths in each case were really, as shown by the Registrar-general's annual reports, more than double the numbers in the bills, being 33,875 in 1839, and 33,143 in 1841.

If then it is necessary, as we have seen, to correct the bills in the eighteenth century by an addition of from 39 to 44 per cent. to the recorded burials, it is necessary in the nineteenth century, or at any rate from 1832 onwards, to make a much larger correction, culminating, in the years when the Registrar-general's reports begin, in an addition of more than 100 per cent.

I say from 1832 onwards, because it is from 1832 that the strongest evidence is forthcoming of negligence on the part of the parish clerks, the total number of burials, which had on the whole increased year by year up to that date, having rapidly declined after it.

It is then abundantly evident that, even if it be allowed that the amount of error in the old bills, as stated in the foregoing remarks, may have been somewhat over-estimated, it is still so large that the utmost caution must be used in drawing any inferences whatsoever from this interesting series of documents; and especially is it plain that these imperfect records of burials supply no trustworthy basis for a comparison between the past and present mortality in London.

APPENDIX A.

A copy of the earliest known Weekly Bill of Mortality.
British Museum.   Egerton MSS. 2603, f. 4.

Syns the xvj[th] day of November unto the xxiij day of the same month ys deed.   In the citie and fredom yong and old thes mayny folowyng of the plage and oder dyseases.

> In primys benetts grace churche j of y[e] plage
> S buttolls without bysshops gate j corse
> S nycholas flesshammuls[25] j of y[e] plage
> S peturs in cornell j of the plage
>   Mary Wolnorth j corse
> All halowes barkyng. ij corses
> Kateryne colmane j of the plage
> Mary aldermanebery j corse
> Michaels in cornelle iij one of y[e] plage
> Alle halowes y[e] moore ij   j of the plagee
> S gylez iiij corses iij of the plage
> S dunstons in y[e] west iiij of y[e] plage
> Stevens in colmane strete j corse
> Alle halowys lumbert strete j corse
> Martens owute whiche[26] j corse
> Mergett moyses j of the plage
> Kateryne crechurche ij of the plage
> Martens in y[e] vyntre ij corses
> Buttolls without algate iiij corses
> S olavus in hert strete ij corses
> S Andros in holborne ij of y[e] plage
> S peters at powls wharff ij of y[e] plage
> S ffeythes j corse of y[e] plage
> S alphes j corse of the plage
> S Mathews in fryday strete j of the plag
> Aldermary ij corses
> Sepulcres iij corses j of the plage
> S thomas appostells ij of the plage
> S leonerds faster lane j of y[e] plage
> Michaels in y[e] ryalle ij corses
> S alborowes j corse of the plage
> Swytthyns ij corses of y[e] plage
> Mary somersetts j corse

[25] *I.e.*, flesh shambles.   [26] *I.e.*, Outwich.

S bryds v corses j of the plage
S benetts powls wharff j of the plage
Alle halows in yᵉ walle j of yᵉ plage
Mary Hylle j corse

sum of yᵉ plage xxxiiij persons
sum of oder sekenes xxxij persons
the holle sum i̽ij and vj.
and ther is this weke clere.
i̽ij and iij parysh as by thez
bills dothe appere

(The bill is endorsed as follows) the extinte of courses beryed of the plage within the citie of London sens xv

APPENDIX B.

Successive Changes in the Area covered by the Bills of Mortality.

The bills in 1603 included all but 1[27] of the 97 parishes within the walls, and all but 3 of the 16 parishes which were part within the liberties and part without. The following list shows the additions[28] made from time to time to these 109 parishes.

[27] This parish was St. James, Duke Place. That it was not included until 1626 is stated above on the authority of the author (Dr. Birch?) of the "Collection of "Yearly Bills of Mortality from 1657 to 1758" (London, 1759). But there seems some doubt whether it was in reality excluded; at any rate it appears in general bills for 1593 and 1625 given in that same collection, the latter of these bills being that made by the parish clerks to the king.

[28] At various dates parts of parishes already included in the bills were constituted separate parishes. Names so added, which represent no additions to the area included in the bills, are printed in this table in *italics*.

Date.	Additions.	Remarks.
1604....	St. Bartholomew the Great.... Bridewell Precinct .... Trinity in the Minories	These are the three parishes part within and part without the liberties which were excluded at first
	St. Clement Danes .... St. Giles-in-the-Fields........... St. James, Clerkenwell .... St. Katharine by the Tower St. Leonard, Shoreditch .... St. Mary, Whitechapel .... St. Martin-in-the-Fields .... St. Mary Magdalen, Bermondsey	Out parishes
'06....	Savoy Precinct	
'25....	—	The weekly bills first printed, with the number of burials against every parish
'26....	St. James, Duke Place	See footnote 27
	St. Margaret, Westminster	At this date the numbers of christenings, burials, and plague, but not of the other causes of death in St. Margaret, Westminster, were brought into the hall, but it appears doubtful whether they were shown in the bills until somewhat later. They appear in the bill of 1657, but not in that of 1636; the intermediate bills are missing from the collection
'29....	—	Sexes and causes of death first distinguished
'36....	Hackney .... Islington .... Lambeth .... Newington.......................... Rotherhithe .... Stepney	The remark made above as to St. Margaret, Westminster, applies also to these parishes
'47....	*St. Paul, Covent Garden*	Previously a part of the parish of St. Martin-in-the-Fields, which had been added in 1604
'60...	—	The bills remodelled and the causes of death in all the 130 parishes shown in them
'70..	*St. Paul, Shadwell*	Previously part of Stepney, which had been added in 1636
'71....	*Christchurch, Southwark*	Previously part of St. Saviour, Southwark, which was in the bills from the first
'85....	*St. James, Westminster*	Previously parts of St. Martin-in-the-Fields, which had been added in 1604
'86....	*St. Anne, Soho*	
'94....	*St. John, Wapping*	Previously part of Whitechapel, which had been added in 1604
1726....	St. Mary-le-Strand	
'28....	—	Ages first distinguished
'29....	*St. George, Hanover Square*	Previously part of St. Martin-in-the-Fields, which had been added in 1604
	Christchurch, Spitalfields .... *St. George-in-the-East*	Previously parts of Stepney, which had been added in 1636
	St. George the Martyr	Previously part of St. Andrew, Holborn, which had been in the bills from the first

Date.	Additions.	Remarks.
1729....	St. Peter ad Vincula, Tower of London.............................	It was decided in 1730 that this church was not parochial, and it was removed from the bills
'30....	*St. Anne, Limehouse*	Previously part of Stepney, which had been added in 1636
'31....	*St. George, Bloomsbury*	Previously part of St. Giles-in-the-Fields, which had been added in 1604
	St. John Evangelist, Westminster	Previously part of St. Margaret, Westminster, which had been added in 1626
1733....	*St. John, Southwark*	Previously part of St. Olave, Southwark, which had been in the bills from the first
	St. Luke, Old Street	Previously part of St. Giles, Cripplegate, which had been in the bills from the first
'46 ...	*St. Matthew, Bethnal Green*	Previously parts of Stepney, which had been added in 1636
1817....	*All Saints, Poplar*	
'49....	—	The old bills came to an end

No further additions were made to the old bills of mortality. The new bills, which commenced in January, 1840, and were published by the Registrar-general, included all the parishes which had been in the old bills, together with Hammersmith, Fulham, St. Mary Stoke Newington, St. Mary Stratford-le-Bow, St. Leonard Bromley, Camberwell, and the (then) district of Greenwich, comprising the parishes of St. Paul Deptford, St. Nicholas Deptford, Greenwich, and Woolwich. The following additions have since been made:—

Date.	Additions.	Remarks.
1844....	Clapham .... Battersea (exclusive of Penge Hamlet) Wandsworth................................. Putney .... Tooting Graveney (or Lower Tooting).... Streatham	District and poor law union of Wandsworth
1846....	Charlton .... Plumstead..................................... Eltham .... Lee... Kidbrooke .... Lewisham	At that time the district and poor law union of Lewisham

In 1887 the hamlet of Mottingham, in the parish of Eltham, was excluded from registration London, and consequently from the bills of mortality.

APPENDIX C.

Christenings and Births.

The purpose of this article is to deal simply with the returns of mortality in the bills; but it may be permissible to add a note concerning the returns of christenings. It must be remembered that it was of these and not of *births* that the number was given in the bills; and indeed not of all of these, but only of such as took place in the parish churches, and were entered in the parish registers.

But in 1694 (*6th and 7th William III, cap.* 6) an Act was passed " for granting to His Majesty certain Rates and Duties " upon Marriages, *Births*, and Burials, and upon Bachelors and " Widowers, for the term of five years, for carrying on the War " against France with vigour," and the clergy were directed to keep registers of all persons married, buried, christened or *born* in their parishes, under a penalty of 100*l.* for neglect or refusal. It was plainly out of the power of the clergy to carry out this enactment, as they had no information as to infants who were born but were not brought to them for baptism; and consequently in the next year (*7th and 8th William III, cap.* 35) it was further enacted that inasmuch as " divers children who are born within " this Kingdom are not christened according to the usages and " ceremonies of the Church of England, and many are christened " in private houses, nor are the parents of such children obliged " " by the aforesaid Act (*6th and 7th William III*) to give notice to " their respective ministers of the birth of such children, for want " whereof an exact Register of all persons born is not kept. The " parents of every child hereafter to be born shall within five days " after the birth give notice to the vicar of the parish of the day " of the birth of such child, under a penalty of 40*s.*; the vicar " being bound under a like penalty to keep a distinct register of " such children so born and not christened."

These registers of the unbaptised children were called bye-registers, and some few are still in existence. If they were properly kept, which the terms of a later Act in 1706 (*4th Anne, cap.* 12, *sect.* 10) show however not to have been the case, it is plain that the number of births in a parish could be obtained by adding the entries in the bye-register to those in the register of baptisms.

The only bye-register that I have personally examined is that
parish of St. Mary at Reading, which has recently been

published by the Rev. G. P. Crawford. This consists of a certain
number of sheets of paper stitched into the register of baptisms,
and is headed " The By-Register according to Actt of Parllement,
" for Byrths of those that are not baptized by the Minister of the
" Parish in the year of our Lord 1695." The entries commence
with April, 1696, and the total number of births entered in the
course of ten years from that time is 101 ; while the baptisms in
the ordinary register during the same period amount to 488.

If, then, this bye-register may be taken to represent the general
state of things elsewhere than at Reading, we must add 20·7 per
cent. to the number of christenings as given in the bills, in order
to obtain the true number of births in London at the close of the
seventeenth century.

APPENDIX D.

*As in Appendix A a copy is given of the earliest known Bill of
Mortality, so here is appended a copy of the earliest, as I believe,
known census of a London Parish. It is extracted from the Harleian
Society's Registers, vol. vi, pp. 159 and 160. Similar lists for
St. Mary Aldermary, at Ladyday, 1733, and Michaelmas, 1734,
are to be found in the registers of that parish, and have been published
by the Harleian Society in vol. v of their series of registers.*

A LIST OF Yᴱ PARISH OF Sᵀ· THOMAS APOSTLE'S TAKEN ON
LADY DAY, 1733.

William Haggard, Tea Warehouse, to Church family four.
Rayham Reap, South Sea house, to Church. Nᵒ in family eight.
Andrew Beach, Surgeon, to Church, in family four.
Tho. Hill, porter. she washer or Laundress. to Church. family
six.
Taylors Court, Mʳ· Price, Carpenter & Undertaker: to Meeting:
Nᵒ 11.
Mʳ· Baker, Merchᵗ, R.C. Nᵒ 5.
Widow Phillips, to Meeting. family three.
Edmond Morgan, to Church, family eleven.
Marsh Dickenson, Attorney, to Church, family ten.
Robert Ramshire, Undertaker, to Meeting, family four.
Dʳ· Eaton, Physitian, to Meeting.
Widow Meggott, to Church, family nine.
Andrew Wood, Broker, to Church, family ten.
James Perrott, to Church, family three.

Grace Shaw, to Church, family six.
John Parker, Apothecary, to Church, family eight.
Stephen Thompson, Wine Merch^t, to Church, family eleven.
Widow Thompson, Hott Presser, to Meeting, family four.
1 House Empty.
William Curtis, Hott Presser, to Church, family five.
Ja. Rostoe, Manchester Goods, to Church, family three.
John Hoott. Attorney. to Church, family seven.
G. Kent. Kalender Shop, to Church, family four.
Tho. Cole, Livery Stable, to Church, family four.
D. Prew. C.C. Drugget Warehouse, to Meeting, family five.
W. Miller, Carpenter, to Meeting, family four.
Geo. Smyth, Bricklayer, to Church, family four.
Isaac Fryer, Glazier, to Church, family six.
1 House Empty.
Widow Jones, Thread Shop, to Meeting, family three.
Edw. Dauber, Barber, to Church, family four.
Widow Hammond, to Church, family eight.
1 House Empty.
John Denning. Carpenter. to Church, family five.
Jno Horton, Tobacconist, to Church, family four.
Jno Richardson, Dyer, to Church, family three.
Mich. Bradshaw, Upholster, to Church, family eight.
Burford, Distiller, Quaker, family three.
Tho. Walker, Stone Cutter, to Church, family three.
M^r· Greaves, Distiller, to Church, N° 11.
Henry Emmett, to Meeting, family five.
Geo. Tobias Guiguer, Merch^t, to Church, family nine.
Alderman Godschall, Wine Merch^t, to Church, N° 13.
Geo. Pinkney, Chandler Shop, to Meeting family three.
Jabez Harris, Post Office, to Meeting, family five.
Ralph Foster, Apothecary, to Meeting, family five.
Willm Key, Taylor, to Church, family three.
Ten Houses, pull'd down in order to be rebuilt.
Segar Corwin, Chairmaker, to Church, family four.
John Webb, Cooper, to Church, family seven.
Ambr. Harding, Lawyer, to Church, family five.
John Dark, Calendar-Shop, to Church, family four.
Joseph Somner, Sexton, to Church, family five.
Joseph Hudson, Porter, to Church, family four.
Widow Webster, Chandler Shop, to Church, family four.
Widow Baxter, Stocking Presser, to Church, family four.
Widow Somersett, M^r· Moore & his wife & serv^t, to Church.
J. Shrimpton, Plasterer, to Church, family three.
William Watson, Hott Presser, to Church, family three.

Ja. Trevett, Alehouse, to Church, family five.

Widow Gibbons, Cuttler, to Meeting, family three.

Robert Mayio, Barber, to Church, family five.

There are in this place ten Houses empty, some repair'd, others pull'd down and rebuilt.

John Breadcutt, Fruiterer, to Church, family six.

R^d Hooper, Coal Meter, to Church, family two.

Jos. Robinson, Bricklayer, to Church, family three.

Moderick Mead, Bookbinder, to Church, family four.

John Jarratt, Innkeeper, to Church, family nine.

Pierce Yardley, Lapidary, to Church, family three.

S. Westall, Lt Col^l, to Church, family seven.

J. Shuttleworth, Fruiterer, to Masse, family nine.

J. Smyth, Baker, to Church, family six.

W. Boddington, Grocer, to Meeting, family five.

1 House Empty.

J. Whitworth, Oil Merch^t, to Church, family seven.

Widow Merry.

W. Martin, to Church, family six.

1 House Empty.

J. Smyth, Drawer of fine Cloth, to Church, family three.

W. Perry, Whitehorse Alehouse, to Church, family eight.

Widow Bowles, Apothecary's Widow, Church, N° 5.

Fran. Lynch, to Mass, in family five.

William Seward, Clerk at ye South Sea House, to Church, N° 5.

The abovesaid Houses in ye parish of St Thos Ap^e are in N^o One Hundred and Two.

EDW. WATKINSON.

Mr. Watkinson appears to have miscounted the houses in his parish, for according to my reckoning the number of them is 101, not, as stated, 102.

The number of families that attended church, so far as can be judged, seems to have been 57, while 15 attended meeting and 3 went to mass. Combining these figures with those to be got from the census at the same date in St. Mary Aldermary, the total result is that 101 attended church, 33 attended meeting, while 6 attended mass, giving a proportion of 27·8 per cent. that were either non-conformist or Roman Catholic.

On comparing the names in the list of parishioners of St. Thomas the Apostle with the names in the registers of christenings and burials in the same parish, I was surprised to find how widely the two lists differed. Taking the registers from the date of the census down to Lady Day, 1738, that is for a period of five years,

I find there are altogether 101 different surnames among the entries, but of these 101 there are only 33 that are to be found in the parochial census of Mr. Watkinson, and this even when the most liberal allowance has been made for possible vagueness in spelling or in pronunciation, when for instance not only such names as Cole and Coles, Smith and Smyth, Forsiett and Fancitt, are looked on as merely forms for one and the same name, but when similar allowance is made for the more divergent names of Morgue and Morgan, Boheme and Bowen, Winkworth and Whitworth.

Whence then came the other 68 names? The intimate connection between St. Thomas the Apostle and St. Mary Aldermary, made it seem possible that some of these 68 might be parishioners of this latter parish who used the church of St. Thomas as their own, but on examining the names in this other parochial census, I found that such a supposition would only account for 7 more of the names, still leaving 61 not to be found in either census.

Some of these 61 may doubtlessly have been servants or lodgers, whose names are not given in the census, they being reckoned without naming in the "family;" and others may be explained by supposing the 25 empty houses in St. Thomas to have come into occupation by persons with new names; but all these several causes seem inadequate to explain so large a discrepancy as that described. The only explanation that appears possible is that many persons, perhaps former inhabitants, must have used this parish for burials and for christenings, though they no longer actually lived in it; and this accords with a passage already quoted by me (p. 447) from an old writer, that "many are "frequently removed from one parish to be buried in another, that "are both within the bills."

MISCELLANEA.

CONTENTS:

I.—*Proceedings of Section F of the British Association.*

THE section devoted to Economic Science and Statistics has this year certainly been quite as popular as any of the eight sections into which the British Association is divided. The following were the officers:—*President.*—The Hon. Sir C. W. Fremantle, K.C.B. *Vice-Presidents.*—Professor W. Cunningham, D.D., D.Sc., F.S.S.; R. Giffen, C.B., LL.D., F.R.S., F.S.S.; Professor J. E. C. Munro, LL.D.; Professor J. S. Nicholson, M.A., D.Sc., F.R.S.E., F.S.S.; R. H. Inglis Palgrave, F.R.S., F.S.S.; T. Bond Sprague, M.A., F.R.S.E., F.S.S. *Secretaries.*—Professor J. Brough, LL.M.; J. R. Findlay, B.A.; Professor E. C. K. Gonner, M.A., F.S.S. (*Recorder*); H. Higgs, LL.B.; L. L. Price, M.A., F.S.S.

Sir Charles Fremantle delivered his opening address on the morning of Thursday, 4th August. This address is reprinted in full in the present number of the Journal (see p. 415).

On the termination of the address, a very hearty vote of thanks was accorded to the President, on the motion of Mr. R. H. Inglis Palgrave, seconded by Sir Rawson W. Rawson. Papers were then read by Professor P. Geddes on "Methods of Social Inquiry," by M. Demolins on "La Science Sociale et sa Méthode," and by Professor J. Mavor on "Some Notes on the Compilation of Monographs on the Statistics of large Cities, with illustrations from the case of Glasgow." These all dealt with the method of scientific investigation and classification; Professor Geddes pointing out that former learned men divided science into three main heads—human affairs, natural philosophy, and natural history; with time the tendency to specialisation became more prominent, and these main heads were subdivided, whereas now the tendency seemed to be in the opposite direction, towards unification, all science being classed as sociology, biology, and physics, while the interdependence of these three on each other was daily becoming more recognised. M. Demolins strongly advocated Le Play's method of collecting monographs, and classifying every particular concerning each individual. Professor Mavor dealt with the same subject, and illustrated his paper by examples from Glasgow. The reading and discussion of these papers having taken longer than was anticipated, Mr. Smiley's contribution on the "Slums of Manchester" was taken as read.

In the afternoon Mr. C. S. Loch, Secretary of the Charity Organisation Society, read a paper on "Parliamentary Returns on Social and Economic Subjects." In this he dealt with the importance of the returns to the general public, who based their arguments largely upon them when discussing social questions, and he drew attention to the necessity of caution in using them, as fallacious conclusions are constantly based on erroneous assumptions. Taking some examples, he pointed out the incompleteness of certain returns in various particulars, and suggested additions which should make them more easily understood, and which might obviate mistakes. He also suggested that the form of the returns should be settled by a committee after consultation with experts, and insisted upon the need of a complete index to parliamentary returns and papers bearing on sections of social investigation. In the discussion which followed, stress was principally laid on the necessity for the careful study of statistical returns, in order that those who consulted them might thoroughly understand exactly what they were intended to convey.

Thursday's proceedings terminated with a paper by Mr. J. S. Mackenzie, on "The Relation of Ethics to Economics." Mr. Mackenzie held that political economy occupied too much importance at present, from an ethical point of view, and that it should be treated more in subordination to questions of social wellbeing. The moral method in economics "what ought to be," should receive more attention than it does: it should be carefully distinguished from, and should receive greater attention than the historical and analytical methods, which deal with the past, and the tendency in the future. As regards the three chief divisions of economics, again, from an ethical point of view, more importance should be given to distribution and consumption than at present, and less to production. Coming then to applied economics, Mr. Mackenzie went on to say that in applying economics to the guidance of conduct, it is necessary to consider the question of justice. On this subject recent ethical thought has thrown an important light by the introduction of the conception of the organic unity of society. The conception of justice thus reached may be opposed to the conceptions of abstract freedom and abstract equality. The chief thing to be insisted on, from this point of view, is that everyone must be treated both as means and as end. We arrive in this way at two great commandments :—(1) Thou shalt not exploit; (2) Thou shalt not pauperise. The application of these principles in detail is by no means easy. It is a problem that will require the same strenuous application as that which has already been devoted to questions of production and exchange.

The whole of Friday was occupied by a discussion on old age pensions and the poor law. Three papers were read: by the Rev. W. Moore Ede, the Rev. T. W. Fowle, and the Rev. J. Frome Wilkinson. All three agreed that the present poor law system was out of date; the present qualification for relief was complete destitution, and this ought to be abolished; but they differed in the remedies which they proposed. The Rev. W. Moore Ede would give a pension of half-a-crown a week to all who could show that they could maintain themselves decently on such a sum, but as it did not seem necessary to endow every one, this pension should be given only to those whose income was less than 50*l.* per annum. For those who could not live decently with the help of this half-crown, there would still remain the workhouse. The additional cost of this scheme need not exceed 5 or 6 millions annually. Thrift would thus be encouraged by giving a pension—insufficient in itself to support life—to those who had savings, but by sending those who had nothing to the workhouse. Mr. Moore Ede concluded: "The nation now endows destitution, I wish the nation to endow thrift." The Rev. T. W. Fowle's paper was entitled "The Poor Law: Can it be Maintained?" His answer was emphatically no. Sixty years ago, when the evils to be combated were different to what they are now, the law answered the required purpose admirably. He would propose that out-door relief be gradually abolished—a task which should certainly not occupy more than twenty-five years—and the money thus saved should be distributed among such friendly societies as were able and willing to grant pensions to those of its members who were disabled by age or sickness. 3,000,000*l.*, saved in this manner would, at 5*s.* per member, subsidise 12,000,000 people. The Rev. J. Frome Wilkinson, in "Old Age Pensions and Friendly Societies," estimated that about 1 in 15 members of the friendly societies were insured for old age, and he called attention to the difficulty that had been experienced in differentiating between sick pay and old age pay. He examined several proposed schemes, and finally himself advocated the endowment of old age.

Mr. C. S. Loch opened the discussion. As is well known, he is no advocate of any of the suggested reforms, and on this occasion he again brought forward many arguments against the schemes suggested by the three speakers. He contended that it was not shown that, say, half a crown a week would encourage thrift, and that the present system was not unjust. Again, none of the methods considered at all the case of those who were under 65 years of age, and these he maintained were in the majority. He believed far more in the good done by charitable persons, and thought that more was done by trusting to the independence of the individual than there would be by transforming the friendly societies into government departments, which would inevitably be the result of adopting Mr. Fowle's club test. Mr. E. Atkinson said he would deal with the subject from an American point of view. In the United States pauperism was not a State question; it was entirely a municipal one. In his own town (Boston) out-door relief had very nearly ceased. More people over there invested their money in trustee savings banks, in which nearly everyone was represented by name. Another inducement to save in Massachusetts, which was one of the more densely populated States in the union, was the facilities offered for the purchase of land; in consequence, everyone endeavoured to lay by enough for this purpose, and when old age came on each had his own house and little bit of ground. The question of old age pensions does not exist in America, where public opinion is opposed to State interference in this matter. Miss Collet, who spoke next, thought that the average guardian might very well be improved, and recommended caution in any attempt to reform the poor law. Mr. E. W. Brabrook considered that there was no other way than thrift, but he would have the friendly societies allow their depositors to stop their payments and claim their pension whenever they liked, the value of the pension of course varying with the length of time during which a man has continued paying his premiums. Also, if the money, payable at a certain age, is not to be forfeited in the event of death before that age, the annual premium will of course be larger, or the pension smaller. Of the other speakers, Sir Raymond West referred to the conditions in India, where, he thought, the solution of the question had been found in the caste system. He pointed out that there was scarcely any destitution among the Parsees. Mr. Stephen Bourne, Mr. T. B. Sprague, Miss Burton, the Rev. C. Stewart, Mr. MacKnight and Mr. H. Higgs also spoke.

Saturday is only a half day, and the programme was accordingly curtailed so as to leave the afternoon free. Mr. L. L. Price read the first paper, on "Adam Smith and his Relations to Recent Economics." After touching upon the question of plagiarism with which Adam Smith had been charged, Mr. Price proceeded to point out some of the qualities to which the "Wealth of Nations" owes its permanent character. First among these are its literary merits, which materially help to render the book so much more popular than most other works on political economy. One of the causes for this literary merit Mr. Price held to be Adam Smith's love of freedom, which has inspired his language throughout the work. The argument for liberty still appeals to us nowadays, and by every writer Adam Smith is acknowledged to be the parent of modern economics. It is also very noticeable how his conclusions on wages, profits, and even rent hold good at the present time; and the same applies to his inquiries into free trade and money. In the discussion Dr. W. Cunningham called attention to the want of a proper edition of Adam Smith, one which would help the reader to understand the man himself, and how the ideas grew up in his mind. Mr. W. Smart read a paper on "The Effects of Consumption of Wealth on Distribution." After considering the difficulties in the theory of distribution, dependent partly on the constant changes in value, he came to the conclusion that distribution depends not altogether on income received, but on the uses to which income is put, and that, practically, consumption of wealth is dictated by the merchant. Mr. R. A. Macfie also read a paper on "Copyright and Patents," in which he advocated the establishment of a responsible board of referees, who should determine the length of time during which a copyright or patent should run.

On Monday, 8th August, the section met to hear a very

interesting paper by Dr. E. Atkinson, of Boston, U.S.A., on "The Continuance of the Supply of Wheat from the United States with profit to the Western Farmers." He drew attention to the great reductions in transit rates—both railway and ocean—that have occurred during the last twenty years, and which have been the most important factor in enabling the western farmer in the United States to make as much profit by selling his wheat in London at 32*s*. per quarter, as he did in 1873, when the price was 54*s*. Another important factor in the fall of the price of wheat was, he held, the introduction of the self-binder, which saved an enormous amount of manual labour. His conclusions will not be particularly encouraging to the English farmer, as he failed to see any indication of the fall in the price of wheat being checked, nor could he foresee any limit to this fall. In support of this view it must be borne in mind that the whole area under wheat in the States (excluding Alaska) is only 2 per cent. of the country, that farmers have thriven and are thriving in spite of declining prices and advancing wages, and that they are not at all heavily burdened with mortgages. He gave an instance of a farm of 3,000 acres, of which the average yield was 18 bushels per acre, and the cost of labour per bushel less than 2*d*. Wheat, it may be noticed, is not the principal cereal, Indian corn being cultivated to a greater extent.

Professor R. Wallace dealt with a similar subject: "Certain Interesting Features of the Agricultural Situation." He touched first upon the question of competition, especially from America, where inexpensive means had been discovered whereby the crop yield could be increased under a more intensive system of management, and referred to the small chance there was of America's produce being consumed in that country. He thought that the State should endeavour to instruct an agricultural student only in those economic principles which the farmer would not acquire by experience in ordinary farm life; it should be impressed upon him, for instance, that the most satisfactory crop was such an one as could be produced at the lowest cost per unit. Considering allotments, he did not think the recent Act would increase the number of people interested in land; those who would utilise the facilities granted would be the tradesmen in villages and country towns. Professor Fream opened the discussion on the two papers by remarking that Mr. Atkinson proved the superior cheapness of the American corn to be due to the reduction in the cost of production, and not to superior skill; in this he maintained the English farmer to be ahead of all others. The British agriculturist was not dependent on one crop alone; and on this account he thought the American producer was at the mercy of the English consumer. Amongst other speakers, Miss Burton agreed with Professor Wallace that allotments would be entirely taken up by artisans, as agriculture would be a relaxation to them after other work, which would not be the case with farm labourers.

Miss Rosa Barratt read a paper on "Legislation in America and elsewhere on behalf of Destitute and Neglected Children." Her object was to show how far England was behind several other countries in this matter. In France and many States of America laws are in force, by the provisions of which children under 16 years of age can be taken from their parents if they are criminals or drunkards, and placed under the protection of public authority, or, in the case of France, certain approved associations and individuals. In Italy and Germany steps are also being taken in the same direction; and government aid is urgently needed to help voluntary charitable efforts in this country.

Mr. W. M. Acworth contributed "A Plea for the Study of Railway Economics." Three points were especially considered : first, the reduction of passenger fares, such as had been inaugurated two or three years ago with success in Hungary, and had been adopted in Austria. England was very different from Hungary, but Mr. Acworth maintained that the system might be given a trial in Ireland, where the conditions were more similar, owing to the comparative poverty and sparseness of the population; secondly, the complicated question of goods rates required the attention of trained economists; and thirdly, the construction of new railways. Cheap railways were rapidly being made abroad, and Mr. Acworth maintained that it would be much better to have lightly made railways in remote parts of England than none at all. Public opinion at present would not admit of any standard lower than the present high one. The country railway stations were also, he considered, far more expensive than necessary, and he advocated the abolition of platforms, &c., at roadside stations. Professor Dewey (Boston, U.S.A.) in the discussion, could not see why railway economics should not be as carefully studied as monetary economics.

On the last day Mr. W. Cramond read a paper on "Illegitimacy in Banffshire," in which he endeavoured to trace the cause of the remarkably high percentage of illegitimate births in that county, second only to Wigtown in this unenviable competition. He found that the rate was lowest in the seaboard districts, and highest in the purely rural districts, and came to the conclusion that by far the greatest number of parents of illegitimate children were farm servants. The cause of this was, he had gathered, the want of dwelling-house accommodation on farms for married servants and for servants inclined to marry, and in support of this theory he brought forward figures showing that there was much less illegitimacy in the early part of this century, prior to the system of joining farm to farm and demolishing cottages.

Mr. Mark Davidson read a paper on "Taxation of Building Land," in which he considered the taxation of ground rents, the assessment of unoccupied land capable of yielding ground rents, and the acquisition by the community of the unearned increment of land.

Mr. D. F. Schloss followed with an explanation of the various "Methods of Industrial Remuneration." In this he defined the terms time-wage, task-wage, piece-wage, all of which are based upon a more or less definite ratio between time, output, and pay, the price per unit tending to be the same. Progressive wages, under which an employee can earn a premium, were also explained.

Mr. Schloss went on to discuss also individual and collective wages, contract and co-operative work, touching also upon the sweating system, and concluded with a review of product-sharing, profit-sharing, and industrial co-operation. The author's object was to define clearly the meanings of the terms used to designate various forms of remuneration, which are generally very vaguely used.

Dr. J. F. Sutherland read the last paper on "The Criminal and Habitual Offender from an Economic, Statistical, and Social Standpoint." In this attention was drawn to the large number of apprehensions, and the comparatively small number of guilty persons: one offender being sometimes responsible for many apprehensions in the course of a year. It is these habitual offenders, when they have undergone a certain number of convictions, whom Dr. Sutherland would wish to see removed from society for an indefinite period, and placed in a retreat.

At this meeting there was also presented the Report of the Committee appointed for the purpose of continuing the inquiries relating to the teaching of science in elementary schools. In 1890 changes were introduced into the code, with the result that English, which is now optional, at once resulted in a diminution of about 500 departments, while elementary science rose suddenly from 32 to 173. The percentage of passes in specific subjects which, during the past nine years, had reached a minimum in 1887-88, is now somewhat rapidly improving.

A vote of thanks, proposed by Mr. Inglis Palgrave, and seconded by Professor James, to the President and Secretaries, terminated the proceedings of the section.

II.—*On the probable Effect of the Limitation of the Number of Ordinary Fellows Elected into the Royal Society to Fifteen in each Year on the eventual Total Number of Fellows.* By Lieut.-General R. STRACHEY, R.E., F.R.S.

[The following communication was Read before the Royal Society on 12th May, 1892.]

The discussions that arose in connection with the revision of the statutes of the Royal Society during the years 1890 and 1891, led me to endeavour to obtain definite data on which to found a trustworthy opinion as to the effect of the existing limitation of the number of yearly admissions on the eventual total strength of the Society, and the probable result of increasing the number beyond fifteen, the present limit.

The facts bearing on this subject, so far as I have been able to collect them from the records of the Society, are embodied in the tables annexed to this communication, for the proper appreciation of the significance of the figures, as to which a few preliminary explanations are necessary.

The anniversary of the Society being fixed for the 30th November in each year, the customary record of the number of Fellows for any year refers to the number on that date. I have throughout regarded the date to which this number applies as being the 1st January of the following year.

The annual election of Ordinary Fellows usually takes place in the first or second week of June in each year. I have considered the date to be the 1st January of the same year.

The lapses, whether from death or other causes, have been treated as having occurred at the end of the calendar year in which they take place.

These assumptions have been made to simplify the various computations that the investigation required (which have been sufficiently troublesome as it is), and owing to the considerable period dealt with, forty-three years, the results will not, I believe, be sensibly affected thereby.

Unless it is otherwise specifically stated, the numbers refer exclusively to the *Ordinary Fellows*, elected at the regular annual meetings fixed for the purpose.

So far as I have been able to ascertain (for the earlier records in many particulars are defective), the number of Ordinary Fellows elected since 1848 has been 15 in each year, except on four occasions; in two years the number having been 14, and in two years 16; the average, therefore, is 15 yearly.

During the period since 1848, the number of *Royal* and *Honorary* Fellows has been about 5, and the *Foreign* Members about 50; these are included in the total number of Fellows shown in the Annual Reports of the Council, but will not be further considered in what follows.

The rules under which certain privileged classes have been admitted as Fellows, in addition to the *Ordinary* Fellows, have varied somewhat since 1848, but at present, apart from the persons eligible for the classes of Fellows above excluded, the only persons so privileged are Privy Councillors. The total number of *Privileged* Fellows elected since 1848 seems to have been 75, which for forty-three years gives an average of 1·75 per annum.

Table I contains a summary of the available data relating to the total number of Fellows since 1848.

The total number, excluding Royal, Honorary, and Foreign Fellows, at the commencement of 1848 was 768. I am not able to say how many of these were Fellows elected in the ordinary way, and how many were privileged, but this has no importance for my present object. From 1860 onwards the distinction between the three classes, those elected before 1848, Privileged Fellows, and Ordinary Fellows, is exhibited.

At the end of 1890, the total number of Fellows, excluding the Royal, Honorary, and Foreign Classes, was 463; of whom 26 were Fellows elected before 1848; 36 were Privileged Fellows elected since 1848; and 401 Ordinary Fellows elected since 1848.

Hence it appears that the reduction of number of Fellows, of the three classes last referred to, has been 305, and as the number of admissions of the privileged class has not been very materially affected by the changes in the rules relating to them, it follows that virtually the whole of this large reduction is a consequence of the restriction, to 15, of the number of Ordinary Fellows elected yearly.

As the ages of the 768 Fellows who constituted the bulk of the Society in 1848 are not known, and as the conditions of election before that year differed materially from what they have been since, no very useful conclusions can be drawn from the rate of their diminution since 1848.

Assuming, however, that the number of Privileged Fellows in 1848 was, as is probable, about 50, there would remain 718 Ordinary Fellows, of whom in forty-three years 692 lapsed, or at an average yearly rate of 2·24 per cent., that is rather more than 16 a year.   This rate, as I shall show subsequently, does not differ greatly from that which has prevailed among the Ordinary Fellows elected since 1848, and it may therefore be presumed that the average age of the Fellows in that year did not differ greatly from the average age since.

Table II gives, as far as available data admit, the ages at the time of election of all Fellows elected since 1848; and shows the number of years they severally survived, the average age at election, the number and average age of those who were alive in 1891, and the greatest and least ages of Fellows elected in each year.

From this table it will be seen that there has been a gradual small increase in the age at election; the average for the first ten years having been 42·2; for the second ten years, 43·0; for the third ten years, 44·8; and for the last thirteen years, 45·2.

The accuracy of these conclusions may be somewhat affected by the greater number of unknown ages in the earlier years, the age when unknown having been taken at the average of the group of years in which the election took place.

The least age at which any Fellow has been elected is 24, one such case being recorded.   The average minimum at any election is slightly under 30, and the average maximum is rather over 63, one election at an age of 87 is recorded, and several above 70.

The oldest survivor of the Fellows elected since 1848, who alone are dealt with in this table, was 86 years of age in 1891.

The average age at election was 43·9, and the average age of all the Fellows in 1891 was 58·4.

Table III records the numbers of Ordinary Fellows elected in each year, and remaining alive in each year after election, until 1891.

From this it will be seen that during the last ten years the numbers have increased by 46; in the previous ten years the increase was 68, or 22 more; and in the ten years still earlier the increase was 111, or 43 more than the last.   If the decrease of growth for the ten years after 1890 takes place in a similar ratio to that which took place between 1870-80 and 1880-90, we might anticipate an increase of only 11 up to 1900, or probably a smaller number.

In order to obtain a satisfactory comparison between the lives of the Fellows and those of the general population as shown in the accepted life tables, I have calculated, from the known ages of the Fellows at election, and the known dates of the deaths that have occurred among them, the average age of the Fellows remaining alive in each year. From these ages I have computed, from Dr. Farr's tables, the probable number of Fellows that would survive from year to year, assuming the initial number to be 15.

From Table III above referred to, have been ascertained the number of Fellows surviving in each successive year after election, and thence has been obtained the average number surviving from an initial number 15.

The results of these computations will be found in Table IV.

The second column in this table shows the number of lives dealt with for each year after election. The first entry, 645, is the total number of Fellows elected in the whole forty-three years. The next column to the right gives their aggregate ages, and the next their average age, 44·9, in their first year. Following the same line to the right, we find the average number of Fellows elected, and in their first year.

Passing to the second line of the table, 619, immediately below 645, is the total number of Fellows remaining in their second year from the elections of forty-two years; this is succeeded, in the columns to the right, by their aggregate ages in their second year and their average age, and the average number in their second year, out of 15, the average number elected.

The third line gives the same data for the third year of Fellowship, and so on throughout, the last line but one showing that in their forty-second year there remained 6 Fellows from the elections of two years, with an aggregate age of 444 years, and an average age of 74·0, the average number surviving in their forty-second year, out of the 15 elected, being 3.

The sixth column of the table gives the successive sums of the numbers in the fifth column, and therefore indicates the aggregate number of Fellows that will, on the average, be surviving in each successive year of Fellowship, the number elected in each year being always supposed to be 15.

It will be seen that the total for the forty-third year is 397 whereas the actual number surviving, shown in Col. XI, is 401. This difference is of course due to the number 397, representing what the result would be if the average rates of election and decrease prevailed, instead of the actual rates for the separate years; and it is probably sufficiently accounted for by the fact already pointed out, of the gradually increasing age at election in the later years, which will lead to the lives in the earlier years of the series being somewhat better than the average. Col. XI shows the *actual* results for successive years corresponding to the average results given in Col. VI. The differences will be seen to be somewhat irregular, but nowhere to be of importance.

Col. VII gives the aggregate ages of the numbers surviving in successive years, as shown in Col. V, and from it is deduced the average age of the whole number of Fellows shown in Col. VI, 397, which is seen to be 57·7 years, a result differing slightly from that obtained from the actual ages of the Fellows surviving in 1891, which was shown to be 58·4. The cause of this difference has already been indicated.

Cols. VIII and IX supply the results that would be obtained by applying to an initial number of 15, the rates of mortality in Dr. Farr's tables, for the ages in successive years given in Col. IV. Col. X contains the ratio of Col. VI to Col. IX, and indicates that throughout the whole period of forty-three years the actual results are somewhat better than the tabular results, or that the lives of the Fellows are better than the ordinary lives, and that this advantage leads in the forty-third year to the actual number of survivors being rather more than 5 per cent. in excess of that which would be given by the life tables, or of about 20 on a total of 400.

An examination of this table will show that, with the exception of the last six or eight years, in which the number of lives dealt with at last becomes very small, the figures indicate a very regular and consistent progression, and it will practically be quite safe to assume that the series in Col. VI may be extended on the basis of the ordinary life tables, subject to the addition of 5 per cent. on the total amounts obtained from these last.

Hence it will be found that in ten years after 1891 the aggregate number of Fellows is not at all likely to be increased by more than 15, that the final result may be as little as 410, but is not likely to be more than 420, or at the outside 425.

The results of this inquiry are shown graphically in the accompanying diagram, in which the thick line shows the progressive series of actual results contained in Col. VI, and the thin line those in Col. IX derived from the life tables. The prolongation of the thick line in a direction conformable to that of the thin line will be seen almost necessarily to fall below the horizontal line indicating a total strength of 420.

In an earlier part of this paper I mentioned that the rate of decrease of the Ordinary Fellows elected before 1848 did not appear to differ materially from that which has prevailed subsequently.

Taking the number of Ordinary Fellows elected before 1848, and then alive, at 718, it will be found that in twelve years (1860) the number was reduced to 422, which is about 60 per cent. of the original number; after twenty-four years (1872) the number fell to 206, which is about 30 per cent. of the original; and in thirty-six years (1884) there remained only 65, which is about 9 per cent. of the first number.

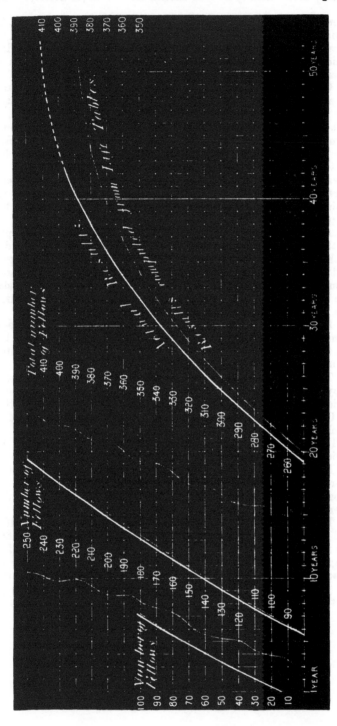

Assuming that the average age of the 718 Fellows elected before 1848, and then alive, was not materially different from (58) the average age of the Fellows elected after 1848 and alive in 1891, when it has probably become nearly stationary, it may be inferred that the lapses among a body of Fellows of that age will correspond to the lapses among the Fellows alive in 1848. Now, from Table IV it will be seen that of the Fellows elected after 1848, the average age in their seventeenth year was 58·3 years, which is almost exactly the average age of the whole body. Further, it is shown that of the supposed original 15 there remained 10·9 in the seventeenth year of the age above mentioned, 58·3. This number was reduced in twelve years to 6·7, which is nearly 60 per cent. of the number in the seventeenth year, and again falls after twelve years more to 3·7, which is not very different from 30 per cent. of the starting number, and after twelve years more the number will be seen to be likely to be less than 1·0, which again will not differ materially from 9 per cent. of the original 10·9. These proportions, it will have been observed, are those above shown to hold in the case of the Fellows elected before 1848.

On the whole it seems to be established that the present restriction of the number of Ordinary Fellows elected in any year to 15 will lead to an eventual maximum number not exceeding 420; and that the ultimate increase of the total strength of the Society for each additional Fellow elected in excess of 15 may be taken at 28, so that an increase of the annual number of Ordinary Fellows elected to 18 would lead to an ultimate total of 500 such Fellows.

TABLE 1.—*Summary of Numbers of Fellows of the several Classes remaining in the Society in each Year from 1848 to 1891.*

Year.	Total at the Commencement of Year.	Privileged Fellows.	Fellows Elected before 1848.	Ordinary Fellows Elected from 1848.
1848	768		768	—
'49	751		737	14
1850	748		719	29
'51	736		692	44
'52	720	Not	661	59
'53	707	separable	636	71
'54	701		616	85
'55	688		588	100
'56	671		556	115
'57	661		535	126
'58	658		517	141
'59	647		495	152
1860	637	51	422	164
'61	621	54	391	176
'62	607	51	368	188
'63	606	49	356	201
'64	602	50	338	214
'65	599	49	324	226
'66	586	49	300	237

TABLE 1 *Contd.—Numbers of Fellows in the Society from* 1848 *to* 1891.

Year.	Total at the Commencement of Year.	Privileged Fellows.	Fellows Elected before 1848.	Ordinary Fellows Elected from 1848.
1867	572	42	281	249
'68	564	40	267	257
'69	548	35	247	266
1870	544	36	229	279
'71	544	38	219	287
'72	542	38	206	298
'73	535	38	197	300
'74	524	38	177	309
'75	525	38	166	321
'76	515	42	148	325
'77	511	42	136	333
'78	505	43	122	340
'79	501	42	116	343
1880	488	42	101	345
'81	486	42	89	355
'82	480	40	82	358
'83	477	43	71	363
'84	473	41	65	367
'85	468	38	60	370
'86	465	36	55	374
'87	464	34	49	381
'88	465	33	45	387
'89	469	36	38	395
1890	466	37	32	397
'91	463	36	26	401

III.—*Homicide in the United States in* 1890.[1]

THE enumeration of the number of prisoners in the jails of the United States at the date of the census (1st June) has been entrusted to Mr. F. H. Wines. The bulletin just issued by him is an investigation into the condition of all persons who, on that one date, were in confinement under sentences or charges of homicide of various degrees, and consequently does not represent the number who were charged during the year. On the contrary, many of those who were enumerated ten years ago, at the last census, reappear, as their term has not yet expired. It must be noticed also that the numbers throughout include all those prisoners who were *charged*—whether convicted or awaiting trial; as some of these latter will probably establish their innocence, the number of homicides is, strictly speaking, exaggerated by that amount. The Hon. R. P. Porter, in his address to the American Statistical Association, delivered last year, states that the information on pauperism and crime was obtained from schedules issued, in the

[1] Census Bulletin No. 182.

5.	16.		Average Age at Election.	Average Age of Survivors in 1891.	Number of Survivors in 1891.	10 Years' Mean of Age at Election.	Least Age at Election.	Greatest Age at Election.	Year of Election.
Life.	Age.	Life.							
—	—	—	42	71	2		26	65	1848
3	—	—	40	77	3		30	50	'49
3	—	—	38	77	4		29	49	1850
1	—	—	37	72	6		26	53	'51
1	—	—	42	73	4	42·2	27	63	'52
12	58	10	43	70	4		26	58	'53
6	—	—	44	76	4		36	58	'54
3	—	—	46	77	5		28	62	'55
2	—	—	47	86	1		36	64	'56
1	—	—	42	70	6		29	63	'57
6	—	—	39	68	7		24	49	'58
—	—	—	43	67	6		28	67	'59
1	—	—	46	70	6		32	66	1860
9	—	—	40	66	9				

TABLE 4.—

Successive years of fellowship.	Num surv in y
I.	
1	64
2	61
3	60
4	57
5	55
6	53
7	51
8	49
9	47
10	44
1	42
2	40
3	38
4	36
5	34
6	31
7	29
8	27
9	25
20	23
1	22
2	20
3	18
4	17
5	15
6	14
7	13
8	11
9	10
30	9
1	8
2	7
3	6
4	

case of the larger institutions, to the officers in charge, while for the smaller, reliance was placed upon the regular enumerators. The authorities in charge of the institutions selected their own enumerators; a plan which was found to work well in practice. The tables have all been worked out with the Hollerith electrical tabulating machine, and the following investigation will give some idea of what has been achieved by its means. It is proposed to deal with all the other crimes in the same way.

Before entering into the special question of homicide, Mr. Wines gives a table of the number of prisoners—under whatever head of charge—in the States. On the 1st June, 1890, there were in the prisons 82,329 men and women (this excludes reformatory institutions for juvenile delinquents), of whom 72,428 had been convicted, 8,889 were awaiting trial, 82 were detained as witnesses, 47 were held for debt, and 883 were lunatics. Classifying them according to colour, 57,310 were white, 24,277 negroes, 420 Chinese,[2] and 322 Indians. By far the greatest number, 11,468, were in New York (which has also the greatest population); Pennsylvania coming next with 6,489; there were fewest in Wyoming (74) and North Dakota (97). Again, of the total, 75,924 were men and 6,405 women.

TABLE 1.—*Prisoners of the United States in 1890, by States and Territories, and by Color and Race.*

	Aggre-gate.	White.			Colored.		
		Native.	Foreign Born.	Nativity Un-known.	Negroes.	Chinese.	Indians.
Maine	512	327	156	18	6	—	5
New Hampshire	321	214	101	4	2	—	—
Vermont	200	145	42	3	10	—	—
Massachusetts	5,227	3,121	1,922	14	161	1	8
Rhode Island	560	338	183	2	37	—	—
Connecticut	1,026	625	329	4	67	—	1
New York	11,468	7,032	3,707	6	701	12	10
„ Jersey	2,455	1,339	792	9	315	—	—
Pennsylvania	6,489	3,979	1,747	23	738	2	—
North Atlantic Division	28,258	17,120	8,979	83	2,037	15	24
Delaware	139	53	15	—	71	—	—
Maryland	1,502	523	133	7	839	—	—
District of Columbia	496	103	35	—	358	—	—
Virginia	2,000	356	24	2	1,618	—	—
West Virginia	450	302	16	2	130	—	—
North Carolina	2,033	399	9	—	1,623	—	2
South „	1,184	117	6	—	1,061	—	—
Georgia	2,938	331	11	—	2,596	—	—
Florida	667	81	15	4	567	—	—
South Atlantic Division	11,409	2,265	264	15	8,863	—	2

[2] This number includes 13 Japanese. Throughout this article Chinese are understood to include Japanese. As a matter of fact, of the 95 Chinese prisoners charged with homicide, only 1 was Japanese.

TABLE 1—*Contd.* *Prisoners, by States and Territories, and Color and Race.*

	Aggre-gate.	White.			Colored.		
		Native.	Foreign Born.	Nativity Un-known.	Negroes.	Chinese.	Indians.
Ohio	2,909	1,978	414	23	481	—	13
Indiana	1,988	1,520	146	55	267	—	—
Illinois	3,936	2,455	972	49	452	6	2
Michigan	2,155	1,339	606	53	141	—	16
Wisconsin	1,118	617	442	19	23	2	15
Minnesota	1,041	606	397	4	24	—	10
Iowa	1,016	710	161	75	70	—	—
Missouri	2,833	1,616	286	23	907	—	1
North Dakota	97	55	36	3	3	—	—
South „	178	119	44	4	2	—	9
Nebraska	655	433	110	46	64	—	2
Kansas	1,928	1,267	315	29	304	—	13
North Central Division	**19,854**	**12,715**	**3,929**	**383**	**2,738**	**8**	**81**
Kentucky	2,110	720	47	170	1,173	—	—
Tennessee	2,451	658	45	30	1,718	—	—
Alabama	2,518	373	44	5	2,096	—	—
Mississippi	1,177	107	11	1	1,058	—	—
Louisiana	1,608	282	83	2	1,238	2	1
Texas	4,747	1,822	605	32	2,270	2	16
Arkansas	1,473	525	29	13	828	—	78
South Central Division	**16,084**	**4,487**	**864**	**253**	**10,381**	**4**	**95**
Montana	432	271	118	8	9	10	16
Wyoming	74	35	9	24	6	—	—
Colorado	902	605	221	18	58	—	—
New Mexico	205	138	41	11	14	1	—
Arizona	250	81	97	—	18	31	23
Utah	269	163	97	2	4	1	2
Nevada	152	55	43	26	6	13	9
Idaho	150	87	49	1	2	9	2
Washington	452	264	129	13	21	12*	13
Oregon	440	293	100	7	10	25	5
California	3,398	1,892	992	63	110	291†	50
Western Division	**6,724**	**3,884**	**1,896**	**173**	**258**	**393‡**	**120**
Total United States	**82,329**	**40,471**	**15,932**	**907**	**24,277**	**420‡**	**322**

* Includes 5 Japanese.   † Includes 8 Japanese.

‡ Includes 13 Japanese.

TABLE 2.—*Prisoners of the United States, Classified according to the Offence.*

Offences.	Total.	Men.	Women.	Offences.	Total.	Men.	Women.
Aggregate	82,329	75,924	6,405	III. Offences against the person	17,281	16,511	770
I. Offences against the government	1,839	1,823	16	Homicide	7,351	6,958	393
				Rape	1,392	1,387	5
Against the currency	389	385	4	Abduction	155	140	15
„ election laws	69	67	2	Abortion	36	25	11
„ postal laws	299	297	2	Assaults, all sorts	8,347	8,001	346
„ revenue laws	290	284	6				
„ pension laws	28	26	2	IV. Offences against property	37,707	36,382	1,325
Against military law	764	764	—				
				Arson	886	806	80
II. Offences against society	18,865	15,033	3,832	Burglary	9,734	9,647	87
				Robbery	2,381	2,350	31
Against public health	11	11	—	Larceny :			
„ justice :				Larceny	8,403	7,978	425
Contempt of court	39	33	6	Grand larceny	6,731	6,411	320
Perjury and false swearing	343	311	32	Petit larceny	3,741	3,475	266
All other	347	338	9	Larceny of horses	1,632	1,627	5
Against public morals :				Receiving stolen goods	487	430	·57
Incest	222	214	8				
Crime against nature	224	223	1	Embezzlement	485	480	5
Bigamy and polygamy	396	373	23	Fraud	395	391	4
Adultery	390	272	118	False pretences	491	477	14
Fornication, &c.	1,014	432	582	Forgery	1,887	1,865	22
Indecency	309	202	107	Malicious mischief and trespass	454	445	9
Gambling	337	330	7				
Violation of liquor laws	844	768	76	V. Offences on the high seas	4	4	—
Public intoxication	5,731	4,695	1,036				
Habitual drunkenness	388	275	113	VI. Miscellaneous	6,633	6,171	462
All other	245	217	28				
Against public peace :				Double crimes	3,449	3,367	82
Breach of the peace	328	259	69	Violation of municipal ordinances	488	388	100
Disorderly conduct	3,827	2,663	1,164	Unclassified	53	53	—
Carrying concealed weapons	512	506	6	Not stated	2,286	2,101	185
All other	277	248	29	Held as insane	291	212	79
Against public policy :				„ witnesses	66	50	16
Vagrancy	2,843	2,451	392				
Incorrigibility	108	94	14				
All other	130	118	12				

Coming now to those charged with homicide, we find their number to have been 7,386, namely, 6,993 men and 393 women. Of these 982 (916 men and 66 women) were awaiting trial. The homicides (*i.e.*, those charged) therefore formed 8·97 per cent. of the entire prison population. The percentage of females charged with homicide, to the total female prisoners, was 6·14, of males 9·21; exactly half as much again. Thirty-five of these prisoners were arraigned under other charges as well, such as arson, &c. These are omitted for the present, leaving only 7,351 to be considered.

BLE **3.**—*Number of Prisoners charged with Homicide, and the Number per Million of the Population in 1890 and 1880, the absolute and relative Increase or Decrease by States and Territories.*

Geographical Divisions.	1890.			1880.			Increase.	
	Population.	Homi-cides.	Ratio.	Population.	Homi-cides.	Ratio.	Abso-lute.	Relative.
The United States....	62,622,250	7,351	117	50,155,783	4,608	92	2,743	25
:h Atlantic	17,401,545	1,087	62	14,507,407	720	50	867	12
aine	661,086	42	64	648,936	29	45	18	19
ew Hampshire	376,530	20	53	346,991	17	49	3	4
ermont......................	332,422	24	72	332,286	11	33	13	39
assachusetts	2,238,943	86	38	1,783,085	83	47	3	— 9
hode Island..............	345,506	15	43	276,531	11	40	4	3
onnecticut	746,258	61	82	622,700	46	74	15	8
ew York	5,997,853	473	79	5,082,871	280	55	198	24
„ Jersey	1,444,933	78	54	1,131,116	63	56	15	— 2
ennsylvania..............	5,258,014	288	55	4,282,891	180	42	108	13
:th Atlantic	8,857,920	1,087	123	7,597,197	663	87	424	36
elaware.......................	168,493	6	36	146,608	8	55	— 2	—19
aryland	1,042,390	84	81	934,943	96	103	—12	—22
istrict of Columbia ..	230,392	10	43	177,624	9	51	1	— 8
irginia	1,655,980	163	98	1,512,565	148	98	15	....
est Virginia	762,794	67	88	618,457	32	52	35	36
orth Carolina	1,617,947	139	86	1,399,750	65	46	74	40
)uth „	1,151,149	158	137	995,577	87	87	71	50
eorgia	1,837,353	347	189	1,542,180	187	121	160	68
lorida	391,422	113	289	269,493	31	115	82	174
:th Central	22,362,279	1,796	80	17,364,111	1,269	73	527	7
hio	3,672,316	217	59	3,198,062	136	43	81	16
diana	2,192,404	225	103	1,978,301	157	79	68	24
nois	3,826,351	362	95	3,077,871	268	87	94	8
chigan	2,093,889	176	84	1,636,937	107	65	69	19
sconsin	1,686,880	127	75	1,315,497	71	54	56	21
nnesota	1,301,826	65	50	780,773	52	67	13	—17
ra	1,911,896	115	60	1,624,615	92	57	23	3
souri	2,679,184	233	87	2,168,380	234	108	— 1	—21
orth Dakota	182,719	12	66	36,909	} 3	} 22	30	{ 44 / { 42
)uth „	328,808	21	64	98,268			9	
ebraska	1,058,910	70	66	452,402	61	135	9	—69
ansas	1,427,096	173	121	996,096	88	88	85	33
:th Central	10,972,893	2,545	232	8,919,371	1,473	165	1,072	67
entucky	1,858,635	439	236	1,648,690	185	112	254	124
ennessee	1,767,518	297	168	1,542,359	180	117	117	51
labama.	1,513,017	336	222	1,262,505	174	138	162	84
' sissippi	1,289,600	217	168	1,131,597	202	179	15	—11
uisiana	1,118,587	328	293	939,946	178	189	150	104
xas	2,235,523	730	327	1,591,749	447	281	283	46
:lahoma	61,834	....	....	....	....	....	....	....
kansas......................	1,128,179	198	176	802,525	107	133	91	43

TABLE 3—*Contd.　Number of Prisoners Charged with Homicide.*

Geographical Divisions.	1890.			1880.			Increase.	
	Population.	Homi-cides.	Ratio.	Population.	Homi-cides.	Ratio.	Abso-lute.	Relative.
Western	3,027,613	836	276	1,767,697	483	273	353	3
Montana.......................	132,159	45	340	39,159	1	26	44	314
Wyoming	60,705	5	82	20,789	5	241	....	−159
Colorado	412,198	76	184	194,327	46	237	30	− 53
New Mexico	153,593	55	358	119,565	14	117	41	241
Arizona	59,620	54	906	40,440	15	371	39	535
Utah	207,905	20	96	143,963	4	28	16	68
Nevada	45,761	41	896	62,266	46	739	− 5	157
Idaho	84,385	26	308	32,610	7	215	19	93
Washington	349,390	42	120	75,116	20	266	22	−146
Oregon	313,767	54	172	174,768	19	109	35	63
California	1,208,130	418	346	864,694	306	354	112	− 8

Table 3 shows the population, homicides, and the number of homicides per million of the population in the different States and territories in 1880 and 1890. It will be noticed that the number has increased by no less than 2,743, or almost 60 per cent. during the ten years, while the population has increased but 24 per cent. In other words, the *relative* increase in the number of homicides (taking account of the larger population) has been 25 per cent. Mr. Porter holds that this " is largely explained by the great length of sentences for homicide, in consequence of which the majority of those reported in 1880 are again reported in 1890, together with those since convicted of the same offence." [But, unless a large increase in the length of the sentences was inflicted on those convicted between 1870 and 1880, a precisely similar remark would apply to the criminals of 1880, which should include the majority of those reported in 1870.] It will be seen that the greatest ratio occurs in the western division. Texas, although having a much greater number of homicides than any other State, has nevertheless not the greatest ratio : Arizona and Nevada stand out far above the others in this respect with nearly 1 per 1,000.

6,958 homicides were men and 393 women. 4,425 were white, 2,739 negroes, 95 Chinese (1 Japanese), and 92 Indians. Of the whites 3,157 were born in the United States and 1,215 abroad. An exhaustive inquiry has been made into the birth places of the parents of the criminals. In this respect Ireland stands out far ahead of all other countries ; the number of Irish parents being considerably more than half as much again as the number of Germans, who take second place, and just four times the number of English, who rank third. Then follow, in order, Mexico, Italy, Canada (English), Scotland, France, &c. Rather less than half the foreign-born prisoners were naturalised. The extreme limits of age for male homicides in prison on 1st June, 1890, were 11 and 86 years, for female homicides, 14 and 74. The greatest number were between the ages of 20 and 29, though in the north-central and western divisions the greatest number were between 30 and 39. It is worth noting the difference in average age of the criminals according to race. Of the homicides, 16·8 per cent. of the Chinese were under 30 years of age; of the foreign born, 21·0 per cent.; percentage under 30 years old of whites with both parents foreign, 43·0; of whites with one parent foreign, 37·5; of whites with both parents native, 37·25. But with the Indians this ratio is 50·5, and among the negroes, 56. Two-thirds of the southerners charged with homicide are negroes, and this will account for the comparative youth of the southern homicide. The average age of the men is 34⅔ years for the whole republic, and 32⅔ years among the women. It must not be forgotten that these are the ages of the prisoners at the time of the census, not at the time they were committed to prison.

The following table shows the degree of education of these homicides :—

TABLE 4.

Degree of Education.	Number.			Percentage.		
	Total.	Males.	Females.	Total.	Males.	Females.
Can neither read nor write	2,457	2,290	167	33·43	32·91	42·49
„ read only	356	329	27	4·84	4·73	6·87
„ both read and write....	4,538	4,339	199	61·73	62·36	50·64
Total..................	7,351	6,958	393	100·00	100·00	100·00

The western and southern divisions are from three to four times as illiterate as the northern. In the south central the percentage of complete illiteracy is 49·68; in the north central it is 12·03. It will be seen also that the women are more illiterate than the men, indeed, in the south central division, only 23 per cent. can both read and write. Of the negroes 56·7 per cent. can neither read nor write, and of the Indians 63. 253—of whom 4 only are women—or 3·44 per cent., have received higher education, half of these again having had a collegiate or professional education. Concerning trade education, only 1,242 men are returned as mechanics or apprentices; as to the remainder, either they were said to have no trade (the great majority), or the question was not answered. It appears that the foreign-born and their children have much more generally acquired a knowledge of a trade than the native white population.

The occupations of 6,958 male prisoners were ascertained : 99 belonged to the professional class; 38 to the official; 1,873 to the agricultural (including 1,386 farmers); 29 were engaged in the lumber trade; 212 were miners; 15 occupied with fisheries; 173 in trade and commerce; 380 in transportation; 1,066 in manufactures and mechanical industries; 446 in personal service; there were 2,194 unskilled labourers; and 17 miscellaneous. 350 female prisoners were returned as having definite occupations, mostly employed in personal service. About one-fifth of the whole number were idle at the time of their arrest.

20 per cent. of the men and 11 per cent. of the women were returned as drunkards, while 19 per cent. of the men and 48 per cent. of the women were total abstainers.

The bulletin contains an elaborate inquiry into the precise meaning in each different State of the words homicide, murder, manslaughter, &c., as laid down by law. Each State in the union has enacted its own laws, and inflicts what penalties it thinks fit for similar offences; as the same term may mean one thing in one State and something else in another, it is consequently difficult to classify the various forms of homicide for which the criminals are under detention. Considering all homicide, broadly, as either murder or manslaughter, it appears that in the United States 76·5 per cent. of the crimes were held to be murder, and 23·5 per cent. manslaughter. The percentage of murders is greater in the western and southern districts; this may mean that the actual murders were more numerous, or that the culprit was more severely judged: it is also greater among women than among men. Even more variable than the definitions are the sentences imposed. For example, the maximum sentence for involuntary homicide in Arkansas, Colorado, or Utah is one year; in Vermont, for precisely the same offence, the minimum is seven years. Rather more than half the sentences were for more than twenty years; the tendency to greater severity increasing slightly from east to west. About 2·5 per cent. were death sentences. The average sentence is greater for men than for women, for negroes than for whites, and the highest of all for Chinamen.

There were 35 other cases of murder or manslaughter, in which the prisoners were also arraigned on other charges, most of these second charges being robbery in various forms.

A circular was issued to all the sheriffs in the United States asking for returns of the number of executions which had taken place in 1890. It appears there were 156: Kentucky having 17, and North Carolina 15. The total number of prisoners under sentence of death on 1st June, 1890, was 165 (158 for murder). In several States a delay of one year after sentence is provided for by law, nor is delay uncommon in other States. This number (165) however represents more than would be the average, owing to the peculiarity of Kansas, where there are no less than 49 awaiting execution. The explanation of this is as follows: The law (in Kansas) provides that, after a criminal is sentenced to death the execution shall take place at such time as the governor, in his discretion, may appoint, not less than one year from the time of conviction. This law took effect in 1872, since which date no governor has ever made an order fixing the date of execution of a convict under sentence of death. While they have therefore capital punishment prescribed by law, it is in effect imprisonment for life. Hence the 49 convicts in Kansas represent those who were condemned during the preceding eighteen years, and who were still alive.

The sheriffs at the same time returned the number of lynchings at 117, of which Mississippi contributed 18. The returns of executions and lynchings are however not believed to be complete.

In conclusion, Mr. F. H. Wines has summed up the impressions gathered in the course of this investigation, as to the effect of severity of punishment upon the volume of crime, and as to the causes of crime. He remarks that it is popularly supposed that the prevalence of crime is chiefly due to inadequate punishment, and that the remedy for it is to be found in harsher laws and a more rigorous administration of them by the courts. He then goes on to say that if this were so, there should be less homicide, relatively to the population in the south central division for example than in any other, as there the average sentence is longer, and points out that the ratio of prisoners charged with homicide in that division is higher than elsewhere. Similarly the number of homicides is greatest in divisions where also the greatest number of executions has taken place. The same remarks apply generally to the States which have least amount of crime, in which also the sentences are not so severe.

As regards the causes of crime, ignorance, ignorance of a trade, idleness, and intemperance all figure largely among the characteristics of the prisoners; but the ratio of each of these to the total is perhaps not so great as might have been expected. For instance, while 19·87 per cent. of the homicides are returned as drunkards, 20·10 per cent. are returned as total abstainers.

IV.—*A Census of Inland Navigation in France.* [Translated from the official publication of the French Ministry of Public Works, 1892.]

It was originally intended by the Government that a census of the number and tonnage of boats on the French rivers and canals should be taken every five years, as this period appeared to meet all reasonable requirements. But various circumstances, among which may be mentioned the important projected law concerning this traffic, and the approaching meeting (in July, 1892) of the fifth International Congress on Inland Navigation, decided the administration to advance by a year the time originally set for the second census.

The census of 1891, like that of 1887, comprises all the ordinary transport and steam boats which frequent the French waterways, except those of a tonnage inferior to 3 *tonneaux* (3 tons nearly[3]); it was taken by the same method as had been already adopted in 1887. The canals and rivers were divided into sections sufficiently short to enable the enumerators to go over them in a few hours. For each boat there was a separate schedule to be filled in; these were distributed on the Friday (15th May), to be collected again the next day. On the 16th the enumerators left

---

[3] One tonneau = 19·7 cwt. For convenience, the word *tonneau* has been translated throughout the article by *ton*, the error being 1 in 67.

their respective posts at 7 in the morning, and on their way, walking towards each other, they collected the schedules from every boat, whether in motion or stationary, which they found in the section assigned to them. A receipt was given to the boatmen for the schedule, which was verified and, if necessary, completed on the spot, all duplication being thus avoided.

In this manner the description of every boat frequenting the French waterways was collected, the only exceptions being those which at the time happened to be travelling out of the country. To arrive at the complete results there were accordingly enumerated at the frontier stations all the boats of this class on their entry into France. This additional census lasted till the end of June.

The schedules were classified in two groups, the first including the ordinary boats, and the second the steamboats, each of these groups being, of course, subdivided. The boats have been classed according to their capacity, and not according to the length as on the first occasion.

I. ORDINARY BOATS.—The census includes all the ordinary boats of a capacity of more than 3 tons, excluding all those craft which, either in motion or stationary, are devoted to industries other than transport, strictly speaking, such as house-boats, washing-boats, baths, dredgers, ferries, lighters, &c.

The total number of transport boats thus counted is 15,925, with a total carrying capacity, when full, of 2,996,230 (French) tons. The number of boats in each class, according to capacity, is as follows :—

	Boats.		Capacity.	
	Number.	Per Cent.	Tonnage.	Per Cent.
Boats of over 300 tons	4,191	26	1,477,860	50
„ 300—200 „	3,297	21	838.652	28
„ 200—100 „	2,459	15	391,733	13
„ 100— 50 „	2,892	18	218,473	7
„ 50— 3 „	3,086	20	69,512	2
	15,925	100	2,996,230	100

Comparing these results with those of 1887, we have an increase in the number of 1 per cent., and of 10 per cent. in the tonnage; it is consequently the average capacity which has increased. As shown by the following figures, however, it is principally in the boats of 38.5 mètres by 5 (42 by 5½ yards), corresponding to the new type laid down by the technical conditions for the principal routes in the law of the 5th August, 1879, that the increase has taken place—

		Total Tonnage.
Number of boats of over 42 yards in 1891	2,016	746,758
„ '87	933	342,933
Increase 1887-91	1,083	403,825

or 54 per cent. in either case.

If we combine the two first categories (boats of over 200 tons, which include the *péniche*, of from 30 to 35 mètres, which predominated on the main routes before their transformation) we have a total of 7,488 boats, with a tonnage of 2,316,512 tons. These figures correspond to 47 per cent. of the number and 78 per cent. of the capacity of all the boats.

8,067 of these boats are decked; these are most numerous on the northern routes: in the other districts the undecked boats are in the majority. Most of the boats are made of wood, 1,051 only being of iron. There were in 1887 858 iron boats; there is thus an increase of 193. The greater number of iron boats are met with on the Seine and on the canals about Paris.

Classified according to nationality the figures are as follows:—

	Boats.		Tonnage.	
	Number.	Per Cent.	Tons.	Per Cent.
French	13,604	85	2,851,259	78
Belgian	1,892	12	562,448	19
German....................................	301	} 3	68,304	} 3
All other (Dutch, Luxemburg, &c.)............................	128		14,219	
	15,925	100	2,996,230	100

It thus appears that the Belgian boats constitute the great majority of foreign craft which habitually frequent the French waterways, contributing alone 82 per cent. of the number of foreign boats and 87 per cent. of the tonnage. The Belgian boats have an average capacity of 300 tons; they belong to the type usually met with on the main routes, being mostly barges or Flemish *péniches*. They are met with on nearly all the large canals and rivers in the northern, eastern, and central districts, but mostly in the frontier departments.

The other foreign craft, which form only an insignificant portion of the total enumerated, average 192 tons. The German boats are the most numerous of these, and have been almost all counted in the eastern region, in the frontier departments of the Ardennes, Meuse, Vosges, and especially Meurthe-et-Moselle.

In 1887 there were 2,098 foreign boats in French waters, i.e., 1,645 Belgian, 280 German, and 173 Dutch and Luxemburg. There is thus an increase of 223 foreign, 247 more Belgian, and 21 German, while the boats of other nations had decreased by 45.

The supplementary enumeration made at the frontier between the 17th May and the 30th June (inclusive), shows a total of 976 boats, which have been included in the general total. Of these 976, 233 French and 542 foreign entered at the Belgian frontier, while 44 French and 167 foreign entered direct from Germany, making a total of 267 French and 709 foreign boats. In 1887, during an equal period of time (15th October to 30th November), the number thus counted was 317—194 coming from Belgium and 123 from Germany.

Nearly all the transport boats possess a cabin, which serves as a domicile for the bargemen, and often for their family, whose sole home it is.   At the time of the census, 13,699 boats were provided with cabins, which sheltered 40,468 persons (19,579 men, 7,917 women, and 12,972 children).   This is an increase of 2,360 persons, or 6 per cent. over the figures of 1887, which included 18,750 men, 7,323 women, and 12,035 children; total 38,108.

It is noteworthy that while the number of boats shows a very small increase (1 per cent.), the tonnage and the population have increased respectively by 10 and 6 per cent.   This must be attributed in great measure to the new type of vessels which now frequent the main routes.

A certain number of barges have also stabling for the animals used in towing.   These amount to 2,094 boats, sheltering 3,106 beasts of burden (1,396 horses, 106 mules, and 1,604 asses).   These figures also show an increase over those of 1887; namely, of 220 in the number of barges provided with stables, and 519 in the number of beasts.   It is principally in the central regions that such boats are found; on other systems, and especially in the north, there are very few of them; in the latter district, these boats number only 33 out of 3,497.

More than half the boats enumerated, 8,460, are navigated by the proprietor himself, and it is among the larger boats that this occurs more particularly, reaching 71 per cent. of the total in the category of boats over 300 tons, as shown by the following figures :—

Of 4,191 boats of over 300 tons, 2,993 are navigated by the proprietor.
  ,, 3,297   ,,   200—300   ,, 1,538   ,,
  ,, 2,459   ,,   100—200   ,, 1,067
  ,, 2,892   ,,   50—100   ,, 1,366
  ,, 3,086   ,,   3— 50   ,, 1,496

These figures bring out the importance of the small proprietors in the water transport industry, as they own more than two-thirds of the boats of the new type which predominate on the main highways.

The census also brings out that the number of French proprietors which possess only one boat is 6,381 out of 8,058 owners (private individuals or companies), *i.e.*, 79 per cent.; the tonnage of their boats is 1,112,983 tons, or 48 per cent.   If we consider the class of small proprietors to be those who possess 1, 2, or 3 boats, their number is 7,706 (95 per cent. of the total), owning boats with a total capacity of 1,648,598 tons (70 per cent. of the total).

As mentioned above, the census was taken on the 16th May, that is to say, at a time when the navigation is generally very active.   It was found that there were—

7,540 boats under weigh, of which 5,393 were laden, and 2,147 empty.
8,385   ,,   at the wharves   ,,   2,675 were being laden, 3,914 were empty and waiting to be laden.
and 1,796 were laden and used as storehouses;

that is a total of 15,925, of which 9,864, or rather more than three-fifths, were actually in use at the time of the census.

II. STEAMBOATS.—On all the waterways there were enumerated 691 steamboats of all kinds.[4] Fully laden their carrying capacity is 43,583 tons, and their horse power 63,913;[5] 217 of these boats are paddle steamers, and 474 screw steamers. These include 40 foreign boats with a tonnage of 3,078 tons, and a force of 7,141 h.p.

This shows an increase since 1887 of 56 boats and 8,543 h.p., principally among the tugs, which in the former year numbered 184, with a total force of 13,278 h.p.; whereas in 1891 they amounted to 237, with 19,397 h.p.

Considering now the use to which these boats are habitually put, we find that 267 are utilised for the conveyance of passengers, 113 for the transport of goods, 237 as tugs, and 74 for hauling, either by working on a chain in the bed of the river, or by cable.

	Number of Steamboats.	Tonnage when fully Laden.	Force of Engines. H.P. of 75 Kilogrammetres.
Passenger boats { paddle	59*	5,852	12,297
screw	208†	11,583	13,678
Total	267	17,435	25,975
Boats used for { paddle	53	12,711	9,380
transport .... { screw	60‡	13,437	5,647
Total	113	26,148	15,027
Tugs .... { paddle	31	—	3,565
screw	206§	—	15,832
Total	237	—	19,397
Towing boats	74	—	3,514

* Including 15 Swiss (force 5,855 h.p.), employed for passengers on the Lake of Geneva.

† One Swiss (130 h.p.), belonging to the same service.

‡ Including 2 Belgian (together 210 h.p.), 1 German (12 h.p.), 2 Swiss (together 200 h.p.), and 2 English (together 300 h.p.).

§ Including 16 Belgian (together 400 h.p.) and 1 Italian (25 h.p.).

The most important depôts for passenger boats are, on the Seine, Paris and Rouen; on the Saône, Lyons; on the Garonne, Bordeaux; on the Loire, Nantes. Those used for the transport of

[4] This number does not include 161 pleasure boats, having a total horse power of 1,917. These pleasure boats are decomposed into 150 French boats of 1,765 h.p., and 11 foreign with a total force of 212 h.p.

[5] This is French horse power. Horse power in France is defined to be the work done in raising 75 kilogrammes through a vertical distance of 1 mètre in one second. It is thus equivalent to about 0·985 English horse power.

goods are more scattered, but are only met with in large numbers
between Paris and Rouen, Lyons and Arles, and St. Jean-de-Losne
and Lyons.   The service of tugs is important only on the Dordogne
below Libourne, the Garonne below Bordeaux, the lower Loire, the
Meuse (in the Ardennes and the northern branch of the Canal de
l'Est), the Rhone below Lyons, the Saône below St. Jean-de-Losne,
and the Seine between Montereau, Paris, Rouen, and Le Havre.
It is on this latter river that the tugs are most frequently met
with.   As for the hauling boats, if we except the government
service at the tunnels on the Burgundy, Eastern, Marne-to-Rhine,
St. Quentin, and St. Martin canals, they are scarcely used, except
on the Yonne between Laroche and Montereau, and on the Seine
between Montereau, Paris, Conflans, and Rouen.   On the Scarpe
and the Deûle these tugs are also used over a part of their course.

Of the 178 proprietors, owning 651 steamboats, 114 own but one
boat, and 78 of which are tugs.   There are 15 proprietors owning
but 1 passenger boat each.

III.—It is well known that the northern, central, eastern, and
south-eastern systems are by far the most important, the traffic on
them amounting to nine-tenths of the total tonnage of the whole
interior navigation in France.   Besides which, considering the
condition of navigation, these four systems form a homogeneous
whole, and the boats which perform the service on them rarely
leave them, as the dimensions and draught of most of them do not
allow of their going up the secondary routes.   In placing the
various systems according to their importance, the foreign boats
have been left out of count.   As was shown above, these latter
frequent almost exclusively the four principal systems, and
especially the northern and eastern, in the departments near the
frontier.   10,082 French boats out of the 13,604 counted, *i.e.*, about
three-fourths, were met with on these four systems; their total
tonnages amounted to 92 per cent. of the total capacity of the
French boats.

*French Boats, classified according to the District in which they were
Enumerated.*

	Total.		Number.	Over 300 Tons.	Number.	200—300 Tons.
	Number.	Tonnage.				
Northern system	3,530	936,843	1,743	606,299	918	250,696
Central ,, ...	4,403	803,897	771	292,016	1,032	241,175
Eastern ,, ...	1,347	295,296	392	133,985	491	123,288
South-eastern system ...	802	118,497	59	20,013	221	53,091
Total	10,082	2,154,533	2,965	1,052,313	2,662	668,250
Other systems	3,522	196,726	5	1,832	31	7,405
Grand total	13,604	2,351,259	2,970	1,054,145	2,693	675,655

French Boats, classified according to the District in which Enumerated—Contd.

	Number.	100—200 Tons.	Number.	50—100 Tons.	Number.	3—50 Tons.
Northern system	357	56,579	229	16,289	283	6,980
Central „	807	142,219	1,528	121,698	265	6,789
Eastern „	162	26,566	91	6,767	211	4,690
South-eastern system	202	32,446	141	9,220	179	3,727
Total	1,528	257,810	1,989	153,974	938	22,186
Other systems	615	85,261	808	57,606	2,063	44,622
Grand total	2,143	343,071	2,797	211,580	3,001	66,808

V.—*Female Labour in New South Wales.*

In the second part of the Census and Industrial Returns Act of 1891 it is provided that "inquiry shall be made into the industrial condition of the people, the hours of labour, the regularity of employment, the wages of workers, and the accommodation afforded by employers for their workpeople, the employment of children and females, the displacement of labour by machinery, the return upon capital invested, the variations in prices, and any other subject on which the Colonial Secretary may deem it expedient to have inquiry made."

Power to accomplish the object in view is conferred by the provision that "it shall be lawful for the government statistician, or any person duly authorised under his hand, to enter any factory, mine, workshop, or place where persons are employed, at any time within reasonable hours, for the purpose of making any inquiries or observations needful for the proper carrying out of this Act."

In accordance with these provisions, an inquiry, of which a first instalment[*] has lately been published, has been made into the conditions of labour in the various industries. Attention has for the most part been confined to the hours of labour, the regularity of employment, the accommodation provided for workers, their wages, the employment of women and children, and similar subjects. The other heads of inquiry mentioned in the Act will be dealt with in a later report.

The present instalment contains reports on the tailoring industry, dressmaking. millinery, whitework and various articles of clothing, the manufacture of woollen cloth, laundries, and shirt making.

1. The tailoring industry employs the greatest number of hands, but a majority of these are out-door, who take work home, the factory system not having yet assumed large proportions in

[*] New South Wales: Census and Industrial Returns Act of 1891 (information respecting).

Sydney. The factories, employed chiefly in the manufacture of "slops," are struggling to oust the English made goods from the markets. The cost of making up the articles is, in Sydney, from 75 to 100 per cent. greater than in London; and it has been found that the people generally prefer the goods made in the colony, which are more suitable in shape and are more to the local taste, so long as the price is not more than 15 per cent. above that of the English goods.

With regard to the earnings, these can only be roughly determined, as the workpeople are paid by the piece, while there are many extras and allowances to be taken into consideration. On the whole, after making due allowance for deductions for irregularity of employment (as to which the opinions of the employers differ essentially from those of the executive officers of the union), the *average* annual wage appears to be 114*l.* or 2*l.* 4*s.* per week, for indoor *employés*, though many earn less, and many much more. The hours of work vary from about 48½ to 51 hours per week, with some few exceptions. The home workers, who are mostly women, earn throughout the year an average of 20*s.* to 22*s.* 6*d.* weekly. It appears that a single girl can maintain herself in moderate comfort on this; but when a woman has children depending on her, she will require some 30*s.*, and this means working 12 to 14 hours daily, not to mention the calls on her time for domestic duties, &c. There is also another large class of outside workers, by whom the work is taken on sub-contract. This is the nearest approach to "sweating" that has been detected.

2. The greatest complaint made by the hands in the dressmaking trade is as to overtime. The nominal hours are, in most cases, 9 till 6, with an allowance for dinner, and till 1 or 2 on Saturdays, but in many establishments these hours appear to be greatly exceeded, and the women are constantly detained up till 9 or even 11 o'clock. It is only in few cases that overtime is paid for, while fines for being late are common. Wages in this trade appear, on the average, to be only about 13*s.* 8*d.* per week; this is exclusive of the small number of highly paid head dressmakers, skirt drapers, and forewomen on the one hand, and the apprentices on the other. Excluding the apprentices only, the average is about 17*s.* 6*d.* per week. In the country the wages are slightly better. Dressmakers working in their own homes usually earn more than they would if employed in shops, for when a connection is once formed, work is fairly plentiful, and sufficiently profitable to afford them a frugal subsistence. The average gross income for 75 houses visited is 65*s.* 5*d.*, but after paying assistants' wages and making allowance for cases where two or more members of a family share in the proceeds, the average net income per head is 39*s.* 9*d.* per week.

Comparing the earnings of home workers employing paid assistants with the earnings of those who employ none, the average net incomes per worker are 47*s.* 4*d.* and 31*s.* 5*d.* per week respectively. The assistants employed number about 2·5 per house, earning an average of 9*s.* 7*d.* each; or, excluding nine unpaid apprentices, 10*s.* 5*d.* each per week. It would therefore appear that the advantage the home workers derive from employing assistants is equal to 15*s.* 11*d.* per employer, and dividing by 2·5, the average number of assistants, this gives a profit to the employer of 6*s.* 4*d.* per week for each assistant employed.

The annual earnings of the workwomen do not, however, on an average, amount to more than 32*l.* or 33*l.*, as during two periods of the year employers grant compulsory "holidays," these periods being those just before the change from winter to summer, and *vice versâ.* These are often felt as a great hardship. Wages are kept low in this trade to some extent by the competition of women who accept work without desiring to earn their living, but who "just want to do something." The apprentices as a rule are not paid, at all events in the city, and the system of apprenticeship is very loose. The girls pick up what they can without being regularly taught, as the employers do not care whether they learn anything or not, for the apprentices frequently leave before their (purely nominal) term is finished. The girls then engage themselves elsewhere, though quite incompetent, as "improvers." These remarks as to apprentices apply equally to the tailoring trade.

3. Millinery is a much more attractive trade; the work is lighter, and the hours of labour (usually 9 a.m. to 6 p m., and 1 p.m. on Saturdays) appear to be strictly observed. This last point is a serious consideration with parents, who prefer to apprentice their girls to this trade, knowing that they will not be compelled to return home alone at almost any time of night. In consequence of these advantages there is a greater demand for employment, and vacancies are easily filled, and it naturally results that wages range lower, so much so that in the lower grades those whose pay in this trade represents their sole income cannot possibly live in any comfort. The majority of the *employées* have other means, and many take to it as a useful accomplishment, the money to them being of very little moment. The pay in the lowest grade ranges from 4*s.* to 15*s.* per week, the average being about 8*s.* In the higher grades the pay is much better, head milliners averaging 3*l.* a week, while many of this class are imported from London and Paris, and are paid at special rates. The apprentices usually serve their time in the same establishment; in some cases they receive a certain wage after having been employed for a certain period.

4. In the "whitework and various articles of clothing" there are two main classes of workers, factory hands and home workers. The former of these are much better off: they are often trained and employed, throughout the regular gradations, in the same establishment, and their pay is better than that of the home workers, who are paid by the piece, and who are for the most part widows, or wives whose husbands earn nothing, and others reduced by misfortune. In the factories a worker is apparently often paid by the piece or by the week, accordingly as either arrangement is most remunerative to the proprietor, *e.g.*, if a worker paid by the week does not produce enough to satisfy her employer, she may be put on piecework, and *vice versâ.* Apprentices average 2*s.* 6*d.* a

week, and machinists about 16s., while improvers and finishers earn
amounts between these two sums. Forewomen and cutters earn
much more, but these are in the highest positions, and are comparatively few in number, the majority being machinists. The
pay of home workers varies immensely, according to the skill of
the individual and the article made; excluding extreme cases, and
deducting the outlay which the *employée* must incur for travelling
and other expenses, the average earnings come out at 11s. 9d. per
head per week. The home workers were formerly much better off,
when there were no factories or middlemen.

5. Considerable difficulty has been experienced in establishing
woollen cloth mills in New South Wales, and the number in
operation at one time has varied considerably. At the present
moment there are five; four of these were formerly flour mills, and
are consequently not so convenient as they might otherwise be.
In four of the five the total number of hands is 145 (75 males and
70 females). The working hours are 54 per week, in which time
the men earn 30s. to 70s. according to their grade, while the women
earn from 15s. to 30s. The mills are too small, and the machinery
too old fashioned to secure any considerable output, that of the
largest mill being only 150,000 yards annually. Most of the mills
are consequently worked in connection with a clothing factory,
which enables the proprietor to gain a certain amount of profit
that he could not possibly make with the mill alone.

6. The most important consideration in the laundry business
in Sydney is drainage, which is in most cases bad, while in many
cases the stables attached to the laundry are not drained at all.
The health of the workpeople is also affected, in some laundries,
by the hot room in which many have to work, while laundry
keepers assert that clothes are sometimes sent to the wash from
sick rooms and hospitals without their having first been disinfected.
Wages vary, on an average, from 12s. 3d.—the earnings of folders
(who generally have more overtime than the others)—to 25s. 9d.,
earned by the starch ironers. Washers earn about 21s. per week,
while sorters, who must be able to read and write, and require
some knowledge of arithmetic, earn about 50s. There is a considerable amount of overtime, which is paid for, and holidays are
rare; while absence, whether from sickness or any other cause,
entails the loss of the wages.

7. Only some 150 hands are employed in the shirtmaking
industry, and there are only four factories, which confine themselves
almost entirely to white shirts of good quality. The other kinds
of shirts mostly come under the head of whitework and sundries.
The hours in this trade average about 44 per week; but among
home workers the average is nearly 60. The wages paid vary from
nothing or 2s. to 7s. 6d. for apprentices, and from 7s. 6d. to 21s. for
machinists, the scales of payment for the others being intermediate between these, except for cutters and forewomen, of whom
there are naturally but few. Home workers average 11s. 6d. per
week.

As regards the accommodation for workers, which has been
carefully studied in the investigations, it varies considerably in the

different trades. In the whitework and shirtmaking it is, on the whole, fairly good, with one or two exceptions. In the tailoring industry the majority of factories are classed as "fair," the remainder as "inferior," none of them being bad; whereas in the workshops attached to retail businesses, "fair" and "inferior" are in nearly equal numbers, while some few are "bad" and "very bad." The points considered were cubic space, floor space, ventilation, cleanliness, approach, sanitary arrangements, and light. In the dressmaking business the accommodation, taken all round, is somewhat inferior to that prevailing in the tailoring industry, and the same remark applies to the millinery, in which, however, heating is mostly absent or inadequate. Attention has already been called to the condition of the laundries, which are by far the worst. On the whole the factories and large establishments have, as might be expected, far better accommodation of every kind than the small retail shops and businesses.

VI.—*Notes on Economical and Statistical Works.*

La Population Française. Par E. Levasseur. Tome troisième. Paris: Arthur Rousseau, 1892.

In this third volume of M. Levasseur's comprehensive treatise on the population of France, the two former volumes of which have been previously noticed in the *Journal*, he proceeds to disengage from the facts and figures which he has collected some laws and principles of a general nature, and to trace the political and economic consequences arising from the condition of affairs thus disclosed. The section of his work, which is contained in the volume, bears the title of the "Laws of Population and the Equilibrium of Nations," and it is divided into two parts, in one of which population is considered in its relation to wealth, while the other treats of the equilibrium of nations and races. The first part naturally commences with that which must almost necessarily be the starting point of all inquiries into the laws of population— the celebrated theory of Malthus, who, as M. Levasseur justly remarks, is more often quoted than read. The place and circumstances of the production of his famous essay, the chief propositions which he sought to establish, and the practical conclusions which he deduced from his facts and reasonings, the anticipations made by other writers, such as Plato and Aristotle, of his doctrines, and, in spite of such forerunners, their essential originality, are duly noticed by M. Levasseur, who then offers some criticisms on the doctrines. The experience of modern times, he maintains, has not confirmed the antithesis, which Malthus set up, between the growth of man and the increase of food. The actual facts of population in Europe, where it has only doubled since the beginning of the century, and has become 360 instead of 175 millions, suggest some doubt of the validity, or, at any rate, of the pertinence, of Malthus' hypothesis of a geometrical ratio of increase; for on that hypothesis in the three generations which have elapsed the population of Europe should have amounted to as much as 700 millions. In fact, in order to realise such an hypothesis, all the adults in a nation should marry and the average number of children to a family should not fall below 7. Demography shows, on the contrary, that all the adults do not marry, and that a proportion of 60 births to 1,000 inhabitants, which is implied by 7 births to a marriage, is far in excess of the actual average of 38 per 1,000 established in Europe for the last thirty years or so. Malthus, indeed, might plead in reply the operation of his check of moral restraint; but the apparent rejoinder would be that these results have occurred without any evidence of extraordinary effort, and simply through the operation of natural and social laws quietly working out their effects. Nor, M. Levasseur contends, does the arithmetical increase of subsistence rest on a surer basis of fact than the geometrical increase of population. It has no precise expression. And so he reaches the conclusion that the laws of population do not admit of being comprised within the narrow limits of a rigid formula. They must rather be expressed in a series of propositions founded on the records of experience—as indeed, we may add, those of Malthus were to a large extent, although they were summarily stated. The propositions are of the following nature : That subsistence, whether produced on the actual soil where the people live, or procured in exchange from abroad, imposes a limit on population. That the limit varies according to the quantity of wealth produced by the people, and the average of individual consumption. That population tends to increase its numbers through births, as it tends also to produce fresh wealth ; but that it is impossible to pronounce off-hand which of the two tendencies will predominate. That a soil fertile for crops, or rich in minerals, permits of a larger population. That, where the production of wealth requires more human labour, population should be more numerous. That industry and intelligence of labour, and abundance of capital, and progressive scientific discovery, and advancing civilisation, allow of greater numbers. That an elevation of the standard of comfort calls for a relaxation of the rate at which population is growing, if the production of food remains stationary. That new countries afford the conditions for a rapid increase of population; and that in old countries manufactures may be easier to establish, and more productive in exchange, and may thus compensate for any additional difficulty felt in such countries in obtaining the products of the soil. That a defective social organisation or a meddlesome government, or inequality of conditions, may check population. That its increase takes place (eliminating the influence of immigration) by the excess of births over deaths, which may be occasioned by an increase of births or a decrease of deaths, or by both causes together. That in the actual state of the world the population of all civilised States exhibits more births than deaths, and is consequently increasing. That both the birth-rate and the death-rate are usually higher in the lower than in the more elevated ranks of society ; and that emigration and immigration help to re-establish the equilibrium of population when it is disturbed. These laws or rules are, M. Levasseur states, based on the facts already collected and examined in the second section of his treatise, or to be investigated in the present volume; and he briefly expresses their general drift by saying that the increase of population depends on the sum of its means of existence and of its needs—that the number of inhabitants borne by a given area is determined, in the first place, by the natural qualities of the soil and climate; in the second, by the quantity of capital, of scientific knowledge, and of energy for work, possessed by the people who inhabit it; in the third, by the facilities for the exchange of its manufactured products for the food products of other countries, and, in the fourth and last, by the average of individual consumption. The first cause accounts for the fact that the polar regions are uninhabited; the second for the larger population of western Europe as compared with tropical Africa; the third for a greater density of population in England and Belgium than in Spain; and the last for a similar greater density in the valley of the Ganges than in France.

These observations, which we have quoted with some detail, will serve to illustrate the general nature of the contents of M. Levasseur's third volume; for he discusses in successive chapters the chief points which he has raised. In the second chapter he considers the relations of population to subsistence, and in the third its relations to wealth. He illustrates, by means of graphic representations, the changes which have taken place in the objects of consumption, and he shows that bread, meat, and other foods and drinks have increased in their production in France far more rapidly than has population, that they have at least doubled, while population has scarcely grown by a third or a quarter, and that consequently the French of to-day eat about one-and-a-half as much again as their grandparents who lived under the Restoration. Nor is this conclusion peculiar to France; it is common to the civilised countries of the globe. And the increase of manufactured commodities, and the improvement in the processes of production and transport, and the accumulation of wealth and diffusion of comfort, have been no less remarkable. The "progress of the working-classes" cannot, in fact, be denied; and the investigations on this point in France only confirm those of Dr. Giffen in England and M. Bodio in Italy, which in their turn show that the stationary state of population existing in France is not a necessary condition for such an advance. If anything, M. Levasseur remarks, the evidence of the nineteenth century has reversed the conclusion formed by Malthus at the end of the eighteenth. The growth in the number of consumers and in that of consumable commodities has been unequal; but it is the latter which has outrun the former, and the past and the present may on this point, even by a sober and not over sanguine inquirer, be treated as a guarantee for the future. There are, however, some signs of misery mingled with those of prosperity, and in his fourth chapter M. Levasseur examines the facts of pauperism and charity. But even here the conclusion is optimistic rather than otherwise; for, if the increase of wealth and well-being does not suppress poverty, it affords the means for its more effectual relief. M. Levasseur traces the history of charitable aid in France during the century with some detail, and in a concluding chapter he contrasts the fecundity of the French population with that of other countries. France occupies the lowest position among European nations as respects its birth-rate, and only a mean position as respects its death-rate, and therefore the fecundity of its population is relatively low. This feature has been noticed during the century by different writers—by Humboldt as early as 1823, and by later writers, such as MM. Bertillon and Loua, who have sounded no indistinct note of alarm. Humboldt brought out the fact of 125 births in France as against 100 deaths, as compared with 137 in England, 166 in Russia, 180 in Western Prussia, and 300 in New Jersey. M. Bertillon, taking the years 1855-74 as the period of observation, pointed out that France exhibited, among other features of population, 173 legitimate births per 1,000 married women of child-bearing age, as against 200 for the other European States, for which he obtained figures, and as much as 305 for Bavaria in particular. M. Levasseur states the various causes which have been assigned for this result, such as delay in marriage, dearness of lodging accommodation, the custom of dowering daughters, the pursuit of official careers, and the diffusion of luxury; and he attributes most influence to what he admits to be the vague circumstance of a change in manners.

To the second section of the volume, which is devoted to the consideration of the equilibrium of nations and races, the limits of space will compel us to give less detailed attention, although, equally with the first, it will, we think, reward the careful study of the economist and statistician. The political questions connected with the balance of power, which may be shifted by a change in the relative numbers of population, and the various matters raised in connection with the migration of peoples—with emigration and immigration, and colonisation—are successively treated, and are copiously illustrated by the graphic method. During the present century the geographical distribution of the area of European territory among the different nations has in many cases undergone important change, and the varying increase of population in the different countries has added to, or taken away from, the effects of these changes on the varying balance of power, while the competition of the military spirit, leading to the huge armies of the present day, has entered into the guiding forces of European politics. Germany has undoubtedly become the preponderating power of Europe. M. Levasseur next reviews the commercial policy of Europe generally, and the internal politics of France in particular, and he then proceeds to trace the movements of population within the limits of different European countries. He shows that the tendency to congregate in towns is a common feature of recent history, and that it is to be found even some distance back; and he considers the influence of foreign immigration into France, where it has raised somewhat similar questions to those with which controversy has busied itself in other countries of the world. In the next chapter he passes to the examination of

European emigration to other continents, and supplies some interesting figures. The course of French colonisation is traced in the following chapter, the progress of the European as contrasted with other races is reviewed in the succeeding chapter, and its supremacy established on the evidence of its wealth, its powerful civilisation, and its wonderful capacity for expansion. Two of the five parts of the globe are inhabited by it. The Chinese race may rival its numbers, but falls immeasurably below in all that contributes to real well-being. In his concluding chapters M. Levasseur treats of the limits to the density of population, and shows how these may vary with varying conditions; and he draws some general demographic, political, and economic conclusions from the immense mass of facts and figures which he has collected and presented in the course of his treatise, while an appendix contains some corrections and additions to this and the preceding volumes. We understand that this is the last volume of his book, and we embrace the opportunity thus afforded to congratulate him on the completion of so laborious and valuable an undertaking as he has now accomplished.

Introduzione allo studio dell' Economia Politica. Di Luigi Cossa. Milano: Ulrico Hoepli, 1892.

Professor Cossa's *Guide to the Study of Political Economy* is favourably known to English economic students, to whom it was introduced by a recommendation from the pen of the late Professor Jevons. Nor, as the distinguished author states in the preface to the present volume, which forms the third edition of the *Guide*, enlarged and revised to date, is it in England alone that its merits have been widely recognised. Two previous editions in Italian attest the place occupied by the work in Dr. Cossa's own country, and the same number of editions in Spanish are one proof of the esteem in which it is held by other foreigners. A glance at the contents of the present edition would suffice to explain and justify, if not to extend and increase, this high reputation. If we take, for example, the section in which the author deals with the writings of English economists, we find that the account he furnishes is as representative and adequate as his information is recent and accurate, and his judgment sound and impartial. In the eighth chapter of the second or historical part of the book he discusses the work of Adam Smith and his immediate successors. He shows how, based as it is largely on the ideas of the physiocratic system, the immortal treatise, as he styles it, of Adam Smith gave the character and dignity of a science to economics. Passing in review the life and writings of the great Scotchman, he supplies in the next place an analysis of the different books of the *Wealth of Nations*, and follows this summary with an account of the author's opponents, his disciples, and his critics. To Adam Smith the names of Malthus and Ricardo naturally succeed, and in either case Dr. Cossa refers to the most recent criticism passed in different countries on the characteristic doctrines of these famous economists. The ninth chapter of this part of his book bears the title of "Political Economy in England," and in this chapter he brings his biblio-

graphical sketch down from Ricardo and Malthus and Adam Smith
to the present time. The popularisation of the classical teaching
by McCulloch and Torrens and Whately and Senior, the immense
and predominant influence of the younger Mill, the numerous
monographs which have appeared in connection with various
departments of economic study, such as those of Wakefield on
colonisation, of Jevons and Bagehot, of Tooke and Newmarch, on
money and prices and banking, of Howell and Holyoake on industrial relations, the criticisms passed on the classical doctrines,
sometimes in a hostile, sometimes in a friendly spirit, the manner
in which those doctrines have been corrected and enlarged by a
succession of writers, whom Dr. Cossa divides for convenience into
three groups, are some of the topics which receive attention in this
chapter. In the first of these groups he places Thornton and
Toynbee, in the second Cliffe Leslie and Dr. Ingram, and in the
third Cairnes and Jevons; and then in the fifth section of the
chapter he proceeds to review the actual state of affairs. Notwithstanding assaults from various quarters, notwithstanding
triumphant predictions of inevitable failure, and gloomy despon-
dent forebodings of early decline, there is still, he remarks, in
England a considerable band of vigorous teachers, surrounded by
no small number of zealous disciples, prosecuting the study of
economics. The "classic home" of economics has not yet forfeited
its early fame. Dr. Cossa shows that he is thoroughly abreast of
the most recent English economic literature. There are few, if
there are any, authors who can fairly complain of omission from
his pages, and he gives a full analysis of the two recent treatises
which may be said to stand out from the rest as evidence of the
vitality of economic science in this country—those of Professors
Marshall and Sidgwick—while the *Economic Journal*, the *Economic
Review*, and the *Dictionary of Political Economy* have not, though
but lately issued, escaped his observant attention.

This detailed account of Dr. Cossa's review of English economics
will serve, perhaps better than anything else, to show the nature
of his book, and to convince those who know the first edition that
it has not deteriorated but, on the contrary, greatly improved in
the interval. It is of course easier to test the accuracy and fulness
of Dr. Cossa's work when he deals with English literature; but
this part may fairly be taken as a sample of the rest. The present
state of economics in France, in Germany, in Spain and Portugal,
in the Scandinavian, the Slavonic, and the Magyar countries of
Europe, in the United States of America, and in Dr. Cossa's own
country of Italy, is similarly reviewed in the later chapters of the
second part, and in a concluding chapter the author considers the
position of theoretic socialism, while he traces in the earlier
chapters the history of economics from its fragmentary beginnings
in ancient and mediæval times down to the empirical systems,
of which the mercantilist writers may be taken as one type, the
liberal reaction against the exclusive and restrictive spirit then
prevalent, the teaching of the forerunners of the scientific conception, and the doctrines of the physiocrats. In the first part of
the book, which is distinguished from the "historical" by the title

of "theoretical," he discusses such preliminary and general points as the object and scope of economic study, its divisions, its various relations, its character, definition and method, its importance, and the answers to objections which have been raised to it in various quarters. We hope, and believe, that it will not be long before English students have the advantage of reading in their own language this improved version of this excellent guide, and the result, we are convinced, will be that their gratitude to Dr. Cossa, already by no means inconsiderable, will be greatly increased.

The Use and Abuse of Money. By W. Cunningham. London: John Murray, 1892.

This book forms one of the earliest issued of a new series intended for University Extension Students; and it has been appropriately intrusted to Dr. Cunningham, who, as he states in the preface, was "one of the pioneers of the University Extension movement in 1874." His experience as an extension Lecturer has led him to prefix a full and useful syllabus, or analysis of contents, in which he divides his subject into three heads, one dealing with "social problems," the second with "practical questions," and the third and last with "personal responsibility." He remarks in the preface that "the subject discussed is *Capital in its Relation to Social Progress;*" and accordingly he examines the nature and work of capital, mainly on traditional lines, so far as the account of its growth, and of the place filled by it in the economic constitution of society, is concerned. "In the present day," he observes, "when capital dominates in so many directions, it is not uninteresting to select this particular factor" (for review) "and consider the part which Capital has played, and its bearing on the material progress of the race." But the title actually given to the book calls attention to the special point of view, which Dr. Cunningham has adopted in his treatment of what is after all a somewhat hackneyed topic in economic manuals; and it is this which gives novelty and interest to his book. He wishes to "lay stress on the element of personal responsibility. Much has been written about the duties of landowners, and it seems worth while to say a little about the responsibilities of moneyed men (or the manner in which they employ their capital and spend their income)." And so, while sketching the position of industry without capital, and tracing the rise and development of the capitalist era, and discussing the formation, investment, replacement, and direction of capital, he also considers the relations of material progress to moral advance, examines the personal responsibility involved in the acquisition and administration of economic influence, and investigates the nature of the duty attaching to the employment of capital, to the return obtained from its use or investment, and, generally, to the enjoyment of wealth. Some of the questions, which he thus raises, are of a nice and difficult character; but they are, without exception, of profound interest, and in no part of the discussion will the student fail to derive stimulus and instruction from Dr. Cunningham's judicious handling.

The Effects of Machinery on Wages. By J. Shield Nicholson. London: Swan Sonnenschein and Co., 1892.

This essay gained some fifteen years ago the first Cobden prize awarded in the university of Cambridge, and Messrs. Swan Sonnenschein and Co. have, we think, done well to reprint it in their *Social Science Series.* They have rendered a real service to economic students; for, though the essay is brief, it is suggestive and original, and the subject of which it treats has not diminished in importance since it was first issued. Professor Nicholson has naturally laid the greater stress on the evils and dangers which are inherent in machinery, as its advantages and benefits had been more fully emphasised by previous writers; but he has not on that account taken an unduly pessimistic view. On the contrary, he has endeavoured, as he remarks, to "put in a clearer light" such good results as the increase of skill, which machinery necessarily requires, and the better division of labour and distribution of labourers, which it occasions. On the other hand, he has called prominent attention to the "fluctuations and precariousness of wages," which are the "inevitable result" of the "system of large industries" encouraged by the use of machinery. After an introduction setting forth the scope of the essay, and defining the terms to be used, and indicating the character of the problem to be solved, he discusses in the first chapter the process by which machinery may be substituted for labour, and shows how the theoretical injury it may undoubtedly occasion is in practice alleviated by the time and method of transition. In the second and succeeding chapters he considers machinery as auxiliary to labour, and as affecting the division of labour, the concentration of labour and capital, and the mobility of capital and labour; and then, in conclusion, he summarises the chief results which have been obtained in the course of the essay.

The Origin of Metallic Currency and Weight Standards. By William Ridgeway. Cambridge: the University Press, 1892.

Professor Ridgeway describes the volume before us as "an attempt to arrive at a knowledge of the origin of Metallic Currency and Weight Standards by the Comparative Method." He has endeavoured to extend the narrow range of observation covered by previous investigators. The numismatists, he remarks, had "confined themselves to the materials presented" "in the earliest money of Lydia, Greece, and Italy," while the metrologists had scarcely passed beyond "the systems of Babylon, Egypt, Greece, and Rome." As the result of this enlargement of view he has been led to criticise certain received doctrines and to advance certain new theories. Amongst the latter he specifies "those on the origin of the earliest Greek coin-types, of the earliest Greek silver coins, of the Greek Obolos, the Sicilian Libra, and Roman As; of the Mina, and its sixtyfold, the Talent." He combats throughout the theory that the weight standards of antiquity have been obtained scientifically. This theory, he remarks, was propounded by Boeckh, and has been accepted by subsequent writers, with scarcely an exception; but, working from the more to the less known, he himself prefers to start with Greece and Rome, where we have abundance of evidence, rather than with the imperfect acquaintance we possess of the Assyrian and Egyptian weight systems, to which the attractive conception of a scientific system has, he thinks, given excessive prominence. Accordingly, in the first chapter he discusses the Homeric units of value—the ox and the talent—and from the connection of the two, and the evidence pointing to the adoption of the cow as the earlier primitive unit, he establishes in the next chapter some important conclusions respecting primitive systems of currency. He adduces abundance of evidence, collected from the most various quarters of the globe, of early systems, and shows that the idea of a "primal convention" with regard to the use of any one particular article as a medium of exchange has as little foundation in fact as the theory in politics of an original "social contract." "Every medium of exchange," on the contrary, "has either an actual marketable value, or represents something which either has, or formerly had, such a value." The ox was a very common unit of value, and its use admitted of the employment of sub-multiples of the standard unit. Of the precious metals, gold, contrary to the received theory, seems to have been discovered before silver or copper; and it was known and played an important part over the same area as the ox, that is to say, over the whole of Europe, Asia, and northern Africa—over the whole district, in short, in which the ancient peoples lived of whom we have historical knowledge. In the fourth chapter of his work Mr. Ridgeway investigates the direction of primæval trade routes, and establishes the fact of "complete intercommunication by means of these routes between the various races of mankind." And hence he concludes that the ox and gold should have the same value throughout the inhabited area, and that, the unit of the latter being fixed on that of the former, the same quantity of gold should be found serving as the metallic unit throughout this area. In the fifth chapter he points out that the art of weighing was first used for gold, and in the sixth that the weight-unit of gold was everywhere about the same value, and that the value of a cow. In the seventh and eighth chapters he considers the question of the way in which these primitive units were fixed, and in the ninth he criticises the old received doctrines. In Part II of the book he considers the growth and development of the various weight standards of the different nations of the world, the origin of which he has thus determined. He examines in succession those of Egypt, Babylon, Lydia, Persia, Greece, Sicily, Italy, and Rome. The whole book contains a great mass of material which has been collected with industry, and it forms a valuable contribution to the literature of the subject with which it deals. If Mr. Ridgeway's arguments are sound, and they certainly appear to be so, an empiric origin must, it seems, be substituted for the scientific conception previously received; and in any case it would be difficult to dispute, and impossible to ignore, the evidence which he has gathered together.

The Land Systems of British India.   By B. H. Baden-Powell.
Oxford: the Clarendon Press, 1892.

It is impossible to do adequate justice to Mr. Baden-Powell's
monumental work on the *Land Systems of British India* within the
narrow limits of space to which a notice in this *Journal* is necessarily
confined.   Three handsome volumes, containing together more than
two thousand pages, are evidence, which it is impossible to dispute,
of abundant knowledge and unflagging industry; and for the
purpose in view, with all its bulk, the book does not seem to be too
long.   Although founded on a *Manual of the Land Tenures and
Land Revenue Systems of British India*, which was written by
Mr. Baden-Powell under the orders of the Government of India
some ten years ago, it is practically a new book; for important
land legislation, which bears more resemblance than might be
suspected to recent legislation in Ireland, so far as it is intended
to define and protect the rights of tenants, has, Mr. Baden-Powell
shows, been passed during the interval.   He aims at giving an
exhaustive and reliable account of the Indian land systems; and,
while these fall into certain broad classes, they also furnish
abundant variety of detail, which cannot be adequately described
without filling many pages of print.   English students are only
too apt to forget, what Anglo-Indians are never tired of repeating,
that "India" is a "geographical expression," and they need to be
reminded that it stretches over a vast area, and that its history
reaches back to distant periods.   There is therefore room for
considerable variety of local practices and customs; and the
succession of conquests, partial or otherwise, to which India has
been so often subjected, together with some experimental legislation
of Englishmen, unacquainted at first with systems, which seemed
different from any they knew in the Western world, has assisted
the rise and decline of various subordinate rights in connection
with the ownership and occupation of land.

The famous Cornwallis Settlement, for example, more perhaps,
as Mr. Baden-Powell shows, by its omissions than by its actual
commissions, by its failure to make a preliminary survey, recording
the rights of the subordinate occupiers of the soil, rather than by
its actual recognition of the Zamindars, undoubtedly altered their
position and introduced a far-reaching and, on the whole, prejudicial
change.   At an earlier time the rise of the Taluqdars in Oude was,
under the Muhammadan rulers, due to revenue exigencies and
arrangements.   All these changes and varieties Mr. Baden-Powell
describes with exhaustive detail; and the future student will
scarcely, we imagine, need to go outside the limits of his book if
he desires full and exact information on the subject.   In this brief
notice we can but indicate the chief divisions of his treatment.
The first volume is divided into two books, one dealing with
introductory matter of a general nature, and the other with the
province of Bengal.   In the general book the author describes the
various provinces and the mode of their creation, and the special
character of Indian legislation, and he then proceeds to a general
view of the land tenures and land revenue systems.   The origin
and nature of the "village" in different districts of India are

shown, and the manner traced in which the English government, after making an avowed mistake, or at least misunderstanding, in the permanent settlement of Bengal, where recognising an existing state of affairs, it sought to stereotype its prominent features, and neglected what was less noticeable but equally important, has since endeavoured in other districts to conform in its revenue systems to actual conditions, dealing with the village, where that is still an entity. as in the north-west, and proceeding by separate individual assessment, where the village is less powerful, as in Madras with its Raiyatwari tenure, or again, as in Oude, utilising the Taluqdars, but everywhere exercising punctilious care in rendering the survey an accurate and full record of all existing rights, and substituting temporary settlement periodically revised for the permanent settlement of Lord Cornwallis. Mr. Baden-Powell next passes on to give a detailed account of that permanent settlement, and of the temporary settlements, which are also found in lands belonging to Bengal that have been acquired subsequently to 1793, or have been resumed, or have lapsed. Volume ii is devoted to the second great division of Indian land tenure, the system of village settlements; and four successive parts deal respectively with the North-Western Provinces and Oude, Ajmer-Merwara, the Central Provinces, and the Panjab. In the third and concluding volume Mr. Baden-Powell passes to the Raiyatwari and allied systems, which are found in Madras, Bombay and Sindh, Berar, Assam, Coorg, and the newly acquired kingdom of Burma. The book is throughout copiously supplied with maps.

Litteraturnachweis über Geld- und Münzwesen. By Dr. Adolf Soetbeer. Berlin, 1892.

This is not merely a guide to the literature on money and coinage, as Dr. Soetbeer entitles this book, but is at the same time a history. Still, it was primarily written as a guide, and this is certainly not the least valuable portion of it, forming, as it does, an index to all the books and articles of any value which have been produced on the subject from the end of the fifteenth century down to the present time. Such a work could not have been undertaken by any one more competent than Dr. Soetbeer, from his life-long acquaintance of the subject, and from the fact that the great majority of the works which he enumerates have passed under his own eye in the preparation of his well-known *Materials for the Illustration and Criticism of the Economic Relations of the Precious Metals,* and other books. The present volume is arranged chronologically, divided into five parts dealing with the periods ending respectively with 1620, 1810, 1850, 1870, and 1891. Each of these is again sub-divided into three parts, dealing with (1) the money question, from the statistical point of view of the quantity of precious metals produced and in use, the relation between gold and silver, &c., and including also a history and discussion of all the acts of governments, recommendations of commissions, &c.; (2) a list of the Acts passed by the administrations of different countries for the regulation of the currency and kindred matters; (3) a list of the works published on money and coinage, including official publications. The book concludes with an exhaustive account of the actual state of the silver question at the beginning of the present year.

Statistical and Economical Articles in Recent Periodicals.

AUSTRIA—
Statistische Monatschrift—
April, 1892—
Die Viehzählung in Oesterreich, 1890: *Dr. J. v. Roschmann-Hörburg.*
Die Selbstmorde in der k. u. k. Armee in 1873-90: *J. Roth.*
Die österreichischen Unfallversicherungsanstalten im Jahre 1890: *Kögler.*
May—June—
Dichtigkeit, Zunahme, natürliche und Wanderbewegung der Bevölkerung Oesterreichs in 1881-90: *Dr. H. Rauchberg.*
Statistik der österreichischen Wassergenossenschaften nach dem Stande des Jahres 1891: *Dr. F. Schmid.*
Die Zuschläge zu den directen Steuern für die autonome Verwaltung Oesterreichs in 1888-90: *Friedenfels.*
Zur Statistik der localen Versicherungsvereine gegen Feuerschäden in Oesterreich in 1890: *H. Ehrenberger.*
Die Feuer- und Hagelschäden Oesterreichs in 1885-89: *K. Krafft.*
July—
Der landtäfliche Grundbesitz in Galizien: *Prof. Dr. Th. Pilat.*
Die Bewegung des Rindviehstandes von 1880-90, in einigen Alpengebieten Oesterreichs: *Prof. Dr. M. Wilckens.*
Die Aufnahmen in den österreichischen Staatsverband und die Entlassungen aus demselben in 1885-89: *J. Thornton.*

FRANCE—
Journal des Economistes—
June, 1892—
Le Budget de 1893: *M. Lacombe.*
Esquisse d'un Cours de Commerce: *M. Courcelle-Seneuil.*
La Banque Agricole de Turquie: *E. F. de Flaix.*
July—
L'Association libre contre le Socialisme d'Etat: *C. Benoist.*
Une expérience de tarifs différentiels [sur les chemins de fer] en Russie: *L. Domanski.*
Les Banques populaires en Italie: *G. François.*
August—
Les lois naturelles de l'Economie Politique et le Socialisme: *G. Du Puynode.*
L'agiotage du temps de Calonne: *C. Gomel.*
L'esprit d'initiative en France. Protectionisme et Exportation: *D. Bellet.*

FRANCE—*Contd.*
Journal de la Société de Statistique de Paris—
June, 1892—
Le rôle de la statistique dans le présent et dans l'avenir :
  A. *De Foville.*
Le crédit des compagnies des chemins de fer français, leurs
  placements et amortissements : A. *Neymarck.*
July—
La vapeur en France depuis 50 années : D. *Bellet.*
Les routes départementales : T. *Loua.*
August—
Le Congo français. Eléments de statistique et d'apprecia-
  tion du pays : M. *Cerisier.*
La Fiscalité sur le combustible à Paris : M. *Bienaymé.*

GERMANY—
Vierteljahrshefte zur Statistik des Deutschen Reichs, 1892. *Heft 3—*
Dampfkessel-Explosionen während 1891.
Anmusterungen von Vollmatrosen und unbefahrenen Schiffs-
  jungen im Jahre 1891.
Religionsverhältnisse nach der Volkszählung von 1890.
Ernte- Statistik für das Erntejahr 1891-92.
Kriminalstatistische Vergleiche in Bezug auf Geschlecht und
  Alter.
Jahrbücher für Nationalökonomie und Statistik, 1892—
Band iii, Heft 6—
Kritik der Marx'schen Werttheorie : P. *Fireman.*
Die Amsterdamer Aktienspekulation im 17 Jahrhundert :
  R. *Ehrenberg.*
Die italienische Valutaregulierung : L. *Sachs.*
Studien zur preussischen Einkommensteuer. Das Einkom-
  men aus Arbeit : J. *Jastrow.*
Die neuere Veterinärgesetzgebung und ihre volkswirtschaft-
  liche Wirkung : *Pütz.*
Die zweite Lesung des Entwurfes eines Bürgerlichen Gesetz-
  buches für das Deutsche Reich : *Jecklin.*
Finanzverhältnisse europäischer Grossstädte : K. T. *Eheberg.*
Band iv, Heft 1—
Der Check- und Clearingverkehr des k.k. österreichischen
  Postsparkassenamtes : E. *Tobisch.*
Die Valutaregulierung in Oesterreich-Ungarn : C. *Men-
  ger.*
Studien zur Preussischen Einkommensteuer : Steuertarif ;
  Fundiertes Einkommen ; Steuererklärung, Steuerhinter-
  ziehung ; Rechtsweg ; Doppelbesteuerung und Reichs-
  kontrolle : *Jastrow.*
Ein Beitrag zur Lohnstatistik (Nordböhmische Arbeiter-
  statistik) : W. *Sombart.*
Band iv, Heft 2—
Die Vermögenssteuer und ihre Einfügung in das preus-
  sische Steuersystem : Dr. J. *Jastrow.*
Zur Lehre von den Lohngesetzen : F. J. *Neumann.*

GERMANY—*Contd.*
Jahrbücher für Nationalökonomie und Statistik—Contd.
   Band iv, Heft 2—Contd.
      Der deutsche Innungs- und allgemeine Handwerkertag vom 14—17 Februar, 1892, und seine Bedeutung für die neuere deutsche Handwerkerbewegung : *T. Hampke.*
      Der Staatshaushalt für das Königreich Preussen im Jahre 1892-93 : *M. von Heckel.*
Allgemeines Statistisches Archiv. Jahrgang II, 1892—
   I Halbband—
      Statistik und Selbstverwaltung : *Dr. E. Mischler.*
      Die Jahresschwankungen in der Häufigkeit verschiedener bevölkerungs- und moralstatistischer Erscheinungen : *Dr. K. Becker.*
      Die Statistik der Zwangsversteigerungen landwirtschaftlicher Anwesen : *Dr. A. Cohen.*
      Die elektrische Zählmaschine und ihre Anwendung insbesondere bei der österreichischen Volkszählung : *Dr. H. Rauchberg.*
      Ueber Sammlung und Verwertung des durch die Arbeiterversicherung gebotenen sozialstatistischen Materials : *Dr. G. v. Mayr.*
      Russlands Bedeutung für den Weltgetreidemarkt : *Dr. O. Mertens.*
      Die Statistik der deutschen Arbeiterversicherung : *Dr. E. van der Borght.*
      Weiteres über die Ergebnisse neuester Volkszählungen : *Dr. G. von Mayr.*
      Die Einrichtung der Bevölkerungsaufnahme, 1890, in den grösseren deutschen Staaten : *G. von Mayr.*
Archiv für Soziale Gesetzgebung und Statistik. Band v, Heft 2—
   Die Reform der deutschen Arbeiterschutzgesetzgebung : *Dr. H. Herkner.*
   Die Sittlichkeitsverbrechen in Deutschland in kriminalstatistischer Beleuchtung : *Dr. H. Lux.*
   Wortlaut des Krankenversicherungsgesetzes vom 15 Juni, 1883, in der Fassung der Novelle vom 10 April. 1892.
   Die Fabrikinspektion in Russisch-Polen : *Dr. S. Daszynska.*

ITALY—
   Giornale degli Economisti—
      June, 1892—
         La situazione del mercato monetario : *X.*
         Considerazioni sui principii fondamentali dell' economia politica pura : *V. Pareto.*
         Il sistema sociologico ed economico di Giovanni Pinna-Ferra : *A. Bertolini.*
         Un extraprofitto consequente all' introduzione di macchine e la sua elisione : *F. Coletti.*
      July—
         La dichiarazione del corso forzoso per sentenza di Tribunale :
         Il problema della popolazione e il socialismo : *F. Virgili.*

ITALY—*Contd.*
Giornale degli Economisti—Contd.
July—Contd.
Sull' organizzazione pubblica del giuoco in Italia nel medio
evo : *L. Zdekauer.*
August—
Gli uffici tecnici di finanza : *L. Perozzo.*
Nota sulla tecnica della statistica criminale : *C. F. Ferraris.*

UNITED STATES—
Annals of the American Academy of Political and Social Science.
Vol. iii, No. 1. *July,* 1892—
School Savings Banks : *S. L. Oberholtzer.*
Geometrical Theory of the determination of Prices :
L. Walras.
American Economic Association Publications, 1892—
Vol. vi, No. 6. State Railroad Commissions, and how they
may be made effective : *F. C. Clark.*
Vol. vii, No. 1. The Silver Situation in the United States :
F. W. Taussig.
Nos. 2 *and* 3. On the Shifting and Incidence of Taxation :
E. R. A. Seligman.
Political Science Quarterly. Vol. vii, No. 2, *June,* 1892—
Tithes in England and Wales : *R. Brown, junr.*
Loria's Landed System of Social Economy : *Prof. U. Rabbeno.*
Local Self-Government in Japan : *E. W. Clement.*
The Exercise of the Suffrage : *Prof. A. B. Hart.*
Quarterly Journal of Economics. Vol. vi, No. 4, *July,* 1892—
Dr. Boehm-Bawerk's Theory of Interest : *F. A. Walker.*
Old Age Pensions in England ; *J. G. Brooks.*
Cantillon's Place in Economics : *H. Higgs.*
Taxation in Japan : *G. Droppers.*

UNITED KINGDOM—
Economic Journal. Vol. ii, No. 6, *June,* 1892—
On International Statistical Comparisons : *R. Giffen.*
On the Origin of Money : *Prof. Menger.*
An Attempt to Estimate the Circulation of the Rupee :
F. C. Harrison.
A " Fixed Value of Bullion " Standard : *A. Williams.*
Thrift in Great Britain : *R. Hamilton.*
A Weakness in the German "Imperial Socialism :" *J. G.
Brooks.*

VII.—*Additions to the Library.*

Additions to the Library during the Quarter ended 15th September, 1892, arranged alphabetically under the following heads :—(a) *Foreign Countries ;* (b) *India and Colonial Possessions ;* (c) *United Kingdom and its Divisions ;* (d) *Authors, &c. ;* (e) *Societies, &c.* (*British*); (f) *Periodicals, &c.* (*British*).

Donations.	By whom Presented.
(a) Foreign Countries.	
Argentine Republic—	
Higiene Publica. Anales de. (Current monthly numbers)	Dr. E. R. Coni
BUENOS AYRES (Province). Mensage del Gobernador de la Provincia leido en la Asamblea Legislativa 1 Mayo, 1892. 8vo.	The Provincial Statistical Bureau
BUENOS AYRES (City). Bulletin mensuel de Statistique municipale. (Current numbers)	The Municipal Statistical Bureau
Instituto Geográfico Argentino. Boletin del, Tomo xii, cuadernos 11 and 12. 1892	The Institute
Sociedad médica argentina. Revista de la, Vol. i, No. 4. 8vo. 1892	The Society
Austria and Hungary—	
Ackerbau-Ministeriums. Statistisches Jahrbuch des k.k., für 1885-90. 13 parts, diagrams, 8vo.	The Ministry of Agriculture
Handel des Zollgebiets. Statistische Uebersichten betreffend den auswärtigen. (Current monthly numbers, and for the first half year of 1892)	The Statistical Department, Ministry of Commerce
Bevolkerung. Bewegung der, im Jahre 1890 Finanzen der Autonomen Verwaltung, 1883-87 Oesterreichisches Statistisches Handbuch. Jahrgang 1891. 8vo. Sanitätswesens. Statistik des, für 1889 Strafanstalten. Statistische Übersicht der verhältnisse der österreichischen, und der Gerichts-Gefängnisse im Jahre 1888 Viehzählung vom 31 Dec., 1890. Ergebnisse der, Heft 1 Statistische Monatschrift. (Current numbers)	The Central Statistical Commission
Vollständiges Ortschaften-Verzeichniss ... nach den Volkszählung, 1890. La. 8vo.	The Registrar-General of England
Prague—	
Bulletin hebdomadaire de la Ville de Prague et des communes-faubourgs. (Current numbers) Die k. Hauptstadt Prag ... nach den Ergebnissen der Volkszählung, 1890. 8vo. Statistischer Bericht über die wichtigsten demographischen Verhältnisse. 8vo. 1887 Statistisches Handbuch der k. Hauptstadt Prag, für 1889. Neue Folge, siebenter Jahrgang. 8vo. Verwaltungsbericht der k. Hauptstadt Prag ... für die Jahre 1887-89. 8vo.	The Statistical Bureau
Belgium—	
Annales des Travaux Publics de Belgique. Tome xlix, cahier 4. Tome l, cahier 1. 8vo. 1892	The Administration of Mines

Donations—Contd.

Donations.	By whom Presented.

(a) **Foreign Countries**—*Contd.*

Belgium—*Contd.*

Annuaire Statistique de la Belgique. 22ᵉ année, 1891
Mouvement Commercial avec les Pays Etrangers.
(Current monthly numbers) ....} **The Bureau of General Statistics**

Brussels. Bulletin hebdomadaire de statistique Demographique et Médicale. (Current numbers) ....} **Dr. E. Janssens**

Chile. Report on the Trade between Chile and Great Britain ... by Agustin Ross ... 8vo. 1892 ....} **The Author**

China—

Customs Gazette. Jan.—March, 1892 ....
Trade, Returns of, and Trade Reports for 1891. Part 2. Reports and Statistics for each Port and for Corea ....} **Sir Robert Hart, G.C.M.G.**

Denmark—

Causes de décès dans les villes de Danemark, 1890. 4to. ....
Comptes Communaux, 1885-89. 4to. ....
Marine Marchande et la Navigation du Royaume en 1891. 4to. ....
Communications de Statistique, 3ᵉ *série.* 8vo.—
   Tome 11. Taille des Conscrits, 1879-88. Récolte en 1890 et 1891. Prix des Céréales en 1890 et 1891
   Tome 12. Recensement de 1890. Population de l'Islande, du Groënland, et des Antilles danoises, 1890 ....} **The Statistical Bureau**

Nationalökonomisk Tidskrift, 1892. (Current numbers) { **The Danish Political Economy Society**

Egypt—

Commerce Extérieur. Bulletin mensuel du. (Current numbers) ....} **A. Caillard, Esq., C.M.G.**
Dette Publique d'Egypte. Compte rendu des Travaux de la Commission pendant 1891. 8vo........................} **Alonzo Money, Esq., C.B.**
Services Sanitaires, &c. Bulletin hebdomadaire. (Current numbers) .. ..} **The Department**

Comité de Conservation des monuments de l'art arabe. Exercice 1891. Fasc. 7. Procès-Verbaux et Rapports. 8vo. ....} **The Committee**
Institut Egyptien. Bulletin. 3ᵉ série, Nos. 2 et 3. Année 1891-92. Plate, 8vo. ....} **The Institute**

France—

Agriculture. Bulletin du Ministère de l'. No. 4. July, 1892 ....} **The Ministry of Agriculture**
Annales du Commerce Extérieur. Années 1887-90. 8vo. **T. J. Pittar, Esq.**
Chemins de Fer. Statistique des, 1888. Documents divers. 1ᵉ Partie, France—Intérêt général. 2ᵉ Partie, France—Intérêt local. Algérie et Tunisie. 2 vols. 4to. ....
Chemins de Fer. Statistique des, au 31 Dec., 1890. Documents principaux. Maps, 4to......................} **The Ministry of Public Works**

Donations.	By whom Presented.

(a) Foreign Countries—*Contd.*

France—*Contd.*

Finances, Ministère des, Bulletin de Statistique et de Législation comparée. (Current monthly numbers) — The Ministry of Finance

Navigation intérieure. Statistique de la—
Relevé général du Tonnage des marchandises. Année 1891. Vols. i et ii. Maps. 4to.
Dépenses de premier établissement et d'entretien concernant les fleuves, rivières et canaux. Documents historiques et statistiques. 4to. 1892 ....
Recensement de la Batellerie, année 1891. 4to. ... — The Ministry of Public Works

Statistique générale de la France. Statistique annuelle. Année 1890. Tome xx. 8vo. ..... — The Ministry of Commerce

Travaux Publics. Ministère des, Bulletin de Statistique et Législation comparée. (Current monthly numbers) — The Ministry of Public Works

SEINE. Aliénés. Rapport sur le service des, du département pendant 1887. 4to. ..... — The Registrar-General of England

L'Economiste Français. (Current weekly numbers)........ — The Editor
Journal des Economistes. (Current monthly numbers).... — „
Le Monde Economique. (Current weekly numbers)........ — „

Polybiblion. Revue Bibliographique Universelle—
Partie Littéraire. (Current monthly numbers)........
   „   Technique. (Current monthly numbers) .... — „

Le Rentier. Journal Financier Politique. (Current numbers) ....
Revue d'Economie Politique. (Current monthly numbers) ....
Revue Géographique Internationale. (Current monthly numbers) .... — „

Ecole Libre des Sciences Politiques, Annales. No. 3. July, 1892 ..... — The Institution

Société de Statistique de Paris, Journal. (Current monthly numbers) ..... — The Society

PARIS. British Chamber of Commerce, Report for 1891. 8vo. 1892 ..... — C. M. Kennedy, Esq., C.B.

Germany—

Handel, Monatliche Nachweise über den Auswärtigen, des deutschen Zollgebiets. (Current monthly returns)
Handel, Auswärtiger, des deutschen Zollgebiets im Jahre 1891. 1 Theil. Darstellung nach Waarengattungen. Heft 1. 4to.
Krankenversicherung der Arbeiter, Statistik der, im Jahre 1890 ......
Seeschiffart, Statistik der, für 1891. Abth. 1. Schiffsunfälle, &c. 4to. ......
Statistisches Jahrbuch für das Deutsche Reich. Dreizehnter Jahrgang, 1892.
Vierteljahrshefte zur Statistik des Deutschen Reichs, 1892. Heft 3. 4to. ..... — The Imperial Statistical Bureau

PRUSSIA. Landesuniversitäten, Statistik der preussischen, für 1887-88, 1888-89, und 1889-90. Fol..... — The Royal Prussian Statistical Bureau

SAXONY. Zeitschrift des K. Sächsischen Statistischen Bureaus, 1891. Heft 1 und 2. Die sächsische Einkommensteurstatistik von 1875-90. Heft 3 und 4. Die sächsische Volkszählung, 1890............. — The Statistical Bureau of Saxony

Donations—Contd.

Donations.	By whom Presented.
(a) Foreign Countries—*Contd.*	
Germany—*Contd.*	
BERLIN. Eheschliessungen, Geburten, Sterbefälle, und Witterung. (Current weekly and monthly numbers)	The Statistical Bureau of Berlin
FRANKFORT. Civilstand. Tabellarische Uebersichten betreffend den, der Stadt im Jahre 1891. 8vo........	—
HAMBURG. Hamburg's Handel und Schiffahrt, 1891. 4to.	The Bureau of Trade Statistics
Archiv für Soziale Gesetzgebung und Statistik. Band v, Heft 2. 1892	The Publisher
Jahrbücher für Nationalökonomie und Statistik. Band iii, Heft 6. Band iv, Hefte 1 und 2. 8vo. 1892	,,
Greece—	
Commerce de la Grèce avec les Pays étrangers pendant 1889 et 1890. 2 vols., fol............	T. J. Pittar, Esq.
Loi sur le Tarif. Tarif des Douanes et décret royal sur la Tare. 4to. 1890.	
ATHENS. Bulletin de mortalité pour la ville d'Athènes. Mars, 1892	The Statistical Bureau
Guatemala—	
Informe por el Director-General de Estadistica correspondiente al año de 1891. 8vo.	..
Italy—	
Annali di Agricoltura, 1892. Le R. Scuole pratiche e speciali di Agricoltura nel triennio 1887-88—1889-90	The Director-General of Agriculture
Annali di Statistica. Statistica Industriale. Fasc. 37. L'Industria della Seta in Italia. 40. Provincia di Genova. 41. Provincia di Ascoli Piceno. 42. Provincia di Macerata. Maps, 8vo. 1892	
Bollettino di Legislazione e Statistica Doganale e Commerciale. (Current numbers)	
Bollettino del Ministero degli Affari Esteri. (Current numbers)	The Director-General, Statistical Department of the State
Bollettino mensile delle situazioni dei Conti degli Istituti d' Emissione. (Current numbers)	
Bollettino di Notizie sul Credito e la Previdenza. (Current numbers)	
Bollettino settimanale dei Prezzi di alcuni dei principali Prodotti Agraria e del Pane. (Current weekly numbers)	
Bollettino Sanitario, Direzione della Sanita Pubblica. (Current numbers)	
Censimento Decennale della Popolazione del Regno. Proposte per il IV°, Raccolta di modelli ed istruzioni per gli ultimi censimenti eseguiti in alcuni stati d' Europa e d' America. 8vo. 1891............	The Registrar-General of England
Movimento Commerciale del Regno d' Italia nell' anno 1891. 2 vols., fol............	The Director-General, Statistical Department of the State
Navigazione nei Porti del Regno. Movimento della, nell' anno 1891. Fol.	
Opere Pie. Atti della commissione reale per l'inchiesta sulle. Vol. ix. 8vo. 1892............	

Donations—Contd.

Donations.	By whom Presented.
(a) Foreign Countries—*Contd.*	
Italy—*Contd.*	
Postale e Telegrafico. Relazione Statistica intorno ai servizi, per 1890-91 ed al Servizio delle casse postali di risparmio per 1890. Fol. Roma, 1892. .... Statistica del commercio speciale di Importazione e di Esportazione. (Current monthly numbers) .... Tasse e diritti comunali, 1887-89. Statistica delle. 8vo.	The Director-General, Statistical Department of the State
L'Economista. (Current weekly numbers) .... Giornale degli Economisti. (Current monthly numbers)	The Editor ˮ
Japan—	
Résumé Statistique de l'Empire du Japon. 6ᵉ année. 4to. 1892 .... Tokio-Fu. Sanitary Annual Report on Tokio-Fu, 1891. Map, 4to.................	The Statistical Bureau The Prefect of Tokio-Fu
Mexico—	
Exportaciones, año fiscal 1891-92. Primer semestre. Fol. .... Movimiento maritimo exterior e interior. Noticias del, en el año fiscal 1889-90. Fol.	The Statistical Bureau
Netherlands—	
Geboorten. Statistik der, en der sterfte naar den leeftijd en de oorzaken van den dood in Nederland, Jan.—June, 1892. Sheets .... Statistiek der Scheepvaart, 1890. Derde Gedeelte	The Netherlands Legation
Annuaire Statistique des Pays-Bas pour 1890. 2ᵉ livraison. Statistique des Colonies .... Bijdragen van het Statistisch Instituut. No. 1, 1892. Diagrams. 8vo.	The Statistical Institute
Roumania—	
Buletin Statistic general al Romaniei. Anul I. April—June, 1892. 8vo. .... Mouvement de la Population de Roumanie pendant 1890	The Director of Statistics
Russia—	
Commerce extérieur par la frontière d'Europe et recettes douanières de l'Empire, 1891	The Department of Customs
Diagram-maps showing prices of Rye and Oats on 1st May and 1st June, 1892, in Russia in Europe. Sheets	The Department of Assessed Taxes
Finland. Société de Géographie de Finlande. Fennia 5. Bulletin de la. Maps, &c. 8vo. 1892	The Society
Servia—	
Recensement de la Population le 31 Décembre, 1890. Tome I, 1—3 Parties. 4to. .... Viticulture. Statistique de la, pour 1889. La. 8vo. Maps	The Statistical Bureau

Donations—Contd.

Donations.	By whom Presented.

(a) Foreign Countries—*Contd.*

Spain—

Comercio Exterior. Resumenes mensuales de la Estadistica del. (Current numbers) .... } The Director-General of Indirect Taxation

Tablas de valores para la Estadistica comercial y el Arancel de Aduanas para 1890 y 1891. 12mo. .... } The Board of Customs

Sociedad Geográfica de Madrid. Boletin. (Current numbers) .... } The Society

Sweden and Norway—

NORWAY. *Norges Officielle Statistik—*
   147. Chemins de Fer publics, 1890-91 ....
   148. Justice civile, 1889.............................
   149. Navigation pendant 1890 ....
   150. Recrutement pour 1891............................
   151. Successions, faillites, &c., 1889..................
   152. Finances des communes pendant 1889 ....
   153. Service vétérinaire en 1890 ....

} The Central Statistical Bureau, Christiania

Switzerland—

Annuaire Statistique de la Suisse. 2ᵉ année, 1892. Map, 8vo. ....
Bulletin hebdomadaire et Bulletin mensuel des mariages, naissances et des décès dans les Villes de la Suisse. (Current numbers.) 8vo. ....
Recensement fédéral du 1ᵉʳ Dec., 1888. Vol. i. Nombre des maisons, ménages et population selon l'origine, le lieu de naissance, la confession et la langue maternelle. Diagram-maps, 4to. ....
Recrues. Résultats de la visite sanitaire des Recrues en Automne, 1890. 4to...........

} The Federal Statistical Bureau

Commerce. Statistique du, de la Suisse avec l'Etranger en 1891. Diagrams, fol. ....
Rapport annuel et Tableau des valeurs moyennes, 1891. 8vo. ....

} The Federal Department of Customs

Régie des Alcools. Rapport concernant la gestion et le compte de la, pour 1891. 8vo. ....

} M. G. E. Milliet, Bern

Schweiz. Handels- und Industrie-Verein. Bericht über Handel und Industrie der Schweiz im Jahre 1891. 4to. ....

} The Association

United States—

Agriculture—
Monthly reports on Crops, &c. (Current numbers)
Report of the Secretary of, 1891. Maps and plates ....
Reports of the Bureau of Statistics of the Department of, (Nos. 81—91), 1891. Maps, &c., 8vo. ....
Special Report of the Statistician, July, 1892. Foreign Crops and Freight Rates ....
Milk Fermentations and their relations to Dairying. 8vo. 1892 ....

} The Secretary of Agriculture

Bureau of American Republics. Bulletin No. 35. March, 1892. Breadstuffs in Latin America. 8vo. } The Bureau

Donations—Contd.

Donations.	By whom Presented.
(a) Foreign Countries—*Contd.*	
United States—*Contd.*	
Census Bulletins. 1890. 173. Fisheries of the Great Lakes. 174, 195. Statistics of Churches. 177. Flax and Hemp. 182. Homicide in 1890. 186, 188. Cereal Production in 1889. 187, 197. Population by color, sex, and general nativity, 1890. 190, 191. Cotton Production. 192. Assessed Valuation of Property, 1890. 193. Artesian wells for irrigation. 196. Manufactures. Operating Telephone Companies. 198. Irrigation in Washington. 198. Colored Population in 1890. 200. Production of Coke. 201. Elements of Population, proportions of the sexes in 1870-80-90. 202. School, militia, and voting ages, 1890 .... Extra Census Bulletin. 22. Statistics of Farms, houses, and mortgages. Mortgages in Missouri	The Superintendent of Census
Consuls. Reports from, No. 139, April, Local Transportation and underground conduits. 140, May. 141, June, 1892. Illustrations, 8vo.	The Bureau of Statistics, Department of State
Education Bureau. Circulars of Information, 1891. 2. Fourth international Prison Congress, St. Petersburg. 4. History of higher education in Michigan. 8. Rise and growth of the Normal-School idea in the U.S. 9. Biological teaching in Colleges of United States	The Bureau of Education
Imports and Exports. Summary Statement of. (Current monthly numbers) .... Imports, Exports, Immigration, and Navigation. Quarterly Reports for the quarters ending 31st Dec., 1891, and 31st March, 1892. [Nos. 2 and 3, 1891-92]	The Bureau of Statistics, Treasury Department
Naval Observatory. Report of the Superintendent for the year ending 30th June, 1891. 8vo.	The Superintendent
Precious Metals in the United States. Report of the Director of the Mint upon production of, during 1891. 8vo.	The Director of the Mint
Prices and Wages. Report on retail, 1892	R. P. Falkner, Esq.
Public Debt and Cash in Treasury of the United States. Monthly statements of. (Current numbers)	The Secretary of the Treasury
Connecticut. State Board of Health— Monthly Bulletins. (Current numbers) .... 14th Annual Report for 1890-91, with registration report for 1890. Diagrams and plans, 8vo.	The Board of Health
HARTFORD. Report of the special committee on Outdoor alms of the town of Hartford, A.D. 1891....	John J. McCook, Esq.
Banker's Magazine. (Current monthly numbers)	The Editor
Bradstreet's Journal. (Current weekly numbers)	,,
Commercial and Financial Chronicle. (Current weekly numbers)	,,
Investor's Supplement to Commercial and Financial Chronicle. (Current numbers)	,,
Political Science Quarterly. Vol. vii, No. 2, June, 1892	The Editors
Quarterly Journal of Economics. July, 1892	The Publisher
The Yale Review. Vol. i, No. 2, August, 1892	The Publishers

Donations—Contd.

Donations.	By whom Presented.

(a) Foreign Countries—*Contd.*
United States—*Contd.*

Actuarial Society of America. Papers and Transactions. No. 7. 1892. (Selection from Contents.) Monetary Mortality-Experience on Annuities in American Life Insurance Companies. Ratios of mortality for number and amount .... — The Society

American Academy of Political and Social Science. Annals. Vol. iii, No. 1, July, 1892 .... — The Academy

American Economic Association. Publications. Vol. vii, Nos. 2 and 3. 8vo. 1892 .... — The Association

American Geographical Society. Bulletin. Vol. xxiv, No. 2, June, 1892. Maps. 8vo. .... — The Society

American Philosophical Society—
    Proceedings. Vol. xxx, No. 138. Plates, 8vo. 1892 ....
    Transactions. New Series, vol. xvii, parts 1 and 2. Plates, 4to. 1892 .... — ,,

Franklin Institute. Journal. (Current monthly numbers) .... — The Institute

International—

Bulletin International des Douanes. (Current numbers.) 8vo. .... — The Board of Trade

Congrès Pénitentiaire Internationale de Saint-Pétersbourg, 1890. Actes du Congrès. Vol. i. Procèsverbaux des Séances. Vol. ii. Rapports sur les questions du Programme de la Section de Droit Pénal. Vol. iii. Rapports sur les questions du Programme de la Section Pénitentiaire. 3 vols. 8vo. 1890-92 .... — Dr. F. J. Mouat, F.R.C.S.

Statistique Internationale. Navigation Maritime. IV. Mouvement de la Navigation; ouvrage rédigé par A. N. Kiær. 4to. 1892 .... — The Compiler

(b) India and Colonial Possessions.
India, British—

Prices and Wages in India. Ninth issue. Fol. 1892 .... — James E. O'Conor, Esq., C.I.E.

Trade by Land with Foreign Countries. Monthly Accounts. (Current numbers) ....
Trade and Navigation. Monthly Accounts. (Current numbers) .... — The Department of Finance and Commerce, Calcutta

Indian Engineering. (Current numbers) .... — The Editor

Asiatic Society of Bengal—
    Journal. Vol. lx; Part I, Nos. 2 and 3; Part II, Nos. 2—4, 1891. Vol. lxi; Part I, No. 1; Part II, No. 1, 1892. Plates ....
    Proceedings. July, 1891—March, 1892 .... — The Society

Bermuda. Births, Marriages and Deaths. Annual Reports of the Registrar-General of, for 1889 and 1890. 2 vols. Fol. .... — The Registrar-General of England

Donations—Contd.

Donations.	By whom Presented.
(b) India and Colonial Possessions—*Contd.*	
Canada, Dominion of—	
Banks acting under Charter, Monthly Statements. (Current numbers)	N. S. Garland, Esq.
Census of 1891. Bulletins, Nos. 10 and 12. Manufactures. 11. Nationalities	Geo. Johnson, Esq.
Sessional Papers, 1891-92. Adulteration of Food. Report for 1890-91. Canal Statistics, 1891. Civil Service Examiners' Report for 1891. Criminal Statistics, 1891. Experimental Farms, Reports on, for 1891. Fisheries, Statements and Inspectors' Reports for 1891. Fisheries, Report of Department of, for 1891. Immigration, Quarantine and Public Health, Reports on, for 1891. Indian Affairs, Report on, for 1891. Interior, Report of Department of, for 1891. Journals of the Senate, vol. xxv, Appendices 1 and 2, Session 1891. Journals of the House of Commons, Session 1891, Appendices, vol. ii. North-west Mounted Police Force, Report for 1891. Public Printing and Stationery, Report on, for 1890-91. Railway Statistics for 1891. Weights, Measures, and Gas, Report on inspection of, 1890-91...............................	J. G. Bourinot, Esq., C.M.G.
MANITOBA. Reports on Crops and Live Stock, (Current numbers)	The Agricultural Department
Insurance and Finance Chronicle. (Current numbers)....	The Editor
Canadian Institute. An appeal to the Canadian Institute on the rectification of Parliament, by Sandford Fleming, C.M.G., &c. (A collection of Papers and Extracts on methods of Election, &c.) 8vo. 1892	The Institute
Cape of Good Hope—	
Census. Results of the Census of the Colony, 5th April, 1891. Diagrams, fol. .... Another copy, bound	The Colonial Secretary
Education. Report of the Superintendent-General of, for 1891. Fol.	The Superintendent
Statistical Register of the Colony for 1891. Diagram, fol.	The Colonial Secretary
Jamaica. Census of Jamaica and its Dependencies, taken on the 6th April, 1891. Fol.	The Registrar-General
Mauritius—	
Births, Deaths, and Marriages. Annual Report of the Registrar-General of, for 1889. Fol.	The Registrar-General of England
Blue Book for the Colony of Mauritius, 1891. Fol.....	His Excellency The Governor
Natal. Durban Chamber of Commerce. Annual Report for 1891. 8vo.	The Chamber of Commerce
New South Wales—	
Agricultural Gazette. (Current numbers)...................	The Director of Agriculture

Donations—Contd.

Donations.	By whom Presented.

(b) **India and Colonial Possessions**—*Contd.*
New South Wales—*Contd.*

Blue Book for 1891 .... { The Agent-General for N. S. Wales

Statistical Account of the seven Colonies, by T. A. Coghlan. Map and diagrams, 8vo. 1892 .... Statistical Register for 1891 and previous years. Part 4. Law and Crime. Part 5. Population and Vital Statistics. Part 7. Agriculture and Minerals. } T. A. Coghlan, Esq., Government Statistician

New Zealand—

Colonial Museum and Laboratory. Twenty-sixth Annual Report, with List of Donations and Deposits during 1890-91. 8vo... ... Geological Explorations. Reports of, during 1890-91. Diagrams, 8vo. .... } The Colonial Museum

Queensland. Supplements to the Government Gazette (containing Vital Statistics). (Current numbers)........ } The Registrar-General of Queensland

South Australia. Census of 1891. Part 3. Conjugal Condition of the People. Fol. .... } The Superintendent of Census

Straits Settlements. The Perak Government Gazette. (Current numbers) .... } The Government Secretary

Tasmania. Census. Results of the Census of the Colony, 5th April, 1891. Parts 5. Education ; 6. Sickness and Infirmity ; 7. Religions of the People. Fol. } The Government Statistician

Victoria—

Census of 1891. Parts 2. Birthplaces of the People. 3. Religions. 4. Ages. Fol. .... } H. H. Hayter, Esq., C.M.G.

Mines. Annual Report of the Secretary of, for 1891. Plates and plans, fol. ... . } The Department of Mines

Statistical Register of the Colony for 1890, and Parts 1, Blue Book ; 2. Population ; 3. Finance, for 1891. Fol. .... Victorian Year-Book for 1890-91. (18th year.) Vol. ii. 8vo. .... } H. H. Hayter, Esq., C.M.G., Government Statist

The Bankers' Magazine and Journal of the Bankers' Institute of Australasia. Vol. v. Nos. 10, May, and 12, July, 1892. Plates, 8vo. .... } G. D. Meudell, Esq.

(c) **United Kingdom and its several Divisions.**
United Kingdom—

Army Medical Department. Report for 1890, with Appendix. Vol. xxxii. 8vo. .... } The Army Medical Department

Board of Trade Journal. (Current monthly numbers.).... The Board of Trade

Customs. 36th Report of the Commissioners of Customs for the Year ended 31st March, 1892. [C-6809.] 8vo. .... } The Commissioners of Customs

Emigration and Immigration from and into the United Kingdom in 1891. (134.) 1892............................... } The Board of Trade

Donations—Contd.

Donations.	By whom Presented.
(c) United Kingdom and its Divisions—*Contd.*	
United Kingdom—*Contd.*	
Railway Returns for the United Kingdom for 1891. [C–6713]	
Statistical Abstract for the principal and other Foreign Countries for 1880 to 1889-90. 18th number. [C-6661.] 8vo.	
Statistical Abstract for the United Kingdom for 1877 to 1891. 39th number. [C-6718.] 8vo.	The Board of Trade
Trade of the United Kingdom with Foreign Countries and British Possessions. Annual Statement for 1891. [C–6676]	
Trade and Navigation. (Current monthly returns)....	
Wages. Return of Rates of, paid by Local Authorities and Private Companies to Police and to Workpeople employed on Roads, &c., and at Gas and Water Works, with Report thereon. [C–6715.] 1892	
Eight Foreign Office Reports on Trade and condition of Labour, &c., in various countries. 1892. 8vo.....	C. M. Kennedy, Esq., C.B.
England—	
Births and Deaths in London, and in twenty-seven other Great Towns. (Current weekly returns)	The Registrar-General of England
Quarterly Return of Marriages to March, Births and Deaths to June, 1892. No. 174. 8vo.	
WEST SUSSEX. 18th Annual Report on the condition of the combined Sanitary District of West Sussex for 1891. 8vo.	Dr. Charles Kelly
London—	
Criminal Returns, Metropolitan Police. 1891. 8vo.	The Commissioner of Police
Metropolitan Asylums Board. Reports for 1891 of the Statistical Committee and the Medical Superintendents of Infectious Hospitals and Imbecile Asylums, &c. Maps and diagrams. 8vo.	The Statistical Committee
Birmingham—	
Abstract of Treasurer's Accounts for the Year ended 31st March, 1892......................................	
"Blue Book." General and Detailed Financial Statement for the year ended 31st March, 1892....	The City Treasurer
Epitome of the Blue Book for the year ended 31st March, 1892. 3 parts, la. 8vo. 1892	
Ireland—	
Census of Ireland, 1891. Part 1. Area, Houses, and Population; also ages, civil or conjugal condition, occupations, birthplaces, religion, and education of the People. Vols. i, Leinster; ii, Munster; iii, Ulster; iv, Connaught. Part 2. General Report, with illustrative maps and diagrams, tables, and Appendix. Fol.	The Registrar-General of Ireland
Births and Deaths in Dublin, and in fifteen of the principal Urban Sanitary Districts. (Current weekly returns)	
Quarterly Return of Marriages to Dec., 1891, and March, 1892, Births and Deaths to March, 1892, and June, 1892. Nos. 113 and 114. 8vo.................	

Donations—Contd.

Donations.	By whom Presented.

(c) United Kingdom and its Divisions—*Contd.*
Scotland—
Births, Deaths, and Marriages in the eight principal Towns. (Current weekly and monthly returns) .... Births, Deaths, and Marriages, Quarterly Return of, for the quarter ending 30th June, 1892. No. 150....} The Registrar-General of Scotland

(d) Authors, &c.

COBB (ARTHUR S.). Metallic Reserves and the Meeting of Parliament. 28 pp., 8vo. 1892 ....} The Author

COSSA (LUIGI). Introduzione allo studio dell' Economia Politica. 3rd edizione. xii + 594 pp., 8vo. Milano, 1892 ....} The Publisher, M. U. Hoepli

Dictionary of Political Economy. Edited by R. H. Inglis Palgrave, F.R.S. Part 3. Chamberlen-Conciliation, Boards of. 8vo. 1892 ....} The Editor

FALKNER (R. P.). Statistics of Prisoners, 1890. 56 pp., 8vo. 1892 ....} The Author

FERRARIS (CARLO F.). Principii di Scienza Bancaria. xi + 445 pp., 8vo. Milano. 1892 ....} The Publisher, M. U. Hoepli

GEISSLER (ARTH). Ueber die Vorteile der Berechnung nach. "Perzentilen Graden." 14 pp., 8vo. Tübingen, 1892 ....} The Author

JEANS (J.S.). On the laws regulating the liability of employers for accidents to workmen in different countries in their bearing on English law and usage. 46 pp., 8vo. 1892 ....} ,,

Juraschek (Dr. Fr. von)—
Otto Hübner's Geographisch - statistische Tabellen aller Länder der Erde. 41 Ausgabe für 1892. Herausgegeben von, vii + 91 pp., obl. 12mo. Frankfurt, 1892 ....
Übersichten der Weltwirthschaft. Jahrgang 1885-89. Lieferung 7. 12mo. 1892 ....}

LEVASSEUR (E.). Note sur la méthode d'enseignement de la géographie. 32 pp., 8vo. [1892] ....} ,,

MAYR (Dr. GEORG v.). Die Statistik auf drei Internationalen Congressen des Jahres 1891. 50 pp., la. 8vo. Wien, 1892 ....} ,,

NICHOLSON (J. S.). The Effects of Machinery on Wages. New and revised edition. x + 143 pp., 8vo. 1892 ....} ,,

OWEN (HUGH, JUN.). The Elementary Education Acts, 1870-73-74, and 1876, with introduction, notes and index, with an Appendix. 14th edition. xv + 600 pp., 8vo. 1879 ....} Dr. F. J. Mouat

(e) Societies, &c. (British).*
Anthropological Institute. Journal. Vol. xxi, No. 4. May, 1892. 8vo. ....} The Institute

* Foreign and Colonial Societies will be found under the various Countries or Possessions to which they belong.

Donations—Contd.

Donations.	By whom Presented.
(e) Societies, &c. (British)—*Contd.*	
British Economic Association. Economic Journal. Vol. ii, No. 6. June, 1892	The Association
Colonial College. Colonia: The Colonial College Magazine. Vol. ii, No. 2. August, 1892. 8vo.	The College
East India Association. Journal. (Current numbers)	The Association
Economic Review. Vol. ii, No. 3. July, 1892	The Publishers
Friendly Society of Ironfounders. (Current monthly reports)	Sir R. W. Rawson
Imperial Institute. Year-Book of the Imperial Institute ... A statistical record of the resources and trade of the Colonial and Indian possessions of the British Empire. First Issue (1892). xiii + 824 pp., map and diagrams, la. 8vo. 1892	The Institute
Institute of Actuaries. Journal. Vol. xxx, Part 2. 1892....	,,
Institute of Bankers. Journal. (Current numbers)	,,
Institute of Chemistry. Register of Fellows and Associates for 1892. 8vo.	,,
Institution of Civil Engineers. Minutes of Proceedings. Vols. cviii—cx, 1891-92. Plates, 8vo.	The Institution
London Chamber of Commerce. Journal. (Current numbers)	The Chamber of Commerce
Royal Agricultural Society, Journal. Third Series. Vol. iii, Part 2. June, 1892	The Society
Royal Asiatic Society, Journal. July, 1892. 8vo.	,,
Royal Colonial Institute. Proceedings. Vol. xxiii, 1891-92. 8vo.	The Institute
Royal Geographical Society. Proceedings. (Current numbers)	The Society
Royal Irish Academy—	
"Cunningham Memoirs." No. 7. Plates, 4to. 1892 Proceedings. Third Series. Vol. ii, No. 2. May, 1892. Plates, 8vo. Transactions. Vol. xxix, Parts 18 and 19. Plates, 4to. 1892	The Royal Irish Academy
Royal United Service Institution. Journal. (Current monthly numbers)	The Institution
Royal Society. Proceedings. (Current numbers)	The Society
Sanitary Institute. Transactions of the, Vol. xii, 1891. Also Report of the Council, &c., March, 1892. Plates, &c., 8vo.	The Institute
Seamen's Hospital Society. General Report of cases under treatment in Hospitals and Dispensaries of the Society during 1891. 8vo.	The Society
Society of Arts. Journal. (Current numbers)	,,
Society for the Propagation of the Gospel in Foreign Parts. Report and Lists for 1891. 8vo.	,,
Statistical and Social Inquiry Society of Ireland. Journal. Vol. ix., part 72. August, 1892	,,
Surveyors' Institution. Transactions. (Current numbers)	The Institution

Donations—Contd.

Donations.		By whom Presented.
(f) Periodicals, &o. (British).*		
Accountant, The	Current numbers	The Editor
Athenæum, The	„	„
Bankers' Magazine, The............................	„	„
British Trade Journal, The	„	„
Building Societies and Land Companies' Gazette, The	„	„
Commercial World, The............................	„	„
Economist, The	„	„
Fireman, The	„	„
Insurance and Banking Review, The	„	„
„ Gazette	„	„
„ Post, The	„	„
„ Record, The	„	„
Investors' Monthly Manual, The	„	„
Iron and Coal Trades' Review, The	„	„
Machinery Market, The............................	„	„
Nature	„	„
Policy-Holder, The	„	„
Review, The..	„	„
Sanitary Record, The	„	„
Shipping World, The	„	„
Statist, The	„	„

* Foreign and Colonial Periodicals will be found under the various Countries
or Colonies in which they are issued.

Purchases.

Authors, &c.—

Cassels (W. R.). Cotton: an account of its Culture in the Bombay
Presidency. xvi ± 347 pp., diagrams and maps, la. 8vo. Bombay, 1862.

Cunningham (W.). The Use and Abuse of Money. xxiv + 219 pp., 8vo. 1891.

Gibbins (H. de B.). The Industrial History of England. 2nd edition.
viii + 240 pp., maps, sm. 8vo. 1892.

Holyoake (George J.). The Co-operative Movement to-day. 198 pp., 8vo.
1891.

Mallet (Sir Louis). Free Exchange. Papers on Political and Economical
Subjects, including chapters on the Law of Value and Unearned Increment. By the late, Edited by Bernard Mallet. xxiv + 356 pp., 8vo.
1891.

Ridgeway (William). The Origin of Metallic Currency and Weight
Standards. xii + 417 pp., illustrations, 8vo. 1892.

Turquan (Victor). Manuel de Statistique Pratique. Statistiques Munici-
pales et Départementales. Statistique générale de la France et de
toutes les branches de l'Administration. Préface de Maurice Block.
xii + 564 pp., la. 8vo. Paris, 1891.

Periodicals, &c.—

Annual Register for 1891.

Palmer's Index to the Times for the first two quarters of 1892.

Publisher's Circular. (Current weekly numbers.)

Vierteljahrschrift für Volkswirtschaft, &c. Band ii, Hälfte 2; Band iii,
Hälfte 1 und 2, 1892.

Parliamentary Papers—

Railway Servants' Hours of Labour. Report on, 1892.

Scotland. Reports of the Registrar-General for 1890 and 1891.

Sea Fisheries of the United Kingdom, 1892.

Vol. LV.]   [Part IV.

JOURNAL

OF THE ROYAL STATISTICAL SOCIETY,

DECEMBER, 1892.

The INAUGURAL ADDRESS *of* CHARLES BOOTH, ESQ., PRESIDENT *of the* ROYAL STATISTICAL SOCIETY. *Session* 1892-93. DELIVERED 15*th November*, 1892.

CONTENTS:

Ladies and Gentlemen,

A PRESIDENT in his address ought, I think, to survey the position, and so far as may be forecast the future of the society or science he represents. As leader for the time being he should recount the triumphs of the past, or from the history of failure draw some salutary warning, and point the way to new conquests; all with the single aim of nerving his fellow workers through confidence and hope to fresh exertions. This is what I should, but alas, am unfit to do, and I must beg your forbearance. I feel very deeply the honour you have done me in choosing me for your President. No one can be more conscious than I am of the importance of statistics in this age of rapid social reconstruction, or of the important part that this Society is well fitted to play in these changes. But it is as a divisional leader that I must address you to-night. Instead of a plan of campaign, all I have to offer is the faithful report of a skirmish. If, next November, I have the honour of addressing you again I hope I may do better.

The losses caused the Society by death in 1891-92 were mentioned in the Annual Report. I wish here especially to refer to that of Sir James Caird, who, by reason of his scientific treatment of economic subjects, stood in the front rank of public servants. We owe to his memory a debt of gratitude, not only for his numerous and valuable contributions to our Proceedings, and the conspicuous ability with which he occupied this Chair, and for his kindness in undertaking the duties of Trustee for our property, but

even more for the example he has set us, and for the proof he
has given the world of the immense value which may attach to
statistical inquiries in connection with the government of the
country.

I have to-night the honour to lay before this Society the results
of an inquiry into the condition of waterside labour in the Port
of London, with some suggestions for its improvement. There is
a good deal in this paper that calls for discussion. In this Society,
by courteous usage, the President's address is not discussed, but I
shall take care to find an early opportunity for hearing the views
and profiting by the criticism of those of my audience who are
interested in the subject.

I.—*London Riverside Labour.*

In 1887, when I was considering dock employment as a principal
East End industry, I found the position to be very hopeless as well
as very unsatisfactory. The employers were content, and the men,
though far from content, were entirely unorganised. The dock
managers accepted the crowd and struggle at the dock gates as an
inevitable phenomenon, which happened to fit in 'well with the
conditions of their trade. They could always be sure of sufficient
labour, and though its quality might be bad, its pay was corres-
pondingly low. The character of the men matched well with the
character of the work and its remuneration. All alike were low
and irregular. The vicious circle was complete. How should it
be broken?

In 1892 all this is changed. The unions, founded under the
greatest difficulties in 1888, have had a wonderful career; and
if some mistakes have been made, and some hopes disappointed,
there yet remains a solid foundation on which much may be
built, and an inspiring record. It may be true that as yet but
little has been done from a purely material point of view to
better the condition of the dock labourer; but what the men have
already achieved through organisation is not to be measured solely
by advantages obtained in pay or the conditions of employment.
By organisation they step into line with other more highly skilled
and more highly paid labour, and so acquire a position of dignity
in the State of the utmost practical value if wisely used. Already
we see the effect of this in the changed attitude of the employers
as to casual employment. It is now generally admitted that more
regular work makes better labourers, and that better labourers are
more satisfactory servants even at higher pay.

Riverside labour consists of the following branches:—

I. Import through the docks.

(1.) Discharging from on board ship in dock.

(2.) Receiving on quay and passing into warehouse.

(3.) Receiving and stowing into lighters.

(4.) Handling in warehouse.

II. Import through the wharves.

(Subject to the same subdivisions as the dock work).

III. Import " over side " from ships lying in the stream.

(The men so employed are termed " shipworkers," and undertake also the loading of coasting vessels).

IV. Export work (both dock and wharf).

Handling goods on quay in preparation for the stevedores.

V. Stowage of cargo (export) by stevedores.

VI. Lighterage of goods.

VII. Handling of coals and ballast (dock, wharf, or stream).

(1.) Discharging coal.

(2.) Loading coal as cargo (by stevedores).

(3.) Coaling steamers.

(4.) Ballast heavers.

VIII. Handling of ships in port.

(1.) Tug boatmen.

(2.) Ship scrapers and painters.

(3.) Riggers and shore gang men.

(4.) Sailors in port.

The labour employed by the dock companies may be considered in two divisions : (1) that of the " joint committee," including the London and St. Katharine, East and West India, Victoria and Albert, and Tilbury Docks, and some warehouses in town : (2) that of the Millwall and Surrey Commercial Docks, which, though on opposite sides of the river, are alike devoted principally to the handling of grain and timber.

Wharf labour may be similarly divided, the men who handle grain and timber being of a different class from the rest, with special aptitude for this work, and a higher rate of pay. The work, however, is not to be obtained all the year round, and those who do it are for the most part unaccustomed to seek any other employment. Some of the grain and timber men, and some of the steamship workers, receive wages as high, and in some cases even higher, than the stevedores (who have 8*d.* an hour), and at this point the spheres of work overlap a little, the Stevedores' Union having one branch consisting of men engaged in the discharge of timber, while some stowage is undertaken by shipworkers.

Apart from this slight element of confusion, the stevedores are a distinct and highly organised body of men, undertaking a distinct division of export work, with very little interference from free labour. The lightermen and watermen also play a distinct part, and are completely organised, there being two bodies, the lighter and watermen proper, and the "non-freemen," or those who have not served a full apprenticeship and so obtained the freedom of the Watermen's Company.

The discharging of coal is done by the "Coal porters' winch-men," a distinct organisation from that of the "National coal "porters," who undertake to coal steamers. The "winchmen" are the successors of the "coal whippers," the change in name following a change in the system of handling the coal. The work is highly paid, but hard and irregular. Up to recent times there has been little outside competition, but an attempt to close the ranks of the union led to the employment of free labour under the management of the Shipping Federation, and although the policy has been abandoned the competition continues. Ballast heaving is very similar work, but is separately organised. Tug boatmen, sailors, &c., have also their unions.

The "import over side" work (Section III) is engaged and paid for by the owners of the vessels lying in the stream to be discharged, these being often also wharf owners; at the Surrey Commercial Docks the shipowners in some instances contract direct with stevedores for the discharge of their cargoes, and at the Victoria and Albert Docks, and in one instance at the St. Katharine's Docks, the shipowners now provide the labour on board and on quay for discharging; otherwise all the labour in Sections I to IV is engaged and paid by the dock and wharf owners.

It is to these sections that what follows will apply. To them only belong the men who are called "dockers." Sections V to VII consist, as we have seen, of distinct bodies of men whose work, though partly interchangeable with that of the dockers, and closely interdependent, is better organised and better paid, and to some extent more skilled. As to Section VIII, seamen in port cannot be considered separately from those at sea, nor the tradesmen engaged in keeping ships in repair separately from those employed in their construction or in other similar work.

II.—*Organisation of the Men.*

In early times the work of the port, then confined to wharves near London Bridge, was in the hands of privileged societies under the jurisdiction of the City; but with the extension of the docks eastward this system broke down, and the only society left is that of "Fellowship Porters," whose numbers are dwindling, and whose claim to certain monopolies is challenged. The abolition of the corn laws brought large imports of grain to the Thames, and the famine in Ireland, happening about the same time, supplied a large number of needy labourers, who, coming to London, got possession of much of the work of handling heavy merchandise, such as grain and timber. There was then no distinction between timber men or corn porters and other dock work, nor between loading and unloading; and all alike was ill paid. But these distinctions began to creep in as the rates of pay rose; the masters refusing to pay the higher rates for the easier and less skilled branches of the work.

After the marked rise of pay secured by the unions established in 1872, the distinction grew sharper, and the men engaged in specially skilled work, as for instance the stowage of cargo and the unloading of grain and timber, became close corporations in the midst of a mass of unorganised labour. For it was only where skill or great strength provided a natural barrier against competition that the unions held together. Thus the General Labour Protection League, established in 1872, with a large number of branches on both sides of the river, practically broke up, only six branches remaining in existence, five of stevedores on the north side of the river, who have continued as the Amalgamated Stevedores' Labour Protection League, and one of corn porters on the south side, who afterwards formed the nucleus of the present South Side Labour League.

In 1888-89 there was a second general upheaval of riverside labour, culminating in the great dock strike of August, 1889, which spread over all classes of dock labour on both sides of the Thames, and affected, by way of "sympathy," most of the interconnected trades. The strike on the north side was largely led by the stevedores' union, and that on the south side by the "over side "corn porters," the leaders of these organisations being the most important components of the strike committees at "Wade's Arms" and "Saye's Court" respectively. As a result of the strike, the two existing unions arose, viz., the "Dock, Wharf, Riverside, and "General Labourers' Union," and the "South Side Labour Protection League." The latter was a revival of the old league—the overside corn porters belonging to both—and like the old league is a decentralised federation of branches which are almost self-governing. The Dockers' Union, on the other hand, like the stevedores, is a centralised organisation, and has followed the example of the Amalgamated Engineers in the method of its spread to other places all over the kingdom.

Under the same impulse the stevedores, while retaining their special organisation, widened its gates so as to include in one union all the members of the trade; and the unions of lightermen, coalies, &c., filled up their ranks; so that for a time nearly the whole labour of the port was included in some organisation or other. Finally, the delegates, who, representing these various unions, had formed the strike committee, developed into the "United Labour Council of the Port of London," an unsuccessful attempt to federate the riverside industries; and this in turn has merged in the present "Federation of Trade and Labour "Unions," from which much has been hoped, but which has so far been attended with only partial success, and which it is to be feared may also end in disappointment.

Under the excitement of the great strike, many who were loafers rather than labourers joined the Dockers' Union and South Side League, thus unduly exaggerating the numbers on the roll. When the strike was over and work began, those who had joined only to claim "strike pay" fell out. That is, they did not pay, or did not long continue to pay, the 2d. a week demanded by the union. Over such as were not really dock labourers at all, the union had no power, and to get rid of them was gain rather than loss. Upon those who actually worked at the riverside, sufficient pressure could be and was exercised, by inspection of "cards," to keep them in the union, whether heartily willing or not. But owing to a change then adopted in the method of engaging men at the docks, this advantage was lost, excepting at the Millwall Dock, at a few of the wharves, and with some lines of steamships, where the employers have been willing to co-operate with the Union. The general result has been a great falling off in the numbers of "financial members."

A member of the union may be as much as six weeks in arrear. If he owes more than six weeks' subscription he ceases to be a "financial member." According to the rules, all levies must also have been paid. But arrears are often forgiven, and levies overlooked, the decision on these points being now left with each branch. Sickness or lack of work are sufficient excuse for remitting arrears, provided a man is ready to pay his current subscription.

It would not be fair to take the financial members as constituting the whole strength of the union, as some members who "pay when they can" are thorough unionists; and there are many others who in a dispute would claim membership and obey the orders of the union, and who must therefore be counted as unionists, even though more ready to draw than contribute to the funds. On the other hand, it would be a mistake to include those who only join under compulsion, and are never at heart loyal members of the union.

After allowing however for those who may still be fairly counted, and for those who never should have been counted at all, there is a considerable diminution in the number of members of the two unions to which I have referred.

The South Side Protection League" consists of seventeen branches, which retain and manage their own funds, paying 3*d.* per member per quarter to the central management fund. In 1890 this contribution amounted to 210*l.*, representing 4,200 members; in 1891 it was 127*l.*, representing 2,500 members. All these would be financial members of the branches; each branch having from 100 to 250 members. Six of the seventeen are branches of corn porters, seven of general wharf labourers, and four are deal porters, ship workers, &c. The entrance fees vary from 2*s.* 6*d.* to 20*s.*, only one branch, that of steamship workers (who are in effect stevedores), being as high as 20*s.* Nearly all these men work on the south side, as do also the members of District IV of the Dockers' Union. There is, as has already been mentioned, a little overlapping of spheres of work on the south side with the stevedores. Where the work is similar, the pay is similar also, and strength of organisation follows invariably a higher rate of pay. Work which any labourer can do is ill paid and difficult to organise.

"The Dock, Wharf, Riverside, and General Labourers' Union" is an organisation which now extends over the whole country. It is divided for London into six districts, with about sixty branches. The number of financial members is not published except in total, and depends for each branch, as we have seen, on the degree of strictness with which a general rule is applied; but the total amount of contributions received by each branch is given in the accounts (which are prepared with great care), and from these amounts a reasonable estimate can be formed (see table below). The contributions received during any period may be diminished by members falling behind, or swollen by the payment of arrears, or by the entrance fees of new members, but on the whole may be accepted as providing a rough measure of the number of financial members. The rate of subscription was 3*d.* per week, or 13*s.* for twelve months (having been raised from 2*d.* to 3*d.* in 1891).

	Branches.	Half-Year to 30th June.	Half-Year to 31st December.	Twelve Months, 1891.
		£	£	£
District I. Town warehouses	10	381	360	741
„ II. Wapping and London Docks	11	492	235	727
„ III. India and Millwall	11	669	461	1,130
„ IV. South side	18	537	560	1,097
„ V. Victoria and Albert	11	1,090	830	1,920
„ VI. Tilbury	4	78	31	109
	60	3,247	2,477	5,724

If each 13*s.*[1] represents a financial member, we should have on
the whole 8,800 for the year, or taking each half year by itself
(at 6*s.* 6*d.* a member) about 10,000, dropping to about 7,500.

I am not able to make a comparison with 1890, because in that
year very considerable sums, included in the accounts, were levied
to assist strikers in Australia, and a further levy (not so well paid)
was made to support a strike at Cardiff, but there is no doubt
that the numbers would show a progressive falling off each half
year—possibly from 15,000 to 12,500, and so to 10,000 and 7,500
in the two years.   On the whole it is not improbable that the two
unions together had within the London District about 20,000
financial members at the beginning of 1890, when nearly all who
were employed could be counted, against about 10,000 now, or
50 per cent. of the total number.

Even if this be so, what remains represents a remarkable
degree of organisation, when the character of the men and the
difficulties of the task are taken into consideration.   It must also
be remembered that if the union has lost some strength in London,
it has gained greatly elsewhere.

III.—*Disputes.*

The main subjects of dispute, whether with the employers or
between the men and their own leaders, have been: (1) the dinner
hour, (2) contract work and the plus system, and (3) the position
of non-unionists.   Of these the first two are complicated by a
tangle of old customs.   The third, concerning the treatment of
non-unionists, is more simple, as the only question is of expediency.   Given the power, and there is no hesitation amongst
unionists as to its use.

Payment for the dinner time is a very old custom.   When the
pay was 2*s.* 6*d.* for a day of eight hours, an interval of a few
minutes was allowed for beer during the morning, and twenty
minutes for dinner, or more properly for lunch, as the dock
labourer made his chief meal, tea and dinner in one, when his
work was done.   These short hours fell in with the customs'
regulations, and if overtime was worked it was paid at 4*d.* an
hour.   On this plan the work at the docks, if ill paid, was fairly
easy.   In 1872 the men struck for and obtained 5*d.* an hour in
place of 2*s.* 6*d.* a day.   The dinner time was still allowed by the
employer, and the men thus received 3*s.* 4*d.* for the full day, but
only 2*s.* 11*d.* in winter, when the day was usually seven hours.   The
overtime rate became 6*d.*   The employers met this advance by

[1] In the report for 1891 the total financial membership is given at 29,140 for
the whole union, and the total of contributions at the various branches 18,784*l.*,
or 12*s.* 11*d.* per head.

taking every advantage of the hour system. Men were not engaged till wanted, and were paid off at any hour if the work was finished. Beyond this, steps were taken by various applications of the contract and plus system to stimulate the men, so as to secure a full amount of work being done in each hour.

The "contract" system consisted of a bargain made with picked men, acting individually or in groups, who employed others at 5*d.* an hour and took for their own remuneration the difference between the money they received, a price per ton, and the wages they paid away. The "plus" system, worked under the dock foremen, attempted to interest every labourer in the expedition of the work by undertaking to pay beyond the regulation 5*d.* a further remuneration, based on a tonnage rate, fixed as for a contract. Wherever these systems could be applied they were adopted. It is not wonderful that they caused a good deal of heart-burning.

From the masters' point of view to "work" is for a man to do his best; to do otherwise is to be an idle fellow, taking money he has not earned. The men would be far from denying that there is such a thing as robbing the employer by loafing and idleness; but they recognise degrees of reasonable honest effort in work, and object, if I may so put it, to give sixpenny or sevenpenny work for 5*d.* The contract system was to them "sweating" —the slave-driving of small masters. It was a system which benefitted the dock company; and the contractors themselves might do very well; but the labourer had no advantage—he sweated that the others might profit.

The plus system, though seemingly more fair, was hardly more satisfactory. It lacked any sound basis, as the men had no voice in fixing the tonnage prices, nor insight into the calculations made, nor was the "plus" equally shared, the largest proportion going to the ganger, whose special interest it thus became to push on the others. There resulted a feeling amongst the men that the whole thing was delusive—a carrot tied in front of the poor donkey's nose to tempt him onwards. This grievance brought about a short strike in the London and India Docks, where chiefly the system applied, ending in the rule being made in 1885 that no labourer should receive less than 6*d.* an hour for contract jobs or for work on the plus system. Many more men than enough could however be had at 6*d.* an hour, and it was complained that in the struggle treating or bribing foremen in order to secure the privilege of work became common, if not customary.

The great strike followed in 1889, having for its objects the uniform 6*d.* rate of pay, the minimum half day's wages (2*s.*), and the abolition of contract. These points were won, but to gain them dinner time pay was abandoned.

We have already seen how, by the excitement of this strike, all riverside workers were brought into line. No sooner was it settled than the divergence of the interests involved became obvious; and the greatest difficulty was in regard to dinner time pay.

At the wharves, where the hours were 6 to 6, or 8 to 6, it had been usual to pay 5*s.* for the long day and 4*s.* 2*d.* for the short day, being 5*d.* an hour over the whole time. The men were allowed for meals 1 hour out of 10, or 1½ out of 12. On the new system they were to get 6*d.* in place of 5*d.* an hour, but instead of gaining 10*d.* or 1*s.* on the day's work, the advantage, by their receiving nothing for meal times, was reduced to 5*d.* or 4½*d.* a day. They had not understood—they thought their interests had been neglected—they would not stand it—they always had been paid for meal times and always would be. So they re-opened the fight at Hay's Wharf, but were finally worsted by the introduction of outsiders engaged permanently on weekly pay.

Nor did the dockers like it, but they did not suffer quite so much on their short dinner time, and the other points in the settlement concerned them more than the wharf men; for the system of taking men on and discharging them short of half a day, which was put an end to, applied principally to the docks, and the contract work objected to was entirely an affair of the docks.

Amongst those working at the different docks there was a similar clashing of interests. The grain and timber men, and the south side workers generally, complained that their interests had been neglected. In this case however the difficulty was settled amicably between the men and their employers.

It is to be remarked that whenever pay is drawn at a minimum or subsistence rate, with a plus to follow according to results, the question of the dinner hour loses its point, assuming there is anything to divide; for the extra wages paid would only reduce the amount to be distributed. When the settlement of 1889 was made, it was agreed that the work might, when desirable, be given to the men at a price per ton, and done under the joint supervision of dock officials and representatives of the men; but the plan did not succeed. Control over the men being nominally shared between the dock foremen and the representatives, was practically lost. The chance of obtaining more than 6*d.* an hour by working hard was to many of the men less attractive than working easy at the minimum rate. The result was that they did not give "sixpennyworth of "work" for the 6d. The representatives of the union could not make their men work properly, but they could and did exclude non-union men from being taken on. There was thus a good deal of friction, and after twelve months' trial the system was put an end to in November, 1890. In place of it the joint committee now allow on most of the work a gratuitous plus over and above the 6d. an hour. This they reckon in their own way, and all who work share in it equally. It varies from nothing to about 3d. an hour, and even where the average earned is lowest, it more than pays for the dinner hour.

At Millwall direct contracts taken by gangs of men work quite well. One man in each gang is leader and spokesman, but all work and share alike. The gang of contractors employ some subordinate labour at 6d. an hour. The work done in this way, handling grain and timber, has a special character.

As a substitute for both contract and plus, an attempt has been made to introduce strict co-operation, and where the conditions are simple, remarkable successes have been made. Yet even so the system does not spread, and seems more likely to die out. It does not seem possible at present to obtain out of the democratic organisation of the men any practical working leadership which shall be able to make bargains, inspire confidence, and enforce discipline.

The last subject of dispute to which I have referred concerns the footing of non-unionists—the claims of free labour, the rights of "blacklegs."

Immediately after the settlement of 1889 there was trouble between union and non-union men, aggravated by very bitter feeling against the men who had been engaged to keep the work going during the strike. The unionists refused to work with non-unionists, and were able generally to enforce this rule. Some of the "blacklegs" left, some obtained permanent places, and some joined the union. This cause of dispute was consequently got over. The power of the union to enforce membership is now very limited, and with the lack of this power has gone one fruitful cause of disputes. On this point there can perhaps never be a hearty agreement between employers and employed. No employer likes to be dictated to, or limited in his choice of those he employs; while the men will never abandon the desire to decide with whom they shall work, and if they have this power will always be tempted to use it to strengthen the weak-kneed and to coerce the unwilling, in the interests, real or supposed, of their organisations.

There was at first some friction between the Dockers' Union and the South Side League, but they now work together, and must be considered as representing jointly docker organisation.

IV.—*Numbers Employed.*

(1.) The whole work, organised or unorganised, is very irregular in character, being affected by the weather and many fortuitous circumstances, as well as by the seasons of the year, and by the occurrence of certain great sales held periodically each year in London. To find enough men at all times involves having many standing idle at other times, and even high rates of pay, such as are received by the men who handle grain and timber, do not produce a satisfactory average income, when little opportunity presents itself, and probably little effort is made, to find supplementary work.

The information collected may be best expressed graphically, and I submit a series of charts and diagrams for this purpose.[2]

Where organisation is complete, as with lightermen, stevedores, and coal porters, the total numbers amongst whom the work is divided are fairly well known, but it is not so with regard to ordinary dock and waterside labour. I am, however, able to show what have been the actual numbers employed day by day in each important branch of the work for the year ending 31st March, 1892. This information, which was collected with the kind co-operation of the dock managers and wharf and steamship owners, in order to be submitted to the Labour Commission, is summarised in the table which follows:—

It will be seen that the greatest number returned as employed on any one day (3rd December, 1891) was 17,994, but the day of maximum employment differs in each division, so that taking the divisions as distinct labour markets, 21,353 men would be required to do the work. The number would be still larger if each small centre of employment were treated separately. The men are mostly known at, and attached to, some particular centre, having their names inscribed, perhaps, on some list which gives preference for employment; and sometimes, if well placed on this list, they will seek work nowhere else. It indeed follows that if they are well known at and constant to one department, they will be unknown at any other. But, within a certain range, there is a great deal of movement, the men flocking wherever work seems most likely to be had, and an imperfect adjustment is thus obtained, which makes it probable that the number of men needed under the present system, though more than the theoretic 18,000, will be less than the addition of the district maxima. The number will probably be somewhere between 18,000 and 22,000, and may be roughly estimated at 20,000. The number of those who regularly compete for the work is larger, and may amount to the full 22,000.

[2] These have been published with the evidence taken by the Royal Commission.

TABLE A.—Number of Men Employed Daily (excluding Tilbury), 1891-92.

Where.	Maximum.			Minimum.			Average.	
	Date.	Number.	Addition.	Date.	Number.	Addition.	Number.	Addition.
London and St. Katharine's Docks	Feb. 5	3,789	} 8,224	Oct. 12	1,249	} 3,092	2,302	} 5,284
East and West India Docks	Jan. 7	2,380		Nov. 11	619		1,317	
Victoria and Albert Docks	Oct. 28	1,107		July 1	611		865	
Town warehouses	Nov. 24	948		May 27	618		800	
Total of Joint Committees' employment (excluding Tilbury)	Feb. 9	7,781	—	Nov. 11	3,553	—	—	—
Shipowners, Victoria and Albert Docks	Nov. 13	2,091	} 7,540	Oct. 19	562	} 3,578	1,322	} 5,443
London Docks	Jan. 28	415		July 4	5		116	
North side wharves and warehouses (except town warehouses)	Sept. 29	3,856		Dec. 24	2,675		3,277	
Millwall Dock	Nov. 14	1,178		Feb. 8	336		728	
Total of other north side employment	Nov. 13	7,084	—	Dec. 24*	4,114	—	—	—
Total north side	Feb. 9	18,305	—	Nov. 11	8,008	—	—	10,787
Surrey Commercial Docks	July 11—17	1,802	} 5,589	March 12—18	621	} 3,222	1,248	} 4,448
South side wharves and warehouses	Nov. 14	3,787		June 30	2,601		3,200	
Total south side	Nov. 4	5,410	—	March 10	3,439	—	—	—
Grand total	Dec. 3	17,994	21,858	Dec. 24*	11,967	9,892	—	15,175

* The smallest number employed being on Christmas Eve, it may be well to give the next smallest, viz.: "Other" north side, March 15, 4,265. Grand total, March 11, 12,200.

(2.) The first chart shows the numbers employed by the joint committee including and excluding the Tilbury Docks. I do not know to what extent men living in the London district go by train to work at Tilbury; or, living at Tilbury, come to work in the London district; but as the distance is great, it seems best to treat Tilbury by itself.

At Tilbury, as over the rest of the dock system, more work is shown from December to March than during the rest of the year; but there are special depressions in May, June, and November not shared by the other districts as a whole. The irregularity of work at Tilbury is very marked, and if we may assume that those who seek their work here are numerous enough to do all that offers at the busiest time, and that they are for the most part out of reach of other chances, then it must follow that many of them are very often necessarily idle.

The line on the chart showing the total numbers employed without Tilbury, is in some ways more satisfactory. In this line we can trace the influence of larger causes, involving less uncertainty than those which make daily and weekly irregularity of work, and there is thus a better chance for finding supplementary earnings. Stated broadly, from the end of April to the middle of November there is a deficiency of work, and this is especially marked after the middle of July, though subject to a temporary rush of work at the end of September.

From July to September is the time of the harvest, and is also the time when the militia, to which many of the men belong, is in training. During these months very many men find work elsewhere. It will be less easy to find supplementary work in October and early in November, and again there will be little to fill up the deficiency shown in March.

The table which follows shows that the maximum number employed on any one day, in all branches of the work of the joint committee (excepting Tilbury), is 7,750, but that on two days only was there work for more than 7,500, on seven days only for any more than 7,000, and on seventeen days only for more than 6,500 men.

TABLE B.—*Particulars of Employment at the Docks under the Management of the Joint Committee (excluding Tilbury).*

		Days.
4,000 { 3,750 men had work for		308—309
250 additional men could have had work for		295—307
5,000 { 250	,, ,,	279—291
250		243—273
250		213—240
250		186—207
6,000 { 250		148—179
250		127—145
250		91—118
250		71— 89
7,000 { 250		45— 62
250		23— 42
250		10— 17
250		7— 9
7,750 { 250		4— 7
250		2— 3
250		1— 2

	Per Cent.
Work done by permanent men	32·2
Other (possible) constant work	35·1
Nearly constant work (necessary deficiency not more than 15 days)	8·4
Irregular work	24·3
	100·0

We have no certainty as to the number of men who make this work their regular business, but we may safely say that 6,500 would be enough, as the 1,000 to 1,250 additional men who are at the most needed would undoubtedly be attracted to the docks at any time by the offer of work.

On the assumption then that 6,500 men take up this work for their livelihood, and have the "first call" for it, and that the surplus labour offering takes up dock work in the intervals of other work, the figures would show that for the 6,500 men, if all shared alike, there would be about four-fifths of full employment (or 250 days work out of a possible 309). But they do not share alike. There are (1) the permanent men; (2) those having first preference (list A), all of whom are now engaged by the week; (3) the second preference (list B); and (4) the third preference (list C): and there may be others who, though not listed, are dock labourers by profession. Moreover, the number who seek their livelihood regularly in this work is certainly more than 6,500.

In the year under review the permanent men numbered 1,780 at the outset, falling to 1,630 at the close. The men on the A list beginning at 850, ended at 1,200. Those on the B list increased from 2,000 to 2,500. Those on the C list—1,300 to 1,400 from April to November, 1891—rose to over 2,000, and including a supplementary list to over 3,000, receding later to between 2,000 and 2,500, at which figure the numbers stood at the end of March. 1892. [The supplementary list seems to have been connected with the wool sales, and probably contained names already listed elsewhere.]

Thus though the total number on the lists up to November, 1891, was from 6,000 to 6,500, the maximum reached in the winter of 1891-92 was 8,500, and the year ends with a total of 8,000. There seems no reason to suppose that any considerable number of men appear on more than one regular list, but it may be that the lists include men who are not regular dock labourers, and are rather to be counted as belonging to some other trade working occasionally at the docks. The great increase in the number on the list during November, 1891, signalised the acceptance by the men of the list method, and it is improbable that there are now many men who seek work regularly at the docks whose names are not on one or other list.

In considering the division of the work amongst these various classes, the following supposititious table may be useful :—

	Men.	Days.	Days' Work.
Permanent men	1,700	294 (309 days, less 5 per cent.)	= 499,800
First preference (A)	1,000	278 (,, 10 ,,)	= 278,000
Second ,, (B)	2,000	247 (,, 20 ,,)	= 494,000
Third ,, (C)	1,800	195 (,, 37 ,,)	= 350,200
	6,500	250 (average)	1,622,000
Occasional labour	1,250	7	8,000
Maximum numbers	7,750	210 (average)	1,630,000

Note.—309 days constitutes the full working year.

It will be seen that for the assumed numbers of each class I have inserted an estimate for lost time : 5 per cent. for the permanent men, 10 per cent. for the A list, and 20 per cent. for the B list, leaving 37 per cent. loss to be borne by the C class if we limit their number to 1,800, and treat the last 1,250 men as taking on the average only seven days each. This result is rather what *might be* than what *is*, and if leaving the 8,000 occasional days to outsiders, we divide the third preference work amongst the residue of the listed men, all of whom may claim to be considered professional dockers, there would be only 106 days' work out of 309, or about one-third work for them, or probably, in truth from one-half to one-fourth work, as the percentage of loss of time is no doubt really a constantly rising one, from one end of the scale to the other.

It is a debateable question whether 4*s*. or 4*s*. 6*d*. or some intermediate sum should be taken as the normal value of a day's work.[3]

If 4*s*. be taken, we get the following average rates of pay:—

				s.	*d.*	
For the A list of 1,000 men	....	21	4	per week.
„	B	„	2,000 „	....	19	-	„
„	C	„	3,300 „	....	8	-	„

If 4*s*. 6*d*. be taken as the basis for translating a day's work into money, the amounts would be one-eighth more.[4]

It is not to be supposed that no earnings would be made by the casually employed men when they are not required at the docks, but such earnings are very precarious, and it would be rash to estimate them at more than 1*s*. a day on the average. If this rate be taken, it would raise the total earnings of Class C by about 4*s*. a week, or from 8*s*. or 9*s*. to 12*s*. or 13*s*. a week on the year's average.

It thus appears that while picked men may make as high an average as 24*s*., the ordinary rank and file of the dockers earn, at their trade, from about 21*s*. at most to about 8*s*. a week, and may supplement this by other earnings, which will probably vary according to the amount of unoccupied time and the use made of it, from 1*s*. to 5*s*. a week. Those who belong, in truth, to other trades, but come at times to the docks, are probably no better off; but their earnings should rather be viewed in connection with the trade to which they are properly accredited.

(3.) At the Victoria and Albert Docks the more regular work is that provided by the Dock Company. That done for the ship-owners varies very much from week to week.

On the whole, there is more work from August to March than during the rest of the year, but during the busiest time there are also the days of least work—a thousand men being put off or taken on according to the weather or the press of work.

The work offered at these docks is desirable: much of it is paid at 7*d*. an hour, and more hours are worked than at the East and West India Docks or London and St. Katharine's Docks. It therefore attracts the best men. There is no very decided busy or slack season. The result is that very few outsiders find employment, those who seek their work here and nowhere else being perhaps enough to meet every demand.

---

[3] See Appendix.

[4] The limits of possible error in these figures are not very wide. If the men on List C make any more than 8*s*. or 9*s*. on the average, so much the less will fall to the men on List B.

TABLE C.—*Particulars of Employment at the Royal Victoria and Albert Docks, April,* 1891, *to April,* 1892.

				Days.
1,500 {	1,200 men had work for.......................................			309
	100 additional men could have had work for			308
	100	,,	,,	306
	100			305
2,000 {	100			300—305
	100			290—294
	100			271—281
	100			245—259
	100			218—229
	100			182—200
	100			147—161
2,500 {	100			109—124
	100			78— 92
	100			54— 67
	100			35— 43
	100			23— 29
3,000 {	100			14— 18
	100			8— 13
	100		,,	5— 7
3,150 {	100	,,	,,	1— 3
	50	,,	,,	1

	Per Cent.
Possible constant work	55·0
Nearly constant work (necessary deficiency not more than 15 days)	20·4
Irregular work..	24·6
	100·0

This table does not show the men with permanent employment, as we have this information only for the Dock Company's employés. The percentage of necessarily irregular work is much the same as for the whole of the joint committee's system—about 25 per cent.

If we assume 3,000 men to be needed, we find that there is on the average 222 days' work for each, and then 150 more men must be attracted to do about three days' work a-piece. Of the 3,000 men we may perhaps assume that 1,000 would not lose over 10 per cent., and another 1,000 not over 25 per cent., and if so the last 1,000 would lose 46 per cent. If, however, there are (as is not improbable) 3,500 men who find their living at these docks, and if the first 2,000 still hold their place in preference, then the last 1,500 would lose 64 per cent.

The average value of a day's work at these docks may perhaps be 4s. 6d., and if so, the earnings of the men divided into three classes as above would be—

		s.	d.	
For 1,000 men	....	24	–	per week.
,,	....	21	4	,,
,,	....	13	1	,,

or, allowing 3,500 men in all, the last 1,500 would earn about 8d. per week.

(4.) The chart showing a year's employment at the East and West India Docks is chiefly noticeable for its "regular irregularity." The fact that on the whole there is most work in the winter is almost disguised by the sharp depressions occurring at the beginning and end of each month; August and March appear to be the worst months. The general character of the line makes it probable that those who rely on this work attend day after day for work which, though very uncertain, may at any time require every man. I am told that the difficulties of those who do not look elsewhere are aggravated by the central position these docks hold: it being comparatively easy for men who are not wanted at the docks lying east and west, or to the south and across the river, to make for the India Docks.

The table which follows shows a maximum of 2,350 men employed on any one day at the East and West India Docks, of whom 300 are permanently engaged. But only on nine days were any more than 1,900 employed, and only on eighteen days any more than 1,800.

TABLE D.—*Particulars of Employment at the East and West India Docks,. April,* 1891, *to April,* 1892.

					Days.
	600	men had work for..			809
	100	additional men could have had work for....			307—808
1,000	100	"	"	....	303—306
	100	"		....	286—299
	100	"	"	....	266—274
	100		"	....	225—251
	100		"	....	195—209
1,500	100			....	162—175.
	100			....	122—140
	100			....	84—105
	100	"		..	54— 71
	100	"	"	..	33— 41
2,000	100	"	"	..	18— 25
	100		"	..	9— 12
	100				6
	100				6
2,350	100				3— 4
	100				1— 3
	50	"			1

	Per Cent.
Work done by permanent men..	21·6
Other (possible) constant work	24·0
Nearly constant work (necessary deficiency not more than 15 days)	18·8
Irregular work..	35·6
	100·0

The Dock Company have about 1,900 men on their lists, viz., 300 permanent, 300 A, 700 B, and 600 C. If these men are all at work they need 500 extra when at the busiest.

If the extra men required on nine days of the year were to be drawn from outside, and if of the 1,600 listed men who divide the work A lose 10 per cent., and B 20 per cent., it would follow that the C class would lose 66 per cent., and taking 4s. as the value of a day's work, A would earn on the average 21s. 4d. per week, B 19s., and C 8s.

The chance of making money out of off-days is perhaps not very good at this dock, as the work, though irregular day by day, is unusually steady week by week, thus demanding the constant attendance of those who make it their regular pursuit.

(5.) The main features of the line of employment shown on the chart for the London and St. Katharine's Docks are explicable by the periodic wool sales, which stand out clearly on the line used to indicate that part of the labour employed in the wool department. The rest of the work rather intensifies than subdues the curve indicating that the work connected with these sales extends beyond the wool department itself to the rest of the dock, as is no doubt the case. There are, however, other agencies at work causing the numbers employed to run up to a considerable height, from time to time, between the sales. The maximum number employed is 4,000 on 5th February, the minimum number is 1,300 on 11th November.

TABLE E.—*Particulars of Employment at the London and St. Katharine's Docks, April,* 1891, *to April,* 1892.

				Days.
	1,300	men had work for		309
1,500	100	additional men could have had work for		306—307
	100	,,	,,	297—305
	100			280—284
	100	. ,,		265—274
2,000	100			244—254
	100			225—236
	100			212—221
	100			201—206
	100			184—195
2,500	100			169—173
	100			145—155
	100			125—135
	100			112—118
	100			95—103
3,000	100			80— 88
	100			69— 77
	100			60— 67
	100			56— 58
	100	,,		49— 53
3,500	100	,,		33— 39
	100	,,		22— 25
	100	,,		17— 18
	100			14— 16
	100			9— 13
4,000	100			8
	100			6— 7
	100	,,	..	1— 3

	Per Cent.
Work done by permanent men	27·1
Other (possible) constant work	27·1
Nearly constant work (necessary deficiency not more than 15 days)	8·2
Irregular work	37·6
	100·0

Any deductions from this table must take into account the peculiarities of the case. The wool sales afford occasional employ-- ment for about 700 extra men; the work is liked, and these men are drawn from all sides. If we could deduct them, and the work they do, from the table, it would be very different. The wool sales occupy in all about 124 days, and assuming that all the additional men needed are outsiders, we get the following result :—

650 permanent men, working 294 days (309, less 5 per cent.)	= 191,100
700 extra men for wool sales, 124 days	= 86,800
2,650 others, average 163 days	= 433,400
4,000	711,300

Of the 2,650 "others," there are 500 who are not wanted more than sixteen days in the year. If these 500 men were obtained from outside, the rest of the work could be performed by 2,150 men, who would have on the average about two-thirds work. There are, however, 2,400 men on the A B and C lists, and the division of the work among them may be about as given below :—

A....	400 men working 278 days (309, less 10 per cent.)........						= 111,200
B....	1,000	„	247	„	(„	20	„)........ = 247,000
C....	1,000	„	71	„	(„	77	„)........ =- 71,000
							429,200
	Occasional work, 500 men averaging 8 days						= 4,200
							433,400

If the C list were reduced to 750, making 2,150 listed in all, each man on the C list might have ninety-five days' work instead of seventy-one as assumed above.[5]

These results, though they may be exaggerated in statement are in accordance with the generally admitted fact that the work at the London and St. Katharine's Docks is for "casualty men," the most casual of any on the river side. It must also be said that it is here especially that we find those labourers who do not desire regular work, and who fall in readily with the off and on employment obtainable at the dock gates, and find means to eke out an existence by many shifts.

(6.) There is a very great similarity between the line on the chart representing the south side wharves and warehouses, and that for the western section of the north side, both showing general

---

[5] It seems probable that in these docks the men on the B list do not obtain so much as 247 days' work. Any reduction of the share allotted to them would by so much increase that of Class C.

features, which are reproduced in a more marked way on the total
line. The same features can just be traced in the line representing the eastern section of the north side, but this line shows on
the whole very great regularity the year through. The variations
from day to day, or week to week, are not very great in any of the
lines.

In the aggregate a surplus of work is shown from September
to Christmas, and a deficiency from March to August, the months
of January and February representing about the mean. Holiday
and fog combined cause a very marked depression in Christmas
week.

TABLE F.—*Particulars of Employment,*[*] *North Side Wharves and
Warehouses.*

			Days.
3,500 {	3,400	men had work for	309
	100	additional men could have had work for	305—306
4,000 {	100	„ „	297—301
	100		287—294
	100		269—282
	100		232—251
	100		179—204
4,500 {	100		127—144
	100		98—112
	100		62— 77
	100		48— 56
	100		26— 40
4,750 {	100		10— 15
	100		3— 7
	50		1

	Per Cent.
Work done by permanent men...	33·9
Other (possible) constant work..	49·6
Nearly constant work (necessary deficiency not more than 15 days)	6·0
Irregular work	10·5
	100·0

In this table the proportion of necessarily irregular work is
only 10 per cent., and doubtless the work at the wharves is less
subject to fluctuation than at the docks; but on the other hand,
there will be less interchange of men between one wharf and
another than between different departments in the same dock.
The figures show that there would be pretty fair work for 4,500
men, but it is not improbable that 5,000 men find their living in it.
There are 1,400 permanent men, and if we divide 3,600 more into

* With the labourers employed in the wharves and other warehouses are here
re-stated those employed in the "town warehouses" managed by the joint dock
committee. The whole form one field of employment, and the masters are mostly
members of an association which holds its meetings at the Dock House.

three classes, we obtain the following not improbable proportion of
work to men :—

1,400 permanent,	294 days (309, less 5 per cent.)........		= 411,600
1,600 first preference,	278 „ („ 10 „).		= 444,800
1,000 second „	247 „ („ 20 „)........		= 247,000
1,000 third „	146 „ („ 53 „)........		= 146,800
5,000			1,249,700

If a day's work is worth 4*s.* 6*d.*, the average weekly earnings
in each class of daily labour would amount to for first preference,
24*s.*; second preference, 21*s.* 4*d.*; third preference, 12*s.* 7*d.* The
permanent men would make about 27*s.* a week, setting overtime
against off days.

TABLE G.—*Particulars of Employment, South Side Wharves and*
Warehouses, April, 1891, *to April,* 1892.

			Days.
	⎧ 2,600	men could have had work for............	309
	⎪ 100	„	.... 302—305
3,000	⎨ 100		.... 288—299
	⎪ 100		.... 258—276
	⎩ 100		.... 232—247
	⎧ 100		.... 193—211
	⎪ 100		.... 161—181
3,500	⎨ 100		.... 124—136
	⎪ 100		.... 85—106
	⎩ 100		.... 42— 61
	⎧ 100		.... 18— 29
3,800	⎨ 100		.... 3— 9
	⎩ 100	„	.... 1— 2

	Per Cent.
Work done by permanent men	37·5
Other (possible) constant work..	43·8
Nearly constant work (necessary deficiency not more than 15 days).	6·1
Irregular work...	12·6
	100·0

The proportion of irregular work is here given as 12¼ per cent.,
3,800 men being needed altogether, of whom 100 are only wanted
on three days, and another 100 only on fifteen days. There is
pretty fair work for 3,500 men, but as with the north wharves, it
is probable that a larger number, not less than 4,000, compete.
There are 1,200 permanent men, and we may make the following table :—

1,200 permanent men,	294 days (309, less 5 per cent.)........		= 352,800
1,200 first preference,	278 „ („ 10 „)........		= 333,600
800 second „	247 „ („ 20 „)........		= 197,600
800 third „	131 „ („ 58 „)........		= 104,800
4,000			988,800

Again taking wages at 4*s.* 6*d.* a day, we get the following for an estimate of the weekly earnings made :—

First preference, 24*s.*; second preference, 21*s.* 4*d.*; third preference, 11*s.* 4*d.*

(7.) *Surrey Commercial and Millwall Docks.*[7]—Taking the docks separately, the chart shows that at the Commercial Dock the highest point is touched about the middle of July, and a fairly high level maintained till the middle of January, with occasional depressions, of which the most marked are at the time of the August bank holiday and at Christmas. From the beginning of April till the middle of July there is not so much work, May being the worst month; and from the middle of January to the end of March there was an almost constant decline in the numbers employed, with the result that on 31st March, 1892, work was found for only 725 men compared to the 1,175 men employed on the 1st April, 1891, when our year began.

At Millwall also, work is best in the autumn and early part of the winter, but the full time does not begin till the end of August. The line is subject to some sharp depressions, due to the weather in October and November, and touches the lowest point at Christmas. May, June, and July show a varying line, but when once the line drops in January there is little to relieve the slackness till the middle of May. The year ends on 31st March, 1892, with employment for 350 men less than it began with on 1st April, 1891, this reduction being due in both docks to the Russian famine and the consequent prohibition of grain export from Russia.

A comparison of the amount of labour employed on handling grain with the total labour employed, shows that it is to grain that the variations must largely be attributed. The number of men on other work varies, however, from 586 at least (on 8th May) to 1,591 at most (on 21st August). From August to January is the period of most work in these as well as in the grain departments. The bulk of this other work consists of handling timber. Special strength and aptitude are required for grain and timber, and it is not possible for outsiders to compete for this work. On the other hand the men who are accustomed to it do not care to take other, less paid, work at all.

[7] For part of the work at the Commercial Dock no record is kept of the number of men employed, and for this work the numbers have been estimated from the wages paid—the proportion of number to wages having been decided by a special inquiry into the facts for a few selected weeks.

TABLE H.—*Particulars of Employment at Surrey Commercial Docks,*
April, 1891, *to April,* 1892.

				Days.
1,000	600 men had work for			309
	100 additional men could have had work for			291—303
	100	"	"	275—281
	100			258—263
	100			242—258
1,500	100			218—230
	100			174—207
	100			144—162
	100			102—132
	100			66— 84
1,800	100			42— 54
	100			18— 42
	100			6

	Per Cent.
Possible constant work	50·2
Nearly constant work (necessary deficiency not more than 15 days)..	8·2
Irregular work	41·6
	100·0

TABLE I.—*Particulars of Employment at the Millwall Docks,*
April, 1891, *to April,* 1892.

				Days.
500	300 men had work for			309
	100 additional men could have had work for			301—308
	100	"	"	262—287
1,000	100			214—240
	100		"	171—193
	100		"	119—134
	100		"	79—103
	100		"	37— 55
1,200	100			14— 24
	100			2— 5

	Per Cent.
Possible constant work	41·1
Nearly constant work (necessary deficiency not more than 9 days)....	13·6
Irregular work	45·3
	100·0

Both of these tables show a greater proportion of irregular
employment than we have found for the docks under the joint
committee.

In neither dock are the permanent men stated separately, nor
are there very many of them. Each dock has its own system of
piece or contract work, and the men of the regular gangs are in
effect preference men. A good deal of money is earned on this
contract work, but the slack seasons affect all hands. Dividing
the men arbitrarily into three classes, according to their chances
for work, they may probably make on the average 30s., 20s., and

10s. a week respectively. As to numbers there is a little interchange between these docks, but on the whole it is not likely that there are less than 3,000 men who seek their living at them.

(8.) The charts include a daily record of the weather, in which red indicates rain sufficient to interfere with work, and black indicates fog. In this record morning is divided from afternoon, and we thus obtain nine varieties of description in each colour. The whole day may be fine, showery, or wet, or a day may begin with any of the three, and change from fine to showery or wet, from showery to fine or to wet, or from wet to showery or fine. Similarly fog, if present at all, may be dense or slight, or may change from one to the other during the day.

The proportion of rainy and foggy days was as follows :—

Rain all day	16	
„　followed by showers	1	
„　in morning only	6	
Showers, followed by rain	1	} days.
Showery all day............................	18	
„　in morning only	22	
Fine, followed by rain	4	
„　　showers	21	

Rainy	89 days.
Foggy	25 „
Fine	195 „
	——
	309
	——

Dense fog all day	4	
„　in morning	7	
Foggy all day................................	3	} days.
„　followed by dense fog	1	
„　morning	6	
Fine, followed by fog	4	

There is no cure for fog; when it is dense work must stop at the docks. But this is not necessarily the case with rain, as the provision of some form of shelter is at least conceivable. A rainy day throws off from 500 to 2,500 men, and costs 4s. a day to each of them. If the interests of masters and men were the same, some means would probably be found to avoid this loss, which in the course of the year must amount to a very large sum. It may be said that the work must be done sooner or later, and the line on the chart shows that in proportion as few men are taken on during rain, additional men are needed when the rain ceases. This, however, does not make up the loss to the men, as the extra demand for men when the rain ceases only brings in additional workers.

(9.) Taking docks, wharves, and warehouses together, it appears that there was work—

Days' Work.

On 302—309 days for 12,500 men (or all the year round) .... = about 8,840,000

„ 298—301   „   500 more (all year except part of March) .... } =   „   150,000

„ 284—297   „   500 „   (all year except part of March, May, and August)........................ } =   „   146,000

„ 260—283   „   500 „   (ditto   ditto) .... =   „   138,000

„ 219—259   „   500 „   (part of March, May, June, July, and August without work) } =   „   125,000

„ 158—218   „   500 „   (no work in August, very little in March, not half work in May and June, and no month without some loss of time) .... } =   „   101,000

    15,000   4,500,000

On 121—157 days for 500 more (no work in March, May, June, or August, and not much in July; half work in April and September) .... } = about   75,000

„   80—120   „   500 „   (no work in March, and practically none 1st May to end of September)........................ } =   „   54,000

„   44— 79   „   500 „   (about half work in November, December, January, and February. No other work except a short spell at the end of September) } =   „   33,000

„   24— 43   „   500 „   (only quarter work in November, December, January, and February) .... } =   „   18,000

„   7— 23   „   500 „   (practically no work, except at end of November and beginning of December) .... } =   „   8,500

    7   „   500 „   (needed at the beginning of December only) .... } =   „   3,500

    18,000   4,692,000

As has been said, it seems probable that in the way the work is now distributed, 20,000 men are actually needed, and that there may be as many as 22,000 professional dockers. This number is made up as follows :—

Usually employed at Victoria and Albert Docks		3,500
„ East and West India		2,000
„ London and St. Katharine		4,000
„ north side wharves and warehouses		5,000
„ south „		4,000
Millwall Docks		1,200
Surrey Commercial Docks		1,800
		21,500[8]

The earnings are also shared by incomers from other trades who seek work at the docks, not because the docks are busy, but because their own trades are slack. How many there are of these at any one time, or altogether, it is not easy to say; but whatever their numbers may be, the work they do must be deducted from that at the disposal of the professional docker. It is the fact of these outsiders coming, not only when needed but at all times, which makes the peculiar difficulty of dock industry.

The improvement in the position of the professional docker might be found in an increase in the number of those who come from other trades to share his work if they were introduced only when the docks were busiest, and if at the same time the number of professional dockers were reduced. There appears to be good work actually for 14,500 to 15,000, or allowing for sickness and unavoidable friction, for about 16,000 men. For these, with strict preference over all outsiders, there would be an average of 281 days out of 309. This calculation assumes that when needed 3,000 more men could be obtained from the unemployed in other trades. The year's work would then be divided somewhat as shown below:—

							Days' Work.
Permanent men....	4,000,	working 294 days (309, less 5 per cent.)				=	1,176,000
First preference....	4,000,	„	287	„	7½	„ =	1,148,000
Second „	4,000,	„	278	„	10	„ =	1,112,000
Third „	4,000,	„	266	„	14	„ =	1,064,000
	16,000 average.						4,500,000
Outsiders	3,000,	working 63 days average					190,000
	19,000						4,690,000

----

[8] The 10,000 financial members of the union may be approximately divided as under among the various docks, &c.:—

London and St. Katharine........	4,000 men, of whom about 700 are organised.			
Victoria and Albert	3,500	„	2,500	„
East and West India .... } Millwall .... }	3,200	„	1,400	„
North side wharves and ware- houses .... }	5,000		1,200	
South side wharves and ware- houses .... } Surrey Commercial Docks.... }	5,800	„	4,200	„
	21,500		10,000	

Figured at 4*s.* a day, the preference men would average 22*s.* 1*d.*, 21*s.* 4*d.*, and 20*s.* 5*d.*, or at 4*s.* 6*d.*, 24*s.* 10*d.*, 24*s.*, and 22*s.* 11*d.* per week. The off-time of the third preference men would fall in the summer, mostly in August, and might be made of some value. If the outsiders, who it will be remembered are wanted mainly in the winter, could be drawn from those trades which are slack at that time, they too might find a sufficient amount of work between two sources of employment for a decent livelihood. This arrangement, if it were feasible, would dispense entirely with the services of 5,000 or 6,000 men. It is not to be supposed that such a change could come about quickly.

The road towards it lies in perfecting the list system and, if possible, deciding over-night the number of men who will be required in each department on the following morning.

Priority of employment, as given in the joint committee's docks, is admitted not only between list and list, but also between man and man, according to the order in which the names stand on the various lists kept. But this inner priority is not absolute, some discretionary power resting in practice, if not in intention, with the foreman, who can pass a name over here, or give an advantage there, when it suits him to do so. This power may be used to favour friends or to give a "drilling" to some man. I believe it is usually exerted to check irregularity of attendance. Men will be told, "you have been playing to please yourself, and " now you can play to please us," or with the same view a man's name may be moved to the bottom of the list. In some form it is a useful, and even necessary power, but it needs safe-guarding if petty tyranny and unfair favouritism are to be avoided.

Every department of the joint dock service has its separate lists, and there are forty-six departments. The numbers enrolled at each vary from 5 to 500. No man is supposed to be on more than one list. Men working in any department other than their own are counted as extra men, exactly as though they were strangers from outside; and as in each department severally the work from day to day fluctuates very much, men even on the A list may not always find work at their "regular call." Of the B men, a considerable proportion have often to try elsewhere. This it is which causes needless rushing to and fro in pursuit of work. The men neither know how many will be required in their particular department, nor what others on the list will decide to do—whether try at home or seek elsewhere—nor do they know what work offers at other departments. Or rather, the knowledge is very vague, and calculated to cause rather than prevent rushes hither and thither. It may therefore happen that a man seeks work elsewhere and does not find it, while if he had stuck to his

proper call he would have been employed; and nearly everywhere
we find extra men taken on, the *habitués* at one place appearing,
evidently, as "extra" men elsewhere. It is no doubt the same at
the wharves.

The statistics of "abstention" from work among men for
whom it was apparently waiting, are consequently very misleading.
There may be cases in which men who, while they complain of
lack of work, do not work when they might, and there will be
other cases when men go elsewhere, deliberately attracted by an
equally good chance of a better job—as for instance in the case of
extra men needed for the wool sales. Lighter work, more "plus,"
and it may be overtime, or a longer run of continuous work, will
constitute a "better job." But in the great majority of cases it
is clear (from an analysis of the dock companies' figures) that the
explanation of the absence of listed men is due to a simple weighing of the chance of work at their own department (with such
preference as they have) against the chance which offers elsewhere
for "extra" men. Amongst extra men it is probable that there
is an unwritten preference for men whose faces are well known,
and it may even be politic for men not to confine themselves too
rigidly to one department. These difficulties would end if the
surplus men at one place could be transferred for preference at the
nearest department which was in need of extra labour, but any
such adjustment would require to be made over-night in such
fashion that the men could go straight where they were booked to
work.

V.—*Possible Regulation of the Work.*

Both masters and men desire to see a reduced proportion of
very casual work, but there is a fundamental difference in the
aims of the two parties, as well as in the methods relied upon to
attain them.

The general policy of the wharf owners is to have as many
permanent servants on weekly wages as possible, and the dock
managers attempt to arrive at the same result by giving a strict
preference for employment day by day to men of their A class, or
as regards the Surrey and Millwall Docks, to the men of the
regular gangs. The employers naturally desire to have a body of
men on whom they can rely, as having too much to lose to engage
without very grave cause in a strike. Beyond this it is their first
interest to secure a sufficient supply of outside labour on which to
draw. Formerly they looked no further, and, as I have said,
accepted the struggle at the dock gates as unavoidable. The great
strike and the public feeling awakened by it have had the effect
of opening their eyes to the close connection which not only ought

to exist but actually does exist between their own welfare and
that of the men they employ. I therefore approach the subject
with the full assurance that any proposal having for its object
an improvement in the condition of the labourers, will receive
a ready and a favourable consideration from the employers.

The ideal of the men is different from that of the masters.
They see in the employment of a permanent weekly staff a
tendency to prevent the free distribution of the work and to
weaken the men's power of combination. They find in it no
solution of the labour question; and while accepting the practice
as inevitable, desire to limit rather than extend its application.
Outside of this body of "permanent" hands they would propose
to form all other professional dockers into a strong ring, the
members of which should be preferred for work to the exclusion
of outsiders. They would wish that all within this ring should
share alike in the chances of work, and would if they could limit
the numbers of those forming it; but this is recognised as impossible at present. The ring is too easily broken. Most of the
work can be done by any labourer, and when men are needed they
must be found. The unions are therefore ready to accept any man
as a member of their organisation, and to allow him to struggle
with the rest for his proportion of the work.

It is questionable whether the men would be content with an
actually *equal* division of the work if that were open to them.
They will no doubt always prefer to do as well as they can for
themselves. They ask only for equal *chances.* On the other hand,
the masters, and especially the foremen, like to pick their men.

Is it possible to find a compromise which shall bring the ideas
of the men sufficiently in line with the policy of the masters?
Each side would need to give way to some extent. It is certain
that men in plenty can be found, who in return for permanent
work will be ready to make their employers' interests their own.
Against this tendency the unions are powerless, and they will do
wisely if they also recognise the superior claim which those who
work regularly have to regular work. On the other hand the
employers may perhaps be willing to accept this simple test of
worth, and abandoning patronage, offer equal chances to all
capable workmen by giving priority of employment strictly
according to regularity of attendance. On this basis an orderly
system of employment seems at least possible if it were adopted,
and I believe that the results would prove beneficial to all
concerned.

Given in rough outline, the plan I would suggest for the better
regulation of dock and wharf labour is as follows :—

(1.) At each place or "call" where men are taken on for work a list should be kept, and periodically adjusted, so that the names of the labourers stand in order of the regularity of their attendance. Each name to have its number.

(2.) These labour "calls" should be grouped conveniently according to district, and each group should have a central office in telephonic communication with all its branches.

(3.) At each place or "call" the number of labourers required should be (so far as practicable) determined on the previous day, and should be posted up in some conspicuous manner, as for instance—"Nos. 1 to 33 wanted here."

(4.) The surplus or deficiency of men at each "call" for the next day should be communicated to the central office of the group, to be there adjusted or "cleared," surplus being set against deficiency. The labour master or foreman at each "call" would then, if in need of extra labourers, be informed as to what men would be sent him, or if he has more men on his own list than he can employ, would be told whether the surplus would be required elsewhere, and if so, where. In the adjustment preference would be given to those whose place of call lay nearest.

(5.) Each place or "call" which did not require all its own men would then add to its announcement "Numbers 34 to 42 " wanted at (so and so)." "No work for numbers 43 to 50" (for example).

(6.) The information as to the next day's labour to be posted at each labour "call" before the men leave work on the preceding day; and also at some convenient common centre, for the benefit of those working at a distance from their usual call.

(7.) The centres of these groups should be themselves in communication, so that, when it happened (as sometimes it might) that every man in some group was employed and more needed, a transfer might be arranged from some other district; or at least that the men not needed in other groups might have information of the demand for men.

For such a plan as this to succeed it would be necessary that the men should recognise the system. They must accept the entering of their names on any list as a contingent engagement. Where they are needed, within the district, there they must go as directed. They can take a day off if they want it, but would be required to give notice beforehand, so that their name might not be counted in for the time. Only by complying with this condition could they expect to retain their preference for work, and I think they would be ready to comply.

The greater difficulty lies on the side of the employers, in having to determine in advance the amount of labour required. lies the crux of the proposal. It will not be a very easy matter, and may even be said to be impossible. On this point I shall be well satisfied if I can arouse practical discussion, as I am inclined to think that the difficulties would be found more imaginary than real.

There are some other obstacles, but most of them may be overcome, or rather whittled away, by reducing the size of the groups, and it must be admitted, by to that extent reducing the efficacy of the plan. But believing as I do, that the principle is right, and that if tried the system would work satisfactorily and tend to perfect itself, I should be content with a very humble beginning. Moreover, gradual action would avoid difficulties and dangers of quite a different character which are involved in any great and sudden changes.

Not only is it unnecessary and even undesirable that, at the outset, the adjustment aimed at should be co-extensive with the whole area of the port, but it need not be adopted by all the employers in any district chosen. An employer who preferred to remain outside could do so, but in that case must by some means provide enough work for his own men, as they would not be able to obtain much elsewhere.

If, however, we for a moment assume that every employer joined—that the districts for groups were made as large as the distance the men were willing to travel allowed—and that the group centres were put into communication with each other so that surplus labour could be transferred, when requisite, from district to district, under some agreement as to travelling expenses —suppose also that the men fell in with the plan, and that all regular dockers registered their names, each at the place of employment he preferred. What then would happen?

Judging by the figures we have been studying, there would usually be more workers than work—not perhaps at every little "labour call," but in any one dock or at any set of wharves. The work done would be shared amongst the enrolled men, with a reasonable self-acting advantage to those most able or most willing to work regularly, but otherwise much as it now is. Against outsiders, however, the door would be shut, excepting in so far as they were actually needed to make good deficiencies in the dockers' ranks. The system would be adverse to two classes—those who do not wish for regular work, and those who come to the docks not because there is any demand for their services as dockers, or because they have chosen that profession, but solely because they have at the time no work to do in their proper trade.

Those who were seldom employed would gradually drop off. The numbers on the lists would grow less. In summer time many would leave. In the winter, when extra men were needed, their names might reappear.

When, with reduced lists, it happened that more men were required than were enrolled, the opening of a supplementary list for temporary employment could be relied on to draw a sufficient supply of good labour. This would probably happen every winter, and would conduce to the systematic dovetailing of seasonal employment.

The varying demand for labour at the docks can be provided for in four different ways: (1) By maintaining at all times a sufficient force to cope with the largest amount of work offering. (2) By working overtime when needed. (3) By drawing upon outside labour for additional hands in busy times. (4) By postponing some of the work. Of these four it is upon the first alone that the employers now rely, and the only mitigation of its hardship is the extent to which the men may themselves find other work in slack times. My present suggestion bears mainly upon the application of the third method here mentioned, *i.e.*, on the introduction when needed (and not at any other time) of outside labour. It may, however, be desirable to use the second and fourth methods to some extent. At times, without causing much delay, it may be possible to spread the work more evenly over the days, or a short pressure of business may be fairly met by overtime, in order to avoid bringing strangers in unnecessarily. If in addition any arrangements could be made for continuing out-door work during rain, it would tend in the same direction by levelling the curve of demand for labour.

If the principal dock and wharf owners were to adopt the system of transferring surplus enrolled men, hither or thither, in accordance with the actual daily demand for their services, 6,000 of those who now call themselves dockers could be (as I have shown) gradually dispensed with, to the lasting benefit of all concerned. It will be asked, what then will become of the displaced men? The answer is that the change would come slowly, and would act more by cutting off the incoming supply of men than in any other way. Among those whose sources of employment would be dried up, there are many who now depend on the earnings of their wives and children, and who work only enough to supply themselves with beer and tobacco. For them little pity need be felt. Beyond this the increased pressure on some lives during the period of change, cannot be weighed against the permanent and growing benefit which would result. I cannot overstate, I cannot even adequately state, how great a blessing more regular work would br ng to some of the poorest parts of London. Of all the causes of poverty and misery, irregular work, coupled, as it always must be, with irregular lives, is by far the greatest. A change in this would effect more than almost anything else could do for the welfare of the people.

APPENDIX.

Daily Wages.

In order to help to determine the ordinary value of a day's work at the docks, the chairman of the Joint Committee of Management has supplied me with his calculations extending half year by half year from 1st January, 1891, to 30th June, 1892.

During this period (which covers the twelve months I have had under review) the value of " piece work " (or work at 6*d.* an hour with a plus) was on the average nearly 5*s.* a day.

The permanent men, when not employed on piece work, were paid on the average 4*s.* 6*d.* per day, and the day labourers when not on piece about 4*s.* There is much more piece work than day work.

Taking the middle period (from June to December, 1891), which is also the middle of the year I have reviewed; we have the following figures:—

				£	Per Day. *s. d.*
An average of	2,890	men on piece received..............		110,619,	or 4 11
„	987	„ permanent (wages)............		34,530,	„ 4 6
„	1,247	„ daily (wages)		89,620,	„ 4 1
Total........	5,124	men		184,769,	or 4 7

I have omitted Tilbury here as elsewhere.

At Tilbury more overtime is worked, and the pay, counted by the day, is higher—piece work and ordinary daily labour figuring for 5*s.* 9*d.* and 4*s.* 4*d.* respectively in place of 4*s.* 11*d.* and 4*s.* 1*d.* elsewhere.

Of the 2,900 men on piece work, many are drawn from the permanent list. I am not sure whether the plus is equally divided, or whether the permanent hands get a larger share than the rest; and even if all share alike it is probable that the permanent hands will be selected for the most responsible and best paid work. It may therefore be right to estimate the average value of the day as follows:—

1,700 permanent men at	5*s.*
3,400 daily labourers at	4*s.* to 5*s.*
5,100 taken together at	4*s.* 7*d.*

The value of the piece work varies very much in the different docks. The London and St. Katharine's Docks represent the average, the East and West India falling below, while the Victoria and Albert Docks and the town warehouses are above the average. It would seem that 4*s*. is the lower and 5*s*. the upper limit of value. The higher value is generally accompanied by longer hours or more strenuous work.

One of the steamship owners, working at the Royal Albert Dock, has also furnished me with some very interesting particulars. These are for the year ending 31st March, 1892. For about half of this time the men were working on the co-operative system, and earned on the average 5*s*. 4*d*. per day for discharging, and 4*s*. 11*d*. for work on the quay. Some of the co-operative work proving unprofitable, the men asked to be, and were, put on time at 6*d*. an hour, and working in this way earned, during the second half of the year, 4*s*. 5*d*. a day for ship and 4*s*. 3*d*. for quay work.

It is remarkable that the cost of working per ton of cargo remained the same. The work done under the pressure of the co-operative system being more efficient in exact proportion as it was better paid; and it seems that the men are as well pleased to give "sixpenny work" for 6*d*. as to give eightpenny work for 8*d*.

Another firm of ship owners working in the same dock has supplied the following particulars :—

			s.	*d.*		*d.*		
Ship work (up to 74 men at most) averaged	4	11	at 6 per hour and plus.
Quay	,,	86	,,	4	6	,, 6	,,	,,
Frozen meat	149	,,	6	1	,, 8	,,	,,

The figures of one large wharf, taken for twelve months, show that a day's work is worth, on the average, fully 5*s*. for the casual men. The permanent hands at the same wharf, not counting foremen, received 28*s*. per week, thus accepting less pay per hour in exchange for the regularity and permanence of their employment.

Longer hours are worked usually at the wharves than at the docks.

Statements made to me by a number of the men give 4*s*. a day as a full average. Taking 7½ hours in summer, and 6½ hours in winter, at 6*d*. an hour, we have 3*s*. 9*s*. and 3*s*. 3*d*. respectively; overtime, the men say, is on the whole balanced by short time— *i.e.*, when the work begins late or ends early on any day; and finally they claim that the "plus" does not do any more than make the money up to 4*s*., taking winter and summer together, on the average of the work done. It is however not denied that large earnings are sometimes made. In the town warehouses, during the wool sales, many men are said to work from 6 a.m. to

10 p.m., earning as much as 50s. in a week. Men working for the feather sales also earn high wages, and for the tea and other sales. A good gang working at frozen meat will make 1s. an hour, &c.

The slight discrepancy which exists between the 4s. as stated by the men as the average value of a day's work and the actual figures shown by the books of the employers, is to be accounted for by the exclusion from or inclusion in the average of large occasional earnings.

So far as all share equally in these extra earnings, they undoubtedly should be included in the ordinary dockers' budget,. but so far as they are in effect a privilege to be enjoyed by a few,. it is misleading to bring them into average. It would be more correct to say that a portion of the day labourers get, like the permanent men, higher pay, as well as more regular work, than the rest.

A census taken by the joint committee of the men employed by them for the week ending 13th July of this year, confirms this view. Those who received over 30s. for the week's work were apportioned as under:—

Permanent men	503 out of 1,418, or 35¼ per cent.
A list	308 „ 1,052, „ 29¼ „
B „	180 „ 1,824, „ 9¾ „
C „	111 „ 1,160, „ 9½ „
Extra	155 „ 2,119, „ 7¼ „

There is a slight error in the numbers of 'B, C and extra men, as those who during the week have worked in more than one department are counted more than once. We may, however, fairly say that not more than one-tenth work at the higher level of pay, taking B, C and extra together, whereas one-third of the permanent hands and men of the A class do so.

While, therefore, the true average value of a day's work at the docks is fully 4s. 6d., it would be rather misleading to use this figure in estimating the position of the ordinary docker. It must, however, be borne in mind if 4s. or even 4s. 3d. a day be taken as the average value of the joint committee's work, that the rule excludes a certain proportion of preferred men who get the cream of the work.

The same applies undoubtedly to part of the wharf and warehouse labour both north and south: some men being able to combine pretty regular work with good and at times high pay. Similarly special work, such as the handling of grain, which from its nature commands an extra price, may be reasonably excluded from the ordinary average.

PROCEEDINGS *on the* 15th NOVEMBER, 1892.

DR. MOUAT, past President, in proposing a cordial vote of thanks to Mr. Booth for his excellent discourse, which was to him a privilege and a pleasure, dwelt upon its merits as a very valuable addition to the series of works in the same direction for which the Society and the public were already indebted to that gentleman. They were an indication that the important labours of the past would bear good fruit in the future in matters of such primary interest, and practical application in their relations to one of the great social and economic questions of the present, as their author was still in the prime of life and activity. Although it was not customary to discuss an inaugural address, it was in strict accordance with precedent and practice to note with approval exceptional excellence such as characterised the paper, to which all present had listened with so much pleasure and profit. He was sure, therefore, that the vote of thanks which he proposed would be received with acclamation.

Mr. ROWLAND HAMILTON said it needed very few words to second the motion of the late President. Mr. Booth had carried them through a most patient and lucid investigation of one of the most difficult problems which occupied those who were interested in social affairs. They might accept it as a type of what might be expected from him hereafter. They would not only cordially thank him for the valuable paper he had given them on his taking the chair, but would look forward, and wish him most hearty God speed in the career which was open to him, as they trusted, for the next two years.

The resolution was then put and carried with acclamation.

The PRESIDENT, after thanking the members for the kind reception he had received, said he had one word to add showing the value which might be found in investigations of this sort. Just at the present time a special inquiry was being made into the real condition of things with regard to the alleged existing distress and lack of employment, and he had been asked if he could say to what extent there was any falling off in the dock employment. With the assistance of Mr. Hubbard, the chairman of the Dock Committee, he had obtained the figures for the present year, and he was happy to say it showed that there was in that business no falling off as compared with last year. He did not doubt that there was a falling off in other trades, but at present there was no falling off in the docks. It was remarkable how closely on the whole the new line beginning at April, 1892, followed the line on the chart for the last year. The principal difference seemed to be due to the moveable feast at Easter. There was a remarkable transference of busy and slack time just then, and it appeared to have to do with the Easter holidays. The rest of the line followed on the whole the same general position up to the present, which might be called the critical point. From this time the curve should be upwards, and they must hope that it would be so this year.

Morbidity and Mortality according to Occupation.

By Dr. Jacques Bertillon, *Chief of the Municipal Statistical Department of Paris.* (Translated from the *Journal de la Société de Statistique de Paris*, October—November, 1892.)

An inquiry into the influence of the occupation upon the sanitary condition of an individual is one of the most difficult which the hygienist or the statistician is called upon to undertake. Below will be found a table of mortality, according to occupation, which has been calculated from documents published in the *Annuaires Statistiques* of the city of Paris (1885-89). This is the first which has ever been calculated in France. It has been preceded abroad by two tables in England and one in Switzerland.

Before commencing an examination in detail of these tables it will be as well to explain clearly how it is that the mortality is the best index of the healthiness of an occupation, and that a study of the morbidity, for example, is not nearly as good a guide.

Insufficiency of morbidity statistics for the purpose of determining the healthiness of an occupation.—There exist but few tables of morbidity, and two only in France; the first, by G. Hubbard (1852), the other, one which I have myself recently drawn up from statistics of the silk workers of Lyons. In Germany, Italy, and Denmark such tables are scarcely more numerous, but in England several have been drawn up by various distinguished actuaries.

In Table VIII (see p. 598) the most important results have been brought together.

We are at once struck with the very considerable differences which appear in them, and which would lead a superficial observer to believe that members of the English friendly societies were far more sickly than the French or Italian. It certainly is not so, and of this we find a sufficient proof in the mortality tables of these same societies: where the morbidity is totally different, the mortality is quite analogous. The discrepancies in the morbidity tables are therefore due not to natural causes, but to differences of definition; the English societies using the word "sickness" in an entirely different sense.

In fact, how are we to distinguish between a real illness, such as would give a right to compensation, and a simple indisposition? The majority of French societies give compensation only in cases where the inability to work has lasted more that five days; this would be a sufficient definition if it were accepted by all societies, but it is not.[1] Then again, by what criterion are we to distinguish between a *chronic illness* and an *infirmity?* Here the problem is much more difficult; the characteristic agreed upon by medical philologists is that an *infirmity* remains in a stationary state, tending neither to heal nor to grow worse. But scientific definitions and the financial administration of a mutual aid society are two very different things.

It would be vain to search the statutes of these societies in order to learn what is considered as a day's sickness; certainly

---

[1] The following are the explanations furnished, for instance, by the President of the Lyons Silk Workers' Mutual Aid Society (*Société de Secours mutuels des ouvriers en Soie de Lyon*) :—

"It is difficult to define the criterion by which the Lyons Silk Workers' Society recognises that a member is suffering under a *chronic* complaint (the medical definition, by the way, has nothing to do with it). The following are the cases where our executive considers itself justified in refusing admission to a new member, or in withholding the daily compensation granted in case of inability to work :—

"Every person desirous of admission into our Society must make a declaration that he is not suffering from any sickness or infirmity which prevents him from performing his habitual or daily work. No medical inspection is required, but before a candidate is proposed to the administrative council, the executive may, on the report, either of the employé who proposes him, or of the visitors whose duty it is to make inquiries as to the occupation, morality, and general health of the candidate, refer the latter to one of the Society's doctors for his opinion. The council, to whom this opinion is submitted, approves or rejects the candidate according as the report of the doctor is doubtful or affirmative on the subject of the incurability of the affection under which he is suffering.

"If, shortly after his admission, the first time a member reports himself sick, the diagnosis justifies the conclusion that, before joining, he was already suffering from the malady, the medical man is required to pronounce upon its nature and gravity, and also give his opinion as to the length of time during which the disease has probably run; and if it appears that before his admission he was suffering from this malady, the council may cancel the admission..

"The daily compensation is not granted after nine consecutive months of incapacity for work. The absences resulting from several different sicknesses are considered as consecutive if not more than three months have elapsed between each. Every member therefore who has received aid during nine consecutive months is held to be suffering from an incurable disease. After these nine months he loses all right to the daily help, and can only henceforth receive extraordinary aid, the granting of which depends upon the resources of the Society, and upon the more or less needy position of the sick person.

"Lastly, in accordance with the provisions of the statutes, the right to compensation may be withdrawn before the expiry of the prescribed nine months, if the member is suffering from a disease reputed incurable, *i.e.*, causing frequent interruptions of work which tend to reproduce themselves periodically, and which the doctor pronounces chronic (in the medical sense). But this regulation is, as a rule, only applied in the case of members who have already cost the Society a great deal, who seemingly desire to abuse their privileges, or to elude the proscriptions by declining, for instance, the compensation, although not yet well, after the number of days when the compensation is reduced, or just before the expiry of the nine months' term, in order to report themselves sick again after another three months."

there are plenty of rules for granting or refusing indemnities, but it will be easily seen that, for the most part, these rules do not explain the differences in different tables. Take the following case: Hubbard, in his table, counts together the days of "sick- "ness" and the days of "infirmity." These figures accordingly appear to include all causes of inability to work; yet the English actuary A. G. Finlaison, omits the cases of chronic illness. Hubbard's figures might thus appear superior to Finlaison's, but the contrary is the case. On the other hand, the tables of mortality drawn up by these two authors show that the health of the persons with whom they dealt was in every way comparable (see Table I).

TABLE I.—*Deaths per Thousand per Annum among Members of certain Friendly Societies.*

Age.	England.						France.		Italy.
	English Friendly Societies.	English Friendly Societies. (Males.)	Manchester Unity of Oddfellows. (Males.)			Foresters. (Males.)	French Mutual Societies.	Lyons Silk-workers. (Males.)	Italian Mutual Societies. (Males.)
	F. G. P. Neison, sen	A. G. Finlaison.	Henry Ratcliffe.			F. G. P. Neison, jun.	Hubbard.	J. Bertillon.	Bodio.
Years	1836-40.	1846-50.	1846-48.	1856-60.	1866-70.	1871-75.	about 1835-49.	1872-89.	1681-85.
20—25...	6·67	7·48	7·40	7·58	6·43	7·43	8·5	13·0	6·3
25—30....	7·26	7·29	7·90	7·48	7·62	7·29	7·5	5·4	5·9
30—35....	7·74	7·96	8·70	8·34	8·18	8·86	9·5	6·4	6·2
35—40....	8·75	8·93	9·16	9·91	9·77	10·92	8·2	6·4	7·8
40—45....	9·92	11·00	11·65	11·78	12·58	12·84	8·9	10·2	9·2
45—50....	12·01	13·06	13·99	14·21	14·29	16·58	15·5	11·8	11·6
50—55....	15·67	16·36	18·61	17·95	19·05	20·45	16·3	20·2	14·9
55—60....	21·20	23·60	28·67	26·19	24·92	29·73	20·3	19·5	22·2
60—65....	27·72	28·55	41·14	35·66	35·37	38·02	29·9	40·7	32·5
65—70....	39·68	43·91	57·21	54·99	52·09	58·43	54·3	67·0	50·4
70—75....	67·32	62·03	70·42	68·25	78·11	80·03	134·3	88·0	73·6
Total all ages }	12·54	12·57	9·75	11·89	12·63	12·14	14·2	23·5	11·7

The fact is that when these societies grant compensation they attach less importance to their regulations than to the state of their till. A rich society gives its help more liberally than a poor one; and this is absolutely the sole cause of the large English societies, which are often very old and generally rich, granting more daily indemnities than the French (for instance), who are obliged to exercise the strictest economy.

If those mutual aid societies which confine themselves to one single occupation would establish the enumeration of their members, and prepare annually statistics of their sick, according to age, science would most assuredly profit by their tables. Up to the present time such statements have been made by one society only (the Lyons silk-workers), but it can easily be believed that the resultant morbidity tables would be more subject to the influence of the prosperity of the society than to the insalubrity or otherwise of the profession. The Statistical Office of Italy has undertaken some researches of this nature; it will be seen later that the results obtained are scarcely such as the mortality tables might lead one to expect. Given what has been said above, this result can hardly surprise us.

In conclusion, a morbidity table, as things at present stand, is not to be compared with a mortality table for purposes of judging of the general health of any community whatever. This results from the fact that the word *death* has but one signification, while *sickness* has many.

Tables of morbidity according to sex, sickness and occupation.—First of all, a statistician must define what he enumerates. But, as we have just seen, those who count the number of days of sickness as a rule do not know what they mean by a day's sickness.

One of the most important considerations is the nature of the diseases which have been the cause of inability to work. If we find mention of such ailments as *pains, indigestion, coryza,* &c., materially contributing to swell the total, we know that the slightest indisposition is counted. If we meet with organic diseases of the heart, liver, kidneys, or lungs, we know that chronic cases have not been omitted, and finally if we find (as we do in certain English offices) blindness, deformity, or loss of a limb, we know that help has been extended to the infirm.[2]

This indication of the nature of the sickness lends a peculiar interest to M. Henri Rauchberg's study of workmen's sick funds in Vienna.[3] A few remarks may however be made concerning the form of the returns which he has been obliged to use. M. Rauchberg is the first to regret that the age of the members is unknown to him, but he points out that this deficiency is the less regrettable, in that the average age of the deceased (and probably

---

[2] I have unfortunately not been able to induce the supervising committee of Friendly Societies to admit the justice of this view. The schedules adopted by this committee distinguish the occupation, but not the nature of the illness: this is depriving the proposed return of the necessary in order to give it the superfluous, for an indication of the disease helps to define what is considered disease, hence it is necessary; whereas the occupation is useless for this purpose, it is therefore superfluous.

[3] *Die Erkrankungs- und Sterblichkeits-Verhältnisse bei der allgemeinen Arbeiter-Kranken- und Invaliden-Casse in Wien (Statistische Monatschrift,* Vienna, 1886). The same author has written an analogous work on the Workmen's Fund in Buda-Pesth *(Statistische Monatschrift,* 1887).

also of the living) is about the same in all the different occupations which come under his notice. These occupations are few in number, and nearly all are industries concerned with metals. The most serious criticism to be made is the manner in which he has grouped the causes of cessation of work: syphilis is included with genito-urinary diseases; measles with skin diseases; diphtheria with diseases of the digestive organs, &c. This grouping would certainly not have been made by any French physician, and it detracts considerably from the value of the figures of the *Arbeiter-Casse*.[4] Fortunately, about a dozen of the headings can be retained as constituting less heteroclite groups. Still, other doubts assail the reader who examines these headings. When we meet with "catarrh of the bronchia and lungs," we think we understand these somewhat oldfashioned terms; but when we learn that this malady, though fairly frequent, never causes death, we find that we have not quite understood the compiler.

Phthisis, much more common in Austrian towns than in any other country, is very constantly met with among the members of the *Arbeiter-Casse* (743 deaths annually per 100,000). The following is the duration of the cases of all kinds during the year 1885.[5]

	Cases.	Cases per Thousand Members per Annum.
1 to 3 days	1,958	44
3 „ 80 „*	14,490	327
1 „ 13 weeks	2,306	52
13 „ 26 „	464	10
Above 26 „	181	4

* Of which 811 were confinements. Since 1885 aid has been given during one week for each confinement. Until 1884 the regulations admitted of no allowance for any illness resulting from confinement until six weeks afterwards.

[4] This is another example of the danger, in nosological statistics, of grouping several diseases under one head. It would be better to consider only the most frequent, keeping each one separate. The grouping in the case of the workmen's fund of Buda-Pesth is less arbitrary.

[5] The following, among the statutes of the societies studied by M. Rauchberg, are those which could have any effect on the figures. Any person above the age of 14 years, irrespective of sex, can belong to the *Arbeiter-Casse*. Single individuals over 55 years of age and those suffering under chronic illnesses are only admitted upon proof that it was impossible for them to have been admitted earlier; in the case when the whole staff of a manufactory or a corporation joins the *Arbeiter-Casse*, this rule may be disregarded. Aid to the sick is not granted until ten weeks after the admission of any member, and is granted even in the shortest cases. After twenty-six weeks the allowance is halved, and after a further twenty-six weeks, except in exceptional circumstances, it ceases altogether. If an individual, within twenty weeks of being pronounced cured of a disease, contracts the same illness a second time, this is held to be a continuation of the first. Women who have been ten months members, receive sick pay during one

Women between 20 and 45 years show a considerably greater morbidity than men of the same age; above 45 their rate approaches that of the men. At least, it is so in the Lyons Silkworkers' Society, in the Italian societies, and (as far as can be judged from a table in which there is no distinction of age) in the Vienna *Arbeiter-Casse*. At the same time it should be noticed that among the Lyons silk-workers not only the morbidity, but also the mortality[6] of females is considerably above that of the males, whereas the opposite holds good with the population as a whole. It is thus at least permissible to enquire whether there be not some peculiarity in this employment which is hurtful to the health of the women engaged in it. The Italian table, which includes a great number of occupations, also brings out a higher rate of morbidity for women than for men, and their mortality at each age (calculated, however, from too small a number of cases) is greater than that of the men.

TABLE II.—*Comparative Morbidity of the Two Sexes.*

Age of the Members.	Lyons Silk-workers (1872-89).						Italian Societies (1881-85). (Corrected Figures.)			
	Annual Average Number of Members.		Morbidity.		Mortality.		Morbidity.		Mortality.	
			Days of Sickness per Annum per Member.		Deaths per Annum per 1,000 Members.		Days of Sickness per Annum per Member.		Deaths per Annum per 1,000 Members.	
Years.	Masc.	Fem.	Masc	Fem.	Masc.	Fem.	Masc.	Fem.	Masc.	Fem.
18 and 19	96	479	1·76	2·18	—	—	—	—	—	—
20—24 ...	607	3,897	3·06	6·37	13·0	10·2	5·0	7·8	6·3	—
25—29	1,481	6,100	3·40	7·49	5·4	9·3	5·4	8·0	5·9	9·1
30—34	2,507	7,377	3·37	7·64	6·4	9·2	5·1	8·9	6·2	10·7
35—39	3,259	8,209	4·32	7·62	6·4	8·9	6·0	7·7	7·8	8·1
40—41	3,442	8,161	5·29	7·64	10·2	9·4	6·2	9·3	9·2	10·0
45—49	3,567	7,720	5·89	8·12	11·8	13·5	6·8	8·2	11·6	8·9
50—54	3,214	6,419	8·04	9·58	20·2	14·3	7·9	9·3	14·9	14·1
55—59 ...	2,964	5,021	8·38	11·01	19·5	21·9	9·2	9·7	22·2	15·9
60—64	2,623	3,795	11·15	14·52	40·7	41·9	11·2	10·0	32·5	—
65—69	1,956	2,617	16·73	18·57	67·0	55·0	13·4	8·2	50·4	—
70—74 ...	999	1,146	19·76	24·48	88·0	85·4	14·7	—	73·6	—
Above 75	878	366	26·90	30·87	148·0	161·0	13·4	—	—	—
Average....	27,093	61,317	7·81	9·39	23·4	17·6	6·6	8·5	11·7	10·7

week in the case of confinements. The weekly subscription varies from 8 to 20 kr.; the sick allowance varies from 22 kr. to 1 fl. 8 kr. (from which is deducted the weekly subscription which is paid even during sickness). The number of members has rapidly increased: it was 6,410 in 1868, 13,813 in 1875, 17,146 in 1880, and 44,372 (8,404 women) in 1885.

   [6] The general mortality of the women (without distinction of age) is on the other hand less than that of the men, while the mortality at each age is greater. To

The tables of the Vienna' *Arbeiter-Casse* point also to the fact that the morbidity of women (526 cases and 9,255 days of sickness per annum per 1,000 women) is above that of men (427 cases and 8,366 days).   In this case we have the further advantage of knowing the cause of the greater amount of sickness among the women.   The conclusion to be drawn from the figures is rather unexpected; we could easily believe that confinements and their consequences, and diseases of the womb are a more frequent cause of absence ; doubtless they contribute to augment the number of cases and of days, but the principal reason of the increase is to be sought for among the very diverse maladies arbitrarily bracketed together under the unsuitable name of "diseases of the digestive "organs."   (Of every 1,000 members of either sex, 966 days of illness among the men, and 1,777 among the women were due to diseases of the digestive organs.)   Yet they do not cause a greater mortality among women than among men, though the duration of these diseases is on the average slightly longer among women than among men (thirteen days against twelve).   It is difficult in running through the list of these, to point to any particular disease as being specially the cause of the greater morbidity among females.   The diseases grouped under this head are as follows: "Angina, diphtheria, constriction of the œsophagus, "gastric fever, diseases of the stomach, diarrhœa, tænia, diseases "of the liver, peritonitis, colics, saturnism, hernia, rectal fistula." Now the diseases of the stomach, often the consequences of alcoholism, we should expect to be more common among men. Peritonitis, it is true, is much more frequent among women, but this terrible disease is fortunately too rare to account for the difference ; besides which it often results in death, and I have already remarked that the excess of morbidity among the women is not accompanied by a corresponding excess of mortality. Possibly it is the indefinite group of diseases comprised under the old name "gastric fever" which is the chief cause.

From calculations based on M. Rauchberg's figures it appears that the "day workmen and factory hands " (in the iron trade) are noted as having a high morbidity due principally to accidents,

explain this apparent anomaly, it is sufficient to consider the first two columns in Table II : it will be seen that nearly half the women (42 per cent.) are under 40 years of age, whilst only a quarter (26 per cent.) of the men are under 40.   The female members being younger, it is not surprising that their general mortality is lower than that of the men, although their mortality at any particular age is greater.

' At Buda-Pesth, according to the *Arbeiter-Casse* of that town, the contrary apparently holds good: of 1,000 workmen there were in one year 309 cases of sickness, of 1,000 workwomen there were only 257. It is true that here confinements were not included.

"rheumatisms and pains," and to diseases of the digestive and respiratory organs. "Blacksmiths and filecutters" have a high morbidity caused chiefly by accidents. "Toy makers and wood-"workers" have a lower rate than the metal workers just considered : accidents are rarer, as are also affections of the eyes and ears (perhaps these are due especially to the dust which constantly lodges in the cornea of workers in iron) and the so-called "diseases "of the digestive system."

Comparison of the four principal tables of mortality according to occupation.—The four tables in question are those of Drs. Farr and Ogle (for England), M. Kummer (for Switzerland), and my own (for Paris), which is the latest. The other statistical writings on this subject have not the same value, because the ages, which are absolutely necessary, are not distinguished. If we calculate, for example, the mortality of landed proprietors, without distinction of age, it will be found to be very high; this is not because their profession is laborious, but simply because landed proprietors are generally more or less elderly people, enjoying in their old age the fortune which they have acquired in their younger days; they thus appear to have a mortality similar to that of aged people. On the other hand, the general mortality of butchers is low, although at each age it is high, the reason being that in order to be a butcher a man must be strong, and consequently young; hence it is that the mortality of butchers as a class is the same as that of young men.

Even a table of mortality according to occupations and age is difficult of interpretation. For a calling which requires force, such as that of a blacksmith, can only be followed by individuals possessing a peculiarly vigorous constitution; if he afterwards gets into bad health he is obliged to take to some other employment, and it is as following this new occupation that he will be registered at his death. When therefore we find a low mortality in certain professions, it is not easy to determine whether this is to be attributed to the daily work demanded by the occupation or to this "selection" of which I have just spoken. On the other hand, sedentary occupations are followed by men who have but a small share of physical force, and who have neither the means nor the will to exert themselves to any great extent. When we find that one of these occupations shows a high mortality, we have accordingly to ask ourselves whether its selection by weaker persons does not swell the number of deaths. This selection by the feeble is especially noticeable in the case of a certain number of trades which require no apprenticeship, and which are the refuge of all who have failed in other branches. Such are the street-criers, itinerant merchants, street porters, &c. These occupations are accompanied by a high death-rate, but it is not fair to assume that they are therefore unhealthy. It is those who follow them who are unhealthy. Neither the preceding considerations, nor the technical difficulties in obtaining from the people exact and precise information concerning their occupation, ought however to prevent us from studying the mortality according to occupation; but they ought to teach us prudence in accepting the conclusions to be drawn from the figures.

Agricultural Industries (*Farmers, Gardeners, Market-gardeners, Nurserymen, Game-keepers*).—In England, as in Switzerland, their death-rate is extremely low, that of the English *gardeners and nurserymen* especially so. At Paris the death-rate of the *market-gardeners*, of whom there are many at Grenelle, is about the average. Attention may be called, in England, to the considerable mortality among young farmers from 15 to 25 years. It is quite constant, and may possibly be due to these young men becoming proprietors at a very youthful age; in other words, having inherited the possessions of their parents when very young, they may have also inherited their health (evidently feeble since the parents died leaving young children), and be carried off by hereditary diseases. Farm servants have also a very low mortality, although slightly superior to that of their masters. English *game-keepers* being picked, vigorous, and suitably paid men, free from all serious care and leading an active out-of-door life, enjoy splendid health. A rather unexpected and improbable result of a study of the Italian tables is that while, according to the English and Swiss tables, agriculturists have a most enviable health, they are in the Italian mutual societies, liable to more days of illness than workmen. This result is the same in both the two periods studied.

In Switzerland, as in England, there are only half the number of cases of phthisis amongst agriculturists and horticulturists as amongst men generally. It appears from the English table that a distinction must be made between farmers and their labourers. Alcoholism is most common among the farmers; and after this come liver diseases and suicide (above the average in this class). The farm-labourers and nursery gardeners either have not the means or have no desire to inebriate themselves so often; liver diseases and suicide are exceptionally rare among this class; but, more exposed to the inclemency of the weather, they succumb oftener to inflammation of the respiratory organs.

Extractive Industries[e] (*Coal-miners, Iron-miners, Cornish miners*).—The *coal-miners* always enjoy an extremely low death-

---

[e] Nearly all the considerations in this section are taken from Dr. Ogle.

rate. All causes of death are rare amongst them, except violent
deaths and inflammatory diseases of the lungs. The figures referring to consumption are very low, and would, Dr. Ogle suspects,
be lower still than appears in the returns, if under this heading
there had not been included a certain number of deaths due to the
disease commonly called "miners' phthisis"—which is apparently
not tubercular. The lowness of the death-rate among coal-miners
is a universal fact, noticed in all the countries in which it has been
investigated;[9] it approaches the mean only in Monmouthshire.
In France the sanitary condition of the miners is equally satisfactory, at least at St. Etienne, as M. Fleury (chief of the Bureau
of Hygiene of that town) showed at the Congress of Hygiene
and Demography held in London last year. Accidents materially
increase the death-rate.

The rare occurrence of consumption among miners has been
noticed by many doctors who were not statisticians,[10] and several of
them, Hirt especially, have concluded that the coal dust and warm
temperature of the mines had the effect of preventing and hindering
the development of tuberculosis. But this conclusion has nothing
to support it. In iron-stone mines, phthisis is no commoner than
in coal mines. Besides, while it is true that phthisis among miners
is not so frequent as among the outside population, it must also be
said that the comparative rarity of other diseases is in the same
proportion. Alcoholism is rarer among English miners than
among the rest of the population, which results, it appears, from
the extreme regularity exacted in the industry, a regularity incom-
patible with drunken habits. The comparative frequency of chest
diseases other than phthisis may doubtless be explained by the
abrupt changes of temperature to which miners are often subjected.
As for the accidents, one half are caused by falls of coal or
stone, &c., another quarter by explosions of fire-damp, and of the
remainder the majority are waggon accidents, which affect especially the boys whose duty it is to bring the coal to the pit's mouth.
Accidents are so frequent as to cause from a fifth to a quarter of

---

[9] It is rare that, either in the census or in the registration of deaths, the word
"coal-miners" is written in full. "Miner" simply is put down, because in any
given district the mines are all of the same nature. They have accordingly been
classed under three heads (coal, iron, and tin lead and copper), the nature of the
mines in the district considered being taken as an index of the kind of mine in
which an individual obtains his livelihood.

[10] François (*Bull. de l'Acad. de Belgique*, 1857); Hervier (*Gazette méd. de
Lyon*, 1859); Riembault (*Ouvriers mineurs*, 1861); Michel Lévy (*Traité
d'hygiène*); Boens Boisseau (*Maladies des houilleurs*, Brussels, 1862); Wilson
(*Brit. Assocn.*, 1863); Hirt (*Staubinhalations - Krankheiten*, Breslau, 1871);
Fleury (*Congress of Hygiene and Demography, Demographic Section*, London,
1891).

the deaths.[11] If these are left out of count, the mortality of miners would be as low as that of agriculturists and gamekeepers. Dr. Ogle inquires whether the extremely low mortality of coal-miners is really due to the healthiness of their calling (which one is not disposed to admit at first sight), or whether it is because the occupation demands considerable vigour and must be abandoned as soon as the workman begins to lose his strength. He rather inclines to this last idea; still he does not fail to notice that many other employments requiring to the full as much strength (black-smiths for example) are yet far from conferring the same health on those following them.

Iron-stone miners have the same low rate as coal miners; there is the same comparative absence of phthisis, and the same frequency of other pulmonary diseases. Accidents are quite as frequent, at least, in spite of the absence of fire-damp. Dr. Ogle attributes their general health to the principle of selection.

The *Cornish miners* (principally tin, and some lead and copper miners) stand out in marked contrast to the others; their mortality being among the highest in the kingdom, and more than double the average death-rate of the county. The chief factors in this high mortality are phthisis and other diseases of the respiratory organs; the rate from the first-named cause being three times that of the other miners, and this malady alone causes ravages among them as great as all diseases combined among English agriculturists. Diseases of the digestive organs are also very frequent, as are also violent deaths, though less so than among other miners. Diseases of the nervous system and organs of circulation are not above the English average, and alcoholism is comparatively rare.

The high mortality of the tin miners was so unexpected, that it appeared desirable to institute a special inquiry to verify the returns. Dr. Ogle points out that the industry had been declining for the last twenty years. Between 1861 and 1871 the number of miners declined by 27 per cent.; at the census of 1881, there was a fresh decrease of 44 per cent. Many Cornish miners had, in fact, gone to seek elsewhere a more remunerative employment. It can easily be supposed that those who had the energy to leave were the best and strongest; but this explanation is certainly quite insufficient, and it is doubtless in a careful examination of the occu-pation and the conditions under which it is carried on, that the real reason, and possibly the remedy, is to be found.

Industries relating to stone, lime, and sand (*Quarrymen,*

---

[11] This great frequency of accidents tends to lower the death-rate from other causes, and especially from phthisis; as a miner may be suffering from consumption and yet would not be included under this head, as he would be in any other industry.

Stonemasons, Masons, Plasterers, Bricklayers, Slaters and Tilers, Sweeps).—The (slate and stone) *quarrymen* have an enormous mortality, although less than that of the Cornish miners. This excess is almost entirely due to phthisis and pulmonary diseases; accidents are also very common, but other causes of death are rare. The occupation of quarryman, like that of miner, and perhaps even more so, demands great physical vigour. They are a good example (and we shall meet with others presently) of the injury done to man by dust, and especially by the hard dusts. *Stone-cutters* and *workers in marble* have in Switzerland a considerable mortality, principally due to phthisis, which rapidly increases with age. Under 20 years of age, it is rarer than among the mass of the population; from 20 to 29 it equals the average, from 30 to 39 it is double, from 40 to 49 it is triple, and from 50 to 59 it is four times the average rate of the Swiss as a nation (Proust: *Traité d'hygiène*). According to the Italian table of morbidity, the "*stone-cutters and* "*pavers*" average fewer days of sickness than the whole population up to 45 years, but considerably more above that age. At Paris, the "*marbriers, praticiens-sculpteurs et mouleurs*" are subject to a high death-rate at all ages.

Builders, masons, and *bricklayers* have in England, according to Dr. Farr, a mortality above the average, according to Dr. Ogle, slightly under. Tuberculosis and other pulmonary diseases are the chief maladies; they are attributed to the dust which they inhale, but this dust is not very injurious, employment being in the open air. Although English masons have the reputation of drinking, alcoholism and diseases of the kidneys and nervous system are infrequent among them; violent deaths are not rare. *Masons* and *plasterers* have in Switzerland a high mortality after the age of 15 years. Here, as among the stone-cutters, phthisis increases with age, but it cannot be considered an important factor in the high mortality alluded to, as it is rare up to the age of 40 years, and exceeds the average only after 50. Judging by the Italian tables, the "*masons* and *whitewashers*" have a few more days' illness than the other members of Friendly Societies. The *Arbeiter-Casse* of Vienna shows that among the "*masons and stone-* "*cutters*" the death-rate is similar to that of workers in iron, *i.e.*, rather high, and the morbidity still greater.

Parisian statistics confirm the above remarks; the death-rate of *masons, stone-cutters,* and *roofers* being, at each age, slightly above the average. In England, the mortality of *slaters and tilers* was in Dr. Farr's tables slightly higher than in Dr. Ogle's, though the latter is high enough. The same applies to *plasterers* and *whitewashers.* Dr. Farr found the death-rate among *chimney sweeps* to be enormous, nor has Dr. Ogle reduced it to any extent.

Metallic industries (*Machine and Boiler-makers, Smiths, Cutlers, File-makers, Needle-makers, Armourers, Locksmiths, Manufacturers of physical, surgical, and mathematical instruments, Watchmakers, Jewellers, Enamellers, &c.*).—In England, *engine and machine makers* and *millwrights* have an average mortality in the tables of both Dr. Farr and Dr. Ogle; the death-rate of *boiler-makers* is exactly the mean. The mortality among *blacksmiths* in England is a little below the average : the only cause of death which is slightly above the mean being diseases of the respiratory organs; while diseases of the nervous system are somewhat rare, and alcoholism is average. The same holds good in Switzerland for *blacksmiths and farriers*, though they have a fairly strong tendency to phthisis between 40 and 60 years. At Paris their death-rate is very low. It must not be forgotten that blacksmiths are chosen from among the most vigorous men.

Mechanicians in Switzerland have an average mortality, and a tendency to consumption above the average up to the age of 40 years. After this age their health is superior to that of the population as a whole.

Cutlers and *file-makers* have an extremely high death-rate, due principally to tuberculosis of the lungs, and diseases of the respiratory system. Metallic dust is the cause of this; and we have already seen the fatal effect produced by hard dusts on the frequency of phthisis: much importance is attached to the stone dust produced by the grindstones. Diseases of the nervous system appear to be numerous among cutlers and file-makers, yet alcoholism does not seem to be very common among them. Lead poisoning is very common among file-makers, because the steel which they are hammering is supported upon a leaden cushion; plumbers and painters only suffer from it to half the extent of the file makers. Contemporaneously with lead poisoning, diseases of the kidneys are developed. Needle-makers, Dr. Farr finds, have a very high death-rate at every age.

The old nomenclature did not distinguish between *makers* and *merchants* of *tools, files, and saws*, and their rate was very high. Similarly in Switzerland, the "*manufacture of machines and* " *tools* " ensures at every age a mortality above the average. Especially noticeable are the ravages of consumption, which annually claims 500 victims per 100,000 living. According to the Parisian figures, the death-rate of persons engaged in the *manufacture or commerce of metals* is low.

Gunsmiths and *gun-manufacturers* have in England but an average death-rate, whereas in Paris the "*manufacturers of hunting weapons and swords*" (*armes de chasse et armes blanches*) are subject (according to observations which are scarcely sufficiently numerous)

to the very high mortality of iron-filers. The two Italian tables
agree in attributing a relatively high morbidity (six to eight days
in the year, according to the age) to "*armourers, blacksmiths, tin-*
"*men, braziers, and farriers.*"

Tin-workers have in England a mortality below the average,
and one which has sensibly diminished. The English include
, *copper, lead, zinc, brass, &c., workers*, under one head: their sanitary condition is not so good as that of the tin-workers, and is
about the average.

The *locksmith's* is in Switzerland the most insalubrious of all
trades (equalled by that of the stone-mason's, with which we shall
deal later). From 15 to 20 years their mortality is nearly double
the average (8·8 per 1,000, instead of 4·8), and at the succeeding
ages it is much above the mean. Phthisis is one of the principal
causes. From 15 to 20 it is three times what it should be (3·4
instead of 1·2); afterwards, contrary to what usually happens
among the population, its frequency increases with age until, at the
age of from 50 to 59 years, it annually carries off 12 per 1,000 of
those engaged in this trade. This frightful figure is also reached
among the stone-masons. At Paris their death-rate is above the
average, but not to the same extent as in Switzerland. This result
may be compared with that which has been found for the makers
of tools, saws, files, and needles, whose business consists, like that
of locksmiths, in filing iron. These workmen succumb to the
accidents described and explained in Proust's *Traité d'hygiène*.
In England, *locksmiths* and *bell-hangers* are grouped with *gasfitters*.
Their mortality was found to be high when Dr. Farr calculated it,
and it is still high, but less so, according to Dr. Ogle.

It appears that in England the mortality of the *makers of
philosophical instruments* is high, and the Parisian returns, too
imperfect on this point to be quoted, seem to bear out this conclusion. Those engaged in the *musical instruments* trade show in
England an average death-rate (rather under than over), while at
Paris the rate is decidedly below the average (but the observations
in the latter case are not sufficiently numerous to be conclusive).
The English *watch* and *clockmakers* have a high mortality between
the ages of 20 and 25; after which it improves from year to year
(it is average between 25 and 35, and low from 35 to 55), and is
again above the mean in old age. In Switzerland, this trade
is less favoured, the mortality is decidedly above the average at all
times, and only approaches the mean after 60. Cases of phthisis
are met with twice as often among them as among the population
generally, and the excess of deaths from this cause is almost
sufficient in itself to account for the great mortality among Swiss
watchmakers.

Engravers and *gilders*, according to the English returns, have a rate above the average.

The Parisian nomenclature, which is the same as the French in 1866, includes under the same head the "*jewellers, goldsmiths,* "*lapidaries, enamellers, watchmakers, gold-beaters, gilders and* "*silverers on wood and metal, artists in bronze, chisellers in metal*." As I have always done, I include with these all who are engaged in the sale of these objects, because it is extremely difficult in practice to distinguish between the manufacturing and merchant jewellers and watchmakers, &c. The final result for these diverse occupations points to a low mortality at every age; a result which is consequently very different from that which obtains in England and Switzerland, but here it should be noticed that the chisellers, jewellers, gilders and goldbeaters are very numerous in Paris, and that the watchmakers only form a small fraction of the total.

The Italian morbidity tables also comprise "*jewellers, goldsmiths,* "*watchmakers, chisellers and engravers*" under a single head. Of all the occupations distinguished by the Italian nomenclature, this is that which shows the least amount of sickness. Watchmaking is one of those sedentary trades which, demanding no strength, and tiring the eyes more than the muscles, attracts more the sickly people and those whose constitution is weakly; by this we may perhaps explain the high death-rate in Switzerland, where this trade is practised even in the country; the strong men devoting themselves to agriculture, the weakly to watchmaking. The fact that the mortality of the Swiss watchmakers is high in youth, and diminishes later, seems to confirm this explanation. In that country the heading includes "*watchmaking and the manufacture* "*of watchmakers' tools*." Evidently the watchmakers' outfit is included; they form thus a fairly diverse group of occupations, but in all the workmen are obliged to file and wear out metals, and to inhale metallic dust. It is perhaps from this cause that the Sw.ss watchmakers' mortality remains always high, instead of decreasing with age like the English.

Wood Industries (*Carpenters and Joiners, Sawyers, Turners, Coopers, Cabinet-makers, Carriage Builders, Ship Builders, Cork Manufacturers*).—*Carpenters and joiners* have, according to English statistics, a low mortality at all ages. All diseases are rare among them. The Swiss figures are less favourable, and bring out a rate about the average or even slightly above; phthisis among them is of average frequency. The Parisian statistics, still more unfavourable, attribute to them a rather high rate from 30 to 50 years of age. The number of days during which the Italian "*joiners, carriage builders,* "*and carpenters*" absent themselves from work is slightly above the average. *Sawyers* have a low death-rate in England. According

to the Parisian figures, the " *coopers, basket-makers,* and *box-makers* "
have a moderate death-rate ; in England the *turners, box-makers,*
and *coopers* are credited with a high rate, both in Dr. Farr's and
Dr. Ogle's tables. The latter is surprised to find the joiners
enjoying much better health than the other workers in wood. He
suspects the coopers of intemperance, and in this his opinion is
borne out by the Swiss returns. The Vienna *Arbeiter - Casse*
attributes to the " *toy-makers and other workers in wood* " a mortality
similar to that of the workers in metallurgy, but much less
sickness.

The important Parisian industry of *cabinet making* is healthy,
the mortality being at all ages below the average. The *upholsterers*
show the same, or even better results. According to the English
tables the mortality of *upholsterers, cabinet-makers, French polishers*
is about the average, or slightly above it.

Shipbuilders in England had according to Dr. Farr, a mortality
rather below the mean until the age of 35, and rather over after.
In 1880-82, it had considerably diminished at all ages, and the
occupation was considered a healthy one.

The *wheelwrights* in England have rather a low mortality, while
the *carriage-builders'* rate is decidedly higher, especially above 45.
This difference, which appears in both tables, is doubtless easily
understood when we consider that the first-named follow their
occupation in the country, and scarcely work any material besides
wood, whereas the carriage-builders' trade is carried on in towns,
and they have to work in wood, iron, varnish, &c. In Switzerland
the " *wheelwrights' trade and manufacture of railway-carriages* " is
most noticeable for a low mortality up to 60 years of age ; consumption occurs very seldom among those following this trade.
At Paris, the same heading includes " *carriage-builders, wheel-*
" *wrights, saddlers, harness-makers, farriers,*" and this group is
apparently subject to a high death-rate at all ages.

The *cork manufacturers* are too few in number in Paris to enable
us to draw any satisfactory conclusion from five years' observation.
I will only say that their mortality appears to be very high at all
ages.

Textile industries (*Spinners, Lace manufacturers, Rope-makers,*
Carpet manufacturers, Tailors, Hatters).—In Switzerland the death-
rate is average, or below the average. Phthisis is rather rare, at
all events up till 50. The statistics of silk mills are more satisfactory than those of cotton mills ; the English figures confirm
this last result, and at the same time give more details. *Cotton-spin-*
ning in Lancashire entails a mortality below the average for the
county (but still high, and certainly above the mean for the whole
of England). The same remark applies to the wool manufacture

in the West Riding: their mortality is only half that of the district, but above that for the whole of England. The *hosiers* of Nottingham and Leicester are in a better condition; their death-rate is much below the English average, but about equal to that of the two counties in question, which have a low rate. It thus appears that in these three occupations, local influences must not be left out of consideration. Lastly the *silk manufacturers*, and especially the *lace makers*, have a very low rate.

Dr. Ogle remarks that these preceding results are not to be explained merely by local influences, but also by the conditions under which the different trades are followed. In cotton-mills, the temperature is tropical and relaxing (according to the official report of Dr. Bridges, October, 1883), and in many the dust is composed of particles of cotton, and of a mineral substance used for sizing. In the wool-factories, there is less heat and less dust. In some of the preliminary operations, it might be produced, but Dr. Greenhow (Third Report of the Medical Officer of the Privy Council) asserts that precautions are taken against this and that very little dust gets about. Both from the point of view of temperature and dust, the silk factories contrast favourably with the cotton and wool-factories, for both dust and heat would be prejudicial to this costly material. The *silk remnant* trade it is true gives rise to a little dust, but this occupies only a few people. Hosiery and lace factories produce dust in the workshops only under exceptional circumstances.

The mortality due to phthisis in the Lancashire cotton mills is rather above the mean of the county (and decidedly above that for the whole country). The disease is less frequent in the woollen factories of Yorkshire, and less still in the stocking trade in Leicestershire and Nottinghamshire; it is true that the general population of these two counties is not susceptible to consumption. On the whole we arrive at the result that the frequency of phthisis among spinners in England is, as in Switzerland, about the average.

The other diseases of the respiratory system are also more frequent among the Lancashire cotton-spinners than the wool-spinners, and more frequent among these than among the Leicester and Nottingham hosiers. In all these three occupations, they are less frequent than among the general population of the district in which each is carried on. Alcoholism appears not to be very common : the contrast is especially noticeable between the cotton-spinners and the rest of the population of Lancashire. Liver diseases are only of average occurrence among the cotton and wool manufacturers, and are unusual among the hosiers. Finally accidents are extremely rare in all three industries. Anthrax,

among wool sorters, should be noticed; of 1,278 deaths of which
the cause is known, 10 are attributed to this disease.

The mortality among *carpet manufacturers* is about the average.
Rope and cord makers, according to Dr. Farr, have a low mortality
up to 45 years of age, and a higher one afterwards; it is much less
according to Dr. Ogle.

For Paris we have not sufficient details to be able to give any
result for *spinners;* the *lace manufacturers*, much more numerous,
have a rate about the average.

MM. Fleury and Reynaud have written an excellent article on
the sanitary condition of the lace-trade at St. Etienne;[12] they
describe the state of the workshops, which are high and well
ventilated, and the motions of the workmen : they note especially
the pressure exerted at each instant on the sternum (pressure
equal to half the weight of the body, which ends by deforming the
sternum, as is proved by anatomical specimens of which they
reproduce photographs). They have noted the cause of death
among them at each age during the ten years 1880-89. Only one
point (unfortunately essential) is wanting, and that is the number
of living at each age, which has not been considered in the
enumeration. From want of this figure, we cannot tell whether
the trade is healthy or no. They only remark that phthisis is not
more common among them than among the other inhabitants of
this city. On the other hand, cancer (particularly of the stomach),
and congestion of the brain are more frequent among them than
among the miners and armourers of St. Etienne. MM. Fleury
and Reynaud believe that the pressure exerted on the stomach
may be a cause of the cancer in that region. The average age at
death of the lace-workers is 56½, which is higher than that of the
miners and armourers : the sanitary condition of the St. Etienne
lace-workers thus appears satisfactory. If by some mechanical
arrangement which will doubtless be discovered, the exaggerated
pressure on the sternum could be removed, this occupation would
probably be rendered even more healthy. The article is a proof
of how interesting would be a study of each occupation compared
with the causes of death which affect the occupation. But in
order that it may be of the greatest value, such an investigation
would require to be accompanied by a census of professions according to age.

The two Italian morbidity tables agree in assigning to *spinners*
and *lace-workers* an average amount of sickness.

The *tailors* in England and Switzerland have a high mortality,
especially at the commencement of their career. Afterwards it is

---

[12] *La Loire médicale*, 15th June, 1890.

nearer the average, but always remains above it. The Swiss table brings out that they are twice as subject to phthisis as the whole population. Although the tailors' occupation is sedentary and is always carried on in a confined and sometimes badly-ventilated space, hygienists have not found any particularly unhealthy feature in it. It is therefore possible that the results which we have just pointed out may be due, not to the occupation, but to a kind of spontaneous selection. Tailoring is one of those sedentary occupations which would naturally attract weakly individuals who have neither the power nor the will to follow a more active trade. Such is also the explanation suggested by Dr. Ogle. Phthisis is frequent among them in England, as in Switzerland; and the other diseases of the respiratory system attain the average (although they are scarcely exposed to the inclemency of the weather). They have, in England, a reputation for drunkenness, borne out by the statistics; while diseases of the liver and nervous system and suicide are fairly frequent. As might be expected, deaths from accident are rare. At Paris the tailors (of whom many are foreigners) are subject to a lower mortality. Up to the age of 40 years the death-rate may be called low, a fact which does not tend to confirm the theory that feeble men select this trade. At a more advanced age the mortality of Parisian tailors is somewhat above the average. The Italian tables, far from showing any great amount of bad health among them, attribute to them a low morbidity: the Vienna *Krankencasse* shows both the morbidity and mortality to be low.

The *manufacturers of metal, ivory, porcelain and other buttons* are liable to a very considerable mortality at Paris. Many of the workmen, especially those who make mother-of-pearl buttons, inhale a hard dust. England and Switzerland have no figures concerning this industry.

Hatters in England have a very high mortality, especially after the 25th year. In certain specialities they are compelled to work in an over-heated atmosphere, but their high mortality is attributed more especially to intemperance and diseases of the liver and nervous system. At Paris on the other hand, *hatters* have a mortality decidedly below the average.[13] In the Italian table, *hatters, umbrella - makers* and *chair - makers* are grouped together; their morbidity seems slightly higher than the average.

Industries concerning Animals (*Cowkeepers, Butchers, Tanners, Curriers, Bootmakers, Saddlers, Persons engaged in the*

---

[13] As has been done wherever possible, the manufacturers and merchants have been added together, because they can scarcely be distinguished in practice; both call themselves *hatters*. According to the census, the manufacturers in Paris are twice as numerous as the merchants.

horsehair, brush and comb trades, Barbers, &c.).—*Butchers* in England have a low mortality up to the age of 25 years, because the most vigorous are chosen, for strength is necessary in order to kill an ox, cut it up rapidly, or carry great quarters of meat at the end of a pole. But the trade appears very unhealthy, since from 25 to 35 years, the mortality of these strong men is already above the average, and it remains so at all the succeeding ages. Phthisis is common among them, but intemperance, and diseases resulting therefrom, are the principal causes of the high mortality among English butchers. Suicide is frequent. Similarly, in Switzerland the death-rate is low until the age of 30 years, after which it is always in excess of the mean. At all ages (except below 20) phthisis is double the average. On the other hand the mortality of Parisian butchers is about the average.

Tanners, curriers, &c., in England show a low mortality up till 35 years of age, then reach the average, and afterwards surpass it the more as age advances. Their mortality is, according to the Parisian tables, moderate at all times. English *saddlers* have a higher mortality than tanners and curriers, though the mortality of both in 1880-82 is less than it was ten years earlier.

Bootmakers and *cobblers* in England enjoy an excellent health, which contrasts strongly with that of the tailors in this country. Phthisis is above the average, and suicide is frequent, though alcoholism is not so. Lung diseases are much below the average. It is the same in Switzerland where the mortality among boot-makers does not surpass the average until after 50, and then only slightly. Their tendency to phthisis also is above the average to any extent only after 50. At Paris their death-rate is above the mean at all ages, especially after 50. In Italy the morbidity of "*cobblers, tanners, saddlers,* and *glove makers,*" is about the average.

Industries concerned with *hair* and *esparto* ("*poils et crins, sparterie*") are subjected, according to the Parisian returns, to a frightful mortality, especially before 30; but the small number of observations, and the paradoxical mortality which results from them, preclude our giving the figures. *Brush and comb makers* are subjected to a mortality almost as high.

Barbers and *wig makers* in England show a very high death-rate at all ages. From an investigation (judged insufficient, however) this would be due more especially to phthisis and the consequences of intemperance. Dr. Ogle remarks that hair-dressers live in a confined atmosphere charged with dust and particles of hair (compare the mortality of brush-makers). At Paris the mortality is lower; it hovers about the mean without going much beyond it.

Industries connected with Vegetable Products (*Millers,*

Bakers). — *Millers* in England have a rather low mortality up to the age of 45 years, and a rather high one afterwards; the same occurs in Switzerland, the increase there taking place about 40. Phthisis is rare among them, as amongst other country-folk, up to 30, average from 30 to 40, then fairly frequent. The Italian tables attribute to the millers, &c. ("*mugnai, brillatori, pastari*"), a low morbidity up to 45, and a high one from 45 to 50. *Bakers* in England and Switzerland present analogous characteristics, though less pronounced than among the millers. In the first-named country, the death-rate is low until 35, average from 35 to 45, and high afterwards. The great cause of death among them is alcoholism and its consequences (diseases of the liver and nervous system, and above all suicide). Phthisis and chest diseases are not above the average. In Switzerland the mortality is slightly under the mean up to 30, then a little above, and very high after 60. Similarly phthisis is of average occurrence up to 40, fairly common up to 60 and exceptionally common after this age. Likewise at Paris, their mortality is average up to 40, and becomes high after 50, and still more so after 60. The sickness of *bakers* in Italy is included with that of *persons exposed to the heat of furnaces* (*smelters, lime burners, &c.*) : this is high.

Chemical Industries (*Manufacture of chemical products dyes colours, Dyeing bleaching and printing of textiles, Candle and soap factories, Glue making, Sugar refining, Paper factories, Binding*).—Dr. Farr finds that the *manufacturers of chemical products, dyes*, and *colours* are subject at all ages to a comparatively high mortality, and Dr. Ogle finds a similar result for *dyers, bleachers*, and *printers of textile fabrics*, especially after 45. *Makers of candles* and *soap* are above the average after 45; *glue* and *manure makers* are even worse off. In Switzerland, on the other hand, the mortality of those under the heading " *Chemical products* " is about the ordinary—rather under than over, in fact. Phthisis is exactly average. At Paris the manufacturers of chemical products—" *bone black, varnish, blacking, gum, madder, colours, oils, soap, oilcloth,* " *india-rubber, &c., &c.*," have an average mortality. *Sugar refiners* (at Paris) have an almost exactly average mortality. In England *paper manufacturers* enjoy a most satisfactory state of health at all ages. Their mortality is still smaller (more particularly under 45) according to Dr. Ogle. The only unhealthy operation in this manufacture is the clipping and sorting of the rags, but this is always performed by women, and I am considering only the death-rate among the men. *Bookbinders* in Paris have a mortality about the average, while in England it is higher than even that of printers; it exhibits, however, a tendency to diminish. The causes of death are not known.

Industries exposing the Workman to Lead-poisoning

(*Glass and earthenware manufacturers, Plumbers, Painters, Printers*).—Of the *file-cutters*—the most exposed of all to lead-poisoning—we have spoken above. (See *Metallic Industries*, p. 571.)

The mortality of *glass makers* is very high at all ages in England after the twenty-fifth year; it is low before this. It is the same with potters, except that their death-rate begins to rise only after the thirty-fifth year. "It is one of the most unhealthy occupations," says Dr. Farr, with figures to confirm his statement. Phthisis and other diseases of the respiratory system are the principal causes of this great mortality. The sanitary conditions under which the potters live vary greatly according to the special nature of the work which they perform. Generally speaking, their high mortality is to be attributed to the fine and very irritating dust which engenders "potter's asthma," *i.e.*, the chronic bronchitis accompanying emphysema, and which may indirectly develop organic diseases of the heart. The abrupt variations of temperature also help to develop affections of the respiratory organs. Deaths from alcoholism are of average occurrence, and those from liver diseases are a little over the average. Dr. Greenhow declares that potters frequently indulge in intemperance, but less than formerly. Saturnism affects the men addicted to a certain branch of this industry, viz., *dipping*. Still, diseases of the nervous system and of the kidneys are not much above the average.

Plumbers, painters of buildings, glaziers have in England good health while young, but their mortality surpasses the average more and more as they get older. From 45 to 55 years of age it is one of the most unhealthy trades in the kingdom. Their mortality, has, however, considerably diminished during the interval which elapsed between the observations of Dr. Farr and those of Dr. Ogle. Phthisis and other diseases of the respiratory organs are not more usual than with the population as a whole. But lead-poisoning, diseases of the nervous system, gout, diseases of the urinary system are extremely frequent. Here, as among the file-makers and potters, we find saturnism accompanied by a great frequency of renal diseases. Alcoholism is common among painters, plumbers, and glaziers; with this are developed liver diseases. Disorders of the circulatory system are often found; and accidents (falls) are almost twice as numerous as amongst masons. At Paris the condition of the painters and glaziers is no better. After the age of 20—29 they are subject to a high death-rate, which increases with age. The "*plumbers, plasterers,* and *floor joiners*" are, at Paris, separately considered; they have also a very high death-rate.

Printers in England, Switzerland and Paris have a considerable mortality at every age. Swiss statistics show that phthisis is twice as common among them as among ordinary persons, at each age. English figures confirm this result, and show us also that this is the sole disease to which their high rate is to be attributed. Doubtless cases of lead-poisoning occur among them, but their number is almost insignificant.[14] Besides, diseases of the nervous system and of the kidneys (which we have seen are constantly met with among painters and those engaged in the other trades exposed to saturnism) are rare among printers, as are also alcoholism, and diseases of the circulatory system and of the liver. Dr. Ogle attributes their high death-rate from phthisis to the confined atmosphere, generally charged with bad smells and dust (metallic, and especially greasy ink which has dried), in which the employment is carried on. The trade is subjected in England to a certain amount of supervision, but it is questionable whether the diminution (which is real, though the mortality is still very high) is due to this inspection.

Transport Industries (*Bargemen, Fishermen, Coachmen, Waggoners, Railway men, Porters, Post and Telegraph employés*).— The health of fishermen, judging by the English figures, is good. Of all the occupations after that of miners, it is the one in which violent deaths occur oftenest. Naturally, drowning claims the greatest number of victims. Phthisis and other diseases of the respiratory organs are only half the average. Alcoholism is infrequent. Diseases of the urinary system are remarkably rare, but the diseases of the circulatory system are frequent, a fact which Dr. Ogle attributes to the violent emotions to which so dangerous an occupation must give rise; it would doubtless be preferable to attribute them to the rheumatism, which the fact of their being constantly wetted and numbed for days together must engender; but the returns do not give any details on the frequency of rheumatism among fishermen.

English *bargemen* seem to have a high mortality—which is also the case with Parisian *watermen* and also with those whose duty it is to keep in repair and look after the canals at Paris; but the figures for this town are not sufficient to justify any very certain conclusions.

Coachmen, waggoners, draymen are subject to a very high mortality to which it may be well to devote a little attention. In England *coachmen, cabmen* (not domestics) are distinguished from *carmen, carriers, carters, draymen*. In both the death-rate is so high, that the occupation may be considered one of the most unhealthy in the country. Of the two that of the coachmen is the

---

[14] I have been told that the type metal used in England is made of a harder substance than on the continent, and that it contains less lead.

worst (the domestic coachman is excluded, for he enjoys very good health), probably because he is obliged to remain on his seat in all weathers and seasons, while the waggoner can walk by his horses and thus keep himself warm.   At Paris, similar results are found. Either occupation has a great mortality, but the cabmen are worse off than the carmen and draymen, whose rate even becomes normal after 50.   The English statistics teach us the causes of death among this class.   Their digestive organs are in good condition, but all the other organs are constantly attacked.   As might be expected, the respiratory organs are most often diseased.   Phthisis is very common; alcoholism is enormously developed, and in its train follow diseases of the liver, urinary organs, nervous and circulatory systems.   Gout is very frequent, and deaths from accidents exceed the average.   In Switzerland "*carting and* "*driving*" give rise to a mortality almost double the average. Phthisis is not the principal factor, for up to 30 years of age it is unusual rather than otherwise among the Swiss coachmen and waggoners; above this age it is over the average, but without reaching anything like the high level we found among stone-masons, locksmiths, and watchmakers, for example.   Although the occupation of coachmen is evidently unhealthy (and it should be noted that a man must be strong and muscular to harness and groom horses, and that selection would tend to diminish the mortality peculiar to this profession), the Italian sickness tables assign to them but few days of illness while they are young.   It is only after 45 that their morbidity is above the average to any great extent.   The English consider "*horsekeepers, grooms, jockeys*" separately; their death-rate is identically the same as that of the coachmen, *i.e.*, is very high.

Railway engine drivers, officers, servants, &c., have in England a very great mortality.   According to the Swiss figures their mortality is rather high only before the age of 30 years, after which it is slight: they have very little tendency to phthisis.

English *messengers, porters*, and *errand boys* have a high death-rate, which again is a little exceeded by that of *dock labourers*. As Dr. Ogle truly remarks, it by no means follows that it is unhealthy to carry loads and run errands.   It results simply from the fact that these employments, needing no apprenticeship, are the refuge of all bad workmen, and those who have fallen from a higher station.   The Italian tables confound "*facchini*" with *bargemen* and *sawyers* under the same heading: they appear to suffer from a large amount of sickness at every age.

Postal and telegraph employés in Switzerland have a mortality corresponding fairly to the mean, at Paris their mortality is rather below the mean.

Commerce of alimentation (*Brewers, Maltsters, Hotel Keepers, Wine Merchants, Innkeepers, Hotel Waiters, Poulterers, Fishmongers, Fruiterers, Confectioners, Ice Makers*).—*Brewers* at Paris, as in England, have a high mortality at all ages. In England, phthisis and the other diseases of the respiratory system constantly occur among them, but the main cause of death is alcoholism and those diseases of the liver and nervous system which result from it. *Maltsters* have on the other hand a low death-rate.

Hotel keepers, innkeepers, wine merchants have in Switzerland a very high rate between the ages of 30 and 60 (especially from phthisis). Under 30, it is average. Paris shows similar results. In England their mortality surpasses that of all the other occupations. Dr. Ogle remarks that his results agree with those of the actuary John Scott, which are based on the experiences of the *Scottish Amicable Life Assurance Society* (1826-76). Naturally, alcohol is the cause of the evil : liver disorders are more common among the innkeepers than is phthisis among the population as a whole. Diseases of the urinary organs and nervous system, gout, and suicide are much in excess of the average. Diseases of the digestive system reach, but do not surpass the average.

Fruiterers (*butter, eggs, milk, cheese, fish, fowl, fruit,* and *vegetable* merchants) have in Paris an extremely low mortality. In England, on the contrary, it is above the average. English tables distinguish *poulterers*, whose mortality is truly enormous, from *fishmongers*, who are scarcely better off.

Grocers in England and Paris have a very low mortality. Phthisis and diseases of the respiratory, circulatory, and nervous systems are unusual, but alcoholism and renal diseases are common in England, and suicide is not rare.

Confectioners, &c., have in Paris a rather high mortality at all ages.

Tobacconists (workmen, and especially vendors) have in England between 20 and 45 years a fairly high death-rate, which afterwards becomes an average one. It is rather lower in Dr. Ogle's table.

Other Commercial Professions (*Bankers, Merchants, and Shopkeepers*).—These occupations are, as we have already pointed out, not clearly defined, owing to the lack of precision in indicating the profession of most commercial men. In the Swiss statistics there is the general heading : "*Commerce properly so-called,* "*bankers' agencies;*" the mortality of this occupation is at all ages slightly higher than the average, phthisis being fairly common. In England the mortality amongst "*commercial clerks and insurance* "*service*" is high at all ages. That of *commercial travellers* is also high, but less than the preceding. Alcoholism is often met

with among English commercial travellers, and consequently
diseases of the liver and of the nervous system, as well as suicide,
are common; gout is fairly frequent; phthisis only slightly
exceeds the average; diseases of the circulatory, respiratory and
digestive organs are comparatively few in number. At Paris,
the mortality of *merchants and employés* (bank, insurance and
general) is, as in England and Switzerland, decidedly above the
average; the same holds good among the employés in the "*lace*
"*and linen-drapers'*" (*nouveautés*) trades. Although the agreement among these different results is worth noting, I have to
confess, for the reasons stated above, that I have not much faith
in them.

The English statistics distinguish eleven varieties of shopkeepers (excluding the spirit merchants, who are not considered
in this category). Generally speaking their health is satisfactory,
but there are considerable differences between each class of shop-
men. The most healthy are the *coal merchants* and *grocers*, whose
rate is very low. Then follow *stationers, drapers, ironmongers*
(who approach the average), *tobacconists, buttermen, druggists* and
fruiterers, who exceed the mean. The causes of death are given in
two cases, for the grocers whose health is satisfactory, and for the
drapers who are more liable to disease (see above the results for
the Paris "*marchands de nouveautés*"). The inferior health of
English drapers is solely due to their tendency to consumption
and other diseases of the respiratory system. For all other
diseases their figures are about the same as those of the grocers,
or even below them, for the latter show an inclination to drink,
and consequently diseases of the liver and kidneys are of more
frequent occurrence.

Professional men (*Clergy, Lawyers, &c., Doctors, Chemists,
Schoolmasters, Musicians, Engineers, Architects*).—The health of the
English *clergy* is most satisfactory; of all professions it is the
one in which the death-rate is lowest. The regularity, certainty
and fairly active life of the profession, doubtless explains this
privileged existence. Although very low according to Dr. Farr,
Dr. Ogle finds the death-rate to be lower still in 1880-82.
English *Catholic priests* have also a low mortality, though higher
than that of the Anglican clergymen. In old age, in fact, their
mortality exceeds the average. Although Parisian statistics are
scarcely sufficient, it should be noted that they completely bear
out the preceding conclusions. The mortality of the Catholic
priests (I am including the secular with the regular clergy, as
their mortality appears practically identical) is very low until the
fiftieth year, after which it attains and even surpasses the mean.
Dr. Farr attributes the higher rate among the Catholics to their

celibacy. In Switzerland, the mortality of the clergy (Protestant and Catholic) is equally small.

The English make a distinction between *barristers*, whose mortality is among the lowest, and *solicitors and attorneys* who, far more numerous than the former, have an average death-rate. From the figures collected at Paris the mortality of barristers (*avocats*) is rather below the mean. That of *public officers and their clerks* is rather above. These results, though they agree with the English, I do not accept with all confidence. *Magistrates* at Paris have a very low mortality, but here again the calculations are based upon too few figures to be accepted without hesitation, although the result is only what we should expect. *Law clerks* in England show a high mortality, and the same may be said of Parisian "*clercs d'officiers ministériels.*"

Doctors and surgeons in England have a very high death-rate at all ages (equal to that of quarrymen), which is not surprising when we consider the insalubrity of their profession. Switzerland shows the same result. Phthisis is however not much more common among them than among the whole population. If, however, they do not profit by their own knowledge of hygiene, their children do, for in no profession (except the schoolmaster's) is the mortality of children under one year so low. At Paris the mortality of doctors is, on the contrary, very low. This result is not so contradictory as might at first sight appear, for the majority of English, and especially Swiss, doctors are naturally country practitioners, obliged to go long distances in the most severe weather, in small open carriages, which they generally drive themselves; it is therefore not surprising that their mortality is high; we have already seen what it is in the case of coachmen. The Paris doctors lead quite a different life, and are much less exposed to the severity of the weather.

English *chemists* and *druggists* had, according to Dr. Farr, a death-rate almost as high as the doctors. Since then, though bad, their health has improved. At Paris *chemists and herborists* seem to have a still lower death-rate than the doctors.

Schoolmasters, &c., have a fairly satisfactory health in England. In Dr. Farr's time it was not so good: low up to 55 years, and above the average afterwards. Precisely the same thing occurs in Switzerland for the *teachers*, their rate, low up till 60, becoming considerable afterwards. Phthisis is average, while their children have an extremely low mortality. The Paris statistics distinguish between *teachers* and "*professors attached to public schools;*" their mortality is one of the lowest at all ages, while that of the *professors of special subjects* (music, dancing, fencing, &c.) is considerable. It is possible that many persons who follow no very

definite occupation return themselves as professors without sufficient right to the title. For the same reason in England the
musicians and music masters have a frightful mortality. The
exercise of this agreeable occupation has however nothing dangerous about it, but music is one of those occupations which serve as
a refuge for the destitute. The English statistics include in this
class even the organ-grinders.

Civil engineers in England have a low mortality up to 45,
becoming average afterwards.

Parisian *architects* have a very low mortality until the fortieth
year, but average afterwards. The English returns group
these under the same heading with *sculptors, engravers and other
artists*. The mortality of this group is very great, but the classification is too vague for us to place very much reliance upon the
result.

CONCLUSION.

In the course of this investigation, I have been obliged to adopt
the order followed in the different nomenclatures of professions as
they appear in the various returns. My conclusions will be more
easily formulated, and will be of a more general character, if I
now exhibit the results in an order more in accordance with
hygienic views. The different occupations considered from the
point of view of their healthiness, may be classified as follows:—[16]

(1.) **Sedentary occupations exposing the person to the
weather.**—Such are especially the occupations of *coachmen*, and
to a less degree, of *waggoners*. We have seen that these are the
most unhealthy occupations.

(2.) **Occupations, not necessarily sedentary, exposing
the person to the weather.**—As the former are dangerous, so
are these generally salubrious; such are the occupations of *farmers,
nursery and market gardeners, gamekeepers, &c.* *Fishermen* and
bargemen, from some points of view, may be included in this
class.

---

[16] Dr. Ogle, before the Congress of Hygiene and Demography held last year in
London, admitted the following seven categories: (1) Labour performed in a
cramped position, and especially such as resists the action of the organs of the
thorax; (2) Overworking, and especially as regards muscular effort, and sudden
movements; (3) Industries in which the workman is exposed to the action of
hurtful substances such as lead, phosphorus, mercury, soiled objects, &c.; (4)
Labour performed in badly ventilated and over heated localities; (5) Temptation
to alcoholic excess; (6) Liability to accidents; (7) Inhalation of dust of every sort.
This division does not differ essentially from my own. Professor Proust *(Traité
d'hygiène)* classifies occupations according to the nature of the pathological
accidents to which they are liable. Although such a classification is very logical,
especially from the medical point of view, I have not been able to follow it here, as
I am considering particularly the noxiousness of each occupation.

(3.) **Out-of-door occupations exposing the workman to inhale hard particles of dust.**—Such is the calling of *stone-masons, marble-cutters, quarrymen,* &c., whose mortality is very high. *Masons, tilers,* and *slaters,* who come to a certain extent in this category, have a rather lower mortality.

(4.) **Occupations exposing the workman to inhale hard particles of dust in a confined atmosphere.**—These cause a mortality at the least as high as the last, whatever be the nature of the dust; be it metallic (*machines and tools, locksmiths, armourers, mathematical and surgical instruments, cutlers, needle-makers,* &c.), stony (*potters,* &c.), or of animal origin (*brush-makers, hairdressers,* &c.).

(5.) **Occupations exposing the workman to inhale soft dust.**—Generally less unhealthy than the preceding (*millers, bakers, spinners, sweeps, &c.*).

(6.) **Occupations exposing the workman to excessive heat, smoke, steam, &c.**—*Blacksmiths* enjoy good health at Paris, less so in England, still less so in Switzerland. *Mechanicians* show an average mortality. *Bakers* without doubt owe their high mortality to the dust they inhale, *glass-makers* and *cutters* to the substance they work in.

(7.) **Occupations exposing the workman to absorb hurtful substances.**—Such are those which engender lead-poisoning (they are, classified according to the frequency of the occurrence of poisoning: *file-cutters, painters, potters, plumbers, printers, &c.*), or in which there is danger of the absorption of phosphorus, mercury, and other mineral poisons, or vegetable poisons (*tobacconists*), or those which bring the workmen into contact with decayed matter (*butchers, tanners, &c.*). The mortality in all these trades is generally high.

(8.) **Occupations exposing the person to the enticements of alcohol.**—In the first place among these must be reckoned *innkeepers* and *wine merchants,* whose mortality at Paris appears less than in Switzerland and England. English *brewers* have a lower rate.

(9.) **Occupations exposing the workman to numerous accidents.**—*Coal* and *ironstone miners* would have an extremely low mortality were it not for the accidents which decimate them, so would also *fishermen.* *Cornish miners* and *quarrymen* are much exposed to accidents, but other causes help greatly to give them their high mortality.

(10.) **Sedentary Occupations.**—Some of these are highly favoured, others are very unhealthy. The sanitary condition of many of them appears to depend on the fact that they are carried on in a confined atmosphere; it also depends on the fact that many of those following these occupations are recruited from amongst the most feeble of the population. Among the sedentary occupations with a low mortality must be mentioned *fruiterers, grocers, &c.;* on the other hand, *linendrapers, fishmongers, &c.,* have an average mortality, while *tailors* have a high one, though this appears to be less than that of *cobblers, watch-makers, engravers, &c.* *Bankers, money changers,* and their clerks, have a mortality exceeding the mean according to the tables, but, as I remarked above, I only accept these figures with due reservation.

(11.) **Professional Class.**—Generally these professions presuppose a certain amount of means; and they are consequently all subjected to but a slight mortality. *Clergymen, magistrates, public schoolmasters,* have a very low death-rate. *Lawyers, public officers,* and their clerks, *architects* and *engineers* are also below the average. *Doctors* in Paris have a low rate of mortality, and a high one in England and Switzerland.

The mortality table according to occupation, which I have calculated for Paris, and which is the first which has been drawn up in France, can only be accepted with caution, being subjected, like all other tables of mortality, to several causes of error. This table confirms in almost every particular the results obtained in England and Switzerland, which, as well as the Italian morbidity tables, are added for comparison.

TABLE III.—**England and Wales.**—*Death-Rates of Males, 25—65 Years of Age, different Occupations, in 1860-1-71 and 1880-82, and their comparative Mortality Figur in 1880-82.*

Reference Number.	Occupation.	Mea per				
		1860-71.				
		Years of Age.				
		25—45.	45—65.	25—45.	45—65	
	All males	11·27	23·98	10·16	25·27	1,000
	Occupied males	—	—	9·71	24·63	967
	Unoccupied males	—	—	32·43	36·20	2,182
	*Males in selected healthy districts	—	—	8·47	19·74	804
1	Clergyman, priest, minister	5·96	17·31	4·64	15·93	556
2	Barrister, solicitor	9·87	22·97	7·54	23·13	842
3	Physician, surgeon, general practitioner	13·81	24·55	11·57	28·03	1,122
4	Schoolmaster, teacher	9·82	23·56	6·41	19·84	719
5	Artist, engraver, sculptor, architect	11·73	22·91	8·39	25·07	921
6	Musician, music master	18·94	34·76	13·78	32·39	1,314
7	Farmer, grazier	7·66	17·32	6·09	16·53	631
8†	Labourer in agricultural counties	—		7·13	17·68	701
9	Gardener, nurseryman	6·74	17·54	5·52	16·19	599
10	Fisherman	11·26	15·84	8·32	19·74	797
11	Cab, omnibus service	15·94	35·28	15·39	36·83	1,482
12	Bargeman, lighterman, waterman	14·99	30·78	14·25	31·13	1,305
13	Carter, carrier, haulier	—	—	12·52	33·00	1,275
14	Groom, domestic coachman	—	—	8·53	23·28	887
15	Commercial traveller	12·28	29·00	9·04	25·03	948
16	Brewer	19·26	36·86	13·90	34·25	1,361
17	Innkeeper, publican, spirit, wine, beer dealer	18·01	34·14	18·02	33·68	1,521
18	Inn, hotel servant	21·91	42·19	22·63	55·30	2,205
19	Maltster	7·04	22·26	7·28	23·11	830
20	Law clerk	18·75	37·05	10·77	30·79	1,151
21	Commercial clerk and insurance service	14·28	28·88	10·48	24·49	996
22	Bookseller, stationer	10·84	21·36	8·53	20·57	825
23	Chemist, druggist	13·92	23·56	10·58	25·16	1,015
24	Tobacconist	13·19	21·76	11·14	23·46	1,000
25	Grocer	9·49	17·15	8·00	19·16	771
26	Draper and Manchester warehouseman	14·34	26·33	9·70	20·96	883
27	Ironmonger	10·38	22·95	8·42	23·87	895
28	Coal merchant	8·83	22·59	6·90	20·62	758
29	General shopkeeper	—	—	9·12	21·23	865
30	Cheesemonger, milkman, butterman	—	—	9·48	26·90	1,009
31	Greengrocer, fruiterer	11·41	24·51	10·04	26·57	1,025
32	Fishmonger, poulterer	15·62	29·21	10·53	23·45	974
33	Shopkeepers, as represented by above eleven (22—32)	—	—	9·04	21·90	877
34	Butcher	13·19	28·37	12·16	29·08	1,170

* The selected healthy districts are all those registration districts in which the mean ann death-rate for persons (males and females together) was under 17·00 per 1000 in 1871-80.

† 8. Labourer in ten agricultural districts, viz., Hertfordshire, Oxon, Bedfordshire, Cambrid shire, Suffolk, Wilts, Dorset, Devon, Herefordshire, Lincolnshire.

III.—**England and Wales.**—*Death-Rates of Males,* 25—65 *Years of Age*—*Contd.*

Occupation.	Mean Annual Death Rates per Thousand Living.				Comparative Mortality Figure, 1880-82.
	1860-71.		1880-82.		
	Years of Age.				
	25—45.	45—65.	25—45.	45—65.	25—65.
Baker, confectioner	10·72	26·39	8·70	26·12	958
Corn miller	9·32	26·65	8·40	26·62	957
Hatter	12·81	31·76	10·78	26·95	1,064
Hairdresser	15·11	30·10	13·64	33·25	1,327
Tailor	12·92	24·79	10·78	26·47	1,051
Shoemaker	10·39	22·30	9·31	23·36	921
Tanner, fellmonger	10·43	26·57	7·97	25·37	911
Currier	11·32	25·09	8·56	24·07	906
Saddler, harness maker	12·29	25·21	9·19	26·49	987
Tallow chandler, soap boiler	11·75	27·24	7·74	26·19*	920
Tallow, soap, glue, manure manufacturer	—	—	7·31	27·57	933
Printer	13·02	29·38	11·12	26·60	1,071
Bookbinder	12·76	31·56	11·78	29·72*	1,167
Watch and clock maker	10·78	24·90	9·26	22·64	903
Watch, clock, philosophical instrument maker, and jeweller	—	—	9·22	23·99	932
Paper manufacture	10·33	20·19	6·48	19·62	717
Glass manufacture	13·19	29·32	11·21	31·71	1,190
Earthenware manufacture	12·59	41·75	13·70	51·39	1,742
Cotton, linen manufacture (Lancashire)	10·65†	27·90†	9·99	29·44	1,068
Silk manufacture	9·89	20·08	7·81	22·79	845
Wool, worsted manufacture (West Riding)	9·35†	23·26†	9·71	27·50	1,032
Carpet, rug manufacture	9·92	25·57	9·48	24·10	945
Lace manufacture	—	—	6·78	20·71	755
Hosiery manufacture (Leicestershire, Notts)	—	—	6·69	19·22	717
Dyer, bleacher, printer, &c., of textile fabrics	11·19	25·99	9·46	27·08	1,012
Rope, twine, cord maker	9·19	29·35	7·95	22·25	839
Builder, mason, bricklayer	11·43	27·16	9·25	25·59	969
Slater, tiler	10·66	30·76	8·97	24·93‡	943
Plasterer, whitewasher	9·50	27·90	7·79	25·07	896
Plumber, painter, glazier	12·48	34·66	11·07	32·49	1,202
Upholsterer, cabinet maker, French polisher	11·09	24·09	9·55	24·77	963
Carpenter, joiner	9·44	21·36	7·77	21·74	820
Sawyer	8·67	21·27	7·46	23·74	852
Wood turner, box maker, cooper	11·80	26·13	10·56	28·55	1,091
Coach builder	10·43	29·57	9·13	24·72	944
Wheelwright	8·40	21·17	6·83	19·21	723
Shipbuilder, shipwright	10·68	26·26	6·95	21·29	775
Locksmith, bellhanger, gasfitter	11·04	27·90	9·15	25·66	967
Gunsmith	10·62	25·32	10·62	25·78	1,031
Cutler, scissors maker	—	—	12·30	34·94	1,309
File maker	16·27	42·30	15·29	45·14‡	1,667

and 47. This rate is based on less than five thousand years of life.

and 55. These figures relate to England and Wales, and not only to Lancashire and the Riding, respectively, as do the figures for 1880-82.

2 and 75. This rate is based on less than five thousand years of life.

TABLE III.—**England and Wales.**—*Death-Rates of Males, 25—65 Years of Age—*

Refer-ence Number.	Occupation.	1860-71.		1880-82.	
		Years of Age.			
		25—45.	45—65.	25—45.	45—65.
76 {	Cutler; scissors, file, needle, saw, and tool maker	11·88*	32·74*	11·71	34·42
77	Engine, machine maker, fitter, millwright ...	—	—	7·97	23·27
78	Boiler maker	—	—	9·27	26·65
79	Last two together (Nos. 77, 78)	10·61	23·81	8·23	23·89
80	Blacksmith	10·07	23·88	9·29	25·67
81	Other iron and steel workers.........	—	—	8·36	22·84
82	Tin workers	10·36	23·67	8·00	24·17
83	Copper, lead, zinc, brass, &c., workers	10·74	26·17	9·15	26·79
84	Metal workers (Nos. 72—83).........	—	—	8·80	25·03
85	Durham, Northumberland, miners.........	11·30ᵃ	22·01ᵃ	7·79	24·04
86	Lancashire　　　,,　　　.........	—	—	7·91	26·30
87	West Riding　　　,,　　　.........	—	—	6·59	21·80†
88	Derbyshire, Nottinghamshire ,,　.........	—	—	6·54	20·23
89	Staffordshire　　　,,　　　.........	11·33ᵃ	30·45ᵃ	7·81	26·50
90	South Wales, Monmouthshire ,,　.........	14·72ᵃ	29·66ᵃ	9·05	30·87
91 {	Coal miners as represented by above six (Nos. 85—90)	—	—	7·64	25·11
92 {	Miner (North Riding and other ironstone districts)	—	—	8·05	21·85
93	Miner, Cornwall	11·94ᵃ	41·73ᵃ	14·77	53·69
94	Stone, slate quarrier	10·88	28·67	9·95	31·04
95	Railway, road, clay, sand, &c., labourer	—	—	11·01	24·80
96	Coalheaver	—	—	10·22	23·77
	Chimney sweep	17·53	42·87	13·73	41·54†
	Messenger, porter, watchman (not Government)	—	—	17·07	37·37
	Costermonger, hawker, street seller	20·09	37·82	20·26	45·33
	General labourer (London)	18·35	40·64	20·62	50·85

* 76. In 1871 only.

ᵃ 85, 89, 90, and 93. These rates are based on a return made to the Commissioners appo to inquire into the condition of all miners in Great Britain, of the miners living at the cens 1861, and of the deaths registered in the three years 1860-62 in certain mining districts i respective counties.

† 97. This rate is based on less than five thousand years of life.

TABLE IV.—England and Wales.—*Comparative Mortality of M*

Occupations.	Diseases of the Nervous System.	Suicide.
All males (England and Wales)	119	14
Farmer, grazier	81	17
Labourer in ten agricultural counties	80	9
Gardener, nurseryman	63	11
Fisherman	81	13
Cab, omnibus service	134	16
Commercial traveller	139	31
Brewer	144	11
Innkeeper, publican, spirit, wine, beer dealer...........	200	26
Grocer	107	17
Draper, Manchester warehouseman	109	5
Butcher..	139	23
Baker, confectioner...................................	136	26
Tailor	144	16
Shoemaker	122	17
Printer	90	8
Earthenware manufacture............	140	†
Cotton, linen manufacture (Lancashire)	142	†
Wool manufacture (Yorkshire)	127	15
Hosiery manufacture (Leicestershire and Notting- } hamshire)... }	114	22
All males, ditto...	*100*	*17*
Builder, mason, bricklayer...............................	88	14
Plumber, painter, glazier	167	21
Carpenter, joiner.......................................	89	17
Cutler, scissors maker...................................	190	†
File maker	262	†
Blacksmith	95	11
Miner (Durham and Northumberland)	88	5
All males, ditto	*114*	*13*
Miner (Lancashire)...................................	83	†
All males, ditto...	*142*	*15*
Miner (West Riding)...................................	60	5
All males, ditto.......................................	*118*	*16*
Miner (Derbyshire and Notts)	64	5
All males, ditto.........................	*99*	*15*
Miner (Staffordshire)...................................	81	3
All males, ditto........	*117*	*13*
Miner (South Wales and Monmouthshire)...............	60	4
All males, ditto .	*97*	*8*
Miner (North Riding and other ironstone districts)	51	11
„ (Cornwall)	117	4
All males, ditto...	*99*	*13*
Stone, slate quarrier	83	11
Costermonger, hawker, street seller	207	44

* The figures in this table are the numbers of deaths that would occur annually in were over 45 years of age.

† The deaths from suicide were not separated in this case from the deaths from n

25—65 *Years of Age, in different Industries, from all and several Causes.**

		Gout.	Plumbism.	Accident.	All other Causes.	
		3	1	67	146	
		2	—	30	107	·63
		1	—	33	117	·70
		1	—	24	105	·59
		—	—	152	115	79
		11	—	84	194	1,48
		6	—	36	95	
		9	—	64	176	1,36
		13	—	45	170	1,52
		2	—	14	100	·77
129	37	2	—	23	121	;88
208	55	5	—	35	160	r,17
186	40	2	—	21	117	·95
186	45	4	—	18	125	1,05
157	44	1	—	17	129	92
166	30	—	5	24	131	
645	49	—	10	24	150	
271	32	—	—	30	151	
205	36	—	—	27	143	
115	42	—	—	16	96	
141	*37*	*1*	—	*51*	*141*	
201	49	3	—	45	134	
185	100	10	21	73	141	
133	39	2	—	38	124	
389	35	—	—	17	132	
350	123	—	41	6	196	
204	44	—	—	49	159	
122	26	—	—	196	125	
155	*30*	—	—	*98*	*145*	
229	24	—	—	198	121	
307	*43*	*1*	—	*82*	*172*	
172	23	—	—	161	99	
213	*36*	*1*	—	*63*	*140*	
138	18	—	—	163	114	
148	*30*	*1*	—	*66*	*135*	
260	38	—	—	172	120	
226	*37*	*2*	—	*75*	*153*	
293	34	—	—	229	111	
209	*39*	*1*	—	*123*	*130*	
·206	23	—	—	206	96	
458	38	—	—	117	206	
165	*29*	*1*	—	*59*	*162*	
274	24	—	—	148	115	
420	69	3	—	53	249	

industry out of 64,641 males, from 25—65 years of age, of whom 41,920 were under and 22,

diseases.

TABLE V.—**Paris.**—*Number of Deaths per Thousand per Annum at each Age, according to Occupation (Males).*

Occupations.	20—29	30—39	40—49	50—59
Whole male population of Paris	11·1	14·9	21·2	31·2
1. Gardeners, nursery and market-gardeners	11·1	13·6	21·6	30·0
2. Various tissues, lace, muslin, haberdashery, gloves, linen	9·1	12·2	20·4	27·8
3. Manufactures of machines of all kinds, stationary and locomotive steam-engines, rails, dies, wrought iron, axles, tyres, heating and ventilating apparatus, agricultural implements, iron, cast iron or zinc portions of buildings, nails, screws, files, pins, needles, wires, &c.	12·7	16·2	21·2	36·0
4. Founders, sword cutlers, ironmongers, coppersmiths, blacksmiths, tin potters, metal turners, cutlers, &c.	9·4	11·4	15·4	22·6
5. Tanners, strap makers, leather dressers, parchment makers, &c.	9·1	10·5	15·9	26·4
6. Coopers, basket makers, trunk makers, box makers	10·9	14·3	17·7	26·1
7. Manufacturers of chemical products for the arts and medicine (acids, soda, potash, alum), bone black, varnish, glue, madder, oils, soap, starch, colours, oilcloths, india rubber, asphalt, sulphur, resin, tar; refiners	13·6	11·3	19·8	27·6
8. Locksmiths	10·9	14·2	23·8	32·9
9. Carpenters and joiners.....................	10·5	18·8	24·3	30·7
10. Masons, stonemasons, slaters	9·5	16·0	23·7	31·4
11. Marble cutters, moulders	20·1	21·2	23·4	39·0
12. Painters, glaziers, plasterers, decorators, whitewashers	14·8	23·0	28·8	42·0
13. Plumbers, floor joiners, &c..................	15·0	22·3	25·2	44·1
14. Cabinet makers, furniture makers, inlayers	9·0	13·6	16·3	24·5
15. Carpet makers, furniture, carpet, curtain, bed, furniture merchants	6·7	10·6	14·5	22·7
16. Hat and cap makers, straw hat makers, hatters	5·9	8·3	15·9	23·6
17. Tailors, ready-made clothiers.................	9·1	11·3	23·4	39·8
18. Boot and shoe makers	13·4	19·2	20·4	35·3
19. Barbers, hairdressers, wig makers	14·8	14·2	18·1	33·2
20. Sugar refiners	7·1	13·7	18·4	24·6
21. Bakers	12·4	16·2	24·4	39·0
22. Butchers (vendors), pork butchers	10·6	14·0	22·2	27·5
23. Butter, egg, milk, cheese, fish, fowl, fruit and vegetable merchants	5·7	9·9	11·8	17·4
24. Grocers	6·6	7·0	8·7	11·4
25. Confectioners, ice merchants, chocolate merchants..............................	15·0	16·5	20·4	25·0
26. Wine and spirit merchants, restaurant keepers, hotel keepers.....................	12·0	21·2	25·7	30·2
27. Carriage builders, wheelwrights, saddlers, harness makers, farriers....	15·9	20·1	25·9	43·8
28. Printers, lithographers, copper engravers, stereotypers	17·8	23·7	26·7	40·6

TABLE V.—Paris.—*Number of Deaths per Thousand per Annum—Contd.*

Occupations.	20—29	30—39	40—49	50—59
Whole male population of Paris	11·1	14·9	21·2	31·2
29. Binders	11·9	14·1	13·2	27·4
30. Jewellers, goldsmiths, lapidaries, enamellers, watchmakers (makers and vendors), gold beaters, wood and metal silverers and gilders, bronze makers, metal chisellers	9·7	14·0	14·9	24·7
31. Waggoners, carters	17·6	21·5	26·7	30·4
32. Directors and administrators, agents, employés of public carriage companies (coaches, omnibuses, cabs, furniture vans), cab proprietors	16·4	20·5	32·0	58·0
33. Postal and telegraph employés	5·7	7·8	10·5	19·3
34. Directors, clerks, agents, &c., of joint-stock banking companies (*Banque de France, Comptoir d'escompte, Crédit foncier, &c.*), of insurance companies, bankers, changers, brokers, auctioneers, agents; merchants and employés without other description	17·5	20·3	28·1	30·7
35. Linen drapers (*commerce de nouveautés*), hosiers	14·8	25·5	40·4	49·4
36. Secular clergy (bishops, canons, priests, curates, chaplains), regular clergy (belonging to religious orders or societies)	5·0	8·2	9·0	30·5
37. Barristers or solicitors of the Court of Commerce	9·8	11·6	11·1	22·8
38. Public officers (attorneys, notaries, ushers, and their clerks)....................	10·3	15·8	22·4	42·2
39. Doctors and surgeons	9·9	11·3	9·8	21·9
40. Chemists and druggists	7·8	9·2	11·1	15·7
41. Directors, professors, masters, bursars, &c., of State, departmental, municipal, or communal schools, &c.	7·0	8·5	5·8	17·0
42. Special professors (music, dancing, drawing, fencing, &c.)....................	19·4	11·8	17·0	55·8
43. Architects	8·6	5·2	17·0	25·8

TABLE VI.—**Switzerland.**—*Mortality according to Occupation* (1879-82). *Number of Deaths from all Causes, per Thousand Living at each Age, per Annum.*

Occupations.	0—1.*	15—19.	20—29.	30—39.	40—49.	50—59.	60—69.	70—79.
1. Mines, turf pits, quarries, and salt mines	—	5·29	7·49	10·42	22·75	31·35	75·56	118·85
2. Agriculture, horticulture, &c.	163·8	3·30	5·71	7·89	12·05	21·66	45·73	112·37
3. Silviculture	—	4·48	5·25	8·74	12·06	21·51	47·51	84·36
4. Hunting and fishing	—	10·75	13·02	8·54	8·26	27·32	67·52	141·51
5. Alimentation (generally)	—	3·68	6·84	12·50	16·98	30·40	64·64	178·65
6. „ millers	—	2·06	6·70	8·39	17·12	33·22	66·86	194·67
7. „ bakers	—	4·15	6·83	11·44	15·92	28·85	72·96	215·16
8. „ butchers and porkbutchers	—	3·18	5·27	17·85	21·45	29·90	64·63	152·10
9. Clothing	—	4·20	8·64	11·26	16·24	29·78	63·82	147·53
10. „ tailors	—	6·14	10·63	11·88	17·86	29·96	60·38	139·76
11. „ bootmakers	—	3·66	7·70	10·01	14·21	29·99	67·24	155·55
12. Construction and furnishing of buildings	177·5	6·00	8·88	12·82	18·38	33·93	64·40	142·29
13. „ stonemasons	—	6·10	8·48	18·14	26·42	45·28	89·56	176·00
14. „ masons and plasterers	—	8·14	9·53	13·12	18·98	34·87	67·40	140·47
15. „ carpenters	—	6·31	6·54	10·14	16·75	30·70	66·34	160·05
16. „ joiners and glaziers	—	5·74	8·24	11·96	15·39	31·60	56·64	135·02
17. „ locksmiths	—	8·78	12·41	15·97	29·68	40·28	69·50	165·76
18. „ coopers	—	2·49	11·27	20·29	22·70	38·92	67·62	122·38
19. Printing	173·8	4·66	10·21	14·33	16·22	26·96	59·86	171·05
20. Textile industries	224·3	4·60	6·20	6·97	12·01	25·79	58·21	134·39
21. „ silk	—	5·76	6·06	6·30	9·87	26·37	56·36	154·93
22. „ cotton	—	4·65	8·03	9·30	13·26	24·91	54·28	119·50
23. „ linen	—	3·54	4·46	6·74	8·79	24·61	59·17	140·00
24. „ embroidery	—	3·90	5·00	5·28	11·46	19·72	44·78	130·43
25. Chemical products	210·3	3·48	5·27	7·68	11·46	25·06	51·85	157·08
26. Manufacture of machines and tools	169·7	4·35	9·23	11·56	17·43	29·54	55·48	131·53
27. „ watchmaking and watch-maker's tools	—	5·35	11·09	13·27	20·12	32·53	52·38	116·56
28. „ mechanicians	—	3·22	7·25	10·09	10·81	20·53	43·78	134·43
29. „ blacksmiths and farriers	—	2·61	6·45	11·25	16·58	32·47	63·56	174·44
30. „ carriage builders and wheelwrights	—	3·43	6·46	9·29	14·00	25·30	57·48	119·81
31. Commerce proper, banks, insurance	154·0	6·29	11·08	14·10	18·67	29·22	55·75	124·22
32. Inns and boarding houses	179·1	3·61	7·77	16·85	24·17	32·76	47·68	145·33
33. „ hotels, restaurants, &c.	179·1	3·67	7·87	17·02	24·39	33·23	48·44	149·35
34. Transport and construction of means of transport	186·4	6·00	8·80	11·24	16·30	28·24	51·41	150·00
35. „ roads and bridges	221·7	6·17	11·08	13·04	18·79	25·32	37·95	124·35
36. „ railways	182·5	6·38	8·36	8·58	11·64	19·94	36·84	131·94
37. „ postal and telegraph service	158·2	6·17	7·11	10·81	13·76	22·49	52·05	107·14
38. „ waggoners and coachmen	—	4·18	10·82	18·31	25·99	51·01	91·67	256·49
39. Public administration and justice	144·1	3·16	9·11	11·23	16·85	34·58	56·91	134·70
40. „ functionaries and public employés	—	2·76	7·30	8·92	17·90	35·49	55·31	133·06
41. Medical science	121·4	3·77	10·90	12·31	20·68	30·36	66·89	139·83
42. Religious professions and public schools	116·0	5·06	7·20	8·20	18·06	23·03	59·06	130·79
43. „ teachers	—	5·37	6·85	8·73	14·80	24·29	63·79	206·82
44. Other professional classes	—	10·06	15·04	14·64	23·39	33·99	70·88	100·61
45. Personal service	—	18·90	18·92	28·21	35·79	48·61	71·61	189·90
46. Without profession or unknown	—	19·78	33·23	42·56	39·19	45·55	56·44	88·05
Average for the whole of Switzerland	178·4	4·78	7·90	10·72	15·31	26·30	51·11	109·22

* Number of children (of fathers following the occupation stated) dying under 1 year of age per 1,000 legitimate births.

Table VII.—**Switzerland.**—*Mortality from* **Pulmonary Phthisis** *only. Number of Deaths per Thousand Living per Annum, according to Occupation and Age.*

Occupations.	15—19.	20—29.	30—39.	40—49.	50—59.	60—69.	70—79.
1. Mines, turf pits, quarries, and salt mines	—	1·86	2·26	5·40	4·50	10·49	2·96
2. Agriculture, horticulture, &c.	0·66	1·48	1·96	2·02	2·37	2·57	2·61
3. Silviculture	—	0·28	3·23	1·71	2·11	2·80	1·28
4. Hunting and fishing	2·69	1·44	2·44	1·18	4·55	9·39	—
5. Alimentation (generally)	0·92	2·72	4·78	4·21	4·75	6·23	4·80
6. „ millers	1·18	0·98	3·68	4·87	4·09	5·21	7·00
7. „ bakers	1·01	2·89	4·05	3·81	4·17	8·32	9·09
8. „ butchers and porkbutchers	0·53	5·59	6·82	5·85	6·29	6·29	—
9. Clothing	1·57	3·60	5·11	4·57	4·91	6·07	4·81
10. „ tailors	2·24	4·89	5·55	5·48	5·54	6·93	2·77
11. „ bootmakers	1·43	2·96	4·41	3·73	5·01	5·45	6·04
12. Construction and furnishing of buildings	1·56	3·61	4·78	5·04	5·66	5·75	4·65
13. „ stonemasons	1·02	3·01	8·65	9·90	12·60	14·05	19·52
14. „ masons and plasterers	1·38	2·80	3·45	4·08	5·59	5·73	4·39
15. „ carpenters	1·27	1·86	3·78	3·41	4·83	6·38	3·31
16. „ joiners and glaziers	2·20	4·67	4·68	5·55	5·92	3·75	5·20
17. „ locksmiths	3·39	5·35	7·29	10·37	11·60	7·70	3·13
18. „ coopers	—	3·32	8·68	7·09	4·55	5·25	4·06
19. Printing	2·00	6·48	7·85	6·56	6·65	7·32	—
20. Textile industries	1·61	2·72	2·66	2·89	4·25	4·80	2·49
21. „ silk	2·81	2·81	2·25	3·06	5·61	4·47	9·68
22. „ cotton	1·51	4·00	3·36	2·68	3·90	4·80	0·53
23. „ linen	1·42	1·91	2·53	1·25	3·80	4·25	2·73
24. „ embroidery	1·06	2·00	2·53	3·55	3·80	11·64	—
25. Chemical products	1·17	3·09	2·94	3·43	4·30	6·95	5·86
26. Manufacture of machines and tools	1·51	5·00	5·21	5·87	5·31	4·02	2·63
27. „ watchmaking and watchmaker's tools	2·28	6·56	6·52	7·32	5·82	3·84	2·55
28. „ mechanicians	0·36	4·50	4·78	3·75	4·02	5·23	2·48
29. „ blacksmiths and farriers	0·76	2·29	4·09	5·57	5·30	3·72	3·96
30. „ carriage builders and wheelwrights	1·14	2·25	3·34	3·19	4·60	1·90	1·33
31. Commerce proper, banks, insurance	1·80	5·75	6·55	4·78	4·42	3·79	2·75
32. Inns and boarding houses	1·21	4·38	6·79	6·04	3·88	1·89	1·08
33. „ hotels, restaurants, &c.	1·23	4·44	6·86	6·11	3·98	1·99	1·17
34. Transport and construction of means of transport	1·20	2·10	2·58	3·40	3·47	4·36	4·80
35. „ roads and bridges	0·62	3·70	2·38	3·78	3·45	4·31	2·72
36. „ railways	1·09	1·38	1·72	2·07	2·99	3·26	—
37. „ postal and telegraph service	3·08	4·08	4·09	3·52	3·04	4·48	5·08
38. „ waggoners and coachmen	0·93	2·74	4·79	5·75	4·46	4·57	14·42
39. Public administration and justice	1·73	4·92	4·77	4·32	6·47	4·01	2·83
40. „ functionaries and public employés	1·11	3·41	3·41	4·45	6·45	5·15	5·60
41. Medical science		4·81	4·67	5·28	3·22	5·01	—
42. Religious professions and public schools	2·52	3·86	3·65	3·65	3·31	4·10	1·17
43. „ teachers	2·67	3·35	3·81	4·57	3·27	6·68	5·01
44. Other professional classes	5·43	8·02	7·29	5·80	6·86	8·12	—
45. Personal service	3·07	6·39	8·96	10·30	9·31	3·00	3·72
46. Without profession or unknown	5·49	12·06	9·38	6·59	5·26	2·85	1·89
Average for the whole of Switzerland	1·26	3·06	3·97	3·54	3·66	3·48	2·60

Table VIII.—*Morbidity. Average Number of Days*

Age.	Highland Society.	London Workmen's Society.	English Friendly Societies.	English Friendly Societies (Males)		Manchester Unity of Oddfellows (Males).			Foresters (Males).
	Charles Oliphant.	J. Finlaison.	Ansell.	F. G. P. Neison, sen.	A. G. Finlaison.	H. Ratcliffe.			
Years.........	1820.	1829.	1835.	1836-40.	1846-50.	1846-48.	1856-60.	1866-70.	
20—25.......	4·0	7·0	5·5	5·99	6·90	4·74	5·80	5·28	5·73
25—30.......	4·2	7·0	5·9	6·23	6·90	5·30	5·74	5·64	5·97
30—35.......	4·6	7·0	6·4	6·42	6·80	5·86	6·01	6·50	6·78
35—40.......	5·0	8·5	7·3	7·25	7·64	6·58	7·02	7·44	8·05
40—45.......	6·0	9·5	8·8	8·92	8·59	8·26	8·68	8·82	9·62
45—50.......	8·3	9·5	10·8	11·42	10·06	10·60	10·81	11·45	11·95
50—55.......	11·4	10·5	14·0	15·26	12·48	14·20	14·10	15·55	15·85
55—60.......	14·9	13·5	19·7	21·32	15·24	22·42	21·20	21·30	22·48
60—65.......	23·0	—	31·8	33·20	21·82	35·40	32·44	33·00	32·13
65—70.......	55·6	—	62·7	70·20	32·39	45·45	50·19	50·60	55·80
70—75.......	—	—	—	115·70	53·65	85·20	84·44	84·50	84·00
Age un-} known }	—	—	—	—	—	—	—	—	—
All ages	—	—	—	13·82	10·11	6·86	9·22	10·46	9·51

Note.—Cols. 1—9. In the English returns the duration of sickness is given in weeks and fractions of weeks; it has here been reduced to days.

Cols. 1 and 3. The figures in these columns refer to the following ages: 21—25, 26—30, 31—35, &c.

Col. 5. A. G. Finlaison states that no account is taken of "chronic cases."

Cols. 10, 11, 12. These are taken from the "Statistica della morbosita," which presents them in a form somewhat different. This form again does not appear to be that of the original. It cannot therefore be guaranteed that the authors' figures are exactly reproduced.

Cols. 14, 15, 16. I am alone responsible for the figures attributed to Hubbard in Cols. 14 and 15, as I have calculated them from statistics which he has collected. Their total (Col. 16) has been published in Hubbard's book, but this is not the portion of his work which is generally reproduced. As generally quoted Hubbard's figures are intermediate between those in Cols. 14 and 15. When he wrote most mutual aid societies only granted to those with "infirmities" one-fourth of the compensation for "sickness." In taking this action they based their arguments principally upon the fact that an acute illness entirely prevents work, whereas a chronic illness or infirmity does not interfere so much with quiet sedentary occupations. Be that as it may, Hubbard, considering the question from a purely financial point of view, calculates in one of his tables four days' infirmity as equivalent to one day's sickness. This is the table usually quoted, and almost invariably without this necessary explanation.

of Sickness per Annum of Members of various Ages.

			14	15	16	17		
				French Tables.				
Leipzig Assurance against Sickness and Invalidity.	Railway Servants.	Travelling Railway Servants.	Twenty-Five Mutual French Societies (*circ.* 1835-49).			Lyons Silk-workers (Males).	163 Italian Mutual Aid Societies (Males).
Heym.	Behm.		G. Hubbard.			J. Bertillon.	Bodio.
1856-75.	1870-77.		Sickness.	Infirmity.	Total.	1872-89.	1866-75.
5·8	8·3	12·6	5·13	0·35	5·48	3·06	6·5
5·1	7·5	11·7	5·33	0·46	5·79	3·40	6·0
5·6	7·7	13·1	4·71	0·46	5·17	3·37	6·1
6·3	9·0	15·2	5·23	0·58	5·81	4·32	6·3
7·8	10·0	16·3	6·21	1·98	8·19	5·29	6·8
7·7	11·3	19·0	6·40	2·01	8·41	5·89	7·1
8·5	14·3	24·2	6·40	2·68	9·08	8·04	7·5
16·3	17·5	30·6	8·85	2·85	11·70	8·38	8·9
12·5	18·1	—	11·03	8·47	19·50	11·15	11·2
18·9	15·0	—	10·63	16·39	27·02	16·73	12·4
—	—	—	12·54	53·50	66·04	19·76	} 11·0
—	—	—	8·29	13·46	21·75	—	
—	—	—	6·21	2·49	8·70	7·80	6·9

Col. 17. These figures are calculated from the "Comptes rendus annuels de la S "ouvriers en soie de Lyon." M. Fontaine is at the present moment working out the at each year of age from these same returns.

Cols. 19 and 20. M. Bodio has applied some very ingenious corrections to Col. 1 rid of the effects of the extreme variety in the regulations adopted by the differen societies.

Besides the above tables the following particulars are found in the statistical publi the French Ministry of the Interior in 1854 and 1855 :—

Number of Days of Sickness per Annum for each Member of a Friendly Societ

	1854.	1855.
From 15 to 35 years	4·9	4·9
„ 35 „ 55 „	6·2	6·0
„ 55 „ 75 „	9·2	10·0
Above 75 years	15·8	16·5
All ages	6·1	6·1

TABLE IX.—Italy.—*Morbidity in the Mutual Aid Societies* (1866-75).

Occupations.	Average Number of Days of Sickness per Member.		
	15—30	30—45	45—60
1. Agriculturists, gardeners	7·3	9·1	10·4
2. Street porters	8·9	7·8	10·9
3. Waggoners	5·1	6·4	9·9
4. Masons	6·6	6·4	7·8
5. Armourers, nailmakers, blacksmiths ...	8·5	5·8	8·0
6. Joiners	5·3	6·6	6·5
7. Bootmakers, tanners, furriers	6·5	7·0	8·6
8. Tailors	5·5	5·3	6·1
9. Jewellers	7·0	2·5	3·7
10. Spinners, weavers	6·3	6·5	7·3
11. Barbers, hatters	5·8	5·3	6·5
12. Millers, bakers	5·5	7·8	9·2
13. Ovenmen, potters	7·0	6·7	12·0
14. Painters, dyers	6·0	6·0	5·2
15. Innkeepers, dealers in comestibles	5·7	6·0	6·7
16. Commercial men, agents	2·8	3·5	4·6
17. Domestic servants, &c.	7·4	6·6	6·7
18. Employés, proprietors	2·8	4·8	6·2

N.B.—Figures in Italics are drawn from less than 100 observations.

TABLE X.—Italy.—*Morbidity in the Mutual Aid Societies* (1881-85).

Occupations.	Average Number of Days of Sickness per Member.		
	15—30	30—45	45—60
1. Agriculturists, horticulturists	5·9	6·1	8·3
2. Labourers, miners	8·0	9·4	11·5
3. Street porters, bargemen, sawyers	6·9	9·4	9·3
4. Stonemasons, pavers	4·5	5·5	10·6
5. Coachmen, waggoners, omnibus conductors ...	4·0	6·1	8·6
6. Masons, whitewashers	4·8	6·2	8·9
7. Armourers, blacksmiths, tinkers, tinmen, farriers	6·1	6·2	8·2
8. Joiners, carriage builders, carpenters	5·6	5·8	8·0
9. Bootmakers, tanners, saddlers, glovemakers	5·7	5·6	7·4
10. Tailors	3·1	4·1	7·0
11. Typographers, lithographers	5·3	5·7	6·4
12. Jewellers, goldsmiths, watchmakers, engravers, chisellers	3·9	3·0	5·4
13. Spinners, weavers, lacemakers	5·6	7·0	7·4
14. Hat, umbrella, and chairmakers	5·3	7·1	7·1
15. Millers, pastemakers	4·1	4·5	9·2
16. Stokers, bakers, founders, ovenmen	5·3	6·3	8·1
17. Mattressmakers, grinders, charcoal burners, sweeps	6·6	7·8	8·7
18. Painters, dyers, photographers, fireworkmakers	8·1	5·5	8·0
19. Innkeepers, brewers, butchers, restaurant keepers	3·6	4·9	7·3
20. Booksellers, ironmongers, druggists, agents	3·2	4·0	4·5
21. Postmen, watchmen, domestic servants	5·1	5·6	8·5
22. Professional men, employés, priests, masters	2·9	3·6	5·0
	5·1	5·8	7·8

CENSUS of IRELAND, 1891.

[THE final returns of the Irish Census, taken under the superintendence of Dr. W. T. Grimshaw, on the night of the 5th April, 1891, have now been published, and we take the following interesting features from the report just issued.]

General Summary of Results.—*Persons.*—The population of Ireland in 1891, including the Navy and Military serving in the country, was 4,704,750 (2,318,953 males and 2,385,797 females). In 1881 it was 5,174,836 (2,533,277 males and 2,641,559 females). There was therefore in the ten years a decrease of 470,086 persons, or 9·08 per cent. (See Tables I and II, and for the density of the population Table V.)

Ages.—There is a marked diminution amounting to 15·7 per cent. of the number of children under 15 years of age in 1891 compared with 1881. There is also a decrease in the number of persons in the age-periods from 20 to 30, and from 30 to 40, amounting to 5·5 and 8·4 per cent. respectively. (See Table III.)

Conjugal Condition.—The number of married persons in 1891 was, males 613,649; females 626,031. In 1881 they were respectively 696,542 and 712,525. Widowers and widows were 91,500 and 232,004 compared with 95,860 and 253,091 respectively in 1881. The unmarried were, males 1,613,804, females 1,527,762; the corresponding figures for 1881 being 1,740,360 and 1,675,737.

Birthplaces.—In 1881 the number of Irish born persons enumerated who did not reside in the county in which they were born, amounted to 10·2 per cent. of the population. In 1891 they amounted to 10·8 per cent., or an increase of 0·6 per cent. In 1881 the number of persons born in England enumerated in Ireland amounted to 69,382; in 1891 the number was 74,523, being an increase of 5,141, or 7·4 per cent.

The number of Scotch in Ireland in 1881 was 22,328; in 1891 27,323, or an increase of 22·4 per cent. The number of persons born outside of the United Kingdom who were in Ireland on the census night in 1881, was 19,792, and in 1891 21,521, being an increase of 9·2 per cent.

Religious Professions. — Roman Catholics decreased from 3,960,891 in 1881 to 3,547,307 in 1891, or 10·4 per cent. Protestant Episcopalians decreased from 639,574 in 1881 to 600,103 in 1891, or 6·2 per cent. Presbyterians decreased 5·5 per cent., their numbers being 444,974 in 1891 as against 470,734 in 1881.

Methodists showed an increase from 48,839 in 1881 to 55,500 in 1891, or 13·6 per cent. "All other" persuasions increased from 54,798 in 1881 to 56,866 in 1891, being an increase of 3·8 per cent.

Education.—In 1891 the number of persons in Ireland 5 years old and upwards who were wholly illiterate, was 18·4 per cent. of the population; in 1881 the percentage was 25·2, showing a decrease in 1891 of 6·8 in the percentage. The number of persons aged 5 years and upwards in 1891 who could read only was 11 per cent. of the population; in 1881 the percentage was 15·5, showing a decrease in 1891 of 4·5 in the percentage.

In 1881 59·3 per cent. of the population aged 5 years and upwards were able to read and write; in 1891 the percentage was 70·6, showing an increase of 11·3 in the decade.

Schools and Scholars: Primary Schools.—In 1891 there were 9,177 establishments for primary instruction, attended by 685,074 pupils. In 1881 the number of establishments was 9,151, and the number of pupils 675,036, showing an increase of 10,038, or 1·5 per cent. In 1891 there were 490 establishments for superior instruction, with 27,769 students. In 1881 the number of *superior schools* was 504, and the number of students 24,693, showing an increase of 3,076, or 12·5 per cent in 1891.

Occupations.—The professional class in 1881 numbered 198,684, or 3·84 per cent. of the population. In 1891 it numbered 214,243, or 4·55 per cent., an increase of 0·71 per cent. The domestic class in 1881 amounted to 426,161, or 8·24 per cent. In 1891 the number was 255,144, or 5·42 per cent. This however is owing to a difference in classification. Had the plan followed on the present occasion been used in 1881, the figures for that year would have been 287,069, or 5·54 per cent. of the population, giving a decrease of 0·12 per cent. during the decade.

The commercial class in 1881 amounted to 72,245 or 1·40 per cent. In 1891 the number was 83,173 or 1·77 per cent., an increase of 0·37 per cent.

The agricultural class in 1881 numbered 997,956, or 19·28 per cent. In 1891 it was 936,759, or 19·92 per cent., an increase of 0·64 per cent.

The industrial class in 1881 was represented by 691,509 persons, or 13·36 per cent. In 1891 it consisted of 656,410 persons, or 13·95 per cent., an increase of 0·59 in the percentage.

The indefinite or non-productive class. The number tabulated in this class for 1881 was 2,788,281, or 53·88 per cent. In 1891 it was 2,559,021, or 54·39 per cent.; but had the composition of the class been the same in 1881 as in 1891, the percentage for the former year would have been 56·75 of the population, showing a decrease of 2·36 in the percentage for the ten years. (See Table IV.)

Families.—The number of families in 1891 was 932,113; in 1881 the number was 995,074, representing a decrease of 6·3 per cent. in 1891.

Houses.—The inhabited houses decreased from 914,108 in 1881 to 870,578 in 1891, or 4·8 less per cent. Houses of the first class increased from 66,727 to 70,740, or 6·0 per cent. Second class houses increased from 422,241 to 466,632, or 10·5 per cent. The number of third-class houses is 312,589, against 384,475 in 1881. This represents a decrease of 71,886, or 18·7 per cent., while fourth-class houses (mud cabins) decreased from 40,665 in 1881 to 20,617 in 1891, or 49·3 per cent.

Rateable valuation.—The rateable valuation of Ireland rose from 13,812,363*l*. 4*s*. 9*d*. in 1881 to 14,034,681*l*. 1*s*. 9*d*. in 1891, or 1·6 per cent.

Births.—From 1st April, 1881, to 31st March, 1891, 1,147,321 births were registered, against 1,391,983 during the preceding ten years.

Marriages.—The marriages registered amounted to 212,256. The number in the previous ten years being 245,968.

Deaths.—The deaths were 879,412, against 969,076 for the previous decade.

Emigration.—The emigration during the decade amounted to 768,105 persons; 393,744 males and 374,361 females.

Sickness.—The sick and infirm of all kinds on census night of 1891 numbered 66,664, or 1 in 71 of the whole population. Of these 35,722 were temporarily diseased, and 30,942 permanently diseased.

In 1881 the number of sick and infirm on census night was 71,328, or 1 in 73 of the whole population. Of these 40,090 were temporarily diseased, and 31,238 permanently diseased.

Blind.—The number of the totally blind in Ireland in 1891 was 5,341. In 1881 the number was 6,111.

Deaf and Dumb.—The deaf and dumb numbered in 1891 3,365; in 1881 their numbers were 3,993.

Dumb, not Deaf.—The number tabulated under this heading in 1881 was 1,143, and in 1891 it was 1,099.

Lunatics and Idiots.—The total number of lunatics and idiots returned in 1881 was 18,413, and in 1891 the number amounted to 21,188. The number of lunatics enumerated on census night of 1891 was 14,945 (7,463 males and 7,482 females), of whom 893 were at large, 11,265 in asylums, and 2,787 in workhouses. In 1881 the number of lunatics was 9,774 (4,857 males and 4,917 females), 943 being at large, 7,547 in asylums, and 1,284 in workhouses.

There were in 1891 6,243 idiots (3,501 males and 2,742 females), of whom 4,077 were at large, 996 in asylums, and 1,170 in workhouses. In 1881 there were 8,639 idiots (4,674 males and 3,965 females). Of these 4,548 were at large, 1,896 in asylums, and 2,195 in workhouses.

It is probable that a portion of the increase in lunatics and decrease in idiots appearing in the figures here given, is due to a difference in classification in the original returns.

Division of Land.—In 1891 the total extent under crops (including meadow and clover) was 4,818,381 acres; in 1881 it was 5,195,377 acres. The extent under grass in 1891 was 10,298,654, acres against 10,075,425 in 1881. Woods and plantation in 1891 occupied 311,554 acres, as against 328,703 acres in 1881, and turf, bog, marsh, barren mountain, roads, fences, &c., represented 4,769,677 acres in 1891, and 4,595,097 in 1881. (See Table V.)

Land under Crops.—In 1891 the extent of land under cereal crops was 1,492,763 acres, under green crops 1,191,424 acres, under flax 74,665 acres, and under meadow and clover 2,059,529 acres. In 1881 the acreage under cereal crops was 1,777,175, under green crops 1,264,223, under flax 147,145, under rape 5,803, and under meadow and clover, 2,001,029 acres.

Live Stock.—The number of live stock in 1891 was as follows: Horses and mules 621,479, asses 216,268, cattle 4,448,516, sheep 4,722,613, pigs 1,367,712, goats 336,337, and poultry 15,276,128. In 1881 the numbers were: horses and mules 574,746, asses 187,143, cattle 3,956,595, sheep 3,256,185, pigs 1,095,830, goats 266,078, and poultry 13,972,426.

Language.—The number of persons returned as speaking Irish only in 1891 was 38,197, or 0·81 per cent. In 1881 the number so returned was 64,067, or 1·24 per cent. The persons who could speak "English and Irish" in 1891 amounted to 642,053, or 13·6 per cent. In 1881 they were 885,765, or 17·1 per cent.

Navy and Military serving in Ireland.—The number of Navy and Military serving in Ireland in 1881 was 26,055, and in 1891 it was 25,725.

Foreigners.—The number of foreigners in Ireland in 1891 was 12,900; in 1881, 11,210 showing an increase of 1,690. The principal feature in connection with this subject is the large immigration of Russian Jews during the latter part of the decade.

Pauperism.—The number of paupers in the workhouses of Ireland on census night in 1891 was 42,348, being 13,482 or 24 per cent. under the number in 1881. The number of persons in receipt of out-door relief in Ireland at the date of the census of 1891 was 62,988. The corresponding number in 1881 was 64,233.

Ages of the People.—The population of Ireland, according
to sexes, in 1881 and 1891, under 1 year, 1 year and under 5, and
in quinquennial periods from 5 years upwards, will be found in
Table III, together with the actual increase or decrease in 1891,
and the proportion per cent. represented by the same.

From this table it will be seen that the number of children
under 15 years of age shows a marked diminution as compared
with the number in 1881 :—

	1881.	1891.	Decrease in 1891.	
			Number.	Per Cent.
Under 1 year	104,965	90,789	14,176	14
1— 5	471,018	379,584	91,434	19
5—10	621,637	508,772	112,865	18
10—15	616,370	549,922	66,448	11

There was a decrease of 21 per cent. in children under 1 year,
and of 9 per cent. in those of 1—5 years in 1881 as compared
with 1871, which would now affect the age-period 10—15, as is
shown in the foregoing statement.   The diminution in the population from 15—20 years in 1891 only amounted to 2 per cent.   At
the reproductive age-period (20 — 55 years), adopted by the
commissioners in 1871, the decrease was 6 per cent., there being
2,112,909 persons in this age-period in 1881, as compared with
1,989,295 in 1891.   Analysing the decrease in this period, we find
a fall of 44,725, or 6 per cent., at 20—30; of 46,796, or 8 per cent.,
at 30—40; and of 47,661, or 15 per cent., at 40—45; with a
slight increase, 5,857, or 3 per cent., at 45—50 ; and an increase of
9,711, or 4 per cent., at 50—55.   At the age 55—60 there was an
increase of 343 persons, or 2 per cent. ; at 60—65 a fall of 33,418,
or 15 per cent. ; at 65—70 of 11,737, or 12 per cent. ; at 70—75 of
10,625, or 9 per cent.; at 75—80 of 363, or 1 per cent.; and at 80 to 85
of 3,104, or 7 per cent.   We then find remarkable increases at the
next two groups of ages (85—90 and 90—95) ; there being 11,329
persons enumerated in 1891 in the former, compared with 8,484 in
1881, an increase of 2,845, or 34 per cent.; and 5,771 in 1891, in
the latter, compared with 4,024 in 1881, an increase of 1,747, or
43 per cent.   We might be inclined to doubt the accuracy of these
figures, were it not that in 1881 we find large increases as compared
with 1871 in the age-periods 75—80 and 80—85.

The population of Ireland was proportionately greater at the
following ages in 1891 than in 1881 :—

Proportion per 100,000 of the Population of Ireland in 1891 and 1881, at each Quinquennial Period, in which there was an INCREASE in 1891.

	1891.	1881.
15 and under 20 years	11,693	10,807
20 „ 25 „	9,451	9,229
25 „ 30 „	6,783	6,399
30 „ 35 „	5,934	5,856
45 „ 50 „ ...	4,312	3,808
50 „ 55 „	5,440	4,760
55 „ 60 „	3,032	2,691
75 „ 80 „	992	909
80 „ 85 „	926	901
85 „ 90 „	241	164
90 „ 95 „	123	77
95 and upwards	43	40

At the following age-periods it was proportionately less :—

Proportion per 100,000 of the Population of Ireland in 1891 and 1881, at each Quinquennial Period, in which there was a DECREASE in 1891.

	1891.	1881.
Under 5 years	10,002	11,137
5 and under 10 years	10,818	12,020
10 „ 15 „	11,693	11,918
35 „ 40 „	4,853	4,858
40 „ 45 „	5,526	5,947
60 „ 65 „	4,073	4,350
65 „ 70 „	1,884	1,940
70 „ 75 „	2,181	2,189

On this basis the general features exhibited are as follows :—

	1891.	1881.
Under 20 years	44,206	45,882
20—55..............................	42,299	40,857
55 years and upwards	13,495	13,261

Thus in every 100,000 of the population we have a *decrease* of 1,676 in the number under 20 years as compared with 1881, and an *increase* of 1,442 in those in the "reproductive period" (20—55), and of 234 in persons aged 55 and upwards.

Under the heading of "ages not specified," there is a decrease of 40 per cent., representing an absolute decrease of 1,210.'

In 1861 the persons whose ages were unspecified amounted to 3,838, in 1871 to 3,769, in 1881 to 2,996, and in 1891 to 1,786. We may take it for granted that so far as regards the domiciled population the enumerators were careful to have all omissions in the returns supplied before transmitting the files to the census office. The cases of unspecified age, therefore, in nearly every instance, we may safely assume, were those of travellers or other persons of shifting residence, whom the enumerators were unable to trace after their departure from the locality where they were living upon the night of the census, some being persons on board ships which left port before full information could be obtained.

The centenarians in 1891 numbered 578 (229 males and 349 females); the number for the year 1881 having been 690 (224 males and 466 females); and for 1871 724 (259 males and 465 females).

It appears that Munster supplies the greatest number of instances of extreme longevity, 91 males and 129 females; Ulster comes next with 85 males and 132 females; Connaught next with 30 males and 57 females; and Leinster last with but 23 males and 31 females. As regards the conjugal condition and education of persons 100 years old and upwards, 57 (18 males and 39 females) were unmarried; 99 (89 males and 10 females) were married; and 422 (122 males and 300 females) were widowed. Only 79 out of the 578 could read and write; 51 could read only, and 448 could neither read nor write. The greatest actual number of centenarians is to be found in Cork, Kerry, Donegal, Galway and Tyrone.

Emigration.—According to returns compiled during the past decade, the number of Irish who left the country during the ten years ended 31st March, 1891, with the intention of permanently settling elsewhere, amounted to 768,105 (393,744 males and 374,361 females). During the previous decade the number was 629,130 (346,869 males and 282,261 females), and the total number for the forty years from the 1st May, 1851 (when the collection of these returns was commenced) to the 31st March, 1891, was 3,415,400 (1,806,256 males and 1,609,144 females).

The following statement shows, by ages, the number of Irish emigrants during the ten *calendar* years 1881-90:—

	Males.	Females.	Total.	Percentage.
Under 5 years	20,387	19,378	39,765	} 9·7
5 and under 10	18,104	16,663	34,767	
10 „ 15	15,592	15,771	31,363	} 24·5
15 „ 20	59,522	97,651	157,173	
20 „ 25	151,394	133,301	284,695	
25 „ 30	61,419	37,576	98,995	
30 „ 35	25,921	18,159	44,080	} 61·3
35 „ 40	11,876	9,952	21,828	
40 „ 45	12,631	10,444	23,075	
45 „ 50	6,863	5,722	12,585	
50 „ 55	6,060	5,724	11,784	
55 „ 60	2,364	2,277	4,641	} 4·4
60 and upwards	2,646	2,272	4,918	
Ages unspecified	519	518	1,037	0·1
	395,298	375,408	770,706	100·0

Table VI shows the number of emigrants from each county in Ireland from the 1st April, 1871, to the 31st March, 1891. The number of emigrants during these twenty years was equal to an average annual rate of 13·7 per 1,000 of the mean population; the rate for the province of Leinster being 9·9; Munster, 16·8; Ulster, 13·3; and Connaught 15·0 per 1,000. From this table it will be observed that in three of the six counties constituting the province of Munster, two of the five counties in Connaught, and one county in Leinster, the rate exceeded 16 per 1,000; that the counties of Kerry, Longford, and Leitrim had the highest rates (20·3, 19·7, and 19·2 respectively) and the counties of Dublin, Wicklow, and Louth the lowest, 5·4, 7·7, and 8·3 respectively.

Since the year 1876 tables showing the destinations of the emigrants have been included in the Emigration Statistics of Ireland, from which we learn that of 770,706 emigrants during the ten years 1881-90, 699,920 or 90·8 per cent. went to the colonies or foreign countries, and 70,786 or 9·2 per cent. to Great Britain. Of the former number 613,508 or 79·6 per cent. of the total emigrants from Ireland went to the United States of America; 39,786 or 5·2 per cent. to Canada; 38,930 or 5·0 per cent. to Australia; 4,599 or 0·6 per cent. to New Zealand; and 3,097 or 0·4 per cent. to other countries, and of those who left for Great Britain, 43,341 or 5·6 per cent. of all the emigrants went to England or Wales, and 27,445 or 3·6 per cent. to Scotland.

Special Inquiry as to Agricultural Holdings.—*Agricultural holdings in 1891, classified according to rateable valuation, with the population, houses, &c., in each class; also the number of holdings according to size.*—In the census report of 1881 tables were included showing the relation between the agricultural population and the holdings upon which they resided. These tables threw a great light upon the social condition and means of subsistence of the occupiers of agricultural holdings in Ireland, and served as useful standards of comparisons between the results published by the Registrar-General in the annual report on the agricultural statistics of Ireland, and the actual condition of the agricultural holdings and their occupiers.

In the Census Report for 1881 the classification adopted was as follows:—

1st class holdings not exceeding 1 statute acre.				
2nd	,,	above 1 and not exceeding 5 statute acres.		
3rd	,,	,, 5	,,	10	,,
4th	,,	, 10	,,	15	,,
5th	,,	, 15	,,	20	,,
6th	,,	, 20	,,	30	,,
7th	,,	,, 30	,,	50	,,
8th	,,	,, 50	,,	100	,,
9th	,,	,, 100	,,	200	,,
10th	,,	,, 200	,,	500	,,
11th	,,	,, 500 statute acres.			

It will be observed that the foregoing grouping was altogether by *acreage.*

During the past decade various inquiries have taken place, and many legislative measures have been brought before Parliament which required special and more accurate information regarding the valuation of agricultural holdings than had hitherto been available. Great difficulty was experienced in obtaining information of this character. We have therefore determined on the present occasion to classify the agricultural holdings not merely by acreage, as was done in 1881, but also by rateable valuation. An attempt has been made to combine as far as practicable the information corresponding to that published in the report of 1881, with the further information regarding the valuation of agricultural holdings.

They have accordingly been grouped, as follows, regarding *valuation :—*

1st class holdings not exceeding 4*l.* in rateable value.

2nd	„	above 4*l.* and not exceeding 10*l.* in rateable value.
3rd		.. 10*l.*	..	15*l.*	..
4th		15*l.*		20*l.*
5th		20*l.*		30*l.*
6th		, 30*l.*		40*l.*
7th		, 40*l.*		50*l.*
8th		„ 50*l.*		100*l.*	„
9th		„ 100*l.*	„	200*l.*	„
10th		„ 200*l.*	„	300*l.*	„
11th		„ 300*l.* in rateable value.

The returns from which these tables were constructed were collected on three forms.

On Form 1, information, as in 1881, was sought as to the number of agricultural holdings, the area and rateable valuation of each, the number of houses and out offices, and the resident population on the night of the census. The valuation referred to is the General Tenement Valuation, commenced in 1852 and completed in 1864 (popularly known as Griffith's); on it are based all public and local assessments, as also are the Parliamentary and municipal franchises.

On Form 2 was made, by the enumerator, a summary by electoral divisions of the particulars contained in Form 1. Form 3 was prepared with a view to provide for those cases where an occupier of land *resident* within the enumerator's district held *two*

or more farms, or had a farm which extended into two or more
adjoining townlands (the townland having been adopted as the
unit of observation with respect to these returns), and on this
form the enumerator entered the name of the townland where each
farm or portion of a farm was situated. Before the general
classification of the holdings was begun in this office, the information given on Form 3 was utilised for the purpose of combining
the several details regarding the different portions of each person's
farm, and the complete farm was subsequently classified according
to rateable valuation in the same manner as if it were an un-
divided holding. The statistical results will be most fully
appreciated by classifying the holdings into groups, above and
below certain definite standards of rateable valuation and acreage.
In the latter, above and below the area of 30 acres as adopted in
the report for 1881, and in the former, above and below the
corresponding value, *i.e.*, above and below 15 guineas. With
regard to acreage, it appears from the tables that, of the 486,865
agricultural holdings, there are 333,464, or 68 per cent., not
exceeding 30 acres. In 1881 such holdings numbered 348,970, or
70 per cent. of the total. Of the holdings in 1891 not exceeding
30 acres in extent, there are 268,530 not exceeding 20 acres,
212,992 not exceeding 15 acres, 150,200 not exceeding 10 acres,
73,797 not exceeding 5 acres, and 18,243 not exceeding 1 acre.
It would be unfair to consider all those as *bonâ fide* agricultural
holdings, having regard to the fact that deduction should be made
for villas standing on small plots of land, situated sufficiently outside large towns to be excluded from town holdings. Again,
certain of those not exceeding 1 acre are merely labourers' holdings. In any case, however, the return shows a vast number of
small agricultural holdings in Ireland, the occupiers of which are
endeavouring to earn a living by the product of the same.

The holdings above 30 acres number 153,401 (or 32 per cent.
of the total, against 30 per cent. in 1881), of which 86,432 were
over 50 acres, 33,504 over 100 acres, 11,150 over 200 acres, and
2,175 over 500 acres.

Comparing the four provinces, it will be found that the
holdings not exceeding 30 acres constitute in Leinster 63·2 per
cent. of the total number, in Munster 50·1, in Ulster 74·9, and in
Connaught 80·4. In the county of Mayo the proportion reaches
83·7 per cent., and in Roscommon 82·5. In the county of Armagh,
where the percentage of those not exceeding 30 acres is 88·0, we find
the highest proportion of small holdings in any county of Ulster.
(See Table VII.)

The average rateable valuation of the holdings included in
these tables is about 10s. 6d. per acre, thus the average value of a

30-acre holding would be 15 guineas; the nearest standard of valuation to this in the table is 15l., therefore the economic condition of the occupiers of smaller holdings may be illustrated in a similar manner in respect to rateable valuation as has already been done with regard to area. Thus classifying the holdings into those of a value not exceeding 15l. and those exceeding 15l. respectively, we find that of the 486,865 holdings; there are 332,556 or 68·3 per cent. not exceeding 15l. in valuation, of these there are 271,690 not exceeding 10l., and 127,098 not exceeding 4l. in rateable value. Similar deductions (as already remarked) would have to be made for holdings not strictly agricultural, as in the case of classification by acreage.

A comparison of these results shows a close correspondence between the area of the poorer districts and the greater subdivision of land into holdings of small area and low value. The holdings valued above 15l. amounted to 154,309, or 31·7 per cent., of which 117,301 exceeded 20l., 40,783 exceeded 50l., 15,210 exceeded 100l., 4,756 exceeded 200l., and 2,190 exceeded 300l. in rateable value. (See Table VIII.)

Comparing the four provinces, it will be found that the holdings not exceeding 15l. in the rateable value constitute in Leinster 57·3 per cent. of the total number of holdings in that province; in Munster 58·3; in Ulster 68·8; and in Connaught 86·6 per cent.

In all the counties in the province of Connaught, the percentage of holdings not exceeding 15l. in rateable valuation is above 80·0; in the county of Mayo the percentage being 92·1; in four counties in the province of Ulster the percentage exceeds 70·0— that for Donegal being 87·2; in the province of Munster the percentage exceeds 70·0 in two counties, viz., Kerry and Clare, in which the percentages are 75·0 and 70·4 respectively; in four counties in Leinster the percentage exceeds 60·0—Longford, Louth, King's, and Queen's, viz., 69·0, 64·1, 63·1, and 63·1 respectively. As stated in the General Report of the Census Commission of 1881 : " These large proportions of smaller holdings in Connaught, " and in some portions of Ulster, point to narrow means of subsis- " tence for such small agriculturists. These deficiencies are, " however, to some extent compensated for in the case of Mayo " and other Connaught counties by the earnings of labourers who " annually visit Great Britain, as shown by the returns of Migratory " Labourers, published annually by the Registrar-General. In the " case of Armagh and other Ulster counties in the north-east of " Ireland, the deficiency is made up by the earnings of hand-loom " weavers in those parts where this industry is still carried on. " Again, the small agriculturists along the coast of the west and " north-west supplement their earnings from farming operations

" by fishing and the manufacture of kelp.   The former occupation
" has been always carried on under great difficulties, and the kelp
" trade has of late years become unremunerative."

The distribution of the population on the agricultural holdings
also points to an excessive struggle for existence in some of the
remote agricultural districts of Ireland.

Thus the proportion of the total population living on agricultural holdings not exceeding 15*l.* in rateable value is for Ireland
34·7 per cent.; for the province of Leinster, 19·7 ; Munster, 29·3 ;
Ulster, 33·5 ; Connaught, 70·6.   In the county of Leitrim the percentage is 78·2 ; in Mayo, 74·6, and in Donegal, 68·0.

The proportion of the population living on agricultural holdings
over 15*l.* in rateable value is for Ireland, 28·4 per cent.; for the
province of Leinster, 28·1 ; Munster, 35·8 ; Ulster, 28·8 ; and
Connaught, 16·3.

Of the population in Ireland on census night of 1891, 36·9 per
cent. did not reside on agricultural holdings ; in Leinster the percentage was 52·2 ; in Munster, 34·9; in Ulster, 37·7 ; and in
Connaught, 13·1.

Comparing the classes of houses, 60 per cent. of the fourth class
houses on agricultural holdings were on holdings not exceeding 15*l.*
in rateable value, in Leinster, 47·0 per cent. ; in Munster, 49·8 ;
in Ulster, 89·9 ; and in Connaught, 82·8.   The percentage in the
county of Donegal is 87·1 ; in Mayo, 86·6 ; in Galway, 84·7 ; and
in Leitrim, 81·5.

TABLE I.—*Population in each County in Ireland,* 1881 *and* 1891.

Counties.	Population.				Increase or Decrease.	
	1891.		1891.	1881.	Total.	Percentage.
	Males.	Females.				
Carlow	20,552	20,384	40,936	46,568	− 5,632	−12·10
Dublin	197,409	221,807	419,216	418,910	+ 306	+ 0·07
Kildare	38,407	31,799	70,206	75,804	− 5,598	− 7·38
Kilkenny	43,468	43,793	87,261	99,531	−12,270	−12·33
King's	33,777	31,786	65,563	72,852	−. 7,289	−10·01
Longford	26,681	25,966	52,647	61,009	− 8,362	−13·70
Louth	35,242	35,796	71,038	77,684	− 6,646	− 8·56
Meath	39,224	37,763	76,987	87,469	−10,482	−11·98
Queen's	38,171	31,712	64,883	73,124	− 8,241	−11·27
Westmeath	33,927	31,182	65,109	71,798	− 6,689	− 9·32
Wexford	54,935	56,843	111,778	123,854	−12,076	− 9·75
Wicklow	31,054	31,082	62,136	70,386	− 8,250	−11·72
Leinster	**587,847**	**599,913**	**1,187,760**	**1,278,989**	**−91,229**	**− 7·13**
Clare	63,138	61,345	124,483	141,457	−16,974	+12·00
Cork	219,988	218,444	438,432	495,607	−57,175	−11·54
Kerry	91,017	88,119	179,136	201,039	−21,903	−10·89
Limerick	78,607	80,305	158,912	180,632	−21,720	−12·02
Tipperary	86,807	86,381	173,188	199,612	−26,424	−13·24
Waterford	48,054	50,197	98,251	112,768	−14,517	−12·87
Munster	**587,611**	**584,791**	**1,172,402**	**1,331,115**	**−158,713**	**−11·92**
Antrim	200,514	227,614	428,128	421,943	+ 6,185	+ 1·47
Armagh	68,370	74,919	143,289	163,177	−19,888	−12·19
Cavan	56,772	55,145	111,917	129,476	−17,559	−13·56
Donegal	91,478	94,157	185,635	206,035	−20,400	− 9·90
Down	126,268	140,791	267,059	272,107	− 5,048	− 1·86
Fermanagh	37,344	36,826	74,170	84,879	−10,709	−12·62
Londonderry	73,260	78,749	152,009	164,991	−12,982	− 7·87
Monaghan	42,727	43,479	86,206	102,748	−16,542	−16·10
Tyrone	84,596	86,805	171,401	197,719	−26,318	−13·31
Ulster	**781,329**	**838,485**	**1,619,814**	**1,743,075**	**−123,261**	**− 7·07**
Galway	108,283	106,429	214,712	242,005	−27,293	−11·28
Leitrim	39,715	38,903	78,618	90,372	−11,754	−13·00
Mayo	107,498	111,536	219,034	245,212	−26,178	−10·68
Roscommon	58,000	56,397	114,397	132,490	−18,093	−13·65
Sligo	48,670	49,343	98,013	111,578	−13,565	−12·16
Connaught	**362,166**	**362,608**	**724,774**	**821,657**	**−96,883**	**−11·79**
Total Ireland	**2,318,953**	**2,385,797**	**4,704,750**	**5,174,836**	**− 470,086**	**− 9·08**

TABLE II.—*Population of Cities and Towns (Urban Sanitary Districts) having more than Ten Thousand Inhabitants.*

	Males, 1891.	Females, 1891.	Total, 1891.	Total, 1881.	Increase or Decrease.	
					Total.	Percentage.
Belfast	118,759	137,191	255,950	208,122	+ 47,828	+ 22·99
Dublin	117,503	127,498	245,001	249,602	− 4,601	− 1·85
Cork	35,427	39,918	75,345	80,124	− 4,779	− 5·96
Limerick	17,699	19,456	37,155	38,562	− 1,407	− 3·65
Londonderry	15,600	17,600	33,200	29,162	+ 4,038	+ 13·84
Rathmines and } Rathgar ....}	11,247	16,549	27,796	24,370	+ 3,426	+ 14·06
Pembroke...................	10,384	13,885	24,269	23,222	+ 1,047	+ 4·51
Waterford	9,908	10,944	20,852	22,457	− 1,605	− 7·15
Kingstown	7,081	10,271	17,352	18,586	− 1,234	− 6·62
Galway......................	6,878	6,922	13,800	15,471	− 1,671	− 10·80
Newry	6,250	6,711	12,961	14,808	− 1,847	− 12·47
Dundalk	6,344	6,105	12,449	11,913	+ 536	+ 4·50
Lisburn.....................	5,597	6,653	12,250	10,135	+ 2,115	+ 20·87
Drogheda	5,619	6,254	11,873	12,297	− 424	− 3·45
Wexford	5,351	6,194	11,545	12,163	− 618	− 5·08
Lurgan	4,911	6,518	11,429	10,755	+ 674	+ 6·27
Kilkenny	5,451	5,597	11,048	12,299	− 1,251	− 10·17
Sligo	4,918	5,356	10,274	10,808	− 534	− 4·94

[*Note.*—It will thus be seen that Dublin is now only the second city in Ireland, so far as concerns the population of urban sanitary districts. The population of the "Dublin Metropolitan Police District" was in 1881, 349,648; in 1891, 352,277; an *increase* of 2,629, or 0·75 per cent.: the population of the "Dublin Registration District" at the same dates was 346,693 and 349,594 respectively, an *increase* of 2,901 or 0·84 per cent. The greatest decrease in the population of the more important towns is shown in *Armagh*, which, from 10,070 in 1881, declined to 7,438 in 1891, or 26·14 per cent. This town and Carrickfergus (10,009 in 1881, now 8,923) thus disappear from the list of towns having over 10,000 inhabitants.]

TABLE III.—*Number of Persons in 1881 and 1891, according to Ages, with the Increase or Decrease since 1881.*

Ages	Males				Females				Total			
	Number 1881	Number 1891	Increase or Decrease, Number	Increase or Decrease, Per Cent.	Number 1881	Number 1891	Increase or Decrease, Number	Increase or Decrease, Per Cent.	Number 1881	Number 1891	Increase or Decrease, Number	Increase or Decrease, Per Cent.
Under 1 year	53,486	46,390	− 7,096	− 13	51,479	44,399	− 7,080	− 14	104,965	90,789	− 14,176	− 14
1 and under 5 years	238,757	192,513	− 46,244	− 19	232,261	187,071	− 45,190	− 19	471,018	379,584	− 91,434	− 19
5 „ 10 „	314,481	258,406	− 56,075	− 18	307,156	250,366	− 56,790	− 18	621,637	508,772	− 112,865	− 18
10 „ 15 „	315,004	280,357	− 34,647	− 11	301,366	269,565	− 31,801	− 11	616,370	549,922	− 66,448	− 11
15 „ 20 „	274,033	276,314	+ 2,281	+ 1	284,923	273,594	− 11,329	− 4	558,956	549,908	− 9,048	− 2
20 „ 25 „	231,754	223,860	− 7,894	− 3	245,542	220,642	− 24,900	− 10	477,296	444,502	− 32,794	− 7
25 „ 30 „	156,149	151,549	− 4,600	− 3	174,783	167,452	− 7,331	− 4	330,932	319,001	− 11,931	− 4
30 „ 35 „	140,155	134,700	− 5,455	− 4	162,695	144,357	− 18,338	− 11	302,850	279,057	− 23,793	− 8
35 „ 40 „	118,082	107,878	− 10,204	− 9	133,165	120,366	− 12,799	− 9	251,247	228,244	− 23,003	− 9
40 „ 45 „	144,572	119,125	− 25,447	− 18	162,957	140,743	− 22,214	− 14	307,529	259,868	− 47,661	− 15
45 „ 50 „	96,183	95,975	− 208	− 0·2	100,736	106,801	+ 6,065	+ 6	196,919	202,776	+ 5,857	+ 3
50 „ 55 „	117,456	121,952	+ 4,496	+ 4	128,680	133,895	+ 5,215	+ 4	246,136	255,847	+ 9,711	+ 4
55 „ 60 „	67,591	71,148	+ 3,557	+ 5	71,551	71,433	− 118	− 0·2	139,142	142,581	+ 3,439	+ 2
60 „ 65 „	104,227	91,933	− 12,294	− 12	120,751	99,627	− 21,124	− 17	224,978	191,560	− 33,418	− 15
65 „ 70 „	50,607	43,884	− 6,723	− 13	49,744	44,730	− 5,014	− 10	100,351	88,614	− 11,737	− 12
70 „ 75 „	55,355	48,578	− 6,777	− 12	57,865	54,017	− 3,848	− 7	113,220	102,595	− 10,625	− 9
75 „ 80 „	24,842	23,822	− 1,020	− 4	22,185	22,842	+ 657	+ 3	47,027	46,664	− 363	− 1
80 „ 85 „	21,997	20,298	− 1,699	− 8	24,651	23,246	− 1,405	− 6	46,648	43,544	− 3,104	− 7
85 „ 90 „	4,207	5,822	+ 1,615	+ 38	4,277	5,507	+ 1,230	+ 29	8,484	11,329	+ 2,845	+ 34
90 „ 95 „	1,734	2,722	+ 988	+ 57	2,290	3,049	+ 759	+ 33	4,024	5,771	+ 1,747	+ 43
95 and upwards	840	875	+ 35	+ 4	1,271	1,161	− 110	− 9	2,111	2,036	− 75	− 4
Ages not specified	1,765	852	− 913	− 52	1,231	934	− 297	− 24	2,996	1,786	− 1,210	− 40
Total	2,533,277	2,318,953	− 214,324	− 8	2,641,559	2,385,797	− 255,762	− 10	5,174,836	4,704,750	− 470,086	− 9

Table IV.—*Occupations of the People.*

	Males.		Total.
ns engaged in the **General** or **Local Government** of the country .... }	27,145	2,539	29,684
Defence of the country	37,674	—	37,674
Professional Occupations (with their immediate subordinates)*.... }	74,152	72,733	146,885
I. PROFESSIONAL CLASS*	138,971	75,272	214,243
II. DOMESTIC CLASS			
ns engaged in **Commercial** Occupations	27,580	1,609	29,189
„ **Conveyance** of Men, Goods, and Messages .... }	53,432	552	53,984
III. COMMERCIAL CLASS	81,012	2,161	83,173
ns engaged in **Agriculture**	824,858	90,940	915,798
„ about **Animals**	20,833	128	20,961
IV. AGRICULTURAL CLASS...................................	845,691	91,068	936,759
ns working and dealing in **Books, Prints**, and **Maps**	6,146	1,576	7,722
„ **Machines** and **Implements**	8,142	117	8,259
„ **Houses, Furniture,** and **Decorations** .... }	50,865	897	51,762
Carriages and **Harness**	5,743	37	5,780
Ships and **Boats**	4,282	2	4,284
Chemicals and **Compounds** .... }	1,659	128	1,787
Tobacco and **Pipes**	900	606	1,506
Food and **Lodgings**	52,218	18,284	70,502
Textile Fabrics...................	46,369	83,515	129,884
Dress	37,695	115,734	153,429
various **Animal Substances** .... }	2,083	645	2,728
„ **Vegetable Substances** .... }	9,340	2,319	11,659
„ **Mineral Substances** .... }	39,927	749	40,676
General or **Unspecified Commodities** .... }	137,836	27,496	165,332
„ **Refuse Matters**...................	950	150	1,100
. INDUSTRIAL CLASS	404,155	252,255	656,410
ERSONS of SPECIFIED OCCUPATIONS and CONDITIONS .... }	1,504,319		
. INDEFINITE and NON-PRODUCTIVE CLASS			

class are included all persons *aged 15 years and upwards* returned as " scholar" or

TABLE V.—*Showing the Total Acreage, the Acreage under Crops and Pasture, th*
of Plantation, Turf, Bog, &c., and the Population to a Square Mile of La
Crops and Pasture, also to a Square Mile of the Total Area.

Area (*Statute Acres*).

Counties. (Rural Districts).	Crops and Pasture.	Plantation, Turf, Bog, &c.	Total.	Persons.	Average Number to a Square Mile under Crops and Pasture.	Aver Squ To
Wicklow	321,089	175,455	496,544	50,159	100	
King's	344,026	146,644	490,670	55,988	104	
Meath	529,952	47,628	577,580	70,597	85	
Galway	915,750	577,077	1,492,827	191,673	184	
Tipperary	858,279	183,179	1,041,458	133,213	99	
Westmeath	360,146	71,975	432,121	56,546	100	
Queen's	352,280	71,064	423,344	57,142	104	
Kerry	683,012	472,210	1,155,222	160,742	151	
Kildare	350,363	61,931	412,294	58,378	107	
Kilkenny	446,619	59,593	506,212	· 75,928	109	
Clare	599,868	166,613	766,481	114,928	123	
Donegal	640,696	548,418	1,189,114	180,844	181	
Wexford	504,464	67,245	571,709	86,810	110	
Mayo	697,332	617,174	1,314,506	207,754	191	
Carlow	190,552	30,277	220,829	35,345	119	
Waterford	314,583	138,826	453,409	72,136	147	
Fermanagh	346,662	70,685	417,347	68,600	127	
Cork	1,379,125	451,807	1,830,932	310,851	129	
Limerick	582,996	76,464	659,460	117,484	129	
Roscommon	465,422	116,969	582,391	107,201	147	
Longford	200,846	56,086	256,932	48,820	155	
Sligo	310,994	137,409	448,403	86,545	178	
Tyrone	573,657	202,939	776,596	154,696	173	
Leitrim	292,246	84,264	376,510	78,618	172	
Londonderry	374,106	135,533	509,639	109,168	187	
Louth	169,650	28,959	198,609	44,649	168	
Cavan	393,765	72,763	466,528	108,949	177	
Monaghan	283,524	34,924	318,448	81,236	183	
Antrim	553,412	134,671	688,083	176,923	205	
Down	510,167	96,487	606,654	184,859	232	
Dublin	177,185	34,968	212,153	66,675	241	
Armagh	269,607	40,675	310,282	107,180	255	
Total rural	14,992,375	5,210,912	20,203,287	3,460,637	148	
Total civic	124,660	—	124,660	1,244,113	6,380	
General total	15,117,035	5,210,912		4,704,750	199	

TABLE VI.—*Showing the Counties arranged according to the Highest Average A*
of Emigration per Thousand of the Population, during the Twenty Years
March, 1891.

County.	Average Annual Rate per 1,000.	County.	Average Annual Rate per 1,000.	County.	Average Annual Rate per 1,000.	County.	A
1. Kerry	20·3	4. Clare	18·7	7. Cavan	16·2	10. Limerick	
2. Longford	19·7	5. Sligo	16·4	8. Galway	15·9	11. Londonde	
3. Leitrim	19·2	6. Cork	16·4	9. Queen's	15·7	12. Tipperar	

ᴇ VI.—*Counties according to the Average Rate of Emigration of the Population—Contd*

unty.	Average Annual Rate per 1,000.	County.	Average Annual Rate per 1,000.	County.	Average Annual Rate per 1,000.	County.	Average Annual Rate per 1,000.
yrone	.... 15·1	18. Roscommon	14·4	23. Armagh........	12·5	28. Down	9·9
ing's	.... 14·9	19. Mayo	14·3	24. Fermanagh .	12·4	29. Kildare	9·3
onegal	.... 14·7	20. Monaghan ..	13·3	25. Westmeath .	11·9	30. Louth	8·3
arlow	.... 14·6	21. Meath	12·7	26. Kilkenny	11·4	31. Wicklow	7·7
aterford	14·5	22. Antrim	12·7	27. Wexford	10·3	32. Dublin	5·4

Province.	Average Annual Rate per 1,000.	Province.	Average Annual Rate per 1,000.
Munster	16·8	Leinster	9·9
Connaught........................	15·0		
Ulster.................................	13·3	Ireland	13·7

ʟᴇ VII.—*Showing by Counties and Provinces the Number of Agricultural Holdings, according to Size, in 1891.*

nties.	Not exceeding 1 Acre.	Above 1 and not exceeding 5 Acres.	Above 5 and not exceeding 10.	Above 10 and not exceeding 15.	Above 15 and not exceeding 20.	Above 20 and not exceeding 30.	Above 30 and not exceeding 50.	Above 50 and not exceeding 100.	Above 100 and not exceeding 200.	Above 200 and not exceeding 500.	Above 500 Acres.	Total Number of Holdings.
....	508	578	396	284	335	501	751	776	323	135	13	4,600
....	487	1,109	697	466	330	373	471	486	384	168	19	4,990
....	668	1,515	901	494	477	500	613	809	606	387	70	7,040
ny	719	1,418	1,070	832	768	1,213	1,899	1,970	808	267	36	11,000
....	588	1,412	1,056	836	728	1,058	1,212	1,033	517	241	76	8,757
rd	212	649	1,131	1,281	1,064	1,347	1,159	547	208	84	15	7,697
....	328	1,100	1,282	786	565	618	568	404	241	112	24	6,028
....	1,067	1,580	1,312	929	764	859	1,001	1,048	817	536	133	10,046
's	428	1,421	1,105	859	730	1,031	1,156	1,008	618	282	60	8,698
eath	809	1,457	1,152	843	868	1,097	1,209	925	424	287	77	9,148
·d	852	1,897	1,440	981	977	1,483	2,252	2,268	918	255	38	13,361
w	235	712	634	451	425	666	995	1,183	684	270	103	6,358
TER	6,901	14,848	12,174	9,044	8,031	10,746	13,286	12,457	6,550	3,024	664	97,725
....	561	1,153	1,315	1,363	1,551	2,597	3,256	2,542	893	390	79	15,700
....	1,207	1,985	2,110	1,860	2,139	3,600	5,802	6,976	3,219	996	125	30,019
....	715	1,807	1,723	1,193	1,443	2,277	3,549	3,575	1,614	624	141	18,661
:k	1,312	1,364	1,099	858	932	1,627	2,424	2,545	1,059	326	48	13,594
....	1,257	2,315	1,836	1,518	1,504	2,398	3,297	3,258	1,421	587	121	19,572
ord	642	1,056	669	428	432	646	1,042	1,401	843	285	41	7,485
TER	5,694	9,680	8,752	7,220	8,061	13,145	19,370	20,297	9,049	3,208	555	105,031
....	289	1,788	2,437	2,221	2,187	3,048	3,381	2,346	662	192	48	18,599
l	541	3,441	4,782	3,018	1,994	1,905	1,327	647	120	28	3	17,806
....	326	1,279	2,991	3,244	3,107	3,239	2,368	1,026	249	52	13	17,894
....	340	2,621	5,194	4,287	3,711	4,190	3,852	2,954	1,004	414	97	28,594
agh	520	3,708	4,929	3,460	2,768	3,094	2,920	1,753	894	101	23	23,669
....	198	914	1,500	1,620	1,621	2,132	2,080	1,218	396	116	24	11,819
derry	172	1,397	2,650	2,326	1,969	2,206	2,215	1,366	440	135	27	14,893
lan	271	1,753	3,526	3,017	2,325	2,216	1,549	586	112	41	9	15,405
....	406	2,320	3,740	3,547	3,288	3,985	8,787	2,370	642	160	51	24,296
R	3,063	19,221	31,679	26,740	22,960	26,015	23,479	14,267	4,020	1,237	294	172,975
....	861	4,253	6,512	4,580	4,308	3,935	3,339	2,096	1,138	690	306	32,018
....	265	804	2,145	2,505	2,383	2,488	1,739	733	189	51	12	13,314
....	546	3,387	8,319	6,496	4,906	4,135	2,649	1,465	679	403	243	33,218
mon	546	1,925	4,013	3,544	2,745	2,467	1,634	863	437	217	68	18,459
....	367	1,436	2,809	2,673	2,144	2,003	1,473	751	293	143	33	14,125
AUGHT...	2,585	11,805	23,798	19,788	16,486	15,028	10,834	5,908	2,736	1,504	662	111,134
RELAND	18,243	55,554	76,403	62,792	55,538	64,934	66,969	52,928	22,354	8,975	2,175	486,865

VIII.—*Showing by Counties and Provinces the Number of Agricultural Holdings according to Rateable Valuation in 1891.*

Classificatio		ldings and Number in each Class.						
Above 10*l.* and not exceeding 15*l.*	Above 15*l.* and not exceeding 20*l.*	Above 30*l.* and not exceeding 40*l.*	Above 40*l.* and not exceeding 50*l.*	Above 50*l.* and not exceeding 100*l.*	Above 100*l.* and not exceeding 200*l.*	Above 200*l.* and not exceeding 300*l.*	Above 300*l.*	Total Number of Holdings.
488	394	361	212	425	198	57	41	4,600
420	310	266	218	665	566	175	127	4,990
599	360	317	261	712	433	142	136	7,040
1,218	990	921	601	1,021	417	86	49	11,000
1,074	751	429	286	504	256	66	65	8,757
1,265	731	291	184	281	141	23	22	7,697
742	449	284	160	368	217	71	67	6,028
993	655	484	370	946	688	274	323	10,046
1,044	688	418	252	602	298	75	55	8,698
1,098	782	522	317	623	326	108	121	9,148
1,500	1,198	1,009	605	1,144	396	72	32	13,361
819	578	436	283	573	300	77	76	6,358
11,260	7,886	5,738	3,749	7,864	4,236	1,226	1,112	97,723
2,497	1,402	602	303	625	234	71	68	15,700
3,783	2,783	2,236	1,453	3,025	1,111	220	159	30,019
2,392	1,411	686	357	549	113	20	16	18,661
1,502	1,185	1,079	703	1,511	611	119	83	13,594
2,305	1,842	1,453	911	1,725	692	176	166	19,572
588	428	531	395	988	401	59	42	7,485
13,067	9,051	6,587	4,121	8,423	3,163	666	523	105,033
2,983	2,279	1,460	935	1,569	445	96	63	18,599
2,796	1,677	788	491	718	177	43	22	17,806
3,416	1,822	562	268	376	104	19	12	17,894
1,962	1,025	534	291	530	181	38	17	28,594
8,306	2,327	1,677	1,043	1,891	577	102	87	23,669
2,144	1,284	584	328	418	109	24	23	11,819
2,348	1,273	674	377	626	180	30	21	14,893
3,064	1,619	567	258	349	98	21	21	15,405
3,938	2,142	1,063	506	731	171	28	25	24,296
25,987	15,448	7,909	4,497	7,208	2,041	401	291	172,975
2,672	1,259	578	353	759	427	117	104	32,018
1,707	701	197	100	153	32	9	4	13,314
2,059	790	278	190	381	181	42	55	33,218
2,274	957	331	208	445	229	74	83	18,459
1,840	916	324	178	340	145	31	18	14,125
10,552	4,623	1,708	1,024	2,078	1,014	273	264	111,134
60,866	37,008	11,942	13,391	25,573	10,454	2,566	2,190	486,865

On the Recent Movement of Labour in Different Countries in Reference to Wages, Hours of Work, and Efficiency.

By J. Stephen Jeans, Esq.

[Read before the Royal Statistical Society, 17th May, 1892.
The President, Dr. F. J. Mouat, LL.D., in the Chair.]

CONTENTS:

APPENDIX.

I.—*Introduction.*

ON the 16th day of December, 1884, I had the honour of reading before this Society a paper on "The Comparative Efficiency and "Earnings of Labour at Home and Abroad." At that time the labour question had not quite come to the front in the prominent manner that it has since done, and consequently there were not so many official and trustworthy sources of information available as to the capacity of workmen in different countries, and the earnings that they are able to command. The bureaus of labour that are now so important and conspicuous a feature of the social and political economy of our own and other countries were comparatively in their infancy. Much had already been done in the United States, mainly under the able guidance and direction of Colonel Carroll D. Wright (then the Commissioner of Labour for the State of Massachusetts, and now the General Commissioner of Labour Statistics for the United States), in the way of throwing light on the industrial conditions of that country; and the census reports of 1870 and 1880 were a mine of wealth, in which rich nuggets of the purest gold were likely to reward the diligent searcher for knowledge of economic facts. In Belgium, moreover, the government had already, for fifty years or more, carried out inquiries into, and published statistical information upon, the conditions of work and wages in that remarkably busy industrial State. Germany, on the other hand, was rather backward in statistics of an industrial character, and France was, if possible, more backward still, although the data that I was able to present in my former paper were perhaps full and explicit enough to indicate the general range of wages and the comparative conditions of work in both countries. In the United Kingdom the Board of Trade had attempted from time to time to collate and to publish in the now defunct "Miscellaneous Statistics of the United Kingdom" what purported to be the rates of wages paid in certain specified industries at different dates, but in such a haphazard way that, on going through these volumes, it is difficult to make a satisfactory comparison of the same industry in the same district or town over any two consecutive periods. With other countries of minor industrial importance we need not concern ourselves.

All this has now been more or less entirely altered. The system of carrying on independent investigations into the conditions of work and wages has been greatly extended in the United States. Voluminous and valuable inquiries have been successfully conducted by bureaus of labour, National and State, into the comparative circumstances of the great industries, as witness the recent portentous work on the cost of production of iron, steel, coal, and iron ores carried out by the United States Commissioner of Labour. While this knowledge has been diligently sought for as regards their people at home, the United States have arranged for the possession of similar information, on the largest possible scale, as to the industrial and economic circumstances of other countries, through the valuable consular reports issued by the Federal Government at regular and frequent intervals, and embracing every conceivable circumstance that is likely to be useful to those who are engaged in such studies. In Germany the State has, within the last few years, undertaken many separate inquiries into the conditions of the industrial population—their hours of labour, their earnings, the cost of living, and the wholesomeness or otherwise of their employment. In France the same spirit of inquiry has been abroad, and has developed various measures of great importance to the welfare of the working population; such as new laws dealing with the improvement of their dwellings, the arrangement of disputes as to wages by arbitration, the placing on a more definite footing of the law that regulates the employer's liability for accidents to his *employé*, the collection of fuller statistics of the hours of labour and the earnings of different classes of workmen, and much else besides. Belgium has been compelled to accommodate her legislation and her systems to the progress made by her neighbours, and the ameliorations that have taken place in the hours of work, the earnings of labour, and otherwise, have been considerable. Even Italy and Spain have entered into the continental competition for improvements in the conditions of labour, and have both shortened the average hours of labour and made important advances in the previous rates of wages. As for Great Britain, the labour question has of late years been more than ever identical with, and the most absorbing feature in, the condition-of-England question. A labour bureau has been established by Mr. Mundella at the Board of Trade, and has been placed ·under the able direction of my old friend Mr. John Burnett. The reports issued by this bureau have been among the most valuable and suggestive that have ever been issued by any department. The Royal Commission to inquire into the condition of trade and industry was largely an inquiry into the circumstances and conditions of labour, and the Royal Commission now sitting to inquire into the labour question is the latest outcome of the same recognition by the State that that question is paramount.

Notable changes have occurred during the same interval, not alone in the amelioration of the condition of the working classes of continental countries, but in the comparative conditions of labour as between those countries and England. The Berlin conference, which did much to give an impetus to the labour question in Germany, did a great deal also to throw light on the differences that distinguished one European country from another in reference to labour matters. I believe the general result of that conference showed that England was ahead of all other countries in reference to the care taken of the army of labour by the inspection of mines and factories, by measures for the avoidance of accidents, by the limitation of the hours of labour, and by the general safety, comfort, and health of the *proletariat*. The progress made by other countries in the interval has been neither more nor less than an attempt to approach, or to catch up, our own advances in these matters, so that if continental countries have now more closely assimilated their hours of work, their scales of wages, and their industrial legislation generally, to our own, they have, to that extent, simply copied the example that England had set before them, as the result of our greater and longer experience of industrial affairs. It is probably too soon as yet to decide how far these changes will alter the respective competitive circumstances of our own and other nations, but it would be unwise to assume hastily that the length of a day's work, or any other single factor, is to alter the relationship hitherto subsisting in this regard. It is by no means satisfactorily proved that a short day means dear labour, or that commodities are higher in price according as the labour employed in their production is highly remunerated.

With such a vast accumulation of material to select from as I have just indicated, the task I have imposed upon myself of endeavouring to compare the comparative efficiency and earnings of labour in different industrial countries, already sufficiently difficult in 1884, becomes much more so in the year 1892. The real rock ahead at the present time is not how to select materials, but how to avoid them. Volume has been piled upon volume to show how one trade or industry compares with another, how far one district or country excels another, and how far it is necessary to make allowances and adjustments in order to bring them abreast. A problem, the full and effective solution of which would occupy many more volumes still without exhausting it, cannot, of course, be adequately considered in the short space of time at my command. The task would be greatly simplified if I were merely to bring up to date the figures presented in my paper of 1884; but even that ray of encouragement does not assist me, inasmuch as the materials on which that paper was largely based—the census returns of our own and other countries—are not yet available for the new censuses of Great Britain and the United States.

II.—*Agricultural Labour.* (A.) *Wages.*

The census returns of the numbers employed in agricultural labour in England, the United States, and the British colonies not yet being available, in order to deal with this important industry at all, we must fall back upon the figures of the census years 1880 and 1881. The United States census of the former year showed that there were 3,320,000 persons employed in agriculture, who earned an average of 50*l.* per annum, as compared with an average wage of 72*l.* 6*s.* for those who were employed in manufacturing industry in the same year. In other words, the manufacturing population averaged fully 44 per cent. per annum more than the agricultural. It is, however, probable that this represents largely a nominal gain, inasmuch as the great majority of the agricultural population would have free land to cultivate, probably free lodgings or houses, and in many cases either whole or partial board. The rate of wages differs greatly in the different groups of States. A recent return by the Commissioner of Agriculture states it was as low as 15 dols. 30 c. per month in the Southern, and as high as 38 dols. 25 c. in the Pacific States.

In England the condition of agriculture has been seriously hampered during the last forty or fifty years by four causes that are specially marked, viz. :—

1. The increased cost of labour.
2. The increase of rates and taxes.
3. The more limited yield of produce.
4. Foreign competition.

With regard to the first of these elements, very striking testimony is borne in the reports of the Assistant Commissioners to the Royal Commission on Agriculture. In Mr. Coleman's Report on Northumberland, there is a statement of the average wages paid to agricultural labourers in each year between 1831 and 1880, of which the following is a summary :—

Year.	Wages Paid per Week to			
	Foreman.	Hind.	Female Workers.	Women Workers in Harvest.
	£ *s.* *d.*	*s.* *d.*	*s.* *d.*	*s.*
1831	— 12 6	11 —	4 —	9
'41	— 14 9	12 —	5 —	9
'51	— 13 —	11 —	5 —	9
'61	— 17 6	16 6	5 —	9
'71	— 18 —	16 6	6 —	12
'80	1 1 —	18 —	7 6	15

It will be noted that the average shown for Northumberland for an ordinary hind comes within 2*s.* per week of the average ascertained by the census of the United States for the same year. It will be understood that the above rates are probably the *maxima* of the United Kingdom, although it is possible that in isolated cases even higher rates have been paid.

In addition to the amount of money specified as wages in the above table, hinds were allowed their cottage and garden rent free, 60 to 80 stones of potatoes, 2 bushels of wheat, 20s. for extra hours in harvest time, and had their coals led free of charge.

In Cheshire the increase of agricultural wages appears to have been much the same in amount as in Northumberland. The Agricultural Commissioners testify that in 1845 the wages of a labourer varied from 8l. to 11l. per annum with food, and of a woman servant from 6l. to 7l. with food. In 1881, however, the wages of the former had risen to 20l., and of the latter to from 12l. to 15l., while their food had doubled in value. The report on Lancashire speaks of the same thing. Wages in 1851 on Lord Winmarleigh's estate were 12s., and in 1881 they were 18s. per week, with extras in hay and harvest times; besides which many had free cottages and gardens.

The effect of this great increase of wages on the profits of farming would have been most serious, if it had been altogether unaided by any other causes of depression. The cost of labour on any farm will, of course, vary in proportion to the relative proportions of arable and pasture land, and to a less degree upon the character of the soil, and the system of farming adopted. Numerous cases are quoted in the reports of the Assistant Agricultural Commissioners, in which the average cost of labour is about 1l. per acre. There are other cases in which the average runs up to as much as 2l. per acre. But if the average is taken at only 20s. per acre, an increase of 50 per cent. to 75 per cent. in the price paid for labour on a farm of any size must be a very heavy item.

Unfortunately this serious increase of outlay entailed by the general movement of wages, has proceeded *pari passu* with another burden which the farming community appear powerless to control. The rateable value of their holdings has in nearly every case been very much increased, and the rates have also been greatly increased. Mr. Coleman mentions the case of a farm of moderate extent in Cheshire, the rateable value of which was increased from 213l. 18s. 10d. in 1844, to 285l. in 1881, while the amount of poor rates paid rose from 7l. 2s. 8d. in the former, to 28l. 10s. in the latter year. Another case is named of a farm of 194 acres, on which the total taxes and tithe paid amounted to 9s. per acre, or 87l. 6s. per annum. Still another case is given in which the poor and highway rates thirty years since amounted to 1s. 3d. in the £, against 4s. 8d. at the present time.[1]

Space does not allow of a comparison of other countries.

[1] Mr. Coleman's "Report on Cheshire," p. 69.

(B.) *Hours of Labour.*

From the character of their employment, it was hardly to be expected that the hours of agricultural labourers should be shortened to the same extent as the hours of labour in manufacturing industry. Nevertheless, there has been a substantial abatement of the hours even of agriculturists during the last thirty years. In Cheshire the average summer hours have since 1860 been reduced from 63 to 59; in Lincolnshire (Lincoln district) from 63 to 60; in East Suffolk from 63 to 59; in Mid Sussex from 57 to 55½; and in North Herefordshire from 59 to 55½. In many other districts the hours of labour have been practically unchanged over the last fifty years.

(C.) *Efficiency.*

There can be little doubt that there is much truth in the farmer's complaint that of late years the average yield of the wheat crops, at any rate, has been under that of earlier times. The reports of the Assistant Agricultural Commissioners prove this fact to the hilt. One of these reports contains a tabular statement of the average yield of wheat per acre between 1844 and 1880. The yield has fluctuated considerably in that time, but the lowest returns are those of the last four or five years in the series. While these adverse circumstances have been in progress, it has been impossible to improve the wages paid in agriculture, as wages have been improved otherwise, consistently with fair profits to the farmer, especially in England. In most continental countries there is a duty levied on imported bread-stuffs, which enables the home producer to command a relatively higher rate than the English grower.

III.—*Mining Labour.* (A.) *Wages.*

In a statement that I recently submitted officially on behalf of the British Iron Trade Association to the Royal Commission on Labour, the following table occurs :—

TABLE I.—*Statement of the Average Daily and Annual Earnings of Coal Miners in different Countries.*

1	2 Under Ground, per Day.	3 Above Ground, per Day.	4 Average Annual Earnings of all Classes.	5 Average Wages Paid per Ton Raised.	6 Average Value of Product per Ton.
	s. d.	*s. d.*	*£ s.*	*s. d.*	*s. d.*
Great Britain	4 4	3 5½	52 –	—	—
United States	10 –	5 5	97 5	3 7	4 8½
Germany	2 8	1 10	38 6	2 2	4 8
France	3 3	2 4	43 12	4 –	8 3
Belgium	2 6	2 1	34 19	3 11	6 9

The rates here given for Great Britain are those shown in the Board of Trade Report on the wages paid in mines and quarries in 1885, and apply to Durham and Northumberland, as typical districts; the other figures are from Government returns. The rates of wages have, however, greatly advanced since then, and as the latest report on trade unions, by Mr. John Burnett, shows, the rates of wages paid to miners in the great northern coalfield were as high as between 6s. and 7s. per day in 1890-91. Unfortunately the question of the maintenance of this, or an approximate rate, has recently been the occasion of one of the most disastrous strikes on record. The rates shown for 1885 are, of course, much more like the normal rates than those recently current.

The average given for the United States is perhaps hardly comparable with that given for Great Britain, inasmuch as it includes a number of remote States where wages were high on account of the scarcity of *employés* or for other reasons. A more exact comparison may be got by taking the Pennsylvania bituminous coalfield alone, and comparing it with the Great Northern coalfield. This gives us the following result :—[2]

Average Annual Earnings of all Classes.

	£
Durham and Northumberland	52
Pennsylvania	59

Average Weekly Earnings.

	Coal Hewers.		Labourers on Surface.	
	s.	*d.*	*s.*	*d.*
Durham and Northumberland	26	–	18	2
Pennsylvania	34	1	20	–

From which it would appear that the Pennsylvania annual rate is only 13·4 per cent. above that of the Great Northern coalfield.

Comparing the United Kingdom with continental countries, it would appear that the average wages paid in our coal mines, as shown above, were :—

34 per cent. higher than in		Germany.
20	,,	France.
49		Belgium.

Of late years, the increase of wages paid, and the general improvement of the condition of the workers, seem to have made

[2] These two coalfields are more alike than any others, alike in the extent of their bituminous coal production, and the numbers they employ. The average productiveness per *employé* is, however, higher in Pennsylvania.

larger progress in Continental countries than in our own. Indeed, it may be questioned whether the average wages of English miners have, on an average, greatly increased during the last twenty-five years, although their circumstances have improved in reference to the hours of labour worked, and other conditions.[3] Happily, the complete returns that are annually collected by some foreign coal-producing countries enable us to bring the matter of their progress to the test of actual figures.

In Belgium the average annual earnings per *employé* have increased over the period of sixty years ending 1890 by 107 per cent., while the average annual output of ·coal per *employé* over the same period has increased by 90 per cent. As in Belgium, so, *mutatis mutandis*, in the principal coalfields of Germany and France. And the advance of wages, although generally considerable, has not often led to any increase in the prices of commodities; but, on the contrary, the prices of commodities have generally shown a marked fall. Increased efficiency and increased industrial earnings have therefore proceeded hand-in-hand.

(B.) *Hours of Labour.*

A Parliamentary return recently published,[4] shows that there has been a remarkable reduction in the hours of labour in the principal coalfields of the United Kingdom during recent years. Comparing 1890 with 1850, it appears that there has been a reduction of 22 hours per week in the Newcastle district, $14\frac{1}{4}$ hours in the Wigan district and in Derbyshire, 18 hours in two of the principal districts of Yorkshire, and 4 to 18 hours in Scotland. These large reductions of the hours of labour are, of course, an equivalent for proportionately higher earnings. In the principal Continental countries the hours continue to be considerably longer than in our own. In France the hewers averaged in 1890 8 hours 13 minutes at the face,[5] as compared with an average of not quite $7\frac{1}{2}$ hours in this country. In Belgium, the average duration of the miner's shift is over 9 hours, and in Germany the time at actual work varies from 8 hours in the Dortmund and Saarbrück coalfields to 10 in Lower, and 12 in Upper, Silesia. In the United States the hours of work vary from $8\frac{1}{2}$ to $9\frac{1}{2}$. Great Britain therefore has shorter hours for mining labour than any other country.

---

[3] The last report of the Labour Correspondent of the Board of Trade shows that in Northumberland the average wages paid to hewers in 1863 was 4*s.* 5*d.*, and that in 1888 it was 4*s.* 6¾*d.*, so that the amount of increase was only 1¾*d.* per day. There had, however, been large variations in the interval.

[4] Mr. Broadhurst's return (375 of 1890).

[5] "Bulletin du Ministère des Travaux Publics," June, 1891.

(c.) *Efficiency of Mining Labour.*

Without quite going the length of saying that the mining labour of Great Britain is less efficient, as measured in terms of annual product, than it formerly was, two things may be asserted with some confidence, namely—

1. That the average productiveness of British labour has not of late years increased so much as it formerly did; and

2. That the average productiveness of labour in Great Britain has not increased during the last thirty years to the extent that is shown in other countries.

Appended is a statement showing the production of coal per workman employed in the principal coal producing countries in 1882 and 1889, including underground and surface labour:—[*]

TABLE II.—*Annual Output of Coal per Employé in different Countries*
1882 *and* 1889.

Country.	1882.	1889.	Increase.	Decrease.
	Tons	Tons	Tons	Tons
Great Britain	310	313	3	—
United States	370*	435	65	—
Germany	274	284	10	—
France	190	215	25	—
Belgium	167	184	17	—

* The figures for the United States refer to the census year 1880.

TABLE III.—*Production of Coal per Miner (Under Ground) in each of the Years* 1882 *and* 1889.

Country.	1882.	1889.	Increase.	Decrease.
	Tons	Tons	Tons	Tons
Great Britain	385	381	—	4
United States	—†	823	—	—
France	265	305	40	—
Belgium	221	246	25	—

† The figures for the United States refer to the census year 1880.

This statement brings out the fact that in foreign countries, and notably in the United States and Germany, the efficiency of labour is improving greatly—that the number of tons produced per man per annum has increased, in spite of shorter hours, so that England is not now in the same relative position that she formerly occupied.

It is however proper to qualify the above comparatively un-

[*] Memorandum submitted to the Royal Commission on Labour by the British Iron Trade Association.

favourable showing for Great Britain, by observing that, taking
ten-yearly intervals from 1861 to 1890, there have been the
following averages :—

Year.	Output per *Employé* (all Classes). Tons
1861	305
'71	316
'81	314
'90	299

These averages are again liable to be qualified, in favour of
British labour, if we take the more important district averages
of ten-yearly periods, as is done in the following statement :—

TABLE IV.—*Average Tons of Coal Raised per Male Worker per Annum.*

District.	Period 1861-69.	Period 1870-79.	Period 1880-90.
	Tons	Tons	Tons
Northumberland and Durham	403	312	332
South Wales	367	277	290
Yorkshire	274	266	300
Scotland	299	276	307
North and East Lancashire	262	274	318

As these five districts or groups represent about 70 per cent.
of the total output of coal in this country in 1890, they may be
regarded as fairly typical of the kingdom generally. It is apparent
that for all districts there has been an increased average output
during the third as compared with the second period, although in
the Great Northern coalfield and in South Wales there appears to
have been a greater average output in the first period than in
either the second or the third.[7]

It has been observed that the average productiveness per
employé appears to have decreased in Great Britain, while it shows
an increase in the United States, Germany, France, and one or two
other countries. This fact, without explanation, would seem to
argue very ill for the present position and future prospects of
England in reference to coal supplies. But as a matter of fact the
figures obtained by dividing the number of workers employed in
any given industry into the total amount of the product are only
a very partial guide to the efficiency of the workers. The output
per man will vary much from one year to another in the same
coalfield, and even in the same mine. This may be quite indepen-

---

[7] In the first of these periods the figures are probably not so reliable as in the
second and third. The second period includes the years of the coal famine,
1872-74, when the miners practised restriction on a large scale.

dent of such accidental disturbing influences as the working of
shorter time, or a strike of the *employés*, or similar occurrences.

In Appendix (A) I have shown the variations in the production
of coal in the United Kingdom as a whole over the last thirty
years. It will be observed that in the United Kingdom generally,
the greatest average output during that period was 320 tons, and
the lowest average was 237 tons, so that the highest was 38 per
cent. more than the lowest. If however we take the country
as a whole for periods of ten years, the average output has not
materially diminished, although there has been a falling-off as
regards individual districts. The tendency has been to set off the
reduction of output which would, under ordinary circumstances,
result from the reduction of the hours of labour that has taken
place during that period, by introducing mechanical improvements
in reference to hauling, winding, and other details of working,
and in some few cases—although this is by no means general—
greater economy has resulted from the introduction of coal-cutting
machinery.

The remarks that have just been made as to the disturbing
elements that affect the *per capita* coal output of the United
Kingdom are equally operative in reference to any estimate of the
comparative efficiency of the coal miners of other countries, as·
measured by individual output. The average output of Germany
has, as will be seen from Appendix (B), varied greatly, like that
of the United Kingdom, although there, as here, there has not, on
the whole, been a reduction of average efficiency, but the reverse.
It is also to be remarked that the average of the principal districts,
when the country as a whole is taken, is liable to be levelled
down by the inclusion of inferior coalfields, in which coal has to be
worked at a greater depth, or as inferior seams. Thus it appears
that over the twelve years ending 1891, the average output per
employé in the Westphalian coalfield, which yields more than
one-half of the total production of Germany, was not less than
287 tons, whereas if we take that Empire as a whole the average
was only 272 tons per workman. The coal output of Germany is
determined, in reference to its competitive position in the markets
of the world, and the comparative efficiency of its workers, by the
Dortmund, or chief Westphalian, coalfield, and hence the importance of this distinction. If we take the other coalfields of
Germany, we find that this adaptability to a large individual production varies greatly, owing in part to the character of the seams,
and partly to the physical structure of the mineral, as well as from
other causes. But the important fact to be borne in mind is that
during recent years the average efficiency of the workmen in the
Westphalian coalfield, as measured in terms of annual output, has

been brought nearly abreast of that of the coal workers of our own country, while their average rate of wages is considerably lower. The other coal-producing countries of Europe are so far behind our own that their power of competition need not be seriously considered.

The remarks as to differences that necessarily exist in the average capacity for a large output of the workers in different districts of the same country, apply, *mutatis mutandis*, to the rates of wages paid. On this point I would ask you to bear in mind two obvious considerations that apply more or less to all earnings, namely :—

1. That the rate of wages per hour or per day affords no necessary clue to the actual annual earnings, and—

2. That as the rate of wages almost invariably differs as between one district and another, it is practically impossible to arrive at a satisfactory general average for any industry, even in regard to the same country.

Taking the United States as a case in point, we find from a recent census *Bulletin* that the rate of wages per hour or per day would, continued over all the working days of a year, give the averages stated in the first column of figures in the following table, whereas the real averages were those stated in the second column :—

	Assumed Average.		Actual Average.	
	s.	*d.*	*s.*	*d.*
Coal hewers	48	10	31	4
Labourers	41	9	32	7
Banksmen	40	–	27	9
Lads on surface	21	6	13	9

In this case we find that the assumed average, based on the actual rate per working day, is about 50 per cent. more than the actual average, the difference being of course accounted for by irregularity of work, or other kindred causes. In a greater or a less degree the same differences will be found in other districts and in other countries.

Many of the remarks that have been applied to coal mining are also more or less applicable to the kindred industry—the mining of iron ore. Table C in the Appendix shows how the annual average output of iron ore has increased in Germany between 1878 and 1891, the average increase in the interval having been 98 tons, or about 50 per cent. ; and Table D shows that in the United States the average annual output of iron ore in the census year 1889 was 379 tons, as compared with 223 tons in 1880—an increase of 156 tons, or about 70 per cent. The averages in both of these cases were greatly liable to be influenced by variations in the quantities of ores mined in different districts, causing a larger proportion of easily-mined ores to be produced at one time than at another, and by other factors; but this would hardly apply to any great extent in the case of Luxembourg, which showed, as between 1881 and 1889, an increase of 166 *tons per employé*, or 28 per cent. I ought to add that the two districts in Continental Europe in which the mining of iron ore is most fairly comparable with our own chief district—that of Cleveland—are those of Luxembourg and Alsace-Lorraine, and that these districts compare as under:—

District.	Production, 1 = 1,000 Tons.	Number of *Employés*.	Average Annual Output per *Employé*.
			Tons
Cleveland	5,657	6,542	864
Luxembourg	3,171	3,964	799
Alsace	2,959	3,439	860

IV.—*Textile Labour.*   (A.) *Wages.*

There is no class of the community whose economic circumstances have undergone greater improvement within recent years than that which is engaged in textile industry, and that, too, in spite of the fact that owing to the exceptionally large number of women and children[8] employed, trades unionism of the ordinary kind is difficult, if not impossible.

Some years ago I published a work[9] in which I cited figures by Mr. R. Montgomery, the President of the Manchester Statistical Society, and Mr. Lord, formerly President of the Manchester Chamber of Commerce, showing the following percentages of increase in the wages paid in textile industries in the county of Lancashire during the previous thirty years:—

	Mr. Montgomery's Figures, 1854 to 1884. Percentage of Increase.	Mr Lord's Figures, 1850 to 1883. Percentage of Increase.
Spinning	63	16·27 to 74·72
Weaving	43	35·16 „ 74·72
Dyeing	16	—
Calico printing	46	50
Calendering	47	40

[8] It is shown in the Board of Trade "Report on the Rates of Wages Paid in "the Principal Textile Trades of the United Kingdom in 1886" (C–5807), that in that year, out of about 143,000 *employés* returned, 44·4 per cent. were women, 16·4 per cent. were girls, and 16·7 per cent. were lads and boys, leaving only 22·5 per cent. of the whole as adult males likely to be capable of combination.

[9] "England's Supremacy." Longmans.

The above advances have of course been coincident with a general reduction of the hours of work—which, instead of being 60 to 65, are now generally 56½ per week—and with a great improvement in the conditions of the workers in other respects.

It is hardly necessary to add that this amelioration has not been confined to the textile trades of our own country. In France, and in other Continental countries, it has been equally marked. The improvement that has taken place in the circumstances of the textile workers of France has been strikingly shown in the following statement of the daily wages paid in the woollen trade of that country in each of the years 1836 and 1872, the wages being in all cases those of men :—[10]

TABLE V.—*Wages Paid to Textile Workers in France*, 1836 *and* 1872.

Description.	Daily Rate of Wages Paid.	
	In 1836.	In 1872.
	s. *d.*	*s.* *d.*
Wool dressers	— 8½	2 2
Carders	— 8½	2 1
Spinners	1 5	2 10
Warpers	— 7¾	2 8½
Hand loom weavers	1 7	2 6¼
Washers	1 1½	2 11
Mechanics	1 —	2 1

Here we have an average increase of wages, all along the line, of considerably over 100 per cent., but the same statement shows that during the same interval the wages of women at the earlier period were more nearly on a level with those of men than they were at the later date—in other words, that men have made much more progress than the other sex. Since 1872, the average range of wages has been more than maintained.

Since the year 1862, particulars as to the wages paid in the textile trades have been carefully collected from a large number of establishments in different parts of Italy. From a summary of such particulars, I have collated the following comparison of the daily earnings of 1862 and 1889 :—[11]

[10] A. Redgrave's " Report on the Cotton, Woollen, and Flax Factories of " France and Belgium, 1873."

[11] " Board of Trade Journal " for April, 1891, p. 413.

TABLE VI.—*Wages Paid to Textile Workers in Italy*, 1862 *and* 1889.

	1862.		1889.	
	s.	*d.*	*s.*	*d.*
Province of Milan—				
Cotton spinners	–	10½	1	6½
„ weavers	1	–¼	1	3¾
Novaro—				
Wool spinners	2	8½	3	5¾
„ carders	1	2½	2	–
Cuneo (women)—				
Silk spinners	–	10	–	11½
„ twisters	–	8	1	–¼

Italy is generally regarded as a type of the more backward countries, from an industrial point of view, so that it need excite no surprise that the progress made in this case is far from equal to that shown for our own country and France. Nevertheless, the position of the textile workers has greatly improved even in Italy—much more so, indeed, than the above figures would seem to indicate. A recent Foreign Office report[12] shows that in order to obtain the equivalent in wages to 100 kilos. of corn, an Italian workman—taking an average of about fifty large factories—had to work only 95 hours in 1889, as compared with 195 hours in 1862, so that, as measured by this test, his circumstances now are twice as good as they were then.

In the United States, the condition of labour has generally been better, estimated by mere wages, than in any European country. Even there, however, there has, within the last forty or fifty years, been a remarkable advance in the general rate of wages. This advance has been well illustrated by a statement drawn up some years ago by my friend, Mr. Edward Atkinson, of Boston, who shows that in a cotton factory that had been carried on continuously for about half-a-century, in one of the Eastern States, the average wages paid per operative per year were:—

	£
In 1840....................................	36·9
„ '84....................................	59·8

being an increase, as between the two dates, of about 62 per cent. If these figures are compared with Mr. Montgomery's, already cited, it will be seen that the increase is about the same as that shown for cotton-spinning in Lancashire for the period 1834-84.

If however we compare Mr. Atkinson's figures with those given in the tenth census of the United States, we find that the

---

[12] No. 195, Miscellaneous series, 1891.

general rate of wages paid in the cotton factories of that country is not so high as in the isolated factory referred to. By dividing the numbers employed in the cotton industry of the United States into the total sum paid as wages in each of the years 1860 and 1880, we get the following averages for all *employés* :—

	£
1860	40·8
'80	50·8

showing an increase of only 10*l.* per *employé*, or 24½ per cent. over the whole period.

The Board of Trade Report on wages in the principal textile trades in 1886[13] gives the average wages paid over all classes of cotton operatives in that year as 36*l.*[14] If this general average is compared with Mr. Atkinson's for 1883, it shows a difference in favour of the United States of 23*l.* 8*s.* per annum, or 66·1 per cent. If it is compared with the general average of the United States for 1880, it shows an increase of only 14*l.* 8*s.* a year, or 41·1 per cent. Of course we must not forget that we are here comparing the year 1880 in the United States, with the year 1886 in this country, but I do not think that, as between 1880 and 1886, there was any considerable rise of wages in either country; and, in any case, the census figures as to the cotton industry for a later date are not yet published, so that the means do not exist for carrying the comparison beyond 1880.

Obviously, in order to give full significance to this comparison, or to any comparison of a like kind, it is necessary to know how many *employés* there were under the several heads of men, women, and children. Such a comparison appears to be favourable to our own country. No fewer than 35 per cent. of the total number engaged in the cotton industry of the United States in 1880 were males above 16 years of age. In the Board of Trade return already cited the number of *employés* returned as *men* was 22·5 per cent. of the whole. The American average therefore appears to have included a considerably larger number of what, from a cotton-trade point of view, would probably be called adult males. It would not be well, however, to attach too much importance to this showing, inasmuch as the Board of Trade report has not given the age at which the *employé* is entered as a man, and obviously if any considerable number of the class described as "lads and boys," as distinguished from men, in that return were over 16 years of age, the percentages of higher-rated male workers above shown would be disturbed.[15]

[13] *Op. cit.*

[14] In two of the most important districts, the average rises to 42*l.* a year.

[15] Mr. Giffen states expressly that " some of these lads and boys are not dis-" tinguishable from young men."

The following comparison of normal wages in the cotton, woollen, worsted, and linen trades, in 1886, is given on the authority of the Board of Trade :—[16]

TABLE VII.— *Wages Paid to Textile Workers in Great Britain in 1886.*

	Cotton.		Woollen.		Worsted.		Linen.	
				ANNUAL.				
	£	*s.*	£	*s.*	£	*s.*	£	*s.*
Men	65	12	60	–	60	13	51	13
Lads and boys	24	4	22	–	16	18	16	4
Women.....................	39	15	34	9	31	–	23	3
Girls	17	17	19	7	16	–	12	17
				WEEKLY.				
	s.	*d.*	*s.*	*d.*	*s.*	*d.*	*s.*	*d.*
Men	25	3	23	2	23	4	19	9
Lads and boys	9	4	8	6	6	6	6	3
Women.....................	15	3	15	3	11	11	8	11
Girls	6	10	7	5	6	2	4	11

The Massachusetts Bureau of Labour Statistics found in 1884, as the result of an exhaustive inquiry into the differences in the rates of wages paid in leading occupations in Great Britain and the United States, that when the earnings were reduced to an hourly rate, the following were the amounts and the higher percentages paid in textile industry in the latter country :—[17]

TABLE VIII.—*Wages Paid to Textile Labour in United Kingdom and United States in 1884.*

	Average Wages Paid per Hour in		Difference by Increase in United States.
	Great Britain.	United States.	
	d.	*d.*	Per cent.
Cotton goods	4·16	5·37	29·0
Woollen „	4·34	5·75	32·4
Worsted „	3·21	6·10	90·0
Hosiery	4·30	5·41	25·8
Clothing	6·25	8·57	37·1

Had this paper been presented to the Society a few months later, I should no doubt have been able to present the average rates of wages in most of the textile industries of the United

[16] " Return of Rates of Wages in the Principal Textile Trades of the United " Kingdom, with Report thereon." (C–5807, 1889.)

[17] " England's Supremacy: its Sources, Economics, and Dangers." By J. S. Jeans. Longmans.

States for the census year 1889-90.   As it is, I have only at command the returns of one industry—that of woollens—for that year.   It appears that, as between 1880 and 1890, there was an increase in the average wages paid to *employés* engaged in the woollen manufactures of the United States from 293 to 347 dols. (61*l*. to 72*l*. 3*s*.), or rather over 18 per cent.   The details are shown for the six principal States in the following table :—

TABLE IX.—*Number of Hands Employed, Total Wages Paid, and Average Wages Paid per Employé in the Woollen Industry of the United States, in the Census Years 1880 and 1890.*

	Total Hands.		Total Wages Paid.		Average Wages Paid per *Employé.*	
	1880.	1890.	1880.	1890.	1880.	1890.
			1 = $1,000.	1 = $1,000.	$	$
Connecticut	12,024	13,047	3,987	4,941	331	378
Illinois	1,749	2,792	388	858	221	307
Indiana......................	2,025	3,109	487	817	240	262
Massachusetts	38,128	43,038	11,636	16,154	305	375
New York	24,286	38,596	7,225	13,058	297	338
Pennsylvania	42,261	55,786	12,338	19,800	291	354
United States	161,557	221,087	47,389	76,768	293	347

The above statement, showing the number of *employés* and the wages paid, may suitably be supplemented by the following table, which shows that the value of the goods produced in 1890 over 1880 had only increased by 26·5 per cent., whereas there had been an increase of 62 per cent. in the total amount of wages paid; and which further indicates the important fact, that, as measured by the quantity of raw materials of all kinds consumed per *employé*, there had been increased efficiency on the part of the workers, in the interval, to the extent of 46 lbs. over the year, or rather under 4 per cent. :—

TABLE X.—*General Comparison of the Woollen Industry of the United States in 1880 and 1890.*

	1880.	1890.	Percentage of Increase.
Number of hands employed	161,557	221,087	36·8
Wages paid................................. $	47,389,087	76,768,871	62·0
Cost of materials used .... $	164,371,551	203,095,642	23·5
Value of goods produced at factory............... $	267,252,913	338,231,109	26·5
Raw scoured wool used............ lbs.	171,880,800	215,001,813	25·1
" per *employé* .... "	1,632	977	—
All materials consumed per *employé* .... "	1,663	1,709	2·8

As between 1880 and 1890, the following characteristics have become apparent in the woollen industry of the United States, and presumably also in other textiles:—

1. A large relative decrease in the number of children employed, the latter being only 7 per cent. of the whole in 1890, as compared with 11·7 per cent. of the whole in 1880.

2. An increase in the relative number of women employed over the age of 15, the latter having been 45 per cent. of the whole in 1890, as compared with 41·6 per cent. in 1880.

3. A decrease relatively to the whole number employed in the males above 16 years of age, who were 44·9 per cent. of the whole in 1890, as compared with 46·8 per cent. in 1880.

(B.) *Hours of Labour in Textile Factories.*

The remarks that have already been made as to the hours of labour in Great Britain being shorter than in other industrial countries will apply as much to textile as to mining labour. In England, as we have seen, the hours in textile factories have been reduced from between 60 and 70 per week in 1850 to an average of 56½ at the present time.[16] These shorter hours have now been enjoyed by our vast textile population for about twenty years, while in the majority of Continental countries 60 to 70 hours per week continues to be the rule, and in many factories 12 hours a day are regularly worked.

It is true that the tendency in foreign countries, following the recommendations made by labour congresses, and acting in the spirit of the Berlin Conference, has recently been to still further reduce the hours of labour, and it is probable that in the future other countries may make efforts in this direction that will do much to secure for their industrial population the same advantages that factory legislation has so long provided for our own.

(c.) *Efficiency of Textile Labour.*

A comparison of the efficiency of labour in the American woollen industry, as between 1880 and 1890, is rendered difficult by the extent to which the consumption of raw wool has been superseded by that of other materials such as shoddy, camel's hair, mohair, and cotton. These latter materials were used to the extent of 164 million lbs. in 1890, while in 1880 they were only used to the extent of 108 million lbs. Taking the materials used as a whole, it appears that in 1890 there was an increase of 46 lbs. per *employé* in the quantities of all raw materials consumed, so that to this extent there appears to have been an increase of efficiency.

---

[16] See Mr. Broadhurst's return (375 of 1890), p. 56 *et seq.*

which was no doubt materially assisted by the fact that the number of establishments at work had been reduced in the interval from 2,689 to 2,503—in other words, there had been a large number of small establishments weeded out, and production had been undertaken on a large scale.   These remarks will apply almost equally to other textiles, although we have not the exact means for determining the influence elsewhere of the changes indicated, that are furnished by the full and specific returns given in the census reports of the United States.

A natural curiosity is likely to be aroused as to whether we have been making as much progress within recent years as we formerly did, or whether we have been making any progress at all.

If we examine the returns collated by the inspectors of factories, we find that in the cotton branch of our textile trades there were 215 spindles of all kinds per *employé*—in spinning factories alone—in 1878, as compared with 217 in 1890.   In this interval of twelve years, therefore, the progress made in our cotton-spinning factories as such would seem to have been stationary.

In the weaving branch of the cotton trade there appears to have been an absolute falling off during the same period, there having been 2·11 looms to each operative employed in 1890, as compared with 2·13 looms in the year 1878.   These figures are for England and Wales only.

Much the same sort of result is brought out by an examination of the woollen and worsted trades.   In regard to the latter, indeed, it appears that the number of spindles of all kinds, in the spinning factories *per se*, per operative employed, was exactly 38 in each of the years 1878 and 1890.

So far as flax is concerned, Scotland during this period shows a large decline, both in absolute and relative production, the average number of spindles per *employé* having been only 14·7 in 1890, as compared with 14·8 in 1878.   On the other hand, Ireland, in the same interval, exhibits the trifling increase of from 21·0 to 21·9 spindles per *employé*.

These facts suggest the reflection that for the time being, at least, if not for altogether, our textile manufactures have almost attained a rest-and-be-thankful stage, and that the future is likely to be more stationary than the past.   This is perhaps what might have been expected, after the very striking progress achieved in the thirty previous years.   But the important question that lies before us is not so much that of the absolute amount of progress we are making, as it is that of the advances which we have made in comparison with other nations.   If they go ahead while we stand still, our relative place in the race must soon become an inferior one.

A remarkable statement was lately published by Mr. Edward Atkinson, showing that in a large factory in the United States, the number of lbs. of cotton worked per operative per day had between 1840 and 1884 increased by 190 per cent.—that is from $10\frac{7.8}{100}$ to $31\frac{2.9}{100}$—while the hours worked per day had concurrently fallen from 13 to 11, or 15 per cent., so that the number of lbs. per operative per hour had increased by 240 per cent. The increase occurred mainly in the additional number of spindles tended, but there was also an increase of efficiency to the extent of 22 per cent. in the number of lbs. of cotton per spindle. A cognate fact of equal significance was that while the wages paid per yard of cotton stuff produced had in this interval fallen by 41 per cent., the wages paid per operative per hour had increased by 96 per cent.

In all probability much the same extent of progress has been achieved within an equally short period in the United Kingdom. I have elsewhere shown,[19] that within a comparatively recent time, the average rate of working spindles has been enormously increased—in some cases from 4,000 to 8,000 revolutions per minute—that improvements in the steam engine have enabled an equal yield of manufactured goods to be obtained with one-half the former consumption of fuel, and that it is no uncommon thing in the most modern mills to see two girls and a man attending to a couple of mules, which, unitedly, have a couple of thousand spindles. It would be wonderful, indeed, if this remarkable progress were to be continued, and while we cannot perhaps prevent other countries from coming up to our own high level, it behoves us, at the stage at which we have now arrived, to take care that other countries do not, in striving after our own standard of attainment, go ahead of us in the race.

V.—*General Labour.*

In my former paper, I showed, from several authorities, that during the previous thirty-five or forty years there had been a very large increase of wages in the principal countries of the world, and in our own more than in any other. This general result has been substantiated by a number of statistics that have since appeared, although not in all cases to the same extent. The evidence of improvement in the economic condition of the workers of the country has generally proceeded from the employers, who have no doubt possessed the most readily available means of showing how matters actually stood, or were tending. It is only fair to add that the evidence that has since been supplied from trades union sources has not shown the same extent of improvement. Indeed,

[19] " England's Supremacy," p. 204.

instead of a general advance of 40 per cent., stated to have occurred in the principal trades of the Manchester district between 1850 and 1883, on evidence supplied by Mr. Lord, and quoted in my former paper (p. 24), a recent trades union report only gives a general rise of from 3s. to 7s. per week in some of the principal trades of the country as between 1850 and 1886, but this latter set of figures, which is appended herewith (Appendices E and F), is rather vitiated by the fact that it is not stated to what particular districts the rates of wages given apply, although it is to be presumed that they will for the most part relate to the metropolis.

The advances in the general rates of wages paid in the United Kingdom, as between 1850 and 1886, have, of course, been coincident with a considerable general reduction in the average hours of labour, so that the improvement in the rates of wages paid is greater than would appear if considered as mere wages alone.

The first important reduction in the hours of labour appears to have come into effect about the year 1870-71, and no doubt it was largely aided by the great 9 hours' strike among the engineers of the North of England. Compositors had their hours of labour reduced from 63 to 60 in 1866, and to 54 in 1872.[20] The reduction in the hours of labour, as between 1850 and 1890, in a number of occupations followed on a large scale, is shown in the Appendix (K). It will be observed that 54 to 56 hours per week now appears to be the rule.

In the United States, the average rate of wages was very low before the war; but the impulse that was given to the demand for commodities generally by that event caused an active inquiry for labour, and consequently raised the general rate of wages, as well as the prices of commodities. It will be seen from the tables (Appendices G and H), selected at random from the volume of the tenth census on wages and the cost of living in the United States, prepared by my friend, Mr. J. D. Weeks, of Pittsburgh, that there was generally a substantial advance of wages between 1860 and 1865; that this advance was maintained and increased up to 1870; that the latter year appears to have reached the high water mark of American wages; and that there was generally a reduction of wages between 1870 and 1875, followed in some cases ·by a recovery, and in others by a further fall about 1880, but in no case

---

[20] My friend Mr. Hanson, of the well-known Ballantyne Press, which has been in existence for nearly a century, has furnished me with returns, from which it would appear that in addition to the reduced hours of labour referred to, the wages of compositors have nearly doubled as between 1784 and 1884. But this has mostly occurred since the year 1864, the advance in the previous eighty years having been only 6s. per week. This is probably a typical example of the improved circumstances within the same interval of skilled labour generally.

coming up to the exceptionally high level of 1870. This applies
equally to skilled and unskilled labour. The figures are unusually
reliable, because they are obtained in each case direct from the
manufacturer, who has gone back over his books for a long series
of years, in order that he may furnish strictly parallel figures.
For unskilled labour the daily rate will be seen to amount to from
5s. to 6s., but this does not of course mean that the sum of a year's
earnings will be 300 or 310 days' of such labour, as the work is in
many cases very irregular. The skilled labour rate appears to be
from 9s. to 10s. per day, as shown in Appendix G, and the
unskilled labour rate from 5s. to 6s. per day, as shown in
Appendix H.

What has been stated as to the generally increased efficiency
of labour in the mining and textile industries will, *ex hypothesi*,
equally apply to the course of labour generally, although it is
obviously impossible that other industries could be considered to
the same extent in this paper. There has been a vast increase of
efficiency, as measured in terms of product, at blast furnaces, steel
works, paper mills, glass works, engineering works, and other
establishments, and this increase has been reflected in the lower
prices of commodities generally, as well as in the greatly improved
condition of labour.

In comparing the returns of production at manufacturing
establishments, it is important to bear in mind the fact that there
have been, in most countries, many more strikes of late years than
there formerly were,[21] and that to this extent the productiveness
of labour in a later period is likely to be unfavourably affected,
so that the additional output, in spite of such interference with
regular working, is all the more cogent evidence of the greater
efficiency of labour.

Before passing entirely from the subject of the recent increased
earnings of workmen in different countries, I would like to call
attention to two remarkable sets of figures recently issued in
reference to France—the first showing the large advances that
have taken place in wages in that country; and the other the
apparent futility of strikes as means of advancing wages.

The average wages paid in the principal coal fields of the Nord

---

[21] It is officially stated that in France strikes were almost unknown until 1874,
when 21 took place in the country as a whole. This number in 1880 had increased
to 65, and in 1882, the number had risen to 182. Between 1874 and 1887, there
were 1,060 strikes in all. It is true that most of them were of short duration.
Of 918 strikes of which particulars are given, 115 lasted for only one day, and
109 more for two days. In 300 cases the workmen concerned numbered less than
50, and only 4 strikes affected between 5,000 and 10,000 men. In England and
in the United States strikes have generally been on a larger scale.

and the Pas-de-Calais in each of the years 1870, 1880, and 1890 have been as under :—

	Nord.		Pas-de-Calais.
	£	s.	£
1870	31	10	27
'80	39	–	41
'90	52	–	52

This advance has been concurrent with a large diminution of the hours of labour, so that, as above indicated, it represents a greater amelioration than appears on the surface.

In his " Annuaire de l'Economie Politique," Block shows that in sixty-two branches of manufacture, of which statistics were supplied by the mayors of the chief towns of France for 1853 and 1887, the average wages paid (not including Paris) were as under :—

Years.	Ordinary.	Maximum.	Minimum.
	frs.	frs.	frs.
1853	1·89	2·36	1·53
'87	3·20	3·90	2·65
Increase	1·31	1·54	1·12
„ per cent.	66·10	64 50	72·00

In reference to France, as in reference to all countries where such a remarkable improvement of the conditions of labour has occurred, we are naturally led to inquire how has this amelioration come about? If we cannot answer this question quite satisfactorily, we can at any rate say how it has *not* come about. Official returns show that out of 1,060 strikes in France between 1874 and 1887, both years inclusive, 474, or 44 per cent., were for a rise of wages, and 267 more, or 22 per cent., were against a proposal for a reduction. Only 247 strikes in all had an issue favourable to the workmen on strike, while 581 had a result unfavourable to them, the remainder having resulted in small concessions or compromises, so that the number of unfavourable results were nearly twice as numerous as the favourable.

It would be interesting, but on this occasion impossible, to enter into the question of what determines the rates of wages paid in different countries, and the cognate inquiry, how far is there in our own and other countries a probability of a further rise of wages, and an assimilation of the wages rates of all countries to a comparatively uniform standard. Our inquiries, so far as they have proceeded, have shown us that the general efficiency of labour has hitherto increased to a greater extent than the increase in the rates of wages paid, qualified by the general reduction in the hours of work, so that although the nominal cost of labour has largely increased, its actual cost, as measured by the value of the commodities produced, has tended to decrease. To suppose that this movement is not likely to be carried farther, would be to assume that finality has been reached in labour-saving machinery, in the discovery of new and cheaper processes, and in mechanical and chemical improvements of different kinds. Such an assumption would not only be very rash, but it would be wholly untenable in view of what has already been stated. At the same time, there must be some, as yet undiscovered, limits beyond which the wages of labour shall not be increased, and the hours of labour shall not be reduced. Hitherto the tendency has been to increase the means of production much more rapidly than consumption.[22] So long as this is continued, it is probable that there may be a margin left for further amelioration in the economic condition of our working population.

VI.—*The Employment of Women and Children, &c.*

The comparative efficiency of labour in different countries is necessarily affected to a greater or less degree by the extent to which the inferior and low-priced labour of women and children is employed. In my former paper I showed that the United States had at that time the largest proportion of juvenile workers, and in this paper I have already shown that as regards one important section of the textile industry—that of woollens—the tendency is to employ a less relative number of children. The same tendency is apparent in other countries, and is especially marked in our own. It will be observed from Table L in the Appendix, that the percentage of the total number of operatives engaged in textile industry in the United Kingdom who were returned as half-timers, fell from 11·33 per cent. of the whole in 1878 to 7·97 per cent. in 1890, and that in the cotton trade the percentage had fallen from 12·63 to 9·10 per cent. In the lace trade the percentage proportion of half-timers had fallen from 11·60 to 2·12 per cent., and in the woollen industry the fall was from over 7·0 to 3·31 per cent.

It is different as regards female labour, which represented, as shown in Appendix M, 56·2 per cent. of our total textile workers in 1890, as compared with 55·5 per cent. in 1878. This slight increase has to be set off against the decrease of half-timers. When this has been done, it is probable that the influence on the average

[22] Mr. Edward Atkinson points out that one operative in a cotton mill now spins and weaves in a year cotton cloth for 250 persons; one operative does the same for 300 persons in a woollen mill; one operative in a boot factory makes two pairs of boots and shoes annually for 800 persons; while one operative in a shirt factory makes four shirts a year for 600 to 800 persons.

efficiency of textile workers generally of the varying proportions of different grades of *employés*, as between the two dates, will be comparatively unimportant.

It is necessary to distinguish between two different forms or aspects of efficiency. There is the efficiency due to sheer strength, brute force, and endurance; and there is the efficiency due to the cultivated and intelligent skill of the trained artizan. There is the efficiency that is born of the improvement of processes and machinery, in which the worker not only generally bears a subordinate part, but in consequence of which he is often transformed from a subtle thinker and a deft worker, into a self-acting tool; and there is the efficiency consequent upon the possession and exercise of higher skill and greater concentration of energy. It is probably not too much to affirm that the greater efficiency of the cotton operatives is more due to the superiority of the machinery at work than to any superiority of the workers themselves, but if the cost of production is reduced the result remains the same. The work of miners and quarriers, on the other hand, although greatly aided by better systems of winding, hauling, &c., as already described, is still largely an increase due to manual efficiency. As regards the latter, as I pointed out in my previous paper, English labour stands very high, due partly to the fact that the climate favours a high degree of physical exertion, and partly to the more persistent energy and doggedness of our workmen.

Lord Brassey appears to hold the opinion, not only that British labour, all things considered, is the most effective in the world, but also that the differences in the rates of wages paid as between English and Continental and other foreign labour is, in general, no more than the measure of the difference in efficiency—in other words, that the actual value of labour, as measured in terms and quality of product, is much the same all over the world. His lordship, in a recent lecture at Toynbee Hall on the labour question, put forward this view of the matter rather pointedly, and, according to a leading article on his lecture in *The Times*, quoted some figures supplied by me in corroboration of his view. I am afraid, however, that the theory in question is less true to-day, if it was ever really justified at all, than it was thirty or forty years ago. Other nations are creeping up to our own standard of efficiency, so that British labour does not enjoy the same incontestably high relative position that it formerly did. But it is probably not to our disadvantage that foreign nations are not only increasing their industrial efficiency but their general range of wages, and that the economic changes in which England has so long led the way are being introduced to a large extent into the factory legislation and arrangements of our competitors.

APPENDIX.

A.—*Statement showing the Production of Coal, the Number of Employés, and the Average Annual Output per Employé in the United Kingdom in 1861 and in each Year from 1864 to 1890.*

Year.	Production of Coal.	Number of *Employés*.	Average Annual Output per *Employé*.
	I = 1,000 tons		Tons
1861	83,635	282,473	305
'64	95,123	307,542	309
'65	98,912	315,451	313
'66	100,729	320,663	314
'67	105,078	338,116	315
'68	104,567	346,820	301
'69	108,003	345,446	312
1870	112,876	350,894	314
'71	117,439	370,881	316
'72	123,394	418,088	295
'73	128,680	471,840	272
'74	126,449	532,780	237
'75	133,178	528,901	251
'76	133,990	508,477	263
'77	134,121	489,113	274
'78	132,482	470,615	281
'79	133,584	470,968	283
1880	146,829	475,397	308
'81	154,051	490,862	314
'82	156,365	499,485	313
'83	163,605	510,454	320
'84	160,635	516,386	310
'85	159,242	516,449	308
'86	157,158	515,757	304
'87	162,013	522,085	310
'88	169,933	530,983	320
'89	176,823	559,708	315
1890	181,612	602,517	299
'91	—	—	—

B.—*Statement showing the Total Production of Coal in Germany, and the Average Annual Output per Miner, 1879, 1883, and 1886 to 1890.*

Year.	Total Production.	Number of *Employés*.	Average Annual Output per *Employé*.
	I = 1,000 tons		Tons
1879	42,025	170,509	246
1883	55,943	207,577	270
'86	58,056	217,581	266
'87	60,334	217,357	277
'88	65,386	225,452	290
'89	67,342	239,954	284
1890	70,237	262,475	267

C.— *Production of Iron Ore in Germany, 1878 to 1889, and Average Output per Employé for each Year.*

	Production of Iron Ore in Germany and Luxembourg.	Number of *Employés*.	Average Output per *Employé*.
	1 = 1,000 tons		Tons
1878....................	5,462	27,745	197
'80....................	7,238	85,814	202
'81....................	7,601	36,891	206
'82....................	8,263	38,783	213
'83....................	8,756	39,658	220
'84....................	9,006	38,914	231
'85....................	9,158	36,072	253
'86....................	8,486	32,137	264
'87....................	9,351	32,969	283
'88....................	10,664	36,009	296
'89....................	11,002	37,762	291

D.—*Statement showing the Average Output of Iron Ore per Employé in the Principal United States in 1889, compared with 1880.*

	1880.			1889.		
	Production.	Number of *Employés*.	Average per *Employé*.	Production.	Number of *Employés*.	Average per *Employé*.
	1 = 1,000 tons.		Tons	1 = 1,000 tons.		Tons
Michigan	1,838	5,562	330	5,856	13,120	444
New Jersey	754	4,811	156	415	1,893	220
„ York............	1,239	4,675	265	1,247	3,178	392
Pennsylvania	1,820	8,733	208	1,560	4,410	353
Virginia	169	839	201	511	2,468	207
Total, United States . ... }	7,065	31,668	223	14,518	38,227	379
Miners only	—	17,928	338	—	12,432	1,167

E.—*Minimum Wages Paid per Week in United Kingdom.*

	1850.	1860.	1870.	1880.	1886.
Working engineers	18/- to 34/-	18/- to 34/-	22/- to 36/-	24/- to 36/-	26/- to 38/-
Carpenters and joiners	—	18/- „ 33/-*	19/- „ 37/8	20/- „ 41/7	20/- „ 42/4½
Steam engine makers	18/- to 34/-†	18/- „ 34/-	22/- „ 36/-	24/- „ 36/-	26/- „ 38/-
Ironfounders	24/6‡	24/6	26/3	26/6	22/3
Bricklayers (winter wages)....	—	18/- to 34/4	18/- to 34/4	24/- to 37/10½	18/- to 37/10½
Compositors (London)	33/-	33/-	33/-	36/-	36/-
Bookbinders „	30/-	30/-	32/-	—	—
Blacksmiths	—	23/-	25/-	28/-	28/-
Stonemasons......................	—	—	18/- to 35/3	22/- to 37/-	22/- to 35/3½

Note.—The above is abstracted from the Board of Trade Report on Trades Unions for 1887.

* 1864.   † 1853.   ‡ 1858.

F.—UNITED KINGDOM.   *Hours of Labour per Week in different Years.*

	1860.	1870.	1880.
Engineers	56 to 63	56 to 60	54
Carpenters and joiners	52 „ 64	50½ „ 62	48½ to 62
Steam-engine makers	57 „ 63	56 „ 60	54
Iron founders	57 „ 63	56 „ 60	54
Coachmakers	56 „ 63	56 „ 63	54 to 62
Bricklayers (winter)	45 „ 58½	45 „ 58½	44 „ 58
Compositors	63	60	54
Bookbinders	60	60	54
Blacksmiths	60	57	54
Cabinetmakers	60	55	55

G.—UNITED STATES.   *Daily Wages Paid in the United States for Skilled Labour (Dollars).*

	States.	1860.	1870.	1880.
Miner	Ohio	—	2·80	2·25
Bleacher	Delaware	0·87	1·50	1·50
Piano case maker	New Hampshire	1·75	2·50	2·00
„	„ York	1·83	2·50	2·66
Pottery and fireman	Ohio	1·75	3·00	2·75
Tanner and currier	New York	1·70	2·50	2·48
Mule spinner	Connecticut	0·83	1·66	2·25
Machinist	„	1·50	2·75	2·50
Cotton dresser	Maine	1·00	1·55	1·52
„ picker	Massachusetts	0·83	1·25	0·80
Wool sorter	Illinois	2·00	2·75	2·75
Carriage body maker	Massachusetts	1·25	2·50	2·30
Wood worker	„	1·25	2·00	2·35
Cabinet maker	Connecticut	2·00	2·25	2·25
Carver	„	2·00	2·50	2·50
Chairmaker	„	1·80	2·00	2 00
Sawyer	Kentucky	1·37	2·50	1·75

H.—*Wages Paid per Day in the United States for Ordinary Unskilled Labour.*

	1860.	1865.	1870.	1875.	1880.
	$	$	$	$	$
Brickmaking (New Jersey), wheeler	1·10	1·50	2·00	2·00	1·35
Brickmaking (Pennsylvania), wheeler	1·20	1·50	2·00	1·75	1·50
Flour mills (Illinois)	1·00	1·50	1·50	1·40	1·25
„ (Indiana)	1·00	1·50	1·54	1·35	1·15
Flint glass (Massachusetts)	1·50	2·50	2·50	2·50	2·50
„ (New York)	1·00	1·50	1·35	1·00	1·25
Stove foundries (Connecticut)	1·25	1·50	1·50	1·25	1·50
Edge tool works (Massachusetts)	0·90	1·50	1·50	1·25	1·15
Machine works (Indiana)	1·00	1·50	1·25	1·25	1·25
Coal mines* (Maryland)	—	1·75	2·00	1·75	1·75

* Outside labourer.

K.—*Statement showing the Hours of Labour Worked in Summer by certain Classes of Workmen in the United Kingdom in 1850 and 1890.*

Note.—In winter the hours of labour are often shorter.

		Hours Worked per Week in	
		1850.	1890.
Dock labourers	Liverpool	46	52½
„	Southampton	63	53 to 54
„	Glasgow	60	60
„	Dublin	59½	55½
Bakers	Manchester	72	54
„	London	56	52½
„	Edinburgh	66	55½
Brickmakers	Stourbridge	62	60
Bricklayers	Leeds	56	50
„	Glasgow	60	51
Carpenters	Liverpool	61	55
Painters	London	60	52½
„	Plymouth	60	56
Plasterers	Liverpool	59	55
Plumbers	Edinburgh	60	51
„	Birmingham	56½	54
Slaters	Newcastle-on-Tyne	61	50
Stonemasons	Cardiff	63	54
Cabinet makers	Birmingham	59	54
„	London	60	54
Shoemakers	Leeds	72 to 84	54
Tailors	Liverpool	72	56
Engineers	Birmingham	60	54

L.—*Half-timers Employed in Textile Factories generally in United Kingdom in 1878 and 1890.*

Factories.	Total *Employés.*		Total Half-Timers.		Percentage of Total as Half-Timers.	
	1878.	1890.	1878.	1890.	1878.	1890.
Cotton	482,903	528,795	61,023	48,133	12·63	9·10
Woollen	134,344	148,729	9,410	4,934	7·00	3·31
Shoddy	5,079	4,503	305	134	6·00	2·97
Worsted	130,925	148,324	21,560	17,872	16·46	12·04
Flax	108,806	107,583	8,032	8,221	7·38	7·64
Hemp	4,780	10,572	348	469	7·24	4·43
Jute	36,354	44,810	3,522	2,948	9·68	6·57
Hair	1,731	2,583	32	25	1·84	0·96
Silk	40,985	41,277	4,260	2,889	10·39	6·97
Lace	10,209	16,930	1,185	359	11·60	2·12
Hosiery	14,992	24,838	1,156	417	7·71	1·67
Elastic	4,438	3,941	400	67	9·01	1·70
All factories	975,546	1,082,885	111,233	86,468	11·33	7·97

M.—*Statement showing the Percentage Proportions of Female Workers Employed in the Chief British Textile Industries in 1878 and 1890.*

Factories.	Total *Employés.*		Total Females over 13 Years Working Full Time.		Percentage of Full Time Females on Total.	
	1878.	1890.	1878.	1890.	1878.	1890.
Cotton	482,903	528,795	264,171	295,176	54·70	55·82
Woollen	134,844	148,729	65.848	76,492	49·01	51·40
Worsted	130,925	148,324	69,784	79,452	53·30	53·56
Flax	108,806	107,583	72,148	70,004	66·30	65·06
Total of above	856,978	933,431	471,951	521,124	55·55	56·20

DISCUSSION *on* MR. JEANS'S PAPER.

THE RIGHT HON. SIR CHARLES DILKE said that he thought it difficult for any one to arrive at a definite conclusion on the subject, on account of its great complexity, and the absence of sufficient information. He agreed with what the lecturer had said as to the Labour Department of the Board of Trade, and he thought it essential that this department must be strengthened. This would have to be one of the first recommendations of the Royal Commission on Labour now sitting. Other countries were doing more in this direction than England, especially the United States, which had a Federal Bureau, and separate State Bureaus. Considering the importance of our foreign trade, England ought to be ahead of other countries instead of behind them. Mr. Jeans was, as he himself was also, an optimist in thinking that it is not proved that either short hours or high wages were necessarily a detriment to the trade of the country which had them. But the facts on which the lecturer based his theories must only be accepted with great caution. It was extremely difficult to arrive at the rates of wages in different countries, and still more difficult to compare the efficiency of labour in different countries. Even in the case of a single employment it was not easy to get at the average hours of labour. In the coal mining industry there were two returns in existence, one prepared by the Government, and another prepared by the men in the various unions, and these two did not agree in the least. He feared that seven and a half hours, as given by the author, was not a scientific average, it was an average arrived at by comparing figures which were not very certain in regard to different parts of the country, without adding up the number of men who worked at the respective hours at different times. One factor could not be taken into account, because there were no statistics bearing on it, and that was the number of days worked

2 x 2

per week. In the house coal mining industry, for instance, four days per week only were often worked in the summer, and sometimes only two or three days. In spite of the work of the Labour Department of the Board of Trade, we had not yet sufficient facts to form a conclusion with regard to our own country; it was obviously much more difficult to arrive at a comparison between different countries. There were elaborate tables in the paper comparing the rates of wages in England and the United States, but there was hardly anything to call attention to the great difference in purchasing power in the two countries. In some years there was such an inflation of currency in the United States, that the purchasing power of wages was extremely small as compared with the nominal amount, and people appeared to be very much better off than they really were. The difference in the rate of wages in the different parts of the States, which the author had pointed out, was greater than the difference between the eastern States and this country. Mr. Jeans had alluded to certain facts as regards France, which he took as a ground for stating a general doctrine with regard to the usefulness of strikes. But the condition of labour on the Continent was very different from what it is here, and French trades unions could not be taken as an example of what might be done by a proper organisation of labour. In France the masters were well organised, whereas the workmen were not. The lecturer said that the large number of small strikes in France had shown the futility of strikes as a means of advancing wages. But he (Sir Charles) believed that where labour was well organised, strikes seldom occurred for the purpose of advancing wages. They were more often employed to resist a fall. When trade was increasing it paid both parties to agree, and good organisation prevented the masters from taking undue advantage of the condition of the markets. He would conclude by expressing a hope that the Labour Department would be well developed in future years by whatever Government might happen to be in power.

Mr. John Burnett said that as so much mention had been made of the Labour Department of the Board of Trade, he might perhaps be allowed to say a few words with regard to it. He agreed with the criticisms which Sir Charles Dilke had passed on the paper, but it must not be forgotten that someone must take the lead in questions of this kind. The paper was necessarily imperfect, and this imperfection was due principally to the fact, which the reader admitted, that it was very difficult to find periods of comparison which would apply equally to all countries; for instance, it was very unsatisfactory to compare 1850, say, in England, with 1860 abroad. Reliable statistics were not obtainable for similar periods in different countries, and this difficulty seemed to point to the fact that there should be not only a national, but an international collection of labour statistics, and that there should be an agreement between nations that all statistics concerning labour should be collected and collated upon certain clearly recognised and well defined principles. In the mining industry, for instance, the author dealt with the relative efficiency of labour in different countries, by comparing the number of tons produced per miner per annum. He thought this was not at all a satisfactory method. The general effect of the argument was that in other countries there was a gradual increase in the production per head, while in England the increase was very much less. He thought this was the natural condition of the mining industry in any country. When a coal industry was being opened up, there was at first a small production per head, then there would be an increase up to a certain maximum, after which, as the coal became more difficult to win, there would be a gradual decrease. Now England was the oldest coal producing country in the world, and it could not therefore be expected that the production from her coal fields, which are becoming exhausted, should increase so fast as the newer fields in Germany or the United States An illustration of this is to be found in the figures referring to England alone. In the Yorkshire district, in the period 1873 to 1876, there was a largely increased production per head, owing to the new coal fields having there been opened up to meet the demand caused by the briskness in the coal trade. Thus if there is an increase in the amount per head produced abroad, it is due to natural causes alone, over which we have no control. As to the textile trades he (Mr. Burnett) considered the figures given in the paper to be too low. He knew it to be a fact in many mills that, instead of the average number of spindles per employé being about 215, it was nearly half as much again. He could quote with absolute certainty the case of the Stalybridge Mill Company, where there were 90,000 spindles running, and where the number of hands—including overlookers, managers and odd hands—was 260, giving an average per operator of 346 spindles. He thought also that the number of revolutions per minute would be found to be nearer 11,000 than 8,000. The figures from which he (Mr. Burnett) was now quoting had been given to him by one of the officials of the chief union of cotton operatives in Lancashire, and he believed them to be very nearly correct. He hoped that when next Mr. Jeans read a paper before the Society, the criticisms passed on the Labour Department of the Board of Trade would be of a somewhat different character. He would venture to say that the statistics given by that department were far more conscientiously collected than those in any other country; and he believed that we had a literature with regard to trades unions which could not be rivalled elsewhere. We had also in England a literature on strikes sufficiently reliable, and so thoroughly representative of the opinions both of operatives and of employers, that in this respect the Labour Department had no equal.

Mr. GEORGE HOWELL, M.P., said that, in acknowledging the admirable paper just read, he hoped that Mr. Jeans on a future occasion would devote a paper more particularly to the iron and steel industries. He thought the examples chosen with regard to agriculture were not quite the best to show the actual condition of that industry, for both Northumberland and Cheshire had advantages which were not possessed by purely agricultural districts. With regard to the iron and steel trades, he thought it possible that more might be done than had been done as regards statistical information; and he would quote from the Annual Reports of Mr. Hey, of the Ironfounders' Society, in order to show that it could be done. In these reports there was a table with regard to the hours of labour and the wages earned which gave an absolute comparison, from actual facts relating to a particular industry from 1831 to the present time. If we could only have a series of such tables for other industries, it would be possible to compare them, and see what real averages meant when applied to those industries. He could not believe the average miner's wage, as given in the paper, in Northumberland and Durham, was high enough; he thought it must be more than 52l. a year. Mr. Jeans was, he believed, one of the first to say a good word for labour, when very few favourable words were spoken for it. He believed that it was not so much the number of hours worked, or the amount paid for the hours worked, which actually determined the cost of production. If they could satisfy the aspirations of the men in many particulars, this would in itself be a stimulus to production; and he thought it possible that a reduction of the hours of labour might take place without lessening the actual cost of production to any considerable extent. He was afraid that Government would not obtain the figures necessary for a comparison, and the Labour Bureau at present could not. Trifling facts on each particular trade in different towns or villages formed the foundation of all statistics on these subjects. Those who neglected what had taken place in the past, could not possibly foretell what would happen in the future; and those who had carefully followed events in the past, looked forward with confidence to the future. Mr. Jeans had said that foreign workmen were catching up with the English, but he (Mr. Howell) thought it would be a long time before they were abreast of us. The competition would then become more equal, as with the increased efficiency of the foreign worker would come higher wages and shorter hours. He rejoiced that the hours of labour were being reduced, as he believed that in proportion as they raised the condition of the people, and increased their wages and the purchasing power of wages, so would they give increased prosperity to the entire country.

Mr. W. H. HEY said he thought there were too few data upon which to found any comparison of real worth. When speaking of the wages of workmen, facts were wanted to show what was the average amount of time lost from every cause, so as to get at the actual net amount that they received. For instance, a man—when fully employed—may have his wages fixed at 30s. a week, but probably 20 per cent. would have to be deducted for loss of time, &c. It will readily be seen that there is a vast difference between the possible and the actual wages income of workmen. The lecturer had remarked that the efficiency or productive power of the working people here was not increasing so fast as it was abroad ; but he thought the efficiency of the English workmen was considerably ahead of that of any other country. It was also a notable fact that the workmen in England were now producing more by working nine hours a day than they did in 1870, when they worked ten hours a day. But in his opinion their productive powers were now strung up to the highest pitch, and he did not see where any further increase in their efficiency could be obtained, only by a further reduction in their hours of labour. All statisticians were agreed that the nation had thriven during the last fifty years, while the hours of labour had been reduced and wages increased, and he believed that if the hours of labour were still further reduced, the country would still go on progressing.

Mr. D. F. Schloss said he thought the statement that foreign efficiency was increasing faster than British, might be accounted for partly by the fact that we used the term efficiency in an ambiguous manner. Labour became more efficient with better organisation and better machinery, irrespectively of the actual effective force of the labourer. Foreign labourers were now better organised and had better machinery than formerly; but there was a limit to efficiency, and Englishmen could not expect to keep so far ahead of other nations for ever. With regard to the decreased efficiency of coal miners, he could carry the figures a little farther than Mr. Jeans had done. In the Midlands the output in 1890 was 412 tons per miner, and in 1891 381 tons, and he thought this decrease very largely accounted for by the explanation given by Mr. Burnett. As the demand for coal increased, more mines were opened. These were easy to work at first, but afterwards became less and less easy. It stood to reason that when a mine was newly opened, the output per miner was much greater than when they got into the deeper workings, and it was also clear that when trade improved, mines would be worked which would not pay when trade was bad, and this decreased the output. He did not think the British workman was decreasing in efficiency. Besides considering the purchasing power of wages, they had also to consider how the wages were spent. In Belgium, as the returns showed, a great deal was spent in spirits. Then there was the climate. In America, for instance, during the greater part of the year the workmen could do with cheap linen clothes, but here cloth was required. To get the best work out of our men we must pay them higher wages than in more favourably situated countries. The question: " What makes a rate of wages ? " involves several difficult problems. How far is it true that high wages are paid, because the labour paid for is more efficient ? How far is it true that the labour is more efficient, because the wages paid for it are higher ? In dealing with the latter subject they must consider not only the amount paid per hour, but also the total annual wages; for nothing told more against efficiency than irregularity of employment. He could give an instance in which a large body of British manufacturers had been enabled to enormously increase the efficiency of labour by introducing machinery which they had declared could not possibly be introduced. Mr. Schoenhof had compared the labour cost of certain operations involved in the production of a specific type of boots in England and America, and had found that while in America the men were paid high wages and worked short hours, the cost of production was less than in east London, where the same operations were being carried out in the sweating dens by men working eighteen hours a day for 3*d.* an hour during five months out of the twelve. After the great strike in the boot trade in 1890, machinery had been introduced into London, and though the operatives in question were now receiving better wages and working much shorter hours, the cost of production had not increased. With regard to the Board of Trade, it was quite true that the reports of the labour department in regard to trades unions and strikes and lock-outs excelled those of any labour bureau. All that was wanted was that it should be increased. The United States spent 30,000*l.* a year on its labour bureau. The French had started one last October, and this year the grant for it was 6,080*l.*, an amount which it was certain would be largely increased in the future. The French bureau started with fifteen persons, and it now had twenty-eight at work. There was also in France a permanent labour commission, and there again he thought England would have to follow her example.

Mr. JEANS, on being called on to reply, said he thought there was very little that it was necessary for him to say, and he would therefore be very glad to give place to Mr. Trow, one of the Royal Commissioners of Labour.

Mr. E. TROW thought the difference in the statements of wages as made by workmen and employers was due to the fact that the workmen, in giving the average, were apt to count every half or three-quarters of a day as a whole day, in order to make their wages appear smaller, while the employers only returned the full day's work. With regard to the difficulty of comparing English and American wages, for instance, he would point out that in America wages increased from 1866 to 1870, and then remained stationary till 1875; while in England wages between 1866 and 1869 reached the lowest point that had been touched for twenty years, and it was only in 1869 that they began to increase. In 1874 they began to go down again, and while English wages were going down, American wages were going up, and *vice versâ*. With regard to the average output of the coal miners in the Midlands in 1891, he thought it required a very careful inquiry to ascertain why the output was less in that year, as it was well known that during the first half of 1891, as far as concerned the iron and steel trades, the Midlands were in a measure paralysed, numbers of works standing, and a large quantity of coal which should have been used was left ungotten there. To calculate the amount per miner per annum, they must therefore consider the number of days worked. Efficiency of labour was in some degree due to machinery; but in puddling and metal work he could say without fear of contradiction that the output during the last twenty-five years had increased 20 per cent., and this was due entirely to the efficiency of the workmen, as the mode of working had been exactly the same during the period. Comparing the tonnage rate now paid to the workmen, it was 20 per cent. below what it was twenty years ago. So far as the steel trade alone was concerned, and there had been no reduction in the hours of labour, the men in the mills now worked twelve hours a day and twelve hours a night (except Saturday) as they had done thirty years ago. In the blast furnaces which Mr. Jeans had mentioned, the men worked twelve hours for seven nights one week and twelve hours for seven days the next. He had no fear of the foreigners being yet able to beat the English out of the market. Increased efficiency, wages and output on this side meant a corresponding increase on the other.

The PRESIDENT, in closing the discussion with the customary vote of thanks, remarked that his personal knowledge of the subject was not such as to induce him to add to the observations of the experts who had addressed the meeting. But he was much struck with the little importance apparently attached to the efficiency of the work resulting from shorter hours and increase of wages, and the evident tendency to the levelling upwards of unskilled labour in productive industry. He remembered a remarkable statement made by the late General Forbes of the Royal Engineers, who devised the magnificent machinery of the Calcutta Mint, on the subject of the relative merits and skill of British and foreign workmen, which question was discussed in his presence by great employers of labour at the table of the late Mr. Bolton, of the celebrated firm of Bolton and Watt, of Manchester. The general tone of the discussion indicated the belief that whilst our workmen were superior to all others in great works demanding more physical force and dogged industry than manual skill, they were inferior in the refinement, artistic taste, and beauty of finish possessed by the artisans of other countries, particularly of France. A gentleman present produced a small dainty sample of a wooden snuff-box, lacquered with Scottish plaid patterns then in use, and said that no English workman could produce so beautiful an example of skilled industry as he then exhibited. Mr. Bolton requested him to send up the box to him, and on examining the outer layer of the lid, showed that it was made by his firm, and by British workmen alone, and that he had thousands of it in his factory. This was long before technical schools were known to us, and proved that there was no inherent deficiency of taste and skill among British workmen, even in that pre-scientific period. The boxes referred to were made in England, sent to France, and brought back again as foreign workmanship of a high order, unobtainable at home, and fetching in consequence a high price in the market at the time. The greatest care should, he thought, be taken to prevent the degradation of skilled labour by legislative or any other more objectionable interference in productive industry on any false economic grounds.

MISCELLANEA.

CONTENTS:

I.—*International Prison Statistics.* By DR. F. J. MOUAT, LL.D. (Report presented to the International Penitentiary Congress, St. Petersburg, 1890.)

>
> (*a.*) Is the compilation of an International Penitentiary Statistic useful?
> (*b.*) Is it possible?
> (*c.*) If it is, to what limit should it be restricted?
> (*d.*) On what system should it be conducted?

IN accepting the honour of being a reporter on the above subject, I find myself in a somewhat difficult position. The matter has been discussed, apparently with little practical result,· at so many congresses devoted to penitentiary and statistical questions, in so complete and exhaustive a manner, as to leave little that is new or has escaped observation to be said. I myself studied it most carefully more than thirty years ago, both theoretically and practically, and constructed a system for the introduction of a complete plan of record into the prisons under my charge, based very much on the resolutions passed by the International Statistical Congress which mèt in London in 1861, under the presidency of the late Prince Consort of England. My plan, with modifications of some details but little change of principle, was introduced in Lower Bengal under the provisions of a special Prison Act in 1864.

Why then has the discussion of the question in Europe been so little successful, as those best acquainted with the matter seem to suppose? It is, I venture to think, because our discussions and resolutions are too formal and academic in character, to carry conviction to the minds of the different legislatures and rulers, who alone possess the authority and power to introduce the plans recommended, in the institutions devoted to the correction of those who have committed, and been convicted of crimes, in their respective countries. It is incumbent on us to show not only what is practicable, but what is in actual operation, upon a sufficiently extended scale, and for a sufficient length of time to admit of its being judged by its results. By no other means can we errors and defects be detected and remedied, and reforms be sanctioned to avoid their recurrence in the future.

It should be borne in mind that although the prison is the key-stone of the judicial arch in dealing with infractions of law in their penological relations, prison discipline is not in itself an end, but a means to an end. In my address as chairman of the Repression of Crime Section of the judicial department of the Social Science Association in 1881, I remarked that what is termed crime, covers an extremely extensive field of knowledge in its range. It embraces the whole subject of morals in their relation to the social organism, and the history of civilisation from the simple savage with his few wants and rude associations, to the complex life of cultivated communities. It includes likewise the study of the entire body of criminal, and a great part of civil law, in the regulation of the public and much of the private lives of the members of every community. It has special regard to the education and training of the young, with a view to the right direction, not only of the offspring of the predatory classes with whom crime is hereditary, but of the children of all who, from the accidents of birth, poverty, and evil surroundings, are liable to acquire irregular habits, culminating in the commission of faults which constitute in the eyes of the law crimes, but which can scarcely be rightly so regarded before the age of real responsibility is reached.

The influence of the prison can only touch the fringe of this great subject; it is as well, therefore, not to expect too much from identity of system, in dealing with the detection and punishment of crime in all countries. Our aim should be to ascertain what is applicable in principle to all, and practicable in all stages and forms of civilisation, and to restrict our recommendations to them, until time and experience leads to the adoption of improved methods of dealing with crime, upon the inductive principle which is so powerful an instrument of progress in physical science.

With this preamble I proceed to the consideration of the questionary, formulated by our distinguished collaborator.

(a.) *Is it useful ?*

In the debate on the question by the Statistical Society of London, in 1876, on the submission of a paper written by me on the subject, the late Dr. Guy, an eminent statist and experienced prison officer, doubted whether the discussion of the question by international conferences was attended by any practical result. At the same time he hoped that the time was not far distant when the criminal would be so followed up and identified, that it would scarcely be worth his while to be a criminal at all. [International action would clearly be necessary for this.]

He did not then foresee how completely his prophecy would be verified by the anthropometric identification of criminals introduced with so much effect in France, by the Messrs. Bertillon, worthy sons of a distinguished father.

I believe that the scientific pursuit of those investigations, and the tabulation of their results in all the countries of Europe, may lead to the discovery of a criminal type—a class of congenital criminals whose physical conformation will tend to place them in the ranks either of the predatory or irresponsible classes, for whom the treatment of a lunatic asylum would be more needed than the discipline of a prison.

General Du Cane, the scientific and distinguished head of the prison department in England, thought that a system of international prison statistics was a step in the right direction, even though all that was desirable was not obtainable from it, for obvious reasons. By aiming at something higher than the object to be attained, some lower mark might be secured more easily. So far as he himself was concerned, he had tried to eliminate from his statistics everything that was useless and misleading, and to retain only that which could be made, and was made absolutely accurate. Whether in the course of time the best principles in dealing with criminals would be established by international statistics, and be generally adopted, he did not know, but it was a result much to be hoped for, and a matter they should all do their best to accomplish.

Most of the other speakers on that occasion concurred generally in my views. Chief among them was the eminent statist Dr. Farr.

I was myself satisfied, from my long and extensive knowledge of prisons in India, of the great usefulness of the interchange of views on the subject by the experts of all nations. In my own prisons, among a daily average population of 20,000, were all sorts and conditions of men, from naked untutored savages, to the most civilised of the indigenous races, and not a few Europeans of many nationalities. I was satisfied then, from personal intercourse with them, and I am convinced now, that once the criminals of all sorts become known to the authorities of their own and other peoples, by photographic, anthropometric. and other means, including similar forms of recording all facts connected with them, a very great advance would be made in formulating the principles best fitted to punish, reform, and return to society as respectable members, those who had offended against it, in all countries. It is, I submit, scarcely prudent to eliminate details of which the immediate use is not perceptible, for correct details are the life of statistics. My own statistics were objected to by the financial advisers of the Government as containing too much, and costing too much money—a doctrine which was emphatically condemned by Lord Brougham at the London Congress. With the aid of convict prisoners, and notably in my chief prison, I was able to prove that their exact cost was 1d. a head, counting all committed to prison during each year.

(b.) *Is it possible ?*

In 1872 I was nominated by the *executive* committee of the Prison Congress held in London in that year, to the office of reporter on the question of International Prison Statistics, and prepared a paper, which was printed, on the subject.

The *international* committee, I presume, not having been made acquainted with it, from an act of omission on the part of the executive committee, assigned the duty to Signor Beltrani Scalia, then and now one of our most distinguished colleagues, and it could not have been in better hands. My report was accordingly neither read nor submitted, and slumbered in peaceful repose until 1876, when the question was revived by the Statistical Society of London, after the publication of Signor Beltrani Scalia's admirable report in 1875, which is by very far the most important landmark in penological progress, in the branch of inquiry to which it relates.

What I shall submit to you now is very much what I thought and wrote then. I see no reason to alter it, as I have in no way retreated from the position I, at that time, took up. Moreover, it seems to me to be desirable never to lose sight of the history of this great question, particularly as the record of the different stages in the inquiry is not generally accessible or available for reference when required. Although some of the resolutions adopted are more or less speculative in character, and represent an ideal perfection which is not attainable, it is best to determine the standard as high and perfect as possible, and get as much as we can from time to time, taking stock of the progress attained at the quinquennial conferences.

In 1863 I submitted a complete scheme of prison regulations and returns to the Government of Bengal. These were submitted for scrutiny and examination to two special committees of judicial officers, and a code of rules for prisons in the whole of India was also drawn up by Lord Lawrence's commission of inquiry in 1864, of which I was a member. All of these were considered by the Government of the Lower Provinces, and a final code, in the preparation of which I was again consulted, was drawn up. This was ordered to be introduced into the prisons under my charge, under the authority vested in the Government of Bengal by Act II of 1864.

I give this historical summary of what, after careful and prolonged official inquiry, was accomplished in India a quarter of a century since, because it is little, if at all, known in Europe, and will show to this Congress the means I had of becoming acquainted with the subject in both its theoretical and practical application, upon a scale that has fallen to the lot of few.

Upon this question then I subsequently placed my views on record in 1872 for the information of the Prison Congress of that year, and in 1876 I submitted them for consideration and discussion by a strictly statistical body. I wrote as follows:—

"Having had a lengthened experience of prison administration on an extended scale, and in circumstances of considerable difficulty, I have naturally given much attention to the best and most simple methods of recording all the facts necessary to throw light upon the system of prison discipline in force in the prisons which were under my general control and supervision from 1855-70."

These are contained in my Annual Prison Reports submitted to the Government, and I endeavoured to present them in a condensed form to the Statistical Society of London, in whose *Journal* they were printed (vol. xxv, pp. 175—218; vol. xxx, pp. 21—106; vol. xxxv, pp. 59—106).

All that has been written and recorded at Prison and Statistical Congresses appears to me to show clearly that an international system of the statistics of prisons is perfectly possible; that to admit of comparison, it requires to be constructed on the same basis; and that it should, as minutely as may be practicable in each country, show the social and general characteristics as well as the antecedents and moral and physical attributes of every individual accused or convicted of crime, prior to incarceration.

In the present uncertain and unsatisfactory state of international judicial statistics, it will probably be sufficient in jail returns to give the name of the crime contained in the warrant of the court by which a prisoner is tried and sentenced, and under the authority of which he is imprisoned, with a special reference to the law, or section of a criminal code relating to it.

This will show whether the offence has been against property or person, or any of the other categories in which crime is at present classified, in the criminal jurisprudence of different countries. More than this cannot, I fear, be attempted at present.

In all other particulars uniformity of system, so far as possibility is concerned, could at once be adopted, and although all facts represented by figures must be interpreted with special reference to the ethnological and other considerations of each nation to which they relate, the basis of comparison being identical, prison statistics would throw much light upon the civilisation of different countries, as represented by their prison populations.

As respects the prisons themselves, the statistics should represent accurately, and in minute detail, all facts regarding their structure, arrangement, government, cost, and scheme of discipline, including labour and instruction, together with the feeding, clothing, and health of the inmates.

The effects of the discipline pursued can only be ascertained by the punishment and good-conduct registers of the prisons, and by following the liberated prisoners into private life, to ascertain what proportion have taken to honest courses, and how many have relapsed into crime. Uniformity of system in collecting and registering all such facts, does not present the same difficulties as an international nomenclature of crime. Hence it appears to me to be most desirable that an international uniform system of prison records and registers should be agreed upon.

By such means alone can light be thrown upon the effects of the penitentiary and reformatory discipline practised in different countries, and by them alone can defects be brought to light with a view to their remedy or removal.

The statistics of criminal lunacy, or the relations of unsound mind to criminal acts, require also to be collected with great care and minuteness. There exists at the present moment considerable divergence of opinion on this important subject. One result of this is constant conflict in England between the bar, the bench, and those who have made a special study of aberrations of mind and their influence on the acts of persons labouring under them, as to the extent to which an individual who has committed a crime, ought to be held legally and morally responsible for the criminal act.

In this inquiry would be contained the collection of facts as to the origin of the disordered mental state of the individual, whether congenital, caused by habitual indulgence in stimulants and narcotics, or in whatever way it is produced.

The constant and careful observation to which persons suspected of being of unsound mind can be subjected in prisons, invests this branch of prison statistics with peculiar interest and value; no pains should therefore be spared to collect and record all particulars connected with it with extreme minuteness.

Prison statistics then, should be divided into four categories, viz., the facts relating to the (1) prisons as buildings, and those relating to the persons confined in them (2) before, (3) during and (4) after their imprisonment.

1. The statistics of prison buildings should contain all particulars connected with their structure, materials and cost, and show the arrangements of the cells, wards, and workshops; the amount of space afforded to each prisoner, cubical and superficial; the nature of the ventilation, drainage, and conservancy; with the provision for guards, warders, and prison officers, together with the kitchens, out-offices, store-rooms, and gardens, if any are attached to the prisons. The hospital accommodation, schoolrooms, provision for religious exercises, &c., should also be given.

While it is probable that too much stress has in some cases been placed upon the mere construction of prisons, and greater cost has been incurred than is really necessary; it is, on the other hand, undeniable that insecure prisons, and those in which inadequate means are provided for the separation, labour, and other conditions required for an effective system of control and discipline, are dear at any price, and render necessary a resort to coercive and other measures of severity, which are not calculated to secure the ends of imprisonment in a satisfactory manner.

The practical result of the careful collection of such statistics would be to show the form, dimensions, and arrangement of prison buildings which combined the greatest security and fitness with the least cost—objects of considerable importance in all countries. Although economic considerations are not of the first importance in such questions, they ought by no means to be overlooked or undervalued.

2. Statistics relating to the prisoners themselves should be collected in three separate categories, viz., prior to imprisonment, during imprisonment, and after discharge from prison.

In the first category should be contained all particulars relating to the age, sex, place of birth, dwelling, religion, education, profession or calling, social status, physical characters, and every circumstance connected with a prisoner that is calculated to throw light upon the cause of his crime.

A detailed and accurate record of his physical characteristics will aid in the collection of statistics on the physical development of man, in circumstances of unusual interest. The minuteness and accuracy with which details can be gathered together in prisons invest the subject with special interest, and imparts to the facts so collected an exceptional value. The criminal population probably affords fair general averages of the population at large, and there is no inquiry relative to physical development to which they cannot be subjected, in the temporary state of bondage in which they have placed themselves by the commission of crime.

Minute particulars regarding the social status of every person convicted of crime are of the utmost importance in relation to the action of the criminal law, to criminal legislation generally, and to such general measures of prevention as the facts and figures collected may show to be most desirable and necessary. Preventive are in all circumstances of greater value than curative measures, for obvious reasons. Crime may well be likened to an epidemic or contagious disease. It is, in truth, a moral disorder peculiarly apt to spread by contagion, and much more easily stamped out *ab origine* than when it has taken hold of individuals or classes.

The first step in prison reform in most, if not in all countries, is probably in the education of the people, and in particular in the early training of all such individuals or classes as are known to be likely to recruit the criminal ranks. Hence in England our ragged schools and reformatories. Provision has been made in the provisional programme for the consideration of this important matter.

3. In the statistics of the prisoner during his detention, equally minute particulars should be collected regarding the abnormal state in which the commission of crime has placed him.

Information respecting his crime, previous convictions, if he has been in prison before, his sentence, his conduct in jail, state of body and mind at the time of and during incarceration, his food, clothing, work, health and sickness in confinement, and state on discharge, should be carefully noted. These particulars cannot be gathered in too great detail, for on their careful and accurate record must in a great measure depend our knowledge of the effects of imprisonment, moral and material.

The statistics of prison officers and establishments, with their cost, mode of appointment, training, and all particulars connected with them, should likewise be given in detail.

I myself attach little comparative importance to personal opinion on questions of this kind, but I place great faith in facts founded on figures, when they are susceptible of illustration by the numerical method, and the figures are vouched for by men of repute and authority. I collected a good deal of information on this point in Bengal, and one result was the establishment of the fact, that in the internal management of jails, prisoners in that country are, when carefully selected after a due course of probation, more trustworthy and of greater value in the maintenance of discipline, than external subordinate paid agency.

It is to the absence of such records as those indicated above, that much of the existing difference of opinion on the results of different systems of prison discipline is due. The provision of such records, carefully digested and conscientiously collated, will do more to promote sound views on the subject than all the discussions of all the congresses that can be gathered together, in the absence of the facts and figures necessary to form a right judgment.

There is probably no branch of social economy in which a careful and correct digest of facts is more necessary for sound legislation, than that relating to crime and criminals.

Fortunately there is none which afford the same facilities for collecting these facts with rigorous exactness, and applying them with almost scientific precision to criminal legislation.

The cost of the prisoner in all particulars should be carefully noted in detail, for details are the life of statistics, and in regard to prisons are of greater importance than gross results. It is comparatively of little consequence to know that it costs the nation 100*l.* to punish a criminal, if we are not made acquainted with the exact nature and distribution of this expenditure. In this way alone can a hard and fast line be drawn between economy, parsimony, and extravagance.

There is no branch of political arithmetic in which greater errors have been committed, in India certainly, and possibly in other countries, than in estimating the cost of prisons, and none certainly in which false economical views have been productive of a greater amount of mischief.

The subject of vital statistics, again, can be investigated with peculiar exactness in prisons, if the necessary trouble be taken and the necessary expense incurred of recording the results.

The vital statistics of the prisons under my charge, which I collected for fifteen years in Bengal with as much minuteness as I could, clearly proved that in a large number of cases, and to many individuals, a brief sentence for a trivial offence proved a sentence of death—a result which cannot be justified by any policy of financial expediency.

The same statistics showed that under very adverse circumstances, which it is not necessary to refer to further, but of which some details will be found in the *Journal* of the Society, a saving of life represented by nearly 40 per 1,000 annually, was effected in the same time and in the same prisons.

It would be difficult to over-estimate the value of such records, and their value depends entirely upon the minuteness, care, and accuracy with which they are collected.

The vital statistics of the jails in Bengal, during the later years of my incumbency, were collected in the forms drawn up with his customary skill and thorough mastery of the subject, by Dr. Farr, of the General Registry Office. They were in all respects more complete than those of any other country that I am acquainted with.

4. The fourth branch of the statistics of criminals is more difficult to collect, and is not so immediately connected with prisons as the two former, yet without it no criminal statistics can pretend to be complete.

The course of the criminal on his restoration to freedom, and his rehabilitation generally, are of the greatest importance as tests of the efficiency of the system of penal discipline to which he has been subjected.

This opens up the whole subject of aids to prisoners in commencing a new career, which being dealt with in other sections, I need not refer to further in this place.

(c.) If so, to what limits should it be restricted ?

If it be conceded that the collection of international prison statistics is both useful and possible, the consideration of the limits in which it is desirable to restrict it, follows in strict logical sequence. The limit fixed by Sir Edmund Du Cane in England is that of securing absolute accuracy in the returns, a factor no doubt of great value and importance in all such inquiries.

When placed, in 1855, in administrative charge of the prisons of all classes in Lower Bengal, representing as we now know the criminals of a population of 60 millions of souls, I had comparatively a *tabula rasa* to deal with. The returns submitted by the prison authorities were not only thoroughly unreliable, but were submitted for different periods, and so varied in detail, as to render comparisons impossible. After visiting and examining carefully every prison, great and small, in the vast area covered by my duties and responsibilities, I submitted special reports of each to my Government, and with the sanction of authority, delayed organising and elaborating any general scheme of prison returns, until I had thoroughly mastered the principles of prison management and control, and ascertained by a visit to Europe the regulations in force in some of the leading prisons of England and France, which I was permitted to visit for the purpose.

Before I had completed my inquiry, I had secured uniformity in the periods for which returns were prepared, similarity of record, and identity of plan of registering such details as are essential in any system that might ultimately be adopted.

And now, as to the history of this particular branch of the question in Europe. It is universally admitted that the basis of the system of repression of crime is the punishment of the offender, his reformation, and therefrom the protection of society. This is common to all countries. To ascertain the results of the particular measures of repression adopted, does not appear to me to present the same difficulties and divergences, as do those of international judicial record generally.

At the first International Statistical Congress, held in Brussels in 1853, no special mention was made of the statistics of prisons as a separate branch of judicial statistics. Many of the facts connected with those convicted of crimes were, however, comprised in some of the categories adopted.

In the second Congress, held in Paris in 1855, a large amount of attention was given to the statistics of penitentiary establishments, and the order and method of classifying and recording the facts connected with them were enumerated in considerable detail, contained in twelve different sections, which I need not enumerate.

At the Congress held in London in 1860, the particulars deemed necessary to record, were formulated in two special resolutions, which in substance were similar to those of Paris.

The Congress of Florence, in 1867, devoted its attention specially to aid to prisoners after release from incarceration.

Of the Prison Congress of London in 1872 I have already spoken, and the great and enlightened consideration given to the matter by the Statistical Congress of St. Petersburg in the same year, must be well known here.

It has since attracted considerable attention at other places, but as yet all the discussions have not produced any appreciable result, except in the case of the first international tables of penitentiary statistics for the year 1872, published by Signor Beltrani Scalia in 1875, which I regard as the leading landmark in the matter.

Of this it is unnecessary for me to make any further mention in his presence.

In all the discussions which I have been able to consult, there is little fundamental difference as to the *principles* which underlie them, and the information desired with regard to them in what I think I am entitled to denominate an *ideal system*, the practical application of which in all countries, must be a question of much time and much reflection.

What I should be disposed to recommend for future adoption with a view to the solution of the question, is, that the prison returns and reports of each year and country should be collected, and the results for the lustrum presented in the manner adopted by Signor Beltrani Scalia, to the Penitentiary Congresses, which will, I hope, be continued every fifth year. Thus resemblances and differences established could then be differentiated and discussed, so as to remove all that was defective, to retain all that was effective, and to eliminate from the whole, the system found to be best adapted for the repression of crime, in the various circumstances of all countries.

(d.) On what system should it be conducted?

I do not quite understand the exact signification of the term system in this portion of the questionary.

If it refers strictly to the manner of framing and keeping prison records with special reference to the figures they can furnish on the different heads of information considered desirable or necessary, the feeling of the Statistical Congress held in London in 1860, is probably the best answer which can be given. The feeling I refer to was, that the exact nature of the information desired respecting crime, its causes and consequences, repression and removal, being given as a basis, each country should collect its statistics in its own way, with special reference to national, local, and ethnological conditions.

The present English plan, so far as I am acquainted with it, is to eliminate all that is regarded as useless or misleading, and to retain only that which can be made absolutely accurate if that is possible.

In the discussion which took place in 1876 in the Statistical Society of London on this question, I dissented somewhat from this view, partly because I believe absolute accuracy in such matters to be unattainable, but chiefly because it would and does, in my opinion, restrict inquiry injuriously. The exclusion of any head of investigation on the ground of its present uselessness is, I think, unwise; inasmuch as it appears to me to be impossible to predicate what detail may or may not be of value for legislative purposes in the constantly changing and advancing conditions of life in association, in this age of progress and rapid intercommunication.

As a system, in the sense which I understand it, that published in Rome in 1875 by our eminently qualified and distinguished colleague who has formulated the questionary, appears to me to be the best. I need not reproduce it in detail, for he is here to explain how far he still retains the views he then expressed, from the subsequent prolonged experience he brings to bear upon all the issues involved.

I have long ceased to have any direct or official connection with prisons, or to have followed with careful attention the progress since made in penology, my time and attention having been devoted to cognate and not less important duties. If my opinions then are considered of any interest or value by this distinguished re-union of experts, it must be in a strictly historical point of view, in furnishing, I trust, not an unimportant link in the chain of working out a system of dealing with crime, its causes and consequence, in the spirit and on the lines initiated by my immortal countryman John Howard, more than a century ago.

II.—*Statistics of the Damage caused by Hail in Austria.*[1]

THE results for the quinquennium 1885-89, when compared with the two preceding equal periods, show that the number of days on which hail fell, as also the area affected, have considerably increased. The damage caused must have been felt to be all the more severe—that is by the agricultural population—as the insurance against such damage is very insufficient. The whole amount of damage caused by hail to fields, meadows, vineyards, kitchen gardens, orchards, and olive groves, amounted on an average during the five years in question to 16,300,000 gulden, while the insurance paid was only 1,890,000 gulden, or 11·6 per cent. of the value of the produce destroyed, leaving some 14·4 million gulden, or 88·4 per cent., uncovered by insurance.

	Damage.	Insurance.	Per Cent. of Damage.
	Gulden	Gulden	
1885	17,957,000	1,951,000	10·9
'86	13,932,000	2,084,000	14·8
'87	9,148,000	1,008,000	11·0
'88	18,273,000	1,751,000	9·6
'89	22,177,000	2,661,000	12·0
1885-89	81,487,000	9,455,000	11·6
'80-84	80,544,000	—	—
'75-79	42,264,000	—	—

[1] From an article by *Karl Krafft* in the "*Statistische Monatschrift*" *herausgegeben* von *der k.k. Statistischen Central-Commission.* Vienna, May—June, 1892.

Showing an increase of 943,000 gulden over 1880-84, and of 39,223,000 gulden, or 92·8 per cent., over 1875-79.

	Damage.		Insurance.	
	Mean of the Five Years 1885-89.	Gulden per Head of the Agricultural Population.	Mean of the Five Years 1885-89.	Per Cent. of Damage done.
	000 gulden.		000 gulden.	
Lower Austria............	1,831	2·89	71	3·9
Upper ,, ...	572	1·54	44	7·7
Salzburg	188	1·53	10·4	7·5
Tyrol and Vorarlberg	1,143	2·02	13	1·1
Carinthia	230	0·96	4	1·8
Steiermark	1,492	1·87	15	1·0
Krain	376	1·11	2	0·5
Maritime districts	794	2·22	0·2	0·0
Dalmatia	453	1·16	0·2	0·0
Bohemia	4,200	1·85	1,023	24·1
Moravia	2,092	2·00	199	9·5
Silesia	598	2·23	29·4	4·9
Galicia	2,218	0·50	402	18·1
Bukowina....................	160	0·39	78	48·7
Austria................	16,297	1·34	1,891	11·6

The area which comes under consideration covers a total of 14·7 million hectares, or 49 per cent. of the whole superficies of Austria. Of this cultivated area, hail fell annually, on the average—

From 1875 to 1879 on 305,076 hectares, or 2·1 per cent.
,, '80 ,, '84 ,, 558,047 ,, 3·8 ,,
,, '85 ,, '89 ,, 633,142 ,, 4·3 ,,

while the number of days on which hail fell increased from an average of 124 during the first period to 143 in the second, and 157 during the last, and the individual hailstorms affected an increasing area, inasmuch as the average number of hectares damaged each day rose from 2,460 in 1875-79 to 3,902 in the following period, and to 4,033 in 1885-89, and more communes were ravaged (1,665, 2,669, and 3,201 annually during the above mentioned periods). With the increase in the extension of the storms however their intensity has somewhat diminished (damage per hectare 27·7, 28·9, and 25·8 gulden annually in 1875-79, 1880-84, and 1885-89 respectively); this decrease is however so slight, that the total damage, as has been already mentioned, has greatly augmented, the increase in the damaged area being in much greater ratio than the decrease in the intensity of the storms; this increase from 1875-79 to 1885-89 being no less than 107·5 per cent.

Summary of Damage caused during the Years 1872-91.

Year.	Number of Days on which Hail fell.	Number of Communes affected.	Number of Hectares Damaged.		Damage.		
			Total.	Per Cent. of Cultivated Land.	000 Gulden.	Gulden per Day on which Hail fell.	Gulden per Hectare.
1872........	132	2,354	407,118	2·78	8,557	64,796	21·0
'73........	138	1,824	267,307	1·82	6,418	46,507	23·8
'74........	115	1,948	375,199	2·56	8,742	76,017	23·3
'75........	110	2,281	419,162	2·86	11,667	106,064	27·8
'76........	126	1,285	184,084	1·26	5,017	39,818	27·3
'77........	135	1,766	352,757	2·41	10,793	79,948	30·6
'78........	124	1,092	176,472	1·20	5,123	41,315	29·0
'79........	123	1,950	392,905	2·68	9,664	78,569	24·6
1880........	140	3,410	819,569	5·59	24,250	173,214	29·6
'81........	126	2,380	433,312	2·96	11,796	93,620	27·2
'82........	150	2,345	504,018	3·44	15,122	100,813	30·0
'83........	136	2,640	551,523	3·76	14,135	103,934	25·5
'84........	161	2,568	481,812	3·29	15,241	94,665	31·6
'85........	156	3,489	682,786	4·66	17,957	115,109	26·3
'86........	158	3,077	524,709	3·58	13,862	87,707	26·4
'87........	158	2,896	433,941	2·96	9,148	57,899	21·1
'88........	157	3,515	772,691	5·34	18,273	116,388	23·6
'89........	154	3,530	751,585	5·18	22,177	144,006	29·5

Table A shows the number of days on which hail fell in each month of the year, with other details, for the year 1889, the latest for which we have particulars :—

TABLE A.—*Damage by Hail in 1889.*

	Number of Days of Hail											Number of Communes Affected	Cultivated Area Affected	Number of Owners Affected	Affected and Insured	Total Damage
	Feb-ruary	March	April	May	June	July	August	Septem-ber	Octo-ber	Nor-ember	Total		Hectares			Gulden
Lower Austria	—	—	2	17	17	13	13	3	—	—	65	181	36,762	13,109	556	1,731,852
Upper „	—	—	—	7	13	3	1	1	—	—	25	60	12,470	2,184	175	567,674
Salzburg	—	—	—	1	4	5	6	2	—	—	18	25	7,463	660	100	121,216
Steiermark	—	—	—	13	15	17	14	6	1	—	66	223	41,599	14,514	266	926,419
Carinthia	—	—	—	—	3	6	5	2	—	—	16	33	9,330	2,516	90	63,749
Krain	—	—	—	6	10	13	9	2	1	—	41	80	24,482	8,556	76	868,826
Maritime districts	—	—	1	3	11	12	9	9	1	—	45	71	55,988	19,461	2	1,031,260
Tyrol and Vorarlberg	—	—	4	3	6	20	17	7	1	—	52	182	74,466	24,249	1	2,026,311
Bohemia	—	—	—	26	29	28	27	1	—	—	115	1,402	273,211	62,150	7,679	9,561,104
Moravia	—	—	—	11	20	17	23	1	—	—	73	377	60,218	24,444	2,338	3,238,561
Silesia	—	—	—	4	7	8	1	3	—	—	21	74	13,516	3,547	320	600,519
Galicia	—	—	—	24	27	28	25	2	—	—	106	759	120,563	47,057	1,009	1,513,898
Bukowina	—	—	—	2	6	6	3	—	—	—	17	46	7,956	8,380	—	128,424
Dalmatia	—	—	1	2	6	5	4	6	—	—	24	17	13,561	9,510	57	296,850
Total, 1889	2	—	8	31	30	31	30	20	4	—	154	3,530	751,585	235,327	12,669	22,176,663
„ '88	—	2	8	22	30	31	31	23	8	—	157	3,515	772,691	226,185	5,511	18,273,386
„ '87	—	1	10	29	30	31	30	23	4	1	158	2,396	433,941	139,465	2,956	9,147,620
„ '86	—	—	6	29	30	31	30	28	3	—	158	3,077	524,709	167,867	8,154	14,071,953
„ '85	—	—	8	29	30	31	31	21	5	1	156	3,489	682,786	223,390	5,508	17,956,933

It thus appears that in 1884 hail fell on more days than during any other year, and with the greatest intensity, yet over a comparatively small area, while the damage caused was somewhat above the average. Whereas in 1880, though there were fewer days of hail and its intensity was less, yet, owing to the large area affected, the amount of damage was the most considerable in any year, though the same figure was nearly reached in 1889. Since 1884 hail has fallen in Austria every day during June and July, and in August in 1885 and 1888; in this latter month in each of the other years one day only was recorded on which none fell.

Only one district (Sechshaus, in Lower Austria) out of the 327 into which Austria is divided, has escaped a visitation during the eighteen years; hailstorms occurred in all the others, and even the highest lying cultivated lands were not spared. For example, Galtür, with 330 inhabitants, in the district of Landeck (Tyrol), at a height of 1,550 metres, where there are only meadows with a little barley and potatoes, was on the 11th and 12th August, 1885, twice visited by hail, and suffered, for this neighbourhood, the excessive damage of 6,065 gulden.

The least damage per head of the agricultural population has occurred in Galicia, but this is in part due to the low estimate of the value of grain customary in that province; it must also be noticed that Galicia, of all the provinces of Austria, shows the densest agricultural population (56 per sq. kilom., or 74·2 per cent. of the whole population), and that the returns from here are less complete than those of other provinces. In Bohemia, as in all thickly populated countries, corn prices are higher; hops are also much cultivated in this kingdom, on which account a relatively greater damage from hail appears there. In Lower Austria, South Tyrol, South Steiermark, Krain and Moravia we have the vine regions, which make the damage appear much heavier; the same holds good in the maritime districts and Dalmatia, in which districts also the damage done to the olives materially raises the amount.

The damage done in any one district is of course subject to great fluctuations; it may be very slight in one year, and excessive in another. For instance, the district of Krems, whose average for the eighteen years is 4 fl. 53 kr. per head, owes this entirely to the year 1880, when the damage caused by hail reached the enormous total of 2,241,000 florins (36 fl. 50 kr. per head of the agricultural population): if we except this year the damage per head is only 2 fl. 65 kr. Again, the district of Dauba had ten years without any hail, in three other years the damage was slight, and it is the year 1889 which, with damage to the amount of 893,000 florins, is answerable for an average of 3 fl. 27 kr. per head, whereas the average for the other seventeen years is 64 kr. per head. A district which has hitherto enjoyed a comparative immunity may thus next year be placed among those which appear to suffer most severely.

It must also be noticed that in those districts in which hail does fall annually, it naturally does not always affect the same communes or proprietors; it rarely happens, as appears from a comparison of several years, that one and the same commune suffers during several consecutive years. In Austria, the Vorarlberg is the least exposed to damage by hail; during the period under review there were five years (1875-76, 1881-82, and 1889) in which none was recorded, and in the other thirteen the damage varied from 400 fl. (1878) to 34,000 fl. (1873), and the average annual damage per head was 8 kr. No other province can point to a whole year without any hail.

The following table shows the greatest and least damage done in a year, and the average in each province :—

	Least Damage.			Greatest Damage.			Average Annual Damage.	
	Year.	Total.	Per Head.	Year.	Total.	Per Head.	Total.	Per Head.
		000 gulden.	Gulden.		000 gulden.	Gulden.	000 gulden.	Gulden.
Lower Austria	1876	174	0·27	1880	5,388	8·49	1,362	2·15
Upper „	'79	23	0·06	'85	1,192	3·21	331	0·89
Danubian provinces	1878	258	0·26	1880	5,701	5·67	1,693	1·68
Salzburg	1874	4	0·04	1885	348	3·87	79	0·88
Tyrol and Vorarlberg	'72	189	0·33	'85	2,181	3·59	922	1·63
Carinthia	'73	61	0·26	'81	540	2·26	247	1·03
Steiermark	'76	400	0·50	'82	2,747	3·45	1,450	1·82
Krain	'79	59	0·17	'80	1,306	3·86	337	1·00
Alpine provinces	1876	1,205	0·59	1880	4,573	2·25	3,085	1·50
Maritime districts	1879	166	0·46	1885	1,695	4·69	554	1·55
Dalmatia....................	'75	81	0·21	'85	1,308	3·36	345	0·89
Maritime provinces	1875	271	0·36	1885	3,003	4·03	899	1·20
Bohemia	1878	426	0·19	1889	9,561	4·25	3,583	1·58
Moravia	'78	41	0·04	'86	3,546	3·40	1,230	1·18
Silesia	'78	1	0·00	'88	2,001	7·47	263	0·98
Sudetic provinces	1878	468	0·13	1889	13,402	3·74	5,076	1·42
Galicia	1878	592	0·13	1883	3,722	0·84	1,848	0·42
Bukowina	'76	17	0·04	'85	252	0·62	110	0·27
Carpathian provinces	1878	629	0·13	1883	3,803	0·79	1,958	0·41
Austria	1879	5,017	0·41	1880	24,249	1·99	12,661	1·04

By bringing the extremes together in this manner, a considerable change for the worse appears in the climatic conditions of the country, as in every single province the minimum occurred prior to 1880, whilst the maximum is noted either in or after that year.

III.—*Population of Bulgaria*, 1888.

THE Census of Bulgaria, taken on the 1st January, 1888, includes that of Eastern Roumelia, which was practically (although such union is not yet recognised by the Powers) joined to Bulgaria proper in 1886. A comparison with the figures for 1881 is therefore only practicable in the case of the older portion of the principality. The population now amounts to 3,154,375; that of Bulgaria proper (2,193,434) having increased during the seven years by 188,515 or 9·4 per cent. The following table shows the population according to *prefectures* in 1888, and, where possible, the increase or decrease since 1881 :—

Population of Bulgaria, 1881 and 1888.

Prefecture.	Population.		Increase or Decrease.	
	1881.	1888.	Number.	Per Cent.
Kustendil	148,031	162,939	+ 19,908	+ 13·9
Lom Palenka	100,885	114,223	+ 18,338	+ 13·2
Lofcha	85,397	119,010	+ 33,613	+ 39·4
Plevna	101,593	92,040	− 9,553	− 9·4
Rahovo	66,882	86,781	+ 19,899	+ 29·7
Rasgrad	122,374	122,370	− 4	0·0
Roustchouk	132,009	154,434	+ 22,425	+ 17·0
Sevlievo	91,750	93,948	+ 2,198	+ 2·4
Shoumla	183,847	175,709	− 8,138	− 4·4
Silistria	101,137	107,637	+ 6,500	+ 6·4
Sistovo	41,898	90,876	+ 48,978	+ 116·9
Sofia	159,580	182,247	+ 22,667	+ 14·2
Tirnovo	217,523	205,344	− 12,179	− 5·6
Trn	64,662	76,051	+ 11,389	+ 17·6
Varna	169,091	206,664	+ 37,573	+ 22·2
Vratza	122,434	87,462	− 34,972	+ 28·6
Widdin	103,826	115,699	+ 11,873	+ 11·4
Bulgaria Proper	2,007,919	2,193,434	+ 185,515	+ 9·4
Bourgas	....	110,363	....	....
Eski-Zagra	....	203,396	....	....
Hasskeui	....	123,168	....	....
Philippopolis	....	226,013	....	....
Slivno	....	161,303	....	....
Tatar-Pazarjik	....	136,698	....	....
Eastern Roumelia	....	960,941	....	....
Total Bulgaria	....	3,154,375	....	....

Since 1881, certain changes have been made in the boundaries of some prefectures, as Vratza, Widdin, and Varna; too much importance must consequently not be attached to apparent fluctuations in the population of the respective prefectures.

As regards the nationalities, the Bulgarians number 2,326,224; the Turkish speaking Mussulmans, 607,372; the Greeks, 58,326; and the total is completed by 162,453 "various," who may be considered as being composed of Vlachs (Roumanians), Jews, gipsies, Slavs of non-Bulgarian race, and other Europeans; their respective numbers being in the order named. The Turkish population is densest in the Danubian prefectures of Shoumla, Varna, Silistria, Roustchouk, and Rasgrad, in each of which the Mussulman element forms the great majority of the inhabitants of the prefecture. Bourgas (in the Aido-Balkan), Eski-Zagra (in the Kezanlik district), Hasskeui, and Philippopolis have each a compact Turkish population. The Greek population is important only in Slivno and Philippopolis—where the Greek districts of Kavakli in the former and Stanimaka in the latter, help to swell their numbers—and in the maritime prefectures of Bourgas and Varna. It should be remarked that a process of Bulgarisation, quite voluntary in nature, has for some time past been going on among that large class which is half Greek and half Bulgarian, and that, especially since the union of the two provinces, the natives of this category describe themselves, and are described, as Bulgarians. In the prefectures of Widdin, Varna, and Rahovo, there are large settlements of Wallachians.

The Bulgarian population has steadily increased by nearly 17 per cent., while the Mussulmans have decreased by 46,691 or 9 per cent. (which figure probably represents the Mussulman emigration during the time), the falling off being greater in the prefectures of Tirnovo, Shoumla, Rasgrad, and Plevna; on the other hand, Varna, Silistria, Sistovo, and Roustchouk show an increase. The Greek population has declined 4¼ per cent.

The chief towns are as follows :—

	Population.		Increase.	
	1881.	1888.	Number.	Per Cent.
Philippopolis	—	33,032	—	—
Sofia	20,501	30,428	9,927	48·4
Roustchouk	26,163	27,194	1,031	3·9
Varna	24,555	25,256	701	2·5
Shoumla	23,093	23,161	68	0·3
Slivno	—	20,893	—	—
Eski-Zagra	—	16,039	—	—
Tatar-Pazarjik	—	15,659	—	—
Widdin	13,714	14,772	1,058	7·7
Plevna	11,474	14,307	2,833	24·7
Hasskeui	—	14,191	—	—
Rasgrad	11,625	12,974	1,349	11·6
Sistovo	11,540	12,482	942	8·1
Stanimaka	—	12,191	—	—
Silistria	10,640	11,414	774	7·2
Tirnovo	11,247	11,314	67	0·6
Yamboli	—	11,241	—	—
Chirpan	—	11,024	—	—
Kustendil	9,590	10,689	1,099	11·5
Bourgas	—	5,749	—	—

IV.—*Population of Ceylon, 1891.*

In this island, as well as in India, the census was taken not on the night of the 5th April, the date of the census in the other parts of the United Kingdom and its colonies, but on that of the 26th February. This earlier date was found preferable on account of the considerable migration which takes place about the month of April. The population of the whole island is now 3,007,789; the increase during the decade being just 9 per cent. The greatest increase is shown in the eastern province (6·4 per cent.), while in *Uva* there is a decrease of 3·9 per cent. The following table shows the population of the provinces:—

General Statement of the Area and Population (exclusive of the Military and Shipping).

	Area. Square Miles.	Females.	Persons.	Increase. Number.	Increase. Per Cent.	Persons per Square Mile, 1891.
estern Province....	1,432	364,071	762,533	91,033	13·5	532
baragamuwa ,,	1,901	116,871	258,626	32,797	14·5	136
orth-western ,,	2,997	145,415	320,070	26,743	9·1	107
entral ,,	2,300	211,836	474,487	818	0·2	206
va ,,	3,155	71,067	159,201	−6,491	−3·9	50
orth Central ,,	4,002	83,988	75,333	9,187	13·9	19
orthern ,,	3,363	158,935	319,296	16,796	5·5	95
tern ,,	4,037	71,063	148,444	20,889	16·4	37
thern ,,	2,146	241,167	489,799	56,279	13·0	228
'otal CEYLON....		1,414,413	3,007,789		9·0	119

There are some remarkable changes in the rate of variation during the last two decades. For instance, between 1871 and 1881 the Europeans *increased* by 48·5 per cent.; in the last decade they *decreased* by 3·2 per cent. Similarly the Veddahs *increased* by 9·8 per cent. during the period 1871-81, and *decreased* by 44·8 per cent. between 1881 and 1891. The following table shows the population according to nationality:—

	Population, 1881.	Increase since 1871. Number.	Increase since 1871. Per Cent.	Population, 1891.	Increase or Decrease since 1881. Number.	Increase or Decrease since 1881. Per Cent.
Europeans	4,836	1,577	48·5	4,678	−158	−3·2
Eurasians and Burghers	17,886	2,551	16·6	21,231	3,345	18·7
Singhalese	1,846,614	182,155	10·9	2,041,158	194,544	10·5
Tamils	687,248	149,434	27·8	723,853	36,605	5·3
Moormen	184,542	20,813	12·7	197,166	12,624	6·8
Veddahs	2.228	198	9·8	1,229	−999	−44·8
Malays	8,895	} 2,630	19·1	{ 10,133	1,238	13·9
Others	7,489			8,341	852	11·4
Total	2,759,738	359,358	14·9	3,007,789	248,051	9·0

The greater increase in the first of the two decades is probably in part accounted for by the fact that the census taken in 1871 was the first enumeration made for forty years, and was thus looked upon with suspicion by the natives, and the returns for that year would consequently in all probability be too low. It appears also that another cause of the slighter increase in 1881-91 is the falling off in the immigration; the excess of immigrants (who are especially Tamils and Moormen) over emigrants amounting in 1871-81 to 201,006, and in the succeeding decennium to only 54,543. The decrease in the Europeans (males only, the females having slightly increased) is attributed to the speculations which attracted many about 1875, and to the destruction of the coffee crop since. The Veddahs apparently put themselves down as Tamil or Singhalese according to the language spoken by them.

It may be noticed that in Ceylon, as in India, the males predominate; they number 1,593,376 against 1,414,413 females. This applies to all nationalities, the proportion of males per 1,000 of the population being as follows in 1891 :—

Europeans 637, Burghers 496, Singhalese 521, Tamils 547, Moormen 554, Malays 531, Veddahs 531, others 648, all Ceylon 529·7.

From the following table, giving the chief towns, it will be seen that the population of Negombo (a port to the north of Colombo) has doubled itself during the last decade :—

| | 1881. | 1891. | Increase or Decrease. | |
			Number.	Per Cent.
Colombo	110,502	126,825	+ 16,323	+ 14·8
Jaffna	39,855	43,179	+ 3,324	+ 8·3
Galle	31,743	33,590	+ 1,847	+ 5·8
Kandy	22,026	20,375	− 1,651	− 7·5
Negombo	9,141	18,933	+ 9,792	+107·0
Trincomalee	9,731	11,596	+ 1,865	+ 19·2
Kalutara	10,211	10,864	+ 653	+ 6·4

V.—*The Silver Census.*

[THE following is taken from the *Journal of the Institute of Bankers*, October, 1892, vol. xiii, part 7.]

Considerable discussion has arisen from time to time as to the redundancy or deficiency of silver coin in the kingdom, and the Council therefore at their meeting in June last decided to endeavour to ascertain the holdings in silver of the banks on a fixed day— Wednesday, 20th July, being chosen for the purpose.

In pursuance of this decision, the following circular letter, with forms of return, was sent to every bank in the kingdom :—

INSTITUTE OF BANKERS, 34, CLEMENT'S LANE,
DEAR SIR, *7th July*, 1892.

We beg to inform you that, at a meeting of the Council, held on 15th June, it was resolved:—"That an inquiry as to the amount of silver held by banks in Great Britain and Ireland, be made on Wednesday, 20th July."

The object of making this inquiry is to arrive at an approximate conclusion as to whether the silver currency is in excess of the requirements of the country, or of any particular district, or the contrary; and it is hoped that the doing so may lead to arrangements being made for assisting banks in the circulation of silver.

In pursuance of the above resolution, we beg to inclose forms available for making the return, which we ask you to be good enough to complete (including your branches, if any), and to forward to the Institute.

If you prefer to send separate returns from each branch without summarising the particulars, pray do so. The returns will, of course, be treated as confidential. The Council trust that a cordial co-operation on the part of the various banks will render the returns as complete as possible. It is proposed to publish only the general results, as in the case of the inquiry as to the amount of gold made by the Institute in 1883.

We are, dear Sir, yours obediently,
THOS. SALT, *President.*
W. TALBOT AGAR, *Secretary.*

(Copy of Form of Return.)

Name of Bank,_____

Silver on hand at the close of business on Wednesday, July 20th, 1892, £_____

In relation to our ordinary average requirements the above amount is:—

In *excess* by £_____
Deficient by £_____

Note.—Information (1) as to excess or deficiency of any particular coin, and (2) as to the amount of silver *in transitu* would be valuable.

The results of these circulars are embodied in the table given below. It is gratifying to note that the returns may be said to comprise, with some unimportant exceptions, all the bank offices of the United Kingdom, and the Council gladly avail themselves of this opportunity to thank the managers and officials of the various banks, whose hearty co-operation has made so complete a return possible:—

Summary of Silver Census. Returns of Silver on hand at the Close of Business on Wednesday, 20th July, 1892.

Class of Banks.	Number of Bank Offices.		Amount of Silver.	In Excess of Average Requirements.	Deficient of Average Requirements.
	Returns Received.	Not Received.			
			£	£	£
English private and joint stock banks*	2,959	92	3,289,797	928,663	31,089
Isle of Man banks	15	—	9,355	5,600	—
Irish banks	537	—	534,566	180,114	—
Scotch banks	986	—	715,057	108,168	10,396
Total United Kingdom	4,497	92	4,548,775	1,222,545	41,485

* Including the amount in the banking department of the Bank of England.

It has not been found possible to collect, on a similar scale, information as to the excess or deficiency of any particular coin, or as to the amount of silver *in transitu*, but as far as evidence has been given, it may be said that the crown, and more especially the four-shilling piece, is an unpopular coin, while there is very frequently a scarcity of sixpences, and, in some few places, of shillings. On the other hand, the amount of three-penny pieces is, in many places, in excess of requirements. The information as to the amount of silver *in transitu* is too meagre to base any opinion on it.

VI.—*Notes on Economical and Statistical Works.*

The Hygiene, Diseases and Mortality of Occupations. By J. T. Arlidge. London: Percival and Co., 1892.

This is a large book on a vast and important subject. Dr. Arlidge calls attention in his preface to the magnitude of the task which he has here attempted, and to the significant fact that few British physicians had previously studied the question, and "no treatise had been written upon it for a long series of years." His own book, he tells us, originated in a course of lectures which were delivered in 1889 at the Royal College of Physicians, but in those lectures the question was strictly confined to the "consideration of diseases consequent upon the inhalation of dust." Since then the scope of the book has been enlarged, and the material of the lectures is in the main reproduced in a single chapter. But even the pathology of dust inhalation forms an extensive topic when treated with the care which Dr. Arlidge has bestowed upon it; and this chapter occupies about half of the volume, and fills some three hundred pages. The occupations, with which he deals, are divided into eight main groups; and the basis of the classification followed is etiological, according to the different modes in which the presence of dust may occasion disease. The generation of dust itself, the employment of noxious or poisonous materials, the evolution of noxious vapours, the action of excessive temperatures, of electricity, and of abnormal atmospheric pressure, excessive use, friction or strain, and exposure to infection and contagion, form the headings of the different groups. The first heading is subdivided into two classes, according as the dust provocative of disease is of mineral or organic origin, and these two subdivisions are in their turn subject to a further bifurcation— in the first case, according as the dust is metallic or non-metallic, and, in the second, according as it is of vegetable or animal origin.

In the previous chapter Dr. Arlidge deals in succession with the occupations which he does not treat in this fifth chapter. These he classifies in the first instance as those occupations which do, and those which do not, raise new wealth from the earth. The former, which are treated last, comprise the work of agriculture and agricultural labourers and of gardeners and nurserymen. They form a class comparatively unimportant for the purposes of the book, as a general experience shows that the healthiness of an occupation bears a correspondence, easy to detect, to the extent to which it is pursued in the open air. The other class is more diversified, and requires minuter attention. It is subdivided into traders and non-traders. The non-traders include the professional classes, which Dr. Arlidge dismisses with comparative brevity. Among them, as is well known, clergymen occupy the most favoured position. The traders are considered in seven sections, devoted respectively to retailers of food and drinks, chemists and druggists, the clothing trades, stationers and booksellers, dealers in metallic and miscellaneous articles, and hairdressers and wig-makers. A sub-class is also constituted of the mechanical trades, consisting of three sections, the first including artisans using mineral materials, such as builders, masons and slaters, the second comprising artisans employing the metals, whether iron, like blacksmiths or engineers, or other metals, such as watchmakers, or printers, or engravers, and the third and last section containing those artisans who use materials of organic origin, whether of an animal or of a vegetable character.

From the account we have given of the classification followed in these two chapters, which form the bulk of the work, it will be seen how thoroughly Dr. Arlidge has dealt with his subject; and in the course of his treatment he has arrived at some conclusions which might surprise those unacquainted with the facts. It is, for example, somewhat astonishing to learn that there is no evidence of any distinct injurious influence exercised on the eye-sight by the minute detailed work of a watchmaker. On the other hand Dr. Arlidge has shown how grievous are some of the evils occasioned, and how desirable it is to enforce such precautions as may be possible and yet neglected. And, if these later chapters afford evidence of the pains with which he has executed his design, the earlier chapters testify to the admirable and cautious spirit in which he has conceived it. In the first, which is introductory and historical, he defines carefully the scope and object of the inquiry on which he is entering. "The problem," he states, "to be solved, is to determine not merely the mortality and relative prevalence of particular diseases in the several occupations, but to discover what, if any, pathological consequences are rightly assignable to them, and what, when such are found, are their causes. It is not sufficient to analyse the returns of sickness and mortality. To arrive at a correct estimate of the effects positively attributable to an occupation, it becomes necessary to eliminate all factors of disease not truly incident to it—a proceeding of great difficulty even when practicable." This statement of the conditions of the problem will commend itself to every candid statistician; and in his second chapter Dr. Arlidge is careful to emphasise the secondary, or collateral, or accidental circumstances which may attend particular kinds of labour. "Every definite employment," he remarks, "involves some circumstances which may give rise to disease." But an investigation of so comprehensive a character is manifestly beyond the power of any single student. In looking for material he will find the greatest abundance to be of Continental origin; but the difference of race, and of conditions of employment, whether as respects the hours of work or the sanitary state of the factories and workshops, and the distant date of publication of many of the most important treatises, detract to no small extent from their value.   In his own historical sketch of the literature of industrial diseases Dr. Arlidge pays a deserved tribute to the work in England of Dr. Farr and his successor, Dr. Ogle; but he also calls attention to a difficulty, noted by many social inquirers, in the defective condition of the occupations returns of our census, and after considering in his second chapter the various *incidental* and *accidental* circumstances of a general nature which affect the healthiness of different occupations, he proceeds in his third chapter to examine the amount of reliance which can be safely placed on the statistical evidence available, and to insist on the mischievous fallacies into which the hasty and careless interpretation of this evidence may easily lead the unwary student.

A History of the Custom-Revenue in England.   By Hubert Hall. London: Elliot Stock, 1892.

Mr. Hubert Hall's history of the custom-revenue is well known to economic students, who will welcome its appearance in a cheaper form.   It is one—and by no means the least important of its class—of a number of books which have in recent years attested the zeal and industry of economic historians, and the special attention, which these inquirers have given to the economic aspect of affairs, and to particular phenomena, has enabled them to correct the hasty generalisations which have sometimes disfigured the writings of economic theorists, and also—and this is a more unexpected but not less important result—to amend some of the conclusions of general historians.   Mr. Hall, for example, calls in question the opinions of so careful an inquirer as Bishop Stubbs; and the argument of the first part of his book may be said to be generally opposed to the contention, which eminent historians have countenanced, and their followers have been content to adopt without question, that the Tudor and Stuart monarchs acted unconstitutionally in the matter of taxation.   Mr. Hall, on the contrary, shows that they could scarcely be said to be infringing the constitution, or enlarging the prerogative, which they were admitted by usage to possess.   And he adduces reasons in support of his views, the validity of which it is difficult to dispute; for he has, as he states on his title page, compiled his history from "original authorities," and his official position in the Record Office has at once given him easy access to many of these authorities, and familiarised him with their proper use and value.   In the first part of his book he deals with constitutional history, with the customs of the middle ages, with those of personal monarchy, with royalist and parliamentarian customs, and finally with the constitutional question which was last raised in English history in connection with the colonial customs.   He points out the immense difficulty which necessarily attends any endeavour to ascertain the exact scope and origin of the prerogative admitted by immemorial usage to belong to the crown.   There is an absence of any recorded financial history prior to the reign of Henry II. "Indistinctly" in that reign, and distinctly in that of Richard I, we know that a "customary revenue was collected for the Crown at the seaports and in other places adapted for the survey of mercantile shipping or transport." Slightly later there is abundant evidence to prove a right of pre-emption, or purveyance, on the part of the Crown, "extending to all commodities within its land and jurisdiction," a further right of "restraining the export or import of any native or foreign commodity" at its mere discretion, and, thirdly, "an official supervision in connection with the Exchequer" "exercised at every available point of observation" on the sea-coast, as well as at certain inland stations. From these various origins—all reducible to the right of purveyance—Mr. Hall traces the history of the Customs. The *Antiqua Custuma*, levied on staple exports at a commuted rate, the *Nova Custuma*, representing any advance on those rates, the Subsidy and the "desperate expedient" of an extraordinary custom upon the chief staple commodities exported from the Kingdom, invidiously described as a "maltolte" (or "mala tolta"). Throughout he tests accepted and traditional opinions by the evidence of original authorities, and convicts them not infrequently of error or extravagance. Throughout he shows that the action of the Crown has been often misrepresented, that the powers of the prerogative were large, and were exerted to recover what had been lost rather than claim what was new, that in the early Tudor period they were approved by the people, and that the Commonwealth did not in practice diminish the vexatious burdens of the Stuart monarchs. In his second part he deals with what he distinguishes as the fiscal history—with the ports, the "customers," the "prises," "captions" and "emptions," in which the prerogative of the Crown was first asserted, with the tolls or prise-commutations, with the antiqua and nova custuma, with the subsidy, which supplemented these, with the "maltolte," and with the assignments, by which the Crown discharged its obligations to one set of individuals by giving them a lien—possibly never to be realised—on the revenue to be collected from another. In the appendices to both the parts the authorities for the statements in the text are furnished.

Manuel de Statistique Pratique. Par Victor Turquan. Paris: Berger-Levrault et Cie., 1891.

The author of this manual is the distinguished statist who presides over the *Bureau de la Statistique Générale de France;* and he has prepared the manual for the guidance of officials engaged throughout the country in the collection, preparation, and digestion of statistics. In the execution of this design, as M. Block remarks in a preface to the work, he has sought to combine practical usefulness with a full recognition, and wide dissemination, of an adequate knowledge of the theory of the subject. By making each official acquainted with the general bearing of the inquiries to which he may be contributing his quota, by explaining the difficulties which commonly present themselves, and the methods which should be adopted for their satisfactory solution, he has hoped to secure that uniformity and correctness of procedure which is so essential a quality, if statistics are to be of any real value. Some data, as M. Block observes, present themselves with automatic exactness and require little exertion on the part of officials. Those which relate to the finances, to the army, to the administration of justice, belong to this class, together with the registration of births, marriages, and deaths. They are collected in accordance with the general laws of the country; and all that is needful is to secure uniformity of procedure. But the greatest difficulties have to be met where the statistics are not thus automatically produced. Even the taking of the census—that primary statistical act of an enlightened government—was at first conducted by imperfect methods, and presented abundant *lacunæ*. It is only by the more profound and scientific study of statistics, and the diffusion of sounder knowledge and more accurate practice, that these earlier faults have been amended; and M. Turquan now seeks to place at the general disposal of French officials the latest and most approved results of statistical inquiry. In an introduction he describes the plan which he has followed. The first book is devoted to an account of the official organisation established in connection with statistics in France and other countries. The administrative arrangements, the various undertakings attempted, and the character of the different publications issued, are described in detail. The book is divided into four parts, in the first of which a historical sketch is given of the position of official statistics in France at different periods—before the Revolution, during the first Republic, the Empire, the Restoration, the July Monarchy, the second Republic, the second Empire, and the third Republic. Since the year 1870 there has been especial progress, for, M. Turquan remarks, statistics are a necessary instrument of government in free societies. Parliament requires information to be gathered and conveyed by numerous well-constructed channels; the popular representatives are sensible at once of an appetite and obligation which impels them to be curious and inquisitive, and the administration on its part has no secrets to screen from public knowledge. And so in the second part of the book M. Turquan runs through the different departments of the French government, and notes the various kinds of statistics with which they are severally concerned. The Ministry of Foreign Affairs, the Ministry of Justice, of the Interior, of Finance, of War, of Commerce, of the Navy, of Public Instruction, of Public Works, and of Agriculture, are successively considered; and the chapter concludes with the statistics of the municipality of Paris. M. Turquan then passes abroad to the United Kingdom, Germany, the Scandinavian States, Russia, Belgium, Italy, Spain, the other European countries, America, and Australasia, and reviews the statistical organisations which the governments of these various countries possess; and in the fourth and concluding part of the book he notices the statistical commissions of other countries and his own. The thoroughness, characteristic of his treatment in this first book, is maintained throughout the manual, and we may proceed to a more summary account of the remaining contents. The second book is described by M. Turquan as being especially practical, and deals with the preparation of the different annual statistics in the various divisions—the *mairies*, the *préfectures*, and *sous-préfectures*—according to which the subordinate administration is organised in France. The third book relates to the sanitary statistics required by the Minister of the Interior ; the fourth furnishes precise and detailed directions for the taking of the census; the fifth, based to a large extent on M. Levasseur's important work, the completion of which was noticed in the last part of this *Journal*, furnishes an account of the actual state of the population in France, and some summary observations on the science of demography. This book, as M. Turquan remarks, may be said to rest on the basis of the material contained in the three previous books. Finally, in the sixth book a rapid glance is cast over French statistics, following the information given in official documents. The area and population of France, the movement of the population—which reveals a decreasing birth-rate and the seemingly rapid approach of a stationary state—the statistics of religion, of crime, of civil actions, and of prisons, of public charity, of insurance, of private beneficence, of public instruction—which has made remarkable progress under the third Republic—of agriculture, and commerce, and industry, of wages—which in France, as elsewhere, have risen—of shipping and fishing, of transport, communication and credit, electoral and military statistics, statistics of finance and taxation, of the octroi, and of consumption, are successively summarised. M. Turquan's manual certainly cannot be said to err on the side of omission ; and, on the other hand, it is difficult for such a publication to include anything which can fairly be deemed unnecessary. It promises to be of the greatest use to those officials for whom it is intended; and it seems admirably calculated to promote the attainment of that high level of statistical practice which it is its chief endeavour to foster.

The Sweating System in Europe and America. Papers read at the Saratoga meeting of the American Association, 1892, and printed in the *Journal of Social Science*, No. xxx, October, 1892.

Among the subjects discussed at the meeting in September last of the American Association at Saratoga, the "sweating system" occupied a prominent place. Various well-known statistical authors read or sent papers detailing the state of those of the working classes who are generally considered to be most liable to be "sweated" in England, Germany, New York, and Massachusetts. All were agreed as to the difficulty of defining exactly what was meant by the term, and in maintaining that the system, *as a system*, did not exist. As regards Germany, the Rev. J. G. Brooks holds that especial hardship is only met with in those industries which are dying out, or in those which, formerly carried on in the workers' own homes, are now being transferred, more or less gradually, to the factories. Mr. D. F. Schloss reviews the working of the "Factory and Workshop Act" and "Public Health (London) Act" of 1891: his conclusion is that "the position of the workpeople employed under 'the sweating system' is, save in a comparatively small number of instances, no better to-day than it was when, more than two years ago, the select committee upon 'the sweating system' made its final report." In the United States "sweating" and "tenement-house labour" seem to be almost convertible terms. Dr. Anna S. Daniel has made an investigation into the condition of many of the tenements visited by her in her professional capacity of out-door visiting physician of a New York hospital, and draws a terrible picture of the dirt and overcrowding in these places, never visited by factory inspectors. The two most interesting contributions on this subject are those by Mr. H. G. Wadlin and Mr. Joseph Lee, who endeavour to estimate the nature and remedies of the evil. Mr. Wadlin's paper deals with Massachusetts. There is less "sweating" in Boston than in New York, owing partly to the smaller number of ignorant and unskilled immigrants in the former city, and partly to the better laws and stricter inspection in force in the State of which it is the capital. Yet that "sweating" is possible in the larger city, prevents wages from being much higher in Boston, as nearly one-sixth of the clothes (which are especially considered) contracted for in this city are made in New York. Mr. Joseph Lee has carefully gone through the evidence given in the House of Lords' committee, and he entirely absolves the middleman from blame (which he is inclined to lay upon the consumer). In fact, he adduces evidence to prove that the middleman himself only makes a bare margin of profit, and that those philanthropic individuals or associations which have endeavoured to get the work done without the intervention of the middleman either fail financially or pay their workpeople at a rate below the average. One of the evils complained of in the system of sub-contract (the *pros* and *cons* of which Mr. Lee discusses at length) is the danger of infection, but of this there is very little proof. Considering the conditions necessary in order that there may be "sweating," Mr. Wadlin shows that the method of paying the superintendent out of profits (so that he has every incentive to grind down wages to the lowest point) must *co-exist* with an absence of organisation on the part of the workmen. Mr. Lee, in an appendix, summarises and discusses the legislation of Massachusetts, New York, and Chicago: in this respect, the former appears to be far ahead of the other States. A licence is now necessary to work in tenements in Boston; this law, although quite recent, seems to have already produced good effects as regards sanitation. In New York and Boston all tenement-made goods are required to have a tag sewn on them, on which must be legibly printed the name of the State and town in which it was made. The general conclusion arrived at is that "sweating" is a result of the competition of unskilled and uneducated workmen, more especially of immigrants, and that the remedy is to be found in a better inspection of the factories (including workshops and tenements) on the part of the State, and in organisation on the part of the men. Much could also be done in America by enforcing the education of the children, who are worked to the utmost from the very earliest possible moment, and consequently remain ignorant all their lives.

Handbuch der Verwaltungs-Statistik. Von Ernst Mischler. (Erster Band.) Stuttgart: T. G. Cotta, 1892.

This is one of the publications, increasing in number, which testify to the growing importance of statistics, and to the more scientific spirit in which the study is now happily prosecuted. The handbook is marked by all the thoroughness which is characteristic of German writers, whether they are engaged on manuals or on more extensive work; and this single volume. which forms only the first part of the manual, contains over three hundred pages, dealing with the subject from a variety of theoretical standpoints, besides supplying considerable information on matters of fact. The first section of the book is devoted to the connection between statistics and administration, and the second to the actual organisation of administration-statistics during the present century in the different countries of the world. The second part is thus concerned with an account of actual fact—and the account is full and exact—while the first may be said to be, by contrast, more theoretical. The statistical functions of administration, and the administrative functions of statistics, are successively examined. The various aspects, from which these statistics may be regarded, according as we look at the question from the point of view of the investigator or the investigated, are next fully treated, and the constitution and duties of statistical boards, and the different parts of statistical work, whether this be the collection, or arrangement, or the elaboration, or publication of figures, are, lastly, reviewed. In fact Dr. Mischler has been as exhaustive in his treatment of the subject as he seems to have been careful and impartial.

Salaires et Budgets Ouvriers en Belgique au Mois d'Avril, 1891. Bruxelles: P. Weissenbruch, 1892.

This volume contains the answers furnished by the Belgian *conseils de l'industrie et du travail* in response to a Government inquiry respecting the average wage, the price of the necessaries of life, and the household budgets, of working-men. Printed forms, to be filled up, were issued to the different sections of the different *conseils,* and, by limiting the inquiry to a single month, it was thought that the difficulties, which might have rendered a year's account impossible, or at any rate untrustworthy, might be successfully overcome. Especially was it deemed desirable to reduce the difficulties of the task to the narrowest limits, as the inquiry was practically the first intrusted to the *conseils.* Patterns of the different schedules are furnished in the earlier part of the volume, and the returns actually made are contained in the latter portion. A great amount of information has certainly been brought together on a topic, which is demanding, and receiving, increased attention every year; and it is but recently that the researches of Le Play and his school on the matter of workmen's budgets have attracted notice in England. English students will therefore feel a special interest in the volume. The forms seem to have been carefully prepared, and the results to be fairly reliable. On the wages schedules the number of workers of different ages and sexes is specified, the average number of hours

worked per day, and of days worked during the month selected
for investigation—that of April, 1891. On the schedule relating to
the necessaries of life, the quantity taken as the basis of calculation
is given in the case of each article which figures on the list; and
in the third and last particular of which information was required
—that of the household budget—the composition by age, by sex,
and by occupation, of the family, is furnished. The receipts are
next given, whether in the shape of wages, or of supplementary
earnings, obtained by each member of the family, together with
the days of labour in the case of the wages, and the origin of the
receipts in the case of those which are supplementary in character,
arising it may be, from some bye-occupation, or from property of
any description, or from charitable assistance or insurance; and
then, finally, the expenditure is classified under three separate
heads—the first including that on material objects, such as food,
drink, lodging, clothing, warming, and taxation, the second referring
to the religious, moral, and intellectual order, and the third to
luxuries, such as tobacco, sports and amusements. This information is followed by an appendix containing some observations on
the part played by the *conseils*, which supplied the media for conducting the inquiry, in the promotion of industrial conciliation,
and interesting examples are furnished of the intervention of different *conseils* in matters at issue between, or affecting the interests
of, employers and employed. In Belgium, as elsewhere, amid much
that may discourage, there is also not a little to afford encouragement, and to foster a hope that rational modes of avoiding or
settling disputes may gain ground, as time passes, on the violent
haphazard methods of strikes and lock-outs.

Trade Unionism: New and Old. By G. Howell. London:
Methuen and Co., 1892.

This little book forms the first volume of a series, which is
now being issued by Messrs. Methuen and Co., under the title of
Social Questions of To-day. The subject and the author are alike
fitted for the commencement of such a series. The topic of trades
unionism is in the forefront of popular discussion, especially in
connection with the new unions formed during the last few years
among unskilled labourers; and Mr. Howell is probably as well
qualified as any man to write on the history of the older unions,
and on the feelings with which some of their most prominent
officials have regarded the claims and methods of action of the
new unionists. He presents in a compact shape in this book some
of the facts and description, which he has given at greater length
in his larger book on the *Conflicts of Capital and Labour,* and he
expresses in no measured terms his condemnation of the language
and designs of the new leaders. From the standpoint of a convinced individualist he objects to their socialistic inclinations; and
he considers that they are too violent in their language, and
aggressive and ambitious in their aims. His own opinions may not
be entirely free from the failings which he thus detects in the
utterances of others, and his whole book is perhaps more remarkable for racy vigour than judicial calmness; but this characteristic

is calculated to increase rather than otherwise its literary attractiveness, and the views of so prominent and experienced a writer on his special subject demand attention even where they do not bring conviction.

An Introduction to Political Economy. By Richard T. Ely. London: Swan Sonnenschein and Co., 1891.

The annual gatherings in America at Chatauqua bear some resemblance to the Summer Meetings, which have of recent years taken place in this country in connection with the University Extension Movement; and, in preparing a text book for the Chatauqua Literary and Scientific Circle, an author is engaged on a work of no ordinary or light responsibility, for he is writing, as Professor Ely remarks in the volume before us, for a "truly immense public." Professor Ely is well known in America, and, to some extent, in England also. He has, we believe, exercised no small influence in stimulating the minds of his pupils to the earnest consideration of social problems, and this quality is present in the book before us, which is divided into eight parts. In Parts II—VI the ordinary topics handled in economic manuals, under the titles of production, exchange, distribution, consumption, and public finance, are treated very much on the ordinary lines. In the other parts, which deal with the growth and characteristics of industrial society, and the nature and evolution of political economy, the historical tendencies and ethical leanings of the author are more apparent. But even here there is little that the straitest economist of the most orthodox school would not accept: for, as Dr. Ingram justly observes in a suggestive preface, quoting from the French economist M. Gide, the change, which has been occasioned in economics by the new forces and movements, may be fittingly described as an *un grand dégel* (a great thaw), and this has affected the old school as well as the new. And so Professor Ely, while undoubtedly an adherent of the historical school, and claimed by Dr. Ingram as such, does not reject, but only seeks to amend, the teaching of the economists of the past.

Statistical and Economical Articles in Recent Periodicals.

AUSTRIA—
  Statistische Monatschrift—
    August—September, 1892—
      Die Heimatsverhältnisse der Bevölkerung Oesterreichs nach den Ergebnissen der Volkszählung vom 31 Dec., 1890: Dr. H. Rauchberg.
      Die Zahl der Vorschussvereine Oesterreichs im Jahre 1891: H. Ehrenberger.

AUSTRIA—*Contd.*
　Statistische Monatschrift—Contd.
　　October—
　　　Die Molkerei-Genossenschaften und andere gemeinschaft-
　　　liche Unternehmungen zur Verwerthung der Molkerei-
　　　producte in den im Reichsrathe vertretenen Königreichen
　　　und Ländern nach den pro 1891 vorliegenden Daten:
　　　A. Freiherrn v. Hohenbruck.
　　　Die Ergebnisse der Strafrechtspflege im Jahre 1889:
　　　Dr. W.
　　　Bericht über die Thätigkeit des Statistischen Seminars an
　　　der k.k. Universität Wien im Wintersemester 1891-92:
　　　Dr. H. v. Schullern-Schrattenhofen.

FRANCE—
　Journal des Economistes—
　　September, 1892—
　　　La réaction protectionniste: *G. de Molinari.*
　　　Sociétés Coopératives en Italie: *V. de Pareto.*
　　October—
　　　Les travaux parlementaires de la Chambre des Députés
　　　1891-92: *A. Liesse.*
　　　Le nouveau régime douanier des Colonies: *A. Bouchié de
　　　Belle.*
　　　Les assurances contre le chomage par suite d'incendie:
　　　E. Rochetin.
　　November—
　　　La Réforme de la Propriété Foncière: *Y. Guyot.*
　　　Les Impots arabes en Algérie: *A. Bochard.*
　　　L'état actuel de la question monétaire: *G. François.*
　　　Le mouvement agricole: *G. Fouquet.*
　　　Le prix du Bétail et les droits de douane: *D. Zolla.*
　Journal de la Société de Statistique de Paris—
　　September—
　　　La Population française: *E. Levasseur.*
　　　Les Irrigations. Etude economique et statistique: *F.
　　　Bernard.*
　　　La Répartition de la propriété foncière en Prusse.
　　October and November—
　　　De la Morbidité et de la Mortalité par profession: *Dr. J.
　　　Bertillon.*
　Revue d'Economie Politique—
　　September—
　　　Les Sociétés Coopératives en Allemagne: *Dr. H. Crüger.*
　　　Idée de l'Etat: *M. Barckhausen.*
　　October—
　　　Observations sur la Sémiologie économique. 1re Partie
　　　Système de l'Indice unique et système Totalisateur:
　　　M. Pantaleoni.
　　　Essai sur la législation de la France. La police des manu-
　　　factures de papier: *Marc Sauset.*
　　　Le rôle sociale de la grande industrie: *W. Lotz.*

FRANCE—*Contd.*
  Revue d' Economie Politique—Contd.
    November—
      Les Sociétés Coopératives en Espagne et en Pórtugal :
        J. P. Hurtado.
      Essai historique sur la législation industrielle de la France :
        M. Sauzet.
      Les tormes d'industrie : *E. Schwiedland.*

GERMANY—
  Jahrbücher für Nationalökonomie und Statistik—
    Band iv, Heft 3—
      Zur Reform der Gemeindebesteuerung in Preussen : *Dr. R.
        Friedberg.*
      Die Kolonisation und die Agrarverfassung der Insel Nan-
        tucket im 17 und 18 Jahrhundert : *A. Sartorius von
        Waltershausen.*
      Zur Lehre von den Lohngesetzen : *F. J. Neumann.*
      Die Litteratur der Unfall- und Krankenversicherung in der
        Schweiz : *E. Heitz.*
      Haushalts-Etat für das Deutsche Reich im Jahre 1892-93 :
        M. von Heckel.
      Reichsversicherungsanstalt oder Berufsgenossenschaften als
        Träger der Unfallversicherung : *C. Hampke.*
    Band iv, Heft 4—
      Die Stundenzonenzeit : *W. Streckert.*
      Ueber den Einfluss des elterlichen Alters auf die Lebens-
        kraft der Kinder : *J. Körösi.*
      Das Elend der Philosophie : *Karl Marx.*
      Der Zucker-Terminhandel : *A. Buyerdörffer.*
    Band iv, Heft 5—
      Von der Theorie des Arbeitslohnes : *Prof. de Ridder.*
      Die industriellen Etablissements der geistlichen Stifter
        in Schlesien unter Friedrich dem Grossen : *H.
        Fechner.*
      Das "Interstate Commerce"-Gesetz in den Vereinigten
        Staaten : *J. A. Hill.*
      Gleiche oder verschiedene Tarifierung von Getreide und
        Mehl im deutschen Eisenbahnverkehr : *C. Hampke.*
  Vierteljahrschrift für Volkswirtschaft, &c.—
    Band iii, Hälfte 2, 1892—
      Die Goldvorräte der russischen Regierung : *T. Buck.*
      Über die russische Handelsbilanz : *N. Syrkin.*
    Band iv, Hälfte 1—
      Die Schweizer Eisenbahnfrage : *E. Ramsperger.*
      Studienreisen eines jungen Staatsmannes in England am
        Schlusse des vorigen Jahrhunderts.
    Band iv, Hälfte 2—
      Das grossbritannische Weltreich als Zollverein : *E.
        Fitger.*
      Die Verbreitung der Protestanten in Kärnten : *Dr. F.
        Pichler.*

Viert_ljahrshefte zur Statistik des Deutschen Reichs—
  Heft 4, 1892—
    Bergwerke, Salinen, und Hütten während 1891.
    Verunglückungen deutscher Seeschiffe in 1890 und 1891.
    Schiffsunfälle an der deutschen Küste während 1891.
    Schulbildung der im Ersatzjahre 1891-92 eingestellten
      Rekruten.
    Verbrechen und Vergehen gegen Reichsgesetze 1886-91.
      Vorläufige Mittheilung.
    Das Salz im Deutschen Zollgebiet.

ITALY—
  Giornale degli Economisti—
    September, 1892—
      La nazione armata. Studio di un nuovo ordinamento dell'
        esercito (contd.—concluded in Oct. and Nov. numbers):
        T. Squilletta.
      Sulle dottrine economiche di Antonio Serra: R. Benini.
      Le intromissioni del governo nelle casse di Risparmio
        libere:
      La classificazione dei dati in Statistica: G. B. Salvioni.
    October—
      Monografie di alcuni operai braccianti nel Comune di
        Ravenna: M. Pasolini.
      Monte de pietà ed opere Pie: P. Sitta.
    November—
      Monografie di alcuni operai braccianti nel Comune di
        Ravenna: M. Pasolini.
      L'industria del corallo in Italia: C. Ghidiglia.
    December—
      Gli elementi per risolvere il problema della Popolazione:
        F. Virgilii.

SWITZERLAND—
  Journal de Statistique Suisse—
    2° Livr., 1892—
      Zwei Haushaltungsbudgets aus dem Kanton Thurgau:
        Dr. E. H fmann.
      Statistik der Todesfälle des Amtes Oberhasli im Jahrzehnt
        1876-1885: J. Renggli.
      Statistik der in der Schweiz erscheinenden Zeitungen,
        Zeitschriften und ähnlicher periodischer Publikationen:
        Dr. W. Barh.
      Das Schweizer bürgerrecht (cont. in 3me livraison): Dr. W.
        Reiser.
      Die Ordnung des Gemeinde- Rechnungs- und Kassawesens,
        als Grundlage einer schweiz. gemeinde-Finanzstatistik:
        Näf.
    3° Livr., 1892—
      Procès-verbal de la Conférence de la Société Suisse de
        Statistique et des délégués officiels des administrations
        féderale et cantonales à Lugano.

UNITED STATES—
Annals of the American Academy of Political and Social Science.
   Vol. iii, No. 2.   September, 1892—
      Economic Causes of Moral Progress: *S. N. Patten.*
      Influence on Business of the Independent Treasury: *D. Kinley.*
      Preventivo Legislation in relation to Crime: *C. H. Reeve.*
   Vol. iii, No. 3.   November, 1892—
      Effects of Consumption of Wealth on Distribution: *W. Smart.*
      Standard of Deferred Payments: *E. A. Ross.*
      Social Work at the Krupp Foundries: *S. M. Lindsay.*
American Economic Association Publications, 1892—
      Vol. vii, Nos. 4 and 5.   Sinking Funds: *E. A. Ross.*
Political Science Quarterly.   Vol. vii, No. 3, September, 1892—
      Asylum in Legations and in Vessels (contd.) : *Prof. J. B. Moore.*
      The Utility of Speculation in Modern Commerce: *A. C. Stevens.*
      Usury in Law and in practice: *G. K. Holmes.*
      Control of National Expenditures: *N. H. Thompson.*
      The Crown and Democracy in England: *Prof. J. Macey.*
      Irish Land Legislation (contd.): *W. A. Dunning.*
Quarterly Journal of Economics.   Vol. vii, No. 1, October, 1892—
      Legal Tender Notes in California: *B. Moses.*
      Reciprocity: *F. W. Taussig.*
      Insurance and Business Profit: *J. B. Clark.*
      The Bank Note Question: *C. F. Dunbar.*
      Colonial Tariffs: *W. Hill.*
Yale Review.   Vol. 1.
   August, 1892—
      Immigration: *F. A. Walker.*
      The Confederate Foreign Loan.   An Episode in the Finan-
         cial history of the Civil War: *J. C. Schwab.*
      Prussian Ministers and Imperial Rule: *E. V. Raynolds.*
      Chinese and Mediæval Gilds: *F. W. Williams.*
   November—
      The Ultimate Standard of Value: *J. B. Clark.*

UNITED KINGDOM—
   Economic Journal.   Vol. ii, No. 7.   September, 1892—
      The Australian Strike, 1890: *A. Duckworth.*
      Profit-Sharing and Co-operative Production: *L. L. Price.*
      Fancy Monetary Standards: *R. Giffen.*
      A new Standard of Value: the late *Walter Bagehot.*
      Capital and Labour: their relative strength: *Prof. J. S.
         Nicholson.*
      The perversion of Economic history: *Rev. W. Cunningham.*
      A reply: *Prof. A. Marshall.*
   The Economic Review.   Vol. ii, No. 4.   October, 1892—
      What attitude should the Church adopt towards the aims and
         methods of Labour Combinations?: *Rev. Canon H. Scott
         Holland.*
      The present position of the "Sweating System" Question in
         the United Kingdom: *D. F. Schloss.*
      Co-operative Credit-banking in Germany: *H. W. Wolff.*

VII.—*Additions to the Library.*

Additions to the Library during the Quarter ended 15th December, 1892
arranged alphabetically under the following heads :—(a) *Foreign
Countries;* (b) *India and Colonial Possessions;* (c) *United Kingdom
and its Divisions;* (d) *Authors, &c.;* (e) *Societies, &c. (British);*
(f) *Periodicals, &c. (British).*

Donations.	By whom Presented.

(a) Foreign Countries.

Argentine Republic—

Comercio Exterior. Datos trimestrales del, año 1892. No. 74, 8vo. ...... — The National Statistical Department

Higiene Publica. Anales de. (Current monthly numbers) — Dr. E. R. Coni

BUENOS AYRES (Province). Policia. Memoria del Departamento de, correspondiente al año 1891 ...... — The Police Department

BUENOS AYRES (City). Bulletin mensuel de Statistique municipale. (Current numbers) ...... — The Municipal Statistical Bureau

Austria and Hungary—

Ackerbau-Ministeriums. Statistisches Jahrbuch des k.k., für 1891. Heft 2. Lief. 1 und 2. Bergwerks-Production im Jahre 1891. — The Ministry of Agriculture

Civilrechtspflege in den im Reichsrathe vertretenen Königreichen und Ländern. Die Ergebnisse der, im Jahre 1888. Fol. ...... — The Central Statistical Commission

Handel des Zollgebiets. Statistische Uebersichten betreffend den auswärtigen. (Current monthly numbers) ...... — The Statistical Department, Ministry of Commerce

Oesterreichisches Statistisches Handbuch für 1887 ....
Statistische Monatschrift. April, May, Aug., and Sept., 1888. April and Oct., 1889. March, 1890. Nov. and Dec., 1891; and current numbers for 1892 — Dr. K. T. Inama-Sternegg

Volkszählung. Die Ergebnisse der, vom 31st Dec., 1890. Heft 1. Die summarischen Ergebnisse der Volkszählung. Fol. ...... — The Central Statistical Commission

HUNGARY. Ungarns Waarenverkehr mit Oesterreich und anderen Ländern für 1891. La. fol. ...... — The Royal Hungarian Statistical Bureau

PRAGUE. Bulletin hebdomadaire de la Ville de Prague et des communes-faubourgs. (Current numbers) .... — The Statistical Bureau

Belgium—

Mouvement Commercial avec les Pays Etrangers. (Current monthly numbers) ...... — The Bureau of General Statistics

Salaires et Budgets ouvriers en Belgique au mois d'avril 1891. Renseignements fournis par les Conseils de l'Industrie et du Travail. 8vo. ...... — The Ministry of Agriculture

BRUSSELS. Bulletin hebdomadaire de statistique Démographique et Médicale. (Current numbers) ...... — Dr. E. Janssens

Bulgaria—

Commerce de la Principauté avec les Pays Etrangers pendant 1891. 4to. ......
Dénombrement de la Population. Résultats généraux du, de la Principauté de Bulgarie le 1er Janvier, 1888. Sm. 4to. — The Statistical Bureau

Chile. Sinopsis Estadistica y Geografica de la Republica en 1891. 8vo. ...... — The late C. T. Maude, Esq.

Donations—Contd.

Donations.	By whom Presented.
(a) Foreign Countries—*Contd.*	
China. Customs Gazette. April—June, 1892. 4to.....	Sir Robert Hart, G.C.M.G.
Denmark—	
Importation et exportation, production d'eau de vie et de sucre de betteraves en 1891. 4to.	The Statistical Bureau
Nationalökonomisk Tidskrift, 1892. (Current numbers)	The Danish Political Economy Society
Egypt—	
Commerce Extérieur. Bulletin mensuel du. (Current numbers) ... '	A. Caillard, Esq., C M.G.
Services Sanitaires, &c. Bulletin hebdomadaire. (Current numbers)	The Department
Institut Egyptien. Bulletin. 3ᵉ série, No. 3. 8vo. 1892	The Institute
France—	
Agriculture. Ministère de l'. Bulletin. No. 5, Sept., and No. 6, Oct., 1892 (containing "Statistique Agricole Annuelle." 1891). Plate, la. 8vo.	The Ministry of Agriculture
Chemins de Fer Français. Statistique des, au 31 Décembre, 1889. Documents divers. 1ᵉ Partie, France—Intérêt Général	The Ministry of Public Works
Commerce de la France. Tableau Général du, avec ses Colonies et les Puissances Etrangères pendant 1891. 4to.	The Director-General of Customs
Enfants. Rapports par M. Théophile Roussel faits au nom de la Commission chargée d'examiner 1° la Proposition de loi ayant pour objet la Protection des Enfants, abandonnés, delaissés ou maltraités. 2° le Projet de loi sur la Protection de l'Enfance. Vols. i et ii. 4to. 1882-83	Dr. F. J. Monat, LL.D., F R.C.S.
Finances, Ministère des, Bulletin de Statistique et de Législation comparée. (Current monthly numbers) ....:..................	The Ministry of Finance
Travaux Publics. Ministère des, Bulletin de Statistique et Législation comparée. (Current monthly numbers)	The Ministry of Public Works
Paris. Annuaire Statistique de la Ville de Paris. Xᵉ année, 1889. Diagrams, &c., la. 8vo.	Dr. J. Bertillon
L'Economiste Français. (Current weekly numbers)........	The Editor
Journal des Economistes. (Current monthly numbers)	,,
Le Monde Economique. (Current weekly numbers).......	,,
Polybiblion. Revue Bibliographique Universelle. Parties Littéraire et Technique. (Current monthly numbers)	,,
Le Rentier. Journal Financier Politique. (Current numbers)	
Revue d'Economie Politique. (Current monthly numbers) ... .:......	
Revue Géographique Internationale. (Current monthly numbers)	:.

Donations—Contd.

Donations.	By whom Presented.
(a) Foreign Countries—*Contd.*	
France—*Contd.*	
Ecole Libre des Sciences Politiques, Annales. No. 4, 1892	The Institution
Société de Statistique de Paris, Journal. (Current monthly numbers)	The Society
Germany—	
Handel des deutschen Zollgebiets. Monatliche Nachweise über den Auswärtigen. (Current monthly returns)	The Imperial Statistical Bureau
Prussia—	
Ernteertrages im preussischen Staate. Die Ergebnisse der Ermittelung des, für 1891. Diagrammaps, fol.	•
Sterblichkeit nach Todesursachen und Altersklassen der Gestorbenen sowie die Selbstmorde und die tödlichen Verunglückungen im preussischen Staate während 1890	The Royal Prussian Statistical Bureau
Zeitschrift des K. Preussischen Statistischen Bureaus. 1890, Heft 4. 1891, Heft 3 und 4. Diagram, fol.	
SAXONY. Kalender und Statistisches Jahrbuch für 1893. 8vo.	The Statistical Bureau of Saxony
Berlin—	
Eheschliessungen. Geburten, Sterbefälle, und Witterung. (Current weekly and monthly numbers)	The Statistical Bureau of Berlin
Die Lohn-Verhältnisse in Berlin im September, 1891. 4to.	
Frankfort—	
Jahresbericht über die Verwaltung des Medicinalwesens die Kranken-anstalten und die oeffentlichen Gesundheitsverhaeltnisse der Stadt. Jahrgang 1891. 8vo.	The Statistical Bureau
Statistische Beschreibung der Stadt Frankfurt am Main und ihrer Bevölkerung. Theil 1. Die äussere Vertheilung der Bevölkerung. Diagram and maps, 8vo. 1892..........................	The Geographical and Statistical Society
HAMBURG. Hamburgs Handel und Schiffahrt, 1891. 4to.	The German Consul-General
Jahrbücher für Nationalökonomie und Statistik. Band iv, Hefte 3—5. 1892	The Publisher
Greece—	
Commerce special de la Grèce. Bulletin mensuel du, Jan.—June, 1892	T. J. Pittar, Esq.
ATHENS. Bulletin de mortalité pour la ville d'Athènes. (Current monthly numbers)	The Statistical Bureau
Italy—	
Annali di Agricoltura, 1892—	
194. Zootecnia. Provvedimenti a vantaggio della Produzione equina negli anni 1891-92	The Director-General of Agriculture
195. Atti della commissione consultiva per la Fillossera. Map. 1892	

Donations—Contd.

Donations.	By whom Presented.

(a) Foreign Countries—*Contd.*
Italy—*Contd.*
  Annali di Statistica—
    Ruoli organici delle Amministrazioni civili e militari del Regno al 1º Luglio, 1891, confrontati con quelli degli antichi Stati Italiani al 1 Gennaio, 1859 Statistica Industriale. Fasc. 43. Provincia di Brescia. 1892..
    Tavole della Frequenza e durata delle Malattie osservate nelle persone inscritte a Società di mutuo soccorso. 1892 ....
    Bollettino di Legislazione e Statistica Doganale e Commerciale. (Current numbers) ....
    Bollettino del Ministero degli Affari Esteri. (Current numbers) ....

The Director-General, Statistical Department of the State

    Bollettino mensile delle situazioni dei Conti degli Istituti d' Emissione. (Current numbers) ....
    Bollettino di Notizie sul Credito e la Previdenza. (Current numbers) ....
    Bollettino settimanale dei Prezzi di alcuni dei principali Prodotti Agraria e del Pane. (Current weekly numbers) ....
    Bollettino Sanitario, Direzione della Sanita Pubblica. (Current numbers) ....
    Statistica del commercio speciale di Importazione e di Esportazione. (Current monthly numbers) ....

  L'Economista. (Current weekly numbers) .... **The Editor**
  Giornale degli Economisti. (Current monthly numbers) .... „

Mexico—
  Exportaciones. Año fiscal de 1891-92. Segundo semestre. Fol. 1892 .... **The Statistical Bureau**
  Maritimo. Noticias del Movimiento, exterior e interior en el año fiscal de 1890-91. Fol. Mexico, 1892 ....

Netherlands—
  Geboorten. Statistik der, en der sterfte naar den leeftijd en de oorzaken van den dood in Nederland. Sheets. (Current monthly numbers) .... **The Netherlands Legation**
  Scheepvaart. Statistiek der, 1891. Gedeelte 1, 2. 4to. .... **The Ministry of Commerce**
  Statistiek van den In—, Uit—, en Doorvoer over het Jahr 1891. Gedeelte 1 and 2. 2 vols., la. fol. .... **Dr. Verkerk Pistorius**

  Annuaire Statistique des Pays-Bas pour 1891. Livr. 1. Statistique de la Métropôle. 8vo. .... **The Statistical Institute**
  Bijdragen van het Statistisch Instituut. No. 2, 1892. 8vo. ....

Russia—
  Agricultural Year Book for 1892. Part 2. Maps, 8vo. (In Russian).. **The Department of Agriculture**
  Commerce extérieur par la frontière d'Europe et recettes douanières de l'Empire, 1891. (Current monthly numbers) .... **The Department of Customs**

Donations—Contd.

Donations.	By whom Presented.
(a) Foreign Countries—*Contd.*	
Russia—*Contd.*	
Diagram-maps showing prices of Rye and Oats in Russia in Europe on 1st July, 1st Sept., and 1st Oct., 1892. Sheets....................	The Department of Assessed Taxes
Servia—	
Recensement de la Population, 31 Décembre, 1890. 2ᵉ et 3ᵉ Parties. Fol. .... Viticulture. Statistique de la, pour 1889. La. 8vo. Maps.....................	The Statistical Bureau
Spain—	
Aranceles de Aduanas para la Peninsula e Islas Baleares. Edicion oficial. La. 8vo. 1892	The Director-General of Customs
Comercio Exterior. Resumenes mensuales de la Estadistica del, (Current numbers).....................	The Director-General of Indirect Taxation
Instituto Geográfico y Estadistico. Memorias del, Tomos 8 y 9. Map and plates, la. 8vo. 1889-92....	The Institute
Sociedad Geográfica de Madrid. Boletin. (Current monthly numbers)	The Society
Sweden—	
Banking, &c. Monthly Statements of. (Current numbers) .... Kapital-Konto till Riks-Hufvud-Boken, 1891. 4to..... Öfversigt af Sveriges Riksbanks ställning, 1891. 4to. .... Riksstat för år 1893. Sm. 4to..................... Statistisk Tidskrift. Nos. 2, 3, 1892. 8vo. .... Trade. Monthly returns of. (Current numbers)	The Central Statistical Bureau
Switzerland—	
Bulletin hebdomadaire et Bulletin mensuel des mariages, naissances et des décès dans les Villes de la Suisse. (Current numbers.) 8vo. .... Examen Pédagogique de Recrues en automne 1891. Map, 4to. Journal de Statistique Suisse, 1892. Quartal-Hefte 2, 3. Maps and diagrams, 4to.	The Federal Statistical Bureau
United States—	
Agricultural Department. Monthly reports on Crops, &c. (Current numbers).....................	The Secretary of Agriculture
Census Bulletins. 1890. 199, Colored Population in 1890. 203, Statistics of Churches. 204, Inmates of Juvenile Reformatories. 205, 208, 216, Population by color, sex, and general nativity, 1890. 206, Annual Interest charge on bonded indebtedness. 207, Cotton Production. 210, 240, Cereal Production in 1889. 211—317, Statistics of Manufactures, 1890, in Cities. Index to Bulletins..... .... Extra Census Bulletins, 1890. 23, Irrigation. 25, 26, Statistics of Farms, Homes, and Mortgages	The Superintendent of Census
Consular Reports for July and August, 1892. 8vo.....	The Department of State

Donations—Contd.

Donations.	By whom Presented.
(a) Foreign Countries—*Contd.*	
United States—*Contd.*	
Imports and Exports. Summary Statement of. (Current monthly numbers)	The Bureau of Statistics, Treasury Department
Imports, Exports, Immigration, and Navigation. Quarterly Report for the three months ending 30th June, 1892. [No. 4, 1891-92]	
Internal Commerce of the United States. Report on, for 1891. Commerce of the Great Lakes, the Mississippi River and its tributaries. Map, 8vo.	
Observations made during 1888 at the U. S. Naval Observatory. Diagrams, 4to. 1892	The U. S. Naval Observatory
Public Debt and Cash in Treasury of the United States. Monthly statements of. (Current numbers)	The Secretary of the Treasu
CONNECTICUT. State Board of Health. Monthly Bulletins. (Current numbers)	The Board of Health
Massachusetts—	
Manufactures. Annual Statistics of, 1891. 8vo. .... Labor. 22nd Annual Report of the Bureau of Labor Statistics. March, 1892. (Tenement House Census of Boston. Rooms, Rents)	The Bureau of Statistics of Labor
WISCONSIN University. School of Economics, Political Science, and History. Announcement for 1892-93. 8vo.	Professor R. T. Ely, Ph.D.
BROOKLYN. Annual Report of the Department of Police and Excise for 1891. 8vo................................	The Superintendent of Police
Banker's Magazine. (Current monthly numbers)	The Editor
Bradstreet's Journal. (Current weekly numbers)	,,
Commercial and Financial Chronicle. (Current weekly numbers)	--
Investor's Supplement to Commercial and Financial Chronicle. (Current numbers)........	,,
Political Science Quarterly. Vol. vii, No. 3, Sept., 1892	The Editors
Quarterly Journal of Economics. Vol. vii, No. 1, Oct., 1892	The Publishers
The Yale Review. Vol. i, No. 3. Nov., 1892	,,
Actuarial Society of America. Papers and Transactions. No. 8. 8vo. 1892	The Society
American Academy of Arts and Sciences. Proceedings. New Series. Vol. xviii, 1890-91. Plates, 8vo.	The Academy
American Academy of Political and Social Science. Annals. Vol. iii, Nos. 2 and 3, 1892	
American Economic Association. Publications. Vol. vii, Nos. 4 and 5. Sinking Funds, by *E. A. Ross.* 1892	The Association
American Geographical Society. Bulletin. Vol. xxiv, No. 3, 1892. Plates	The Society
American Statistical Association. Quarterly Publications. June, Sept., 1892. (Statistical Inquiry concerning Domestic Service): *L. M. Salmon.* 8vo.	The Association
Franklin Institute. Journal. (Current monthly numbers)	The Institute
Smithsonian Institution. Smithsonian Contributions to Knowledge. Vol. xxviii. Plates, 4to. 1892	The Institution

Donations.	By whom Presented.
(a) Foreign Countries—*Contd.*	
Uruguay. MONTEVIDEO. Censo municipal del Departamento y de la Ciudad de Montevideo. Edificacion, Escuelas, Poblacion e Industrias, 1889-90. Maps, plans, and diagrams, la. 8vo.	The Bureau of General Statistics
International—	
Bulletin International des Douanes. (Current numbers.) 8vo.	The Board of Trade
Congrès Pénitentiaire International de Saint-Pétersbourg, 1890. Actes du. Vols. iv and v. 8vo. 1892	Dr. F. J. Mouat
(b) India and Colonial Possessions.	
India, British—	
Sanitary Measures in India. Report on, in 1890-91. Vol. xxiv. [C–6735.] 1892	The India Office
Statistical Abstract relating to British India from 1881-82 to 1890-91. 26th number. [C–6736.] 1892	
Trade by Land with Foreign Countries. Monthly Accounts. (Current numbers)	The Department of Finance and Commerce, Calcutta
Trade and Navigation. Monthly Accounts. (Current numbers)	
Trade. Review of the, of India in 1891-92. 1, Foreign Sea-borne Trade. 2, Trans-frontier Trade. 3, Coasting Trade. Fol.	J. E. O'Conor, Esq., C.I.E.
Indian Engineering. (Current numbers)	The Editor
Asiatic Society of Bengal—	
Journal. Vol. lxi, Part 1, No. 2, and Part 2, No. 2, 1892. Plates	The Society
Proceedings. April—July, 1892	
Canada, Dominion of—	
Census of 1891. Bulletin No. 13. Manufactures, Wages. 8vo.	George Johnson, Esq.
Agriculture and Colonisation. Report of Select Standing Committee, 1892	J. G. Bourinot, Esq., C.M.G.
Canals Revenue Branch of Department of Railways and Canals. Report for 1890-91	
Dairy Commissioner. 2nd Annual Report for 1891-92	
Debates of the House of Commons, Session 1892. Vols. 1 and 2	
Horses. Trade with Great Britain in, 1892	
Insurance. Report of Superintendent of, for 1891	
Steamboat Inspection. Report on, for 1891	
Banks acting under Charter. Monthly Statements. (Current numbers)	N. S. Garland, Esq.
Loan Companies and Building Societies. Report on, for 1891. 8vo.	
Statistical Year-Book of Canada for 1891. Seventh year of issue.	The Compiler
Insurance and Finance Chronicle. (Current numbers)	The Editor
Royal Society of Canada. Proceedings and Transactions for 1891. Vol. ix. Plates, maps, 4to.	The Society

Donations—Contd.

Donations.	By whom Presented.
(b) India and Colonial Possessions—*Contd.* **Canada, Dominion of—*Contd.***	
Toronto University. The Benefactors of the University, after the Great Fire of 11th February, 1890. Plate, 8vo.	The University
Cape of Good Hope. Port Elizabeth Chamber of Commerce. 27th Annual Report for 1891.· 8vo.	The Chamber of Commerce
Ceylon— Census of Ceylon, 1891. Vol. i, General Report. Vol. ii, Area and Population, age, nationality, birthplace, education, religion, and occupation. Vol. iii, List of Towns and Villages, with houses, families, and population therein. 3 vols., map, fol.	Lionel Lee, Esq., the Superintendent of Census
Railways. Report of the General Manager of the Ceylon Government Railways for 1891. Fol.	J. C. Farquharson, Esq.
Jamaica— Annual Report of the Registrar-General for the eighteen months ended 31st March, 1891. Fol. .... Causes of Death. Tables showing, at different periods of Life, in the eighteen months ended 31st March, 1891. Fol.	The Registrar-General of Jamaica
New South Wales— Agricultural Gazette. (Current numbers).....................	The Director of Agriculture
Aborigines. Report of the Board for the Protection of, for 1891. Fol. .... Agriculture. Report of the Department of, for 1891 Fisheries of the Colony. Report of the Commissioner for 1891. Fol. .... Mines and Agriculture. Annual Report of the Department for 1891. Maps and plans, fol. .... Postmaster-General. Annual Report of the, for 1891 Railways and Tramways. Annual Report of the Railway Commissioner for the year ending 30th June, 1892. Diagrams and map, fol.	The Agent-General for N. S. Wales
Census and Industrial Returns Act of 1891. (Information respecting.) The Coal Mining Industry. Census of 1891. Part 1. Ages of the People. 4to. .... Statistical Register for 1891 and previous years. 8vo.	The Government Statistician
New Zealand— Government Insurance Department. Quinquennial Investigation, 1890. Third Division of Profits. Annual Report, 1891. 4to.	The Commissioner
Official Handbook, 1892. Map and diagram, 8vo.	Registrar-General
New Zealand Institute. Transactions and Proceedings, 1891. Vol. xxiv. Plates, 8vo.	The Institute
Queensland— Friendly Societies, Building Societies, and Trade Unions. Sixth report of the Registrar of, for 1890-91. Fol.	The Registrar of Friendly Societies

Donations—Contd.

Donations.	By whom Presented.
(b) India and Colonial Possessions—Contd.	
Queensland—Contd.	
Statistics of the Colony for 1891. Fol. .... Supplements to the Government Gazette (containing Vital Statistics). (Current numbers).....................	The Registrar-General of Queensland
South Australia—	
Births and Deaths. Monthly Statements of. (Current numbers)............... Births, Deaths, and Marriages. Annual Report of the Registrar-General for 1891. Fol........................	The Registrar-General of S. Australia
Agricultural and Live Stock Statistics for the year ending 31st March, 1892, with Report...................... Census of 1891. Part 4. Education of the People. Fol.	L. H. Sholl, Esq., Under Secretary and Government Statist
Straits Settlements. The Perak Government Gazette. (Current numbers)	The Government Secretary
Tasmania—	
Census. Results of a Census of Tasmania, 1891. Part 8. Occupations of the People. Fol.	The Government Statistician
Railways. Report on the Tasmanian Government Railways for 1891. Fol.	Frederick Back, Esq.
Victoria—	
Census of Victoria, 1891. Parts 5. Conjugal Condition; 6. Education; 7. Sickness and Infirmity; 8. Occupations. Fol..................... Statistical Register of the Colony for 1891. Part 4. Interchange; Part 5. Vital Statistics. Fol.	H. H. Hayter, Esq., C.M.G., Government Statist
Public Library, Museums, and National Gallery of Victoria. Report of Trustees for 1891. 8vo. .... Catalogue of Newspapers, Magazines, &c., received at Melbourne Public Library. 8vo. 1891..................	The Trustees
Royal Society of Victoria. Proceedings. Vol. iv. New series. Part 1. Plates, 8vo. 1892	The Society
(c) United Kingdom and its several Divisions.	
United Kingdom—	
Agricultural Returns. Statistical Tables, showing acreage under crops and grass, and the number of horses, cattle, sheep, and pigs in the United Kingdom. 1892. 8vo.	The Board of Agriculture
Allotments Acts. Acquisition of Land by local authorities. (310.) 1892.................. County Council Elections, 1892. Cost. (268.) 1892 Elementary Education. (Schools receiving special grants.) (336.) 1892 .... Friendly Societies, Reports on, for 1891. Part A. (187.) 1892 .... Joint Stock Companies. (119.) 1892 .... Labourers (Ireland) Acts. (Cottages.) (334.) 1892 Local Taxation. Licences, 1891-92 (323.) 1892	T. J. Pittar, Esq.

Donations—Contd.

Donations.	By whom Presented.

(c) United Kingdom and its Divisions—*Contd.*
United Kingdom—*Contd.*

Local Taxation Returns, England, 1890-91. Part 1.
(269.) 1892 ....
Local Taxation Returns, Scotland, 1890-91. Parts 1—6.
(309.) 1892 ....
Metropolitan Hospitals, &c. Third Report from Select
Committee on. (321.) 1892 ....
Parliamentary Elections. (Illiterate voters.) (319.)
1892 .... } T. J. Pittar, Esq.
Paupers. (England and Wales.) (266.) 1892 ....
Pilotage Returns for 1891. (212.) 1892 ....
Poor Relief. (England and Wales.) (270—C.) 1892
Public Works Loan Board, 1891-92. Seventeenth
Annual Report. (242.) 1892...................................
Savings Banks Returns for 1891. (347.) 1892 ....
Workhouses. Consumption of Spirits, &c. (292.) 1892

Board of Trade Journal. (Current monthly numbers.).... The Board of Trade
Local Government Board. Twenty-first Annual Re- } The Board
port, for 1891-92. [C-6745.] 8vo. ....
Railways. Summary of Statistics of, for 1881 and } J. Shillito, Esq.
1887-91. Sheets...
Railways. General Report on Share and Loan Capital,
Traffic in Passengers and Goods, &c., for 1891. } The Board of Trade
[C-6714] ....
Trade and Navigation. (Current monthly returns)....
Woods, Forests, and Land Revenues. Seventieth Re- } The Commissioners
port of Commissioners. (355.) 1892......................

England—
Births and Deaths in London, and in twenty-seven
other Great Towns. (Current weekly returns) .... } The Registrar-Gene-
Quarterly Return of Marriages to June, Births and } ral of England
Deaths to Sept., 1892. No. 175. 8vo. ....
British Museum. Catalogue of Printed Books. } The Trustees of the
11 parts, 4to. 1892 .... } Museum
LONDON. Wandsworth District. Thirty-sixth Annual
Report of the Board of Works for 1891-92, with } The Board of Works
the report of Medical Officers of Health for 1891.
8vo. ......
MANCHESTER. Public Free Libraries. Annual Report } The Chief Librarian
for 1891-92. 8vo. ....

Ireland—
Births and Deaths in Dublin, and in fifteen of the
principal Urban Sanitary Districts. (Current } The Registrar-Gene-
weekly returns) .... } ral of Ireland

Scotland—
Births, Deaths, and Marriages in the eight principal
Towns. (Current weekly and monthly returns) .... } The Registrar-Gene-
Births, Deaths, and Marriages, Quarterly Return, for } ral of Scotland
the quarter ending 30th Sept., 1892...................
GLASGOW. The Mitchell Library. Eleventh General } The Library
Report, 1889-91. 8vo. ....

Donations.	By whom Presented.
(d) Authors, &c.	
BOURGADE LA DARDYE (Dr. E. DE). Paraguay: The Land and the People, natural wealth and commercial capabilities. English edition edited by E. G. Ravenstein. xiv + 243 pp., map and plates, 8vo. 1892	E. G. Ravenstein, Esq.
COOPER (JOSEPH). Tabular guides to ordinary and Industrial Life Assurance, &c. Folded sheets. 1892	The Author
DALLA VOLTA (RICCARDO). Camere e Borse del Lavoro. 20 pp., 8vo. Firenze, 1892	..
DE BROË (O.). Le métal méprisé. [L'argent-métal]. 32 pp., 8vo. 1892	
EDGEWORTH (F. Y.). Mathematical Psychics, an essay on the application of mathematics to the moral sciences. viii + 150 pp., 8vo. 1881....	,,
ELLISON (THOMAS). A Centennial Sketch of the Cotton Trade of the United States. 28 pp., 8vo. New York, 1892	Messrs. Ellison & Co.
FISHER (Dr. IRVING). Mathematical Investigations in the Theory of Value and Prices. 124 pp., 8vo. [New Haven.] 1892.....................	The Author
GIBSON, (GEORGE R.). The Vienna Bourse. 33 pp., plate, 8vo. New York. 1892	::
GOW WILSON and STANTON (Messrs.). Annual Reports on the Tea Trade during 1889-90, and 1891, and also current weekly reports. Diagrams, fol. 1890-92.......	A. G. Stanton, Esq.
HENRY (JAMES). Aeneides, or critical, exegetical, and aesthetical remarks on the Aeneis. Indices. 188 pp., 8vo. Meissen. 1892.....................	The Trustees of the Author
HEWINS (W. A. S.). English Trade and Finance chiefly in the seventeenth century. xxxv + 174 pp., sm. 8vo. 1892	The Author
HOWARD (LUKE). The Climate of London deduced from Meteorological observations made in the metropolis and at various places around it. 2nd edition. 3 vols., diagrams and plates, 8vo. 1833	Dr. G. B. Longstaff
JOHANNIS (A. J. DE). Le Monopole de la Production de l'Argent. 16 pp., 8vo. Florence, 1892.....................	The Author
JURASCHEK (Dr. FRANZ VON). Übersichten der Weltwirtschaft. Lief. 8. 12mo. 1892.....................	
MISCHLER (Dr. ERNST). Handbuch der Verwaltungs-Statistik. Band 1. Allgemeine Grundlagen der Verwaltungs-Statistik. xx + 323 pp., 8vo. Stuttgart, 1892	The Publishers
MORTIMER (THOMAS). General Dictionary of Commerce, Trade, and Manufactures, exhibiting their present state in every part of the world. 8vo. 1810.....................	Dr. G. B. Longstaff
PLATT (JAMES). Excelsior. 208 pp., 8vo. 1892	The Author
Priestley (Joseph)— Historical account of the navigable rivers, canals, and railways of Great Britain as a reference to Nichols, Priestley and Walker's new map of Inland Navigation. xiv + 702 + viii pp., maps, 8vo. 1831 .... Also large Map of Inland Navigation and Railroads, in case. 4to.....................	Dr. G. B. Longstaff
RAFFALOVICH (ARTHUR). Note sur les stocks d'or du Trésor et de la Banque de Russie. 22 pp., 8vo. Paris, 1892	The Author

Donations—Contd.

Donations.	By whom Presented.
(d) Authors, &c.—*Contd.*	
SCHULZE-GÄVERNITZ (Dr. GERHART VON). Der Grosbetrieb, ein wirtschaftlicher und socialer Fortschritt. Eine Studie auf dem Gebiete der Baumwollindustrie. vi + 281 pp., 8vo. Leipzig, 1892	The Author
STREET'S List of Newspapers published in Great Britain and Ireland. xlvii + 231 pp., map, 8vo. 1892	Messrs. Street Bros.
THOMPSON (HERBERT M.). The Theory of Wages and its application to the eight hours question and other labour problems. xxiv + 140 pp., 8vo. 1892	Messrs. Macmillan & Co.
TRAILL (H. D.). Central Government. viii + 162 pp., 8vo. 1892	,,
WALPOLE (SPENCER). The Electorate and the Legislature. viii + 163 pp., 8vo. 1892	,,
WALRAS (LEON). The Geometrical Theory of the Determination of Prices. 64 pp., 8vo. Philadelphia, 1892	The Author
WELLS (DAVID A.). Four pamphlets (1) A Primer of Tariff Reform, 1892. (2) McKinley's views and statesmanship. (3) A Tariff for Revenue, what it really means. (4) The Plutocratic Revolution. 8vo. 1892	The Hon. David A. Wells
(e) Societies, &c. (British). *	
Anthropological Institute. Journal. Vol. xxii, Nos. 1 and 2. Plates. 8vo. 1892	The Institute
British Economic Association. The Economic Journal. Sept., 1892. Vol. ii, No. 7	The Association
Economic Review. Vol. ii, No. 4. 8vo. 1892	The Publishers
Cobden Club— Annual General Meeting, 1892. Report. 12mo. Fiscal Federation of the Empire, by G. W. Medley. 12mo. 1892	The Club
East India Association. Journal. (Current numbers)	The Association
Friendly Society of Ironfounders. (Current monthly reports)	Sir R. W. Rawson
Howard Association. Report. October, 1892, and Leaflets with regard to Pauperism and Crime, &c.	The Association
Imperial Federation League. Imperial Federation, the [monthly] Journal of the League. (Current numbers)	The League
Institute of Bankers. Journal. (Current numbers)	The Institute
Institution of Mechanical Engineers. Proceedings, May, 1892. Plates. 8vo.	The Institution
London Chamber of Commerce. Journal. (Current numbers)	The Chamber of Commerce
Manchester Literary and Philosophical Society. Memoirs and Proceedings. 1891-92. Fourth series. Vol. v, No. 2. 8vo.	The Society
Royal Agricultural Society, Journal. Third Series. Vol. iii, Part 3. 1892 (contains "Allotments and Small Holdings," by Sir J. B. Lawes and J. H. Gilbert)	,,
Royal Asiatic Society. Journal. October, 1892. Plates, 8vo.	,,

* Foreign and Colonial Societies will be found under the various Countries or Possessions to which they belong.

Donations.	By whom Presented.
(e) Societies, &c. (British)—*Contd.*	
Royal College of Surgeons of England, Calendar for 1892. 8vo.	The College
Royal Geographical Society. Proceedings. (Current numbers)	The Society
Royal Irish Academy. Transactions. Vol. xxx. Parts 1 and 2, plates, 4to. 1892	The Academy
Royal Society of Edinburgh— Proceedings. Vol. xviii, Session 1890-91. 8vo. 1892 Transactions. Vol. xxxvi. Parts 2 and 3. Session 1890-91. Plates, 4to. 1891-92	The Society
Royal United Service Institution. Journal. (Current monthly numbers)	The Institution
Royal Society. Proceedings. (Current numbers)	The Society
St. Bartholomew's Hospital. Statistical Tables of the Patients under Treatment in the wards during 1891. 8vo.	The Hospital
Society of Arts. Journal. (Current numbers)	The Society
Surveyors' Institution. Transactions. (Current numbers)	The Institution
University College, London. Calendar. Session 1892-93. Plans, 8vo.	The College

(f) Periodicals, &c. (British). *		
Accountant, The	Current numbers	The Editor
Athenæum, The	„	„
Bankers' Magazine, The........................		
British Trade Journal, The	„	„
Building Societies and Land Companies' Gazette, The	„	„
Commercial World, The........................	„	„
Economist, The	„	„
Fireman, The	∷	∷
Insurance and Banking Review, The	„	„
„ Gazette, The		
„ Post, The	„	„
„ Record, The	„	„
Investors' Monthly Manual, The	„	„
Iron and Coal Trades' Review, The	„	„
Machinery Market, The........................	--	--
Nature	„	„
Policy-Holder, The	„	„
Review, The........................	„	„
Sanitary Record, The	„	„
Shipping World, The........................	„	„
Statist, The	„	„
Trade Circulars for the Year 1892 *of Messrs.—*		
Boutcher, Mortimore, & Co., London (Leather)................		The Firm
Durant & Co., London (Silk)........................		„
Eaton (H. W.) & Sons, London (Silk)........................		„
Ellison & Co., Liverpool (Cotton)........................		„

* Foreign and Colonial Periodicals will be found under the various Countries or Colonies in which they are issued.

Donations—Contd.

Donations.	By whom Presented.
Trade Circulars for the Year 1892 of Messrs.—Contd.	
Gooch & Cousens, London (Wool)	The Firm
Gow, Wilson, & Stanton, London (Indian, &c., Tea)	,,
Helmuth, Schwartze, & Co., London (Wool)	,,
Page & Gwyther, London (Bullion).......................	,,
Pixley & Abell, London (Bullion)	,,
Powell (T. J. & T.), London (Leather)	,,
Ronald & Rodger, Liverpool (Wool)	,,
Thompson (W. J. & H.), London (China Tea)	,,
Urmson, Elliot, & Co., Liverpool (Tobacco)	,,

Purchases.

Authors, &c.—

Arlidge (J. T.). The Hygiene, Diseases, and Mortality of Occupations. xx + 568 pp., 8vo. 1892.

Du Cane (Col. Sir E. F.). The Punishment and Prevention of Crime. vi + 235 pp., 8vo. 1885.

Düsing (Dr. C.). Das Geschlechtsverhältnis der Geburten in Preussen. 82 pp., diagrams, 8vo. Jena, 1890.

Ely (Richard T.). An Introduction to Political Economy, with Preface by John K. Ingram, LL.D. 358 pp., 8vo. 1891.

Fowle (T. W.). The Poor Law. vi + 175 pp., 8vo. 1890.

Hall (Hubert). History of the Custom-Revenue in England from the earliest times to the year 1827. Part 1, Constitutional History. Part 2, Fiscal History. 327 + 288 pp., map, 8vo. 1892.

Haupt (Ottomar). The Monetary Question in 1892. x + 179 pp., 8vo. 1892.

Howell (George, M.P.). Trade Unionism new and old. xv + 235 pp., 8vo. 1891.

Mansion House Council. The Dwellings of the Poor. Report of the Council for 1891. 87 pp., plan, 8vo. 1892.

Nouveau Dictionnaire d'Economie Politique. 19e Livraison. Table des auteurs. Table méthodique et Table analytique. La. 8vo. 1892.

Periodicals, &c.—

Annuaire de l'Economie Politique et de la Statistique. 1892.

Co-operative Wholesale Societies' Annuals for 1889, 90, and 1892. 3 vols., plates and maps.

Palmer's Index to the Times for the third quarter of 1892.

Publishers' Circular. (Current weekly numbers.)

Vierteljahrschrift für Volkswirtschaft, &c. Band iv, Hälfte 1 und 2. 8vo. 1892.

Parliamentary Papers—

Army. Annual Return for 1891. [C–6722.] 8vo. 1892.

Bankruptcy. Report of Board of Trade on, [C–6825.] 1892.

Building Societies that have ceased to exist. (239.) 1892.

Finance Accounts for 1891-92. (274.) 8vo. 1892.

Judicial Statistics (England and Wales) for 1891.

Purchases—Contd.

Parliamentary Papers—*Contd.*
> Judicial Statistics (Scotland) for 1891.
> Judicial Statistics (Ireland) for 1891.
> Labour Commission. 1st Report, 1892.
> Local Taxation Accounts, 1891-92. (341.) 1892.
> Lunacy Commissioners' Report for 1891. (320.) 8vo. 1892.
> National Debt. Report on the, 1786-1890. [6539.] 1891.
> Police, Foreign Countries. [C–6749.] 1892.
> Prisons (Military). Report for 1891. 8vo.
> Prisons (Scotland). Report for 1891-92.
> Railway Servants (Hours of Labour). (125), (246). 1892.
> Reformatory and Industrial Schools, Great Britain. Report for 1891. 8vo.
> Shipping Casualties during 1890-91. [C–6717.] 1892.
> Trade. Index to F.O. Reports on, 1886-92. 8vo.
> Vaccination Commission. 5th Report, 1892.

INDEX to Vol. LV,

YEAR 1892.

	PAGE
CAIRD (Sir James), obituary notice of	1
(see also *Booth*, inaugural address, p. 521.)	
CENSUSES:	
Bulgaria (1888)	674-5
Ceylon (1891)	676-7
France. A census of inland navigation (1891)	482-8
India. Religious census of India (1891)	88
Ireland (1891)	601-19
General Summary of results: Persons, Ages, Conjugal Condition, Birth-places; Religious Professions	601
Education; Schools and Scholars; Primary Schools; Occupations	602
Families; Houses; Rateable Valuation; Vital Statistics; Emigration; Sickness; Blind, Deaf, and Dumb; Lunatics and Idiots	603
Division of Land; Land under Crops; Live Stock; Language; Navy and Military; Foreigners; Pauperism	604
Ages of the People	605
Emigration	607
Agricultural Holdings	608
Holdings classified according to acreage	610
Holdings classified according to rateable valuation	610
Table I. Population in each County in Ireland, 1881 and 1891, with the increase or decrease during the decade	613
—— II. Population of Cities and Towns having more than 10,000 inhabitants, with the increase or decrease since 1881	614
—— III. Number of Persons in 1881 and 1891 according to ages, with the increase or decrease since 1881	615
—— IV. Occupations of the People	616
—— V. Total Acreage, Acreage under Crops and Pasture, Acreage of Plantation, Turf, Bog, &c.; and the Population to a square mile of Land under Crops and Pasture, also to a square mile of the total area	617
—— VI. Showing the Counties arranged according to the Highest Average Annual Rate of Emigration per 1,000 of the Population during the twenty years ended 31st March, 1891	618
—— VII. Showing by Counties and Provinces, the number of Agricultural Holdings, according to size, in 1891	618
—— VIII. Showing by Counties and Provinces the number of Agricultural Holdings, according to rateable valuation, in 1891	619
United States. Homicide in 1890	474-82
—— Summary of the statistics collected in 1890	326-33
CEYLON, census (1891)	676-7
CLEARING, London. *Periodical Returns*	183
COIN. Withdrawal of pre-Victorian gold (see *Fremantle*)	416
COMMERCIAL history and review of 1891	88-109
Foreign trade (imports and exports)	88
Traffic returns of railways	90
Prices of imports and exports	91
Pauperism in England and Wales	93
Consumption of dutiable articles	94
Savings banks	94
Agriculture	94
Protection in foreign countries	95
Prospects for 1892	96
Finance	97
Cash reserves held by banks. One pound notes	100
The money market	101
European rates of discount	102
Silver	103
Effects of the crisis of 1890	104
Appendix I. Our foreign trade of 1891 compared with that of 1890	106
—— II. Railway traffic receipts in 1891 and 1890	108
CONSOLS. *Periodical Returns*	165
CORN, average prices of British. *Periodical Returns*	180-81
COUNCIL, annual report of the. See *Report of the Council*	369
CURRENCY, reform of the, in Austria-Hungary	333-9
DEATHS. *Periodical Returns*	163, &c.
DOCK Labour (see *Booth: Inaugural address*)	521
ECONOMIC articles in recent periodi	503, 688
ELECTRICAL tabulating machine	326

PAGE

APPENDIX.
(Corrected to 31st December, 1892.)

ROYAL STATISTICAL SOCIETY.

(FOUNDED 1834. INCORPORATED 1887.)

9, ADELPHI TERRACE,
STRAND, W.C., LONDON.

Contents.

LONDON:
PRINTED FOR THE SOCIETY,
BY HARRISON AND SONS, 45 AND 46, ST. MARTIN'S LANE,
Printers in Ordinary to Her Majesty.

1893.

ROYAL STATISTICAL SOCIETY.

No. 9, Adelphi Terrace, Strand, W.C., London.

NOTICES TO FELLOWS.

December, 1892.

THE Council desire to call the attention of the Fellows to the fact that notwithstanding the change in the name of the Society by the addition of the word "Royal," they are still, in using letters after their names, signifying the membership of the Society, only entitled under Rule 6, to use the letters F.S.S.

ANNUAL Subscriptions are due in advance, on the 1st of January in each year. A Form for authorising a Banker or Agent to pay the Subscription Annually will be forwarded by the Assistant Secretary, on application. When convenient, this mode of payment is recommended. Drafts should be made payable to the order of "The Royal Statistical Society," and crossed "*Drummond and Co.*"

To be included in the Ballot at any particular Ordinary Meeting, the Nomination Papers of Candidates for Fellowship, must be lodged at the Office of the Society, at least six days before the date of such Meeting.

FELLOWS who may desire to receive Special and Separate Notices of each Paper to be read before the Society at the Ordinary Meetings, should indicate their wishes to the Assistant Secretary.

THE Ordinary Meetings of the Society are now held, by permission of the Lords of the Committee of Council on Education, in **The Lecture Theatre of the Museum of Practical Geology, 28, Jermyn Street, S.W.**

THE Library and the Reading Room are open daily for the use of Fellows from 10 A.M. to 5 P.M., excepting on Saturdays, when they are closed at 2 P.M. The Society's Rooms are entirely closed during the month of September, but books required by Fellows can be obtained from the Library on application.

FELLOWS borrowing books from the Library are requested to be good enough to return them with as little delay as possible, but without fail at the expiration of a month, and without waiting for them to be recalled. (See p. 71.)

FELLOWS changing their Addresses are requested to notify the same to the Assistant Secretary, so that delay in forwarding communications, or the *Journal*, may be avoided.

BY ORDER OF THE EXECUTIVE COMMITTEE.

A 2

CALENDAR FOR THE SESSION 1892-93.

1892	MON.	TUES.	WED.	THURS.	FRI.	SATUR.	SUN.	1893	MON.	TUES.	WED.	THURS.	FRI.	SATUR.	SUN.
NOV.	...	1	2	3	4	5	6	MAY	1	2	3	4	5	6	7
	7	8	9	10	11	12	13		8	9	10	11	12	13	14
	14	**15**	16	17	18	19	20		15	**16**	17	18	19	20	21
	21	22	23	24	25	26	27		22	23	24	25	26	27	28
	28	29	30						29	30	31				
DEC.	...	...	...	1	2	3	4	JUNE	...	...	...	1	2	3	4
	5	6	7	8	9	10	11		5	6	7	8	9	10	11
	12	13	14	15	16	17	18		12	13	14	15	16	17	18
	19	**20**	21	22	23	24	25		19	**20**	21	22	23	24	25
	26	27	28	29	30	31	...		26	27	28	29	30		
1893								JULY	...	...	...	...	...	1	2
JAN.	...	...	...	...	...	...	1		3	4	5	6	7	8	9
	2	3	4	5	6	7	8		10	11	12	13	14	15	16
	9	10	11	12	13	14	15		17	18	19	20	21	22	23
	16	**17**	18	19	20	21	22		24	25	26	27	28	29	30
	23	24	25	26	27	28	29		31						
	30	31						AUG.	...	1	2	3	4	5	6
FEB.	...	...	1	2	3	4	5		7	8	9	10	11	12	13
	6	7	8	9	10	11	12		14	15	16	17	18	19	20
	13	14	15	16	17	18	19		21	22	23	24	25	26	27
	20	**21**	22	23	24	25	26		28	29	30	31			
	27	28						SEP.	...	...	...	...	1	2	3
MAR.	...	...	1	2	3	4	5		4	5	6	7	8	9	10
	6	7	8	9	10	11	12		11	12	13	14	15	16	17
	13	14	15	16	17	18	19		18	19	20	21	22	23	24
	20	**21**	22	23	24	25	26		25	26	27	28	29	30	
	27	28	29	30	31			OCT.	...	...	...	...	...	...	1
APR.	...	...	...	...	...	1	2		2	3	4	5	6	7	8
	3	4	5	6	7	8	9		9	10	11	12	13	14	15
	10	11	12	13	14	15	16		16	17	18	19	20	21	22
	17	**18**	19	20	21	22	23		23	24	25	26	27	28	29
	24	25	26	27	28	29	30		30	31					

The dates of the Ordinary Meetings of the Society, at which Papers are read and discussed, are marked in the Calendar above by **Black Figures**.

The Chair will be taken at 7.45 p.m., precisely.

These Meetings are now held, by permission of the Committee of Council on Education, in **The Lecture Theatre of the Museum of Practical Geology, 28, Jermyn Street, S.W.**

THE ANNUAL GENERAL MEETING

WILL BE HELD ON THE 27TH JUNE, 1893, AT 5 P.M., AT 9, ADELPHI TERRACE.

ROYAL STATISTICAL SOCIETY.

Programme of the Session 1892-93.

THE

MONTHLY MEETINGS

ARE HELD ON THE

THIRD TUESDAY IN THE MONTHS OF NOVEMBER—JUNE

In the LECTURE THEATRE of the MUSEUM OF PRACTICAL GEOLOGY,

28, JERMYN STREET, S.W., at 7·45 p.m.

Tuesday,	Nov.	15	Tuesday,	March	21
,,	Dec.	20	,,	April	18
,,	Jan.	17	,,	May	16
,,	Feb.	21	,,	June	20

The following Papers have been read (Dec., 1892):—

The President's Inaugural Address. (Dock Labour.) By CHARLES BOOTH, Esq. (Delivered 15th November.)

"Distribution and Movement of the Population in India." By J. A. BAINES, Census Commissioner for India. (Read 20th December, 1892.)

The following Papers have been offered; and from these and from others that may yet be offered, a selection will be made by the Council:—

"Progress of the Export and Import Trade of the United Kingdom." By STEPHEN BOURNE.

"Income Tax and Population." By F. B. GARNETT, C.B.

"Workmen's Budgets." By HENRY HIGGS, LL.B.

"On Rural Depopulation, so-called." By G. B. LONGSTAFF, M.A., M.D., F.R.C.P.

"Railway Rates, and the Cost of Railway Carriage and Terminals." By R. PRICE-WILLIAMS, M.Inst.C.E.

"The Reorganization of our Labour Department." By DAVID F. SCHLOSS.

"Electoral Statistics and Theories of Representation." By JAMES PARKER SMITH, M.P.

"Observations on Mental and Physical Conditions of Children." By FRANCIS WARNER, M.D., F.R.C.P

ROYAL STATISTICAL SOCIETY:

AN OUTLINE OF ITS OBJECTS.

THE *Royal Statistical Society* was founded, in pursuance of a recommendation of the British Association for the Advancement of Science, on the 15th of March, 1834; its objects being, the careful collection, arrangement, discussion and publication, of facts bearing on and illustrating the complex relations of modern society in its social, economical, and political aspects,—especially facts which can be stated numerically and arranged in tables;—and also, to form a Statistical Library as rapidly as its funds would permit.

The Society from its inception has steadily progressed. It now possesses a valuable Library of more than 27,000 volumes, and a Reading Room. Ordinary meetings are held monthly from November to June, which are well attended, and cultivate among its Fellows an active spirit of investigation; the Papers read before the Society are, with an abstract of the discussions thereon, published in its *Journal*, which now consists of fifty-five annual volumes, and forms of itself a valuable library of reference.

The Society has originated and statistically conducted many special inquiries on subjects of economic or social interest, of which the results have been published in the *Journal*, or issued separately.

To enable the Society to extend its sphere of useful activity, and accomplish in a yet greater degree the various ends indicated, an increase in its numbers and revenue is desirable. With the desired increase in the number of Fellows, the Society will be enabled to publish standard works on Economic Science and Statistics, especially such as are out of print or scarce, and also greatly extend its collection of Foreign works. Such a well-arranged Library for reference, as would result, does not at present exist in England, and is obviously a great *desideratum*.

The Society is cosmopolitan, and consists of Fellows and Honorary Fellows, forming together a body, at the present time, of over *one thousand* Members.

The Annual Subscription to the Society is *Two Guineas*, and at present there is no entrance fee. Fellows may, on joining the Society, or afterwards, compound for all future Annual Subscriptions by a payment of *Twenty Guineas*.

The Fellows of the Society receive gratuitously a copy of each part of the *Journal* as published Quarterly, and have the privilege of purchasing back numbers at a reduced rate. The Library (reference and circulating), and the Reading Room, are open daily, for the convenience of Members.

Nomination Forms and any further information will be furnished, on application to the *Assistant Secretary*, 9, *Adelphi Terrace*, *Strand*, *W.C.*, *London*.

ROYAL STATISTICAL SOCIETY.

LIST OF THE SOCIETY'S PUBLICATIONS.

Note.—Sets—or Copies of any number—of the *Journal*, or of the other Publications of the Society (if not out of print), can be obtained of the publisher, E. Stanford, 26 and 27, Cockspur Street, Charing Cross, London, S.W., or through any bookseller.

	Price.
Proceedings— 308 pp. 1 vol. 8vo. 1834-37	(Out of print)
Transactions— Vol. 1, part 1. 148 pp. 4to. 1837	,,
Journal (published quarterly)— Vols. 1—55. 8vo. 1838-92	5s. each part*
General Analytical Index to Vols. 1—50 of the Journal (1838-87). In 4 parts. 8vo.— (i) For the First Fifteen Volumes (1838-52) (ii) For the Ten Volumes (1853-62)................ (iii) For the Ten Volumes (1863-72)................ (iv) For the Fifteen Volumes (1873-87)	8s. 6d. each part
First Report of a Committee on Beneficent Institutions. I. The Medical Charities of the Metropolis. 68 pp. 8vo. 1857........................	2s. 6d.
Catalogue of the Library— iv + 142 pp. 8vo. 1859........................	(Out of print)
Statistics of the Farm School System of the Continent (reprinted from the *Journal*, with a Preface and Notes). 63 pp. 8vo. 1878	1s.
Catalogue of the Library (New)— iv+573 pp. Cloth, super royal 8vo. 1884	10s.
Index to the Catalogue of 1884— i + 372 pp. Cloth, super royal 8vo. 1886	10s.
Jubilee Volume— xv + 372 pp. Cloth, 8vo. 1885...............	10s. 6d.
List of Fellows, Rules and Bye-Laws, Regulations of the Library, and Outline of the Objects of the Society, &c. Corrected annually to 31st December. 8vo.	Issued gratuitously

Price of back Numbers of the Journal, &c., to Fellows only.

Fellows only, can obtain sets—or single copies of any number—of the *Journal,* or copies of the other Publications, at the Society's Rooms, 9, Adelphi Terrace, Strand, W.C.

By different resolutions of the Council, the prices charged to Members are as follows :—(a.) back numbers of the *Journal* of the Society, three-fifths of the publishing price; (b.) each part of the General Index to the *Journal,* 2s. 6d. ; (c.) the Jubilee Volume, 5s.

NOTE.—One or two numbers of the *Journal* are now out of print.

* Before 1870 the price varied.

CONTENTS OF VOL. LV

OF THE

Royal Statistical Society's Journal

FOR THE YEAR 1892.

ROYAL STATISTICAL SOCIETY.

Founded 15th March, 1834, Incorporated 31st January, 1887.

LIST OF THE FORMER

Patron and Presidents

OF THE SOCIETY.

Patron.

	Period.
HIS ROYAL HIGHNESS THE PRINCE CONSORT, K.G.	1840–61

Presidents.

	Period.
The Most Noble the Marquis of Lansdowne, F.R.S.	1834–36
Sir Charles Lemon, Bart., M.P., LL.D., F.R.S.	1836–38
The Right Hon. the Earl Fitzwilliam, F.R.S.	1838–40
The Right Hon. the Viscount Sandon, M.P.	1840–42
(afterwards Earl of Harrowby.)	
The Most Noble the Marquis of Lansdowne, K.G., F.R.S.	1842–43
The Right Hon. the Viscount Ashley, M.P.	1843–45
(afterwards Earl of Shaftesbury.)	
The Right Hon. the Lord Monteagle	1845–47
The Right Hon. the Earl Fitzwilliam, F.R.S.	1847–49
The Right Hon. the Earl of Harrowby	1849–51
The Right Hon. the Lord Overstone	1851–53
The Right Hon. the Earl Fitzwilliam, K.G., F.R.S.	1853–55
The Right Hon. the Earl of Harrowby, K.G., D.C.L.	1855–57
The Right Hon. the Lord Stanley, M.P.	1857–59
(now Earl of Derby.)	
The Right Hon. the Lord John Russell, M.P., F.R.S.	1859–61
(afterwards Earl Russell.)	
The Right Hon. Sir J. S. Pakington, Bart., M.P., G.C.B.	1861–63
(afterwards Lord Hampton.)	
Colonel W. H. Sykes, M.P., F.R.S.	1863–65
The Right Hon. the Lord Houghton, D.C.L., F.R.S.	1865–67
The Right Hon. W. E. Gladstone, M.P., D.C.L.	1867–69
W. Newmarch, F.R.S., Corr. Mem. Inst. of France	1869–71
William Farr, M.D., C.B., D.C.L., F.R.S.	1871–73
William A. Guy, M.B., F.R.S.	1873–75
James Heywood, M.A., F.R.S., F.G.S.	1875–77
The Right Hon. George Shaw Lefevre, M.P.	1877–79
Thomas Brassey, M.P.	1879–80
(now the Right Hon. Lord Brassey.)	
The Right Hon. Sir James Caird, K.C.B., F.R.S.	1880–82
Robert Giffen, C.B., LL.D., F.R.S.	1882–84
Sir Rawson W. Rawson, K.C.M.G., C.B.	1884–86
The Right Hon. George Joachim Goschen, M.P., LL.D., F.R.S.	1886–88
T. Graham Balfour, M.D., F.R.S., F.R.C.P.	1888–90
Frederic J. Mouat, M.D., LL.D., F.R.C.S.	1890–92

LIST OF FELLOWS.

Year of Election.	
1888	Ackland, Thomas, G., F.I.A., *St. Mildred's House, Poultry E.C.*
1888	Acland, The Right Hon. Arthur Herbert Dyke, M.A., M.P., *35, Cadogan-terrace, S.W.*
1862	Acland, Sir Henry Wentworth, Bart., K.C.B., M.D., F.R.S., *Oxford.*
1869	Acland, The Rt. Hon. Sir Thomas Dyke, Bart., F.R.G.S., *Killerton, Exeter ; and Athenæum Club, S.W.*
1892	Acworth, William M., M.A., *47, St. George's-square, S.W.*
1879	Adam, Robert (*City Chamberlain*), *City Chambers, Edinburgh.*
1891	Addington, Right Hon. Lord, *24, Princes-gate, S.W.*
1867	Addison, John, *Colehill Cottage, Fulham Palace-road, S.W.*
1890	Adler, Marcus Nathan, M.A., F.I.A., *1. Bartholomew-lane, E.C., and 22, Craven-hill, W.*
1884	Agius, Edward Tancred, *90, Belsize-park-gardens, N.W.*
1886	Ainslie, William George, *23, Abingdon-street, S.W.*
1876	Aitchison, William John, *2, Princes-street, E.C.*
1885	Aitken, Thomas, *131, West Regent-street, Glasgow.*
1879	Akers-Douglas, The Right Hon. Aretas, M.P., J.P., *Chilston Park, Maidstone, Kent.*
1876	Aldwinckle, Thomas Williams, *1, Victoria-street, S.W.*
1887	Allard, Alphonse, *52, Avenue Louise, Brussels, Belgium.*
1889	Allen, Frank, J.P., *Guildford-terrace, off Hill-st., Thorndon, Wellington, N.Z.*

Year of Election.	
1876	Allen, John T. R., 18, *York-road, Hove, Brighton.*
1877	Allen, Joseph, 18, *Crossley-street, Halifax, Yorkshire.*
1871	Anderson, Sir James, F.R.G.S., F.G.S., 50, *Old Broad-street, E.C.*
1889	Anderson, John Andrew (Alderman), *Faversham, Kent.*
1886	Andras, Henry Walsingham, F.I.A., 25, *Pall Mall, S.W*
1890	*Andrews, Henry, 18, *Essex-street, Strand, W.C.*
1871	Angus, R. B., *Montreal, Canada.*
1890	Ann, Alfred E., F.R.G.S., *The Oaks, Snaresbrook, Essex.*
1884	Anning, Edward James, 78, *Cheapside, E.C.*
1872	*Archibald, William Frederick A., M.A., 4, *Brick-court, Temple, E.C.*
1892	Argyle, Jesse, 74, *Lordship-road, Stoke Newington, N.*
1888	Asch, William, 4, *Albert Mansions*, 118, *Victoria-street, S.W.*
1883	Aschenheim, Gustav, 27, *Mincing-lane, E.C.*
1891	Ashman, Rev. Joseph Williams, M.A., M.D., *Harrow, and National Club*, 1, *Whitehall-gardens, S.W.*
1884	Ashwell, Henry, *Woodthorpe Grange, Sherwood, Notts.*
1888	Atkinson, Charles, *Benhilton, St. Saviour's-road, Croydon.*
1871	Atkinson, George W., 1, *Regent-street, Barnsley.*
1892	Atkinson, Robert Hope, *Equitable Life Ass. Soc. of United States, Sydney, N.S.W.*
1870	Avery, Thomas, *Church-road, Edgbaston, Birmingham.*
1872	*Babbage, Major-General Henry Prevost, *Mayfield, Lansdown-place, Cheltenham*
1890	Back, Frederick, *Hobart, Tasmania.*
1872	*Backhouse, Edmund, *Bank, Darlington.*

Year of Election.	
1892	Bacon, George Washington, F.R.G.S., 127, *Strand, W.C.*
1879	Baden-Powell, Sir George, K.C.M.G., M.P., 8, *St. George's-place, Hyde Park Corner, S.W.*
1855	BAILEY, ARTHUR HUTCHESON, F.I.A., 7, *Royal Exchange, E.C.*
1890	Bain, William Whyte, 23, *Castlereagh-street, Sydney, New South Wales.*
1881	Baines, Jervoise Athelstane, I.C.S., *India Office, S.W.*
1887	Baldwin, Altred, M.P., J.P., *Wilden House, near Stourport.*
1878	Balfour, The Right Hon. Arthur James, M.P., LL.D. 4, *Carlton-gardens, S.W.*
1848	Balfour, General Sir George, K.C.B., D.L., 6, *Cleveland-gardens, Bayswater, W.*
1886	Balfour, Gerald William, M.P., 67, *Addison-road, Kensington, W.*
1873	Balfour, Jabez Spencer, M.P., 28, *Whitehall-court, S.W.*
1886	Barker, W. E., B.A.,
1884	Barlow, William Henry, F.R.S., C.E., 2, *Old Palace-yard, S.W.*
1887	Barnes, Joseph Howard, F.I.A., 70, *Lombard-street, E.C.*
1889	Barr, Andrew Wallace, *Copthall House, Copthall-avenue, E.C.*
1885	Barratt, Thomas J., 75, *New Oxford-street, W.*
1887	*Barrett, Thomas Squire, F.Z.S., M.A.I., F.R. Hist. Soc., *High-street, Berkhampstead.*
1888	Barron, Thomas Walter, M.A., M.B., M.R.C.S., &c., 10, *Old Elvet, Durham.*
1888	Barrow, Alfred, *Weston-street, Southwark, S.E.*
1878	Barry, Francis Tress, M.P., *St. Leonard's-hill, Windsor.*
1888	*Bartlett, Frederick W., 82, *Camberwell Grove, S.E.*
1889	Bastable, Professor C. F., M.A., 74, *Kenilworth-square, Rathgar, Co. Dublin.*
1873	Bate, George, 258, *Waterloo-road, Burslem, Staffs.*
1877	BATEMAN, ALFRED EDMUND, C.M.G. (*Hon. Secretary*), *Board of Trade, Whitehall-gardens, S.W.*
1888	Batten, John W., 3, *Harcourt Buildings, Temple, E.C.*
1877	Bayfield, Arthur, 95, *Colmore-row, Birmingham.*

Year of Election.	
1873	*Baynes, Alfred Henry, F.R.G.S., 19, *Furnival-street, Holborn, E.C.*
1871	*Baynes, William Wilberforce, F.I.A., *Pickhurst Wood, Bromley, Kent.*
1875	*Beardsall, Francis E. M., 25, *Booth-street, Manchester.*
1875	*Beaufort, William Morris, F.R.A.S., F.R.G.S., 18, *Piccadilly, W.*
1882	*Beazeley, Michael Wornum, M.A., 8, *St. Paul's-road, Thornton Heath, Surrey.*
1883	Beckingham, James Horace, *Westwood House, Ryton-on-Tyne, Co. Durham.*
1884	Bedford, James, *Woodhouse Cliff, Leeds.*
1889	Beecroft, William Henry, *Guildhall, Westminster, S.W.*
1882	*BEETON, HENRY RAMIE (6a, *Austin Friars, E.C.*) ; 9, *Maresfield-gardens, Hampstead, N.W.*
1886	Begg, Ferdinand Faithfull, *Bartholomew House, E.C.*
1890	Bell, Frederick, F.I.A., 9, *King-street, Cheapside, E.C.*
1892	Bell, Frederick William, *P.O. Box 916, Johannesburg, S. Africa.*
1880	Bell, Sir Isaac Lowthian, Bart., J.P., F.R.S. *Rounton Grange, Northallerton, York, N.R.*
1884	Bell, James T., *Northcote, Dowanhill, viâ Glasgow.*
1888	Bellew, Thomas Acheson, 65, *Tower Buildings, Liverpool.*
1888	*Benson, Godfrey R., M.P., *Oxenford Hall, Oxford.*
1884	*Bentley, Richard, F.R.G.S., *Upton, Slough, Bucks.*
1884	Berg, Wilhelm, 37, *Mincing-lane, E.C.*
1890	Berry, Arthur, M.A., *King's College, Cambridge.*
1891	Berry, Oscar, *Monument-yard, E.C.*
1875	Bevan, Thomas, *Stone Park, near Dartford, Kent.*
1869	*Beverley, The Hon. Mr. Justice Henry, 42, *Chowringhee, Calcutta.*
1879	*Bickford-Smith, William, J.P., D.L., *Trevarno, Helston, Cornwall.*
1891	Biddle, Daniel, M.R.C.S., L.S.A., *Gough House, Kingston-on-Thames.*
1886	Biggs, Thomas Hesketh, (*Comptroller*), *Royal Colonial Institute, Northumberland-avenue, S.W.*

Year of Election.	
1888	Billinghurst, Henry F., 41, *Lothbury, E.C.*
1883	Binney, William, 13, *St. Helen's-place, E.C.; Hillfield, Hampstead, N.W.*
1888	Binns, Richard William, F.S.A., *Diglis House, Worcester.*
1884	Birch, Robert W. Peregrine, M. Inst. C.E., 5, *Queen Anne's-gate, Westminster, S.W.*
1892	*Birkmyre, William, M.P., *Reform Club Chambers, Pall Mall, S.W.*
1890	Bishop, Frederic Sillery, M.A., J.P., *Glanrafon, Sketty, Swansea.*
1881	Bishop, George, 113, *Powis-street, Woolwich.*
1883	Blades, R. H., 23, *Abchurch-lane, E.C.*
1884	Boileau, John Peter H., M.D., &c. (*Brigade-Surgeon Lieut.-Col.*) *Medical Staff, Meerut, Bengal.*
1881	Bolitho, Thomas Robins, *Pendrea, near Penzance.*
1887	Bolling, Francis, 2, *Laurence Pountney-hill, E.C.*
1890	Bolton, Edward, *Clifton House, Beverley-road, Hull.*
1880	Bolton, Joseph Cheney, M.P., *Carbrook, Larbert, Stirlingshire.*
1885	*Bonar, James, M.A., LL.D., *Civil Service Commission, Westminster, S.W.*
1887	Bond, Edward, *Elm Bank, Hampstead, N.W.*
1885	BOOTH, CHARLES (*President*), 2, *Talbot-court, Gracechurch-street, E.C.*
1885	Bordman, Emanuel Linden, *Victoria House, Trinity-street, Southwark, S.E.*
1879	Bordman, Thomas Joseph Clarence Linden, LL.D., *Victoria House, Trinity-street, Southwark, S.E.*
1888	Bottomley, George, *Arbourfield House, Derby.*
1871	BOURNE, STEPHEN, *Abberley, Wallington, Surrey.*
1885	Bovell, The Hon. Henry Alleyne, LL.B. *Chelston, Barbados, West Indies.*
1876	Bowen, Horace George, *Bank of England, E.C.*
1879	Bowley, Edwin, F.I.A., 78, *South Hill Park, Hampstead.*
1886	Boyle, Sir Courtenay, K.C.B., *Board of Trade, Whitehall-gardens, S.W.*
1888	Braby, Frederick, F.C.S., F.G.S., *Bushey Lodge, Teddington.*

Year of Election.	
1875	Braby, James, J.P., *Maybanks, Rudgwick, Sussex.*
1888	Bramwell, Sir Frederick J., Bart., D.C.L., F.R.S., 5, *Great George-street, Westminster, S.W.*
1873	BRASSEY, THE RIGHT HON. LORD, K.C.B. (*Honorary Vice-President*), 4, *Great George-street, S.W.; and* 24, *Park-lane, W.*
1864	*Braye, The Right Hon. Lord, *Stanford Hall, Rugby.*
1884	Breckon, John Robert, 53, *John-street, Sunderland.*
1888	Broad, Harrington Evans, M.P., 1, *Walbrook, E.C.*
1876	Brodhurst, Bernard Edward, F.R.C.S., 20, *Grosvenor-street, Grosvenor-square, W.*
1883	Brooke, C. B., 16, *Leadenhall-street, E.C.*
1874	Broom, Andrew, A.C.A., 2, *De Crespigny-terrace, Denmark-hill, S.E.*
1878	Brown, Alexander Hargreaves, M.P., 12, *Grosvenor-gardens, S.W.*
1890	Browne, Edward William, 33, *Poultry, E.C.*
1875	Browne, Thomas Gillespie C., F.I.A., 11, *Lombard-street, E.C.*
1892	Bruce, Lord Charles Frederick B., (*Hyde Park Court, S.W.*) *Wolfhall Manor House, Marlborough.*
1886	Bruce, Lord Henry Brudenell, M.P., 36, *Eaton-place, S.W.*
1886	*Brunner, John Tomlinson, M.P., *Druid's Cross, Wavertree, Liverpool.*
1883	Buck, Sir Edward Charles, C.S.I., *Revenue and Agricultural Department, Simla, India.*
1865	Bunce, John Thackray, *Longworth, Priory-road, Edgbaston, Birmingham.*
1880	*Burdett, Henry Charles, *The Lodge, Porchester-square, W.*
1878	*Burdett-Coutts, The Right Hon. the Baroness, 1, *Stratton-street, W.; and Holly Lodge, Highgate, N.*
1884	Burdett-Coutts, William, M.P., 1, *Stratton-street, Piccadilly, W.*
1885	Burridge, Arthur Francis, F.I.A., *Equitable Assurance Office, Mansion House-street, E.C.*
1886	Burrows, Abraham, J.P., *Green Hall, Atherton, near Manchester.*
1880	Burt, Frederick, F.R.G.S., *Woodstock, Crouch End, N.*
1872	*Burton, The Right Hon. Lord, (*Chesterfield House, *Mayfair, W.*); *Rangemore, Burton-on-Trent.*

Year of Election.	
1886	Bush, Baron William de, F.C.S.,
	20, *Artillery-lane, Bishopsgate-street, E.C.*
1891	Butler, Arthur J.,
	Dale Close, Mansfield, Notts.
1888	Byrom, William Ascroft, F.S.A.A.,
	Savings' Bank, Wigan, Lancashire.
1892	Byworth, Charles Joseph,
	Vestry Office, Battersea Rise, S.W.
1877	Campbell, George Lamb,
	Market-street, Wigan.
1879	Campbell-Colquhoun, Rev. John Erskine,
	Chartwell, Westerham, Kent.
1889	Cannan, Edwin, M.A.,
	24, *St. Giles', Oxford.*
1891	Cannon, Henry W. (*Chase National Bank*),
	15, *Nassau-street, New York, U.S.A.*
1888	Carbutt, Sir Edward H., Bart., M. Inst. M.E., M. Inst. C.E.,
	19, *Hyde Park-gardens, W.*
1881	Carden, Lionel Edward Gresley,
	H.M. Consul, Mexico.
1872	*Carillon, J. Wilson, F.S.A., F.R.G.S.,
	The Chimes, Richmond, Surrey.
1887	Carmichael, Charles H. E., M.A.,
	Earlsmuir House, Mirabel-road, Fulham, S.W.
1885	Carmichael, Thomas D. Gibson,
	Castlecraig, Dolphinton, N.B.
1888	Carr, Ebenezer,
	24, *Coleman-street, Bank, E.C.*
1888	Carruthers-Wain, William J.,
	Linden Lodge, Thornton Heath, Surrey
1890	*Carter, Eric Mackay, A.I.A., F.C.A.,
	33, *Waterloo-street, Birmingham.*
1883	Carter, Joseph Robert,
	185, *Tottenham Court-road, W.*
1878	*Casley, Reginald Kennedy, M.D.,
	Northgate-street, Ipswich.
1885	Casson, William A.,
	4, *Reigate-villas, Leatherhead.*
1880	Castle, Robert,
	18, *Merton-street, Oxford.*
1883	Cater, J. J.,
	39, *Lombard-street, E.C.*

Year of Election.	
1883	Cattarns, Richard, *Gresham Club, King William-street, E.C.*
1881	Causton, Richard Knight, M.P. *12, Devonshire-place, Portland-place, W.*
1858	Chadwick, David, *The Poplars, Herne Hill, Dulwich, S.E.*
1869	CHADWICK, JOHN OLDFIELD, F.R.G.S., *95, Finsbury-pavement, E.C.*
1884	Chailley, Joseph, *9, Rue Guy de la Brosse, Paris.*
1888	Challis, William H. *Enfield, Middlesex.*
1880	*Chamberlain, The Right Honourable Joseph, M.P., F.R.S. *40, Prince's-gardens, S.W.*
1886	Chamberlain, Richard, *89, Cadogan-square, S.W.*
1886	Chapman, Samuel, *c/o Inter-Oceanic Railway, Mexico City (viâ New York).*
1892	*Chatham, James, F.I.A., F.F.A., *Inverleith Park House, Edinburgh.*
1851	*Cheshire, Edward, *3, Vanbrugh Park, Blackheath, S.E.*
1853	Chisholm, David, F.I.A., F.S.A., *9, Rillbank-terrace, Edinburgh.*
1886	*Chisholm, George Goudie, M.A., B.Sc., F.R.G.S., *26, Dornton-road, Balham, S.W.*
1869	Chubb, Hammond, B.A., *Bickley, Kent.*
1849	Clark, Gordon Wyatt, *10, James-street, Buckingham-gate, S.W.*
1886	Clark, Henry James (*Government Statist of Trinidad*). *Port of Spain, Trinidad.*
1856	Clark, Sir John Forbes, Bart., *Tillypronie, Tarland, Aberdeen.*
1868	Clarke, Charles Goddard, *Ingleside, Elm Grove, Peckham, S.E.*
1871	Clarke, Ebenezer, *Grove-road-villas, Walthamstow.*
1882	*Clarke, Ernest, F.L.S., F.S.A., *10, Addison-road, Bedford-park, Chiswick.*
1877	*Clarke, Henry, L.R.C.P., *H.M. Prison, Wakefield, Yorks.*
1890	Clarke. Henry, *Cannon Hall, Hampstead. N.W.*
1856	*CLARKE, HYDE, *32, St. George's-square, S.W.*
1869	Cleghorn, John, *8, Spring-gardens, S.W.*
1853	Clirehugh, William Palin, F.I.A., *66, Cornhill, E.C.*

B

Year of Election.	
1888	Clough, Walter Owen, 89, *Gresham-street, E.C., and The Ridgway, Enfield*
1889	Coate, James, *East Villa, Lyme-road, Axminster.*
1873	Cockle, Captain George, F.R.G.S., 9, *Bolton-gardens, South Kensington, S.W.*
1884	Cockshott, John James, 24, *Queen's-road, Southport.*
1887	Cohen, Nathaniel Louis, 31, *Throgmorton-street, E.C.*
1888	Coleman, Harry, 34, *Golden-square, W.*
1859	Coles, John, F.I.A., 39, *Throgmorton-street, E.C.*
1892	*Coliet, Miss Clara Elizabeth, M.A., 7, *Coleridge-road, Finsbury Park, N.*
1887	Collet, Sir Mark Wilks, Bart., 2, *Sussex-square, W., and St. Clere, Sevenoaks, Kent.*
1883	Collmann, John S.,
1882	*Collum, Rev. Hugh Robert, M.R.I.A., F.R.C.I., *Leigh, near Tunbridge, Kent.*
1867	Colman, Jeremiah James, M.P., *Carrow House, Norwich.*
1878	Colomb, Captain Sir John C. R., K.C.M.G., M.P., J.P., *Droumquinna, Kenmare, Kerry.*
1889	Compton, The Right Hon. Earl, M.P., 51, *Lennox-gardens, S.W.*
1888	Connell, Arthur Knatchbull, M.A., 20, *Elmtree-road, N.W.*
1891	Cooper, Joseph, 60, *Park-street, Farnworth, near Bolton.*
1874	Corbett, John, 20, *Hertford-street, Mayfair, W.*
1888	Corgialegno, M., *George-yard, Lombard-street, E.C.*
1873	Cork, Nathaniel, F.R.G.S., 18, *Birchin-lane, E.C.*
1889	Cornwallis, Fiennes Stanley Wykeham, M.P., *Linton-park, Maidstone, Kent.*
1890	Cotton, F. Carter, *Vancouver, British Columbia.*
1862	Courtney, The Right Hon. Leonard Henry, M.A., M.P., 15, *Cheyne Walk, Chelsea, S.W.*
1882	Cowen, Charles, *Johannesburg, Transvaal, South Africa.*
1888	Craggs, John George, C.A., *Stone House, St. John's, S.E.*
1874	CRAIGIE, MAJOR PATRICK GEORGE (*Hon. Secretary*), 6, *Lyndhurst-rd., Hampstead, & 4, Whitehall-place, S.W.*

Year of Election.	
1870	Craik, George Lillie, 29, *Bedford-street, Strand, W.C.*
1889	Cramp, Charles Courtney, C.E., 28, *Boscombe-road, Uxbridge-road, W.*
1890	Crawford, Richard Frederick, 4, *Whitehall-place, S.W.*
1891	*Crawley, Charles Edward, *Treasury-buildings, Calcutta, India.*
1878	Crewdson, Ernest, *Platt Abbey, Rusholme, Manchester.*
1892	Cripps, Charles Alfred, Q.C., 32, *Elm Park-gardens, S.W.*
1886	Crispin, Edward, *Royal Insurance Buildings, Dale-street, Liverpool.*
1890	Croal, David Octavius, 15, *York-buildings, Adelphi, W.C.*
1885	Cropper, James, *Ellergreen, Kendal.*
1887	Culley, George, C.B. 2, *Whitehall-place, S.W.*
1875	Cunningham, David, C.E., *Works' Office, Harbour-chambers, Dundee.*
1883	CUNNINGHAM, REV. WILLIAM, M.A., D.D., 2, *St. Paul's-road, Cambridge.*
1884	Curtis, Charles Edward, 6, *Barron's Court-road, West Kensington, S.W.*
1879	Curtis, Robert Leabon, F.S.I., J.P., 120, *London Wall, E.C.*
1878	Czarnikow, Cæsar, *Effingham-hill, Dorking, Surrey.*
1886	Dale, David, *West Lodge, Darlington.*
1888	Dangerfield, Athelstan, A.C.A., 17, *Basinghall-street, E.C.*
1884	Daniell, Clarmont J., *Constitutional Club, S.W.*
1880	Danvers, Frederick Charles, *India Office, Westminster, S.W.*
1878	Danvers, Sir Juland, K.C.S.I., 108, *Lexham-gardens, Kensington, W*
1886	Darrell, Charles, *Sidcup, Kent.*
1892	Dash, William Lawson, J.P., 301, *Pitt-street, Sydney, N.S.W.*

Year of
Election.

1890	Davey, Robert Williams, B.A.,
	7, *Mincing-lane, E.C., and Junior Athenæum Club, S.W.*
1869	Davies, James Mair,
	75, *West Regent-street, Glasgow.*
1874	Davies, William Henry,
	51, *Trequnter-road, West Brompton, S.W.*
1890	Dawson, A. L. Halkett, M.A., F.R.G.S.,
	Molesworth Chambers, Melbourne, Victoria.
1888	Dawson, G. J. Crosbie, M. Inst. C.E., F.G.S.
	North Staffordshire Railway, Stoke-upon-Trent.
1880	Debenham, Frank,
	26, *Upper Hamilton-terrace, St. John's Wood, N.W.*
1885	De Broë, Emile Conrad De Bichin,
	Walden Lodge, College Park, Wandsworth-common, S.W.
1879	*De Ferrieres, The Baron Du Bois, J.P.,
	Bay's-hill House, Cheltenham.
1883	*De Keyser, Sir Polydore (Alderman),
	Chatham House, Grove-road, Clapham Park, S.W.
1877	Deloitte, William Welch,
	4, *Lothbury, E.C.*
1891	Denne, William,
	Statistical Department, Custom House, E.C.
1873	Dent, Edward,
	Fernacres, Fulmer, near Slough, Bucks.
1887	Dent, George Middlewood,
	13, *Chambres-road, Southport.*
1855	*DERBY, THE RIGHT HON. THE EARL OF, K.G., F.R.S., D.C.L.
	(*Honorary Vice-President*),
	St. James's-square, S.W.; Knowsley, Prescot, Lancashire.
1889	De Rothschild, Leopold, J.P., D.L. (Alderman),
	5, *Hamilton-place, Piccadilly, W.*
1892	De Smidt, Henry (*Permanent Under-Secretary*),
	Cape Town, Cape Colony.
1877	Dever, Henry,
	4, *Lothbury, E.C.*
1892	Dewar, William Nimmo,
	163, *Queen-street, Melbourne, Victoria.*
1889	De Woolfson, Louis Estevan Green,
	St. John's-hill, Shrewsbury.
1877	De Worms, The Right Hon. Baron Henry, M.P., F.R.A.S.,
	Carlton Club, Pall Mall, S.W.
1885	Dibley, Captain George,
	4, *St. George's-square, S.W.*
1890	Dickinson, Willoughby Hyett,
	4, *Culverden-road, Balham, S.W.*
1866	*Dilke, The Right Hon Sir C. Wentworth, Bart., M.P., LL.M.,
	76, *Sloane-street, S.W.*
1873	Dixon, George, M.P.,
	The Dales, Edgbaston, Birmingham.

Year of Election.	
1889	Double, Alfred, 25, *Jewin-crescent, Cripplegate, E.C.*
1889	Doubleday, William Bennett, 123, *Tulse-hill, S.W.*
1889	Douglas, J., *E.I. Railway House, Dalhousie Square, Calcutta.*
1875	Doxsey, Rev. Isaac, 186, *The Grove, Camberwell, S.E.*
1878	Doyle, Patrick, C. E., F.G.S., M.R.A.S., *Calcutta.*
1890	Drummond, Charles James, 21, *Dalmore-road, West Dulwich, S.E.*
1875	Dun, John, *Parr's and Alliance Bank, Bartholomew-lane, E.C.*
1886	Dundonald, The Right Hon. the Earl of, 34, *Portman-square, W*
1878	*Dunraven, The Right Hon. The Earl of, K.P., *Kenry House, Putney Vale, S.W.*
1885	Dyer, William John, 17, *Montpelier-row, Blackheath, S.E.*
1888	Earnshaw, Jacob, 36, *South King-street, Manchester.*
1887	Ebbsmith, Joseph, 86, *St. James's-streeet, S.W.*
1888	Eckersley, J. C., M.A., F.R.G.S., *Standish Hall, Wigan.*
1883	EDGEWORTH, PROFESSOR FRANCIS YSIDRO, M.A., D.C.L., 5, *Mount Vernon, Hampstead, & Balliol College, Oxford.*
1869	Edmonds, William, *Annesley House, Southsea.*
1880	Egerton of Tatton, The Right Honourable Lord, 7, *St. James's-square, S.W.*
1872	Elliot, Sir George, Bart., M.P., *Park-street, Park-lane, W.; 23, Gt. George-street, S.W.*
1885	Elliot, William Henry, 122, *Mansion House-chambers, Queen Victoria-street, E.C.*
1888	Elliott, Henry W., *Elmfield, Selly Oak, near Birmingham.*
1885	ELLIOTT, THOMAS HENRY (*Vice-President*), *Board of Agriculture, 4, Whitehall Place, S.W.*
1885	Elliott, William, 22, *St. George's-street, Cape Town.*

Year of Election.	
1877	Emmott, W. T., *New Bridge-street, Manchester.*
1888	Emson, Reginald Embleton, ————. *Hazelmere, Glen Eldon-road, Streatham, S.W.,*
1889	Erhardt, William, *7, Bury-street, Bloomsbury, W.C.*
1882	Essex, Benjamin Smily, *48, Pall Mall, S.W.*
1879	Evans, Henry Jones, J.P., *Greenhill, Whitchurch, Cardiff.*
1890	Evill, John Percy, *32, Abingdon-villas, Kensington, W.*
1892	Faber, Harald, *Fiona, Lennard-road, Penge, S.E.*
1875	Faraday, Frederick J., *17, Brazennose-street, Manchester.*
1888	Farlow, A. R. King, *4, King-street, Cheapside, E.C.*
1889	Farnworth, Edward James, *20, Cannon-street, Preston.*
1891	Farquharson, J. C., *Railway Department, Colombo, Ceylon.*
1878	Farren George, J.P., M.Inst.C.E., *Carnarvon.*
1878	Farrer, Sir Thomas Henry, Bart., J.P., *27, Bryanston-square, W.; Abinger Hall, Dorking.*
1890	Faulks, Joseph Ernest, B.A., F.I.A., *187, Fleet-street, E.C.*
1882	Fell, Arthur, M.A., *46, Queen Victoria-street, E.C.*
1864	Fellows, Frank Perks, *8, The Green, Hampstead, N.W.*
1888	Fellows, James I., *Saxon Hall, Palace-court, Kensington Gardens, W.*
1887	Fenton, James J., *Office of the Government Statist, Melbourne, Victoria.*
1885	Ferguson, Ronald Crawfurd Munro, M.P., *Raith, Kirkcaldy, N.B.*
1888	Finckenstadt, Edmund Ernest, *6, King-street, Cheapside, E.C.*
1880	Findlay, Sir George, (*General Manager L. & N. W. R.*), *London and N. Western Railway, Euston Station, N.W.*

Year of
Election.

1880	Finlaison, Alexander John, C.B., F.I.A.,
	19, *Old Jewry, E.C.*
1889	*Finlay, Major Alexander,
	The Manor House, Little Brickhill, Bletchley, Bucks.
1884	*Finnemore, Robert Isaac, J.P., F.R.G.S.,
	Durban, Natal, South Africa
1892	Fisher, George,
	House of Representatives, Wellington, N.Z.
1888	Fisher, Walter Newton, F.C.A.,
	4, *Waterloo-street, Birmingham.*
1892	Fitzgerald, Lieut.-Colonel R. Purefoy, J.P.,
	North Hall, Basingstoke.
1885	*Fitz-Gerald, Lt.-Col. Wm. G., M.A., F.R. Hist. S., F.R.S. L.,
	47, *Crosby-buildings, Crosby-square, E.C.*
1882	Foley, Patrick James, M.P.,
	Pearl Ins. Co., Adelaide-place, London Bridge, E.C.
1889	Foot, Alfred,
	Bedford-villas, Penge-road, South Norwood.
1841	Fortescue, The Right Honourable Earl,
	Castle Hill, South Molton, Devon.
1888	Forwood, Sir William B., J.P.,
	Blundell Sands, Liverpool.
1884	Fosbery, William Thomas Exham,
	The Castle-park, Warwick.
1888	Foster, Harry Seymour, M.P., F.R.G.S.,
	City Carlton Club, St. Swithin's-lane, E.C.
1868	Fowler, William,
	43, *Grosvenor-square, W.*
1890	Fox, Charles Allen, M.R.C.S.,
	Martock, Somerset.
1878	Foxwell, Professor H. Somerton, M.A.,
	St. John's College, Cambridge.
1888	Frampton, Albert Tom,
1887	Frankland, Frederick William, F.I.A.
	92, *Cheapside, E.C.*
1886	Fream, Professor William, B.Sc., Lond., LL.D., F.L.S., F.G.S.,
	The Vinery, Downton, Salisbury.
1887	Freeman, T., F.G.S.,
	35, *Whitehall-park, N.*
1890	Freestone, John,
	West Bridgford, Nottingham.
1884	Frith, Walter Halsted,
	69, *Lombard-street, E.C.*
1886	Fuller, George Pargiter, M.P.,
	Neston-park, Corsham, Wilts.
1878	Fuller, William Palmer,
	Portland House, Basinghall-street, E.C.

Year of Election.	
1879	Gairdner, Charles, *Broom, Newton Mearns, Renfrewshire.*
1852	Galsworthy, Sir Edwin Henry, J.P., *26, Sussex-place, Regent's-park, N.W.*
1873	*Galton, Capt. Sir Douglas, K.C.B., D.C.L., **LL.D., F.R.S.,** *12, Chester-street, Grosvenor-place, S.W.*
1860	Galton, Francis, F.R.S., F.R.G.S., *42, Rutland-gate, S.W.*
1887	Garcke, Emile, *21, Priory-road, Bedford-park, Chiswick.*
1889	Garland, Nicholas Surrey, *Finance Department, Ottawa, Canada.*
1881	Garnett, Frederick Brooksbank, C.B. *4, Argyll-road, Kensington, W.*
1881	Garraway, The Hon. David G., *Castries, St. Lucia, West Indies.*
1879	*Gassiot, John Peter, J.P., *The Culvers, Carshalton, Surrey,*
1883	Gates, Jacob S., *St. George's House, Eastcheap, E.C.*
1880	*Gates, John Benjamin, A.C.A., *47, Warwick-street, Regent-street, W.*
1881	*Gatty, William Henry, *Market Harborough, Leicestershire.*
1885	Gibb, George S., *North-Eastern Railway Company, York.*
1872	Gibb, Thomas Eccleston, *16, Lady Margaret-road, N.W.*
1874	Gibbs, Alban George Henry, M.P. *82, Portland-place, W.*
1871	Gibbs, George Sleight, *45, Northgate, Darlington.*
1889	Gibson, George Rutledge, *55, Broadway, New York City, U.S.A.*
1867	*GIFFEN, ROBERT, C.B., LL.D., F.R.S. (*Hon. Vice-President*), *44, Pembroke-road, Kensington, W.*
1877	Gilbert, William H. Sainsbury, *62, Old Broad-street, E.C.*
1878	*Glanville, Silvanus Goring, *39, Vicar's-hill, Lewisham, S.E.*
1860	Glover, John, J.P., *88, Bishopsgate-street Within, E C.*
1888	Goad, Charles E., M. Am. Soc. C.E., M. Can. Soc. C.E., *53, New Broad-street, E.C., and Montreal, Canada.*
1884	*Gonner, Professor Edward C.K , M.A., *University College, Liverpool.*
1877	Good, Alfred, *57, Moorgate-st., E.C.; Downe Lodge, Beckenham, Kent.*
1886	Goodrich, Harry St. Aubyn, *5, Herbert-crescent, Hans-place, S.W.*

Year of Election.	
1885	Goodsall, David Henry, F.R.C.S., 17, *Devonshire-place, W.*
1892	Goodwin, Alfred, M.A., 2, *Charles-road, St. Leonards, Sussex.*
1868	GOSCHEN, THE RIGHT HON. GEORGE JOACHIM, M.P., (*Honorary Vice-President*), 69, *Portland-place, W.*, and *Seacox-heath, Hawkhurst.*
1855	*Gosset, John Jackson, *Thames Ditton, Surrey.*
1885	Goulding, William Purdham, F.S.I., 41, *Moorgate-street, E.C.; and 18, Mercers-road, N.*
1887	Gover, Frederic Field, *Casino House, Herne Hill, S.E.*
1853	Gover, William Sutton, F.I.A., 4, *Queen-street-place, Southwark Bridge, E.C.*
1885	Grant, Thomas Rennie, 10, *Harrington-gardens, Kensington, S.W.*
1887	Graves, The Rev. Michael, B.A., *Sir W. Borlase's School, Great Marlow.*
1847	Gray, Thomas, 84, *Fenchurch-street, E.C.*
1888	Green, Joseph Shaw, 18, *King Street, Warrington.*
1887	Gribble, George J., 25, *Hans-place, S.W.*
1883	Griffin, Josiah, *Vanbrugh Park, Blackheath, S.E.*
1868	Griffith, Edward Clifton, 1, *Waterloo-place, S.W.*
1884	Griffith, His Honour T. Risely, C.M.G., *Government House, Mahé, Seychelles, vid Marseilles.*
1889	Grigsby, William Ebenezer, M.A., LL.D., 7, *King's Bench Walk, Temple, E.C.*
1883	Grimshaw, Thomas Wrigley, M.D., M.A., (*Registrar-General of Ireland*), *Priorsland, Carrickmines, Co. Dublin.*
1886	GRIMSTON, THE RIGHT HON. VISCOUNT, *Cell Barnes, St. Albans.*
1889	Grosvenor, George, *Holywell, Streatham-common, S.W.*
1888	Grosvenor, The Hon. Norman de l'Aigle, 58, *Green-st., Grosvenor-sq.; Moor-park, Rickmansworth.*
1883	Gunther, Charles, 9, *Fenchurch-avenue, E.C.*
1875	Gunn, Arthur, 31, *Gloucester-road, Gloucester-gate, Regent's-park, N.W.*
1878	Guthrie, Charles, F.C.A. *London Chartered Bank of Australia, Melbourne, Victoria.*
1885	Guthrie, Edwin, *Victoria Park, Manchester.*

1887   Guyot, Yves (*Depute*),
         9, *Rue de Seine, Paris.*

1880   *Gwynne, James Eglinton A., J.P., F.S.A.,
         97, *Harley-st., W. ; Folkington Manor, Polegate, Sussex.*

1887   Gwyther, John Howard,
         34, *Belsize-park-gardens, N.W.*

1884   Haas, Hendrik Christiaan,
         32, *Fenchurch-street, E.C.*

1892   Haddan, Herbert John,
         66, *Victoria-st., S.W., & 18, Buckingham-st., Strand, W.C.*

1892   Hadfield, Robert A.
         Fairfield, Sheffield.

1884   Hadley, Joseph,
         5, *Argyll-place, Regent-street, W.*

1888   Hadrill, Henry John,
         60, *Mark-lane, E.C.*

1873   *Haggard, Frederick T.,
         1, *Broadwater Down, Tunbridge Wells.*

1884   Hague, John,
         King-street, Toronto, Canada.

1887   Haldeman, Donald Carmichael,
         Claremont, Gypsy Hill, S.E.

1883   Hall, Sir John, K.C.M.G.,
         Hororata, Canterbury, New Zealand.

1890   Hall, Joseph Castle,
         89, *Gresham-street, E.C.*

1878   Hallett, Thomas George Palmer, M.A.,
         Claverton Lodge, Bath.

1887   Hamilton, Edward W., C.B.,
         The Treasury, Whitehall, S.W.

1873   Hamilton, The Right Hon. Lord George Francis, M.P.,
         17, *Montagu-street, Portman-square, W.*

1883   Hamilton, James Thomas,
         22, *High-street, Southampton.*

1879   HAMILTON, ROWLAND, (*Vice-President*),
         Oriental Club, Hanover-square, W.

1887   Hamilton, Thomas, J.P.,
         46, *Parliament-hill-road, Hampstead, N.W.*

1884   *Hammersley, Hugh Greenwood,
         14, *Chester-square, S.W.*

1888   Hammond, Robert,
         117, *Bishopsgate-street Within, E.C.*

Year of Election.	
1885	*Hancock, Charles, M.A.,
	2 *Cloisters, Temple, E.C.; and Reform Club, S.W.*
1875	Hankey, Ernest Alers,
	91, *St. Ermin's Mansions, Victoria-street, S.W.*
1876	Hansard, Luke,
	68, *Lombard-street, E.C.*
1871	*Harcourt, Right Hon. Sir William Vernon, Q.C., M.P., F.R.S.
	Reform Club., S.W.
1886	*Hardcastle, Basil William,
	Beechenden, Hampstead, N.W.
1886	Hardcastle, E. J.,
	Oriental Club, Hanover-square, W.
1877	Harding, Colonel Charles, F.R.G.S.,
	10, *St. Swithin's-lane, E.C.*
1883	Harding, G. P.,
	La Chaumière, Trouville S./M. France.
1884	Hardy, George Francis, F.I.A.,
	5, *Whitehall, S.W.*
1883	Hardy, William Henry, F.C.A.,
	5, *Great Winchester-street, E.C.*
1891	Harris, Arthur Wellesley, M.R.C.S., L.S.A., D.P.H.,
	High-street, Southampton.
1868	Harris, David,
	Caroline Park, Granton, Edinburgh.
1887	Harris, William A., F.R.S.S.A.,
	Phœnix Chambers, Exchange, Liverpool.
1882	Harris, William James,
	Halwill Manor, Beaworthy, N. Devon.
1890	Harrison, Rev. Arthur, B.A., F.R.S.L.
	Colan Vicarage, St. Columb, Cornwall.
1889	Harrold, Major Arthur Lucas,
	Adelaide, South Australia.
1887	Harrold, Leonard F., F.R.G.S.,
	29, *Great St. Helens, E.C.*
1884	Hart, James,
	16, *Philpot-lane, E.C.*
1881	Harvey, Alfred Spalding, B.A.,
	67, *Lombard-street, E.C.*
1884	Harvey, Thomas Morgan,
	Portland House, Basinghall-street, E.C.
1876	Hawkins, Alfred Templeton, F.R.G.S.,
	22, *Budge-row, Cannon-street, E.C.*
1879	Hawksley, Thomas, C.E., F.R.S., &c.,
	30, *Great George-street, Westminster, S.W.*
1880	Hazell, Walter,
	15, *Russell-square, W.*
1887	*Heap, Ralph, jun.,
	1, *Brick-court, Temple, E.C.*
1884	Hedley, Robert Wilkin,
	31a, *Colmore-row, Birmingham.*

1870   Hefford, George V.,
         Rugby.

1883   Heilgers, Robert Philip,
         22, *Great St. Helens, E.C.*

1889   *Hemming, Arthur George, F.I.A.,
         46, *Comeragh-road, West Kensington, W.*

1865   Hendriks, Augustus, F.I.A.,
         7, *Cornhill, E.C.*

1855   *HENDRIKS, FREDERICK, F.I.A.
         7, *Vicarage-gate, W., and* 1, *King William-street, E.C.*

1888   Heriot, George,
         1, *Whittington House, Leadenhall-street, E.C.*

1881   Hewat, Archibald, F.I.A., F.F.A.,
         22, *George-street, Edinburgh.*

1890   Hewins, W. A. S., B.A.,
         26, *Leckford-road, Oxford.*

1892   Hey, William Henry,
         200, *New Kent-road, S.E.*

1834   *HEYWOOD, JAMES, M.A., F.R.S., F.G.S.
         (*Honorary Vice-President and Trustee*),
         26,*Palace-gardens,Kensington,W.; Athenæum Club,S.W.*

1886   Hibbert, H. F.,
         8, *Park-road, Chorley, Lancashire.*

1869   Hickson, Sir J., J.P. (*General Manager Grand Trunk Ry.*),
         Grand Trunk Railway, Montreal, Canada.

1892   Higgs, Henry, LL.B.,
         164, *Brixton-hill, S.W.*

1878   *Hill, Frederick Morley,
         22, *Richmond-road, Barnsbury, N.*

1878   Hillingdon, The Right Hon. Lord,
         Camelford House, Park-lane, W.

1890   Hinde, Frederick,
         63, *Leopold-street, Leeds.*

1884   Hoare, Alfred,
         37, *Fleet-street, E.C.*

1879   Hoare, H. N. Hamilton,
         37, *Fleet-street, E.C.*

1870   *Hoare, Henry,
         22, *Bryanston-square, W.*

1889   Hogg, Quintin (Alderman),
         5, *Cavendish-square, W.*

1892   Hole, James,
         1, *Great College-street, S.W.*

1888   Hollams, John,
         52, *Eaton-square, S.W.*

1888   Hollington, Alfred J.,
         Aldgate, London, E.

1884   Hollond, John Robert,
         Reform Club, S.W.

Year of Election.	
1891	Hooker, Sir Joseph Dalton, K.C.S.I., F.R.S., &c., *The Camp, Sunningdale.*
1879	Hooper, George Norgate, *Elmleigh, Hayne-road, Beckenham, Kent.*
1878	Hooper, Wynnard, *13, Sumner-place, Onslow-square, S.W.*
1887	Hopkins, John, *Hayes Court, Hayes, Kent.*
1890	Howarth, William, F.R. Hist. S., *102, Malpas-road, Brockley, S.E.*
1888	Howell, Edward J. *Kingston House, Caterham Valley, Surrey.*
1883	Howell, Francis Buller, *2, Middle Temple-lane, E.C.*
1883	Howell, George, M.P., *Hampden House, Ellingham-road, Shepherd's Bush, W.*
1864	Hudson, Thomas, *22, Sudbourne-road, Brixton-hill, S.W.*
1878	Hughes, John, *3, West-street, Finsbury-circus, E.C.*
1872	Humphreys, George, M.A., F.I.A., *79, Pall Mall, S.W.*
1874	HUMPHREYS, NOEL ALGERNON, *Census Office, Charles-street, Westminster, S.W.*
1883	Hunt, Richard Aldington, A.I.A., *Moor-street, Birmingham.*
1888	Hunter, George Burton, *Wallsend-on-Tyne.*
1885	Hunter, William Alfred, LL.D., M.P., *2, Brick-court, Temple, E.C.*
1857	Hurst, George, *King's Brook House, St. Mary's, Bedford.*
1890	Huth, Ferdinand M., *12, Tokenhouse-yard, E.C.*
1888	Hyde, Clarendon G., B.L., *4, Pump-court, Temple, E.C.*
1887	Hyde, Henry Barry, *5, Eaton-rise, Ealing, W.*
1874	*Ingall, William Thomas Fitzherbert Mackenzie, *6, Drapers'-gardens, E.C.*
1869	*Inglis, Cornelius, M.D., *Athenæum Club, S.W.*
1888	*Ionides, Alexander A., *1, Holland Park, W.*

Year of Election.	
1887	Irvine, Somerset William D'Arcy, J.P., *Equitable Life Office of United States, Brisbane.*
1864	*Ivey, George Pearse, 39, *Denmark-villas, West Brighton.*
1885	Jackson, Henry, 158, *The Common, Peckham Rye, S.E.*
1880	*Jackson, The Right Hon. William Lawies, M.P., *Chapelallerton, Leeds.*
1879	Jamieson, George Auldjo, 37, *Drumsheugh-gardens, Edinburgh.*
1872	JANSON, FREDERICK HALSEY, F.L S., 41, *Finsbury-circus, E.C.*
1878	Jeans, J. Stephen, *Victoria Mansions, Victoria-street, Westminster, S.W.*
1890	Jepson, John,
1881	*Jersey, The Right Hon. the Earl of, P.C., 3, *Great Stanhope-street, W.*
1892	Johnson, Charles Henry, B.A., 4, *Parkhurst-road, Bowes Park, N.*
1881	Johnson, Edwin Eltham, 16, *Albany-villas, West Brighton.*
1891	Johnson, George, 113, *Victoria-road, Darlington.*
1888	Johnson, John Grove, 23, *Cross-street, Finsbury, E.C.*
1880	Johnson, Walter, *Rounton Grange, Northallerton.*
1872	Johnston, Francis John, *Lamas, Chislehurst.*
1891	Johnston, Robert M., F.L.S.,(*Government Statist of Tasmania*), *Hobart, Tasmania.*
1888	Johnston, Thomas, *Broomsleigh-park, Seal, Sevenoaks.*
1878	Johnstone, Edward, *Nightingale-lane, Clapham-common, S.W.*
1884	*Jones, Edwin, J. P., 141, *Cannon-street, E.C.*
1878	Jones, Henry R. Bence, B.A., *Board of Trade, Whitehall-gardens, S.W.*
1874	Jones, Herbert, 15, *Montpelier-row, Blackheath, S.E.*

Year of Election	
1888	Jones, J. Mortimer,
	153, *Highbury New-park, N.*
1887	Jones, John Walter,
	58, *Cheapside, E.C.*
1887	Jones, Lewis Davies,
1877	Jones, Theodore Brooke,
	70, *Gracechurch-street, E.C.*
1888	*Jordan, William Leighton,
	25, *Jermyn-street, S.W.*
1858	Jourdan, Francis,
	14, *Gledhow-gardens, South Kensington, S.W.*
1890	Joyner, Robert Batson,
	Poona, India.
1889	Justican, Edwin, F.I.A.,
	St. Mildred's House, Poultry, E C.
1873	Kay, Duncan James,
	Drumpark, Dumfries, N.B.
1877	Kealy, James William,
	26, *Moorgate-street, E.C.*
1885	Keen, William Brock,
	3, *Church-court, Old Jewry, E.C.*
1874	Kelly, Charles, M.D., F.R.C.P.,
	Worthing, Sussex.
1884	Kelly, Edward Festus,
	51, *Great Queen-street, Lincoln's-inn-fields, W.C.*
1867	Kelly, Edward Robert, A.M.,
	51, *Great Queen-street, Lincoln's-inn-fields, W.C.*
1883	KELTIE, JOHN SCOTT, F.R.G.S.,
	52, *Cromwell-avenue, Highgate, N.*
1884	Kemp, John,
	46, *Cannon-street, E.C.*
1889	Kempson, William (Alderman),
	Leicester.
1884	*KENNEDY, CHARLES MALCOLM, C.B.,
	Foreign Office, S.W., and 27, *Kensington-gate, W.*
1886	Kennedy, John Gordon,
	Foreign Office. S.W.
1878	Kennedy, J. Murray,
	New University Club, St. James's-street, S.W.
1881	*Kennett-Barrington, Sir V. Hunter, M.A., LL.M.,
	65, *Albert Hall Mansions, S.W.*

Year of Election.	
1883	*Keynes, John Neville, M.A., D.Sc. 6, *Harvey-road, Cambridge.*
1887	Kidd, Benjamin, *Inland Revenue Office, Somerset House,* W.C.
1884	Kimber, Henry, M.P., 79, *Lombard-street,* E.C.
1852	Kimberley, The Right Honourable the Earl of, M.A., P.C., 35, *Lowndes-square,* S.W.
1883	*King, Bolton, B.A., *Toynbee Hall,* 28, *Commercial-street,* E.
1888	King, John, F.S.A.A., 59, *St. Thomas's-road, Chorley, Lancashire.*
1884	Kirby, Horace Woodburn, F.C.A., 19, *Birchin-lane,* E.C.
1888	*Kitson, Sir James, Bart., M.P., J.P., *Gledhow Hall, Leeds.*
1889	Kloetgen, W. J. H., 16, *Watling-street.* E.C.
1889	Klugh, Arthur George, F.S.A.A., 3, *Newgate-street,* E.C.
1878	*Kusaka, Yoshio, *First National Bank, Tokio, Japan.*
1885	Latham, Baldwin, M. Inst. C.E., 7, *Westminster-chambers,* S.W.
1892	Latham, Stanley A., A.C.A., 6, *Adelphi-chambers,* W.C.
1874	Lawes, Sir John Bennett, Bart., LL.D., F.R.S., F.C.S., *Rothamsted-park, St. Albans.*
1878	Lawrence, Alexander Macclesfield, 18, *St. Helen's-place,* E.C.
1891	Lawrence, James, 8, *Tenter-terrace, Morpeth.*
1873	Lawrie, James, F.R.G.S., *Bellefield, Lanark, N.B.*
1873	LAWSON, ROBERT, LL.D. (*Inspector-General of Army Hospitals*), 20, *Lansdowne-road, Notting-hill,* W.
1891	Lawson, Robertson, 34, *Old Broad-street,* E.C.
1890	Lawson, William Ramage, 57, *Fitzjohn's-avenue, Hampstead,* N.W.
1883	*Leadam, Isaac Saunders, M.A., 1, *The Cloisters, Temple,* E.C., *and Reform Club,* S.W.

Year of Election.	
1890	Leakey, James, 256, *Burdett-road, E.*
1886	Leathes, Stanley M., *Trinity College, Cambridge.*
1883	Lee, Henry, *Reform Club, S.W.*
1886	*Lee, Sir Joseph C., *Mosley-street, Manchester.*
1884	Lee, William, *Fairlands, Worplesdon, Guildford, Surrey.*
1879	*Leete, Joseph, 36, *St. Mary-at-hill, E.C., & Eversden, S. Norwood-park.*
1877	LEFEVRE, THE RIGHT HON. GEORGE SHAW, M.P., M.A., J.P. (*Honorary Vice-President*), 18, *Bryanston-square, W.*
1877	*Leggatt, Daniel, LL.D., 5, *Raymond-buildings, Gray's-inn, W.C.*
1880	Leighton, Stanley, M.P., *Sweeney Hall, Oswestry, Salop.*
1887	Leitch, Alexander, 17, *King William-street, E.C.*
1892	Leon, Herbert Samuel, M.P., *Bletchley Park, Bletchley, Bucks.*
1888	*Le Poer-Trench, Col. The Hon. W., R.E., J.P., 3, *Hyde Park-gardens, W.*
1887	*Le Roy-Lewis, Herman, B.A. (*Trinity College, Cambridge*), *Westbury House, Petersfield, Hants.*
1889	Lescher, Herman, 6, *Clement's-lane, Lombard-street, E.C.*
1862	Lewis, Robert, 1, *Bartholomew-lane, E.C.*
1888	*Liberty, A. Lasenby, 13, *Cornwall-terrace, Regent's-park, N.W.*
1877	Ligertwood, Thomas, M.D., F.R.C.S., *Royal Hospital, Chelsea, S.W.*
1884	*Lines, William Edward, c/o *R. S. Lines, Noel House, Hertford.*
1892	Llewelyn, Sir John T. D., Bart., *Penllergare, Swansea.*
1878	Lloyd, Thomas, 20, *Bucklersbury, E.C.*
1879	Lloyd, Wilson, M.P., F.R.G.S., *Myvod House, Wood-green, Wednesbury.*
1888	LOCH, CHARLES S., B.A. (*Vice-President*), *Hedge Row Cottage, Queen Anne's-gardens, Bedford-park.*
1882	*Longstaff, George Blundell, M.A., M.D., F.R.C.P., *Highlands, Putney Heath, S.W.*
1888	Lord, John, 54, *Springfield-road, South Hampstead, N.W.*

1876 | *Lornie, John Guthrie, J.P. (*of Birnam and Pitcastle*),
Rosemount, Kirkcaldy, N.B.

1892 | Lough, Thomas, M.P.,
Bedford Park.

1834 | Lovelace, The Right Honourable the Earl of, F.R.S.,
East Horsley-park, Ripley, Surrey.

1886 | *Low, Malcolm,
22, Roland-gardens, S.W.

1889 | Lowles, John,
Hill-crest, Darenth-road, Stamford-hill, N.

1865 | LUBBOCK, THE RIGHT HON. SIR JOHN, BART., M.P., F.R.S.
(*Trustee*),
High Elms, Beckenham, Kent.

1878 | Lucas, Sir Thomas, Bart., J.P.,
37, Great George-street, Westminster, S.W.

1885 | Luckie, David Mitchell, J.P.,
Wellington, New Zealand.

1875 | *Mabson, Richard Rous
20, Bucklersbury, E.C.

1873 | *Macandrew, William, J.P.,
Westwood House, near Colchester.

1873 | McArthur, Alexander, M.P.,
79, Holland-park, W.

1890 | McAuslane, James (*Dunster House, Mincing-lane, E.C.*),
Glenrose, Balham Park-road, S.W.

1891 | MacBrayne, John Burns,
Lilybank House, Hillhead, Glasgow.

1884 | McCabe, William, LL.B., F.I.A.,
17, Clarence-square, Toronto, Canada.

1888 | McCankie, James,
34, St. Andrew's-square, Edinburgh.

1867 | M'Clean, Frank.
Rusthall House, Tunbridge Wells.

1892 | McCleery, James C.,
11, Dale-street, Liverpool.

1873 | McDermott, Edward,
Hill Side, Grove-park, Camberwell, S.E.

1887 | Macdonald, Andrew J.,
40, Threadneedle-street, E.C.

1872 | Macdonell, John,
Room 183, The Royal Courts of Justice, Strand, W.C.

Year of Election.	
1873	*McEwen, Laurence T.,
	c/o. R. A. McLean, 1, Queen Victoria-street, E.C.
1890	McKay, Andrew Davidson,
	13, York-street, Liverpool.
1886	*Mackenzie, Colin, F.R.G.S.,
1878	McKewan, William,
	Elmfield, Bickley, Kent.
1876	*McLean, Robert Allan, F.R.G.S.,
	1, Queen Victoria-street. E.C.
1863	*Maclure, John William, M.P., J.P., D.L.,
	Carlton Club; The Home, Whalley Range, Manchester.
1888	McNiel, Henry
	5, Cross-street, Manchester.
1875	Macpherson, Hugh Martin, F.R.C.S. (Inspector-General),
	14, St. James's-square, S.W.
1887	Macpherson, Walter Charles Gordon,
	Howrah, E.I.R., Bengal, India.
1883	Macqueen, Robert Davidson Barkly,
	20, Upper Addison-gardens, Kensington, W.
1882	MacRosty, Alexander,
	13, King's Arms-yard, E.C.; West Bank, Esher.
1889	McVail, John C., M.D., &c.,
	2, Strathallan-terrace, Dowanhill, Glasgow.
1891	Maidment, Thomas,
	1, Gloucester-terrace, Southsea.
1887	Makower, Maurice,
	11, Randolph-crescent, Maida Vale, W.
1887	Malleson, Frank R.,
	Dixton Manor House, Winchcombe, Cheltenham.
1887	Mann, William Edward,
	23, Jewin-street, E.C.
1884	*Manson, Frederick William,
	Wellfield, Muswell Hill, N.
1888	Manuel, James,
	c/o The London and Provincial Bank, Cardiff.
1877	*Maple, Sir John Blundell, M.P.,
	8, Clarence-terrace, Regent's-park, N.W.
1889	Marks, Harry H.,
	Loudoun Hall, N.W.
1875	Marsh, Alfred,
	85, Gracechurch-street, E.C.
1880	*Marshall, Professor Alfred, M.A.,
	Balliol Croft, Madingley-road, Cambridge.
1887	Marshall, W. Bayley, M.Inst.C.E., M.Inst.M.F.,
1887	Martin, James,
	4, King-street, Cheapside, E.C.

Year of Election.	
1874	*MARTIN, JOHN BIDDULPH, M.A., F.Z.S. (*Trustee and Foreign Hon. Secretary*), 17, *Hyde-park-gate, S.W.*
1872	*MARTIN, RICHARD BIDDULPH, M.P.. M.A. (*Treasurer*), 68, *Lombard-street, E.C., and Chislshurst.*
1876	*Martin, Thomas Jaques, 84, *Collins-street West, Melbourne, Victoria.*
1879	Martin, Waldyve Alex. Hamilton, *The Upper Hall, Ledbury, Herefordshire.*
1884	Mason, William Arthur, 81a, *Colmore-row, Birmingham.*
1875	*Mathers, John Shackleton, *Hanover House, Leeds, Yorkshire.*
1883	Mathieson, Frederic Coxhead, *Beechworth, Hampstead, N.W.*
1891	Maxwell, Robert George, *P.O. Box, 299. Cape Town.*
1882	Medhurst, John Thomas, *Clay-hill, White Hart-lane, Tottenham.*
1888	*Medley, George Webb, 21, *Park-street, Park-lane, W.*
1853	*Meikle, James, F.I.A., 6, *St. Andrew's-square, Edinburgh.*
1890	Merriman, Hon. John Xavier, *Cape Town, Cape of Good Hope.*
1884	Merton, Zachary, 18, *Chesham-place, S.W.*
1873	Millar, William Henry, *Cleveland Lodge, New Park-road, Brixton-hill, S.W.*
1890	Miller, Gordon William (*Admiralty, Spring Gardens, S.W.*), 37, *Granville-park, Lewisham, S.E.*
1877	Miller, Robert Ferguson, *Ramsden-square, Barrow-in-Furness.*
1879	Miller, William, 67, *Queen Victoria-street, E.C.*
1888	Mills, Sir Charles, K.C.M.G., C.B., 7, *Albert Mansions, Victoria-street, S.W.*
1889	Mills, Major Henry Farnsby, *Junior United Service Club, Charles-street, S.W.*
1892	Milner, Alfred, *Inland Revenue Office, Somerset House, Strand, W.C.*
1882	Milnes, Alfred, M.A , 22a, *Goldhurst-terrace, S. Hampstead, N.W.*
1874	*Mocatta, Frederick D., F.R.G.S., 9, *Connaught-place, W.*
1878	Moffat, Robert J., *Cherry Hinton Hall, near Cambridge.*
1888	*Molloy, William R. J., M.R.I.A. (*National Education Board*), 17, *Brookfield-terrace, Donnybrook, Dublin.*

Year of Election.	
1879	Moore, Alfred, C.E., *Queen's Chambers, 2, Ridgfield, Manchester.*
1887	Moore, Arthur Chisholm, *28, Essex-street, Strand, W.C.*
1874	Moore, Charles Kendall, *137, Brockley-road, Lewisham-road, S.E.*
1878	*Moore, John Byers Gunning, *Loymount, Cookstown, Ireland.*
1874	*Morris, James, M.D., F.R.C.S., *13, Somers-place, Hyde-park-square, W.*
1888	Morris, John (17, *Throgmorton-avenue, E.C.*), *13, Park-street, Grosvenor-square, W.*
1891	Morrison, Rev. William Douglas, *6, Heathfield-road, Wandsworth-common, S.W.*
1877	Mort, William, *1, Stanley-crescent, Notting-hill, W.*
1885	*Mosley, Tonman, *Bangors, Iver, Uxbridge.*
1847	*Mouat, Frederic John, M.D., F.R.C.S., LL.D. (*Honorary Vice-President*), *12, Durham-villas, Kensington, W.*
1886	Mowbray, Robert Gray Cornish, M.P. *10, Little Stanhope-street, S.W.*
1886	Moxon, Thomas B., *Manchester and County Bank Limited, Manchester.*
1889	Muir, Robert, jun., *Clydesdale, Wolseley-road, Crouch-end, N.*
1888	Muirhead, Henry James, *Oakwood, Farquhar-road, Upper Norwood, S.E.*
1880	Mulhall, Michael George, *Standard Office, Buenos Ayres.*
1890	Mumby, Bonner Harris, M.D., *Portsmouth.*
1878	*Mundella, The Right Hon. Anthony John, M.P., F.R.S. *16, Elvaston-place, Queen's-gate, S.W.*
1891	Murphy, Shirley Foster, M.R.C.S., *41, Queen Anne-street, Cavendish-square, W.*
1878	Murray, Adam, *Hazeldean, Kersal, Manchester*
1890	Musgrave, James, *Brookland, Heaton, Bolton.*
1892	Naoroji, Dadabhai, M.P., *National Liberal Club, S.W.*
1888	Narraway, W. F., *Crooms Hill House, Greenwich, S.E.*

Year of Election.	
1889	Nash, William, M.D., M.R.C.S. (*Brigade-Surgeon*), 18, *Victoria-street, S.W.*
1878	*Nathan, Henry, *Dashwood House, New Broad-street, E.C.*
1854	Neild, Alfred, *Mayfield Print Works, Manchester.*
1869	NEISON, FRANCIS GUSTAVUS PAULUS, F.I.A., 98, *Adelaide-rd., S. Hampstead, & 19, Abingdon-st., S.W.*
1885	Nelson, Edward Montague, J.P., *Hanger Hill House, Ealing, W.*
1877	Nevill, Charles Henry, 11, *Queen Victoria-street, E.C.*
1862	Newbatt, Benjamin, F.I.A., F.R.G.S., 15, *St. James's-square, S.W.*
1883	Newmarch, Mrs. Elizabeth, *Mulnanth, 5, Harrold-road, Upper Norwood, S.E.*
1889	Newsholme, Arthur, M.D., 15, *College-road, Brighton.*
1889	Newton, Henry William (Alderman), 2, *Ellison-place, Newcastle-on-Tyne.*
1878	Nicholson, Professor J. Shield, M.A., D.Sc., *University of Edinburgh.*
1858	Nightingale, Miss Florence, 10, *South-street, Park-lane, W.*
1877	Nix, Samuel Dyer, F.C.A., 3, *King-street, Cheapside, E.C.*
1871	*Noble, Benjamin, F.R.A.S., *North-Eastern Bank, Newcastle-on-Tyne.*
1883	Norfolk, J. Ernest Walter,
1877	Norman, H.E. General Sir Henry Wylie, K.C.B., G.C.M.G. (*Governor of Queensland*), *Brisbane, Queensland.*
1878	Northbrook, The Right Hon. the Earl of, G.C.S.I., D.C.L., 4, *Hamilton-place, Piccadilly, W.*
1878	Notthafft, Theodor, *c/o Discount Bank, St. Petersburg.*
1888	Oakley, Sir Henry (*General Manager, G.N.R.*), 37, *Chester-terrace, Regent's-park, N.W.*
1891	Oates, John, F.S.A.A., 10, *Saltoun-road, Brixton, S.W.*
1884	Odgers, William Blake, LL.D., 4, *Elm-court, Temple, E.C.; & Fitzjohn's-avenue, N.W.*

Year of Election.

1880	*Oelsner, Isidor,
1862	Ogbourne, Charles Henry, A.I.A. 29, *Dalhousie-square, Calcutta.*
1885	OGLE, WILLIAM, M.A., M.D., F.R.C.P., &c. *General Register Office, Somerset House, W.C.*
1885	*Oldham, John, *River Plate Telegraph Company, Montevideo.*
1884	Oldroyd, Mark, M.P., *Hyrstlands, Dewsbury, Yorkshire.*
1892	Onslow, The Right Hon. the Earl of, G.C.M.G., 7, *Richmond-terrace, S.W.*
1878	Oppenheim, Henry, 16, *Bruton-street, Bond-street, W.*
1877	Ormond, Richard, 24, *Grainger-street West, Newcastle-on-Tyne.*
1889	Oung, Moung Hla, 45, *Lansdowne-row, Calcutta.*
1887	Owen, Evan F., A.I.A., *Office of Government Statist, Melbourne, Victoria.*
1887	*Page, Edward D., (*Box* 3382,) c/o *Faulkner, Page, & Co., New York City, U.S.A.*
1886	Pain, James, *St. Mary's-street, Ely.*
1866	*PALGRAVE, ROBERT HARRY INGLIS, F.R.S., *Belton, Great Yarmouth, Norfolk.*
1879	Palmer, George, J.P., *The Acacias, Reading.*
1884	Palmer, Joseph Thomas 8, *Wine Office-court, Fleet-street, E.C.*
1887	Pankhurst, Richard Marsden, LL.D. (5, *New-inn-square, W.C.*), 10, *St. James's-square, Manchester.*
1888	Pannell, William Henry, *Library-chambers, Basinghall-street, E.C.*
1878	Park, David Francis, C.A., F.F.A., A.I.A., 17, *Change-alley, Cornhill, E.C.*
1887	Parker, Archibald, *Camden-wood, Chislehurst, Kent.*
1878	Parry, Thomas, *Grafton-place, Ashton-under-Lyne.*
1879	Partridge, Henry Francis, L.D.S., &c., *Sussex House, Sussex-place, South Kensington, S.W.*

Year of Election.	
1883	Paterson, John, 1, *Walbrook, E.C.*
1888	Pattullo, James Durie, 31, *St. Swithin's-lane, E.C.*
1877	Paul, Henry Moncreiff, 12, *Lansdowne-crescent, Notting-hill, W.*
1878	Paulin, David, 44, *Moray-place, Edinburgh.*
1884	*Peace, Walter, 21, *Finsbury-circus, E.C.*
1857	*Pearson, Professor Charles Henry, M.A., c/o *Lady Pearson, 75, Onslow-square, S.W.*
1880	*Pease, Sir Joseph Whitwell, Bart., M.P., *Hutton Hall, Gisborough, Yorks.*
1876	*Peek, Sir Henry William, Bart., *Wimbledon House, S.W.*
1886	Pembroke, The Right Hon. the Earl of, *Wilton House, Salisbury.*
1880	Pender, Sir John, G.C.M.G., M.P., 18, *Arlington-street, S.W.;* 50, *Old Broad-street, E.C.*
1891	Penn-Lewis, William, 8, *Halford-road, Richmond, Surrey.*
1887	Percival, William, *Constitutional Club, S.W.*
1888	Perratt, William Henry, A.I.A., 193, *The Grove, Hammersmith, W.*
1890	Peters, John Wyatt, *The Gables, Grove-road S., Southsea.*
1883	Petheram, Frederick William, F.C.A., 61, *Gracechurch-street, E.C.*
1886	Peto, Sir Henry, Bart., M.A., *Fleet House, Weymouth.*
1887	Phelps, Major-General Arthur, 23, *Augustus-road, Edgbaston, Birmingham.*
1886	*Phelps, The Rev. Lancelot Ridley, M.A., *Oriel College, Oxford.*
1874	Phené, John Samuel, LL.D., F.S.A., 32, *Oakley-street, S.W.*
1879	Philips, Herbert, 35, *Church-street, Manchester.*
1877	Phillipps, Henry Matthews,
1887	Phillips, Charles H., J.P. (*Registrar-General of Trinidad*), *Court House, Port of Spain, Trinidad.*
1888	Phillips, John Orwell, *Horseferry-road, Westminster, S.W.*
1871	*Pickering, John, F.R.G.S., F.S.A., 86, *Thicket-road, Anerley, S.E.*
1885	Pierrard, Paul, 24, *Coleman-street, E.C.*

Year of Election.	
1878	*Pim, Joseph Todhunter, *Rinnamara, Monkstown, County Dublin.*
1886	Pink, J. Francis, *62, Chandos-street, Strand, W.C.*
1890	Pittar, Thomas J, *H.M. Custom House, E.C.*
1879	Pixley, Francis William, *23, Linden-gardens, W.*
1881	Planck, Charles, M.R.C.S. (*Deputy Surgeon-General*), *Allahabad, India.*
1883	Platt, James, *Rookwood, Hampstead, N.W.*
1861	PLOWDEN, SIR WM. CHICELE, K.C.S.I. (5, *Park-crescent, Portland-place, W.*); *Wyke Hall, Gillingham, Dorset.*
1888	Plumb, Benjamin M.,
1869	Pochin, Henry Davis, J.P., *Bodnant Hall, Eglwysbach, R.S.O., Denbighshire.*
1888	Pollard, James, J.P. *Chamber of Commerce, Edinburgh.*
1884	Polson, John, *West Mount Paisley, N.B.*
1891	Pope, Henry Richard,
1891	Potter, Henry, *Folkestone Villa, Elm-grove, Peckham, S.E.*
1879	*POWELL, SIR FRANCIS SHARP, Bart., M.P. (*Horton Old Hall, Bradford*), 1, Cambridge-square, Hyde Park, W.*
1888	Powell, James Heslop, *33, Cornhill, E.C.*
1871	Power, Edward, *6, Crosby-square, E.C.*
1877	*Prance, Reginald Heber, *Frognal, Hampstead, N.W.*
1877	Praschkauer, Maximilian, *109, Fenchurch-street, E.C.*
1867	*Pratt, Robert Lindsay, *80, Bondgate, Darlington.*
1891	Preston, Sydney E., *54, Coleman-street, E.C.*
1888	Price, Henry Sherley, *49, Queen Victoria-street, E.C.*
1887	*PRICE, L. L., M.A., *Oriel College, Oxford.*
1877	PRICE-WILLIAMS, RICHARD, M.INST.C.E., *32, Victoria-street, S.W.*
1887	Probyn, Leslie Charles, *79, Onslow-square, S.W.*
1889	Probyn, Major Clifford, *55, Grosvenor-street, Grosvenor-square, W.*

Year of Election.	
1884	*Proctor, William, 89, *Corporation-street, Manchester.*
1886	Provand, Andrew Dryburgh, M.P., *Lloyd's House, Manchester.*
1871	Puleston, Sir John Henry, 2, *Bank-buildings, Princes-street, E.C.*
1886	Pulley, Joseph, 90, *Piccadilly, W.*
1885	Purvis, Gilbert, *Ingle Neuk, Brackley-road, Beckenham, Kent.*
1874	Quain, Sir Richard, Bart., M.D., F.R.S., F.R.C.P., 67, *Harley-street, W.*
1888	Quirk, William Henry, 9, *Gracechurch-street, E C.*
1883	Rabbidge, Richard, F.C.A., 32, *Poultry, E.C.*
1872	*Rabino, Joseph (*Chief Manager*), *Imperial Bank of Persia, Teheran.*
1888	*Radcliffe, Sir David, J.P., *Thurstaston Hall, near Birkenhead.*
1858	*Radstock, The Right Honourable Lord, *Mayfield, Woolston, Southampton.*
1888	Rae, George, *Redcourt, Birkenhead.*
1885	RAE, JOHN, M.A.(*Vice President*), 15, *Werter-road, Putney, S.W.*
1887	Raffalovich, His Excellency Arthur, 19, *Avenue Hoche, Paris.*
1877	Raikes, Lieut.-Col. George Alfred, F.S.A., F.R. Hist. Soc., 63, *Belsize-park, Hampstead, N.W.*
1860	Ramsay, Alexander Gillespie, F.I.A., *Canada Life Assurance Co., Hamilton, Canada West.*
1885	Randell, James S., 19, *Alfred-street, Bath*

Year of Election.	
1880	Rankin, James, M.P., 85, *Ennismore-gardens, Prince's Gate, S.W.*
1881	Raper, Sir Robert George, *Chichester.*
1884	Raphael, Alfred, 87, *Alexandra-road, N.W.*
1859	Rathbone, P. H., *Greenbank Cottage, Liverpool.*
1878	Rathbone, William, M.P., 18, *Prince's-gardens, Prince's-gate, S.W.*
1884	*Ravenscroft, Francis, *Birkbeck Bank, Chancery-lane, W.C.*
1874	*RAVENSTEIN, ERNEST GEORGE, F.R.G.S., 91, *Upper Tulse-hill, Brixton, S.W.*
1889	Rawcliffe, Henry, J.P. (Alderman), *Beechwood, Rock Ferry, Birkenhead.*
1886	Rawlins, Frederick, *Southport, Queensland.*
1877	*Rawlins, Thomas, 45, *King William-street, E.C.*
1835	RAWSON, SIR RAWSON W., K.C.M.G., C.B. (*Honorary Vice-President*), 68, *Cornwall-gardens, Queen's-gate, S.W.*
1888	Read, Thomas William, 80, *Castle-street, Liverpool.*
1890	Reade, Herbert, 10, *Herbert Crescent, Hans-place, S.W.*
1889	*Reed, Thomas, F.C.A., 63, *King-street, South Shields.*
1888	Reid, Herbert Lloyd, *Ardentinney, Balham Park-road, Balham, S.W.*
1888	Rew, Robert Henry, 8, *Wharton-road, West Kensington, W.*
1886	Rhens, Robert, 20, *Fussett-square, Dalston, E.*
1888	Rhodes, George Webber, 131, *Wool Exchange, E.C.*
1879	Rhodes, John George, 46, *St. George's-road, S.W.*
1890	Richards, Fred., 29, *Northampton-square, E.C.*
1892	Richards, Westley, J.P., *Ashwell, Oakham, Rutland.*
1892	Richardson, Hubert, *Biddick Hall, Tyne Dock, Co. Durham*
1888	Richardson, J. H., 8, *Finch-lane, Cornhill, E.C.*
1888	Richmond, Edwin, *Gladstone-buildings, Sheffield.*

Year of Election.	
1891	Ridge, Samuel H., B.A., F.R.G.S., F.R. Hist. S. 257, *Victoria Parade, E. Melbourne, Victoria.*
1878	Ripon, The Most Hon. the Marquess of, K.G., F.R.S, &c., 9, *Chelsea Embankment, S.W.*
1889	Rippon, Robert Whitfield, LL.B., 2, *The Cloisters, Temple, E.C.*
1892	Rivington, Francis Hansard, 44, *Connaught-square, W.*
1887	Roberts, Arthur Herbert, F.C.A., F R.G.S., *Caledonian Chambers, St. Mary-street, Cardiff.*
1882	Roberts, Edward, F.R.A.S. (*Nautical Almanac Office*), 3, *Verulam-buildings, Gray's Inn, W.C.*
1890	Roberts, Sir William, M.D., F.R.S., 8, *Manchester-square, W.*
1885	Robertson, Thomas Stewart, 1, *Market-bldngs., Collins-street, W., Melbourne, Victoria.*
1887	Robinson, Henry James, *St. John's Villa, Woodlands, Isleworth, W.*
1885	Rodger, Adam Kier, 81, *Renfield-street, Glasgow.*
1886	Roechling, Herman A., A.M. Inst. C.E., 23, *Highfield-street, Leicester.*
1880	*Ronald, Byron L., 14, *Upper Phillimore-gardens, W.*
1878	*Rosebery, The Right Hon. the Earl of, LL.D., F.R.S., 38, *Berkeley-square, W.*
1892	Ross, Charles Edmonstone, 2, *Raymond-buildings, Gray's-inn, W.C.*
1891	Ross, Frederick William Forbes, M.B , C.M., *New Brighton, Cheshire.*
1865	Ruck, George Thomas, *The Hawthorns, Dorville-road, Lee, S.E.*
1890	Ruffer, Marc Armand, M.A., M.D.. B.Sc., 19, *Iddesleigh Mansions, Westminster, S.W.*
1888	Rusher, Edward Arthur, F.I.A., 142, *Holborn Bars, E.C.*
1886	Russell, Arthur B., A.C.A., 11, *Ludgate-hill, E.C.; 20, Beacon-hill, Camden-rd., N.*
1878	Russell, Richard F., 8, *John-street, Adelphi, W.C.*
1887	Russell, Thomas, C.M.G., 59, *Eaton-square, S.W.*
1890	Rutherford, Frederick William, 12, *King-street, Cheapside, E.C.*
1878	Rutherford-Elliot, J. G., *Elphinstone, Tyndall's Park-road, Clifton, Bristol.*

Year of Election.	
1887	Sacré, Alfred Louis, C.E., 60, *Queen Victoria-street, E.C.*
1873	*Salisbury, The Most Hon. the Marquess of, K.G., P.C., F.R.S., 20, *Arlington-street, W.*
1881	Salmon, James, *Tower Chambers, Finsbury Pavement, E.C.*
1875	*Salomons, Sir David Lionel, Bart., J.P., *Broom-hill, Tunbridge Wells.*
1876	Salt, Thomas, M.P., *Weeping Cross, Stafford.*
1892	Samuel, Charles, 176, *Sutherland-avenue, Harrow-road, W.*
1868	Samuelson, Sir Bernhard, Bart., M.P., F.R.S., 56, *Prince's-gate, Hyde-park, S.W.*
1888	Sandell, Edward, F.C.A., 181, *Queen Victoria-street, E.C.*
1889	Sandell, Frederic David, 181, *Queen Victoria-street, E.C.*
1891	Sarda, Pandit Har Bilas, B.A., M.R.A.S., *Government College, Ajmere, India.*
1886	Sauerbeck, Augustus, 4, *Moorgate-street-buildings, E.C.*
1877	Saunders, Charles Edward, M.D., *County Asylum, Hayward's Heath, Sussex.*
1852	Saunders, James Ebenezer, F.G.S., J.P., 9, *Finsbury-circus, E.C.*
1888	Sawyer, Lucian Willard,
1887	*Scarth, Leveson, M.A., *Keverstone, Manor-road, Bournemouth.*
1883	Schidrowitz, Samuel, 102, *Oxford-gardens, Notting-hill, W.*
1877	Schiff, Charles, 22, *Lowndes-square, S.W.*
1891	Schloss, David F., 1, *Knaresborough-place, Cromwell-road, S.W.*
1891	Schooling, John Holt, 19, *Abingdon-street, Westminster, S.W.*
1883	*Schwann, John Frederick, *Oakfield, Wimbledon, S.W.*, and 6, *Moorgate-street, E.C.*
1883	Sclanders, Alexander, 10, *Austin Friars, E.C.*
1892	Scofield, Ernest Frank, B.A., 65, *Carlyle-road, Cambridge.*
1885	Scott, James Henry, *St. Mildred's House, Poultry, E.C.*
1885	Scott, Rev. John Davidson, M.A., *The Vicarage, Cholmondeley, Malpas.*
1888	Scotter, Charles (*General Manager, L. & S.W. R.*), *Waterloo Station, Waterloo-road, S.E.*

Year of Election.	
1887	Seaton, Edward, M.D., Lond., F.R.C.P., 56, *North-side, Clapham-common, S.W.*
1880	*Seeley, Charles, M.P., *Sherwood Lodge, Nottingham.*
1886	Selwyn, Captain Charles W.. 21, *Lowndes-square, S.W.*
1886	Seyd, Ernest J. F., 38, *Lombard-street, E.C.*
1878	Seyd, Richard, 38, *Lombard-street, E.C.*
1892	Shand, Hans George Leslie, *Treasury, Whitehall, S.W.*
1888	Shaw, James Charles, 35, *Leinster-gardens, Hyde Park, W.*
1879	Shepheard, Wallwyn Poyer Burnett, M.A., 15, *Old Square, Lincoln's-inn, W.C.*
1885	Sherwin, Joseph Henry, 16, *Whitehall-place, S.W.*
1888	Shillcock, Joshua, B.A., *Bank of England, West Branch, Burlington-gardens, W.*
1888	Shuttleworth, Thomas G., *Queen's Insurance-buildings, Church-street, Sheffield.*
1871	Sidgwick, Professor Henry, M.A., *Trinity College, Cambridge.*
1886	Silver, Stephen William, 3, *York-gate, Regent's-park, N.W.*
1878	Simmonds, G. Harvey, 1, *Whitehall, S.W.*
1892	*Sinclair, Captain John, M.P., 76, *Jermyn-street, S.W.*
1850	Singer, Charles Douglas, *Silverton, Silver-street, Enfield Town.*
1886	Sitwell, Sir George Reresby, Bart., M.P., J.P., *Renishaw Hall, Chesterfield.*
1882	Skinner, Charles Weeding, *Hill Crest, Theydon Bois, Essex.*
1881	Skrine, Francis Henry, J.P., *c/o Messrs. King, Hamilton, and Co., Calcutta, India.*
1888	Slade, Alfred Thomas, *Wardrobe-chambers, Queen Victoria-street, E.C.*
1888	Slade, Francis William, 17, *Victoria-street, Westminster, S.W.*
1883	Sly, Richard Stevens, F.R.G.S., *Fern Villa, Queen's-road, New Cross Gate, S.E.*
1869	Smee, Alfred Hutcheson, M.R.C.S., *The Grange, Wallington, Surrey.*
1886	*Smith, Arthur Manley, 29, *Lincoln's Inn-fields, W.C.*
1878	*Smith, Charles, M.R.I.A., F.G.S., Assoc. Inst. C.E., *c/o Dr. Gilbert, F.R.S., Harpenden, St. Albans.*

Year of Election.	
1888	*Smith, The Hon. Sir Donald A., K.C.M.G., LL.D., 1157, *Dorchester-street, Montreal, Canada.*
1871	Smith, E. Cozens, 1, *Old Broad-street, E.C.*
1889	Smith, George Armitage, M.A., 26, *Regent's Park-road, N.W.*
1878	*Smith, George, LL.D., C.I.E., *Serampore House, Napier-road, Edinburgh.*
1888	Smith, H. Llewellyn, B.A., B.Sc. 49, *Beaumont-square, E.*
1877	Smith, Howard S., A.I.A., F.F.A. 37, *Bennett's Hill, Birmingham.*
1878	*Smith, James, *South Indian Railway, Trichinopoly, Madras Presidency.*
1891	Smith, James Parker, M.P., *Jordanhill, Partick, N.B.*
1877	Smith, John, 8, *Old Jewry, E.C.*
1883	Smith, Samuel, M.P., 7, *Delahay-street, Westminster, and Reform Club, S.W.*
1890	Smith, William Alexander, 21, *Castlereagh-street, Sydney, New South Wales.*
1888	Smith, Walter J., 19, *West Smithfield, E.C.*
1887	Snell, Arthur Henry, 27, *Mincing-lane, E.C.*
1855	Sowray, John Russell, *Office of Woods, Forests, &c.,* 1, *Whitehall-place, S.W.*
1889	Spackman, J. Woolsey. *The Daltons, St. Albans.*
1889	Speirs, Edwin Robert, 8, *Theobalds-road, W.C.*
1891	Spence, James, 20, *Chepstow-place, W.*
1867	*Spencer, Robert James, 175, *King's-road, Southsea.*
1892	Spender, John Alfred, M.A., 29, *Cheyne-walk, S.W.*
1883	Spicer, Albert, *Woodford, Essex, and* 50, *Upper Thames-street, E.C.*
1856	*Sprague, Thomas Bond, M.A., F.I.A., 26, *St. Andrew-square, Edinburgh.*
1872	Spriggs, Joseph, *Foxton, near Market Harborough.*
1882	Stack, Thomas Neville, *Crosby-bldngs., Crosby-square, E.C.,* 1, *St. Andrew-st., Dublin.*
1889	Stanton, Arthur G., 13, *Rood-lane, E.C., & 70, Granville-park, Blackheath, S.E.*
1877	Staples, Sir Nathaniel Alexander, Bart., *Lissan, Cookstown, Tyrone, Ireland.*

Year of Election.	
1880	Stark, James, 17, *King's Arms-yard. E.C.*
1880	Stephens, William Davies, J.P., 4, *Abbotsford-terrace, Newcastle-on-Tyne.*
1882	*Stern, Edward D., 4, *Carlton-house-terrace, S.W.*
1885	Stevens, Marshall, *Highfield House, Urmston, near Manchester.*
1877	Stone, William Alfred, 90, *Cannon-street, E.C.; Hayton, Bramley Hill, Croydon.*
1889	Stow, Harry Vane, *National Liberal Club, Whitehall-place, S.W.*
1865	Strachan, Thomas Young, F.I.A., 88, *Cannon-street, E.C.*
1872	Strachey, General Richard, R.E., C.S.I., F.R.S., 69, *Lancaster-gate, W.*
1880	Strutt, Hon. Frederick, *Milford House, near Derby.*
1891	Stuart, Harold A., *Glenview, Ootacamund, Madras Presidency, India.*
1884	*Sugden, Richard, *The Farre Close, Brighouse, Yorkshire.*
1880	*Summers, William, M.P., *Reform Club, Pall Mall, S.W.*
1881	Sykes, George Samuel, 1, *Grant's-lane, Calcutta, India.*
1859	*Tait, Patrick Macnaghten, F.R.G.S., 37, *Charlotte-street, Portland-place, W.*
1889	Tarling, Charles, *Stoneleigh House, Warltersville-road, Crouch-hill, N.*
1889	Tattersall, William, *Hazelwood, Hale, Cheshire.*
1889	Tayler, Stephen Seaward (Alderman), 151, *Brixton-road, S.W.*
1887	Taylor, R. Whately Cooke, 8, *Spencer-road, Coventry.*
1888	*Taylor, Theodore Cooke, J.P., *Sunny Bank, Batley, Yorkshire.*

Year of Election.	
1884	Tempany, Thomas William, F.R.H.S., 25, *Bedford-row, W.C.*
1888	Temperley, William Angus, jun., 2, *St. Nicholas-buildings, Newcastle-on-Tyne.*
1890	Tenney, John, *Exchequer and Audit Department, Somerset House, W.C.*
1891	Terrey, William. *Sheffield Water Department, Sheffield.*
1888	Theobald, John Wilson, 75, *Palmerston-buildings, E.C.*
1889	Thodey, William Henry, 479, *Collins-street, Melbourne, Victoria.*
1888	Thomas, David Alfred, M.P., *Llanwern, near Newport, Mon.*
1887	Thomas, John, 18, *Wood-street, E.C.*
1879	Thomas, W. Cave, 8, *Fitzroy-street, Fitzroy-square, W.*
1864	*Thompson, Henry Yates, 26a, *Bryanston-square, W.*
1868	Thomson, James, 35, *Nicholas-lane, E.C.*
1871	Thomson, Thomas D., 57, *Moorgate-street, E.C.*
1890	Thring, The Right Hon. Lord, K.C.B., 5, *Queen's Gate-gardens, S.W.*
1889	Tims, James, 6, *Queen Anne-terrace, Battersea-park, S.W.*
1882	Tinker, James, *Hordlecliff, Lymington, Hants.*
1879	Tipping, William, *Oakfield House, Ashton-under-Lyne.*
1889	Touch, George Alexander, 47, *Goldhurst-terrace, N.W.*
1868	*Treatt, Frank Burford, J.P., *Fernmount, Bellenger River, New South Wales.*
1868	Tritton, Joseph Herbert, 54, *Lombard-street, E.C.*
1892	Trobridge, Arthur, *Bloxcidge House, Langley Green, near Birmingham.*
1888	Trotter, John Townley, 27, *Brazennose-street, Manchester.*
1887	Tunley, George, 8, *Foley-avenue, Hampstead, N.W.*
1878	Turnbull, Alexander, 118, *Belsize park-gardens, N.W.*
1890	*Turner, Rev. Harward, B.Sc., F.R.M.S., 27, *Quai d'Austerlitz, Paris.*
1885	Turner, William, *Board of Trade, Cardiff.*

D

Year of Election.	
1892	Tyler, Edgar Alfred, 55, *Charing-cross, S.W.*
1841	Tyndall, William Henry, F.I.A., *Morlands, Oxford-road, Redhill.*
1877	*Urlin, Richard Denny, 22, *Stafford-terrace, Phillimore-gardens, W.*
1888	Van Raalte, Marcus, 22, *Austin Friars, E.C.*
1884	Veevers, Richard, *Woningworth, Fulwood-park, Preston.*
1890	Venn, John, D.Sc., F.R.S. (*Caius College, Cambridge*), *Chine-crescent-road, Bournemouth.*
1889	Venning, Charles Harrison, 22, *Great George-street, S.W.*
1888	Verdin, William Henry, J.P., *Winsford, Cheshire.*
1886	Vernon, The Right Hon. Lord, *Sudbury Hall, Derby.*
1876	Vigers, Robert, 4, *Frederick's-place, Old Jewry, E.C.*
1885	Vincent, Frederick James, A.I.A., 38, *Queen's-road, South Hornsey, N.*
1877	Vine, Sir John Richard Somers, 6, *Adelphi-terrace, W.C.*
1890	Walford, Ernest L., 2, *Shorter's-court, E.C.*
1890	Walkley, William Henry, *Hope House, Elthorne-road, Hornsey Rise, N.*
1868	Wallis, Charles James, 93, *Brecknock-road, Camden-road, N.*
1880	Wallis, E. White, 49, *Clifton-hill, St. John's Wood, N.W.*

Year of Election.	
1888	Walmsley, Frederic, 49, *Hanging Ditch, Manchester.*
1876	Walter, Arthur Fraser, *Finchampstead, Wokingham, Berks.*
1850	Walter, John, 40, *Upper Grosvenor-street, W.*
1879	Wansey, Arthur H., *Sambourne, Stoke Bishop, Bristol.*
1888	Ward, Henry, 103, *Cannon-street, E.C., and Eaton-road, Sutton*
1888	Warren, Reginald Augustus, J.P., *Preston-place, near Worthing.*
1888	Wartnaby, William Wade, *Market Harborough, Leicestershire.*
1886	Waters, Alfred Charles, *General Register Office, Somerset House, Strand, W.C.*
1865	Waterhouse, Edwin, B.A., A.I.A., F.C.A., 44, *Gresham-street, E.C.*
1892	Wates, C. Marshall, 17, *Radford-road, Lewisham, S.E.*
1888	Watson, T. Wilkinson, 183, *West George-street, Glasgow.*
1883	Watson, William Livingstone, 7, *Wetherby-gardens, South Kensington, S.W.*
1885	*Watt, William, 17, *Queen's-road, Aberdeen.*
1888	Webb, Henry Barlow, 7, *Warrior-square-terrace, St. Leonards-on-Sea.*
1887	Weir, Archibald, M.A. *Bendarroch, Ottery St. Mary, Devon.*
1873	*Welby, Sir Reginald Earle, K.C.B., *The Treasury, Whitehall, S.W.*
1874	Welch, Charles, F.S.A., *Guildhall, E.C.* (*Representing the Library Committee of the Corporation of the City of London.*)
1890	Weller, William Hamilton, *Roseleigh, Tolworth, near Surbiton, Surrey.*
1889	Wells-Smith, Henry, A.C.A., 8, *Norfolk-row, Sheffield.*
1855	Welton, Thomas Abercrombie, *Rectory Grove House, Clapham, S.W.*
1879	Wenley, James Adams, *Bank of Scotland, Bank-street, Edinburgh.*
1879	*Westlake, John, Q.C., LL.D., *The River House, 3, Chelsea Embankment, S.W.*
1882	*Whadcoat, John Henry, F.C.A. 18, *Highbury-crescent, N.*
1883	*Whadcoat, William Edward, 112, *Grosvenor-road, Highbury New Park, N.*
1878	Wharton, James, *Edgehill, Netherhall-gardens, FitzJohn's-avenue, N.W.*

Year of Election.	
1887	Whinney, Frederick, 8, *Old Jewry, E.C.*
1859	Whitbread, Samuel, M.P., 10, *Ennismore-gardens, Princes-gate, S.W.*
1887	*White, The Rev. George Cecil, M.A., *Nursling Rectory, Southampton.*
1863	White. Leedham, 25, *Cranley-gardens. South Kensington, S.W.*
1871	White, William, 23, *Wynell-road, Forest-hill, S.E.*
1888	Whitehead, Sir James, Bart., M.P., J.P., D.L. (Alderman), 9, *Cambridge-gate, Regent's-park, N.W.*
1892	Whitelegge, Benjamin A.. M.D., *St. John's, Wakefield.*
1884	Whiteley, William, *Westbourne-grove, Bayswater, W.*
1879	*Whitwill, Mark, J.P., *Bristol.*
1884	Wightman, Charles, 1, *Fenchurch-avenue, E.C.*
1888	Wilkinson, James H.,
1875	Wilkinson, Thomas Read, *Manchester and Salford Bank, Manchester.*
1860	Willans. John Wrigley, *The Woodlands. Kirkstall, Leeds.*
1864	Williams, Frederick Bessant, 46, *Leicester-square, W.C.*
1881	*Williams, Henry Maunder, 188, *New Cross-road, S.E.*
1870	Williams, Henry Reader, 6, *Lime-street, E.C., and The Priory, Hornsey, N.*
1888	*Williams, Robert, Jun., 20, *Birchin-lane, E.C.*
1888	Williamson, John W., 5, *Stone-buildings, Lincoln's Inn, W.C.*
1888	Wills, John Tayler, B.A., F.R.G.S., 273, *Vauxhall Bridge-road, S.W., and Esher, Surrey.*
1891	Wilson, Henry Joseph, M.P., *Osgathorpe Hills, Sheffield.*
1884	Wilson, James (*Deputy Commissioner*), *Shahpur, Panjab, India.*
1874	*Wilson, Robert Porter, 5, *Cumberland-terrace, Regent's-park, N.W.*
1890	Winter, Alexander,
1884	Wishart, G. D., 8, *Livingstone-avenue, Sefton-park, Liverpool.*
1889	Woodford, Ethelbert G., *Pretoria, Transvaal, South African Republic.*

Year of Election.	
1887	Woodhouse, Coventry Archer, 30, *Mincing-lane, E.C.*
1888	Woolfe, Thomas Rodriques, A.C.A., 65, *Watling-street, E.C.*
1838	Woolhouse, Wesley Stoker Barker, F.R.A.S., *Alwyne Lodge, Alwyne-road, Canonbury, N.*
1890	Woollcombe, Robert Lloyd, LL.D., F.I. Inst., M.R.I.A., 14, *Waterloo-road, Dublin.*
1890	Worroll, Charles, *Colonial Mutual Life Office, Adderley-street, Cape Town.*
1878	Worsfold, Rev John Napper, M.A., *Haddlesey Rectory, near Selby, Yorkshire.*
1888	Worsfold, William Basil, M.A., *St. Stephen's Club, S.W.,* and 1, *Elm-court, Temple, E.C.*
1887	Worthington, A. W., B.A., *Old Swinford, Stourbridge.*
1880	Wren, Walter, M.A. 7, *Powis-square, W.*
1879	Yeats, John, LL.D., 7, *Beaufort-square, Chepstow.*
1886	Yerburgh, Robert Armstrong, M.P., 27, *Princes Gate, S.W.*
1888	*Yglesias, Miguel, 2, *Tokenhouse-buildings, E.C.*
1877	*Youll, John Gibson, *Jesmond-road, Newcastle-on-Tyne.*
1882	Young, E. M., 13, *Leadenhall-street, E.C.*

*** *The Executive Committee request that any inaccuracy in the foregoing list may be pointed out to the* ASSISTANT SECRETARY, *and that all changes of address may be notified to him, so that delay in forwarding communications and the publications of the Society may be avoided.*

HONORARY FELLOWS.

HIS ROYAL HIGHNESS THE PRINCE OF WALES, K.G.
Honorary President.

Argentine Republic.

1890. **Buenos Ayres..** FRANCISCO LATZINA, Director General of Statistics; late Astronomer of the Observatory, and late Professor of Mathematics at the University, of Cordoba; Honorary Member of the National Department of Hygiene; Member of the International Statistical Institute, of the Geographical and Statistical Societies of Paris, of the Society of Commercial Geography of Paris, and of the Argentine Geographical Institute, &c.

Austria and Hungary.

1890. .**Vienna** .... KARL THEODOR VON INAMA-STERNEGG, Doctor of Political Economy; President of the Imperial and Royal Central Statistical Commission; Professor at the University.

1877. .... MAX WIRTH, Economist; formerly Director of the Federal Statistical Bureau of Switzerland.

Belgium.

1879. **Brussels** ...... EUGÈNE JANSSENS, Doctor of Medicine; Chief Inspector of the Board of Health of the City of Brussels; President of the Federal Committee of Health of the Brussels District; Member of the Central Statistical Commission and of the Superior Council of Health; Knight of the Belgian Order of Leopold and of the French Legion of Honour; Officer of the Italian Order of SS. Maurice and Lazare; Civic Cross of the 1st Class; Officer of the Academy of France; Associate of the Statistical Society of Paris and of the International Statistical Institute; Member of the Royal Academy of Medicine, and of the Local Medical Commission.

China.

king ...... SIR ROBERT HART, G.C.M.G., LL.D., Inspector-General of Imperial Maritime Customs, China.

Denmark.

penhagen .. VIGAND ANDREAS FALBE - HANSEN, Member of the "Folkething;" Professor of the University of Copenhagen.

.. PETER ANTON SCHLEISNER, Doctor of Medicine, State Councillor; Knight of the Order of the "Dannebroge," and of the Swedish Order of the North Star; President of the Royal Danish Institute of Vaccination; Member of the Royal Danish General Board of Health.

France.

ris .... JACQUES BERTILLON, Doctor of Medicine; Chief of the Statistical Department of the City of Paris; Member of the Superior Council of Statistics; of the Consultative Committee of Public Hygiene of France; and of the Statistical Society of Paris.

,, ... MAURICE BLOCK, Knight of the Legion of Honour, and of Orders of Sweden, Russia, Prussia, Bavaria, Austria and Hungary, Greece, Italy, Spain, and Portugal; Member of the Institute of France, of the Society of Political Economy of Paris, and of many Academies and Scientific Societies.

,, ... ARTHUR CHERVIN, Doctor of Medicine and Surgery; Director of the Paris Institute for Stammerers; Member of the Superior Council of Statistics and of the International Statistical Institute, &c.

,, ... MAXIMIN DELOCHE, Honorary Director of the General Statistics of France; Commander of the Legion of Honour; Officer of the Order of Public Instruction; Commander of the Austrian Order of Francis Joseph; Member of the Institute of France, and of several learned societies.

, ... ALFRED DE FOVILLE, Chief of the Statistical Bureau of the Ministry of Finance; Professor at the National Conservatoire of Arts and Trades (Chair of Industrial Economy and Statistics); Knight of the Legion of Honour; Laureate of the Institute of France; Past President of the Statistical Society of Paris; Member of the International Statistical Institute and of the Superior Council of Statistics.

Germany—*Contd.*

1877. **Strassburg** .. DR. GEORG VON MAYR, Ex-Under Secretary of State in the Imperial Ministry for Alsace-Lorraine; formerly Director of the Royal Statistical Bureau of Bavaria; Associate of the Statistical Society of Paris.

1860. **Munich** .... DR. GEORG KARL LEOPOLD SEUFFERT, formerly Chief Inspector and Director of the Royal Custom-House at Simbach; Knight of the Bavarian Order of St. Michael, 1st Class.

1876. **Frankfort** .... THE PRESIDENT (for the time being) OF THE GEOGRAPHICAL AND STATISTICAL SOCIETY OF FRANKFORT.

Italy.

1879. **Rome** .... GEROLAMO BOCCARDO, Senator; Councillor of State; Doctor of Laws; late Professor at the University and at the Superior Naval School of Genoa; Grand Officer of the Order of SS. Maurice and Lazare; Knight of the Order of Civil Merit; Member of the Academy "dei Lincei," of the Academy of Naples, of the Institutes of Science of Milan, Venice, and Palermo; and of the Cobden Club, of the International Statistical Institute, of the Academy of Madrid, and of the Deputation of National History, &c.

1874.   ,, ... LUIGI BODIO, Doctor of Laws; Professor at the University of Rome; Director-General of the Statistical Department of the State.

1880. **Pavia** .... LUIGI COSSA, LL.D.; Professor of Political Economy; Commander of the Order of the Crown of Italy; Officer of the Order of SS. Maurice and Lazare; Member of the Superior Council of Public Instruction, and of the Cobden Club; Honorary Member of the American Economic Association; Ordinary Member of the Academy "dei Lincei" and of the Royal Institute of Sciences of Milan; Correspondent of the Royal Academies of Lisbon, Modena, Turin, Naples, &c.

1845. **Venice** .... FRANCESCO FERRARA, Senator; Professor and Director of the Royal Superior School of Commerce at Venice; late Minister of Finance; Member of the Academy "dei Lincei."

1880. **Rome** .... ANGELO MESSEDAGLIA, Senator; Professor of the Royal University of Rome.

1868.   ,, ... THE MARQUIS ERMENEGILDO DEI CINQUE QUINTILI, Advocate; General Secretary of the Hospitals Commission of Rome.

Russia.

1878. **St. Petersburg** HIS EXCELLENCY MONS. PIERRE SEMEN-
OFF (SEMENOW), Senator; Privy Councillor to
His Imperial Majesty; President of the Imperial
Statistical Council; President of the Imperial
Geographical Society; Honorary Member of the
Academy of Sciences in St. Petersburg; Associate
of the Statistical Society of Paris.

1890.   ,,   HIS EXCELLENCY MONS. NICOLAS TROÏ-
NITSKY, Former Governor; Privy Councillor;
Director of the Central Statistical Committee of
the Ministry of the Interior; Life Member of the
Statistical Council; Member of the Imperial Geo-
graphical Society of Russia, of the International
Statistical Institute, and of the Statistical Society
of Paris.

Spain.

1845. **Madrid**........ HIS EXCELLENCY SEÑOR DON JOSÉ
MAGÁZ Y JAYME, Advocate, and Member of
the Council of State; Ex-Deputy of the Cortes;
Ex-Senator; Ex-Director-General of Treasury;
Ex-Under-Secretary of the Ministry of Finance;
·Grand Cross of the Order of Isabella Catolica;
Commander of the Order of Carlos 3°.

Sweden and Norway.

1858. **Christiania....** THORKIL HALVORSEN ASCHEHOUG, Doctor
of Laws; Professor of Political Economy at the
University of Christiania; Assessor Extraordinary
of the Supreme Court of Norway; Commander of
the First Class of the Swedish Orders of St. Olave
and of the North Star; and of the Danish Order of
the "Dannebroge;" Corresponding Member of the
Institute of France; Member of the Institute of
International Law, of the International Statistical
Institute, and of the Academies of Christiania,
Trondhjem and Upsala, also of the Royal Historical
Society of Denmark.

1874.   ,,   .. ANDERS NICOLAI KIÆR, Director of the Central
Statistical Bureau of Norway; Associate of the
Statistical Society of Paris.

1860.   ,,   .. THOMAS MICHELL, Esq., C.B., Her Majesty's
Consul-General for Norway.

1890. **Stockholm....** ELIS SIDENBLADH., Ph.D., Director in Chief of
the Central Statistical Bureau of Sweden; Presi-
dent of the Royal Statistical Commission; Commander, Officer, and Knight of several Swedish and
Foreign Orders; Member of the Royal Academies
of Sciences and of Agriculture, at Stockholm;
Honorary and Corresponding Member of several
foreign learned Societies.

Switzerland.

Year of
Election.

1890. **Bern**.......... LOUIS GUILLAUME, Doctor of Medicine; Director of the Federal Statistical Bureau; Secretary of the International Penitentiary Commission.

United States.

1878. **Albany, N.Y.** .. THE HON. WILLIAM BARNES, Lawyer; Ex-Superintendent of the Insurance Department, State of New York.

1881. **Washington** .. JOHN SHAW BILLINGS, Esq., A.M., M.D., LL.D., Edinburgh and Harvard; D.C L., Oxon; Surgeon, U.S. Army; Member of the National Academy of Sciences, &c.

1890. **New York** .... RICHMOND MAYO-SMITH, Esq., M.A., Ph.D., Professor of Political Economy and Social Science in Columbia College; Vice-President of the American Statistical Association; Member of the International Statistical Institute, and of the National Academy of Sciences.

1870. **Taunton, Mass.** THE HON. JOHN ELIOT SANFORD, Lawyer; Speaker of the House of Representatives; Insurance Commissioner; Chairman of the Board of Harbour and Land Commissioners.

1876. **Boston, Mass.** .. FRANCIS AMASA WALKER, Esq., Ph.D., LL.D., formerly Superintendent of the United States Census; President of the Massachusetts Institute of Technology; President of the American Statistical Association, and of the American Economic Association; Member of the National Academy of Sciences; Corresponding Member of the Central Statistical Commission of Belgium.

1870. **Norwich, Conn.** THE HON. DAVID AMES WELLS, D.C.L., LL.D., Economist. Late Special Commissioner of Revenue of the United States; Chairman of Commission for the Revision of Taxes of the State of New York; Lecturer on the Principles and Practice of Taxation, Harvard University, Cambridge, United States; Member of the Board of Arbitration of American Railways; Corresponding Member of the Institute of France; President of the American Social Science Association; and of the American Free Trade League; Chairman in 1883 of the Department of Finance of the American Social Science Association.

1877. **Washington** .. EDWARD YOUNG, Esq., A.M., Ph.D., formerly Chief of the Bureau of Statistics, United States America.

India.

1886. **Calcutta and Simla** JAMES EDWARD O'CONOR, Esq., C.I.E., Assistant Secretary with the Supreme Government, India, Department of Finance and Commerce.

Dominion of Canada.

1876. **Toronto** ...... JOHN LANGTON, Esq., M.A., late Auditor-General.

New South Wales.

1876. **Sydney**........ EDWARD GRANT WARD, Esq., J.P., Registrar-General ; Chairman of Board of Land Titles Commissioners.

New Zealand.

1876. **Wellington**.... SIR JAMES HECTOR, K.C.M.G., M.D., F.R.S.S., L. and E., F.G.S., &c. Director of the Geological Survey, of the Meteorological Department, and of the New Zealand Institute, &c.

Tasmania.

1876. **Hobart**........ EDWIN CRADOCK NOWELL, Esq., J.P., Clerk of Executive and Legislative Councils of Tasmania ; late Government Statistician ; Clerk to the Federal Council of Australasia in its first three Sessions.

Victoria.

1875. **Melbourne** .... HENRY HEYLYN HAYTER, Esq., C.M.G., Government Statist of Victoria ; Officer of the French Order of Public Instruction ; Chevalier of the Order of the Crown of Italy ; Honorary Member of the Statistical and Social Inquiry Society of Ireland, of the Statistical Association of Tokio, of the Royal Society of Tasmania, and of the Intercolonial Medical Congress of Australasia ; Honorary Corresponding Member of the Society of Arts, London, of the Statistical Society of Manchester, of the American Statistical Association, Boston, of the Commercio-Geographical Society of Berlin, of the Geographical Society of Bremen, and of the Royal Society of South Australia ; Honorary Foreign Member of the Statistical Society of Paris ; Fellow and Honorary Corresponding Secretary for Victoria of the Royal Colonial Institute ; Member of the International Statistical Institute.

1858.   „   .... WILLIAM HENRY ARCHER, Esq., K.S.G., F.I.A., F.L.S., &c., Barrister-at-Law.

Great Britain and Ireland.

Year of
Election.

1876. **Manchester** .. THE PRESIDENT (for the time being) OF THE MANCHESTER STATISTICAL SOCIETY.

1876. **Dublin** .... THE PRESIDENT (for the time being) OF THE STATISTICAL AND SOCIAL INQUIRY SOCIETY OF IRELAND.

NOTE.—The Executive Committee request that any inaccuracies in the foregoing List of HONORARY FELLOWS may be pointed out, and that all changes of address may be notified to the Secretary, so that delay in forwarding communications and the publications of the Society may be avoided.

ROYAL STATISTICAL SOCIETY.

Copy of Charter.

Victoria, by the Grace of God of the United Kingdom of Great Britain and Ireland Queen, Defender of the Faith.

To all to whom these Presents shall come, Greeting :—

Whereas Our Right trusty and entirely beloved cousin, Henry, Third Marquess of Lansdowne, Knight of the Most Noble Order of the Garter, Charles Babbage, Fellow of the Royal Society, John Elliott Drinkwater, Master of Arts, Henry Hallam, Fellow of the Royal Society, the Reverend Richard Jones, Master of Arts, and others of Our loving subjects, did, in the year One thousand eight hundred and thirty-four, establish a Society to collect, arrange, digest and publish facts, illustrating the condition and prospects of society in its material, social, and moral relations; these facts being for the most part arranged in tabular forms and in accordance with the principles of the numerical method, and the same Society is now called or known by the name of " The " Statistical Society."

And Whereas it has been represented to Us that the same Society has, since its establishment, sedulously pursued such its proposed objects, and by its publications (including those of its transactions), and by promoting the discussion of legislative and other public measures from the statistical point of view, has greatly contributed to the progress of statistical and economical science.

And Whereas distinguished individuals in foreign countries, as well as many eminent British subjects, have availed themselves of the facilities offered by the same Society for communicating important information largely extending statistical knowledge; and the general interest now felt in Statistics has been greatly promoted and fostered by this Society.

And Whereas the same Society has, in aid of its objects, collected a large and valuable library of scientific works and charts, to which fresh accessions are constantly made; and the said Society has hitherto been supported by annual and other subscriptions and contributions to its funds, and has lately acquired leasehold premises in which the business of the said Society is carried on.

And Whereas in order to secure the property of the said Society, to extend its operations, and to give it its due position among the Scientific Institutions of Our kingdom, We have been besought·to grant to Sir Rawson William Rawson, Knight Commander of the Most Distinguished Order of St. Michael and St. George, and Companion of the Most Honourable Order of the Bath, and to those who now are Members of the said Society, or who shall from time to time be elected Fellows of the Royal Statistical Society hereby incorporated, Our Royal Charter of Incorporation for the purposes aforesaid.

1. **Now Know Ye** that We, being desirous of encouraging a design so laudable and salutary, of Our especial grace, certain knowledge and mere motion, have willed, granted, and declared and Do by these Presents, for Us, Our heirs and successors, will, grant, and declare that the said Sir Rawson William Rawson, Knight Commander of the Most Distinguished Order of St. Michael and St. George, and Companion of the Most Honourable Order of the Bath, and such other of Our loving subjects as now are Members of the said Society, or shall from time to time be elected Fellows of "The Royal Statistical Society" hereby incorporated according to such regulations or bye laws as shall be hereafter framed or enacted, and their successors, shall for ever hereafter be by virtue of these presents one body politic and corporate, by the name of "**The Royal Statistical Society,**" and for the purposes aforesaid, and by the name aforesaid, shall have perpetual succession and a common seal, with full power and authority to alter, vary, break, and renew the same at their discretion, and by the same name to sue and be sued, implead and be impleaded, answer and be answered, unto and in every Court of Us, Our heirs and successors.

2. **The** Royal Statistical Society, in this Charter hereinafter called "The Society," may, notwithstanding the statutes of mortmain, take, purchase, hold and enjoy to them and their successors a hall, or house, and any such messuages or hereditaments of any tenure as may be necessary, for carrying out the purposes of the Society, but so that the yearly value thereof to be computed at the rack rent which might be gotten for the same at the time of the purchase or other acquisition, and including the site of the said hall, or house, do not exceed in the whole the sum of Two thousand pounds.

3. **There** shall be a Council of the Society, and the said Council and General Meetings of the Fellows to be held in accordance with this Our Charter shall, subject to the provisions of this Our Charter, have the entire management and direction of the concerns of the Society.

4. **There** shall be a President, Vice-Presidents, a Treasurer or Treasurers, and a Secretary or Secretaries of the Society. The Council shall consist of the President, Vice-Presidents, and not

less than twenty Councillors; and the Treasurer or Treasurers and the Secretary or Secretaries if honorary.

5. **The** several persons who were elected to be the President, Vice-Presidents, and Members of the Council of the Statistical Society at the Annual Meeting held in the month of June, One thousand eight hundred and eighty-six, shall form the first Council of the Society, and shall continue in office until the first Election of officers is made under these presents as hereinafter provided.

6. **General** Meetings of the Fellows of the Society may be held from time to time, and at least one General Meeting shall be held in each year. Every General Meeting may be adjourned, subject to the provisions of the Bye Laws. The following business may be transacted by a General Meeting, viz.:—

    (*a.*) The Election of the President, Vice-Presidents, Treasurer or Treasurers, Secretary or Secretaries, and other Members of the Council of the Society.

    (*b.*) The making, repeal, or amendment of Bye Laws.

    (*c.*) The passing of any proper resolution respecting the affairs of the Society.

7. **Bye Laws** of the Society may be made for the following purposes, and subject to the following conditions, viz.:—

    (*a.*) For prescribing the qualification and condition of tenure of office of the President; the number, qualifications, functions, and conditions of tenure of office of the Vice-Presidents, Treasurers, Secretaries, and Members of Council, and Officers of the Society; for making regulations with respect to General Meetings and Meetings of the Council and proceedings thereat, and for the election of any persons to be Honorary Fellows or Associates of the Society, and defining their privileges (but such persons, if elected, shall not be Members of the Corporation), and for making regulations respecting the making, repeal and amendment of Bye Laws, and generally for the government of the Society and the management of its property and affairs.

    (*b.*) The first Bye Laws shall be made at the first General Meeting to be held under these presents, and shall (amongst other things) prescribe the time for holding the first election of officers under these presents.

8. **The** General Meetings and adjourned General Meetings of the Society shall take place (subject to the rules or bye laws of the Society, and to any power of convening or demanding a

Special General Meeting thereby given) at such times and places as may be fixed by the Council.

9. **The** existing rules of the Statistical Society, so far as not inconsistent with these presents, shall be in force as the Bye Laws of the Society until the first Bye Laws to be made under these presents shall come into operation.

10. **Subject** to these presents and the Bye Laws of the Society for the time being, the Council shall have the sole management of the income, funds, and property of the Society, and may manage and superintend all other affairs of the Society, and appoint and dismiss at their pleasure all salaried and other officers, attendants, and servants as they may think fit, and may do all such things as shall appear to them necessary or expedient for giving effect to the objects of the Society.

11. **The** Council shall once in every year present to a General Meeting a report of the proceedings of the Society, together with a statement of the receipts and expenditure, and of the financial position of the Society, and every Fellow of the Society may, at reasonable times to be fixed by the Council, examine the accounts of the Society.

12. **The** Council may, with the approval of a General Meeting, from time to time appoint fit persons to be Trustees of any part of the real or personal property of the Society, and may make or direct any transfer of such property so placed in trust necessary for the purposes of the trust, or may, at their discretion, take in the corporate name of the Society conveyances or transfers of any property capable of being held in that name. Provided that no sale, mortgage, incumbrance, or other disposition of any hereditaments belonging to the Society shall be made unless with the approval of a General Meeting.

13. **No** Rule, Bye Law, Resolution, or other proceeding shall be made or had by the Society, or any meeting thereof, or by the Council, contrary to the general scope or true intent and meaning of this Our Charter, or the laws or statutes of Our Realm, and anything done contrary to this present clause shall be void.

In witness whereof We have caused these Our Letters to be made Patent.

Witness Ourself, at Westminster, the thirty-first day of January, in the fiftieth year of Our Reign.

By Warrant under the Queen's Sign Manual,

MUIR MACKENZIE.

ROYAL STATISTICAL SOCIETY.

Index to Rules and Bye-Laws.

RULES AND BYE-LAWS OF THE ROYAL STATISTICAL SOCIETY.

Objects of the Society.

1. The objects of the Royal Statistical Society are to collect, arrange, digest and publish facts, illustrating the condition and prospects of society in its material, social and moral relations; these facts being for the most part arranged in tabular forms and in accordance with the principles of the numerical method.

The Society collects new materials, condenses, arranges, and publishes those already existing, whether unpublished or published in diffuse and expensive forms in the English or in any foreign language, and promotes the discussion of legislative and other public measures from the statistical point of view. These discussions form portions of the published Transactions of the Society.

Constitution of the Society.

2. The Society consists of Fellows and Honorary Fellows, elected in the manner hereinafter described.

Number of Fellows and Honorary Fellows.

3. The number of Fellows is unlimited. Foreigners or British subjects of distinction residing out of the United Kingdom may be admitted as Honorary Fellows, of whom the number shall not be more than seventy at any one time.

Proposal of Fellows.

4. Every Candidate for admission as a Fellow of the Society shall be proposed by two or more Fellows, who shall certify from their personal knowledge of him or of his works, that he is a fit person to be admitted a Fellow of the Society. Every such certificate having been read and approved of at a Meeting of the Council, shall be suspended in the office of the Society until the following Ordinary Meeting, at which the vote shall be taken.

Election of Fellows.

5. In the election of Fellows, the votes shall be taken by ballot. No person shall be admitted unless at least sixteen Fellows vote, and unless he have in his favour three-fourths of the Fellows voting.

Admission of Fellows.

6. Every Fellow elect is required to take the earliest opportunity of presenting himself for admission at an Ordinary Meeting of the Society.

The manner of admission shall be thus:—

Immediately after the reading of the minutes, the Fellow elect, having first paid his subscription for the current year or his composition, shall sign the obligation contained in the Fellowship-book, to the effect following:—

"We, who have underwritten our "names, do hereby undertake, each for "himself, that we will endeavour to "further the good of the Royal Statis- "tical Society for improving Statistical "Knowledge, and the ends for which "the same has been founded; that we "will be present at the Meetings of the "Society as often as conveniently we "can, and that we will keep and fulfil "the Bye-laws and Orders of this "Society: provided that whensoever "any one of us shall make known, by "writing under his hand, to the Secre- "taries for the time being, that he "desires to withdraw from the Society, "he shall be free thenceforward from "this obligation."

Whereon the President, taking him by the hand, shall say,—"By the "authority, and in the name of the "Royal Statistical Society, I do admit "you a Fellow thereof."

Upon their admission Fellows shall have the right of attaching to their names the letters F.S.S., but not in connection with any trading or business advertisement other than the publication of any book or literary notice.

Admission of Honorary Fellows.

7. There shall be Two Meetings of the Society in the year, on such days as shall be hereafter fixed by the Council, at which Honorary Fellows may be elected.

No Honorary Fellow can be recommended for election but by the Council. At any Meeting of the Council any Member thereof may propose a Foreigner or British subject of distinction residing out of the United Kingdom, delivering at the same time a written statement of the qualifications of, offices held by, and published works of, the person proposed; and ten days' notice at least shall be given to every Member of the Council, of the day on which the Council will vote by ballot on the question whether they will recommend to the Society the election of the person proposed. No such recommendation to the Society shall be adopted unless at least three-fourths of the votes are in favour thereof.

Notice of the recommendation shall be given from the chair at the Meeting of the Society next preceding that at which the vote shall be taken thereon. No person shall be elected an Honorary Fellow unless sixteen Fellows vote and three-fourths of the Fellows voting be in his favour.

The Council shall have power to elect as Honorary Fellows, the Presidents for the time being of the Statistical Societies of Dublin, Manchester, and Paris, and the President of any other Statistical Society at home or abroad.

Payments by Fellows.

8. Every Fellow of the Society shall pay a yearly subscription of Two Guineas, or may at any time compound for his future yearly payments by paying at once the sum of Twenty Guineas.*

Defaulters.— Withdrawal of Fellows.

9. All yearly payments are due in advance on the 1st of January, and if any Fellow of the Society have not paid his subscription before the 1st of July, he shall be applied to in writing by the Secretaries, and if the same be not paid before the 1st of January of the second year, a written application shall again be made by the Secretaries, and the Fellow in arrear shall cease to receive the Society's publications, and shall not be entitled to any of the privileges of the Society until such arrears are paid; and if the subscription be not discharged before the 1st of February of the second year, the name of the Fellow thus in arrear shall be exhibited on a card suspended in the office of the Society; and if, at the next Annual General Meeting, the amount still remain unpaid, the defaulter shall, unless otherwise authorised by the Council, be announced to be no longer a Fellow of the Society, the reason for the same being at the same time assigned. No Fellow of the Society can withdraw his name from the Society's books, unless all arrears be paid; and no resignation will be deemed valid unless a written notice thereof be communicated to the Secretaries. No Fellow shall be entitled to vote at any Meeting of the Society until he shall have paid his subscription for the current year.

Expulsion of Fellows.

10. If any Fellow of the Society, or any Honorary Fellow, shall so demean himself that it would be for the dishonour of the Society that he longer continue to be a Fellow or Honorary Fellow thereof, the Council shall take the matter into consideration; and if the majority of the Members of the Council present at some Meeting (of which and of the matter in hand such Fellow or Honorary Fellow, and every Member of the Council, shall have due notice) shall decide by ballot to recommend that such Fellow or Honorary Fellow be expelled from the Society, the President shall at its next Ordinary Meeting announce to the Society the recommendation of the Council, and at the following Meeting the question shall be decided by ballot, and if at least three-fourths of the number voting are in favour of the expulsion, the President shall forthwith cancel the name in the Fellowship-book, and shall say,—

" By the authority and in the name " of the Royal Statistical Society, I do

* Cheques should be made payable to "The Royal Statistical Society," and crossed "Messrs. "Drummond and Co."

" declare that A. B. (naming him) is no " longer a Fellow (or Honorary Fellow) " thereof."

And such Fellow or Honorary Fellow shall thereupon cease to be of the Society.

Trustees.

11. The property of the Society may be vested in three Trustees, chosen by the Fellows. The Trustees are eligible to any other offices in the Society

President, Council, and Officers.

12. The Council shall consist of a President and thirty Members, together with the Honorary Vice-Presidents.

From the Council shall be chosen four Vice-Presidents, a Treasurer, the Honorary Secretaries, and a Foreign Secretary, who may be one of the Honorary Secretaries. The former Presidents who are continuing Fellows of the Society shall be Honorary Vice-Presidents. Any five of the Council shall be a quorum.

Election of President and Officers.

13. The President, Members of Council, Treasurer, and Honorary and Foreign Secretaries shall be chosen annually by the Fellows at the Annual General Meeting.

The Vice-Presidents shall be chosen annually from the Council by the President.

The President shall not be eligible for the office more than two years in succession.

Six Fellows, at least, who were not of the Council of the previous year, shall be annually elected; and of the Members retiring three at least shall be those who have served longest continuously on the Council, unless they hold office as Treasurer or Honorary or Foreign Secretary.

Nomination of President, Council, and Officers.

14. The Council shall, previously to the Annual General Meeting, nominate, by ballot, the Fellows whom they recommend to be the next President and Council of the Society. They shall also recommend for election a Treasurer and the Secretaries (in accordance with Rule 12). Notice shall be sent to every Fellow whose residence is known to be within the limits of the metropolitan post, at least a fortnight before the Annual General Meeting, of the names of Fellows recommended by the Council.

Extraordinary Vacancies.

15. On any extraordinary vacancy occurring of the Office of President, or other Officer of the Society, the Honorary Secretaries shall summon the Council with as little delay as possible, and a majority of the Council, thereupon meeting in their usual place, shall, by ballot, and by a majority of those present, choose a new President, or other Officer of the Society, to be so until the next Annual General Meeting.

Committees.

16. The Council shall have power to appoint Committees of Fellows and also an Executive Committee of their own body. The Committees shall report their proceedings to the Council. No report shall be communicated to the Society except by the Council.

Auditors.

17. At the first Ordinary Meeting of each year, the Fellows shall choose two Fellows, not being Members of the Council, as Auditors, who, with one of the Council, chosen by the Council, shall audit the Treasurer's accounts for the past year, and report thereon to the Society, which report shall be presented at the Ordinary Meeting in February. The Auditors shall be empowered to examine into the particulars of all expenditure of the funds of the Society, and may report their opinion upon any part of it.

Meetings Ordinary and General.

18. The Ordinary Meetings of the Society shall be held monthly, or oftener, during the Session, which shall be from the 1st of November to the 1st of July in each year, both inclusive, on such days and at such hours as the Council shall declare. The Annual General Meeting shall be held on such day in the month of June of each year as shall be appointed by the Council for the time being.

Business of Ordinary Meetings.

19. The business of the Ordinary Meetings shall be to elect and admit Fellows, to read and hear reports, letters, and papers on subjects interesting to the Society. Nothing relating to the bye-laws or management of the Society shall be discussed at the Ordinary Meetings, except that the Auditors' Report shall be presented at the Ordinary Meeting in February, and that the Minutes of the Annual General Meeting, and of every Special General Meeting, shall be submitted for confirmation at the next Ordinary Meeting after the day of such Annual or Special General Meeting. Strangers may be introduced to the Ordinary Meetings, by any Fellow, with the leave of the President, Vice-President, or other Fellow presiding at the Meeting.

Business of Annual General Meeting.

20. The business of the Annual General Meeting shall be to elect the Officers of the Society, and to discuss questions on its bye-laws and management. No Fellow or Honorary Fellow shall be proposed at the Annual General Meeting. No Fellow shall propose any alteration of the rules or bye-laws of the Society at the Annual General Meeting, unless after three weeks' notice thereof given in writing to the Council, but amendments to any motion may be brought forward without notice, so that they relate to the same subject as the motion. The Council shall give fourteen days' notice to every Fellow of all questions of which such notice shall have been given to them.

Special General Meetings.

21. The Council may, at any time, call a Special General Meeting of the Society when it appears to them necessary. Any twenty Fellows may require a Special General Meeting to be called, by notice in writing signed by them, delivered to one of the Secretaries, specifying the questions to be moved. The Council shall, within one week of such notice, appoint a day for such Special General Meeting, and shall give at least one week's notice of every Special General Meeting, and of the questions to be moved, to every Fellow

within the limits of the metropolitan post, whose residence is known. No business shall be brought forward at any Special General Meeting other than that specified in the notice convening the same.

Duties of the President.

22. The President shall preside at all Meetings of the Society, Council, and Committees which he shall attend, and in case of an equality of votes, shall have a second or casting vote. He shall sign all diplomas of admission of Honorary Fellows. He shall admit and expel Fellows and Honorary Fellows, according to the bye-laws of the Society.

Duties of the Treasurer.

23. The Treasurer shall receive all moneys due to, and pay all moneys owing by, the Society, and shall keep an account of his receipts and payments. No sum exceeding Ten Pounds shall be paid but by order of the Council, excepting always any lawful demand for rates or taxes. The Treasurer shall invest the moneys of the Society in such manner as the Council shall from time to time direct.

Duties of the Honorary Secretaries.

24. The Honorary Secretaries shall, under the control of the Council, conduct the correspondence of the Society; they or one of them shall attend all Meetings of the Society and Council, and shall duly record the Minutes of the Proceedings. They shall issue the requisite notices, and read such papers to the Society as the Council may direct.

Powers of the Vice-Presidents.

25. A Vice-President, whether Honorary or nominated, in the chair, shall act with the power of the President in presiding and voting at any Meeting of the Society or Council, and in admitting Fellows; but no Vice-President shall be empowered to sign diplomas of admission of Honorary Fellows, or to expel Fellows or Honorary Fellows. In the absence of the President and Vice-Presidents, any Member of Council may be called upon by the Fellows then present, to preside at an Ordinary or Council Meeting, with the same power as a Vice-President.

Powers of the Council.

26. The Council shall have control over the papers and funds of the Society, and may, as they shall see fit, direct the publication of papers and the expenditure of the funds, in accordance with the provisions of the Charter.

27. The Council shall be empowered at any time to frame Regulations not inconsistent with these bye-laws, which shall be and remain in force until the next Annual General Meeting, at which they shall be either affirmed or annulled; but no Council shall have power to renew Regulations which have once been disapproved at an Annual General Meeting.

28. The Council shall have the custody of the Common Seal. The Common Seal shall not be affixed to any instrument, deed, or other document, except by order of the Council and in the presence of at least two Members of the Council, and in accordance with such other regulations as the Council shall from time to time prescribe. The fact of the seal having been so affixed shall be entered on the minutes of the Council.

29. No Dividend, Gift, Division, or Bonus in money shall be made by the Society, unto or between any of the Fellows or Members, except as hereinafter provided.

30. The Council shall publish a Journal of the Transactions of the Society, and such other Statistical Publications as they may determine upon, and may from time to time pay such sums to Editors and their assistants, whether Fellows of the Society or not, as may be deemed advisable.

31. All communications to the Society are the property of the Society, unless the Council allow the right of property to be specially reserved by the Contributors.

REGULATIONS OF THE LIBRARY.

1. The Library and the Reading Room are open daily for the use of Fellows from 10 a.m. till 5 p.m., except on Saturdays, when they are closed at 2 p.m.

2. Fellows of the Society are permitted to take out Books on making personal application, or by letter addressed to the Librarian, all expenses for carriage being paid by the Fellows.

3. Fellows are not to keep any books longer than one month. Any Fellow detaining a book for more than a month shall not be permitted to take another from the Library until the book detained shall have been returned.

4. Scientific Journals and Periodicals are not circulated until the volumes are completed and bound.

5. Cyclopædias and works of reference are not circulated, but may be lent on the written order of an Honorary Secretary for a period not exceeding *seven* days. The Assistant Secretary or Librarian is allowed at his discretion to lend works of reference for a period not exceeding *three* days, reporting at the same time to the Honorary Secretaries. If works so lent be not returned within the specified time, the borrower shall incur a fine of one shilling per day per volume for each day they are detained beyond the time specified.

6. Any Fellow damaging or losing a book, either replaces the work, or pays a fine equivalent to its value.

7. Books taken from the shelves for reference, are *not* to be replaced but must be laid on the Library table.

8. The Librarian shall report to the Council any infringement of these regulations, and lay upon the table at each regular Meeting (*a*) a List of any "Works of Reference" that may have been borrowed, and (*b*) a List of Books that have been out more than a month.

DONORS TO THE LIBRARY.

(a) Foreign Countries.

Argentine Republic—
General Statistical Bureau.
National Health Department.
Buenos Ayres, Provincial Statis-
              tical Bureau.
      ,,   Provincial Police
              Department.
      ,,   Municipal Statis-
              tical Bureau.
Argentine Geographical Institute.
    ,,   Medical Society.

Austria and Hungary—
Central Statistical Commission.
Ministry of Agriculture.
Statistical Department of the
    Ministry of Commerce.
Bukowina Statistical Bureau.
Hungarian Statistical Bureau.
Prague Statistical Bureau.

Belgium—
Bureau of General Statistics.
Administration of Mines.
Brussels Bureau of Hygiene.
Hasselt, The Burgomaster of.
Royal Academy of Sciences.

Bulgaria. Statistical Bureau.

Chili. Department of Commercial
Statistics.

China—
Imperial Maritime Customs.
Royal Asiatic Society's Branch.

Denmark—
Royal Statistical Bureau.
Political Economy Society.

Egypt—
Director-General of Customs.
Egyptian Institute, Cairo.

France—
Director-General of Customs.
Ministry of Agriculture.
       ,,   Commerce.
       ,,   Finance.
       ,,   Justice.
       ,,   Public Works.
Paris Statistical Bureau.
Economiste Français, The Editor.
Journal des Economistes, The
    Editor.
Monde Economique, The Editor.
Rentier, Le, The Editor, Paris.
Revue Bibliographique Univer-
    selle, The Editor, Paris.
Revue d'Economie Politique, The
    Editor, Paris.
Revue Géographique Interna-
    tionale, The Editor, Paris.
Statistical Society of Paris.
Free School of Political Science.
Suez Canal Company, Paris.

Germany—
Imperial Statistical Bureau.
German Consul-General, London.
Prussian Royal Statistical Bureau.
Saxony Royal Statistical Bureau.
Berlin Statistical Bureau.
Dresden Statistical Bureau
Frankfort Chamber of Commerce.
      ,,   Statistical Bureau.
Hamburg Chamber of Commerce.
      ,,   Statistical Bureau.

During the Year 1892—*Contd.*

(a) Foreign Countries—*Contd.*

Germany—Cont.
Archiv für Soziale Gesetzgebung, &c., The Editor. Tubingen.
Geographical and Statistical Society of Frankfort.

Greece. Statistical Bureau.

Guatemala. Statistical Bureau.

Italy—
Director-General, Statistical Department of the State.
Director-General of Agriculture.
Director of Public Health.
Economista, The Editor, Florence.
Giornale degli Economisti, The Editor, Bologna.

Japan—
Bureau of General Statistics.
Central Sanitary Bureau.
Tokyo Statistical Society.
  „ The Prefect of.

Mexico. Statistical Bureau.

Netherlands—
Department of the Interior.
Director of P. O. Savings Banks.
Legation, London.
Ministry of Commerce & Industry.
Statistical Institute.

Paraguay. Statistical Bureau.

Roumania. Statistical Bureau.

Russia—
Agricultural Department.
Central Statistical Committee.
Customs Statistical Bureau.
Department of Assessed Taxes.
Ministry of Finance.
Finland Geographical Society.

Servia. Statistical Bureau.

Spain—
Board of Customs.
Director - General of Indirect Taxation.
Geographical & Stat. Institute.
Geographical Society of Madrid.

Sweden. Central Statistical Bureau.

Norway—
Central Statistical Bureau.
Christiania Statistical Bureau.

Switzerland—
Federal Statistical Bureau.
  „ Department of Customs.
Aargau Statistical Bureau.
Geneva Public Library.
Statistical Society.
Swiss Union of Commerce and Industry.

United States—
Bureau of American Republics.
Bureau of Education.
Commissioner of Labor.
Comptroller of the Currency.
Department of Agriculture.
  „ of State.
Director of the Mint.
Marine Hospital Service.
Naval Observatory.
Secretary of the Treasury.
Superintendent of Census.
Surgeon-General, U. States Army.
Statistical Bureau, Treasury.

Connecticut State Board of Health.
Illinois Bureau of Labor Statistics.
Massachusetts—
Board of Health, Lunacy, &c.
Bureau of Statistics of Labor.
Michigan State Board of Health.
New York State Library.
  „ Bureau of Labor.

During the Year 1892—*Contd*

(a) **Foreign Countries**—*Contd.*

United States—*Contd.*
Wisconsin. State Board of Health.
Bankers' Magazine, New York.
Bradstreet's Journal, New York.
Commercial and Financial Chronicle of New York.
Forum, The, The Editor.
Political Science Quarterly, Columbia College.
Quarterly Journal of Economics, The Editor, Boston.
Academy of Arts and Sciences.
Academy of Political and Social Science.

United States—*Contd.*
Actuarial Society of America.
Economic Association, Baltimore.
Geographical Society, New York.
Philosophical Soc. of Philadelphia.
Statistical Association, Boston.
Astor Library, New York.
Columbia College, New York.
Cooper Union, New York.
Franklin Institute, Philadelphia.
Smithsonian Institution.
Yale University.

Uruguay. Statistical Bureau.

(b) **India, and Colonial Possessions.**

India, British—
Census Commissioner.
Finance and Commerce Depart.
Lieutenant-Governor of Bengal.
Indian Engineering, The Editor.
Asiatic Society of Bengal.
Bombay Branch of the Royal Asiatic Society.

Canada—
Department of Agriculture.
The High Commissioner, London.
Manitoba Agricultural Depart.
Insurance and Finance Chronicle. The Editor, Montreal.
Canadian Institute.
Royal Society of Canada.
Toronto University.

Cape of Good Hope—
Colonial Secretary.
Director of the Census.
Superintendent-General of Education.
Port Elizabeth Chamber of Commerce.

Ceylon. The Supt. of Census.

Jamaica. Registrar-General of.

Mauritius—
H.E. The Governor of.
The Colonial Secretary.

Natal. Durban Chamber of Commerce.

New South Wales—
Agent-General, London.
Government Statist, Sydney.
Director of Agriculture.

New Zealand—
Government Insurance Department.
Registrar-General.
Department of Mines.
Colonial Museum, Wellington.
New Zealand Institute.
Wellington Harbour Board.

Queensland. Registrar-General of.

Saint Lucia. Colonial Secretary.

During the Year 1892—Contd.

(b) India and Colonial Possessions—Contd.

South Australia —
   The Chief Secretary.
   The Government Statist.
   The Registrar-General.
   Public Library, &c., Adelaide.

Straits Settlements. The Government Secretary, Perak.

Tasmania—
   Government Statistician, Hobart.
   Royal Society of Tasmania.

Trinidad—
   Registrar-General.
   Government Statist.

Victoria—
   Department of Mines.
   Government Statist.
   Royal Society of Victoria.
   Public Library, &c., Melbourne.

(c) United Kingdom and its several Divisions.

United Kingdom—
   Admiralty Medical Department.
   Board of Agriculture.
   Army Medical Department.
   Board of Trade.
   British Museum.
   Customs, Commissioners of.
   Home Office.
   India Office.
   Local Government Board.
   Metropolitan Asylums Board.
      „   Fire Brigade.
      „   Police.
   Royal Mint.
   Woods, Forests, &c., H.M.

England—
   Registrar-General of England.

England—Contd.
   London County Council.
   London. Board of Works for Wandsworth District.
   Birmingham Medical Officer.
      „   Library.
      „   City Treasurer.
   Liverpool Free Public Library.
   Manchester Free Public Library.

Ireland—
   Registrar-General of Ireland.
   Dublin Commissioner of Police.

Scotland—
   Registrar-General of Scotland.
   Edinburgh City Chamberlain.

(d) Authors, &c.

Ashley, Profesor W. J., Toronto.
Baak, M. E., Netherlands.
Back, F., Esq., Tasmania.
Bailey, W. F., Esq., Dublin.
Baines, J. A., Esq., London.
Baker, Dr. H. B., Lansing, U.S.A.
Becker, Dr. Charles, Berlin.
Berthold, Dr. G., Berlin.
Bertillon, Dr. J., Paris.

Billings, Dr. J. S., Washington.
Birt, W., Esq., London.
Blackwood & Sons, Messrs., Edinburgh.
Blenck, Herr E., Berlin.
Blomfield, Rear-Admiral R.M., Alexandria.
Bockh, Dr. R., Berlin.
Bohmert, Dr. V., Dresden.

During the Year 1891—*Contd.*

(d) **Authors**, &c.—*Contd.*

Bodio, Professor Luigi, Rome.
Boinet, A., Bey, Cairo.
Bolles, Albert S., Esq., New York.
Booth, Charles, Esq., London.
Bosco, Signor A., Florence.
Bourinot, J. G., Esq., C.M.G., LL.D.
Boutcher, Mortimore, & Co., London.
Bouteron, M. Ed., Cairo.
Brachelli, Dr. H. von, Vienna.
Caillard, A., Esq., Cairo.
Campbell, Patrick, Esq., Brooklyn.
Cannon, H. W., Esq., New York.
Carter, J. R., Esq., London.
Cernuschi, M. Henri, Paris.
Clarendon Press, Oxford.
Cobb, Arthur S., Esq., London.
Coghlan, T. A., Esq., Sydney.
Cohn, Professor Gustav.
Coni, Dr. E. R., Buenos Ayres.
Cooper, Joseph, Esq., Farnworth.
Craigie, Major P. G., London.
Cunningham, Rev. W., M.A.
Dalla Volta, Signor R., Florence.
Danvers, F. C., Esq., London.
Dawson Bros., Messrs., Montreal.
De Broë, C., Esq., London.
Dodge, J. R., Esq , Washington.
Doyle, Patrick, Esq., Calcutta.
Durant & Co., Messrs., London.
Eaton & Sons, Messrs. H.W.,London.
Edgeworth, Prof. F. Y., Oxford.
Elliott, T. H., Esq., London.
Ellis, G. H., Esq., Boston.
Ellison & Co., Messrs., Liverpool.
Engel, Dr., Cairo.
Falkner, R. P., Esq., Philadelphia
Farquharson, J. C., Esq., Ceylon.
Fenton, James J., Esq., Melbourne.
Ferraris, Professor Carlo F., Venice.
Findlay, Sir George, London.
Finnemore, R. I., Esq., J.P., Natal.
Fischer, Herr Gustav, Jena.
Fisher, Dr. Irving., New Haven, U.S.A.

Folger, Herbert, Esq.
Foville, M. A. de, Paris.
Fremantle, Hon. Sir C. W., K.C.B.
Fyfe, Peter, Esq., Glasgow.
Gad, M. Marius, Copenhagen.
Garland, N. S., Esq., Ottawa.
Geissler, Herr A., Tübingen.
Gibson, G. R., Esq., New York.
Gooch & Cousens, Messrs., London.
Gow, Wilson & Stanton, Messrs.
Granville, E., Esq., J.P., Sydney.
Grimshaw, Dr. T. W., Dublin.
Gruber, Dr. Ignaz, Vienna.
Guillaume, Dr. Louis, Bern.
Guyot, M. Yves, Paris.
Halton, W. F., Esq., Cairo.
Haggard, F,. Esq., Tunbridge Wells.
Hague, George, Esq., Ottawa.
Hamer, John, Esq., London.
Hardy, Ralph P., Esq., London.
Hart, Sir Robt., G.C.M.G., Peking.
Hayter, H. Heylyn, Esq., C.M.G.
Hazell, Watson, and Viney, Messrs.
Hector, Sir James, K.C.M.G., F.R.S.
Helmuth, Schwartze & Co., Messrs.
Henry, Mr., The Trustees of the late.
Hewins, W. A. S., Esq., Oxford.
Hoepli, Signor U., Milan.
Howell, E. J., Esq., London.
Inama-Sternegg, Dr. K. T., Vienna.
Ishibashi, M. S., Tokio.
Janssens, Dr. E., Brussels.
Jeans, J. S., Esq., London.
Johannis, M. A. J. de, Florence.
Johnson, C. H., Esq., B.A., London.
Johnson, Geo., Esq., Ottawa.
Johnston, R. M., Esq., Hobart.
Jones, H. R. Bence, Esq., London.
Jordan, W. L., Esq., London.
Juraschek, Dr. F. v., Vienna.
Kardorff-Wabnitz, Herr W., Berlin.
Keleti, Dr. C., Vienna.

During the Year 1892—*Contd.*

(d) **Authors,** &c.—*Contd.*

Kelly, Charles, Esq., M.D., F.R.C.P.
Keltie, J. Scott, Esq., London.
Kennedy, C. M., Esq., C.B., London.
Kiær, M. A. N., Christiana.
Körösi, M. Joseph, Budapest.
Kummer, M. J. J., Bern.
Lang, R. H., Esq., C.M.G., Cairo.
Latzina, Dr. F., Buenos Ayres.
Leemans, M. H., Brussels.
Levasseur, M. Emile, Paris.
Littledale, Ragg, & Co., Liverpool.
Loch, C. S., Esq., London.
Longstaff, Dr. G. B., London.
MacCook, J. J., Esq., Hartford, U.S.A.
Macmillan & Co., Messrs., London.
Martin, J. B., Esq., M.A., London.
Mathieson, Messrs. F. C. & Sons, London.
Maude, C. T., Esq., Santiago.
Mayr, Dr. G. von, Munich.
Meudell, G. D., Esq., Melbourne.
Milliet, M. E. W., Bern.
Molinari, M. G., Paris.
Molloy, W. R. J., Esq., Dublin.
Money, Alonzo, Esq., C.B., Cairo.
Mouat, Dr. F. J., LL.D., London.
Moxon, Th. B., Esq., Manchester.
Neison, F. G. P., Esq., London.
Neymarck, M. Alfred, Paris.
Nicholson, Prof. J. S., Edinburgh.
Nierop, M. A. H. van, Netherlands.
Nixon, W. J., Esq., London Hospital.
O'Conor, J. E., Esq., C.I.E., India.
Page, Edward D., Esq., New York.
Page & Gwyther, Messrs., London.
Palgrave, R. H. I., Esq., F.R.S.
Patten, Prof. S. N., Philadel., U.S.A.
Petersen, Aleksis, Esq., Copenhagen.
Pierson, Israel C., Esq., New York.
Pistorius, Dr. Verkerk, The Hague.
Pittar, T. J., Esq., London.
Pixley & Abell, Messrs., London.
Platt, James, Esq., London.
Porter, Hon. R. P., Washington.

Powell, Messrs. T. J. and T., London.
Rabino, J. Esq., Teheran.
Rae, John, Esq., London.
Raffalovich, His Ex. A., Paris.
Ravenstein, E. G., Esq., London.
Rawson, Sir R. W., K.C.M.G., C.B.
Rentoul, Dr. R. R., Liverpool.
Richards, Admiral Sir G. H., K.C.B.
Roberts, A. L., Esq., London.
Ronald & Rodger, Messrs., Liverpool.
Ross, Agustin, Esq., London.
Roustan, M. H., Montevideo.
Rusk, Hon. J. M., Washington.
Russell, Dr. J. B., Glasgow.
Schloss, David F., Esq., London.
Schulze-Gävernitz, Dr. Gerhart von, Germany.
Scott-Moncrieff, Col. Sir C. C., Cairo.
Seligman, Prof. E. R. A., New York.
Shillito, J., Esq., York.
Sidenbladh, Dr. K., Stockholm.
Simonds, J. Sexton, Esq., London.
Stanton, A. G., Esq., London.
Street, Bros., Messrs., London.
Supan, Herr A., Germany.
Thompson, W. J. and H., London.
Troinitsky, M. N., St. Petersburg.
Tupper, Sir Charles, Bart., London.
Turquan, M. V., Paris.
Urmson, Elliott, & Co., Liverpool.
Vannacque, M., Paris.
Venn, Dr. J., F.R.S., Bournemouth.
Virgilii, Signor F., Milano.
Wadlin, H. G., Esq., Boston, U.S.A.
Wagner, Dr. H., Gotha.
Walras, M. Léon, Switzerland.
Wells, The Hon. D. A., D.C.L.
Whitaker, W., Esq., Plymouth.
Wood, Sir Henry, M.A., London.
Woolston & Beeton, London.
Wright, Hon. C. D., Washington.
Yacoub, Artin, Pacha, Cairo.
Yakchitch, M. V., Belgrade.
Yvernès, M., Paris.

During the Year 1892—Contd.

(e) Societies, &c. (British).

Accountants & Auditors, Society of.
Actuaries, Institute of.
Anthropological Institute.
Arts, Society of.
Bankers, Institute of.
British Association.
    „   Economic Association.
    „   Iron Trade Association.
Chartered Accountants, Institute of.
Civil Engineers Institution of.
Cobden Club.
East India Association.
Friendly Society of Ironfounders.
Glasgow Philosophical Society.
Howard Association.
Imperial Federation League.
Imperial Institute.
International Statistical Institute
Liverpool Lit. and Phil. Society.
London Chamber of Commerce.
    „   Hospital.
Manchester Literary and Philosophical Society.
    „   Statistical Society.
Mechanical Engineers, Institution of.

Middlesex Hospital.
Mitchell Library, Glasgow.
Peabody Donation Fund.
Royal Agricultural Society.
    „   Asiatic Society.
    „   College of Physicians.
    „   College of Surgeons.
    „   Colonial Institute.
    „   Geographical Society.
    „   Institution of Great Britain.
    „   Irish Academy.
    „   Med. and Chirurgical Society.
    „   Nat. Life Boat Institution.
    „   Society, Edinburgh.
    „   Society, London.
    „   United Service Institution.
St. Bartholomew's Hospital.
Sanitary Institute of Great Britain.
Society for Propagation of the Gospel in Foreign Parts.
Statistical and Social Inquiry Society of Ireland.
Surveyors' Institution.
Travelling Tax Abolition Committee.
University College, London.

(f) Periodicals, &c. (British). *The Editors of—*

Accountant, The, London.
Athenæum, The, London.
Bankers' Magazine, The, London.
British Trade Journal, The, London.
Building Societies, &c., Gazette, The.
Commercial World, The, London.
Darkest Russia, London.
Economic Review, The, London.
Economist, The, London.
Fireman, The, London.
Insurance and Finance Leader, The.

Insurance Post, The, London.
    „   Record, The, London.
Investors' Monthly Manual, The.
Iron and Coal Trades' Review, The
Machinery Market, The, London.
Nature, London.
Policy-Holder, The, Manchester.
Review, The, London.
Sanitary Record, The, London.
Shipping World, The, London.
Statist, The, London.

JOURNAL

OF THE

ROYAL

STATISTICAL SOCIETY.

Founded 1834.

Incorporated by Royal Charter 1887.

VOL. LV.—PART IV.

DECEMBER, 1892.

LONDON:

EDWARD STANFORD, 26 AND 27, COCKSPUR STREET,
CHARING CROSS, S.W.

1892.

ROYAL STATISTICAL SOCIETY,

No. 9, Adelphi Terrace, Strand, W.C., London.

NOTICES TO FELLOWS.

December, 1892.

The Council desire to call the attention of the Fellows to the fact that notwithstanding the change in the name of the Society by the addition of the word "Royal," they are still, in using letters after their names, signifying the membership of the Society, only entitled under Rule 6, to use the letters F.S.S.

Annual Subscriptions are due in advance, on the 1st of January in each year. A Form for authorising a Banker or Agent to pay the Subscription Annually will be forwarded by the Assistant Secretary, on application. When convenient, this mode of payment is recommended. Drafts should be made payable to the order of "The Royal Statistical Society," and crossed "*Drummond and Co.*"

To be included in the Ballot at any particular Ordinary Meeting, the Nomination Papers of Candidates for Fellowship, must be lodged at the Office of the Society, at least six days before the date of such Meeting.

Fellows who may desire to receive Special and Separate Notices of each Paper to be read before the Society at the Ordinary Meetings, should indicate their wishes to the Assistant Secretary.

The Ordinary Meetings of the Society are held, by permission of the Lords of the Committee of Council on Education, in **The Lecture Theatre of the Museum of Practical Geology, 28, Jermyn Street, S.W.**

Fellows are entitled to a copy of the Catalogue of the Library and of the Index to the Catalogue. They may be had on personal application at the office, or will be forwarded upon the payment of carriage (1s. per parcel post). Fellows residing abroad or in the colonies are requested to send the necessary amount to cover postage, according to postal circumstances. (Weight, 3 lb. 14 oz. and 2 lb. 10 oz. respectively.)

The Library and the Reading Room are open daily for the use of Fellows from 10 A.M. to 5 P.M., excepting on Saturdays, when they are closed at 2 P.M.

Fellows borrowing books from the Library are requested to be good enough to return them with as little delay as possible, but without fail at the expiration of a month, and without waiting for them to be recalled.

Fellows changing their Addresses are requested to notify the same to the Assistant Secretary, so that delay or error in forwarding communications, or the *Journal*, may be avoided.

By Order of the Executive Committee.

2

ROYAL STATISTICAL SOCIETY:

AN OUTLINE OF ITS OBJECTS.

THE *Royal Statistical Society* was founded, in pursuance of a recommendation of the British Association for the Advancement of Science, on the 15th of March, 1834; its objects being, the careful collection, arrangement, discussion and publication, of facts bearing on and illustrating the complex relations of modern society in its social, economical, and political aspects,—especially facts which can be stated numerically and arranged in tables;—and also, to form a Statistical Library as rapidly as its funds would permit.

The Society from its inception has steadily progressed. It now possesses a valuable Library of more than 27,000 vols. and a Reading Room; Ordinary Meetings are held monthly from November to June, which are well attended, and cultivate among its Fellows an active spirit of investigation; the Papers read before the Society are, with an abstract of the discussions thereon, published in its *Journal*, which now consists of fifty-five annual volumes, and forms of itself a valuable library of reference.

The Society has originated and statistically conducted many special inquiries on subjects of economic or social interest, of which the results have been published in the *Journal*, or issued separately.

To enable the Society to extend its sphere of useful activity, and accomplish in a yet greater degree the various ends indicated, an increase in its numbers and revenue is desirable. With the desired increase in the number of Fellows, the Society will be enabled to publish standard works on Economic Science and Statistics, especially such as are out of print or scarce, and also greatly extend its collection of Foreign works. Such a well-arranged Library for reference, as would result, does not at present exist in England, and is obviously a great *desideratum*.

The Society is cosmopolitan, and consists of Fellows and Honorary Fellows, forming together a body, at the present time, of over *one thousand* Members.

The Annual Subscription to the Society is *Two Guineas*, and at present there is no entrance fee. Fellows may, on joining the Society, or afterwards, compound for all future Annual Subscriptions by a payment of *Twenty Guineas*.

The Fellows of the Society receive gratuitously a copy of each part of the *Journal* as published quarterly, and have the privilege of purchasing back numbers at a reduced rate. The Library (reference and circulating), and the Reading Room, are open daily for the convenience of Members.

Nomination Forms and any further information will be furnished, on application to the *Assistant Secretary, 9, Adelphi Terrace, Strand, W.C., London.*

ROYAL STATISTICAL SOCIETY.

Binding of the Journal.

Arrangements have been made with the Printers to bind the annual volumes of the *Journal* in cloth (in the style of the Catalogue and Index to the Library), at a cost of One Shilling per volume, conditionally on six to twelve volumes being sent at a time. Fellows wishing to have their *Journals* thus bound, should therefore send them (carriage prepaid) to the *Offices of the Society*, 9, Adelphi Terrace, Strand, W.C. (*not* to the Printers). To avoid delay, Fellows are requested to send their *Journals* to the offices *as soon as possible*, as they will only be forwarded to the Binders when there are six copies ready to be bound.

These terms apply to the binding of the present and of preceding volumes.

Fellows who wish to avoid the trouble of sending their *Journals* to London, can have the cases sent down to them at the same price (exclusive of carriage). The weight of one single cover is about 5 ounces.

Fellows who desire it, can have the several parts of the *Journal* retained and forwarded annually, bound in a single volume, at their expense. Or, by special instruction from any Fellow, the December part only may be retained and bound up with the other parts when received from the Fellow.

5

ROYAL STATISTICAL SOCIETY.

LIST OF THE SOCIETY'S PUBLICATIONS.

Note.—Sets—or Copies of any number—of the *Journal*, or of the other Publications of the Society (if not out of print), can be obtained of the publisher, E. Stanford, 26 and 27, Cockspur Street, Charing Cross, London, S.W., or through any bookseller.

Price.

Journal (published quarterly)—
Vols. 1—55. 8vo. 1838–92 .... } 5*s.* each part*

General Analytical Index to Vols. 1—50 of the
Journal (1838-87). In 4 parts. 8vo.—
  (i) For the First Fifteen Volumes (1838-52)
  (ii) For the Ten Volumes (1853-62) ....
  (iii) For the Ten Volumes (1863-72) ....
  (iv) For the Fifteen Volumes (1873-87) ... } 3*s.* 6*d.* each part

First Report of a Committee on Beneficent Institutions. I. The Medical Charities of the
Metropolis. 68 pp. 8vo. 1857 .... } 2*s.* 6*d.*

Statistics of the Farm School System of the
Continent (reprinted from the *Journal*, with a
Preface and Notes). 63 pp. 8vo. 1878 ... } 1*s.*

Catalogue of the Library (New)—
iv + 573 pp. Cloth, super royal 8vo. 1884 } 10*s.*

Index to the Catalogue of 1884—
i + 372 pp. Cloth, super royal 8vo. 1886 } 10*s.*

Jubilee Volume—
xv + 372 pp. Cloth, 8vo. 1885 .... } 10*s.* 6*d.*

List of Fellows, Rules and Bye-Laws, Regu-
lations of the Library, and Outline of the
Objects of the Society, &c.
Corrected annually to 31st December. 8vo. } Issued gratuitously

---

Price of back Numbers of the Journal, &c., to Fellows only.

Fellows only, can obtain sets—or single copies of any number—of the *Journal*, or copies of the other Publications, at the Society's Rooms, 9, Adelphi Terrace, Strand, W.C.

By different resolutions of the Council, the prices charged to Members are as follows:—(a.) back numbers of the *Journal* of the Society, three-fifths of the publishing price; (b.) each part of the General Index to the *Journal*, 2*s.* 6*d.*; (c.) the Jubilee Volume, 5*s.*

NOTE.—One or two numbers of the *Journal* are now out of print.

* Before 1870 the price varied.

PRINTERS IN ORDINARY TO HER MAJESTY & BOOKSELLERS TO H.R.H. THE PRINCE OF WALES.

HARRISON & SONS

45, 46, & 47, St. Martin's Lane, Charing Cross, London.

14, 15, 16, 17, 18, 19, & 20, GREAT MAY'S BUILDINGS.

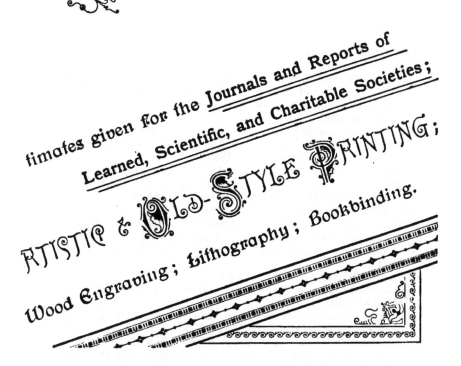

Estimates given for the Journals and Reports of Learned, Scientific, and Charitable Societies;

ARTISTIC & OLD-STYLE PRINTING;

Wood Engraving; Lithography; Bookbinding.

ROYAL STATISTICAL SOCIETY'S LIBRARY.

DESIDERATA.

The following is a List of some of the Odd Numbers, Parts, and Volumes, of Works wanting in the Library. They are arranged under the following heads:—(a) *Foreign Countries;* (b) *India, and Colonial Possessions;* (c) *United Kingdom and its Divisions;* (d) *Authors, &c.;* (e) *Societies, &c. (British);* (f) *Periodicals, &c. (British).*

Donations of any portion thereof will be acceptable, and will be duly acknowledged by the Society.

[The Dates and Numbers are in all cases inclusive.]

(a) Foreign Countries.

Argentine Republic—
Educacion Comun. Informe sobre el estado, durante 1885-90.
Buenos Aires—
Annuaire Statistique de la Province de, Année 1889, *et seq.*
Registro Estadistico de la Provincia de, for 1872, and for earlier years except 1854.

Austria and Hungary—
Austria—
Ackerbau-Ministeriums. Statistisches Jahrbuch des k.k. Heft 1, 2, and Lief. 1 of Heft 3 of 1882; Lief. 2 of Heft 3 of 1885; Lief. 1 and 2 of Heft 3 of 1886; Lief. 2 of Heft 3 of 1887; Heft 2 of 1890.
Entwicklung von Industrie und Gewerbe in Österreich, 1848-88 herausg. von der Kommission der Wiener Jubiläums- und Gewerbe Ausstellung. Wien, 1888.
Handel. Ausweise über den auswärtigen, der Oesterreichischen Monarchie. 1866, 1871, 1875, and Abth. 2, 3 of 1880.
Oesterreichisches Statistisches Handbuch. 1882-84.
Sanitätswesens. Statistik des, für 1887. Fol.
Seeschiffahrt. Statistik der, und des Seehandels in den Oesterreichischen Häfen in 1889 and for earlier years.
Statistisches Jahrbuch der Oesterreichischen Monarchie für 1863-68. 8vo.
Statistische Monatschrift. 1875-83.
Strafrechtspflege. Ergebnisse der, Heft 2 of 1884; Hefte 2 and 3 of 1886.
Hungary. Statistisches Jahrbuch für Ungarn. 1874, Heft 12 of 1875; Title page, &c., of 1881; Title page, &c., of 1888; Hefte 2, 7, 8, 10, 11, 12 of 1889; Hefte 1, 2, 4, &c., of 1890.
Vienna. Statistisches Jahrbuch der Stadt Wien, für 1883 and earlier years, 1885, *et seq.*

Belgium—

Annuaire Statistique de la Belgique. 1ᵉ année, 1870.

Bulletin de la Commission Centrale de Statistique. Vols. v—vii (*cir.* 1852-59).

Chemins de Fer. Compte-Rendu des Opérations pendant 1843, 1860, 1861, 1863, 1864, 1868, 1884.

Documents statistiques recueillis et publiés par le Ministre de l'Intérieur. 4ᵉ et 5ᵉ publications (*cir.* 1840).

Instruction Primaire. Rapport Triennal pour 1873-75, 1882-84, 1885-87.

Justice Criminelle et Civile. Résumé Statistique. 1860 and for earlier years.

Population. Relevé de la, 1ᵉʳ Janvier, 1831.

Population. Recensement de la, en 1866.

Population. Relevé proportionnel des naissances, des mariages, et des décès 1841-67.

Population. Mouvement de l'Etat Civil et de, en 1885, *et seq.*

Situation des provinces et des communes de Belgique. Résumé du Rapport sur la, 1830-40.

Situation du Royaume. Exposé de la, 1831-40; 1841-50.

Sociétés de Secours Mutuels. Rapports, 1860 and for earlier years, 1862, 1864.

Travaux Publics. Renseignements Statistiques recueillis par le Departement des—, for 1856, 1861, 1868, *et seq.*

Bruxelles. Annuaire Démographique et Tableaux Statistiques des causes de décès. No. 10, 1871; No. 18, 1879.

Brazil—

Agriculture. Renseignements sur l'. 1874.

Institutions de prévoyance. Notice sur les. 1883.

Instruction Primaire. Statistique de l'. 1882.

Population de l'Empire. Rapport de la Commission de Statistique sur la. 1827.

Chile—

Annuaire Statistique du Chili. 1860-79.

Estadistica Comercial, 1881-83, 1885 and 1886.

China— *Imperial Maritime Customs.*

  I. *Statistical Series—*

No. 3. [Annual] Returns of Trade for 1859-70, 1873-75.

„ 4. [„] Reports on Trade for 1864-70.

  II. *Special Series—*

No. 1. Native Opium, 1864.

„ 2. Medical Reports, No. 1, 1871.

„ 9. Native opium, 1887.

„ 10. Opium, crude and prepared, 1888.

„ 11. Tea, 1888.

„ 12. Silk statistics, 1879-88.

Royal Asiatic Society. North China Branch. Journal. Series I, 1858-63; No. 9, 1875; and No. 12, 1878, of the new series, and title page, &c., of vol. 21, 1886.

Mémoires concernant l'histoire des Chinois, par les Missionaires de Pekin. Vol. xvi, *et seq.* 1776-91.

Colombia. Annuaire Statistique des Etats de Colombie. 1875 et 1876.

Costa Rica—
Anuario Estadistico de la Republica de Costa-Rica. Año de 1885.
Estadistica del Comercio Exterior de Costa Rica, for 1885 and for 1887, *et seq.*

Denmark—
Statistisk Tabelværk—
Ældste Række, 1835-47. (All the series.)
Ny Række. Bind 2—11, and 20—26, 1851-64.
Tredie Række. Bind 1—26, 1863-73.
Meddelelser fra det statistiske Bureau. Samling vi, 1861.
Statistiske Meddelelser. Bind 1—13, 1862-77.
Sammendrag af Statist. Oplysninger ang. Kongeriget Danmark.
Nr. 1—5, 1869-73.

Danmarks Statistik. En Haandbog af V. Falbe-Hansen og Dr. Will. Scharling (the whole series).

Egypt—
Institut Egyptien—Bulletin. 1ᵉ Serie. Nos. 1, 7, 10—12.
Mémoires. Tome i, 1888.

France—
Abolition de l'Esclavage dans les Colonies anglaises, Enquêtes sur, vols. i et ii, 1840-41.
Album de Statistique Graphique de 1879, et 1881-83.
Agriculture. Statistique de la France. 2ᵉ série. Statistique Agricole. 1858-59. L'Introduction, et 1ᵉʳᵉ Partie.
Agriculture. Ministère de l'. Bulletin. 1882, 1883; No. 3 of 1884, Nos. 3, 8 of 1888, No. 1 of 1889.
Annuaire du Bureau des Longitudes. 1795-1813, 1815-17, 1828, 1833-34, 1837-40, 1843, 1845-55, 1857-61, 1863-68, 1874-77, 1880, *et seq.*
Armée. Compte rendu sur le Recrutement pendant 1887, and for earlier years except 1851 and 1866.
Armée. Statistique médicale en 1885, and for earlier years.
Atlas Graphique et Statistique du Commerce de la France.
Atlas Statistique de l'Administration des Forêts de la France.
Caisses d'Epargne. Rapports pour 1872, 1874-77, 1880.
Cabotage. Tableau Général du, pendant 1874, 1877, 1878, 1883, et 1887.
Commerce. Tableaux Généraux du, pendant 1846, 1847, 1850, 1868—1876, et 1879.
Chemins de Fer Français. Situation au 31 Déc. pour 1875, 1877, 1878, 1880, 1883.
Chemins de Fer. Documents Statistiques pour 1867, 1869, 1873-75, 1877, 1883.
Colonies. Statistiques Coloniales pour 1883-85, 1887.
Denombrement de 1886. 2ᵉ Partie Algérie, et recensement des Français à l'étranger. La. 8vo.
Enquête sur la Circulation Monétaire et Fiduciaire. Vol. vi. Paris, 1867.

France—*Contd.*

Exposé de la situation de l'Empire. 1868.
Marine Marchande. Enquête sur la, 4to. 1878.
Pénitentiaires. Statistique des etablissements, pour 1887.
Police Militaire. Compte rendu pour 1886, and earlier years.
Religion. Statistique des cultes, 1888-90.
Revue Maritime et Coloniale. Tome 88, 294ᵉ Livraison, 1886.
Sociétés de Secours Mutuels. Rapports pour 1875, 1877, 1878, 1882, *et seq.*
Statistique générale de l'Algérie. 8vo. 1878-82.
PARIS. Recherches Statistiques sur la Ville de Paris et le Département de la Seine. Vol. vi. Années 1837-56.

Annuaire de l'Economie Politique et de la Statistique, pour 1844-55, 1866 et 1884.
Economiste Français. 1877, No. 35; 1879, Nos. 30 and 31; 1889, No. 11; 1890, No. 28; contents, &c., of vol. 2 of 1891.
Journal des Economistes. 1ᵉ Serie. Vols. i—xxi, 1842-48. 2ᵉ Serie. Vol. xxiii, Juillet, 1859.
La Réforme Economique. Tome I, 2ᵉ livraison, 1875; 4ᵉ livraison *et seq.*
Marseilles. Société de Statistique de. Répertoire des Travaux. 8vo. Vols. i—xviii, 1840-58.
Société Internationale des Etudes pratiques d'Economie Sociale. Les Ouvriers des Deux Mondes. Vol. ii. Paris, 1857.

Germany—

Eisenbahnen. Statistik der im betriebe befindlichen, Betriebsjahr 1889-90.
Justice. Statistics of the administration of Civil, (The whole series.)
Seeschiffahrt. Statistik der, im 1876; im 1881, abth. 2.
Waarenverkehr des Zollgebiets mit dem Auslande im 1882, Theil 1.
Report of the Vaccination Commission, presented to the Reichstag in April, 1885.
Baden—
Beiträge zur Statistik des Grossherzogthums Baden. Bände 8, 9 (1ᵗᵉˢ Heft), 17—21, 23, 24, 30, 1860-68
Statistisches Jahrbuch für 1868-77.
BAVARIA. Mittheilungen des Statistischen Bureaus der Stadt München. Bände i, ii; Hefte 2—4, Band iv; Hefte 2—4, Band v, *et seq.*
MECKLENBURG-SCHWERIN. Beiträge zur Statistik Mecklenburgs. 1860-74, 1877.
OLDENBURG. Statistische Nachrichten herausgegeben vom Statistischen Bureau. Hefte 1—12, 14, 16, 1857-76.
Saxony—
Jahrbuch für Statistik und Staatswirthschaft, 1854.
Kalender und Statistisches Jahrbuch für 1873.
Mittheilungen des Statistischen Vereins für das König. Sachsen. Hefte 1—5 (*cir.* 1830-34), 7, 1836; 19, 1850, *et seq.*
Zeitschrift des k. sächsischen statistischen Bureaus. 1855-67; Hefte 1—6, and 10—12 of 1874; Hefte 1—3 of 1875.

Germany—*Contd.*

BREMEN. Jahrbuch für die Amtliche Statistik des bremischen Staats. 1868-74.

Almanach de Gotha. The first ninety-six volumes, 1763-1859.

Jahrbücher fur Nationalökonomie und Statistik, 1891 and earlier years.

Greece. Recensement Général de 1889. 1ᵉʳᵉ Partie.

Guatemala—

Censo General de la republica de Guatemala 1880.

Movimiento de poblacion habido en los pueblos de la republica, durante 1890.

Hawaii—

Census of Hawaii, 1884.

Hawaiian Statistical Directory. 1880.

Italy—

Annali del Ministero di Agricoltura Industria e Commercio. Nos. 1—46, 48—50, 52—65, 67—69, 72—78, 80—82, 84, 90—96, 98, 99, 101, 102, 104, 105, 107.

Annali di Agricoltura. 2ᵉ serie. Nos. 1, 3, 24.

Giornale della Societa Italiana d'Igiene. An IIᵒ, Nos. 1 e 2, 1880.

L' Italia Economica. 1868—1870. 8vo.

Rivista Europea, Rivista Internazionale. Vols. .i—iii, 1877; Vol. xxiii, 1881.

Japan—

Trade. Returns of Foreign Trade for 1890.

Transactions of the Asiatic Society of Japan. 1872, *et seq.*

Mexico—

Comercio Exterior de Mexico, 1887, and earlier years.

Estadística de la Republica Mexicana. 1880.

Statistique descriptive et historique des Etats Mexicains, 1889.

Boletin de la Sociedad de Geografia y Estadistica de la Republica Mexicana. 1ª Epoca. Tomo iii; iv, No 1; v, Nos. 1, 2. 2ª Epoca. Tomo i. 3ª Epoca. Tomo vi, Nos. 4, *et seq.*

Netherlands—

Census of 1889. Results of the,

Résumé Statistique des Pays Bas. No. 3. 1884.

Orange Free State. Census of 1880.

Portugal—

Annuario Estadistico de Portugal. 1877-83, 1886, *et seq.*

Commercio do Reino com Paizes Estrangeiros nos anno de 1881 (and earlier years), 1888, *et seq.*

Movimento da População nos 1887, *et seq.*

Boletim da Sociedade de Geographia de Lisboa. 1ᵉ Serie, Nos. 1, 2, 1879; 3ᵉ Serie, No. 9, 1882; 5ᵉ Serie, No. 6, *et seq.*, 1885.

12

Roumania. Commerce avec les puissances étrangères pendant 1887, *et seq.*

Russia—
Annuaire des Finances Russes. 1872, 1873, 1884, *et seq.*
Commerce extérieur de la Russie de 1861 à 1878. 1 vol., 8vo.
Minérale. Aperçu preliminaire de l'Industrie, en 1889.

Servia. Statistique de la Serbie. 4to. Belgrade, 1875-80.

Spain—
Estadistica general de Comercio exterior de España en 1885, (and for earlier years, excepting for 1856, 1882, and 1884).
Estadistica General de primera enseñanza correspondiente al decenio que termino, 1880.
Ferro-carriles. Situacion de los, en 1891.
Mineral, Estadistica, de España, año 1888.

Sweden and Norway—
SWEDEN. *Bidrag till Sveriges Officiela Statistik—*
C. Bergshandtering, 1859-63, 1867, 1868.
D. Fabriker och Manufakturer, for 1859-63, 1867.
E. Inrikes Handel och Sjöfart, 1859-63, 1865, 1867.
F. Utrikes Handel och Sjöfart, for 1859-62.
G. Fangvarden, for 1862.
I. Telegrafvasendet, for 1863, 1867, 1868.
K. Helso och Sjukvarden, 1861, 1863-64, 1867.
N. Jordbruk och Boskapsskotsel, 1867.
O. Landtmateriet, for 1867.
Statistisk Tidskrift. Häftet 1—16, 1862-67; Häftet 19—25, 1868-70. Title page, &c., for 1872.
NORWAY. *Norges Officielle Statistik—*
C. 1b. Folkemængdens Bevægelse. 1866.
C. 6. Beretning om den Höiere Landbrugsskole i Aas. 1875-76.
D. 1a. Indtægter og Udgifter. 1863.
Statistisk Årbog. Heft 1, 3. 1867-69.

Switzerland. Statistique de la Suisse. Nos. 1, 8, 32, 49, 1860-81.

United States—
Agricultural Department. Special Reports. [Old Series.] Nos. 1—9, 11, 12, 18, 22, 26, 28—31, 33—36, 40, 41, 44, 45, 48, 50, 53, 56, 58, 62, 63. Title Page and Table of Contents of vols. of Monthly Reports for 1884, 1885, 1886.
Fisheries and Fishery Industries of the United States. Vols. 1, 2, 4—7. 1889.
Interstate Commerce. Report of Senate Select Committee on, 1886.
Mineral Resources of the United States for 1882 to 1886.

American Association for the Advancement of Science. Proceedings. 1848, *et seq.*

United States—_Contd._

American Geographical Society—
   Bulletin. Parts 2 _et seq._ of vol. i, vol. iii (_cir._ 1858).
   Journal. Nos. 4 _et seq._ of vol. i, Nos. 1 and 3 _et seq._ of vol. ii,
      vol. iii (_cir._ 1872).
   Proceedings. Vol. i, Nos. 2 and 5 _et seq._ of vol. ii (_cir._ 1863),
      et seq.

American Philosophical Society—
   Transactions. Vols. i—xi; vol. xii, Part 1, 1861; vol. xiv,
      Parts 1 and 2, 1870.
   Proceedings. 8vo. Vols. i—ix; vol. x (1—296 pp.); vol. xii,
      No. 88.

_American Social Science Association—_Journal, containing the
   Transactions. Nos. 4, 1872, and 18, 1884, _et seq._

Charities. Reports of the Proceedings of the Conferences of—.
   1st, 1874; 5th, 1878; 10th, 1883, _et seq._

Philadelphia Society for the Promotion of National Industry.
   Addresses of the. 12mo. 1820.

Prison Discipline Society. Boston. Annual Reports. Nos.
   1—23; No. 26, 1851; No. 28, _et seq._

Smithsonian Institution. Annual Reports of the Regents. The
   first three for 1846-48.

Annual Statistician (McCarty's), San Francisco, Cal., 1877-85.

Bankers' Magazine. New York. The first twenty volumes, comprising the second and third series. Series 3, No. 7 of vol. ii,
   No. 2 of vol. v, Nos. 5 and 7 of vol. vii, No. 6 of vol. viii, 1868-73.

Uruguay—
   Anuario Estadistico, for 1888.
   Commercio Exterior de la Republica Oriental del Uruguay.
      1885, and for earlier years.
   Direccion de Estadistica General de la Republica O. del Uruguay.
      Nos. 1—3, 9, 10, 12, 15.

Venezuela—
   Estadistica Mercantil. 8vo. 1883.
   Segundo Censo de la República, 1881.
   Statistical Annuary of the U. S. of Venezuela. Caracas, 1885-86.

Statistique internationale—
   Actes du Congrès Penitentiaire International de Rome. Part 1
      of Vol. ii, 1885.
   Congrès International de Statistique. IXᵉ Session, à Budapest,
      1876. Part 3.
   International Monetary Conference, Paris, 1878. Report of
      Proceedings, &c.
   Programmes du travail statistique international sur le territoire,
      la navigation fluviale, et sur les mines et usines. St. Péters-
      bourg, 1872.
   Statistik der Binnenschiffahrt. Programm für die Bearbeitung
      der internationalen Statistik der Binnenschiffahrt im westlichen
      Europa. Im Auftrage des kaiserl. stat. Amtes des Deutschen
      Reiches aufgestellt von A. Meitzen. Berlin, 1875. (Inland
      Navigation.)

(b) India and Colonial Possessions.

India—

Agricultural Statistics of British India for 1885-86, *et seq.*

Finance and Revenue Accounts for 1860-61, 1863-64, 1866-67.

Home Accounts for 1841, 1843-54, 1856, 1857, 1865, 1867-69, 1870, 1877.

Maritime Trade for 1878-79, and previous years.

Railways in India. Reports for 1862-63.

Sanitary Commissioner with the Government of India. Twenty-Second Annual Report for 1885.

Statistics of British India for the Judicial and Administrative Departments subordinate to the Home Department for 1886-87, 1887-88, 1889-90, *et seq.*

BERAR. Census of, 1867.

PUNJAB. Selections from Records of the Government of the Punjab. New series. Nos. 19, 20, 23, 1882.

Asiatic Society of Bengal—

Asiatic Researches. Vols. x—xx, 1810-39.

Gleanings in Science. Vols. i—iii, 1829-31.

Journal. Vols. i—xvi, 1832-47.

Bengal Social Science Association. Transactions. Vol. i, Part 2, 1867, *et seq.*

Royal Asiatic Society. Journal of the Bombay Branch. Vols. i—vi, 1841; Nos. 23—28.

Mauritius—

Almanac and Colonial Register, Nos. 1—4, 1869-72.

Census of Mauritius and its Dependencies. 1871.

New Zealand Institute. Transactions. Vols. ii, iii, 1869-70.

Straits Branch of the Royal Asiatic Society. Journal. 1878, *et seq.*

Tasmania. Royal Society of Tasmania. Papers and Proceedings previous to 1848, for 1849, and for 1860-62, 1864, 1866-73.

(c) United Kingdom and its Divisions.

United Kingdom—

Banks of Issue. First Report of the Select Committee of Secrecy on. No. 366, 1841.

Children's Employment Commission. Third Report, 1864 [3414-I].

Civil Establishments. 1st Report of Royal Commission on, [C-5226.] 1887.

Coal Commission. Vols. 1—3 of the Reports of the—; also the volume of maps and sections. 1871.

Colonial Possessions. Reports on the Past and Present State of, for 1852, 1855, 1857-58, 1860, 1864-69.

Colonial Possessions. Papers relating to, for 1871, part 2 of 1874 and 1877 [C-1869].

Finance Accounts for 1883-84 and 1884-85.

United Kingdom—*Contd.*

House of Commons. Catalogue of Reports, 1696-1834, continued to 1837.

House of Lords. General Index to Sessional Papers for 1801-59 and 1859-70.

Investments for the Savings of the Middle and Working Classes. Report from the Select Committee on. (No. 508.) 1850.

Labouring Classes. Reports on Sanitary Condition of Residences of the. Nos. 5 and 13, 1842.

Mineral Statistics of the United Kingdom for 1875-77. 8vo.

Mint. Reports of the Deputy Master, 1st—5th, 7th—9th, and 11th Reports, 1870-80.

Monetary Conference, Paris, 1878. Report of Commissioners representing H.M.'s Government at the—. [C-2196.] 1879.

Parliamentary Papers. List for the year 1873. 8vo.

Railway Accidents. First Report on, for 1853.

Record Commission Publications. Acts of the Parliaments of Scotland. Vol. i, 1124-1424. Fol.

Water Supply for Metropolis and large Towns. Minutes of Evidence, appendix, maps, plans, and index to the Report of the Commissioners. 1868-69 [4169-I-II].

Great Britain—

Prisons, Home District. Reports of Inspectors. 16th, 17th, 19th, 20th, 1850-57.

Prisons, Northern and Eastern District. Reports of Inspectors. 5th—7th, 18th, 19th, 21st, 22nd, 1840-58.

Prisons, Southern and Western District. Reports of Inspectors. 19th, 21st, 22nd, 1854-57.

Prisons, Scotland, Northumberland, and Durham. Reports of Inspectors. 7th, 1842; 20th—22nd, 1855-57.

Reformatory and Industrial Schools in Great Britain. Reports of the Inspector. 6th, 26th, 1862-83.

Veterinary Department. Annual Reports for 1871-74, 1876-80, 1882, *et seq.*

England and Wales—

Charity Commissioners. 1st, 2nd, 5th—20th, 22nd, 25th, 26th, 28th, 30th, 31st, Reports, 1854-84.

Convict Prisons. Reports of Directors for 1858.

Local Taxation Returns for 1870-71, and 1873-74.

Military Prisons. Reports on discipline and management of, for 1855, 1857, and 1867.

Population of Counties and Divisions, and of Parliamentary Cities and Boroughs in England and Wales in 1821, 1831, and 1861. Number of Electors in 1832 and 1862 ... 1866 (259).

Prisons, Midland District. Reports of Inspectors. 23rd, 1859, to 27th, 1862.

Prisons, Northern District. Reports of Inspectors. 23rd—28th, 1857-63; 31st, 1866; 41st, 1877.

Prisons, Southern District. Reports of Inspectors. 23rd—29th, 1857-64; 31st, 1866.

Prisons. Report of the Surgeon-General of, 1856. [2147.]

England and Wales—*Contd.*
Prisons. Annual Reports of the Commissioners of, 5th, 1882.
Registrar-General for England—
Annual Summaries of Weekly Returns for 1850-54.
Tables of Mortality, No. 41 of 1841.
Weekly Returns of Births, &c. Nos. 43—51, 1879.
London School Board—
Annual Statements of the Chairman, to the Board. (All the
statements, except those for 1878 and 1889.)
Reports of the Statistical Committee for 1874-77, and 1879-88.
Metropolitan Police. Criminal Returns for 1836.

Ireland—
Convict Prisons. Reports of Directors. 2nd—4th, 1855-57;
7th, 1860; 9th—12th, 1862-65; 14th, 1867; 15th, 1868;
19th, 1872.
Prisons. Inspector-General's Reports. First, 1823; 2nd, 1824;
6th, 1828; 7th, 1829; 20th, 1842; 34th, 36th, 37th, 40th, 43rd.
Reformatory and Industrial Schools, Ireland. Reports of
Inspector. 7th and 8th, 1867-68.
Registrar-General's Weekly Returns of Births, &c., for 1864-71.
Dublin Metropolitan Police. Statistical Tables for 1843-59 and
1870.

Scotland—
Agricultural Surveys. By the Board of Agriculture. The
vols. for Kirkcudbright and Lanark. (*Circa* 1795-1816)
Prisons. Reports of General Board of Directors, 17th—22nd,
1856-61.
Prisons Administration Act. Reports of Managers under the,
23rd—31st, 1862-70; 38th, 1877.
Glasgow—
Reports [Annual] upon the Vital, Social, and Economic Statis-
tics of Glasgow, for 1862, 1867, 1873-75, 1877, 1879.
Report on Enteric Fever, 1880, by Dr. James B. Russell.

(d) Authors, &c.
ACHARD (M. A.). Influence des Taxes que frappent les obligations
sur leur prix d'après un taux d'intérêt determiné. (Journal des
Actuaires Français, tome iv, Janvier, 1875). Paris.
ACHENWALL (Gottfried). Abriss der Staatswissenschaft der
Europäischen Reiche. Statistik als Wissenschaft, 1808
ALDAMA-AYALA (G. de). Compendio geographico- estadistico de
Portugal e sus posesiones ultramarinas. 8vo. Madrid, 1880.
ANCILLON (Frédéric). Du Juste-Milieu, ou du rapprochement
des extrêmes dans les opinions. Vol. i. 12mo. Brux., cir. 1837.
AUBERT (V. S.). La Republique Sud-Africaine. Situation écono-
mique et commerciale en 1889. Paris, 1889.
AUDIFFRET (Marquis d'). Etat de la fortune nationale et du credit
public de 1789 à 1873. 8vo. Paris, 1875.
BARBERET (J.). Le Travail en France. Tome I. 8vo. 1886.
BEHM und WAGNER. Die Bevölkerung der Erde. No. 1 (cir. 1872).

BELOCH (Jules). Die Bevölkerung der griechisch-römischen Welt. Leipzig, 1886.

BERARDI (D.). Le funzioni del governo nelli economia sociale. Florence, 1887.

BEENARD (Aug.). De l'Origine et des Débuts de l'Imprimerie en Europe. 1ᵉʳᵉ Partie. 8vo. Paris (*cir.* 1852).

Block (Maurice)—
L'Espagne en 1850. Paris, 1851.
Charges de l'Agriculture dans divers pays de l'Europe. 1851.
Statistique de la France comparée, &c. 2nd edit. Paris, 1875.
Les Communes et la liberté. 8vo. Paris, 1876.
Traité théorique et pratique de Statistique. 2nd edit. Paris, 1886.

Boccardo (Gerolamo)—Dizionario dell' Economia politica e del Commercio. 4 vols. 4to. 1857.
Dizionario Universale della Economia Politica e del Commercio. 8vo. Milano, 1874.
Applicazione dei Metodi Quantitativi alle Scienze Economiche Statistiche e Sociali. 1875.

BŒHM-BAWERK (Dr. E.). Kapital und Kapitalzins. Abth. 1. Geschichte und Kritik der Kapitalzins-Theorien. 8vo. 1884.

Bolles (Albert S.)—
The Financial History of the United States from 1774 to 1789, and from 1789 to 1860. 2 vols. 8vo.
The Industrial History of the United States.
The Conflict between Labor and Capital.

BORDAS. De la Mésure de l'Utilité des Travaux Publics. (Annales des Ponts et Chaussées, 1847. 2ᵉ série, tome xiii). 8vo. Paris.

BRENTANO (Lujo). La question ouvrière, traduit de l'Allemand par L. Caubert. 16mo. 1885.

BRISSON (B.). Essai sur la Navigation. Paris, 1802.

BUQUOY (G. Graf von). Theorie der Nationalwirthschaft, hierzu 3 Nachträge. Leipzig, 1816-18.

BURDETT (H. C.). Official Intelligence of British, American, and Foreign Securities. For 1884, 1885, 1887, *et seq.*

BUTTE. Statistik als Wissenschaft (1808).

CANARD (Nicolas François). Principes d'Economie Politique. 8vo. Paris, 1802.

CAUWÈS (Paul). Précis du Cours de l'Economie politique. Vol. ii *et seq.* 8vo. 1879.

CHAMBERLAYNE (Edward). Angliæ Notitia: or the present state of England. Copies of editions ranging from 1667 to 1707. 12mo.

CHAMBERLAYNE (John). Magnæ Britanniæ Notitia: or the present state of Great Britain. Copies of editions ranging from 1708 to 1755, except those for 1741, 1743, and 1755. 8vo.

COBBETT (W.). Paper against Gold: on the History and Mystery of the Bank of England. 470 pp. 4th edition, 1821.

COKE (C. A.). Statistical Summary of England and Wales, 1865.

COLLE (E.). La France et ses Colonies au xixᵉ Siècle. 8vo. 1878.

CONRING (Hermann). "Notitia rerum politicarum nostri ævi celeberrimarum" (*cir.* 1660).

COUMAILLEAU (Louis). Etude sur le mouvement de la Population en France. 4to. 1886.

18

Land Concentration and Irresponsibility of Political Power, as causing the Anomaly of a wide-spread state of Want by the side of the Vast Supplies of Nature. [Anon.] 8vo.

Lang—
Historische Entwickelung der Deutschen Steuerverfassung. 1793.
Ueber den obersten Grundsatz der Politischen Oeconomie. 8vo. Riga, 1807.

Laurent (H.). Démonstration simple du Principe de M. Ménier. (Journal des Actuaires Français, tome iv, Janvier.) 1875.

Lavergne (Léonce de)—
Les Assemblées provinciales sous Louis XVI. 1 vol., 8vo.
Etudes économiques et agricoles. 1 vol., 18mo.
Rural Economy of England, Scotland, and Ireland. Translated from the French; with notes by a Scottish Farmer. 8vo. 1855.

Lefevre (H.). Principes de la Science de la Bourse. 8vo. Paris, 1874.

Léon (M.). De l'accroissement de la Population en France et de la doctrine de Malthus. 8vo. Paris, 1866.

Leroy-Beaulieu (Paul). De la Colonisation chez les peuples modernes. 3ᵉ edition. 8vo. 1886.

Levi (Leone)—
Annals of British Legislation. Summary of Bills, Accounts and Papers, Reports, &c., of Parliament. First Series, 1856-65. Vols. 8—14. New Series, 1866-68. Vols. 1, 3, and 4.
Chart of the principal Commercial Countries of the World, 1851.
Law of Nature and Nations as affected by Divine Law. 8vo. 1855.

Macgregor (John)—
Civil Statistics of all Nations. 5 vols., 8vo. 1844-50.
Commercial Statistics. Vol. iv, 1847.

Macleod (Henry Dunning)—
Theory and Practice of Banking. Third edition, in 2 vols.
Economics for Beginners. The 1st—3rd editions. Sm. 8vo.
Principles of Economical Philosophy. The first edition, and Part 2 of vol. ii of the second edition.
Elements of Banking. The 1st, 2nd, 3rd, 5th, 6th and 7th editions.

Malouet (V. P.). Collection des mémoires et correspondances officielles sur l'administration des colonies. Vols. vi et vii. 8vo. 1802.

Martin (E. D.). Estudios sobre politica y administracion financieras. Madrid, 1887.

Mayhew (Henry)—
London in the Olden Time. The White Book of the City of London; compiled A.D. 1419, during the Mayoralty of Richard Whittington; describing the Social, Political, and Criminal Condition of the City in the Middle Ages. 1 vol., 4to.
London Labour and London Poor. Vol. iii of the 1851 edition.

Menendez (D. B.). Manuel de Geografia y estadistica del Peru. 12mo. Paris, 1862.

Meyer (Dr. R.). Der Emancipations-Kampf der vierten Standes. Band I.

Michelsen (Edward H.). The Ottoman Empire and its resources. 8vo. 1854.

MILLET (Réné). La Serbie économique et commerciale. 8vo. Paris, 1889.

MINARD. Usage gratuit des Constructions établies aux Frais de l'Etat. (Annales des Ponts et Chaussées.) 1850.

MONTCHRETIEN (A. de). Traité de l'Economie Politique. 1615.

Moreau (César)—

Industrie britannique vue dans ses exportations pour chaque pays, de 1698 à 1826.

Etat de la navigation marchande intérieure et extérieure, de la Grande-Bretagne, de 1787 à 1827.

Aperçu du Commerce de la Grande-Bretagne de 1821 à 1827 ...

Commerce général, en trois tableaux, du royaume de France ... pour 1827 et 1828.

Situation détaillée et comparée des cinquante-trois principales branches de commerce français ... en 1827 et 1828, avec l'Europe, l'Asie, l'Afrique, et l'Amérique ...

Commerce de la France avec tous les pays du monde, depuis 1815 jusqu'à 1829.

Aperçu statistique du commerce français, de 1825 à 1829.

Tableau comparatif du commerce de France avec toutes les parties du monde avant la révolution et depuis la restauration.

MORPURGO (Emilio). La finanza italiana dalla fondazione del Regno fino a questi giorni. 8vo. Roma, 1874.

MOSSER (François). L'Esprit de l'Economie Politique. 2nd edition, 1879.

Mulhall (M. G.)—

Rio Grande do Sul and its German Colonies. 8vo. 1873.

Handbook of the River Plate. 8vo. 1885.

Progress of the World from 1800. 8vo. 1880.

NEUMANN-SPALLART and G. A. SCHIMMER. Die Reichsraths-Wahlen vom Jahre 1879 in Oesterreich. 8vo. 1880.

NEWCOMB (Simon). Review of Cairnes' Logical Method of Political Economy. (N. American Review, No. 249.) 1875.

Nicolai (Edmond)—

Chemins de Fer de l'Etat en Belgique, 1834-84. 8vo. 1885.

Tribunaux de Commerce en Belgique, 1840-81. Etude Statistique. 8vo. 1886.

NILES (Hezekiah). Journal of Proceedings of Friends of Domestic Industry, in Convention, at New York, 1831.

NOIROT (N. J. E.). L'Art de Conjecturer, appliqué aux Sciences Morales et Politiques. 8vo. Paris, 1851.

NORTON (C. E.). Considerations on some Recent Social Theories. 12mo. Boston, 1853.

OBEDENARE (M. G.). La Roumanie Economique. Paris, 1876.

OLDENBURGER (P. A.). Itinerarium Germaniæ Politicum (*cir.* 1675).

OUSELEY (William G.). Remarks on the Statistics and Political Institutions of the United States. 8vo. Philadelphia, 1832.

PALMER'S Index to the Times, 1847 to 1865, and the first two quarters of 1866.

Pantaleoni (Maffeo)—

Dell' ammontare probabile della richezza privata in Italia. 8vo. Roma, 1884.

Teoria della pressione tributaria. Roma, 1887.

PATTON (Jacob H.). Natural Resources of the United States.
New York, 1888.

PERY (G. A.). Geographia e estatistica geral de Portugal e
colonias. 8vo. Lisbon, 1875.

PHILLIP (Henry, jun.). Historical Sketches of the Paper Currency of the American Colonies, prior to the Adoption of the
Federal Constitution; and Continental Currency. 2 vols.,
sm. 4to. Roxbury, 1865.

PHILLIPS (W. A.). Labour, Land, and Law : a Search for the
Missing Wealth of the Working Poor. 12mo. New York.

PILLON (F.). Année philosophique. Etudes critiques sur le mouvement des idées générales dans les divers ordres de connaissances.
1869, *et seq.* 12mo.

Platt (James)—
Leaseholds. 120 pp. 8vo.
Mammon. 208 pp. 8vo.

POLITANUS (Helenus). Microscopium Statisticum (*cir.* 1672).

POOR (Henry V.). Manual of the Railroads of the United States.
(For any years except 1874 and 1875.)

PORTER (G. R.). The Progress of the Nation. Sections 3 and 4
of the edition of 1836. 8vo.

PORTER (R. P.), (H.) Gannett and (W. P.) Jones. The West,
from the Census of 1880. Chicago, 1882.

RAFFALOVICH (Arthur). Les Finances de la Russie depuis 1876-83.
Paris, 1883.

RATCLIFFE (Henry). Observations on the Rate of Mortality and
Sickness amongst Friendly Societies. 8vo. Manchester, 1850.

RAU (Karl Heinrich). Grundsätze der Volkswirthschaftslehre.
8e Ausgabe, 1ste Abtheilung, 368 pp. 8vo. Leipzig, 1868.

RECHERCHE sur la méthode à adopter pour la discussion des éléments
de la Statistique. (Journal des Actuaires Français, vol. ii. 1873.)

RECK (Hugo). Geographie und Statistik der Republik Bolivia.
4to. Gotha, 1865.

REDEN (Baron F. W. von). Allgemeine vergleichende Finanz-Statis-
tik. Band i, Abtheilung 1, 2. Band ii, Abtheilung 1. 8vo. 1851.

RICKARDS (R.). India, or Facts to illustrate the Character and
Condition of the Native Inhabitants. Part 4 (*cir.* 1830).

SASKI (Theodor). Jahrbuch für das gesammte Versicherungs-
wesen in Deutschland, 1865, *et seq.* La. 8vo.

SAY (LÉON). Les solutions démocratiques de la question des
Impôts. 2 vols., 8vo. 1886.

Scherzer (Dr. K. von)—
Statistisch- commerzielle Ergebnisse einer Reise um die Erde.
8vo. Leipzig, 1867.
Die wirthschaftlichen Zustände im Süden und Osten Asiens'.
8vo. Stuttgart, 1871.

SCHMOLLER (Gustav). Jahrbuch für Gesetzgebung, Verwaltung
und Volkswirthschaft im Deutschen Reich. 8vo. Leipzig,
1877-80, 1882-85.

SCHÖNBERG (Dr. Gustav). Handbuch der Politischen Oekonomie.
Band i—iii. 8vo. Tübingen, 1885.

SCRATCHLEY (A.). Treatise on the Enfranchisement of Copyhold,
Life-Leasehold, and Church Property. Part 2. 1859.

Schubert (F. W.). Handbuch der Statistik (*cir.* 1835).

Scully (William). Brazil, its Provinces and chief cities. Agricultural, Commercial, and other Statistics. 8vo. 1868.

Sève (E.). La situation economique de l'Espagne. Bruxelles, 1887.

Seyd (Richard). Record of Failures and Liquidations ... in the United Kingdom from 1877. (In continuation of a former volume giving the failures from 1865 to July, 1876.)

Shadwell (J. L.). System of Political Economy. 8vo. 1877.

Sittewald (Philander von). Somnium Itinerarium Historico Politicum (*cir.* 1649).

Smith (Adam)—
Wealth of Nations. Edited by J. R. McCulloch. Vol. i, 1828.
Ueber die Quellen des Volkswohlstandes. Neu bearbeitet von Dr. C. W. Asher. First vol. 8vo. 1861.

Strachey (Sir John). Finances and Public Works of India from 1869 to 1881. 8vo. 1882.

Tarassenko-Otreschkoff. De l'Or et de l'Argent. Vol. ii. Paris, 1856.

Thomas (E.). Histoire des Ateliers Nationaux. 12mo. Bruxelles, 1848.

Thomson (Dr.). History of the Royal Society. 1812.

Thurmann. Bibliotheca Statistica (*cir.* 1701).

Tozer (John)—
Mathematical Investigation of Effect of Machinery on Wealth and on the Fund for Payment of Wages. (Cambridge Philosophical Transactions, vol. vi, 4to.) 1838.
Effect of Non-Residence of Landlords, &c., on Wealth of a Community. (Cambridge Philosophical Transactions, vol. vii.) 1840.

Tucker (George). Progress of the United States in Population and Wealth in Fifty Years. 12mo. New York, 1855.

Visschers (A.). Nouvelle étude sur les Caisses d'épargne, 1861.

Vührer (M. H.). Histoire de la Dette Publique en France. Paris, 1886.

Walras (Auguste). Nature de la Richesse et Origine de la Valeur. 8vo. Paris, 1831.

Walras (L.). Nuovo Ramo della Matematica dell' applicazione delle Matematiche all' Economia Politica. 8vo. 1876.

Wappœus (Dr. J. E.). Handbuch der Geographie und Statistik von Brasilien. 8vo. Leipzig, 1871.

Warden (D. B.). Statistical, Political, and Historical Account of the United States. 3 vols., 8vo. Edinburgh, 1819.

Wayland (Fr.). Elements of Political Economy. 3rd edit., 12mo. Boston, 1840.

Weld (Charles Richard) and Banfield (T. C.). Statistical Companion for 1850. 8vo.

Westergaard (Harald). Den Sandsynlige Lov for den Internationale Telegraftrafik Anmeldt af—. 8vo. Copenhagen, 1878.

Whewell (William)—
Mathematical Exposition of the Leading Doctrines in Mr. Ricardo's "Principles of Political Economy and Taxation." (Cambridge Philosophical Trans. Vol. iv.) 4to. 1851.
Mathematical Exposition of some Doctrines of Political Economy. (Cambridge Philosophical Trans. Vol. iii.) 4to. 1829.

WHITE (William). The Insurance Register for 1865, 1870, 1873, 1874, 1876, 1881. 8vo.

WIRTH (Max). Allgemeine Beschreibung und Statistik der Schweiz. 3 vols., 8vo. Zürich, 1871-75.

WOLKOFF (M.). Lectures d'Economie Politique Rationelle. 12mo. Paris, 1861.

WOLOWSKI (Louis F. M. R.). L'Or et l'Argent. 2ᵉ Partie, *et seq.* 8vo. 1868.

ZEDLITZ-NEUKIRCH (L. von). Der Preussische Staat in allen seinen Beziehungen. Vol. i. 8vo. 1836.

(e) **Societies, &c. (British).***

Aborigines Protection Society. Publications. Vol. iii, 1842, *et seq.*

Arts, Society of. Journal, No. 1652, of vol. 32, 1884.

Association of Chambers of Commerce of the United Kingdom, Annual Reports. Nos. 2, 3, and 6, 1862-63 and 1866.

Central Chamber of Agriculture, Annual Reports for 1866-67.

Chamber of Commerce Journal. (Issued by London Chamber of Commerce.) . No. 6, for August, 1882.

Co-operative Wholesale Societies' Annual for 1891. 8vo.

East India Association. Proceedings. No. 6 of vol. xvii. No. 6, and title page, &c., of vol. xx.

Financial Reform Almanack for 1865.

Iron and Steel Institute, Journal for 1872, 1885, *et seq.*

Labourer's Friend. Nos. 230, 1869, and 231, 1870.

Liverpool Literary and Philosophical Society, Proceedings. Nos. 1—5, 1844-45 to 1848-49.

Literary and Philosophical Society of Manchester:—
　Memoirs. The first series of five vols.; second series, vols i (*cir.* 1812) and xiii, 1857 ; third series, vol. vi, *et seq.*
　Proceedings. 8vo. Vols. i, ix, xii, xiii and xiv, 1857, *et seq.*

Manchester Statistical Society. Transactions for 1854-55.

Philosophical Society of Glasgow. Proceedings. First six volumes, and Nos. 1 and 2 of vol. vii, 1871.

Royal Asiatic Society. Journal. Old series, vol. xiv, 1853-54; New series, vol. xiv, parts 2 and 4, 1882; vol. xv, parts 1 and 2, 1883.

Royal Colonial Institute. Proceedings. Vol. iii, 1872.

Royal Irish Academy—
　Proceedings. Series 1, vols. vii—x. Series 2 (Science), vol. i; Series 2 (Polite Literature and Antiquities), vol. i, Nos. 1—11.
　Journal, vol. viii, *et seq.* Transactions, vols. i—xxiv.

Royal Medical and Chirurgical Society. Transactions. Vols. i—xxviii.

Royal Society of Edinburgh. Proceedings. Vols. i and ii. Transactions. Vols. i—xiv.

Royal Society, London—Proceedings. No. 201, 1880.
　Indexes to the Philosophical Transactions. 4to. Parts 1—3.
　Catalogue of Scientific Papers. Vols. i—viii. 4to.

* Foreign and colonial societies will be found under the various countries or possessions to which they belong.

Social Science Association. Sessional Proceedings. Table of Contents and Title Page of vol. viii, 1875; No. 6, &c., and Table of Contents, &c., of vol. xiii, 1880; No. 7, &c., and Table of Contents, &c., of vol. xiv, 1881; No. 6, &c., and Table of Contents, &c., of vol. **xv**, 1882.

Statistical Society, London—Proceedings of the—, 1834-37. Any odd numbers. Lists of Fellows, &c., *ante* 1872. Any back numbers of the *Journal*.

(f) Periodicals, &c. (British).*

Athenæum. The first four vols. 1827-31, viz., Nos. 1—218.

Economist—
The vol. for July—Dec., 1844; also the Numbers for 13th Nov. and 18th Dec., 1847; for 15th July, 26th Aug., 9th and 30th Sept., and 2nd Dec. of 1848; for 3rd Feb. and 11th Aug. of 1849; for 19th Jan. and 21st Dec. of 1850; for 4th Jan. and 24th May of 1851; for 1st Jan. and 26th Feb. of 1853; for 11th Feb., 15th April, and 30th Dec. of 1854; for 7th April, 1855; 27th Dec., title page and index, of 1856; for 3rd, 10th, 17th, and 31st Jan., and 17th Feb. of 1857; and title page and index for 1863.
Commercial History and Review of 1872, 1882, 1883, 1884, 1885, and 1886.

Investors' Monthly Manual—
The whole of the first series, 1865-70.
New series, first three volumes of the, 1871-73.

Literary and Statistical Magazine for Scotland. Vol. i, 1817; and vol. iv, 1820, *et seq.*

Nature. Vols. i—vii.

Pamphleteer, The (London, 1813-28). Vols. **xvi, xxvii—xxix.**

Post Magazine, Almanack and Insurance Directory for the years 1842-45, 1856, 1868-71, 1873, 1876, 1880, 1883, 1885-88.

Railway Intelligence (Slaughters's). Nos. 1—9, 11—15, 18, 1875, and 19, 1877.

Sanitary Record. New series. Vol. i, 1880.

Simmond's Colonial Magazine. Vols. i—iii, 1844; x—xii, 1847; and No. 2 of vol. xvi, 1849, *et seq.*

Social Science Review. New series, 1864. Vol. vi, Sept., Oct., Nov., Dec., 1866, and table of contents; and 1867, *et seq.*

The Daily Universal Register (afterwards the "Times"). Several odd numbers for 1785 and 1786.

The Times—For the years 1801, 1802.

Wheat Trade. Annual Review, &c., for 1883, *et seq.* La. 8vo.

* Foreign periodicals will be found under the various countries in which they are issued.